POWER AND PRINCIPLE IN INTERNATIONAL AFFAIRS

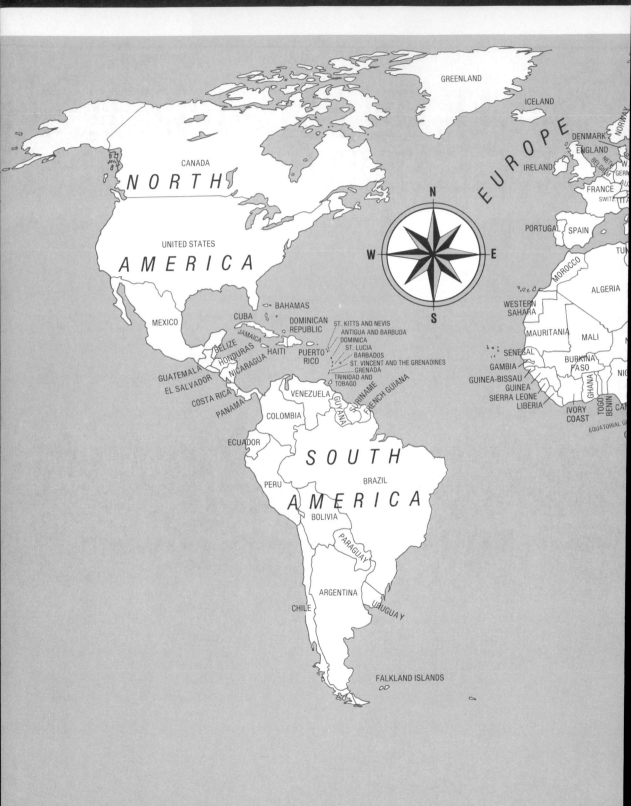

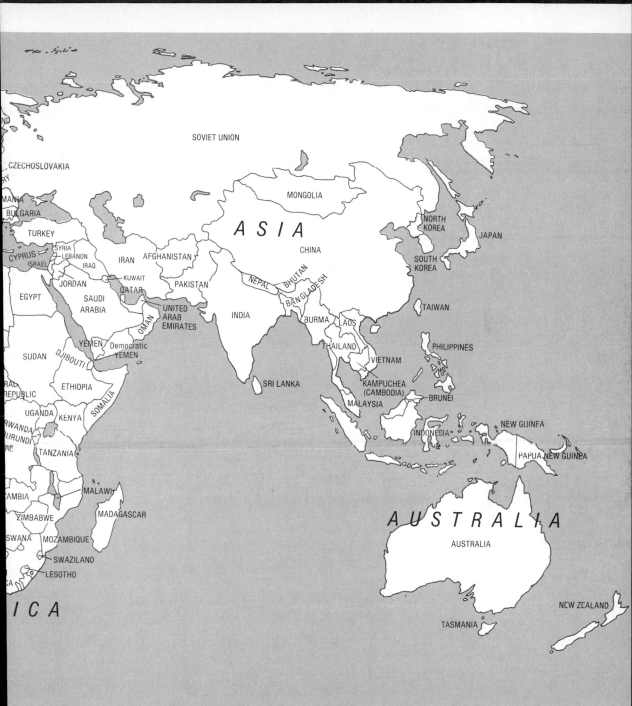

POWER AND PRINCIPLE IN INTERNATIONAL AFFAIRS

GORDON C. SCHLOMING

Lewis & Clark College

HARCOURT BRACE JOVANOVICH, PUBLISHERS

San Diego   New York   Chicago   Austin   Washington, D.C.
London   Sydney   Tokyo   Toronto

PREFACE

It is always with great humility that an author approaches the acknowledgment of his intellectual debts. Having taught international relations for twenty years, I must credit my students at Amherst College, the University of Portland, Pomona College, and Lewis & Clark College with the main stimulus to my thinking. Many ideas first took form in the enthusiasm of the classroom or surfaced from the deep spring of dialogue with students. I am also indebted to the many scholars who have dedicated their lives to mastery of a specialized subject and have set down their ideas in countless books and articles. My own inclinations are those of a generalist nourished over the years by eclectic reading and writing across the boundaries of disciplines and specialties. However, generalists are a rare breed these days, and few scholars apply themselves to the task of writing a textbook for undergraduates that presents a clear, comprehensive, and sophisticated rendering of international affairs. I leave it to students and instructors to judge whether I have succeeded in my aim: to communicate in an attractive style, without obscure jargon or simplifications that insult the intelligence.

Although the realist – idealist approach I have adopted is fairly traditional and the coverage of topics is standard, I have included features that the instructor will find useful to recent trends in the field. The pro-and-con discussion section that concludes each chapter should act as a stimulus to critical thinking, so students will not accept the point of view of the author as settled wisdom. I have tried hard to make both sides of the argument convincing, which may confuse some students (in a creative way) and press them to examine the focus of the argument, the controlling assumptions, and the selection of facts. Many of the discussion questions address issues in American foreign policy because they were most likely to be familiar and interesting to students. It is my hope that these sections will serve as springboards for papers or class discussions. Extensive bibliographies, presented by topic, are included to support subjects that the book touched only lightly. Special attention has been given to recent changes in the Communist world, to international political economy, to problems of the global commons, and to North – South relations, particularly issues of dependency and development in the Third World. Methodological, historical, and ethical concerns also receive greater emphasis than in most textbooks. A variety of maps help to acquaint the student more fully with world geography.

One of my greatest professional pleasures has been the opportunity to teach in a number of small liberal arts colleges where I have had the freedom to offer courses on dozens of subjects in international relations. One of my regrets is that these modest departments rarely provided the wide professional contacts that foster lively and extensive discussion within specialized subfields. Conferences and professional meetings have helped, but when the writing begins, the circle of contacts necessarily closes to a few intimates. If the writing of this book has been more lonely than I anticipated or wished — partly by the advent of a sabbatical leave and a Fulbright Fellowship in Peru — I have still enjoyed the benefit of specific comments and criticisms from several colleagues. Bob Mandel and Rich Peck, fellow faculty members at Lewis & Clark College, read major portions of the manuscript, with invariably helpful insights. Tsuneo Akaha discussed with me its analytic organization and shared generously his classroom experience regarding student response to different approaches. Miroslav Nincic provided helpful comments on Chapter 3. I received fine institutional support from the international affairs and political science departments of Lewis & Clark College, and intellectual inspiration from its Faculty Seminar on International Development. I also wish to thank my colleagues who reviewed the book proposal for the publisher: Richard Foster, Idaho State University; Benjamin Most, University of Iowa; and James Peterson, Valdosta State College.

I am grateful to Robbie Roy, Karen Jenner, Karen Nairn, and Susan Kirschner for assistance in preparation of the manuscript. Herman Asarnow generously agreed to read the galley proofs, lending his graceful sense of style. Above all, I have been steadfastly and creatively supported by my editors at Harcourt Brace Jovanovich. Drake Bush, who proposed this project in the first place and shared fully his confidence, patience, experience, friendly manner, and competence, kept me going in the years-long effort of producing such a work. Cathy Fauver managed to streamline a very long manuscript with remarkable skill, commenting helpfully on matters of substance as well as style. Her meticulous work improved the book immensely. The rest of the book team also contributed a superb effort. These include Tracey Engel and Mary Allen, production editors; Linda Wooton Miller, designer; Louise Sandy, art editor; and Mary Kay Yearin, production manager.

I extend very special thanks to my family. My son Galen offered daily diversions that lifted my spirits and reminded me, always, that being a father was my most important job. My wife, Jennifer, gave the kind of endless support — far beyond any reasonable limit — that only a loving spouse can. A good book could not have been written without the coauthorship of such a sterling and steadfast partner.

Many unnamed individuals must be credited as well, though their contributions have occurred in such an indirect manner that I cannot trace the lineage of their ideas or distinguish them clearly from my own. Because the field of international affairs is so vast, and because so much of the actual writing took place in relative isolation, there are sure to be mistakes of fact and interpretation. I trust that students and scholars in the field will be generous enough to correct my errors or challenge my ideas, just as I have freely shared my own opinions regarding the various issues treated in this book. By such means, it will become a better book, and a model for the truth-telling dialogue that keeps us from being prisoners of our own perspective.

Gordon C. Schloming

CONTENTS

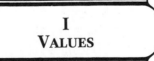

I
VALUES

II
STRUCTURES

5
EAST-WEST CONFLICT   201

6
NORTH-SOUTH CONFLICT   292

III
ACTORS

7
NATION-STATES   393

Introduction: Thinking Analytically About International Relations

Events on the international stage are often complex and difficult to understand, with motive forces easily hidden from the public eye. Diplomatic relations are conducted in private, and even the occasional well-publicized event is likely to occur far from our shores, in a political or cultural setting quite different from our own. Sensational newspaper headlines frequently obscure important details of events, and nightly news broadcasts rarely give any in-depth analysis or sense of continuity from one event to another. We are left largely to our own devices when it comes to interpreting world affairs.

One important purpose of this book is to set out some organizing concepts that can help us understand otherwise disconnected facts and events in terms of the wider forces at work in the world. Careful readers will be able to trace the roots of current problems in the historical development of the international system. They will become familiar with the many players on the field of international politics, and with the forces that shape their perspectives and control their actions. Readers will gain a better understanding of why a particular crisis occurred, what is likely to be its long-term outcome, and which factors represent enduring influences in international affairs.

But simply to understand what is happening is not enough. We also need to be able to think critically about international issues, so that we can make intelligent choices in those arenas in which we actually participate. World trade, terrorism, satellite transmissions, foreign travel, the constant threat of nuclear destruction, and a thousand other international influences on our daily lives have brought the era of national isolation to an end. All parents want to know what they can do to reduce the risk of war, so that their children will inherit a planet at peace. Business people cannot make intelligent decisions if they are ignorant about the international economy and the political forces that shape international financial flows, technology transfers, and the global exchange of goods and services. Even international travelers can enrich their experiences tenfold if they understand the political and cultural differences they will encounter. On the national level, in an era when a revolution or regional war can cut off our access to vital raw materials or threaten our basic security, we must be attentive to those factors that are constantly transforming our relations with the rest of the world. And, as citizens of a country that is a leading influence in world politics, we have a responsibility to participate meaningfully in the public debate and political decisions of foreign policy.

In-depth understanding and informed participation are the twin goals of this book. It is designed to encourage the capacity for independent thought and to help the careful reader become aware of the analytic approaches, underlying values, and basic assumptions that shape the information presented in, say, a presidential address, a news commentary, or a textbook such as this one. Pro-and-con discussion questions are provided in every chapter as a particular stimulus to this kind of critical thought. But let us begin with a brief overview of the concepts around which the book is organized and then go on to a consideration of the kinds of analytic distinctions that will inform our discussions throughout the book.

ORGANIZING CONCEPTS

Looking at a rapidly moving, complex series of events, we usually can focus on only one or two factors at a time. So it is with the study of international relations. We must start with a "slice" of reality, a "freeze-frame" view of a single aspect at one moment in time. As we go on, we will learn to take several of these slices and edit them together to create a more sophisticated picture of reality. The four slices, or concepts, on which this book focuses are the values, the structures, the actors, and the instruments of international affairs — the subject matter of the book's major divisions.

The most fundamental of these concepts, for both the actor and the analyst, is *values*. Though intangible and sometimes difficult to discern, values shape the goals and outlooks of each individual, organization, and nation-state. The ideological conflicts between East and West, communism and capitalism, dictatorship and democracy are rooted in basic value differences that define the characters of the competing societies. National interests deemed vital to the preservation of a country's way of life can be understood only in terms of the core values of its people and their leadership. Core values determine the organizing principles of a political community and the distinct perspective through which a nation views international affairs. Important value differences within each state result in controversies over basic issues of foreign policy as well as domestic affairs. Even scholars of international relations, who share a common commitment to the truth, can fall into serious controversies that reflect their differing values and approaches.

The *structures* of international relations consist of the patterns of interaction and the institutions that provide an organized context within which individuals and states pursue their goals. In the political arena, relations among states are structured by a balance of power, whose form changes over time in response to historical trends and to the efforts of individual actors to shape the international order to their own advantage. In economics, exchanges take place through various market mechanisms that reflect different principles of organization and different degrees of competitiveness or interdependence. Cultural relations of greater or lesser intensity are another element of community within the international system. To the degree that relations become habitual and fixed, they comprise the structures that define the nature of the international system at a given time. These structures express the historic conflicts of the moment and provide the opportunities and restraints that influence the behavior of states, political leaders, and other international actors.

The principal *actors* on the world stage are individual leaders, states, transnational corporations, intergovernmental organizations, like the United Nations, and a variety of groups and organizations with international interests. Each actor operates as a coherent unit and has a distinctive character, interests, and activities. Since there always will be individuals carrying out particular actions, it is important to distinguish when someone is acting as a private individual and when as a representative of a larger organization or entity. Diplomats and soldiers are typically agents of the state, their actions shaped by an official role and a public agenda. Nonetheless, at times political leaders will have a personal or private agenda as well as a public responsibility and may be playing several roles at once. State bureaucracies empowered to act on behalf of the national interest often become independent actors as well, seeking to further their own organizational fortunes while also acting for the state. Much of the drama of international relations is contained in its individual actors — in powerful personalities and conflicts between private and public interests, for example, or in the force with which some leaders can drive the larger organizations to which they are attached symbolically and emotionally.

But actions in the international arena most often coalesce around the decisions of nation-states on key issues. The most fateful of these, with the largest and most obvious impact on international relations, is the decision for war, which we will explore shortly. The nation-state is thus the most prominent international actor, not only because it holds most of the instruments of power and makes the decisions for war and peace, but also because it has established elaborate internal decision-making mechanisms for conducting foreign relations. Other prominent actors are certain intergovernmental institutions (the European Economic Community is one) and nongovernmental organizations (multinational corporations, for example) whose permanent officials and bureacratic apparatus allow them to exercise influence on the international scene.

Power, diplomacy, and law are the *instruments* international actors employ to accomplish their aims. In the highly competitive arena of world politics, power is the main instrument, and the state has become the dominant actor because of its capacity to control a vast panoply of power resources and mobilize them on an enduring basis. Restraints on power are achieved through diplomacy and international law, which seek to adjust competing interests by such means as arbitration, negotiation, or participation in international organizations. Diplomacy and law are alternatives to power as instruments for resolving conflicts between states, individuals, or such nongovernmental actors as multinational corporations.

Of course, each of these conceptual "slices" will reveal only one aspect of international relations; no single focus can do justice to the complexity of actual events. Like a surgeon, we cut into reality, at the risk of killing live tissue, because it is the only way we can reveal the inner forces at work. We employ the analytic knife in order to simplify, but a time will come when we must stitch our concepts back together so that they will acquire a larger coherence. The pro-and-con discussions provide this kind of holistic integration as it applies to a particular problem or policy arena. Thus, we dissect international relations to see more clearly the character of each aspect, while always keeping in mind that the factors interact. To put it another way, actors in international affairs hold certain values, operate within given structures of conflict and cooperation, employ instruments of power, diplomacy, organization, and law to reshape those structures to their benefit, and make policy decisions that reflect their goals, values, and capabilities.

These concepts are only some of the tools to understanding, however. Readers may want to invent concepts of their own or reorganize the material they are studying along lines that suit them better. One risk of an analytic approach such as this book takes is that reality gets broken down into its constituent elements but is never reassembled. Another is that it may focus too narrowly on the given categories and slight the integrative process of continually relating analysis in one section to discussion in another. Robert Pirsig's *Zen and the Art of Motorcycle Maintenance: An Inquiry into Values* contains a warning about analytic descriptions: they suffer from the classical problem of focusing on underlying form at the expense of reality. By appearing to be detached and "objective," such descriptions hide the point of view of the observer or author and tend to wash out value judgments or bury them beneath a mountain of facts. Pirsig cautions us always to keep an eye on the author's choice of organizing concepts, for

> There is a knife moving here. A very deadly one; an intellectual scalpel so swift and so sharp you sometimes don't see it moving. You get the illusion that all those parts are just there and are being named as they exist. But they can be named quite differently and organized quite differently depending on how the knife moves. . . .
>
> When analytic thought, the knife, is applied to experience, something is always killed in the process. But what is less noticed . . . something is always created too. And instead of just dwelling on what is killed it's important to see what's created and to see the process as a kind of death-birth continuity that is neither good nor bad, but just *is*. (pp. 72, 77)

So we must be self conscious about our analytic categories and modest about the degree to which our schematic description captures the flesh and blood of world affairs. We will hope to avoid assassination by the analytic knife and will try always to wield it with the careful skill of the surgeon.

MAPS AND MENTAL IMAGES

Maps provide a concrete illustration of the way analytic perspective controls our picture of the world. Maps depict a supposedly objective reality — the land masses, oceans, and physical contours of the earth — and we take their accuracy for granted. But in fact they reflect many hidden assumptions. First, there is the not-so-simple choice of projection, the means by which the three-dimensional globe is tranposed onto a flat, two-dimensional surface. Cartographers have a striking variety of projections to choose from, and those choices strongly reflect (and affect) our perceptions about which areas are most important. The traditional choice for world maps is the Mercator projection, which is centered on the United States and enlarges the Northern Hemisphere by placing the equator almost two-thirds of the way down the page; Antarctica, largely because it is uninhabited (except for a few hundred visiting scientists), is considered so unimportant that it often does not even appear on the map. As international events have shifted power and attention away from Europe and the West, however, our world maps have been modified to reflect a more balanced view, literally enlarging the presence of Third World nations and the Southern Hemisphere. Figure 1-1 compares a Mercator map with a map drawn in one of the newer projections, the Peters Equal Area Projection. Another of the equal-area projections, the Robinson, is used for the maps inside the front and back covers of this book.

A second dimension of maps relates to the political, economic, social, or cultural features the mapmaker chooses to emphasize. Most maps define the world in terms of its political divisions, enshrining the nation-state by those ever-present lines that mark territorial boundaries. But one could just as easily see the world in terms of its major religions or its population distribution and climatic zones, as in Figures 1-2 and 1-3. And now the age of rocketry and extraterrestrial travel is giving us new maps of the earth as an interdependent ecology. Satellite photos like Figure 1-4, which shows the ozone hole over Antarctica, are making us increasingly aware of planet Earth's unity, finiteness, and fragility.

Geopolitical perspective is a third dimension reflected in maps of the world. The dominance of the North and the Eurocentric focus on the Atlantic Ocean that we find in almost all our maps are products of the age of navigation, when European explorers "discovered" the world. The New World took its meaning by reference to the Old, just as Portuguese and Spanish sailors took their bearings from the north magnetic pole. European mapmakers naturally put the features that were most important to them at the top of the page,

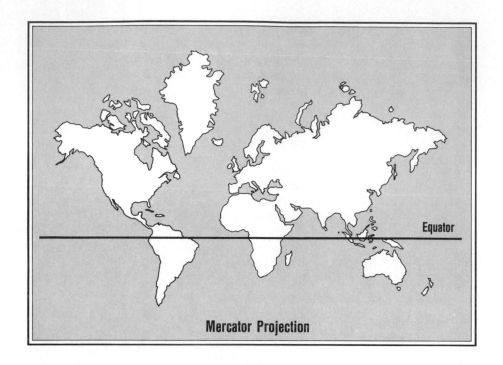

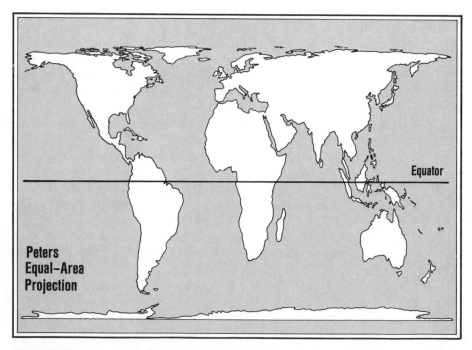

FIGURE 1-1
COMPARISON OF MERCATOR AND EQUAL-AREA PROJECTIONS

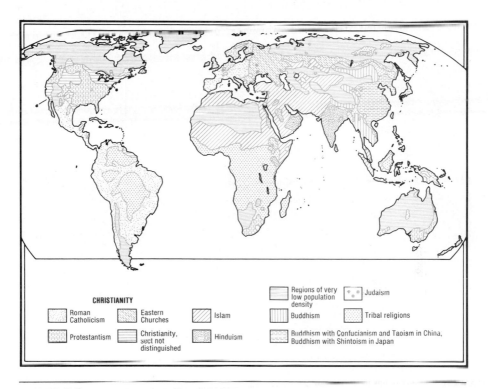

CHRISTIANITY

	Roman Catholicism
	Protestantism
	Eastern Churches
	Christianity, sect not distinguished
	Islam
	Hinduism
	Regions of very low population density
	Buddhism
	Buddhism with Confucianism and Taoism in China, Buddhism with Shintoism in Japan
	Judaism
	Tribal religions

FIGURE 1-2
THE WORLD AS DIVIDED BY RELIGION

reflecting the cultural practice of reading from the top down. But it might be just as valid today to view the world "upside down" or from the point of view of individual nation-states. Compare, for example, the maps inside the front and back covers of this book to imagine a world with a Southern orientation and a Pacific focus. Every state views its security, its external relations, and its interests in terms of its physical location on the globe, and these views can have a striking impact on foreign policy, as we will chronicle in Chapter 7, in the discussion of nation-states. For the moment, it is helpful simply to compare the several views shown in Figure 1-5, which depicts the world from the geopolitical perspective of the United States, the Soviet Union, China, and Argentina. This important dimension of geopolitical perspective is highlighted by the variety of maps used throughout the book.

The example of maps represents only one of many kinds of mental images that influence our perceptions of international affairs. Each of us has an interior landscape of hidden categories and unconscious and untested assumptions. To guard against having these control our analysis, and to enrich our perspective, we must adopt self-conscious conceptual tools that will force us to look at our reality in new terms. Levels of analysis is one such tool that is particularly applicable to the problems of international affairs.

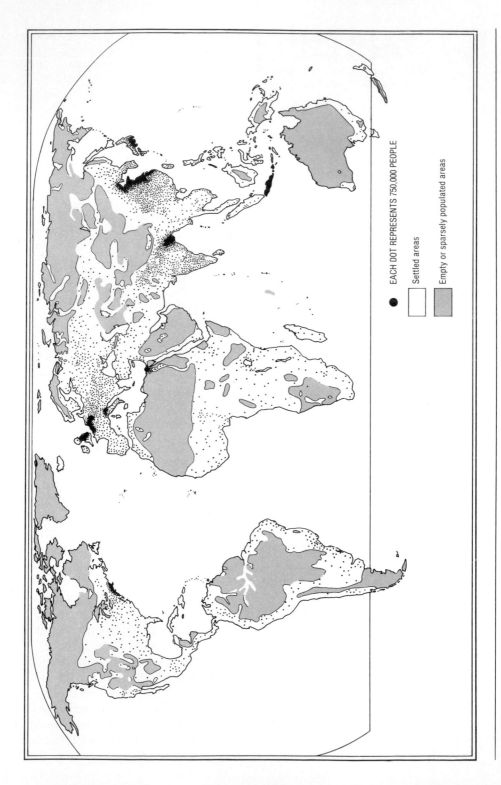

FIGURE 1-3   POPULATION DISTRIBUTION AND CLIMATIC ZONES OF THE WORLD

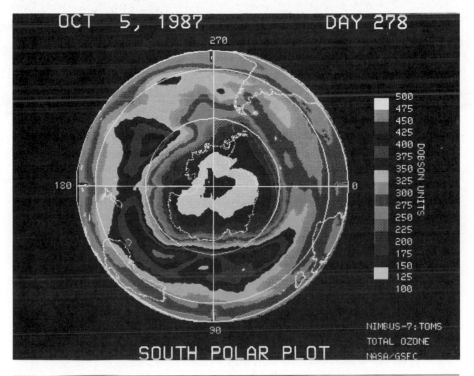

FIGURE 1-4
PLANET EARTH: SOUTH POLAR PLOT WITH OZONE HOLE
This NASA satellite photo shows the most serious ozone depletion ever recorded. The light area in the center of the photo shows the perimeter of the ozone hole. The dark center is the area of greatest depletion.

LEVELS OF ANALYSIS

The *levels of analysis* method allows us to study international relations either from a *macro-* perspective, which views the international system as a whole, or from a *micro-* perspective, which dissects the system into its constituent units. If we classify actors along an ascending scale of size and complexity, we immediately see that it breaks into three levels: (1) the persons who are the actual decision makers, (2) nation-states, and (3) transnational actors. Each of these levels presumes a shift in perspective and in the locus of decision. Of course, these units, or subsystems, do not operate in isolation from one another. Each unit is also embedded in a larger system. Individual actors operate within group and organizational settings. Organizations interact according to the structure of national decision making. National actors both cooperate in intergovernmental organizations and compete with each other within a larger balance-of-power system. Transnational actors are members of a global society

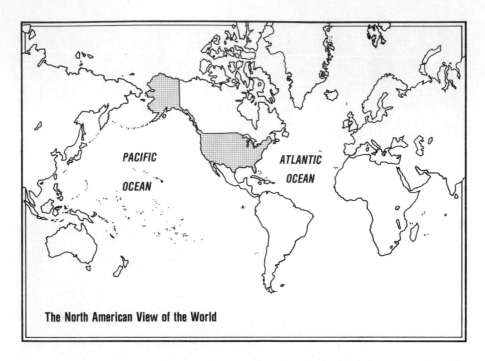

The North American View of the World

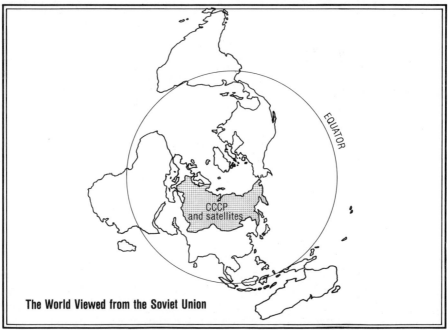

The World Viewed from the Soviet Union

FIGURE 1-5
A VARIETY OF GEOPOLITICAL PERSPECTIVES

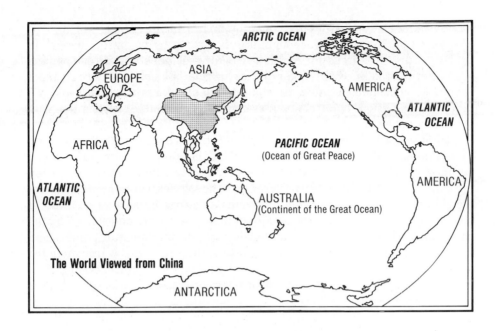

The World Viewed from China

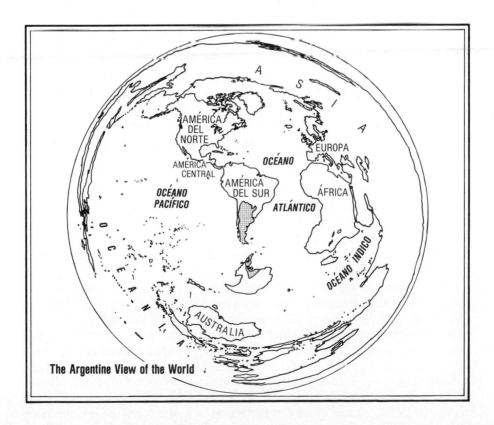

The Argentine View of the World

with systemic characteristics that constrain their behavior. Thus, explanations of international relations vary significantly simply by virtue of changes in analytic focus. In a discussion of agent-structure relationships, we can emphasize either the qualities of the actor or the characteristics of the environment of action. For example, treating the state as relatively autonomous leads to a different conclusion than treating it as embedded in a larger system that constrains its behavior.

Different analytic focuses or levels of analysis predominate in various parts of this book. The treatment of actors divides them into the three levels just outlined — individual leaders, nation-states, and transnational actors — and explains their actions largely by reference to the self-defined and self-determining characteristics of each actor. Individuals emerge because of qualities of personality and leadership. The actions of nation-states are determined by the power and will of the nation, the national character, bureaucratic politics, and the decision-making processes that operate within the state. A transnational organization is understood in terms of its organizational features and its motivating forces. The section on international structures, on the other hand, takes a systemic perspective, on the assumption that international actors — whether individuals, states, or transnational organizations — are bound by the rules of the national or international framework within which they operate. At this level, the personal, programmatic, or ideological goals of individual units are modified by their participation in the processes of national policy making and international diplomacy. Nation-states or multinational corporations may desire to act independently, but they are caught up in systems of power and interdependence that limit their options. Conflicts between nations are shaped by the dominant cleavages in the international system. The changing status of multinationals or of intergovernmental decision-making bodies like the United Nations is a function of changing conditions in the international arena. In short, this part of the story is told from the viewpoint of the system as a whole, not of its individual units.

But no explanation of international affairs can be complete without utilizing several levels of analysis and looking at events from the perspectives of both actors and systems. In fact, some analysts employ six or more levels, distinguishing between the individual and his or her role or group affiliation, between government proper and society as a whole, between interstate or transnational relations and the world system itself. For our purposes, the simple three-level division will be sufficient.

At the individual level, we look for any physical or psychological attributes of a decision maker that might serve as important influences or constraints, as well as for qualities of personal leadership and factors that might determine when or under what circumstances the decision maker acts rationally or irrationally. The behavior of statesmen is examined from the point of view of their offices, roles, and public images. Individuals are evaluated in terms of their membership in an elite that shares an operational code or set of organizational attitudes. In turn, group settings are studied for the way they shape individual decisions. Decision makers are categorized according to personality type, education, socialization, career path, and formative experiences. Within the decision-making group, we look for psychological factors strong enough to determine the group's perceptions, motivations, and structure. Biographies and memoirs are invaluable tools for uncovering the factors at work at this individual level of analysis.

At the nation-state level, we focus on the way different forms of government and society shape both the aims and the instruments of foreign policy. Democratic and authoritarian states are far apart in their styles and structures, giving their leaders distinctive sets of opportunities and limits. Capitalist and socialist states also differ fundamentally in foreign policy aims, though ideologists disagree over which system is peace loving and which inherently imperialistic. Each state's unique geographical and historical position creates another set of national interests that help to define its foreign policy agenda, as do its resource base and power capabilities. In addition, a state's actions and perceptions are filtered through a national character or ideology rooted in the broad formative experiences of its history. Political cultures, national security bureaucracies, political economies — all national in character — form the "personality" of the nation-state and explain its behavior. At this level, we study decision making not as the interactions of individuals but as a process driven by the policies and sociopolitical dynamics of the state. The motive forces transcend individuals and constrain them to behave in ways delimited by institutional interests, governmental politics, and the bureaucratic process itself.

At the global level — what we might call a "god's-eye" view of the system as a whole — both individuals and states are embedded in a larger matrix with its own set of opportunities and constraints. In this evolving international system, distinctive forms of organization have marked different historical periods. Old balance-of-power systems have been succeeded, in part, by forms of interdependence that have altered the way international actors relate to one another. Relations between rich and poor states, between the strong and the weak, add their unique pieces to the pattern. International arms races display technological dynamism and action-reaction responses that take on a life of their own. Networks of alliances shape the foreign policy agendas of participating states, which are controlled by their past commitments and future expectations. Transnational flows of technology, ideas, population, and pollution compel states to take these global issues into account. From an ecological perspective, all international actors are undergoing environmental changes that are reshaping their behavior. In all these areas, the behavior of states can be understood only in terms of the determining power of the international system itself.

J. David Singer's study, "The Level of Analysis Problem in International Relations," reviews the different insights each level provides. The systemic perspective has the advantage of a comprehensive overview of the patterns of interaction, the creation and dissolution of coalitions, the stability of specific power configurations, the international impact of changes in global political institutions, and the norms or folkways that spring up within international society. However, this approach has disadvantages as well. It tends to exaggerate the impact of the system on national actors, discounting the capacity of states to form or control their own environment of action. It also assumes a high degree of uniformity in the nature of states, postulating that all the inter-acting units possess roughly the same motives, operational codes, and patterns of conduct. The nation-state perspective, on the other hand, highlights national differences, emphasizing that states are not "interchangeable" and that some international outcomes are the result of the unique response of one national actor. But the national perspective may tend to exaggerate the cultural or political differences between states and to ignore the conditions and constraints that affect all states. It can also personify the state and attribute to it goals, motives, or perceptions that rightly belong only to individuals. Thus, the indi-vidual level of analysis is essential for understanding the human, subjective factors that influence the conduct of political decision makers. This level also permits us to examine the details of the decision-making process, making us aware that states are not always fully coherent entities expressing a single interest. To understand better the insights to be gained from levels of analysis, we will apply the method to one of the core issues of international affairs, the causes of war.

The Causes of War

A discussion of the causes of war highlights the central problem of world politics: there exists no legitimate source of authoritative decisions and no law enforcement mechanism to compel the peaceful resolution of conflicts. Conse-quently, international actors always operate under the potential threat of war, however remote it may seem at any given moment. No wonder that the last 3,500 years have seen only 270 years of peace, by the estimate of Lynn Mon-tross in his *War Through the Ages.* For the late 1980s alone, Figure 1-6, "The World at War," lists some twenty contemporary wars. As the Greek philoso-pher Plato remarked: "Only the dead have seen the end of war."

War may be defined as the organized conduct of armed hostilities between states or between organized social groups within a state or territory. The level of hostilities may range from total war, utilizing weapons of mass destruction, to limited war, employing unconventional means and guerrilla tactics. What-ever its form, the causes of war are many and complex, requiring a knowledge of biology, psychology, anthropology, sociology, and economics as well as the more familiar disciplines of history and politics. Kenneth Waltz's *Man, the State, and War* is one systematic attempt to understand the causes of war through the use of levels of analysis. Waltz classifies various theories of war according to whether they locate its motive forces in the nature of human beings, the nature of the state, or the nature of the system of states. His analysis provides the basis for the following discussion.

Individual Causes of War

Many theorists believe the causes of war lie in enduring tendencies in the makeup of the human species. They assume that, no matter how elaborate the international schemes of control or how strong the rational incentives to cooperation, human nature is so flawed by evil and by aggressive impulses that humankind will inevitably turn to war. The parable of the Frog and the Scorpion captures this image of the controlling influence of human nature:

> One day a frog and a scorpion, bitter enemies by nature, found themselves confronting one another on a river bank. Frog wanted to pass over the stream, but Scorpion stood in the way, insisting that Frog give him a ride across. Frog refused, protesting that he was likely to be stung to death by his mortal enemy. But Scorpion, who was an expert in the logic of deterrence, appealed to Frog's reason, suggesting that he could jump on Frog's back after he had already entered the water. If Frog was stung, then they would both drown, since Scorpion could not swim. Frog, trusting in rational restraint and Scorpion's self-interest in survival, consented to carry his enemy across the river. Frog waded in, Scorpion jumped on, and they proceeded out into the river. About halfway across, the glistening flesh of Frog began to tempt Scorpion, and after a few moments of inner struggle, he plunged his stinger into Frog's plump back. As they both went down, Frog cried out: "Why have you stung me? Now we will both die!" Scorpion stammered: "I . . . I don't know. . . . Perhaps it is my nature to sting!"

At the most basic level, then, war arises out of the desires, emotions, and irrational impulses of individuals. Foremost among these impulses is *instinctual aggression,* a propensity to violence such as we see in the unfettered aggression of young children, the elaborate playing out of macho fantasies in sport, cinema, and popular culture, and the viciousness of criminals. It is easy enough to see war as an organized extension of such behavior. As Albert Einstein remarked in a letter to Sigmund Freud: "Man has within a lust for hatred and destruction. . . . It is a comparatively easy task to call this into play and raise it to the level of a collective psychosis."

Konrad Lorenz's research in animal behavior has led him to conclude that war can be traced to instinctual impulses. By the process of natural selection, the most aggressive animals survive, mate, and pass along their aggressive traits. So might human evolution have encouraged the propensity to fight — a propensity that is functional so long as destructive means are limited and war can confer a substantial advantage on the victor. Lorenz's animal experiments have shown that among the lower species, aggression plays an important role in self-defense, the rationing of food resources, and the selection of mates. But it is always bounded by an instinctual inhibition against unlimited violence toward one's own species. The inhibition is biologically triggered when the victim of an attack gives the appropriate signal of submission, and the power of the inhibition is in direct proportion to the lethality of the species. Human beings lack lethal natural weapons like teeth, claws, and poison stings, so their

---

FIGURE 1-6

THE WORLD AT WAR

The Americas	Africa
Guatemala Central America's bloodiest war. Military fights leftist guerrillas living among the nation's Indian peasants. Right-wing death squads seek to annihilate rebel sympathizers. **War since 1966** **Deaths: 138,000 (72% civilian)**	**Sudan** Civil war between Sudanese People's Liberation Army, representing Christian, animist southerners, and military government backed by Islamic, Arab northerners. **War since 1983** **Deaths: 506,000 (99% civilian)**
El Salvador Leftist Farabundo Martí National Liberation Front fighting to overthrow Salvadoran Government. U.S. military and economic aid to government exceeds $3 billion. **War since 1979** **Deaths: 73,000 (70% civilian)**	**Burundi** Government troops dominated by minority Tutsi tribe, massacred thousands of majority Hutu tribe, rekindling ethnic conflict. **War since 1988** **Deaths: 5,000 (100% civilian)**
Nicaragua Three years after leftist Sandinistas overthrew Somoza family dynasty, *contras* with U.S. support launched civil war. U.S. military aid to *contras* stopped in 1988. Cease-fire reached June 1990. **War since 1981** **Deaths: 25,000 (40% civilian)**	**Somalia** Civil war along the Ogaden desert border with Ethiopia as Issaq tribe seeks overthrow of government led by President Mohamed Siad Barre. **War since 1988** **Deaths: 55,000 (91% civilian)**
Colombia Criminal syndicates terrorize democratic government and operate global cocaine-traffic network from Colombia. Leftist guerrillas and at least 140 death squads add to the havoc. **War since 1986** **Deaths: 22,000 (64% civilian)**	**Ethiopia** Secessionist rebels from five regions battle Marxist government, most prominently in Eritrea. War-induced famine a major factor in casualties. **War since 1974** **Deaths: 570,000 (88% civilian)**
Peru Ultra-leftist Shining Path guerrillas seek overthrow of democratic government, now control much of Peru's coca-growing peasantry in league with cocaine traffickers. **War since 1983** **Deaths: 17,000 (53% civilian)**	**Angola** Civil war over tribal, ideological differences followed independence from Portugal. U.S. and South Africa support rebels; Soviet Union and Cuba back Marxist regime. **War since 1975** **Deaths: 341,000 (94% civilian)**
	Mozambique End of Portuguese colonialism brought civil war between new Marxist regime and Renamo rebels backed by Rhodesia and South Africa. Famine worsened by the war. **War since 1975** **Deaths: 1,050,000 (95% civilian)**

instinctual inhibition against violence is weak. Unfortunately, humankind has been able to fashion weapons of destruction that go far beyond the feeble limits of instinct. Thus, according to Lorenz, the aggressive urge has escaped the bounds of natural design, allowing humans to kill their own species without mercy or limit.

In a similar manner, sociobiologist Edward O. Wilson argues that human beings are biologically programmed for "unreasoning hatred" and a violent

Middle East	Asia	
Lebanon Multisided civil war started in 1975 between Muslims, Maronite Christians and Druse Lebanese, joined by Syrians, Iranians and Palestinians. Israel invaded in 1982. **War since 1982** **Deaths: 63,000** **(65% civilian)**	**Afghanistan** Communist military overthrow of civilian government sparked insurrection among Islamic guerrillas. Soviets intervened, lost 15,000 soldiers before leaving in 1989. **War since 1978** **Deaths: 1,300,000** **(62% civilian)**	**Cambodia** Vietnam ousted ultra-leftist Khmer Rouge, established puppet regime. Khmer Rouge and two other groups launched guerrilla campaign against Vietnam-backed government. **War since 1978** **Deaths: 65,000** **(22% civilian)**
Iran (Two wars) Iran and Iraq waged all-out war to overthrow each other's governments; cease-fire reached July 1988. **War since 1980** **Deaths: 1 million** **(10% civilian)** Islamic revolution toppled monarchy in 1979, but violence continues between religious and secular dissidents. **War since 1978** **Deaths: 88,000** **(80% civilian)**	**India** Sikh religious separatists seek independent theocracy in the Punjab. Police and Sikh militants both accused of widespread use of terror. **War since 1983** **Deaths: 14,000** **(79% civilian)** **Sri Lanka** Tamil separatists fighting Sinhalese-dominated government. India intervened to disarm Tamils after government concessions, Sinhalese fighters seek to expel Indians and nullify Tamil gains. **War since 1984** **Deaths: 30,000** **(60% civilian)**	**Indonesia** End of Portuguese colonial rule followed by Indonesian invasion and annexation of East Timor island. East Timorese continue to resist. **War since 1975** **Deaths: 150,000** **(67% civilian)** **Philippines** (Two wars) Communist New People's Army fights classic guerrilla insurgency to overthrow the government. **War since 1972** **Deaths: 40,000** **(50% civilian)**
Iraq After cease-fire with Iran, Iraq set out to crush rebellious Kurdish minority. Government has used poison gas. **War since 1988** **Deaths: 10,000** **(90% civilian)**	**Burma** Frontier rebels from 11 ethnic groups fight for autonomy from military regime. Pro-democracy Burmese students joined rebels after 1988 military crackdown. **War since 1985** **Deaths: 9,000** **(67% civilian)**	Muslim insurgency directed by the Moro National Liberation Front aimed at achieving autonomy for southern islands in the Philippines. **War since 1972** **Deaths: 35,000** **(57% civilian)**

Note: War, as defined by William Eckhardt, Lentz Peace Research Laboratory, is "any armed conflict, involving at least one government, and causing at least 1,000 deaths per year."

response to perceived threats to their safety or possessions. Because power and privilege have gone to those with no inhibitions about killing their fellows, violence has become a learned behavior, expressed in the tendencies to separate people into friends and aliens, to fear deeply the actions of strangers, and to solve conflict by aggression. By persisting over hundreds of thousands of years, Wilson maintains, such behaviors have become genetically embedded in the human species.

Sigmund Freud, the founder of modern psychology, believed that the human species lives in a precarious balance between the instinctual impulses of the unconscious and the civilizing prohibitions of conscience. Within everyone's unconscious mind, according to Freud, is the urge to break free of civilized restraints, by violence if necessary, to fulfill one's primal needs. Along with this urge goes a kind of death wish whose purpose is to relieve the tensions of such a psychically divided existence. Collectively, these unconscious impulses are the fuel for war. Peace depends on how well the conscience can repress or redirect them, as when parents discipline their children, institutions socialize individuals, states police and order their societies, or cultural conditioning restrains aggressive behavior.

Individual *psychic disorders,* such as neurosis and megalomania, also contribute to destructive political behavior. Both Woodrow Wilson and Adolf Hitler, although motivated very differently, acted in self-defeating ways that were rooted in mental illness. The need of both to combat an "inner enemy" led them to justify their decisions for war in terms of a Manichean worldview that established rigid distinctions between friend and enemy, between the absolute morality of one's own acts and the absolute evil of a depersonalized other. Even ordinary citizens tend to project their inner fears on an outer enemy, attributing to foreigners the aggressive impulses they refuse to acknowledge in themselves. Personal insecurities take political form when military conflict can serve as a proving ground for one's manhood or when military objects can be treated as unconscious sexual surrogates. For example, just as Madison Avenue sells liquor, cars, and cigarettes through sexual innuendo that suggests their manliness, the Pentagon has appealed to the latent machismo of legislators in trying to sell them on the MX missile. Just before one decisive debate, it placed in the lobby of Congress scale models of large Soviet rockets next to smaller (though technologically superior) American rockets; the implied message was that if the United States would build the larger and heavier MX, it would have at last something "bigger" with which to compete. The psychological dimension surfaced as well during the Vietnam War in President Lyndon Johnson's personalizing of the conflict. He spoke often of "my war," persistently referred to the Vietnamese in belittling and demeaning stereotypes, and stated with pride and vehemence that "I am not going to lose in Vietnam." In like manner, one of his secretaries of defense gloated to newspaper reporters, after an American bombing of Hanoi: "We cut their peckers off." Harold Lasswell, in *Power and Personality,* explains this kind of powermongering as psychological compensation for personal insecurity and low self-esteem. In his view, many political leaders, particularly those with aggressive or authoritarian tendencies, are attracted to politics just because it is an arena in which they can satisfy their cravings for recognition and control. For them, international relations becomes a competitive domain in which they exercise power without principle or limit in a violent struggle for glory.

Still other individual motivations for violence are feelings of *vanity, greed, insecurity,* or *alienation.* Theologians from St. Augustine to Reinhold Niebuhr have put forward interpretations that blame war on the human propensity for sin. To quote Kenneth Waltz's *Man, the State, and War:*

> Man is a finite being with infinite aspirations, a pigmy who thinks himself a giant. Out of his self-interest, he develops economic and political theories and attempts to pass them off as universal systems; he is born and reared in insecurity and seeks to make himself absolutely secure; he is a man but thinks himself a god. The seat of evil is the self, and the quality of evil can be defined in terms of pride. (p. 21)

Hans Morgenthau, a proponent of the "realist" philosophy of international relations, argues similarly that evil and aggression cannot be removed from human action because of humankind's ineradicable lust for power, a lust so strong that it has transformed churches into political organizations, revolutions into dictatorships, and love of country into imperialism. As Jonathan Swift once said: "The very same principle that influences a bully to break the windows of a whore who has jilted him, naturally stirs up a great prince to raise mighty armies, and dream of nothing but seiges, battles, and victories" (cited in Waltz, p. 4).

The great English philosopher Thomas Hobbes, in his *Leviathan,* has described the state of nature as a condition in which "every man is enemy to every man," with "continual fear, and danger of violent death," and human life is "solitary, poor, nasty, brutish, and short." This condition proceeds from such universal emotions as envy (competition and the search for gain), fear (the search for safety), and pride (the search for glory or reputation), which, according to Hobbes, can be overcome only by the imposition of an absolute authority that holds everyone in awe.

Erich Fromm, in *The Anatomy of Human Destructiveness,* makes a distinction between "defensive" and "malignant" forms of aggression. A violent attack may provoke an aggressive response that is rational and adaptive, or defensive, as opposed to the malignant aggression of those who initiate the violence. Such persons, often alienated or members of groups that have substituted hatred of outsiders for authentic bonds of community, are psychologically separated from their fellow human beings and thereby are driven irrationally to avenge their feelings of loneliness and impotence through sadistic or "godlike" acts of destruction. Like Hobbes, Fromm acknowledges a human propensity to aggression, but he sees it as rooted more in social conditions than in innate predisposition. The impulse varies dramatically from individual to individual, Fromm believes, and in even the most violent it is affected by social conditioning and triggering mechanisms related to basic political and economic conditions. Thus, Fromm is more hopeful than Freud or Hobbes that violence can be curbed by nonrepressive means.

Many social psychologists locate the motivation for war — especially revolutionary wars — in a *frustration-aggression dynamic* that emerges whenever an individual encounters substantial interference with the attainment of strongly desired objectives. Such frustration invites intense anger, which is vented on the persons who are considered the obstacles to fulfillment. When long-standing grievances accumulate within a group, or when one group comes to see another as standing in the way of its most basic objectives, the potential for war increases substantially. This kind of violent response is particularly prevalent in undemocratic societies, in which government indifference and repression increase the sense of frustration. Sometimes the tendency to search for scapegoats causes the frustration to be redirected outward, against persons who are seen as alien. Any deterioration of social conditions in a group consequently increases the probability of conflict with out-groups. For example, some scholars trace the aggressive attitude among declining middle-class elements in Germany before World War II, and their support for German fascism, to the desire of these marginal groups to find a scapegoat for the dislocations of a modernizing economy. Although war could not restore their power, it did serve to vent their frustrations.

Most revolutionary wars arise from the universal human desire for *freedom from oppression*. Any structure of exploitation or domination, with grossly unequal distribution of status and rewards, can be expected to provoke a violent effort to achieve equality and social justice. Twentieth-century history is filled with revolutions and civil wars aimed at overthrowing oppressive elites, often of foreign origin or with distinct racial identities. Such internal wars occur when a sense of grievance or injustice and a perception of relative deprivation arise among the majority population, when rising expectations outpace the actual level of satisfaction. The concept of *relative deprivation* helps explain the paradox of why very poor traditional societies have remained stable, while the great revolutions of Europe and the Third World have come at times when conditions were actually improving. Revolutionary violence is a product of the spread of political and economic ideas that change the expectations of ordinary citizens about their lives, coupled with their frustrations over the temporary setbacks that are bound to occur in a transitional phase. Revolutionary wars are not only a device of emancipation but a symptom of the turmoil a society undergoes in the process of modernization.

Pessimists — or realists, to use the conventional term of political theory — see no end to war because injustice will always exist and aggressive impulses can never be more than temporarily curbed. How, then, to account for peace and respect for social order? If human aggression is always present, we are left with no explanation for those moments when individuals choose peaceful relations or refrain from aggressive acts. Inequalities of power that might tempt an aggressor have existed in all times and places, but they have not always led to war. Governments take repressive actions every day, but rebellious responses do not always follow. The potential for aggression is constantly present in everyone's instinctual endowment, yet war is intermittent. Biologically and psychologically, the human species is assumed to be relatively stable, while the character of war has changed over the centuries, from religious and dynastic wars to nationalist and revolutionary/ideological wars. If human nature has not changed over time but the nature of war has, then the immediate causes of particular wars must lie outside the realm of the individual.

Why do the human traits that can cause international wars not find an outlet instead in war within a state? At least one reason is that the state is effectively organized to channel aggression, to provide alternative avenues of conflict resolution, and, with its legitimate monopoly of violence, to suppress all those who would challenge the present order by force. But if those mechanisms can encourage us to act peacefully some of the time, why not all the time? Because, as Seyom Brown points out in *The Causes and Prevention of War,* the mechanisms themselves can be repressive, leading to unhappiness, neurosis, irrational behavior, and aggressive outbursts.

The success of collective inhibitions to violence may depend, therefore, on the character of the culture. Some countries and cultures are more aggressive than others because their patterns of socialization redirect rather than dissipate aggressive impulses. Both Germany and Russia, which developed along highly repressive and authoritarian lines, have long histories of militarism. Some analysts blame their propensities to war on the special way in which these cultures have permitted the aggressive instinct to take organized expression — through the glorification and ideological justification of violence. Another example of such glorification of war is the impact of Fascism on the behavior of Italians under dictator Benito Mussolini, who exhorted his people in these terms:

> War alone brings up to their highest tension all human energies and puts a stamp of nobility upon the people who have the courage to meet it. All other trials are substitutes, which never really put a man in front of himself in the alternative of life and death. A doctrine, therefore, which begins with a prejudice in favor of peace is foreign to Fascism.

Clearly, then, war is more likely when the human aggressive drive is harnessed by cultural mechanisms to a national purpose or belief system.

Optimists — the idealists of political theory — take the existence of civil order as testimony to the civilizing power of social institutions. They believe the individual can be reformed through education, psychosocial readjustment, and the channeling of aggression. While conceding that human aggression and psychological maladies can be contributing causes of war, they argue nonetheless that there are social cures for these personal causes. Then the question becomes: Can societal restraints be carried over to an international scale? This depends on how states are organized and whether they are able to prevent aggressive individuals from gaining the reins of power. Peace also depends on whether states have the same incentives to restrain their use of violent means abroad as they do at home. To answer this question, we must pass on to analysis at the level of the nation-state.

So far, from our analysis at the individual level, we can assert that wars always begin with the individual acts of leaders. They do not simply happen, but are initiated by individuals who feel compelled to use violence; the truly accidental or catalytic war is rare. We have found that certain biological and psychological forces shape the outlook of decision makers who risk violent means, as do their particular motivations and attitudes. But these explanations all assume that the decision for war is basically emotional or irrational. What can explain why individuals *rationally* choose war, even at known risk to their own lives? For this, we must look to the individual's identification with a higher cause, a decision-making role, or a set of national interests, and to the larger institutional setting within which the decision for war is taken. Explanations of war at the level of the individual may be the most basic (aggression) and the most immediate (the individual act), but they cannot be separated from larger forces working on the individual. Moreover, it is difficult to suppress underlying human instincts or to manipulate the motivations of individual actors at the moment of decision except through institutional restraints and more systematic efforts. So we must seek the cure as well as the causes of war at a higher level of social organization than the individual.

National Causes of War

The anthropologist Margaret Mead has described war as a cultural invention. Although organized warfare between social entities is widespread, a few societies can be found that do not rely on war as a device for resolving conflict. War is unknown, for example, among the Eskimo peoples, the Zuni Indians of the American Southwest, the !Kung Bushmen of the Kalahari Desert, the Arapesh of New Guinea, the Semai of Malaysia, and the Lepchas of Sikkim. It is not simply that they have chosen peace over war, but that their societies lack altogether the idea that disputes can be resolved by the organized use of force. The Pueblo Indians, a gentle people, nonetheless have employed defensive warfare because they have learned the art of war from their more aggressive neighbors. The Lepchas, on the other hand, having no idea of warfare, cannot organize to defend themselves and merely submit to invaders. Robert Knox Dentan describes the peaceful Semai people of Malaysia in similar terms:

> The Semai are not great warriors. As long as they have been known to the outside world, they have consistently fled rather than fight. . . . They had never participated in a war or raid until the Communist insurgency of the early 1950s, when the British raised troops among the Semai. . . . Initially, most of the troops were probably lured by wages, pretty clothes, shotguns, and so forth. Many did not realize that soldiers kill people. When I suggested to one Semai recruit that killing was a soldier's job, he laughed at my ignorance and explained, "No, we don't kill people, brother, we just tend weeds and cut grass." (cited in Brown, p. 5)

War is therefore a product of a particular form of social organization. This becomes clear if we trace the ways in which changing political forms have altered the nature of violent conflict. Under feudalism, conflict took the form of duels, blood feuds, knight errantry, and religious crusades. The rise of consolidated monarchies and empires brought dynastic wars and colonial wars. The last two centuries have witnessed nationalist wars, revolutionary wars of independence or liberation, and ideological wars. Thus, the causes of war have shifted as the nature and aims of states have changed. The crucial assumption we make from this is that states are the principal actors in international affairs and that reasons of state provide the principal motives for war, with individuals involved merely as agents of a larger political entity.

From this focus on social forms and institutional interests, it appears that most modern wars are the product of *nationalism,* which expresses itself in wars of territorial defense, unification, ethnic rivalry, separatism, and irredentism. The idea of the nation-state assumes that political boundaries should correspond to cultural, linguistic, or ethnic identity, making each people into a self-governing community. Both Otto von Bismarck and Adolf Hitler launched wars based on nationalist appeals for the unification of the German-speaking people. The Kurds, divided between Iraq, Iran, Turkey, and the USSR, have fought for centuries to escape domination by alien cultures and to unite as an autonomous people. Palestinians, scattered among dozens of countries, have employed the most extreme of terrorist methods to regain a lost homeland in the Middle East. Nigeria experienced severe civil conflict in the 1960s as its various tribal groups (Ibo, Yoruba, Hausa, and others) fought among themselves for control over or separation from the artificial state entity created by the British colonial occupation. In 1972, the East Pakistanis, separated from the dominant West Pakistanis by both geography and religion, waged a successful war of secession to create the state of Bangladesh. In any state established as an empire or federation, with distinct minority populations, the potential for violence exists. Nationalist sentiments fueled many wars of independence during the era of decolonization. More recently, nationalism has inspired revolutionary movements to separate the Basques from Spain, the Croatians from Yugoslavia, the Sikhs from India, the Irish Catholics of Ulster from Britain, the Tamils from Sri Lanka, the French-speaking Quebecois from Canada, the Namibians from South Africa, and the Eritreans from Ethiopia, to name but a few. Figure 1-7 gives a full listing of contemporary nationalist movements.

A related cause of war is the struggle to gain *internal cohesion and political control* through external conflict. War against a common enemy can sometimes bind together a disunited people and channel the aggression that might otherwise express itself in intragroup conflict. Jean Bodin, the famous French theorist of state sovereignty, has said: "The best way of preserving a state, and guaranteeing it against sedition, rebellion, and civil war is to keep the subjects in amity one with another, and to this end, to find an enemy against whom they can make common cause" (quoted in Waltz, p. 81). Such scapegoating and political manipulation of a foreign threat frequently contributes to hostile relations between states. Anticommunism and exaggeration of the Soviet threat were used regularly in the Cold War to unite opposing parties in the United States behind a bipartisan defense budget, subordinating better relations with the Soviets to domestic political considerations. The Soviets used the same tactic, binding together a multiethnic empire by appealing to the need for a common defense against imperialism and capitalist encirclement. Opposition to an external enemy was a strong force during the anticolonial struggles, when hatred of the European imperial power became a unifying focus for African or Asian peoples who otherwise lacked a common identity. This kind of synthetic

FIGURE 1-7

SEPARATIST AND IRREDENTIST MOVEMENTS

Recent Wars of Secession

Movements in Eritrea, Tigre, and Ogaden regions of Ethiopia (1961–present)
Biafran independence struggle by the Ibos of Nigeria (1966–70), failed
Secession of East Pakistan to create the state of Bangladesh (1971–72), successful
Black Sudan People's Liberation Army vs. Arab government of Sudan (1984–present)
The Dhofar region of Oman, failed
The Kurds in Iran (since 1946) and Iraq (since 1961)
Revolt of Bakongo and Shaba/Katanga province of Zaïre (1960–present)
Arab secessionist movement vs. black regime in Chad (since 1965)
Namibian (Southwest Africa) independence movement vs. South Africa (1968–88), successful
The Polisario Front in Western Sahara vs. Morocco (1975–1989)
The Karens, Kachins, Shans, Chins, Mons, Arkanese in Burma (1948–present)
Separatists in Punjab (Sikhs), West Bengal, Assam, Mizoram, and Nagaland vs. India (1984–present)
Revolts against Indonesian rule in East Timor, Moluccas, Sumatra, Celebes (since 1975)
The New People's Army and the Moro National Liberation Front in the Philippines (since 1969)
Tamil separatists in Sri Lanka (since 1984)

Other Separatist Movements

Basques and Catalans in Spain
Croatians and Albanians in Yugoslavia
Quebecois in Canada
Bretons and Basques in France
Ulster Irish Catholics, Welsh, and Scots in the United Kingdom
Latvians, Estonians, Lithuanians, Ukrainians, Armenians, and others in the USSR
Jura region of Switzerland
Tibet and Sinkiang province of People's Republic of China
Baluchis in Pakistan
Bugandans in Uganda
Independistas in Puerto Rico
Palestinian Intifada in Israel
Miskito Indians in Nicaragua

States and Regions Subject to Irredentist Claims

Togo, claimed by Ghana on grounds of Ewe unification
Mauritania, regarded by some as part of Morocco
Spanish Sahara and Tindouf regions of Algeria, claimed by Morocco
Djibouti (former French Somaliland), claimed by Somalia
Northern Frontier District of Kenya, claimed by Somalia
Palestine (Israel), claimed by Arab nationalists and the Palestine Liberation Organization
Kuwait, claimed by Iraq
Gambia, claimed by Senegal
Cyprus, claimed by both Greece and Turkey
Taiwan, claimed as part of Communist China
Guyana, regions claimed by Venezuela and Surinam
Mongolia and parts of the Soviet Far East, claimed by China
Sabah region of Malaysia, claimed by Indonesia and the Philippines
Kashmir region of India, claimed by Pakistan
Northern Ireland (Ulster), regarded by the Irish Republican Army as part of Ireland
North and South Yemen both claim parts of the other's territory

Unification Movements

North and South Vietnam, divided in 1954, successfully reunited (by force) in 1975
East and West Germany, divided in 1945, officially in 1949; reunited in 1990
North and South Korea, divided in 1948

nationalism may explain why so many new states whose leaders have a fragile grasp on the reins of power have initiated wars that seem irresponsible and unaffordable. For example, it is alleged that Sukarno provoked conflict with Malaysia over West Irian only to consolidate his control in Indonesia. Likewise, considerations of domestic unity and the maintenance of political control are thought to be important factors in the war between Iran and Iraq.

The *economic or material interests* of states are another significant cause of wars. Beyond defense of their territory, groups and states will fight to secure profits, investments, or access to resources. Among primitive peoples, neighboring groups commonly fought over territory and resources. Thomas Malthus, the eighteenth-century English political economist, argued that the pressure of population growth on a declining resource base can prompt a state to wage war for additional living space (with the war also serving as a direct limit on surplus population). A century later, Vladimir Lenin maintained that the cause of all wars is economic competition between advanced capitalist states. The great European empires were created out of capitalism's search for new resources and markets. Once the globe was divided, however, colonial rivalries inevitably led to increasingly violent conflict between the imperial powers, culminating in World War I. Three decades later, the event that precipitated the Japanese attack on Pearl Harbor was an economic decision of the U.S. government — the freezing of Japanese assets and an embargo on the shipment of oil to Japan. Moreover, war production (if not always war itself) has been an important economic stimulus to industrial economies. World War II contributed greatly to America's recovery from the Great Depression; in the postwar era, defense spending became the most reliable means, under Keynesian economic theory, of maintaining aggregate demand through public investment. Where living standards are dependent on particular forms of foreign economic or trade relations, states do not hesitate to go to war to advance or preserve their well-being. Secretary of State Henry Kissinger, for example, would not rule out the use of force against the oil-producing countries of the Middle East if their control over supply or price threatened to produce a "strangulation of the industrialized world." President Jimmy Carter, in like manner, proclaimed the right of the United States to use force to protect its economic interests in the Persian Gulf.

The propensity to war is also stimulated by the presence of a *military-industrial complex* and powerful elites who will profit personally from war. Large industries that stand to benefit from defense production gain access to government decision makers through campaign contributions, lobbying, and the like. For the same reason, defense industries maintain a special relationship with the armed forces, the advocates for most military spending. As the defense sector grows, so also does its influence over such public policy decisions as levels of public spending, arms control proposals, and other matters likely to affect its flow of profits. When the interests of a multinational corporation are involved, a government may go so far as to intervene, either directly or covertly, to protect overseas investments or access to strategic raw materials. Many students of world affairs see the military industrial complex as having a direct interest in promoting antagonisms between states and exaggerating military threats to justify additional spending—behavior that can increase international tensions to the point of war. This kind of manipulation for selfish economic interests can occur in a socialist state as easily as in a capitalist one when the institutional interests of the professional military coincide with those of the state managers in the military sector.

Political and ideological interests provide an additional motive for states to fight one another. The threat of subversion by a rival state may bring a regime to defend its political sovereignty by force. Considerations of national honor may provoke a government to use force to defend its citizens abroad (the official justification for the U.S. invasion of Grenada), to protect its overseas property (President Gerald Ford's intervention with the U.S. Marines to rescue the freighter *Mayaguez*), or to trumpet the power of the state (President Ronald Reagan's bombing of Tripoli, Libya, in retaliation for Moammar Khadafy's terrorist attack on a West Berlin discotheque). Competition between religious faiths has spilled enormous amounts of blood over the centuries. Christian states launched holy crusades against the Muslim infidel during the Middle Ages and then fought continuously among themselves in the sixteenth and seventeenth centuries. Muslim tradition has its own holy war, or *jihad,* which has played itself out most recently in the eight-year war between Sunni Iraq and Shi'ite Iran. The modern equivalent of wars of religion is the ideological competition between capitalist and socialist states. In these conflicts over fundamental religious or ideological differences, involving the very identity of a people or the survival of their way of life, the basic moral objectives of the two sides can be so incompatible that force is the only arbiter.

This willingness to risk war for one's religion, ideology, freedom, or autonomy, even when defeat seems certain, may appear irrational, but it is one of the most insoluble causes of war. Thucydides makes this point in relating an encounter between the Melians and the Athenians during the Peloponnesian War. The invading Athenians tried to persuade the weaker Melians to capitulate by appealing to their prudence and self-interest—the realpolitik argument that self-preservation was the highest value and no dishonor lay in surrendering to a superior force. The Athenians were operating on the principle that states should stand up to their equals, behave with propriety toward their superiors, and treat their inferiors fairly. By such rules, Melos could avoid an unnecessary war. Surrender would be treated with magnanimity, but resistance would bring utter defeat. However, the Melians did not perceive the conflict as one of self-interest, which could be adjusted by reason. They saw it as a conflict of honor. They argued that a free people could not willingly submit to slavery without destroying their very identity, and therefore the outcome was not something that could be bargained for, but only decided by force. We have seen the same kind of conflict in core principles in Cold-War Soviet-American relations and, to a still higher degree, in the Hindu-Muslim conflict over Kashmir, the Turkish-Greek conflict in Cyprus, the Arab-Israeli conflict, the civil war in Lebanon, and the struggle between Iran and Iraq in the 1980s. In some of these instances, the incompatibilities have been so extreme that the warring parties have seemed unable even to talk to one another to adjust their differences except by resort to violent means.

Nationalism, economic interests, and ideological principles are all causal factors that explain war principally by reference to how the state is organized. Two of our most important traditions of political thought, liberalism and Marxism, agree that war's basic cause is the structure and nature of states. The American revolutionary Thomas Paine argued that absolute monarchy, because it lacked popular restraint, tended inevitably toward war. In the same spirit, the French moralist Jean de La Bruyère asked: "How does it serve the people and add to their happiness if their ruler extend his empire by annexing the provinces of his enemies; how does it help me or my countrymen that my sovereign be successful and covered with glory, that my country be powerful and dreaded, if, sad and worried, I live in oppression and poverty?" (quoted in Waltz, p. 98). As Waltz comments, the transitory interests of royal houses may be advanced in war, but the real interests of all peoples are furthered by peace. The majority suffers in war merely to enrich the few and allow them to indulge their kingly ambitions. Woodrow Wilson extended this idea to all forms of arbitrary or authoritarian government, on the assumption that when the people have the opportunity to speak, they as a rule decide for peace. Consequently, liberals view democracy as the uniquely peaceful form of government. While Lenin would agree that a people's government is the only safe guardian of peace, he and other Marxists would add that only socialist systems qualify as truly democratic. In their theory, capitalism is controlled by an exploitative elite that is quite willing to allow common proletarians to die in wars of imperialism that protect the capitalists' interests and profits. Critics of Marxism counter that a principal cause of war in the twentieth century has been the expansive and subversive influence of Communist states committed to world conquest by revolutionary means.

Each of these perspectives locates the cause of war in a particularly aggressive type of state that must somehow be restrained. Thomas Paine advocated revolution against monarchy, to end once and for all wars of empire and dynastic interests. Wilson called for a League of Nations based on the universal principle of self-determination and fought a "war to end all wars" in the hope that victory in World War I would "make the world safe for democracy." Lenin proposed a revolutionary movement of socialist liberation that would overthrow capitalism, unite proletarians around the world, and at one stroke put an end to nationalism, exploitation, and war. In each case, the cure for national or sociopolitical causes of war was the internal reorganization of the state. But few states see themselves as evil or in need of reform to curb their own militaristic tendencies. For this reason, almost all analyses that locate the cause of war in the disordered constitutions of nation-states turn to revolution or external restraint for a cure. So Mao Tse-tung remarked: "War, that monster of human fratricide, will inevitably be wiped out by man's social progress and this will come about in the near future. But there is only one way to do it—war against war" (cited in Waltz, p. 112). Thus, it appears that peace will come only by a war of extermination or by resort to some form of international organization that will restrain "bad" states. Ironically, partisans of world government and realpolitik advocates of the balance of power both look to the systemic level to solve the problem of war. Just as individual aggressions can be curbed only within the civilizing restraints of the state, national aggression occurs only when there is no international community or law to curb violent behavior. Without the latter, the sole device of order left for peace-loving states is to remain armed and maintain a balance of power that can contain aggressive states.

Systemic Causes of War

At the level of the international system, it can be argued that the most basic cause of war is the condition of anarchy that characterizes relations between states. No state desires war, but every state must nonetheless be prepared to resort to it whenever there is a risk that another state may prevail by force. The absence of institutions of international order poses a predicament for individual states: whether to rely on cooperative solutions, through peaceful means, at the risk of losing one's sovereignty, or to look to one's own selfish interests, at the risk of alienating other states and forcing them to arm. The weakness of collective solutions in the absence of enforcement mechanisms is captured well by the French philosopher Jean Jacques Rousseau's parable of the stag and the hare:

> Five men gather together to hunt for food. Each of them can be satisfied by the small part of a stag or the whole of a hare. Since the capture of a deer would more than satisfy everyone, they agree to cooperate in the hunt. Success depends, however, on each man playing his part, without sacrificing the group aim to his own selfish interest. A dilemma emerges when one of them spies a rabbit and is forced to decide whether to satisfy his own hunger immediately or continue in a collective endeavor that may (or may not) bring greater benefit to everyone in the long run. He ponders but a moment, and then snatches the hare and goes off to satisfy his hunger.

As the parable illustrates, someone who is starving to death is very likely to make the selfish choice. By analogy, when a state's survival is perceived to be dependent on protection by its military forces, it is likely to resist disarmament and to choose a go-it-alone option, even at the risk of war. Some insist this is the only *rational* course, given the self-serving nature of existing relations of anarchy. Individuals or states that operate from self-interest will gain, while the altruistic ones will go hungry or suffer defeat. And the more individuals or states that are involved, the more likely it is that deceit or a selfish act by any one of them will bring a tragic result for all. Self-protective responses may assure one's own survival, but they are bound to bring conflict with those who are committed to cooperation and thus feel betrayed. Without some form of sanction or punishment for self-regarding behavior, any cooperative scheme is tragically fated to collapse.

This dynamic lies behind the escalating worldwide accumulation of arms and the competitiveness of international behavior, with outcomes determined by a balance of power rather than by an authoritative system of arbitration or decision. Rousseau has summarized the dilemma in these terms:

> It is quite true that it would be much better for all men to remain always at peace. But so long as there is no security for this, everyone, having no guarantee that he can avoid war, is anxious to begin it at the moment which suits his own interest and so forestall a neighbour, who would not fail to forestall the attack in his turn at any moment favourable to himself, so that many wars, even offensive wars, are rather in the nature of unjust precautions for the protection of the assailant's own possessions than a device for seizing those of others. However salutary it may be in theory to obey the dictates of public spirit, it is certain that, politically and even morally, those dictates are liable to prove fatal to the man who persists in observing them with all the world when no one thinks of observing them towards him.

In short, "to be sane in a world of madmen is in itself a kind of madness." To survive in the jungle of international affairs, the civilized person or nation adopts the tooth-and-claw tactics of the primitive even if that brings the regrettable necessity of fighting wars.

Thus, in the systemic perspective, the principal cause of war is a *change in the balance of power*—that is, a shift in the relative capabilities of states to coerce one another. The classical view is that aggression takes place whenever the distribution of power is *unbalanced*, tempting a potentially dominant power to dictate forcefully to the weak or to fill the power vacuum. Thucydides blamed the Peloponnesian War, for example, on the failure of Sparta and other states to counter the rising power of Athens. The assumption is that competition for power is a basic drive in all societies, that occasions and issues for conflict always exist, and that the immediate cause of wars is the failure to maintain a symmetrical balance of power among states. Recent studies have shown, however, that the most stable periods have been those presided over by a hegemonic power enjoying a position of unchallenged dominance and, conversely, that a relatively even distribution of power may foster competition for the dominant role and occasion frequent wars of adjustment. The international system appears to be most war-prone under circumstances of a *power transition*, when an aspiring but dissatisfied state has acquired new power capabilities and challenges the international status quo. The rise of Napoleonic France and the emergence of Soviet dominance after the collapse of Europe in World War II are two often-cited instances of such a destabilizing shift in power. Some theorists see the competition for power and the tendency for nations to expand as a kind of fundamental social principle that guides all relations between organized groups. Social Darwinists and fascists are among those who see war this way—as a struggle for the survival of the fittest, an evolutionary instrument for facilitating the advancement of civilization by favoring the powerful and vital states over the weak and decadent.

Balance-of-power relations tend to provoke wars over what Seyom Brown calls *derived interests*. These are interests —not vital in themselves— whose loss might erode the power position of a state or its future ability to protect valuable assets or a sacrosanct way of life. States have gone to war, for example, to secure a strategic position or protect an important geopolitical interest, as Britain and France did when Egypt's Gamal Abdel Nasser announced the nationalization of the Suez Canal in 1956. States have fought on behalf of allies, even when they were not directly attacked. The German attacks on Belgium and on Poland precipitated British entry into World Wars I and II not simply because of alliance obligations but because the British perceived that German domination of the continent would eventually jeopardize the security of the British Isles. States have used force to convince an enemy of their credibility and political will — apparently the main motivation behind British Prime Minister Margaret Thatcher's forceful defense of the Falkland Islands against Argentine attack in 1982. States go to war over relatively minor issues or over territory of little intrinsic value because they perceive that the contest is linked to a larger potential threat to their national security. The "domino theory," which held that one country after another would fall to Communism unless it was contained early, offers a classic example of how derived interests can lead to war. The theory encouraged the United States to fight in both Korea and Vietnam, even though their loss posed no vital threat in itself. It was the fear of more falling dominoes that caused American presidents to draw the line before the appetite of the aggressor could be whetted by easy victories.

An inevitable source of friction at the international level is the diversity of cultures, values, and perceptions found among independent states. The narrow interests, parochial attitudes, and partisan vision fostered by a system of competing states are bound to create suspicion and hostility. Thus, another systemic cause of war is *misperception and miscommunication.* Viewing the world through national or ideological lenses causes many distortions of perception. Simplistic images of both socialism and capitalism have exaggerated the imperialist tendencies of each system in the eyes of the other. The judgments of both individuals and groups can be clouded by the psychological stresses involved in making the fateful decision to go to war and by the perceptual distortions that come with trying to interpret the behavior of others from a distance. For example, Irving Janis's *Groupthink* shows how distorted information and group pressures for conformity under crisis conditions created misperceptions among White House decision makers that led to the fiasco of the Bay of Pigs invasion of Cuba in 1961. On the other hand, in the Cuban Missile Crisis of 1962, both President John F. Kennedy and Soviet Premier Nikita Khrushchev accurately perceived the stakes, and each was able to view the situation from his adversary's vantage point, leading to deescalation of the crisis. Rational individuals may nevertheless hold stereotyped images of the enemy as the result of national prejudices or a particularly traumatic historical experience. Negative feelings toward the Japanese have long outlived the events of Pearl Harbor, and the Soviets still conjure the image of a German threat, based on repeated past invasions. Bitter memories die hard, and suspicious expectations, even when unjustified, tend to be self-fulfilling. In times of crisis, old attitudes resist change and threatening messages often drown out conciliatory statements. These problems are compounded by the tendency of political leaders, in an era of mass publics and global communications, to engage in propaganda wars, in which verbal and symbolic politics replaces the private efforts of professional diplomacy. Rhetoric escalates and facts are deliberately distorted to gain political advantage at home or abroad. The net effect is to make all parties disbelieving and mistrustful. A prime example of such misperception occurred in the tense final moments before World War I, when genuinely conciliatory telegrams between Germany's Kaiser Wilhelm and Russia's Czar Nicholas were interpreted as tricks designed to gain them time and advantage in the mobilization for war. Of course, it may be that wishful or irrational thinking precedes all wars. But if power relations could be accurately perceived, outcomes would be predictable and no state that was militarily inferior would dare to fight.

Advanced technology is a new element in communications failures among nations that makes *accidental war* ever more possible. Guided missiles, computer programs, and complex communication networks all have the potential for running out of control. The speed and highly destructive character of modern weapons also put a premium on rapid response, allowing little time for deliberation or a careful assessment that might minimize misunderstanding. Arms races are a perfect example of a pattern of hostility that combines mutual misperception with technical dynamism. A state fears for its security, and those fears cause it to arm defensively, setting off a reciprocal pattern of fear and armament in an adversary. Every increment of arms is interpreted by an adversary as an aggressive rather than a defensive act; what one state considers its margin of safety is viewed by the other as military superiority. One state's decisive technological breakthrough or rapid mobilization can be an overpowering incentive for another state to deploy its own weapons or troops in defense. The cycle of mutual fear spirals ever upward. The miscommunication between heads of state at the outbreak of World War I was reinforced by a long train of earlier misperceptions fostered by entangling alliances, arms races, and interlocking mobilization schedules that made it impossible for the major powers of Europe to step back from the brink of a war no one really wanted. A more recent example of failed communications was the crisis over the Soviet shooting down of Korean airliner KAL 007, which had strayed into Soviet airspace, apparently because its on-flight navigation computer had failed. Suspicious Soviet decision makers, however, assumed that the intrusion was an intelligence-gathering ploy designed to test their air defense capability. Neither Japanese nor Soviet air traffic controllers managed to communicate with the airliner pilot, and failures in the Soviet response capability led to a hasty decision to shoot the plane down just moments before it exited Soviet airspace. The subsequent recriminations on both sides raised hostilities and replayed old Cold War stereotypes, without any acknowledgment of the degree to which the incident was the tragic result of technical failures and miscommunication in the hurried, hostile atmosphere in which the decision making took place.

Structures of domination and *relations of inequality,* the source of many revolutions and anticolonial wars on the national level, are also present as systemic forces that can lead to war. Immanuel Wallerstein speaks of the development of a modern world system in which the technological dynamism of core areas in Europe encouraged their expansion into and control over less-developed areas in the global periphery. The racism of the "white man's burden," the missionary impulses of a "superior" people, and pretensions to empire are not the only explanations for the growth of dominant-dependent relations between states. The same forces that create a dynamic economy at home (one that benefits rather than exploits the people) are responsible for economic expansion overseas, and direct imperial control complements economic dominance wherever a state's resources and military technology give it the political advantage. These dominant states may not by nature be more militaristic or exploitative in their social organization than other states, or be ruled by leaders who are more greedy or power hungry. They are simply enjoying the fruits of hegemony that fall to states upon which fate and historical processes have conferred a technological advantage.

Finally, the resort to war appears to be inevitable so long as the international system lacks alternative conflict resolution mechanisms. Given the conflictual nature of the system, it is no wonder that groups or states turn to *calculated and instrumental uses of violence,* as a device of self-defense or an instrument of last resort for protecting vital interests. Where core values are at stake or groups have mutually exclusive territorial claims, force may be the only way to resolve the dispute. Even when peaceful means are not fully exhausted, leaders may nonetheless prefer war to other options, based on a careful, logical calculation of the costs and benefits. Thus, both the Soviet Union and the United States have undertaken wars of intervention as a means of protecting their security, consolidating a sphere of influence, or gaining political advantage in a contested area. The idea that war can serve as a rational instrument of decision and that political leaders adopt it by choice is disturbing and, to some, morally repugnant. But it is perhaps the most general and comprehensive explanation of why wars occur. Beyond such expedience, "just war" theory provides moral and theological justification for the use of force in self-defense, to protect the innocent, and in pursuit of a righteous cause whose benefits exceed the costs of violence.

If impulses to war lie in the very nature of the international system, what solutions do we have? Since there is no higher level of social organization to which one can appeal, reforms will have to come from within the system. But that road tends to be closed off by the very institutions, habits, and patterns that have shaped the system. Idealists hope for the emergence of an international society whose institutions and incentives will curb selfish national behavior and reverse the negative spiral of hostility and misunderstanding. They look also to technological developments that will improve global communication and erode the national and cultural barriers that foster competition between narrow interests. They call on the human capacity for self-analysis and critical reflection to help us curb the temptation to war, which is becoming ever more costly and less rational, no matter how powerful the selfish incentives. The more pessimistic realists take the fateful view that humankind is helplessly trapped in a predicament that no one state or individual can escape. They say the best we can hope for is a kind of enlightened self-interest that utilizes the balance of power as a systemic device to monitor the peace.

CONCLUSION

Levels of analysis can help us understand more fully the causes of war, but they should not be used slavishly to seek a unique cause of war at a particular level. It is clear from our review that several causes may be present in any given conflict. The German impulse to war in 1939 involved Hitler's psychological disorders, a cultural propensity to aggression, German nationalism, shifts in the balance of military power, misperceptions of Soviet and British resolve, scapegoating, frustration over the economic inequities imposed by the Versailles Peace Treaty, and more. Soviet-American hostility stems from several root causes, including stereotyping of the enemy, mutual misperceptions in the arms race, competition for global preeminence, nationalist appeals, and fundamental ideological differences. The causes of revolutionary war might be located in any one of the three levels — in the workings of relative deprivation (individual focus), the imperialist impulses of capitalism (national focus), or the structural dependencies of an expanding world economy (systemic focus). In some cases, a cause may be operating on several levels at once. Failed communications, for example, can involve distortions introduced by individual irrationality as well as by the systemic influences of technological complexity. The aggressive instincts of individuals can be activated by cultural and ideological mechanisms at the national level. Always we must be careful to look for the way in which our analytic knife slices a complex reality.

Having divided reality analytically, can we unite it again now to arrive at a more adequate explanation? One possibility is to think of war in terms of a basic underlying cause (human motives), a permissive condition (power resources and historic opportunities), and a direct or precipitating cause (conflicting principles or interests). This also permits us to view different levels of analysis interactively. The underlying cause is located in the individual — the fundamental desires of potential antagonists augmented by the universal human propensity for aggression. But every desire of an aggressor cannot be fulfilled; prudence will often dictate that individuals or states take up violence only when there is some promise of success. Access to power and opportunities for aggression — the permissive conditions of the international system — can spell the difference between war and peace. For the realist, warlike impulses can be contained only so long as there is a balance of power. Unassailable deterrent forces can make even the most aggressive individuals behave more reasonably. On the other hand, the idealist interprets the permissive condition as the absence of alternative, nonviolent means of conflict resolution, which forces the naturally peace-loving individual into a reluctant armed defense of vital interests and core values. Violent, aggressive outbursts express the frustrations of actors confronting a system that is unresponsive to their needs and lacking in effective tools for the management of conflict. Thus, (individual) aggression expresses itself intermittently, depending on (systemic) shifts in power, military technology, social organization, and the like. As for precipitating causes, they comprise the transitory issues of state conflict. They do not matter much to the realist, since they only camouflage the underlying impulse to power of all states and serve as mere rationalizations. The idealist sees these immediate causes as the real motives for war — differences in values and interests that invite war whenever channels for nonviolent resolution are lacking. Which of these explanations is more convincing depends on the controlling philosophies of the actors as well as on the value perspective of the onlooker. Chapter 2 will explore such values and how they affect both the events of international affairs and our understanding of them.

QUESTION FOR DISCUSSION (PRO AND CON)

Can war be abolished?

☞ **PRO**

To speak of abolishing war will seem to some ridiculously utopian or impossibly broad. But that attitude only indicates what a powerful grip war has on the imaginations of modern men and women. The war system is so deeply institutionalized — in our budgets, our bureaucracies, our educational systems, our ways of thinking — that it is difficult for us to accept the fact that war is nothing but a cultural invention rooted in social and political patterns with the potential for change. Slavery and absolute monarchy are two traditional institutions that were accepted for centuries as inevitable, natural, even divinely ordained. Then a few abolitionists began to imagine a world without slavery, and that idea spread, along with the democratic notion that no one is permanently endowed with the right to rule over others. In the end, both slavery and the divine right of kings were cast into the dustbin of obsolete social institutions. In like fashion, we can abolish war if we can only begin to imagine a world beyond war. One form of war — revolution — has already been effectively banished from advanced industrial societies. The efficiency of modern governments and their patterns of mass participation have removed any realistic prospect of violent social revolution. Scattered civil violence may still occur, but great revolutions seem likely only in those underdeveloped or authoritarian societies in which the catalytic mobilization of disfranchised masses is still possible. War between the industrial democracies also seems to have atrophied, given their shared political values and high degree of economic interdependence. If a working peace system exists for hundreds of millions of people dispersed over more than thirty distinct states and cultures, why can't it be widened to encompass the entire globe?

Democracy has played a powerful role in institutionalizing nonviolent forms for resolving conflict. Although it is clear that conflict can never be banished totally, we have devised methods of processing it so that grievances can find legitimate, peaceful expression. The existence of systems of law proves that our claims to certain selfish rights are not absolute. We willingly sacrifice complete freedom or autonomy for order. Every day we accept government restraints on our personal sovereignty on behalf of a cooperative social order. All of us may want more power or perfect freedom of action, but that does not mean we are prepared to war with our neighbors to get it. Why should we insist on such conditions of absolute sovereignty for nation-states in the international arena? Moreover, if our individual material interests are largely accommodated through the mechanism of the free marketplace, why can't the international economy prosper without the distorting intervention of national governments? Surely there are compelling reasons, in an era of economic interdependence, to move from a competitive mercantilism, which depends on a nation's willingness to use force to protect its markets, to an unfettered global market system. Such a cooperative orientation has brought more economic benefits and technological advances than has economic outlawry or a go-it-alone philosophy that preserves for states the right to war for narrow national ends. The United States of America was created out of a weak confederation largely for economic reasons, as was the European Economic Community. There is no reason why such economic incentives cannot work on a global scale to reinforce peaceful relations.

Not only is global economic interdependence eroding the bases for war; so is the modern turn toward democratic values in capitalist and socialist systems alike. A non-Communist government in Poland, free elections in Hungary, and the dismantling of the Berlin Wall in East Germany are recent signs of these democratizing impulses within the Communist bloc. The rise of popular access to decision making has gone far to reduce the incentives for both civil and international wars. Apart from the few who are motivated by glory, medals, and other combat-related rewards, individual soldiers have little to gain from fighting, as compared to the risk to their personal well-being. Ordinary citizens can be moved to kill remote strangers only through a command-and-obedience structure reinforced by elaborate ideological justification and the threat of punishment if they shirk their national "duty." Except in cases of invasion or civil war, even the leader's reason for fighting is tied closely to personal status or career and to an identification with a national entity whose power and prerogatives are being defended. If this defense could succeed without war, and if a more thoroughgoing democratization could rob leadership of the opportunity to gain personally from a war pursued at someone else's expense, then the use of violent means could be dramatically curtailed.

Of course, the abolition of war will require more than keeping our political elites accountable. We will also have to change the perceptions and judgments of opposing national leaders that have so often engendered misunderstanding and hostility. While it may be impossible to eliminate all national rivalries and diplomatic wrangling (even between allies), there is every hope that the opening up of communication between East and West will lay old stereotypes to rest. The Cold War was marked by tremendous ignorance and suspicion on both sides, largely for lack of knowledge about the true intentions of either leadership. As a result, defensive fears were translated into expectations of aggression. Today, the Soviet Union is absorbed in internal economic reforms and a program of *perestroika* (political restructuring) that require genuine coexistence with the West if the reforms are to succeed. The Soviet state is experiencing a historic transition from revolutionary challenger to a relatively conservative, bureaucratically entrenched member of the international status quo. It is competing on power terms to protect its superpower interests, but it no longer displays the revolutionary zeal of an orthodox Communist state. If the United States and the Soviet Union can arrive at a stable structure of coexistence, the most basic current source of international tension will be laid to rest. The Soviet leader, Mikhail Gorbachev, shows every sign of serious commitment to an enduring détente and a wide-ranging program of verifiable arms control. If the two superpowers can devise a mutually secure arrangement of arms control and de-escalate the arms race, they will also have disarmed the fears and the self-fulfilling rhetoric of enmity that pave the way to war.

Even where hostile motives and fundamental divisions cannot be removed, we can prevent them from being expressed in armed conflict by removing or limiting the military means. All states have a self-interest today in reaching agreements to restrain the weaponry of large-scale conflict — weapons so destructive that they are useless as devices of conflict resolution. Before nuclear weapons existed, the casualty rate in Europe for the first quarter of this century exceeded the total of war casualties for all preceding centuries combined. Technological developments have led to a tenfold increase in war deaths every fifty years; at that rate, another world war would kill practically the entire population of the globe. This deadly trend has not been lost on the leaders of the world, who have learned from two cataclysmic world wars that they cannot afford a World War III. The horrifying lessons of Hiroshima and Nagasaki have also struck home; they have brought a degree of restraint to superpower relations despite intense ideological antagonism. All this is testimony to the human ability to alter the most deeply ingrained patterns of conduct. Something similar occurred when our self-destructive behavior threatened to deplete the world's petroleum reserves. As oil became scarcer and more expensive, we developed new consumption habits and alternative sources of energy. In like manner, the growing destructiveness of war has brought changes in our behavior consistent with the belief that the human species is highly adaptive. Between 1945 and 1980, major wars became fewer, and wars of all kinds became shorter and more geographically confined, with fewer participants and fewer casualties. The Iran-Iraq War and the Soviet intervention in Afghanistan pushed the casualty rate up after 1980, but successful peace efforts or significant deescalation since 1988 have eased both of those apparently intractable conflicts. The negotiation of a wide range of arms control treaties and the rise of international organizations for the regulation of peace have given impetus to the growing number of formal agreements among contending parties. Once we have passed over a certain threshold of experience and confidence building, there is no reason we cannot agree to abolish war itself, not just particular classes of arms.

Modern science has been responsible for the increased destructiveness of weapons, but it also has brought advanced communications and technological improvements in intelligence-gathering capabilities. Societies that were once closed are becoming transparent. Copy machines and satellite broadcasts are making it impossible for authoritarian elites to control public opinion as they once did. Cultures that were formerly bound in self-reinforcing patterns of national perception are becoming exposed to international influences. Scientific advances in verification techniques have made feasible the effective policing of arms testing, production, and deployment. As the political leadership on each side takes advantage of these techniques, confidence will grow that arms limitations can be made reliable. In an era of industrial economies and mass politics, these limitations do not have to be very stringent, for modern societies are not easily invaded or held forcibly by a foreign power. If every leader knows that an adversary, no matter how intense the dispute, cannot afford to resort to armed means, then the incentives to war are completely undercut. If political leaders once considered war a tolerable device for getting their way, the current level of destructiveness makes such a Machiavellian concept morally obsolete. Today, major interstate conflicts occur not so much out of raw aggression as from interacting fears that compel even peacefully inclined leaders to resort to schemes of military defense so long as there is the chance of armed means being used against them. Once such military systems are in existence, with their built-in suspicions and elaborate war planning, periods of crisis can easily set them in motion. If we can dismantle the war machines and improve our crisis communications, then the conflicts that inevitably occur can be resolved, or tolerated, without war.

☞ CON

War can never be abolished because it is rooted in aggressive impulses of human nature that are impossible to reform or eliminate. The process of growing up necessarily engenders deep conflicts in the human psyche; the reconciliation of our animal natures with civilized behavior involves powerful repressive mechanisms that cannot be kept forever and everywhere under control. Political leaders sometimes display a higher-than-average degree of the aggressive tendencies that are normal for most adults. Adolf Hitler rose to the top of one of the most civilized, technically advanced, and highly institutionalized states without ever being screened out for his irrational tendencies. So long as political leaders possess the ordinary frailties and psychological deformities of the species, they will be tempted to war, for personal reasons as well as reasons of state.

Moreover, the selfish motives of political leaders are primary, overpowering all good intentions and rational peace-keeping arrangements. War will cease only if we can create a world in which no single leader has an incentive to choose war over peace. Unfortunately, deep grievances and fundamental conflicts in national interests are sufficiently common that some leaders will invariably choose war no matter what conflict resolution mechanisms or arms controls are present. This is so, first, because we are genetically programmed to fight over territory. Second, it is because, in the Darwinian struggle for survival, the strong and the aggressive will choose the competitive path for which they are best fitted, and that is war. Also, some individuals will not settle for a merely "just" reward if there is a chance that they can gain still more by mobilizing others to fight on their behalf. Third, peace is not valued for its own sake if the price of peace is the sacrifice of some fundamental value. Ideological or religious attachments can be so strong that they erase all considerations of prudence, as we readily see in the various Middle East conflicts. Perpetuation of the social community and its core values appears to be the overriding aim of all governments, even at the risk of their annihilation in wars of self-defense. Some governments will court war for considerably lesser values — the reinforcement of in-group bonding, for example, by directing animosity toward out-groups and foreigners.

Coercion theorists have pointed out that all societies, despite the rhetoric of democracy, are organized around the control of some groups by others and around control of the masses by an elite. Karl Marx has pointed out that liberal democratic societies tend to preserve the ownership privileges of the propertied classes, who exert control over foreign policy. Thus, even so-called democracies will go to war to protect markets, resources, investments, and the interests of the military-industrial complex. Even if there are no economic interests at stake, democracies still suffer from an elitism that enshrines a class of national security managers who make a profession of war and thereby encourage its occurrence. Robert Michels, a German sociologist, in a study of the most democratic party organizations of Europe, concluded decades ago that every society suffers from an "iron law of oligarchy." Milovan Djilas, a prominent Yugoslav Communist, has pointed out that Russian socialism showed the same tendency toward elitism and the degeneration of democratic controls. He has criticized the Soviet Communist party for becoming a new ruling class with the same old Russian tendencies for class exploitation, national chauvinism, and war. Chinese students were making the same judgment when they rallied by the thousands in Tiananmen Square in Beijing in 1989 to demand reform of the Communist party and democratization of the system — a movement the party elite put down by force.

In sum, war is rooted in the ineradicable desire of some to dominate others. So long as we have attempts at domination, even peoples like the Swiss and the Swedes, who are committed to neutrality and the resolution of conflict without war, must have strong military establishments. This is the prudent concession peace-loving nations have to make in a world filled with aggressive and evil actors. Even those who look to a better future in which power is democratically shared must remain willing to fight those who seek special power and privilege. War was a necessary tool of justice in the American Revolution and dozens of other liberation struggles, and no doubt such just wars will continue to be fought so long as the impulse to tyranny exists.

Many of those who imagine a world without war look to the creation of a world government that will be able to control conflict on the model of domestic societies. But even domestic governments employ forceful constraints. Every stable social order is based on an implicit social contract that empowers a sovereign enforcer to keep the social peace — by curbing criminal tendencies that might threaten social order, for example. But in international relations, the potential lawbreakers are in the majority, and only through the efficiency of arms can the minority control them. World government will consequently look more like empire than like domestic order. If states do manage to come together voluntarily, their confederated global institutions are sure to differ fundamentally from the unified political structure of a nation-state. The member states will not share the same principles of governmental legitimacy, and so the international system is unlikely ever to become the kind of integrated social system that is built on cultural bases of consent. Nor will it have a centrally controlled economic system through which it can reward conformity and compliance with the law. In short, the conditions of civil society simply cannot be re-created on a global scale. We must realize that the civil order we enjoy is based on a government's legitimate monopoly of the means of force and its control of plentiful sources of patronage — in plain language, on arms and economic benefits. But no state will consent to a global planning mechanism for allocating its ever more scarce resources. As for arms, even if nuclear disarmament succeeds, a thorny problem of arms control will remain: how, in a nuclear-disarmed world, are we to distinguish the armed forces that are necessary to maintain order within a state, particularly a dictatorship, from the forces of aggression?

Finally, it is not East-West tensions that are the main source of war today, but the deeply rooted and ineradicable problems of the Third World. Soviet-American détente will not solve the problems of underdevelopment, nor will it calm the intense ethnic, religious, and national rivalries that divide three-quarters of the globe. With many new states struggling for sovereignty, how will we be able to tell an internal civil conflict from an international war? The main causes of war today are various forms of civil violence and revolution. To abolish war, we would have to forbid or repress all these violent movements for social change, or wait until all the revolutionary impulses of the modern world are spent. For war is rooted not only in individual irrationality, the fight for territory, the sense of nationality, and the striving of elites for control. It is also rooted in the poverty and inequality of three-quarters of the human race. To eliminate these conditions, and the revolutionary violence they give rise to, is impossible so long as the world is divided between rich nations and poor. So long as we suffer global scarcities that breed a life-or-death competition for basic resources, we will have war. In sum, the main motives for war today cannot be compromised or solved nonviolently because they involve fundamental questions of identity, self-rule, and control of territory or resources that nations are unwilling to share. People will settle for less only after risking their very lives in wars to secure that which they feel, deeply and passionately, is theirs by right. War is an inevitable fact of political life.

SOURCES AND SUGGESTED READINGS

On Concepts and Levels of Analysis

Bergesen, Albert. "From Utilitarianism to Globology: The Shift from the Individual to the World as a Whole as the Primordial Unit of Analysis" in Albert Bergesen, ed., *Studies of the Modern World-System.* New York: Academic Press, 1980, pp. 1–12.

Dougherty, James E., and Robert Pfaltzgraff, Jr. *Contending Theories of International Relations.* Philadelphia: Lippincott, 1971.

Knorr, Klaus, and James Rosenau, eds. *Contending Approaches to International Politics.* Princeton, N.J.: Princeton University Press, 1969.

Maul, William. "The Level of Analysis Problem Revisited." *Canadian Journal of Political Science* (September 1973).

Morgan, Patrick M. *Theories and Approaches to International Politics.* San Ramon, Calif.: Consensus Publishers, 1972.

Nye, Joseph S., Jr., and Robert Keohane. "Transnational Relations and World Politics: An Introduction." *International Organization,* vol. 25 (Summer 1971), pp. 329–49. (Also in Robert Art and Robert Jervis, eds., *International Politics,* pp. 497–518.)

Pirsig, Robert. *Zen and the Art of Motorcyle Maintenance.* New York: Bantam Books, 1974.

Schelling, Thomas C. *Micromotives and Macrobehavior.* New York: Norton, 1978.

Singer, J. David. "The Level of Analysis Problem in International Relations" in James Rosenau, ed., *International Politics and Foreign Policy.* New York: Free Press, 1969.

Waltz, Kenneth. *Man, the State, and War.* New York: Columbia University Press, 1954.

Wendt, Alexander. "The Agent-Structure Problem in International Relations Theory." *International Organization,* vol. 41, no. 3 (Summer 1987), pp. 335–70.

On the Nature and Causes of War

Alland, Alexander, Jr. *The Human Imperative.* New York: Columbia University Press, 1972.

Ardrey, Robert. *The Territorial Imperative.* New York: Atheneum, 1966.

Art, Robert J., and Kenneth N. Waltz, eds. *The Use of Force.* Boston: Little, Brown, 1971.

Ashley, Richard K. *The Political Economy of War and Peace.* New York: Nichols, 1980.

Bandura, Albert. *Aggression: A Social Learning Analysis.* Englewood Cliffs, N.J.: Prentice-Hall, 1973.

Barnet, Richard. *The Roots of War: The Men and Institutions Behind American Foreign Policy.* New York: Atheneum, 1972.

Beer, Francis A. *Peace Against War: The Ecology of International Violence.* San Francisco: W. H. Freeman, 1981.

Beitz, Charles R., and Theodore Herman, eds. *Peace and War.* San Francisco: W. H. Freeman, 1973.

Berkowitz, Leonard. *Aggression: A Social Psychological Analysis.* New York: McGraw-Hill, 1962.

Blainey, Geoffrey. *The Causes of War.* New York: Macmillan, 1975.

Boulding, Kenneth E. *Conflict and Defense: A General Theory.* New York: Harper Torchbook, 1962.

Bramson, Leon, and George W. Goethals, eds. *War: Studies from Psychology, Sociology, Anthropology,* rev. and enl. ed. New York: Basic Books, 1968.

Brodie, Bernard. *War and Politics.* New York: Macmillan, 1973.

Brown, Seyom. *The Causes and Prevention of War.* New York: St. Martin's, 1987.

Bueno de Mesquita, Bruce. *The War Trap.* New Haven, Conn.: Yale University Press, 1981.

Calvocoressi, Peter, and Guy Wint. *Total War: Causes and Courses of the Second World War,* rev. ed. New York: Viking, 1989.

Choucri, Nazli, and Robert North. *Nations in Conflict: National Growth and International Violence.* San Francisco: W. H. Freeman, 1975.

Clark, Ian. *Waging War: A Philosophical Introduction.* Oxford: Clarendon Press, 1988.

Claude, Inis. *Power and International Relations.* New York: Random House, 1962.

Coser, Lewis. *The Functions of Social Conflict.* New York: Free Press, 1956.

Davies, James C., ed. *When Men Revolt and Why: A Reader in Political Violence and Revolution.* New York: Free Press, 1971.

Dedring, Juergen. *Recent Advances in Peace and Conflict Research: A Critical Survey.* Beverly Hills, Calif.: Sage Publications, 1976.

Djilas, Milovan. *The New Class: An Analysis of the Communist System.* New York: Praeger, 1957.

Dollard, John, Leonard Doob, Neal Miller, et al. *Frustration and Aggression.* New Haven, Conn.: Yale University Press, 1939.

Eckhart, William, and Edward Azar. "Major World Conflicts and Interventions, 1945–1975." *International Interactions,* vol. 5 (January 1978), pp. 75–110.

Eckstein, Harry, ed. *Internal War: Problems and Approaches.* New York: Free Press, 1964.

Eibl-Eibesfeldt, Irenaus. *The Biology of Peace and War: Men, Animals, and Aggression.* New York: Viking, 1979.

Fabbro, David. "Peaceful Societies." *Journal of Peace Research,* vol. 15 (1978), pp. 67–83.

Falk, Richard A., and Samuel S. Kim. *The War System: An Interdisciplinary Approach.* Boulder, Colo.: Westview Press, 1980.

Farrar, L. L., Jr., ed. *War: A Historical, Political, and Social Study.* Santa Barbara, Calif.: ABC-Clio Press, 1978.

Farrell, John, and Asa Smith, eds. *Image and Reality in World Politics.* New York: Columbia University Press, 1968.

Feierabend, Ivo, Rosalind Feierabend, and Ted Gurr, eds. *Anger, Violence, and Politics: Theories and Research.* Englewood Cliffs, N.J.: Prentice-Hall, 1972.

Frank, Jerome. *Sanity and Survival: Psychological Aspects of War and Peace.* New York: Vintage, 1968.

Freud, Sigmund. *Civilization and Its Discontents.* New York: Norton, 1963.

Fromm, Erich. *The Anatomy of Human Destructiveness.* New York: Holt, Rinehart & Winston, 1973.

Gochman, Charles S., and Zeev Maoz. "Militarized Interstate Disputes, 1816–1976: Procedures, Patterns, and Insights." *Journal of Conflict Resolution,* vol. 28 (December 1984), pp. 585–616.

Gurr, Ted Robert. *Why Men Rebel.* Princeton, N.J.: Princeton University Press, 1970.

Haas, Michael. *International Conflict.* Indianapolis, Ind.: Bobbs-Merrill, 1974.

Houweling, Henk, and Jan Siccama. "Power Transitions as a Cause of War." *Journal of Conflict Resolution,* vol. 32 (1988), pp. 87–102.

Howard, Michael E. *The Causes of War.* Cambridge, Mass.: Harvard University Press, 1983.

————. *War in European History.* New York: Oxford University Press, 1976.

Huntington, Samuel P. "Arms Races: Prerequisites and Results." *Public Policy,* (1958), pp. 41–83.

Intrilligator, Michael, and Dagobert Brito. "Arms Races Lead to the Outbreak of War." *Journal of Conflict Resolution,* vol. 28 (1984), pp. 63–84.

Janis, Irving L. *Groupthink,* 2nd ed. New York: Houghton Mifflin, 1982.

Jervis, Robert. *Perception and Misperception in International Politics.* Princeton, N.J.: Princeton University Press, 1976.

Kara, Karel. "On the Marxist Theory of War and Peace." *Journal of Peace Research,* vol. 6, no. 1 (1968), pp. 1–27.

Kidron, Michael, and Dan Smith. *The War Atlas: Armed Conflict—Armed Peace.* New York: Pluto Press/Simon & Schuster, 1983.

Koistinen, Paul. *The Military-Industrial Complex: A Historical Perspective.* New York: Praeger, 1980.

Lafore, Laurence. *The Long Fuse: An Interpretation of the Origins of World War I.* New York: Lippincott, 1971.

Lalman, David. "Conflict Resolution and Peace." *American Journal of Political Science,* vol. 32 (1988), pp. 590–615.

Lasswell, Harold. *Power and Personality.* New York: Norton, 1976.

Levi, Werner. *The Coming End of War.* Beverly Hills, Calif.: Sage Publications, 1981.

Levine, R. A., and D. T. Campbell. *Ethnocentrism: Theories of Conflict, Ethnic Attitudes, and Group Behavior.* New York: Wiley, 1972.

Levy, Jack S. "Declining Power and the Preventive Motivation for War." *World Politics,* vol. 40 (1987), pp. 82–107.

———. "Misperception and the Causes of War." *World Politics,* vol. 35 (October 1983), pp. 76–99.

———. "Organizational Routines and the Causes of War." *International Studies Quarterly,* vol. 30 (June 1986), pp. 193–222.

———. *War in the Modern Great Power System, 1495–1975.* Lexington, Ky.: University Press of Kentucky, 1983.

Lewontin, R. C., Steven Rose, and Leon J. Kamin. *Not in Our Genes: Biology, Ideology, and Human Nature.* New York: Pantheon, 1984.

Lorenz, Konrad. *On Aggression.* New York: Bantam Books, 1970.

Magdoff, Harry. *Imperialism: From the Colonial Age to the Present.* New York: Monthly Review Press, 1978.

Mead, Margaret. "Warfare Is Only an Invention—Not a Biological Necessity." *Asia,* vol. 40, no. 8 (August 1940), pp. 402–05. (Reprinted in David Brook, ed., *Search for Peace: Readings in International Relations,* New York: Dodd, Mead & Co., 1973.)

Melko, Matthew. *Fifty-two Peaceful Societies.* Canadian Peace Research Institute, 1973.

Melko, Matthew, and John Hord. *Peace in the Western World.* Jefferson, N.C.: McFarland, 1984.

Michels, Robert. *Political Parties.* New York: Free Press, 1959.

Midlarsky, Manus I. *On War.* New York: Free Press, 1975.

Moas, Zeev. *Paths to Conflict.* Boulder, Colo.: Westview Press, 1982.

Mommsen, Wolfgang. *Theories of Imperialism.* Chicago: University of Chicago Press, 1982.

Montagu, Ashley, ed. *Man and Aggression.* New York: Oxford University Press, 1973.

Montross, Lynn. *War Through the Ages.* New York: Harper & Row, 1960.

Morgenthau, Hans J. *Politics Among Nations: The Struggle for Power and Peace,* 6th ed., revised by Kenneth W. Thompson. New York: Knopf, 1985.

Mosley, Leonard. *On Borrowed Time: How World War II Began.* New York: Random House, 1969.

Nelson, Keith L., and Spencer C. Olin, Jr. *Why War?: Ideology, Theory, and History.* Berkeley: University of California Press, 1979.

Nelson, Stephan D. "Nature/Nurture Revisited: A Review of the Biological Bases of Conflict." *Journal of Conflict Resolution,* vol. 18 (June 1974), pp. 285–335.

Nettleship, Martin, ed. *War: Its Causes and Correlates.* Beresford Book Service, 1975.

Niebuhr, Reinhold. *Moral Man and Immoral Society: A Study in Ethics and Politics.* New York: Scribner, 1932.

Nieburg, H. L. *Political Violence: The Behavioral Process.* New York: St. Martin's, 1969.

Nomikas, Eugenia, and Robert North. *International Crisis: The Outbreak of World War One.* Toronto: McGill-Queen University Press, 1976.

O'Connell, Robert L. *Of Arms and Men: A History of War, Weapons, and Aggression.* New York: Oxford University Press, 1989.

Organski, Λ. F. K., and Jacek Kugler. *The War Ledger.* Chicago: University of Chicago Press, 1980.

Prosterman, Roy L. *Surviving to 3000: An Introduction to the Study of Lethal Conflict.* Belmont, Calif.: Duxbury Press, 1972.

Quester, George H. *Offense and Defense in the International System.* New Brunswick, NJ: Transaction Books, 1988.

Reeves, Emery. *The Anatomy of War.* New York: Viking, 1947.

Richardson, Lewis. *Arms and Security.* Pittsburgh, Pa.: Boxwood Press, 1960.

Rosecrance, Richard. *International Relations: Peace and War.* New York: McGraw-Hill, 1973.

Rosen, Steven, ed. *Testing the Theory of the Military-Industrial Complex.* Lexington, Mass.: D. C. Heath, 1973.

Rummel, Rudolph. *Understanding Conflict and War.* 4 vols. Boulder, Colo.: Sage, 1975–79.

Russett, Bruce, ed. *Peace, War, and Numbers.* Beverly Hills, Calif.: Sage Publications, 1972.

Schellenberg, James A. *The Science of Conflict.* New York: Oxford University Press, 1982.

Simmel, Georg. *Conflict and the Web of Group Affiliations,* trans. Kurt Wolff. New York: Free Press, 1955.

Singer, J. David. "Accounting for International War: The State of the Discipline." *Journal of Peace Research,* vol. 18, no. 1 (1981), pp. 1–18.

Singer, J. David, ed. *The Correlates of War.* New York: Free Press, 1979.

Singer, J. David, et al. *Explaining War.* Beverly Hills, Calif.: Sage Publications, 1979.

Singer, J. David, and Melvin Small. "War in History and in the State of the World Message" in William D. Coplin and Chas. W. Kegley, Jr., eds., *Analyzing International Relations*. New York: Praeger, 1975, pp. 220–48.

Siverson, Randolph, and M. Tennefoss. "Interstate Conflicts: 1815–1965." *International Interactions*, vol. 9 (July 1982), pp. 147–48.

Small, Melvin, and J. David Singer. *Resort to Arms: International and Civil Wars, 1816–1980*. Beverly Hills, Calif.: Sage Publications, 1982.

Small, Melvin, and J. David Singer, eds. *International War: An Anthology and Study Guide*. Homewood, Ill.: Dorsey Press, 1985.

Smoke, Richard. *War: Controlling Escalation*. Cambridge: Harvard University Press, 1977.

Snyder, Glenn H., and Paul Diesing. *Conflict Among Nations: Bargaining, Decision Making, and System Structure in International Crises*. Princeton, N.J.: Princeton University Press, 1977.

Stagner, Ross. *Psychological Aspects of International Conflict*. Belmont, Calif.: Brooks-Cole, 1967.

Stoessinger, John. *Why Nations Go to War*, 4th ed. New York: St. Martin's, 1985.

Thompson, William R. *On Global War: Historical-Structural Approaches to World Politics*. Columbia: University of South Carolina Press, 1988.

Tilley, Charles. *From Mobilization to Revolution*. Reading, Pa.: Addison-Wesley, 1978.

Van Creveld, Martin. *Technology and War: From 2000 B.C. to the Present*. New York: Free Press, 1989.

Vasquez, John A. "The Steps to War: Toward a Scientific Explanation of Correlates of War Findings." *World Politics*, vol. 40 (1987), pp. 108–45.

Vigor, P. H. *The Soviet View of War, Peace, and Neutrality*. London: Routledge & Kegan Paul, 1975.

Von der Mehden, Fred R. *Comparative Political Violence*. Englewood Cliffs, N.J.: Prentice-Hall, 1973.

Wallerstein, Immanuel. *The Modern World System I: Capitalist Agriculture and the Origins of the European World-Economy in the Sixteenth Century*. New York: Academic Press, 1974.

Waltz, Kenneth. *Man, the State, and War*. New York: Columbia University Press, 1954.

Wilson, Edward O. *On Human Nature*. Cambridge: Harvard University Press, 1978.

Woito, Robert. *To End War: A New Approach to International Conflict*. New York: Pilgrim Press, 1982.

Wright, Quincy. *A Study of War*. Chicago: University of Chicago Press, 1964.

I
VALUES

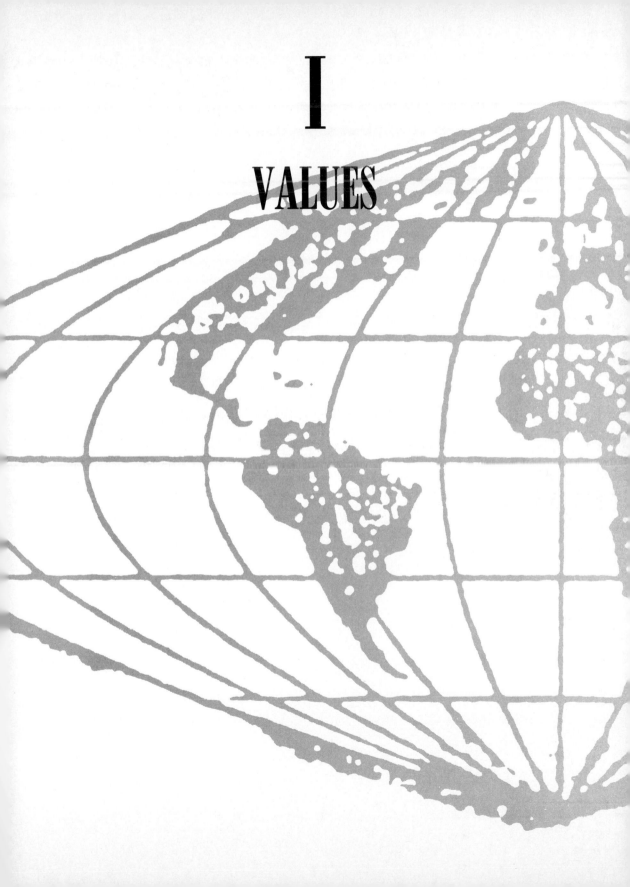

VALUES IN THEORY AND PRACTICE

Power has traditionally been the dominating feature of international relations—power exercised openly and vigorously by political leaders preoccupied with increasing their influence. But the accumulation or exercise of power is not a self-justifying activity, nor is power a concrete entity that can be stockpiled, like oil or money. Power is more accurately viewed as an instrument of *exchange* whose nature we cannot understand without knowing *who* the participants in the exchange are, *why* they have acted as they have, and *what* they perceive to be at stake. That is, power is a relationship of influence involving perceptions, motivations, and conflicting aims. Despite the occasional claim that everyone craves power for its own sake, it is most useful to evaluate power in terms of the *values* or interests it serves.

Value conflicts lie at the center of international affairs. Politics, by its nature, deals with questions that have at least two right answers, with problems that are not amenable to objective or technical solutions. "Right" answers depend on what each side values the most and whether it can achieve those values through a given political solution. The lack of an accepted consensus on values is what makes sovereign states resort so often to force: they lack institutional means for collective decision-making and, more fundamentally, the community of values that allows common institutions to arise and function effectively. Contested values—underlying conflicts in interests and perceptions—are the real motive forces of international relations.

Value conflicts are apparent in the different terms states and ideologies use to define themselves. Political leaders express the cultural values and orientation of the societies in which they are raised—even in authoritarian systems, which do not formally represent the values of the citizenry. The decisions leaders make are based on different perceptions of their adversaries, competing definitions of the national interest, and conflicting personal and political priorities. In fact, the reason states and politicians seek power is as a means of protecting their values or imposing them on others.

Values condition individual perceptions as well. Ordinary citizens all have prejudices and preferences about foreign events, to which they respond with interest or outrage, depending on their value frameworks. Even ignoring international affairs is a value statement in itself, since it places politics below business or sports in the hierarchy of values. The actions a citizen approves or disapproves depend almost entirely on that person's nationality, party affiliation, or political values, and rarely on a dispute over the facts.

Yet even the "facts" of international affairs are influenced by the values of those who report them. A news reporter must sort out a complex set of data to arrive at a coherent account of events. The order thus imposed on a chaotic happening is already an act of interpretation reflecting the values and judgments of the one attempting the description. The filtered or biased nature of the news is obvious in *Pravda,* the official Soviet Communist party newspaper, but such bias occurs, in more subtle forms, everywhere in the world, even when complete objectivity is intended. If a reporter's "angle" or "slant" can itself lead to conflicting interpretations and reactions, it is no wonder there is such controversy today about bias in the media.

If reporters and readers interpret events differently, it should be no surprise that scholars of international relations do also. Their differences over both policy and methods reflect the value commitments of various schools of thought. We will discuss some of the problems that emerge from the conflicting values of the *traditional,* the *Marxist,* and the *behavioral* approaches in the next part of this chapter. Then we will consider the tension between the "ideological" and "pragmatic" orientations in international diplomacy. Two predominant, and opposing, value perspectives — *realism* and *idealism* — shape the actions of diplomats and political leaders. These terms refer, of course, to contrasting "ideal types" — a sort of caricature of the actual positions of statesmen or scholars. Few of us represent an extreme or pure type; most of us move along a continuum, closer to one type or another depending on the issue. These ideal types nonetheless provide a convenient framework for uncovering the way in which values shape both the theories of international affairs and the actions of decision makers.

The Role of Values in Analysis

A question of much dispute among scholars is whether it is possible to study international relations scientifically. Behavioral scientists have challenged the traditional forms of scholarship for being insufficiently systematic and objective, and the Marxist school also lays claim to a scientific method, criticizing even the behaviorists for hidden bias and for employing incorrect categories of analysis. To evaluate these competing claims, let us start by looking at some of the strengths and weaknesses of the traditional approach.

The Traditional Approach

In the classical, or traditional, school of thought, ethical questions are regarded as central, and scholars must employ both judgment and intuition to make sense of human phenomena that do not lend themselves to quantifiable, objective, or unique conclusions. Human beings are complex and unpredictable by nature. Moreover, most political questions are so essentially contested that they cannot be resolved in a detached manner that rules out bias or underlying value considerations. According to the traditionalist, the scientific method — creation of abstract, value-free models and investigation only of matters that can be precisely measured — ignores the most important elements of international affairs and leaves the scientist proving the obvious or the trivial.

Traditional scholars believe that philosophy, law, and ethics are the appropriate, even essential, tools for dealing with international relations, since these fields accept moral reason as a common human faculty and an arbitrator of political differences. Only after Machiavelli and Hobbes did statecraft (mistakenly) come to be considered apart from ethics, moral questions, and value conflicts; likewise, today's scientific worldview sees facts and values as two distinct entities. Historically, theory and practice were not widely separated, so that studies of international affairs tended to be commentaries on diplomatic history or analyses of institutions with an eye to successful political action. Even Niccolo Machiavelli, the political philosopher widely regarded as the founder of a modern "science" of international relations, was a professional diplomat, and the principles of statecraft outlined in his famous *The Prince*, completed in 1517, were written as practical advice to a reigning monarch. The traditional approach, strongly rooted in political philosophy and history, does not divorce the question of what is morally right from what is politically useful. Its judgments require events ("facts") to be placed in a value context for proper interpretation.

Contemporary scholars who have adopted the traditional approach argue that international relations is too subjective and multifaceted to lend itself to scientific analysis. How does one quantify power, for example? To focus on a specific historical context: evaluating the bases of Vladimir Lenin's power at the time of the Bolshevik Revolution involves an extremely complex set of events and a very subtle leader-follower relationship. We would have to begin by examining the historical conditions that created the potential for revolutionary turmoil. Then we would have to explain why Lenin, more than any other person, perceived this historic opportunity and possessed leadership attributes that appealed to important revolutionary elements. We would also have to explain how his charisma, his organizational skills, and his ideological appeals were able to overpower not only the Czarist regime but the numerous non-Bolshevik opposition groups that actually constituted a majority at the time. A thorough treatment might even require the traditionalist to employ some modern scientific methods, utilizing psychobiography, for instance, to explore the personal qualities that made Lenin a great revolutionary figure. But at some point the imperfections of the science of psychology would impose limits; the very choice of a psychological model—say, Freudian analysis—involves a judgment. There is no consensus among the behaviorists themselves about the validity of their various analytic tools. Evaluations as broad as the Lenin example inevitably encounter a tangled train of historical events and a great number of intangible psychological factors whose interpretation requires the scholar to make suppositions, offer judgments, and hazard guesses, sophisticated and well informed though they may be.

Another kind of question the classicist might raise is this: Could the Russian Revolution have occurred without Lenin? The behavioral scientist is likely to reject such a question as too speculative and hypothetical, since we cannot experiment with history in the same way as the scientist experiments in the laboratory by removing certain variables and substituting others. But it is precisely such hypotheses that help us unravel the chain of cause and effect, and so the traditionalist must pose them, even if the character of politics and history does not allow for scientific controls.

To continue with the example of Lenin's rise to power, the question raises problems for the Marxist theoretician as well as for the behaviorist. A key to Lenin's success was his charisma, a great revolutionary force in that tradition-bound epoch. It gave him a personal domination over events and marked him as a leader who defied predictions and made the unexpected happen. Lenin was able to stand Marxism on its head, exchanging its economic determinism for a program of political voluntarism by a self-conscious elite that launched a socialist revolution in the most backward country in Europe. That directly contradicted Marx's theory of how history works and his prediction that Communist revolution would occur first in the most advanced capitalist state.

Passing from the question of Lenin's power to an evaluation of the power of an entire nation-state leads us into a still more complex domain. The traditionalist argues that state power cannot be adequately described by the methods of the Marxist or the behavioral scientist. The behaviorist is inclined to exaggerate the effect of those concrete variables that can be measured—such as population, geography, economic and military forces—and to ignore intangible factors that are difficult to assess objectively—ideology, political will, quality of leadership, public morale, national reputation, organizational effectiveness. In fact, the classicists point out, many a war has been lost by an "objectively superior" power because it underestimated the impact of these latter forces—a mistake the United States made in the Vietnam War. Marxist analysis also has its blind spots. The Soviets became stuck in a terrible Vietnam-like stalemate in Afghanistan because Marxist theory did not give sufficient weight to the power of religion and the role of Islamic fundamentalism. Likewise, Marxist-Leninist predictions about capitalist wars and Third World revolutions, based on class analysis, have been consistently upset by the influence of modern nationalism, which has proved to be the most potent force of the twentieth century. For adequate judgments about world events, there seems to be no substitute for the eclectic, qualitative, and necessarily subjective methods of the traditionalist.

The Marxist Approach

Marxists criticize the traditional approach as description without explanation. To recount diplomatic history without introducing class analysis or the dialectical forces that drive history is to engage in mere chronology. At its worst, the Marxists say, traditional scholarship serves only as rationalization, covering up the true motivations of political actors and hiding the prejudices of scholars even from themselves. So Machiavelli could set out rules of prudence for a powermongering prince without understanding the authentic economic bases for power in a modern state or the motivation of statesmen to protect the property rights of the ruling class. Likewise, moralists discuss standards of conduct under international law without recognizing that these standards are rules of the game imposed on weak states by the powerful. Moreover, such standards embody conceptions of morality that reflect the cultural and political prejudices of capitalist states eager to protect the status quo.

Karl Marx, the nineteenth-century philosopher and political economist, felt that the traditional approach lacked sufficient rigor in not supplying a *systematic* explanation for the behavior of the ruling classes. He also desired to articulate certain laws of history that he believed gave a predictive power to his generalizations about political and economic affairs. In this sense, Marx was one of the first to attempt a scientific explanation of international affairs. He nonetheless preserved the classical school's integration of theory and practice, finding it impossible to separate facts and values or to divorce the actor from the political and ideological prejudices imposed by his social history and class position.

Marxist scholars claim to be more scientific than their behavioral colleagues because, they say, the typical Western scholar is nothing but an apologist for capitalist values and does not possess insight into the objective laws of history. Skeptics will certainly want to examine carefully the grounds on which any scholar, Marxist or behaviorist, claims to be scientific. The dispute does show us that in our technological era, in which science has become the legitimizing worldview of modern culture, many groups are competing for the prestige of being called scientific.

Lenin extended Marxist ideas more fully into the international sphere. Marx argued that the state had emerged as a special apparatus for coercion in the context of the class society, which consisted of a ruling group in control of the forces of production and the exploited majority, whose labor was appropriated for the benefit of the few. Marx originally had predicted that this class division would become so acute in advanced industrial societies that the societies would break down in revolutionary turmoil. Lenin's contribution was to show how capitalism had temporarily smoothed over these internal contradictions through an imperialism that enslaved whole peoples for the benefit of the colonizing power. This internationalization of the class system, and the creation of a system of dominant and dependent states, took place through competition between capitalist states for investment opportunities, overseas markets, and cheap sources of raw materials. By such means did Europe and America reduce the whole of the non-Western world to colonial or dependent status within an international market economy systematically rigged to favor rich and powerful states. According to Marxists, this competition lies at the root of all modern wars, whether they be the world wars of European states struggling for economic preeminence or the wars of colonial domination and national liberation in the Third World.

A predominant theme in all Marxist-Leninist thought is the inevitable rise of revolutionary impulses as the exploited seek to escape their condition by the only means available to them — force. Marxists claim to offer a systematic, scientific explanation for the patterns of monopoly, indebtedness, trade imbalance, cultural and political imperialism, military intervention, and social unrest that give rise to revolution in the Third World. The subordination of the Third World to the power centers of the advanced economies, they say, can be understood only through class analysis and the dynamic of imperialism as the last stage of capitalist development. Marxists are skeptical of the analyses of non-Marxist scholars, who say underdevelopment or revolution may be due to cultural, technological, or political factors within the poor societies themselves. To the Marxist, such factors are only symptoms of the exploitative process that, through five centuries of imperial domination, has enriched the advanced capitalist economies.

Marxists also blame economic motives within the capitalist ruling class for exaggerating the character of the Soviet threat and helping to sustain the arms race. American leaders, for example, employ nationalist or religious appeals and other forms of "false consciousness" to hold the support of groups that have nothing to gain from growing defense budgets or potentially catastrophic nuclear rivalry with the Soviets. Weapons systems are purchased because they serve the interests of an entrenched political class and funnel profits to the powerful defense monopolies that control the military appropriations process. When the Soviet Union comes forward with realistic arms control proposals, pressures from defense contractors force the "people's" representatives to sacrifice the public desire for peaceful coexistence to the special interests of the military-industrial complex.

According to Marxist theory, the majority of Western scholars have class prejudices that color their interpretations. In addition, the traditional and the behavioral approaches both lack the methodology needed for a truly scientific understanding of the world. Most Western social scientists either count numbers or spin abstract explanations, which miss the mark precisely because they are cut off from class analysis that would focus attention on the most important issues and lend significance to otherwise random facts.

The Behavioral Approach

Behavioral scientists argue that they have distinctive tools for producing an objective, systematic, value-free view of international affairs. They base their work on logical or mathematical proofs, on strictly empirical procedures of verification. Their investigations begin with carefully formulated hypotheses, which are then made operational so that measurable data can be gathered to either prove or disprove them. Where discrete data are unobtainable, the behaviorists fashion logical models of reality through which they attempt to define relationships between variables. These models are conceptual abstractions with carefully defined components that function within certain theoretical parameters — simplified rules of operation that the analyst imposes on the system for the purpose of isolating key variables. They are a kind of mental experiment that helps us understand the logical landscape of a complex situation. By modifying the variables until the model approximates reality, a skeletal theory is transformed into a flesh-and-blood picture of real events. The behavioral approach tends to rule out investigator bias by formulating its propositions in a way that permits other scholars to examine their assumptions and reproduce, or replicate, similar results. Following standard, formal procedures also encourages a more systematic accumulation of knowledge, since it allows for the verification of cause-and-effect relationships through comparative studies that apply the same methodology to new data bases.

Although these modern methods cannot explain the psychology of individuals, they can make useful statements about the tendencies of whole systems, in which individual idiosyncracies generally cancel one another out. We can create a theoretical model that is stable and predictable, while the historical system we are attempting to describe is not — an indication that some factor is operating which the theory does not adequately take into account. The traditionalist would take this as an excuse for discarding model building as irrelevant; the behavioral scientist sees it as a need to adapt or refine the model. If the hypotheses or models seem rather artificial, it is because the scientist tries to use precise, neutral language and make all assumptions explicit. This, the behaviorists say, avoids one of the problems of traditionalist and Marxist analysis, that of scholars imparting their own prejudices into their work, often in a hidden way, so that other scholars cannot possibly come to the same conclusions unless by chance they share the same biases. If modern social scientists can explain only a limited range of international phenomena, it is because they are modest about the limits of their rigorous method in its present early phase of development.

Traditional and Marxist scholarship have both yielded important ideas, but we cannot be sure of their validity without putting them to the proof of statistical verification. Take the example of the Marxist theory of dependent development, which the conscientious scientist must regard as hypothesis rather than revealed truth. Behavioral science would search for relationships that can be tested empirically — for example, the impact of foreign investment on Third World income distribution and social policy. A scientist might study the correlation between the percentage of capital in foreign hands and various measures of underdevelopment — net flow of profits, employment rates, technology transfers, shifts in income distribution, patterns of monopoly versus competition, the rise of indebtedness. Critics argue that such statistical indexes do not truly measure the dependency relationship, since it also has psychological and cultural dimensions. The behavioral scientist nevertheless continues to search for measurable items—operational variables—that will eventually yield an accurate picture of the wider forces at work.

Cross-cultural and cross-temporal research—comparisons between nations or over time—is a method that has helped behaviorists wash out temporary or parochial forces and identify laws of behavior that are constant and universal. For example, comparative studies of civil violence have shown a close correlation between the degree of political instability and a government's ability to satisfy newly forming social wants and keep public expectations from outstripping the society's economic capacities. This research lends support to the traditional frustration-aggression hypotheses, which had remained intuitive speculations until scientific methods provided independent confirmation.

One of the most important advantages of scientific theory building, especially in its present early stage, is as a heuristic, or problem-solving, aid to discovery. It can generate fruitful new hypotheses that can then be explored by more traditional methods. A good theory always raises new questions and opens our eyes to novel ways of seeing things. Thus, the systems analyst's various models of the international system have, for example, refined our understanding of the balance of power and the rules by which it is maintained. As a result, we now see more clearly how shifts in technology, ideology, and the number of states led to the breakdown of the traditional European balance of power. Likewise, games theorists, through logic and mathematics, have revealed some of the hidden dynamics in the psychology of deterrence and the bargaining strategies of allies and adversaries. Such approaches have also encouraged us to think more rigorously about international relations as a distinctive arena with forces and features of its own that set it apart from domestic politics. In other words, the behavioral scientists help us think in terms of those analytic slices of reality, or levels of analysis, that were discussed in Chapter 1 and are reflected in the overall structure of this book.

It is worth remarking that the debate over a science of international relations has moderated in recent years, mostly because no one school has been able to prove that its method is the best. Scholars, as a practical matter, have come to depend on one another's work. The behavioral school itself has called for a post-behavioral revolution that would encourage scientists to abandon their ivory towers of specialized research in favor of work with greater relevance for concrete policy concerns. This policy-science orientation echoes more traditional concerns for the integration of theory and practice, while also asking the behavioral scientist to confront the messy moral and political dilemmas of practical diplomacy. In this conception, science must be wed to common sense; knowledge does not exist for its own sake, but should be used responsibly in trying to improve the human condition. Scientists cannot ignore value implications, if only because scholars are not mere technical experts or intellectual "guns for hire." They must be concerned about the application of their knowledge, the fundamental value assumptions in which it is rooted, and the degree of control that the predictive power of science at its best can confer on political decision makers. Finally, scientists cannot remain detached from taking sides on political questions because their commitment is to the truth and to the preservation of the conditions of free inquiry that make science possible.

THE ROLE OF VALUES IN DIPLOMACY

Turning to the world of practice, we see that policy makers as well as theorists exhibit dramatically different perspectives and values. They hold conflicting ideas about human nature, politics, and the international system. They express different attitudes about human aggression, the prospects for controlling war, and the possibility of developing cooperative institutions to regulate international affairs. They disagree over what the proper tools of diplomacy are and whether it is ever appropriate to use evil means to achieve good ends. They have different conceptions of national security and the bases of state power. These conflicting perspectives fall into two schools of diplomacy, which we label *realist* and *idealist.* We turn now to a detailed portrait of each school and to the Machiavellian or Utopian attitudes it represents.

Realism and the Machiavellian Outlook

The realist sees politics as a fundamental struggle for power. Even in an environment of abundance, competition is inevitable because human beings are fearful and possessive. Pride and the desire for recognition stimulate a competition for power such that one person's gains are the losses of another, leaving many losers feeling aggrieved or deprived. No arrangement can satisfy everyone, and so governments can impose their dominion and preserve the rule of law only by achieving a legitimate monopoly of force.

The realist's pragmatic orientation responds to common experience and past practice, not to principle or theory, which tend to incorporate wishful thinking. Realists have more faith in institutional realities than in constitutional ideals; they practice bureaucratic prudence rather than pursuing intellectual perfection; and their conservative orientation tends to place them toward the right of the political spectrum. They prefer to keep the policy process free of controversial moral considerations and to celebrate practical wisdom over the puritan impulses of the moral absolutist.

The realist attitude stems from a general pessimism about human nature and our ability to control historical events. There is no expectation that the human condition will steadily improve along some irreversible path of progress. Self-interest and greed are the mainsprings of all action, and cooperation is always tactical, temporary, and ineffective in the long run. Competition creates flawed political institutions: most of them cannot rise much above the limits of the selfish individuals who operate them. The genius of the American system is its ability to overcome that very selfishness by rendering it harmless, or occasionally productive, through the constitutional system of checks and balances and the competitive market. On the other hand, Utopian systems such as communism, which are built on the assumption that human beings are basically good and that workers will sacrifice for the benefit of the state or their fellow citizens, are doomed to fail, the realists say. The ideological bonds of communism have not prevented international competition based on national interest. The Soviets have fought border skirmishes with their presumed ideological allies the Chinese Communists, the Chinese have warred with the Vietnamese, and the Vietnamese with the Cambodians. What better evidence is there that national self-interest is more powerful than principles, Marxist or otherwise?

The realist believes that the resort to force in international politics is inevitable, that war is an ever-present reality which states will ignore at their peril. Because human nature is innately aggressive, the best one can hope for is peace through strength. Realists are not warmongers but skeptics — and sometimes cynics — about the ability to achieve peace through accommodation, which they feel is often a disguised form of appeasement that only encourages an unscrupulous state to capitalize on the good intentions of others.

Power is paramount in the realist view of international relations. Every foreign policy aim is subordinate to the primary task of accumulating and reinforcing the power assets at the state's disposal, both to protect vital domestic interests and to realize policy goals abroad. But maximization of power must be accompanied by a realistic assessment of the limits of one's power, so that policies do not exceed the state's capacity to implement them prudently. In short, foreign policy makers must avoid extravagant commitments and Utopian goals that they do not have the power to sustain.

A state's power is measured in such tangible assets as military hardware, troop numbers, and strategic resources. Of secondary importance are psychological, political, and cultural factors that contribute to the effective use of tangible assets. Statesmen also must accommodate their behavior to the realities of geography, economic capacity, military readiness, and the like, which are the ultimate determinants of the international hierarchy. In addition, a prudent foreign policy will take account of the power and interests of one's opponents, so that a state can avoid becoming involved in ideological crusades that unnecessarily threaten the security interests of another state.

Acording to the realists, history has demonstrated that stable relations between states are possible only on the basis of a balance of power. States are sovereign units that interact like billiard balls in a pattern of action-reaction determined by the relative force each state exerts. Threats to security emerge when any one state or group of states accumulates a preponderance of power. "Peace-loving" states — even democracies — may rationalize that they have to accumulate power in order to preserve international order, but an excess of power invariably invites abuse. Consequently, reason and prudence dictate that potentially vulnerable states must protect themselves by arming or entering alliances. But the realist principle on alliances is: "No permanent enemies, no permanent friends." Ideological affinity may influence the formation of an alliance, but it cannot be counted on as the basis for enduring cooperation. Conversely, ideological hostility should never stand in the way of an alliance that is convenient for other reasons. The realist measures the diplomatically prudent act with a dispassionate eye for the long-term benefits to the state, believing that overzealous attachment to ideological concerns can blind a state to its true interests and limit its freedom of maneuver.

The introduction of nuclear weapons has not basically changed the balance-of-power equation; expensive arms races still express the same old impulses to protect the sovereignty of the state. The anarchy of the international system has forced every nation to look out for itself in providing a means of defense. Nuclear weapons have merely extended classical military means to the ultimate in destructive potential, while reducing the number of states that can afford to stay in the competition. Small states become allies, or satellites, of superpowers on the basis of what they can contribute. In exchange, they receive aid and the protection of a nuclear umbrella. But it is a pragmatic relationship that is likely to be abandoned as soon as a state has its own deterrent force, as occurred with China and France. As long as nuclear weapons exist, we have to take seriously the prospect that they will be used. To say that they have made war obsolete is to mistake hope for reality; technology of itself has no power to change human nature.

In the economic sphere, traditional mercantilism and economic nationalism prevail even among apparent allies, as evidenced in current relations between the United States and Japan. In the Third World, the spread of allegedly transnational ideologies like democracy, capitalism, or communism has done little to curb fierce national competition, which has sparked massive arms races among countries too poor to afford them. To the realists, existing power relations between the most underdeveloped states only prove their point that technological advances make arms competition inevitable and give the advantage to the states with the best-prepared power resources.

Realists make a strict separation between domestic and foreign affairs. They think idealists are wrong in believing that political and ethical principles operating within governments can be applied equally to relations between states. In fact, domestic political institutions are not exportable, they say, because foreign tastes differ so fundamentally. Where there is no consensus on values, power becomes the sole arbitrator, and where there is no single governing body with a monopoly of power, there can be no international rule of law. The anarchic and purely competitive character of foreign affairs makes it impossible to employ even those limited tools of civility that are available to a sovereign nation-state within its own borders.

In particular, this makes fruitless any attempts to organize a nation's foreign policy democratically or to insist that it observe particular ethical or moral restraints. The foreign policy establishment should be professionalized, the realists maintain, and the executive given decisive control, since only the chief of state can embody the interests of the entire nation. Successful diplomacy must be prudent, discrete, often secret, and conducted by a professional elite dedicated to serving a clearly defined national interest. The state must speak with one voice, avoiding the temptation of democratic societies, in particular, to have as many foreign policies as they have special interest groups.

In balance-of-power diplomacy, ethical concerns are subordinate to survival. International organizations lack the power to protect people, and international law cannot institute democracy or human rights when it has no means of enforcement. At its best, international law can define conditions of sovereignty and assist in protecting the rights of states, not individuals. Because the standards of conduct in international affairs are set by the most aggressive and least principled actors, foreign policy must be pragmatic, even Machiavellian. The state that imposes moral restraints on itself is sure to be at a diplomatic disadvantage against those states that are less scrupulous. Power, not moral purity, is the implement of influence in world politics. States may choose to practice morality at home, but abroad they must be prepared to compete in the power dimension, doing whatever is required to avoid becoming subjects of an alien power for whom morality is irrelevant.

From this realist perspective, the test of an effective diplomacy is its ultimate impact on the security and power position of the state. Individuals can afford to be altruistic and self-sacrificing, but political leaders have a special responsibility to act in a way that protects the public interest at all costs. Foreign policy is to be judged by what Max Weber, in "Politics as a Vocation," has called an ethic of consequences, not an ethic of ultimate ends. The road to defeat, like the road to hell, is paved with good intentions. A policy maker may desire a noble outcome and may pursue it by ethically exacting means, but if the net outcome is a loss of power to the state, the policy will be judged a failure. For the realist, motivations mean nothing: good intentions do not excuse bad policy, as measured in terms of its effect on national security. To be sure, self-aggrandizement in high office can place a nation's foreign policy at risk, but not half so much as wishful thinking that denies the military realities and unnecessarily sacrifices the national interest. A preoccupation with power can cause a state to waste resources on unneeded military security, but well-intentioned do-gooding can place the entire state in jeopardy. Appeasement or concessions offered in a liberal spirit give the appearance of weakness and invite aggression.

The realist's value orientation leads to particular policy emphases. Since military power is considered the biggest threat, the realist worries more about East-West issues and superpower competition than about North-South matters of development, trade, aid, and technology transfer. Likewise, environmental and global resource issues are of lesser concern than arms races and military rivalry. These policy emphases flow naturally from the assumption that each state's responsibility is to look out for itself, not to get involved in fruitless or self-defeating efforts to aid the development of other states or improve the global "commons." Moreover, the realist believes that the most likely source of international instability is aggression by an established power, either by direct attack or by subversion. Consequently, conflicts in the Third World are assessed in terms of their impact on the bipolar balance of power and the competition between capitalism and communism, rather than as localized struggles of underdevelopment, ethnic rivalry, or regional power interests. The realist sees every conflict as a potential destabilizing force and a threat to the status quo. If intervention is required, deception and covert activities are justified as effective means of maintaining or favorably altering the balance of power.

Idealism and the Utopian Outlook

For the idealist, politics is a community-building enterprise in which values play a central role. Rather than seeing the state as an imperial creature of power, idealists see it as a cooperative decision-making apparatus for, in David Easton's words, "the authoritative allocation of values." Although conflicts are inevitable, it is the civilizing mission of politics to provide avenues for common solutions and compromise. At bottom, the state is a community of common values based on consent. This is true even for the Soviet Union, which is so immense and complex that a monopolistic party could not rule it effectively without the patriotic cooperation or passive consent of the majority. The idea that a policeman's gun lies behind the law, in any society, takes the extreme case for the rule. Most societies are held together by the voluntary compliance of the people, who maintain a collective existence without the intervention of the state.

This idealist image of politics is rooted in the assumption that human beings are naturally social creatures motivated by ideals, principles, and, occasionally, genuine altruism and that they often will subordinate their self-interest to a higher cause. Patriotism, with its call for citizens to sacrifice their lives in time of war, is a potent reminder of the power ideals and principles can exert in political life. But the nation-state is not the only form of community to which individuals adhere. The political community itself has undergone an astounding expansion over history, from village or tribe to modern state, brought about mostly by developments in communications, economy, culture, and other peaceful means. This is testimony to the institution-building capacity of politics, and to the likelihood that someday another, possibly higher form of community will replace the nation-state. Already we see a level of cooperation among the Western industrial democracies, despite their different cultures and economic interests, that has made wars between them obsolete. The ideological glue of capitalism and democracy and the complex economic interdependence of these industrial societies have created a functioning peace system between powers that only five decades ago were engaged in a deadly world war.

Idealists are optimistic about the human capacity to shape history, which they view as a progressive unfolding of human possibilities. This vision of history celebrates the free will of individuals to plan for and create their own future. If expectations can be self-fulfilling, then we will inherit the future we have imagined; every one of us plans today in terms of what we hope to realize tomorrow. Even the Marxist-Leninists, who describe themselves as material-ists and determinists, have discovered the need for a voluntarist philosophy as a means of motivating individuals to accept responsibility for revolutionary acts and as a promise that the efforts of this generation will bear fruit for the next. They also embrace the theory that ideology can control human behavior, as shown by their practice of propagandizing people into a false consciousness that causes them to act contrary to their objective class interests. Indeed, the Great Proletarian Cultural Revolution in China, as well as numerous other thought-reform movements in Communist states, was based on the notion that progress could be achieved only by changing the ideas, the expectations, the consciousness of the majority of citizens.

While the pragmatist assesses each policy option for its immediate advan-tage, the idealist insists that a proper foreign policy must make principles paramount, in order to have a consistent standard by which to judge outcomes. Besides, idealists say, every policy option embodies a choice about basic values as well as about actions. To avoid the test of principle is to court disaster, for no state — least of all a democracy — can survive for long if it pursues policies that contradict its constitutional principles. The latter will have a demoralizing impact at home, eroding the state's bases of legitimacy. Abroad, they will bring a loss in credibility, in ideological appeal, and finally in power. For military power is not the only basis for influence. A good reputation and considerations of justice, fairness, honesty, faithfulness, and consistency also count as a kind of power, protecting the solidarity of alliances and cultivating the kind of image at home and abroad that will bring friends to one's defense.

The idealist celebrates theory over practice and planning over improvisa-tion. An effective policy should always begin with a clear intellectual concep-tion of what it is to accomplish. Otherwise, foreign policy becomes a prisoner of the pressures of the moment or of the bureaucratic interests of those who are implementing it. The good policy maker, the idealist says, will also take into account the influence of psychology, political culture, and ideology on the conduct of political leaders, who are not dependent on arms alone. Ethical considerations also play an important role, especially in preserving the integ-rity of the policy process and ensuring that bureaucrats do not become mere empire builders and powermongers. Political office is a public trust in which citizens will have confidence only if the persons who hold that trust display integrity and truthfulness. Rare is the leader who can practice a Machiavellian and calculating diplomacy abroad while remaining honest and frank with those at home.

The idealist also believes that war is an unnecessary social invention, the unfortunate consequence of particular sets of political circumstances. No one willingly courts the enormous human costs of war unless he or she feels powerfully threatened and insecure or is the emotionally unbalanced product of a disturbed social order. The solution to war, then, is to reorganize social and political life so that states will feel more secure and individuals will receive the care and emotional nourishment they need to bring out their naturally social and loving human characteristics. War is a social institution that desperate people turn to in the absence of a better means to security; aggressive attitudes and the macho ethic are learned behaviors, which can be curbed through appropriate changes in socialization and education.

For these reasons, idealists are strong believers in peace programs, arms control schemes, and international organizations as global and lawful solutions to human problems. To them, the example of domestic politics *is* relevant: in socialist and democratic capitalist systems alike, there are many functioning governments that peacefully regulate the domestic conflicts of hundreds of millions of people. Where tribes, races, classes, and religions used to war, there now are systems of law and order. Why can't these systems prove just as effective on a wider scale? To say that it has not happened yet is no proof that it cannot happen in the future. The idealist does not surrender to the conservative, constricting possibilities of the past, but has faith in progress. That optimism is what makes most idealists tend to the left of the political spectrum and advocate programs of radical reform or progressive social change.

The idealist also is optimistic about the twentieth-century trend toward creating international institutions to bridge national interests and curb destructive competition. Both the North Atlantic Treaty Organization (NATO) and the Warsaw Pact, formed in the Cold War, became potent economic and ideological alliances whose members were more fully integrated than ever in the past. The European Economic Community, despite a variety of problems, has provided tangible economic benefits for member states that chose to subordinate some of their separate interests. The European Parliament, although not yet given the attributes of sovereignty, is proving to be a useful first step in enabling nations to experiment with transnational government. The League of Nations and the United Nations have served this same purpose, articulating principles of international conduct to which almost all states subscribe, in word if not always in deed. Such agreement in principle is no small feat. Although the UN's peacekeeping functions have worked only occasionally, it has had some success in mediating a variety of disputes and has performed valuable services in fostering socioeconomic cooperation. Even in the institution-poor Third World, almost every region has its political body (the Organization of American States, the Association of Southeast Asian Nations, the Organization for African Unity), and in some cases functioning trade and tariff agreements.

The idealist has no doubt that balance-of-power politics is being superseded by relations of complex interdependence that have woven nation-states into a kind of "cobweb" model of the international system. Particularly in the economic sphere, global trade and investment have expanded so dramatically that advanced industrial states can no longer survive without vital raw materials from the Third World, while the diffusion of industrial technology to less-developed states has made them equally dependent. Acid rain, toxic wastes, and radioactive fallout pass back and forth with utter disregard for national boundaries, as do satellite transmissions, scientific technologies, political ideas, the fish in the oceans, and migrant workers. Ecologically, the globe has shrunk to a kind of planetary village in which neighbors are forced into cooperating if they hope to improve their standard of living or solve any of the problems of the global commons.

Nuclear weapons, economic interdependence, global communications, international ideologies, and revolutionary technological advances have all changed the nature of international relations fundamentally and irreversibly, making military force no longer the decisive implement of influence or the principal means for a state to achieve lasting security. The era of the territorial state with its invulnerable protective shield is dead, say the idealists. Nuclear-tipped missiles can penetrate any shield at any moment, and all military leaders can do to deter them is to promise an irrational revenge — a nuclear retaliation that would come too late to make any difference. Any sizable nuclear attack, with its risk of setting off a "nuclear winter" that would alter the world's climate irreversibly, could prove to be a kind of indirect suicide. Nuclear weapons have forever redefined the meaning of national security, since the mere accumulation of weapons can no longer promise protection.

The growing scope of the political community, expanding horizons of personal and national identification, the mobility of individuals, and the primacy of transnational forces have all tended to make the nation-state counterproductive if not obsolete. As such integration and interdependence increase, domestic principles of order become more and more appropriate in the idealist model for international society. None of this is to say that cultures or states need sacrifice their identities or political autonomy in significant areas (individual states have retained important powers under the U.S. federal system). But a global federalism that provides common security for all can be imagined today as never before. As with all creative processes, the step from idea to reality will be difficult, but human ingenuity can do remarkable things — particularly when there is the promise of practical improvements in one's own economic and physical well-being through such a cooperative scheme.

In foreign policy, idealists insist that diplomats follow the political principles of the domestic system. For the United States, this would mean a decentralized and democratized foreign policy apparatus strictly accountable to the popular will. Diplomacy is to be pursued through "open covenants, openly arrived at," and guided by a pluralistic conception of the national interest as a democratic summation or consensus of constituent interests within the state. The U.S. government would also be bound to support international law, which would protect the rights of individuals as well as states. As at home, there are times in international affairs when a state must accept limits to its sovereignty. The idealist recognizes that international law has a role to play in regulating such actors as multinational corporations, which lie outside strictly national jurisdiction. In this sense, international law is properly transnational in character, something more than a cosmetic instrument that states manipulate for their own selfish ends.

Ethical standards are the same for policy makers and ordinary citizens. In Utopian theory, politics is where conscience and power meet, where enlightened leaders make policies that serve the national interest and the human interest at once. Both democracy and capitalism attest to the practical wisdom that well-functioning institutions survive only where self-interest and the general welfare converge. Hence, ethical considerations should govern the choice of both means and ends. The idealist believes that certain aims — those core values that define the basic character of a people and its political system — cannot be compromised, no matter the cost. The choice of means is also crucial, since means and ends cannot be easily separated. The decision, for example, to betray an ally in order to control the source of a strategic raw material may be justified in terms of national self-sufficiency and short-term gains, but it will have powerful consequences for long-term security. Thus, the character of a nation and its foreign policy are shaped as much by the choice of means as of ends. Finally, good intentions are worth something, despite realist criticism. They show a nation's good faith and its expectations for the future, which may turn out to be self-fulfilling. If a state is unwilling to aim at good ends simply because the short-term prospects for achieving them are slim, what hope is there that any good will ever emerge?

We may seem dangerously naive, the Utopians say, but our naïveté is not half so dangerous as a pragmatism without direction or purpose. If foreign policy is reduced merely to a struggle for advantage and the accumulation of power, egoists and manipulators will rise into the main decision-making roles, with self-fulfilling consequences that will never let us escape the deadly competition of warring powers. Or a regime of conservatives, whose only aim is to preserve the status quo, might turn the state into a reactionary force for holding the world's dynamism in check. Such an effort is doomed to fail, with disastrous consequences for the repressive and imperialist status quo power.

In the realization that lasting security requires global equity and justice, and a remedy for the development dilemmas of the non-Western majority, the idealists place their policy emphasis on North-South issues. Another world war is most likely to break out in the Third World, they believe, where tensions reflect both the high level of deprivation and the self-assertiveness of newly liberated peoples. A rational diplomacy will attend to the global agenda and to the multipolar rivalries of the postcolonial era, rather than becoming preoccupied with the Soviet-American rivalry. The idealist, feeling that too many resources are wasted on nonproductive arms races, prefers to spend the money on foreign aid, in the expectation that technological intervention will speed the development process. Moreover, each state, especially the powerful and the privileged, has an ethical obligation toward the well-being of all other states.

The idealist generally views military intervention as inadvisable and is skeptical about the ability to alter complex societies by force alone. For this reason, as well as from ethical concerns, the idealist opposes covert action, lies, and "dirty tricks" as inappropriate means of conducting foreign policy. Besides, the probable sources of global catastrophe go far beyond military aggression. Revolutionary upheavals in poor and oppressed states can threaten national security. Wars can occur by accident or through misperception, as the unintended consequences of arms competition. Or global security can be damaged by an ecological catastrophe brought on by neglect. In short, policy makers should not become so preoccupied with immediate political and military threats that they fail to confront the more serious long-term problems of the global commons, which can only be resolved collectively.

QUESTION FOR DISCUSSION (PRO AND CON)

Should American foreign policy be guided by realism? In particular, should the United States use covert operations to protect its interests and extend its influence?

☞ PRO

American foreign policy should be based on a realistic assessment of the international environment and should take whatever actions are necessary—covert or otherwise—to protect U.S. sovereignty and our primary interests. Although some critics say realists are motivated solely by aggressive intent and a will to power, in fact their main motivation is the security of the state. Any responsible political leader will treat national security as a kind of public trust, which does not permit the luxury of a soft heart or an attitude of self-sacrifice when the very life and future of the state are at stake. The resort to arms or covert operations as security devices is not a response to militaristic attitudes so much as to the perennial insecurity that the existing system of competitive states imposes on every nation. Paramount national security interests also require America to ally itself, from time to time, with nondemocratic regimes. Preserving the balance of power is more important than consistency in our ideological affiliations, since we cannot practice our values unless we can maintain our freedom and independence.

Moreover, when a state is dealing with immoral powers, whether allies or adversaries, it has to sacrifice its own morals if need be for the good of the nation. The realist does what *has* to be done, fights fire with fire. This is because the statesman acts in a public context, with special responsibilities. In private affairs, dishonesty, infidelity, selfish behavior, and other immoral acts do not generally have broad consequences for a nation's survival. In international affairs, on the other hand, hostile acts by an adversary—violation of a treaty, covert sponsorship of an insurgency—have an impact on national security that goes well beyond the immoral act of lying or breaking one's commitment. In private life, infidelity may lead to divorce; in public affairs, it leads to war, which imposes its costs on many innocent persons. Idealists take all this as reason for still higher moral standards in public life. But their calls for ethical perfectionism are motivated more by the dramatic and violent consequences of war than by the immorality of foreign policy makers, whose acts are neither more evil nor more morally impeachable than those of the average citizen. Ethical compromises result from the awful responsibilities and special burdens of public office and the power of states as actors, not from the moral failings of political leaders.

International politics, like all politics, operates within a domain of conflicting values in which civility is possible only through compromise and give-and-take. If nations and persons cannot be stereotyped as either angels or devils, and if no solution can self-righteously be declared the final one, then we must often settle for half a loaf or the lesser of two evils. The essence of diplomacy is accommodation; it cannot avoid coalition building, strange bedfellows, temporary alliances, and occasional concessions to purely selfish concerns. If we insist on an inappropriate moral standard, we simply encourage hypocrisy. Politicians will often attempt to justify their practical and selfish acts in high-flown moral language that suggests an unreachable standard of moral conduct. The resulting gap between appearance and reality may lead to public disillusionment, then to cynicism and worse.

It is much better for international relations to be conducted on a frank and realistic basis, with open acknowledgment of conflicting moral claims and of the prudent, if selfish, grounds on which they are to be reconciled. Real solutions lie always in the domain of converging interests, with each nation gaining something. The Marshall Plan for aid to Europe after World War II, for example, was successful because the American people understood they had a selfish interest in reconstructing the economies of their European trading partners and ensuring their protection from Communist penetration. The policy could not have been half so generous or so firm if it had been characterized solely as a moral obligation. The main reason there is little public support for foreign aid to the Third World today is that most Americans do not understand how it would serve the national interest. Our foreign aid policies have therefore remained vacillating and weak. We may talk altruistically about development assistance, but the bottom line for an effective policy is to make a tangible connection between aid and the protection of American security. When that connection has been made, as it was in Taiwan and South Korea, American aid has played a generous and productive role in economic development.

It is the idealist, not the realist, who tends to be isolationist and parochial, by virtue of trying to impose on a complex and diverse world the narrow standards of American domestic politics. The role of the United States as a superpower and our economic and technological integration into a global market system require us to be flexible in adapting our behavior, and our moral standards, to conditions *as we find them* around the world. We could afford to be purists when the exercise of American power was confined largely to the Western Hemisphere. Today, when we bear a large part of the responsibility for global stability and play a central role in maintaining the balance of power, we cannot afford to let moral scruples stand in the way of an effective policy.

The realist knows that prestige comes from the steady, effective exercise of power. A strong nation that is unwilling to use its force will quickly lose its credibility and influence. In the nuclear era, which has ruled out many forms of overt warfare, a superpower is necessarily reliant on acts of manipulation and covert operations to protect its interests and indicate its resolve. The existence of nuclear weapons has forced these unconventional tactics not only on the superpowers but on Third World revolutionary guerrillas as well. Such tactics constitute a kind of compromise in the use of force, the alternatives being overt conflict or outright surrender to tyranny. At a time when global media coverage has made random terrorism the calling card of the weak and lawless, civilized states cannot maintain law and order unless they are prepared to engage in equally ruthless counterterrorism. This takes a strong stomach and the frank admission that force, in all its forms, is a necessary tool of any great power.

The idealist would ban the use of force altogether, or would employ it only under the special circumstances of a moral crusade. That kind of diplomacy slips too easily into impotence or fanaticism. It divides states into good and evil and then proposes to establish permanent peace by exterminating the evil state — demanding total victory — forgetting that the blame rarely lies all on one side. When the idealist intervenes with force, it tends to take on a messianic self-righteousness fortified by extravagant justifications and unwarranted hopes. The realist has a political and moral duty to combat such tendencies, to observe prudence in international conduct, and to see international relations as they are — a mix of motives and interests. A state should not become so self-righteously preoccupied with its own virtue and national values that it ignores the legitimate interests of competing states. From such fanaticism comes more war, not peace.

As Raymond Aron, the French scholar of international relations, has remarked, in his *Peace and War:*

> All [idealists] set law in opposition to force. Might, they say, cannot make right. But the law resulting from agreements between states is based upon force, since without it the states would not exist. To declare that force is intrinsically unjust is to decree the original injustice of all juridical norms, inconceivable without the existence of states. Hence the ultimate alternative: either there is a right of force, or the whole of history is a web of injustice. . . . No great state has been established without recourse to coercion, without absorbing smaller collectivities. If the use of force is absolutely culpable, all states are branded by a brand of original sin. . . . What [the idealist] forgets is that the non-use of force belongs to one moral-legal system, that of the United States, and to one philosophy, that of the contract and of consent, not to the Soviet system or to Marxist philosophy. Hence it is not respect for an international law whose authority they do not acknowledge which will incite the Kremlin leaders not to use force outside their borders, but prudence. And prudence will not forbid them all uses of force, but only open war, crossing of frontiers by regular armies. By the same token we leave the universe where peace by law prevails, and re-enter the real world where the absence of war is due to fear rather than to a common will, and in which the secret games of subversion are played. . . . States constitute a society of a unique type which imposes norms on its members and yet tolerates recourse to armed force. As long as international society preserves this mixed and, in a sense, contradictory character, the morality of international action will also be equivocal. (pp. 604–08)

From such a realist perspective, it is clear that the most basic problems in international affairs do not yield to peaceful solutions. Religious and ideological incompatibilities, the very definition of the community, the reconstruction of nationalities, political self-preservation, and the protection of the international equilibrium from the threat of a would-be hegemonic power — these are all problems lacking any means of resolution but force. If states are justified in fighting open wars over such goals, they can certainly employ any covert means necessary to secure the same ends. To argue otherwise is to impose polite and self-annihilating rules of "fair" competition on basic struggles for survival in which actions can be identified as prudent but not necessarily "just."

This is why the United States must be prepared to use covert operations, deception, even "dirty tricks" to defend its interests. Secrecy is essential in keeping faith with revolutionary freedom fighters attempting to overthrow tyrannies around the world. The Soviets could never have been pressured into leaving Afghanistan, for example, if the United States had not supplied covert arms aid to the opposing *mujahedeen* guerrillas. Open American support for subversives makes it difficult for them to gain the domestic support they need to win power, and revelations about the operations of clandestine organizations help dictatorial governments identify and get rid of opposition forces. Also, there are times when, for purely domestic political reasons, an American president cannot openly support a government or a movement whose success is important to American security. In such cases, covert operations are essential.

At times, too, a president must keep information from his own people, for fear of jeopardizing a delicate diplomatic operation by too much publicity. Negotiating positions harden if they are exposed prematurely or if a nation's prestige becomes publicly committed to a given position or outcome. A purely public diplomacy would rule out back-channel approaches, off-the-record briefings, and "trial balloon" proposals, all of which can be valuable in testing the negotiating atmosphere. Compromise often requires the use of face-saving formulas or secret compensation to keep certain aspects of a conflict or its solution below the surface. This was the case with the private assurances President John F. Kennedy gave to Soviet Premier Nikita Khrushchev in their negotiations for the withdrawal of Soviet missiles from Cuba in 1962. There are also occasions when a president wants to mislead an enemy and can do so only through public statements that are less than candid. In circumstances in which vital intelligence information and methods are at stake, the president may have to tell a direct lie to avoid revealing information that might compromise national security. This was what happened in 1960, when President Dwight D. Eisenhower publicly denied that the United States was conducting aerial surveillance of the Soviet Union at the very moment the Soviets were shooting down Gary Powers in an American U-2 spy plane.

It has been widely reported that the United States has used a variety of "dirty tricks" and covert measures in an effort to destabilize the regime of Moammar Khadafy in Libya. A disinformation campaign spread false rumors of a Libyan plot to assassinate President Ronald Reagan, and unspecified secret intelligence information was cited as justification for a bombing raid on Tripoli following a terrorist attack on a West Berlin nightclub frequented by U.S.

Marines. The bombing operation even called for an attack on Khadafy's home and family, in the hope that he might be killed or intimidated into taking a more compliant posture. Assassination plots, although expressly forbidden by U.S. law, have been mounted against Cuba's Fidel Castro and the Congo's Patrice Lumumba, both Communist leaders who had severely threatened U.S. interests. In such cases, when foreign leaders have openly attacked U.S. policy or have conducted overseas operations against our allies, we are justified in using whatever means are necessary to topple those leaders from power. Khadafy's connection to state-sponsored terrorist organizations was clear, even if his direct involvement in the Berlin nightclub bombing has not been conclusively proved. Castro himself has claimed the right to send Cuban troops to Africa to support Communist regimes and to fight in Communist insurgencies. If he claims the right to use force to reshape the political complexion of regimes beyond his borders, we have an equal right, if not an obligation, to use force to frustrate his revolutionary designs. While a small power can afford to flaunt its challenge to the status quo, however, a great power must act with discretion, for fear its actions in one area will adversely affect a complex set of relations in another.

Congressional critics of the covert operations apparatus say it is out of control in its failure to report faithfully to Congress. But the legislative oversight process is conducive to leaks and breaches of security, which naturally drive the Central Intelligence Agency (CIA) and other agencies to shield sensitive covert operations. Unfortunately, the fiascos of the CIA are splashed over the front pages, while its successes are never made public. So it has acquired an unwarranted reputation for skulduggery. The Iran-Contra scandal and the "basement diplomacy" operations run by the CIA and the National Security Council (NSC), which caused so much public outcry, ought to be put in perspective. Such operations are the result of attempts by Congress to place unnecessarily strict limitations on the president's discretion. Foreign policy cannot be formed, let alone implemented, by 535 bickering members of Congress. The "illegal" actions of the NSC staff were the product of meddling laws and overzealous congressional supervision. Congress, which can keep scarcely any secrets for more than a few hours, should not be in the position of supervising sensitive operations. It should get out of the foreign policy business and leave it to the president. Only our top executive possesses the truly national perspective, the capacity for action, the information, and the discretion required for mounting the foreign policy operations — covert or not — that our national security requires.

☞ CON

American foreign policy should reflect the idealism and the democratic values embodied in our Constitution and in our domestic political practices. Faithfully following the Constitution in our foreign policy would have saved the United States from the three worst political mistakes of our postwar national life. The first was the anti-Communist crusade of Senator Joseph McCarthy in the early 1950s, when scores of government officials and ordinary citizens were harassed and deprived of their legal rights in a zealous witchhunt. Until McCarthy's censure by the Senate in 1954 for abuse of power, his activities caused thousands of innocent people to lose their jobs, intimidated two administrations, and launched an exaggerated anti-Soviet paranoia that persists to this day. The second mistake stemmed from the Vietnam War, which induced at least three presidents to ride roughshod over the constitutional separation of powers and congressional authority in order to maintain executive control over the war effort and public debate about it. Illegal attempts to squash domestic dissent over the Vietnam War were also at the root of the Watergate caper, which ended in the jailing of a number of high government officials and President Richard Nixon's resignation under threat of impeachment. More recently, the Iran-Contra operation represents a third major effort to circumvent Congress and duly constituted legal procedures in the name of overriding national security interests. In this case, a few individuals in the National Security Council and the CIA undertook on their own a secret operation to sell arms to Iran, ransom hostages, and divert the profits into military support for the anti-Sandinista Nicaraguan *contras.* In doing so, they were violating their own executive's professed policy of not dealing with terrorists. They also violated the Boland Amendment, the Intelligence Oversight Act of 1980, and the Neutrality Act and lied systematically to the public, to government officials, and perhaps to the president himself. As in the two earlier crises, these individuals, whose actions undermined the Constitution and damaged the credibility of the U.S. government in the eyes of both the American public and international opinion, represented their efforts as purely patriotic.

National prestige is not just the awe inspired by a powerful arsenal. It is the product of one's moral reputation, an influence as important as arms in preserving a nation's international position — especially a nation that styles itself democratic and above pure power politics. In the name of prudence, we must recognize that some forms of power are necessary. But a military success purchased at the expense of credibility, fidelity to alliance commitments, domestic well-being, economic competitiveness, or any other national interest constitutes a defense burden, not a strength. The idealist does not propose to abolish power, but to exercise it on behalf of collective security goals, so that one nation need not fear the accumulation of power by another.

The realist attitude toward power tends to self-destruct, not only through its excessive emphasis on competitive national interests, but also because realist politicians have difficulty drawing the line between self-regarding Machiavellian behavior that protects the nation and similar behavior that protects only the power interests and policy preferences of an elite. The realist operates negatively, out of fear and distrust, which lead to overreaction and unwarranted hostility. The self-defeating spiral of the arms race is symptomatic of the degree to which suspicion has triumphed over good sense.

Idealists do not focus on whether the balance of arms is exactly equal, but on the underlying causes of the arms race. They define the national interest in broader terms than the preservation of one's position in the international power hierarchy. While encompassing the protection of our enduring principles, U.S. interests are very often compatible with a wider human interest. To the idealist, such wider issues as human rights, protection of the global environment and resources, and support for international institutions like the United Nations, the International Court of Justice, and the Law of the Sea belong high on the foreign policy agenda. Likewise, security is a problem to be solved by mutual and verifiable arms control, not by a competitive arms race. Economic issues should be treated not within the framework of simple gains to the nation, but in terms of mutual benefit in a world market. Concern for the general welfare and for an end to the underlying causes of war impels the idealist to support foreign aid and economic development efforts that address the problems of Third World poverty. The idealist does not view these as giveaway programs but as investments in the future security and prosperity of the globe.

Realists falsely criticize idealists for being naive and weak, arguing that their idealistic schemes for collective security, like the League of Nations, fail to take account of power relations between states and the necessity of curbing aggression by force. Such naïveté, they allege, contributed to the appeasement of Adolf Hitler at Munich, which made it more difficult to contain him and thus set the stage for World War II. The idealist would counter that the seeds of World War II were sown at Versailles in 1918, when the victorious Allied powers imposed on Germany a punitive peace. At the same time, the Allies refused to implement a League of Nations effective enough to have frustrated the likes of Hitler and Benito Mussolini. The League's signatories would have had only to commit seriously to collective security and to the upholding of a sanctions policy, at some modest short-term cost to their national interests. But Italy attacked Ethiopia, Japan invaded Manchuria, and, finally, Germany rearmed and swallowed the Sudetenland without any effective protest from the League of Nations. Everyone's national interest was appeased, and each state, including Hitler's Germany, was free to calculate its own power interests, ultimately leaving only two unfortunate alternatives — appeasement or war. Because the aims of the League of Nations were never implemented, it brought no significant restructuring of international relations. In the realist argument, this is exactly the point: national self-interest does not allow for the sacrifice of sovereignty to a higher ideal. And yet, if men and women were not willing to curb their selfish interests to achieve broader social goals, people would never sacrifice their personal independence to the nation. Nor could such institutions as the North Atlantic Treaty Organization and the European Economic Community have come into existence. If we will accept such limits to sovereignty for economic gain and personal security, why not for the security of the globe itself, to avoid another, even more catastrophic, world war?

The realist says that the national interest is too sacrosanct to be sacrificed to any transnational interest. But the national interest is compromised every day in domestic politics, with one group or another claiming to speak or act for the nation. A multinational corporation seeks access to and protection of its overseas market. A domestic firm demands tariff barriers or import quotas to keep out competing foreign goods. A defense corporation seeks a government contract by promoting its new weapons system as necessary to national security. A labor union demands stricter import regulations for offshore industries that are taking jobs away from Americans. If the national interest can accommodate competing internal demands like these, all of which claim to serve the general welfare as well as the aims of particular groups, why can't national interests be similarly compromised for international goals that serve us all?

The idealist demands a higher degree of morality in international affairs precisely because of the tendency to subordinate the public interest to private aims. As Arnold Wolfers has said, in his essay entitled "Statesmanship and Moral Choice":

> International politics offer some opportunities and temptations for immoral action on a vast and destructive scale; these opportunities tend to present themselves in the guise of "necessity of state." Statesmen in command of the machinery by which public opinion is manipulated may make it appear as if they were acting for the sake of objectives to which the people attach high value when in fact they are out to serve personal material interest or to satisfy personal ambitions for power. Where men wield as much power as they do in international politics there is room for an infinite variety of abuses for which the "necessity of state" can serve as a convenient cloak. (*Discord and Collaboration,* p. 61)

Nowhere is the claim of national security more commonly invoked than in the keeping of official secrets and the telling of official lies. The realist argues that our leaders have to withhold information, mislead the public, and sometimes lie in order to deceive the enemy. But our enemies have sophisticated intelligence apparatuses that tell them what is going on; it is the American public that remains in the dark. Government by consent cannot proceed from official lies. If anything, we should err on the side of keeping the public fully informed, even at the risk of disclosing security information that might be marginally helpful to an adversary. If our government cannot give us timely and accurate information or acquires a reputation for not telling the truth, it loses the trust of the people. Without such trust, democracy withers. (A few Americans have become so cynical that they believe the lunar landing was faked, to further our scientific reputation and allow us to say we had "won" the space race, and that the CIA was responsible for the assassinations of President Kennedy and other prominent political figures.) Moreover, lies are like drugs: they induce a dependency on further lies. Psychologists say that persistent lying indicates low personal self-esteem. What does this say about our country's self-esteem? An individual's effectiveness is based on self-confidence, openness, and a reputation for honesty. Why shouldn't this be true for our country too? In personal situations, illicit acts are kept under control by the most moral party, which simply abstains from behavior it considers unacceptable rather than surrender to a moral inferior. Why should it be different in foreign affairs? Do we need to behave like delinquent teenagers just to please the international "gang," instead of remaining faithful to our own moral system?

The realist invokes self-defense as a common justification for unsavory acts. But what is being defended? Covert action to save democracy is a contradiction in terms. We engage in a sort of self-assassination if we compromise our core values in the name of security. Mere survival never has been the primary policy of a great state; nor has a great power long endured if it relied on purely Machiavellian impulses, with no regard for the cost to its citizens or its principles. Few actions in international affairs are determined exclusively by considerations of power and security. Most states are animated by higher goals, by ideological considerations, by value constraints, all of which count as powerful forces in shaping foreign policy. Many states have willingly fought to secure their independence or risked the safety of the regime to protect values they consider sacred. To fight simply to win, without demanding that the means be consistent with the ends, is to pry war out of its political matrix and turn it into a kind of amoral gladiatorial contest of military prowess.

Dirty tricks are unnecessary when policy is based on genuinely popular political movements. Moreover, an enlightened idealism is actually more effective in protecting long-term national interests. The United States should long ago, for example, have pressed the governments of Pakistan and South Korea to democratize, even though that might have compromised some of our short-term strategic and economic interests, like our ability to sustain steady military pressure on North Korea or on the Soviets in Afghanistan. But the long-term security of both South Korea and Pakistan would have been enhanced immeasurably if they had fully democratic regimes enjoying wide popular support. The United States should openly support genuinely popular governments, rather than aiding unpopular regimes through covert means that become an embarrassment at home and a destabilizing factor abroad.

CIA operations, *because they are secret,* always tend to run out of control. We have ample evidence of this in the testimony of former agents and in incidents like the Iran-Contra scandal. Covert operations destroy our reputation as a fair and friendly power committed to the principle of self-determination. They undermine democratic control of our foreign policy and threaten the democratic character of our domestic political system. Even from a pragmatic point of view, covert operations are almost never successful instruments of policy, particularly when the costs are measured against long-run benefits. Secret CIA interventions have usually been mounted either to rescue a failed policy or to launch a questionable policy that will not bear the full light of public scrutiny. Their aim has been not so much to subvert dictatorships as to discredit leftist governments of any kind, including some that were popular, well entrenched, and vastly superior to the corrupt right-wing governments they had replaced. The CIA experienced short-term successes in overthrowing three such leftist regimes, all democratically elected: in Iran (Mohammad Mossadegh was replaced by the Shah in 1953), in Guatemala (Jacobo Arbenz was replaced by the right-wing Colonel Carlos Castillo Armas in 1954), and in Chile (Salvador Allende was overthrown by General Augusto Pinochet in 1973). But the long-term results have proved disastrous for American policy, precisely because we installed repressive governments that suppressed popular nationalist forces. Instead of supporting free elections, decolonization, land reform, and social justice for the poor — all consistent with our democratic ideals — we attempted to impose stability from the outside to protect so-called American interests — in fact, the economic interests of U.S. corporations — by means that brought more oppression, polarization, and violence to the three countries. This only increased the probability of long-term revolutionary ferment. More than thirty years later, the three countries are all less stable than before and American interests in worse jeopardy, whether measured in political, military, or economic terms. Meanwhile, U.S. policy throughout the Third World has been severely discredited. Such covert operations, which have earned us an imperialist reputation, should be abandoned in favor of an American foreign policy that is fully open, accountable, and consistent with our democratic way of life.

SOURCES AND SUGGESTED READINGS

Classical Sources

Aristotle. "The Relation of War and Peace." *The Politics.* Book I, ch.1; Book VII, chs. 1, 14, 15.

Clausewitz, Karl von. *On War,* Book I, ch 1.

Freud, Sigmund. "Thoughts on War and Death" in *The Collected Papers of Sigmund Freud.* Vol. 4, pp. 273–304. New York: Basic Books, 1959.

Gallie, W. B. *Philosophers of Peace and War.* Cambridge: Cambridge University Press, 1978.

Hobbes, Thomas. *The Leviathan.* Part I, chs 1–21 (esp. 13 14, 17–18, 21).

Lijphart, Arend, ed. *World Politics: The Writings of Theorists and Practitioners, Classical and Modern,* 2nd ed. Boston: Allyn & Bacon, 1971.

Locke, John. *Second Treatise of Government* esp. Sections 3–4, 6–7, 14, 87, 88, 143–148, 175–176.

Machiavelli, Niccolo. *The Prince* and *The Discourses* (esp. chs. 5, 14–19, 21, 25–26 of *The Prince*).

Roosevelt, Theodore. *The Strenuous Life: Essays and Addresses.* New York: Century Co., 1905, pp. 1–21.

Thucydides. "The Melian Dialogue" in *The Peloponnesian War.* Book V, chs. 84–116. (See also Book I; Book II, chs. 1–10, 19–23, 28–30, 59–65; Book III, chs. 1–9, 25–26.)

Tooke, J. D. *The Just War in Aquinas and Grotius.* Naperville, Ill.: Allenson, 1965.

Treitschke, Heinrich von. "The State and the Value of War" in *Politics.* Vol. I, pp. 15–16, 27–32, 63–66. London: Constable & Co., 1916.

Tucker, Robert, ed. *The Marx-Engels Reader,* 2nd ed. New York: Norton, 1983.

Vasquez, John A. *Classics of International Relations.* Englewood Cliffs, N.J.: Prentice-Hall, 1986.

Weber, Max. "Politics as a Vocation" and "Science as a Vocation" in H. H. Gerth and C. Wright Mills, eds., *From Max Weber: Essays in Sociology.* New York: Galaxy Books, 1958, pp. 77–128, 129–56.

Wilson, Woodrow. "The World Must Be Made Safe for Democracy," "The Fourteen Points," "The Final Triumph," and "Collective Security vs. the Balance of Power" in James Brown Scott, ed., *President Wilson's Foreign Policy: Messages, Addresses, Papers.* New York: Oxford University Press, 1918.

On Theoretical Approaches

Aron, Raymond. *Peace and War: A Theory of International Relations.* Garden City, N.Y.: Doubleday, 1966.

Beitz, Charles R. *Political Theory and International Relations.* Princeton, N.J.: Princeton University Press, 1979.

Bobrow, Davis B. *International Relations: New Approaches.* New York: Free Press, 1972.

Bull, Hedley. *The Anarchical Society*. New York: Columbia University Press, 1977.

Buzan, Barry, and R. J. Barry Jones, eds. *Change in the Study of International Relations: The Evaded Dimension*. London: Francis Pinter, 1981.

Dougherty, James E., and Robert Pfaltzgraff, Jr. *Contending Theories of International Relations*, 2nd ed. New York: Harper & Row, 1981. (See especially chapters on political realism and theories of international integration.)

Easton, David. *A Framework for Political Analysis*. Englewood Cliffs, N.J.: Prentice-Hall, 1965.

Farrell, John C., and Asa P. Smith, eds. *Theory and Reality in International Relations*. New York: Columbia University Press, 1967.

Holsti, K. J. *The Dividing Discipline: Hegemony and Diversity in International Theory*. Winchester, Mass.: Allen & Unwin, 1985.

Hopkins, Terence K., Immanuel Wallerstein, et al. *World Systems Analysis*. Beverly Hills, Calif.: Sage Publications, 1982.

Kaplan, Morton A. *System and Process in International Politics*. New York: John Wiley & Sons, 1957.

Kaplan, Morton A., ed. *New Approaches to International Relations*. New York: St. Martin's Press, 1968.

Kegley, Charles W., Jr., and Eugene R. Wittkopf, eds. *The Global Agenda: Issues and Perspectives*. New York: Random House, 1984. (See especially articles by Henkin and Puchala.)

Keohane, Robert O., and Joseph S. Nye. *Power and Interdependence: World Politics in Transition*. Boston: Little, Brown, 1977.

Knorr, Klaus, and James N. Rosenau, eds. *Contending Approaches to International Politics*. Princeton, N.J.: Princeton University Press, 1969.

————. *The International System: Theoretical Essays*. Princeton, N.J.: Princeton University Press, 1961.

Lerche, Charles O., Jr., and Abdul A. Said. *Concepts of International Politics*. Englewood Cliffs, N.J.: Prentice-Hall, 1963.

Lieber, Robert J. *Theory and World Politics*. Cambridge, Mass.: Winthrop Publishers, 1972.

Mansbach, Richard W., and John A. Vasquez. *In Search of Theory: A New Paradigm for Global Politics*. New York: Columbia University Press, 1981.

McClelland, Charles A. *Theory and the International System*. New York: Macmillan, 1966.

Morgan, Patrick M. *Theories and Approaches to International Politics: What Are We To Think?* 3rd ed. New Brunswick, N.J.: Transaction Books, 1981.

Olson, William C., ed. *The Theory and Practice of International Relations*, 7th ed. Englewood Cliffs, N.J.: Prentice-Hall, 1987. (See especially articles by Wight, Guerrieri, Knorr, Thompson, Howard.)

Rosenau, James N. *The Scientific Study of Foreign Policy*. New York: Nichols, 1980.

Rosenau, James N., ed. *International Politics and Foreign Policy*, rev. ed. New York: Free Press, 1969. (See especially articles by McClelland, Singer, Levi.)

Smith, Steve, ed. *International Relations: British and American Perspectives*. Oxford: Blackwell, 1985.

Snidal, Duncan. "The Game *Theory* of International Politics." *World Politics*, vol. 38 (October 1985), pp. 25–57.

Stegenga, James A., and W. Andrew Axline. *The Global Community: A Brief Introduction to International Relations*, 2nd ed. New York: Harper & Row, 1982.

Taylor, Trevor, ed. *Approaches and Theory in International Relations*. New York: Longman, 1978. (See especially articles by Suganami, Taylor, Hodges, Goodwin.)

On Realism and Idealism

Ashley, Richard K. "The Poverty of Neorealism." *International Organization*, vol. 38 (Spring 1984), pp. 255–86.

Bainton, Roland H. *Christian Attitudes Toward War and Peace: A Historical Survey and Critical Reevaluation*. Nashville: Abingdon, 1978.

Bozeman, Adda B. "American Policy and the Illusion of Congruent Values." *Strategic Review*, vol. 15 (Winter 1987), pp. 11–23.

Carr, Edward H. *The Twenty Years' Crisis, 1919–1939: An Introduction to the Study of International Relations*. New York: Harper & Row, 1964.

Cohen, Marshall, Thomas Nagel, and Thomas Scanlon, eds. *War and Moral Responsibility*. Princeton, N.J.: Princeton University Press, 1974.

Cohen, Sheldon M. *Arms and Judgment: Law, Morality, and the Conduct of War in the Twentieth Century*. Boulder, Colo.: Westview, 1989.

Dennis, Robert D. "Human Rights Policy: A Call for a New Sense of Realism." *Global Perspectives*, vol. 3 (Spring 1985), pp. 6–22.

Doyle, Michael. "Kant, Liberal Legacies, and Foreign Affairs," parts I and II. *Philosophy and Public Affairs*, vol. 12, nos. 3, 4 (Summer and Fall, 1983), pp. 205–35, 323–53.

Falk, Richard. *The End of World Order: Essays on Normative International Relations*. New York: Holmes & Meier, 1983.

———. *A Study of Future Worlds*. New York: Free Press, 1975.

Frost, Mervyn. *Towards a Normative Theory of International Relations*. Cambridge: Cambridge University Press, 1986.

Galtung, Johan. *The True Worlds: A Transnational Perspective*. New York: Free Press, 1980.

Gilpin, Robert. "The Richness of the Tradition of Political Realism." *International Organization*, vol. 38 (Spring 1984), pp. 287–304.

Hehir, J. Bryan. "Morality and Foreign Policy: A Sketch of the Issues." *America*, vol. 156 (Jan. 31, 1987), pp. 64–68.

Herz, John. *Political Realism and Political Idealism*. Chicago: Chicago University Press, 1951.

Hoffmann, Stanley. *Duties Beyond Borders: On the Limits and Possibilities of Ethical International Politics*. Syracuse, N.Y.: Syracuse University Press, 1981.

———. "Realism and Its Discontents." *The Atlantic*, November 1985, pp. 131–36.

Johnson, James Turner. *Can Modern War Be Just?* New Haven: Yale University Press, 1984.

Kegley, Charles W., Jr. "Neoidealism: A Practical Matter." *Ethics and International Affairs*, vol. 2 (1988), pp. 173–97.

Keohane, Robert O., ed. *Neo-Realism and Its Critics*. New York: Columbia University Press, 1986.

Kipnis, Kenneth, and Diana Meyers, eds. *Political Realism and International Morality: Ethics in the Nuclear Age*. Boulder, Colo.: Westview Press, 1987.

Krauthammer, Charles. "The Poverty of Realism." *The New Republic*, vol. 194 (February 17, 1986), pp. 14–22.

Lackey, Douglas P. *Moral Principles and Nuclear War*. London: Rowman & Allenheld, 1984.

Lanyi, George A., and Wilson C. McWilliams, eds. *Crisis and Continuity in World Politics: Readings in International Relations*, 2nd ed. New York: Random House, 1973.

Maghroori, Ray, and Bennett Ramberg, eds. *Globalism Versus Realism: International Relations' Third Debate*. Boulder, Colo.: Westview Press, 1985.

McNeil, William H. *The Pursuit of Power*. Chicago: University of Chicago Press, 1982.

McSorley, Richard. *New Testament Basis of Peacemaking*. Washington, D.C.: Georgetown University Center for Peace Studies, 1979.

Miller, Lynn H. *Global Order: Value and Power in International Politics*. Boulder, Colo.: Westview Press, 1985.

Morgenthau, Hans J. *Politics Among Nations: The Struggle for Power and Peace*, 6th ed., revised by Kenneth W. Thompson. New York: Knopf, 1985.

———. *Scientific Man Versus Power Politics*. Chicago: The University of Chicago Press, 1946.

Nardin, Terry. *Law, Morality, and the Relations of States*. Princeton, N.J.: Princeton University Press, 1983.

Niebuhr, Reinhold. *Christian Realism and Political Problems*. New York: Scribner's, 1953.

———. *Moral Man and Immoral Society*. New York: Scribner's, 1947.

Novak, Michael. *Human Rights and the New Realism: Strategic Thinking in a New Age*. New York: Freedom House, 1986.

Nye, Joseph S., Jr. "Neorealism and Neoliberalism." *World Politics*, vol. 40 (1988), pp. 235–51.

———. *Nuclear Ethics*. New York: Free Press, 1986.

Osgood, Robert E. *Ideals and Self-interest in America's Foreign Relations*. Chicago: Chicago University Press, 1953.

Phillips, Robert L. *War and Justice*. Norman: University of Oklahoma Press, 1984.

Ramsey, Paul. *The Just War: Force and Political Responsibility*. New York: University Press of America, 1983.

Rothstein, Robert L. "On the Costs of Realism." *Political Science Quarterly*, vol. 83 (September 1972), pp. 347–62.

Sheils, W. J., ed. *The Church and War*. Oxford: Basil Blackwell, 1983.

Shue, Henry. *Basic Rights: Subsistence, Affluence, and U.S. Foreign Policy*. Princeton, N.J.: Princeton University Press, 1980.

Smith, Michael J. *Realism as an Approach to International Relations*. Baton Rouge: Louisiana State University Press, 1987.

———— . *Realist Thought from Weber to Kissinger.* Baton Rouge: Louisiana State University Press, 1986.

Spegele, Roger D. "Three Forms of Political Realism." *Political Studies* (Oxford, Eng.), vol. 35 (June 1987), pp. 189–210.

Swomley, John M., Jr. *American Empire: The Political Ethics of Twentieth-Century Conquest.* New York: Macmillan, 1970.

"Symposium on the New Realism." *International Organization*, vol. 38 (Spring 1984), pp. 225–327.

Thompson, Kenneth W. *Ethics, Functionalism, and Power in International Politics: The Crisis in Values.* Baton Rouge: Louisiana State University Press, 1979.

———— . *Masters of International Thought: Major Twentieth Century Theorists and the World Crisis.* Baton Rouge: Louisiana State University Press, 1980.

———— . *Political Realism and the Crisis of World Politics.* Princeton, N.J.: Princeton University Press, 1960.

Tucker, Robert. "The Purposes of American Power." *Foreign Affairs* (Winter 1980/81).

Vasquez, John A. *The Power of Power Politics: A Critique.* New Brunswick, N.J.: Rutgers University Press, 1982.

Vincent, R. J., ed. *Foreign Policy and Human Rights.* Cambridge: Cambridge University Press, 1986.

———— . *Human Rights and International Relations.* Cambridge: Cambridge University Press, 1986.

Waltz, Kenneth N. *Theory of International Politics.* Reading, Mass.: Addison-Wesley, 1979.

Walzer, Michael. *Just and Unjust Wars: A Moral Argument with Historical Illustrations.* New York: Basic Books, 1977.

———— . *Obligations: Essays on Disobedience, War, and Citizenship.* Cambridge, Mass.: Harvard University Press, 1970.

Wolfe, Alan. "Crackpot Moralism, Neo-realism, and U.S. Foreign Policy." *World Policy Journal*, vol. 3 (Spring 1986), pp. 251–75.

Wolfers, Arnold. *Discord and Collaboration: Essays on International Politics.* Baltimore: Johns Hopkins Press, 1962.

Woolsey, R. James, ed. *Nuclear Arms: Ethics, Strategy, and Politics.* San Francisco: Institute for Contemporary Studies, 1984.

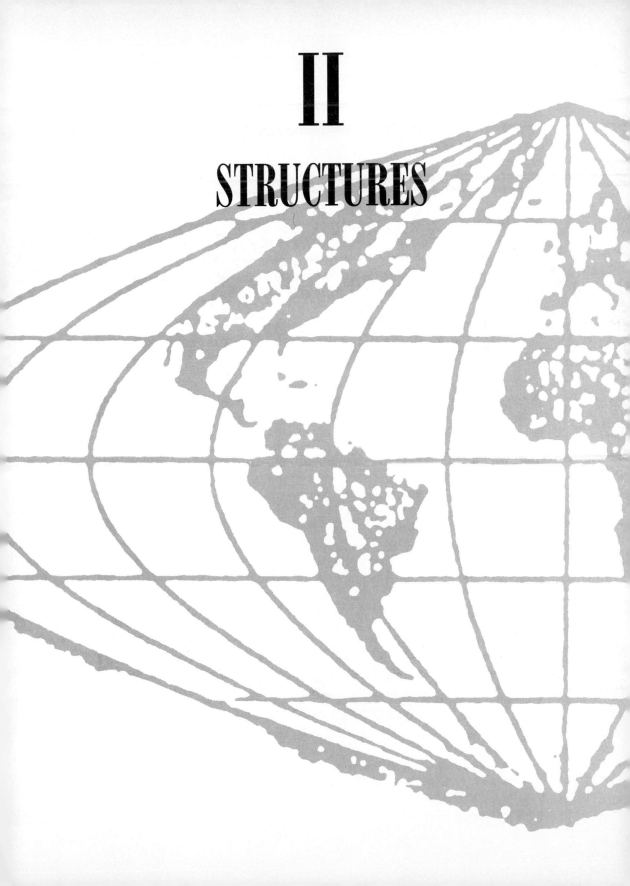

II
STRUCTURES

3

POLITICAL-MILITARY STRUCTURES AND THE BALANCE OF POWER

THE NATURE OF INTERNATIONAL SYSTEMS

The *structure* of international relations is the framework within which states and transnational actors attempt to realize their values. It is not fixed, but changes in response to shifts in the economy, communications, military technology, political organization, ideas, and the like. This structure is composed of intertwined political, economic, and cultural systems, or collections of entities united by a regular pattern of interaction or a characteristic form of control. In this book, we are primarily concerned with three kinds of systems: (1) relations of *power,* which deal with conflict resolution and decision making; (2) relations of *exchange,* which allocate resources in the marketplace; and (3) relations of *community,* which define membership in a society by virtue of shared values and interdependence.

These three types of relationship correspond roughly to the three faces of power described by Kenneth Boulding (1989). As he writes, the kind of power most typically identified with international affairs studies is the *threat* power of deterrence relationships, which depend on the destructive or coercive capacity of weaponry. This type of power relation dominates when there is a struggle over who shall rule or when voluntary agreement is impossible. But Boulding argues that economic power and integrative power are just as important. *Economic* power defines relations of ownership and production. It also involves exchange relations that arise voluntarily when the parties see a mutual economic advantage. *Integrative* power lies in the capacity to evoke love or respect. These qualities confer legitimacy and social power on leaders or governing institutions, giving them resources they might otherwise have to extract through threats or bargaining. In a community, integrative power coalesces in cultural habits, communication links, voluntary associations, overlapping memberships, and common values and ideas that establish a focus of loyalty and a shared identity. In sum, the international system as a whole is shaped by these three interacting subsystems: the distribution of power — whether imperial, hegemonic, or dispersed; the character of exchange relations — whether autarkic, dependent, or interdependent; and the level of integration — the sense of global community versus regional, national, or subnational identities. Power relations are the subject of this chapter; relations of exchange and community are taken up in Chapter 4.

International structures develop when individual actors have an interest in creating a stable, orderly arrangement within which to realize their goals. If a particular pattern of relationships, or structure, proves useful, it becomes perpetuated by custom or formal agreement into a system. The system then exerts a reciprocal influence on the actors who created it, constraining or regulating any behavior that deviates from its norms. Should one or more participants come to perceive the system as offering more obstacles than opportunities, they might try to overthrow it, perhaps by means of a political attack on the institutions, agreements, or principles of legitimacy that have sustained the system. Their aim would be to disrupt the customary pattern of relations — by the withdrawal of one actor, a violent attack on another actor, or some other action — and to reorganize the system on terms more favorable to the dissatisfied party.

The entities that make up a system can be individuals, states, multinational corporations, private associations, intergovernmental organizations, or any other of the many actors in international affairs. The type of actor that is dominant within a particular system obviously affects its character, or structure. For example, nation-states are territorial entities whose primary interest is the protection of their national security through the accumulation of power, and the members of this state system typically interact in a competitive struggle for power. The rules that govern the interactions of states range from very informal to highly institutionalized. The competition may become violent and unstable, with few "rules of the game" to restrict behavior. Or it may become highly ritualized, expressing itself in formal treaties, trade agreements, membership in international organizations, and elaborate codes of conduct institutionalized in international law.

When the dominant actors are economic entities like multinational corporations or private entrepreneurs, whose interests lie in furthering mutually advantageous market exchanges, the patterns of interaction naturally change, since the structure of a market is quite different from that of a balance-of-power system. Instead of arms races and wars over territory, which result in gains and losses that tend to cancel each other out (zero-sum), economic competition weaves the actors into a web of interdependence in which all partners to the exchange stand to gain (positive-sum). Also, the market system has a common disciplinary mechanism — prices — to keep out inefficient producers. However, the structure of the international economic system is affected, as well, by the unequal level of development among economic actors and the uneven distribution of resources. Instead of a free-market model of perfect competition, we may encounter oligopoly and dominance-dependence relations, just as we do in the balance-of-power system.

In real life, the political and economic systems are never completely separate. Multinational corporations enter the political realm by attempting to influence both domestic legislation and foreign governments. Governments enter economic markets, using foreign aid, diplomatic influence, or military intervention to gain access to strategic resources or a friendly reception for overseas investments. The distinction between the state system and the market system is simply an analytic device to help us understand international relations more clearly.

Later in this chapter and the next, we will analyze international systems through the use of various *models,* ranging from simple images — the billiard-ball interactions of the balance of power versus the cobweb of economic interdependence — to more formal deductive systems. Such models are not sets of closely interrelated hypotheses, but are more in the nature of simple conceptual abstractions that help us see the dominant features. Each model will emphasize a different aspect of an integrated, larger, and more complex international reality.

DOMESTIC AND INTERNATIONAL POLITICS COMPARED

In domestic politics, the relations of power, community, and exchange are highly integrated. State power derives its authority from a consensus on procedures for achieving the right to rule. The state's decision-making authority is utilized frequently and accepted willingly and peacefully. Domestic authority also usually reflects an underlying balance of social forces, a widely shared sense of community, and well-developed relations of communication and exchange, which make state intervention largely unnecessary in regulating internal conflicts or satisfying basic needs.

At the international level, however, the relations of power, exchange, and community constitute separate systems that interact less frequently and are more likely to arouse conflicting interests. Political authority is weak, because economic and national actors do not yet perceive that a global regime might be able to protect or further their interests. Global political integration has not developed as quickly as global trade relations, communications, and cultural intercourse. Modern technology can penetrate a cultural system without requiring changes in its political organization, and so the modern world is much more united in its material values and scientific knowledge than it is in principles of political legitimacy. The sovereignty of the state is jealously guarded, largely because it is the only security community that has proved reliable in the traditional international environment. However, the high costs of arms races, the threats of nuclear annihilation and environmental decay, and the advantages of a more integrated global market have eroded the attractiveness of the state as a security community and the principal locus of authoritative decisions.

Throughout the second half of the twentieth century, global relations of exchange and community have grown with the diffusion of modern values and technologies, so that we can speak today of an international society knit together by communications, economic ties, and a rising ecological interdependence. Integration theorists speak of a possible spillover effect whereby common markets and closer trade relations may lead to a higher level of political integration. But divisive ethnic, national, religious, and ideological identities continue to work against the development of a common political culture or a community of values consistent with a collective decision-making apparatus. So far, functional integration has allowed only limited political cooperation, through a variety of intergovernmental organizations whose decisions are not yet treated as authoritative and who lack the enforcement powers of domestic politics.

Any international system may be classified somewhere along a continuum between pure anarchy and world government. At one pole is a system of perfect competition between autonomous states that share neither economic nor cultural ties, are motivated purely by self-interest, and respond primarily in terms of military power. At the other pole is a legitimate, stable system of world government with fully integrated political, economic, and cultural relations, similar to the kind of integration found in a highly developed nation-state today. Most analysts would place the contemporary international system somewhere in the middle of the spectrum, with a fairly dispersed system of power, a somewhat higher degree of economic interdependence, and cultural relations sufficiently strong that we can begin to speak of a global community. Realists say that the international system has always teetered on the brink of anarchy; idealists argue that it is evolving inevitably toward world government. Neither may be right (anarchy and world government may not define the appropriate range of possibilities), but these opposing ideal types are useful theoretical yardsticks against which to measure different versions of the international system. In the remainder of this chapter, we examine the concept of balance of power and various other political models of the international system. The following chapter discusses the concept of interdependence, presents various economic and cultural models, and assesses their impact on transnational political integration.

THE BALANCE OF POWER DEFINED

No organizing concept in international relations has been more important than the idea of *balance of power*. It has been defined in so many ways, however, that it has become an ambiguous and often contested idea. Used objectively or descriptively, the term indicates the relative distribution of power among states into equal or unequal shares. Traditionally, it refers to a state of affairs in which no one power predominates over others. Prescriptively, it refers to a policy of promoting a power equilibrium, in the recognition that unbalanced power is dangerous. Prudent states that are at a disadvantage in the balance of power will (or at least should) form alliances against a potentially hegemonic state or take other measures to enhance their ability to restrain a possible aggressor. Also, one state may opt for a self-conscious "balancing" role, changing sides as necessary to preserve the equilibrium. A balance-of-power policy requires, as well, that a state moderate its independent quest for power, since too much power for one state will bring self-defeating reactions of fear, hostility, and compensating power adjustments by other states.

Hans Morgenthau, a prominent realist theoretician, has described the balance of power as a restraining structure within which states compete for power and attempt to realize their aims. To him and other realists, it is the very law of life for independent units, enabling them to preserve their sovereignty and freedom of action. As Morgenthau has written in his *Politics Among Nations*:

> The aspiration for power on the part of several nations, each trying either to maintain or overthrow the status quo, leads of necessity to a configuration that is called the balance of power and to policies that aim at preserving it. We say "of necessity" advisedly. For here again we are confronted with the basic misconception . . . that men have a choice between power politics and its necessary outgrowth, the balance of power, on the one hand, and a different, better kind of international relations on the other. It insists that a foreign policy based on the balance of power is one among several possible foreign policies.
>
> It will be shown . . . that the international balance of power is only a particular manifestation of a general social principle to which all societies composed of a number of autonomous units owe the autonomy of their component parts; that the balance of power and policies aiming at its preservation are not only inevitable but are an essential stabilizing factor in a society of sovereign nations. (3rd ed., p. 167)

In this realist conception, statesmen are motivated principally by the desire for power, the only reliable instrument of security. Further, power can be restrained only by countervailing power, since no state is willing to limit itself and unbalanced power inevitably leads to abuse. An increase in one state's power is always countered by a compensating accumulation of power among rival states, so long as their leaders are acting rationally and prudently. War breaks out whenever irresponsible statesmen allow one power to outclass its rivals and dictate its will by force.

The assumption that states constantly seek to maximize their power seems to contradict the very idea that they can follow a policy of maintaining a balance. The realists respond that balance emerges through the constant adjustments of a kind of "invisible hand," which brings peace as an unintended consequence. However, the stability of the balance is subject to the realities of mobilized power, technological capacity, geography, and the distribution of resources more than to the good intentions of statesmen. Neorealists contend

—as Kenneth Waltz argues in his *Theory of International Politics* —that states have no choice about playing balance-of-power politics: their behavior reflects the structural constraints of the international system, not the power motivations of statesmen (as the classical realists maintain). Although states may differ in ideology and organization, Waltz says that they imitate one another in foreign policy and so have become socialized into the power system of which they are potential victims. So long as this system is characterized by dispersed power and anarchic competition, foreign policies will respond only to differences in national capability, and balance-of-power policies will result.

Ironically, idealists might fault the realists for their excessive optimism about the automatic character of the balance and their unwarranted expectation that the accidents of history (the structural or systemic variables) favor stability over instability. Idealists also point out that the balance of power is not the only organizing principle available: international law and organization, nuclear deterrence, and economic interdependence are others. Some of these objections will be explored further, but let us first define more fully the characteristic features of the balance-of-power model.

Every balance-of-power system has certain conditions in common: (1) a multiplicity of sovereign actors unconstrained by any legitimate central authority; (2) continuous but controlled competition over scarce resources or conflicting values; (3) an unequal distribution of status, wealth, and power potential among the political actors that make up the system. Inequality and the ever-present threat of violence combine to give the dominant and the subordinate powers a shared (although not equal) interest in preserving the order of the system, whose equilibrium protects their sovereignty. The balance of power is a kind of compromise among states, which find its credible order preferable to absolute chaos, even though it is a system that favors the stronger and more prosperous states, at the expense of justice and sovereign equality for all. On the other hand, the equilibrium serves to protect large and small states alike from expansionist or revisionist threats.

Great powers—or superpowers, to use today's term—play the leading roles in a balance-of-power system, by virtue of their preponderant military force and control of key technologies. A dominant or hegemonic power will often try to buttress its position by appeals to legitimacy—a so-called "right to rule," usually resting on three factors, as Robert Gilpin notes in *War and Change in World Politics* (p. 34). First, the superpower's demonstrated ability to enforce its will is codified in formal treaties that define the status quo. Second, the dominant power frequently can provide certain public goods, such as a beneficial economic order or international security. Third, the dominant power may be supported by ideological, religious, or other values that are common to a set of states, permitting appeals to a common culture, informal agreements on alliance management and other "rules of the game," and perhaps the embodiment of those values in international law.

Great powers reap a disproportionate share of the benefits of the system, but they also bear a greater responsibility as its regulators. When their hegemony has come through leadership rather than conquest, the dominant powers have an acknowledged voice in determining issues that affect the peace and security of the international system as a whole. They have a corresponding duty to be restrained in their exercise of power and to modify their policies in light of their managerial responsibilities. In *The Anarchical Society,* Hedley Bull suggests that great powers contribute to international order in two ways: by managing their relations with one another, and by exploiting their preponderance in such a way as to impart a degree of central direction to the affairs of international society as a whole. They preserve the general balance of power by avoiding or controlling crises among themselves, by policing conflicts within their respective spheres of influence, and by engaging in joint actions to preserve the status quo from attacks by revolutionary aspirants. The balance of power breaks down as a regulatory system when one or more of the great powers seek world dominance, when they sponsor the rise of powerful international authorities, when they question the internal legitimacy of another great power, or when a general war erupts.

Bull goes on to suggest several important distinctions about the balance of power. First is the distinction between a simple and a complex balance. A simple balance is one between two states or blocs of states roughly equal in power. They compete by augmenting their intrinsic strengths — expanding in territory or population, developing their industrial or military organizations, introducing new military technology. In the modern era, arms races are the typical equilibrating mechanism in a simple balance of power. A complex balance is based on alliance relationships among at least three competing powers. In this case, one state's greater military and economic strength does not necessarily give it preponderance, because the weaker powers can always combine against it. Thus, a complex balance opens up additional possibilities for power maneuvers among states, by absorption, partition, or the formation of alliances.

A second distinction is between regional or local balances and the balance of power in the international system as a whole. Although historians have often spoken of the European balance of power as if it were the whole of international politics, this was effectively true only for the brief period when European states dominated the rest of the globe. Before the rise of Europe, several balances existed in different parts of the world, and today we have a number of complex regional balances overlaid by a global pattern that reflects both Soviet-American competition and Third World efforts to balance the dominating influence of the superpowers.

Finally, there is the difference between a subjective and an objective balance. Power does not achieve its deterring or balancing effect unless one's adversary perceives it as doing so. Calculations of power are complex, with plenty of opportunity for misperception; what seems barely enough to one state may appear overwhelming to a potential adversary. A true balance is always difficult to strike, and is subjective, because every state desires not just equality but a margin of safety. Power is all the more difficult to estimate when one must take into account not only military forces in being but economic potential, the capacity for rapid mobilization, the degree of domestic support, and the politi-

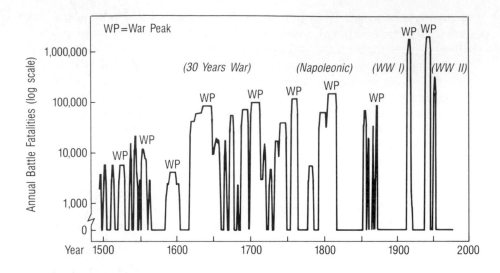

FIGURE 3-1

GREAT POWER WAR SEVERITY, 1495–1975

Cycle	Peak Wars	Annual Fatality Rate at Peak (in thousands)
1	First and Second Wars of Charles V (Ottoman War v. Hapsburgs)	13
2	Fifth War of Charles V (Ottoman War v. Hapsburgs)	22
3	War of the Armada (Austro-Turkish War)	11
4	Thirty Years' War: Swedish/French Phase	88
5	War of the Spanish Succession	107
6	Seven Year's War	124
7	Napoleonic Wars	156
8	Franco-Prussian War	90
9	World War I	1,934
10	World War II	2,158

cal will to use force. The United States, for example, possessed superior military force in Vietnam but not the capacity to use it effectively or the political base at home to sustain the state's war-making potential. And Japan has arrived at great-power status on the basis of its technological dynamism and industrial capacity, despite the absence of significant military forces. In like manner, the Arab oil-producing states were able to alter the balance of power dramatically through their economic control of oil exports to states that were militarily more powerful. In such circumstances, the statesman does not have an easy time discerning when a balance has actually been reached. The only real test is war itself, the very condition the balance of power is meant to prevent.

In actuality, the balance of power has often served as a pretext for war or coercive action by states attempting to maintain or correct the balance. Historically, it has preserved the modern state system against conquest and transformation into a universal empire. It has protected the independence of small states by discouraging their absorption or domination by their neighbors. And it has sustained an equilibrium in which other institutions of international order (diplomacy, international law, great-power management) have been able to operate. But the chief function of the balance of power has been to preserve the existing system of autonomous states, not to preserve the peace. Attempts to adjust the balance have resulted in a succession of wars, interventions on behalf of the great powers at the expense of the small, and violations of international law. (For a picture of the cyclical recurrence of major wars in the modern European state system, see Figure 3-1.) These are paradoxical outcomes, which raise questions about the stability of the balance-of-power system and about the motivations on which it is based.

CRITICISMS OF THE BALANCE OF POWER

As A. F. K. Organski has pointed out in his *World Politics*, power is only one of several objectives of a state. Many domestic priorities compete for the finite resources of the state — the classic guns-versus-butter trade-off — and some states choose not to engage in the power competition at all. Finland, Costa Rica, Switzerland, and Japan, all states that do not possess military forces consistent with their power potential, have decided that the risks and the costs of unrestrained power competition outweigh the risks of remaining neutral or of playing a passive role in a power coalition. Isolationism — as in the United States before World War II and in China during much of its history — is also inconsistent with the notion that there is something inevitable or automatic about the balance of power. States often behave in ways that disregard the requirements of a balance of power. We cannot conclude, therefore, that power maximization is an iron law of international affairs or that it is essential to the preservation of one's sovereignty.

Balance-of-power theory also tends to focus on the great powers and their patterns of interaction at the expense of smaller states on the periphery. It is a center-oriented theory that relegates Third World states to the status of pawns in the power competition. This focus obscures the various structures of domination that exist within spheres of influence and ignores altogether regional dynamics and the conditions of dependency and underdevelopment that shape international conflict as fully as great-power relations do.

Another criticism of the balance-of-power system is that it has failed to supply the international stability it promises. Balanced power has often been the accidental result of intersecting impulses to aggrandizement, rather than the intended consequence of restraint or direct attempts to attain a balance. Rarely has a state appeared to prefer parity in power over a favorable disequilibrium — at least when it had a choice. Although many historians have argued that British policy in the eighteenth and nineteenth centuries self-consciously pursued a balancing role, others have pointed out that this policy flowed from national self-interest, furthered Britain's imperial designs, and eventually placed the British in a predominant position worldwide.

Even when equilibrium is the aim, it is not necessarily the outcome, given the constant shifts in power and the conditions of perpetual change to which all societies are subject. In a revolutionary world, efforts to maintain a balance of power often end up as frustrated defenses of the status quo. Wherever reactionary powers forcibly resist progress, any apparent balance is bound to prove temporary and unstable. If states genuinely aimed at balancing power, a dominant but declining state would make way willingly for a rising power, welcoming a readjustment that restored equilibrium even though that meant giving up some of its own privileges. In practice, no state cooperates in its own eclipse. In a dynamic world, efforts to maintain a fixed distribution of power only encourage, and serve to justify, wars of repression and intervention, intermixed with the revolutionary attacks of the rising powers on an order they perceive as inflexible and unjust.

Organski and Jacek Kugler, in *The War Ledger,* point out that prolonged periods of peace have actually accompanied control by a single preponderant power, while equal distributions of power have tended to encourage conflict. The eighteenth century, the "golden age" of the balance of power, saw constant wars. In the last two centuries, general war has been absent only in those periods presided over by the Pax Britannica or the Pax Americana, when one hegemonic power was the arbiter of peace. On the two occasions when German power rose to challenge British preeminence, world wars broke out. And the most violent conflicts of the Cold War — whether the American containment effort in Vietnam or Soviet adventurism in Angola, Afghanistan, and Nicaragua — took place *after* the Soviets had acquired nuclear parity with the United States. Before then, the Americans did not need to fight to maintain their preeminence, and the Soviets — during the Berlin blockade and the Cuban missile crisis — chose to back down rather than enter a war on unfavorable terms. These events show that dominant powers are rarely challenged at the height of their strength, when it clearly would be foolish for a weaker power to try to force change. Rather, states fight only when they believe they have a reasonable chance of winning — that is, when the two sides are fairly evenly matched. Consequently, a balance of power is as likely to increase the chance of war as to contribute to peace.

International economic stability has likewise been a product of hegemony, not balance. Stephen Krasner, whose "State Power and the Structure of International Trade" takes the traditional state-centric approach, nevertheless argues that free trade has prospered not when power was dispersed, but when there was a hegemonic power to enforce open trade. Robert Keohane, in both "The Theory of Hegemonic Stability and Change in International Economic Regimes" and *After Hegemony,* has extended Organski's theory of hegemonic stability to a great variety of international "regimes" in the areas of trade, energy, and monetary relations. Keohane concludes that these regimes — regularized cooperation between states and adherence to stable "rules of the game" in particular areas of issue conflict — have been the product of hegemonic structures of power, that is, domination by one country. Fragmentation of political power between relatively equal competing countries (a condition of balance), however, has led to challenges to existing international regimes and a decline in stability.

Only a dominant state, Keohane continues, has the power to enforce adherence to rules and the resources to provide benefits to those who cooperate. Smaller states are willing to collaborate with the hegemon in order to maintain a flow of aid, gain the benefits of stability, and win the "free ride" that comes with the collective goods (such as stable money or favorable access to trade) provided by the hegemon. As power and resources become more equally distributed and the hegemon declines, it is likely to try to shift the costs of leadership (aid and enforcement expenditures) to its allies ("burden sharing"). At the same time, the secondary states will become powerful enough to reduce their support for the international regimes and may attempt to rise in status by reshaping existing rules and arrangements to their own interests. The rise of challengers and the decline of the hegemon's capability describe well the circumstances under which U.S. leadership has eroded since 1967, bringing instability to the world petroleum market, the international monetary order, foreign trade, and alliance relations.

These studies point to a still broader criticism of balance-of-power theory: it is too narrow in its concept of power and too mechanistic in its description of how the international system operates. Marxists and world-system theorists both argue that economic forces are just as important as the balance of military power. (For representative views of the Marxist school, see the bibliographic citations under "On the World System, Imperialism, and Dependency" at the end of Chapter 4.) Economic exploitation and trade dependency, these critics say, affect national well-being as much as threats of aggression do. The balance of power may have accurately described certain mechanisms of adjustment among the European powers themselves, but when these dominant states began to act on the larger global stage, they created a colonial system and patterns of trade and investment whereby weak states became part of a core-periphery relationship that served the interests of the dominant states.

Liberal political economists agree that contemporary international relations, characterized by complex interdependence, cannot be described simply in terms of the balance of power. (For representative views of the liberal school, see the bibliographic citations under "On Interdependence" in Chapter 4.) Military force is no longer the chief source of power, nor do security and relative power position constitute the only or the overriding goals of states. Keohane and Joseph S. Nye, Jr., in their *Power and Interdependence* and *"Power and Interdependence" Revisited*, cite four reasons for the diminishing influence of force: nuclear weapons increase the risks of escalation; revolutionary nationalism and unconventional means of warfare make resistance easier in poor or weak countries; economic interdependence and the vulnerability of resources make the use of force more costly; and the mobilization of public opinion produces popular opposition to the human costs of war. Thus, the Eisenhower administration could intervene in Iran, Guatemala, and Lebanon with little difficulty because the desired outcomes were dictated largely by traditional balance-of-power considerations. But the Reagan administration, despite a more self-assertive and forceful policy, encountered much greater difficulty in launching interventions in the same regions in the 1980s because by then relations had become more complex and the legitimacy of great power interventions had been called into question, considerably altering the utility of American power as a tool of diplomacy.

The rise of multiple issue areas and the absence of hierarchy among them mean that outcomes are dictated not by a single, central balance but by bargaining within the issue areas and trade-offs or linkages between them. The influence a state has over a given issue depends on factors that go beyond the overall power structure or the distribution of capabilities. These new factors include economic and technological change, the distribution of power and leverage within the issue area, and the presence of international networks of relationships, norms, and institutions that raise the cost of coercive or go-it-alone strategies. The growth of nonstate actors and multiple channels of contact between societies has also reduced the ability of governments to monopolize or control interstate relations. States are no longer billiard balls or unitary actors: the boundaries between domestic and international politics have broken down, giving rise to "intermestic" issues. Governments are as often constrained by the potential political or economic impact of a policy or action at home as by military threats emanating from abroad. In sum, an adequate explanation of outcomes in conflict situations today must take account of the economic structures of interdependence as well as the power-political dimensions of the international system.

In addition to the structural elements of the balance of power that we have been discussing, there are certain political *processes,* both domestic and international, that influence state behavior. The distribution of power provides the overall opportunities and contraints, but we also must know something about the preferences and motivations of statesmen if we are to understand why they adopt certain strategies and actions. For example, Germany was in a roughly comparable geopolitical position within the European balance of power in 1886, in 1914, and in 1936, but its foreign policies were dramatically different, due to the contrasting strategies of its leaders — the conservatism of Otto von Bismarck, the muddled diplomacy of Kaiser Wilhelm, and the revolutionary, hegemonic aspirations of Adolf Hitler. As W. W. Rostow has noted, in an article entitled "Beware of Historians Bearing False Analogies," it does make a difference whether states have a revisionist or a status quo orientation, whether they pursue hegemony or take the role of balancer, even though their power capabilities may be the same. In short, balance-of-power theory wrongly assumes that all states *use* their power resources to roughly the same degree.

Another important influence of the political process is the perceptions of political elites. Events can dramatically alter these perceptions of the national interest, as the failed interventions in Vietnam and Afghanistan clearly did in the United States and the Soviet Union. The Soviet-American arms race is another example; it has passed from one decade to another without altering the power equation or upsetting the equilibrium, but it has incurred economic costs and created networks of strategic interdependence that have altered elite beliefs about the value of further accumulations of arms. Also, an election, a coup, or generational evolution can lead to the replacement of leaders holding one set of beliefs by leaders with quite different perceptions, as Soviet President Mikhail Gorbachev's rise to power clearly testifies. Although Soviet power capabilities changed little after 1985, the Soviet military threat diminished substantially and Soviet diplomacy became remarkably more effective. The influence of domestic politics, the intensity of economic interdependence, the degree of institutionalization of international rules or regimes, the ability of states to communicate and cooperate effectively, the skill of diplomats and the goals of political leaders, the ability of elites to learn from past mistakes — all these factors influence international outcomes quite independently of the balance of power.

Additional discussion of hegemonic stability, international regimes, imperialism, and interdependence as alternatives to the balance of power concept will be found later in this and in the next chapter. First let us examine two balance-of-power models and historical examples of each.

TYPES OF BALANCE-OF-POWER SYSTEMS

Raymond Aron, in his *Peace and War,* lists three features that distinguish the various balance-of-power systems: (1) the nature of the units in conflict, (2) the distribution of power, and (3) the nature of military organization. The transformation of a balance occurs with changes in the power configuration, shifts in military technology, or the rise of a new type of state that appeals to different principles of legitimacy. The rise of Napoleonic France marked an especially important transition because several of these factors converged. Revolutionary nationalism fired France's citizen army and challenged the aristocratic principles of the day, while Napoleon's imperial designs, military genius, and state-sponsored weapons development threatened to upset the power balance. World War II was another point of critical change, marking the collapse of Europe after two exhausting world wars and initiating a decolonization that broke up all the major European empires. The war also witnessed the invention of nuclear technology and the emergence of the United States and the Soviet Union as dominant powers competing on the basis of ideological principle.

Interstate conflict has changed dramatically in its evolution from aristocratic warrior and mercenary soldier to citizen-conscript, professional officer, and guerrilla insurgent. Feudal, dynastic, and religious struggles have been replaced largely by disputes over colonial policy, national identity, and political-economic organization. The unit in conflict has also shifted, from the city-state or empire to the nation-state or ideological bloc. Both nuclear technology and unconventional guerrilla warfare have altered the character of power and the balance mechanism. Still, the distribution of power capabilities — whether multipolar, bipolar, or hegemonic — and the character of alliances are to most theorists the enduring determinants of the structure of a balance-of-power system. Morton Kaplan's *System and Process in International Politics* identifies the classical balance of power and the loose bipolar system as the two main historical variants of the balance-of-power system, and we will now look at these two systems in detail.

The Classical Balance of Power

The classical balance of power is a model derived from the history of the European state system between the Treaty of Westphalia (1648) and the outbreak of World War II (1939). The system began to develop with the emergence of the modern state, which coincided with broader social transformations that were altering the late medieval order and introducing new patterns of international behavior. The unity of medieval Christendom was shattered by commercial and secular impulses that robbed the Papacy and the Holy Roman Empire of their power to regulate political affairs. Renaissance thinkers like Niccolo Machiavelli, spawned in the brawling atmosphere of the Italian city-state system, articulated a philosophy of statecraft that justified the accumulation and exercise of power outside traditional religious bounds. Consolidating monarchies mobilized their growing resource bases through systems of taxation that allowed them to mount large armies to serve the state's national and secular goals *(raisons d'état)*. The chivalrous medieval knight gave way to the massed power of mercenaries, commanded by a sovereign whose control over the affairs of state, both domestic and foreign, could not have been imagined in the feudal era. For a time, the emerging states contended bitterly over religious issues, but after the Peace of Westphalia affairs of state became centered around dynastic concerns and a search for territory and resources — matters that could be accommodated through diplomacy and limited wars. The presence of a vast colonial frontier facilitated the adjustment of conflicting state interests; monarchs could exercise claims and offer compensations that did not strike at the core national interests of others. Also, a common cultural orientation united the ruling classes of Europe, whose aristocratic values were reinforced by intermarriage and by the spread of Enlightenment learning to all the royal courts. Once the compromise was struck in 1648 on religious questions, Europe became a diversity of states regulating their own affairs through a rational diplomacy of alliances and balance of power. Wars did not cease, but they were mostly ritualized and limited. The absence of any nationalistic identification between the prince and his people served to moderate conflict. Ordinary citizens played no role in politics or in war, leaving professional diplomats free to adjust state interests with relative ease. Since Europe's cosmopolitan ruling aristocracy shared the same political and economic principles of legitimacy, with no fundamental division into status quo and revolutionary states, major wars would only have brought mutual disadvantage to the ruling elites, and therefore they were avoided.

Ludwig Dehio, in *The Precarious Balance,* describes the system that emerged from this particular geopolitical context as an equilibrium in which expanding continental powers were periodically balanced by the countervailing influence of peripheral states. Alliances were freely made and unmade in a constant effort to maximize the independence and freedom of maneuver of competing states. Whenever a potentially dominant power threatened to conquer all of Europe, however, a general coalition would form in opposition, restoring the continent to its condition of "ordered anarchy" and preserving the sovereignty of individual states. Six such general threats to the European order occurred over four centuries: twice from Hapsburg princes (Charles V and Philip II), twice from the French (Louis XIV and Napoleon), and twice from the Germans (Kaiser Wilhelm II and Hitler). Each time the decisive role was played by a balancing power that enjoyed the advantages of geographical distance and naval superiority — the Turks, the Dutch, the British, and finally the Americans (although the U.S. intervention brought a basic shift in the balance from continental to global).

As Han Morgenthau has remarked in *Politics Among Nations* (p. 489), the classical European balance depended on three factors. The first was the existence of a moral consensus within the European community. This was reflected, in the nineteenth century, in a flourishing movement to establish an international law of war, a codification of restraints on violent behavior. Foreign affairs were managed in accordance with a diplomatic code of conduct that reinforced a sense of personal responsibility among kings and foreign ministers. When the sovereign himself made commitments of state, he could be held accountable to a universal ethical standard applied by identifiable individuals. Monarchs had an interest in safeguarding their honor and reputation, so as not to jeopardize their standing in the eyes of other rulers or damage their ability to form alliances. They shared a common moral code, by virtue of noble birth and Enlightenment education, and this international morality was buttressed by family ties, a common diplomatic language (French), a common life-style, and a shared standard of gentlemanly conduct.

The diplomatic corps was transnational in character. At the Congress of Vienna in 1815, for example, Alexander I of Russia had as his foreign affairs ministers or advisers two Germans, one Greek, one Corsican, one Swiss, one Pole, and one Russian. It was not uncommon for two states to bid for the services of the same military officer, as when the Duke of Brunswick, in 1792, refused the supreme command of the French forces and chose, instead, to lead the Prussian army against the French. As late as 1862, on the eve of his appointment as Prussian prime minister, Bismarck was offered service in the Russian diplomatic corps. In the twentieth century, even to consider such an offer would be regarded as treasonous, but Bismarck reported that he declined "courteously," flattered by what was then looked on as a routine business proposition — the transfer of a diplomat's loyalties from one monarch to another for a fee. In classical balance-of-power diplomacy, it was both proper and common for a government to pay a foreign diplomat a pension (or "bribe") as a means of facilitating treaty negotiations. Like the code of aristocratic conduct, money was a universal coin that helped moderate the intensity of international conflict and soften the rigidities of dynastic or national loyalty.

A second factor in maintaining the power balance was the geopolitical configuration of Europe and its relationship to the vastness of the colonial frontier. Expansion abroad became an attractive alternative to expansion at the expense of a powerful neighbor. Moreover, states could draw their new territories into the game as counterweights against any bids for European supremacy. Two potentially powerful players, the United States and Russia, stayed apart from the European balance altogether, spending their energies instead on gaining political control of the "empty" spaces in their continental backyards. On the continent itself, not yet consolidated into nation-states, shifting boundaries helped to preserve flexibility. Poland underwent three major partitions between 1772 and 1795, testimony to the dominance of imperial diplomacy over Polish national interests. Germany and Italy were not unified until the latter half of the nineteenth century, while the Austro-Hungarian Empire, a shifting collection of diverse peoples, held together until 1914.

Once the chessboard of Europe was occupied, square by square, there remained the vast domains of Africa and Asia, which the great powers could parcel out among themselves, thereby avoiding direct conflict. The fate of Africa was decided at the Berlin Colonial Conference of 1885, at which statesmen bargained, laid rulers on maps, and carved out the arbitrary boundaries of their imperial domains. Europe's dominant military and economic power was increasingly spent on a race for colonial possessions and for pieces of the declining empires of Spain, Turkey, China, and Persia.

The third factor that helped preserve the classical balance of power, particularly in its later phases, was a succession of brilliant statesmen who were masters of the arts of compromise and realpolitik diplomacy. One of the earliest was Cardinal Wolsey, who, in the reign of Henry VIII, is credited with devising for England the role of balancer, articulating a principle of prudent diplomacy that served English interests well for more than three centuries. The policy's success was due in large part to its execution by a long line of gifted statesmen. Perhaps the most important of them were Viscounts Castlereagh and Canning, who helped fashion the concert of great powers that policed the peace of Europe after the Congress of Vienna in 1815. Castlereagh also supported Britain's participation in the Holy Alliance, a conservative bulwark against revolutionary France, while Canning successfully turned the growing national and liberal movements to British purposes as counterweights in the continental balance. Equally important to the success of arrangements reached at the Congress of

Vienna—a kind of international government of the great powers—was the Austrian ambassador, Prince Clemens von Metternich. Like most of the statesmen who participated in the Vienna settlement, Metternich was a conservative and did not foresee the strength of the ideas and forces—nationalism, liberalism, socialism—that would remake the map of Europe over the next century. But he did have a clear notion about the vital necessity for establishing an equilibrium among the great powers, and his diplomatic skills set in motion a system that survived the buffeting forces of fundamental change for almost a hundred years.

Although this traditional balance-of-power arrangement was threatened by the popular, and ideologically inspired, revolutions of 1848, it broke down only once, briefly, during the Crimean War of 1854–56. Then another brilliant statesman, Prussia's Otto von Bismarck, kept it alive for a half century longer. Seeking German unification under an absolutist government, Bismarck pursued an active, though essentially conservative, policy whose aim was to preserve the aspiring state's freedom of maneuver. He was wise enough not to tackle the revolutionary popular movements of the era head on, but instead undercut them by taking over those parts of their programs that he could reconcile with the interests of the state. He ultimately achieved his objective of unification through a series of tactical alliances, limited wars, and strategic shifts in Prussian policy—a complex system of checks, balances, and alliances whose only flaw was that it required a statesman as brilliant as Bismarck to manage it. As Henry Kissinger has remarked, in his study entitled "The White Revolutionary: Reflections on Bismarck":

> Statesmen who build lastingly transform the personal act of creation into institutions that can be maintained by an average standard of performance. This Bismarck proved incapable of doing. His very success committed Germany to a permanent tour de force. It created conditions that could be dealt with only by extraordinary leaders. Their emergence in turn was thwarted by the colossus who dominated his country for nearly a generation. Bismarck's tragedy was that he left a heritage of unassimilated greatness. . . . When the novelty of Bismarck's tactics had worn off and the originality of his conception came to be taken for granted, lesser men strove to operate his system while lacking his sure touch and almost artistic sensitivity. As a result, what had been the manipulation of factors in a fluid situation eventually led to the petrification of the international system which produced World War I. (p. 319)

As we can see from the preceding discussion, certain conditions are essential for the successful functioning of the classical balance of power. The system must have a large enough number of independent states to form and dissolve alliances readily. Military technology must be such as to inhibit rapid mobilization for war, prevent prolonged wars, and reduce the possibility of annihilation. Wars must be limited in an ideological sense as well. In the classical balance, wars are not waged to annihilate an enemy or deny a major power the right to exist under its own principles of legitimacy; they are an adjustment mechanism to prevent one powerful state from dominating the entire system. Alliances are struck on the basis of interests and capabilities, not friendship, loyalty, or ideology, and ideological differences must not be so severe as to prevent a moral consensus on the rules of war and diplomacy. The classical balance also presumes a system that is either geographically limited or divided into spheres of influence that enable the major powers to police their colonial domains, maintain regional balances, and ensure that peripheral or subordinate states do not challenge the stability of the central balance. Finally, diplomacy must be unconstrained by international organizations or by domestic public opinion; the great powers must be free to make decisions about alliances and intervention without the need to calculate domestic costs and without the risk of compromising a state's status in an international forum.

The classical balance of power in Europe drew its stability from these historical factors: rough equality among the five or more principal powers; comparability in the kind of power each employed; a substantial ideological consensus among a cadre of professional diplomats; a clear separation of the central balance from the problems of colonial empire; a clear distinction between great powers and small; and a preponderance of power in the hands of a balancer, Britain, which had no aspirations to continental conquest. This stability was disturbed whenever power shifted into the hands of a continental monarch with imperial pretensions, as was the case with Napoleon in France and Kaiser Wilhelm II in Germany. Napoleon's nationalist crusade, which reflected many of the underlying forces that were beginning to erode the equilibrium at its base, proved only temporary and was defeated by a coalition of conservative states. But the consolidation of German power after Bismarck, coupled with the long-term erosive effects of nationalism and liberalism, set off a pattern of disintegration that by 1914 could no longer be held in check by traditional balance-of-power methods. With the decay of the European balance, new ideological, geopolitical, and technological trends introduced a new form of the balance of power, at once bipolar and nuclear.

The Loose Bipolar System

The loose bipolar balance-of-power model describes a system in which nuclear capabilities and an intense ideological rivalry reduced international conflict to a contest between two main antagonists and their allies. This model is also historically based, corresponding roughly to the bipolar global balance that existed from 1945 until the collapse of the Cold War. Its origins may be traced to the forces that brought an end to the classical balance.

First, the industrial revolution made the technology of warfare vastly more destructive. States began to mobilize their entire economies in arms races unaccompanied by any formal declarations of war. The "technical surprises" of World War I, in which the devastating effects of mechanized warfare were first felt, forced the warring parties to mobilize vast conscript armies and inflate their ideological rhetoric; only by making it a total war between conflicting ways of life could they justify their heavy human losses. In World War II, production centers and civilian populations became military targets, erasing the distinction between soldiers and noncombatants. This tendency reached its ultimate in Vietnam, where guerrilla warfare permeated every aspect of society. Nuclear weapons, which threatened the survival of entire peoples, raised the stakes of conflict even higher. The United States and the Soviet Union, the first great powers to possess such weapons, also developed nearly instantaneous intercontinental delivery systems able to penetrate the hard shell of the territorial state, and in consequence both of the threatened societies went on a permanent war footing. Peacetime security pacts, like the North Atlantic Treaty Organization (NATO) and the Warsaw Pact, sprang up as protection against the awesome war machines.

Second, the twentieth century became an age of ideology. Mass nationalist movements swept away the polite forms and limited commitments of aristocratic diplomacy, and foreign policy became an armed crusade between mutually exclusive ideologies. Liberalism awoke from its peaceful economic pursuits to fight a "war to end all wars" and rid the world forever of autocracy. Communism set out on a worldwide crusade to cast off the exploiting shackles of capitalism. Democracy fought a war to the death against fascism, and capitalism launched a lengthy cold war against the infecting bacillus of socialism. These campaigns of ideas changed the whole tone of international relations, making the power of governing elites, and their freedom of maneuver, subject to the active consent of the masses. Nationalism became the new morality, destroying any vestiges of an international code of conduct and subordinating the interests of both citizen and diplomat to the axiom "My country, right or wrong." Popular participation in political life encouraged governments to indoctrinate their citizens with propaganda images of the enemy, so that the populace would be inoculated against subversive ideas and willing to sacrifice their blood and treasure for the nation. The fight was no longer for territory or resources, but for truth, freedom, and survival itself.

Each nation conceived its particular ideology as having universal application. Both liberal democrats and socialists thought their creeds could unite the world and bring global peace, when in fact they led only to a fundamental ideological division. Alliances became fixed on the basis of principle and doctrinal conformity, and the complete loyalty of one's allies became paramount. Given the nature of the nuclear threat, arrangements of security had to be stable, protection absolute. A change of alliance was a betrayal. Friends were no longer sought for reasons of prudence or convenience, but to prove the legitimacy and worthiness of one's way of life.

A third force in the transition from the classical to the bipolar balance was a series of geopolitical shifts. The number of great powers in Europe had been gradually declining for centuries. At the end of the Thirty Years' War, the German empire was composed of 900 sovereign states. The Treaty of Westphalia reduced these to 355, Napoleon eliminated 200 more, and the Germanic Confederation of 1815 comprised only 36 sovereign states. Bismarck's unification in 1871 made the remaining 24 German states into one. This reduction in the number of independent players in the center of Europe naturally reduced the opportunities for alliances and flexible diplomacy — a trend that became

FIGURE 3-2
EUROPE IN 1648

global after 1815. At the end of the Napoleonic wars, Europe was dominated by eight great powers — Austria, Prussia, France, Great Britain, Russia, Portugal, Spain, and Sweden. The last three were replaced over the next hundred years by Italy, Japan, and the United States, leaving again eight great powers at the outbreak of World War I. (Figures 3-2 and 3-3, maps of Europe in 1648 and in 1914, give a sense of the changing national boundaries.) By the end of World War II, however, there were only two great powers — the United States and the Soviet Union — with Britain, France, and China great powers in name only. For all practical purposes, the two nuclear superpowers were so preponderant that an alliance switch by one of the secondary powers would have made little difference in the global balance.

As the number of great powers declined, the balance of power was expanding to global proportions, due to the growth of global commerce and transportation and the disappearance of the colonial frontier. This expansion began with the imperial conquests of Spain, Holland, France, and England, which spread European interests around the world. Britain, the champion of a free-trade economy, used its naval supremacy to reach into every part of the globe. European capital began to develop the colonial regions, creating markets and sources of supply that were tied to the mother country. Then, in the 1870s, the advent of the iron steamship made maritime traffic speedy, safe, and cheap. But

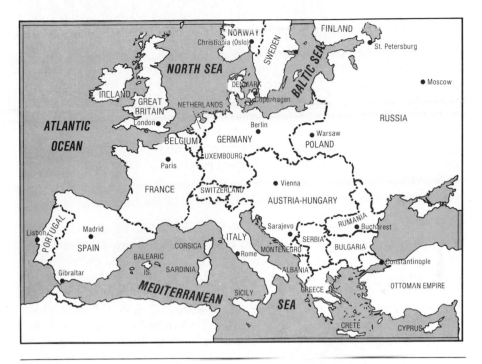

FIGURE 3-3
EUROPE IN 1914

the flows of capital and colonists were also spreading liberal ideas about self-government that ultimately brought a migration of power. The American Revolution, in 1775, was only the first of the blows struck by restless colonial peoples against European power centers. Within a few decades, the Latin American states rebelled against the imperial domination of Spain and Portugal, leaving an entire hemisphere outside Europe's direct control. The shift of power eventually reached the heart of Europe itself, with the dissolution of the Ottoman and Austro-Hungarian empires—the consequence of a self-consuming rivalry among the great powers, whose empires had no further room to expand in Africa and Asia. World War I was set off by the intersection of these imperial rivalries and a nascent nationalism, which came together in the struggle over the Balkans. What began as a strictly European war finally drew in the United States, whose wealth and power proved decisive. To paraphrase Winston Churchill, the New World stepped forth to rescue the Old. After a period of renewed separation and isolation, the pattern was repeated in World War II, the point at which the balance shifted irreversibly toward the two non-European superpowers.

Several events symbolized America's new global role: Commodore Matthew Perry's forcible entry into Japan in 1854; the annexation of the Philippines after the Spanish-American War of 1898; Secretary of State John

Hay's declaration of an open-door policy for China; U.S. mediation during the Russo-Japanese peace conference at Portsmouth in 1905; and, finally, the American intervention in the two world wars. After World War II, only the Soviet Union remained powerful enough to challenge the United States, and Europe became just one of many regional power systems in a balance controlled by the two global superpowers. Their dominion was sealed by the postwar colonial revolutions. Independence movements throughout the Third World deprived the European powers, already weakened by two world wars, of any advantages remaining from their former military, political, and economic domination of the non-West. A key moment was the 1954 defeat of the French at Dienbienphu, in Indochina (Vietnam), which symbolized the end of empire and marked a new turn in the global rivalry between the United States and the Soviet Union.

The traditional role of a balancer disappeared in the bipolar system. Although decolonization after World War II once again increased the number of sovereign states, none had sufficient wealth or power to play the role of balancer, let alone become a new challenger. All the Third World states together were too poor and disunited to balance the superpowers, especially since they lacked a comparable nuclear capability. As a result, Third World nations have suffered repeated interventions by the Soviet Union and the United States, each seeking to expand its sphere of influence or gain an ideological ally. Some nonaligned states, such as Egypt and India, have made successful use of their neutrality, or of tactical shifts in their allegiances, to win concessions from both sides. But the disparities in economic development and military power were so great that the Third World's regional conflicts have remained apart from or subordinate to the interests of the two nuclear giants. Third World states have been useful mainly as minor coalition partners or as proxies through which the superpowers sought to avoid direct nuclear conflict.

The advanced industrial states continued to be important international players, but only as subordinate members of the competing blocs, which were split by ideology, political economy, and system of government. These relations were formalized in a series of peacetime security pacts that removed any prospect of independent military action by the members of the blocs. The American global alliance system was embodied in the Organization of American States (the Rio Pact of 1947), the North Atlantic Treaty Organization (1949), the Anzus Pact with Australia and New Zealand (1951), the Southeast Asia Collective Defense Treaty, or SEATO (1954), the Central Treaty Organization, or CENTO (1959), and a series of bilateral security treaties with Japan (1951), the Philippines (1951), South Korea (1953), and Taiwan (1954). These agreements involved the United States in institutionalized military alliances with forty-two governments on every continent. The postwar recovery of Western Europe and Japan revived a number of the earlier great powers, but only in economic terms, not militarily, and they remained dependent on the predominant military force of the United States. Japan relied entirely on the American nuclear umbrella to shield it from Soviet attack. Likewise, Japan and Western Europe depended on the United States and its approximately 336 overseas military bases to police their interests in Europe, Asia, and the Third World. For example, the U.S. Navy and the Rapid Deployment Force (RDF) protect access to the Persian Gulf oil fields, which supply 80 percent of Japan's needs and 50 percent of Europe's, but only 7 percent of the United States'.

The Soviet Union similarly institutionalized its dominant role in Eastern Europe, through the Communist Information Bureau, or Cominform (1947), the Council for Mutual Economic Assistance, or Comecon (1949), the Warsaw Pact (1955), and the Brezhnev Doctrine (1968), which claimed for the Soviet Union the right to safeguard the collective interests of the socialist bloc even by military intervention in the internal affairs of a fraternal state. (For comparative data on the Warsaw Pact and NATO as of 1982, see Figure 3-4.) Soviet relations with China were cemented by the Sino-Soviet Treaty of 1950, although effective cooperation between these two historical and ideological rivals lasted less than a decade. Close military and economic relations were established with Mongolia (1936), North Korea (1953), and Cuba (1960); treaties of friendship and mutual assistance were signed with Yemen (1955), Congo-Brazzaville (1968), Egypt (1971, abrogated in 1976), India (1971), Iraq (1972), Somalia (1974, renounced in 1977), Syria (1976), Angola (1976), Mozambique (1977), Vietnam (1978), Ethiopia (1978), Afghanistan (1978), the People's Democratic Republic of Yemen (1979), and Libya (1982). Soviet participation in the world economy, on the other hand, was slight. The Soviet Union preferred close economic ties among the sixteen states with Communist governments, to keep their planned economies insulated from the influence of international capitalism. The Soviet military presence in the Third World was correspondingly small, consisting primarily of arms aid to certain client states and limited basing rights for the growing Soviet blue-water navy.

Despite the polarization of the globe into two main blocs, the balance remained relatively loose, exhibiting a constant tendency toward pluralism. (The Cold War divisions and realignments between 1947 and 1982 are shown in Figure 3-5.) The Soviet Union experienced steady difficulty in keeping its satellite states in tow. Yugoslavia, which had defeated the wartime Nazi occupation with entirely local Communist forces, defected from the Soviet bloc in 1948 because its leader, Marshal Tito, who was as much a nationalist as a Communist, insisted on Yugoslavia's right to pursue an independent socialist path. Tito accepted aid and loans from the West and permitted economic practices substantially more liberal than Joseph Stalin found acceptable. Independent impulses and nationalist unrest subsequently occurred throughout Eastern Europe. General strikes and armed revolts in East Germany (1953), Hungary (1956), Czechoslovakia (1968), and Poland (1980) were all repressed by Soviet troops or influence, but at the price of greater Soviet tolerance for diversity and autonomy in intrabloc relations. In the 1970s and '80s, Communist parties in Western Europe, once faithful to Moscow, also declared their political and ideological independence. After the advent of Mikhail Gorbachev's policy of *glasnost* ("openness") in 1985, liberalization within the Communist camp proceeded rapidly, with the recognition of non-Communist parties and independent trade unions throughout Eastern Europe. The Polish

FIGURE 3-4

THE WARSAW PACT AND NATO

Warsaw Pact

Members (year of accession: 1955)	Population (thousands, mid-1983)	Armed Forces (thousands, mid-1983)
Bulgaria	8,944	162
Czechoslovakia	15,420	205
German Democratic Republic	16,724	167
Hungary	10,691	105
Poland	36,356	340
Romania	22,649	189
USSR	272,308	5,050

Area: 9 million sq. mi.
　(USSR = 8.7 million sq. mi)
Population: 369 million (1978)
　(USSR = 261 million)
GNP: $1.3 trillion (1978)
GNP per capita: $3,500
Share of world GNP: 16%
Share of world trade: 8% (1979)
Chief international economic affiliations: All are members of Council for Mutual Economic Assistance.
Percentage of crude oil imported: 0%
Essential items imported from other areas: Idustrial machinery and technology (largely from NATO countries and Japan), grains
Total military personnel in place in Europe: 4,000,000

Note: Albania withdrew in 1961.

NATO

Members (with year of accession)	Population (thousands, mid-1983)	Armed Forces (thousands, mid-1983)
Belgium (1949)	9,865	95
Canada (1949)	24,882	83
Denmark (1949)	5,115	31
France (1949)	54,604	493
Germany, Federal Republic of (1955)	61,543	495
Greece (1952)	9,898	185
Iceland (1949)	236	no forces
Italy (1949)	56,345	373
Luxembourg (1949)	366	0.7
Netherlands (1949)	14,374	103
Norway (1949)	4,131	43
Portugal (1949)	10,008	64
Spain (1982)	38,234	347
Turkey (1952)	49,115	569
United Kingdom (1949)	56,006	321
United States (1949)	234,193	2,136

Area in Europe: 1 million sq. mi.

Population: 566 million (1978); (323 million in Europe)

GNP: $4.4 trillion (1978)

GNP per capita: $8,302

Share of world GNP: 51% (1979)

Share of world trade: 59% (1979)

Chief international economic affiliations: All are members of Organization for Economic Cooperation and Development; Belgium, Denmark, France, W. Germany, Greece, Italy, Luxembourg, Netherlands, Portugal, Spain, and the United Kingdom are in the European Economic Community; Norway, and Iceland, are in the European Free Trade Association.

Percentage of crude oil imported: 79% (all by sea routes)

Essential items of transatlantic trade: Grains and other agricultural products from the United States

Essential items imported from other areas (excluding fuel): Nonfuel minerals (some from Warsaw Pact countries)

Total military personnel in place in Europe: 2,600,000 (excludes French forces—France withdrew its forces from NATO's international commands in 1966 but remains a member of the alliance)

Note: Figures in the third column do not include Spain, which became a member of NATO on May 30, 1982.

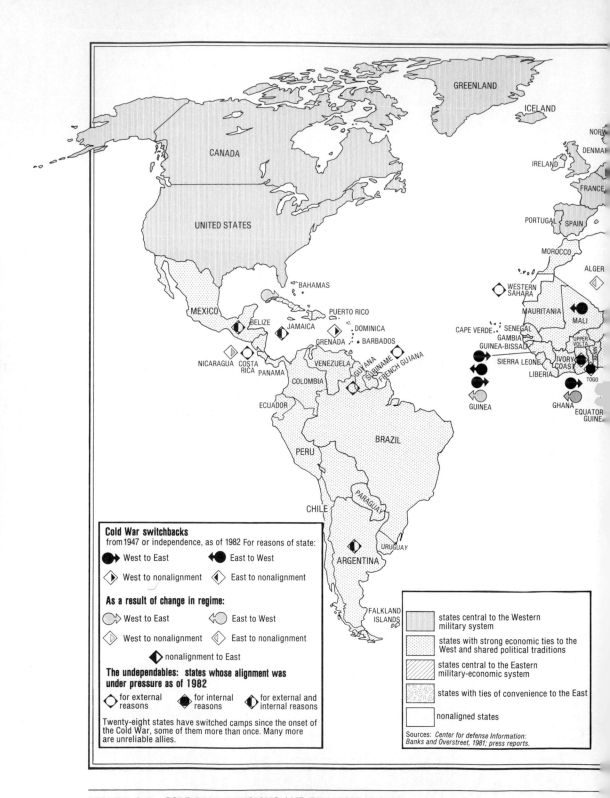

FIGURE 3-5   COLD WAR DIVISIONS AND REALIGNMENTS

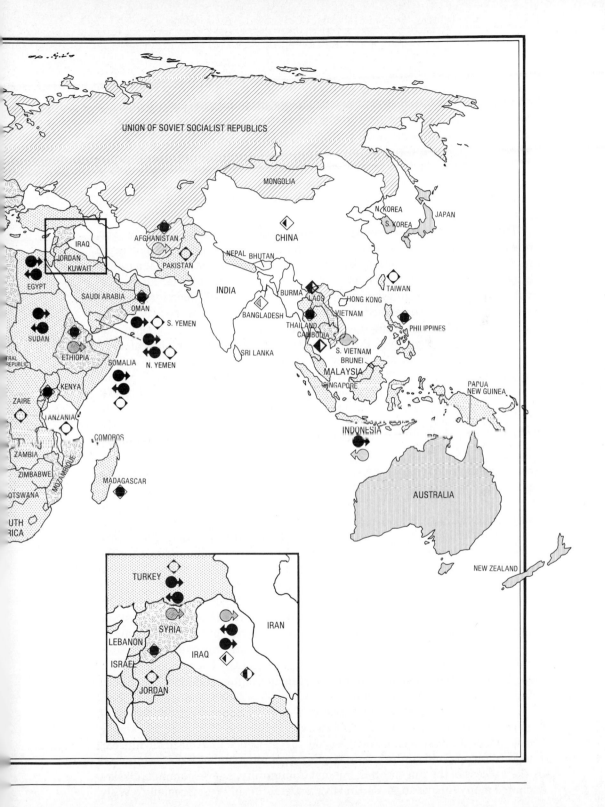

union, Solidarity, was legalized in 1989 and shortly thereafter formed the first independent non-Communist government in the socialist bloc. By 1990, revolutions had taken place in every Eastern European country except Albania, and open multiparty elections had been held in both Poland and Hungary. In Romania, the ruling Communist party was overthrown and declared illegal. In East Germany, Czechoslovakia, and Bulgaria, the Communist party's constitutional monopoly on power was officially rejected and important measures of democratization set in motion. Whether these newly free states of Eastern Europe will continue to define themselves as socialist remains an open question in the 1990s.

The earliest, and most enduring, challenge to Soviet leadership, however, came from the Chinese Communists. Stalin had never given his wholehearted support to the Chinese Communist leader, Mao Tse-tung, fearing that a united China would represent a serious military threat and a potential ideological rival. Following the Chinese Communist victory in 1949, doctrinal and national differences were patched over for a time, in the face of intense Cold War pressures from the West, and the conflicts in Korea and Vietnam kept formal Sino-Soviet cooperation alive. But the underlying hostilities were growing, and by 1963 the Sino-Soviet split had emerged full-blown, setting off ideological disputes within the socialist bloc, rivalry for influence in Third World communist movements, and several military engagements, between 1969 and 1971, along the disputed Sino-Soviet border. Then, in 1979, the Soviet Union's invasion of Afghanistan began a series of setbacks for it in the Third World. The Soviets intervened in Afghanistan to overthrow a Marxist radical and install their own, more moderate client, but after sending in more than 100,000 troops and fighting for almost a decade, they had still not succeeded in stabilizing the country or removing the threat of an Islamic fundamentalist revolution on their southern border. They were forced to withdraw from Afghanistan in 1989. Other countries where the Soviets lost influence or control include Albania, Indonesia, Egypt, Iraq, Somalia, Mali, Guinea, Sudan, and South Yemen. Laos and Cambodia (Kampuchea) joined the socialist camp after the American defeat in Vietnam, but the region has remained under the local influence of the consolidated Vietnamese regime in Hanoi, rather than under Moscow's influence. In 1978, the Vietnamese Communists threw out the Chinese-backed Pol Pot regime in Cambodia, setting off a brief border war between China and Vietnam, but in 1988 the Hanoi government agreed to withdraw its troops from Kampuchea. That opened the way to an improvement in Sino-Soviet relations. In 1989, the Soviet leader, Mikhail Gorbachev, and China's Deng Xiaoping held a historic summit meeting in Beijing, although Sino-Soviet relations remain somewhat cool.

In the West, NATO's solidarity was called into question by the defection of the French, who created an independent nuclear force in 1966, and by a strong European peace movement that resisted the presence of American nuclear weapons, troops, and control. Western Europe's independence was reinforced by the success of the European Economic Community, whose common market excluded many American goods, and by the *Ostpolitik* of West Germany's Willy

Brandt, which opened trade ties with the Soviet Union and Eastern Europe. American influence in other areas gradually diminished. U.S. economic leadership has been strongly challenged by Japan, Germany, France, and other members of the capitalist bloc, including the newly industrialized countries of Taiwan and South Korea. U.S. dominance in the United Nations, symbolized by the UN's formal sponsorship of American peacekeeping forces during the Korean War, was stripped away by the new Third World member nations that gained their independence in the 1960s. Latin America, a U.S. sphere of influence since the Monroe Doctrine of 1823, began to take nonaligned positions with increasing frequency, and the appearance of socialist or left-leaning governments in Guatemala (1954), Cuba (1958), the Dominican Republic (1965), Chile (1970), Nicaragua (1979), and Grenada (1980) also marked the loss of American influence there. America intervened militarily, by direct or covert means, against all these regimes, successfully in most cases. But, despite strenuous U.S. efforts, Cuba and Nicaragua cemented their ties with the Soviet Union. The military defeat in Vietnam marked at least the temporary end of an active American containment policy and permitted countries like Zimbabwe (formerly British Rhodesia), Bangladesh, and Peru to experiment with radical measures without suffering American sanctions or being forced to seek Soviet protection. The rise of the OPEC oil cartel gave the Arab states of the Middle East important independent leverage, and the fall of the Shah in Iran, civil war in Lebanon, and the growth of state-sponsored terrorism have further eroded American control in that region.

Despite the diminished ability of the two superpowers to enforce political orthodoxy and alliance solidarity, the distribution of military capabilities in 1990 still favored a roughly bipolar balance. A power center with the potential for outweighing one of the rivals, or at least controlling the outcome of a direct struggle between them, did not yet exist. Acquisition of nuclear capability by China and India and the emergence of independent Third World regimes only made the loose bipolar arrangement somewhat looser. Japan and Western Europe, because of their economic growth, had become increasingly influential in international trade and finance. And on global regime issues, such as the environment, the multipolar diffusion of power was apparent. But on the key political-military questions   alliance relations, nuclear arms control, intervention in Third World revolutions — the superpowers were still dominant. A definitive transition from a bipolar military balance to a multipolar political-economic balance will depend on a number of outcomes associated with the end of the Cold War: successful democratization in the Eastern bloc, the reunification of Europe, radical cuts in the superpower arsenals and overseas bases, integration of the Soviet economy into the world market, and continued affirmation by both socialist and capitalist states that universal human values take precedence over ideological divisions.

Now let us summarize the essential features of the loose bipolar system. It consists of institutionalized alliances based on ideological interests that are perceived as both permanent and mutually antagonistic. The bipolarity is reinforced by the industrial capacity and conventional military strength of two superpowers. Both possess nuclear arsenals with an invulnerable retaliatory capability, which creates a system of stable deterrence while providing incentives for nonnuclear powers to seek the protection of one of the giants. Ideological rivalry and competition for the allegiance and resources of Third World states support the tendency toward a division into two mutually antagonistic blocs. Nonetheless, the system accommodates nonbloc actors — international organizations as well as nonaligned states. The balance is not maintained by the dissolution and formation of alliances or by one nation's taking the role of a balancer; rather, adjustments take place through arms races or the mediation of nonbloc members or international agencies. Hostility between the blocs and the absence of any integrating cultural norms largely remove equilibrium as an explicit goal of the system. Instead, each superpower aims at defeating the rival bloc, while the secondary powers aim at belonging to the dominant coalition. Massive nuclear retaliation is the strategy devised for policing such a maximally hostile power arrangement, but the very threat of nuclear destruction leads to a tacit agreement not to provoke a direct military confrontation between the blocs. Large-scale wars have consequently been replaced by arms races and by limited wars fought through surrogates or client states.

Some scholars question whether a bipolar system is capable of maintaining a stable balance. Mutual antagonisms between unified and dynamic blocs, they argue, have historically tended to intensify into war. The cause of World War I, for example, is often said to have been the polarization of the flexible nineteenth-century alliance system into the rigid and ideologically antagonistic Triple Alliance and Triple Entente. Traditionally, bipolar systems that have not ended in war or the complete dominance of one side have undergone a diffusion of power that has re-created the conditions of the classical balance of power.

But nuclear weapons may have fundamentally changed the dynamics of the bipolar system. Research on the relationship between polarity and stability has produced evidence that a bipolar balance may be less war-prone, although its wars are likely to be longer and more severe. It is clear that nuclear deterrence has made both of today's superpowers exceedingly cautious about exercising force in areas of vital interest to the rival power. The destructiveness of nuclear retaliation has also tended to override other differences in capabilities, so that American economic predominance and NATO's military superiority, say, cannot be translated into the capacity to compel changes in Soviet policy. The reduction of the great powers to two has simplified power calculations, removing the uncertainties of alliance commitments such as existed under the traditional balance of power. In a bipolar setting, the origin of a threat is readily identifiable, and the resources for response are under one's own control. From their constant interaction over several decades, the two superpowers have become familiar with the adversary's likely responses and have improved their mechanisms for crisis management. On all these counts, the bipolar system may be more stable than the multipolar balance — particularly because bipolarity does not rely on frequent trials of strength to ensure that no nation has grown disproportionately strong.

Both of the superpowers have a strong incentive for keeping wars in the Third World localized, limited to the periphery, and nonnuclear. Also, their control of large power blocs makes them relatively immune to the adventures of third parties, which under the traditional system often embroiled an alliance partner in war. The loose bipolar system has been able to survive a number of conflicts within the Western bloc — the several Arab-Israeli wars, squabbles in Central America, the conflict between Turkey and Greece over Cyprus, the war between Britain and Argentina over the Falkland Islands (Las Malvinas) — precisely because these wars had little effect on the balance between the two main contenders. Such sizable powers as Yugoslavia, China, France, and Iran could withdraw from alliances or even switch sides without upsetting the basic postwar equilibrium. Finally, the zero-sum competition of a bipolar world, in which one bloc's loss is the gain of the other, encourages rigid alignments and the fierce protection of the most minor of allies, for fear the conquest of one might set off a domino effect that would threaten the solidarity of the whole bloc. On the other hand, the intensity of the competition encourages the great powers to respond promptly to unsettling events, to police carefully their respective spheres of influence, and, most often, to resolve conflicts at a lower level of crisis than war.

ALTERNATIVES TO THE BALANCE OF POWER

The Imperial System

The hierarchical, or imperial, model of international order is one in which power is highly skewed toward one dominant entity. It is not a balancing system, since its stability depends exclusively on one power's ability to dominate all others. (If Napoleon had succeeded in conquering all of Europe or Hitler had won World War II, we might have witnessed a global imperial system.) Conquest does not necessarily bring an end to conflict, however. Imperial systems inevitably suffer from separatist tendencies, resulting in civil wars that the imperial power must suppress, with greater or lesser success. In practice, global domination could not last long unless it was buttressed by devices of legitimacy and ties of community or economy, and these would convert it into the more complex and stable form of a world government.

The Roman Empire is the only historical example of a hierarchical system that successfully encompassed the whole of the Western world. It was founded on Rome's military power, which first unified the empire by force. That was soon followed by political, economic, and cultural integration, which allowed the ruling group to conserve its power resources. Roman citizenship was offered to local elites in the conquered territories, facilitating the assimilation of culturally diverse populations. Roman law, the *jus gentium,* codified the principles held in common by many of the peoples and became a kind of international law. It was administered by a class of international civil servants who became, in effect, a cosmopolitan ruling class. The Roman army defended the empire's frontiers, but local regions had great political autonomy. At the apex of this conglomerate structure was the emperor, the focus of loyalty. Even so, the empire's cohesion was always in question. War was perpetual; a consistent 14 percent to 20 percent of the adult male population was in army service at all times. As the empire grew in wealth and size, its ruling class became increasingly dependent on the administrative competence and extractive powers of a centralized state apparatus. Leadership, subject to the accident of birth, varied dramatically in quality. As with most empires, the ruling elite soon began to live beyond its means, and weak and decadent emperors consumed state resources faster than they were being created. Even under competent leadership, cultural change and divisive tendencies made it difficult to hold the empire together. Later emperors tried to use Christianity—a creed they had once persecuted ruthlessly—as a kind of religious glue to stop the decay. Still, it was a remarkable achievement for the Romans to perpetuate their hierarchical system of world government over several centuries.

Later imperial systems were more limited in their geographical reach. The Russian and the Ottoman empires, two other examples of multiethnic hierarchical systems, were created by conquest, and the single ruling group's military power was the principal force uniting entities that were not culturally or economically interdependent. Once the coercive power of the centralizing state began to decay, as happened in Ottoman Turkey at the end of the nineteenth century and in Soviet Russia after 1980, the empire was bound to come apart. In sum, an imperial state is dependent on a hegemonic power's ability to consolidate its control within a regional power balance—a feat that is difficult and rarely enduring.

Consequently, the prospects are slim for a worldwide imperial system in the modern era. Imperialism is not well suited to a nationalist age marked by the secessionist desires of cultural minorities. Ethnic unrest in the Soviet Union and Eastern Europe gives ample evidence of the truth of that statement. In light of today's high level of political consciousness and widely shared norms of popular legitimacy, powerful elites cannot easily take control by force. A modern empire would require a transcultural legitimizing principle. Marxism-Leninism has performed this function within the Soviet empire, but with only limited success, and it is an ideology that is hardly likely to find global acceptance. The Romans secured their control through administrative practices that coopted conquered elites, and their military and communications technology was far advanced over that of the subordinate states they were policing. Even so, Roman emperors eventually had to resort to deification and other devices of religious justification to maintain their authority. In the modern age, with its widespread literacy, global dissemination of advanced technology, and competing ideologies of all sorts, the formation of an imperial state seems practically impossible. Neither capitalism nor socialism has proved to be a strong enough ideology to erase national differences; the widely accepted principle of self-determination still locates sovereignty in a well-defined cultural community. Nor is there a technology so powerful that it can confer control in the face of the resistant forces of nationalism and subversive terrorist and guerrilla tactics. While there are many practical restraints against the creation of a global empire, the hierarchical model is nonetheless a useful ideal type against which we can measure the tendencies of a system.

The Nuclear Proliferation Model

At the opposite theoretical extreme from a hierarchical system is the possibility of such a complete proliferation of nuclear weapons throughout the world that every state or group could claim sovereignty unto itself. Current members of the nuclear club include the United States, Great Britain, France, the USSR, and China. Countries suspected of having operational nuclear devices include India, Israel, and South Africa. Potential nuclear powers — states with the resources, technical skill, and motivation to develop such weapons — include, at a minimum, Argentina, Brazil, Chile, Iran, Iraq, Libya, Pakistan, South Korea, and Taiwan. Of course, Japan and all the industrial societies of Europe are capable of developing nuclear weapons as well, but currently lack the incentive to do so, given their membership in collective security arrangements with the superpowers. If nuclear technology becomes widespread, along with the incentive to deploy such weapons, we will have what Morton Kaplan calls a *unit-veto* system.

In this model, nuclear deterrence is universal, meaning that every state could credibly threaten to retaliate against any attack. The international hierarchy would be radically equalized. Small states would become indigestible "porcupines" with nuclear quills to deter the great powers that formerly would have swallowed them up. Interventions would be avoided as far too risky, and war in general would cease to play a conflict-resolving role. The high probability of nuclear escalation would give each state a potential veto on the actions of all others, so long as its threat of nuclear retaliation was believable. Alliances would recede in importance, and hegemonial ambitions would be curbed. Each power would exist in isolated self-sufficiency, rejecting all outside pressures, even from international organizations.

It is a matter of debate whether such a system would be highly stable or highly unstable. Some theorists imagine that widespread nuclear proliferation might cause a sort of cold-war peace to descend on the whole planet — a generalized form of the present deterrent relationship between the United States and the Soviet Union. However, the stalemate between these superpowers is based on a power equivalence that goes well beyond nuclear capacity. Moreover, the size and dispersal of their nuclear forces and their huge geographical size give them a relative invulnerability that small states would not possess. Other factors also make it unlikely that the unit-veto system would be a stable one. The more primitive technology of new nuclear states would be prone to accident; have-not nations with little to lose might be more willing to risk nuclear confrontation; anonymous terrorist groups, immune to counterattack because they have no geographical base, could use nuclear weapons as devices of intimidation and revenge. The chances of nuclear war through accident, miscalculation, irrationality, or fanaticism would be extremely high.

Universal nuclear proliferation does not rule out the possibility of other power gradations. France, China, India, and Israel have not become super-powers, despite their acquisition of nuclear bombs. Also, the self-canceling effects of deterrence could bring into play other instruments of influence by which states might swing the balance of power in their favor. Conventional weapons, economic and political pressures, ideological alliances, diplomatic maneuvers — any of these might succeed in altering the status quo dramatically, even in the presence of complete nuclear proliferation. The preservation of international order and of a balance of power depends, therefore, on other factors than nuclear technology and the number of states with access to it.

The Collective Security System

Two additional models are the collective security system and the multibloc system. They share with the traditional balance-of-power model the assumption that power continues to be dispersed in sovereign units and that international order depends on containing aggressors by force. In the collective security system, power is exercised in accordance with a substantial consensus on and adherence to international law. In the multibloc model, relations are stabilized through regional confederations.

The collective security model is the archetype for international order that President Woodrow Wilson was championing in his advocacy of a League of Nations. In this model, sovereignty continues to reside in individual nations, but all states pledge to join collectively in resisting aggression, no matter what the source. No central authority or peacekeeping force is needed, since the states voluntarily coordinate their forces and abide by self-imposed moral and legal obligations to uphold the collective peace. Military force as an ordinary instrument of policy is forbidden, and standing alliances, whether long- or short-term, do not exist. Nations ally themselves only at the moment of aggression, when they join in economic and military sanctions to punish the use of force.

To be feasible, a collective security system must meet certain conditions: (1) there must be widespread agreement that the status quo is just and therefore worth defending; (2) the collective system must be able to muster at all times such overwhelming power that any potential aggressor or coalition of aggressors is dissuaded from challenging it; (3) war must be a realistic option for the system, with a technology that makes its threat of a "war to end war" believable; (4) aggression must be clearly identifiable as such; (5) political leaders must believe that the interests of peace transcend their particular national interests; (6) all significant international actors must be members of the collective security league.

These conditions are difficult to meet at present. Nuclear technology, by rendering war less imaginable and less feasible, has made it almost impossible for even the strongest of coalitions to compel a nuclear-armed state to alter its behavior. Collective security also tends to generalize war, turning each act of aggression into an occasion to mobilize the entire system rather than letting normal diplomacy pursue its goals of keeping wars localized and limited. Collective security, though it aims to abolish war, is pledged to use force against states that reject this prohibition; since a few such states are likely always to be present, a system whose intent is to enforce peace on an imperfect world ends by making war universal and, in the nuclear era, possibly fatal to everyone. Aggression has become more difficult to identify unambiguously, with the spread of guerrilla insurgencies, covert operations, terrorist operations, and other forms of indirect aggression. In addition, the ferment associated with modernization and radical social change has led to civil violence on an unprecedented scale, and the frequent involvement of outside forces in these revolutionary movements makes it very difficult to separate interstate conflict from domestic violence. Collective security tends to support the entrenched interests of the status quo, often leaving violence as the only means of satisfying frustrated claims for justice or reform.

A major problem of the collective security model is its reliance on voluntary agreement among members to punish aggression by the imposition of sanctions. Sanctions fly in the face of traditional sovereignty and freedom of choice, while reducing the diplomatic flexibility that often can resolve disputes. In fact, conditions that would permit the effective imposition of sanctions constitute one of the prerequisites for world government. If the vast majority of states ever achieved a clear consensus on sanctions or other procedures limiting their use of violence and restraining their sovereignty, they would already have reached a sufficient level of trust to create a central authority. This goes far beyond the narrow scope of collective security, which attempts to respond to aggression by imposing special rules on the balance-of-power system at no sacrifice to the principle of national sovereignty. Such rules seem basically incompatible with the nature of balance-of-power politics. The refusal of only one moderately powerful state — the United States — to become a member was enough to torpedo the League of Nations, the first experiment in collective security. Noncompliance by key powers has also undercut the efforts of both the League and the United Nations to impose economic sanctions: against Italy in the 1930s for its aggression in Ethiopia, and against South Africa today for its racist policy of apartheid. It is difficult to achieve universal compliance with a sanctions mechanism when implementation is left up to individual states.

The Multibloc Model

The multibloc model, another theoretical modification of the balance of power, is a system consisting of consolidated regional federations or blocs with mutually exclusive spheres of influence organized around five or more major power centers. A real-world example of one such bloc would be a politically consolidated Western Europe whose existing economic cooperation under the

Economic Community was complemented by a united and self-sufficient security arrangement. Along the same lines, security-political organizations similar to NATO or the Warsaw Pact could grow around groups of states in the Third World or East Asia. Rules would be established to prevent one region from interfering in the internal affairs of another region, and the multiplicity of power centers would serve to restrain any impulses of the nuclear superpowers toward global empire.

Joseph Nye, in *Peace in Parts,* posits five characteristics of regional integration that connect it to an enhanced degree of international order. First, a multibloc division of power would work against two dangers of the current bipolar system—the possibility of domination by one superpower or of a catastrophic structural breakdown. Advocates of a European community, for instance, see their region as presently divided by ideological rivalry and manipulated or vulnerable because of its military dependence on the superpowers. Second, small or weak states that are sovereign in name only could become more powerful and secure by joining together. It was in this spirit that Kwame Nkrumah, the first president of Ghana, championed pan-African unity, arguing that regional consolidation would reduce neocolonialism and remove temptations for foreign intervention. Third, the creation of institutions at a level somewhat above the nation-state would assist in the transition to global order by curbing some of the powers of sovereign states. Fourth, tying contiguous states together in a tight web of economic, social, and cultural relations would lead to regional interdependence and inhibit any resort to war by one of them—a regional variant of the functionalist approach to world order, with its assumption that cooperative socioeconomic relations will spill over into restraints on violence. Fifth, the regional federations or blocs would be better at policing order in their domains than a remote actor would, since they understand better the causes of conflict and the conditions under which it can likely be resolved. The claim is made, for example, that the Contadora Group is the best mediator of a negotiated settlement in Nicaragua and throughout Central America, since the Latin American states understand the roots of the conflicts better than the superpowers do and, besides, have a stake in insulating their region from outside influence.

Critics argue that the multibloc model is impractical because it fails to take into account that most conflicts occur between neighboring states, which do not necessarily share common interests. A history of conflict marks relations between India and Pakistan, Israel and Syria, Vietnam and Cambodia, Peru and Chile, China and Taiwan, and dozens of other regional rivals. Franco-German frictions, which manifested themselves in more than a half-dozen major wars, have largely been put to rest by regional cooperation, but the European experience appears unique and not likely to be repeated elsewhere. Historically, regional consolidations have come mainly through conquest, which may be a more reliable means of subordinating separate sovereignties but is hardly a formula for international order.

Both the collective security and the multibloc models assume that sovereign entities will adopt a certain level of cooperation in defense of their security.

Such explicit collaboration, while not wholly borne out in reality, does indicate the degree to which all systems of international order are a combination of peace by power and peace by law or satisfaction (consent). Even in the classical balance of power, stability depends not only on countervailing military forces but on agreed-upon international norms that allow the great powers to take concerted action to protect their shared stake in the system. Relations of pure power exist only in the mind of the foreign policy theorist. Every balance-of-power system is in fact modified to some extent by elements of international community that create a consensus on certain rules of the game. When these rules become institutionalized to the degree that they place significant restraints on the exercise of sovereign powers, we have what we call international regimes.

International Regimes

John Ruggie, in "International Responses to Technology," defines an international regime as "a set of mutual expectations, rules and regulations, plans, organizational energies and financial commitments which have been accepted by a group of states" (p. 570). According to Stephen Krasner's *International Regimes* (p. 2), the principles and norms that constitute a regime include shared values, common expectations, and a sense of legitimacy, which take form in statements of belief and definitions of rights and obligations. At the organiza tional level, a regime adopts rules that specifically prescribe or prohibit certain actions and implements these rules through established decision-making procedures.

Such a regime, or "pattern of regularized cooperative behavior," in Krasner's words, may spring up in an issue area like trade, monetary relations, civil aviation, telecommunications, or some other functional concern. For example, the General Agreement on Trade and Tariffs (GATT) has established a conference procedure for drawing up sets of rules to govern international trade. Currencies and exchange rates are regulated through the International Monetary Fund (IMF), supplemented by the joint decision making of central banks and economic summit conferences of the so-called Group of Seven (the leading industrial nations). Or an international regime may focus on geographical jurisdiction, such as joint use of Antarctica or fisheries in the North Pacific. A regime's scope of action may be fairly narrow — for example, managing the supply of a particular commodity. Or it may be quite broad — like the United Nations' conflict management regime, which encompasses the Disarmament Commission, formal peacekeeping operations, and many informal devices of conflict resolution. An international regime typically draws its authority from a variety of public and private sources: treaties, executive agreements, and other instruments of international law; the charters, regulations, resolutions, and practices of international governmental organizations; the domestic laws of states as they bear on foreign policy; and the practices of multinational corporations and other nongovernmental organizations. Initially, common need defines the arena of decision; over time, habit becomes the glue holding the loose decision-making amalgam together. Thus, authority is dispersed, but expectations converge on certain rules and common understandings that encourage regular compliance. The Law of the Sea is a regime embodying such a mix of rules and procedures, which define territorial waters, codes of conduct on the high seas, and the management of common ocean and seabed resources.

International regimes function best when states face common problems that require a cooperative solution but are reluctant to sacrifice their sovereignty to a more permanent decision-making body. Robert Keohane, in *After Hegemony,* sees regimes as a device for mediating the "crucial tension between economics and politics: international coordination of policy seems highly beneficial in an interdependent world economy, but cooperation in world politics is particularly difficult" (p. 49). Regimes facilitate agreement on matters of substance within particular issue areas when ad hoc joint action will not suffice. For example, states prefer to provide foreign aid and loans bilaterally, so they can dictate the terms of repayment, but when debt problems became so large as to threaten the stability of international financial markets, they quickly devised collaborative schemes. States seek order and security, but when these cannot be obtained by the traditional devices of sovereignty, self-interest encourages states to turn to the decision-making structure of an international regime.

The hardest problems international regimes confront are those involving the "commons," or what are sometimes called collective-goods problems. Everyone benefits from controls on arms, resource depletion, pollution, energy consumption, and the like, but an individual state can gain an advantage by remaining exempt from the controls that all other states observe. For example, the hunting of whales has been severely restricted to avoid their rapid depletion, but Japan and Iceland, which have refused to obey the international prohibition on whaling, can profit from whaling for decades, so long as they are the only violators. The dilemma: how to get everyone to go along with a common solution when each has an incentive for cheating.

A related problem is the temptation to become a "free rider" on the efforts of others. If Switzerland introduces controls on toxic chemical spills at the headwaters of a polluted river that crosses its national boundary, those controls will redound to the benefit of Germany, but they also will increase costs for the Swiss chemical manufacturers. If Brazil restricts logging in its tropical rain forests, the entire planetary ecosystem will benefit, although Brazil alone must bear the immediate cost in reduced exports and slowed economic growth. The free-rider dilemma arises from the nature of collective goods: they cannot be supplied to one member of a group without being supplied to all. A primary function of government taxing agencies is to make sure everyone shares in the cost of collectively consumed items, such as national defense, public schools, highways, and clean air and water. Deterrence, democracy, and political stability are collective goods that are supplied to everyone, even those unwilling to pay for arms, participate in the democratic process, or fight for their freedoms. The benefits of a security community or alliance are also collective goods, and every coalition member faces the temptation of letting its partners pay the costs of collective action, such as the deployment of nuclear arms, an embargo against a joint enemy, or trade subsidies. International regimes are a device for negotiating the sharing of the burden among partners who stand to realize joint gains. They "bind the members of the international community to rules of conduct, to which they agree, and which will restrain each member from free riding, and allocate burdens equitably, as a matter of international legal commitment," writes Charles Kindleberger in "Dominance and Leadership in the International Economy" (p. 252). Thus, a newly industrializing country like China may be persuaded to join a global ban on ozone-depleting chlorofluorocarbons only if the advanced industrial states will agree to supply China with alternative technologies in return.

A variety of means are used to achieve joint action on collective goods. A more powerful state can administer rewards or punishments to its junior partners to persuade them to become members of a regime. The United States, for example, can offer to subsidize United Nations programs or pay for new NATO deployments; it can likewise withhold dues to an international organization or threaten to withdraw troops from Europe. Offers of aid, arms, or favorable trade status are other measures for cementing a regime. Since states are unequal in power and resources, and since the benefits of collective action are rarely distributed evenly, it is not surprising that few regimes are based on purely voluntary agreement. Most arise through the leadership of a hegemonic power with the diplomatic and military clout to enforce their regulations and the resources to subsidize reluctant partners. A hegemonic power has a stronger interest in maintaining orderly international arrangements and benefits from them disproportionately, making it willing to provide certain collective goods even when it must bear most of the cost and support a few free riders.

Idealists and realists disagree on whether international regimes are primarily a response to growing interdependence, with its need for greater policy coordination, or to the leadership of preeminent stability-seeking states able to translate their hegemony into new norms and procedures of international order. It is more likely that a push-pull phenomenon is at work, with interdependence creating shared conditions and interests and hegemonial leadership providing the impetus for states to pass over the threshold from independent to coordinated action. In the case of European integration, American support clearly facilitated the process, as did the role played by leading states in the core area. American leadership was also important in the creation of the Bretton Woods international economic structure and the more liberal postwar trade regime. (European integration and the Bretton Woods system are discussed more fully in the next chapter.) Initially, the United States was powerful enough to set the rules, enforce them, and effectively veto any that it opposed. However, such dominance is not necessarily tyrannical manipulation or exploitation, as Marxists and world-system theorists often imply. Whatever privileges hegemony may confer on the leading power (and they are many), hegemonial relations can have important side benefits for international order. Conversely, many regime theorists hypothesize that the present decline in American power may be accompanied by a decay in the international regimes so painstakingly constructed since 1945. Indeed, some instability has already surfaced in monetary relations, in international finance, in the petroleum trade, and at the United Nations. The fear now is that the decay will spread into the trade arena as American protectionist sentiments grow.

Regimes may persist, however, in spite of a decline in the hegemon's influence. As regimes become institutionalized, they acquire a life of their own; maintaining them is not as difficult as forming them. If the regime was truly a response to a collective dilemma and was the product of leadership rather than domination by the hegemon, there remain important incentives for keeping it in place. In such a case, the decline of the hegemon does not leave a power vacuum or an exploitative structure that invites revolt. What is lost is the power of the hegemon to provide a collective good on favorable terms, but if other states can jointly pick up the burden, the regime may endure.

There is a point at which a regime may become so powerful and enduring as to be considered a formal international governmental organization and thus one of the incipient institutions of world government. Moreover, the shared political principles, interdependent economic interests, and sociocultural ties that regimes foster may become so strong as to relegate power relations and traditional diplomacy to a secondary status as regulators of international affairs. We will explore the role of the United Nations and other international agencies in Chapter 8; interdependence and socioeconomic factors are examined in the next chapter.

LONG CYCLES, HEGEMONY, AND TRANSFORMATION IN THE INTERNATIONAL SYSTEM

A common criticism of both regime analysis and the balance of power is that they give too static an image of international affairs. Organized around order and equilibrium, they perhaps overemphasize structural determinants at the expense of national and subnational factors. (A discussion of domestic determinants of foreign policy is to be found in Chapter 7, on nation-states.) Such a criticism can be made of any model of the international system that does not take into account the dynamics of national decision making or historical elements of continuity and change over time.

One approach toward uncovering patterns of change in the international system is *long-cycle theory,* which Joshua Goldstein has summarized in his *Long Cycles.* While the research falls into several schools of thought, all long-cycle theorists agree that international relations since about 1500 have alternated cyclically between periods of war and periods of peace, though they disagree about the nature, causes, and length of the cycles. There appear to be two types of cycles. Economic long waves, or Kondratieff cycles, are phases of economic expansion and stagnation that repeat about every 50 years and affect all countries more or less simultaneously. Hegemony cycles, lasting between

100 and 150 years and marking out the rise and decline of nations, alternate between periods of rivalry and war and periods of domination or leadership by a preeminent power. Most theorists agree that the political and economic cycles interact in some way—there is a strong historical correlation between the economic long waves, price fluctuations, and severe great-power wars—but there is no consensus about causal relationships.

Four main theories have been advanced to explain the economic cycle. The capital investment theory argues that economic long waves arise out of massive investment in and depreciation of long-lived capital goods, such as railroads, canals, and factories. The innovation theory holds that clusters of innovation in leading sectors drive economic growth, which is followed by a period of investment and profit taking and then by stagnation in innovation and gradually diminishing returns. The capitalist crisis school, following Marxist theory, describes a boom-and-bust cycle resulting from the internal contradictions of capitalism and the tendency of the profit rate to decline. Capitalist states periodically escape the economic consequences of the class struggle through imperial expansion, discovery of new natural resources, or suppression of the labor movement, which temporarily restores profits and favorable conditions of capital accumulation. The war theory maintains that major wars give periodic shocks to the economy and set off inflationary cycles.

The hegemony cycle is associated with a major military victory that gives one state an unrivaled position in the international system, a position from which it eventually falls by dint of challenge from another would be hegemonic power. George Modelski's *Long Cycles in World Politics* identifies five such cycles in the modern era: the dominant role of Portugal after 1517, the Netherlands after 1609, Britain after 1714 and 1815, and the United States after 1945 (see Figure 3-6). Modelski believes that the leadership of a hegemonic power is essential for ordering and maintaining global-level interactions. It provides a structure for resolving the most pressing problems of world politics (not the least being the threat of war itself) and therefore is viewed as more or less legitimate by the other members of the state system. They defer willingly to the hegemon, at least in the initial period of its ascendancy, because it acts with restraint, builds on the common interests of all states, and projects an appealing vision of world order—and also because the preceding cycle of war has reminded all powers of the costs of anarchy.

Historically, the hegemonic power has been a liberal one. It has introduced more open trade relations, has served as a "lead polity" for other states to imitate, and has disseminated important innovations in administration, diplomacy, and military strategy. It invariably has been the dominant economic center and the source of technological innovation. As Modelski says, in his study entitled "Long Cycles and the Strategy of U.S. International Economic Policy":

> Upon reflection, the linkage between world power and lead economy is not really surprising. A lead economy requires the political stability and international protection afforded by the services of the quality and the dimension

FIGURE 3-6

FIVE LONG CYCLES OF WORLD LEADERSHIP

Cycle	Duration	Global Powers	Hegemonic Powers	Principal Challengers	Global War
I	1517–1608	England, France, Portugal, Spain, Netherlands	Portugal	Spain	(Italian wars 1494–1516) Spanish wars 1581–1609
II	1609–1713	England, France, Spain, Netherlands	Netherlands	France	Wars of Louis XIV 1688–1713
III	1714–1815	Britain, France, Spain, Russia, Netherlands	Britain	France	Revolutionary and Napoleonic wars 1792–1815
IV	1816–1945	Britain, France, Germany, Italy, Japan, Russia, United States	Britain	Germany	World Wars I & II 1914–18, 1939–45
V	1945–	United States, USSR	United States		

afforded by the world power. Each world power has been, in its time, the area of the greatest security of rights and entitlements, and of lowest transaction costs and superior global information services, and therefore also most frequently, the economy of refuge. On the other hand, world power is also costly and cannot be maintained without the support of an active and growing economy. Operations of global reach and global wars in particular cannot be conducted on the cheap. Hence a lead economy built upon a global flow of activities becomes a *sine qua non* of world power. (p. 104)

The hegemonic power's dominance does not come primarily from naked force or a cumbersome political superstructure of direct imperial control. Rather, it constructs and supervises orderly relationships between politically independent societies through a combination of diplomacy, hierarchies of control, and the operation of markets. As Robert Keohane notes, in *After Hegemony:* "Hegemony rests on the subjective awareness by elites in secondary states that they are benefiting, as well as on the willingness of the hegemon itself to sacrifice tangible short-term benefits for intangible long-term gains" (p. 45).

Eventually, the power of the hegemon begins to decline. Of the three main theories about the rise and fall of great powers, Modelski belongs to the leadership cycle school, which emphasizes the role of political innovation by the leading power and its acquisition of preeminence less by economic means than by providing order and collective goods that benefit everyone. The world-system school embraces the Marxist assumption that political change flows from the dynamics of the capitalist mode of production; periodic wars are a result of the struggle for hegemony among core states and their competition for control of the periphery and the world economy. The power transition school, based on realist theory, holds that the recurrence of war is a symptom of the power-seeking behavior of nation-states. Shifts in national capabilities incite ambitions and introduce uncertainties into the power calculation; a rapid rise in one state's power increases the likelihood of friction because the newly powerful state has not yet acquired respect or status and the declining power feels threatened by the very pace of the change.

Quincy Wright attributes the war/hegemony cycle to three factors — systemic, economic, and psychological:

> Fluctuations in the intensity of war in the history of a state would tend to assume a definite periodicity if the international system exerted a persistent pressure toward war and if the economic and technological period necessary to recover from a severe war and to prepare for another were identical with the psychological and political period necessary to efface the anti-war sentiment after such a war and to restore national morale. (*A Study of War,* p. 231)

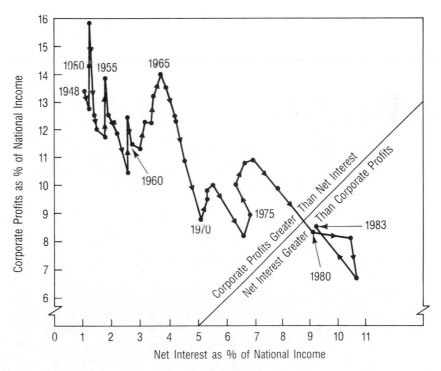

Note: Data from National Income and Product Accounts.

FIGURE 3-7
U.S. CORPORATE PROFITS AND NET INTEREST

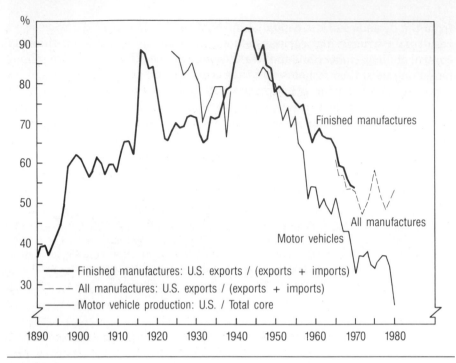

FIGURE 3-8
THE RISE AND DECLINE OF U.S. PRODUCTION HEGEMONY

Goldstein's own explanation of hegemonic cycle follows Wright closely, with particular emphasis on the role of production and its impact on national capabilities. A significant factor is the cost of war; the biggest wars have occurred only after sustained periods of economic growth, when the core countries could afford them. Indeed, prosperity tends to create an aggressive, expansionist psychology that is conducive to war; but when the treasury is empty and the economy depressed, a people's self-confidence erodes, making the ruling order more vulnerable to attack. Periods of increased production, at higher levels of technology, are accompanied by lateral pressures for increased trade and colonial expansion. These lead to heightened competition for resources, markets, and strategic territories, which increases the probability of international conflict. On the other hand, war itself has a dampening effect on long-term production growth, while the social memory of war prevents its recurrence for at least a few generations. In sum, alternating periods of enthusiasm and war-weariness intersect with cycles of innovation, investment, and economic decline.

Paul Kennedy, in *The Rise and Fall of the Great Powers,* argues that great powers decline because of "imperial overstretch." A hegemonic power becomes overcommitted politically and militarily, increases its defense spending, neglects the foundations of its power, and experiences a gradual erosion of its economic base. The great power's exercise of its hegemony only strengthens nationalist resistance, which increases the cost of expansion beyond the impe-

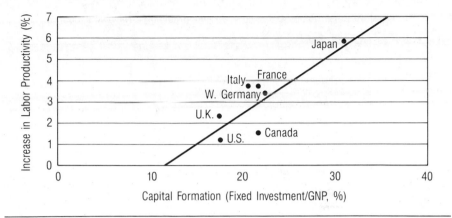

FIGURE 3-9
INTERNATIONAL PRODUCTIVITY GROWTH AND CAPITAL FORMATION, 1960–83

rial power's economic capacity — a self-defeating cycle that inevitably ends in failure. The rise of more vigorous rivals, unencumbered by empire or heavy defense spending, brings strong economic competition, the delegitimization of the hegemon's authority, and a global deconcentration of power. Both Kennedy and Goldstein say that America's relative decline in power and economic position in the late twentieth century fits this long-cycle pattern. A steady drop in U.S. economic productivity, capital formation, corporate profits, financial reserves, and share of world manufactured exports correlates with high defense spending (in relation to that of its economic competitors) and vigorous political-economic challenges in both the core and the periphery. (Figures 3-7 through 3-10 are various statistical indicators of the U.S. economic decline.) The United States, like all other great powers through history, seems to have contracted what Robert Keohane calls "a disease of the strong": the refusal to adjust to change. Small states have no choice but to respond to external demands and challenges; powerful states can postpone their adjustments. Thus, for Spain in the sixteenth century, the discovery of gold and silver in the New World proved disastrous; for Britain in the nineteenth century, the retreat into empire fatally delayed an effective national response to industrial decline. For the United States, the overwhelming economic superiority of the 1950s and '60s allowed domestic interests to accumulate privileges and postponed the processes of investment and reform that might have countered the economy's sclerotic tendencies.

According to long-cycle theory, the world is currently moving from a period of strong hegemony, following the global wars of 1914–45, to one of declining hegemony that may stretch over many decades. The economic long wave is in a period of stagnation as regards production, war, and prices. Reinvigorated world economic growth is projected for sometime around 1995 to 2020, followed by an increasing likelihood of war and inflation. If the cycles

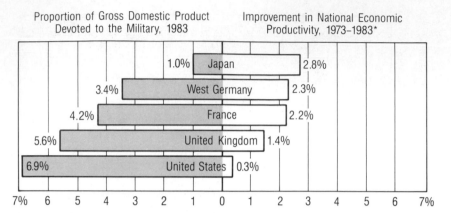

Proportion of Gross Domestic Product Devoted to the Military, 1983

Improvement in National Economic Productivity, 1973–1983*

*Average annual increases in productivity, measured as Gross Domestic Product per employed person.

Note: Data from Stockholm International Peace Research Institue and President's Commission on Industrial Competitiveness.

FIGURE 3-10

MILITARY SPENDING AND PRODUCTIVITY

recur as they have over the past five centuries, the early twenty-first century could witness another catastrophic world war, brought on by the dangerous combination of economic expansion and declining hegemony. Goldstein concludes:

> Only major changes in the nature of world politics can temper these dangers. Some of these changes have already occurred with the advent of nuclear war; others are beginning to develop in such areas as the information revolution, the conquest of space, and the development of new international regimes. Evolving patterns of international relations are bringing a globalization in which the only security is common security. The next world order will have to be built around this common security, not power politics, if the cycle of great power war is finally to be broken. (p. 17)

QUESTION FOR DISCUSSION (PRO AND CON)

Is the balance of power obsolete in an era of nuclear weapons and global interdependence?

☞ PRO

Many signs point to a revolutionary restructuring of international affairs. The war-inhibiting impact of nuclear weapons and ties of trade and investment among the major powers are only the two most important of these signs.

International politics has also been reshaped by monetary disorder, resource depletion, environmental deterioration, debt accumulation, overpopulation, arms proliferation, terrorism, revolutionary nationalism, and decolonization. These forces have all led to a global diffusion of power and limits on productive potential that may make it impossible for the traditional system of great-power rivalry to continue. In any case, war appears to be less profitable and hegemonic domination less likely today than ever before.

The conditions for a classical balance of power no longer exist, and for a number of reasons they cannot be re-created in our contemporary international system. First, industrialization and democracy in the more advanced countries have woven them into a web of economic interdependence that has broken down the traditional system of state rivalries. Domestic political and economic priorities control foreign policy as never before, and modern communications have made public opinion a significant domestic restraint, especially in democracies. For some influential groups, state security is no longer the most important goal of foreign policy. Liberal groups often place human rights ahead of national concerns; socialists advocate class solidarity; business, labor, religious, ethnic, and racial groups all attempt to influence foreign policy in ways that are irrelevant to the balance of power or are contrary to the state's security interests. Moreover, the global arena is proliferating with nonstate actors—multinational corporations, international organizations, private groups with international agendas—that maintain no military forces and exercise power in ways that cannot be measured or balanced in traditional terms.

With the modern economy integrated around a grid of common information and global transfers of scientific innovation, changes in power potential are not so likely to be concentrated within one leading state, nor are they so easily adjusted through traditional balance-of-power mechanisms. The very bases of power have been changing, so that it can no longer be measured by deployments of military forces. For example, trade ties and overseas investments give a nation influence, but they also restrain its freedom of action in ways that are difficult to calculate in pure power terms. Likewise, it can be argued that advanced communications and shared political ideas have spread a "world public opinion," which has made states more conscious of the need to preserve their reputations and credibility. This is a genuine consideration in shaping a state's conduct, else diplomats would not spend so much effort propagandizing about images and perceptions. But how does one plug such intangibles into the power equation?

In the second place, the basic nature of alliances is changing. The solidarity of the Western alliance has so reduced the perception of threat that increases in the power of member states are welcomed rather than resisted. The rise of American preeminence did not immediately awaken suspicion in all quarters that such power would be abused. The Americans claimed, and many people everywhere believed, that the United States possessed constitutional checks on the abuse of power that dictatorships did not have. American power also seemed to be safeguarded by good intentions and a certain virtue. Although the United States has succumbed often to the temptations of Machiavellianism and a quasi-imperial role, one can nevertheless say that it has exercised its power within a different moral framework and with different results than those of a pure power-politics model. The United States self-consciously promoted European economic recovery and the rehabilitation of the defeated powers after World War II out of prudent balance-of-power considerations: it was afraid of the Soviet military threat. But the Americans also supported democracy in the restored states in the hope that their augmented power could be made benign. Some statesmen, both American and European, imagined that the balance of power could be replaced by an Atlantic community tied together by bonds of economy and ideology that would set aside calculations of power. Despite renascent European nationalism, one can see signs of success in this endeavor.

Third, nuclear weapons have created an altogether different kind of power relationship. Their potential for devastation has made wars both too expensive and too risky. The balance-of-power system was based on force and the efficacy of its threatened use. All actors regarded violence as a rational tool of diplomacy that could resolve disputes either by inducing compromise or by compelling concessions. In the nuclear age, superpowers cannot afford to go to war with each other, even over the most vital interests. Deadlocked negotiations no longer bring them to war as the arena of last resort. As for the small powers, they can defy the nuclear giants almost at will. "Renegade" behavior is rampant, and small powers thumb their noses at the great powers as never before because the nuclear giants are helpless to initiate the kind of forceful control they wielded in the past. Nuclear deterrence, with its capacity to utterly destroy the civil society of the competing superpower, has erased the distinction between domestic and foreign affairs and tied the hands of traditional diplomacy. It is not so much a system of balance conducive to international order as a situation of superpower stalemate that has created a fundamental division of interests between great and small powers. The stalemate is so precarious, moreover, that it presents the spectre of an instantaneous, perhaps accidental, breakdown in the international system.

The fourth condition that makes the balance of power obsolete is the global diffusion of power. Accompanied by economic and ideological changes, this diffusion has destroyed the world's diplomatic unity and any idea of a central balance policed by the great powers. A two-tiered hierarchy — between the communist East and the capitalist West on ideological issues and between an industrialized North and an underdeveloped South on economic issues — has been replaced, as the Cold War fades, by a more complex set of divisions. NATO and Warsaw Pact forces have maintained their formal alliance commitments, despite the changes in Eastern Europe, but political, economic, and technological change has been transforming the relationships of power within the blocs. Current conflicts cannot be adjusted by military means, particularly nuclear ones. The Soviets, despite the prospect of losing control altogether, have concluded that the evolution of Eastern Europe cannot be guided by force. In the Third World, Muslim fundamentalism has placed power in the hands of ideological fanatics and terrorists, but countervailing power can do nothing against them. The economic development efforts of the Third World are still burdened by the weight of traditional values, old patterns of dependency, trade imbalances, debt, inappropriate technology, and cultural imperialism, but the old means of armed force and competition for power between states are irrelevant to solving these kinds of problems.

The political monopoly of the nuclear superpowers and the traditional dominance of Europe in the global system are under challenge from more than a hundred self-assertive states that have appeared during the process of decolonization. The problems of these lesser powers and their patterns of interaction are not just a by-product of the central balance, but something different. Revolutionary nationalism in the less-developed countries and the rise of unconventional warfare—from guerrilla armies to nuclear-armed minipowers—have brought complex new sets of international relations that are out of superpower control. Political outcomes in Vietnam, Iran, Nicaragua, Lebanon, Angola, and elsewhere have been determined by local conditions and forces. Indigenous forces, not superpower interventions, create or restrain modern revolutions. No amount of military coalition building in the West would have altered outcomes in Czechoslovakia, Afghanistan, or Poland. No coalition of adversaries could have prevented the United States from moving into the Vietnam quagmire, nor could any simple augmentation of American power have extricated us from it. Such fragmentation of global power has also made it impossible to reach any cultural or moral consensus on norms of international behavior. Widespread terrorist activity, the inability of the superpowers to control revolutionary upheavals in small states like Vietnam, Afghanistan, and Iran, and the regular violation of so elementary a principle as diplomatic immunity are all signs that the traditional balance of power has broken down irretrievably.

The end of the Cold War brings the balance-of-power era to a close. The advanced states are united by ideology and economics as never before. The underdeveloped states remain in turmoil, but their fundamental problems—national identity, economic modernization, political autonomy—cannot be solved by force. Revolutionary upheavals will disrupt the international system; they cannot be managed or suppressed by balance-of-power policies. One can imagine the resurrection of a traditional balance of power only under one of these three conditions: (1) the rise of a new ideology to challenge liberal democracy as the ruling creed of the twenty-first century; (2) a collapse of the international free trade regime and its attendant conditions of interdependence, caused either by a great depression or by the onset of extreme protectionism; or (3) the rise of a new great-power challenger through the rapid modernization of one of the underdeveloped giants. However, a new ideological division of the globe is unlikely. Fascism and communism are old and dying ideas; Islamic fundamentalism is on the rise but is not likely to become transcendent in a state that also has the strength to challenge the international consensus. Japan is powerful enough to challenge the system, but it is hemmed in by its interdependence and by the fact that any purely nationalist Japanese policy would not make sense unless the international market utterly collapsed—an outcome that would badly hurt a resource-poor trading power like Japan and, at the same time, would erode its capacity to implement imperial pretensions. China and possibly Brazil might have the right combination of radical ideology, size, and economic self-sufficiency that would incline them toward a policy of competitive nationalism. But rapid modernization in either country is unlikely, and radical ideologies can well lose credibility as the countries reach a level of affluence that makes participation in the global market more attractive and antidemocratic policies more costly.

☞ CON

The element of continuity is by far the most powerful feature of world politics. States still arm themselves to preserve their national security. Violence is still prevalent as a device for adjusting differences between states. Political leaders still seek to insulate their economies, through protectionism, resource self-sufficiency, or outright imperialism, from the vagaries of global interdependence. Nationalist sentiments, cultural chauvinism, and territorial attachments are still strong. And the international system is still characterized by the traditional hierarchies of power: the divisions between the strong and the weak, the rich and the poor, the resource-rich and the resource-dependent. Nothing can explain these structural inequalities except the balance of power, which permits the haves to predominate over the have-nots.

To argue that the balance of power is dead is to pretend that politics itself is dead. So long as international entities of any kind continue to have conflicts that can be resolved by the exercise of power, the balance of power will play an important role. Ironically, the diffusion of power and the rise of powerful new economic actors have actually assisted in the resurrection of a pentagonal balance, which resembles the classical balance of power more closely than it does the purely bipolar balance of the 1950s. The ascent of China, Japan, and a renascent Europe to the status of great powers has restored a kind of traditional diplomacy that has stabilized Soviet-American relations while softening the effect of their nuclear dominance. President Richard Nixon and his secretary of state, Henry Kissinger, self-consciously articulated such a vision of a restored balance in the so-called Nixon Doctrine. Subsequent events have confirmed the tendency of regionally dominant powers to police their own spheres of influence while coexisting in a great-power concert to maintain global peace.

However, the general balance of power that exists today is infinitely more complex than the traditional one. We now must differentiate between the "high politics" of the military balance and the "low politics" of the international political economy. The state that is dominant in nuclear arms may not control the institutions of international finance. Coalitions that come together on questions of the environment or population control may not match those dealing with human rights or international trade. Actors in the various issue areas do not line up consistently on the same side of the balance. But this does not mean that coalition building and power considerations do not still count. In superficial respects, the classical balance of power is gone: the great powers are no longer equal in strength; their power cannot be precisely quantified; they do not exercise control in collaboration; they are not united by a common culture; nor do they have much alliance flexibility. But the balance of power fulfills the same basic functions. A global balance does exist, calculated in a complex trade-off of military, economic, and political power that prevents the system of states from being dominated by any single power. Local balances, in addition, prevent the emergence of a regional power to challenge the great powers. Together, these balancing mechanisms provide the conditions that make possible the maintenance of order and permit the functioning of international law, traditional diplomacy, and great-power management of the international system. In this sense, a balance-of-power system is alive and well, even if it is not a strictly traditional one.

Economic interdependence, by making states more vulnerable to external events, has only spurred them to acquire the tools of influence they need to control their own fates. Even very poor states, for instance, place a high priority on acquiring modern weapons as the guarantors of their sovereignty. Also, the two most powerful states in the international system—the Soviet Union and the United States—are quite self-sufficient. They are only slightly influenced by considerations of interdependence, and then mainly with respect to maintaining their access to strategic minerals and avoiding the global catastrophe of nuclear war. Even in states heavily dependent on foreign trade, security remains a higher priority than economic welfare. Besides, the search for a powerful role in the international economy is simply another version of power politics. Japan is more interdependent today than ever before, but also more powerful. It pursued economic preeminence because a variety of international restraints blocked the military route to great-power status. Its global economic ties have made it an indispensable player in the international balance. These ties do not restrain the Japanese so much as they do Japan's rivals. As for China, though it is still less interdependent than the Soviet Union, it has played a crucial balancing role in the Soviet-American relationship. Both superpowers have courted China, quite against ideological prohibitions on each side—concrete evidence of the continuing presence of balance-of-power calculations.

Moreover, nuclear weapons have not changed the balance of power in any fundamental way. First, nuclear capacity does translate into a traditional hierarchy of influence, with the Soviet Union and the United States dominating all others precisely because of the sophistication of their nuclear arsenals. If rated on the basis of economy alone, the Soviet Union would be considered a second-rate power and Japan would rival America. Second, nuclear deterrence is a means for using power to balance power, not for making power itself obsolete. Military means have become more important, not less; states have fallen out of the competition simply because they do not have the industrial base or the resources to develop an array of power sufficiently broad to challenge one of the nuclear giants. Third, nuclear weapons have brought an unparalleled period of peace between the major powers. Only the restraining influence of the nuclear threat—a tangible power factor—can explain why the intense hostilities of the Cold War never broke out in general war. The alliance structure of the Cold War created mutual defense pacts under competing nuclear umbrellas as much as under different ideological flags. The superpowers have been able to translate their nuclear power into assurances to their allies, as well as into an intimidating influence in their dealings with nonnuclear powers.

The claim that nuclear weapons have made violence obsolete is reckless and wishful. No one can deny the possibility that some future statesman will be daring or desperate enough to employ nuclear war for political ends. Even if arms cuts bring peace between the superpowers, the proliferation of nuclear weapons to the Third World threatens a new era of arms races, in a setting in which the relative restraint of the Cold War is not likely to be reproduced. It is historic happenstance, not a law of international relations, that nuclear weapons have utility only as a deterrent. In fact, they were used at Hiroshima and Nagasaki and could well be used again. Also, we must not discount conventional military power. Nuclear deterrence has encouraged restraint in superpower confrontations, but it has not inhibited the traditional use of force by the great powers within their own spheres of influence or in their competition for control of lesser powers. Arms races remain an important device for maintaining equilibrium, particularly in the Third World. The looseness of the bipolar structure leaves plenty of room for diplomatic maneuver and changes of heart among nonaligned states. If allies really did not matter, the superpowers would not court them so ferociously with economic and arms aid. Since nuclear weapons tend to be self-canceling, it is still the alliance ties and nonnuclear military capacities of a state that give it global influence. Knowledge of nuclear physics does not make a superpower. That takes an immense resource base, a sizable territory and population, an industrial economy, sophisticated technology, a strategic location, and diplomatic clout with lesser powers — all traditional factors that continue to play a role in the modern balance of power.

SOURCES AND SUGGESTED READINGS

Domestic and International Politics Compared

Boulding, Kenneth. *Three Faces of Power.* Newbury Park, Calif.: Sage, 1989.
Farrell, Barry R., ed. *Approaches to Comparative and International Politics.* Evanston: Northwestern University Press, 1966.
Knorr, Klaus, and James N. Rosenau, eds. *The International System: Theoretical Essays.* Princeton, N.J.: Princeton University Press, 1961.
Masters, Roger D. "World Politics as a Primitive Political System." *World Politics,* Vol. 16 (July 1964), pp. 595–619.
Wesson, Robert G. *State Systems: International Pluralism, Politics, and Culture.* New York: Free Press, 1978.

On Balance of Power

Aron, Raymond. *The Century of Total War.* Boston: Beacon Press, 1954.
————. *Peace and War: A Theory of International Relations.* Garden City, N.Y.: Doubleday, 1966.
Baldwin, David. "Power Analysis and World Politics: New Trends vs. Old Tendencies." *World Politics,* vol. 31 (January 1979), pp. 169–94.

Becker, Harold S. "Conflict and Accommodation: The Future of the Balance of Power." *The Futurist*, June 1982, pp. 21–25.

Bell, Coral. "Kissinger in Retrospect: The Diplomacy of Power-Concert." *International Affairs* (London), vol. 53 (April 1977), pp. 202–16.

Boulding, Kenneth E. *Conflict and Defense: A General Theory.* New York: Harper & Row, 1962.

Bull, Hedley. *The Anarchical Society: A Study of Order in World Politics.* New York: Columbia University Press, 1977.

Burns, Arthur L. "From Balance to Deterrence: A Theoretical Analysis." *World Politics*, vol. 9 (July 1957), pp. 494–529.

Chi, Hsi-sheng. "The Chinese Warlord System as an International System." In Morton Kaplan, ed., *New Approaches to International Relations*, New York: St. Martin's, 1968. Pp. 405–35.

Claude, Inis L. *Power and International Relations.* New York: Random House, 1962.

Cottam, Richard W., and Gerald Gallucci. *Power: The Rehabilitation of Power in International Relations.* Pittsburgh: University Center for International Studies, University of Pittsburgh, 1978.

Craig, Gordon A., and Alexander L. George. *Force and Statecraft: Diplomatic Problems of Our Time.* New York: Oxford University Press, 1983.

Dehio, Ludwig. *The Precarious Balance: Four Centuries of the European Power Struggle.* New York: Vintage, 1962.

Deporte, Anton W. *Europe Between the Superpowers: The Enduring Balance.* New Haven: Yale University Press, 1979.

Deutsch, Karl W., and J. David Singer. "Multipolar Power Systems and International Stability." *World Politics*, vol. 16 (April 1964), pp. 390–406.

Doran, Charles F., and Wes Parsons. "War and the Cycle of Relative Power." *American Political Science Review*, vol. 74, no. 4 (December 1980), pp. 947–65.

Franke, Winfried. "The Italian City-State System as an International System." In Morton Kaplan, ed., *New Approaches to International Relations*, New York: St. Martin's, 1968. Pp. 426–58.

Gulick, Edward V. *Europe's Classical Balance of Power.* Ithaca: Cornell University Press, 1955.

Haas, Ernst B. "The Balance of Power: Prescription, Concept or Propaganda?" *World Politics*, vol. 5 (July 1953), pp. 442–77.

Haas, Michael. *International Conflict.* Indianapolis: Bobbs-Merrill, 1974.

———. "International Subsystems: Stability and Polarity." *American Political Science Review*, vol. 64 (1970), pp. 98–123.

Haas, Richard. "The Primacy of the State, or Revising the Revisionists." *Daedalus*, vol. 108, no. 4 (Fall 1979).

Hanreider, Wolfram F. "The International System: Bipolar or Multi-bloc?" *Journal of Conflict Resolution*, vol. 9 (1965), pp. 299–308.

Healey, Brian, and Arthur Stein. "The Balance of Power in International History." *Journal of Conflict Resolution*, vol. 17 (March 1973), pp. 33–62.

Herz, John H. *International Politics in the Atomic Age.* New York: Columbia University Press, 1959.

Hinsley, F. H. *Power and the Pursuit of Peace: Theory and Practice in the History of Relations Between States.* Cambridge: Cambridge University Press, 1963.

———. "The Rise and Fall of the Modern International System." *Review of International Studies*, vol. 5, no. 1 (1982), pp. 1–8.

Holborn, Hajo. *The Political Collapse of Europe.* New York: Knopf, 1965.

Hopkins, Raymond, and Richard Mansbach. *Structure and Process in International Politics.* New York: Harper & Row, 1973.

Kaplan, Morton A. "Some Problems of International Systems Research." In *International Political Communities: An Anthology*, Garden City, N.Y.: Anchor, 1966. Pp. 469–86.

———. *System and Process in International Politics.* New York: John Wiley & Sons, 1957.

Kegley, Charles W., Jr., and Gregory A. Raymond. *When Trust Breaks Down: Alliance Norms and World Politics.* Columbia: University of South Carolina Press, 1989.

Kissinger, Henry. "The White Revolutionary: Reflections on Bismarck." In Dankwart Rustow, ed., *Philosophers and Kings: Studies in Leadership*, New York: Braziller, 1970. Pp. 317–53.

———. *A World Restored.* New York: Grosset & Dunlap, 1964.

Knorr, Klaus, ed. *Historical Dimensions of National Security Problems.* Wichita: University Press of Kansas (National Security Education Program), 1976.

Kratochwil, Friedrich V. *International Order and Foreign Policy: A Theoretical Sketch of Post-War International Politics.* Boulder, Colo.: Westview Press, 1978.

Levy, Jack. *War in the Modern Great Power System, 1495–1975.* Lexington: University of Kentucky Press, 1983.

Liska, George. *Quest for Equilibrium: America and the Balance of Power on Land and Sea.* Baltimore: Johns Hopkins University Press, 1977.

Mandelbaum, Michael. *The Nuclear Revolution: International Politics Before and After Hiroshima.* New York: Cambridge University Press, 1981.

Midlarsky, Manus I. "The Balance of Power as a 'Just' Historical System," *Polity,* vol. 16 (Winter 1983), pp. 181–200.

Modelski, George. *Principles of World Politics.* New York: Free Press, 1972.

——— . *World Power Concentrations: Typology, Data, Explanatory Framework.* Morristown, N.J.: General Learning Press, 1974.

Morgenthau, Hans J. *Politics Among Nations: The Struggle for Power and Peace,* 6th ed., rev. Kenneth W. Thompson. New York: Knopf, 1985.

Nogee, Joseph L. "Polarity: An Ambiguous Concept." *Orbis,* vol. 28 (Winter 1975), pp. 1193–1224.

Organski, A. F. K. *World Politics.* New York: Knopf, 1958.

Organski, A. F. K., and Jacek Kugler. *The War Ledger.* Chicago: University of Chicago Press, 1980.

Osgood, Robert E., and Robert W. Tucker. *Force, Order, and Justice.* Baltimore: Johns Hopkins Press, 1967.

Quester, George. *Offense and Defense in the International System.* New York: John Wiley & Sons, 1977.

Rosecrance, Richard. *Action and Reaction in World Politics.* Boston: Little, Brown, 1963.

——— . "Bipolarity, Multipolarity, and the Future." *Journal of Conflict Resolution,* vol. 10 (September 1966), pp. 314–27.

Russell, Greg. "Balance of Power in Perspective." *International Review of History and Political Science,* vol. 21, no. 4 (November 1984), pp. 1–16.

Russett, Bruce M. "Toward a Model of Competitive International Politics." *Journal of Politics,* vol. 25 (May 1963), pp. 226–47.

Seabury, Paul, ed. *Balance of Power.* San Francisco: Chandler Publishing, 1965.

Simowitz, Roslyn L. *The Logical Consistency and Soundness of the Balance of Power Theory.* Denver, Colo.: Graduate School of International Studies, University of Denver, 1982.

Siverson, Randolph, and Michael P. Sullivan. "The Distribution of Power and the Onset of War." *Journal of Conflict Resolution,* vol. 27, no. 3 (September 1983), pp. 473–94.

Snyder, Glenn H. "The Balance of Power and the Balance of Terror." In Dean G. Pruitt and Richard C. Snyder, eds., *Theory and Research on the Causes of War,* Englewood Cliffs, N.J.: Prentice-Hall, 1969. Pp. 114–26.

Thucydides. *The Peloponnesian War,* ed. T. E. Wick. New York: Modern Library College Editions, 1982.

Tucker, Robert W. *The Inequality of Nations.* New York: Basic Books, 1977.

Waltz, Kenneth N. "International Structure, National Force, and the Balance of World Power." *Journal of International Affairs,* vol. 21, no. 2 (1967), pp. 215–31.

——— . *Theory of International Politics.* Reading, Mass.: Addison-Wesley, 1979.

Wight, Martin. "The Balance of Power." In *Diplomatic Investigations: Essays in the Theory of International Politics,* Cambridge: Harvard University Press, 1968. Pp. 149–75.

Woodruff, William. *The Struggle for World Power, 1500–1980.* New York: St. Martin's Press, 1981.

On Alternatives to the Balance of Power

Axelrod, Robert, and Robert Keohane. "Achieving Cooperation Under Anarchy." *World Politics,* vol. 38 (October 1985), pp. 226–54.

Bull, Hedley, and Adam Watson. *The Expansion of International Society.* New York: Oxford University Press, 1984.

Geiger, Theodore. *The Future of the International System.* Boston: Unwin Hyman, 1988.

Gilpin, Robert. *The Political Economy of International Relations.* Princeton, N.J.: Princeton University Press, 1987.

Gowa, Joanne. "Anarchy, Egoism, and Third Images." *International Organization,* Winter 1986.

Haas, Ernst B. "Why Collaborate?" *World Politics,* April 1980.

Hopkins, Terence K., Immanuel Wallerstein, et al. *World Systems Analysis.* Beverly Hills, Calif.: Sage Publications, 1982.

Jervis, Robert. "From Balance to Concert: A Study of International Cooperation." In Kenneth Oye, ed., *Cooperation Under Anarchy*, Princeton, N.J.: Princeton University Press, 1986.

Johansen, Robert C. *Toward an Alternative Security System: Moving Beyond the Balance of Power in the Search for World Security.* New York: World Policy Institute, 1983.

Keohane, Robert O. *After Hegemony: Cooperation and Discord in the World Political Economy.* Princeton, N.J.: Princeton University Press, 1984.

Keohane, Robert O., and Joseph S. Nye, Jr. *Power and Interdependence: World Politics in Transition.* Boston: Little, Brown, 1977.

———. *"Power and Interdependence* Revisited." *International Organization*, vol. 41, no. 4 (Autumn 1987), pp. 725–53.

Kothari, Rajni. *Footsteps into the Future: Diagnosis of the Present World and a Design for an Alternative.* New York: Free Press, 1974.

Krasner, Stephen. "State Power and the Structure of International Trade." *World Politics*, vol. 28, no. 2 (April 1976), pp. 317–47.

Lipson, Charles. "International Cooperation in Economic and Security Affairs." *World Politics*, vol. 37 (October 1984), pp. 1–23.

Liska, George. "Concert Through Decompression." *Foreign Policy*, vol. 63 (Summer 1986), pp. 108–30.

Nye, Joseph S., Jr. *Peace in Parts.* Boston: Little, Brown, 1971.

Olson, Mancur. *The Logic of Collective Action.* Cambridge: Harvard University Press, 1971.

Oye, Kenneth. "Explaining Cooperation Under Anarchy." *World Politics*, October 1985.

Oye, Kenneth, ed. *Cooperation Under Anarchy.* Princeton, N.J.: Princeton University Press, 1986.

Rosenau, James. "Before Cooperation: Hegemons, Regimes, and Habit-Driven Actors in World Politics." *International Organization*, vol. 40, no. 4 (Autumn 1986), pp. 849–94.

———. "A Pre-Theory Revisited: World Politics in an Era of Cascading Interdependence." *International Studies Quarterly*, vol. 28 (1984).

Wesson, Robert G. *The Imperial Order.* Berkeley: University of California Press, 1967.

On International Regimes & Collective Goods

Dolman, Antony J. *Resources, Regimes, World Order.* New York: Pergamon Press, 1981.

Froelich, Norman, Joe Oppenheimer, and Oran Young. *Political Leadership and Collective Goods.* Princeton, N.J.: Princeton University Press, 1971.

Haas, Ernst B. "Regime Decay: Conflict Management and International Organizations, 1945–1981." *International Studies*, vol. 37 (1983), pp. 189–256.

———. "Words Can Hurt You; Or Who Said What to Whom About Regimes." *International Organization*, Spring 1982.

Haggard, Stephan, and Beth A. Simmons. "Theories of International Regimes." *International Organization*, vol. 41, no. 3 (Summer 1987), pp. 497–517.

Hardin, Garrett, and John Baden, eds. *Managing the Commons.* San Francisco: W. H. Freeman, 1977.

Jervis, Robert. "Security Regimes." *International Organization*, vol. 36 (Spring 1982), pp. 357–78.

Krasner, Stephen D., ed. *International Regimes.* Ithaca, N.Y.: Cornell University Press, 1983.

Kratochwil, Friedrich, and John G. Ruggie. "International Organization: A State of the Art on the Art of the State." *International Organization*, vol. 40 (Autumn 1986), pp. 753–75.

Nye, Joseph S., Jr. "Nuclear Learning and U.S.-Soviet Security Regimes." *International Organization*, vol. 41 (Summer 1987), pp. 371–402.

Oppenheimer, Joe. "Collective Goods and Alliances." *Journal of Conflict Resolution*, vol. 23 (1979), pp. 387–407.

Ruggie, John Gerard. "International Responses to Technology: Concepts and Trends." *International Organization*, vol. 29, no. 3 (Summer 1975), pp. 557–84.

Russett, Bruce M., and John D. Sullivan. "Collective Goods and International Organization." *International Organization*, vol. 25 (1971), pp. 845–65.

Smith, Roger K. "Explaining the Non-Proliferation Regime: Anomalies for Contemporary International Relations Theory." *International Organization*, vol. 41 (Spring 1987), pp. 251–81.

Snidal, Duncan. "Public Goods, Property Rights, and Political Organizations." *International Studies Quarterly*, vol. 23 (1979), pp. 532–66.

Starr, Harvey. "Collective Goods Approaches to Alternative World Structures." In Bruce Russett and Harvey Starr, *World Politics: The Menu for Choice,* 2nd ed., San Francisco: W. H. Freeman, 1985. Pp. 506–19.

Strange, Susan. "Cave! Hic Dragones: A Critique of Regime Analysis." *International Organization,* vol. 36 (Spring 1982), pp. 479–96.

Tetreault, Mary Ann. "Regimes and Liberal World Orders." *Alternatives,* vol. 13 (1988), pp. 5–26.

Young, Oran. "International Regimes: Problems of Concept Formation." *World Politics,* vol. 32 (April 1980), pp. 331–56.

———. "International Regimes: Toward a New Theory of Institutions." *World Politics,* vol. 39 (October 1986), pp. 104–22.

Zacher, Mark W. "Trade Gaps, Analytical Gaps: Regime Analysis and International Commodity Trade Regulation." *International Organization,* vol. 41 (Spring 1987), pp. 173–202.

On Cycles, Hegemony, & Transformation

Avery, William P., and William Rapkin. *America in a Changing World Political Economy.* New York: Longman, 1982.

Bergesen, Albert. "Modeling Long Waves of Crisis in the World System." In A. Bergesen, ed., *Crises in the World-System,* Beverly Hills, Calif.: Sage, 1983. Pp. 73–92.

Boswell, Terry, and Albert Bergesen, eds. *America's Changing Role in the World System.* New York: Praeger, 1987.

Bousquet, Nicole. "From Hegemony to Competition: Cycles of the Core?" In Terence Hopkins and Immanuel Wallerstein, eds., *Processes of the World-System,* Beverly Hills, Calif.: Sage, 1980. Pp. 46–83.

Calleo, David P. *Beyond American Hegemony: The Future of the Western Alliance.* New York: Basic Books, 1987.

Cox, Robert W. "Social Forces, States and World Orders: Beyond International Relations Theory." *Journal of International Studies/Millennium,* vol. 10, no. 2 (Summer 1981), pp. 126–55.

Friedman, Edward, ed. *Ascent and Decline in the World-System.* Beverly Hills, Calif.: Sage, 1982.

Gaddis, John Lewis. "The Long Peace: Elements of Stability and Instability in the Postwar International System." *International Security,* vol. 10 (Spring 1986), pp. 99–142.

Gilpin, Robert. *War and Change in World Politics.* New York: Cambridge University Press, 1981.

Goldstein, Joshua S. *Long Cycles: Prosperity and War in the Modern Age.* New Haven: Yale University Press, 1988.

Holsti, Ole R., et al., eds. *Change in the International System.* Boulder, Colo.: Westview Press, 1980.

Jacobs, Jane. "The Dynamic of Decline." *Atlantic Monthly.* vol. 253 (April 1984), pp. 98–114.

Kaldor, Mary. *The Disintegrating West.* New York: Hill & Wang, 1978.

Keal, Paul. *Unspoken Rules and Superpower Dominance.* New York: St. Martin's, 1983.

Kennedy, Paul. "The (Relative) Decline of America." *Atlantic Monthly,* vol. 260 (June 1987), pp. 29–38.

———. *The Rise and Fall of the Great Powers: Economic Change and Military Conflict from 1500 to 2000.* New York: Random House, 1987.

Keohane, Robert O. "Hegemonic Leadership and U.S. Foreign Economic Policy in the 'Long Decade' of the 1950s." In William Avery and David Rapkin, eds., *America in a Changing World Political Economy,* New York: Longman, 1982. Pp. 49–76.

———. "The Theory of Hegemonic Stability and Change in International Economic Regimes, 1967–1977." in Ole Holsti et al., eds., *Change in the International System,* Boulder, Colo.: Westview Press, 1980. Pp. 131–62.

Kindleberger, Charles P. "Dominance and Leadership in the International Economy." *International Studies Quarterly,* vol. 25 (1981).

Liska, George. "Continuity and Change in International Systems." *World Politics,* vol. 16, no. 1 (October 1963).

McCormick, Thomas. "'Every System Needs a Center Sometimes': An Essay on Hegemony and Modern American Foreign Policy." In Lloyd C. Gardner, ed., *Redefining the Past,* Corvallis: Oregon State University Press, 1986.

Mead, Walter Russell. *Mortal Splendor: The American Empire in Transition.* Boston: Houghton Mifflin, 1987.

Modelski, George. "The Long Cycle of Global Politics and the Nation-State." *Comparative Studies in Society and History,* vol. 20 (April 1978), pp. 214–35.

———. "Long Cycles and the Strategy of U.S. International Economic Policy." In William Avery and David Rapkin, eds., *America in a Changing World Political Economy,* New York: Longman, 1982. Pp. 97–116.

———. *Long Cycles in World Politics.* Seattle: University of Washington Press, 1987.

Modelski, George, ed. *Exploring Long Cycles.* Boulder, Colo.: Lynne Rienner, 1987.

Modelski, George, and Robert Benedict. "Structural Trends in World Politics." *Comparative Politics,* vol. 6, no. 1 (October 1963).

Olson, Mancur. *The Rise and Decline of Nations: Economic Growth, Stagflation, and Social Rigidities.* New Haven: Yale University Press, 1982.

Peterson, Peter. "The Morning After." *Atlantic Monthly,* October 1987, pp. 43ff.

Rasler, Karen, and William R. Thompson. "Global War, Public Debts, and the Long Cycle." *World Politics,* vol. 35 (1983), pp. 489–516.

Rosecrance, Richard. "Long Cycle Theory and International Relations." *International Organization,* vol. 41, no. 2 (Spring 1987), pp. 283–301.

Rostow, W. W. "Beware of Historians Bearing False Analogies." *Foreign Affairs,* vol. 67 (1988), pp. 863–68.

Ruggie, John Gerard. "Continuity and Transformation in the World Polity: Toward a Neorealist Synthesis." *World Politics,* vol. 35, no. 2 (January 1983), pp. 261–86.

Russett, Bruce. "The Mysterious Case of Vanishing Hegemony: Or, Is Mark Twain Really Dead?" *International Organization,* vol. 39 (Spring 1985), pp. 207–31.

Snidal, Duncan. "The Limits of Hegemonic Stability Theory." *International Organization,* vol. 39, no. 4 (Autumn 1985), pp. 579–614.

Stein, Arthur A. "The Hegemon's Dilemma: Great Britain, the United States, and the International Economic Order." *International Organization,* vol. 38, no. 2 (Spring 1984), pp. 355–86.

Strange, Susan. "The Persistent Myth of Lost Hegemony." *International Organization,* vol. 41, no. 4 (Autumn 1987), pp. 551–74.

Thompson, William R. *On Global War: Historical-Structural Approaches to World Politics.* Columbia: University of South Carolina Press, 1989.

———. "Polarity, the Long Cycle, and Global Power Warfare." *Journal of Conflict Resolution,* vol. 30 (1986), pp. 587–615.

———. "Uneven Economic Growth, Systemic Challenges, and Global Wars." *International Studies Quarterly,* vol. 27 (1983), pp. 341–55.

———. "The World-Economy, the Long Cycle, and the Question of World-System Time." In Pat McGown and Charles W. Kegley, Jr., eds., *Foreign Policy and the Modern World System,* Beverly Hills, Calif.: Sage. 1983. Pp. 35–62.

Tucker, Robert W. "America in Decline: The Foreign Policy of 'Maturity.'" *Foreign Affairs,* vol. 58, no. 3 (1980), pp. 449–84.

Wallerstein, Immanuel. "The Three Instances of Hegemony in the History of the Capitalist World-Economy." *International Journal of Comparative Sociology,* vol. 24, nos. 1–2 (1983), pp. 100–08.

Whitman, Marina V. N. "Leadership Without Hegemony." *Foreign Policy,* vol. 20 (1975), pp. 138–60.

Wright, Quincy. *A Study of War.* Chicago: University of Chicago Press, 1942. (Reprinted 1964.)

ECONOMIC-SOCIAL STRUCTURES AND INTERDEPENDENCE

The most remarkable international development of the twentieth century has been the growth of an interdependent society reaching into every corner of the globe. It is embodied most concretely today in the global market economy.

This world system began with the European age of discovery and the imperial conquests of the early modern era, which over five centuries carried Western colonists, capital, and ideas everywhere. Even countries that successfully resisted conquest, like Russia, Turkey, and Japan, were able to maintain their independence only by adopting the military and industrial technology of Europe. As Arnold Toynbee has pointed out in his essay *The World and the West,* technology was the initial wedge that pried loose the foundations of traditional societies and opened them to more profound processes of Westernization. Any remaining islands of isolation were quickly wiped out by the competition among the great powers for colonial dominion, markets, and resources to sustain their rapidly expanding capitalist economies. Decolonization and the Cold War division of the world between the Soviet Union and the United States exacerbated competition in the Third World, spreading Western arms and influences still further. However, once political power had shifted decisively to the rimlands of Russia and America, the Western industrial democracies began a new process of economic integration, ending the self-consuming capitalist competition that had fed imperialism and world war. If the European colonial era created the outlines of a global economy, structured along lines of dominance and dependence, the postwar political collapse of Europe, decolonization, and the emergence of American economic leadership permitted the construction of a different kind of international political economy, this time along more interdependent lines.

To understand the degree to which the new conditions of dependence and interdependence have modified balance-of-power politics, we will briefly review the history of the global economy since World War II and describe its main institutional features. Then we will examine three competing images of the international economy: the interdependence model of the liberal, the mercantilist model of the economic nationalist, and the imperialism-dependency model of the Marxist and the world systems analyst. Although the emphasis in this chapter is on economics, we should not lose sight of the political and social matrix in which it is entangled. International history has been profoundly affected by interactions between political and economic interests, whether they are the mercantilist policies of the early European states, imperial competition in the nineteenth century, or the role of trade, investment, and technology in elevating Britain and the United States to hegemony and in integrating Europe.

Today, economic pressure is an integral tool in the arsenal of international diplomacy. Through financial manipulation, a state can diminish the value of an opponent's currency or stabilize the value of its own. By economic penetration of a weaker country, a state can gain control over its government or an important strategic advantage, such as military basing rights. Conversely, military interventions may be mounted to gain economic advantages — concessions on access to resources or favorable terms for foreign investment. Other economic strategies states exploit are price fixing, the dumping of surplus goods at artificially low prices, and the imposition of quotas and exchange controls. Trade embargoes and other forms of economic boycott have become powerful weapons against unfriendly countries, while allies are courted by means of foreign aid, economic subsidies, and even bribes. Vulnerable states hide behind tariff barriers or stockpile strategic resources; strong ones institutionalize their dominance in favorable trade arrangements or in control of the international organizations that regulate economic affairs. Every political action today is scrutinized for its impact on a state's economic position, and economic policies are tailored to the state's overriding political and security interests. The whole diplomatic calculus of modern statecraft is bound up in an inseparable strategic mix of political and economic ends.

The international economy has become an alternative decision-making arena. A state's power may depend as much on control of markets, resources, exchange rates, technology transfers, capital flows, and terms of trade as on arms or territory. Ideological divisions reflect more than a competition between democracy and dictatorship or between conflicting security systems; they reflect the competing political-economic principles of capitalism and socialism. Economic relations affect alliance solidarity, the convergence of state interests, and the prospects for political and cultural integration. It is indisputable that the state has become a primary economic actor, in foreign policy as in domestic affairs, and that states are profoundly constrained today in the exercise of their power by their networks of economic ties. The only questions are whether these global economic ties are beneficial or exploitative, whether they make for peace or war, whether they erode everyone's national sovereignty or enhance the power of some states at the expense of others.

The Evolution of the International Economy Since World War II

In 1945, after the traumatic experiences of the Great Depression and World War II, it was clear to all the major capitalist powers that they needed a new means of stabilizing their relations and stimulating economic recovery. The Soviet Union, newly dominant in Eastern Europe, was the only major power to resist a new economic order. For reasons of ideology, the Soviets did not believe advanced capitalism could maintain a stable global economy or match socialist goals for equity and planned social change, so they were reluctant to expose their newly industrialized economy to a capitalist international market. In practical terms, the Soviet Union and Eastern Europe were afraid that they would have to conform to the economic leadership of an arch-rival, the United States, which would have been unpalatable politically. The Western allies had an equally strong fear of further Communist penetration of their weakened societies; Marxist parties that had been important in the resistance movements in Nazi-occupied Europe already were strong partners in postwar coalition governments, in France and Italy in particular. The Soviets themselves proved uncooperative in the postwar interallied commissions, choosing to administer their sector of occupied Germany as a separate entity, taking heavy reparations, even transporting whole factories back to war-devastated Russia. As a consequence of all these factors, Europe was breaking down economically along the East-West lines of the military occupation.

The United States stepped in at once with loans and technical assistance to buttress the fragile economies of Western Europe. It sent over $3 billion in immediate relief funds, and almost $4 billion in loans to Great Britain, while rebuffing Soviet requests for economic aid. In 1948, a massive American assistance program was formalized in the European Recovery Program, or Marshall Plan. The Soviets were invited to join, but only on the condition that they open their economy to external controls, and they refused. This left a strictly Western economic bloc, consolidated at first around the Organization for European Economic Cooperation (OEEC) and expanded in 1960 to include virtually all the free-world market economies under the rubric of the Organization for Economic Cooperation and Development (OECD). Moscow, for its part, organized a corresponding bloc of socialist states, the Council for Mutual Economic Assistance (CMEA or Comecon), thus completing the institutionalization of Cold War patterns of economic exchange. Because socialist economics is autarkic and relies on central planning, the Comecon states would remain largely isolated from Western trade and finance until the late 1980s. With the exception of Yugoslavia, whose Marshal Tito had an early falling out with Joseph Stalin, the socialist states also refused to participate in many of the economic organs sponsored by the United Nations, such as the International Monetary Fund and the World Bank. Some of these organs had weighted voting schemes based on a country's financial contribution, which gave the United States an overwhelming advantage, and the East bloc countries concluded they had nothing to gain from such a one-sided arrangement.

After 1948, the global economy was dominated by an alliance of capitalist powers with an enormously high level of industrial and technical development and pursuing a policy of relatively unrestricted world trade. Joan Spero, in *The Politics of International Economic Relations,* summarizes the immediate post-war economic developments in these terms:

> During and after World War II, governments developed and enforced a set of rules, institutions, and procedures to regulate important aspects of international economic interaction. For nearly two decades, this order, known as the Bretton Woods system, was effective in controlling conflict and in achieving the common goals of the [Western industrial] states which had created it. The political bases for the Bretton Woods system are to be found in the coincidence of three conditions: the concentration of power in a small number of states, the existence of a cluster of important interests shared by those states, and the presence of a dominant power willing and able to assume a leadership role. (p. 23)

Management of the global economy was concentrated in the developed states of North America and Western Europe, which imposed their decisions on other states. The less-developed regions of Asia, Africa, the Middle East, and Latin America remained economically subordinate within the still-existing imperial structure. Their trade was oriented to the Northern metropoles, on which they depended for most new capital investment. Consequently, mining, manufacturing, and large-scale agriculture were almost all under the ownership of European or American corporations, and monetary decisions were monopolized by the leading banks of London, Paris, and New York, which also controlled the dominant exchange currencies. New states in the Third World would not be an important force until the 1960s, and Japan would remain subordinate and outside the Bretton Woods management system for several decades.

The non-Communist states embraced America's dominance of the new system, not only because they needed American aid but also because they shared a commitment to the same kind of liberal, capitalist world order. All had suffered during the Depression years of the 1930s from exchange controls, high tariffs, competitive devaluations, and a disastrous breakdown into regional trade and monetary blocs, and all the advanced states were now agreed on the need for a more open, interdependent system, to further both economic welfare and the prospects for peace. They wanted some modest government intervention in the economy—a mixed, or welfare state, economy at home and, abroad, publicly managed institutions to remove trade barriers and create a stable monetary system.

American Economic Leadership and the Creation of the Bretton Woods System

The two principal institutions of the new economic order were established at an international conference held at Bretton Woods, New Hampshire, in July 1944. They were the International Monetary Fund (IMF), to stabilize currencies, and the International Bank for Reconstruction and Development (IBRD), or World Bank, to finance the postwar recovery and expand trade. The IMF fashioned a system of fixed exchange rates, pegged to the value of gold, with freely convertible currencies. It oversaw changes in exchange rates and could make loans to members with temporary balance-of-payments deficits. Such deficits, which occur when a nation imports more than it exports or sends more money abroad (as investments, loans, grants, or military payments) than it receives, were a particular problem in postwar Europe because of the wartime disruption of its extensive overseas markets, coupled with skyrocketing imports to meet reconstruction needs; at the same time, the United States was accumulating tens of billions of dollars in reserves from its trade surpluses. The World Bank was given an initial loan fund of $10 billion for capital projects, and it was also authorized to issue securities, raise new funds, and underwrite private loans. Together, the IMF and the IBRD operated as a kind of central bank for the international system. The World Bank, however, soon proved unable to meet all the urgent needs for greater liquidity, emergency loans, and new capital, and it fell to the United States, as the world's leading economy, to fulfill many of these functions. Between 1948 and 1953, the United States deliberately incurred balance-of-payments deficits in sending overseas $17 billion in Marshall Plan aid, plus billions more in loans, investments, and payments to support its armed forces around the world. The United States rescued the hard-pressed economies of Europe and Japan, reversing their balance-of-payments difficulties and making the dollar a new international reserve currency. For the next twenty-five years, U.S. economic leadership, in conjunction with the IMF and the IBRD, brought stable monetary relations, expanded world trade, economic growth, and political harmony to the world's developed market economies.

The Marshall Plan and U.S. reconstruction aid to Germany and Japan were aimed at cementing transnational economic ties and creating an unbreachable security community, immune both to intramural struggles, like the Franco-German rivalries of two world wars, and to Soviet penetration and subversion. Although U.S. postwar aid was an act of unprecedented generosity, it was largely precipitated by the near-bankruptcy of the allied economies. The Americans knew that a European economic and political collapse could only redound to the benefit of the Communists. The United States also made the practical judgment that it needed healthy European trading partners as a market for its rapidly growing exports. For these combined economic and political reasons, the United States strongly supported the development of a self-sufficient European economic community.

Europe had taken its first steps toward economic integration in 1944, when Belgium, the Netherlands, and Luxembourg (Benelux) formed a customs union to reduce tariffs and quotas between their countries. A more daring venture was the European Coal and Steel Community (ECSC), launched in 1951 under the visionary leadership of France's Jean Monnet. In 1957, six continental European states (the Benelux countries plus France, Italy, and West Germany) made the historic decision to join in a Common Market — officially, the European Economic Community (EEC) — aimed at creating an integrated economic community and, eventually, a United States of Europe. To the latter end, the ECSC, the EEC, and the European Atomic Energy Community — the main economic organs — were supplemented by a ten-member Council of Ministers, a Commission of the European Communities, a Court of Justice, and a European Parliament composed of 434 elected representatives. Although the hopes for political integration have never been fully realized, European economic cooperation has been a great success, with the EEC's membership growing by 1986 to twelve states — all the major economies of Europe.

The United States preserved its leadership, and avoided the discriminatory costs of the common European tariff barrier, by heavy private investment in the newly revitalized European economies. Multinational corporations also played a leading role in extending American influence in the Third World, particularly in the decaying colonial empires of Britain and France. Using direct investment, U.S. firms secured oligopolistic control of such extractive industries as petroleum and minerals, and there was a massive overseas expansion in manufacturing. This thrust in foreign investment was fed by the rapid growth of the U.S. economy in the 1950s and '60s. By 1970, U.S. firms had assets abroad of $31 billion, which represented about 12 percent of the book value of all U.S. companies; by 1984, U.S. direct investment abroad amounted to $233 billion, a seven-fold increase in a decade and a half. U.S. foreign trade also expanded rapidly in this period, making America the world's largest market for raw materials and the leading supplier of technology to Europe, Japan, and the less-developed countries.

World trade in general expanded dramatically in these years. Between 1950 and 1980, the volume of world trade grew about six times and its value (in real terms) about twenty times; world production rose from $1.1 trillion in 1955 to $10.8 trillion in 1980. The basis for the trade growth was the liberalized rules adopted in 1947 at Geneva, Switzerland, in the General Agreement on Tariffs and Trade (GATT). GATT established guidelines for free trade and a commercial code and set up procedures for fashioning an international consensus on trade. It provided for a series of multilateral conferences, or rounds, at which the principal trading partners could negotiate tariff reductions. These reductions were then to be extended to all parties adhering to GATT's "most-favored nation" principle of nondiscrimination, which stated that tariff preferences or other trade privileges granted to one nation must be granted to all other nations trading in the same product. Of course, most of the socialist bloc states were not parties to the GATT agreement, and it also made exceptions for existing preferential systems, such as Britain and France had with their colonial dependencies, and for any future customs unions or free-trade associations. Still, GATT's effect on the liberalization of world trade was substantial. It established international trade norms for its member states and enshrined the central free-trade principle of reciprocity, or mutually advantageous tariff reductions.

Six rounds of tariff negotiations occurred between 1947 and 1967, concluding with the highly productive Kennedy Round, which replaced item-by-item negotiations with across-the-board percentage cuts. Although most nations continued to protect their agricultural products out of domestic political considerations, large gains were made in liberalizing trade in manufactured goods. Most quotas and exchange rate barriers were eliminated, and regulations were placed on subsidies and dumping (selling below cost to gain control of a foreign market). The liberal trade practices adopted under GATT were one of the principal forces behind the rapid economic recovery of Japan and Western Europe.

The United States could afford to tolerate balance-of-payments deficits and asymmetrical trade benefits as long as its economic growth remained vigorous. America's increasing military presence and political influence more than compensated for short-term economic losses. Also, the United States had a free hand in the Third World, realizing substantial economic gains on the heels of the British and French withdrawal. Soviet competition in the Third World and the risk of revolutionary upheavals in underdeveloped regions led the United States to expend large sums in foreign aid, particularly to the Republic of China (Taiwan), South Korea, and South Vietnam — key countries in the U.S. effort to contain Communism in Asia. However, the Soviet political-military presence in the Third World in the first postwar decade was quite limited and economic assistance almost nil, as the Soviets focused on reconstructing their own damaged economy. The result of all these factors was to make the United States the dominant economic force in every region of the globe.

The Breakdown of the Bretton Woods System

The two decades between 1960 and 1980 witnessed dramatic changes in the structure of the global economy, and in America's role in particular. Rapid growth and expanding investment and trade had knit the global economy into a system that was beginning to restrict the ability of states to act independently. Monetary interdependence, for example, made it less easy for national governments to control their own money supply through adjustments in interest rates and other traditional fiscal and budgetary tools. Exchange rates were dramatically affected by speculation in the currency markets or by a foreign bank's decision to sell large dollar reserves. High interest rates, which once had a dampening effect on inflation, now simply attracted large amounts of foreign capital. Deficit financing introduced to stimulate a sluggish U.S. economy set off unwanted inflationary pressures elsewhere. It was the same with trade: if

America sneezed, the whole world caught a cold. A recession in the United States could be an economic disaster for economies heavily dependent on the U.S. market. In a less-developed country, a 5 percent drop in U.S. imports could have a catastrophic effect of 50 percent on its exports. On the other hand, a dramatic increase in U.S. imports of Japanese cars and electronics, say, would send American employment plummeting and capital scurrying overseas in search of cheap labor. The very success of economic interdependence was breeding instability and renewed nationalist tendencies. Political leaders began to search for economic policies that would shield their citizens from the less desirable effects of the international market.

In the United States, domestic constituencies were demanding that the government protect them from cheap offshore labor and shield well-established industries from the inroads of foreign imports. The long period of growth without substantial foreign competition had created huge U.S. industries in textiles, autos, steel, footwear, ship construction, and the like, many of them with large overseas markets, foreign subsidiaries, and multinational sources of supply and sales. But corporations were finding that the benefits of an integrated global market could be as easily withdrawn as they had been gained. From the standpoint of comparative advantage and pure market efficiency, domestic production does not automatically respond to changing international conditions. Political considerations enter in, often forcing a government to restrict free trade, in the national interest or perhaps on behalf of a particularly well-entrenched domestic industry or other vested interest.

One common device for protecting a nation's industry is import quotas, which limit the quantity of a particular product that can be imported, thereby raising the product's domestic price and stimulating its production (or production of a substitute) at home. The United States imposed import quotas on oil and sugar in the 1950s, arguing that they were necessary to protect American producers. But political motives were involved as well — the desire to isolate Fidel Castro's Cuba, which was a major sugar supplier, and to reduce dependence on foreign oil. States can also bypass GATT's prohibitions on tariff barriers by negotiating a variety of bilateral export restraints. Thus, the United States forced voluntary export restrictions from Japan in the 1980s to reduce the flood of Japanese autos and give the American industry time to adjust to the shift toward smaller, more fuel-efficient cars. Likewise, voluntary restrictions and orderly marketing arrangements were negotiated with a number of Asian textile producers in order to control their exports to the United States and Europe. Health and safety standards, grading restrictions, tax incentives, government subsidies, and various kinds of regulations are other devices for restricting trade or protecting private industry from foreign competition. All these nontariff barriers effectively circumvented the GATT guidelines and achieved neomercantilist goals of increased domestic production and employment, expansion of exports, and a positive balance of trade.

The breakdown of the GATT guidelines on free trade was matched by the failure of the Bretton Woods system of fixed exchange rates. In the immediate postwar years, international liquidity had been sustained by the outflow of U.S.

dollars in the form of foreign aid, military assistance, and investments, financed by the deliberate policy of balance-of-payments deficits. By the late 1960s, however, American dollars were no longer so badly needed abroad, and the payment deficits, once a reflection of American strength, now had become a necessity. Largely due to military overcommitments and a growing weakness in productivity and exports, U.S. government expenditures began to exceed the growth capacities of the economy, eroding the confidence of the foreign banks that held large dollar reserves. The U.S. balance-of-payments deficit doubled in a decade. In 1971 it soared to $10.6 billion, and U.S. imports exceeded exports for the first time in the twentieth century. U.S. gold stocks were being steadily reduced to maintain the dollar's value at the fixed rate of $35 per ounce. The magnitude of this shift can be appreciated only in retrospect. In 1947, the United States held 70 percent of the world's total official monetary gold stock; by 1984, it had dwindled to 8 percent. Likewise, as late as 1965, total external claims against the dollar amounted to only $12 billion; by 1987, these had soared to over $1,000 billion ($1 trillion).

The U.S. domestic budget rose dramatically during Lyndon Johnson's presidency, due to the costs of his Great Society programs and the Vietnam War, and this overheated the American economy. The resulting inflation quickly spread abroad because the Bretton Woods system prevented a downward adjustment of the dollar, which normally would have accompanied a weakening economic position. This left foreign governments holding large amounts of unwanted dollars in reserve just at a time when skepticism about the dollar's convertibility to gold was growing and there was great volatility in the currency markets. Foreign banks feared that an American devaluation, a run on the dollar, or a rise in the price of gold could substantially cut the value of their reserves. In the United States, domestic political pressures caused two successive administrations (one Democratic, one Republican) to attempt to shift the burden of adjustment to America's allies, rather than face the political costs of a painful deflationary policy. But the size of the "dollar overhang," or Eurodollar pool, had become so immense that the Europeans saw no reason to continue in an economic arrangement that gave the United States a privileged position. Moreover, the initiation of trade with some of the Eastern bloc countries and an emerging atmosphere of détente told the Europeans that they had less need for U.S. protection. Sharpening differences over U.S. policy in Vietnam also made America's allies increasingly reluctant to bear the indirect financial burden of the war-related deficits.

The monetary crisis came to a head in 1971, when President Richard Nixon took measures to shore up the American economy that unilaterally put an end to the Bretton Woods system. On August 15, 1971, he declared his New Economic Policy, which imposed domestic wage and price controls and a 10 percent surcharge on imports. He also ended the U.S. commitment to convert dollars to gold and called for new multilateral negotiations on trade and monetary reform. However, two successive devaluations of the dollar were not enough to save the system of fixed exchange rates. By March of 1973, rising inflationary pressures had led to the adoption of floating exchange rates for all the major world currencies, to insulate them from externally induced inflation. The death of the gold standard and fixed exchange rates left the international monetary system subject to the forces of the market and to whatever minor adjustments the central bankers could agree on.

The final test of the Bretton Woods system, over its commitment to free trade, did not come until the 1980s, when the United States' deepening balance-of-payments crisis forced it to end preferential relations with Europe and Japan. For several decades, the American economy had been strong enough to tolerate some discrimination against U.S. exports and direct overseas investment, especially since the United States openly monopolized Third World markets. But by 1987 the U.S. trade deficit was at an all-time high of $170.1 billion. This, along with friendlier relations with the Soviet Union and a rising economic capacity in both Europe and Japan, resulted in American demands for its allies to maintain more open markets and share a greater part of the defense burden. There were frictions with the Europeans over the restrictive EEC policies on U.S. agricultural exports and with the Japanese over barriers to U.S. direct investment. But the allies proved reluctant to assume the economic burdens of a more liberal international order, and the American response was correspondingly nationalist and protectionist. Its rapidly deteriorating trade position pushed the United States gradually away from liberal principles, even under the Reagan administration's staunch free-trade philosophy. In the process, the United States has passed from being a champion of economic interdependence, under Presidents Nixon and Carter, to being an advocate of greater national independence and self-sufficiency today.

Before 1971, the overvalued dollar and its privileged position as a reserve currency had saved the U.S. economy from the domestic austerity measures that its declining international role would otherwise have required. However, between 1970 and 1987, the United States was transformed from the world's largest creditor nation to the largest debtor nation. At the end of 1986, America owed more than $264 billion abroad, well over double the total of the previous year and more than twice the $108 billion foreign debt of Brazil, the previous leader. The causes of the accumulating balance-of-payments deficit were many: large amounts in foreign military assistance, including the special economic burdens of the Vietnam War and a vast overseas military complex; rising trade deficits, reflecting low productivity, high labor costs, and an end to cheap oil; loss of earnings from the "technological rents" that went with U.S. postwar industrial preeminence. Foreign indebtedness was aggravated by high interest rates, themselves the result of domestic deficits that even the fiscally "conservative" Republicans could not control. High interest rates refueled the demand for dollars, overvaluing them once more in relation to America's real productive capacity, and this only compounded the swelling U.S. trade deficit of the 1980s (see Figure 4-1). At the same time, lower earnings on overseas investments, lagging debt repayments from the Third World, increased global competition, and altered terms of trade with the Third World were cutting further into the export sector.

America's reaction to these negative trends was to shift away from free trade and become the leader in a new phase of protectionism. Domestic pressures behind the call for trade restrictions included runaway industry, high unemployment, the shock of the oil crisis, monetary instability, and the vulnerabilities of interdependence. Recession added its cyclical pressures to the more basic structural problems of certain industries, such as steel, textiles, shipping, and light-engineering products, in which U.S. technological innovation, capital investment, and labor productivity lagged far behind the levels in Japan and in the dynamic export-oriented economies of several newly industrializing countries. And so the temptation was irresistible for the United States to improve its payments imbalance through trade measures that restricted imports.

This changing economic environment is well summarized by David Blake and Robert Walters in *The Politics of Global Economic Relations:*

> The post-Bretton Woods system of flexible exchange rates has tremendous political-economic implications for the United States. Specifically, alterations in the exchange rate of the dollar have created a much closer link between America's international payments position and the performance of its domestic economy than was the case prior to 1973. International monetary policies used to be consistently subordinated to domestic economic policies and to the goal of maintaining American autonomy from international monetary constraints. Now the United States sometimes finds it necessary to subordinate domestic economic policy to developments in its international economic relations. The timing of President Carter's decision in November 1978 to increase interest rates dramatically (thereby inviting higher unemployment) was dictated by a precipitous decline in the value of the dollar. America's economic growth and staggering

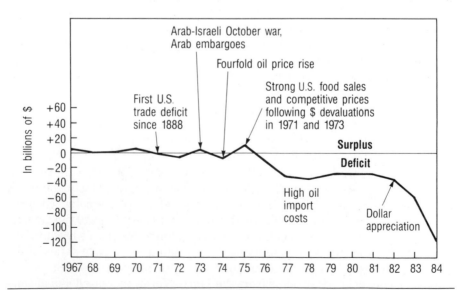

FIGURE 4-1

U.S. MERCHANDISE TRADE BALANCE, 1967–84

government budget deficits during the mid-1980's were being financed largely by massive inflows of foreign capital whose sudden withdrawal could produce a financial crisis and a collapse of the dollar's value. There was widespread concern that, quite apart from domestic economic policy preferences, the United States would be compelled to increase interest rates to sustain the flows of capital from abroad upon which its domestic economy was relying. In such circumstances international capital flows would dictate American domestic monetary policy. Clearly, the United States [was] losing much of its autonomy in the international monetary system and the role of the dollar within it. (pp. 74–75)

New Challenges to American Economic Leadership

The dissolution of the Bretton Woods system was associated with a gradual decline in America's economic leadership. One challenge to U.S. preeminence came from the newly independent countries of the Third World. Increasingly aware of the degree to which their patterns of trade and investment favored the former colonial powers, they began to demand reforms that would strip the advanced industrial states of these advantages. A formal agenda embodying the Third World demands was presented at the United Nations Conference on Trade and Development (UNCTAD) in 1964 and in subsequent special sessions of the UN General Assembly in 1974 and 1975. The oil crisis of 1973 shocked the advanced industrial states into some degree of cooperation with the Third World's demand for a New International Economic Order (NIEO), and the immense transfer of resources to oil-exporting nations encouraged the growth of a group of middle-income states able to challenge American and West European dominance of Third World commodity markets. Also, by the 1970s, some newly industrializing countries, like the Republic of China (Taiwan), South Korea, Hong Kong, and Singapore, were beginning to compete effectively in exports of such finished goods as textiles and electronics. U.S. industry was soon losing sales, and eventually jobs, to the highly disciplined and efficient labor markets of East Asia.

As their production surpassed prewar levels, Europe and Japan no longer had economic reasons for bowing to American political dominance, and the United States no longer needed to bear the economic costs of leadership for reasons of security. The biggest challenge to American economic hegemony came from the European Econonomic Community, which had become a dynamic and powerful trading bloc. The disappearance of internal barriers to trade among the West European states had created the largest single market anywhere in the world (almost 300 million consumers, as of 1986), importing and exporting more goods than the United States and Japan combined. The EEC's customs union, with a common tariff wall, had a decidedly negative impact on U.S. trade. Its Common Agricultural Policy (CAP), adopted in 1966, set artificially high farm prices that served to exclude American agricultural goods from the European market, just when the United States had become the world's leading exporter of farm products and a principal trading partner of the EEC countries. And the EEC market was growing progressively larger

(Denmark, Ireland, and the United Kingdom joined in 1973, Greece in 1981, Spain and Portugal in 1986). Moreover, it had negotiated a series of preferential trade agreements with the states of the European Free Trade Association (EFTA) — Austria, Finland, Iceland, Norway, Sweden, and Switzerland — and with more than seventy countries of the Third World, most of them former colonies of EEC member states.

By the late 1960s Japan was also becoming an economic rival. Its gross domestic product grew at an astonishing rate, rising from $44 billion in 1960 to $1,040 billion in 1980, a *twenty-five-fold* increase in only two decades. In the same period, U.S. production increased five-fold (from $507 billion to $2,587 billion), and EEC production rose ten-fold (from $271 billion to $2,756 billion). The annual growth rate for Japanese exports reached 17.2 percent in the 1960s, while that for U.S. exports remained at a moderate 6 percent. Despite Japan's rise to the rank of third largest economic power, after the United States and the USSR, it remained outside the Bretton Woods system and pursued a policy of economic nationalism that collided head-on with the prevailing free trade. Import quotas and administrative regulations were employed to bar competition in agriculture and such industries as computers, electronics, heavy machinery, and automobiles, all of which were heavily subsidized to stimulate exports. Also, a consistently undervalued yen, which made Japanese goods comparatively cheap in foreign markets, contributed to balance-of-trade surpluses.

The Japanese achieved their economic miracle by joint government-business management of the economy, with scant respect for traditional laissez-faire principles. Naturally, when this philosophy was carried into the burgeoning foreign trade sector, it brought Japan into direct conflict with American tariff policies. American businesses and workers consistently complained that they were not competing on a "level playing field," that the Japanese were tilting the game in their own favor by export subsidies and by a host of bureaucratic barriers to the entry of foreign goods. If trade could no longer be purely *free*, at least it could be *fair*. American critics thought the Japanese government ought to scale back its involvement in the export sector and end nontariff barriers to the entry of American goods. It remains an open question, however, whether the United States can convert Japan to its arms-length approach to government regulation or whether, in the face of low productivity and declining competitiveness, the United States will decide to adopt reindustrialization measures, in imitation of Japan's policy of a prominent entrepreneurial and developmental role for the state.

In this same period, many of the socialist bloc states of Eastern Europe began to express a desire to participate more fully in the international economy. East-West trade had started early with Yugoslavia and then progressed to Hungary and Czechoslovakia in the 1960s, following the economic liberalization and decentralization of Soviet Premier Nikita Khrushchev's de-Stalinization campaign. West Germany, no longer dependent on its American patron and spurred by Chancellor Willy Brandt's *Ostpolitik,* opened the East German market in the 1970s. After 1974, the Eurocurrency markets were overflowing with recycled petrodollars (deposits from oil exporters seeking the safety of European banks), and the East Europeans found them an attractive and rapidly increasing source of loans. In just five years, the total Western debt of the East bloc countries grew from $22 billion to $64 billion. In fact, trade and monetary interdependence grew so quickly that by 1979 Poland alone owed $20 billion and was spending 92 percent of its earnings from East-West trade on debt service.

Under Premier Leonid Brezhnev, the Soviets themselves began to reassess the price of their isolation from the technologically dynamic global capitalist economy. Their growth rate was slowing dramatically, and Brezhnev needed new technology from abroad to make Soviet industry more efficient. The computer boom and the scientific-technical revolution were threatening to pass the Soviet Union by, yet Brezhnev was reluctant to introduce the material incentives, the decentralization, or the free exchange of information that might spur domestic innovation. His solution was to expand trade with the West and use the Soviet hard-currency earnings to pay for the latest in Western technology. But Soviet crop failures, coupled with a chronically unproductive collectivized agriculture, led to massive expenditures for foreign grain. Also, the Soviets were increasingly burdened by their subsidies to restless East European satellites, which were eager for more economic liberalization and could be held in line only by maintaining their standard of living at a higher level than that of the Soviets themselves. To keep political control at home and among its allies, the Soviet Union found itself gradually increasing its role in the international economy. At the same time, the rising power of Japan was pressing the USSR in its Asian sphere, where the Soviets were learning well that nuclear weapons were not enough to ensure their superpower status — that a great power must hold a dominant stake in the global economy if it is to command all the levers of modern diplomacy.

Secretary-General Mikhail Gorbachev's new policies of *perestroika* ("restructuring") and *glasnost* ("openness"), entailing domestic reforms and improved relations with the West, were primarily motivated by economic considerations. The USSR has begun to debate its role in the Far East and the possibility of participating fully in the growing Pacific Rim economy. It also must decide whether the resource-rich Siberian frontier should serve socialist self-sufficiency and European Russia or, with the help of Japanese and Western technology, the global market. So far the political reformers have seemed solidly in control, with Deputy Premier Leonid Abalkin, head of the State Commission on Economic Reform, arguing for a market-oriented economy with a convertible currency by 1995. The People's Republic of China, despite the setbacks associated with its repression of the prodemocracy student movement in 1989, is in the throes of a similar opening to Western investment, trade, and technology. For all the states of the socialist bloc, internal economic reform and growth have appeared to be intimately bound up with an end to their ideological and economic isolation. The more relaxed political relations of today will likely permit resources to be redirected from the military sector and a largely obsolescent heavy industry to consumer goods, high technology, and other more productive sectors. But this will require the socialist states to enter more fully into the global economy, both for access to technology and capital and for export markets.

THE GLOBAL ECONOMIC PREDICAMENT

The rising economic power of the Third World, Japan, the European Economic Community, and the socialist bloc has begun to eclipse American economic power. Although in 1983 the United States still had a $3 trillion-plus economy that accounted for more than 30 percent of global output, its relative position has declined sharply since 1945, spawning a global as well as a national dilemma: without American leadership, and without a substitute for the Bretton Woods system, the international economy threatens to regress into a more protectionist phase. Nationalist rivalries play themselves out in the global economic arena today as fully as they do in the more traditional arenas of arms races and diplomatic wrangling. In fact, among OECD member countries, which are united ideologically, economic rivalry is the principal source of conflict. North-South tensions have also centered on such vital economic issues as oil and food. Simply put, interdependence has outstripped the capacity of the present informal system to manage it. This poses a basic choice for every country: either withdraw from the entangling confines of the international market, with the economic losses this might entail, or augment the collective management of the international system by making some sacrifices in political and economic sovereignty. The global economy has continued to expand, despite the protectionist flavor of the Tokyo Round of Multilateral Trade Negotiations (the seventh GATT conference) held between 1975 and 1979. The dollar recovered its strength for a time in the 1980s, largely because of an end to double-digit inflation and a resumption of growth. This restored confidence in the international money markets and convinced foreign bankers that it was safe to continue holding huge dollar reserves. Meanwhile, the deficit-induced rise in U.S. interest rates made the dollar and the U.S. market attractive once again to foreign investors.

However, the growth of the 1970s and '80s was bought at the price of a huge expansion in international indebtedness. International reserves (held mostly in dollars) rose from $129 billion in 1971 to over $700 billion in 1983. The Eurocurrency market (foreign currency deposits reloaned outside the country of origin) grew from $85 billion in 1971 to $2,200 billion in 1984. As a result, the United States has effectively lost control of its own currency. The dollar's value fluctuated wildly in the 1980s, in spite of the best efforts of U.S. treasury secretaries to work with foreign central bankers in stabilizing currency markets. The huge pool of dollars outside U.S. control has funded extensive borrowing by states hard-hit by oil price hikes and runaway inflation. This growth in credit/debt and reserves allowed many states, including the United

States, to finance their balance-of-payments deficits without having to undergo painful domestic political and economic adjustments. But such actions have simply deferred basic reforms and made the international economy a hostage to the stability and creditworthiness of debtor nations. Nagging doubts remain about the U.S. ability to impose a long-term solution to its trade deficit problem without setting off a new global recession, and the Third World's inability to meet debt repayments could also place the international banking system in jeopardy.

Criticism of unregulated market exchanges is growing. Many states have doubts about the basic stability of the post-Bretton Woods system, and most seem to want a more decisive management of what has become a crisis-prone capitalist order. The real question is whether the management should be national or international. Many of the less-developed countries feel that the system of free trade is rigged against them and have called for international management. Advanced capitalist countries whose national markets are being penetrated by foreign goods or whose industries are exporting capital and jobs overseas have called for more regulation and protection by their own governments. All states are finding it more difficult to counter the international forces that interfere with domestic control; national economies have become increasingly vulnerable to external influence at the very time when the legitimacy of modern government depends more than ever on its ability to deliver economic benefits. Interdependence has contributed to prosperity, but it also has created conditions that states can no longer manage by the traditional means of market adjustment and bilateral diplomatic bargaining.

In the search for new institutions of global economic management, UNCTAD, the series of UN-sponsored conferences on North-South issues, and the Group of Seventy-seven's call for a New International Economic Order have voiced Third World concerns. The Western industrial democracies have attempted to discipline debtor nations and induce the IMF and the World Bank to take a stronger role in debt rescheduling. The IMF has been coordinating private and public responses to requests for new loans from the Third World and imposing domestic reforms as a condition for rescheduling unfulfilled debt obligations. In many Third World states, this has resulted in severe austerity programs, deflationary policies, cutbacks in welfare and government services, and across-the-board wage reductions, all mandated by the creditor nations acting through the IMF. Since 1975, annual economic summit meetings among the seven leading nations of the OECD (the United States, Britain, France, West Germany, Japan, Canada, and Italy) have sought joint action on pressing political-economic issues. The EEC has also searched for new management institutions to substitute for the defunct Bretton Woods system; the most important has been the European Monetary System (EMS), which coordinates monetary policies and stabilizes exchange rates among EEC members.

Today, the international economy appears poised on the brink of a historic transition. Socialist powers are entering the international market, instability continues in the advanced capitalist bloc, and the Third World and the newly industrializing countries are pressing for greater participation. But it is uncertain what the future will bring: more integration and cooperation in managing growing prosperity and interdependence; or a general withdrawal from interdependence, renewed assertions of sovereignty, a relative decline in exchange and growth, new protectionism, and a breakdown into rigidly defined national or regional blocs. Crucial to the transition is the shifting leadership role of the United States. As Robert Gilpin has argued, in *U.S. Power and the Multinational Corporation,* "the modern world economy has evolved through the emergence of great national economies that have successively become dominant" (pp. 40–41). While the United States was supplying enormous military and economic support to its allies, matched by vigorous domestic growth and technological innovation, it was able to serve as the enforcer in a contentious yet interdependent world. The United States could fashion a consensus on trade and monetary policy by economically constraining any states that attempted to deviate from the prevailing international order. However, once the United States began to decline in productivity and primacy, and therefore to manipulate the international economy strictly for short-term American advantage, Japan and the EEC states were bound to call the Bretton Woods scheme and America's leadership into question.

Who will become the successor and how the new international economic order will be regulated are unclear. Also unclear is whether traditional nationalist policies will adjust to the requirements of a newly interdependent world political economy. The collapse of a dominant economy has been associated with political disaster in the past, the two most dramatic examples being the economic decline of the Roman Empire, whose fall brought on the Dark Ages of medieval Europe, and the Great Depression of the 1930s, which followed on the economic destruction of World War I and the end of Britain's leading role in the international economy.

If a new economic leader or a collective management regime does not emerge, "the common interest of an overwhelming majority of states can be frustrated, almost at will, by individual governments, some of whom are compelled to comply with the erratic wishes signalled periodically by unpredictable electorates, some free to do as they please. Under the circumstances, only the power of persuasion of a superior economy backed by matching military capability can prevent the system, such as it is, from being pulled down by its component parts," writes Henry Bretton, in *International Relations in the Nuclear Age* (p. 204). Bretton lists these requirements for a world economic leader: (1) the ability to maintain a freely convertible currency that states are willing to hold as a reserve currency, the same as if it were gold; (2) economic policies and practices, at home and abroad, that are outer-directed, including restraints on government spending, deficits, and interest rates; (3) a resilient, productive, and powerful growth economy; (4) the strength to curb domestic protectionist pressures in order to absorb exports from trading partners experiencing payments difficulties and from less-developed countries whose survival depends on their breaking into the established market; (5) the ability to flatten out fluctuations in the capitalist business cycle by playing a kind of global

Keynesian role as a regulator of the international economy and a sponsor of welfare-state spending to aid the system's weakest members; (6) substantial economic reserves, backed by the banking and lending structures of all its trading partners, that allow it to act as lender of last resort in times of severe economic crisis. These are formidable requirements, which the United States possessed only in the best of times and perhaps will not be able to recover, even should deficit reduction, reindustrialization, and domestic economic reform prove successful. And it is unlikely that Japan, Germany, or any other advanced industrial state can ever occupy such a commanding position. This leaves the fate of the international political economy in the hands of cooperative management strategies if it is to escape the anarchical tendencies of the balance-of-power system. We face once again the collective decision dilemma of Rousseau's parable of the stag and the hare, except that this time the scope is global and the economic consequences potentially earth-shattering.

At stake are the stability and interdependence of the advanced capitalist states, the hopes for development and greater equity in North-South relations, and the prospects for integrating the East bloc economies into the international system. Both capitalism and socialism will be tested for their long-term ability to deliver prosperity, stability, and equity. The advanced capitalist states face the historic question of whether they can function within a global system without using recessionary measures, protectionism, manipulation of the world banking system, or exploitation of the Third World to sustain their economic growth. The capitalist states will also be tested for their ability to subdue national competition for economic control—which issued in such breakdowns as the colonial rivalries that led to World War I and the beggar-thy-neighbor policies of the Great Depression—in favor of collective forms of international management. The socialist states face the question of whether their historically closed, command economies can make the adjustments necessary to gain them greater access to new technology and a competitive position in the international market. They will also be tested on the crucial issue of state socialism's ability to incorporate increasingly democratic and decentralized forms of management. The Third World states have perhaps the most difficult decision of all: should they enter the interdependent international economy as secondary players, or should they seek economic self-sufficiency by imitating the socialist or mercantilist paths to modernization that the European powers followed in their early phases of development? Whatever the choice, most of the late-modernizing states will have to reform their political systems fundamentally before they can perform effectively as development agents and independent international actors, instead of remaining the victims of external manipulation or self-serving elites. In this sense, the Third World states provide a clear instance of the impact of interdependence: the successful pursuit of international economic goals is dependent on effective state institutions; but ending corruption and political turbulence in the "soft states" of the Southern Hemisphere requires, beyond internal reform, the cooperation of the advanced states in creating a more equitable international economic order.

Three Models of the International Political Economy

The postwar international changes that we have just outlined were accompanied by changes in our patterns of thought. As military means of implementing foreign policy began to give way to economic measures, the balance-of-power concept was no longer an adequate explanation for international relations. States had become drawn into a complex web that mixed elements of cooperation and competition, and analysis in terms of pure power politics had to be supplemented by attention to the effects of economic interdependence. International relations theory, once almost exclusively concerned with political relations and military competition, now began to focus on nonstate actors and socioeconomic influences. One important theorist, Robert Gilpin, in *The Political Economy of International Relations,* gives us three competing models of the formative forces that have shaped the emerging international political economy. These three schools of thought are liberalism, Marxism, and economic nationalism.

Liberalism emphasizes free trade, comparative advantage, and the growth of mutually beneficial relations of *interdependence.* In this model, the emergence of close ties among the advanced capitalist states is seen as a positive step toward joint management of the global economy. Interdependence has forced the hitherto warring states to cooperate in order to maintain their shared stake in a stable international system.

Marxism focuses on the exploitative character of relations between the imperial power centers and their peripheral colonial states. According to this view, the growth of the modern world economy has created relations of *dependency* and inequality that have subsidized the development of the industrialized states at the expense of the poor peoples of the Third World. Indeed, Third World poverty, in the Marxist view, was caused by the domination of the European capitalist states and is perpetuated even today by neocolonial ties and unfair trade relations.

Economic nationalism gives the state the dominant role in international economic relations. The world political economy reflects the prevailing distribution of state power, and economic policies are guided by national self-interest. Indeed, economic interests have become more important as a constituent of state power because of every state's need for advanced technology and a wider resource base. In other respects, states have continued to follow the traditional principles of *mercantilism,* which aim at maximizing state power and economic independence. Economic nationalists downplay the role of transnational economic ties, arguing that reasons of state remain the motive forces in the international economy and that the world market is merely a by-product of national drives for self-sufficiency or domination.

In the remainder of this chapter, we will explore each of these models in detail and see how they affect our understanding of international affairs.

INTERDEPENDENCE DEFINED

We have used interdependence so far in the loose sense of a growing interconnectedness in the modern world system. Now we need to define it more precisely, as a condition of *mutual dependence* in which individuals and states are
reciprocally affected by transnational forces. We measure the degree of interdependence by the number of international transactions and their relative
impact — whether symmetrical or skewed — on the participating countries or
actors. Flows of money, goods, people, and information across international
boundaries, which have increased dramatically since World War II, are all
signs of global interconnectedness. So are revolutionary ideas and the arms to
implement them, which move rapidly from one part of the world to another.
The deadly AIDS virus is carried from one continent to another. International
trade puts exotic fruits and foreign perfumes in the hands of the ordinary
consumer. Satellite communications spread television coverage of sports
events, political rallies, and foreign wars. But such interconnectedness does
not by itself constitute mutual dependence. True global interdependence exists
only when states' political-economic systems are so fully organized around
international transactions that they suffer significant losses if the connections
are disrupted. The constraints of interdependence include not only the threat of
harmful acts by a foreign power — economic sanctions leveled by one state
against another or the mutual vulnerability of the nuclear superpowers. They
also include many unintended consequences of global relatedness, like "culture
shock," international terrorism, demonstration effects (such as rising expectations in the Third World), global pollution, resource depletion — the collective
costs that accompany the benefits of a global communications net, an international trading system, or the worldwide transfer of industrial technology.

This *vulnerability* to outside influences makes it clear that interdependence
has costs as well as benefits. Typically, the benefit sought is an economic one
and the cost is a loss of political sovereignty. At the beginning, the weaker states
bore the direct costs of global interrelatedness in the form of their dependence
on the expanding, technologically dynamic imperial powers. Any costs to the
dominant powers were greatly outweighed by the benefits of the highly asymmetrical colonial relationship. But eventually the great powers began to lose
control, as an indirect, long-term consequence of the global diffusion of culture
and technology that they themselves had initiated as a device for maintaining
control. Every state today is subject to the entangling influence of a global
structure of socioeconomic relations. The quality of interdependence is just as
important as the quantity of transactions: a state's vulnerabilities are the real
measure of its dependence on international transactions. For example, any
state that trades extensively is sensitive to the effects of trade disruptions, but a
state is vulnerable only if it cannot substitute an internal resource or find an
alternative source of supply. Although decolonization and the growing volume
of world trade have tended to spread the benefits of interdependence more
evenly, some states remain more vulnerable than others, with poor countries

FIGURE 4-2

U.S. MERCHANDISE IMPORTS, 1984 (IN BILLIONS OF $)

Total	**341**
Western Europe	75
Canada	67
Japan	60
Asia (excl. Japan and OPEC)	55
Latin America and Caribbean (excl. OPEC)	41
OPEC	28
Africa (excl. OPEC and South Africa)	5
Oceania	4
South Africa	3
USSR and Eastern Europe	2
Other	1

and small states at an obvious disadvantage in their range of options. Nonetheless, even the most powerful states have found it necessary at times to sacrifice elements of political autonomy in exchange for access to an expanding and more productive global economic system. (Figures 4-2 and 4-3 show, for example, America's growing dependence on imports and its trade deficit with Japan.)

Interdependence does not presume, therefore, a perfectly mutual, noncompetitive relationship, but a condition of interrelatedness in which a state's actions and interests are subject to varying degrees of external restraint. Such dependency may offer a state incentives for cooperation, but it may as easily

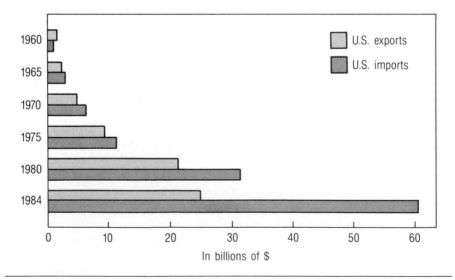

FIGURE 4-3

U.S. MERCHANDISE TRADE WITH JAPAN

cause the state to react competitively to its vulnerability by seeking greater control or independence of action. What distinguishes the structure of interdependence from the balance of power is its mix of cooperative and conflictual relations and the fact that its conflicts stem directly from the benefits of a more complex and closely related system. They are conflicts that cannot be resolved simply by coercing or punishing an adversary; the nature of interdependence is such that an attack on any one member of the system bears negative consequences for all. Discrete national identities are submerged in a larger web of relations, and autonomous sources of power are hard to mobilize. Still, if the benefits of interdependence become highly skewed, or if a state desires autonomy above all other values, the structures of interdependence can come under attack. And even when everyone gains, states may fight over their relative shares. On the other hand, states may cope with these strains by resorting to new methods of collective decision making. For example, the thirteen American states that made up the early Confederation were economically interdependent far beyond the capacity of their embryonic political organization to manage. Their patterns of trade imposed on them costs of "alliance management" and "international" coordination of policies. The U.S. Constitution was the political device they adopted, after winning their independence, to manage their interdependence more efficiently.

Our survey of the international political economy since World War II has also shown that interdependence often involves the *codetermination* of political and economic aims. A state's security is no longer defined solely in terms of military policy, and domestic prosperity cannot be separated from interests of state. The American standard of living cannot be sustained without international ties, while an event abroad — a war in the Middle East affecting oil supplies, say — can have a fundamental impact on American security and well-being. Thus, the United States has sought to protect both its economic and its military interests through the Marshall Plan and other programs of foreign economic assistance. At the same time, such military measures as the stationing of U.S. troops in Europe, the building of a 600-ship navy, the creation of a Rapid Deployment Force (RDF), and the placement of constabulary forces in the Third World — at a cost exceeding the U.S. strategic nuclear forces budget — have been aimed at protecting American investments, trading partners, and other economic interests. The struggles in South Africa, Rhodesia/Zimbabwe, and Angola have been as much over access to scarce strategic minerals as over apartheid, Marxism, and the political complexion of those regimes. When the Cold War divided the globe into a bipolar diplomatic-security system, it also divided it into two separate economic blocs. When détente and ideological pluralism softened these dividing lines, they also changed the patterns of East-West trade. We can even say that the Reagan-Gorbachev round of peace initiatives beginning in 1986 was fundamentally motivated by domestic economic considerations: the desire of each side for relief from the burdens of the arms race. Today, America's power profile in the world depends significantly on its economic decisions, and its balance-of-payments position vitally affects what kind of defense it can afford to mount abroad. Such entanglements of economic and political aims are one of the most powerful ways in which interdependence impacts on foreign policy.

Another important phenomenon of interdependence is the *interpenetration* of domestic and international affairs, or the breakdown of traditionally impervious national borders, as symbolized by the invasive power of missile technology and the mass media. Economically, this interpenetration is evident in the growth of foreign trade and in the mutual vulnerability of global economic exchange. National economic policy, once made in isolation, is now influenced by the OECD, the IMF, GATT, and literally thousands of other international governmental organizations. Moreover, the rise of such nonstate actors as multinational corporations has created a whole new constituency of transnational interests to press the levers of domestic politics in furtherance of their international aims. Likewise, foreign trade policy is suddenly subject to the influence of domestic groups, like organized labor, whose impact on foreign economic decisions has never been so great. U.S. presidents used to get elected by promising to make pocketbook issues the basis of their domestic economic agenda, but foreign policy has entered into election politics as never before, and voters now rate a president's ability to deliver the economic goods in terms of his effective management of the international system. A change in nuclear strategy and a strong commitment to new weapons procurement in the Reagan years, for example, added so many billions to the U.S. deficit that the economic legacy will shape domestic politics for decades. Just as Japan's spectacular economic recovery has catapulted it into international prominence, so will America's power position and international competitiveness in the coming years be determined by how effectively the United States deals with domestic reindustrialization, education, and technological innovation. Just as America's economy has expanded far beyond its own borders, so U.S. foreign policy is not restricted to events outside those borders: international politics no longer stops "at the water's edge." David Blake and Robert Walters, in *The Politics of Global Economic Relations,* review some of the typical ways in which political-economic issues have spilled out of their traditional national compartments:

> The International Labor Organization sets labor standards strengthening the bargaining position of domestic labor unions with management and with the state (e.g., Poland). National trade unions in Europe seek to influence EEC law requiring companies to share plans with unions twice a year. The Council of the Americas tries to modify provisions of the investment code of the Andean Common Market. The United Nations attempts to draw up a code of conduct regulating activities of multinational corporations. Belgium attempts to change EEC ruling on the inappropriateness of its investment incentives. The EEC seeks to legitimize and also limit the emergency measures of Italy to overcome balance-of-payment problems in 1974. The International Metalworkers' Federation works against the antitrade union policies of the Chilean government. South Korea pursues policies designed to attract multinational corporations. Unions from Germany and the Netherlands apply pressure to a European multinational chemical firm. Henry Ford visits the United Kingdom and urges the British people to adopt measures to improve the chaotic labor relations climate in the United Kingdom. The UAW pressures the U.S. government to restrict the inflow

of Japanese automobiles. The French government assures its farmers that, in return for their support of the EEC, policies will be adopted to inhibit competition from American agricultural imports. (p. 236)

The complexity of interdependence violates many of the assumptions of the realist vision of world politics. Realism has regarded states as coherent units whose primary instrument is force and whose relations are regulated by a balance of power that places the "high politics" of military security above the "low politics" of social and economic affairs. But, as Robert Keohane and Joseph Nye, Jr., have pointed out in their seminal work, *Power and Interdependence,* actors other than states participate directly in world politics today, no clear hierarchy of issues exists, and force is often ineffective as an instrument of policy.

They speak of *multiple channels* connecting modern societies: informal ties between governmental elites to complement official diplomatic relations; face-to-face interactions and extensive personal communications among nongovernmental elites; and transnational exchanges among such organizations as multinational banks and corporations. International organizations have also become more prominent in facilitating the resolution of problems of interdependence. For instance, in the 1970s, the United Nations sponsored a series of international conferences on the environment, food, population, law of the sea, water resources, and technology transfer. The most remarkable thing about them was that traditional power-political divisions did not control the outcomes; in fact, the Soviet Union and the United States found themselves on the same side of the fence on many issues. Thus, with interdependence, North-South issues of economic development and social justice have come to rival East-West concerns about security and ideology.

Keohane and Nye perceive an *absence of hierarchy* among issues, such that military security no longer consistently dominates the agenda. General shifts in the distribution of capabilities do not automatically translate into a clear change in a single hierarchy of power. Nuclear powers can remain preeminent in the arms race while slowly losing their control of the international economy. Nonnuclear powers, such as the oil-rich states, can become powerful in certain areas without any significant augmentation of their military capability. Japan or one of the newly industrializing countries can make rapid economic gains that do not translate directly into military power.

Foreign policy now deals with the more complex and more diverse problems of energy, resources, environment, population, trade, and technology, and these problems compete with military security, ideology, and territorial rivalry for the attention of policy makers, who no longer occupy just the traditional offices of foreign affairs. For example, U.S. Treasury Secretary James Baker played a central role during the second Reagan administration in the making of America's foreign economic policy, launching a formal plan for coordinating the economies of the OECD countries. Likewise, the U.S. Departments of Agriculture, Labor, and Commerce and many other agencies have extensive international commitments. Also, different issues generate different coalitions, within governments and across them; certain agenda items can threaten the interests of powerful domestic groups without threatening those of the nation as a whole, leaving many voices to compete for the privilege of defending the "national interest" and adding to the difficulty of arriving at a clear and consistent national policy.

A third characteristic of complex interdependence, according to Keohane and Nye, is the *minor role of military force.* The resolution of economic differences among members of the major alliances does not typically reflect their military capabilities. Japan has gained significant economic concessions from the United States and has maintained economic dominance despite its military dependence on U.S. forces. The Soviet Union could use its military dominance to enforce economic control on Hungary and Czechoslovakia in 1956 and 1968, but that policy has failed with Poland and other East European states since 1979. Likewise, states that are dominant militarily may be vulnerable on a variety of economic issues. Where popular opposition to prolonged military conflict is high, where conventional forces are of limited use in controlling socially mobilized populations, where force is disruptive, costly, and uncertain, military power becomes much less attractive and effective as an instrument of diplomacy.

It is the combination of multiple channels of interaction and the depreciation of power politics that makes the idealist hopeful about the peaceful, integrative impact of increasing interdependence. When the nation-state was an enclosed, self-sufficient military and economic unit, self-interest dictated a purely nationalist policy. Now that the state has become permeable and disaggregated, with global economic and security ties, protection of the national interest requires a more complex balancing act that takes into account the economic vitality and security of allied states and the interests of many nongovernmental entities, both subnational and transnational. Where a militarily dominant state could once dictate to its coalition partners, it must now negotiate and cajole. Even a weak state can often use its control of a vital resource or its voice in an intergovernmental forum to protect or impose its interests in a limited issue area. Where national policy makers once dictated to domestic interests and international organizations, they must now adapt to multinational organizations, both private and public. Where a state used to speak with one voice in foreign policy, it now must listen to a thousand organizations pursuing their own interests. Balance-of-power politics encouraged an essentially reactive foreign policy, or at best a policy that anticipated only those problems that could be met by the single-minded pursuit of maximum military power. The politics of interdependence requires a state to look to the future, to expend effort in building multi-issue coalitions and controlling the formation of the international agenda. The new ecological issues, in particular, call for investment and planning, not just crisis management; they require strategies for collective action and the management of complex alliances, not just national self-assertion.

It is conceivable that interdependence may eventually be expressed in norms and institutions shared by an international system that is bound together by common cultural forces and intertwined economic interests. Between the realist conception of warring states and the cosmopolitan universalism of the idealist, there is the third possibility of a society of states held together by common rules and institutions. Such a society would neither abolish the state altogether nor surrender to purely competitive, amoral relations among states, but would recognize that interdependence has made international politics partly conflictual, partly cooperative. Today's international society already encourages states to coexist through a mix of military prudence, economic cooperation, and moral imperatives. The state is not about to destroy itself or become obsolete, but it may be able to thrive only by adopting international norms of behavior that will facilitate free and peaceful social and economic interchanges between all countries.

Hedley Bull, in *The Anarchical Society,* points out that this idea of international society has its intellectual roots in the natural law tradition of the early modern period, when such thinkers as Francisco de Vitoria, Francisco Suárez, Alberico Gentili, Hugo Grotius, and Samuel von Pufendorf envisioned a Christian society based on self-evident rules of conduct that bound all civilized states. In the eighteenth and nineteenth centuries, European secular theorists substituted the law of nations for divinely ordained natural law. Any moral consensus that exists today for an international society rests on the common values of "modernity" propagated worldwide by the dominant Western powers; on the universal principles embodied in such institutions as the United Nations and the International Court of Justice; and on the spirit of cooperation that impels adherence to the rules of international regimes in a variety of issue areas. Although these values and institutions do not have the degree of universality and legitimacy that lend authority to the agencies of a nation-state, they do provide a constraining matrix for the conduct of international relations. Because states are not recognized as sovereign unless they are members of international organizations, they tend to adhere at least formally to such international norms as the United Nations Declaration on Human Rights. If often violated, these declarations are nonetheless a useful device in persuading recalcitrant states to conform. Membership in a variety of functional international organs also serves the pragmatic purpose of facilitating international commerce.

Urbanization and growing literacy have contributed toward an international culture and a common life-style marked by a high degree of Westernization and a more homogeneous elite culture — at least among the 40 percent of the world's population that is urban and the 66 percent that is literate. While presently lacking any binding moral authority or extensive value consensus, international society does display some common intellectual elements — a shared tradition of science, English as a lingua franca, egalitarian and democratic norms (though variously defined), merit-based bureaucratic procedures, and common aspirations for economic and technological development. Harold Jacobson, in *Networks of Interdependence,* argues that the ideas spread by the network of international organizations have resulted in a limited consensus on certain issues: the need to prevent nuclear holocaust, the illegitimacy of using military force to resolve disputes or alter established territorial boundaries, the need to eliminate colonialism and racial discrimination, and the common interest of all states in the continued smooth functioning of the global economy.

These areas of consensus are reinforced at the practical level by the thousands of international organizations, both governmental and nongovernmental, that have sprung up over the last century. According to Jacobson, by 1972 there were 289 international governmental organizations, more than the total number of states. Every sovereign state was a member of at least a few of these organizations, and their concerns ran the gamut from social security for Rhine boatmen and the production of various commodities (with separate organizations for peanuts, tea, tin, lead, zinc, coal, steel, coffee, wine, tuna, copper, rice, olive oil, furs, cotton, wheat, sugar, rubber, and wool) to nutrition, navigation, telecommunications, fisheries, health, criminal justice, and civil aviation. International nongovernmental organizations numbered 2,470 by 1972, including, for example, professional societies, advocates of human rights, famine relief and welfare organizations. And more than 7,000 corporations were conducting transnational operations through more than 27,000 subsidiaries. Between 1939 and 1967, subsidiaries of the leading U.S. manufacturers grew from 715 to 3,646. By 1974, the world's 50 largest multinationals (half of them U.S.-owned) had sales amounting to more than 8 percent of the gross world product, and they employed about 2 percent of the world's population.

As this explosive growth of multinational organizations shows, the modern economy requires international trade to achieve the most efficient economies of scale. Perhaps only the United States, the Soviet Union, China, and India are large enough to be at once specialized and self-sufficient national markets. In 1976, only these 4 out of roughly 160 sovereign states had populations of more than 200 million, and only 32 had populations of more than 20 million. It is no accident that the most successful modernizers, early or late, have been export oriented. Even the socialist bloc states have discerned the necessity of participating in the global economy if they are to gain from economies of scale, technical specialization, and comparative trade advantages. The management of the negative side of industrial technology — acid rain, radioactive wastes, water pollution, toxic chemicals, deforestation, and the depletion of nonrenewable mineral resources — also requires an increasing degree of international cooperation.

Although sovereign states have not been superseded as the principal actors in world politics by the various transnational ties we have been discussing, their monopoly on value formation and decision making has been rapidly eroding. For reasons of prudence rather than principle, states are less free to make unilateral decisions. But the declining monopoly and authority of the state have not been vested in a new center of global decision making. Instead, they have passed to the decentralized mechanisms of the global market and to the informal coordination of public and private international organizations, with their sophisticated devices of global communication. Ernst Haas, in "International Integration: The European and the Universal Process," has described the creation of "infinitely tiered multiple loyalties" in which overlapping jurisdictions erode the central authority of the state without replacing it by some more highly integrated structure of world government. It may be that the global political system is approaching the problem of international decision making and coordination through the back door of the common values and shared institutions of socioeconomic interdependence. (Whether interdependence may lead to more complete political integration is addressed in a subsequent section of this chapter entitled "Interdependence and Integration.")

CRITICISMS OF INTERDEPENDENCE

One criticism of the interdependence model is that it has been inconsistently applied to several different patterns of interaction. The nuclear superpowers may be mutually dependent on each other to show restraint, and such interdependence may become global, through nuclear proliferation and the dread of planetary contamination. But this is very different from the economic interdependence that has resulted from expanding world trade. The nuclear powers' common interest in controlling arms has been imposed on them because their survival is at stake; their interdependence is symmetrical and absolute, but it remains secondary to the intense rivalry that led to the arms dilemma in the first place. Economic interdependence, on the other hand, is voluntary and asymmetrical; some states benefit substantially more than others, yet most have great freedom of choice in the degree of dependence to which they are subject. Economic relations can be readily adjusted to suit national preferences: states need accept trade restraints only so long as they seem beneficial overall. In sum, there is nothing inherently cooperative in the desire of two competing nuclear superpowers to stay alive, nor anything inevitable or irreversible about world economic integration.

Second, some critics argue that true interdependence exists only among the advanced industrial states, and perhaps among the countries of the Soviet bloc, but not in the global system as a whole. In fact, they point out, the international economy is sharply divided into three main groups, the OECD states, the Comecon states, and the less-developed countries, each with its separate concerns and each gaining quite different benefits from its participation in the global economy. (Figure 4-4 is a map of the world's three most important economic blocs.) The socialist countries have never been interdependent with the West, and their relationship with the USSR has been more a dependent than an interdependent one. The advanced capitalist states, the only countries that even approximate a relationship of mutual economic dependency, are tied together as much by security and ideology as for purely economic gain. As for the less-developed countries, they trade little with one another and are at a huge disadvantage in their economic exchanges with more advanced states. Except for a few dramatic instances of rich states almost totally dependent on a strategic resource from the Third World, the North-South relationship is still one of dependency rather than interdependence. (An extended discussion of the

FIGURE 4-4
THE WORLD'S THREE MAJOR ECONOMIC BLOCS

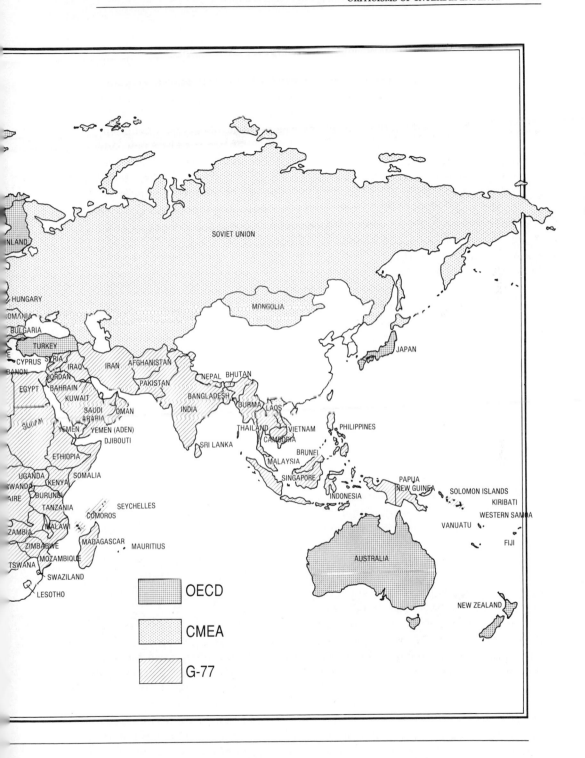

Marxist argument against interdependence appears in the final section of this chapter, "Imperialism and Dependency.")

Robert Gilpin has argued that the efficiencies of a world market economy and an international division of labor have brought sustained economic growth and moderated international conflict, at least among the industrial democracies. But he also points out that the old imperial patterns of exclusive economic spheres carved out by military power have simply been replaced by a new kind of competition for economic control. The strong protectionist reaction of recent years gives evidence that interdependence has indeed begun to erode national sovereignty. But the fundamental division between rich states and poor remains, and economic interdependence is less widespread geographically than it was in the late nineteenth century. Governments are more concerned today about the economic welfare of their citizens, and thus more sensitive to any costs they may incur from the economic policies of their neighbors. Expectations have risen, and with them the potential for violent response to negative linkages or to the limits imposed by interdependence. Also, rapid growth has created powerful vested interests that resist redistributive change. In this sense, there may be a threshold beyond which interdependence cannot pass without engendering contradictory nationalist tendencies. The search for economic efficiency may have replaced the struggle for territorial aggrandizement, but it has not ended national competition for a larger share of the growing world product.

K. J. Holsti maintains that a trend toward separatism, international fragmentation, and renewed nationalism has been more powerful in the late twentieth century than the growth of global interconnectedness and transnationalism. In fact, these disintegrative tendencies may well be a direct product of the economic forces that have brought the nations of the world into closer proximity. Far from building mutual understanding and tolerance, the growth of international communications may have reinforced cultural differences and sparked a more vigorous national self-assertion. The experience of nation-states (less than 10 percent of which can be described as ethnically homogeneous) shows that communication does not always reinforce intergroup solidarity; in many ethnically mixed countries, increased contacts between minority groups have led instead to intense conflict and secessionist movements. Even the transnational spread of democracy has reinforced the principle of national self-determination, not global solidarity.

Governments often seek to counter global homogenizing forces through policies designed to control, reduce, or eliminate a wide range of foreign influences and transnational processes. The assumption that international transactions will automatically cause states to adapt cooperatively rather than resist is unwarranted. Many states perceive interdependence as a threat to their national values and will take steps, at considerable economic cost, to reduce external penetration and preserve their autonomy. The fact of increasing interconnectedness is not in dispute, but its consequences are open to question. In many cases, it has simply led to greater conflict, exploitation, and dependency. Surprisingly few international connections are genuinely mutual or supply any basis for an authentic global community. More often, interdependence is a euphemism for a structure of domination or penetration through which a few nations expand their global influence and control. Interdependence is not an inevitable process leading to uniquely desirable outcomes shared by all. (For a fuller discussion of the nationalist argument against interdependence, see "Economic Nationalism and Neomercantilism" later in this chapter.)

The growth of scientific knowledge will not necessarily generate cooperative efforts to see that it is commonly shared; nations frequently compete fiercely for control of new technologies. Ecological problems may heighten our consciousness of "spaceship earth" and the planetary limits to growth, but a burgeoning population and dwindling resources could breed a neo-Malthusian struggle for survival of the fittest rather than collective schemes for managing the global "commons."

In a similar vein, European imperialism spread common values of modernity, but the anticolonial struggle has stirred up Third World nationalism and made us aware that the physical unity of the globe is not matched by a moral or political unity. The revival of Islamic fundamentalism, terrorism's rejection of the Western diplomatic code, and the proliferation of regional conflicts (Libya-Chad, India-Pakistan, Turkey-Greece, Vietnam-Cambodia, Ethiopia-Somalia, Tanzania-Uganda, Angola-South Africa, Syria-Israel, Iraq-Iran, China-Vietnam, Nicaragua-Honduras) make it clear that the present limited degree of global interdependence has not papered over deep divisions of race, religion, wealth, and ideology.

Economic integration without the benefits and controls of political integration may in fact be the worst of worlds, by making states vulnerable and less autonomous without giving them decision-making structures to mitigate the intrusive or exploitative impact of global economic change. Governments that once had only to defend territory now must regulate an immense range of economic forces or risk losing their political legitimacy. If interdependence is to become the foundation for a global community, it must go beyond converging economic interests and attack basic national identity itself. Clearly the global system has both integrative and disintegrative tendencies, and perceptions of which tendency is likely to prevail in the long run may reflect the "half-empty/half-full" phenomenon.

Kenneth Waltz, in his *Theory of International Politics,* offers one of the strongest criticisms of the idea that the contemporary global system is highly interdependent. The great powers were much more interdependent in the late nineteenth and early twentieth century, Waltz says. Capital and labor moved freely within a single Atlantic community of nations, whose volume of trade and immigration was much higher than today, in proportion to domestic population and production. In the period from 1909 to 1913, foreign trade took between 33 percent and 52 percent of the gross national product (GNP) of Britain, France, Germany, and Italy. In 1975, the Soviet Union and the United States traded only 8 percent and 14 percent, respectively, of their GNP. In 1910, the total value of British investment abroad was one and a half times larger than national income. In 1973, the total value of American investment abroad was only one-fifth of national income. In 1910, Britain's return on investment abroad amounted to 8 percent of national income; in 1973, American overseas investment earned only 1.6 percent of national income. Before 1914, Germany was highly interdependent with its European neighbors — the best customer of six European states and the largest source of supply for ten. Britain, France, Russia, Italy, and Germany had the highest degree of economic interdependence that any great powers have ever known, yet it did not prevent them from going to war or stave off the subsequent disintegration into relatively insulated, self-sufficient national economies.

Waltz argues that the global economy, like national economies, works within a structure that is politically maintained and thus must be measured not solely in the volume of economic interactions but in the capacity of states to use their power resources for protecting their economic position. The United States provides an instructive example. It has huge investments abroad (over $300 billion dollars), but they are highly diversified by country and are primarily in stable manufacturing industries in the advanced states, making them relatively safe and little affected by expropriation or instability. Weaker nations are unlikely to agree to economic sanctions against the most powerful nation on earth, and this makes American overseas investments secure, even if particular American firms are not. In addition, though American exports and imports account for a large proportion of world trade, they make up only a small percentage of the U.S. national product. For example, the Middle East oil boycott of 1973 threatened between 40 percent and 60 percent of the energy supply of Japan and Western Europe, but only 2 percent of America's; the United States consequently did not have to appease the Arab states but could maintain its freedom of action. Another factor is multinational firms, whose decentralized operations camouflage the underlying reality of centralized control: most of these economic giants are based in the United States, employ American technology, and have Americans as their top managers. It is obvious from all this that the United States' very size and power protect its trade. It can absorb great losses and still remain independent; it can force access to important resources, use its leverage to obtain alternative supplies, or simply get along without. In short, the interdependence of nations varies with their power capabilities, and in today's international system these are less equally distributed than ever before.

Waltz argues further that interdependence cannot be an element of an international system if it does not include the great powers. But the United States and the Soviet Union both act with an independence unknown to an earlier era. They are economically self-sufficient, dependent neither on one another nor on their principal allies. The total volume of Soviet imports from the capitalist countries amounted to less than 1.5 percent of its gross social product in 1976. A global economy does exist, but only the two superpowers are in a position to bear the costs of nonparticipation. Many states are dependent on trade with their bloc leader, but this is largely a one-way street. A narrow concentration of power gives the few states at the top of the power hierarchy both a larger interest in exercising control and a greater ability to do so. Even when joint solutions to global problems are necessary, their costs will be borne disproportionately by the leading economic powers, and those who pay the bills will naturally insist on a larger voice in the so-called collective management. This has been true at the United Nations, where the United States for years funded over 25 percent of the total operating budget. It explains why the UN has become progressively less powerful as its dominance by the United States has declined, and why America withdrew from the United Nations Educational, Scientific, and Cultural Organization (UNESCO) in 1985, when it could no longer control the agenda. If Third World states are beginning to act on such environmental concerns as deforestation, it is only because the United States has made this a condition of its approval of IMF loans. As Waltz says: "All nations may be in the same leaky world boat, but one of them wields the biggest dipper. In economic and social affairs, as in military matters, other countries are inclined to leave much of the bailing to us" (p. 210). Increased interconnectedness may have led to an increased need for collective management, but this has only tended to reinforce the role of the superpowers as global police and regulators of the system's stability. It has not produced genuine interdependence, which presumes relationships of equality.

INTERDEPENDENCE AND INTEGRATION

Despite the debate over the meaning and extent of interdependence, liberals insist that it is the single most useful model for describing contemporary international affairs. The transition from a subsistence economy to the modern industrial economy has by definition created more complex networks of exchange. No one can wish away the steady growth in international trade, investment, monetary relations, and technology exchange. For example, U.S. receipts from the sale of technology abroad rose from $362 million in 1956 to more than $3 billion in 1987. On the other hand, U.S. dependence on imported minerals rose dramatically in the same period, with nearly 100 percent of its aluminum, chromium, manganese, columbium, arsenic, strontium, industrial diamonds, and metals in the platinum group coming from foreign sources. America is heavily dependent (between 50 percent and 80 percent) on imports of such basic industrial commodities as cobalt, asbestos, tungsten, chromium, nickel, tin, zinc, antimony, and cadmium. The transnational flow of resources has placed Third World producers at the mercy of growth rates and recessions in the industrialized world and has made First World consumers vulnerable to interruptions caused by political conflict and instability among their raw-material suppliers. All parties thus have a common interest in supporting international institutions that can ensure peace, a system of managed growth, and orderly trade relations.

It is also clear that the efficient utilization of many modern technologies requires vast markets and the economies of scale that go with internationalized production. Lester Brown's *World Without Borders* offers these examples:

Production costs for nitrogen fertilizer are about a third less for plants that use a technology requiring the production of at least 200,000 tons annually, but only an immense export market can justify the construction of such plants (outside of the very few countries with large domestic markets). Electric power grids tying the countries of Western Europe together have reduced the total generating capacity below what was formerly needed to supply the countries individually. Likewise, Paraguay and Brazil have constructed huge hydroelectric generating facilities that make economic sense only if energy can be exported to neighboring states, like Argentina. New discoveries in superconducting materials are likely to increase still more the appeal of long-distance, interdependent power grids that can distribute peak loads over widely separated time zones. Capital outlays and research and development costs in automobiles, aviation, computers, rocketry, and satellite communications, among many other products, are so high that they can be justified only for industries with access to international markets.

The value assumptions of liberals come into play when they argue that these trends *necessarily* erode national control of economic affairs and transfer sovereign powers to transnational institutions like multinational corporations and international agencies. The liberals assume that when national sovereignty interferes with economic efficiency, the global dissemination of technology, or the attainment of a higher standard of living, political leaders will choose a higher degree of integration over a decline in prosperity. In the liberal view, reason and self-interest come together to place sovereignty at bay. Driving integration forward is a socioeconomic revolution that has raised material expectations and made domestic economic goals predominant in the hierarchy of national goals. To maintain its global market ties, a government may even be willing to relinquish its traditional military prerogatives. Saburo Okita of the Japan Economic Research Center is one who believes that the pursuit of global military power is not cost effective. If Japanese assets should be expropriated, he argues, the government would be better off to compensate the investors directly, rather than spending immense sums on a military force whose ability to protect international economic assets is doubtful.

The liberal argues further that the perennial antagonisms of rich and poor states are being steadily eroded by international forces that favor the Third World. As the economies of developed countries have become more service oriented, as their trade balances and access to raw materials have worsened, and as their labor costs have risen, manufacturing has migrated to the less-developed countries. This process is transferring capital, technology, and managerial know-how from rich to poor in a pattern of international specialization that favors all parties. Although benefits will continue to be distributed unequally, the principle of comparative advantage, operating in a global market, will maximize the efficient allocation of resources. As long as the tide of economic growth is rising, it will lift all boats.

At the heart of liberal thought is the notion that peace and political integration will be by-products of expanding socioeconomic ties. The most optimistic expression of this idea is *world federalism,* which envisions authoritative international institutions with jurisdiction over well-defined areas or issues. Sovereignty would be divisible; nation-states would coexist with international authorities whose powers were derivative and limited, though binding. This closer worldwide political cooperation might arise for reasons of economy and security, as it did among the infant American states. The theory is not so naive as to assume a transfer of all authority to a world government, given the immense diversity of constituent cultures. Rather, it sees a progressive global federalism whose member states would find it increasingly advantageous to surrender elements of their sovereignty to intergovernmental organizations better able to protect the environment, allocate scarce resources, and monitor the global economy. The integration of states around the regional security regimes of NATO and the Warsaw Pact has shown that states can cooperate even in military affairs. Given recent changes in Eastern Europe and the prospect of German reunification, it is not impossible to imagine that the agreement to remove nuclear missiles from Europe might grow into an international inspection entity to which all states would surrender some measure of sovereignty in the interests of mutual security.

The greatest weakness of federalist theory is its inability to explain exactly how loyalty, legitimacy, and effective enforcement powers would be transferred to the various international entities in the absence of territorial consolidation or a formally ratified division of jurisdictions. World federalists assume that the reasons for cooperation will be self-evident. But realists say that political integration cannot happen without a political authority to exercise effective control over the use of violent means. Historically, they add, political consolidations of separate cultural entities have most frequently come about through the use or threat of force. For the realist, the only model of global integration is empire.

The liberals counter by pointing to the long-standing peaceful relations among the world's liberal democracies, which, they say, prove that integrated security communities are possible without the cumbersome apparatus of an international bureaucracy or a global police. Integration may arise out of utilitarian motives — the prospect of common economic gain — or it may be the result of an increasing similarity in the political and economic structures of interacting states. To the liberal, global interdependence will enhance both the sense of shared values and the expectation of joint rewards or penalties. At first there may be only a small elite that perceives these gains. But as the national actors become more tightly linked, large numbers of ordinary citizens will shift their expectations and eventually their loyalties to the new centers of political and economic decision.

Integration theorists trying to define the circumstances under which this process of integration and consolidation of political loyalties might take place fall into two bodies of thought, *communications theory* and *functionalism*. The communications, or *transactional*, model was pioneered by Karl Deutsch in his studies of nationalism in North Atlantic communities. Taking countries as clusters of population united by grids of communications and transport, he analyzed how such transactions as trade, migration, mail, telephone, and radio gave rise to complementary habits, shared experiences, and common symbols. Economic ties, he found, intensified the communication flows and resulted in joint policy making and the growth of shared political and administrative capacities. Under conditions of high volume, expanding substance, and continuing reward, these interactions led over time to social-psychological processes that assimilated the peoples into a more highly integrated community. Thus, a shared pattern of communication seems to be an important prerequisite to integration: the creation of community must precede the organization of state.

Deutsch stresses that an amalgamated security community like the modern nation-state emerges only under these conditions: (1) mutual compatibility of major values; (2) a distinctive cultural identity; (3) expectations of joint rewards that exceed the burdens of amalgamation; (4) a marked increase in the political and administrative capabilities of at least some of the participating units; (5) superior economic growth for some participating units, which then become core areas around which the weaker units coalesce; (6) unbroken links of social communication, both between geographical regions and between different social strata; (7) a broadening of the political elite; (8) personal mobility, particularly among the politically relevant groups; and (9) a multiplicity of communications and other transactions. Although such conditions are rare on an international scale, some of them are present in the pluralistic security communities that the modern industrial democracies have created, such as those between the United States and Canada, the United Kingdom and Ireland, France and Germany. Here the conditions for integration are in effect reduced to three: compatibility of values among the decision-making elites, mutual responsiveness, and predictability of behavior, including the central expectation that disputes will be settled peaceably. Such integration, while not involving the same level of shared institutions or the formal sacrifice of political sovereignty that the liberal idealists envision, is nonetheless viewed as a significant step toward global community.

The *functional* model is based on the proposition that states can cooperate in limited technical spheres and that these functional ties will spill over into a higher degree of political integration. David Mitrany, an early exponent of functional theory, argued that the growth of modern technology and the intensification of mass demands for a higher standard of material welfare worked together to pressure governments into a higher degree of technical and economic cooperation. The dramatic twentieth-century increase in the number of international governmental organizations with specific purposes was taken as evidence that governments could segregate technical problems from political ones. The assumption was that these functionally specific organizations, staffed by specialists rather than diplomats, would breed a politically detached class of international civil servants with a shared professional ethic and technocratic criteria for assessing performance. They would gradually enmesh states in a functional cooperation that would erode the incentives to war. In Mitrany's words, "Every activity organized in that way would be a layer of peaceful life, and a sufficient addition of them would create increasingly wide strata of peace — not the forbidding peace of an alliance, but one that would suffuse the world with a fertile mingling of common endeavor and achievement."

Early functionalist theory has been called unrealistic in its expectation that technical and political issues could be successfully separated. Decisions that were once viewed as narrowly technical have come to have a large impact on security matters. Scientists, who had been expected to adhere to universal intellectual standards and international values, instead became prime movers in the military-industrial complexes of both superpowers. Debates about trade and monetary policies have been just as acrimonious as those over security policy. Ernst Haas and other neofunctionalists have tried to bypass these objections by arguing for a linkage strategy that takes explicit account of the political dimension. In fact, neofunctionalists believe that cooperation on economic projects of great national significance will generate pragmatic incentives among key economic elites toward further political integration. According to Haas, solutions at a lower level generate an "expansive logic of sector integration" that impels national actors to "upgrade their common interests." Integrative lessons learned in one functional context or sector will spill over into others, with technical problems becoming gradually more politicized. In this vein, Jean Monnet, when he was president of the newly formed European Coal and Steel Community, insisted that distortions in coal and steel prices could be eliminated if the member countries would integrate their social security and transport policies. Since the economic gains stood to be considerable, the deed was done, and the European elites went on to tackle effectively a whole range of other problems whose resolution was similarly facilitated by a greater degree of integration.

Haas argues that power stakes and political loyalties are not so much ends in themselves as indexes of satisfaction with the performance of governments in generating and allocating material benefits. It was widely perceived in Europe that political integration would further social welfare aims, and thus there were no inherent obstacles to the spillover effect of economic cooperation. Spillover is possible because states are not single units but collections of competing elites and autonomous groups with particular interests that can be enlisted on behalf of supranational goals. In other words, putting together attractive "package deals" of economic benefits that can be gained only by sacrifices of sovereignty may lead to transnational coalitions supporting international integration.

ECONOMIC NATIONALISM AND NEOMERCANTILISM

The concepts of interdependence, integration, and economic development by which liberals describe the processes of international change are assumed to be linear, automatic, irreversible, and beneficial. Neomercantilist critics respond that the influence of economics on politics is not so simple and deterministic, is not a one-way street, and is not inevitably benign. Economic issues, they say, can divide states, and politicians can commit their nations to schemes of international integration or torpedo those schemes with equal ease.

For example, the great success of European economic integration has been interrupted by significant disintegrative episodes and recalcitrant nationalist sentiments; it was not the simple result of spillover from economic interdependence, as the neofunctionalists imagined. The European Economic Community, whose initial impetus came from the powerful leadership of such figures as Robert Schuman and Jean Monnet, was nearly derailed several times by the nay-saying nationalism of Charles de Gaulle and Margaret Thatcher. At the same time, external political factors such as the global balance of power and the politics of the Western alliance were important in encouraging its growth. The United States had a powerful role, at once enlightened and self-interested, in furthering European unity and economic recovery. West Germany saw European integration as a device both for regaining the respect of the Western nations and for furthering German economic leadership. And the Cold War certainly pressed all the Western Europeans into closer cooperation than might otherwise have occurred. In short, the functional spillover of incremental decision making in the economic and technical sectors was powerfully affected by the "high politics" of diplomacy, strategy, and national security. The findings of integration scholar Jacob Viner underline this point. His study entitled *The Customs Union Issue* concludes that most cases of economic unification are politically motivated. Thus, the functioning of the international economy and long-term prospects for integration cannot be understood without attention to the political forces of nationalism.

Curiously enough, both liberals and Marxists try to wish away the influence of the state in the conduct of international economic relations. Classical liberalism argues that the requirements of economic rationality ought to determine political relations, while Marxism holds that the mode of production determines the political superstructure. In both cases, economic factors are seen as contributing to the decline of nationalism and to a higher degree of political unification. Neomercantilists — conservatives and realists — believe that political and security considerations are still primary, even in the era of global technologies, and they challenge the basic liberal assumption that free trade benefits everyone and generates political commitment to a growing level of international cooperation. The neomercantilists are quick to point out that so-called "free" trade primarily benefits those states that hold a dominant market position and have well-developed technologies, transport, and trade relations. Liberal economics has always thrived during periods when a hegemonic power such as Britain or the United States championed a free-trade regime because it served their imperial designs or their narrow economic interests. When conditions changed, each of these powers was quick to abandon its commitment to liberal principles. In short, the neomercantilist sees economic nationalism not interdependence or integration, as the main motive force shaping international society. Robert Gilpin summarizes this school of thought in *The Political Economy of International Relations:*

> [T]ransnational [economic] actors and processes are dependent upon peculiar patterns of interstate relations. Whether one is talking about the merchant adventurers of the sixteenth century, nineteenth-century finance capitalists, or

twentieth-century multinational corporations, transnational actors have been able to play an important role in world affairs because it has been in the interest of the predominant power(s) for them to do so. As political circumstances have changed due to the rise and decline of nation-states, transnational processes have also been altered or ceased altogether. Thus, . . . the world economy did not develop as a result of competition between equal partners but through the emergence and influence of great national economics that successively became dominant.

Patterns of investment also reflect national priorities, according to the neomercantilist school of thought. Multinational corporations, far from being impartial agents of international exchange, are instruments of the nation-states in which they are headquartered. Any contributions they have made to interdependence have been as agents of their home governments, which thereby have gained greater power over international economic affairs. It was only during a transitional period, when local markets, regional spheres of influence, and exclusive imperial arrangements were breaking down, that internationalization of production appeared to be a counterforce to nationalism. Now that the market is truly a global one and new market shares must be carved out at someone's expense, an intense new national competition is arising over exports, investment outlets, and sources of raw materials. Migration of labor and industry has taken place, but it has engendered a fierce protectionist reaction that maintains national barriers to the free transfer of finished goods and factors of production.

The prevailing philosophy in international economics today is mercantilism, which may be defined as governmental manipulation of economic arrangements in order to maximize such national interests as security and autonomy, even at the expense of economic efficiency. With their similar goals of domestic stability, full employment, and national security, both socialist planning and Keynesian policies have tended to encourage a regional breakdown of the international economy and the reassertion of national controls over trade and capital flows. Socialist and capitalist states alike have sacrificed their internationalist pretensions to preserve domestic legitimacy.

The rapid growth and rising interdependence of the international economy after World War II rested on certain special conditions: (1) cheap energy and raw materials, which temporarily subsidized economic expansion; (2) American technological dominance, which forced other states to accommodate American trade policies if they wanted access to American goods and investments; and (3) the Third World's continuing quasi-imperial dependence on the economies of the former colonial powers. Poverty and political divisions robbed most Third World states of their ability to bargain effectively with multinational corporations; if they wanted any jobs for their people, or had any hope of immediate improvement in their standard of living, they had to accept foreign investment on the multinationals' terms. No wonder the multinationals appeared to be so powerful. But their ability to hold sovereignty at bay was strong only when they were dealing with new and weak states that desperately needed access to narrowly concentrated foreign capital. More recently, access to technology and investment capital has become more diversified, and the global balance of economic power has shifted from the owners of capital toward the owners of natural resources. This shift was symbolized by the OPEC oil cartel's ability to hold many of the advanced states hostage to its political aims, and it has been reinforced by a growing awareness that the pool of nonrenewable resources is finite and dwindling rapidly. Now that parts of the Third World are more independent economically and U.S. hegemony has been challenged by Japan and others, a new struggle for control of the international economy is in prospect. The struggle will likely issue in commercial and imperialist competition very similar to that among the major capitalist powers before World War I, which marked the end of the era of British dominance.

The renewed economic nationalism associated with the decline of American hegemony supports the neomercantilist perspective. Once the United States became vulnerable to the competition embodied in liberal economics, unrestricted flows of capital and goods did not look so attractive. America's loss of economic autonomy brought powerful changes in foreign policy, whose aim now was to use U.S. political-military clout to restructure the international economy along more favorable lines. Foreign aid declined dramatically, and the government began to take an active role in promoting foreign military sales and the export of nuclear power technologies, sometimes at the expense of nonproliferation agreements. The United States exercised its veto in the World Bank and the International Monetary Fund for political ends, seeking to force debtor nations to conform to U.S. foreign policy aims. These actions resulted in the destabilization of the Marxist government of Salvador Allende in Chile in the early 1970s and put significant pressure on the new democratic government of Alan García in Peru in the mid-1980s. President Ronald Reagan's invocation of the Carter Doctrine to defend America's special interests in the Persian Gulf demonstrated U.S. willingness to use its naval supremacy to protect the economic interests of the Western alliance. At the same time, NATO countries were being pressured politically to make larger financial contributions to the common defense. Disputes arose among the allies over trade and technology transfers with countries of the Eastern bloc. One development that testified perfectly to the primacy of national considerations over liberal principles was President Reagan's boycott of the French for selling natural-gas pipeline technology to the Soviets at the same moment as he was lifting President Jimmy Carter's embargo on the sale of American wheat to the USSR. Only politics and the primacy of national considerations could explain the inconsistency. To the mercantilist, these changes in America's postwar foreign economic policy are proof of their proposition that politics is in control, that the structure of the international economy is determined by competing national interests and the prevailing balance of power.

IMPERIALISM AND DEPENDENCY

Marxism, a third major model of the international political economy, emphasizes the role of imperialism and the relations of inequality that imperialism spawns. The Marxist, while granting that international society has systematic ties, says they are ties of dependency, not interdependence. The state is important, but only as an agent of the ruling and exploiting classes; as an economic force, nationalism is secondary to the profit motive and property interests. And behind the state are various nonstate actors that have represented the dominant economic modes of their times. The preeminent actor in the twentieth century is the multinational corporation, which expresses what Stephen Hymer has called the Law of Increasing Firm Size and the Law of Uneven Development. Since the beginning of the industrial revolution, the tendency has been for the typical firm to increase in size from the workshop to the factory to the national corporation to the multidivisional corporation to the multinational corporation. Geographical scope and monopoly power were matched by a qualitative increase in the firm's capacity to plan economic activity and vertically integrate all elements of production and exchange. Penetrating national boundaries and wresting control from local elites, the multinational corporation tore at the social and political fabric of the nation-state in order to fashion an international division of labor suited to the economic aims of its own corporate elite. In the process, a regime of multinationals

> would tend to produce a hierarchical division of labor between geographic regions corresponding to the vertical division of labor within the firm. It would tend to centralize high-level decision-making occupations in a few key cities in the advanced countries, surrounded by a number of regional sub-capitals, and confine the rest of the world to lower levels of activity and income, i.e., to the status of towns and villages in a new Imperial system. Income, status, authority, and consumption patterns would radiate out from these centers along a declining curve, and the existing pattern of inequality and dependency would be perpetuated. The pattern would be complex, just as the structure of the corporation is complex, but the basic relationship between different countries would be one of superior and subordinate, head office and branch plant. (Hymer, in Modelski, ed., *Transnational Corporations and World Order*, p. 387)

The main consequence of such a system is the simultaneous production of poverty and wealth. The capitalist elites of the center and the periphery conspire to subordinate the national productive capacity to their joint domination, creating in the process a variety of marginal and dependent classes. Development takes place, but it is very lopsided. Traditionally self-sufficient agriculture is destroyed in favor of capital-intensive technologies monopolized by elites in the urban financial and industrial cores of the dominant economies. Development and underdevelopment occur simultaneously — the two faces of the historical evolution of a global capitalist system. The advancement of the industrializing Northern states was and is contingent on their ability to impose an unequal pattern of exchange on the Southern states, as the producers of primary commodities or the consumers of the products of Northern subsidiaries.

It is a kind of dual society, at both the national and the international level, compartmentalized by race and wealth and linked by parasitic relations of economic dependence. (Figure 4-5 graphically depicts the North-South economic divide.) The human impact is captured by Frantz Fanon in his *The Wretched of the Earth:*

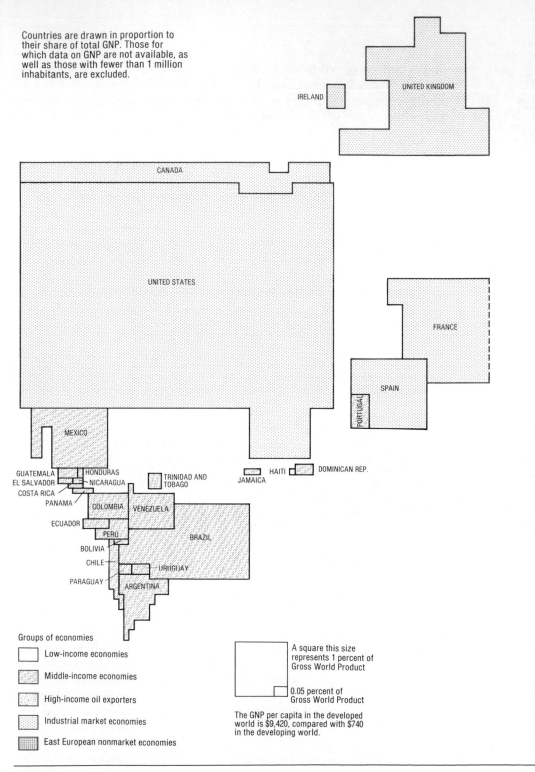

Countries are drawn in proportion to their share of total GNP. Those for which data on GNP are not available, as well as those with fewer than 1 million inhabitants, are excluded.

IRELAND

UNITED KINGDOM

CANADA

UNITED STATES

FRANCE

SPAIN

PORTUGAL

MEXICO

HAITI   DOMINICAN REP.

GUATEMALA   HONDURAS
EL SALVADOR   NICARAGUA
COSTA RICA
PANAMA

JAMAICA

TRINIDAD AND TOBAGO

COLOMBIA   VENEZUELA

ECUADOR

PERÚ

BRAZIL

BOLIVIA

CHILE

URUGUAY

PARAGUAY   ARGENTINA

Groups of economies

Low-income economies

Middle-income economies

High-income oil exporters

Industrial market economies

East European nonmarket economies

A square this size represents 1 percent of Gross World Product

0.05 percent of Gross World Product

The GNP per capita in the developed world is $9,420, compared with $740 in the developing world.

FIGURE 4-5
DISTRIBUTION OF PRODUCT AMONG SELECTED COUNTRIES, 1982

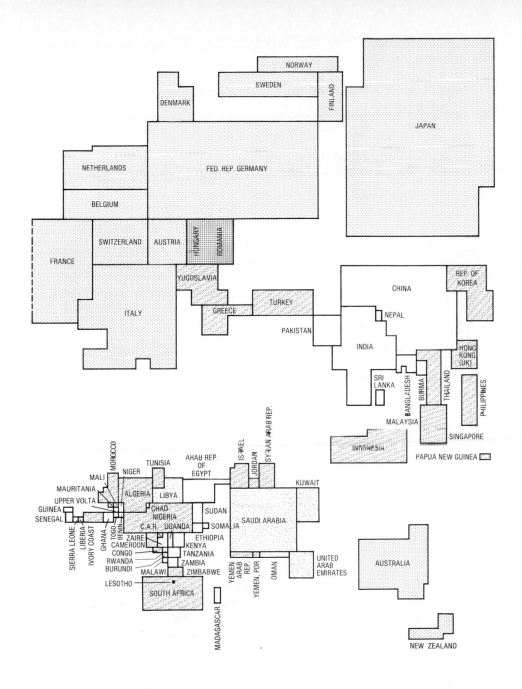

The settlers' town is a strongly built town, all made of stone and steel. It is a brightly lit town; the streets are covered with asphalt, and the garbage cans swallow all the leavings, unseen, unknown and hardly thought about. The settler's feet are never visible, except perhaps in the sea; but there you're never close enough to see them. His feet are protected by strong shoes although the streets of his town are clean and even, with no holes or stones. The settler's town is a well-fed town, an easygoing town; its belly is always full of good things. The settlers' town is a town of white people, of foreigners.

The town belonging to the colonized people, or at least the native town, the Negro village, the medina, the reservation, is a place of ill fame, peopled by men of evil repute. They are born there, it matters little where or how; they die there, it matters not where, nor how. It is a world without spaciousness; men live there on top of each other, and their huts are built one on top of the other. The native town is a hungry town, starved of bread, of meat, of shoes, of coal, of light. The native town is a crouching village, a town on its knees, a town wallowing in the mire. It is a town of niggers and dirty Arabs. The look that the native turns on the settler's town is a look of lust, a look of envy; it expresses his dreams of possession. (p. 39)

Where colonialism has been formally abolished, a native exploitative elite has taken the imperialist's or settler's place. Though the faces may be black or brown, the outlook and class interests are white and wealthy, for this new elite can maintain its neocolonial position only by serving the new imperialism. As Tony Smith points out, in "Requiem or New Agenda for Third World Studies?," the structures of international capitalism encourage, even dictate, this symbiotic relationship, in which the dominant Third World groups derive their power from serving as intermediaries between the imperialist managers and the local peoples. Although this collaborating class may have local concerns and display a variety of national and cultural differences, its participation in the world economic system ultimately establishes a common identity and a uniformity of conduct; it can survive as a ruling class only by remaining dependent on, and faithful to, the rhythms of the international economic order.

Often this client elite comes from a wealthy landowning class whose relationship to the poor majority is essentially feudal, though the landowners themselves may be tied to the international economy through exports of agricultural products and imports of Western consumer goods. As this traditional semifeudal elite comes to play a more modern entrepreneurial role, it transfers food-producing land into mining or plantation-grown crops, like bananas, coffee, cocoa, cotton, and other primary products, that are exported to the advanced countries. The Third World economies therefore are highly vulnerable to fluctuations in the market demand for their commodities, and many countries that were once self-sufficient must import food from the West. Often, the dependent Third World elite is militaristic or bureaucratic, playing no productive or entrepreneurial role, and thus is doubly parasitic on the indigenous society. Military regimes are, of course, powerfully tied to the more developed economies by their perceived need to import advanced military technology, and the external debts they incur to finance these imports only subordinate their economies still further. Where a national business class does exist, it is secondary to the foreign multinationals, which own the bulk of manufacturing and extractive industries, monopolize even local sources of credit and capital, and control key technologies.

This penetration by foreign firms often accelerates growth rates, but only for the benefit of the minority who participate in the cash economy. Capital-intensive activities expand, but so do unemployment and the disruption of the traditional labor-intensive sector. Consumption levels go up for the wealthy 5 percent to 20 percent, who ape the life-styles of the West, but for the bottom 60 percent life becomes increasingly marginal and often real income declines. Profits flow abroad in the form of remissions, royalties, debt service, patent or franchising fees, and other payments. Measured by net capital flows, the poor states actually subsidize the rich ones (see Figure 4-6). According to a World Bank report released in 1989, the seventeen most highly indebted countries of the Third World gave rich countries and multinational lending agencies $31.1 billion more than they received, triple the amount in 1983. For all of the Third World, net payments to industrial countries were estimated at $43 billion, up from $38.1 billion in 1987. By contrast, in 1982, when the global debt crisis first erupted, developing countries were taking in $18.2 billion more than they paid out. Total outstanding debt has doubled since 1982, reaching more than $1,035 billion (see Figure 4-7). Latin America, where Western capital invest-ment has been most heavily concentrated, has the heaviest debt burden — a per capita debt of $986, more than half the annual per capita GNP. Development in the poor countries, which need new capital most desperately, is significantly impeded by these large net transfers of funds to richer nations.

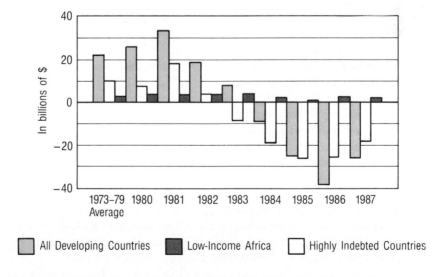

Note: Net resource transfers are defined as disbursements of medium- and long-term external loans minus interest and amortization payments on medium- and long-term external debt.

FIGURE 4-6

NET RESOURCE TRANSFERS TO DEVELOPING COUNTRIES, 1973–87

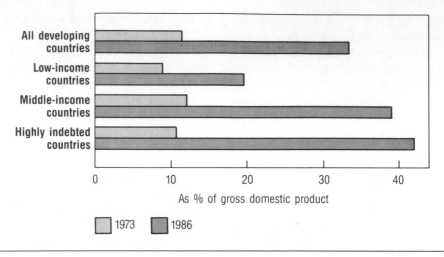

FIGURE 4-7
GROWTH OF PUBLIC DEBT

The governments of the advanced states, which have had to intervene in their own economies to stimulate business expansion, now do the same for the corporate interests they represent transnationally. It may look like old-fashioned mercantilism, but economic interests are in the driver's seat. The leading capitalist states support and subsidize their foreign investments in the Third World through security expenditures and interventions that protect property and access to resources. They also gain dominance indirectly, through tied loans, technical aid, tariffs, and a variety of bilateral preferential arrangements between "friendly" governments. And the bilateral ties and financial obligations are policed by the Western-dominated IMF, World Bank, and other international economic organizations.

Occasionally, a radical nationalist elite has come to power and overthrown foreign domination. No matter what its social class, political aims, or ideological orientation, it has been instantly branded as "Communist" or "Soviet-dominated," since the socialist bloc is the one economic force outside the control of international capitalism. A Cold War polarization and militarization immediately set to work to isolate the would-be independent state and force it to choose between dependency on East or West. In rare cases, a neutral power has been able to float temporarily in the backwaters of the global balance of power, but it cannot claim genuine independence until it has managed to restructure its economy to eliminate dependent state capitalism. Osvaldo Sunkel, in "Big Business and 'Dependencia,'" describes the task in these terms:

> Having taken over the control of the state, these [radical nationalist] groups face three essential tasks in correcting the main malformation inherited from the historical process of interaction with the international system: in the first place, this means transforming the agrarian structure, which is the fundamental root of inequality, marginalization and stagnation; second, using the primary export

sector, which represents an underdeveloped country's most important source of capital accumulation, to support the expansion of heavy and consumer industries; and, finally, the reorganization of the industrial sector, essentially in order to orient it away from satisfying the conspicuous consumption of the minority into satisfying the basic needs of the majority. (In Modelski, ed., *Transnational Corporations and World Order*, p. 224)

Obviously, this is a radical program, but dependency theorists see it as necessary to any authentic development process. The drives for self-sufficiency and equity reflect the radical's judgment that the existing capitalist order, even when it works through free markets and democratic systems, naturally favors the powerful and the rich. Poor states begin with so many disadvantages that they can never become equal partners. The elephant and the mouse may walk the same path in the economic jungle, but the small inevitably must accommodate to the big.

Immanuel Wallerstein's *The Modern World System,* which extends Lenin's theory of imperialism as the highest stage of capitalism, has contributed much to dependency theory. Wallerstein emphasizes the polarization between rich and poor states that accompanies capitalist expansionism. (Figure 4-8 shows the highly inequitable character of this international stratification.) He argues that states can escape some of the costs of the contraction phase of the capitalist economic cycle by raising their level of technological development, increasing their exploitation of labor, or expanding to incorporate new direct producers in wider zones of the world economy. To escape painful economic adjustments at home, the more powerful states ("the core") have naturally sought to exercise their power abroad (in "the periphery") — one of the simplest survival strategies available. However, there is a limit to the number of new states and households that can be subjected to exploitation and incorporation into market relations of imperialism and dependency. That is, the world capitalist system can go only so far toward attaining stability through expansion. Also, dependent elites, lacking authentic indigenous bases of political support, are notoriously weak at home, and this forever locks the rich states into a policy of intervention to shore up their client elites in the periphery. So dependent development suffers from the built-in self-contradiction of tending to elicit challenges from marginal groups led by radicals who place nationalism, socialism, autonomy, and equality above other political-economic goals. In short, the capitalist world system has spawned its own global antisystemic movement.

Although Marxist thinkers are the most prominent advocates of the dependency model, it is important to recognize that many non-Marxists also embrace this theory. They have, for example, used dependency theory to describe the inequalities between the USSR and its satellites in Eastern Europe and the Third World. Certainly Cuba has been tied to the Soviet economy so deeply as to become a kind of client state utterly dependent on its imperial patron. Johan Galtung, for one, has set out a general structural theory of imperialism that does not follow the Leninist definition of a strictly economic relationship motivated by private capitalism's need for expanding markets. Instead, Galtung gives the name of imperialism to any system of center-periphery relations in

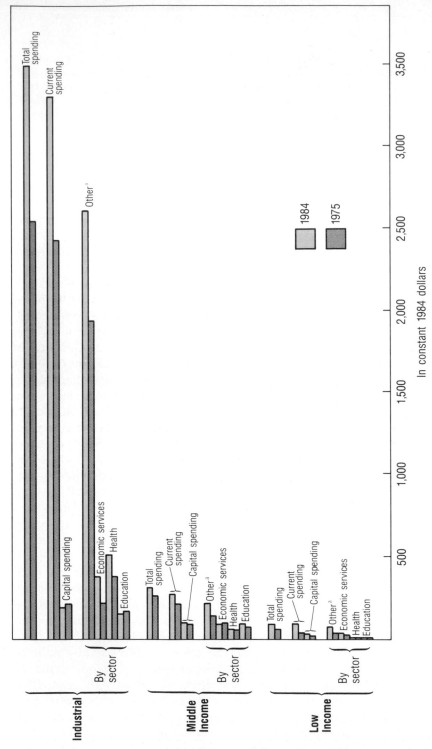

FIGURE 4-8
CENTRAL GOVERNMENT SPENDING PER CAPITA, 1975 AND 1984

which the states are unequal, some having a shared interest in reducing the autonomy and living conditions of the others.

A feature common to the theories of both Lenin and Galtung is the ability of imperial elites to coopt the political class in the Third World and to use imperialism's benefits to expand the state's economic powers. Within capitalist countries in particular, the dominant elite can satisfy its own people and reduce inequality at home by increasing inequality abroad. Thus, the class conflicts that might otherwise divide the rich countries are deflected onto poor states by widening the geographical scope of exploitation. The global system as a whole then breaks down into a conflict between rich and poor states — between the peasant masses of the South, or "countryside," and the urban elites of the North, or "city." Galtung sees such a center-periphery, city-country relationship in all forms of imperialism. The more perfect the imperial system, the less dependent it is on direct violence. Feudal-style relations in the poor countries accomplish the same ends, perpetuating unequal exchanges, political disorganization, and repressive regimes whose self-interests are tied to the maintenance of dependency between their own countries and their imperial patrons.

In dependency theory, a global international system centered on economic forces does exist, but these forces are not the mutually beneficial commercial relations of integration theory. Consequently, the liberal is mistaken in thinking that the nation-state has become subordinate to international markets or to cosmopolitan community norms. Both the Marxists and the mercantilists argue that the state has been increasingly assertive in determining the flow of benefits from international transactions, but the mercantilist errs in regarding the state as an autonomous agent unaffected by economic interests. At root, the Marxists say, the actions of national elites are controlled by domestic class interests that have been reshaped profoundly by the internationalization of production, which has expanded global interconnectedness but has also pushed states into an imperial role.

Whether a global system characterized by equality and integration of political values can evolve in the future is an open question. The economic nationalists remain skeptical. The more optimistic Marxists say yes, but only through global revolution and a transition from capitalist monopoly to socialist democracy. The liberals continue to insist that a global system will emerge, but by a more peaceful, evolutionary route such as that taken by the EEC.

QUESTION FOR DISCUSSION (PRO AND CON)

Is the international system evolving, both in the size of the political community and in the level of integration, toward world government? In particular, is the European Economic Community (EEC) a step in this direction?

☞ PRO

There can be no doubt that the political community has grown dramatically larger over time. Its horizons have widened from family or tribe to village to city to nation-state. If citizens can give their primary political allegiance to an impersonal bureaucratic entity whose scope goes far beyond their personal knowledge, then they can just as easily attach their loyalties to an entity of global scope. It is a matter of perception and problem solving. The nation-state is the current vehicle for common socialization and communication, and its control of taxing and decision powers is presently seen as essential to prosperity and security. But the nation-state has not always performed these important functions, and it need not in the future. As problems arise that the state cannot solve, and as communication patterns become more globally integrated, they are likely to bring new opportunities for decision-making institutions of world government.

One problem that can never be solved except on a global scale is environmental protection. Acid rain, deterioration of the ozone layer, water pollution, depletion of fossil fuels, and destruction of the world's forests and fisheries are but a few of the issues that have sparked cooperative efforts to regulate the international environment. To deal with these problems, we have such organizations as the International Council of Scientific Unions, the International Union for the Conservation of Nature and Natural Resources, the Worldwatch Institute, and several agencies of the United Nations, including the Food and Agricultural Organization and various scientific committees. To cite a specific example, the decline in ocean fish stocks has prompted agreement on a limitation act that will preserve adequate breeding stocks. Other fisheries problems are being resolved, with increasing success, by the International Whaling Commission and the newly codified International Law of the Sea. (The United States is one of the few states that have refused to ratify the Law of the Sea Treaty, because of temporary political pressures. But we took the lead in its negotiation and are likely to observe almost all the guidelines in any event.) The dangers of massive deforestation and ozone destruction may lead us still further toward enforceable international solutions, since these problems represent more than mere economic losses. They risk the destruction of the planetary matrix that sustains all life.

It is also clear that only large-scale economic entities can compete effectively in the global market economy. Their territorial size is what has given the United States and the USSR the capacity to be superpowers. Continental integration is what has given the European Economic Community a leading role in the international economy. Those multinational corporations that have become authentic transnational agents already embody an incipient form of world government, with decision-making powers that rival those of many states. If such multinationals are to be held politically accountable, we must have a countervailing power at a transnational level. The United Nations has attempted a modest kind of regulation in proposing an ethical code for multinational investors — a far cry from world government, but a great advance over the notion that national markets should be autonomous. Archaic nationalist forces are still battling to limit the effects of growing interdependence, but they are fighting a losing battle, since it is the most backward sectors of the economy that are seeking protection and the most advanced that are being forced to internationalize further in order to compete.

Since traditional military-political means are insufficient to protect complex modern economies, all the most advanced states, including the USSR, have a direct incentive for maintaining peaceful relations. Their populations will not consent to impoverishment as the price of national chauvinism. As security threats gradually diminish, the state will leave the cocoon of national security in favor of more open and efficient institutions of world government. What form these will take is unclear. But it is apparent that economic development has been carrying us toward more centralized (though less authoritarian) forms of political authority for several centuries. If the state has become more powerful as an economic actor and regulator of society today than in the past, why won't the same imperative work toward central global regulation?

The tendency toward global integration becomes clearer still when we examine the ideological dimension. Communities are cohering around ever more universal sets of values, in science, in economics, and in politics. Although they still maintain separate armies, the Western industrial democracies have become so integrated in their values that they constitute what Karl Deutsch calls a pluralistic security community. For them to fight a modern war with one another would mean their physical, moral, and economic suicide. Socialist systems, while less mature in their development and less united, are also integrated around ideological and economic values that transcend the nation-state. Moreover, socialism, still in an adolescent and authoritarian phase, is slowly being democratized, much as autocratic capitalist states were transformed in an earlier era. Already the requirements of the modern economy have carried Eastern Europe, China, and the USSR toward market socialism, political liberalization, and a progressive incorporation of their states into the international legal and economic order. The differences between communist and liberal-capitalist societies hide a more profound dissemination of common values—those of democracy, the modern scientific worldview, and secular-materialist culture. In short, we are witnessing the rise of a much more uniform world culture, whose main division is the cultural gap between modern and traditional ways of life. This North-South division may seem as deep and irresolvable as the East-West split once appeared to be, but it is testimony that modernization can progressively alleviate the value conflicts that are at the heart of global political divisions.

Skeptics will point to the newly rampant nationalism in the Third World as evidence that the nation-state has not yet outlived its appeal. But we must recognize that nationalism has been a modernizing and integrating force within the traditional framework of peasant or tribal society. It should be no surprise that the Third World, several hundred years behind Europe in economic development, is just entering the integrative phase that marked Europe's transition from feudalism to modern society and government. Attacks on the nation-state by subnational ethnic and linguistic groups, even in the advanced states, should not be taken as reasons for pessimism about global integration. The state is under attack from above *and* below, and allegiances must be withdrawn from it before they can be conferred on any transnational entity. It is a matter of our perspective on time: we see national power being exercised daily, but it has taken decades and centuries for the national community to evolve. Could the American colonist of 1700 have foreseen the creation of the United States of America a brief seventy-five years later, let alone the powerful and integrated transcontinental colossus of 200 million people some two centuries later?

The experience of the European Economic Community confirms all the arguments we have just been discussing. The Treaty of Rome, signed in 1958, put relations between the states of Europe on a new footing and established the indispensable preconditions for their modernization. Politically, the founders of a united Europe set out to abolish any possibility of another European civil war, like those between France and Germany in 1870, 1914, and 1939. Today, France and Germany regard each other as the most reliable of allies. German money has financed French technological developments, such as the Airbus and the Ariane rocket. Former German Chancellor Helmut Schmidt proposed that France's nuclear forces be enlarged to defend the Federal Republic of Germany and that a joint Franco-German army be formed, under a French supreme commander. In the most vital area of weapons procurement, the French have a panoply of world-class designs that they cannot afford to build and deploy except on a Europe-wide basis, and so they have launched coproduction ventures with the Germans. Economically, the Franco-German relationship is the backbone of the European Community. Together they make most EEC decisions and, with Britain, provide the lion's share of the funds to support agricultural subsidies and regional economic development in the other member states. As Eastern European states have departed the Communist camp, Germany and France have also provided massive resources to the new regimes in East Germany, Poland, and Romania. That the wealthier states are willing to sacrifice financially to create or maintain a political union is proof of their deep commitment to the concept of a united Europe.

Of course, all EEC members have benefitcd greatly from the second main purpose of the founders, the creation of a single market for all of Europe. A veritable explosion of trade occurred between 1958 and 1982; EEC exports and imports increased thirteen-fold, and trade within the Community grew at double that rate. Foreign trade has created cohesion within the EEC and has made it the world's leading trade bloc and a power no other country can ignore. In addition, the Rome Treaty created a commission that has taken over from the national governments the responsibility for commercial policy; it negotiates trade pacts and cooperative accords for all of Europe.

Another sign of the EEC's strength is the steady expansion of its membership, rising from six nations in 1958 to twelve in 1986. The European community is now united, from the Middle East to the Arctic Circle, in a Greater European Free Trade Zone that encompasses even the nonaligned states of Europe. Two rounds of negotiations at Yaoundé, in Cameroon, and two at

Lomé, in Togo, subsequently expanded EEC ties to more than sixty African, Caribbean, and Pacific countries. Several states on the borders of Europe — Turkey, Cyprus, and Morocco — are eager to join, showing that the union's attractions go beyond a European cultural context. The power of a united Europe has both symbolic and practical expressions. Many Europeans now choose to carry a European passport rather than a national one. Three universities, in England, France, and Germany, recently agreed on a common international curriculum that would confer the first European diploma. It is now possible for most European professionals (doctors, lawyers, architects, teachers) to practice in any EEC country. There is free movement of workers in all fields: Italian writers in London, British teachers in Spain, Portuguese domestic help in France, Greek mechanics in Germany, and young people in odd jobs in every neighboring state.

Integration is tightening as well. The European Parliament, the ultimate authority on the Community's budget, is now directly elected, and others of its powers have been strengthened. In 1986, it adopted the Single European Act, which committed the EEC to achieve by 1992 a single internal market without barriers of any kind. Some critics point to certain still-existing nontariff barriers as signs of the Community's failure to erase nationalist residues, but the clearing away of these hurdles has the emphatic support of government heads of state. Even the reluctant Margaret Thatcher, Britain's conservative prime minister, was persuaded in 1989 to accept a common European currency and to harmonize British economic policies with the planning procedures of the European Community. The EEC's ability to preserve its progress in free trade during one of the worst recessions in history is clear evidence that the European union has passed the point of no return. It has formulated policies on a range of subjects that boggles the mind: customs procedures, the harmonization of standards, taxation, capital movements, transport, research and development on new technologies, subsidies for small business, common agricultural practices, environmental protection, monetary regulation, public works contracts, free competition in public procurement, legal protection of patent rights, public health measures, and dozens more. The member states' confidence in the successful implementation of this ambitious agenda is demonstrated by the move from unanimous to majority decisions in the European Council.

The Europeans have patched over their differences and pressed forward in even the most contentious and sensitive areas. The Common Agricultural Policy (CAP), a point of strong friction from the beginning, provides for the free and unrestricted distribution of farm produce among member states, at uniform prices guarded from world market fluctuations by a commonly financed fund. As world food prices have plummeted, the subsidy for these agricultural preferences has come to more than two-thirds of the common EEC budget, the bulk of it paid out to just a few states. Timely adjustments in CAP policies have preserved the commitment to unity while meeting the original goals of increased agricultural productivity, a fair standard of living and a reasonable income for farmers, stability of produce markets, and the guaranteed availability of supplies. National differences have been successfully reconciled, too, in the formation of the European Monetary System, an institution not provided for in the Rome Treaty. This system has created a European Currency Unit (ECU), has established an intervention mechanism to harmonize exchange rates, and has set up extensive facilities for credit, monetary support, and financial assistance. The deep recession of the early 1980s pressed hard on this infant institution, but it made structural adjustments and went on. ECU bond issues have attracted so many private investors that the ECU now ranks as the third most important currency in world markets, after the dollar and the deutsche mark — another clear sign that a united Europe is here to stay.

☞ CON

Advocates of global integration see world politics and economics as tightly linked. But the EEC has made it possible for Europeans to enjoy the fruits of a large market and a customs union without giving up any of their cultural identity or political autonomy. Economic integration can coexist with national power, can sometimes even reinforce it, and thus should not be cited as a stepping stone to transnational government. Economic interdependence can as easily become a point of political friction; trade does not necessarily make friends, and common economic aims do not necessarily spill over into shared political values.

Global conditions do not supply either the required degree of consent or the required centralization of coercive capacity for effective world government. In fact, the last half century has seen such a multiplication of ideologies and governments that both the capitalist and the socialist blocs are fractionated into some 160 competing national entities. Decolonization marked not only the end of European control but the death knell of the arrogant Western assumption that its values were universally desirable. With the end of the European state system came what Hans Morgenthau has called the twilight of international morality. More than ever before, the globe is divided into conflicting political cultures. Until education and socialization can wean us from these national cultures, there can be no larger political community or transnational roles.

Existing international organizations, because they are *inter*governmental institutions whose authority and enforcement capacities flow from the member states, cannot be considered precursors to world government. The League of Nations and the United Nations have failed dismally when attempting to transcend the national powers from which they derive their legitimacy. The UN has succeeded in exercising a quasi-global sovereignty only in exceedingly narrow technical fields in which there was no controversy whatsoever. Its inability to transfer a cooperative functional relationship into the political field is good evidence that spillover does not readily occur. Surveys of senior civil servants in domestic policy-making bureaucracies also indicate that the majority give low or no priority to transnational solutions, even on issues with an acknowledged degree of interdependence. In the case of energy interdependence, for one, they actually viewed global interconnectedness as risky and undesirable.

We greatly underestimate the factors that encourage global *dis*integration. Among them could be listed (1) mutually exclusive military commitments; (2) increasing participation by previously passive groups; (3) the growth of ethnic and linguistic differentiation; (4) protests by disadvantaged minorities in times of economic decline or stagnation; (5) efforts by formerly privileged groups to reassert their dominance; (6) revolutionary movements aimed at opening up closed political elites; and (7) protest movements in the face of failed reforms. To highlight only one type of disintegrative behavior, the twentieth century has been filled with secessionist efforts, even in highly advanced countries — the Soviet Union, Canada, Spain, France, Portugal, the United Kingdom — whose integrative powers are formidable. In the Third World, secessionist movements number in the hundreds, and they often are sparked not by the most backward but by educated leaders reacting against Western cultural domination while championing the modern value of political self-determination. At times, entire governments have responded to asymmetrical dependence on the Western imperial powers by withdrawing into a more self-reliant pattern of development. In Burma, Bhutan, Cambodia, Iran, Iraq, Peru, Tanzania, and China, greater communication and transaction flows led not to higher integration or better understanding, but to strong nationalist reassertions of their political autonomy, at significant economic cost.

The most remarkable case of failed integration is the relationship between the United States and Canada. If the spillover thesis were correct, transaction flows and common economic interests should long since have led to amalgamation between these two states. They share the longest unguarded frontier in the world, as well as a variety of cooperative defense arrangements institutionalized in such forms as North American Air Defense (NORAD). Socially homogeneous, they are similar in ethnic background, language, social mobility, educational level, literacy, and political and social values. Whether measured in tourism, migration, imports, capital flows, ownership of investments, telecommunications, media programming, or educational exchanges, the United States and Canada have the highest score in the world in those transaction indicators that presumably are the basis for a shared community.

But tightening economic interdependence has not been followed by a rise in sentiment for *political* amalgamation. On the contrary, by the mid-1960s, the Canadians were becoming greatly concerned that they might be absorbed by the United States. Acceding to a nationalist trend in public opinion, the Canadian government decided after 1968 to resist further integration, and it withdrew from many U.S.-Canadian institutions of policy coordination. The Canadian Radio and Television Commission required all broadcasting facilities to present a specified percentage of Canadian content. Canadian advertisers had to produce their own commercials, rather than import them from the United States. Divestiture guidelines were set up to reduce U.S. ownership in Canadian corporations; broadcast companies, for example, were required to reduce U.S. participation to less than 20 percent. Canadian universities, hitherto staffed heavily by Americans, began the preferential hiring of Canadians, and Canadian trade unions systematically reduced their ties to U.S. labor organizations. Nationalist reaction to one issue alone, the free-trade pact negotiated by Prime Minister Brian Mulroney and President Ronald Reagan, nearly unseated the Conservative government in the 1988 elections. Nothing in the U.S.-Canadian relationship supports the notion that the world is headed inevitably toward a higher level of integration, let alone toward world government.

The European Economic Community offers further confirmation of this finding. The EEC was a necessary response to the eclipse in the power of the European states after World War II. It was a pragmatic solution to a power-political calculus, not a commitment to principles of regional or world government, and it succeeded because the members saw integration as the only effective path to recovery for their industrialized economies. The EEC was embraced politically because it offered hope of preserving a distinct European identity against the threat of Soviet aggression and the smothering grip of the all-powerful American ally.

Nonetheless, from beginning to end, the European Community has been troubled by disruptive episodes. Proposals for a European Defense Community and a European Political Community failed in 1954. France's Charles de Gaulle vetoed British membership in 1963 and then, two years later, boycotted Community institutions in a struggle over the allocation of decision-making powers. In 1967, Britain's membership application failed a second time. In 1972, the Norwegians voted against membership because they feared that economic integration would destroy their traditional small farming and fishing sectors and would compromise Norwegian social values. Though the Arab oil boycott of 1974 left Europe vulnerable, the EEC was unable to forge a common response to it. The subsequent inflation and monetary instability were treated largely through unilateral national actions rather than concerted policies.

In short, European integration has seen considerable ups and downs. The failure of spillover in Western Europe may be attributed, among other things, to the diversity of the national units and their conflicting foreign policy responses to the postwar bipolar international system. France and Germany could amalgamate their coal and steel industries, but they could not agree on whether to support American policy in Vietnam, on East-West trade, or on the virtues of making Europe a kind of neutral third force between the superpowers.

Robert Ball, in a 1983 article in *Fortune*, pointed to some more specific EEC failings. Since 1980, intra-Community trade had actually declined as a percentage of member states' total trade, and Europeans were increasingly looking elsewhere for investment opportunities. A study by the Community's Commission listed fifty-six different categories of nontariff barriers that were preventing a true internal market, ranging from discrimination in government procurement contracts through national health and technical regulations to sheer chicanery at national customs borders. Karl-Heinz Harjes, a Commission member, says: "Instead of thinning out, the jungle of national laws and administrative rules, which frequently have a clearly inhibiting aim, is becoming increasingly impenetrable and dense. . . . After 25 years, formalities and inspections at internal Community frontiers are virtually identical with those carried out at frontiers with nonmember countries." Customs formalities are estimated to cost more than $10 billion — a substantial hidden tariff, perhaps as high as 10 percent of the value of the goods being traded. Capital investment within the Community has also fallen. West Germany's investment in the United States is more than double its investment in the EEC, and the shift in French investment patterns is even more striking. In 1963, France invested 54 percent in the EEC and only 6 percent in the United States; by 1983, French investment was evenly divided, at 28 percent each.

Finally, the expansion of EEC membership from six to twelve states has made its decision-making institutions more cumbersome. Since any major change in the level of policy coordination requires unanimous agreement (and an election is always looming somewhere), it has been easier to patch together expedient compromises than to overhaul major programs. For example, Denmark continues to be influenced by its traditional Scandinavian ties with nonmembers Norway and Sweden, and the neutralist ideology of Greece's ruling socialists has restrained further Greek commitments to integration. Many governments are troubled by the prospect of admitting new members, particularly if it should put the EEC in the middle of the Greco-Turkish dispute or bring in a state with a majority Islamic population. As a result, there is little likelihood that a regionally integrated Europe can become the core of a larger political community.

In summarizing the lessons of European integration, Ernst Haas has pointed out that decisions made by the same officials, in organizations with a stable membership, in a nonrevolutionary socioideological setting with compatible institutional characteristics, nevertheless have varied sharply in their integrative impact. Most often, no consensus was achieved on the upgrading of shared interests. The best they could manage was to "split the difference," or compromise on a minimum common denominator. If the impulse to integration is so weak in the European Community, in which the background factors of social structures, acceptance of pluralism, level of urban-industrial development, and ideological affinity are so favorable, then integration is less likely still in a group so large and diverse as, say, the United Nations. There is little prospect that the Third World states, with their considerably lower level of development, will ever possess comparable prerequisites to integration; most Third World nations have not yet reached the level of transaction flows that characterized Europe in the nineteenth century. Even in the EEC, which can be declared a moderate success, integration has reinforced national and regional solidarity and removed any incentives to surrender sovereignty to a global regime. If the EEC has set any precedent, it is for a loosely integrated confederation, not world government.

SOURCES AND SUGGESTED READINGS

On Interdependence and the International Political Economy

(Political-economic issues are also treated in Chapters 6 and 8, on North-South conflict and transnational actors. See bibliographic entries on development and underdevelopment, trade, food and population, energy and resources, debt, foreign aid, and multinational corporations.)

Abbott, Charles C. "Economic Penetration and Power Politics." *Harvard Business Review,* vol. 26 (1948), pp. 410–24.

Avery, William P., and David P. Rapkin, eds. *America in a Changing World Political Economy.* New York: Longman, 1982.

Baldwin, David A. *Economic Statecraft.* Princeton, N.J.: Princeton University Press, 1985.

⸻. "Interdependence and Power: A Conceptual Analysis." *International Organization,* vol. 34 (1980), pp. 471–506.

Beres, Louis Rene, and Harry R. Targ. *Reordering the Planet: Constructing Alternative World Futures.* Boston: Allyn & Bacon, 1974.

Beres, Louis Rene, and Harry R. Targ, eds. *Planning Alternative World Futures.* New York: Praeger, 1975.

Bergsten, C. Fred, and Lawrence B. Krause, eds. *World Politics and International Economics.* Washington: Brookings Institution, 1975.

Blake, David H., and Robert S. Walters. *The Politics of Global Economic Relations,* 3rd ed. Englewood Cliffs, N.J.: Prentice-Hall, 1987.

Block, Fred L. *The Origins of International Economic Disorder.* Berkeley: University of California Press, 1977.

Blumenthal, Michael. "The World Economy and Technological Change." *Foreign Affairs,* vol. 66, no. 3 (1987/88), pp. 529–50.

Brandt, Willy. *Common Crisis: North-South Cooperation for World Recovery.* Cambridge: MIT Press, 1983.

Bressand, Albert. "Mastering the Worldeconomy." *Foreign Affairs,* vol. 16 (1983), pp. 747–72.

Bretton, Henry L. *International Relations in the Nuclear Age: One World, Difficult to Manage.* Albany: State University of New York Press, 1986.

Brown, Lester R. *World Without Borders.* New York: Vintage, 1972.

Brown, Seyom. *New Forces in World Politics.* Washington: Brookings Institution, 1974.

Calleo, David P. *Beyond American Hegemony.* New York: Basic Books, 1987.

Calleo, David, et al. "The Dollar and the Defense of the West." *Foreign Affairs,* vol. 66, no. 4 (Spring 1988), pp. 846–62.

Camps, Miriam. *The Management of Interdependence.* New York: Council on Foreign Relations, 1974.

Caporaso, James A. "International Political Economy: Fad or Field?" *International Studies Notes,* vol. 13 (Winter 1987), pp. 1–8.

Cassen, Robert, et al., eds. *Rich Country Interests and Third World Development.* London: Croom Helm for the Overseas Development Council, 1982.

Chase-Dunn, Christopher. "Interstate System and Capitalist World-Economy: One Logic or Two?" *International Studies Quarterly,* vol. 25 (March 1981), pp. 19–42.

Cline, William R. *International Debt and the Stability of the World Economy.* Washington: Institute for International Economics, 1983.

Cohen, Benjamin. "Europe's Money, America's Problem." *Foreign Policy,* vol. 35 (Summer 1979), pp. 31–47.

⸻. *Organizing the World's Money: The Political Economy of International Monetary Relations.* New York: Basic Books, 1977.

⸻. "Trade and Unemployment: Global Bread-and-Butter Issues." *Worldview,* vol. 26 (January 1983), pp. 9–11.

Cooper, Richard. "Economic Interdependence and Foreign Policy in the Seventies." *World Politics,* vol. 24, no. 2 (January 1972), pp. 159–81.

⸻. *Economic Policy in an Interdependent World.* Cambridge: MIT Press, 1986.

Dell, Edmund. *The Politics of Economic Interdependence.* New York: St. Martin's, 1987.

Deyo, Frederic C., ed. *The Political Economy of the New Asia Industrialism.* Ithaca, N.Y.: Cornell University Press, 1987.

Diaz-Alejando, Carlos F., and Gerald K. Helleiner. *Handmaiden in Distress: World Trade in the 1980's.* Washington: Overseas Development Council, 1982.

Drucker, Peter. "The Changed World Economy." *Foreign Affairs,* vol. 64 (Spring 1986), pp. 768–91.

Falk, Richard. *A Global Approach to National Policy.* Cambridge: Harvard University Press, 1975.

Frieden, Jeffry, and David Lake, eds. *International Political Economy: Perspectives on Global Power and Wealth.* New York: St. Martin's, 1987.

Friesen, Connie M. *The Political Economy of East-West Trade.* New York: Praeger Special Studies, 1978.

Gasiorowski, Mark J. "Economic Interdependence and International Conflict: Some Cross-National Evidence." *International Studies Quarterly,* vol. 30 (March 1986), pp. 23–38.

Geiger, Theodore. *The Future of the International System: The United States and the World Political Economy*. Boston: Allen & Unwin, 1988.

Gill, Stephen, and David Law. *The Global Political Economy: Perspectives, Problems, and Policies*. Baltimore: Johns Hopkins University Press, 1988.

Gilpin, Robert. *The Political Economy of International Relations*. Princeton, N.J.: Princeton University Press, 1987.

———. "Three Models of the Future." *International Organization*, vol. 29 (Winter 1975), pp. 37–60.

Graham, Thomas R. "Revolution in Trade Politics." *Foreign Policy*, vol. 26 (Fall 1979), pp. 49–63.

Helleiner, Gerald K. *International Economic Disorder: Essays in North-South Relations*. Toronto: Toronto University Press, 1981.

Holsti, Ole R., Randolph Siverson, and Alexander George, eds. *Change in the International System*. Boulder, Colo.: Westview Press, 1980.

Hoogvelt, A. M. M. *The Third World in Global Development*. London: Macmillan, 1982.

Huntington, Samuel P. "Trade, Technology, and Leverage: Economic Diplomacy." *Foreign Policy*, vol. 32 (Fall 1978), pp. 63–80.

Jacobson, Harold K. *Networks of Interdependence: International Organizations and the Global Political System*. New York: Knopf, 1979.

Jones, R. J. Barry. *Conflict and Control in the World Economy*. Atlantic Highlands, N. J.: Humanities Press, 1986.

Jones, R. J. Barry, and Peter Willetts, eds. *Interdependence on Trial: Studies in the Theory and Reality of Contemporary Interdependence*. New York: St. Martin's, 1985.

Katzenstein, Peter, ed. *Between Power and Plenty*. Madison: University of Wisconsin Press, 1981.

Keohane, Robert O. *After Hegemony*. Princeton, N.J.: Princeton University Press, 1984.

Keohane, Robert O., and Joseph S. Nye, Jr. *Power and Interdependence: World Politics in Transition*. Boston: Little, Brown, 1977.

———. "*Power and Interdependence* Revisited," *International Organization*, vol. 41, no. 4 (Autumn 1987), pp. 725–53.

Keohane, Robert O., and Joseph S. Nye, Jr., eds. *Transnational Relations and World Politics*. Cambridge: Harvard University Press, 1972.

Kindleberger, Charles P. *America in the World Economy*. Headline Series 237. New York: Foreign Policy Association, 1977.

Krasner, Stephen. "Transforming International Regimes: What the Third World Wants and Why." *International Studies Quarterly*, vol. 25 (March 1981), pp. 119–48.

Lavigne, Marie, ed. *East-South Relations in the World Economy*. Boulder, Colo.: Westview, 1988.

Lewis, W. Arthur. *The Evolution of the International Economic Order*. Princeton, N.J.: Princeton University Press, 1978.

Lindblom, Charles E. *Politics and Markets: The World's Political-Economic Systems*. New York: Basic Books, 1977.

Luard, Evan. *The Management of the World Economy*. New York: St. Martin's Press, 1983.

———. *Types of International Society*. New York: Free Press, 1976.

MacEwan, Arthur, & William K. Tabb, eds. *Instability and Change in the World Economy*. New York: Monthly Review Press, 1989.

Modelski, George. "Agraria and Industria: Two Models of the International System." *World Politics*, vol. 14, no. 1 (October 1961), pp. 118–43.

Morse, Edward. *Modernization and the Transformation of International Relations*. New York: Free Press, 1976.

Nau, Henry R. "Trade and Deterrence." *The National Interest*, vol. 7 (Summer 1987), pp. 48–60.

Rosecrance, Richard, et al. "Whither Interdependence?" *International Organization*, vol. 31 (Summer 1977), pp. 425–71.

Rosecrance, Richard, and Arthur Stein. "Interdependence: Myth or Reality?" *World Politics*, vol. 26 (October 1973), pp. 1–27.

Rosenau, James. "A Pre-Theory Revisited: World Politics in an Era of Cascading Interdependence." *International Studies Quarterly*, vol. 28 (1984).

Rosenau, James, ed. *The Study of Global Interdependence: Essays on the Transnationalization of World Affairs*. New York: Nichols, 1980.

Rothstein, Robert. *Global Bargaining: UNCTAD and the Quest for a New International Economic Order*. Princeton, N.J.: Princeton University Press, 1979.

Ruggie, John Gerald. "Political Structure and Change in the International Economic Order: The North-South Dimension." In John Gerald Ruggie, ed., *The Antinomies of Interdependence*, New York: Columbia University Press, 1983. Pp. 423–89.

Russett, Bruce M., ed. *Economic Theories of International Politics*. Chicago: Markham, 1968.
Sandler, Todd, ed. *The Theory and Structures of International Political Economy*. Boulder, Colo.: Westview, 1980.
Schott, Kerry. *Policy, Power, and Order: The Persistence of Economic Problems in Capitalist States*. New Haven: Yale University Press, 1984.
Scott, Andrew M. *The Dynamics of Interdependence*. Chapel Hill: University of North Carolina Press, 1982.
Spero, Joan Edelman. *The Politics of International Economic Relations*, 4th ed. New York: St. Martin's Press, 1990.
Stewart, Michael. *The Age of Interdependence: Economic Policy in a Shrinking World*. Cambridge: MIT Press, 1984.
Strange, Susan, ed. *Paths to International Political Economy*. London: George Allen and Unwin, 1984.
Toynbee, Arnold. *The World and the West* and *Civilization on Trial*. New York: Meridian, 1958.
Vernon, Raymond. "International Trade Policy in the 1980s: Prospects and Problems." *International Studies Quarterly*, vol. 26 (December 1982), pp. 483–510.
———. *Sovereignty at Bay: The Multinational Spread of U.S. Enterprises*. New York: Basic Books, 1971.
Winham, Gilbert R. *International Trade and the Tokyo Round Negotiation*. Princeton, N.J.: Princeton University Press, 1986.
World Bank. *World Development Report*. New York: Oxford University Press. Issued annually.
Yarbrough, Beth and Robert. "Cooperation in the Liberalization of International Trade: After Hegemony, What?" *International Organization*, vol. 41, no. 1 (Winter 1987), pp. 1–26.
Yergin, Daniel, and Martin Hillenbrand. *Global Insecurity*. Boston: Houghton Mifflin, 1982.

On Integration, Functionalism, and the European Community

Angell, Robert Cooley. *The Quest for World Order*. Ann Arbor: University of Michigan Press, 1979.
Ball, Robert. "The Common Market's Failure." *Fortune*, Nov. 14, 1983, pp. 188–98.
Brown, Seyom. "The World Polity and the Nation-State System: An Updated Analysis." *International Journal*, vol. 39 (Summer 1984), pp. 509–28.
Bull, Hedley, and Adam Watson. *The Expansion of International Society*. New York: Oxford University Press, 1984.
Caporaso, James A. *Functionalism and Regional Integration: A Logical and Empirical Assessment*. Beverly Hills, Calif.: Sage, 1972.
Clark, W Hartley. *The Politics of the Common Market*. Westport, Conn.: Greenwood Press, 1975.
Deutsch, Karl W. *Nationalism and Social Communication: An Inquiry into the Foundations of Nationality*, 2nd ed. Cambridge: MIT Press, 1966
Deutsch, Karl W., et al. *Political Community and the North Atlantic Area*. Princeton, N.J.: Princeton University Press, 1957.
Doose, Douglas, David Gowland, and Keith Hartley, eds. *The Collaboration of Nations: A Study of European Integration*. New York: St. Martin's, 1982.
Eastby, John. *Functionalism and Interdependence*. Lanham, Md.: University Press of America, 1985.
El-Agraa, Ali M., ed. *The Economics of the European Community*. New York: St. Martin's, 1980.
Etzioni, Amitai. *Political Unification: A Comparative Study of Leaders and Forces*. New York: Holt, Rinehart and Winston, 1965.
Falk, Richard A., and Saul H. Mendlovitz, eds. *Regional Politics and World Order*. San Francisco: Freeman, 1973.
Feld, Werner J. *The European Community in World Affairs*. Sherman Oaks, Calif.: Alfred, 1976.
Haas, Ernst B. *Beyond the Nation-State*. Stanford: Stanford University Press, 1964.
———. "International Integration: The European and the Universal Process." *International Organization*. vol. 15, no. 3 (1961), pp. 366–92.
———. *The Uniting of Europe*. Stanford: Stanford University Press, 1958.
Haas, Michael. "A Functional Approach to International Organization." *Journal of Politics*, vol. 27 (August 1965), pp. 498–517.
Jacob, Philip E., and James Toscano, eds. *The Integration of Political Communities*. Philadelphia: Lippincott, 1964.
Kerr, Anthony J. *The Common Market and How It Works*. Elmsford, N.Y.: Pergamon Press, 1977.
Kitzinger, Uwe W. *The Politics and Economics of European Integration*. Westport, Conn.: Greenwood Press, 1976.

Lindberg, Leon N. *The Political Dynamics of European Economic Integration.* Stanford: Stanford University Press, 1963.

Lindberg, Leon, and Stuart Scheingold. *Europe's Would-be Polity: Patterns of Change in the European Community.* Englewood Cliffs, N.J.: Prentice-Hall, 1970.

Lodge, Juliet, ed. *Institutions and Policies of the European Community.* New York: St. Martin's, 1983.

Mitrany, David. *A Working Peace System.* Chicago: Quadrangle Books, 1966.

Owen, Nicholas. *Economies of Scale, Competitiveness, and Trade Patterns Within the European Community.* New York: Oxford University Press, 1983.

Pryce, Roy. *The Politics of the European Community.* Totowa, N.J.: Rowman & Littlefield, 1973.

Puchala, Donald J. "The Integration Theorists and the Study of International Relations." In Charles Kegley, Jr., and Eugene Wittkopf, eds., *The Global Agenda,* 2nd ed., New York: Random House, 1988. Pp. 198–265.

Saunders, Christopher, ed. *Regional Integration in East and West.* New York: St. Martin's, 1983.

Sewell, James P. *Functionalism and World Politics.* Princeton, N.J.: Princeton University Press, 1966.

Soroos, Marvin S. *Beyond Sovereignty: The Challenge of Global Policy.* Columbia: University of South Carolina Press, 1986.

Taylor, Paul. "Intergovernmentalism in the European Communities in the 1970s: Patterns and Perspectives." *International Organization,* vol. 26 (Autumn 1982), pp. 741–66.

———. *The Limits of European Integration.* New York: Columbia University Press, 1983.

Tsoukalis, Loukas, ed. *The European Community: Past, Present, and Future.* Oxford: B. Blackwell, 1983.

Viner, Jacob. *The Customs Union Issue.* New York: Carnegie Endowment for International Peace, 1950.

Wolf, Peter. "International Organization and Attitude Change: A Re-examination of the Functionalist Approach." *International Organization,* vol. 27 (Summer 1973), pp. 347–71.

On the State, Economic Nationalism, and Neomercantilism

Baldwin, David A. *Economic Statecraft.* Princeton, N.J.: Princeton University Press, 1985.

Bertsch, Gary, and John McIntyre, eds. *National Security and Technology Transfer: The Strategic Dimensions of East-West Trade.* Boulder, Colo.: Westview Press, 1983.

Bull, Hedley. "The State's Positive Role in World Politics." *Daedalus,* vol. 108 (Fall 1979), pp. 111–23.

Calleo, David, and Benjamin Rowland. *America and the World Political Economy: Atlantic Dreams and National Realities.* Bloomington: Indiana University Press, 1973.

Claude, Inis L., Jr. "Myths About the State." *Review of International Studies,* vol. 12 (January 1986), pp. 1–11.

Cohen, Stephen D. *The Making of United States International Economic Policy.* New York: Praeger, 1989.

Destler, I. M. *American Trade Politics: System Under Stress.* Washington: Institute for International Economics, 1986.

Destler, I. M., and John S. Odell. *The Politics of Antiprotection: Changing Forces in United States Trade Politics.* Washington: Institute for International Economics, 1987.

Eayrs, James. "The Outlook for Statehood." *International Perspectives: The Canadian Journal of International Affairs,* March-April 1987, pp. 3–7.

Fromkin, David. *The Independence of Nations.* New York: Praeger, 1981.

Gilpin, Robert. *U.S. Power and the Multinational Corporation: The Political Economy of Foreign Direct Investment.* New York: Basic Books, 1975.

Gowa, Joanne. *Closing the Gold Window: Domestic Politics and the End of Bretton Woods.* Ithaca, N.Y.: Cornell University Press, 1983.

Hanreider, W. F. "Dissolving International Politics: Reflections on the State." *American Political Science Review,* vol. 72 (December 1978), pp. 1276–87.

Holsti, K. J. "The Necrologists of International Relations." *Canadian Journal of Political Science,* vol. 18 (December 1985), pp. 675–95.

Keohane, Robert. "Theory of World Politics: Structural Realism and Beyond." In Ada Finifter, ed., *Political Science: The State of the Discipline,* Washington: American Political Science Association, 1983.

Krasner, Stephen. *Defending the National Interest.* Princeton, N.J.: Princeton University Press, 1978.

————. "State Power and the Structure of International Trade." *World Politics*, vol. 28, no. 2 (April 1976), pp. 317–47.

————. "The Tokyo Round: Particularistic Interests and Prospects for Stability in the Global Trading System." *International Studies Quarterly*, vol. 23 (December 1979), pp. 491–531.

Liska, George F. *Nations in Alliance: The Limits of Interdependence*. Baltimore: Johns Hopkins Press, 1962.

Mann, Michael. "The Autonomous Power of the State." *European Journal of Sociology*, vol. 25, no. 2 (1984), pp. 185–213.

Morse, Ronald. "Japan's Drive to Preeminence." *Foreign Policy*, vol. 69 (Winter 1987/88), pp. 3–21.

Ronen, Dov. *The Quest for Self-determination*. New Haven: Yale University Press, 1979.

Rosecrance, Richard. *The Rise of the Trading State: Commerce and Conquest in the Modern World*. New York: Basic Books, 1986.

Schoultz, Lars. "Politics, Economics, and U.S. Participation in Multilateral Organizations." *International Organization*, Summer 1982, pp. 537–74.

Strange, Susan. "Protection and World Politics." *International Organization*, vol. 39, no. 2 (Spring 1985), pp. 233–60.

Tivey, Leonard, ed. *The Nation-State: The Formation of Modern Politics*. New York: St. Martin's, 1981.

Vernon, Raymond, and Debora Spar. *Beyond Globalism: Remaking American Foreign Economic Policy*. New York: Free Press, 1989.

Waltz, Kenneth. "The Myth of National Interdependence." In Charles P. Kindleberger, ed., *The International Corporation*, Cambridge: MIT Press, 1970. Pp. 205–23.

————. *Theory of International Politics*. Reading, Mass.: Addison-Wesley, 1979.

On the World System, Imperialism, and Dependency

Amin, Samir. *Accumulation on a World Scale: A Critique of the Theory of Development*. 2 vols. New York: Monthly Review Press, 1974.

Becker, David. *The New Bourgeoisie and the Limits of Dependency: Mining, Class, and Power in "Revolutionary" Peru*. Princeton, N.J.: Princeton University Press, 1983.

Bodenheimer, Susanne. "Dependency and Imperialism: The Roots of Latin American Underdevelopment." In K. T. Fann and D. C. Hodges, eds., *Readings in U. S. Imperialism*, Boston: Porter Sargent, 1971. Pp. 155–82.

Brown, Michael Barratt. *Economics of Imperialism*. New York: Penguin, 1974.

Caporaso, James. "Dependency Theory." *International Organization*, vol. 34, no. 4 (Autumn 1980), pp. 605–28.

Caporaso, James, ed.. "Dependence and Dependency in the Global System." *International Organization* (Special Issue), vol. 32 (Winter 1978), pp. 1–300.

Caporaso, James, and Behrouz Zare. "An Interpretation and Evaluation of Dependency Theory." In H. Muñoz, ed., *From Dependency to Development*, Boulder, Colo.: Westview, 1981.

Cardoso, Fernando. "Associated-Dependent Development: Theoretical and Practical Implications." In Alfred Stepan, ed., *Authoritarian Brazil*, New Haven: Yale University Press, 1973.

————. "The Consumption of Dependency Theory in the United States." *Latin American Research Review*, 1977, pp. 7–24.

Cardoso, Fernando, and Enzo Faletto. *Dependency and Development in Latin America*. Berkeley: University of California Press, 1979.

Chase-Dunn, Christopher, and Richard Rubison. "Toward a Structural Perspective on the World-System." *Politics and Society*, vol. 7, no. 4 (1977), pp. 453–76.

Chirot, Daniel, and Thomas D. Hall. "World-System Theory." *Annual Review of Sociology*, vol. 8 (1982), pp. 81–106.

Cockcroft, J., Andre Gunder Frank, and D. Johnson, eds. *Dependence and Underdevelopment*. Garden City, N.Y.: Doubleday, 1972.

Cohen, Benjamin. *The Question of Imperialism: The Political Economy of Dominance and Dependence*. New York: Basic Books, 1973.

Collier, David. "Industrial Modernization and Political Change: A Latin American Perspective." *World Politics*, vol. 30, no. 4 (July 1978), pp. 593–614.

Denemark, Robert, and Kenneth Thomas. "The Brenner-Wallerstein Debate." *International Studies Quarterly*, vol. 32, no. 1 (March 1988), pp. 47–66.

Doyle, Michael. *Empires.* Ithaca, N.Y.: Cornell University Press, 1986

Duvall, Raymond. "The State and Dependent Capitalism." *International Studies Quarterly,* March 1981.

Emmanuel, Arghiri. *Unequal Exchange: A Study of the Imperialism of Trade.* New York: Monthly Review Press, 1972.

Evans, Peter. "After Dependency." *Latin American Research Review,* vol. 20, no. 2 (1985), pp. 149–60.

———. *Dependent Development: The Alliance of Multinational, the State, and Local Capital in Brazil.* Princeton, N.J.: Princeton University Press, 1979.

Fagen, Richard. "Equity in the South in the Context of North-South Relations." In Roger Hansen, ed., *Rich and Poor Nations in the World Economy,* New York: Mc Graw-Hill, 1978.

Fanon, Frantz. *The Wretched of the Earth.* New York: Grove Press, 1968.

Farnsworth, Clyde H. "Financial Drain Reaches Record in Third World." *The Oregonian,* Dec. 19, 1988, p. A11.

Freeman, Edward, ed. *Ascent and Decline in the World-System.* Beverly Hills, Calif.: Sage Publications, 1982.

Galtung, Johan. "A Structural Theory of Imperialism." *Journal of Peace Research,* vol. 8, no. 2 (1971), pp. 81–117.

Gereffi, Gary. *The Pharmaceutical Industry and Dependency in the Third World.* Princeton, N.J.: Princeton University Press, 1983.

Hopkins, Terence K., and Immanuel Wallerstein, eds. *Processes of the World-System.* Beverly Hills, Calif.: Sage Publications, 1980.

Kolko, Gabriel. *The Limits of Power.* New York: Harper & Row, 1972.

Magdoff, Harry. *The Age of Imperialism.* New York: Monthly Review Press, 1969.

McGowan, Patrick. "Imperialism in World-System Perspective." *International Studies Quarterly,* vol. 25 (March 1981), pp. 43–68.

Modelski, George, ed. *Transnational Corporations and World Order.* San Francisco: W. H. Freeman, 1979.

O'Brien, Philip. "A Critique of Latin American Theories of Dependency." In Oxaal, Barnet, and Booth, eds., *Beyond the Sociology of Development,* London: Routledge & Kegan Paul, 1975. Pp. 7–86.

Olson, Gary L. *How the World Works: A Critical Introduction to International Relations.* Palo Alto, Calif.: Scott, Foresman, 1984.

Palma, Gabriel. "Dependency." *World Development,* vol. 6, no. 7/8 (1978).

Payer, Cheryl. *The Debt Trap: The International Monetary Fund and the Third World.* New York: Monthly Review Press, 1974.

Petras, James F., et al. *Capitalist and Socialist Crises in the Late Twentieth Century.* Totowa, N.J.: Rowman & Allanheld, 1983.

Pfister, Ulrich, and Christian Suter. "International Financial Relations as Part of the World-System." *International Studies Quarterly,* vol. 31 (September 1987), pp. 239–72.

Rhodes, Robert I., ed. *Imperialism and Underdevelopment.* New York: Monthly Review Press, 1970.

Seers, Dudley, ed. *Dependency Theory.* London: F. Pinter, 1981.

Skocpol, Theda. "Wallerstein's World Capitalist System: A Theoretical and Historical Critique." *American Journal of Sociology,* vol. 82 (March 1977), pp. 1075–90.

Slater, Jerome. "Is United States Foreign Policy 'Imperialistic' or 'Imperial'?" *Political Science Quarterly,* vol. 91 (Spring 1976), pp. 63–87.

Smith, Tony. "The Logic of Dependency Theory Revisited." *International Organization,* vol. 35 (Autumn 1981), pp. 755–76.

———. "Requiem or New Agenda for Third World Studies?" *World Politics,* vol. 37 (July 1985), pp. 532–61

———. "The Underdevelopment of Development Literature: The Case of Dependency Theory." *World Politics,* vol. 31 (January 1979), pp. 247–88.

Valenzuela, Samuel and Arturo. "Modernization and Dependency: Alternative Perspectives in the Study of Latin American Underdevelopment." *Comparative Politics,* vol. 10, no. 4 (1978), pp. 535–57.

Wallerstein, Immanuel. *The Capitalist World-Economy.* New York: Cambridge University Press, 1979.

———. *The Modern World System I: Capitalist Agriculture and the Origins of the European World-Economy in the Sixteenth Century.* New York: Academic Press, 1974.

————— . *The Modern World System II: Mercantilism and the Consolidation of the European World-Economy, 1600–1750*. New York: Academic Press, 1980.

————— . "The Rise and Future Demise of the World Capitalist System: Concepts for Comparative Analysis." *Comparative Studies in Society and History*, vol. 16 (September 1974), pp. 387–415.

Wallerstein, Immanuel, ed. *The Politics of the World-Economy: The States, the Movements and the Civilizations*. Cambridge: Cambridge University Press, 1984.

EAST-WEST CONFLICT

World War II wrote the epitaph to five centuries of European domination of the international system and set the scene for a great struggle between the United States and the Soviet Union for control of a divided Europe, and eventually the globe. This *East-West* conflict, a Cold War marked by more than four decades of intense Soviet-American rivalry, has been the dominant axis of global conflict since 1945. It has been marked by revolutionary military technologies, total ideologies, and a bipolar competition between rival political-economic systems.

A second axis of conflict, between the imperial powers and the colonized countries, between the rich and the poor, the North and the South, was also set off by the destructive consequences of world war. This *North-South* conflict took expression in anticolonial nationalism that spread through Asia, Africa, and the Middle East and reconstructed the political geography of the Third World in the decades after World War II. It was marked by revolutionary movements struggling for both modernization and self-determination. With the Chinese-Soviet rift after 1960, the socialist world as well as the capitalist was split between its have and have-not states, between the dominant powers and the dependent satellites that wished to emancipate themselves.

The two axes of conflict have often intersected, in such locales as Cuba, Vietnam, Angola, Afghanistan, and Nicaragua, and the "high politics" of the East-West struggle has affected the Third World's agenda of political independence and economic development. Both superpowers have given arms and economic assistance to their client states, and both have been drawn into the Third World's social revolutions. In some cases, superpower involvement accelerated economic development or the liberation struggle; in others, it destroyed governments, deformed economies, and subordinated indigenous politics to the concerns of the superpower patrons.

It is difficult to say which has been the more compelling issue of our time: the struggle between communism and capitalism, the arms race, and the risk of nuclear war between the Soviet Union and the United States; or anticolonial nationalism, social revolution, and the struggle of the Third World to escape poverty and dependency. This chapter, on the East-West conflict, and Chapter 6, on the North-South conflict, will examine these two great axes of global conflict and their points of intersection.

THE ORIGINS OF THE COLD WAR

Although Russia and the United States experienced a long period of friendly relations between 1776 and 1917, and they were temporary allies in the wartime antifascist coalition between 1941 and 1945, their relations have been largely hostile ever since America's armed intervention in the Bolshevik Revolution. From 1918 onward, the propaganda war between socialism and capitalism was vociferous. The United States refused to recognize the new Soviet regime until 1933, and even then the Stalinist purges made Americans skeptical about the prospect for normal relations with such a dictatorship. Their worst fears were apparently confirmed by the signing of the Nazi-Soviet Non-Aggression Pact in 1939, which divided Poland between the two dictatorships and left Adolf Hitler free to launch a war on the Western front without fear of Soviet attack. The Soviets further alienated themselves by declaring war on Finland and occupying the Baltic states of Latvia, Lithuania, and Estonia.

The Nazi-Soviet Non-Aggression Pact is a prime illustration of the way diametrically opposed interpretations of one event can sow lasting distrust. The Western allies saw it as a device whereby Joseph Stalin "cleverly contrived to turn Hitler against the democracies in the expectation that they would bleed one another white, while he emerged supreme" (Bailey, p. 709). Stalin saw the pact as a necessary self-protective response to the Western appeasement of Hitler at Munich, which had aimed his expansion eastward, at Russia's expense. Stalin was also playing for time to build up the Soviet economy, severely hurt by both the collectivization of agriculture and his purges, which had cost the country millions of its most productive citizens. The division of Poland gave the Soviets additional breathing space — territory they could sacrifice in the event of a German attack. Still, Stalin was sure that Hitler would not be so irrational as to hazard a second front — so sure that he refused to believe ample intelligence information that an attack was imminent in June 1941. Stalin's refusal to face reality was reinforced by his deep suspicions of the British and by his wishful thought that the pact might give Russia the several more months, perhaps years, it needed to prepare adequately for war. In the event, Hitler's attack threw Stalin into the arms of the Western capitalist powers he so fiercely distrusted, for Allied aid was essential in a ferocious campaign that cost more than a million Russian troops and placed the Germans at the gates of Moscow within four short months.

Wartime Alliance and the Seeds of Conflict

In the subsequent years of the war, the Soviets and the Americans came to disagree on three major issues — the question of a second front, the postwar division of Europe outlined at the Yalta Conference, and Soviet participation in the invasion and occupation of Japan — all of which contributed to their postwar animosities. Britain's Prime Minister Winston Churchill and U.S. President Franklin D. Roosevelt, although they had differing assessments of Stalin's trustworthiness, were agreed that a second front should be deferred until quite late in the war. Churchill, eager to protect Europe from a Soviet-dominated peace, advocated a southern European campaign that would drive north and join up with Soviet forces well to the east, effectively sparing most of Europe from Red Army occupation. Roosevelt, primarily concerned with saving American lives, argued for a well-prepared amphibious invasion from the west. They compromised on a North African campaign and an invasion of Italy, with the major invasion, at Normandy in France, delayed until June 1944. Meanwhile, from 1941 on, Stalin had repeatedly been begging the Allies to open a major offensive that would relieve the intense German pressure on Soviet forces. Still, by May of 1943, the American and British forces were facing only twelve German and eight Italian divisions in a limited campaign, while the Soviets were fighting along a thousand-mile front against 258 divisions of Axis troops. It is not surprising that the Soviets, who bore the brunt of the fighting, should have interpreted the Anglo-American behavior as a conspiracy to crush Soviet Communism by means of the Nazi panzer divisions. Marxist-Leninist ideology encouraged such a conspiratorial view of capitalism. Remarks like this one by then Senator Harry S Truman added fuel to the fire: "If we see that Germany is winning the war we ought to help Russia, and if Russia is winning we ought to help Germany and in that way let them kill as many as possible."

The Yalta Conference of February 1945 was the high point of Soviet-American wartime cooperation. Eventual victory in Europe seemed assured, but the United States still faced the prospect of a bloody invasion of the Japanese home islands. Roosevelt, who did not yet know if the fledgling Manhattan Project would be successful in developing the atomic bomb, was anxious to have the Soviets participate in the invasion. He also wanted to avoid any possibility of a separate German-Soviet peace settlement in Europe, along the lines of the Nazi-Soviet Non-Aggression Pact. Russian forces had already liberated Poland and East Prussia and were moving on Vienna, while the British-American forces were still recovering from the German counteroffensive of the Battle of the Bulge. FDR consequently consented at Yalta to the joint Allied administration of occupied Germany, the division of Europe into spheres of influence that acknowledged Soviet preeminence in Eastern Europe, and the recognition of Soviet territorial claims in the Far East. In exchange, he received the promise of free elections in Eastern Europe ("broadly representative of all democratic elements in the population") and a Soviet declaration of war against Japan within ninety days after a European armistice. It was also agreed "as a basis for discussion" that Germany would pay $20 billion in reparations, half to the USSR.

Orthodox interpretations of the origins of the Cold War hold that the Soviets, by their aggressive behavior in Eastern Europe and occupied Germany, betrayed the spirit of Yalta. The Soviets were charged with manipulating the Polish resistance forces in order to eliminate non-Communist leadership in Poland; as early as 1940, the Soviets had massacred a large number of Polish officers in the Katyn Forest, and then, in 1944, during the Warsaw uprising, Stalin had stalled his troops on the outskirts of the city, apparently to give the withdrawing Nazis time to suppress the indigenous resistance forces. Differences also emerged over how to define the "democratic elements" referred to in the Yalta understanding on free elections. The Soviets said it meant the exclusion of all anti-Communist elements, while Churchill and Truman conceived of elections in terms of Western-style democracy and pluralism. In addition, the Americans were dismayed by the unilateral Soviet reparations policy in East Germany, which was systematically stripped of its economic assets. Postwar cooperation was further complicated by Soviet intransigence on various interallied commissions, which came to a head in the attempt in 1948–49 to block Allied access to Berlin. The Berlin blockade, following shortly on a Soviet coup in Czechoslovakia, confirmed for many the need for an active policy to contain Soviet aggression.

Revisionists say that Stalin remained remarkably faithful to the spheres of influence hammered out at Yalta. He withdrew Soviet support for the Communist insurgency in Greece and, under prodding from President Truman, finally removed Soviet troops from Iran. He recognized the Kuomintang nationalists in China and grudgingly acceded to the independence of the Communist party in Yugoslavia. More important, he accepted coalition governments in Eastern Europe and refrained from encouraging subversion by the West European Communists (who had made up the bulk of the wartime resistance movements in France and Italy), accepting instead a patriotic, nationalist, parliamentary orientation among West European Communist parties.

In Stalin's eyes, it was the West that betrayed the Yalta agreement. The Germans, knowing that defeat was inevitable, surrendered as much territory as they could to the advancing Anglo-American troops on the Western front, paring down the Soviet Union's hard-won right to a substantial zone of occupation. Worse still, the British and the Americans, conspiring to arrange a separate peace favorable to the West, tried to exclude the Soviets from armistice negotiations. Lend-lease aid to the Soviets was suspended immediately upon the signing of a European armistice on May 7, 1945, despite the standing Soviet pledge to aid the United States in the invasion of Japan. President Truman, inexperienced and belligerent, then seized on the atomic bombing of Hiroshima and Nagasaki, on August 6 and 9, 1945, as a Machiavellian tactic for cutting the Soviets out of the fruits of victory. Far from being necessary to induce Japan to surrender, the dropping of the A-bombs was aimed at intimidating the Soviets and excluding them from their agreed role in the Japanese occupation. The United States went on to participate in the economic reconstruction of Japan and Germany, the defeated fascists, while refusing loans to the USSR and putting a stop to reparations from West Germany to the Soviet Union.

In the orthodox interpretation, these measures were necessary to the war effort; the cancellation of lend-lease hurt Britain as much as it did the Soviet Union, and the Soviet exclusion from a cooperative postwar alliance was the self-imposed result of its own distrust, secretiveness, and belligerence. Revisionists answer that Stalin's wartime behavior was essentially defensive and nationalist and that his main objective was the protection of Soviet security.

Although excesses occurred in occupied Germany, the Soviets exerted pressure only in traditional zones of Russian interest, and Stalin accepted gracefully his exclusion from a significant role in Italy and Japan, in spite of wartime promises to the contrary. He even withdrew from Iran, despite its strategic location on the Soviet southern border. Finally, they say, it was the Western powers that initiated NATO and the militarization of Europe, which left Germany permanently divided, and the Soviet Union that remained faithful to the Yalta formula of a neutralized Germany under four-power control.

Revisionist scholars see America's betrayal of promises made at Yalta as part of a pattern of anti-Communist antagonism aiming at isolating and encircling the Soviet Union. They point to the role of opinion leaders in whipping up periodic "Red scares" and to the perennial interest of the military-industrial complex in keeping the Cold War hot enough to justify continuing arms procurement. Although these factors may have been important later in sustaining the arms race, many scholars do not accept them as a satisfactory explanation of the origins of Soviet-American hostility. The Cold War cannot be blamed solely on U.S. imperialism, economic expansionism, or counterrevolutionary motives, as the revisionists often allege, even if the United States, paradoxically, was more nearly the power with a global ideological vision and the Soviet Union was only following classical balance-of-power politics.

More moderate historians of the Cold War say its origins cannot be reduced to a devil theory that blames one side or the other. The United States may genuinely have desired an arrangement of shared power, for example, and might even have agreed to surrender its atomic weapons to an international agency. But postwar differences in the United Nations and over the Baruch plan for the international management of atomic energy showed that the Soviets were reluctant to surrender sovereignty (including the right of on-site inspection) to organizations that were dominated by the United States and its allies. This is not the fault of Stalin's paranoia or Marxist-Leninist zeal, but is the simple prudence that any great power displays in protecting its national interests. Stalin, for all his flaws, had shown himself to be a cautious statesman and a masterful practitioner of balance-of-power diplomacy. If Roosevelt was less canny at Yalta and yielded too many concessions, it may well have been the result of his poor health (he died two months later), misguided American zeal, or Roosevelt's naïveté in not paying sufficient attention to the war's political aims. In the latter respect, the United States was handicapped by Roosevelt's idealism and personalism, by American isolationist tendencies, and by the inclination to rely on quick military fixes ("leave war to the generals"). Roosevelt had counted on his considerable charm and diplomatic skills to overcome differences with Stalin and preserve Allied solidarity in the new United Nations, but he did not live to see his postwar designs realized, and the new president, Harry Truman, was more skeptical about the Soviets. If Stalin took advantage of his wartime gains to extend Soviet influence throughout Eastern Europe, the United States relied too heavily on empty moralism and wishful thinking, rather than on raw balance-of-power calculations. When the American public demanded the quick return of U.S. troops after the war, the

European theater was left open to the influence of the Red Army and the more persevering Soviet diplomacy.

From the preceding discussion, we can identify several fundamental sources of the Cold War and Soviet-American animosity, each of which we will consider in turn: (1) deeply rooted cultural and historical differences that antedate the Bolshevik Revolution of 1917; (2) ideological differences that can be traced to the antagonisms of 1917; (3) geopolitical differences arising from the circumstances of World War II; and (4) mutual misperceptions and misunderstandings after the war. By itself, no one factor is sufficient to have engendered the Cold War, but taken together, in a kind of layered effect, they account for the intensity of the hostility that dominated Soviet-American relations for four decades.

Cultural and Historical Differences

The two societies have had contrasting cultural and historical experiences that generated different worldviews. First, there are dissimilar constitutional experiences. The United States began as a democratic society, with an educated middle class and a large population of enterprising, self-sufficient yeoman farmers. It inherited from England a liberal tradition that provided the foundation for a constitutional republic, and it has no history of radical revolution based on European socialist theory. Russia, on the other hand, has always suffered extremes of wealth and poverty. It was ruled by an oppressive aristocracy and a czarist autocracy, under which anarchic and revolutionary impulses found expression in frequent peasant rebellions and the flowering of Marxist thought. Before the Revolution of 1905, which established a provisional parliament, or duma, Russia's only experiment in representative government had been a short-lived token body in the sixteenth century. The Soviet political tradition is authoritarian and collectivist, the American consensual and individualist.

Second, the two societies have had contrasting economic histories. Russia was a society of peasants leading an austere life in an inhospitable climate, suspicious of change, and dragged into the twentieth century only with enormous effort and suffering. America began as a thriving commercial culture sustained by a particularly favorable physical milieu; it amassed great wealth rapidly and took its continuing progress for granted.

Finally, the two countries' different geopolitical settings gave them sharply contrasting experiences of war. Russia, a land power, was vulnerable to repeated invasions and suffered traumatic military defeats and centuries of foreign occupation. America, a sea power, enjoyed a hemispheric isolation that brought it unparalleled success in war. All these different experiences and attitudes were bound to create misunderstanding between two strongly ethnocentric peoples, as the French historian Alexis de Tocqueville foresaw as early as 1832:

There are, at the present time, two great nations in the world, which seem to tend towards the same end, although they started from different points: I allude to the Russians and the Americans. Both of them have grown up unnoticed; and whilst the attention of mankind was directed elsewhere, they have suddenly assumed a most prominent place amongst the nations; and the world learned their existence and their greatness at almost the same time. All other nations seem to have nearly reached their natural limits, and only to be charged with the maintenance of their power; but these are still in the act of growth: all the others are stopped, or contine to advance with extreme difficulty; these are proceeding with ease and with celerity along a path to which the human eye can assign no term. . . . The Anglo-American relies upon personal interest to accomplish his ends, and gives free scope to the unguided exertions and common sense of the citizens; the Russian centres all the authority of society in a single arm; the principal instrument of the former is freedom; of the latter, servitude. Their starting-point is different, and their courses are not the same; yet each of them seems to be marked out by the will of Heaven to sway the destinies of half the globe. (*Democracy in America,* vol. 1, pp. 521–22)

Ideological Differences

The Soviet-American ideological estrangement goes back to the Bolshevik Revolution of 1917. This rivalry had several dimensions: capitalism versus socialism as an economic system; a belief in consensus and the self-evident character of natural rights versus the inevitability of class conflict and revolutionary liberation; the atheism and secular humanism of the Marxist versus the Puritan ethic and a Judeo-Christian heritage. Both the United States and the Soviet Union, with their diametrically opposed ideologies, saw themselves as offering a light to humanity, a crusading vision, a model for the future. Each self-righteously declared that its principles of political economy had universal application, that only the extermination of the other's ideology could bring peace and freedom. Both claimed to represent true democracy and to have the right to intervene on behalf of any people's struggle for self-determination.

These pretensions to a universalist ideology are well captured in the figures of Woodrow Wilson and Vladimir Lenin, the leaders of the two countries in the important formative years just after the Bolshevik victory. Wilson envisioned the League of Nations as a world order constructed on the principles of Western-style democracy and centered in the right of self-determination — but he was not above intervening in the Mexican Revolution or in the Russian Revolution, lest these supposedly self-evident principles be overlooked. Lenin, a believer in the Marxist theory that the Bolshevik Revolution was a first step in the progressive liberation of the capitalist world from the shackles of wage slavery, was not above helping history along by working assiduously to export the revolution to societies in which it was supposed to take place spontaneously. Thus, both systems displayed idealistic and imperialistic impulses that were bound to bring them into conflict.

An American propaganda campaign following the Bolshevik coup d'état sharpened the conflict. Publications characterized the Russian Communists as ruthless barbarians who participated in satanic orgies. Chamber of Commerce speeches played up Communist attacks on the family and on private property, decrying at once the despotic and the anarchic elements of the Russian Revolution, in the hope of strangling the illegitimate "monster" while it was yet in the crib. Then, in the closing months of World War I, President Wilson was persuaded to join the British and the French in an Allied military intervention in Russia, ostensibly to protect war supplies at Murmansk and to rescue some stranded Czech soldiers who were needed in the war effort. The intervening troops inevitably drifted into support for the counterrevolutionary "Whites" in the ferocious civil war raging in Russia. The Bolsheviks naturally took the intervention as proof that the West was implacably hostile to socialism and was bent on encircling and destroying the infant Soviet state. A long dispute over czarist debts and the United States' continuing nonrecognition only compounded Soviet suspicions. These initial antagonisms were exacerbated by Stalin's duplicitous pact with Hitler, which proved (at least in American eyes) that dictatorship was a more powerful principle than all others and that the Communists would stoop to anything to defeat the West. So World War II, which elevated both the United States and the Soviet Union to the position of leading powers, merely amplified an existing rivalry.

The United States looked on World War II as a ratification of its power and virtue. Frustrated in its earlier efforts to impose its liberating vision on a recalcitrant world, it saw an opportunity to reform an evil system, to put an end to balance-of-power politics, to make good on the Wilsonian promise of a reconstructed world order via the United Nations. Successful reforms in Germany and Japan under the American occupation were seen as proof of the benign character and inherent superiority of the American constitutional and economic model. With the U.S. economy revitalized (war production had finally ended the Great Depression), Americans felt hopeful. The only obstacle they saw to world peace was the risk of Soviet aggression, of Communism on the march. The competition with the Soviet Union, the first challenger to America's newly acquired status as a world power, came to have a traumatic and fixative quality that led to deep disillusionment once the wartime alliance began to unravel.

The United States tended to view every aspect of its new world role in strongly ideological terms. The Europeans regarded Hitler as a reprise of the old "German problem"; to the United States, he was the epitome of evil. An even plainer example is the different Soviet and American reactions toward the Communist victory in China. The Soviets, who might have been expected to eagerly embrace a fraternal socialist state, were ambivalent, out of fears of a new geopolitical threat. The Americans, on the other hand, adopted the defeated Chiang Kai-shek as one of their own, as a kind of Christian patriot, and interpreted the "loss" of China as a "stab in the back" by Communist sympathizers and softheaded liberals in the State Department. The hysterical quality of the ensuing anti-Communist witchhunt by Senator Joseph McCarthy and others testified to America's insecurity over its newfound global responsibilities and to the profound influence of ideology in both foreign and domestic politics. In short, ideological themes have played through Soviet-American relations from beginning to end.

Geopolitical Competition

A third influence on the Cold War was the geopolitical competition between the two states for influence in the global balance of power after 1945. Political realists would argue that great powers will always fight for dominance, regardless of ideology, and that the Cold War was inevitable, given the armed might of the Soviet Union and the United States and their monopoly of nuclear weapons technology. In this sense, World War II, by destroying all their rivals, was the immediate cause of the Soviet-American split, and ideology's only role was to justify each power's actions in protecting its national interests. When the wartime alliance had required them to subordinate their ideological animosities, they had done so. When the Yalta spheres of influence approach broke down afterward, because of the unprecedented power vacuum in Europe and the rapid decay of European control over unstable zones in the Third World, national interests dictated that the two superpowers challenge one another directly.

The two states' different geopolitical situations had thrust them into different military roles in the war. The Soviets' land-based forces were their protection against the ever-present German menace. The United States relied on a sea and air power consistent with its technological superiority and the "Fortress America" attitude fostered by its hemispheric isolation. Masses of Soviet troops ground out victory in scorched-earth campaigns that affected every Russian family, displacing tens of millions from their homes and killing one out of four adult Russian males. The Americans, leaving the safety of their own untouched territory, went abroad to rescue others. Although many a GI Joe died in the foxholes, the predominant American images of the war were of naval battles in the Pacific and air raids over Germany. Psychologically speaking, death was administered from a distance; the A-bomb attacks perfectly symbolized this attitude. Technology could substitute for manpower, saving countless American lives. These contrasting experiences have shaped the strategic concepts of the two powers ever since, the Soviets emphasizing land-based conventional forces of tanks, artillery, and tactical aircraft, the United States emphasizing a blue-water navy, intercontinental bombers, and a nuclear arsenal. In the realist view, geography is destiny, and geography dictated this rivalry between a land power controlling the European heartland and a sea and air power in control of the surrounding rimlands.

The security conceptions of the two superpowers have reflected these geopolitical differences. The United States has always negotiated about arms on the basis of parity, or equal numbers of forces. The Soviets have consistently responded that this leaves them at a distinct disadvantage, since the United States is technologically superior, territorially less vulnerable, and subject to attack from only one source. The Soviets have therefore negotiated on the basis of equal security, which takes into account their need to garrison a long land frontier with hostile neighbors. In fact, they claim to be threatened from all four directions, including attacks over the North Pole by intercontinental missiles. (For the Soviet perception of its encirclement, see Figure 5-1.)

The Soviets look back on World War II as a near disaster in which socialism barely escaped defeat by Nazism. To them, their victory justified, in retrospect, the forced industrialization and Stalinist sacrifices of the 1920s and '30s, which built up the heavy industry that proved essential to Soviet security and great-power status. The Great Patriotic War, in which a multiethnic empire unified itself around a Soviet core in defense of Mother Russia, was the central formative event of the new Soviet state. Even today, World War II is replayed more often in Soviet films than the Bolshevik Revolution is; it has shaped Russian consciousness in the same way as western films and the experience of the frontier have shaped American consciousness. For the majority of Soviets, it was not Marxism-Leninism but the patriotic nationalism of the Great War that glued their country together. The postwar subordination and dismemberment of Eastern Europe were viewed as a just reward for the monumental and desperate Soviet sacrifice. The Soviet occupation of satellite states was only to re-create a buffer zone, or cordon sanitaire, along traditional balance-of-power lines (remember the many partitions of Poland in the eighteenth and nineteenth centuries) and to restore lands "stolen" by the Germans in 1917, recouping the losses of the czarists and Mensheviks. In this view, the East European policies that contributed so much to postwar differences had little to do with betrayal and deceit and everything to do with the balance of power and traditional Russian interests.

Mutual Misperception

The mutual misperceptions that emerged from different Soviet and American wartime experiences were a fourth contributing factor in the Cold War. Both physically and psychologically, the war was much more traumatic for the Soviets than for the United States. The Soviets suffered 20 million dead, versus 300,000 for the United States. The Russian economy was completely devastated; the U.S. economy was regenerated. After the war, the Soviets rebuilt with assets confiscated from Eastern Europe, while America sent Marshall Plan aid to Western Europe and supported a self-sufficient European Economic Community. The Eastern bloc was consolidated around a Soviet empire and the dependent Comecon relationship; the Western alliance evolved into relations of equality and interdependence. In spite of their huge armed forces, the war left the Soviets feeling extremely vulnerable, and from 1945 to 1985 they exhibited a defensive paranoia and an excessive concern for military preparedness. The United States, on the other hand, felt that the war had ratified its virtue; it had become a great power through selfless acts, not out of imperial designs, and destiny or divine providence had given it a special role as the guardian of world peace. In sum, Soviet feelings of insecurity, military encir-

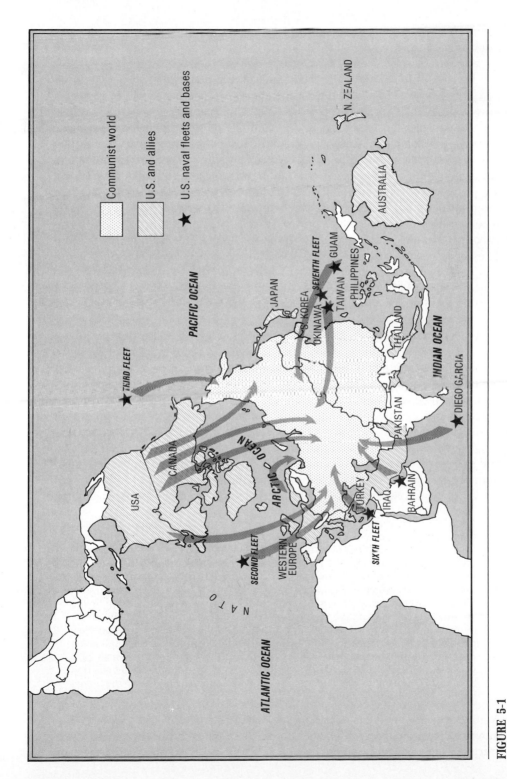

FIGURE 5-1

THE SOVIET UNION'S PERCEPTION OF ITS ENCIRCLEMENT BY THE U.S. AND ITS MILITARY ALLIES (1950–55)

clement, and diplomatic isolation, in contrast to U.S. economic confidence, nuclear superiority, and world leadership, gave the Soviets an "inferiority complex" they have been pressing to shed ever since.

Both sides fell victim to distorted images and ideological stereotypes that had little basis in fact. Mutual fears, compounded by ignorance, gave rise to a long series of false alarms about arms "gaps," perpetuating what might otherwise have been short-term misunderstandings over the sharing of postwar power. In actuality, objective conflicts in the national interests of the two powers have been few. They do not share contiguous borders, except in the Arctic, and have never gone to war with one another or disputed over territory. They have no ongoing competition for resources, trade, or colonies. Their two economies are not interdependent or mutually vulnerable. They do not compete for allies among the major powers, except perhaps in China, whose influence has actually brought about a degree of Soviet-American reconciliation. They occupy quite separate spheres of influence a hemisphere apart.

Their mutual misunderstandings were largely rooted in the domestic idiosyncrasies of each regime. For the Russians, it was an orthodoxy and an Iron Curtain mentality that had kept them isolated since before the Renaissance and had led to the Kremlin's excessive secrecy. For the United States, it was the provincial dynamic of its democratic politics, which overstated the Soviet threat in its opportunistic appeals to the votes and pocketbooks of an ill-informed and isolationist public. On each side, domestic conditions exaggerated the degree of distrust in the other — a distrust compounded by each society's unprecedented vulnerability to the nuclear firepower of the other. This context of fear and distrust engendered mirror images in which one side epitomized virtue, the other evil. The dire consequences of nuclear attack fostered planning in which each side projected upon its adversary the worst of intentions, and such projections then became self-fulfilling, since only the most diabolical of intentions can justify an immense arms establishment in the absence of war.

As George Kennan wrote, each side misread the other's postwar actions:

> The Marshall Plan, the preparations for the setting up of a West German government, and the first moves toward the establishment of NATO, were taken in Moscow as the beginnings of a campaign to deprive the Soviet Union of the fruits of its victory over Germany. The Soviet crackdown on Czechoslovakia (1948) and the mounting of the Berlin blockade, both essentially defensive . . . reactions to these Western moves, were then similarly misread on the Western side. Shortly thereafter there came the crisis of the Korean War, where the Soviet attempt to employ a satellite military force in civil combat to its own advantage, by way of reaction to the American decision to establish a permanent military presence in Japan, was read in Washington as the beginning of the final Soviet push for world conquest; whereas the active American military response, provoked by this move, appeared in Moscow . . . as a threat to the Soviet position in both Manchuria and in eastern Siberia. ("The United States and the Soviet Union, 1917–1976," pp. 683–84)

Neither power saw itself as having imperial designs, but each felt forced to mount an increasingly military response to pressure from the other. What started as political containment became military confrontation. What began as a strategy of regional security became a striving for global hegemony. Because the wartime collaboration had fostered unrealistic expectations of postwar harmony, the dashed hopes brought a strong overreaction on both sides.

Stanley Hoffmann has described the early stages of the Cold War as a paradoxical consequence of the interaction of defensive universalisms. Soviet security, interpreted in Communist terms as entailing socialist regimes in Eastern Europe, seemed threatening to the United States, while the American vision of an open world, without arms, vetoes, or Iron Curtains, seemed threatening to the Soviets. To the Soviets, the United States, a capitalist power, was by definition an offense to socialism; to the United States, the Soviet Union was a revolutionary renegade whose purpose it was to undermine the international system. In Hoffmann's words,

> This is where the stuff of tragedy . . . can be found. The Soviet Union saw the United States as being far more deliberate and far more vigilant than the United States actually was. And the United States saw the Soviet Union as being far more ambitious and more in control of everything than the Soviet Union actually was. This can be confirmed by anybody who works in the field of perceptions: each side always tends to see his antagonist as being infinitely more cunning, centralized, controlling, and competent than he is. . . . The Soviet Union's policy was to a large extent defensive and cautious, but was pursued so vigorously that to many Americans and West Europeans, it looked like the policy of Genghis Khan reincarnate. On the other side, the United States had a policy which it viewed as defensive, but in some ways its own vision of the future was highly universal and implicitly imperialistic, in the sense that it wanted to see a world which would look much like the United States. And of course the United States, undevastated and indeed strengthened by the war, had the biggest weapons available to any nation in history. ("Revisionism Revisited," in Miller and Pruessen, pp. 16–18)

And so we must conclude that the Soviet-American conflict was inevitable. No one side was to blame, and all four of the factors we have considered were important in reinforcing and widening the early divisions, until the hostility reached a point beyond which effective cooperation was impossible.

As the Cold War heated up, it came to be waged in two main arenas: geopolitical competition over spheres of influence, and the arms race. The first arena involved struggles over the Third World, as well as periodic tests of the solidarity of the adversary's alliance system. Each superpower intervened, directly or indirectly, in neighboring countries whose alliance commitments or stability were in question. The United States invaded Cuba (1961), the Dominican Republic (1965), Grenada (1983), and Nicaragua (via the *contras*) and used covert action to overthrow left-leaning regimes in Guatemala (1954) and Chile (1973). The Soviet Union sent troops into Hungary (1956), Czechoslovakia (1968), and Afghanistan (1979) to reinforce crumbling socialist regimes and used a combination of political and military pressure to keep control in East Germany (1954) and Poland (1980). Each superpower also attempted to extend its influence into areas beyond its strictly regional security needs. For the Soviet Union, this involved probes in such places as Southeast Asia, Southern Africa, the Caribbean, and Central America. For the United States, it was the effort to create a structure of containment completely surrounding the Soviet Union. In many of these efforts, the superpowers acted through surrogates among their client states and Third World allies. Although American troops (in Korea, Vietnam, Cambodia, and Lebanon) and Soviet arms and military advice (in Cuba, Angola, Syria, Egypt, Libya, Ethiopia, and Nicaragua) played a significant role, none of these contests led to face-to-face conflict between the two powers. Their direct competition largely took the form of an ever-escalating arms race and the progressive development of strategic nuclear doctrines designed to forestall direct attack on one's home territory or on a vital military ally. The next sections will examine the policy of containment, the arms race, and Soviet-American rivalry in the Third World.

Containment in Europe and Asia

The Truman Doctrine and the Militarization of Containment

By March of 1947, when President Truman made his famous speech pledging American military and economic support against Soviet pressure in Greece and Turkey, the U.S.-Soviet split was irreparable. The language of this Truman Doctrine vividly dramatized the division: The United States must "help free peoples to maintain their free institutions and their national integrity against aggressive movements that seek to impose upon them totalitarian regimes." Every nation faced a choice between two antithetical ways of life, one based on freedom, the other on coercion, Truman said. The United States had an obligation to intervene wherever there was "attempted subjugation by armed minorities or by outside pressures." Peace and world order were inseparable goals; it was essential to maintain the internal stability of friendly regimes to prevent their becoming targets of aggression. These, Truman said, were the lessons of Munich. At the same time, Undersecretary of State Dean Acheson gave an alarming briefing to Congress in which he called the Soviets "an eager and ruthless opponent" whose acts had brought the two nations to the point of "Armageddon." Unless America stepped into the breach, "the corruption of Greece would infect Iran and all to the east. It would also carry infection to Africa through Asia Minor and Egypt, and to Europe through Italy and France." The eastern Mediterranean, Acheson continued, was at "a point where a highly possible Soviet breakthrough might open three continents to Soviet penetration."

Truman's speech cemented American perceptions of a hostile Soviet intent and launched a policy of military and political *containment* of the Soviet Union. With the concomitant failure of the Baruch plan to neutralize the nuclear threat and prevent a new arms race, the Soviets turned their energies toward acquiring a nuclear arsenal to match that of the United States. The Cold War had begun in earnest.

President Roosevelt had hoped to restore normal relations with the Soviet Union after the war, either by integrating it into the United Nations or by bilateral quid pro quo bargaining. Such an openhandedness and a clear recognition of the Soviet right to a great-power role would presumably have overcome earlier Soviet mistrust. But the Soviets, slow to adapt, remained relatively impervious to external influences, and it was the argument of George Kennan, American chargé d'affaires in Moscow, that the Kremlin leaders were too bound up in their suspicions ever to trust the West. They depended on a hostile attitude abroad to justify their repression at home. Consequently, concessions would not generate good will with the Soviets. In the short run, the only logic they were sensitive to was the logic of force. They could not be expected to respond to any form of rational persuasion or assurance. The best course for the United States to follow was to deal openly with the inevitable disagreements, maintaining an attitude of self-confidence and patience. The United States should show its determination to defend vital European interests. If the United States remained firm, the Soviet regime might mellow over time.

Kennan's advice was to abandon any universalist pretensions for restructuring the international order and to pursue instead a more realistic policy based on maintaining equilibrium. This would not bring harmony, but it could preserve America's security, by defining the national interest more prudently (and more modestly) and backing it by a firm commitment to maintain a balance of power. The Soviet Union, exhausted by the war, did not at the time pose a military threat in Europe, and Kennan's main concern was that neighboring regimes, in the throes of reconstruction, would become demoralized and fall prey to Communist propaganda or subversion. The United States therefore needed to support these countries politically and economically to make them resistant to Soviet influence.

But Kennan's advice became transposed, in implementation, from a defensive policy of economic aid and moral support into a strategy of military confrontation. The policy of containment metamorphosed from a commitment to America's vital interests in the European heartland, consistent with limited U.S. capabilities and a low interest in overseas engagement, into a strategy for policing the global peace wherever a threat to stability occurred. What began as an effort to support independent centers of power in Europe and Asia ended in dividing the world into Soviet and American spheres of influence. A policy aimed at inducing the Soviets to negotiate realistically on outstanding issues was replaced by a strategy of encircling the USSR with military alliances. Kennan's belief that reconciliation was not possible short of a change in the nature of the Soviet system was interpreted to mean that the United States could, and should, demand internal reforms as a condition of coexistence. In the depths of the Cold War, many zealots — including President Eisenhower's secretary of state, John Foster Dulles — went so far as to say that the United States should "roll back" Communism from Eastern Europe right to the Kremlin itself. Such a confrontational and unrealistic goal was bound to exacerbate differences between the two superpowers.

Several factors contributed to this expansion of the containment concept and the hardening of the Cold War. First, the Truman administration overemphasized the severity of the Communist threat, in order to combat American isolationist tendencies and to ensure a national defense budget adequate to meet America's new global responsibilities. A case in point is the famous National Security Council Memorandum NSC-68, which painted a very stark picture of the Soviet-American rivalry and had the unfortunate consequence of seeming to treat the whole world as a vital arena in the competition. Such an expansive definition of American national security actually put the Soviets in control and cast U.S. policy in a reactive mode. By exerting pressure in a part of the world where they enjoyed a local advantage, the Soviets could compel the United States to expand its commitments far beyond the limits of prudence. The result was a temptation to Soviet adventurism and a formula for fruitless conflict in areas of secondary importance.

Certain U.S. actions between 1948 and 1950 that stepped beyond mere defensive counterpressures aroused new Soviet insecurities and suspicions. These included the formation of the North Atlantic Treaty Organization (NATO), the creation of an independent West German state, the permanent stationing of U.S. military forces in Japan, and the decision to develop the hydrogen bomb. On the other hand, the fall of China to the Communists and the invasion of South Korea by Communist North Korea, which had Stalin's backing if not his blessing, aroused in Americans an enduring fear of Soviet expansionism. The invasion of South Korea, in June of 1950, confirmed American suspicions, and U.S. forces were quickly mobilized, under UN auspices, to defend South Korea. The United States suffered 142,886 casualties in Korea before an armistice was negotiated in July 1953. (Figure 5-2 depicts the military course of the war.) The Korean War marked the end of American isolationism and initiated permanent peacetime mobilization, setting off a pattern of reciprocal arms aid to the Third World to match the ever-swifter race in nuclear weapons and strategic bombers.

Misperceptions played as powerful a role at this stage of the Cold War as they had at the beginning. Soviet motives were extremely difficult to decipher; they seemed to oscillate between extreme belligerence and conciliation, particularly in the unstable years between the death of Stalin and Leonid Brezhnev's consolidation of control. The United States, each time it was challenged, felt compelled to respond with a compensating action or deployment aimed at creating a "situation of strength" from which it could extract Soviet concessions. From the Soviet perspective, this appeared to be an American effort to restore strategic superiority and deny the Soviet Union its rightful position of superpower equality. For example, the hydrogen bomb project — although it pushed the United States ahead in the arms race — was primarily America's anxious reaction to the shock of an earlier-than-expected Soviet atomic test. Such mutual insecurities constantly stimulated overreactions on each side. To work as Kennan had conceived it, containment required America to show self-confidence. Instead, Americans were frightened by the prospect of falling dominoes in Asia and by Soviet technological breakthroughs in the arms race. For deterrence to work, American military power had to be sufficiently strong to convey the U.S. determination to resist, without displaying aggressive intentions — a fine distinction that the Soviets, with their ideologically conditioned suspicions of capitalism, never appreciated.

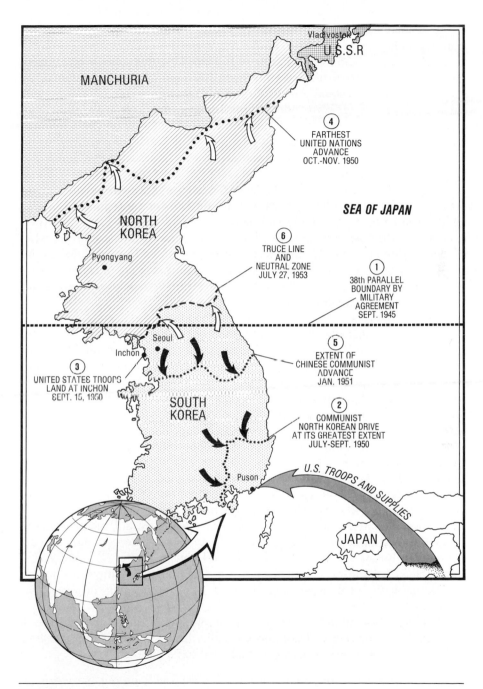

FIGURE 5-2
THE KOREAN WAR

A mismatch in strategy and military forces compounded the misunder-standings. The United States had no desire to match in manpower the consider-able Communist land forces, and so it turned to a doctrine of *massive retaliation*—the threat of direct nuclear retaliation against Communist ag-gression. Unable to equal America's technological capabilities, the Soviets chose to increase their conventional forces (redoubling American suspicions) and to engage in acts of deception, bluster, and bluff to hide their military inferiority. It was this pattern that tempted Nikita Khrushchev into putting intermediate-range nuclear missiles in Cuba in 1962 and the United States into its posture of "brinkmanship" in Cuba and elsewhere (such as the 1955 and 1958 confrontations over the islands of Quemoy and Matsu in the Taiwan Strait). The rivalry also began to express itself more and more in a rhetoric in which negotiating positions were taken for their propaganda value rather than in hope of any real agreement. The actual balance of power was not so critical as the *perception* of it. Soon, allies were being courted and arms added to the superpower arsenals less for their own sake than to protect or augment one power's image, prestige, and credibility. A long train of hostile encounters and failed disarmament negotiations was to follow.

Defense budgets in the Eisenhower years had remained somewhat limited. The policy of strategic deterrence was buttressed by the dispatching of tactical nuclear weapons to Europe, along with additional American ground forces to serve as a "trip wire," letting the Soviets (and the West Europeans) know that the United States was committed to defending NATO. But nuclear weapons were considered too risky and too blunt a tool to use in the Third World, where independence movements and guerrilla armies—only some of them Soviet backed—were challenging European colonial positions. Moreover, Third World revolutions seemed to be relatively immune to nuclear threats. Conse-quently, the United States sent arms, advisers, and in some cases troops into Indochina (Laos, Cambodia, Vietnam) and the Middle East (Egypt, Lebanon) to contain Communism, and it conducted covert operations in Iran, Guatemala, Indonesia, Cuba, and the Congo to restrain radical nationalist movements. The 1950s became famous for the U.S. policy of "pactomania," the creation of SEATO, CENTO, and other military alliances to form a deterrent ring around Communist Russia and China. As the Nixon Doctrine would do two decades later, these Eisenhower "New Look" strategies abetted indigenous forces in dealing with local aggression, without the commitment of American manpower.

Although the containment policy was largely successful in the two decades between 1947 and 1967, John Lewis Gaddis, in *Strategies of Containment*, singles out several features that eventually led to its failure:

1. It relied excessively on military means, and especially on nuclear weapons as the primary instrument of deterrence, thereby narrowing the range of feasible responses to aggression.

2. It failed to deter revolutions in the Third World or to make an adequate distinction between Soviet-backed subversion and indigenous nationalism.

3. It permitted the Soviet and Chinese Communists to set the terms of conflict and determine its locale.

4. It did nothing to promote arms control or to inhibit Soviet efforts to match the U.S. strategic delivery capability.

5. Based on the false premise of a monolithic Communism, it encouraged a policy of confrontation that was inappropriate, particularly after Khrushchev's de-Stalinization campaign and the Sino-Soviet split.

As a result, opportunities for the negotiated resolution of Soviet-American differences were neglected. Two decades later, George Kennan, the architect of containment, judged the implementation of his policy in these terms:

> [I]f the policy of containment could be said in later years to have failed, it was not a failure in the sense that it proved impossible to prevent the Russians from making mortally dangerous encroachments "upon the interests of a peaceful world" (for it did prevent that); nor was it a failure in the sense that the mellowing of Soviet power . . . failed to set in (it did set in). The failure consisted in the fact that our own government, finding it difficult to understand a political threat as such and to deal with it in other than military terms, and grievously misled, in particular, by its own faulty interpretation of the significance of the Korean War, failed to take advantage of the opportunities for useful political discussion when, in later years, such opportunities began to open up, and exerted itself, in its military preoccupations, to seal and to perpetuate the very division of Europe which it should have been concerned to remove. It was not "containment" that failed; it was the intended follow-up that never occurred. (*Memoirs, 1925–1950*, p. 365)

Vietnam and the Failure of Containment in Asia

Presidents John F. Kennedy and Lyndon Johnson set out to remedy some of the deficiencies of containment by introducing the element of *flexible response* into American strategy. But their notion of flexibility was largely confined to the choice of military options and was never effectively applied in the diplomatic arena. In particular, it involved the strengthening of nonnuclear military options. The crises in Berlin and Cuba had demonstrated the ongoing importance of conventional forces, and the growing U.S. commitment in Laos and Vietnam encouraged the creation of special counterinsurgency units that could be deployed in the Third World. The United States wanted to have a more symmetrical set of forces available to respond to Soviet threats, as well as a more diverse array of containment instruments, including political and economic programs to stimulate progressive change. The hope was that such massive projects as the Peace Corps and the Alliance for Progress could forestall revolutionary instability. Also, President Kennedy was beginning to consider the virtues of a negotiated solution to the Cold War, thanks to the chastening influence of the Cuban Missile Crisis (1962) and the promise of improved relations embodied in the Partial Nuclear Test Ban Treaty (1963). But then came President Johnson's decision to commit American troops in Vietnam, bringing a renewed emphasis on military containment that overshadowed any efforts at reconciliation. (For a picture of the military confrontation in Indochina, see Figure 5-3.)

Vietnam became the test case for the American containment policy, and the point at which the policy's flawed assumptions were most strikingly revealed. Containment had worked reasonably well in Europe because the conditions of conflict suited the policy. America's vital interests were clear and unmistakable, and public support at home was strong. The main instruments of containment in Europe were political and economic aid; the indigenous governments were reasonably stable, popular, and strong enough to fight on their own behalf, if given supplemental support. The risk of external aggression was real; the adversary (the Soviet Union) was clearly identifiable and subject to direct deterrence. None of these conditions were present in Southeast Asia.

Ostensibly the United States was fighting to preserve "democracy" in South Vietnam, whose defense was thought to be important to American power, prestige, and credibility. Besides, if the Vietnam domino fell, it would be the first in a long line of Communist victories that would threaten world order. If the United States could not successfully resist Soviet or Chinese aggression in Southeast Asia, then America's alliance commitments around the world would be brought into question. In fact, the South Vietnamese regime was a notoriously corrupt, incompetent, unstable, and unpopular military dictatorship, and the attack on it came from a largely indigenous force, the Viet Cong, which was fighting a popular nationalist crusade for control of the country. The Communist faction in this civil conflict clearly received outside support, but it was not controlled by any single source, no matter what the Americans said about everything being "Soviet-inspired aggression from North Vietnam." The Viet Cong received arms and economic aid from Eastern Europe, China, and the Soviet Union, but North Vietnamese troops did not become involved until late in the war. In any event, the North Vietnamese leader, Ho Chi Minh, was an independent and popular figure who would surely have won majority support if the democratic elections mandated by the Geneva Accords of 1954 had ever taken place. The United States, regarded in Vietnam as the neocolonial successor to the French imperialists, had refused to support this negotiated resolution, which had followed France's defeat by Vietnamese insurgents at Dien Bien Phu. Instead, the United States recognized a weak and hastily constructed alternative government under Ngo Dinh Diem. This government, its support confined to large cities and a few isolated pockets, was propped up by massive infusions of American dollars, advisers, and eventually troops.

Never in the course of the conflict was it clear who the United States was fighting or what vital interests it was trying to protect. After two decades, at the cost of half a million troops and hundreds of billions of dollars, America's main goal was to avoid the humiliation of defeat. However obscure, trifling, or mistaken the initial involvement had been, the United States had raised the stakes of the conflict so high as to affect perceptions of American power around the world. With the U.S. bombing of Laos and the invasion of Cambodia in 1971, the domino theory had become self-confirming: if the United States lost in Vietnam, it would lose the whole of the Indochinese peninsula to the Commu-

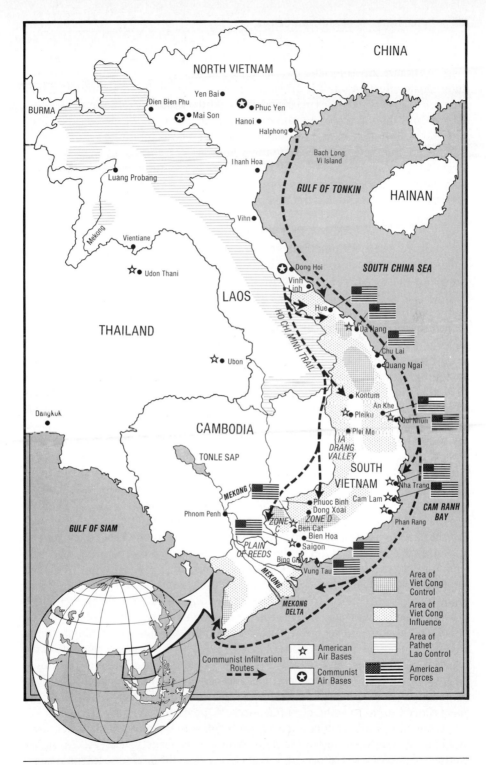

FIGURE 5-3
THE VIETNAM WAR (1965)

nists. At home, the American public's growing ambivalence about the war was making the effective pursuit of containment in Asia still more difficult. More than once, electoral politics provided a powerful temporary impetus for wading deeper into the swamp of Vietnam in the hope of eventual victory. But four successive administrations were not able to produce a convincing rationale for American involvement, and long-term support for the costly war was not forthcoming. American ignorance about Vietnamese affairs made it difficult to rally public support and impossible to fight the war effectively.

Preoccupation with Vietnam kept President Johnson from pursuing possible areas of agreement with the Soviets or Chinese and from taking strategic advantage of the developing Sino-Soviet split. The emphasis on global confrontation prevented the United States from appreciating the limits of its resources, power, and understanding. The rhetoric of containment obscured the weaknesses of the Soviet regime and the systemic factors that ruled against any policy of global hegemony. For more than a decade after Communism's permanent division, America's assumptions about Vietnam kept alive the notion of a monolithic Communism. A false model of external aggression prevented America from coming to terms with radical nationalism in the Third World and from assimilating the lessons of decolonization, which, ironically, had converted the Europeans into critics of the misguided affair in Vietnam. In addition, the staggering cost of the war impeded the U.S. effort to maintain its strategic nuclear superiority. In the period between the Cuban Missile Crisis (1962) and America's negotiated withdrawal from Vietnam (the Paris Agreements of 1973), the Soviets dramatically increased their land-based missile forces, bringing them up to effective strategic parity.

In sum, the United States was mistaken in trying to apply the lessons of European containment to Asia and the Third World generally. It treated a complicated social revolution and independence struggle as if it were a simple case of Communist expansion, to be contained by conventional military means. Communism played a different, and more genuinely popular, role in backward peasant societies than it did in the developed democracies of Europe, and the Communist forces in Asia were relatively free of direction from Moscow. Moreover, the United States did not possess the same capacity for stabilizing underdeveloped societies that were experiencing profound and rapid changes in their values and social structures. Consequently, anticommunism proved unreliable as a formula around which to rally faithful allies or establish stable governments in the Third World. In a diverse world undergoing revolutionary transformations, not all sources of instability could be attributed to the single cause of Soviet aggression. Sweeping commitments and vast expenditures were no substitute for a prudent calculation of U.S. national priorities and for policies tailored to the specific circumstances of the country involved.

Ironically, while Indochina eventually fell under Communist control, the original objectives of the containment policy were largely achieved. A global balance of power was restored in Europe and Asia, although due less to American military efforts than to the fragmentation of Communism and the revitalized economies of Japan and Western Europe. The Communists made no significant additional gains in the Third World except in Angola and Mozambique, where Portuguese colonial power had been particularly repressive and resistant to change. The Soviet Union's geopolitical influence in the Third World remained limited, and perhaps even diminished after 1975. And the Soviets were becoming more moderate and pragmatic, more willing to discuss such issues as arms control and détente. Their international posture did indeed mellow considerably, in the transition from Stalin to Khrushchev to Brezhnev to Mikhail Gorbachev, to the point of accepting diversity in the socialist camp and peaceful coexistence with capitalism. But before we examine the movement toward détente, let us explore another facet of Soviet-American rivalry, the arms race.

THE ARMS RACE

The overwhelming military capacity of the Soviet Union and the United States is by far the most important of all the factors that have marked them as the superpowers of the second half of the twentieth century. They have held a near monopoly of nuclear weapons and the complex intercontinental systems for delivering them, and this nuclear preponderance has made every other state vulnerable to them and dependent on one or the other for its security. Both powers were able to extend an umbrella of military protection over a large number of allies, due to their wide variety of conventional forces and to their invulnerable nuclear retaliatory capabilities. Although such military assets have allowed the United States and the Soviet Union to dominate their allies and client states, the fact that these two powers alone possess the nuclear capacity to destroy one another makes each uniquely vulnerable and highly sensitive to the arms procurement policies of the other. The mutual and mortal character of the nuclear threat joined the two countries in that relentless symbiotic competition we call the arms race.

The arms race began officially in August 1949, when the Russians exploded their first atomic weapon — a plutonium bomb of an advanced design that they developed almost half a decade earlier than expected. This atomic test exploded any illusions about a U.S. nuclear monopoly and spurred American development of a hydrogen (or thermonuclear) bomb. The decision reflected President Truman's initial impulse after Potsdam — to treat nuclear weapons as a trump with which to win diplomatic objectives that the United States had not been able to secure during the difficult wartime collaboration with the Soviets. But the decision, interacting with Soviet insecurities and xenophobia, also set off an action-reaction pattern of arms competition that has continued to this day.

While it no longer was the sole possessor of the secrets of the atomic bomb, the United States was able to preserve its nuclear dominance until 1957, largely because it had the largest number of operational bombs, an overwhelming superiority in delivery capability, and overseas bases in Europe and Asia within range of Russian territory. This was the period of the strategy called massive retaliation. For a decade after 1957, the United States remained predominant, but its lead was slowly eroding. The launching of the first earth satellite, *Sputnik,* in 1957 symbolized the rising Soviet challenge, but the real turning point was the Cuban Missile Crisis of 1962. Khrushchev had made the daring decision to compensate for Soviet inferiority "on the cheap," by secretly placing intermediate-range nuclear missiles in Cuba. U.S. intelligence discovered the missile sites only days before they were to become operational, and the United States demanded an immediate Soviet withdrawal. It threw up a naval blockade against the ships transferring the missiles, and the Joint Chiefs of Staff contemplated a "surgical" air strike against the Cuban emplacements. After thirteen tense days during which, in President Kennedy's words, the odds of nuclear war were "somewhere between one out of three and even," the Soviets backed down, in exchange for assurances that the United States would not invade Cuba. The missile crisis dramatized to the Soviets the weakness of their diplomatic bargaining position so long as their strategic—that is, intercontinental—nuclear delivery capability remained inferior. From the time of the humiliating retreat from Cuba, Khrushchev had to cater to the Kremlin hard-liners, who were committed to securing military equality with the United States no matter what the cost to the domestic economy.

After 1965, Soviet military spending rose steadily, and within a few years the Soviets had deployed enough rockets to create a situation of mutual deterrence. Although the two powers' strategic forces were by no means equal, the United States could no longer be sure it would not suffer unacceptable damage in retaliation for an attack on the Soviet Union. By 1971, the steady deployment of Soviet land-based missiles had brought an essential equivalence in the two powers' intercontinental ballistic missile (ICBM) forces. Overall parity, or rough equality, was reached in about 1980, by which time the Soviets matched the United States in all categories of nuclear weapons except cruise missiles and various tactical devices. (Figure 5-4 compares the U.S. and Soviet strategic nuclear forces.)

Differences of opinion in the late 1970s over which superpower held the nuclear advantage were more a reflection of the values of the analysts and their criteria than of an objective description of the respective forces. Many factors have made it difficult to compare the two arsenals. Because of the deployment lag, various components of the forces were in different stages of modernization, and deployment was affected by differences in the two countries' geography and technology. The Soviets' rockets and warheads were bigger, but the Americans' were more accurate. The Soviets concentrated on land-based forces; the Americans put most of their warheads in submarines. The effectiveness of weapons also had to be evaluated in light of the differing strategies and intentions of the two superpowers. Presumably the United States, which had no aggressive designs, did not need certain types of offensive weapons. On the other hand, the Soviets had to take account of nuclear threats from France, Britain, and China, which made their legitimate defensive requirements far more complex. The Americans believed in limited nuclear war and a first-use

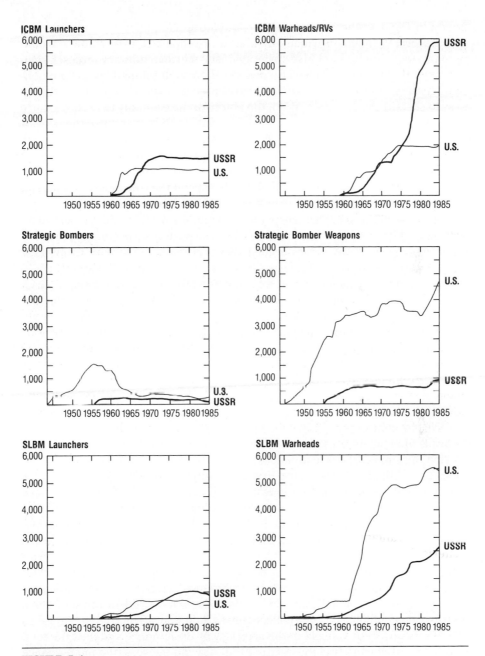

FIGURE 5-4
U.S. AND SOVIET STRATEGIC NUCLEAR FORCES

policy in Europe; the Soviets adopted a no-first-use policy but articulated a counterforce strategy in which any kind of threatened nuclear attack would precipitate a direct preemptive strike against American military forces. Calculations of the nuclear balance also depended on such intangibles as "momentum" in the arms race, the reliability of exotic technologies, the public's willingness to sustain the defense burden, the ability of the economy to produce more weapons, and the will of political decision makers to buy and use them.

The strategic nuclear balance was a central issue in the 1980 American presidential campaign. With Reagan's victory, the issue was resolved in favor of a new American arms buildup, to counter recent Soviet gains in strategic forces. The Reagan administration pledged to spend the sum of $1.8 trillion on a 600-ship navy, the deployment of Pershing II and cruise missiles in Europe, development of the MX/Peacekeeper missile and the B-1B bomber, research on a strategic defense system, or Star Wars, and the beefing up of defenses in many other categories. Many critics argued that this massive increase in military spending, particularly the purchase of so many new strategic weapons, could not be sustained in the long term, since it made little provision for spare parts, maintenance, and other support services. There were also complaints that the programs were being pressed too quickly, that production bottlenecks would occur and shortcuts in design and testing would exacerbate an already serious problem of technological failures. Nonetheless, the psychological and symbolic impact of the Soviet Union's having achieved parity, after so many years of American superiority, brought intense pressure from the public and from political leaders to restore America's "margin of safety" — testimony to the powerful effect of perceptions and prestige on the arms race.

Despite continuing U.S. technological dominance, periodic war scares and an occasional Soviet breakthrough have fed the anxieties of U.S. war planners and led the United States to initiate almost all the major escalations of the arms race. The United States was the first (and only) power to employ a nuclear weapon in actual war, the first to test a hydrogen bomb, the first to develop a bomber of transcontinental range, the first to deploy ICBMs in force, the first to put short-range nuclear weapons in Europe, the first to deploy submarine-launched ballistic missiles (SLBMs), the first to add multiple warheads (MIRVs), and the first to test and deploy cruise missiles. America holds a technological lead in such areas as computers, satellite reconnaissance, silent submarines, antisubmarine warfare techniques, tactical nuclear weapons (such as the neutron bomb), and the wide variety of anti-ballistic missile (ABM) and space technologies known collectively as Star Wars. The United States has also been consistently ahead in the accuracy of its guidance systems, the total number of warheads, and the overall reliability of its forces (the maintenance and readiness factor). The Soviets, on the other hand, were the first to test successfully an ICBM, an ABM, and an antisatellite weapon (ASAT), and they have been consistently ahead in the throw weight of their rocket launchers and in the total megatonnage of their warheads (because of their larger bombs and larger, if somewhat less reliable, liquid-fueled rockets). Since about 1970, the Soviets have also fielded a greater overall number of missile launchers, although deficiencies in their MIRV technology have kept them inferior in the number of warheads.

If the Soviets have led in relatively few areas, the psychological impact of those leads has nonetheless been very powerful. For example, their launching of *Sputnik* in 1957 indicated that they had the capacity for delivering intercontinental weapons via rocket and had transcended in one leap what had appeared to be a serious deficiency in long-range bombers. It was the first time that the Soviet Union beat the Americans in testing a technology. However, it was a very narrowly based crash program, benefiting from the concentration of resources possible in a centrally directed economy. Self-consciously planned as a propaganda coup, at a time when the Soviets still felt highly vulnerable, it came at the expense of more solid research in missile propulsion and design. Nonetheless, it catalyzed American research and jolted the United States into deploying a thousand Minuteman ICBMs early in the Kennedy administration.

The same pattern was repeated twenty years later in space technology. The Soviets' early research on lasers and their development, ahead of the United States, of an ASAT weapon, in conjunction with their suspected cheating on the Anti-Ballistic Missile Treaty, aroused great fear in the United States that they were about to make a breakthrough in Star Wars technology, or ballistic missile defense (BMD). However, the Soviet "killer satellite" program experienced a high number of test failures (more than 50 percent), even though its technology was relatively primitive. The United States, though slower to reach the testing phase, came up with a more sophisticated and reliable ASAT, which could be launched from an aircraft and could attack a target without going into orbit. Nonetheless, the timing of the Soviets' program, plus uncertainties about their intentions and the secrecy of their research, set off a vigorous debate over whether the United States was losing the space race.

As these two episodes make clear, the arms race is very much shaped by perceptions: short of war, there is no way to test who is in fact ahead. Some say that it is foolish to count missiles and warheads, once each superpower has a few hundred, since the level of destruction is so high. President Kennedy's secretary of defense, Robert McNamara, estimated that 200 megatons (roughly 200 to 400 warheads) was enough to destroy 75 percent of Soviet industry and 35 percent of the Soviet population. Under such conditions, aptly called mutual assured destruction (MAD), any additional weapons would seem to be superfluous. Also, Carl Sagan and other scientists have hypothesized that the explosion of even a few hundred nuclear bombs would so contaminate the atmosphere that the resulting "nuclear winter" would threaten the entire globe. Given that NATO and the Warsaw Pact *each* had over 11,500 strategic nuclear warheads by 1987, the level of overkill is considerable. The total number of warheads worldwide is roughly 50,000, including tactical and shorter-range nuclear weapons — an explosive yield of approximately 1 million Hiroshima bombs or 13 billion tons of TNT, about 3 tons for every man, woman, and child on earth.

The reason for so many weapons is the search for redundancy, the safety that comes from great numbers and a diversity of delivery systems. Redundancy has traditionally been found in the so-called strategic triad of land-based

ICBMs, sea-based SLBMs, and long-range bombers (see Figure 5-5). More recently, the triad has been augmented by the nuclear-tipped cruise missile, which can be launched from air, sea, or ground. Defense establishments on both sides have searched constantly for ways to make their nuclear arsenals more reliable and less vulnerable to a first strike or surprise attack. New generations of weapons have incorporated improvements in mobility, hardening, and communications, command, and control (called C^3). Advocates of modernization continue to argue for new procurements even if this swells the total number of warheads far beyond the threshold of minimum deterrence, or MAD.

Strategists prominent in the Reagan administration argued that such arms purchases were necessary to support a variety of new nuclear-war-fighting strategies, or nuclear utilization targeting strategies (NUTS). The most basic of these, variously called the damage-limiting or countervailing strategy, was meant to achieve two goals: prevent escalation and terminate hostilities in the event deterrence failed, or actually fight and prevail in a protracted nuclear conflict. In either case, the arms requirements were quite similar and involved matching the Soviets at every possible level, from tactical weapons (like nuclear-tipped artillery shells and mines) to intermediate-range or "theater" weapons (the U.S. Pershing II) to intercontinental missiles (the U.S. Minuteman III, MX, and Trident missiles). Such strategies relied on nuclear weapons that could launch an offense under adverse circumstances and could target military objectives (counterforce) or industry and population centers (countervalue). And the counterforce weapons had to be speedy, accurate, and fielded in sufficient numbers to convince the Soviets that the warhead-to-target ratio remained unfavorable to them, no matter what type of attack or defense they mounted.

Of course, as the Soviets have hardened their missile silos, increased the mobility of their rockets (by placing them on railway cars, for example), and improved their ballistic missile defense capability, the United States has multiplied its number of attacking warheads. Only by launching several warheads per target, presumably, can it ensure a "decapitating" blow in a preemptive first strike or deliver "assured destruction" in second-strike retaliation. The most significant step in raising the warhead-to-target ratio was the MIRV, or multiple independently-retargetable reentry vehicle, which placed multiple warheads (as many as twelve or fifteen) on a missile that hitherto had carried only one—thereby improving the weapon's "prompt hard-target kill capability." Other weapons, such as the slower but highly accurate cruise missile and manned long-range bombers, have given nuclear forces greater versatility and a recallable striking power. Also essential to a successful nuclear-war-fighting capability, many strategists say, are civil defense programs (to improve the survivability of industry and population centers), ABMs (to improve the survivability of retaliatory forces), and hardened communications, command, and control facilities (to permit the waging of a protracted nuclear war)—all measures that are unglamorous and low priority and have not received adequate funding. Thus, advocates of the countervailing strategy maintain that the

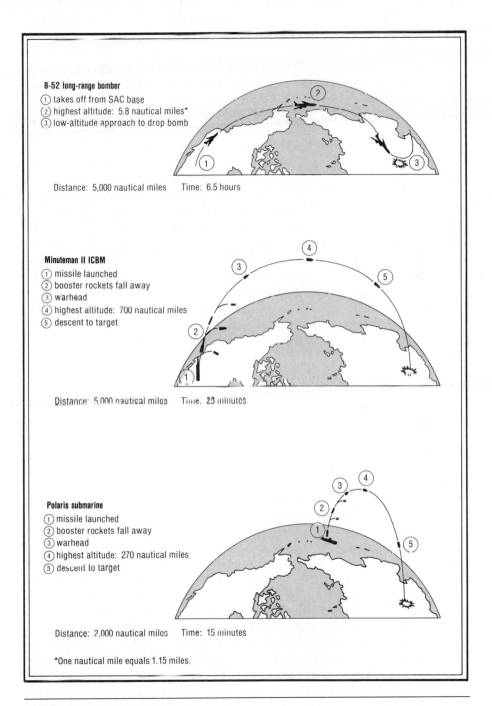

B-52 long-range bomber
① takes off from SAC base
② highest altitude: 5.8 nautical miles*
③ low-altitude approach to drop bomb

Distance: 5,000 nautical miles   Time: 6.5 hours

Minuteman II ICBM
① missile launched
② booster rockets fall away
③ warhead
④ highest altitude: 700 nautical miles
⑤ descent to target

Distance: 5,000 nautical miles   Time: 25 minutes

Polaris submarine
① missile launched
② booster rockets fall away
③ warhead
④ highest altitude: 270 nautical miles
⑤ descent to target

Distance: 2,000 nautical miles   Time: 15 minutes

*One nautical mile equals 1.15 miles.

FIGURE 5-5
THE TRIAD: THE THREE DELIVERY SYSTEMS OF THE U.S. STRATEGIC NUCLEAR FORCE

United States, for all its large number of weapons, is still inadequately defended.

Strategy and technology have always been interlinked in the arms race. It is difficult to separate the causal relationship between these two important factors. Most American strategic innovations, however, have involved shifts toward a counterforce targeting that could employ existing "excess" warheads and take advantage of ongoing advances in missile accuracy, and in this sense technology has driven strategy. The only area in which new strategic concepts have clearly preceded weapons technology is space warfare—Reagan's Star Wars program. His administration authorized the spending of approximately $25 billion over three years for "concept development" alone, with the aim of shifting to an absolutely fail-safe defensive strategy. This sum is equal to what typically was spent for an entire weapons system, start to finish. The aspiration was grand, but the scientific consensus was that prospects for a "hard shell" defense of the entire country were extremely poor. What seems more likely, though still unproved, is that more sophisticated versions of existing ABM technologies can be developed to protect America's increasingly vulnerable land-based missile forces. This would be a repetition of the more typical pattern, in which strategy comes afterward, as a justification for the deployment of a technology that exists in the defense industry's laboratories.

Both superpowers have strong military-industrial complexes that constantly pressure their decision makers to approve new weapons. At the most cynical level, these individuals and organizations have a self-interest in profits, career advancement, bureacratic entrenchment, and political power. More altruistically, the lobbying of the defense establishment reflects the conservative estimates that military professionals are obliged to make in safeguarding national security. On both sides, the arms race has been perpetuated by worst-case planning, which adopts the most pessimistic scenario possible and always imputes aggressive intentions to an adversary, even when an increase in military capability has been defensively motivated. The severity of the nuclear threat causes planners to exercise extreme caution in protecting against all possible threats—but caution in assessment means extravagance in expenditures. And escalation in arms procurement has become self-perpetuating, especially when one power's defense acts can so easily be interpreted by the enemy as aggressive. Secrecy is another complicating factor in the making of accurate strategic assessments: the Soviets' secretiveness in concealing or inflating their military capability has flagrantly distorted Western perceptions.

The length of time required for research and development (R&D) programs in advanced military technologies—ten years or more from conception to deployment—has served to keep the arms race going. One power started with a half-decade lead, and the two rivals have been playing technological leapfrog ever since. Typically, American weapons have reached the field first, but the compensating Soviet weapons often have incorporated more modern features that have aroused fears of Soviet momentum and American obsolescence—and then worst-case planning sets off a new round of U.S. R&D, which sends a signal to the Soviets that they dare not let up yet. Thus, arms control (discussed later in this chapter) is not only a matter of agreements on numbers of weapons but of halting the momentum of weapons research.

Of course, there have been times when diplomats have added their own calculations to those of the defense professionals. Both sides are concerned about being perceived as powerful, in an era when the danger of nuclear war rules out many of the traditional displays of "gunboat diplomacy." The caution induced by nuclear weapons makes the superpowers "helpless giants" and explains, in part, why they have lost limited wars with such secondary powers as Vietnam or Afghanistan. Nuclear capability is not readily translatable into diplomatic clout. All the weapons in the world will not deter an enemy who does not believe you will deliver on your threat. It is the determination to compete, to match the adversary arm for arm, that has the most powerful impact on superpower prestige and credibility. That is why the MAD threshold makes little difference; arms acquisitions are their own self-justifying indicators of a superpower's status and resolve. The danger, clearly, is that weapons acquired for political or psychological reasons will lose any rational relationship to a military or strategic purpose beyond making the other side look bad.

Herbert York, in *Race to Oblivion: A Participant's View of the Arms Race,* characterizes the arms race as fueled by "overreactions and technical excesses" motivated by "patriotic zeal, exaggerated prudence, and a sort of religious faith in technology" (p. 107). Nothing in four decades of Soviet-American arms rivalry, however, has been more powerful than fear and misperception. Throughout the Soviet thrust to superpower status — a halting effort in the 1950s, a more serious challenge in the '60s and '70s — there were repeated false alarms about the Soviets gaining the upper hand. Secrecy, Cold War fears, and politically motivated intelligence findings fueled these Red scares and led to successive new rounds of spending and weapons research. In each case — the bomber gap of the mid-1950s, the missile gap of the Kennedy-Nixon presidential campaign, the spending gap of the Ford administration, the window of missile vulnerability in the Reagan-Carter campaign, and the Star Wars gap — the Soviet threat has proved nonexistent or exaggerated. (For a detailed analysis of these false alarms, see Chapters 3 and 4 of the author's *American Foreign Policy and the Nuclear Dilemma.*) The Soviets have never had the capacity to outrun the United States in the arms race, nor have they seriously threatened to do so. They have pressed hard, however, in the geopolitical competition (Cuba, Vietnam, Angola, Nicaragua) and have taken conventional military measures that raised suspicions of an aggressive intent. These include the invasions of Czechoslovakia (1968) and Afghanistan (1979), the downings of the U-2 spy plane (1960) and Korean airliner KAL 007 (1983), and the use of Soviet military equipment, advisers, and Cuban troops in Angola (1975) and Ethiopia (1977). Regarding them as inflammatory acts, the United States responded with a military buildup that effectively ended the emerging strategic nuclear parity — showing the difficulty of disentangling the issue of nuclear arms, in which the superpowers have a mutual self-interest in restraint, from other areas of competition marked by a direct clash of interests. Soviet-American competition in the Third World has been a central source of such frictions.

SOVIET-AMERICAN RIVALRY IN THE THIRD WORLD

Soviet-American competition in the Third World falls into several distinct stages. At the beginning of the Cold War, the United States and the existing colonial powers had things largely to themselves. With its capacity for global power projection, the United States was readily able to impose itself on a South that was still in a colonial or neocolonial status. Challenges to the status quo were directly linked to the East-West struggle, and Third World regimes became pawns in the containment policy. American covert interventions in Iran and Guatemala in 1954 typified superpower dominance, and the one major conventional struggle of this early period, the Korean War, was fought by forces under the direct command of outside powers. Even Cuba, whose revolution began under independent leadership, fell quickly into the status of a Soviet satellite — evidence of the strictly bipolar division of the globe at this stage of the Soviet-American rivalry. Soviet support for Third World revolutions was largely rhetorical, however, with direct military assistance going only to countries with Communist governments.

The Soviet Union adopted a more visible and vigorous Third World role after the stalemate in Korea and the death of Stalin. Khrushchev saw a common interest between national liberation movements and Soviet foreign policy, and between 1954 and 1964 the Soviet Union sent abroad more than $2.7 billion in arms, 80 percent of them to non-Communist nations. Indonesia, for example, received about $1 billion in weapons to back Sukarno's foreign policy in the Sumatran rebellion (1958–60), his fight with the Dutch over West Irian (1961–62), and the "Crush Malaysia" campaign of 1963–65. At the same time, the United States was extending its formal alliance structure to provide collective security guarantees to South Korea, Taiwan, the Philippines, Thailand, Pakistan, Turkey, Iran, and others. As independence movements blossomed, the two superpowers actively courted the new states.

Once a superpower had found compelling reasons to enter a Third World conflict, it tended to expand what had been a regional dispute into a geopolitical or ideological test of the global balance, a dynamic that persisted in some locales into the 1970s and '80s. Angola and Nicaragua, for example, are two strategically located Southern states whose civil conflicts became symbolic arenas for the testing of superpower intentions, and in both places the Northern involvement showed how vulnerable the weaker Southern states still were. A new regime that was strongly opposed by one superpower was unlikely to survive without the help of the other; if one faction in a civil war received significant outside arms aid, all the other factions were compelled to seek outside patrons as well. Since the superpowers' credibility was tested by their wins and losses in the Third World, the North tried to impose its own strategic agenda on civil or regional struggles in the South. Thus, Angola became the centerpiece of Soviet initiatives in Africa aimed at maintaining the global military and diplomatic momentum stemming from the Communist victory in Vietnam. For the United States, Nicaragua became the focus of Reagan's "rollback" anti-Communist strategy and a test of America's determination to support "freedom fighters" around the world. (Figure 5-6 shows the American-Soviet balance in the Caribbean at the end of the Reagan presidency.)

After 1962, however, instances of direct Soviet-American confrontation were the exception. The Cuban Missile Crisis and the Sino-Soviet split altered strategic perceptions and introduced caution into Soviet decision making. Khrushchev's unpredictable adventurism was replaced by the pragmatism of Leonid Brezhnev and Aleksey Kosygin. The humiliation of the nuclear showdown in Cuba had demonstrated to the Soviet leadership that nuclear parity was a precondition to a forward policy in the Third World. They continued to

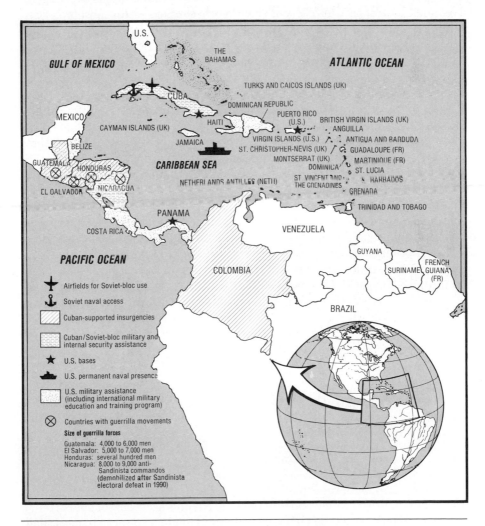

FIGURE 5-6
SOVIET-AMERICAN RIVALRY IN THE CARIBBEAN BASIN

seek global allies, exporting $6.5 billion in arms between 1965 and 1972, but they imposed no ideological litmus test, and, for old-fashioned balance-of-power and geopolitical reasons, much of the aid went to military governments and conservative regimes. In this realpolitik diplomacy, the Soviets were careful not to interpose forces beyond their immediate sphere of influence. In fact, from 1945 to 1979, no Soviet ground troops saw combat outside the boundaries of the Warsaw Pact.

The United States, on the other hand, became bolder after the Cuban crisis and the defection of Communist China from the Soviet bloc. President Kennedy adopted an active counterinsurgency policy aimed at preventing any more takeovers like Castro's in Cuba. Both he and Johnson committed covert operatives and U.S. troops in a variety of Third World conflicts—the most important being Vietnam. The Soviets, meanwhile, were preoccupied with their succession struggle and with internal divisions in their own bloc. When they invaded Czechoslovakia in 1968 and became embroiled in border conflicts with the Chinese in 1969–71, the United States chose to remain aloof. Even in this period of active U.S. interventionism, the specter of nuclear war introduced caution in direct Soviet-American dealings. The October War of 1973 in the Middle East reinforced the lesson that the superpowers could become entangled in supporting their erstwhile clients far beyond the point at which their own interests were affected—a lesson taught still more painfully by the U.S. decision to abandon its commitment in South Vietnam.

The fall of Saigon marked the end of an era. The U.S. defeat in Vietnam shattered perceptions around the world about American invincibility and demonstrated to the Third World that a military alliance with a nuclear superpower was no absolute guarantee of security. Quite the contrary, nuclear parity after 1973 made it increasingly risky for one superpower to engage its prestige or its military forces in an arena where it might encounter direct opposition from its rival. Indeed, since 1962, nearly all the direct U.S.-Soviet military confrontations in the Third World have been the result of entrapment or miscalculation; neither the USSR nor the United States has planned or initiated an intervention where it expected active resistance from the other. Nonetheless, confrontations have been all too frequent.

DÉTENTE, ARMS CONTROL, AND EAST-WEST TRADE

Facing defeat in Vietnam and the prospect of further conflict in the Third World, the Nixon administration launched a serious effort in the 1970s to contain the Soviet Union by less confrontational means. For economic and survival reasons, both superpowers had a stake in arms control, which became the cornerstone of the new policy of détente. Nixon's secretary of state, Henry Kissinger, who devised the policy, hoped that it might also serve to deescalate competition in the Third World.

The first serious effort at arms control goes back to the Cuban Missile Crisis of 1962, which dramatized the unique risks of the nuclear era and demonstrated to the superpowers that they had a mutual interest in nuclear restraint. Before then, negotiations between them had centered around the vaguely defined goal of "complete and universal disarmament" — so all-encompassing as to guarantee the sterility of the talks. The United Nations Disarmament Subcommittee had become the scene of a propaganda battle in which the two nuclear giants bashed one another with an unrelenting exchange of unrealistic proposals. The most they managed to agree on was the multilateral Antarctic Treaty of 1959, which prohibited military uses of that frozen and unpeopled continent. After 1962, however, the Soviet Union and the United States began to bargain seriously. Early in 1963 they signed a hot-line agreement giving them the ability to communicate rapidly in a crisis, and this was quickly followed by the Limited Test Ban Treaty of 1963, which banned nuclear testing in the atmosphere, in outer space, and under water.

The Limited Test Ban Treaty was successful for several reasons. It responded to sustained public outcry and overwhelming scientific evidence about the harmful effects of radioactive fallout. It could easily be monitored by technical means that did not require intrusive on-site inspections. It increased security by introducing uncertainty into the superpowers' deterrence calculations; without precise testing, neither side could know, for example, the effect of electromagnetic pulses on communications, the true utility of hardened silos, or the possibility of "fratricide" (one exploding warhead triggering others). Other multilateral agreements followed: the Outer Space Treaty of 1967, which prohibits nuclear weapons in space or on celestial bodies; the Treaty Prohibiting Nuclear Weapons in Latin America (signed at Tlaltelolco, Mexico, in 1967); and the Nuclear Non-Proliferation Treaty of 1968, which sought to prevent the spread of nuclear weapons beyond those countries already possessing them and called for arms control among the existing nuclear powers.

A more intensive bilateral pursuit of arms control ensued, in the period between 1971 and 1979, marked by a Cold War thaw and the policy of détente. On the U.S. side, the immediate impetus for improved relations came from the failure of containment in Vietnam and the Nixon administration's desire to enlist Soviet cooperation in an "honorable" American withdrawal. The Vietnam War had brought home two points: Third World nationalist regimes, Communist or not, were not going to be the stooges of either superpower, and the costs of involvement in civil wars on the periphery, successful or not, far exceeded any likely strategic gains. On the Soviet side, deployment of the first generation of land-based ICBMs was complete, and the Soviets needed to shift resources into the hard-pressed consumer sector. In particular, they wanted to open up trade with the West, in order to alleviate their critical grain shortage and to gain Western capital and technology for developing Siberian oil and natural gas.

Changing American Attitudes and Interests

On both sides, fundamental changes of attitude were paving the way for détente. Richard Barnet, who has chronicled the changes in *The Giants: Russia and America,* points out that Vietnam was but one act in the larger drama of America's decline. Economic problems were making it more difficult to extract the sacrifices required by an all-out arms race, let alone the costly war in Indochina. De Gaulle in France and Willy Brandt in Germany were challenging traditional American prerogatives. The United States was beginning to confront an anti-American majority in the General Assembly of the United Nations, where the new states of the Third World were moving toward neutralism and nonalignment. Instability continued in Latin America, once an American preserve; particularly threatening was the election of a Marxist, Salvador Allende, as president of Chile in 1970. The Soviet position was likewise deteriorating, due to a declining domestic economy and international opposition from independent Communist movements in China and Eastern Europe. The conjunction of these forces was shifting the balance of power from a predominantly bipolar to a multipolar one.

The United States saw all this as an opportunity to seek improved relations with the Communist world, at a time when it needed a respite from skyrocketing defense budgets and overextended commitments in the Third World. The Nixon doctrine, as set forth by the president and his chief foreign policy adviser, Henry Kissinger, concluded that the United States no longer possessed the power or the will to police "gray areas" of the world. The doctrine advocated the Vietnamization of the war in Southeast Asia, as part of a larger process of having local forces assume the responsibility for regional stability, freeing the nuclear superpowers to compose their differences at the strategic level. Kissinger also believed that the Sino-Soviet dispute indicated that the Soviet Union had converted from a revolutionary state into a revisionist, status quo power. In December 1969, Kissinger stated that the United States has "no permanent enemies" and that "we will judge other countries, including Communist countries, . . . on the basis of their actions and not on the basis of their domestic ideology." Soviet-American relations should move beyond the balance-of-power competition, he said, toward a more interdependent relationship rooted in the "habits of mutual restraint, coexistence, and, ultimately, cooperation."

In short, a policy of global confrontation with Communism had become too expensive and too risky; containment and the arms race should be replaced by a policy of détente. In the Kissinger view, U.S. interests would be better served by an opening to China, to create a triangular balance, and by arms control agreements that would limit the Soviet threat to American security. Opposition to the Vietnam War had destroyed the foreign-policy consensus that had been the basis for containment. Consequently, the Russians were more likely to be "contained" through political and economic inducements that brought them into the family of nations and gave the Soviets a stake in maintaining international order. The economic warfare associated with containment had only sealed the Soviet Union ever more firmly behind its Iron Curtain; perhaps more liberal trade could serve as the entering wedge for a flow of information and ideas that would break down the closed Soviet system. Besides, the United States was suffering from an unprecedented trade imbalance and could profit handsomely from the untapped market of more than a billion potential customers in the Communist bloc. Credits, technology, and long-term economic relationships could be incentives to good political behavior and might set up a "linkage" between the Soviet interest in expanded trade and the U.S. interest in restraining Soviet adventurism. Moreover, the Soviets' interest in parity and a cap to the arms race could lead them to moderate their posture in regional disputes.

Kissinger also was well aware that Third World nationalism was working against the interests of both superpowers. Egypt, for example, had accepted a large contingent of Soviet troops after its defeat in the 1967 Arab-Israeli War, but in 1972 it kicked them out, largely because of a fear of Soviet meddling in domestic affairs. Given this passion for nonalignment, the United States had decided it could safely support a Marxist guerrilla leader, Robert Mugabe, in Zimbabwe (formerly British Rhodesia) so long as he remained an independent nationalist outside the Soviet orbit. Kissinger feared that efforts to control revolutionary movements by force would only lead to more Vietnams and push insurgents into military and economic dependency on the Soviet Union. Left alone, he thought, radical nationalists would gravitate naturally toward neutralism.

Changing Soviet Attitudes and Interests

The death of Stalin and the succession of Khrushchev had brought important changes in the Soviet Union. Domestically, Khrushchev was a reformer, liberal by Soviet standards. His far-reaching changes, aimed at establishing socialist legality and ending Stalinist terror, converted the former totalitarian system into a more pragmatic authoritarian regime. Khrushchev also introduced important changes in foreign policy and in the Marxist-Leninist interpretation of relations between socialism and capitalism. Despite his reputation for bluster and erratic behavior, he articulated a doctrine of peaceful coexistence that attempted to adapt socialist thought to the realities of nuclear annihilation. He continued to declare that the victory of socialism was inevitable and that the Soviet Union had a right to support liberation in the Third World. But he emphasized that the socialist victory would not come via nuclear war and did not require the exercise of Soviet military power abroad. Later, under Brezhnev and Kosygin, the leadership became at once more bureaucratic, more collectivized, and more responsible, though the ruling elite remained relatively narrow. The regime became more cautious in foreign policy and progressively more preoccupied by the faltering domestic economy. Khrushchev's aggressive economic measures had failed; his ambitious "virgin lands" campaign, designed to end perennial agricultural shortfalls, was a disaster. By 1972, after a series of bad harvests, Brezhnev was forced to purchase grain abroad — $250 million worth from the United States. Khrushchev's adventures in Berlin and Cuba had also resulted in Soviet humiliation. As a consequence, Brezhnev adopted a policy of strategic arms buildup at home and restraint abroad.

The Soviet Union's less zealous ideological posture reflected both the maturity of the regime, which had acquired many vested interests, and divisions within the international Communist movement. To keep any influence over the changing Eurocommunist parties, for instance, the Soviets had to accept their nonrevolutionary, parliamentary orientation. There were constant difficulties with the socialist bloc states in their own backyard. East Germany, Hungary, Czechoslovakia, and Poland experienced steady turmoil from the 1950s on. The invasions of Hungary in 1956, Czechoslovakia in 1968, and Afghanistan in 1979, far from showing expansionism, were evidence that the Soviet grip on its satellites was eroding. Each was a desperate last-ditch effort to salvage Soviet prestige and prevent a neighboring Communist state from departing the socialist camp altogether. In the case of Afghanistan, always well within the Russian sphere of influence, the Soviet leadership badly miscalculated the American reaction and was genuinely surprised to find the issue threatening the whole fabric of détente. But perhaps it had been misled by Western acquiescence in the 1968 invasion of Czechoslovakia, which had had little effect on the emerging U.S. interest in détente.

Meanwhile, shifts in the strategic balance were bringing the Soviets their first fleeting moments of parity. With some hard bargaining on arms control, they might be able to head off a new round of weapons procurement that their sluggish economy could ill afford. From the Soviet point of view, the United States had used its nuclear superiority as a strategy to neutralize disadvantageous shifts in other global forces. Domestically, the arms race had saved capitalism (temporarily) by boosting production and absorbing excess capital. Internationally, the arms race had reinforced America's tendency to react militarily to economic, political, and ideological challenges. If the Soviet Union could get the United States to agree to arms restraint, the West would lose its most powerful weapon. And the Soviet Union, besides winning recognition as a coequal, would be relieved of the awful threat that nuclear war could rob socialism of its inevitable victory. It is unclear whether the Soviet leadership considered détente as offering a breathing spell while socialism gathered its strength for a final push, or whether it took the more pessimistic (and revisionist) view that Soviet Communism was losing the scientific-technical revolution. In either case, the short-term effect was to reinforce the Soviet interest in improved political and economic relations with the West.

The Soviets had also begun to fear a nuclear attack from a new quarter. China, their historical enemy, had exploded both fission and fusion bombs and had tested its first intercontinental ballistic missile between 1964 and 1967. The Chinese then installed nuclear weapons on submarines they had received from the Soviets in the years before the Sino-Soviet split. By 1965, the Chinese were denouncing the Soviet state as a "socialist imperialist" power and a traitor to the cause of Marxism-Leninism. Meanwhile, long-festering territorial claims were reopened publicly, and in 1967 the Soviet embassy was physically attacked. A further provocation was a series of border disputes along the Ussuri and Amur rivers between 1969 and 1971, in which several hundred troops lost their lives. The Soviets were alarmed enough to consider a preemptive strike against China's infant nuclear facilities. But eventually their desire to defuse this new threat without risking war between the two leading socialist states pressed the Soviets toward stabilizing their relations with the United States. They also began to call for global limits on the arms race — pushed along by the adroit diplomacy of Kissinger's visit to China as a preface to the Moscow summit of 1972.

On the positive side, the Soviets were feeling more secure, because of their missile buildup and because the U.S. blunder in Vietnam had, at least temporarily, shifted the Third World balance in their favor. They were optimistic about their long-term prospects in the Third World and were showing a new sophistication toward the outside world. On the negative side was a stodgy and inefficient economy, in which all important groups were accommodated but output faltered. An overcentralized concentration of resources on military production was causing the Soviets to fall further and further behind in high technology. Consumer goods were in very short supply, and the chronically deficient system of collectivized agriculture was absorbing most new capital investment, with scant results. With ideological fervor waning, the authoritarian regime could manage public unrest only by delivering improvements in the standard of living or by returning to Stalinist methods. But the Stalinist legacy of excessive secrecy persisted as a stultifying factor on Soviet technical innovation. So Brezhnev faced a difficult choice: liberalize the regime at home or seek the necessary technology and grain abroad through a more liberal trade policy. The latter seemed by far the less risky route. At the Twenty-fourth Party Congress, in 1971, Brezhnev made a public commitment to détente, staking his prestige on a policy of strategic arms limitations and "peaceful entanglement" with the United States.

The Substance of Détente

Détente came to be defined through a series of agreements on four subjects. The first was the status of Germany, particularly Berlin, and the resolution of Soviet-American differences in Europe. A four-power agreement, signed on September 3, 1971, guaranteed Western access to Berlin, normalized relations between East and West Germany, and recognized the Oder-Neisse Line as the border between Poland and East Germany. The agreement constituted an implicit mutual recognition of the postwar status quo in Europe. The 1975 Helsinki Accords extended the settlement of outstanding East-West issues. This Conference on Security and Cooperation in Europe officially recognized the division of Germany and the legitimacy of the Communist regimes in Eastern Europe, in exchange for a Soviet commitment to protect human rights and permit the freer exchange of persons and information between the blocs. It also implemented certain "confidence-building measures," such as the obligation of the NATO and Warsaw Pact countries to give each other advance notice of military maneuvers.

A second area of agreement involved expanded trade and scientific and cultural exchanges. There were the joint *Apollo-Soyuz* ventures in space and the exchange visits of the Bolshoi Ballet and American jazz and rock performers. More important was the trade expansion. U.S. exports to the Soviet Union grew from $100 million in 1971 to almost $2.5 billion by 1976, and American business ventures began to crack the Soviet market, in which the French, Germans, and Japanese had already made serious inroads. Soviet petroleum and natural gas flowed west, in exchange for grain sales that benefited U.S. farmers. In 1972, for example, Occidental Petroleum concluded a $3 billion deal for the exploitation of Siberian natural gas, while the Soviets purchased more than $1 billion worth of American grain. At the same time, a long-standing economic grievance was settled by the Soviet agreement to pay $722 million over twenty-nine years on its old lend-lease debt.

Third, the superpowers reached several agreements on improved bilateral relations and crisis resolution. In 1971 they signed an updated hot-line agreement and an Agreement to Prevent Accidental Nuclear War. At the Moscow summit in May of 1972, Nixon and Brezhnev laid out ground rules for peaceful coexistence, in the form of a Statement of Basic Principles — especially important to the Soviets because it was the first document to recognize them as a legitimate coequal power with the United States. A subsequent Agreement on the Prevention of Nuclear War obliged the two superpowers to consult in "situations capable of causing a dangerous exacerbation of their relations" and charged them with "a special responsibility. . . . to do everything in their power so that conflicts or situations will not arise which would serve to increase international tensions."

The heart of détente, however, lay in the fourth area: arms control. An early breakthrough came in the Strategic Arms Limitation Talks (SALT), in May 1971, when each side made major concessions that paved the way for several subsequent treaties. The Soviets agreed not to count the U.S. forward-based systems, such as aircraft carriers and jet fighters based in Europe — all capable of delivering nuclear payloads to Soviet soil. The Americans dropped their insistence on strict numerical equality in launchers, permitting the Soviets to retain their three-to-two advantage in long-range missiles. In 1972, the two powers signed an Interim Agreement to Limit Offensive Strategic Arms, which established specific ceilings on the number of missile launchers in each arsenal. The Soviet ceilings were higher, but the treaty excluded long-range bombers, in which the United States held a decisive advantage, and placed no limits on MIRV technology or on the number of warheads, in which the United States was also ahead. Though critics said otherwise, and it was difficult to compare two very different arsenals, SALT appeared to be a codification of rough equality between the superpowers. To protect the stability of deterrence, an Anti-Ballistic Missile Treaty prohibited the deployment of a nationwide defense that might challenge the penetration capabilities of the other side's retaliatory forces. Ongoing negotiations also yielded a Threshold Test Ban Treaty in 1974, which banned underground tests larger than 150 kilotons, and a Peaceful Nuclear Explosions Treaty in 1976, which regulated the use of nuclear devices in mining, excavation, and other peaceful pursuits. A follow-on agreement on offensive strategic weapons was negotiated between 1974 and 1979. This SALT II Treaty set aggregate limits on the number of launchers and warheads, a ban on construction of certain types of launchers, limits on future deployments, and verification procedures. It established a Standing Consultative Commission to arbitrate disputes over interpretation and enforcement. Again each side compromised: the agreement excluded both U.S. ground-launched cruise missiles and Soviet Backfire bombers because of a controversy over defining them as strategic delivery vehicles. These aside, SALT II established equal aggregate limits on all types of intercontinental nuclear delivery systems, with sublimits on the number of MIRVed launchers. Other multilateral accords reached during this period include: the Seabed Arms Control Treaty (1971), the Biological Weapons Convention (1972), the Environmental Modification Convention (1977), and the Convention on the Physical Protection of Nuclear Material (1980).

The Decline of Détente

Although the arms control effort carried through to the end of the Carter administration and beyond, détente began to fade with Kissinger's departure from government in 1976. His skill in diplomacy had been a prime factor in crafting the delicate new web of relations, and his realpolitik, balance of-power philosophy had proved ideal for bridging the gap between the Soviet and American concepts of détente. But the different images of international affairs that had kept the two powers apart for decades remained, to become one of the underlying factors in the erosion of détente. Soviet ideologues viewed peaceful coexistence within the Marxist frame of an ongoing competition between social systems. Although the Soviets did not believe that war is necessary to the advance of socialism, they never expected détente to further remove ideological or class contradictions or to establish harmony between the competing systems. To them, détente was a strategic acknowledgment of the nuclear realities and a tactical adaptation to economic circumstances. Since nuclear technology was here to stay, some features of détente might be extended indefinitely, but no convergence or fundamental reconciliation of the two systems was possible. To the Soviets, détente did not imply any commitment to liberalize their internal political system or to abandon their world revolutionary aspirations. The two superpowers could recognize one another's legitimate national interests and agree to resolve their own disputes peaceably, but meanwhile the Soviets would give political, economic, and moral support to liberation struggles around the globe and await the verdict of history.

Détente took on a distinctly different cast in American eyes. The range of public opinion was broader with respect to its virtues (or vices), and much more polarized. Die-hard anti-Communists criticized it from beginning to end as a Machiavellian ruse in line with Lenin's dictum of "Two steps forward, one step back." Some conservatives saw the Soviets' interest in détente as a sign of their weakness and a tacit admission that they could not compete with the

United States in the arms race; consequently, it was not a time for concessions, but for pressing all the harder to drive the Soviets into submission. But the majority, showing the kind of idealism that has so marked American foreign policy, were prepared to believe that peace was at hand. In this respect, the pragmatism of the policy-making elite was out of step with the more naive mood of the public. Most Americans expected détente to be the beginning of friendship and the end of Cold War. Kissinger's more limited view was that of classical diplomacy: one great power cannot afford to ignore another, whatever their ideological differences may be. In 1974, Kissinger described détente as "a process of managing relations with a potentially hostile country in order to preserve peace while maintaining our vital interests." Though conflicts were inevitable, détente was a mode for defusing the nuclear threat and moderating the Soviet exercise of power until such time as the forces of liberty and truth could work their will. This was not so far from the Soviet concept of peaceful coexistence, though the theories diverged, of course, in the judgment about which side was favored by God, history, or nature. But, as a former U.S. ambassador to the Soviet Union, Malcolm Toon, has remarked, the idea of détente sometimes engendered "uncritical and heedless euphoria" in the minds of Americans, who thought "a millennium of friendship or mutual trust has arrived."

Détente could survive as long as the realpolitik faction was in charge of both governments. But once détente became the subject of political controversy, as was bound to occur, its pragmatic basis was undercut by critics on both sides with ideological axes to grind. A prime example is the effect the Jewish emigration issue had on U.S.-Soviet trade, one of the key elements of détente. Important to the Soviet Union in its economic relations with the United States was the granting of most-favored-nation status, which would have placed Soviet goods on a competitive par with all other U.S. imports. But Senator Henry Jackson, a Democrat from Washington and an unremitting Cold Warrior, insisted that such status be tied to a more liberal Soviet policy on Jewish emigration. To this end, in 1974 he introduced the Jackson-Vanik amendment, which set a minimum annual emigration quota of 60,000 Jews as a condition for the trade liberalization. Between 1970 and 1973, to court American favor, the Soviets had unilaterally loosened Jewish emigration, which leaped from 230 to more than 35,000 annually. After the Jackson amendment was introduced, however, they sharply curtailed exit visas and repudiated the Soviet-American trade agreement, contending that the United States was interfering in their internal affairs. Kremlin hard-liners accused the United States of betraying the spirit of détente and violating long-recognized principles of national sovereignty. Feelings were sufficiently intense that the Soviets swallowed a considerable economic loss rather than let their emigration policy appear to be dictated by the United States.

The Jewish emigration issue also became embroiled in differing interpretations of the human rights provisions of the Helsinki Accords. The Americans stressed the traditional rights of liberalism — the political rights of individuals and the procedural rights of a democratic pluralist society. The Soviets emphasized the economic rights that attach to membership in a socialist collective, including the rights to food, clothing, housing, education, medical care, and employment. Free emigration fell in the category of procedural rights, which the Soviets considered secondary. To Americans, however, the Soviet emigration restrictions appeared to be a violation of the Helsinki Accords and confirmed their old suspicions that the Russians could not be trusted.

One paradox of détente was that the Soviets' increasing contacts with the West made the Soviet party elite more repressive in combating the domestic impact of liberalized relations. Increased communication, trade, and cultural exchanges were bound to bring profound changes to the closed Soviet society — as the dramatic pace of change in the Gorbachev era displays ever more emphatically. But Brezhnev was determined to limit the effects of détente to foreign affairs, and as a result, elements of Stalinist orthodoxy were resurrected. They did much to defeat the Soviet effort to establish normal relations abroad, since they sent confusing signals about the regime's motives. In both societies, internal political disputes generated double messages that were read differently by domestic and foreign audiences. But the problem was particularly striking on the Soviet side, where Brezhnev, in order to hold off the Kremlin hard-liners, periodically had to reaffirm the orthodoxy of his ideological credentials. Was a particularly hard-hitting speech intended only for domestic consumption, leaving pragmatism to reign in foreign policy, or did it indicate he was using détente as one more Marxist tactic to lull the West into complacency?

In America, President Nixon's impeccable anti-Communist credentials largely saved him from backbiting and second-guessing by his domestic opposition. But President Ford, facing a vigorous challenge within his own party from the conservative Ronald Reagan, had to back away publicly from détente, even while his secretary of state continued to practice it. Kissinger struggled, too, caught in a delicate balancing act abroad that was difficult to interpet to the public back home, where opponents could readily trot out the old ideological rhetoric. Since he was a master of public relations and skillful in dealing with the press, he was able to "sell" détente with consummate success in the short run. But it was often at the cost of repeating clichés, arousing false expectations, and catering to millennial hopes for an end to the Cold War. Still, it seems unfair to fault him for his failure to alter, in only a few years, anti-Communist attitudes that had been built up over decades. His initial overtures to China and Russia were accepted enthusiastically by a public eager to exit Vietnam and responsive to all the diplomatic hoopla, but the Nixon-Kissinger team could never have hoped to sustain this level of support through the preoccupations of Watergate. Kissinger's popularity and the effectiveness of his personal shuttle diplomacy helped to keep détente alive, even in the midst of regional crises that called its assumptions into question, but once Kissinger and his sustaining diplomatic vision were gone, détente began to come apart.

One critical area of misunderstanding was the question of linkage. Although Kissinger himself was ambivalent on this point, most Americans felt that détente implied a commitment to restraint in all aspects of Soviet-

American competition. Consequently, arms control agreements (which many American conservatives accepted reluctantly) came to be linked explicitly to Soviet good behavior in the Third World. Only if the Soviets refrained from pressing revolution or expansionism could they be trusted to uphold treaties limiting them militarily. Critics of détente cite the Middle East as one arena in which Soviet backsliding occurred almost from the beginning. For example, when Egypt, then a close Soviet ally, was preparing to attack Israel in October 1973, many Americans said that, under the rules of détente, the Soviet Union should have prevented the attack, or at least notified the United States that it was impending. Instead, the Soviets first stalled and then deceptively attempted to impose a superpower solution that would have institutionalized a Soviet supervisory role in the whole of the Middle East.

The Soviets contended that they had never accepted the notion of linkage as basic to détente and that they could not accede to a status quo in the Third World that institutionalized American neocolonial supremacy. In Soviet eyes, the Americans defined their national interests so expansively as to justify intervention anywhere around the globe. Their capitalist economy ostensibly needed a worldwide naval presence "to protect trade routes," but the United States had, besides, a global constabulary, a network of military bases in the Third World, and effective economic domination of the nonsocialist world — all in the name of free markets, protecting access to vital resources, and securing sea lanes. In "self-defense," capitalism might seek to preserve the status quo, and with it American hegemony in the Third World, the Soviets said, but no reasonable person could conclude that the Soviet commitment to limit strategic arms included a complacent acceptance of this American domination.

The SALT process was able to stand on its own, since both superpowers needed a reprieve from the arms race and they had a mutual interest in avoiding nuclear war. Any linkage of SALT to Third World issues — such as Soviet support for a peace process that would permit a graceful American exit from Vietnam — occurred out of American necessity and Soviet restraint, not from any negotiated quid pro quo. If linkage was essential to détente, and applied equally to both powers, then Brezhnev would never have sat down with Nixon in May of 1972, ten days after the American mining of North Vietnam's Haiphong harbor, to sign SALT I and initiate a thaw in bilateral relations. From the Soviet perspective, instability in the Middle East, in Indochina, or in any other part of the Third World is a sign of structural problems resulting from a history of Western domination; wars of liberation and anti-American reactions are the result of indigenous nationalism and strong anticolonial sentiment, not Soviet "meddling." Even Kissinger's top aides agreed that it was unrealistic to expect the Soviets to be able to control all their clients, since alliances with Third World countries often turned out to be maneuvers by the presumably dependent power to secure a greater level of aid and involvement. In the Egyptian case, the Soviets had steadfastly opposed the attack on Israel as reckless (it was one reason Sadat booted out the Soviet technicians and advisers in 1972), but when faced with a fait accompli, the Soviets went along rather than lose all their influence in the region.

The controversy over linkage and the rules of détente in regional disputes was played out in Angola, which became a litmus test of Soviet intentions. The Soviet Union had always been careful to commit itself in conflicts only when there was a high probability of victory and little likelihood of a vigorous U.S. response. Thus, the isolationist mood in America brought on by the Vietnam defeat encouraged the Soviets to take the offensive in Africa in the 1970s. Even then, they intervened only where the issues and the local balance of forces were in their favor. Demonstrating better strategic instincts and a more detailed knowledge of local conditions than the United States did, they rarely backed the losing side.

In Angola, three main groups had launched anticolonial liberation struggles against the Portuguese. All three factions were radical in approach, but they were separated by differences in leadership, tribal loyalties, regional bases, and sources of arms patronage. The Soviets might have backed any one, but they sent arms primarily to the Popular Movement for the Liberation of Angola (MPLA), led by Agostinho Neto. Yet the Soviets cautiously delayed committing their prestige or sending military advisers until the MPLA faction already had the upper hand politically. They did not increase their weapons deliveries dramatically until after December 1975, when the U.S. Senate voted to block all further American aid. Between March 1975 and February 1976, the Soviets sent $300 million in military equipment and assisted in the transfer of 11,000 Cuban troops to Angolan soil. They were partly motivated, ironically, by their fear of the Chinese Communists, who were giving considerable aid to two of the three factions. The Soviets also feared the South Africans, who had intervened militarily in the civil war.

Soviet and Cuban aid brought victory for the MPLA, the best-organized faction and the one most representative of the modern urban elite. It was also relatively moderate, at least in its willingness to deal with Western business interests. But its Soviet backing called forth all the old Cold War overtones. America rushed aid to the opposition factions, and this strong reaction tended to invest a local struggle with global significance. At the Twenty-fifth Party Congress, Brezhnev gave this explanation for the Soviet actions in Angola:

> Détente does not in the slightest abolish, and cannot abolish or alter, the laws of the class struggle. . . . No one should expect that because of détente Communists will reconcile themselves with capitalist exploitation or that monopolists become followers of the revolution. . . . We make no secret of the fact that we see détente as the way to create more favorable conditions for peaceful socialist and communist construction. This only confirms that socialism and peace are indissoluble.

Privately, Brezhnev assured Kissinger that Angola was a special situation and not likely to be repeated. Nonetheless, the situation soured many Americans on détente.

American policy makers soon concluded that Soviet actions in the Third World were eroding U.S. influence there. Between 1975 and 1979, the USSR had logged steady gains, intervening to back armed takeovers by pro-Soviet regimes in South Vietnam, Laos, Angola, Ethiopia, Afghanistan, South Yemen, and Cambodia. The response from the United States was predictable — a slow return to the policy of engagement to protect its Third World interests. In May 1978, the United States supported an airlift of Moroccan and Egyptian troops to Zaire to help Mobutu Sese Seko combat an internal rebellion in the sensitive and economically vital Shaba province (bordering Angola). By 1979, the convergence of Soviet aggression in Afghanistan and disturbing events in Nicaragua and Iran had finally shaken the United States out of its post-Vietnam apathy. Under the Nixon Doctrine, a favored U.S. ally like Iran was supposed to be acting as a surrogate gendarme to maintain the regional balance and police American interests. But the Ayatollah Khomeini's sudden rise to power and the accompanying disruption of oil supplies demonstrated how vulnerable the United States was, politically and economically, to any Third World custodian of its vital interests. Linkage, intended to bring moderation to Soviet behavior in regional conflicts, was instead bringing the whole policy of détente into question.

Congressional support for détente and the SALT process was undermined, after 1976, by shifts in public opinion associated with a spending-gap controversy and a scare over the stationing of a Soviet brigade in Cuba. Unlike the Soviet pressure in Angola, which represented a new geopolitical thrust, these two events later proved to be false alarms, fabricated by misunderstandings and resurrected Cold War fears. They nonetheless had a negative influence on Soviet-American relations and hastened the decline of détente. The spending-gap debate was set off by President Ford's politically motivated order, in 1976, for a review of CIA intelligence findings on Soviet levels of defense spending. A routine review — Team A — had indicated that the Soviets were not increasing their military forces, and subsequent CIA analyses in the 1980s confirmed that this initial assessment had been correct — that, in fact, Soviet spending had *declined* after 1975, from a growth rate of 4 or 5 percent to less than 2 percent. But the Team B assessment mandated by Ford, under the direction of the conservative Richard Pipes, spread alarming claims of a dramatic Soviet buildup — a conclusion based on flawed accounting procedures, inflated assessments, and dubious assumptions that the CIA itself repudiated in 1983. The Team B findings were trumpeted around the country, however, by the Committee on the Present Danger, just at the time when the Soviet-Cuban involvement in Angola seemed to be breaking the rules of détente. Although the Soviet actions in Africa were unrelated to Soviet nuclear capabilities or military spending, and very likely posed no threat to America's vital interests, the American public was frightened.

Then, in 1979, the Carter administration "discovered" a new Soviet brigade in Cuba and publicly denounced the Soviets for escalating their presence in Latin America, traditionally an American security zone. It subsequently came out that the brigade was a Russian training unit, it had been in Cuba for more than a decade, and it represented no new Soviet challenge to the rules of détente. But it did become a rallying point for a Democratic administration that was under attack from the Republicans for being "soft" on Communism. President Carter's get-tough attitude was in response to a perennial pressure — the fear of right-wing reaction against policies viewed as too liberal toward the Soviets. Both these scares illustrate the difficulties of pursuing détente with an ideological adversary, which tempts opposition elements to capitalize on a confrontationist foreign policy.

Although American critics had been vociferous in their attacks on détente from the beginning, the hope for an enduring thaw in Soviet-American relations did not finally die until late in 1979, when the Soviets invaded Afghanistan. President Carter retaliated with an embargo on grain sales and a boycott of American participation in the 1980 Moscow Olympics. Sales of high technology to the Soviet Union were suspended and Soviet fishing rights in American waters severely restricted. Carter also withdrew the SALT II Treaty from ratification proceedings in the Senate, although he continued to observe its provisions, as did President Reagan. Zbigniew Brzezinski, Carter's national security adviser, referred to the Soviet invasion as the first step toward a stranglehold on the Western oil lifeline in the Persian Gulf. The Soviet intervention in this "arc of crisis" prompted the proclamation of the Carter Doctrine, which promised to use a newly created Rapid Deployment Force (RDF) to protect American access to the Persian Gulf. The crisis in Afghanistan, which constituted a serious challenge from Islamic fundamentalists and threatened Soviet control of a Marxist ally, had a more direct impact on policy than did Carter's own encounter with the Islamic radicals who had taken Americans hostage in the U.S. embassy in Iran. A new crack in the solidarity of the Soviet bloc was elevated into a new line of confrontation in the Cold War. Détente was dead.

REAGAN AND THE RUSSIANS

The disillusionment with détente and the conservative reaction that swept America in the 1980 election can be traced to two intersecting trends: the perception of growing Soviet military strength and U.S. political-economic weakness. During the 1970s, the Soviet Union had reached parity in the arms race and also had established a new military presence in the Third World, sending advisers to dozens of countries and acquiring overseas bases to service its growing blue-water navy. Although this presence was still greatly inferior to the well-established U.S. position, the United States felt increasingly insecure about the new geopolitical challenges. (Figure 5-7 compares the U.S. and Soviet military presence in the Third World.) Americans were still not psychologically prepared to grant the USSR equal status as a great power; they harbored ideological suspicions and grave doubts about Soviet intentions and feared that the momentum of the buildup would carry the Soviets to a position of superiority. In the same decade, the United States, while retaining an overall military dominance, was becoming weaker politically and economically, due to a variety of internal and external forces. The most important economic

FIGURE 5-7

U.S. AND SOVIET MILITARY PRESENCE IN THE THIRD WORLD (1987)

Soviet Military Personnel in the Third World

Latin America (including Cuba)	8,165
Asia (including Vietnam)	3,500
Middle East/North Africa	10,600
Sub-Saharan Africa	5,250
Afghanistan	116,000

Cuban Military Personnel in the Third World

Latin America	2,000
Middle East/North Africa	550
Sub-Saharan Africa	42,000

U.S. Military Personnel in the Third World

Latin America/Caribbean	34,820
East Asia and Pacific	143,800
Middle East/North Africa	11,090
Sub-Saharan Africa and other	1,500

Total Soviet Naval and Marine Forces

Personnel	477,000
Attack and cruise missile submarines	360
Principal surface combatants	274

Total U.S. Naval & Marine Forces

Personnel 583,800 (Navy) + 199,600 (Marine Corps) =	783,400
Attack submarines	96
Principal surface combatants	237

Warsaw Pact Naval Forces Outside of European Waters

Aircraft carriers	2	Cruisers, destroyers, frigates	52
Naval aviation	378	Other combatant ships	322
Submarines (excluding strategic nuclear forces)			70

NATO Naval Forces Outside of European Waters

Aircraft carriers	13	Cruisers, destroyers, frigates	142
Naval aviation	970	Other combatant ships	60
Submarines (excluding strategic nuclear forces)			42

Soviet military bases in the Third World (including access rights)	16
U.S. military bases in the Third World (including access rights)	89

Note: Figures for 1987 are typical of Soviet-American forces abroad throughout the 1980s. U.S. figures, however, do not reflect its superior airlift/power projection capability and exclude the Rapid Deployment Force (about 200,000 troops in 5 divisions, 350 aircraft, 20 to 30 ships). After 1989, the Soviet Union withdrew all its forces from Afghanistan, along with substantial cuts in troop levels in Eastern Europe and Mongolia. Likewise, almost all Cuban troops stationed in the Third World were repatriated after 1989.

challenge, ironically, was from close U.S. allies—Japan and Western Europe —but OPEC, the oil cartel, and the newly industrializing countries also contributed to an overall decline in America's trade position. The most important political challenge came from the Third World. The defeat in Vietnam had marked the end of America's ability to preserve the privileges it inherited from the old European empires and initiated a general trend toward multipolarity and a greater show of independence by postcolonial regimes. Neither superpower could preserve the solidarity of its own bloc, let alone the sanctity of its traditional sphere of influence. Soviet troubles in Poland and Afghanistan were echoed by American difficulties in Chile, Peru, Grenada, El Salvador, and Nicaragua. The Iranian crisis—which saw the Ayatollah Khomeini's Islamic loyalists hold U.S. hostages for more than a year while they thumbed their noses at America — symbolized the strong anti-Americanism that was alive in all countries where the United States had attempted to preserve its power by imposing repressive right-wing dictatorships.

The 1980 election was a barometer of the American mood and a test of public perceptions regarding the causes of America's decline. In foreign policy, the election became an indirect referendum on Vietnam and détente. Had Americans become "soft" and surrendered to Communist pressures in Indochina and in the arms race? Or had the world become a more complex place, in which peaceful coexistence required a recognition of the limits to American power? The first diagnosis would blame the Soviets (and the liberal Democrats). It would junk détente and take the revivalist road: if we but rearmed and reasserted America's will, Soviet power could be curbed and American preeminence restored. The second diagnosis would blame a naive and fickle American public (and the conservative Republicans). It would call for patience and take the road of compromise: if we only held out the hand of peace steadfastly, relinquishing our imperial pretensions and our self-contradictory diplomacy, we could restore satisfactory relations with the Soviets. Ronald Reagan won the presidency largely on the basis of the former position, which was, after all, a much easier message for a frustrated public to accept. But a complete analysis of the decline in Soviet-American relations must ascribe blame to both sides and confront the untidy consequences of multipolarity.

Much of American foreign policy since 1945 has been shaped by an initial reluctance to accept the new requirements of a global role, followed by insecurity when the United States was forced to relinquish its newfound dominance so rapidly. After World War II, the United States enjoyed a moment of supreme preeminence, leading in every indicator of national strength, dominating every political arena. But this was only temporary, the result of the war's immense destruction. The United States was bound to be restrained eventually by a reconstructed global balance, once the Soviet Union, Japan, and Europe had recovered and the realigning effects of decolonization were fully felt. In the relatively short period of America's postwar dominance, its foreign policy oscillated between the zealous idealism of a public that neither understood nor supported an imperial role and the professional realism of an elite trying to protect American power. Americans accepted their leadership of the free world with the enthusiasm of reformers determined to avoid the great-power sins of the past. But in the end they were forced to wield power like any other state, and to hide their covert operations and the soiled hands of secret diplomacy even from themselves. Having enjoyed a monopoly of power and pictured itself in such an exemplary role, the United States found it hard to share power with the Soviet Union and adapt to a global balance in which neither superpower was dominant.

The dilemma in 1980 was how to regain a position of strength in the global balance when the conditions of American "exceptionalism" had been gone for more than a decade. Reagan's appeal lay in his claim that America had lost its position not through the natural evolution of the reconstructed global balance but through Democratic incompetence and a failure of nerve, in Vietnam and in the arms race alike. He promised what the American people were eager to hear: that the world was amenable to U.S. control and that the golden era of the 1950s could be restored if America would just rearm and stand up to the Soviets. The shortsightedness of this view was apparent in Iran, Lebanon, the Persian Gulf, and Nicaragua, where ostensibly the Reagan administration was showing a fortitude that would counteract the debilitating effects of Vietnam but actually was repeating many of the mistakes of that tragic war. In Lebanon, the United States sent Marines into a civil war whose historical roots it barely understood, in an attempt to solve a deep political and religious crisis with troops and arms aid. In the Persian Gulf, America's commitments escalated, and so did its military deployments, largely because it viewed a complex regional conflict exclusively in terms of the Soviet threat and superpower competition for influence. The decision to offer American naval protection to reflagged Kuwaiti tankers was spurred by a Russian offer to the Kuwaitis, not by any real threat to Western oil supplies. The embarrassing diversion of funds and arms-for-hostages deals of the Iran-Contra scandal demonstrated that American foreign policy had not yet escaped the grasp of provincial attitudes, self-righteous crusading, and black-and-white thinking. Amateur high jinks and covert actions actually jeopardized American interests in the Middle East and the Persian Gulf, regions of the globe where the United States has fundamentally misunderstood local events and forces. And in Nicaragua, Soviet influence increased precisely because U.S. boycotts and armed intervention forced the Sandinista regime into greater dependence on the Soviets for both economic and military aid. The 1990 electoral defeat of the Sandinistas reflected popular disillusionment and pressure from the Soviets and neighboring Central American states for a negotiated settlement, not the success of the American-backed *contras,* who never established themselves as politically legitimate or militarily viable. The failures of American diplomacy in Central America — even the United States' Latin American allies did not support its policy in Nicaragua — lay in the perennial tendency to interpret every complex civil conflict in terms of Soviet aggression and the stereotypes of the Cold War.

The harsh rhetoric of President Reagan showed the persistence of Cold War attitudes (though the rhetoric moderated in his second term). In his first press conference, in 1981, he accused the Soviet leadership of reserving unto themselves "the right to commit any crime, to lie, to cheat." This theme was echoed in his famous address to a conference of Christian fundamentalists, in 1983, in which he characterized the USSR as the "focus of evil in the modern world . . . an evil empire." Reagan's antipathy emerged most clearly when, in an unguarded moment while testing his voice before a radio broadcast, he jokingly said: "My fellow Americans, I am pleased to tell you I just signed legislation which outlaws Russia forever. The bombing begins in five minutes." And strong words were mixed with strong measures. Reagan initiated economic sanctions against the Soviet Union, in conjunction with a European gas pipeline controversy, amid revelations that the Soviets were conducting widespread industrial espionage. Relations took a still stronger downturn in September 1983, after the Soviet shooting down of a Korean airliner with 269 persons aboard. The Soviets claimed that KAL 007 was an "American spy plane" that had violated the "sanctity of Soviet air space." President Reagan called it a cold-blooded act of "barbarism" by an international "outlaw." Although the Politburo had not authorized the decision to shoot down the as-yet-unidentified plane—a result of poor communications and a serious failure of Soviet air defenses—the Kremlin leadership refused to apologize. It turned instead to name-calling, comparing Reagan to Hitler and declaring that the Soviet Union would continue to defend its air space against American "provocateurs and spies." Soviet-American relations deteriorated to a level not seen since the darkest days of the Cold War.

The first Reagan term also marked a reassertion of U.S. willingness to intervene in the Third World. The more aggressive use of American troops and arms was accompanied by a new Reagan Doctrine giving support to Third World anti-Communist resistance groups. President Carter had emphasized diplomatic and economic incentives to contain radical regimes and encourage them to disengage from Soviet influence. Reagan abandoned this policy of arms restraint and limited cooperation in favor of the overthrow of radical regimes, or of bleeding them white as a warning to others. Accordingly, several billions were spent annually to fund "freedom fighters" trying to unseat Marxist governments in Nicaragua, Afghanistan, Angola, and Cambodia. Covert military aid to the Afghan rebels, for example, amounted to over $500 million in 1987, almost five times the amount budgeted for military assistance to the Philippines. The sophisticated Stinger antiaircraft missiles supplied by the United States dramatically reduced the effectiveness of Soviet air support for Afghan government troops and contributed directly to the Soviets' decision to cut their losses and leave. Where internal opposition could not be mobilized against a radical regime, the United States found other measures. Against Libya's Moammar Khadafy, Reagan started with economic and diplomatic pressures. In May 1981, Libyan diplomats were expelled, and in March 1982 an embargo was placed on all oil imports from and high technology exports to Libya. Then military aid was offered to Libya's neighboring rivals—Chad, the Sudan, and Tunisia. Next came military actions in the Gulf of Sidra in 1981 and 1985, followed in 1986 by a direct attack on Khadafy's headquarters in Tripoli by eighteen F-111 fighter-bombers. Clearly, Reagan was signaling that the United States was prepared to "get tough" and would no longer remain passive in the face of direct or indirect challenges to U.S. interests.

Arms control suffered in the chilling atmosphere. The Kremlin leadership was preoccupied by a series of succession crises: the death of Brezhnev in November 1982; of his successor, Yuri Andropov, only fifteen months later; and of an aged interim figure, Konstantin Chernenko, in March 1985, after serving slightly more than a year. Only after Mikhail Gorbachev had consolidated his power behind a reform coalition did the Soviet Union begin to signal a serious interest in arms reduction and a thaw in relations. The Reagan administration was highly skeptical about the value of arms control in enhancing American security—at least until the United States was well on the road toward Star Wars and a refurbished strategic arsenal. Reagan was more eager to correct a perceived imbalance in ICBM forces and to match Soviet deployments of intermediate-range nuclear weapons in Europe. The United States submitted a Strategic Arms Reduction (START) proposal, but it was so one-sided that it was never taken seriously. Many proposals were floated on both sides, but all contained "jokers" that were sure to get them rejected. Negotiations fell once again to the level of propaganda wars. Then the Reagan administration decided to abrogate its (unofficial) compliance with the SALT II Treaty by increasing cruise missile deployments and pressing forward with ASAT testing and other modernization measures. At the same time, it publicized a series of reports on Soviet violations of the SALT and ABM treaties. Arms control was at a standstill.

Even in the best days of détente, arms control had done no more than restrain the pace of the buildup and steer new arms development into predictable channels. SALT I did not stem the race in warheads and new technology; its limits on launchers were outflanked by MIRV technology and a great variety of other improvements. SALT II suffered the same fate. By the time it was signed, it was obsolete, and it did nothing to restrain the moves toward nuclear-war-fighting strategies, ballistic missile defense, and the incorporation of new technologies in both theater and conventional military forces. In answer to Reagan's claim that arms control had failed, some critics argued that it had never really been tried.

Although political tensions temporarily eased, the 1970s had witnessed a continuing buildup in conventional armed forces in Europe, which talks on Mutual and Balanced Force Reduction (MBFR), beginning in 1973, utterly failed to curb. After Vietnam, the United States sent three additional army divisions and four air force wings to Europe, making a total of 300,000 U.S. military personnel there, at an annual cost of $35 billion. (For a comparison of NATO and Warsaw Pact conventional forces, see Figure 5-8.) A "two-track" decision by NATO had put off the deployment of new intermediate-range nuclear missiles (IRBMs), pending negotiations with the Soviets on the removal of their SS-20s. Reagan was pursuing a zero-option policy aimed at persuading the Soviets to trade their missiles in place for an American promise not to deploy missiles in the future. But it was difficult to reconcile the assymetries between the NATO and Warsaw Pact forces. The American proposal excluded French and British nuclear forces, amounting to several thousand warheads, on the premise that the United States could not negotiate for its allies. The Soviets could have created a symmetrical situation, but only by allowing a dangerous proliferation of weapons in the hands of their East European allies. The geography of Europe created confusion over the definitions of theater and strategic weapons, since the Pershing II and cruise missiles introduced by the United States in 1983 could reach Soviet targets, whereas the Soviet SS-20s could not reach the United States. Arms control advocates complained that the Reagan administration had intentionally stalled the Intermediate Nuclear Forces (INF) talks until the Pershing and cruise missiles were deployed. The administration responded that it was the Soviets who had torpedoed the talks

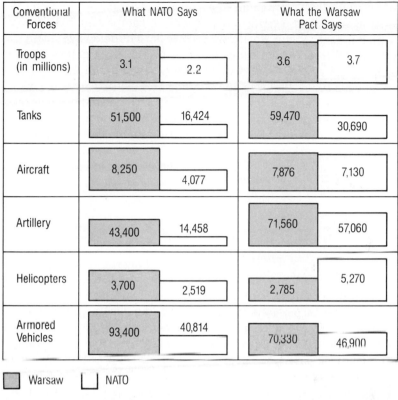

Conventional Forces	What NATO Says		What the Warsaw Pact Says	
Troops (in millions)	3.1	2.2	3.6	3.7
Tanks	51,500	16,424	59,470	30,690
Aircraft	8,250	4,077	7,876	7,130
Artillery	43,400	14,458	71,560	57,060
Helicopters	3,700	2,519	2,785	5,270
Armored Vehicles	93,400	40,814	70,330	46,900

▨ Warsaw   ☐ NATO

Warsaw Pact figures from communique by Ministers of Defense Committee, Jan. 30, 1989.
NATO figures from "Conventional Forces in Europe: the Facts," published by NATO, November 1988.
NATO manpower figures do not include naval personnel in European theater.

FIGURE 5-8

NATO AND WARSAW PACT CONVENTIONAL FORCES

(they walked out in 1984), in the expectation that European public opinion, at first sharply divided, would eventually swing behind a growing movement for disarmament and disengagement from NATO. This was a Soviet miscalculation. Most European governments finally agreed to accept new American arms, and the Eurostrategic balance was less favorable to the Soviets than ever.

The arms talks having broken down at all levels, the Soviets made matters worse by boycotting the Los Angeles Olympics in 1984, in retaliation for the American boycott of 1980, on the trumped-up excuse of a concern over security. Meanwhile, Reagan was pressing ahead with his military buildup. He secured congressional support for his Strategic Defense Initiative (SDI), or Star Wars, and for several new strategic weapons, including the B-1B bomber and the MX, or Peacekeeper, missile. The MX, more powerful than any weapon then in the U.S. arsenal, carried ten MARV (maneuvering reentry vehicle) warheads of increased accuracy. Since it was to be deployed in a vulnerable mode (in refurbished Minuteman silos), the Soviets regarded it as a first-strike threat. They also were skeptical about what a comprehensive anti-ballistic missile system such as Star Wars was meant to be; if its defensive shield was not 100 percent foolproof, then its main value would be in deflecting a Soviet retaliatory attack after an American first strike. In addition, loose talk among Reagan officials about "fighting and winning" a nuclear war was making the Soviets apprehensive about the possibility that the United States was trying to achieve a preemptive first-strike (counterforce) capability. All these fears eventually brought the Soviets back to the negotiating table, but by then relations had so soured that little progress was made. The sole arms accord of the first Reagan term, signed in July 1984, was an updating of the hot line agreements of 1963 and 1971.

GORBACHEV AND "NEW THINKING"

Soviet-American relations warmed significantly after 1985, due in large measure to the dramatic changes initiated by the new Soviet leader, Mikhail Gorbachev. His policies of *perestroika* and *glasnost* launched a program of fundamental reform that rivaled the revolutions of Lenin and Stalin. The old guard in the Soviet politburo was swiftly retired and measures set in motion to dismantle the stranglehold of party control over a centralized and still-Stalinist bureaucracy. Though Gorbachev's reforms were slowed by widespread resistance, both official and popular, to radical measures such as profit incentives, market mechanisms, abolition of quotas, a return to various forms of private property and individual responsibility, there were no effective challenges to his leadership or his democratizing agenda. Widespread cynicism and inertia reflected the stultifying economic and cultural effects of decades of repression, but everyone conceded that problems were so severe that the old system must be sacked. The costs of empire had become prohibitive and the domestic economy was nearly at a standstill.

Insofar as Gorbachev's popular legitimacy could not be buttressed by immediate gains in Soviet living standards, his reforms depended on the prestige and momentum garnered from liberalization in both domestic and foreign affairs. *Glasnost* would empower reform-minded allies at home, while disarming Cold War critics abroad. It would cement the support of the intelligentsia while holding the bureaucracy to account, exposing corruption, incompetence, and inefficiency. Political openness would permit Gorbachev to reconstruct Soviet foreign policy. His "new thinking" imagined peaceful relations between capitalism and socialism, sustained by common human values. Avoiding war and global ecological catastrophe outweighed the struggle between classes. Gorbachev sought, and needed, more than the breathing space of a temporary détente; he wanted a new world order in which the Soviet Union was a full participant, economically vital, politically legitimate. Only thus could the Soviet Union gain enduring access to trade and advanced technology; only by dismantling the Soviet empire and putting an end to the arms race could sufficient resources be freed to reconstruct the failing socialist economy. Over the next four years, this new thinking was reflected in new human rights policies, liberalized emigration, increases in scientific and cultural exchange, a welcoming attitude toward foreign investment and expanded trade, and revised press policies that ended the heavy veil of secrecy in both domestic and national security affairs. Most dramatically, Gorbachev cut the defense budget, announced unilateral troop withdrawals, renounced the Brezhnev doctrine, and offered concessions that spurred the process of arms control.

U.S. observers, however, were slow to give credence to Gorbachev's reform efforts, not least because authoritarian habits were so entrenched and concrete economic gains so slow in coming. Though Gorbachev was thought sincere, his political power nonetheless depended on the support of a party apparatus that was still conservative. Moreover, his popular support, fuelled by his considerable charismatic qualities, would wane in the end if he could not deliver the goods. Democratization and decentralization also gave voice to restless minorities who began to demand greater autonomy. By 1989, this had bred open defiance of the Kremlin and separatist movements led by the Communist leadership itself in Armenia, Azerbaijan, the Ukraine, and the Baltic Republics of Latvia, Lithuania, and Estonia. Given the rapid pace of change, President Reagan, and Bush after him, adopted a cautious "wait-and-see" attitude that reflected a reluctance to abandon Cold War categories and a recognition that the Gorbachev reform agenda, real though it may be, was not yet institutionalized and irreversible.

Nonetheless, U.S. policy did began to shift after 1985. The waning of the anti-Communist crusade permitted the U.S. to abandon right-wing dictators in favor of democratic movements, even where this might mean a decline in U.S. control and a less sure guarantee of U.S. interests. Points of U.S.-Soviet confrontation in the Third World began to be defused. President Reagan had not succeeded in restoring the pre-Vietnam consensus for intervention, and the Soviets had quickly learned in Afghanistan how risky it was to commit troops to quell a Third World insurgency. The Grenada intervention was popular because it had been short and successful, but there was strong opposition throughout the 1980s to the Reagan policy in Nicaragua. Ironically, some of the strongest opposition to foreign interventions came from the U.S. professional military itself. It clearly had learned some lessons from Vietnam: that force should be employed only when there was a strong public consensus behind it and only when the military was permitted to win a quick and decisive victory by whatever means it found necessary. On this basis, Secretary of Defense Caspar Weinberger had adamantly opposed the presence of U.S. Marines in Lebanon in 1982–84. Similarly, the chairman of the Joint Chiefs of Staff, Colin Powell, counseled President Bush to embrace an all-or-nothing position in the Persian Gulf crisis of 1990. Either the United States should refrain from intervening against Iraqi president Saddam Hussein's annexation of Kuwait, or it should enter massively, with troops, tanks, and naval deployments that would assure U.S. superiority.

The Democrats, who regained control of Congress in 1984, favored a more restrained foreign policy, and they began to press the arms control agenda. In an unusual series of legislative initiatives, the Congress used its funding authority to bar the president from testing an antisatellite weapon and imposed a brief nuclear test moratorium. The latter was in response to an unprecedented Soviet initiative, Gorbachev's declaration of a total nuclear test moratorium, which he extended for more than nineteen months. The Soviets also made concessions at the resumed INF talks, with Gorbachev accepting in all important respects the Reagan zero-option proposal of 1983. The Soviets then proposed a 50 percent across-the-board reduction in strategic arsenals, but only in exchange for a limit on Star Wars research. Reagan, for his part, insisted on linking progress in the arms talks with improvements in Soviet foreign policy, especially in the Third World. Gorbachev largely removed this obstacle to better relations by pressing his allies in both Eastern Europe and the Third World to follow the same process of *perestroika* that was proceeding so rapidly within the Soviet Union. Peace talks eventually led to the withdrawal of Soviet, Vietnamese, and Cuban troops from Afghanistan, Cambodia/Kampuchea, Angola, and Namibia.

Gorbachev and Reagan held their first summit encounter in November 1985 at Geneva, and it was followed by a second summit meeting at Reykjavik, Iceland, in October 1986. The Geneva summit was largely a goodwill session, although it laid the groundwork for future meetings. The Reykjavik summit, impromptu and hastily prepared, began with an apparent breakthrough in which the two leaders agreed to dismantle their entire nuclear arsenals step by step — so breathtaking a prospect that both negotiating teams spent the rest of the summit backing away from the initial agreement and maneuvering to make the other side look responsible for the breakdown.

We can draw a number of conclusions from the Soviet-American encounter at Reykjavik. The first is that the U.S. commitment to the Strategic Defense Initiative was a big stumbling block to arms control. As Reykjavik made clear, SDI was a nonnegotiable issue in the eyes of Ronald Reagan, a true believer in the technological effectiveness of the system. Gorbachev did not share this view, but feared that SDI would set off a new race in offensive technologies designed to defeat the Star Wars defense, or that perhaps it was simply a U.S. ruse to secure public support for more military spending and a new arms race in space. The Soviets also were hard-pressed economically and recognized that they could not compete effectively in the area of high technology.

Second, the U.S. security community was itself strongly divided over whether arms control and coexistence were in America's best interests. Hardliners and moderates joined in a summit bargaining strategy of offering massive cuts. But when Gorbachev surprised them by accepting, the conservatives took it as a sign that the Soviets were in desperate economic straits and could be either bullied into further concessions or pushed to exhaustion in a costly arms race. Thus, the conservative majority within the Reagan administration continued to oppose controls on strategic weapons. Once again, it was clear that the professional diplomats had won only half the battle by coming up with a common definition of Soviet and American national interests. The gap still had to be bridged between liberals and conservatives, détenteniks and Cold Warriors, within the domestic political establishments of both states.

Third, the Reykjavik summit brought confusion and renewed questioning about the basic doctrine of nuclear deterrence. In a moment of distraction, idealism, or just plain honesty, both sides had agreed to abolish all nuclear weapons, but, that done, nobody was sure any longer if nuclear armament was essential or what nuclear weapons were good for, apart from deterring other nuclear weapons. However fleetingly, the suggestion had been voiced that it was possible to denuclearize superpower relations without altering the fundamental balance.

Although mutual recriminations were the immediate result of Reykjavik, the summit did serve to break up a hardened consensus against arms control that had been present in the Reagan administration ever since the president's decisions not to ratify SALT II or to renew the promising Comprehensive Test Ban Treaty (CTBT) talks in 1981. The way was open for new proposals — hastened along by the Iran-Contra scandal and Reagan's lame-duck status as his second term neared its end. Reagan, like all presidents before him, had an eye on the history books. A peace agreement with the Soviets would restore lustre to his badly tarnished foreign policy and would provide a fitting legacy in foreign affairs to go with a quite remarkable shift in America's domestic agenda.

Following Gorbachev's agreement to the complete dismantling of all intermediate nuclear weapons in Europe and his compliance with Reagan's demands for strict on-site verification, the INF talks progressed rapidly. The treaty, signed at the Washington summit of December 1987, marked the first occasion on which the two superpowers agreed to actually destroy existing nuclear weapons and reduce the level of armaments. This Treaty on the Elimination of Intermediate-range Nuclear Forces banned all Soviet and American ballistic missiles and American ground-launched cruise missiles with ranges between 500 and 5,500 kilometers, and it called for the destruction of existing weapons in the banned categories under strict verification procedures that included foreign inspection of both production and disposal facilities. The United States eliminated a total of 841 missiles (including Pershing IIs), the USSR a total of 1,746 missiles (including SS-20s) — a cut of about 4 percent in overall nuclear arsenals.

Unresolved issues remained in the areas of conventional and strategic nuclear weapons, where the problems of establishing a formula for cuts and instituting trustworthy verification measures proved more difficult. The American INF negotiating team, which had pressed hard for intrusive verification measures, in the end was reluctant to accept Soviet inspectors at American defense facilities. Ironically, the Soviets appear to have concluded that open verification will gain them as much in security and intelligence as they will lose by moderating their old policy of secrecy; Gorbachev's *glasnost* had brought a surprising switch. Nonetheless, successful arms control depended on a variety of other factors. Domestic economic constraints in both countries continued to favor it, but the history of Soviet-American enmity was long and bitter. The INF agreement launched the new era of détente, but mutual security, and a lasting peace, could not be achieved without deeper cuts (in troops as well as arms) and an end to the technological dynamic that fed the arms race.

By 1990, the Bush administration appeared to accept Gorbachev's fundamental changes as irreversible. The positive signs were numerous. The new Soviet openness was apparent, for instance, in U.S. press coverage of an unprecedented range of events within the USSR and the Eastern bloc. In a typical few days in March 1989, Americans learned about ethnic dissidence and independence movements in the Baltic states, expressions of alarm over the AIDS epidemic, a Soviet agreement to submit human rights disputes to binding arbitration in the World Court, presummit talks between U.S. Secretary of State James Baker and Soviet Foreign Minister Eduard Shevardnadze, Lech Walesa's announcement of Solidarity's official recognition by the Polish Communist government, Soviet acknowledgment of responsibility for the Katyn Forest massacre of World War II, popular outrage over the Soviet government's handling of the Chernobyl nuclear cleanup, and a Soviet proposal for massive conventional arms cuts in Europe. The range of information and opinion, and the Soviet Communist leadership's willingness to admit mistakes, was breathtaking. In June 1989, the first Congress of People's Deputies, summing up the new climate in its concluding manifesto, called for speedier economic reforms, cuts in military spending, and the drafting of a new constitution incorporating the dramatic political changes of the past two years, including further decentralization within a federal structure, judicial reform, freedom of religious belief, freedom of the press and association, greater protection for individual rights, and clearer limits on the authority of the government and the ruling Communist party. In the same week, an officially sanctioned article accused Lenin of being a dictator and a terrorist, calling into question for the first time the Soviet view that only Stalin was to blame for the perversion of socialist democracy.

Most dramatic of all, in February 1990, the Central Committee of the Communist Party of the Soviet Union agreed, with only a single dissenting vote, to abandon its constitutional monopoly on power and make way for a multiparty system. The party issued a far-reaching manifesto that affirmed the state's responsibility to respect all the traditional rights of liberal democracy (see Figure 5-9). A few weeks later, the Congress of People's Deputies embraced a new constitution, modeled on the French and American examples, with a "superpresidency" that shifted effective power from Communist party organs to a popularly elected executive. Gorbachev was elected by the Congress to fill the first four-year term, although about a third of the deputies, in the new spirit of democracy, dissented vigorously because he had not stood for a direct vote before a national electorate.

The democratic possibilities of the new Soviet system were expressed in a number of dramatic developments. In March 1990 the Baltic republic of Lithuania declared its formal independence. It recalled its youth from the Soviet

Army, formed its own citizen's militia, and initiated new border procedures. Soviet troop movements, tactics of intimidation, and a boycott of energy and resource supplies indicated how seriously the Kremlin took this challenge to the integrity of the Union of Soviet Socialist Republics. The new republic called for negotiations, but Moscow refused to talk until the declaration of independence was revoked, although Foreign Minister Shevardnadze and President Gorbachev indicated their commitment to resolve the dispute peacefully. Despite severe shortages induced by the partial economic blockade, Lithuania refused to comply with Moscow's demands. The crisis was finally resolved when Lithuania agreed to "suspend" its declaration of independence in exchange for a Kremlin promise of formal negotiations over the full range of issues. Within months, Latvia, Estonia, Armenia, and the Russian republic (which contains 52 percent of the Soviet population and three-quarters of its land mass) issued their own declarations of sovereignty, although in a somewhat less defiant mode. Meanwhile, Moldavia and Georgia appeared likely to follow the secessionist route.

Within the party itself, Gorbachev's position of primacy began to be eroded by more progressive voices who took him to task for dilatory half-measures and resistance to decentralization. Radicals were elected as party leaders in Moscow and Leningrad, and the maverick populist Boris Yeltsin, a personal rival that Gorbachev purged from the Politburo in 1987 for daring to complain about the slow pace of national renewal, returned to power as the democratically elected president of the Russian republic. Yeltsin called for the immediate resignation of the Soviet government of Prime Minister Nikolai Ryzhkov and the separation of the post of president from that of Communist Party secretary general (which would force Gorbachev to abandon his dual bases of power). He also appealed for an end to the economic boycott of Lithuania, declaring that the Russian republic itself should be free from central control. Yeltsin envisioned the rapid transformation of the Soviet Union into a loose confederation of sovereign republics, each pursuing its own foreign and domestic policies, with republican laws taking precedence over federal legislation. Each republic would reclaim control over its own resources, and private property would be legalized for all farms, small factories, and businesses. Yeltsin's policies were quickly endorsed by Anatoly Sobchak, the radical mayor of Leningrad, who was also touted as one of the few leaders within the Soviet Union to rival Gorbachev's personal popularity.

Gorbachev's economic reform proposals, calling for an end to food subsidies and a phasing in of free market prices, were caught between popular resistance — panic buying and consumer complaints over higher prices forced him to scrap a proposed referendum on the measures — and criticism from economic experts that the proposals did not go far enough. Once the arbiter between conservative and liberal factions of the party, Gorbachev increasingly came under attack from both extremes — impatient democrats and old-fashioned ideologues. A skillful balancing act threatened to disintegrate into isolation and indecision, confronting a public that was at once polarized and confused. Gorbachev's June summit with President George Bush took place under

---

FIGURE 5-9
SOVIET COMMUNIST PARTY AGENDA

The following are excerpts from the platform adopted by the Soviet Communist Party in February 1990, as translated by Tass.

The Soviet Communist Party stands for the earliest formulation of legal acts guaranteeing the rights and freedoms of citizens. The recognition of personal liberty as the key and vital value and a volte-face to guarantee the entire complex of human rights is perestroika's most important accomplishment. Now it is necessary to consolidate these rights, to rest them on a solid material, legal, and political foundation.

The party will uphold

Reliable legislative protection of a citizen's personality and honor, the immunity of his home and property, the secrecy of correspondence and telephone conversations;

Stronger guarantees to realize the right to work, including payment according to the quantity and quality of work done and its results;

The development and strengthening of the political rights of citizens: participation in running the affairs of the society and the state; freedoms of speech, the press, meetings and demonstrations; and the formation of public organizations;

Freedom for creative activities and attitude to talent as a national asset;

Man's free self-determination in the spiritual sphere, the freedom of conscience and religion;

A higher role of the court of law in protecting civil rights, the establishment of public-state commissions exercising law-enforcing activities.

＊　＊　＊　＊　＊

The party advocates an effective finance recovery program, including such measures as the encouragement of deposits in savings banks at increased interest rates, the development of the insurance business, the distribution of state loan bonds on advantageous terms, the selling of dwellings, advance payments by the population for durable goods they plan to buy in the future, and the selling of stocks and other securities. . . .

The creation of a full-fledged market economy requires the formation of markets of consumer products, capital goods, securities, investment, currencies, and research and development, and an early reform of the financial, monetary, and credit systems.

＊　＊　＊　＊　＊

The protection of nature is the protection of man. Toward the close of the 20th century, environmental protection has become a categoric imperative for preserving life on the earth. We must introduce world standards in this country and take an active part in international ecological cooperation. . . .

The party's policy proceeds from the recognition of the sovereign will of the people as the only source of power. The rule-of-law state of the whole people has no room for dictatorship by any class, and even less so for the power of a management bureaucracy. . . .

The electoral system should be brought in line with the principles of universal, equal, direct suffrage. We wish elections to become an honest competition between representatives of all the sections of society, of individuals and ideas submitted to the judgment of voters by the party, public organizations and movements, and individual candidates.

★ ★ ★ ★ ★

The development of society does not preclude the possibility of forming parties. The procedure for their formation will be established by law and reflected in the Constitution of the USSR.

The Soviet Communist Party does not claim a monopoly and is prepared for a political dialogue and cooperation with everyone who favors the renewal of socialist society.

The Soviet Communist Party holds that the separation of legislative, executive, and judiciary powers is fundamentally important to the Government's efficiency. In Lenin's words, we should combine the advantages of the Soviet system with the advantages of parliamentarianism.

A rule-of-law state presupposes effective political guidance of the defense, the accountability of the military department to the supreme civil authorities, and maximum openness in the activity of the military department, taking into account the level of confidence among states. . . .

★ ★ ★ ★ ★

Remaining vital to the maintenance of public order, interior and state security bodies should operate strictly within the law and under control of elective government bodies.

The principle of the self-determination of nations in a renewed Soviet federation presupposes the freedom of national-state entities to choose forms by which to structure life, institutions, and symbols of statehood. Our ideal is not unification but unity in diversity.

The party reaffirms its commitment to Lenin's principle of the right of nations to self-determination, including secession, and favors the adoption of a law on a mechanism for the exercise of this right. At the same time we are convinced that the weakening and disruption of reciprocally diverse and interrelated ties could lead to negative consequences for all peoples — to say nothing about individual destinies — consequences that are very difficult to foresee. That is why we resolutely oppose separatist slogans and movements that would lead to the destruction of the great multiethnic democratic state.

There is a need for rethinking the principle of democratic centralism. It should no longer be treated in such a way that it can be used to implement barrack-room, hierarchical discipline.

There is no other way to overcome Communists' dissatisfaction with their role in the policy and activity of the party. There is no other way to restore in each of them a sense of dignity and inner freedom.

the shadow of his declining control over domestic affairs. The eclipse of Gorbachev's authority could be traced both to the failure of his reforms to deliver any concrete economic gains and to his lack of legitimacy. Only popular election could give the kind of mandate that would allow Gorbachev and his party to weather the bold and risky reforms that are essential to Soviet economic renewal. Opposition movements had proven their strength at the polls, with attractive, nationally recognized leaders who were building an increasingly united coalition of peasant farmers, junior military officers, independent trade unionists, intellectuals, and Russian nationalists. Within the Communist party itself, divisions became so deep on fundamental issues — ranging from market reforms to sovereignty for the republics — that many leading members (including Yeltsin) resigned from the party at its 28th Congress in July 1990. By all signs, a 70-year-old political system was crumbling. The Soviet regime was facing the necessity for a new power-sharing arrangement; Gorbachev might remain head of state, but only at the price of a multiparty Cabinet.

In foreign affairs, equally striking changes were taking place. The 1988 Reagan-Gorbachev summit in Moscow marked a new era of good feelings: When asked about his "evil empire" remark, President Reagan disavowed it, saying that Gorbachev had changed everything. Even the hard-bitten realists in the American delegation spoke euphorically about the changes they had witnessed and the new candor of their Soviet counterparts. Gorbachev clearly recognized the need for "mutual security," admitting publicly that the unilateral Soviet search for a self-sufficient security posture had fuelled the arms race and led to greater distrust. In an interdependent world, the Soviets could not be secure unless the Americans were too. This focus on interdependence was reflected in a new Soviet emphasis on the global environment, with a prominent United Nations speech urging cooperative measures. Recognizing the collective dimensions of European security as well, the Soviets announced a new doctrine of "nonoffensive defense," accompanied by a restructuring of Warsaw Pact forces that reduced forward deployments and the capacity for surprise attack. They unilaterally demobilized 500,000 troops (10 percent of Soviet forces) and 10,000 tanks. At the same time, Gorbachev launched a peace initiative with the Chinese, attending a 1989 summit meeting in Beijing with the Communist leadership.

This flurry of pronouncements and summit diplomacy was soon matched by events that radically altered the socialist bloc and relations between the superpowers. The collapse of the Communists' monopoly of power began in August 1989 in Poland, where Solidarity leader Tadeusz Mazowiecki formed the first reform government in Eastern Europe. In Hungary, the Communist party renounced its monopoly on power, changed its name to the Hungarian Socialist Party, and resurrected the old national flag of the Republic of Hungary. Within a year, it was replaced in multiparty elections, despite its new social democratic orientation. In Czechoslovakia, dissent playwright Vaclav Havel passed from jail to the nation's presidency in a matter of months. The Civic Forum opposition movement led a peaceful revolution against Communism, marked by massive demonstrations that were echoed throughout Eastern Europe. Alexander Dubcek, the reform Communist who had been ousted by the Soviet invasion in 1968, was rehabilitated and elected speaker of the Czech Parliament. Although Hungary and Czechslovakia remained within the Warsaw Treaty Organization, like other reform governments that emerged in Eastern Europe, they elicited from Gorbachev a commitment to withdraw all Soviet troops.

In December 1989, a bloody uprising in Romania followed on the brutal suppression of mass demonstrations. The army defected and a newly formed National Salvation Front executed the Communist leader, Nicolae Ceausescu, and his wife after a summary trial. Multiparty elections in May 1990 secured a popular mandate for the National Salvation Front, although Communists remained dominant within it, reforms were limited, and harassment of opposition parties continued. Bulgaria soon followed the reform path, abolishing the Communist party's official monopoly on power, but full-fledged democratization was also slow in coming. By mid-1990, Bulgaria and Romania retained ruling Communist parties, after internal reform and reasonably free elections had given the party a new sense of popular legitimacy.

The truly decisive step in the reconstruction of the Soviet bloc was taken in East Germany, where the hard-liner Erich Honecker was replaced by reformer Hans Modrow. He promptly formed a coalition with the non-Communist opposition and lifted all emigration restrictions. Tens of thousands poured across the border into West Germany. On November 9, 1989, the government began to demolish the Berlin Wall, that most concrete of Cold War symbols. West German Chancellor Helmut Kohl called for reunification talks, and party alliances emerged that spanned the East-West divide. Monetary union was proposed, and the great powers, meeting in Ottawa, Canada, embraced a "two-plus-four" formula for negotiations on German unification under a European collective security arrangement. Elections in East Germany ratified a speedy reunification process, putting Lothar de Maiziere at the head of a three-party Alliance for Germany, led by the Christian Democratic Union. In July 1990, the West German deutschemark became the official currency of the East German economy, marking the first step toward a reunited nation. The East German parliament soon voted to join West Germany by means of all-German elections, and the Soviets withdrew their objection to German membership in NATO. By December, Germany rejoined the ranks of the great powers as a united, fully sovereign state.

By mid-1990, the winds of change were blowing everywhere. In March, Mongolia became the first Asian Communist country to follow the path of perestroika. Pro-democracy protests forced a wholesale renewal of party cadres and the new rulers vowed to conduct free, multiparty elections. Open, competitive electoral contests were held throughout Eastern Europe, turning out Communist governments and parties in favor of new faces and forces. Albania remained the lone bastion of Communist orthodoxy, though it launched some limited reforms as well.

Further steps in the arms control process were taken at the Bush-Gorbachev summit in June 1990, when the two superpowers agreed, in principle, to deep cuts in strategic nuclear arsenals. They resolved their differences on cruise missiles and Moscow dropped its demand for a ban on Star Wars technology, at a time when declining support in the U.S. Congress was likely to place de facto limits on testing and deployment anyway. The proposed Strategic Arms Reduction Treaty (START) would reduce long-range nuclear warheads on land-based missiles, aircraft and submarines to a ceiling of 6,000 each — a cut of about 30 percent. (Figure 5-10 describes the superpower inventories at the time of the summit.) A formal START agreement would be accompanied by strong verification measures, including an "open skies" agreement and limits on the encoding of missile-test data. Although the Soviets agreed to reduce by half their force of SS-18 missiles, the Bush administration still insisted on further concessions regarding multiple warhead mobile missiles, the Soviet Backfire bomber, and testing of the SS-18 heavy missiles.

A preliminary outline for a Conventional Forces in Europe (CFE) Treaty was negotiated between the foreign ministers of the two superpowers before the summit. It called for the U.S. and the Soviets to reduce tanks, artillery, and aircraft in Europe. Troops were limited to 195,000 on each side in Central Europe, with the Americans entitled to an extra 30,000 elsewhere, such as in Greece and Turkey. These cuts amounted to a 65 percent reduction for the Soviets and 26 percent for the Americans. Once again asymmetrical cuts and Soviet concessions cleared the path, indicating that Gorbachev was eager to cement friendly relations with the United States and free both resources and attention for pressing domestic concerns. The emergence of independent non-Communist regimes in Eastern Europe also sped the process, since nationalist sentiments there were pressing the Soviets toward withdrawal of their occupying forces.

At the summit itself, however, a formal agreement could not be signed. The Soviets were reluctant to make any reductions without first settling the future military status of Germany. Unification was taken for granted by all, but the Soviets wished to put German security within a larger European framework. Gorbachev proposed that both the NATO and Warsaw pacts be discarded, thus removing the troops and weapons that had militarized Germany and made war in Central Europe possible. Germany would be obliged to renounce the use of force, along with the production, possession, or stationing of weapons of mass destruction in its territory, in exchange for dissolution of the set of military and political decisions — including the Potsdam agreement that defined four-power administration of Germany — that had hitherto divided Germany and impeded its sovereign right to self-determination. President Bush and German Chancellor Helmut Kohl refused to accept German neutrality or any limits on German defenses, but they did pledge to strengthen the authority of the 35-member Conference on Security and Cooperation in Europe. The U.S. secretary of state, James Baker, promised that the reunification of Germany would not take place at Soviet expense, reassuring the Warsaw Pact nations that "they will not be left out of the new Europe." The prospects for a pan-European framework of security guarantees appeared promising after post-summit meetings of the two alliances declared an end to the Cold War. The Warsaw Pact issued a statement calling for "constructive cooperation" with NATO and a transformation of the Soviet-dominated military structure into "a treaty of sovereign states with equal rights, formed on a democratic basis." NATO Secretary General Manfred Woerner, extending "the hand of friendship and cooperation" to the Soviet Union and its former satellites, said: "We do not see ourselves as a bloc in a confrontational system. We are moving beyond confrontation to become a partner in the new European peace order."

The Bush-Gorbachev summit did reach accord on the verification of two nuclear test ban treaties and on a comprehensive ban on chemical weapons. The two nations agreed to stop all production and to reduce their chemical weapons stockpiles by about 80 percent, to 5,000 tons each. The two leaders called for the complete abolition of these weapons, following approval of a worldwide treaty. The summit also produced a significant commitment by President Bush to liberalize trade and promote most-favored-nation status for the Soviet Union, conditional on Soviet passage of a law permitting unfettered emigration. Practically speaking, trade between the two countries was unlikely to grow rapidly, partly because the Soviets produce little that Americans want to buy and cannot afford what America sells, and partly because Congress was sure to make ratification of new trade measures conditional on Soviet recognition of Baltic sovereignty. But Gorbachev lobbied hard for the commitment nonetheless, as a symbol of amity and a political step toward a new relationship. He argued, successfully, that the United States should be prepared to offer the Soviet Union the same trade benefits that the Bush administration had extended to China. The two leaders also signed agreements on grain sales, fisheries, maritime transportation, expanded airline service, cultural exchanges, and scientific projects. They pledged joint efforts to end the civil war in Ethiopia and to cooperate on environmental questions.

Although the summit did not accomplish as much as was hoped by way of formal agreements on arms control and European security, it set a new tone in the Soviet-American dialogue. Both sides pledged to meet more frequently, in annual working meetings that would dispense with the ceremony and political expectations of a formal summit conference. Gorbachev took time to travel the country, wooing both the public and private investors. He made it clear that he welcomed Western capital and technology by signing multimillion-dollar deals with Chevron and IBM. Addressing students at Stanford University, Gorbachev declared "a military economy is ultimately a dead end" and encouraged the superpowers to learn some lessons from such economic success stories as Japan. He said: "I would take as a point of departure the fact that the Cold War is now behind us. And let us not wrangle over who won it. . . . To avoid finding ourselves on the sidelines in the Pacific as well as in Europe, we ought to think about the speediest way to abolish political-military rivalry." Clearly the Soviets wanted to end their isolation from the world's banking and trading system and increase their participation in such global economic forums as the General Agreement on Tariffs and Trade (GATT) and the International Monetary Fund (IMF). President Bush, who had initially opposed observer status for the Soviet Union at GATT, now appeared willing to cooperate to this end.

FIGURE 5-10

THE STRATEGIC NUCLEAR BALANCE, 1990

Current U.S. Strategic Forces Under SALT and START Counting Rules

Counting rules	SALT/START	SALT		START	
	Launchers deployed	Warheads/launcher	Total warheads	Warheads/launcher	Total warheads
ICBM Minuteman II	450	1	450	1	450
Minuteman III	500	3	1,500	3	1,500
MX	50	10	500	10	500
Subtotal (ICBM)	1,000		2,450		2,450
SLBM Poseidon C-3	224	14	3,136	10	2,240
Trident C-4	384	8	3,072	8	3,072
Subtotal (SLBM)	608		6,208		5,312
Bombers B-1B	97	12	1,164	1	97
B-52G/H (non-ALCM)	69	12	828	1	69
B-52G (ALCM)	98	20	1,960	10 (12)	980
B-52H (ALCM)	96	20	1,920	10 (20)	960
Subtotal (bombers)	360		5,872		2,106
TOTAL	1,968		14,530		9,868

Current Soviet Strategic Forces Under SALT and START Counting Rules

Counting rules		SALT/START	SALT		START	
		Launchers deployed	Warheads/ launcher	Total warheads	Warheads/ launcher	Total warheads
ICBM	SS-11	400	1	400	1	400
	SS-13	60	1	60	1	60
	SS-17	138	4	552	4	552
	SS-18	308	10	3,080	10	3,080
	SS-19	350	6	2,100	6	2,100
	SS-24	30	10	300	10	300
	SS-25	165	1	165	1	165
Subtotal (ICBM)		1,451		6,657		6,657
SLBM	SS-N-6	240	1	240	1	240
	SS-N-8	286	1	286	1	286
	SS-N-17	12	1	12	1	12
	SS-N-18	224	7	1,568	7	1,568
	SS-N-20	100	9	900	10	1,000
	SS-N-23	80	10	800	4	320
Subtotal (SLBM)		942		3,806		3,426
Bombers	Bear (ALCM)	75	20	1,500	10 (8)	750
	Bear (non-ALCM)	100	2	200	1	100
	Blackjack	20	12	240	1	20
Subtotal (bombers)		195		1,940		870
TOTAL		2,588		12,403		10,953

After the 1990 summit, each side took steps in a pattern of restraint that made unilateral measures and tacit cooperation as important as formal agreements in ending the superpower rivalry. Mikhail Gorbachev met with South Korean President Roh Tae-woo in an effort to "melt down the ice" that makes the Korean peninsula a frigid remnant of the Cold War. Their meeting restored diplomatic relations between the two countries, expanded trade, and gave a boost to prospects for reunification. The Soviets also announced they would withdraw a portion of their short-range nuclear weapons from Central Europe "in order to create favorable conditions" for future talks. The Soviets may have made a political virtue of a military necessity, since the collapse of the Warsaw Pact as a military alliance was forcing the Soviets to withdraw their troops, and their battlefield nuclear weapons, from Eastern Europe anyway. But the United States faced the same dilemma regarding the modernization of NATO's short-range Lance missiles, which President Bush canceled in the face of strong German opposition to the deployment of any additional nuclear weapons. NATO also announced a decision to revamp its military strategy, including reconsideration of its dependence on the first use of nuclear weapons. Defense secretary Dick Cheney, in the first indication that the Bush administration would consider deep reductions in military spending, ordered the Pentagon to prepare a plan for cutting troops, ships, and air wings by 25 percent over five years. On the trade front, the United States and other major industrial powers, meeting in the Coordinating Committee on Multilateral Export Controls, agreed to a sharp reduction of restrictions on high-technology exports to Warsaw Pact nations. Liberalization extended to controls on machine tools, computers, and telecommunications, and applied to all Communist countries, with no conditions attached.

The Cold War was winding down, bringing an end to direct Soviet-American competition in the Third World as well. By 1990, the signs of the new order were everywhere. In Chile, General Augusto Pinochet was replaced by the democratically elected Patricio Aylwin Azócar. In Nicaragua, the Sandinista government of Daniel Ortega was peacefully overturned by an electoral coalition led by Violeta Chamorro. In South Africa, a reform-minded president, F. W. de Klerk, replaced Pieter Botha and began to dismantle apartheid. He freed African National Congress (ANC) leader Nelson Mandela, legalized the ANC, and lifted the state of emergency. In Namibia, de Klerk gave his blessing to the newly independent government of erstwhile Marxist guerrilla, Sam Nujoma. In Afghanistan, President Najibullah Ahmadzai called on his ruling Communist party to surrender its monopoly on power and rewrite the constitution to permit the participation of fundamentalist Moslems who spearheaded the guerrilla opposition. Extremist regimes on both the left and the right were increasingly isolated, and norms of nonaggression in international affairs received sweeping endorsement. The extent of this new international consensus became clear in August 1990 when the Soviet Union voted in the UN Security Council to permit the use of force by member states to uphold the UN's economics blockade of Iraq, a former Soviet ally.

However, several events gave pause to optimistic predictions. In Communist China, a decade of political and market reforms had introduced a surprising degree of vitality and pluralism, including social criticism in the arts and media, debate over a wide spectrum of political models (even parliamentary and multiparty systems), discussion of alienation and humanism in a socialist country, and contention over the economic meaning of "socialism with Chinese characteristics," to the point of abandoning socialism altogether. But a violent crackdown and conservative backlash, after rapid reform of the economy had stimulated student demands for democratization, gave an ominous warning to those who took liberalization in the Communist bloc for granted. The party's armed suppression of student demonstrators in Tiananmen Square in June 1989 brought about the removal of reform leader Zhao Ziyang, along with a temporary break in relations with the United States. At the opening session of the National People's Congress in 1990, Chinese Communist Premier Li Peng hailed the defeat of the "counterrevolutionary rebellion" as a triumph of order and Maoist orthodoxy over the forces of "chaos." Li upheld the necessity for political dictatorship, centralized planning, self-reliance, and a fight against subversion from abroad, though he proclaimed that Beijing would continue its open-door economic policy and maintain normal relations with all countries, including the new reform governments of Eastern Europe. Trade and foreign investment continued to grow, but so did the size of China's military budget, which jumped 15 percent—an obvious reward for the military's loyalty in the repression that followed the Tiananmen protests. Despite these measures by the hardliners, passive resistance from a sullen population has obstructed central control, and conservatives have been unable to effect a major purge. Advocates of change continue to call for price liberalization, stock markets, privatization of housing, property auctions, and other measures to restructure the economy. Beset by factional struggles, the Chinese political system appears to be stalemated. Deng Xiao-ping and the "gang of elders" are likely to pass from power soon, simply by dint of age, inaugurating a generational transition and a new period of turmoil. For the moment, patriotism and party loyalty are the watchwords; all talk of reform is suppressed in the name of protecting the ideological fabric of a socialist China.

Meanwhile, in Central America, President Bush deployed U.S. troops in December 1989 to oust Panamanian General Manuel Noriega, who had invalidated election results and defied an American economic boycott. Critics lambasted the United States for indulging in old-fashioned interventionist habits, but the vitriol obscured the shifting grounds of action. There were no Cold War issues at stake and tellingly few repercussions from the Third World. (Latin American states uniformly opposed the U.S. action as illegal, but privately acquiesced in the forceful liquidation of a regime they all disliked.) It was the first U.S. intervention to overturn a right-wing dictator and the first in decades that depended for its legitimacy on something other than anti-Communism. Nonetheless, the intervention underscored the reality of continuing instability in the Third World, even after withdrawal of Soviet support for revolutionary insurgencies. An end to the Cold War would not solve chronic problems of dependency and poverty or completely defuse strong anti-American feelings; nor would it prevent great powers from intervening against governments that jeopardize their interests. This became doubly clear with the Iraqi invasion of Kuwait and the massive American military response. These events did not disrupt superpower relations, but they did testify to a marked shift in the lines of conflict from East-West to North-South.

Although democratic capitalism has been declared the victor in the Cold War, threats to world peace and liberal democratic principles are likely to continue, and perhaps proliferate, in the unstable societies of the Third World. Preoccupation with the Soviet Union and the nuclear arms race has obscured a continuing transfer of arms to the Third World that produced a global power shift of unprecedented proportions. The militarization of the Third World can be chronicled in shocking statistical detail. Between 1950 and 1990 world military expenditures have grown (in constant dollars) from $200 billion to almost $1 trillion. Since 1960, the less developed countries increased their arms outlays more than sixfold. In this same period, U.S. arms sales leaped from $1 billion to $21 billion per year. If the world as a whole spends 6 percent of its GNP on the military, the Third World spends almost 20 percent. More than 50 Third World nations have acquired a nuclear weapons production capability or nuclear capable aircraft and missiles through the mechanisms of the free market. Several states, such as Iraq and Libya, have also acquired chemical weapons. In short, the escalation of Third World conventional conflicts or the use of their newly acquired nuclear or chemical weapons capabilities is the most likely route to general war today.

Regional conflicts (and the arms supply relationships that go with them) are likely to continue to inflame international relations, especially because the superpowers are selling other nations the weapons that are being demobilized under recent arms control treaties. For example, the United States is selling Egypt 700 M-60 tanks no longer needed by U.S. forces in Europe. As the Soviet Union and the United States disengage from regional conflicts, Third World nations feel a greater need to build up their own military establishments. For the superpowers themselves, foreign arms sales are viewed as a way to increase the security of overseas allies, as a source of hard currency earnings, as a substitute for foreign aid, and as a way to keep military production lines open at a time when military budgets are being cut.

Moreover, the factors that have brought peaceable superpower relations today are not reproduced in the foreign policies of radical nationalist states in the Third World. Without nuclear weapons to supply a structure of restraint, Third World governments have killed more than 20 million persons in conventional war since 1945. Gorbachev has been persuaded to end the Cold War because of domestic economic imperatives associated with a maturing (and failing) socialist economy, the heavy costs of empire, and the generally dismal record associated with Soviet attempts to install socialist regimes in the Third World. He also belongs to a generation of Soviet leaders that are better educated, more technically skilled, more moderate, less ideological. Sharing a common European culture, a common nuclear threat, and common incentives to peace, the Soviets and the Americans can now reconstruct their relationship along more cooperative lines. But conflict in the Third World is still fueled by rabid nationalism, ideological thinking, ethnic tensions, social ferment, and intense anti-imperial sentiments which have a strong prospect of taking violent expression, well supplied by the arms exports of the developed states.

Finally, de-escalation of the East-West struggle has not freed Europe of all its troubles. Ethnic rioting in Romania, Yugoslavia, and the Soviet Union has exposed the ancient nationalities problem, indicating that Communism might well be replaced by chaos rather than democracy. Precisely because of its repressive character, the Soviet empire had placed in abeyance the ethnic rivalries which so inflamed the Russian empire, the Balkans, and Central Europe before World War I. With democratization and an end to suppression, these hostilities are re-emerging. In January 1990, rioting between Moslem Azerbaijanis and Christian Armenians, set off by the controversy over control of the Nagorno-Karabakh region, forced Gorbachev to declare martial law in the southern republic of Azerbaijan. Invading tanks and troops quelled the ethnic unrest, but not without bringing attacks on the central authorities and the legitimacy of Gorbachev himself. One Azerbaijani enclave in Nakhichevan went so far as to declare independence. Periodic rioting has also erupted between Uzbek and Kirghiz factions in Central Asia, compounding the disintegrative tendencies of the Soviet system. Despite martial law, the central authorities were unable to quell these ethnic tensions. In Romania, the Hungarian minority came under violent attack, while Serbs and Croatians battled in Yugoslavia. In Bulgaria, the Turkish minority began to flee the country in the wake of rioting. The democratization movement in Eastern Europe seemed to open a Pandora's box of ethnic unrest. If history is any guide, some of these conflicts are sure to lead to repressive measures, perhaps martial law and a reimposition of dictatorial controls. Multiparty coalitions in fragile new democracies are not likely to stand the strain.

The fate of the Soviet Union itself is uncertain. Perestroika, democracy, and the future of the Soviet Communist party all hang in the balance. Despite strenuous efforts at reform, many conservative and authoritarian tendencies exist. Unprecedented progress in the human rights field has opened the Soviet Union to monitoring by the International Helsinki Federation, for example, but their public hearings in Moscow, held without official interference, still revealed a pattern of human rights abuses that echoed the old regime. The opposition press continued to be harassed, restraints were still imposed on the right of emigration, religious persecution surfaced from time to time, mobility within the country was severely restricted, and political prisoners were still being held. Given these atavistic tendencies, and the fact that the populace as a whole still had not swallowed the bitter pill of economic reform, the Soviet Union seems fated for further upheaval. The emerging pattern of East-West aid, economic cooperation, and détente — justified by support for budding democracy — may well be slowed or disrupted.

If a lasting shift in East-West relations is to be achieved, the Soviet Union must avoid any explosive breakdown and the repressive policies that violence is likely to bring. Eastern Europe must navigate successfully the rocky transition to democracy. The two superpowers will have to agree to a formula for common security in Europe and put an end to their rivalry in the Third World, defusing regional disputes before they reach the point of military confrontation and superpower intervention. An enduring thaw in Soviet-American relations will depend on Gorbachev's ability to hold together his reform coalition in the Politburo and successfully implement the painful process of market reforms. At the same time, he must convince American skeptics, by his actions, that the Soviet Union will continue to behave as a responsible and pragmatic member of the international community, free from any revolutionary ideological aspirations.

Additional problems may lie in the very success of East bloc reforms: perestroika could bring a more dynamic economy and a more self-confident Soviet leadership, reconstructing the bases for a more aggressive role in world politics. A reunited Germany, buttressed by new economic ties to Eastern Europe, might well pose a threat to the equilibrium in Europe, so long rooted in the EEC and a now-vanishing American military presence. But these are threats formed around old images and categories. Given the new forces of interdependence and the common yearning for freedom, old patterns need not be repeated, even if the success of democracy cannot be assured everywhere. Perhaps the greatest remaining challenge to democracy is an internal one: having won the Cold War, liberal capitalism has yet to cure many of the inequalities and market abuses that made socialism an attractive alternative in the first place. Freed from its preoccupation with an external enemy, America can now put its energy and resources to the challenge of building a more humane society at home.

QUESTION FOR DISCUSSION (PRO AND CON)

Has the reform of Communism ended the East-West rivalry? In particular, should the United States liberalize trade, investment, and credit with the Soviet Union, presuming the Cold War is over?

☞ PRO

The historic changes that we have witnessed under Gorbachev are not simply the product of one man or the reform efforts of a half decade: the Soviet Union has become steadily less ideological and more moderate, internally and externally, ever since the death of Stalin. Moreover, both Soviet strategy and Marxist doctrine have adjusted to the realities of deterrence and the risk of nuclear annihilation. Economic troubles at home and political resistance abroad have given the Soviets pragmatic incentives to improve relations with the United

States. There is every evidence that these changes are irreversible and that they can benefit both countries, if the United States is willing to abandon old habits of thinking, curb military spending, and open new ties of trade and investment.

An objective assessment of postwar Soviet geopolitical influence shows that the socialist bloc has not expanded significantly since 1948. In fact, the Soviets have been losing influence steadily since 1968, among both Marxist allies and neutrals. Soviet foreign policy has not been particularly successful in China, Afghanistan, Eastern Europe, or the Third World. The Kremlin's control of Communist parties in Western Europe ended in the 1970s, when the Eurocommunist movement pushed toward a fully democratic, parliamentary orientation. Military repression kept the East European states in the Soviet bloc for a time, but recent defections from the socialist camp have left very few orthodox Communist states in power. Those that remain are weak and divided among themselves. Long-standing ideological and nationalist frictions with China encouraged the Soviets to court more friendly relations with the United States as a counterbalance to the Chinese threat. Afghanistan has been the Soviet Union's Vietnam — a costly blunder and an embarrassment. Its military occupation was a sign of Soviet weakness, not strength, and the total withdrawal of Soviet troops, in February 1989, was accompanied by an official acknowledgment that the invasion had been a mistake. All these setbacks have forced the Soviets to revise their revolutionary aspirations and confine their energies, in the main, to the preservation of the Soviet system itself. If they once had expansionist or imperialist designs, the Soviets now accept détente as the best policy for protecting their declining fortunes abroad and renewing their economy at home.

The realities of the nuclear threat have also modified the Marxist assumptions of the Soviet regime. The superpowers' ability to tolerate outstanding differences is based on the pragmatic judgment, shared by both sides, that the mutual possession of nuclear weapons makes it impossible for one country to control the other, short of risking the destruction of the planet itself. Once each superpower possessed the minimum invulnerable force needed for retaliation, mutual deterrence encouraged restraint on both sides, no matter how intense the conflict. In this sense, the Cold War was already a kind of enforced détente; in any previous historical era, Soviet-American clashes of interests would have resulted in general war. The entrenched power positions of the two nuclear giants make their task one of embracing coexistence with confidence and moving from a grudging to a willing acceptance of peace. Détente does not require that we always like or trust one another, only that we find it prudent to coexist rather than risk nuclear extermination. Under détente, we need do no more than establish rules of engagement whereby conflicts can be resolved without resorting to arms. The United States and the Soviet Union may not share the same principles of legitimacy or the same moral standards, but they can meet on the common ground of balance-of-power calculations and their mutual interest in self-preservation.

Gorbachev has led the way from a policy of confrontation to one of joint security. Speaking before the UN in February 1989, he said, "Force or the threat of force neither can nor should be instruments of foreign policy. . . . It is clear even today that no country can achieve omnipotence, no matter how much it builds up its military might. Furthermore, emphasis on might alone will in the final analysis undermine other aspects of that country's national security." After the June 1990 summit, he gave a blunt distillation of his new thinking: "We are proceeding from the assumption that anything that is not good for the United States . . . will not be good for us either." As an indication of its new commitment to globalism, the Soviet Union paid the UN $200 million in arrears and put increased emphasis on cooperative measures to protect the environment. New Soviet policies on the peaceful resolution of conflict, disarmament, nonintervention, and participation in the world economy mark an important ideological departure. As a result, the American public no longer perceives the Soviet Union as a serious military threat. The percentage of Americans saying the world is likely to get into a nuclear war in the next ten years declined from 47 percent in 1981 to 18 percent in 1990. In 1950, 81 percent of the public thought the Soviet Union was trying to dominate the world; in 1990, less than a third expressed this view. The new mood was echoed even by American conservatives, such as James Kilpatrick, who said in his syndicated column of June 7, 1990:

> Given the collapse of the Warsaw Pact and the revolutionary changes in Europe, the maintenance of huge nuclear arsenals becomes all the more pointless. Surely strategic sufficiency could be preserved with a few hundred verifiable weapons apiece. Total nuclear disarmament is out of the question, but it is insane—wastefully, dangerously insane—to talk of spending an additional $100 billion over the next decade on such stupidities as two mobile missile systems, four more Trident submarines and 75 B-2 bombers for which there is no plausible mission.

Nuclear arms control is particularly promising in the present moment because we are at a hiatus in technological development. The first generation of warheads and delivery systems has reached the limits of refinement, and we are still a decade away from the widespread deployment of such completely new systems as precision-guided conventional munitions, chemical-bacteriological weapons, ballistic missile defense, or space-based technologies. Immediate changes in the U.S. strategic arsenal will largely involve modernization (for example, stealth technology) and mobility (the Midgetman missile). Gains in security will be quite marginal in relation to cost, and there is a fairly widespread public perception that the two superpowers already have more weapons than they need to protect their basic security. If the diplomats can seize this window of opportunity, they may be able to effect a comprehensive freeze in nuclear testing and weapons production, one that would still be verifiable by existing national technical means. As miniaturization progresses, as the line between nuclear and conventional weapons is steadily erased, as ballistic missile defense and Star Wars make it increasingly difficult to distinguish between offensive and defensive technologies, unambiguous agreements will become more and more difficult to negotiate. A comprehensive freeze— unlike the earlier SALT treaties, which only limited certain categories of arms —could bypass the constant squabbling over what constitutes "modernization" and could impose limits so severe that either side would be able to spot cheating in any of the six stages of weapons development: budget decision, research, development, testing, production, or deployment. From this kind of mutual, verifiable freeze, we could move toward deep cuts in the two arsenals until we arrived back at an affordable minimum deterrent of just a few hundred invulnerable nuclear systems. These mutual gains in national security can be reinforced by gains in trade and domestic prosperity that will give future generations a positive stake in maintaining détente.

Domestic conditions affect the warmth or hostility of Soviet-American relations as never before. For détente to succeed, there must be converging pressures within both countries that lead them to a mutually advantageous strategy of cooperation. We are at such a historic moment today. Mikhail Gorbachev has taken dramatic initiatives on behalf of détente, recognizing that Soviet foreign policy must be completely reconstructed in order to rescue the struggling economy from the burden of nonproductive military expenditures. In 1988, he said, grimly: "Perestroika is our last chance. If we stop, it will be our death." After more than a decade of stagnating growth, agricultural failures, and lagging technological innovation, the Soviet leadership is convinced that state socialism as it has been organized cannot compete effectively with the West, nor can it satisfy rising internal demands for consumer goods. When asked what was the first thing the country needed to do to improve their lives, 71 percent of the Soviet public responded, in a 1989 poll published in *Literaturnaya Gazeta*, that it should severely curtail military spending. In their first competitive elections in seventy-odd years, Soviet citizens defeated party bosses and military brass in favor of candidates advocating military cuts. Given these domestic political-economic pressures, it is safe to say that real reductions in military spending will take place. Today, the Soviet people know their standard of living compares unfavorably with the West, and Gorbachev knows that only material incentives, not ideological exhortations, can induce the people to work harder. Improved Soviet-American relations are necessary if Gorbachev is to cement a reform coalition at home that will disarm and decentralize, if not completely democratize, the process of economic decision making.

Détente will remain attractive to the Soviets over the long run for these reasons: first, their economic difficulties are structural and will take decades to solve. Even if Gorbachev's aim is to rebuild socialism rather than destroy it, the effect of perestroika is to dismantle Soviet-style communism. Tolerance in the Kremlin is not so important as impotence: by necessity as much as by choice, Gorbachev has adopted a "triage strategy" to salvage the Soviet Union by the only means possible — market reforms and the surrender of a politically indigestible and economically burdensome empire. Second, democratization in Eastern Europe will provide a steady stream of liberal influences and political-economic incentives to reform. Marxist systems all over the world are turning to non-Communist ways in production, trade, aid, and alliance relations. The Soviets not only have acquiesced in this trend but have imitated it for themselves. Third, China will remain as a long-term threat to Soviet security, which can be balanced only by friendlier relations with the United States, along with arms control on a global scale to restrain the Chinese nuclear buildup. Fourth, now that Third World extremists have begun to target the Soviets as well as the United States, the two superpowers have a common interest in restraining terrorism and maintaining traditional rules of the diplomatic game.

In the United States, budget deficits have pushed both fiscal conservatives and advocates of social programs toward sharp cuts in defense spending. Both idealists and realists have come to support détente. Optimists view the Gorbachev era as something utterly new and different — a generational change that amounts to a revolution from within. Realists, such as former President Richard Nixon, say that the Reagan military buildup gave us the ability to negotiate from strength and to pursue a patient diplomacy. They also realize that changes in the Soviet Union are erupting from sources too deep to permit their suppression even if Gorbachev's tenure turns out to be relatively brief. Soviet retrenchment is dictated by economic and strategic necessities. With regard to ideological differences, we need simply to adopt the pragmatic policy of live-and-let-live that we have shown toward Communist China, whose Marxism is more orthodox than Moscow's and whose record on human rights and totalitarian practices is worse than the Soviets'. The Soviet Union is viewed as more dangerous because of the size of its nuclear arsenal and its role as a great-power competitor. If we can defuse the nuclear threat through arms control, the only remaining obstacle to détente will be our power impulses — and perhaps our reluctance to abandon an image of "the enemy" that makes us feel virtuous and gives us a scapegoat. These are poor reasons for hanging on to an adversarial relationship.

Détente holds much promise for the United States in the area of expanded trade relations. Apart from our grain sales, the main beneficiaries of the trade liberalization that began in 1974 have been Japan and the European Economic Community, which have offered the Soviet Union credits and nondiscriminatory trade terms without suffering a trace of economic subversion or "Finlandization." The United States has paid a high price for the outmoded notion that trade is a privilege that we should withhold from our ideological adversaries: export controls have cost U.S. firms between $7 billion and $9 billion annually. Expanded economic exchanges between the United States and the USSR could immensely benefit both sides while creating a basis for more stable relations. Gorbachev has openly courted a marriage of Western capital with the vast natural resources of Siberia, promising privileged access to firstcomers, foreign control of joint ventures, and the right to repatriate profits. The Soviet Union would like to import entire factories, fertilizer plants, petroleum and natural gas facilities, power-generating systems, transport and distribution systems. It desperately needs U.S. managerial know-how, high technology, computer hardware and software in nonmilitary areas. The United States, having run spectacular trade deficits for more than a decade, needs new markets. Why should we suffer a self-imposed economic isolation that puts us at a competitive disadvantage against other industrial societies? Granting the Soviet Union most-favored-nation status and giving it access to Export-Import Bank credits would normalize economic relations between our two countries.

The Soviets have proved themselves creditworthy and scrupulously reliable in fulfilling their commercial commitments. The time is ripe for détente on the trade front.

On the question of linkage — whether trade, arms control, human rights, and Soviet good behavior in the Third World ought to be tied together — it would be better to allow each issue to stand alone, so that cooperation in one arena will not be infected by continuing competition in another. In the spirit of free trade, economic relations should not be linked to political considerations. We should permit an unfettered exchange in every area that promises mutual benefits, so that economic relations will be a self-supporting, and consequently more stable, arena of cooperation. Trade that is politically motivated simply distorts the market and makes both economies unnecessarily vulnerable to crises and to the ideological climate of the moment. Most vital of all, we should give up the idea that improved economic relations are contingent on internal reforms in the Soviet system. Steady investment, stable market relations, and a growing dependence on world trade are the surest guarantees of moderation in Soviet foreign policy, even if domestic turmoil brings a return to more repressive measures at home. Besides, diplomacy is by definition the management of conflict between states that do not share the same political language and that differ in the character of their domestic regimes. To insist that relations be liberalized on one side or the other's terms is to defeat the purposes of diplomacy and the very principle of reciprocity, the core of any enduring policy of coexistence.

☞ CON

Despite liberal hopes for an end to the Cold War, East-West competition will continue for some decades to come. The Soviet Union remains a potent military threat and continues to seek, by the path of reform, a strengthened great power position. Perestroika and glasnost have been pressed upon the Kremlin leadership by economic necessity, not by virtue of any conversion from socialism to capitalism; they are designed to refurbish the Soviet economy, enhance national security, and advance their global influence. We see a tactical retreat in Afghanistan and Eastern Europe, where the burdens of empire have become too costly, but we do not see an end to great power rivalry or a decline in the pace of modernization in Soviet strategic forces. We see an abandonment of Marxism-Leninism, but not of militaristic habits, authoritarian tendencies, bureaucratic rigidities, or anti-democratic impulses in Russian culture. Even if the reform efforts are sincere and peacefully directed, they have touched off a turbulent process of social change that will not issue in a stable regime, let alone liberal democracy, for many years to come. We will be wise to contain our enthusiasm for Gorbachev until he has weathered the storms of transition which are already breaking apart a beleaguered empire. Given the history of animosity and the size of existing arsenals (despite recent arms reductions), the United States should adopt a cautious "wait-and-see" policy toward the Soviet Union.

Nuclear weapons do not create any automatic confluence of interests between the Soviet Union and the United States. In fact, the threat of utter destruction is one factor that has inflamed superpower relations beyond their traditional bounds. Such an apocalyptic threat inevitably arouses suspicions, and any prudent political leader will maintain a healthy skepticism toward a nuclear adversary, no matter what arms control regime may have been negotiated. Add to the military threat a revolutionary agenda in the Third World and the Soviet Union remains a fearsome competitor. Perennial misunderstandings and conflicts are built into the very structure of superpower relations.

Gorbachev's announcement of sweeping troop, artillery, and armor cuts has stirred neutralist tendencies in Europe, pulled at the ties that bind NATO, and inclined many Americans to conclude that it is safe to pull out of Europe and cut the defense budget. But the Soviet conventional military advantage is still better than two-to-one, and the 600 miles from the Soviet border to the heart of Germany is not a sufficient obstacle to aggression. Withdrawal must be matched by demobilization of forces if the West is to be secure, given the inherent geopolitical advantages enjoyed by the Soviets. New "defensive" military doctrines may be propounded, but they are not yet matched by cuts in force structure, resources, or deployments. The USSR continues to improve its strategic rocket forces, both in mobility and accuracy. They are modernizing their nuclear-powered, ballistic-missile submarine force, the world's largest, with Typhoon and Delta IV deployments. They are enhancing their bomber forces with the introduction of the Blackjack, the world's largest and heaviest bomber, and the addition of longer-range AS-15 cruise missiles to an already potent fleet of Bear bombers. The Soviets have also upgraded their tank forces, their fleet of missile destroyers and attack submarines, their air defenses and tactical aircraft wings. NATO's retiring secretary general, Lord Carrington, warned in 1988 that "the Soviet . . . military machine is still, so far, operating at exactly the same level as it was in the days before perestroika and glasnost." Moreover, ethnic unrest and separatist movements in the Soviet Union appear to have increased the influence of the military and slowed the momentum of arms control, as indicated by the meager results of the June 1990 summit.

Détente is dangerous because it obscures the basic conflict and lulls the West into complacency: it is the opiate of democracy. The détente of the Nixon-Kissinger era was a diplomatic and ideological snare by which the Soviet Union gained U.S. recognition of Communist hegemony in Eastern Europe without having to give any reciprocal recognition of U.S. interests in Latin America or elsewhere. Détente was a cosmetic formula to cover American retreat from Vietnam and the Third World generally. If détente means the recognition of equal status for competing principles of legitimacy or of the Soviets' right to global influence, then it equates dictatorship with democracy and legitimizes Soviet domination of others. A democracy that accepts such a state of affairs does not long survive. A détente that contributes to a general weakening of America's power and resolve should be rejected.

Glasnost is a new version of détente—a Potemkin Village designed to attract Western aid, in the tradition of Lenin's New Economic Policy (NEP) of the 1920s. The alleged "new thinking" arouses liberal optimism but it disguises the regime's ongoing predicament and the Soviet propensity to deception. Properly understood, "peaceful coexistence" is just another term for class struggle on a global scale. In the 1950s, Soviet Premier Khrushchev described this coexistence as a decadent marriage between a rich old woman (the United States) and a vigorous young man (the USSR). The old woman would grow weaker as she lost more and more influence over the world. The young man would have affairs in the Middle East, Africa, and Latin America. Eventually she would stop caring. When this happened, the Soviet Union would not have to wait for her to die in order to inherit her global pre-eminence; the United States would have surrendered it meekly. Perhaps today the roles are reversed, but the inherent conflicts of interest and ideology still remain.

In the era of perestroika, Marxist dogma may be dead, but we still have to contend with Soviet inclinations to militarism. The Russian threat has a long historical record, going back to the expansionist tendencies of the czars. Karl Marx himself described the Russian imperial impulse in several newspaper dispatches he wrote in the 1850s:

> The Russian frontier has advanced: towards Berlin, Dresden and Vienna . . . towards Constantinople . . . towards Stockholm . . . towards Teheran. . . . The total acquisitions of Russia during the last 60 years are equal in extent and importance to the whole Empire she had in Europe before that time. . . .
> And as sure as conquest follows conquest, and annexation follows annexation, so sure would the conquest of Turkey by Russia be only the prelude for the annexation of Hungary, Prussia, Galicia, and for the ultimate realization of the Slavonic Empire. . . . The arrest of the Russian scheme of annexation is a matter of the highest moment.

Around the same time, a State Department dispatch characterized the diplomatic goals of the Russian Empire in these terms: "A strange superstition prevails among the Russians, that they are destined to conquer the world." Of the deceptiveness of Russian diplomacy, President Theodore Roosevelt said, during the Russo-Japanese War of 1905: "Russia is so corrupt, so treacherous and shifty . . . that I am utterly unable to say whether or not it will make peace, or break off negotiations at any moment." Russia's "Iron Curtain complex" began as early as the Renaissance, when its political and religious orthodoxy led it to cut off cultural contact with the West. And militarism is just as deeply rooted in Soviet soil. A search for secure frontiers, rail access, and warm water ports has pitted the Russians against every single state that has ever had the misfortune to border the Russian Empire. The marriage of imperialism and militarism over centuries of Russian history makes it doubly unlikely that the Soviets will experience a change of heart at this late date.

As former President Richard Nixon notes, all Gorbachev's actions have been directed toward two geopolitical goals: to revive his moribund economy via access to Western capital and technology; and to divide his adversaries and thereby end the political isolation of the Soviet Union. The aim of détente in Soviet eyes has always been to detach the Europeans from the U.S. security zone and thereby neutralize the largest center of economic production and military potential in the world. As long as Western Europe remains under American political and military protection, the Soviets will never feel safe. This is why they propagandized so hard to persuade the Europeans to reject the U.S. deployment of Pershing II and cruise missiles. Although thousands joined in peace marches in 1983, the Reagan administration held to its tough position, the missiles were deployed in Europe, and the Soviets were forced back into negotiations. These eventually led to the INF treaty and the withdrawal of a whole class of nuclear missiles. The lesson is clear: it was not détente that brought concessions, but America's willingness to arm and to negotiate from strength. Détente in the 1970s turned out to be a device for restraining American arms development while the Soviets ran pell-mell to catch up. The SALT agreements did not serve American security well. We would have done better to begin the Reagan buildup back in the 1970s, rather than to lose a decade to our self-imposed disarmament stance. Moreover, the NATO alliance can well afford to run an arms race with the Russians, since its resources and economic potential vastly outweigh the Soviet Union's accumulated assets.

On the trade front, the West is in danger of selling the Soviets the rope with which they will hang us. Already the Japanese, the Norwegians, and the French have sold them the computers and machine tools they needed to match us in silent submarine technology. Capitalism has propped up the Soviet regime from the beginning, when Lenin's New Economic Policy conspired to use foreign capital and economic concessions to rebuild Russia after the ravages of war and the Bolshevik Revolution. A careful study of foreign investment in the postrevolutionary years shows that by 1930 there was not one important industrial process that did not derive from transfers of Western technology. Then, after a wave of autarky and expropriation, came another infusion of Western capital, through wartime lend-lease and the postwar transfer of $10 billion worth of German industrial and military equipment. When the Soviet economy began to stagnate once more in the 1960s, Brezhnev turned again to the import of foreign technology, the perennial savior of the Soviet economy. There is no doubt that present desire for access to revolutionary Western innovations in computers and electronics is a critical factor in the Soviet conversion to détente. From 1981 to 1985, there was practically no economic growth; per capita income actually declined. Since January 1986, when Gorbachev's new five-year plan was launched, growth has been less than 2 percent per year, half the plan's target rate. The Soviet economy under perestroika has been a disaster. It has lost whatever meager discipline and rationality was imparted by the old system, without the vitality of really thoroughgoing reforms, because these would threaten the control of the party and the security of the elite, including Gorbachev himself. So he must follow the strategy of the NEP: to use capitalism against itself, by offering economic concessions to gain foreign investment and technology. But, as former Defense Secretary Frank Carlucci has noted (in Karen Swisher, *The Superpowers,* p. 186), "If the . . . result is that . . . the Soviet Union modernizes its industrial and technological base, and if sometime in the 1990s it . . . can produce enormous quantities of weapons even more effectively than it does today, then we will have made an enormous miscalculation."

The one-sided character of trade liberalization is noted by Carl Gershman ("Selling Them the Rope: Business and the Soviets," *Commentary* [April 1979], pp. 35–45): "The asymmetry of the technological 'exchange' relationship is reinforced by the Soviet Union's obsession with secrecy and by its unabashedly predatory approach." Furthermore, the industrial espionage of the Soviets has been unprecedented, as they seek to steal the technology they cannot buy or invent for themselves. And Western businesses have acquiesced in a pattern of trade that favors the Soviet propensity for economic isolation: the transfer of whole factories ("turnkey" plants), along with the training of Soviet personnel to make the plants self-sufficient. This has hardly brought the linkage or the interdependence imagined by Western economic liberals. In fact, Western trade has often been the source of vital military technologies that have strengthened the Soviet defense posture. This was true of Germany's military assistance in the 1920s, and it is more true of technology transfers today. Even imports of civilian technology indirectly aid Soviet defense, by modernizing the economy and freeing scarce talent and resources for military purposes. Thus, American goods actually serve to sustain the Communist state. If greater liberalization and decentralization of the Soviet system are among the goals of détente, they might better be achieved by strict controls on the transfer of foreign technology, which would force the Soviets to loosen the political reins which stifle their own innovative capacities. This point is made by Judy Shelton, in a speech given to the National Press Club on March 14, 1989:

> In short, the two inputs the Soviet system needs to break out of its financial and economic conundrum—consumer goods to motivate workers, technology to increase productivity—must come from outside the Soviet Union. If the West does not furnish them, Gorbachev (or his replacement) will be forced to make a fundamental and wrenching change within the Soviet system to transfer resources out of the military sector, which is basically unproductive, and into manufacturing for the consumption sector, which is the source of real economic production. The alternative is to permit the Soviet economy as a whole to deteriorate, and, in so doing, incur the grave risk of social and political unrest.
>
> In light of this analysis, it becomes apparent that deliveries from the West of consumer goods and technology, financed with Western credits, have the effect of relieving . . . the internal economic pressure that is the compelling force behind perestroika; it enables Soviet authorities to continue to devote scarce internal resources to the military as before. Thus, aid from the West has the effect of forestalling the very transition process we presumably would like to see taking place in the Soviet Union: a switch in priorities from military spending to improving the quality of life for the Soviet people.

If gullible Western banks and investors give the green light to freer trade, they may divert so many resources to Soviet projects and joint ventures that they deprive other needy nations of capital, driving up the cost of funds to everyone. Reverse leverage could come into play, just as it has on Third World debt, making the Soviet threat of default or nationalization a potentially destabilizing factor in the world economy. The Western banks' painful over-exposure in Eastern Europe, especially in Poland, should breed a healthy suspicion of putting too many eggs in the Soviet basket. On the other hand, if the United States is willing to adopt a tough trade policy and cut Soviet access to hard currency and Western technology, the Soviet empire will collapse without our spending $300 billion on defense or firing a single shot.

For the Soviet Union to receive Western assistance, Richard Nixon recommends six conditions:

> First, Moscow must establish a free-market economy. Second, Eastern European countries must complete their transition to full independence. Third, NATO and the Warsaw Pact must establish parity in conventional arms. Fourth, the United States and the Soviet Union must conclude a verifiable START agreement ensuring stable nuclear deterrence. Fifth, Gorbachev must cease his aggressive policies in the Third World. Sixth, the Soviet Union must adopt a political order that respects human rights and reflects the wishes of people expressed in free elections. (*In the Arena: A Memoir of Victory, Defeat, and Renewal*)

These conditions are far from being fulfilled. Communism may have lost the Cold War, but the West has not yet won it. The victory still must be consolidated in geopolitical terms. In the meantime, we must remember that the Soviets have broken their promises before, on arms control, trade, emigration, human rights. The prudent course is to pay the closest attention to the hardest of facts and keep our powder dry.

SOURCES AND SUGGESTED READINGS

General Works on Soviet-American Relations

See also references cited in Chapter 7 on U.S. and Soviet foreign policies.

"American Strength, Soviet Weakness." *The Defense Monitor*, vol. 9, no. 5 (1980).

Arbatov, Georgi, and Willem Oltmans. *The Soviet Viewpoint*. New York: Dodd, Mead, & Co., 1983.

Bender, Peter. "The Superpower Squeeze." *Foreign Policy*, vol. 65 (Winter 1986/87), pp. 98–113.

Bethlen, Steven, and Ivan Volgyes, eds. *Europe and the Superpowers: Political, Economic, and Military Policies in the 1980s*. Boulder, Colo.: Westview Press, 1985.

Bronfenbrenner, Urie. "Mirror-Image in Soviet-American Relations." *Journal of Social Issues*, vol. 17, no. 3 (1961), pp. 45–56.

Brzezinski, Zbigniew. *Game Plan: How to Conduct the U.S.-Soviet Contest*. Boston: Atlantic Monthly Press, 1986.

Cohen, Richard, and Peter A. Wilson. "Superpowers in Decline? Economic Performance and National Security." *Comparative Strategy*, vol. 7 (1988), pp. 99–132.

Cohen, Stephen F. *Sovieticus: American Perceptions and Soviet Realities*, rev. ed. New York: Norton, 1987

Collins, John M., and Anthony Cordesman. *Imbalance of Power: Shifting U.S.-Soviet Military Strengths*. San Rafael, Calif.: Presidio Press, 1978.

Dallin, Alexander. *Black Box: KAL 007 and the Superpowers*. Berkeley: University of California Press, 1985.

Dean, Jonathan. *Watershed in Europe: Dismantling the East-West Military Confrontation*. Lexington, Mass.: Lexington Books, 1987.

De Tocqueville, Alexis. *Democracy in America*, 2 vols. New York: Schocken, 1961.

Gaddis, John Lewis. *Russia, the Soviet Union, and the United States: An Interpretive History*. New York: Wiley, 1978.

Garthoff, Raymond. *Détente and Confrontation: American-Soviet Relations from Nixon to Reagan*. Washington, D.C.: Brookings Institution, 1985.

George, Alexander, ed. *Managing U.S.-Soviet Rivalry: Problems of Crisis Prevention*. Boulder, Colo.: Westview Press, 1983.

George, Alexander, et al., eds. *U.S.-Soviet Security Cooperation: Achievements, Failures, Lessons.* New York: Oxford University Press, 1988.

German, Robert K., ed. *The Future of U.S.-U.S.S.R. Relations: Lessons from Forty Years Without World War.* Austin: University of Texas at Austin, 1986.

Gray, Colin. *The Geopolitics of Superpower.* Lexington, Ky.: University Press of Kentucky, 1988.

Herman, Robert. "After the INF Treaty: The Road to Deep Cuts." *Nucleus,* vol. 9, no. 4 (Winter 1988), pp. 1–4.

Hoffmann, Stanley. "Coming Down from the Summit." *The New York Review of Books.* (Jan. 21, 1988), pp. 21–25.

Holbraad, Carsten. *Superpowers and International Conflict.* New York: St. Martin's, 1979.

Hyland, William G. *Mortal Rivals.* New York: Random House, 1987.

Jönsson, Christer. *Superpower: Comparing American and Soviet Foreign Policy.* New York: St. Martin's, 1984.

Kaplan, Fred M. *Dubious Specter: A Second Look at the "Soviet Threat."* Washington, D.C.: The Transnational Institute, 1977.

Krauss, Melvyn B. *How NATO Weakens the West.* New York: Simon & Schuster, 1986.

Lafeber, Walter. *America, Russia, and the Cold War, 1945–1980,* 3rd ed. New York: Wiley, 1980.

Larson, Thomas B. *Soviet-American Rivalry.* New York: Norton, 1978.

Liska, George. "Concert Through Decompression." *Foreign Policy* (Summer 1986), pp. 108–29.

———. "From Containment to Concert." *Foreign Policy* (Spring 1986), pp. 3–23.

Luttwak, Edward. *The Grand Strategy of the Soviet Union.* New York: St. Martin's Press, 1983.

Nincic, Miroslav. *Anatomy of Hostility: The US-Soviet Rivalry in Perspective.* New York: Harcourt Brace Jovanovich, 1989.

Nye, Joseph S., Jr., ed. *The Making of America's Soviet Policy.* New Haven: Yale University Press, 1984.

Pipes, Richard. *Survival Is Not Enough.* New York: Simon & Schuster, 1984.

Savigear, Peter. *Cold War or Détente in the 1980s: The International Politics of American-Soviet Relations.* New York: St. Martin's, 1988.

Schmookler, Andrew B. "US-USSR: Are We Angling Toward a Shoot-Out at the OK Corral?" *Political Psychology.* vol. 6, no. 2 (June 1985), pp. 275–90.

Schwartz, Morton. *Soviet Perceptions of the United States.* Berkeley. University of California Press, 1978.

Shulman, Marshall D. "Four Decades of Irrationality: U.S.-Soviet Relations." *Bulletin of the Atomic Scientists* (Nov. 1987), pp. 15–25.

Steele, Jonathan. *Soviet Power,* rev. ed. New York: Touchstone/Simon & Schuster, 1984.

Stoessinger, John G. *Nations in Darkness: China, Russia, and America,* 4th ed. New York: Random House, 1986.

Talbott, Strobe. *The Russians and Reagan.* New York: Vintage-Council on Foreign Relations, 1984.

Ulam, Adam. *The Rivals: America and Russia Since World War II.* New York: Viking, 1971.

———. "U.S.-Soviet Relations: Unhappy Coexistence." *Foreign Affairs* (Jan. 1979), pp. 555–71.

White, Ralph K. *Fearful Warriors: A Psychological Profile of U.S.-Soviet Relations.* New York: Free Press, 1984.

Wildavsky, Aaron, ed. *Beyond Containment: Alternative American Policies Toward the Soviet Union.* San Francisco: Institute for Contemporary Studies, 1983.

On the Cold War and Its Origins

Alperovitz, Gar. *Atomic Diplomacy: Hiroshima and Potsdam—The Use of the Atomic Bomb and the American Confrontation with Soviet Power,* rev. ed. New York: Penguin, 1985.

Bailey, Thomas A. *America Faces Russia.* Ithaca, N.Y.: Cornell University Press, 1950.

Bernstein, Barton. "Roosevelt, Truman and the Atomic Bomb, 1941–1945: A Reinterpretation." *Political Science Quarterly,* vol. 90 (Spring 1975), pp. 23–62.

Brands, Jr., H. W. *Cold Warriors: Eisenhower's Generation and American Foreign Policy.* New York: Columbia University Press, 1988.

Carlton, David, and Herbert M. Levine, eds. *The Cold War Debated.* New York: McGraw-Hill, 1988.

Deporte, A. W. *Europe Between the Superpowers.* New Haven, Conn.: Yale University Press, 1979.

Divine, Robert A. *Eisenhower and the Cold War.* New York: Oxford University Press, 1981.

Feis, Herbert. *Churchill, Roosevelt, Stalin: The War They Waged and the Peace They Sought*, 2nd ed. Princeton, N.J.: Princeton University Press, 1967.
———. *From Trust to Terror: The Onset of the Cold War, 1945–1950*. Princeton, N.J.: Princeton University Press, 1970.
Fenno, Richard F., Jr., ed. *The Yalta Conference*. Boston: D.C. Heath, 1955.
Gaddis, John Lewis. *The United States and the Origins of the Cold War, 1941–1947*. New York: Columbia University Press, 1972.
Graebner, Norman A., ed. *The Cold War: A Conflict of Ideology and Power*, 2nd ed. Boston: D.C. Heath, 1976.
———, ed. *The National Security: Its Theory and Practice, 1945–1960*. New York: Oxford University Press, 1986.
Grosser, Alfred. *The Western Alliance*. New York: Vintage, 1982.
Halle, Louis. *The Cold War as History*. New York: Harper & Row, 1967.
Harbutt, Fraser J. *The Iron Curtain: Churchill, America, and the Origins of the Cold War*. New York: Oxford University Press, 1986.
Herken, Gregg. *The Winning Weapon: The Atomic Bomb in the Cold War, 1945–1950*. New York: Vintage, 1981.
Kennan, George F. *American Diplomacy, 1900–1950*. New York: Mentor, 1952.
———. *Russia and the West Under Lenin and Stalin*. New York: Mentor, 1961.
———. "The United States and the Soviet Union, 1917–1976." *Foreign Affairs*, vol. 54 (1976), pp. 673–94.
Kolko, Gabriel. *The Politics of War*. New York: Random House, 1968.
Lafeber, Walter, ed. *The Origins of the Cold War, 1941–1947*. New York: Wiley, 1971.
Maddox, Robert J. *The New Left and the Origins of the Cold War*. Princeton, N.J.: Princeton University Press, 1973.
Maier, Charles S., ed. *The Origins of the Cold War and Contemporary Europe*. New York: New Viewpoints, 1978.
Miller, Lynn, and Ronald Pruessen, eds. *Reflections on the Cold War*. Philadelphia: Temple University Press, 1974.
Paterson, Thomas. *Meeting the Communist Threat: Truman to Reagan*. New York: Oxford University Press, 1988.
———. *Soviet-American Confrontation: Postwar Reconstruction and the Origins of the Cold War*. Baltimore: Johns Hopkins University Press, 1973.
———, ed. *The Origins of the Cold War*. Boston: D.C. Heath, 1970.
Schlesinger, Arthur, Jr. *The Cycles of American History*. Boston: Houghton Mifflin, 1986.
Sivachev, Nikolai, and Nikolai Yakovlev. *Russia and the United States: U.S.-Soviet Relations from the Soviet Point of View*. Chicago: University of Chicago Press, 1979.
Spanier, John. *American Foreign Policy Since World War II*, 9th ed. New York: Holt, Rinehart & Winston, 1983.
Thomas, Hugh. *Armed Truce: The Beginnings of the Cold War, 1945–46*. New York: Atheneum, 1987.
Thompson, Kenneth W. *Cold War Theories*. Baton Rouge, La.: Louisiana State University Press, 1981.
Wolfe, Alan. *The Rise and Fall of the Soviet Threat: Domestic Sources of the Cold War Consensus*. Boston: South End Press, 1984.
Yergin, Daniel. *Shattered Peace: The Origins of the Cold War and the National Security State*. Boston: Houghton Mifflin, 1977.

On Containment, Korea, and Vietnam

Berman, Larry. *Planning a Tragedy: The Americanization of the War in Vietnam*. New York: W. W. Norton, 1982.
Berman, William C. *William Fulbright and the Vietnam War: The Dissent of a Political Realist*. Kent, Ohio: Kent State University Press, 1988.
Billings-Yun, Melanie. *Decision Against War: Eisenhower and Dien Bien Phu, 1954*. New York: Columbia University Press, 1988.
Blair, Clay. *The Forgotten War: America in Korea, 1950–53*. New York: Times Books, 1988.
Braestrup, Peter, ed. *Vietnam as History: Ten Years After the Paris Peace Accords*. Washington, D.C.: University Press of America, 1984.

Deibel, T. L., and John L. Gaddis, eds. *Containment: Concept and Policy*, 2 vols. Washington, D.C.: National Defense University Press, 1986.

Draper, Theodore. *Abuse of Power*. New York: Viking, 1967.

Fall, Bernard. *The Two Vietnams*, 2nd rev. ed. New York: Praeger, 1967.

Fitzgerald, Frances. *Fire in the Lake: The Vietnamese and the Americans in Vietnam*. New York: Vintage, 1972.

Foot, Rosemary. *The Wrong War: American Policy and the Dimensions of the Korean Conflict*. Ithaca, N.Y.: Cornell University Press, 1985.

Franklin, David, and James Chace. "The Lessons of Vietnam?" *Foreign Affairs* (Spring 1985), pp. 722–46.

Fulbright, J. William. *The Arrogance of Power*. New York: Vintage, 1967.

Gaddis, John Lewis. *The Long Peace: Inquiries into the History of the Cold War*. New York: Oxford University Press, 1987.

————. *Strategies of Containment*. New York: Oxford University Press, 1982.

Gardner, Lloyd C. *Approaching Vietnam*. New York: Norton, 1988.

————, ed. *The Korean War*. New York: Quadrangle, 1972.

Gelb, Leslie, with Richard Betts. *The Irony of Vietnam: The System Worked*. Washington, D.C.: Brookings Institution, 1979.

Gibbons, William C. *The U.S. Government and the Vietnam War*. Princeton, N.J.: Princeton University Press, 1987.

Goodrich, Leland M. *Korea: A Study of U.S. Policy in the United Nations*. New York: Council on Foreign Relations, 1956.

Guttmann, Allen, ed. *Korea and the Theory of Limited War*. Boston: Heath, 1967.

Halberstam, David. *The Best and the Brightest*. New York: Random House, 1972.

Hellmann, John. *American Myth and the Legacy of Vietnam*. New York: Columbia University Press, 1986.

Herring, George C. *America's Longest War: The United States and Vietnam, 1950–1975*. New York: Wiley, 1986.

————. "The 'Vietnam Syndrome' and American Foreign Policy." *Virginia Quarterly Review*, vol. 57 (Fall 1981).

Hess, Gary. *The United States' Emergence as a Southeast Asian Power, 1940–1950*. New York: Columbia University Press, 1987.

Hoffmann, Stanley, et al. "Vietnam Reappraised." *International Security*, vol. 6 (Summer 1981), pp. 3–26.

Hoopes, Townsend W. *The Limits of Intervention*. New York: David McKay, 1969.

Horowitz, David, ed. *Containment and Revolution*. Boston: Beacon Press, 1967.

Kahin, George M. *Intervention: How America Became Involved in Vietnam*. Garden City, N.Y.: Anchor/Doubleday, 1987.

Kahin, George M., and John W. Lewis. *The United States in Vietnam*, rev. ed. New York: Delta (Dell), 1969.

Kaiser, David E. "Vietnam: Was the System the Solution?" *International Security*, vol. 4 (1980), pp. 199–218.

Karnow, Stanley. *Vietnam: A History*. New York: Penguin, 1983.

Kattenburg, Paul M. *The Vietnam Trauma in American Foreign Policy, 1945–75*. New Brunswick, N.J.: Transaction Books, 1980.

Kaufman, Burton I. *The Korean War: Challenges in Crisis, Credibility, and Command*. Philadelphia: Temple University Press, 1986.

Kennan, George F. *Memoirs, 1925–1950*. Boston: Little, Brown, 1967.

Kolko, Gabriel. *Anatomy of a War: Vietnam, the United States, and the Modern Historical Experience*. New York: Pantheon, 1986.

Kolko, Gabriel, and Joyce Kolko. *The Limits of Power*. New York: Harper & Row, 1972.

Lewy, Guenter. *America in Vietnam*. New York: Oxford University Press, 1980.

Lowe, Peter. *The Origins of the Korean War*. London: Longman, 1986.

Lyons, Gene M. *Military Policy and Economic Aid: The Korean Case, 1950–1953*. Columbus: Ohio State University Press, 1961.

MacDonald, Callum A. *Korea: The War Before Vietnam*. New York: Free Press, 1987.

May, Ernest. *Lessons of the Past: The Use and Misuse of History in American Foreign Policy*. New York: Oxford University Press, 1973.

Nardin, Terry, and Jerome Slater. "Vietnam Revised." *World Politics*, vol. 33 (1981), pp. 436–48.

Oglesby, Carl and Richard Shaull. *Containment and Change: Two Dissenting Views of American Foreign Policy*. New York: Macmillan, 1967.

Paige, Glenn D. *The Korean Decision, June 24–30, 1950.* New York: Free Press, 1968.
Palmer, Jr., Bruce. *The Twenty-Five-Year War: America's Military Role in Vietnam.* Lexington: University Press of Kentucky, 1984.
Paterson, Thomas, ed. *Containment and the Cold War.* Menlo Park, Calif.: Addison-Wesley, 1973.
Pike, Douglas. *History of Vietnamese Communism, 1925–1976.* Palo Alto, Cal.: Hoover Institution Press, 1978.
Pike, Douglas. *Vietnam and the Soviet Union: Anatomy of an Alliance.* Boulder, Colo.: Westview, 1987.
Podhoretz, Norman. *Why We Were in Vietnam.* New York: Simon & Schuster, 1982.
Rotter, Andrew. *The Path to Vietnam: Origins of the American Commitment to Southeast Asia.* Ithaca, N.Y.: Cornell University Press, 1987.
Stillman, Edmund, and William Pfaff. *Power and Impotence: The Failure of America's Foreign Policy.* New York: Random House, 1966.
Thompson, Jr., James C. "How Could Vietnam Happen? An Autopsy." *Atlantic Monthly,* vol. 221 (1968), pp. 47–53.
Thompson, Sir Robert. *No Exit from Vietnam.* New York: McKay, 1969.
Thompson, W. Scott, and D. D. Frizzill, eds. *The Lessons of Vietnam.* Philadelphia: Crane Russak, 1977.
Tillema, Herbert K. *Appeal to Force: American Military Intervention in the Era of Containment.* New York: Thomas Crowell, 1973.
Tucker, Robert. "The Two Containments: An Argument Retraced." In Robert Tucker, *The Purposes of American Power: An Essay on National Security.* New York: Praeger, 1981.

On Soviet-American Rivalry in the Third World

See also references cited in Chapter Six, under the heading "U.S. Intervention in the Third World."
Bender, Gerald. "Angola, the Cubans, and American Anxieties." *Foreign Policy,* (Summer 1978), pp. 3–33 (with comment by Chester Crocker).
Bender, Gerald, et al., eds. *African Crisis Areas and U.S. Foreign Policy.* Berkeley: University of California Press, 1985.
Bernstein, Alvin H. "Insurgents Against Moscow: The Reagan Doctrine Can Put Soviet Imperialism on the Defensive." *Policy Review,* vol. 41 (Summer 1987), pp. 26–29.
Bertram, Christoph, ed. *Third World Conflict and International Security.* London: Macmillan, 1982.
Bodie, William R. "The Reagan Doctrine." *Strategic Review,* vol. 14 (Winter 1986), pp. 21–29.
Brown, James, and William P. Snyder, eds. *The Regionalization of Warfare.* New Brunswick, N.J.: Transaction Books, 1985.
Calvocoressi, Peter. *World Politics Since 1945,* 4th ed. New York: Longman, 1982.
Carpenter, Ted Galen. "U.S. Aid to Anti-Communist Rebels: The 'Reagan Doctrine' and Its Pitfalls." *Cato Institute Policy Analysis,* vol. 74 (June 24, 1986).
Copson, Raymond W., and Richard P. Cronin. "The 'Reagan Doctrine' and Its Prospects." *Survival* (London), vol. 29 (Jan./Feb. 1987), pp. 40–55.
Davis, Nathaniel. "The Angolan Decision of 1975." *Foreign Affairs* (Fall 1978), pp. 109–24.
Dominguez, Jorge I., and Marc Lindenberg. *Central America: Current Crisis and Future Prospects* (Headlines Series No. 271, November/December). New York: Foreign Policy Association, 1984.
Dominguez Reyes, Edme. *Soviet and Cuban Interests in Central America.* Boulder, Colo.: Westview, 1989.
Donaldson, Robert H., ed. *The Soviet Union in the Third World.* Boulder, Colo.: Westview, 1981.
Duncan, W. Raymond, and Carolyn McGiffert Ekedahl. *Moscow and the Third World Under Gorbachev.* Boulder, Colo.: Westview, 1989.
Duncan, W. Raymond, ed. *Soviet Policy in the Third World.* New York: Pergamon, 1980.
Evron, Yair. *The Middle East: Nations, Superpowers, and Wars.* New York: Praeger, 1973.
Feinberg, Richard E. *The Intemperate Zone: The Third World Challenge to U.S. Foreign Policy.* New York: W. W. Norton, 1983.
Fukuyama, Francis. *Moscow's Post-Brezhnev Reassessment of the Third World.* Santa Monica, Cal.: Rand, 1986.
———. *U.S.-Soviet Interaction in the Third World.* Santa Monica, Cal.: Rand, 1985.
Gavshon, Arthur. *Crisis in Africa: Battleground of East and West.* Middlesex, Eng.: Penguin, 1981.
Heikal, Mohammed. *The Road to Ramadan.* New York: Quadrangle, 1975.

——. *Sphinx and Commissar: The Rise and Fall of Soviet Influence in the Arab World*. London: Collins, 1978.

Heilbroner, Robert L. "Counterrevolutionary America." *Commentary* (April 1967), pp. 31–38.

Hosmer, Stephen T., and Thomas W. Wolfe. *Soviet Policy and Practice Toward Third World Conflicts*. Lexington, Mass.: D. C. Heath, 1983.

Hough, Jerry F. *The Struggle for the Third World: Soviet Debates and American Options*. Washington, D.C.: Brookings Institution, 1986.

Johnson, Robert H. "Exaggerating America's Stakes in Third World Conflicts." *International Security* (Winter 1985/86).

Kaplan, Stephen S. *Diplomacy of Power: Soviet Armed Forces as a Political Instrument*. Washington, D.C.: Brookings Institution, 1981.

Kaplan, Stephen S., and Barry M. Blechman. *Force Without War: U.S. Armed Forces as a Political Instrument*. Washington, D.C.: Brookings Institution, 1978.

Katz, Mark N. "Anti-Soviet Insurgencies: Growing Trend or Passing Phase?" *Orbis*, vol. 30 (Summer 1986), pp. 365–91.

——. "Soviet Third World Policy." *Problems of Communism*, vol. 35 (July/Aug. 1986), pp. 87–92.

Kenworthy, Eldon. "Central America: Beyond the Credibility Trap." *World Policy Journal*, vol. 1, no. 1 (Fall 1983), pp. 181–200.

Kiernan, Bernard P. *The United States, Communism, and the Emergent World*. Bloomington: Indiana University Press, 1972.

Kirkpatrick, Jeanne. "Dictatorship and Double Standards." *Commentary* (Nov. 1979).

Kolodziej, Edward, and Roger Kanet. *The Limits of Soviet Power in the Developing World*. Baltimore: Johns Hopkins University Press, 1988.

Kwitney, Jonathan. *Endless Enemies: The Making of an Unfriendly World*. New York: St. Martin's Press, 1984.

Lafeber, Walter. *Inevitable Revolutions: The United States in Central America*, rev. ed. New York: Norton, 1984.

Laquer, Walter. *Confrontation: The Middle East War and World Politics*. London: Wildwood House, 1974.

Layne, Christopher. "Requiem for the Reagan Doctrine." *SAIS Review* (Winter-Spring, 1988).

Liska, George. "The Reagan Doctrine: Monroe and Dulles Reincarnate?" *SAIS Review*, vol. 6 (Summer/Fall 1986), pp. 83–98.

Litwak, Robert S., and Samuel F. Wells, Jr. *Superpower Competition and Security in the Third World*. Boston: Ballinger, 1988.

Lowenthal, Abraham F. *Partners in Conflict: The United States and Latin America*. Baltimore: Johns Hopkins University Press, 1987.

MacFarlane, S. Neil. *Superpower Rivalry and Third World Radicalism: The Idea of National Liberation*. London: Croom Helm, 1985.

Marcum, John. "Lessons of Angola." *Foreign Affairs* (April 1976), pp. 407–25.

Middlebrook, Kevin J., and Carlos Rico, eds. *The United States and Latin America in the 1980s: Contending Perspectives on a Decade of Crisis*. Pittsburgh: University of Pittsburgh Press, 1986.

Morley, Morris H. *Imperial State and Revolution: The United States and Cuba, 1952–1986*. New York: Cambridge University Press, 1987.

Papp, Daniel S. *Soviet Policies Toward the Developing World During the 1980s*. Maxwell Air Force Base, Ala.: Air University Press, 1986.

Petras, James, and Morris H. Morley. *The United States and Chile: Imperialism and the Overthrow of the Allende Government*. New York: Monthly Review Press, 1975.

Porter, Bruce D. *The USSR in Third World Conflicts*. New York: Cambridge University Press, 1984.

Price, Robert M. *U.S. Foreign Policy in Sub-Saharan Africa: National Interest and Global Strategy*. Berkeley, Cal.: University of California Institute for International Studies, 1978.

Quandt, William B. *Camp David: Peacemaking and Politics*. Washington, D.C.: Brookings Institution, 1986.

——. *Decade of Decisions: American Policy Toward the Arab-Israel Conflict, 1967–1976*. Berkeley, Cal.: University of California Press, 1977.

Saivetz, Carol R. *The Soviet Union and the Gulf in the 1980s*. Boulder, Colo.: Westview, 1989.

Saivetz, Carol R., and Sylvia Woodby. *Soviet-Third World Relations*. Boulder, Colo.: Westview, 1985.

Schulz, Brigitte, and William W. Hansen, eds. *The Soviet Bloc and the Third World: The Political Economy of East-South Relations*. Boulder, Colo.: Westview, 1988.

Sewell, John W., Richard Feinberg, and Valeriana Kallab, eds. *U.S. Foreign Policy and the Third World.* New Brunswick, N.J.: Transaction Books, 1985. (One of a series published by the Overseas Development Council)

Shulman, Marshall D., ed. *East-West Tensions in the Third World.* New York: W. W. Norton, 1986.

Sigmund, Paul E. *The Overthrow of Allende and the Politics of Chile, 1964–1976.* Pittsburgh: University of Pittsburgh Press, 1978.

"Soviet Geopolitical Momentum: Myth or Menace?" *The Defense Monitor,* vol. 9, no. 1 (1980).

Tillman, Seth. *The United States in the Middle East.* Bloomington: Indiana University Press, 1982.

Trofimenko, Henry. "The Third World and the U.S.-Soviet Competition: A Soviet View." *Foreign Affairs,* vol. 59, no. 5 (Summer 1981), pp. 1021–40.

Whelan, Joseph G., and Michael J. Dixon. *The Soviet Union in the Third World: Threat to World Peace?* Washington, D.C.: Pergamon-Brassey's, 1986.

Wolfe, Charles, et al. *The Costs of Soviet Empire.* Santa Monica, Cal.: Rand, 1983.

Working Group on Security Affairs. *After Afghanistan—The Long Haul: Safeguarding Security and Independence in the Third World.* Washington, D.C.: The Atlantic Council, 1980.

On Nuclear Conflict, the Arms Race, and Arms Control

See also references listed in Chapter 9 under the heading "Deterrence and Nuclear War-Fighting Strategies."

Abel, Elie. *The Missile Crisis.* Philadelphia: Lippincott, 1966.

Aron, Raymond. *The Great Debate.* New York: Doubleday, 1965.

Bernstein, Barton J. "The Cuban Missile Crisis." In Lynn Miller and Ronald Pruessen, eds., *Reflections on the Cold War,* pp. 108–42. Philadelphia: Temple University Press, 1974.

Bundy, McGeorge, et al. "Nuclear Weapons and the Atlantic Alliance." *Foreign Affairs,* vol. 60 (Spring 1982), pp. 753–68.

Carlton, David, and Carlo Schaerf, eds. *Reassessing Arms Control.* New York: St. Martin's Press, 1985.

Cockburn, Andrew. *The Threat: Inside the Soviet Military Machine,* rev. ed. New York: Vintage Books, 1984.

Craig, Paul, and John Jungerman. *Nuclear Arms Race: Technology and Society.* New York: McGraw-Hill, 1986.

Dean, Jonathan. "American Approaches to Arms Control: Contentious, Erratic, and Inadequate." *Harvard International Review* (May/June 1987), pp. 14–16.

Dinerstein, Herbert S. *The Making of a Missile Crisis: October 1962.* Baltimore: Johns Hopkins Press, 1976.

Draper, Theodore. *Present History: On Nuclear War, Détente, and Other Controversies.* New York: Random House, 1983.

Ehrlich, Robert. *Waging Nuclear Peace.* Albany: State University of New York Press, 1985.

Freedman, Lawrence. *The Evolution of Nuclear Strategy.* New York: St. Martin's Press, 1983.

Frei, Daniel. *Perceived Images: U.S. and Soviet Assumptions and Perceptions in Disarmament.* Totowa, N.J.: Rowman & Littlefield, 1986.

Garfinkle, Adam M., ed. *Global Perspectives on Arms Control.* New York: Praeger, 1984.

Garthoff, Raymond L. *Reflections on the Cuban Missile Crisis.* Washington, D.C.: Brookings Institution, 1987.

George, Alexander L. "The Cuban Missile Crisis, 1962." In Alexander George et al, *The Limits of Coercive Diplomacy.* Boston: Little, Brown, 1971.

Gervasi, Tom. *The Myth of Soviet Military Supremacy.* New York: Harper & Row, 1986.

Gottfried, Kurt, and Bruce Blair, eds. *Crisis Stability and Nuclear War.* New York: Oxford University Press, 1988.

Gray, Colin S. "NATO's Nuclear Dilemma." *Policy Review,* vol. 22 (Fall 1982), pp. 97–116.

———. "Nuclear Delusions: Six Arms Control Fallacies." *Policy Review,* vol. 37 (Summer 1986), pp. 48–53.

———. *The Soviet-American Arms Race.* London: Saxon House, 1976.

Haley, P. E. et al, eds. *Nuclear Strategy, Arms Control, and the Future.* Boulder, Colo.: Westview Press, 1985.

Hanreider, Wolfram, ed. *Technology, Strategy, and Arms Control.* Boulder, Colo.: Westview Press, 1985.

Harris, John, and Eric Markusen, eds. *Nuclear Weapons and the Threat of Nuclear War.* San Diego: Harcourt Brace Jovanovich, 1986.

Holloway, David. *The Soviet Union and the Arms Race,* 2nd ed. New Haven: Yale University Press, 1984.

Horelick, Arnold. "The Cuban Missile Crisis: An Analysis of Soviet Calculations and Behavior." *World Politics,* vol. 16 (April 1964).

Howard, Michael. "Illusions That Fuel Pressure for Arms Control." *Atlantic Community Quarterly,* vol. 24 (Summer 1986), pp. 119–21.

Ikle, Fred Charles. "NATO's 'First Nuclear Use': A Deepening Trap." *Strategic Review,* vol. 8 (Winter 1980), pp. 18–23.

Kahan, Jerome. *Security in the Nuclear Age: Developing U.S. Strategic Arms Policy.* Washington, D.C.: Brookings Institution, 1975.

Kegley, Charles, Jr., and Eugene Wittkopf, eds. *The Nuclear Reader: Strategy, Weapons, and War,* 1st and 2nd eds. New York: St. Martin's Press, 1985, 1989.

Kennan, George F. *The Nuclear Delusion: Soviet-American Relations in the Atomic Age,* rev. ed. New York: Pantheon Books, 1983.

Kennedy, Robert F. *Thirteen Days: A Memoir of the Cuban Missile Crisis.* New York: New American Library, 1969.

Kincade, W. J., and Jeffrey Porro, eds. *Negotiating Security: An Arms Control Reader.* Washington, D.C.: Carnegie Endowment for International Peace, 1979.

Kolkowicz, Roman, and Neil Joeck, eds. *Arms Control and International Security.* Boulder, Colo.: Westview, 1984.

Kolkowicz, Roman, and Ellen Propper Mickiewicz, eds. *The Soviet Calculus of Nuclear War.* Lexington, Mass.: Lexington Books, 1986.

Krepon, Michael. *Strategic Stalemate: Nuclear Weapons and Arms Control in American Politics.* New York: Macmillan, 1985.

Kruzel, Joseph. "From Rush-Bagot to START: The Lessons of Arms Control." *Orbis,* vol. 30 (Spring 1986), pp. 193–216.

Kurtz, Lester R. *The Nuclear Cage: A Sociology of the Arms Race.* Englewood Cliffs, N.J.: Prentice-Hall, 1988.

Lee, Admiral John. *No First Use.* Boston: Union of Concerned Scientists, 1983.

Lens, Sidney. *The Day Before Doomsday: An Anatomy of the Nuclear Arms Race.* Boston: Beacon Press, 1977.

Levine, Herbert, and David Carlton, eds. *The Nuclear Arms Race Debated.* New York: McGraw-Hill, 1986.

Long, Franklin, et al., eds. *Weapons in Space.* New York: Norton, 1986.

Mandelbaum, Michael. *The Nuclear Question: The U.S. and Nuclear Weapons, 1946–76.* New York: Cambridge Univesity Press, 1979.

McNamara, Robert S. *Blundering into Disaster: Surviving the First Century of the Nuclear Age.* New York: Pantheon, 1987.

Mearsheimer, John J. "Nuclear Weapons and Deterrence in Europe." *International Security,* vol. 9 (Winter 1984/85), pp. 19–46.

Molander, Earl, and Roger Molander. *What About the Russians—And Nuclear War?* New York: Pocket Books/Ground Zero, 1983.

Myrdal, Alva. *The Game of Disarmament: How the United States and Russia Run the Arms Race,* rev. ed. New York: Pantheon, 1982.

Nacht, Michael. *The Age of Vulnerability: Threats to the Nuclear Stalemate.* Washington, D.C.: Brookings Institution, 1985.

Nerlich, Uwe, and James A. Thomson, eds. *Conventional Arms Control and the Security of Europe.* Boulder, Colo.: Westview, 1988.

Nincic, Miroslav. *The Arms Race: The Political Economy of Military Growth.* New York: Praeger, 1982.

O'Keefe, Bernard J. *Nuclear Hostages.* Boston: Houghton Mifflin, 1983.

Parrott, Bruce. *The Soviet Union and Ballistic Missile Defense.* Boulder, Colo.: Westview Press (Johns Hopkins Foreign Policy Institute), 1987.

Porro, Jeffrey, ed. *The Nuclear Age Reader.* New York: Knopf, 1989.

Powaski, Ronald E. *March to Armageddon: The United States and the Nuclear Arms Race, 1939 to the Present.* New York: Oxford University Press, 1987.

Prins, Gwyn, ed. *The Nuclear Crisis Reader.* New York: Vintage, 1984.

Russett, Bruce. *The Prisoners of Insecurity: Nuclear Deterrence, the Arms Race, and Arms Control.* San Francisco: W. H. Freeman, 1983.

Russett, Bruce, and Bruce Blair, eds. *Progress in Arms Control?* San Francisco: W. H. Freeman, 1979.

Schloming, Gordon. *American Foreign Policy and the Nuclear Dilemma.* Englewood Cliffs, N.J.: Prentice-Hall, 1987.

Schroeder, Dietrich. *Science, Technology, and the Nuclear Arms Race.* New York: Wiley, 1984.

Scott, R. T., ed. *The Race for Security: Arms and Arms Control in the Reagan Years.* Lexington, Mass.: Lexington/D.C. Heath, 1986.

Seaborg, Glenn T. *Kennedy, Khrushchev, and the Test Ban.* Berkeley: University of California Press, 1981.

Singer, J. David. *Deterrence, Arms Control, and Disarmament.* Washington, D.C.: University Press of America, 1984.

Smoke, Richard. *National Security and the Nuclear Dilemma.* Menlo Park, Calif.: Addison-Wesley, 1984.

Stein, Jonathan B. *From H Bomb to Star Wars: The Politics of Strategic Decision-Making.* New York: Heath, 1984.

Steinbruner, John, and Leon Sigal, eds. *Alliance Security: NATO and the No-First-Use Question.* Washington, D.C.: Brookings Institution, 1983.

Talbott, Strobe. *Deadly Gambits: The Reagan Administration and the Stalemate in Nuclear Arms Control.* New York: Vintage, 1985.

Turner, John, and SIPRI. *Arms in the '80s: New Developments in the Global Arms Race.* Philadelphia: Taylor & Francis, 1985.

U.S. Arms Control and Disarmament Agency. *Arms Control and Disarmament Agreements: Texts and Histories.* Washington, D.C.: U.S. Arms Control & Disarmament Agency, 1982.

U.S. Department of Defense. *Soviet Military Power.* Washington, D.C.: U.S. Government Printing Office, 1985.

USSR Ministry of Defense. *Whence the Threat to Peace.* Moscow: Military Publishing House, 1982.

Wieseltier, Leon. *Nuclear War, Nuclear Peace.* New York: Holt, Rinehart & Winston, 1983.

York, Herbert. *Race to Oblivion: A Participant's View of the Arms Race.* New York: Simon & Schuster, 1970.

Zuckerman, Lord Solly. *Nuclear Illusion and Reality.* New York: Viking, 1982.

————. *Star Wars in a Nuclear World.* London: William Kimber, 1986.

On Détente

Barnet, Richard J. *The Giants: Russia and America.* New York: Touchstone/Simon & Schuster, 1977.

Bell, Coral. *The Diplomacy of Détente: The Kissinger Era.* New York: St. Martin's, 1977.

Brzezinski, Zbigniew. *Power and Principle.* New York: Farrar, Straus & Giroux, 1983.

Friedland, Edward, et al. *The Great Détente Disaster: Oil and the Decline of American Foreign Policy.* New York: Basic Books, 1975.

Gaddis, John Lewis. "The Rise, Fall, and Future of Détente." *Foreign Affairs* (Winter 1983/84).

Gati, Charles, and Toby Trister Gati. *The Debate Over Détente.* Washington, D.C.: Foreign Policy Association, 1977.

Goldman, Marshall I. *Détente and Dollars: Doing Business with the Soviets.* New York: Basic Books, 1975.

Hersh, Seymour M. *The Price of Power: Kissinger in the Nixon White House.* New York: Summit Books, 1983.

Hess, Gary R., ed. *America and Russia: From Cold War Confrontation to Coexistence.* New York: Crowell, 1973.

Hoffmann, Stanley. "Détente." In Joseph S. Nye, ed., *The Making of America's Soviet Policy.* New Haven, Conn.: Yale University Press, 1984.

Kissinger, Henry. *The White House Years.* Boston: Little, Brown, 1979.

Litwak, Robert S. *Détente and the Nixon Doctrine.* New York: Cambridge University Press, 1986.

Neal, Fred Warner, ed. *Détente or Debacle: Common Sense in U.S.-Soviet Relations.* New York: Norton, 1978.

Newhouse, John. *Cold Dawn: The Story of SALT.* New York: Holt, Rinehart & Winston, 1973.

Nixon, Richard. *RN: The Memoirs of Richard Nixon.* New York: Grosset & Dunlap, 1978.

Nutter, G. Warren. *Kissinger's Grand Design.* Washington, D.C.: American Enterprise Institute, 1975.

Pranger, Robert J., ed. *Détente and Defense.* Washington, D.C.: American Enterprise Institute, 1976.

Sokoloff, Georges. *The Economy of Détente: The Soviet Union and Western Capital.* New York: St. Martin's, 1987.

Smith, Gordon B., ed. *The Politics of East-West Trade.* Boulder, Colo.: Westview, 1984.

Stoessinger, John G. *Henry Kissinger: The Anguish of Power.* New York: Norton, 1976.

Talbot, Strobe. *Endgame: The Inside Story of SALT II.* New York: Harper & Row, 1979.

Wolfe, Thomas. *The SALT Experience.* Cambridge, Mass.: Ballinger, 1979.

On Gorbachev and New Thinking

Adelman, Kenneth L. "Is the Soviet Threat Over?" *The Intercollegiate Review* (Spring 1990), pp. 3–12.

Adomeit, Hannes. "What's Happening in Moscow?" *National Interest,* vol. 8 (Summer 1987), pp. 18–22.

Bialer, Seweryn, and Michael Mandelbaum, eds. *Gorbachev's Russia and American Foreign Policy.* Boulder, Colo.: Westview, 1988.

Brown, Archie. "Change in the Soviet Union." *Foreign Affairs,* vol. 64 (Summer 1986), pp. 1048–65.

Bukovsky, Vladimir. "Glasnost: Genuine Change or Illusion?" *The Heritage Lectures* (no. 113). Washington, D.C.: Heritage Foundation, 1987.

Cracraft, James. "The Gorbachev Regime After Two Years." *Bulletin of the Atomic Scientists,* vol. 43 (May 1987), pp. 31–33.

Dahlburg, John-Thor. "Official Soviet Article Calls Lenin Dictator, Terrorist." *The Oregonian* (June 29, 1989), p. A10.

Gati, Charles. *The Bloc That Failed: Soviet-East European Relations in Transition.* Bloomington: Indiana University Press, 1990.

Gorbachev, Mikhail. *Perestroika: New Thinking for Our Country and the World.* New York: Harper & Row, 1987.

Hough, Jerry F. *Russia and the West: Gorbachev and the Politics of Reform.* New York: Simon & Schuster, 1988.

Kaiser, Robert G. "The Soviet Pretense." *Foreign Affairs,* vol. 65 (Winter 1986/87), pp. 236–51.

Kilpatrick, James J. "A Conservative View: Adding to Nuclear Stockpile Meaningless, Insane." *The Oregonian* (June 7, 1990), p. D9.

Lewin, Moshe. *The Gorbachev Phenomenon: A Historical Interpretation.* Berkeley: University of California Press, 1988.

Nixon, Richard M. *1999: Victory Without War.* New York: Simon & Schuster, 1988.

———. *In the Arena: A Memoir of Victory, Defeat and Renewal.* New York: Simon & Schuster, 1990.

Oreskes, Michael. "Poll Finds Fewer Americans See Soviet Union as Threat." *The Oregonian* (May 30, 1990), p. A11.

Parks, Michael. "Soviets Quicken Reform Pace with Manifesto." *The Oregonian* (June 25, 1989), p. A8.

Shelton, Judy. "The Western Economic Response: Should We Help Gorbachev?" Speech given to the National Strategy Information Center at the National Press Club, March 14, 1989.

Swisher, Karin. *The Superpowers: A New Détente—Opposing Viewpoints.* San Diego, Calif.: Greenhaven Press, 1989.

Talbott, Strobe, and Michael Mandelbaum. *Reagan and Gorbachev.* New York: Vintage, 1987.

Yanov, Alexander. *The Soviet Challenge and the Year 2000.* New York: Basil Blackwell, 1987.

6

NORTH-SOUTH CONFLICT

The rise to self-assertion of Third World peoples has altered the whole tone of international affairs. Over a hundred of new states—most of them with deep political and economic problems—have emerged in the Middle East, Africa, Asia, and Latin America in the aftermath of decolonization. We cannot understand the main sources of international instability today without understanding this ferment in the Third World.

We use the term *Third World* to refer to all the less-developed nations outside the advanced capitalist and the Communist blocs, but it is a term coined by the West and is somewhat misleading in that it lumps together many states of great diversity. Although most of the Third World experienced colonialism or Western domination, some countries, such as Iran, Thailand, and Ethiopia, escaped European conquest. Latin America is set apart by its geographic location, by the distinctive nature of Spanish and Portuguese colonialism, and by its gaining of independence early in the nineteenth century. Israel, South Africa, Australia, and New Zealand are geographically a part of the Third World, but unique circumstances have given all of them a standard of living (at least, for their citizens of European ancestry) well above that of the typical Third World state. The oil states of Saudi Arabia, Kuwait, Oman, Qatar, Libya, Bahrain, and the United Arab Emirates have a gross national product (GNP) per capita of between $5,000 and $25,000, comparable to that of the advanced industrial countries, yet they remain traditional societies. Despite their wealth, they are not industrialized, and they possess many social and political features common to the remainder of the Third World, whose per capita income ranges more typically between $120 and $3,000 per year. The average per capita GNP for all developing economies, as measured by the World Bank in 1986 dollars, was $610. A number of states that belong in the Third World socially and economically have Communist governments and can hardly be considered nonaligned; among them are Cuba, the People's Republic of China, North Korea, Vietnam, Laos, and Kampuchea. On the other hand, several newly industrializing countries (NICs), such as South Korea and the Republic of China (Taiwan), are aligned firmly with the Western capitalist bloc. Because of their export-oriented strategies of development, they more closely resemble the developed West than do such neighboring countries as the Philippines or India.

For all these differences, "Third World" is the common shorthand term for the less-developed Southern two-thirds of the globe, which does have many features in common. The majority of the states are new actors in international affairs, having come to independence only after World War II. Most of them are poor, politically unstable, and nonaligned, that is, outside the formal East-West alliance structure. Moreover, their development models are neither those of the First World of industrial democracy nor of the Second World of centralized state socialism. They have been forced to search out their own path to modernization, and they aspire to new political-economic models that fit their own indigenous traditions — a "third way" that is autonomous, politically neutral, and a mix of capitalist and socialist elements.

In this second great axis of global conflict, the developed democracies of Japan, Western Europe, and North America, along with the Soviet Union and the advanced socialist states of Eastern Europe, are the privileged or "have" nations of the North, whose power and wealth give them control over the "have-nots" of the South. The developed states hold a veto power in the United Nations, dominate the international economy, have overwhelming military power, and monopolize advanced technology. In reaction, the Third World states have coalesced politically to exert joint power in various ways — in the United Nations, in cooperative economic agendas, in independent coalitions (like the Contadora group) to mediate local conflicts. Individually, poor states have sought to manage their relations with the developed North in such a way as to serve their own development priorities without compromising their political sovereignty. The political leaders of the new states have struggled to catch up with the North both economically and politically, and they also have tried to achieve the military prowess and technology that confer international stature. As new nations have modernized and become armed, they have affected both regional stability and the global balance of power.

Commentators often refer to the Third World as an "intemperate zone" or an "arc of crisis." Its instabilities are the result of several factors that we will examine in this chapter: (1) decolonization and the independence movements of the postwar period; (2) an appalling poverty; (3) revolutionary upheavals, military coups, and other internal struggles for power; (4) the military interventions and proxy wars of the East-West conflict. The North-South dimension, with its immense problems of underdevelopment, poverty, and insecurity, is high on the agenda of international concerns. As Third World governments have struggled with conditions of dependence and vulnerability, they have increasingly affirmed that both the sources of underdevelopment and their solutions are global in character. Civic strife cannot be stifled so long as it is kept alive by the arms, agents, and meddling interests of the superpowers. Third World poverty has its roots in colonialism and dependency, which is perpetuated even today in disguised forms of neocolonialism. Problems of technology transfer, capital formation, population control, food production, access to resources, pollution control, and regulation of trade are incapable of being resolved except on a global, multilateral basis. The South has thus constellated itself as a diplomatic unit, bargaining for concessions and institutional reforms that will allay the problems of the Third World as a whole. The North-South conflict is yet another indicator of an interdependent world economy and a global balance of power.

THE PROBLEM OF UNDERDEVELOPMENT

Tradition Versus Modernity

The dilemmas of development in the new states of the Third World may be grouped around four main themes. The first of these is the tension between tradition and modernity. Much of this tension is the consequence of imperialism, which saw the powerful conquering states impose their technology and the more dynamic values of modernity on tradition-bound tribal or peasant societies. A similar clash of cultures occurred in those societies that were able to escape colonial occupation by means of "defensive" modernization. Contact with the West compromised the cultural integrity of the Third World peoples and forced them to search for distinctive identities of their own.

Arnold Toynbee, in *The World and the West,* tells of the poignant attempt of Mehmed Ali Pasha, the Ottoman governor-general of Egypt in 1839, to protect his country from the predations of the great powers by obtaining Western arms for himself. But he could not hire Western naval architects without agreeing to bring their families, and the families would not come without their doctors, so Mehmed Ali Pasha hired them, too. The doctors, energetic and public-spirited, had little work to do, since the contingent of Westerners was small, so they decided to help out the local population by organizing a maternity hospital within the precincts of the naval arsenal. Very soon it filled up with poor Islamic peasant women who had learned of its lifesaving potential. As Toynbee's story continues, the contact with Western technology and ideas quickly spread well beyond the medical realm:

> The moral of this story is the speed with which, in cultural intercourse, one thing can lead to another, and the revolutionary length to which the process may go. Within the lifetime of all concerned, the traditional seclusion of Muslim women from contact with men outside their own household had still been so strictly enforced that in eighteenth-century Turkey, even when one of the Sultan's most dearly beloved wives was so ill that her life was in danger, the most that the Islamic code of manners would allow a Western doctor to do for this precious imperial patient was just to feel the pulse of a hand held out timidly between the tightly drawn curtains of the invisible lady's bed. . . . And now, within the same lifetime, Muslim women were boldly venturing inside the precincts of an outlandish arsenal to avail themselves of the services of infidel Western obstetricians. This dire breach with the traditional Islamic conceptions of decency in the social relations between the sexes had been a consequence of the Pasha of Egypt's decision to equip himself with a navy in the Western style; and this undesigned and, at first sight, remote social effect had followed its technological cause within the span of less than half a lifetime.

> This piece of social history, which is piquant but not unrepresentative, gives the measure of the degree to which those nineteenth-century Ottoman statesmen were deluding themselves when they imagined that they would be able to fit their country out with adequate Western armaments and then to arrest the process of Westernization at that point. (pp. 284–85)

History's verdict was clear: the tradition-minded Ottomans could not preserve both their cultural integrity and their political independence; Westernization was progressing too fast for them to maintain their isolation and too slow for them to create a power center of sufficient vitality to resist conquest. Among the Ottoman domains, only Turkey escaped foreign domination, and that was largely through the modernizing reforms of a Western-educated army officer, Mustafa Kemal Ataturk. China's history followed a similar course. Only a modernizing revolution could overcome the backwardness of the doddering Manchu dynasty and rescue China from the opium trade, the unequal treaties, and the economic dependency that the Western imperial powers had imposed. In their roles as nationalist leaders, both Sun Yat-sen and Mao Tse-tung adopted Western ideas, techniques, and principles of political-economic organization as the best means of freeing their country from poverty and colonial subjugation. Though this emulation of the most advanced states carries no guarantee of success, isolation or a retreat into traditionalism do not appear to be possible, either. The penetrating power of the developed states — militarily, economically, culturally — forces the Third World to adapt in some way to modern values. Its leaders are caught between an impulse to imitate the advanced states and a fear that too close a relationship, and too rapid a pace of change, will damage their countries' cultural roots, political legitimacy, and economic independence.

The Struggle for Political Stability

A second theme in the development dilemma is the struggle for political stability, as manifested in the tension between rapid social mobilization and poorly developed political institutions. It is the problem of balancing order and change. Samuel Huntington, in *Political Order in Changing Societies,* has suggested that the process of socioeconomic modernization, with its profoundly disturbing impact on traditional societies, releases new energies but not always the political capacity to channel those energies constructively. Modernization is a two-fold process of destroying the old order and creating a new one. Colonialism and other contacts with foreign governments and technologies, which set the process going, have a profoundly erosive impact on traditional societies. But legitimacy and grass-roots political organization, the essential ingredients of a stable modern polity, cannot be imported from abroad. Indigenous institutions must arise to manage the forces of change, or instability results. Backwardness itself is not the cause of disorder in the Third World; the traditional societies, though poor and exploited, were quite stable. The fault lies in an incomplete and uncontrolled modernization. And the problem is heightened when there has been rapid economic penetration by a technology well suited to production for the foreign market but badly suited to the needs and cultural habits of local peoples.

Dankwart Rustow, in *A World of Nations: Problems of Political Modernization* (pp. 1–31), emphasizes that a new state cannot achieve economic development without the corresponding development of a modern political consciousness. This sociopolitical transformation depends in turn on the state's having a distinctive national identity to cement its legitimacy. Foreign technologies can be begged, borrowed, or bought, but nation building is a homegrown enterprise, to be done with one's own hands. Above all, governments must plan for or cooperate in the process of development, without becoming parasites on it.

Third World governments typically are dominated by traditional patron-client relationships. And the political elite itself is not cohesive, but is often split into factions led by figures whose influence is based on personal loyalty rather than political belief. This personalism breeds nepotism, with government positions awarded to friends and family members instead of the most competent. Personalist tendencies are reinforced where the population is largely illiterate and has no direct identification with the central government, which tends to be viewed as the same kind of alien force as its colonial predecessor. Many new states lack effective party organizations and professional bureaucracies and have fragile political identities. Their governments are often mere networks of patronage held together by the distribution of rewards within the personal fiefdoms of their leaders. In effect, the leaders are colonizing their own governments and becoming parasites on them. This kind of patrimonialism has fed corruption and factionalism throughout the Third World.

Another source of political instability is the top-heavy position government occupies in many postcolonial economies. Colonialism, statist in character and with economic planning centered in the imperial metropole, discouraged the development of an independent entrepreneurial class. Native elites worked for the colonial bureaucracy or, occasionally, as junior managers in foreign firms. A private sector or an indigenous middle class was almost nonexistent. After independence, most governments simply perpetuated the statist and centralizing practices of the colonial regime, but without the same level of skills and resources and with few limits on the recruitment of the local population into their burgeoning bureaucracies. Economic modernization was likely to consist of no more than increasing the state's exports of cash crops and its imports of foreign capital, aid, and loans. This put substantial resources at the state's disposal, but, in an otherwise poor economy, it also generated intense struggles for control of the government, a ready source of patronage and one of the few avenues of rapid upward mobility.

Merle Kling has elaborated a theory of power and political instability in Latin America in which he argues that repeated coups and factional struggles are symptoms of the importance attached to state power, which is the only significant resource the people of an underdeveloped society have to compete for. This is especially the case in states whose agriculture, mining, or other economic bases of power are controlled by traditional elites or foreigners. When the economy has remained essentially neocolonial and static, an exceptional premium attaches to control of the apparatus of government as a dynamic route to wealth and power. When foreign capital and political influence are also present, it is no surprise to find ambitious elites choosing to ally themselves with the powerful expatriate elements, rather than undertake the difficult tasks of entrepreneurial enterprise or coalition building and party organization at the grass roots. Politicians who do play popular politics tend to appeal to traditional communal and ethnic ties, which generate strong pressures on modern institutions; under simultaneous attack from outside and in, the newly created national institutions simply crumble.

Corrupt, backward, and lacking in firm bases of popular support, many Third World governments represent what Gunnar Myrdal has termed the phenomenon of the "soft state." In some of the poorest African states, more than 25 percent of the national budget goes for government salaries, keeping alive a vast bureaucracy of questionable productivity. Hernando de Soto, in *The Other Path*, speaks of mercantilist states in Latin America in which government regulation has stifled the private sector and elites compete for access to centrally controlled resources, encouraging the proliferation of bureaucratic red tape, patronage, and black-market activities. In most underdeveloped countries, individuals and businesses must spend a significant portion of their incomes on routine bribes, tips, and official "protection" just to survive. The government becomes a predator on the productive enterprises, and the "informal" (which is to say illegal) sector expands rapidly among groups with no access to government patronage. Corruption and nepotism keep a system running that might otherwise collapse. But the pattern also makes governments inefficient and vulnerable to penetration and breakdown, and political institution building becomes all the more impossible.

When government control is a valuable prize, the struggle for it can be a highly personal one in which political leaders will use all the levers of power to suppress opposition. In developed countries, losing opposition groups can easily retreat to the private sector, to foundations or think tanks, to the professional bureaucracy, or to sinecured party posts. In an underdeveloped country, without an independent middle class, there is no place for a defeated opponent or a critic of the government to go except to jail or into exile. Political conflict is therefore more intense, opposition voices more strident, and "solutions" more violent. When civilian institutions are weak and popular support insecure or factionalized, leaders will often seek to strengthen their hold on power by turning to the military — especially if the military is serving as a constabulary force to suppress guerrilla movements or revolutionary challenges. Conversely, military leaders are often tempted to intervene, in the name of patriotism and national unity, to overthrow corrupt, divided, or inefficient governments. (For the extent of internal military rule in the Third World, see Figure 6-1.)

The dominant role of the military in many Third World countries is only the most obvious sign of what Huntington calls a "praetorian" society — one in which social groups of all kinds have become intensely politicized but lack any

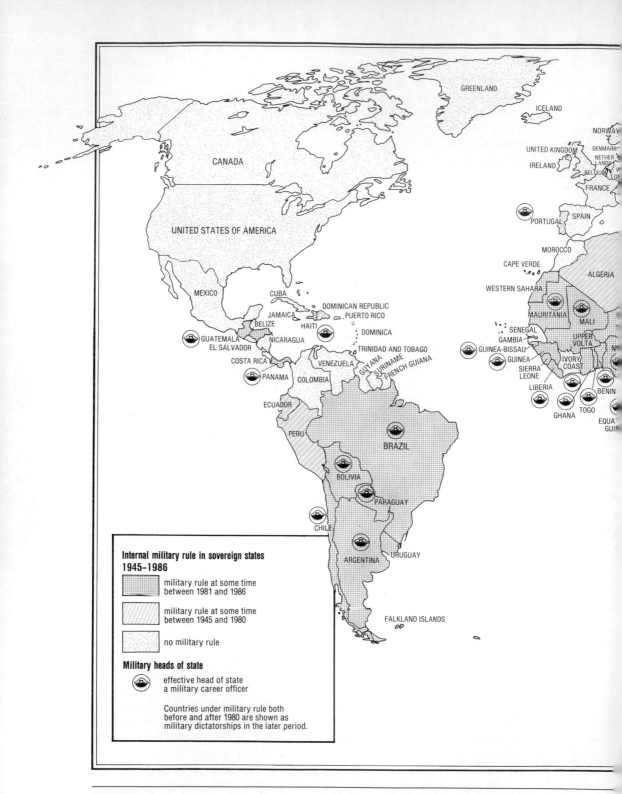

FIGURE 6-1
MILITARY REGIMES

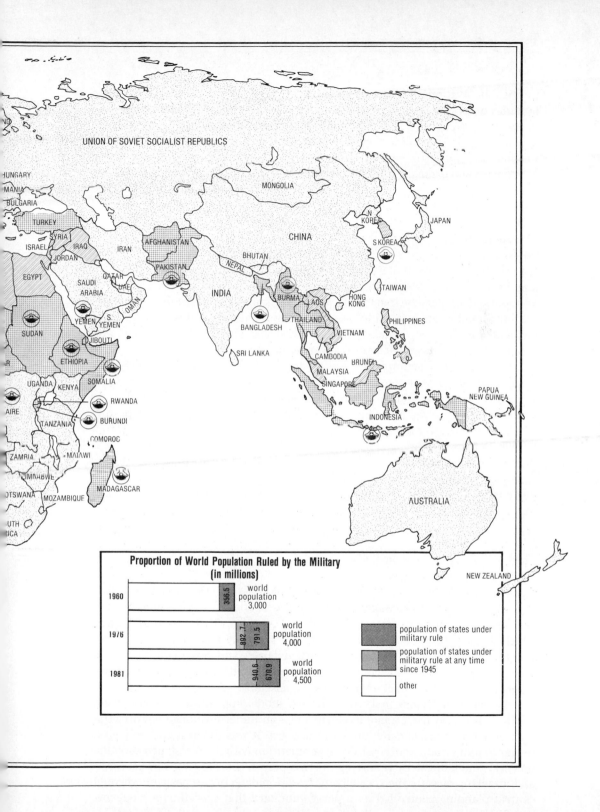

UNION OF SOVIET SOCIALIST REPUBLICS

HUNGARY
MANIA
BULGARIA
TURKEY
SYRIA
ISRAEL   IRAQ
JORDAN
EGYPT
QATAR
SAUDI   UAE
ARABIA   OMAN
YEMEN S.
YEMEN
SUDAN
JIBOUTI
ETHIOPIA
SOMALIA
UGANDA KENYA
ZAIRE
RWANDA
TANZANIA BURUNDI
COMOROC
ZAMBIA MALAWI
ZIMBABWE
BOTSWANA MOZAMBIQUE
MADAGASCAR
UTH
ICA

MONGOLIA

N
KOREA   JAPAN
S KOREA
CHINA
TAIWAN

AFGHANISTAN
IRAN
PAKISTAN
NEPAL BHUTAN
INDIA
BURMA LAOS HONG
KONG
BANGLADESH THAILAND
VIETNAM PHILIPPINES
SRI LANKA
CAMBODIA BRUNEI
MALAYSIA
SINGAPORE
PAPUA
NEW GUINEA
INDONESIA

AUSTRALIA

NEW ZEALAND

Proportion of World Population Ruled by the Military
(in millions)

1960 — 356.5 — world population 3,000

1976 — 892.7 — 791.5 — world population 4,000

1981 — 940.6 — 670.9 — world population 4,500

population of states under military rule

population of states under military rule at any time since 1945

other

political institutions capable of mediating, refining, or moderating their group action. Power is fragmented, political allegiances shift rapidly from one group to another, high office is easily acquired — and as easily lost — and violence pervades all. In the absence of a well-defined public interest and of institutional mechanisms that can aggregate interests and expand loyalties, every group approaches government from the standpoint of its own narrow interests and in ways that reflect its own nature and capabilities. In Huntington's words, "The wealthy bribe; students riot; workers strike; mobs demonstrate; and the military coup" (p. 196).

Such a praetorianism has international implications. When the military is dominant, budgets are skewed away from domestic development and toward the purchase of more modern equipment for the armed forces. Civilian leaders stay in power by placating the military's demands, and often by displaying a xenophobic nationalism that directs popular animosities and the energies of the military against an ostensible outside enemy. This might take the form of strident anti-Western attacks, regional rivalries, or border skirmishes and territorial aggrandizement against a weaker neighbor. Often, a foreign government encourages a faction of the military to direct its power inward, against its own people and government. Coups and insurrections often are supported by a superpower patron. Officer training programs and arms aid also serve as levers of influence and insurance policies for a superpower that cannot predict who will be in power next. Elections have been overturned or made irrelevant when a Southern politician has gained office who does not particularly suit the interests of a Northern power. Whether or not there is a self-conscious effort to destabilize an unwanted regime, civil strife tends to invite outside interference and covert intervention. In all these ways, military domination of governments in the Third World leads to a further militarization of North-South relations.

Capitalism Versus Socialism

Another major theme in Third World development is the tension between capitalism and socialism as models for modernization. The United States and the Soviet Union have each attempted to export its own model, and Third World leaders face a choice between the existing arrangements of capitalist economics, which now dominate international trade and most of their domestic markets, and the planned economies of socialism, which might give their governments stronger control over their own assets.

A variety of factors make the socialist model appealing. One is that the Soviet Union was itself a late modernizer — an underdeveloped country that took only fifty years to catch up with the West. It was the first and only great power to industrialize successfully in competition with the developed capitalist powers. And it did so by removing the free play of spontaneous market forces and attacking directly the recalcitrant traditionalism of the peasants through central planning controlled by a party vanguard that served as a modernizing elite.

These features of the Soviet model have many parallels in the Third World today. The desperate poverty lends an urgency that is incompatible with the evolutionary gradualism of capitalism; no Third World leader has the 200 or so years it took the West to prepare the way for modernization. Many of the new states have a statist bias left over from their colonial bureaucracies, which were incipient planning agencies controlled from above. In addition, socialism provides a rationale for the expropriation of domestic assets still controlled by foreigners. It promises to give emerging political elites greater autonomy and control over the setting of economic priorities and affords a workable model for self-sufficient economic development.

The Soviet model is also appealing for political reasons. Most of the new states are one-party authoritarian systems, and socialism's theory of the vanguard offers a justification for such control by a few in the name of modernization. Socialism puts a premium on the controlled mobilization of latent forces to smash old exploitative aristocracies and revolutionize a backward social order. The political determinism of Leninism, in particular — as the Soviet experience has demonstrated — posits the power of modern institutions to transform society, the power of political control to generate new economic power. Socialism provides a potent body of ideology that taps anti-Western and anticolonial feelings, while substituting a modern political religion for traditional values. In its break with capitalist domination of international markets, socialism reinforces the emergent nationalism of the new states. A socialist vanguard party, with its monopoly of political participation, could provide an organizational framework and an idoological formula for overcoming the divisive regional and ethnic animosities that democracy, in the context of underdevelopment, only tends to inflame.

There are many practical obstacles, however, to the implementation of a socialist system in an underdeveloped society. Few people are equipped by training, experience, or education to manage a planned economy. The governmental infrastructure inherited from colonialism, already weak, can easily collapse under the complex burdens of state socialism, with its self-defeating tendency to have bureaucracies perform tasks that private entrepreneurs could do better (and have). In several instances, African states have tried to take over the distribution sector by replacing traditional "market mamas" and traders. Socialism has also placed an inappropriate emphasis on heavy industry, despite the lack of capital, a developed infrastructure, or a domestic market for heavy manufactures. Likewise, state-planned farming has employed large-scale mechanized methods, which are capital intensive (despite a plentiful labor supply) and often poorly suited to the local terrain. Small farmers have tended to return to subsistence farming rather than be bullied into joining the state-controlled enterprises, which to them are no improvement over the old colonial plantations, with their impressment of labor. The positive inducements of a small-scale, indigenous capitalism and the prospect of a rise in real income are what more likely will bring the marginal peasant into the money economy.

Capitalism has powerful appeal for urban elites as well. Soviet-style socialism has been successful in developing heavy industry and an advanced military sector, but its successes stop there. Socialism is still basically Spartan, and Western life-styles are enormously more attractive to most of the Third World. Capitalism's productive capacities are unsurpassed, and almost all the states wealthy enough to provide the needed development capital and new technology are capitalist. Socialism may carry the symbol of revolutionary transformation, but capitalism offers the symbol of dynamic growth. As Peter Berger has pointed out, in *Pyramids of Sacrifice,* these symbols embody competing "myths" that motivate the respective camp followers, and for the moment capitalism has proved to be the more effective salvationist ideology when it comes to delivering the goods. Also, its liberal democratic ideals hold out the promise of a gradual, reformist approach to the resistance from traditional sectors. Rather than smashing the old order, liberal capitalism would try to realize the modernizing potential in traditional elements. It would focus on adaptability and reconciliation, on the knitting together of pluralistic elements, and on a blunting of the explosiveness of rapid social change through greater political participation and economic opportunity.

Unfortunately, as Berger goes on to say, neither system has lived up to its ideals, and both have exacted a terrible human price. China and Brazil, Third World states that embody the respective strategies, have each sacrificed an entire generation in the name of national development. In China, ideological zealots conducted a harsh campaign of political persecution against peasants, "bourgeois" elements, and anyone else who opposed their Maoist philosophy of radical modernization and central party control. Yet the modernizing potential of a party vanguard was never realized: doctrinal purity triumphed over pragmatic economic considerations. A party elite entrenched itself in the military and the bureaucracy, development was straitjacketed, and the majority languished in economic backwardness. In Brazil, the indifference of the free marketplace generated a lopsided pattern of growth in which the real income of the bottom 60 percent declined in the midst of an unprecedented expansion in GNP. The democratic promise of the capitalist path was not fulfilled: a tiny minority became wealthy, while urban slums proliferated and the rural majority starved. Neither the socialist ideologue nor the capitalist technician succeeded.

Dependency and the Struggle for Sovereignty

Is there any option other than capitalism or socialism as a humane and effective avenue of development? Is there any way the Third World can avoid being drawn into the polarizing political-economic competition of the leading powers? These problems express the fourth theme in the development dilemma, the struggle to escape dependency. A complete analysis of North-South relations must ask an important historical question: could Europe have industrialized without the fruits it received from imperialism? The question has contemporary significance because it defines the economic limitations of the Third World states, whose own development is taking place in precisely the opposite context, that of subordinate status in an existing international hierarchy. Put from the perspective of the Third World, the question becomes: can Third World poverty be successfully attacked by direct economic means in collaboration with the North, or does development require an overturning of the international hierarchy and the relations of dependency inherited from imperialism? Some answers have been emerging over the last four decades of North-South relations.

When development was first placed on the policy agenda, it was regarded as a simple matter of technology transfer, capital accumulation, and incremental increases in per capita GNP. However, such a narrowly economic approach did not take account of the internal political and cultural obstacles to successful technology transfers or of the ways in which traditional social systems, marked by gross disparities of wealth and power, could funnel resources away from those needs that an objective observer would see as the most basic. Within a decade, this approach was discredited. After the frustrations experienced by the first UN Development Decade and the Alliance for Progress, Northern development experts grudgingly had to acknowledge that perhaps modernization was not possible without changes in political structures, social systems, and basic values.

Dependency theorists turned for a solution to an analysis of the economic consequences of colonialism and the debilitating impact of cultural imperialism via Westernization. They argued that Third World poverty stemmed from a process of global development through which rich nations gained their wealth by the progressive enslavement of others. Jawaharlal Nehru, the first prime minister of an independent India, says, in *The Discovery of India*, that when England and India first came into contact, they were roughly comparable in their level of development. India had an advanced civilization, literate elites, a thriving commerce, a sophisticated banking system, a productive textile industry, and attractive cities that were as livable as any in England. What the British possessed was superior political and military organizations and a navy that permitted them to conquer India and despoil the country economically. In Nehru's words,

> The British had power and wealth but felt no reponsibility for good government or any government. The merchants of the East India Company were interested in dividends and treasure and not in the improvement or even protection of those who had come under their sway. In particular, in the vassal states [where the British ruled indirectly through local princes] there was a perfect divorce between power and responsibility. . . .
>
> A significant fact which stands out is that those parts of India which have been longest under British rule are the poorest today. Indeed some kind of chart might be drawn up to indicate the close connection between length of British rule and progressive growth of poverty. . . . Bengal had the first full experience of British rule in India. That rule began with outright plunder, and a land revenue system which extracted the uttermost farthing. . . . The outright plunder gradually took the shape of legalized exploitation which, though not so obvious, was in reality worse. . . . Indian goods were excluded from Britain by legislation, and as the [British East India] company held a monopoly in the

Indian export business, this exclusion influenced other foreign markets also. This was followed by vigorous attempts to restrict and crush Indian manufactures by various measures and internal duties which prevented the flow of Indian goods within the country itself. British goods meanwhile had free entry. The Indian textile industry collapsed, affecting vast numbers of weavers and artisans. . . . The classic type of modern colonial economy was built up, India becoming an agricultural colony of industrial England, supplying raw materials and providing markets for England's industrial goods.

The liquidation of the artisan class led to unemployment on a prodigious scale. . . . India became progressively ruralized. . . . The crisis in industry spread rapidly to the land and became a permanent crisis in agriculture. Holdings became smaller and smaller, and fragmentation proceeded to an absurd and fantastic degree. The burden of agricultural debt grew, and ownership of the land often passed to moneylenders. The number of landless laborers increased by the million. . . .

It may be said that a great part of the costs of transition to industrialism in western Europe were paid for by India, China, and the other colonial countries whose economy was dominated by the European powers. (pp. 187, 208–13)

In the view of Nehru and of dependency theory in general, the expansion of the Western systems was itself a central cause of underdevelopment in the colonized regions of the globe. Thus, any modern attempts at technology transfer were bound to fail so long as they operated in the framework of neocolonial patron-client relations, in which parasitic and dependent local elites exploited the technology for their own benefit rather than the well-being of the nation. Further, since technology cannot be separated from the values it serves, the export of Western models of development invariably served to Westernize the Third World and reshape it in a foreign image, to the detriment of indigenous values.

Ivan Illich, in an article entitled "Outwitting the 'Developed' Countries," has suggested that an important aspect of underdevelopment is an attitude among Third World elites that their problems cannot be solved except by prepackaged, high-tech solutions from the West. Illich describes this as a reification of consciousness, or "the hardening of the perception of real needs into the demand for mass manufactured products . . . the translation of thirst into the need for a Coke." Rich nations have benevolently imposed a straitjacket of traffic jams, hospital confinements, and classrooms on the poor nations and declared this to be "development."'

In fact, the technologies of the North rarely suit the real needs of the South. Each imported car on the road denies fifty people good bus transportation. Each refrigerator in a rich home reduces the chance to build a community freezer that would serve an entire village. Every dollar spent on doctors, hospitals, high-priced surgery, and heart-lung machines imported from America costs a hundred lives that could have been saved by spending the dollar on paramedics, basic sanitation, and safe drinking water. Each person sent abroad for a Western-style university education deprives hundreds at home of the opportunity to acquire basic literacy. What the Third World farmer needs is a 1920s mechanical donkey — a basic tractor of simple design that will last a generation and can be repaired locally by someone who has been trained in a few hours. What he gets, if he is one of the wealthy few who can pay to import it, is a refined technological marvel suited to Western standards and budgets — a fancy tractor that goes 70 miles an hour on the highway, has a canopy, upholstered seats, and electric windshield wipers, and requires frequent servicing, with imported parts, by a Western-educated mechanic.

So long as the Third World blindly seeks to imitate the technological solutions of the developed world, the demand for modern goods will always exceed the resources of the poor states. Illich's solution is a revolution in institutions and expectations that would permit Third World countries to unplug themselves from the technological handouts and planned obsolescence of the North. Once elitist assumptions have been questioned and the need for imports curtailed, their vast resources can be freed to meet the needs of their poor majorities. But first the South must stop wanting to be like the North and must start searching for indigenous solutions to its basic human problems.

However, no Third World state has dared to adopt such a radical approach. Tanzania, under the leadership of Julius Nyerere, tried something akin to it in what was called "Ujamaa socialism." But the Tanzanian economy was too closely tied to international capitalism and too dependent on outside aid and investment to be able to wean itself away. Moreover, many members of the urban elite were unwilling to make the sacrifices in status and life-style required by such a self-sufficient redistributive strategy. Communist China tried a similar kind of bootstrap revolution after it cut its ties with the Soviet Union. But China has discovered — as has the Soviet Union itself — that in a backward economy autarky means isolation from the stimulus of trade, investment, advanced technology, and the latest scientific knowledge. Such isolation may be no handicap for a nation that simply wishes to feed its people, but it does not afford the growing wealth and innovation that are essential for a state that wishes to compete internationally in military weaponry or world trade. And these latter objectives have proved just as important for Third World states as meeting the basic needs of their populations.

The present asymmetrical distribution of international power gives Third World states strong incentives for seeking the protection of great-power patrons. The North is their main source of loans, investments, and arms. A superpower can provide technical expertise and the know-how for implementing development, whether capitalist or socialist. Rapid modernization may well require dependency on the resources of developed states. Yet relations between economically unequal partners are almost invariably exploitative. Moreover, modernization involves a substantial degree of Westernization, which many Third World leaders perceive as a kind of cultural imperialism.

Even the Soviets, who like to pose as champions of anticolonialism, have found themselves resented when they have tried to replace neocolonial capitalism with their own version of Westernization and subordination. Anwar Sadat of Egypt, attempting to emancipate his country from Western influence, accepted extensive Soviet aid and allowed Soviet troops to be stationed on Egyptian soil. But when the Soviets, displaying their own cultural arrogance and pursuing their own foreign policy agenda, tried to control Sadat's independent exercise of power in the Middle East, he chose to break his ties with them and kicked out the Russian troops and advisers, insisting that Egypt must retain control of its own political and economic destiny. This exercise of autonomy obviously incurred some short-run economic sacrifices, for Egypt very soon was turning back to the United States for essential military and economic aid.

Most Third World states face the same kind of smothering embrace, from one superpower or the other. Geographic proximity, military threats, or economic realities may dictate their continued reliance on the patronage or protection of a big brother to the North. Few are strong enough to keep their freedom of maneuver and diplomatic flexibility while walking the tightrope between the Soviet Union and the United States, and rarely are the superpowers willing to let them be neutral and independent. Cuba, now a virtual satellite of the Soviet Union, only exchanged one form of dependency for another, despite Fidel Castro's best efforts to preserve a measure of self-determination. Mexico, for all its large size and relative wealth and stability, has not been able to escape Americanizing pressures and a top-heavy pattern of capitalist development that leaves its rural poor open to revolutionary appeals. Salvador Allende's Chile and Sandinista Nicaragua both aspired to an independent version of democratic socialism; neither was able to escape the extremes of reactionary capitalism or Soviet sponsorship.

India and China are among the few Third World countries to maintain a relatively high degree of autonomy in international affairs. Interestingly enough, neither has been neutral in its choice of a development strategy. India is predominantly capitalist but has protected its political neutrality through a long-standing treaty of friendship with the Soviet Union. This alliance has served India well in its regional rivalries with Pakistan and China while allowing it to solicit foreign aid from both East and West. China is decidedly socialist economically, but the deep Sino-Soviet split has pushed China into more friendly relations with the United States, preserving a triangular leverage that comes of its equidistance between the superpowers. Moreover, China's security fears and historic rivalry with the Soviet Union have been fed by recent doubts about the economic efficiency of the Stalinist model, causing China to welcome capitalist investment and open up its traditionally closed borders. The Communist Chinese have concluded that they can escape isolation and the new "social imperialism" of their more powerful and dynamic Soviet neighbor only by closer relations with the West and that they cannot vitalize their peasant economy except by incorporating the profit incentive, the decentralized decision making of the market, and some other elements of capitalism. These economic reforms continue to be viewed as necessary despite the party leadership's resistance to political liberalization. The freedom of action China and India have displayed, rare in North-South relations, is partly due to their immense size, as well as to their development of an independent nuclear capability.

In most Third World countries, internal economic conditions have strengthened dominance-dependence relations. Colonial occupation and uneven patterns of growth have generally created a dual society marked by a huge gap between the modern and the traditional sectors. In agriculture the division is between subsistence farming and export-oriented cash-crop agriculture. There also tends to be a strong urban-rural split, with few of the benefits of modernization passing beyond the capital city and its urban satellites. The resulting pressures on the marginal rural population, such as famine or land-lessness, have combined with the urban concentration of capital and opportunity to spark an explosive urban growth.

On an international scale, the city-countryside splits translate into a dependence of Third World elites on First World markets and sources of capital, technology, and support. The upper classes frequently have stronger ties to international capitalism than to their own countries. With currencies unstable and governments unpredictable, Third World capitalists often invest their profits in the safe haven of the industrial North. This problem of capital flight leaves the less-developed countries (LDCs) still more heavily dependent on loans and investments from the North, whose multinational corporations (MNCs), constantly on the search for sources of cheap labor and raw materials, tend to invest only where there are high profits, concessionary terms, and local government guarantees of stability. A heavy burden of external debt ensures that the governments will remain committed to export commodities, which generate the foreign currencies they need to service their debt.

Not surprisingly, revolutionary nationalists (who may be neither socialists nor Communists) will try, from time to time, to break the pattern of dependency by expropriating foreign-owned industries, ousting the international "bour-geoisie," and reclaiming control of national resources. Local movements for land reform or social justice almost always spill over into attacks on those social and economic elites whose position is buttressed by their ties to foreign capital, and the Northern governments often are pressured into intervening to suppress these attacks or to protect the profits, employees, and other interests of their multinationals. Capitalist governments fear that the instability of revolutionary turmoil might give a foothold to Soviet influence. In addition, repudiation of Third World debt, now substantial, risks destabilizing the entire infrastructure of international banking and commerce.

Some Third World governments would like to get out of the revolving door of debt, dependency, and foreign intervention. Nationalism has been a powerful impetus in their efforts to secure political autonomy and domestic legitimacy — although it sometimes has so inflamed popular feeling that it has forced Third World leaders into defiance of the superpowers, at considerable risk and cost to themselves. Economic self-sufficiency is attractive for a number of reasons. It affords the opportunity for infant industries and more appropriate indigenous technologies to develop. It can wean a country from dependence on foreign imports, whether luxury items for the nonproductive elite or foodstuffs for the general population. Other measures aimed at self-sufficiency, like land reform, investment in the rural sector, and redistribution of wealth, can go some way toward closing the glaring, and politically destabilizing, internal gap between rich and poor, even if they reduce the flow of foreign investment or temporarily curtail a rise in aggregate national income.

Having outlined the four developmental dilemmas of the Third World, we will now explore their historical origins in the colonial era, the crucial formative period for today's North-South relations.

Colonialism, Resistance, and the Rise of the Third World

The Age of Imperialism

Spain and Portugal were the dominant actors in the earliest stages of European imperialism. Seeking spices, gold, territory, and religious converts in the unexplored regions of the globe, they conquered much of the New World and also established an influence in Africa, the East Indies, and the South Pacific. The Netherlands, England, and France quickly followed, their commercial and political rivalry in Europe stimulating a competition for control of the Americas in particular. This first phase of Western colonialism arose out of a variety of motives, most of which survived into the twentieth century. One important stimulus was straightforwardly economic—the search for precious metals, foodstuffs, raw materials, and manpower (the slave trade played a particularly important role in Africa and the Caribbean). Equally important was the geopolitical rivalry, with colonies sought for reasons of prestige, strategic location, and the weight they could lend in the overall balance of power. Since all the early imperial powers relied on large navies, control of the seas was another important reason for acquiring colonies. Britain, for instance, took over Hong Kong, Aden, Malta, Gibraltar, and the Falkland Islands as outposts to service its extensive navy.

Secondary motivations included religious and cultural impulses and the pressures of surplus population. Certainly science and technology spurred the Age of Discovery by providing improved instruments of navigation and more effective military weapons. The Spanish and the Portuguese pursued a religious crusade, with a zeal that is attested by the enduring influence of Roman Catholic culture in Central and South America today. The French believed that their language, culture, and religion were among the great fruits of civilization, and their missionaries spread throughout North America, Africa, and Asia carrying an assimilationist philosophy that would later contribute to the strong resistance of the French, along with the Portuguese, to modern movements toward independence. Population pressures were never severe, but Britain and France did send large numbers of religious nonconformists, convicts, debtors, and other "undesirables" to Australia and the Americas. Among settler populations, the search for opportunity fueled expansion across the United States and Russia and left significant white enclaves in Algeria, Kenya, Rhodesia, and South Africa. As late as the 1930s, the Japanese sought control of Manchuria in part as a potential outlet for their surplus population. More often, however, religious conversion and European settlement followed from imperial expansion undertaken for more fundamental economic and geopolitical reasons. (For the extent of European expansion in this first phase, see Figure 6-2.)

The successful revolt of the British colonies in North America and the independence movement among the Spanish and Portuguese colonies in the New World ended the first phase of European colonialism. By the middle of the nineteenth century, the whole of the Americas, with the exception of a few small dependencies, was free of European control. After 1860, however, the industrial revolution spurred a new competition for overseas empire. Industrialization required increased supplies of raw materials and economies of scale that could be realized only by the expansion of trade into overseas markets. Industrial expansion also generated surplus profits in search of new investment opportunities.

As Tony Smith writes, in *The Pattern of Imperialism,* several factors intensified the economic rivalry in the latter part of the nineteenth century. First, Europe fell into a long-term depression lasting from 1873 to 1896. "This downturn in the business cycle made foreign ventures all the more attractive and encouraged business and finance to rely more and more on their governments to promote their interests" (p. 37). Even the free-trade philosophy of the British was replaced by a more neomercantilist, protectionist approach that emphasized the annexation of territory and direct political control of key markets.

Second, as the European alliance systems grew more unstable and great power rivalries came to the fore, the acquisition of colonies became a matter of "high" policy. Britain, in the four decades before World War I, expanded its imperial holdings from 9.1 million to 12.6 million square miles, making vast acquisitions throughout Africa and Asia. France expanded from 200,000 to 4.35 million square miles, taking over much of West Africa, Tunisia, Morocco, and Indochina. Although Russia had no overseas empire (it sold Alaska to the United States in 1867), it acquired vast stretches of contiguous territory, including more than 1 million square miles in Asia. Japan defeated both China (1895) and Russia (1905) to win control of Korea and Manchuria. Austria-Hungary gained mandates in the Balkans. In the scramble for Africa, the Belgians got the Congo (now Zaire); the Germans, Togo, Cameroon, Tanganyika, and Southwest Africa; and the Italians, Libya and the Horn (Eritrea and Somalia). The Dutch retained their control of the East Indies (now Indonesia), and the Portuguese held Macao, Goa, Guinea, Angola, and Mozambique. Spain, although it lost Cuba, the Philippines, and Puerto Rico to the United States after the Spanish-American War in 1898, still held colonial enclaves in North and West Africa. After World War I, the German colonies in Africa were parceled out anew, as the Italian colonies would be after World War II. In the Middle East, the dismembered Ottoman Empire was divided largely between England (Egypt, Palestine, Trans-Jordan, Iraq) and France (Syria, Lebanon). It should be noted that all the peoples coming under colonial rule in this second period of empire were non-Western and nonwhite. (For the extent of European expansion by 1914, see Figure 6-3.)

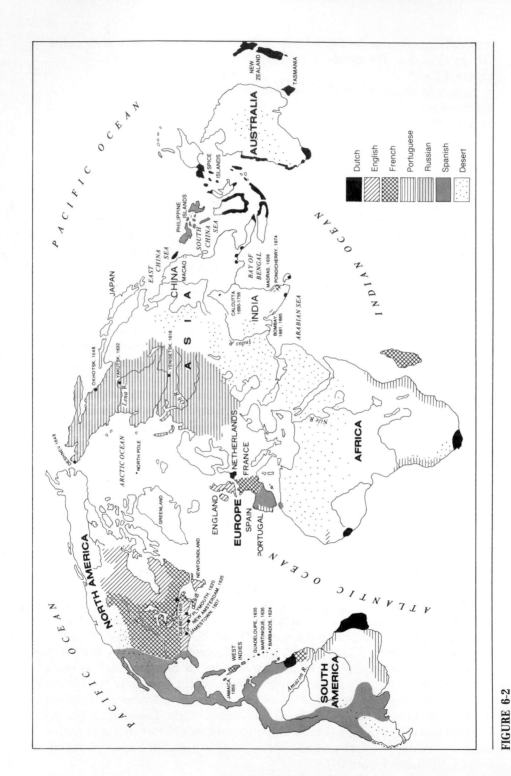

FIGURE 6-2
EUROPEAN OVERSEAS EMPIRES, CIRCA 1700

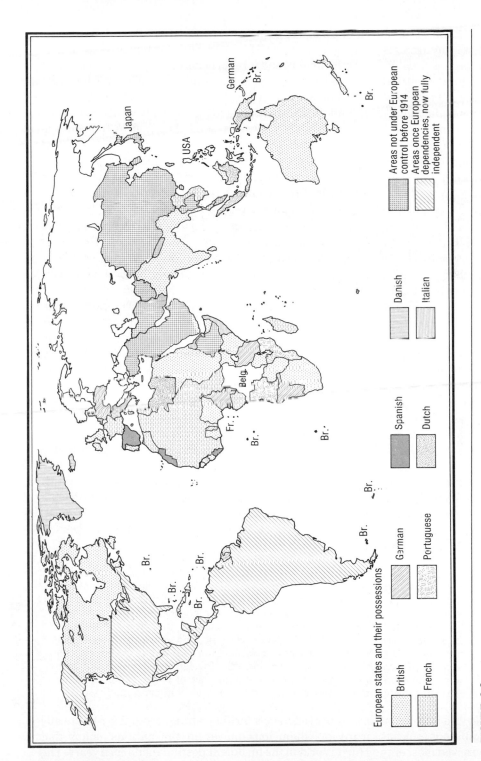

European states and their possessions

British
French
German
Portuguese
Spanish
Dutch
Danish
Italian

Areas not under European control before 1914
Areas once European dependencies, now fully independent

FIGURE 6-3
THE COLONIAL EMPIRES, 1914

A third stimulus to this stage of imperial expansion was the relative weakness of indigenous regimes in Asia and Africa. These areas had already undergone considerable domestic turmoil and foreign penetration, making it difficult for local authorities to deal with rising socioeconomic tensions. The weaknesses of the old Ottoman and Manchu dynasties excited great-power interventions in the Middle East and China. In tropical Africa, already weakened by the slave trade, traditional aristocracies were being eroded further by the penetration of European traders and missionaries into the hinterlands. With political authority crumbling, the imperial powers pressed all the harder to fill the vacuum they had helped create. To old-fashioned economic imperialism was added a political struggle for direct control, as each great power sought to ensure that another would not infringe on its sphere of influence.

This second, more active phase of European expansion was brought to an end by the two world wars and by the reassertion, especially after World War II, of political vitality among the colonized peoples. However inadequate or exploitative the colonial systems of education and economic development were, they gave the colonies a substantial number of individuals who were familiar with European ideas, techniques, and institutions. This Western-educated minority was soon in direct competition with the whites for control of their societies. In Africa there emerged such leaders as Jomo Kenyatta in Kenya, Nnamdi Azikiwe in Nigeria, Kwame Nkrumah in Ghana, Hastings Kamuzu Banda in Malawi, Léopold Senghor in Senegal, and Félix Houphouet-Boigny in the Ivory Coast. All these nationalist leaders learned the ways of representative government, as well as their revolutionary ideas, from the Europeans themselves, and their feelings against racism and imperialism were strengthened by the two world wars. In other countries, militant European-style labor movements served as a spawning ground for such leaders as Tom Mboya of Kenya and Sékou Touré of Guinea.

World War II's impact on the Third World was particularly powerful. It was felt in the widespread recruitment of native troops and in the social disruptions wrought by battles waged across extensive regions of the Middle East, Africa, and Asia. The situation in Africa is well described by Rupert Emerson and Martin Kilson in *The Political Awakening of Africa:*

> Not until a decade after the war in Africa did the full effects of the war become inescapably evident, but the inner changes which it stimulated were immense. The denunciations of racialism and the declarations of Allied leaders as to the virtues of freedom and the right of peoples to a freely chosen self-government could not help but be turned by the African nationalists to their own purposes. Presumably of even greater importance were the contacts with Western cultures established by African troops and civilians abroad, and by the presence in several African countries of American and other foreign armed forces. Furthermore, the drive to increase production of a number of products for Allied or African consumption also stimulated change and development. (p. 13)

Service in colonial armies proved to be a fertile training ground for politically ambitious officers, many of whom took power in the military coups that wracked most of the Third World in the turbulent postindependence years. The

Japanese occupation in China sparked nationalist revolt and abetted the Chinese Communist effort to form an independent party organization among the rural peasantry. Elsewhere in Asia, the Japanese occupation had a similar effect in erasing the colonial control of the French in Indochina and of the Dutch in Indonesia. Also, ironically, the Japanese showed that a nonwhite, non-European power could defeat a predominantly white nation in combat.

Of course, anti-imperial and anti-Western revolutionary precedents had already been set by Francisco Madero in Mexico (1910), Sun Yat-sen in China (1912), Mustafa Kemal Ataturk in Turkey (1908–23), Vladimir Lenin in Russia (1917), Mahatma Gandhi in India (1920), and Saad Zaghlul Pasha in Egypt (1922). In the interwar years, eight Third World states emerged from colonial domination—the first successful independence movements since the early 1800s. After World War II, decolonization took on an increasing momentum, releasing sixty-eight new states from imperial dependency between 1945 and 1980. The Communist victory in China in 1949 and the USSR's attainment of superpower status after World War II lent impetus and ideological ammunition to the anticolonial struggle. After the Japanese defeat, Korea was partitioned and granted dual independence. The Dutch withdrew from Indonesia and the Italians from their overseas possessions in Ethiopia, Libya, and Somalia. In 1946, the United States granted independence to its principal colony, the Philippines. The dismantling of the two largest empires, those of Britain and France, followed in short order. The process is chronicled in Robert Clark's *Power and Policy in the Third World:*

In 1945, the largest empire in the world was Great Britain. More than one fourth of the world's population, about 600 million people, were governed from London. By 1948, about two thirds of this total were living in independence. In these years, the nations of South Asia—India, Pakistan, and Ceylon (now Sri Lanka)—were created. Burma, Egypt, Iraq, and Jordan also successfully asserted their independence. Following the partition of Palestine, Israel claimed its independence and, by the early 1950's, informed British opinion recognized the inevitability of the disintegration of its empire. In 1956 and 1957, the granting of independence to the Sudan, Malaya (Malaysia), and Ghana initiated the process of emancipation in large scale. Today, the British Empire consists of a few scattered islands in the Western Hemisphere (such as Bermuda) and a handful of strategic posts that Great Britain refuses to yield [Gibraltar and the Falkland Islands are the most important]. . . .

The second largest empire in 1945 was France and, although France fought much harder than Great Britain to retain its colonial holdings, the outcome was the same. In the mid-1940's, Syria and Lebanon were given their independence and, in 1954, after the disastrous French-Indochina War, Cambodia (now Kampuchea), Laos, and the two halves of Vietnam left the French sphere. In 1956, Tunisia and Morocco were freed after agitation and guerrilla war. In 1958, after Charles de Gaulle's return to power, France's African holdings were reduced —first Guinea (1958) and later (1960) the remainder of her French Equatorial and West African possessions as well as Madagascar were liberated. Algeria was the possession that France was most reluctant to release, probably because of its proximity to the mother country and because of the many French citizens living in Algeria. But, by 1962, the violence and destruction of the Algerian war had so weakened French resolve that the nation's possessions there were terminated as well. As of the middle of the 1970's, French possessions include some scattered holdings in the Western Hemisphere (French Guiana, Guadeloupe, and Martinique) and some islands in the Pacific. (pp. 24–25)

The collapse of the European empires was presided over by the United Nations, which displayed a far greater interest in the problems of colonialism than had its predecessor, the League of Nations. Through a mandate system, the League had loosely supervised only a few colonial domains; the UN's trusteeship system represented a marked tightening of international supervision. In 1960, the General Assembly unanimously adopted a condemnation of colonialism that asserted the right of all peoples to self-determination (the United States, Britain, and France abstained). The UN also played an important peacekeeping role in the civil conflict that followed on Belgium's abrupt departure in 1960 from the Congo (now Zaire). Independence soon followed (in 1962) for the other Belgian possessions, Rwanda and Burundi. The last African colonies to be liberated — Spanish Sahara (now under Morocco's control), Río Muni (now Equatorial Guinea), Portuguese Guinea (now Guinea-Bissau), Angola, and Mozambique — were those belonging to countries ruled by dictatorships at home, Spain and Portugal.

The Colonial Experience and the Problems of New States

Two factors determined the character and stability of the postcolonial regimes: the type and length of the colonial rule and the nature of the decolonization process. The Latin American states experienced a typical pattern of praetorianism and military intervention after winning independence, but they had the initial advantage of being able to work out their fates outside the orbit of great-power competition. Because of the many years of independence and because European political ideas were implanted early, during the lengthy colonial occupation, Latin American political parties have been more highly developed. But Latin American societies have suffered from a deeply entrenched racial and cultural dualism between their Indian populations and the descendants of the Spanish and Portuguese settlers. And economic problems have been deepened by the fact that Latin America has undergone two colonial epochs: the initial Iberian conquest and the later neocolonial domination under the big-stick and dollar-diplomacy policies of the United States, which introduced new factors of political instability and economic dependency.

In Africa and Asia, the successor regimes were shaped by the strongly contrasting policies of the colonizing powers regarding education, assimilation, and preparation for self-government. The British maintained a strong color bar but went the furthest in educating an indigenous elite and permitting them to participate in incipient representative institutions. The British also favored, where traditional authority was strong, an indirect form of colonial rule that preserved some degree of local autonomy. They were the first to recognize that decolonization was inevitable and were astute enough to groom their successors and implant institutions of democratic accountability. Although the British, like all colonial authorities, used nationalist divisions to their advantage in bargaining over the transfer of power, independence was arrived at amicably in most cases, and the former colonies' relations with the imperial ruler have remained relatively harmonious. Many of the former British colonies were also wealthy enough to maintain a high degree of economic independence. The result of the British policies is that India, Sri Lanka, Malaysia, Singapore, Hong Kong, Sierra Leone, Gambia, Ghana, Nigeria, Botswana, Zambia, Zimbabwe, Malta, Belize, Jamaica, Trinidad and Tobago, Barbados, and the Bahamas — all former British colonies — make up almost the entire list of Third World countries that have had extended periods of parliamentary rule. Only in Latin America, which has seen a wave of free elections in the 1980s, are there other postcolonial states with any history of democratic government — although democracy has been a relatively recent antidote to extended periods of dictatorship and military rule (with the exception of Costa Rica, always a democracy, and Chile, a long-time democracy, which lapsed into military dictatorship in 1973).

The former colonies of France, Belgium, and Portugal have tended almost uniformly toward authoritarian government, due to colonial policies that favored direct rule, scant education beyond basic literacy, and assimilation into the imperial tongue and culture for the few natives who rose to positions of responsibility. Political reforms were granted only so long as they preserved colonial rule; demands beyond that were strongly repressed. In a few instances, mainly in French Africa, independence was achieved peacefully, but only in the context of a French "community" that kept the former colonies, already very poor, economically dependent. Most of these colonies were poorly prepared for self-government. The Belgian Congo literally fell to pieces after the abrupt departure of the Belgians. No more than a handful of persons were competent to manage a ministry or an industry. Many of the states have fallen under the control of a dominant personality and are still without well-developed parties of any kind. This has been true of Sékou Touré's Guinea, Houphouet-Boigny's Ivory Coast, François Duvalier's Haiti, and Mobutu Sese Seko's Zaire. The rest have been dominated by a single party with a monopoly of power, a tendency encouraged by the reluctance of the French and the Portuguese, in particular, to relinquish control. The liberation struggles, long and violent, forged a high degree of unity in otherwise diverse anticolonial coalitions and allowed revolutionary elites to mobilize mass support among the peasantry. But the long struggles also radicalized the anticolonial movements and discouraged the formation of pluralistic nationalist parties in the struggle for independence. Former French and Portuguese dependencies make up most of the Third World countries that are ruled by Marxist-oriented parties — Vietnam, Laos, Cambodia, Algeria, Congo (Brazzaville), Guinea-Bissau, Angola, and Mozambique.

Regardless of how they came to independence, almost all the new states have experienced profound political and economic upheavals, and the majority have fallen victim to military coups or extraconstitutional changes of government. Multiparty systems, where they existed, were strongly polarized, highly factionalized, or subject to rapid turnover. These political conditions can be attributed largely to the ambivalent character of the colonial legacy, as well as to arbitrary boundaries, ethnic heterogeneity, fragile parties, inexperienced or corrupt leadership, and the overwhelming economic demands that the newly mobilized publics were making on their infant governments.

But the legacy of imperialism is by no means entirely negative. The colonial powers transmitted an immense corpus of political ideas, including the very notions of social equality, political freedom, and national self-determination that the Third World used to throw off the shackles of colonialism. European-style bureaucracies provided the framework for postcolonial governments. They brought modern transportation and technology, hygiene and health care, science and education, commerce and trade. In particular, colonial policies (1) brought together in a single state cultural and ethnic groups that had not previously been united politically and that separately were not economically viable entities; (2) established rationalized governmental bureaucracies staffed, at least in the lower ranks, by indigenous personnel; (3) created legal systems based on European values and codes, including (implicitly) respect for due process, human rights, and personal freedom; (4) organized and trained military and police units manned by local personnel and equipped with modern weapons; (5) introduced a monetary system, a cash economy, and a system of taxation; (6) established Western-style secular education; (7) promoted commercial agriculture and industrial development; and (8) built up infrastructures of ports, roads, railways, airports, and communication facilities.

As Karl Marx himself argued, colonialism was much more than a system of political and economic domination. In his Communist Manifesto , Marx speaks of capitalism's productive power as "more massive and more colossal than . . . all previous generations put together," and he adds that the bourgeoisie, an intellectual as well as a material force, "draws all, even the most barbarian, nations into civilization." In 1853, he summed up Britain's rule in India in these terms:

> We must not forget that these idyllic village communities, inoffensive though they may appear, had always been the solid foundation of Oriental despotism, that they restrained the human mind within the smallest possible compass, making it the unresisting tool of superstition, enslaving it beneath traditional rules. . . . England has to fulfill a double mission in India: one destructive, the other regenerating—the annihilation of old Asiatic society, and the laying of the material foundations of Western society in Asia. The political unity of India, more consolidated, and extending farther than it ever did under the Great Moguls, was the first condition of its regeneration. This unity . . . will now be strengthened and perpetuated by the electric telegraph. The free press, introduced for the first time in Asiatic society, and managed by the common offspring of Hindoo and European, is a new and powerful agent of reconstruction. . . . From the Indian natives, reluctantly and sparingly educated at Calcutta, under English superintendence, a fresh class is springing up, endowed with the requirements for government and imbued with European sciences. Steam has brought India into regular and rapid communication with Europe, has connected its chief ports with those of the whole south-eastern ocean, and has revindicated it from the isolated position which was the prime law of its stagna-

tion. . . . England, it is true, in causing a social revolution in Hindostan, was actuated only by the vilest interests, and was stupid in her manner of enforcing them. But that is not the question. The question is, can mankind fulfill its destiny without a fundamental revolution in the social state of Asia? If not, whatever may have been the crimes of England, she was the unconscious tool of history in bringing about that revolution. (From the New York Daily Tribune, quoted in Kilson, pp. 37–38)

In short, colonialism brought revolutionary social change to preliterate, preindustrial societies. It expressed the dynamism of Western capitalist societies, whose expansion to non-Western societies inevitably resulted in their reconstruction along modern lines. In the Marxist sense of the historical evolution of the forces of production, colonial modernization played a progressive role in the non-West.

In other ways, the colonial heritage was profoundly crippling. The modern transportation networks expedited exports to the imperial metropole rather than overall development within the colony. Transportation grids were sketchy or skewed toward a few urban centers; the hinterland and the coast were linked, to facilitate the flow of raw materials and foodstuffs, but internal links between regions often were nonexistent. Western medicine and public health measures radically reduced death rates, through inoculations, antibiotics, sanitary improvements, maternity care, and the like, but, in the absence of changes in traditional attitudes toward the family and birth control, they also led to massive overpopulation. Imported capital-intensive methods were inappropriate in a society with a plentiful supply of unskilled labor. Cash-crop plantation agriculture increased the productivity of the land, but only in export crops, like coffee, cocoa, sugar cane, bananas, peanuts, tobacco, pepper, hemp, and rubber, which could not feed the indigenous population. New methods in both industry and agriculture swelled dramatically the number of landless and unemployed. A former colony's integration into the world market was likely to be at the cost of its greater vulnerability to fluctuating commodity prices and other external pressures. The most expensive Western import, socially as well as economically, has proved to be military technology, whose legacy has been ambivalent. Imported modern arms helped liberation armies to defeat the imperialists and independent states to defend their security, but the cost was oppression at home and a militarization of the entire planet. Science liberated the colonial peoples from superstition, but it also invited the exploitation of nature. Western communications created an informed public opinion, but also cultural imperialism and a slavish imitation of foreign models. Western education shaped the nationalist elites that rule these countries today, but it also endowed them with feelings of inferiority and cultural ambivalence. Modern legal codes have emancipated the individual from the stifling control of family, clan, and custom, but that emancipation has also allowed traditional communal lands to be sold, alienated, monopolized, and exploited. The Western imperial powers developed urban centers of civilization among "backward" peoples, but the economic and cultural enclaves they left further compartmentalized societies already subject to highly uneven development.

Possibly the most damaging element in the dual legacy has been the problem of nationhood itself. In Europe, where consolidation of the state and economic development preceded democratization, nationalism was a unifying force. In the Third World, where democratization simply gave voice to the diverse religious and ethnic elements of traditional societies, nationalism has been an agent of particularism. The nationalist movements of the South were at first held together by their hatred of imperialism and the wish to be free. But opposition to colonialism was not in itself a program for bridging internal class, regional, and ethnic divisions, nor could it mobilize social forces behind a country's economic development. The dominant groups were precisely those that had adapted best to the colonial system and its modern values. With independence, the omnibus anticolonial coalitions fell apart. Competition emerged for scarce, and dwindling, resources. Leaders who had championed the struggle against foreign domination soon faced internal challenges to their own Westernizing agendas. Many traditional groups found the centralizing power of a national government as alien and imperial as its colonial predecessor had been. Colonialism, in constellating the prerequisites of a modern state, defined its boundaries arbitrarily, turning the dream of modern nationalism into a nightmare of separatist movements. Countries that could have been economically viable in terms of their size and the requirements of the world market were often rendered politically vulnerable in terms of national unity and democratic participation.

The political structures the new states inherited were imported institutions that had been set up as instruments for central control. They were not necessarily well suited to the indigenous cultures or to the task of mobilizing popular support for a newly created national entity. Also, few nationalist leaders had the military resources to secure their position domestically or regionally, and so they looked for stability to a multitude of new ties with the former imperial powers or with the rival superpowers, whose impulses to hegemony were no less a threat to the loose fabric of national sovereignty. National unity quickly eroded under multiple pressures: an untutored and unrestrained exercise of the liberties of democracy; societies sharply divided by the uneven impact of modernization; and the authoritarian tendencies of privileged elites that had inherited power from the colonizers and had a vested interest in preserving the neocolonial character of the new regime.

THE THIRD WORLD IN INTERNATIONAL POLITICS

Multipolarity and the Decline of Great-Power Control

The international role of the new states after 1945 was affected by both the East-West and the North-South conflicts. In the early years of the Cold War, when the competition was largely bipolar, both superpowers extended their influence over the South in the search for allies, opportunities, and resources.

Almost every newly independent state was politically unstable, making interventions both tempting and profitable for the North. The superpowers took advantage of civil conflicts to extend their influence over new governments in the Congo, Laos, Indonesia, Yemen, Nigeria, and Pakistan. The intensity of the Cold War rivalry also pressed them to defend their vulnerable new Third World allies. This is how the Soviet Union and the United States came to be drawn to opposing sides in regional disputes in Korea, China, Vietnam, and the Middle East, which soon became high-stakes arenas of great-power confrontation. (For a comparison of the interventionist tendencies among developed states, see Figure 6-4.)

Once a strong alliance had been established between a superpower and a Third World regime, considerations of prestige made it difficult for the great power to disengage, no matter how high the cost of the relationship. The superpowers often overcommitted themselves and ended up with the apparent proxy calling the tune. They could not use their only lever — the threat to cut off arms and economic aid — for fear of endangering the larger security interests that had motivated the alliance tie. And if a Third World leader could portray his regime as a potential domino likely to fall to Communism or as a potential victim of Western imperialism, he could count on substantial moral and material support from one or the other superpower. The stereotype of the North-South relationship — a poor, insecure Third World state being bullied by a superpower — does not capture the whole reality. Just as often, the superpower has been manipulated by its client into giving arms, economic aid, or diplomatic support that primarily served the interests of the Third World state.

In the early stages of the Cold War, the superpowers tended to intervene in any regional disputes or civil conflicts that might upset the delicate bipolar balance. But bipolarity also gave the Third World states some political leverage in extracting aid or concessions, and eventually, as the South began to exert more independence, the superpower involvement in its conflicts had a frac-

FIGURE 6-4
DEVELOPED COUNTRIES WITH THE MOST FOREIGN MILITARY INTERVENTIONS, 1948–67

Countries Ranked on Total Interventions	Countries Ranked on Interventions per Unit of GNP
1. United States	1. Israel
2. United Kingdom	2. Saudi Arabia
3. Israel	3. New Zealand
4. France	4. Greece
5. Australia	5. United Kingdom
6. New Zealand	6. Australia
7. Greece	7. France
8. Soviet Union	8. Belgium
9. Saudi Arabia	9. South Africa
10. Belgium	10. United States
11. South Africa	11. Soviet Union

tionating impact on the structure of bipolarity. North-South issues began to supplant traditional Cold War concerns and engendered new cleavages in the two blocs. Communist China, identifying with the peasant societies of the South, held itself out as the only authentic Marxist-Leninist model for Third World liberation, and the Sino-Soviet rift, which emerged publicly around 1960, destroyed the ideological solidarity of the socialist bloc. But the conflicting development concerns of the two societies also reflected powerful North-South differences. The ideological and developmental differences together would fuel a growing competition between Soviet- and Chinese-oriented factions within the Third World.

Splits also occurred within the Western alliance. Britain and France, intervening with force in Egypt in 1956, when Gamal Abdel Nasser nationalized the Suez Canal, were opposed by the United States, which had no colonial empire to protect. Anglo-French differences over the budding European Community were exacerbated by divergent colonial interests and a reluctance to abandon special economic ties to the British Commonwealth and the overseas French Community, respectively. North-South issues later became a source of friction in the NATO alliance, but with the roles reversed, the Europeans opposing American policy in Vietnam and Nicaragua. (For a comparison of colonial spheres of influence, the changes wrought by independence, and the contemporary superpower rivalry in the Middle East and Africa, see Figures 6-5 to 6-8.)

The explosion of independence movements in the South shifted the center of gravity in the global balance of power, which became increasingly multipolar and without an integrated hierarchy. Economic relations were revolutionized, although neocolonial influences remained. Politically, the Third World became an arena of intense new competition — between the new states themselves (decolonization sparked many irredentist claims) and among the great powers. Even in the nuclear arms race, the preeminence of the United States and the Soviet Union was being challenged by the British, the French, and the Chinese, all of whom were developing independent strategic nuclear forces, and by the Third World states of India, Pakistan, Israel, Iraq, and South Africa, which were making strenuous efforts to enter the nuclear club.

Several factors were working to limit the ability of either superpower to dictate outcomes in the Third World. By the time of the Vietnam War, the techniques of guerrilla war had given many indigenous regimes a capacity to resist that made them less dependent on outside arms aid and less inclined to accept direction from a superpower donor. In particular, Vietnam demonstrated that a small state fighting for its survival had a considerable advantage over a superpower fighting for limited goals. The Soviet experience in Afghanistan likewise reaffirmed that the superpowers were less able to achieve foreign policy objectives by direct military intervention in the Third World. Civil conflicts in such places as Iran, Mozambique, Peru, El Salvador, and Kampuchea — none of which could be explained in Cold War categories — made it clear that the North could not always control the deciding factors. In Iran, Muslim fundamentalists burned effigies of the Yankee imperialist and the Russian atheist. In Peru, ultraleftists of the Sendero Luminoso bombed both

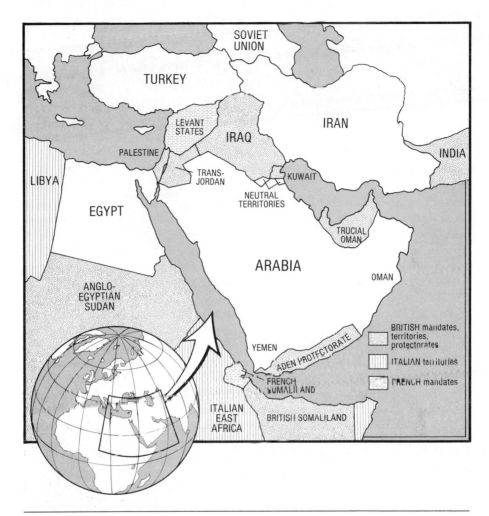

FIGURE 6-5
THE MIDDLE EAST, 1941

the Soviet and the American embassies. An interested superpower that tried to discount indigenous factors or impose its own agenda on such a conflict experienced only frustration, isolation, or expulsion. Even in Angola and Nicaragua, where the superpowers remained important sources of aid and influence, regional powers — South Africa and the Contadora group — were as important in exacerbating or resolving the conflict.

After 1973, it was rare to find a Third World country playing the role of a superpower puppet. Egypt dared to challenge the Russians; Israel defiantly launched policies that the United States openly opposed. Despite heavy Soviet contributions, the victorious Marxist regimes in Vietnam and Angola proceeded with independent foreign policies, sometimes to the direct displeasure

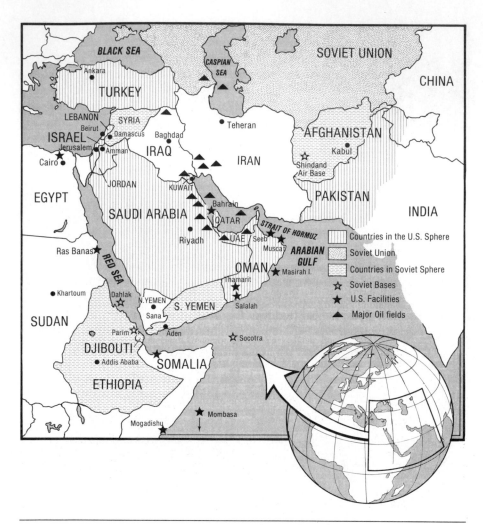

FIGURE 6-6
THE MIDDLE EAST AND THE SUPERPOWERS

of the Soviets. In 1984, Mozambique's Samora Machel, a Marxist who had taken power by revolutionary means (and Soviet arms), signed a nonaggression pact with South Africa's Pieter Botha. Chile's strongman, General Augusto Pinochet, who had seized power in 1973 with the direct assistance of the CIA, refused to bow to strong American pressures in the 1980s for more liberal policies on human rights and democratization. (He finally departed the presidency in 1990, though he retained his position as head of the armed forces.) Panama's General Manuel Antonio Noriega, who had similarly benefited from covert U.S. support, defiantly refused to vacate his office voluntarily, despite

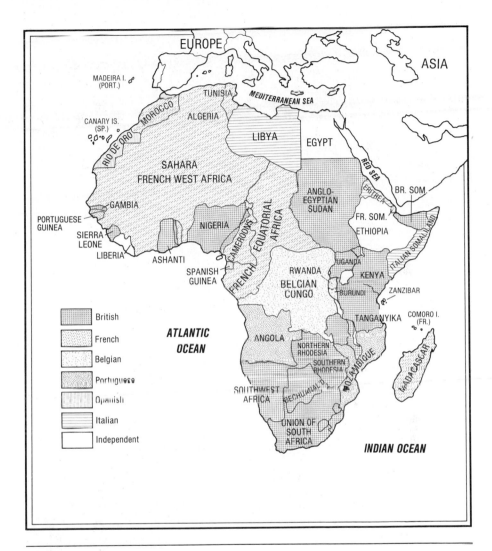

FIGURE 6-7
COLONIAL AFRICA, 1935

immense economic pressure and his indictment in the United States on drug-smuggling charges. (He was ousted by an American invasion in 1989.) Even Cuba's Fidel Castro, heavily dependent on Soviet economic support, has made his own decisions regarding the use of Cuban troops in Africa and has disputed publicly with his Kremlin patrons. In the current climate of North-South relations, the countries of the Third World — whatever their political complexion and no matter how large their debt to a superpower patron — must be taken much more on their own terms.

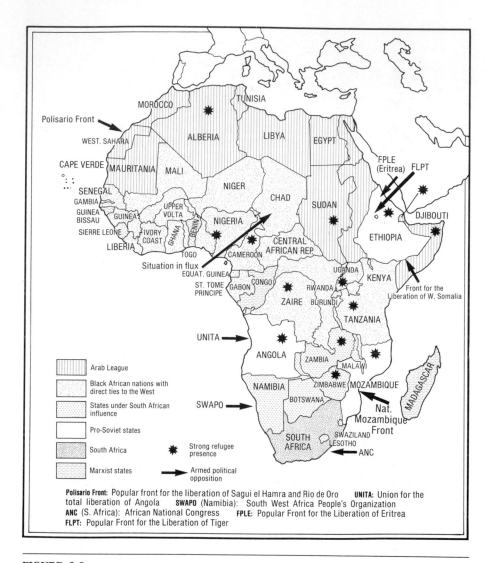

FIGURE 6-8
INFLUENCES AND ARMED STRUGGLES IN AFRICA

Several trends account for this shift in relations. First, many countries of the South are now equipped with modern weaponry, as the result of a long period of arms proliferation. Some — Brazil, South Africa, Israel, China, Vietnam — have developed their own sizable arms industries. Countries that could once have been conquered in a matter of hours by a few airborne battalions can now be pacified only by the commitment of tens of thousands of troops, with attendant casualties. The short, "minor" Falklands war was immensely costly to Britain and Argentina. Britain sent 28,000 men and 125 ships to rescue the islands and their 1,800 inhabitants; 1,000 were killed and many more wounded on both sides.

Second, great-power interventions, whether direct or covert, became less and less acceptable to the rest of the world. A series of UN declarations had established a body of international law that supported the sovereignty and self-determination of the South, and the expansion of global communications had created a world public opinion that tended to condemn realpolitik diplomacy. The human and economic costs of intervention also aroused domestic constituencies in opposition. Certainly the great powers continued to act in self-interested and Machiavellian ways, but the costs were rising.

A third factor was the breakdown of solidarity among both NATO and Warsaw Pact members and a more general dispersal of international political and economic power, giving Third World nations greater freedom to maintain their neutrality. Early in the Cold War, the nonalignment movement had been a haven that provided strength in numbers, its strong rhetoric belying the weakness of the new states. When the collapse of bipolarity made Third World allegiances less crucial to the outcome of East-West disputes, nonalignment or outright defiance of the superpowers could more easily be tolerated.

Fourth, both superpowers suffered military defeats at the hands of Third World powers — a chastening experience for the superpowers and heartening to those resisting imperialism and neocolonialism. Vietnam and Afghanistan, customarily viewed as watershed events in the Cold War, did not actually affect Soviet-American relations half so much as they reshaped North-South relations. In 1981, both the Third Islamic Summit Conference and the Seventh Conference of Non-aligned States condemned Soviet policy in Afghanistan. Also, the use of force to gain new Third World clients was proving expensive, especially for the Soviets. Mozambique and Ethiopia, both Marxist-Leninist governments that came to power with Soviet arms, have become international charity cases, with economic problems that Soviet resources alone have not been able to solve. Declaring the victory of Marxism-Leninism from the seat of government could not create a functioning socialist system any more than paper constitutions and liberal rhetoric could change Central American banana republics into functioning democracies. Cambodia, Ethiopia, Afghanistan, Angola, Mozambique, and Nicaragua have all suffered from costly anti-Communist guerrilla wars — symptomatic of these regimes' narrow political base and lack of legitimacy. Propping up an unpopular elite with imported arms and wholesale aid has been a never-ending no-win proposition for the Soviets, just as it has been for the United States in Vietnam and Nicaragua.

Finally, the problems of the Third World have proved not to be very manageable. In particular, no amount of arms aid or direct military control has brought political stability. As the superpowers came to appreciate the complexities of development and the limits to the transferability of Northern technologies and institutions, they have been more inclined to leave the South to its own resources — an inclination that grew stronger when the developed states began to experience problems of lagging economic growth and political dissent within their own camps.

The Search for New Political-Economic Relations

For all its internal problems and the ambivalence of new states toward their former colonial masters, the Third World has become an important force in the international political economy. The challenge from the South grew slowly, as individual states escaped from Northern economic control and as the bloc learned to engage in joint diplomacy. By 1960, the Third World had coalesced into a more united and self-conscious group, marked by greater voting power in the United Nations and by the increased militancy of the pronouncements issuing from the periodic conferences of the nonaligned states. The first formal challenge to the existing system came in September 1961 at the Belgrade Conference of Nonaligned Countries, which issued a demand for a UN-sponsored international conference on trade and development. This resulted in the United Nations Conference on Trade and Development (UNCTAD), which convened in Geneva in 1964. To present a common front there, the Southern states formed the Group of Seventy-seven (G-77), which expanded eventually into a permanent body representing the economic interests of more than 120 states. They also were able to establish UNCTAD as a permanent UN organization, with a secretariat, a Trade and Development Board, and triennial conferences. But UNCTAD's ability to force reforms on the North was limited by the South's marginal economies, its declining importance in the great-power competition, and its internal political and ideological divisions. The North, which possessed almost all the material and political resources necessary to implement the reforms, could simply ignore them.

In the 1970s, however, the growing Northern dependence on raw materials from the South gave the Third World increased bargaining power. Steady economic growth in the advanced industrial states had dramatically increased their consumption of basic commodities which were becoming depleted or more expensive. At the same time, the South was placing new political restrictions on the North's access to cheap Southern exports. The North, increasingly vulnerable to price hikes and interruptions in supply, and still the object of much anti-imperial sentiment, was finding it far more difficult to intervene politically or militarily to protect its economic interests.

The North-South economic battle line was drawn in earnest in October 1973, when war in the Middle East set off an embargo by the Arab oil-producing states on exports of oil to the United States and the Netherlands. There followed the general restriction of worldwide oil production negotiated by the Organization of Petroleum Exporting Countries (OPEC), the cartel that came to monopolize the world's supply of oil. OPEC engineered a dramatic increase in the price of petroleum, which quadrupled within a year; in 1974 alone, more than $70 billion was transferred from oil-consuming countries, primarily developed market economies, to the oil-producing states. This set off a period of rapid global inflation and indebtedness, which continued through a second period of severe oil shortages and price hikes associated with the Iranian Revolution of 1978 and the beginning of the Iran-Iraq War in 1980. The oil crisis showed the Northern states how vulnerable they were to Southern threats to withhold raw materials. Even the United States, whose dominant and largely self-sufficient economy had made it the least sensitive to Third World demands, responded, at the seventh special session of the UN General Assembly, in September 1975, with a call for international economic reforms and cooperative management of commodity supplies.

Playing on the prospect that OPEC's success might be imitated with other commodities, the Third World began to issue more general demands for a New International Economic Order (NIEO). It pushed its demands at the Third World Conferences of 1974–76; at special sessions of the UN General Assembly in 1974, 1975, and 1980; at the Conference on International Economic Cooperation (CIEC) of 1975–77; and at UNCTAD IV in 1976 and UNCTAD V in 1979. The inequities that NIEO was designed to cure were summarized by Mahbub ul Haq, a Pakistani official at the World Bank. His first argument was that the international order, like national governments in the Third World, favored a privileged minority in its distribution of benefits, credit, services, and decision-making authority. Once such a disparity existed, the free market mechanism ceased to function equitably, since it was weighted heavily in favor of the rich, who had the purchasing power to bend the market to their own interests. The favored rich states, with only 20 percent of the world's population, controlled over 96 percent of international currency reserves. Control of the International Monetary Fund (IMF) and the international banking community also meant that a country like the United States could finance its balance-of-payments deficits simply by expanding its own national reserve currency. Southern states, on the other hand, must come begging to the Northern banks, public and private, for loans and credit.

The second argument was that the LDCs received too small a portion of the final price paid in international markets for their goods, because rich states controlled most of the processing, shipping, and marketing. Of the $200 billion paid in 1976 by final consumers for primary exports from the Third World (excluding oil), the LDCs received only $30 billion. The rest went to Northern-controlled middlemen.

Third, the protective trade barriers of the developed countries shut off Third World products from a fair opportunity to compete in international markets. In 1976, the value of this lost market was reflected in more than $26 billion collected in tariffs and $20 billion spent on farm subsidies by member countries of the Organization for Economic Cooperation and Development (OECD), far larger than the $13.8 billion they gave in foreign aid and development assistance. Clearly, allowing Third World states more access to the international market and a fair price for their commodities would benefit them more than uncertain handouts and burdensome loans from the rich.

The fourth argument was that the terms of contracts, leases, and concessions negotiated by multinational corporations were inequitable. In Liberia, foreign investors were withdrawing profit remittances annually that amounted to one-quarter of the total GNP. In Mauritania, the government was receiving only about 15 percent of the profits that MNCs were making from iron ore — a nonrenewable national asset — simply because the foreigners controlled the mining technology.

Mahbub ul Haq maintained that basic institutional reform could transfer between $50 billion and $100 billion annually to Third World countries, eliminating their dependence on degrading schemes of foreign assistance. The New International Economic Order, he said, was consistent with Western values and the whole historical evolution toward equality and liberation. It would imitate on the international scale what was already accepted as just at the national level: that governments must actively intervene on behalf of the poorest segments of their populations. Moreover, the NIEO would be a natural second stage in the liberation of the developing countries, adding economic to political independence. Although the NIEO proposals endorsed the UN's guidelines on foreign aid, which called for Northern countries to give 0.7 percent of their GNP in annual aid, the emphasis was on Third World access to economic opportunity and on long-term increases in productivity, not to temporary transfers of income from North to South. The specific goals of the NIEO agenda, as outlined by Mahbub ul Haq, were these:

> 1) Revamping of the present international credit system by phasing out national reserve currencies and replacing them with an international currency; 2) Gradual dismantling of restrictions in the rich nations on the movement of goods and services as well as labor from the poor nations; 3) Enabling the developing countries to obtain more benefit from the exploitation of their own natural resources through greater control over various stages of primary production, processing, and distribution of their commodities; 4) Introduction of an element of automaticity in international resource transfers by linking them to some form of international taxation or royalties or reserve creation; 5) Negotiation of agreed principles between the principal creditors and debtors for an orderly settlement of past external debts; 6) Renegotiation of all past leases and contracts given by the developing countries to the multinational corporations under a new code of ethics to be established and enforced within the United Nations framework; and 7) Restructuring of the United Nations to give it greater operational powers for economic decisions and a significant increase in the voting strength of the poor nations within the World Bank and the International Monetary Fund. (*The Third World and the International Economic Order,* p. 10)

The Third World's challenge brought some concessions from the United States, Japan, and the European Economic Community. Because of growing pressures for protectionism after 1973, it became easier for them to depart from established free-trade principles and recognize Third World claims for preferential trading agreements. The EEC's response was the Lomé Convention, negotiated in February 1975 with forty-six associated African, Caribbean, and Pacific (ACP) states. This, the germ of a new international economic order, was subsequently expanded somewhat, after difficult bargaining at Lomé II in 1979, to cover fifty-eight ACP countries, but the NIEO principles were never fully instituted in the international economy. The Lomé agreements undercut considerably the traditional neocolonial base of North-South economic exchanges, but the Third World did not succeed in its other objectives of a single, integrated international commodities program, with a common fund to stabilize export earnings, or a system for indexing prices and equalizing earnings on raw materials and manufactured products.

The early 1980s brought an unexpected oil glut and the disintegration of OPEC's oil monopoly. This, along with the end of an extended period of stagflation, stiffened the resolve of the rich states to make no further concessions. The conditions that had made the oil cartel effective did not prove enduring or transferable to other commodities. The Third World did not remain as united or confrontational as it had been in the first bloom of the NIEO challenge. Recession, debt, food shortages, and high oil prices all were affecting the Third World states in quite different ways. Rising oil prices associated with the shortages of 1973 and 1979 ended up hurting non-OPEC nations in the Third World more severely than they had hurt the industrialized countries. The high cost of importing fuel and fertilizer (an oil-based product) sent many Third World states' balance of payments into serious deficit, at the same time as petrodollars were swelling the foreign exchange coffers of a privileged few among them. Both political and economic forces began to divide the Third World, to the point that some analysts now spoke of a Fourth World — nations so weak politically and economically that they might never arrive at a developed state. At the other extreme were the newly industrializing countries (NICs), which appeared to be escaping poverty through their utilization of export strategies that operated within the traditional economic framework. Between 1970 and 1978, manufacturing output in Brazil, South Korea, Mexico, Portugal, Singapore, Spain, Taiwan, and Yugoslavia rose at more than twice the rate of the developing world as a whole. The rise of the NICs, while leaving the Third World highly divided, represented a further dispersal of political-economic power in the postwar international order.

CONTEMPORARY ISSUES IN NORTH-SOUTH RELATIONS

By the mid-1980s, the bargaining power of the Third World as a bloc had clearly declined. Economic differences and dozens of regional and territorial squabbles were engendering a new and more strident nationalism. A bloc diplomacy conducted across continents, cultures, and diverse ethnic groups was even more complex than the politics of decolonization had been. And the international economic order dominated by the established industrial states proved much more entrenched and more resilient than expected.

The Third World was particularly vulnerable to the global recession between 1977 and 1983 (see Figures 6-9 and 6-10). Commodity prices plummeted, economic growth rates stagnated, and the level of debt rose dramatically. Even OPEC lost its luster, and a serious oil glut demonstrated how fragile were the hopes that commodity power would be a weapon for forcing the industrialized North into long-term structural reforms in the international economy. Both the OPEC nations and the NICs now had a vested interest in

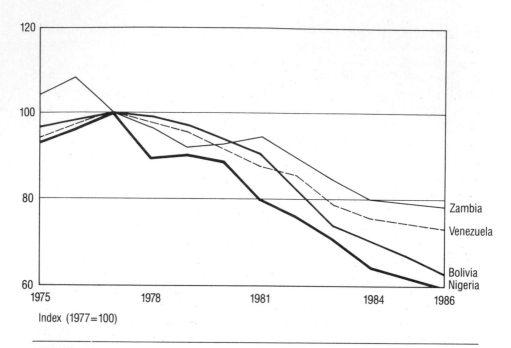

FIGURE 6-9

PER CAPITA GROSS DOMESTIC PRODUCT IN SELECTED COUNTRIES

preserving the status quo, since they were benefiting under the existing rules and their economies were becoming more fully integrated into the global system. The oil-rich states had recycled their petrodollar surpluses of the 1970s into substantial investments in the advanced economies, and the NICs were exporting manufactured and semifinished goods in the open markets of the North. North-South confrontation did not suit either of these subgroups within the Third World.

Many common concerns endure in the Third World, however. Problems of trade, aid, investment, and debt affect a majority of the states, which from time to time retaliate against the North's economic dominance by threatening to nationalize foreign assets, default on debt payments, or cut off access to oil or a strategic mineral. The South suffers perennially from overpopulation, a chronic shortage or maldistribution of food, and mass starvation, but the North's humanitarian aid creates new problems of dependency and disruption of Third World markets. Political differences remain on questions of human rights and democracy, since many of the new regimes feel they can ill afford internal opposition. The global environment is a growing concern among the comparatively wealthy states of the North, but the poor states resist any regulations that might impose higher costs on their infant industries. Conversely, some cooperative management schemes that hold economic promise for the Third World (for example, the Law of the Sea Treaty), have been resisted by

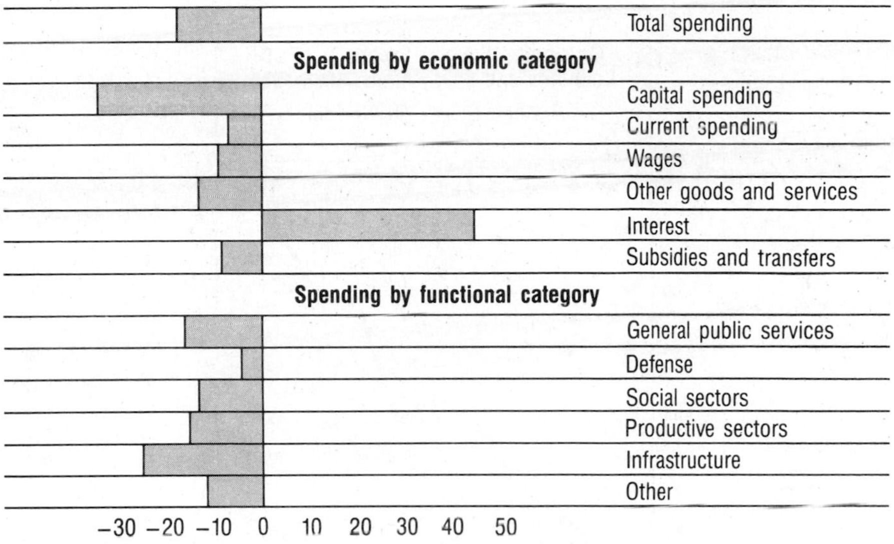

Note: The countries include Argentina, Bolivia, Brazil, Costa Rica, Dominican Republic, Indonesia, Liberia, Mexico, Morocco, Paraguay, Senegal, Sri Lanka, Togo, Uruguay, and Venezuela.

FIGURE 6-10
REAL REDUCTION IN CENTRAL GOVERNMENT SPENDING IN FIFTEEN
COUNTRIES, EARLY 1980s

First World states, which refuse to forgo their present economic and technological advantages. We will survey some of these contemporary North-South issues in the following sections.

The Terms of Trade

The LDCs of the South are heavily dependent on trade with the industrial economies of the North (see Figure 6-11). But the pattern of trade is unequal in several respects. For one thing, the North and South do not exchange comparable products. In 1978, 84 percent of the developed countries' imports from the Third World consisted of primary commodities, mainly agricultural products and minerals, and 82 percent of the Third World's imports from the developed countries were manufactured goods. The technologies for producing or extracting the South's primary goods also come largely from the North, as does most of the finance, shipping, and processing. Export earnings on commodities constitute a large percentage of the GNP in many LDCs, but imported primary goods are a relatively small part of the value of Northern manufactures and only a small fraction of total trade in the North, whose advanced industrial states trade primarily with one another. (The Third World still accounts for

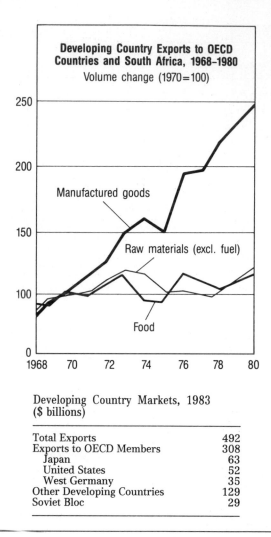

Developing Country Markets, 1983
($ billions)

Total Exports	492
Exports to OECD Members	308
Japan	63
United States	52
West Germany	35
Other Developing Countries	129
Soviet Bloc	29

FIGURE 6-11
DEVELOPING COUNTRY EXPORT GROWTH

only one-fifth of global GNP.) Imports of manufactured goods are essential for developing economies that are trying to industrialize and build up their infrastructures. These, along with aid flows, loans to finance imports of oil and machinery, and investment by multinationals, have kept the South tied to the North economically. And the LDCs, which cannot afford to cut off their trade with the North, are at the mercy of fluctuating demand for their commodities. Trade barriers, changes in consumer tastes, or recession can cause a catastrophic fall in an LDC's export earnings. Worse still, the price of industrial goods has risen steadily, whereas the price of primary commodities reached an all-time low in the 1980s. Thus, the postwar expansion of trade did not do much to improve conditions in the Third World. In fact, the export share of the non-OPEC LDCs fell from 3.6 percent in 1960 to 2.2 percent in 1970, and then to 1.5 percent, in 1977. At the same time, the LDCs doubled their food imports between 1955 and 1970 — increasing their dependence on the North for the one commodity they cannot do without. With the exception of oil and a few key minerals, the South remains asymmetrically dependent on the North.

It is the thesis of Raul Prebisch and other dependency theorists that the colonial pattern of center-periphery relations persists, rooted in unequal terms of trade and in the strikingly different market conditions for exporters of manufactures versus exporters of primary products. Only sixteen Third World states have more than 25 percent of their total production in industrial goods, leaving the majority dependent for export earnings on primary goods that typically suffer from low productivity gains, inelastic demand, and fluctuating prices (see Figure 6-12). Since advanced economies can absorb only a fixed amount of many food products (bananas, coffee, cocoa, and the like), bumper harvests bring gluts and falling prices, not profits, for the LDC producers. First World farmers receive price supports and subsidies from their governments; Third World farmers do not. In the industrial world, powerful labor unions keep wages high, forcing up the prices of finished goods and securing for the workers a fair share of productivity gains. In the Third World, where labor organizations are weak, productivity gains go to management (often Northern

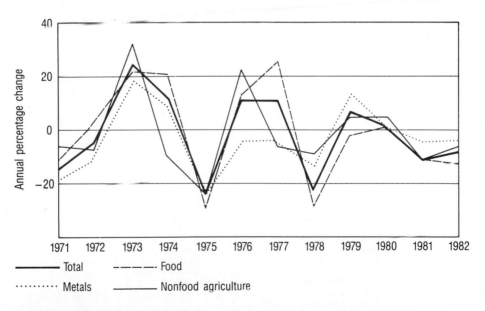

Note: Based on a sample of 33 commodities, excluding petroleum, weighted by current values of developing-country commodity exports, deflated by the manufacturing unit value index.

FIGURE 6-12

ANNUAL FLUCTUATIONS IN DEVELOPING COUNTRY EXPORT PRICES, 1971–82 multinationals), in the form of profits, or are passed on to consumers in the form of lower prices.

Complex economies have a flexibility that allows them to substitute one raw material for another or to defer the consumption of a product. An LDC that exports only one or two commodities does not have a comparable range of choices. (Figure 6-13 lists the forty-seven countries dependent on one commodity for more than 50 percent of their export earnings.) Libya, Sierra Leone, Chile, Bangladesh, Burma, Ethiopia, Ghana, and the Dominican Republic are also heavily dependent on just a few export items. Moreover, world commodity

---

FIGURE 6-13

ONE-COMMODITY COUNTRIES (BASED ON 1980–83 EXPORT AVERAGE, MARKET ECONOMIES ONLY)

Latin America and Caribbean

The Bahamas
 Petroleum products
Bolivia
 Natural gas (1983)
Colombia
 Coffee
Ecuador
 Crude petroleum
El Salvador
 Coffee
Jamaica
 Alumina
Mexico
 Crude petroleum
Netherlands Antilles
 Petroleum products
Suriname
 Alumina
Trinidad and Tobago
 Petroleum and products
Venezuela
 Crude petroleum

Africa

Algeria
 Crude petroleum
Angola
 Crude petroleum
Botswana
 Diamonds
Burundi
 Coffee
Comoros
 Cloves
Congo
 Crude petroleum
Gabon
 Crude petroleum
The Gambia
 Groundnut products
Guinea
 Bauxite
Lesotho
 Diamonds
Liberia
 Iron ore

Libya
 Crude petroleum
Mauritania
 Iron ore
Mauritius
 Sugar
Niger
 Uranium
Nigeria
 Crude petroleum
Rwanda
 Coffee
Seychelles
 Copra
Somalia
 Live animals
Uganda
 Coffee
Zaire
 Copper
Zambia
 Copper

Middle East Asia

Iran
 Crude petroleum
Iraq
 Crude petroleum
Kuwait
 Crude petroleum
Oman
 Crude petroleum
Qatar
 Crude petroleum
Saudi Arabia
 Crude petroleum
Syria
 Crude petroleum
United Arab Emirates
 Crude petroleum
Yemen (Aden)
 Petroleum products

Asia/Pacific

Brunei
 Petroleum and products
Fiji
 Sugar
Indonesia
 Crude petroleum
Papua New Guinea
 Copper
 concentrate
Vanuatu
 Copra

prices are subject to radical fluctuations. Prices varied by an average of 5 percent between 1950 and 1970, fluctuated by more than 12 percent during the 1970s, and were less volatile in the 1980s only because they were depressingly low. If an LDC did realize productivity gains, falling prices often cancelled them. For example, Malaysia managed to raise its productivity in rubber by increasing exports almost 25 percent from 1960 to 1968 while reducing the plantation labor force significantly. But its income from rubber sales declined by about 33 percent in those years, as the result of lower world prices. The productivity gains were passed along to foreign consumers in the form of lower prices, rather than going to Malaysian workers as increases in their wages and living standards.

The complaint of the North is that, in attempting to remove trade inequities, the LDCs have erected barriers to trade that threaten the liberal free-trade philosophy of GATT and the Bretton Woods system. Since World War II, the LDCs have grown faster overall than the advanced industrial countries and have increased their relative share of exports in manufactures. The question is: what have they done with all those foreign exchange earnings? If the earnings have been squandered on nonproductive uses, or eaten up by a prodigious population explosion, or expended on still more Western imports, the North says, then it can hardly be blamed for the South's trade shortfalls. Basic structural problems within the LDCs, not the terms of trade, are at fault. The South argues that this position is historically naive and does not take into account the advantages the North has by being first comer to the development process. An unregulated market will always favor the better organized and those who control the financing and technology. Seeing little to be gained from a liberal regime of unregulated trade, given the huge disparities in size, market share, and bargaining power, many of the new states have imposed tariff barriers to trade with the established economic giants.

They have focused on an inward-looking strategy of import substitution that will give their infant industries the opportunity to develop. Short-term access to cheap imports has been deemed less vital than the long-term goal of creating a self-sufficient national industrial capacity. In theory, the law of comparative advantage should reward equally the LDC that specializes in primary products and the advanced industrial state that exports finished goods. In practice, diversification in exports seems to be a better strategy for weathering the vicissitudes of fluctuating markets and protecting vital domestic interests. But for an LDC suffering from neocolonial dependence and overspecialization, such diversification cannot take place without regulation of the terms of trade.

The North's response to the growth of manufacturing capacity in the South has been basically protectionist. In America, when its strong market position declined, so did its attachment to the liberal trading principles that had marked the early period of GATT. Tariff barriers have recently been rising, as part of a nationalist, neomercantilist reaction to the export successes of the NICs of East Asia. The World Bank has estimated that if the West opened its markets freely to Third World trade, the LDCs could earn an additional $24 billion a year — approximately what they receive today in foreign economic assistance —

although the earnings would go mainly to the few states that have already broken into the world market in finished goods.

The LDCs say that alterations in market relations are essential if they are to be properly represented in the decision-making structures of the global economy. Poor states, an overwhelming majority in the international community and with four-fifths of the world's population, have less than one-third of the votes in the Bretton Woods institutions, such as the IMF and the World Bank, which tend to favor the laissez-faire philosophies and market dominance of the developed states. Not surprisingly, the LDCs advocate more aggressive and interventionist policies for redirecting trade and capital flows to the benefit of Third World development.

One such policy is a generalized system of preferences (GSP) under which the developed nations would abandon the nondiscriminatory most-favored-nation rules of Bretton Woods in favor of preferential trade access for the LDCs. This would meet the capital needs of the poor states indirectly, through increased access to trade, rather than directly, through aid and investment from the North. It would erase the stigma as well as the political controls associated with direct transfers and would introduce a new pattern of economic exchange at once more dignified, more just, and more reliable in generating an ongoing stream of development capital and foreign exchange. The EEC took tentative steps in this direction at Lomé and in the Multilateral Trade Negotiations concluded in Geneva in 1979. But in the 1980s, increasing competition from the NICs caused the developed states to argue for a "graduation" clause that would exclude from the GSP those Third World states with growing exports in manufactures. The Southern states took this to mean that the North's commitment to alter the terms of trade would last only as long as Northern export capacities and market shares in manufactures were not threatened. By definition, any diversification of exports in a primary producer economy requires lower tariff barriers and sectoral shifts in the advanced economies. In theory such changes should not be costly to anyone, but in practice there are always short-term winners and losers and temporary balance-of-payments problems. The rich states, which are better able to cope economically with these pains of transition, are also better organized politically to avoid them.

Price stabilization is a second trade initiative that the LDCs have put forward. If the prices developing nations received for their exports were linked, or indexed, to the prices they paid for imports, the problem of fluctuating commodity prices could be managed without any changes in the overall volume of exports. The effects of inflation or wage increases on the prices of finished goods from the North would be reflected in an equal rise in the prices paid for primary products from the Third World. Strong opposition from the industrialized world has so far prevented the adoption of such price indexation. An alternative proposed by the Group of 77 at the UNCTAD IV meetings, in Nairobi, Kenya, in 1976, led to the adoption of an Integrated Programme for Commodities (IPC), which envisioned a series of international agreements that would create commodity stockpiles, establish a common fund for financing price stabilization, encourage long-term supply and purchase agreements, and expand the LDC role in processing and intermediary services. The Lomé Convention of 1975 had previously launched a pioneering effort to stabilize the export earnings of the forty-six ACP nations through a common financing mechanism known as STABEX, but the EEC received preferential access to the raw materials, making the arrangement more in the nature of a reciprocal trade agreement. The IPC's common fund plan, on the other hand, would have been financed largely by contributions from the commodity consumers — namely, the industrialized states. Consequently, Northern support for commodity stabilization remained lukewarm because it transferred resources to the South, as a disguised form of aid, without offering any significant benefits or controls in return. As might be expected, the North was unwilling to concede to the South any trade advantages that the South could not win for itself by a more direct exercise of its political or economic power.

Food and Population

A major North-South issue is the maintenance of a proper balance between limited global resources and a growing population. The persistence of widespread famine in Africa over the past two decades has vividly illustrated the basic dilemma of multiplying mouths and dwindling food production in the Third World. Many of the world's poor have come to be kept alive by imported food and the aid of such international agencies as the World Food Council, CARE, Oxfam, and the International Fund for Agricultural Development, and this has given food and population issues an important international dimension.

The population explosion in the Third World is partly a consequence of the uneven impact of modernization — a case of good intentions going awry or, more accurately, of partial modernization being worse than none at all. Starting in the colonial period, Western health practices were introduced that rapidly depressed death rates, particularly the rate of infant mortality, but with no corresponding efforts to change the traditional preference for large families. In poor societies, in which life is unpredictable and government assistance to families absent, children are a kind of social security system, a hedge against old age and an uncertain future. In a deprived society, children are a main source of pleasure and status. In a farming culture, they are a ready source of labor. When there has always been a high risk of losing one's children to disease or malnutrition, high birth rates seem logical. Even among better-off urban dwellers, large families remain the custom, despite the decline in death rates. And among the rural poor, large families are a sign that modern benefits and services have not yet penetrated deeply enough to support the survival of smaller families.

The experience of advanced states demonstrates that couples tend to have large families for a reason, not because they are unable to prevent them. In North America, birth rates declined rapidly after 1825, in the absence of government direction and of modern contraceptive techniques, undoubtedly in response to better economic conditions; parents chose to have smaller families because they perceived that the costs of raising more children outweighed the benefits. In a Third World context, this means that family-planning programs can assist parents who choose to have smaller families, but the programs cannot, of themselves, motivate that choice. In both China and India, where population limits were imposed without corresponding changes in education and welfare policies, powerful economic incentives, government intimidation, and strong community pressure were necessary to get couples to practice contraception. If similar restrictions on freedom are to be avoided elsewhere, then development itself may be the best contraceptive, especially when accompanied by changes in the status and education of women. But such changes have been slow in coming and cannot be transferred wholesale from the West. It is much easier to lower death rates by the selective introduction of Western technologies — medical science, agricultural production, public sanitation — than to make the more fundamental political and cultural reforms that would alter a nation's way of life.

Solutions to the Third World's food and population problems are not merely technical, and their consequences are not purely demographic or economic. Many of the technologies are already available, but their effective application is impeded by social or political factors. Imported technologies are expensive and often involve mortgaging the future in some respect — something that is true both of sterilization campaigns among the illiterates of India and of the capital-intensive, high-yield techniques of the Green Revolution, which deplete investment funds, foreign exchange, and the fertility of the soil while boosting food production in the short term. The Green Revolution, which introduced high-yielding "miracle" strains of wheat and rice into the Third World, has raised agricultural output in a number of countries, like Mexico, India, and the Philippines, but it has had a negative political impact on rural stratification. The new grains, requiring heavy use of irrigation, fertilizers, and pesticides, were adopted mostly by wealthy farmers who already had easy access to credit and imports; the capital requirements and mechanized methods encouraged a growth in the size of farms. Though more efficient in producing large crops to feed burgeoning urban populations, the methods of the Green Revolution drove many marginal farmers into bankruptcy, leaving the new grains available only to those with the resources to purchase them in the money economy. The problem of world hunger is more intimately related to prevailing socioeconomic inequities than to failings in agricultural technology. The starving poor do not have the purchasing power to participate in the money sector or redirect the forces that control the market demand for food.

There has always been enough food to feed the world's poor. The problem has been one of distribution, both between nations and within nations. World grain harvests doubled between 1950 and 1975, resulting in a per capita increase of 25 percent in the amount of food available. The present agricultural capacities of the Third World would be sufficient to meet food needs there if existing croplands were appropriately utilized. Yet the United Nations estimated in 1983 that thirty-five developing countries were deficient in food or dependent on imports, and some experts project a rise to fifty-five countries by the turn of the century. The difficulty has been to establish a self-sustaining system of local production to feed a growing population.

Prevailing land-tenure arrangements favor large landowners, who produce cash crops for export, not the small farmer, who raises food for local consumption. Most hunger results from an inability to obtain locally available food supplies or to obtain land that could support subsistence farming. Since chronic malnutrition contributes heavily to high infant mortality rates, inadequate food supplies encourage poor peasants to have large families. In this sense, food shortages lead to rapid population growth, not the other way around. Political and social inequities in the agricultural sector have created a structural poverty that accounts for both rapid population growth and limited food production. Maldistribution of land is a serious problem throughout the Third World — overall, less than 10 percent of the population owns more than half the land — and the skewed pattern of land ownership is particularly severe in Latin America. In Peru, where only about 7 percent of the land is arable, a tiny 1 percent of the landowning aristocracy controls more than 80 percent of the land, most of it held in tenancy or in sharecropping arrangements that give the farmers little incentive to improve productivity. Those large landowners who do cultivate their own land tend to plant cash crops for export, using capital-intensive methods that increase rural unemployment; land is taken out of food production and the landless laborers migrate to the cities, where they become dependent on imported foodstuffs. These practices set up a vicious circle in which the government assists the wealthy export sector to expand further in order to generate the foreign exchange earnings needed to import food to subsidize and pacify the volatile urban poor. So we witness the striking paradox, in both Africa and Latin America, of countries that have sharply increased their production of agricultural goods for foreign markets but cannot provide a minimally adequate diet for the majority of their citizens.

Ecologists have made us increasingly aware that there are limits to the global carrying capacity; we can no longer naively assume that the Third World will simply "outgrow" its poverty. Increasing production is only one part of the equation, and it becomes a negative rather than a positive if it is accompanied by a population explosion that erases the gains. When population outpaces food production, per capita consumption is lowered, but the level of throughput (the rate at which resources are consumed) and the burden on the planet's finite stock of nonrenewable resources are raised. Our technological ingenuity may raise the level of food production in the short term — through irrigation, fertilizers, energy-intensive mechanization — but only at some risk to sustainable yields. Supplies of fresh water, fuel, fertilizer, and top soil are not inexhaustible; all these factors of production are depleted or degraded at a rate that rises in proportion to rising levels of population and economic growth. Thus, the problem in the Third World has not simply been one of insufficient production. On the contrary, domestic productivity and economic growth in the LDCs increased overall, between 1966 and 1986, at a faster rate than growth in the North. But population growth exceeded the expansion of production, and import needs outstripped rising export earnings, making most of the LDCs worse off today than ever. The gap in GNP per capita between rich and poor states is wider than ever. The aggregate annual income of *all* the economies of Africa, Asia, Latin America, and the Middle East amounts to only about half the annual production of the United States alone.

The issue may be a matter of which ought to come first, birth control or wealth control. The conventional view in the North, whose population growth rate is quite low, is that the wealth the South seeks through economic development is impossible without population control. There is no doubt that standards of living in the Third World could be raised by limiting population growth. Sri Lanka, the Indian state of Kerala, and Communist China have all succeeded in lowering their birth rates through a combination of contraception campaigns, vigorous public education, and health and nutrition policies aimed at convincing low-income mothers that traditional causes of infant mortality no longer pose a threat to their children. But many Third World leaders argue that population control can be only marginally effective in the absence of broad-based development that brings literacy and a rising standard of living to the poor majority. They feel it is unrealistic and unfair to expect the Third World to impose population limits by more stringent means than those that operated in the North. Theories of demographic transition suggest that poverty is itself a cause of high birth rates and that population control will follow naturally in the wake of economic development.

What the Third World needs, in the view of its leaders, is aid and reform programs that will help countries reach the takeoff point for launching their own economies into self-sustained growth. It also needs, they say, a commitment from the North to limit its wasteful consumption, so that nonrenewable resources will not be exhausted before future generations in the Third World have had the opportunity to claim their fair share. With the industrialized third of the world's population consuming 70 percent of its natural resources, there is no hope that a China or an India can ever reach economic parity, with or without successful population control. There simply are not enough resources to go around.

The injustice of the skewed pattern of consumption is underlined by the fact that the North's high level of consumption is associated with the nonessential "wants" of superabundance, while the South has difficulty meeting its basic needs. One American consumes more than twenty-five times as much as one Indian; forty Somalis do not make as heavy a demand on the planetary resource base as a single Swiss. Lowering population in the North or limiting its extravagant consumption habits would do more to free resources for the poor than any other measure. At the United Nations Conference on Population held in Bucharest, Romania, in 1974, Nicolae Ceausescu, then the premier of the host country, went so far as to maintain that poor countries must increase their populations to avoid being consigned to a position of inferiority in the international balance of power. A Western scholar, Julian Simon, has argued that human creativity is the ultimate resource and that economic development in the West was preceded by a vigorous population growth that gave it vitality and an abundant supply of manpower. In light of these views, it should not be surprising that only about thirty developing countries have active population-limitation programs. Perhaps it is wrong to blame the Third World for failing to curb its population. If it is to repeat the economic successes of the West, population control appears less important than securing comparable access to global capital and resources.

Nevertheless, realism dictates that the Third World states must put some limits on population growth to avoid the tragic consequences of continuing famine and dependency. Countries that cannot solve their population problems rationally face the unforgiving solutions of nature, and even those that succeed face the time bomb set ticking by past excesses. The Third World will be particularly vulnerable in the years ahead because a large percentage of its people today are children. Populations will continue to swell, even though a country may have achieved a zero net replacement rate (the point at which each couple has only two children or each mother only one daughter), because large numbers of young women born in the boom years will reach childbearing age. Their impact will be felt even if they choose to have small families. In general, population growth is likely to continue for fifty to seventy years after replacement-level fertility is reached, until age groups have become equalized. Latin America, for example, has reduced its population growth rate significantly (to about 2.4 percent in 1984), but it will continue to see the effects of huge numbers of young people entering their reproductive years over the next decade. If current population trends continue, the world could reach a zero replacement rate by the year 2020; the total population will not stabilize, however, until it reaches more than 11 billion, around the beginning of the twenty-second century (see Figure 6-14).

Finally, global interdependence has increased for every nation the foreign policy costs and risks associated with food and population issues. The political-economic stability of many Third World regimes is held hostage to population pressures. When 45 percent of a population is under fifteen years of age, there is a heavy burden on such public services as schools and hospitals. With a relatively small proportion of productive workers, a state must spend its resources on immediate needs, rather than investing in infrastructure. As the young reach working age, they will swell the ranks of unemployed or underemployed, becoming slum dwellers or marginal workers. Shantytowns already house more than 30 percent of the urban population in the Third World, and any growth in urban slums is sure to generate political and social unrest. Food shortages will become an explosive political issue wherever a third or more of a country's population is packed into slums in its capital city. Any large constituency like this, which is subject to immediate social mobilization, puts political order at risk. Urban unrest and structural violence spill over into civil violence, posing threats to neighboring states and to the entire international system. Economic hardship and social disorder swell the number of illegal immigrants and refugees seeking asylum. Aid budgets and the resources of international agencies are stretched to their limits.

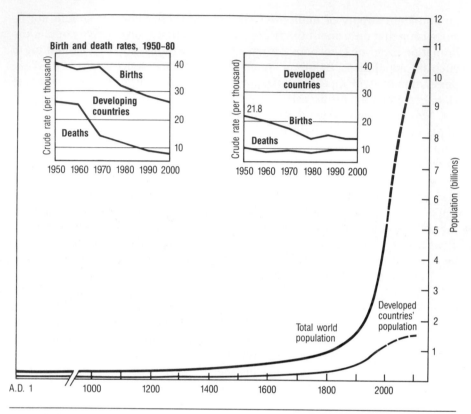

FIGURE 6-14
PAST AND PROJECTED WORLD POPULATION

The Third World's growing dependency on food imports also highlights the asymmetry, and potential fragility, of current patterns of interdependence. By the early 1980s, developing countries were importing nearly 100 million metric tons of cereal grains annually. At the same time, much of the world had come to rely unduly on the United States for food stocks (America's subsidized agriculture produces most of the world's surplus), placing a powerful "food weapon" in the hands of a single state. Canada, Australia, Argentina, and France are the only other significant food exporters; together, the United States and Canada account for 90 percent of total grain exports. Food supplies are so concentrated that the Soviet Union has been able to influence prices and reserves through its large purchases of foreign grain. The combined impact of rising oil prices and massive Soviet grain purchases caused the price of grain to rise 300 percent after 1973, although the shortfall in grain production was only 3 percent. Rising food prices added as much to the global inflation of the 1970s as rising petroleum costs did. The entire planet has become a potential victim of poor harvests in the vital breadbasket of North America — a degree of interdependence that has vastly increased global vulnerability to disruptions from many sources.

Oil, Energy, and Access to Resources

Access to oil, a central point of friction in North-South relations for the past two decades, is symptomatic of the extent to which the developed states have become dependent on resources from the Third World. But the flow of resources, from South to North, is indicative of the industrial world's disproportionate wealth and dominant share of global production. Energy consumption per capita in North America is fifty times that in South Asia, and the industrial North as a whole consumes about ten times as much energy as the underdeveloped South does. In industrial societies, energy is a primary factor of production, which in the early stages of industrialization came mostly from domestic sources. The extension of imperial control over the Third World brought access to more abundant and cheaper supplies of energy and raw materials, which rapid growth, improvements in transportation, and global economic specialization made ever more valuable to the industrial North. However, when the global political balance shifted after decolonization, this resource dependency became a point of vulnerability. Despite the dominant role of Western technology and investment in bringing Third World resources to market, the possibility of national expropriation or embargo stood as a direct threat to the economic lifeline of the West. (Figure 6-15 illustrates the dependence on Third World sources of energy.) The Iraqi attempt in 1990 to control

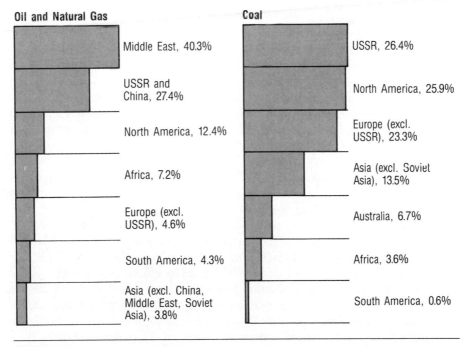

Oil and Natural Gas

Middle East, 40.3%

USSR and China, 27.4%

North America, 12.4%

Africa, 7.2%

Europe (excl. USSR), 4.6%

South America, 4.3%

Asia (excl. China, Middle East, Soviet Asia), 3.8%

Coal

USSR, 26.4%

North America, 25.9%

Europe (excl. USSR), 23.3%

Asia (excl. Soviet Asia), 13.5%

Australia, 6.7%

Africa, 3.6%

South America, 0.6%

FIGURE 6-15
WORLD FOSSIL FUEL DEPOSITS

Kuwaiti oil supplies and its success in raising the price of OPEC oil are dramatic indicators of this continuing vulnerability.

An examination of the United States' oil and energy policies will give some indication of global resource trends. The United States was at one time the world's leading exporter of oil and headquarters to five of the famous "seven sisters"—the MNCs that controlled nearly two-thirds of the world's oil production. These vertically integrated firms once monopolized every aspect of oil production and marketing, from exploration to refining, transport, and retail sale. Their control of Third World sources was virtually complete, making the North the center of energy policy as well as consumption. The MNCs often paid more in taxes to their home governments than they paid in royalties for the oil itself. The ready supply of cheap Third World oil, augmented by the North's own substantial production, helped to fuel industrial expansion and create an energy-intensive infrastructure.

By 1973, the picture had changed dramatically. Energy consumption was still growing, with oil supplying half the energy used across the world every day, but skyrocketing demand and dwindling domestic oil reserves had converted the United States from an exporter of oil to an importer. In 1973, it depended on other countries for 39 percent of its supply (see Figure 6-16). Meanwhile, OPEC, the producers' cartel, was finally succeeding in its efforts to restrict competition, curtail production, and raise prices. Management of the international oil regime passed almost overnight from the Northern based MNCs to Southern producer states: Saudi Arabia, Iraq, Iran, Libya, Kuwait, Qatar, United Arab Emirates, Algeria, Indonesia, Venezuela, Ecuador, Nigeria, and Gabon. The cost of oil more than quadrupled in 1973, rising from $2.59 to $11.65 a barrel. Gas lines formed in the United States, and its GNP fell by 2.5 percent over the next three years. By 1977, U.S. dependency on foreign oil had risen to 48 percent, in spite of still higher prices—a sign that the industrial North could not get along without this precious commodity. The U.S. vulnerability to interruptions in its supplies was confirmed when, in 1979, a second Arab oil embargo, coupled with revolution in Iran, cut production in the Middle East. In 1981, the price per barrel rose to $37, and the U.S. GNP fell by 3.5 percent.

The picture changed again after 1981. A global recession and vigorous conservation efforts were cutting demand for oil, and the exploitation of new reserves in Mexico, Alaska, and the North Sea were boosting supply, even while shipments through the Persian Gulf were curtailed by the Iran-Iraq War. The United States removed price controls on domestic production, and suddenly it had an oil glut. OPEC's share of world production fell from 53 percent to 32 percent. Falling prices forced OPEC to cut its official rate in 1983 and to set a ceiling on aggregate production levels. In 1985, Saudi Arabia made the decision to increase production, in line with an OPEC move to regain its market share, and the price nose-dived to $12 a barrel. In the same year, U.S. dependence on foreign oil reached a temporary low of 31 percent. (Figure 6-17 illustrates the impact of international events on oil prices.) In light of the oil glut and sizable strategic reserves of petroleum, President Reagan abandoned the

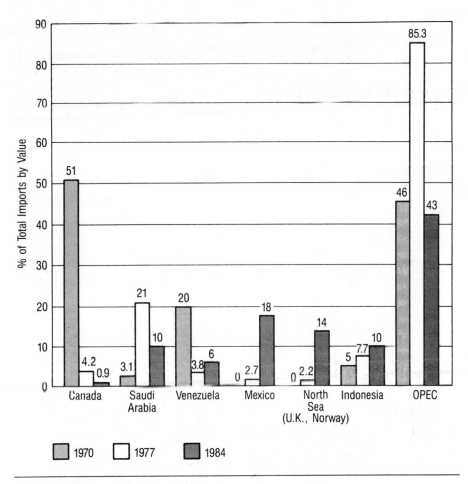

FIGURE 6-16
SOURCES OF U.S. CRUDE OIL IMPORTS

Carter administration's plans for the development of alternative energy sources, and he also set aside President Nixon's Project Independence—the goal of national energy independence—as unrealistic and, for the moment, unnecessary.

Since 1985, however, the trend of declining U.S. dependency has reversed. In 1988, the United States imported 40 percent of its oil, a return to the dependency level of 1973. America consumes approximately 3.5 billion barrels annually, roughly one-fourth of world consumption. With its own sources nearly depleted (the United States possesses only 5 percent of the world's proven reserves), dependency has been rising rapidly. Heavy purchases from the volatile Persian Gulf region have been avoided temporarily; 63 percent of imports are from Mexico, Canada, Venezuela, Nigeria, Britain, and Indonesia. Saudi Arabia remains a major source, however (about 15 percent of imports),

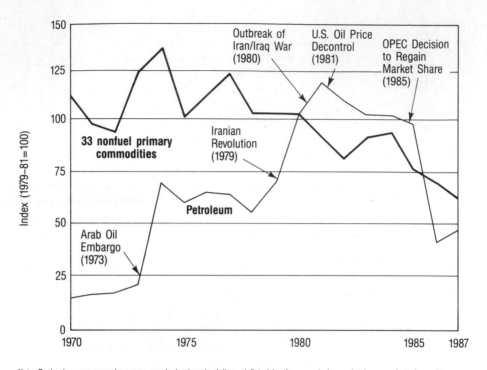

Note: Real prices are annual average nominal prices in dollars, deflated by the annual change in the manufacturing unit value index (MUV), a measure of the price of industrial country exports to developing countries.

FIGURE 6-17

HOW OIL PRICES REFLECT INTERNATIONAL EVENTS

and it is vulnerable to conflicts in the Persian Gulf and to internal unrest from the forces of Islamic fundamentalism. Because over half the world's known oil reserves lie in the Middle East, the United States will almost certainly become more dependent on Persian Gulf oil in the near future.

Several factors make it likely that OPEC's strategic role and the importance of Middle East supplies will continue to grow. First, oil is a finite resource, distributed unevenly around the world, and at current levels of consumption the world's known reserves will be exhausted in sixty years. Since OPEC controls nearly two-thirds of the untapped supply — 80 percent of it under the sands surrounding the Persian Gulf — scarcities are almost sure to bring more production freezes or price hikes. Second, because of OPEC's position as the supplier of last resort, it stands to gain disproportionately from a shift in global demand, just as it lost disproportionately from the oil glut of the 1980s. Then, a 1 percent drop in global energy demand brought a 16 percent decline in OPEC exports. When demand rises, however, the multiplier effect works in reverse, sharply expanding global dependence on OPEC oil. In the third place, alternative sources of energy continue to be less attractive than oil. Nuclear power's high capital costs and environmental effects have slowed its development. Both the United States and the Soviet Union have suffered serious nuclear accidents —Three Mile Island (1979) and Chernobyl (1986)—which have dampened public enthusiasm. Also, concern about nuclear proliferation has discouraged the advanced states from sharing nuclear technology. Fourth, the Soviet Union, now a net oil exporter, will soon become an importer, as its consumption rises with renewed industrial growth. Although the Soviets will probably continue exporting to the West for a time, in order to earn vital hard currency, they will almost surely cut their substantial oil subsidies to Eastern Europe. The overall effect will be to restrict global supplies and increase demand. Finally, the North Sea reserves of Britain and Norway and those in Alaska's North Slope/Prudhoe Bay complex will be exhausted soon, at current levels of production. When they are gone, OPEC will pass from its present position as residual supplier to that of the principal source of oil for the industrial world.

America's allies, Europe and Japan, are even more dependent than the United States is on resources from the Third World, particularly from the volatile oil-producing regions of the Middle East (see Figure 6-18). Japan and Western Europe together account for about 30 percent of world demand for oil, but their domestic production is less than 4 percent. The EEC depends on foreign oil for 60 percent of its total energy needs, 42 percent from the Middle East; the comparable figures for Japan are 78 percent foreign oil, 34 percent of

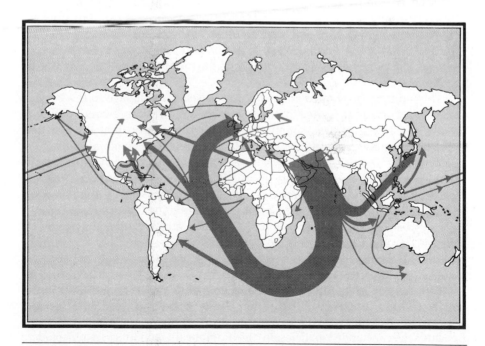

FIGURE 6-18
OIL FLOWS FROM THE MIDDLE EAST

it Arab oil. Japan's dependence on foreign oil offers an interesting history lesson in the economic bases of much foreign policy decision making. In the 1930s, Japan absorbed almost a quarter of America's annual oil exports — oil that was essential to Japan's occupation of Manchuria and military expansion into Southeast Asia. When Roosevelt cut off the exports in 1941, the Dutch East Indies became the most available source of oil to support the imperial ambitions of Japan's Greater East Asia Co-Prosperity Sphere, but U.S. forces in the Philippines and at Pearl Harbor stood in the way of Japan's conquest of Indonesia. The drive to become self-sufficient in oil was thus a major motivation behind the Japanese attack on Pearl Harbor on December 7, 1941.

Supplies of foreign oil have become just as important to the United States today. In 1979, President Carter said that protecting access to Persian Gulf oil was essential to American national security, and his Carter Doctrine declared that "an attempt by an outside force to gain control of the Persian Gulf region will be regarded as an assault on the vital interests of America and such an assault will be repelled by any means necessary, including military force." President Reagan reaffirmed the link between oil and national security when, in 1981, he announced that the United States had an interest in guaranteeing the domestic stability of the oil-producing states of the region, saying, "Saudi Arabia we will not permit to be an Iran." In addition, the 1974 International Energy Program had committed the United States to share its oil with seventeen Western European nations, Japan, and Australia if their oil supplies were disrupted. All these foreign policy commitments took tangible form in Reagan's 1987 decision to provide U.S. naval escorts for reflagged Kuwaiti oil tankers, which sent forty warships and more than 17,000 U.S. servicemen to the Persian Gulf. By 1990, President Bush had sent 100,000 troops to Saudi Arabia and was spending more than $25 million a day to protect American access to Middle East oil.

This military guarantee of the right of access and passage in the Persian Gulf, which made the United States a hostage to the resource vulnerability of the Western alliance, was simply an explicit recognition that the Western industrial nations were just as likely to be threatened by economic strangulation from the Third World as by military attack from the Soviet Union. (It should be said that both these threats are remote ones.) Oil has been cited as a reason for several U.S. interventions. A concern about Soviet-Cuban interdiction of oil supply routes in the Caribbean was one of the principal reasons Reagan gave for the 1983 invasion of Grenada, and U.S. dependence on oil from Mexico and Venezuela also contributed to Reagan's stiff resistance to the Nicaraguan Sandinistas, who, he maintained, were inciting political and economic subversion in Central America.

Different energy vulnerabilities and geopolitical advantages have led to tensions within the NATO alliance and to disagreements over Middle East and Central America policy, and East-West trade. The Europeans strongly opposed Reagan's heavy-handed policies in the Caribbean, and Reagan objected to Europe's provision of capital and technology to the Soviets for the development of a natural gas pipeline to the West. He thought that energy dependency on the

Soviets was no better than dependency on the Arabs; the Europeans apparently found the Soviets less dangerous and diversification of energy dependency more attractive. Different national perspectives also account for a stronger European sympathy toward the Palestinian cause and for a pro-Arab tilt after the October War and the oil embargo of 1973. Less vulnerable economically, the United States could afford to stick solidly behind the Israelis, even after their invasion of Lebanon. The Europeans needed reliable allies in the Middle East and a guaranteed source of oil. America, more inclined to view the Middle East from the perspective of the larger East-West struggle, entered the Persian Gulf war out of a concern over potential Soviet strategic gains rather than European economic losses.

For all these differences, the North has been united in its fear that the OPEC experience might lead to other Third World attempts at monopolization and the restriction of access to resources. This is, no doubt, one of the reasons that the industrial states united in condemnation of Iraqi aggression in the Persian Gulf. An analysis of the OPEC embargo, an early test of the Third World's chances of turning resource dependency to its advantage, may help us see whether those fears are justified.

Certain economic factors favored the success of a cartel, or monopoly, in oil. It was a commodity for which demand was inelastic— that is, the need for it was sufficiently great that consumers would pay almost any price. Furthermore, there were no cheap or ready substitutes for oil, and it was not easy to stockpile. Higher prices did spur exploration for new reserves, but tapping them required a great deal of time and expense. A similar dependency on foreign sources exists for many nonfuel minerals, such as bauxite, chromium, cobalt, copper, iron ore, manganese, nickel, tin, and zinc, but all are easily stockpiled and have a number of ready substitutes, and many can be recycled, unlike oil, which is almost completely consumed during use. Agricultural products are unsuitable for cartel formation because of unpredictable supplies, elastic demand, and a low value as compared to fuels. Finally, none of these commodities—foodstuffs or nonfuel minerals—are as crucial for an industrial economy as petroleum is. Higher prices for them, or dwindling supplies, would have a minimal effect, and most large industrial economies could easily afford to outwait any boycotts or price increases.

Political factors were more important to OPEC's success, however. The largest suppliers, the Arabs, were united by culture, language, and foreign policy objectives. They shared a common hatred of Israel and common political goals. The governments of Saudi Arabia and Kuwait in particular were stable enough to bear the immediate political and economic costs of a cartelization strategy. Traditional sheikdoms with small populations, vast foreign exchange reserves, and few pressing socioeconomic needs, these Arab states could tolerate production quotas that would cut their revenues in the short run, but might give them control in the long run. Most Third World exporters of other commodities are poor, populous states whose foreign exchange revenues are vital to their daily survival; many are politically fragile and can ill afford even a short-term economic disruption. These are factors that work against cartels in the other three products that are controlled exclusively by the Third World: copper (Chile, Peru, Zaire, and Zambia), tin (Bolivia, Indonesia, Malaysia, and Thailand), and bauxite (Guyana, Jamaica, and Surinam). In the case of other nonfuel minerals, there are important suppliers among the industrialized states (for example, Canada and Australia meet many of the United States' needs in strategic minerals), and therefore few incentives for the formation of cartels; the number and diversity of producers works against collaboration across the North-South line. Agricultural commodities, widely produced in the North, are traded mainly among the industrial states. Countries at different levels of development do not have many economic interests in common, except perhaps the principle of free trade itself. Ideological rivalries make some commodity cartels most unlikely; the Soviet Union and South Africa, which control a major share of the world's chromium, gold, platinum, and manganese, can hardly be expected to collude in a cartel when they are so fundamentally divided on political issues.

The policies of the MNCs also contributed to OPEC's success. The major oil companies, far from protecting the interests of the countries in which they were headquartered, proved willing to trade a loss of administrative control for a very large gain in earnings, both for profit and as a means of pacifying the tide of nationalism associated with OPEC's rise. This experience has not been repeated in other markets, however; Northern control of investment capital and extractive technologies has served to keep relations between importers and exporters mutually dependent. When MNCs were confident that they could keep control of a market, as in an agricultural commodity like cocoa, coffee, or bananas, they effectively resisted Third World efforts to form a producers' monopoly. Often, it was a case of one powerful, well-entrenched monopoly fighting off the challenge of another — except that the fragile new Third World coalition hardly qualified as a cartel. Moreover, the MNCs often enjoyed the advantage of political (and sometimes military) support from their home governments, as was the case when Chile attempted to nationalize its American-controlled copper industry. For the most part, such individual instances of nationalization have been the strongest challenges to Northern control of their resources that the Southern states have been able to make.

OPEC's monopoly of the oil trade proved to be short-lived. The temporary ideological consensus among the Middle East producers did not endure past 1979, when Egypt's decision to sign a separate peace with Israel split the Arab world into moderate and radical factions. Iran and Iraq fell to fighting between themselves. Saudia Arabia, Kuwait, and others, unable to absorb the flow of petrodollars into their small economies, found themselves hostage to the heavy investments they had made in the West; any new embargo that threatened the industrial world threatened them too. Mexico's debt crunch forced it to export more oil than the current prices justified. Several of the OPEC countries, like Algeria, Indonesia, and Nigeria, had domestic development projects for which oil revenues were desperately needed, and could not afford to curtail production even temporarily. In short, the different political, foreign policy, and financial needs of OPEC members, along with changing market conditions that even a united OPEC could not control, destroyed the cartel's unity.

The difficulty of using commodity power for political purposes was further underlined by the simultaneous breakdown of the U.S. embargo on grain sales to the Soviet Union. President Carter had declared the boycott after the Soviet invasion of Afghanistan in 1979, but Argentina's right-wing military junta quickly stepped in to fill the gap. Profit and national interest overcame ideological antipathy. Reagan lifted the embargo in 1983, despite his vocal criticism of the Soviet regime, because he concluded that it was hurting the American farmer more than the Soviet leadership. Third World regimes, with their much more precarious economies, have by and large come to similar conclusions about the value of commodity cartels.

The Debt Crisis

The global debt problem had its origins in the 1970s, in a convergence of forces that made it attractive for Third World countries to borrow heavily in the capital market. Most of the LDCs were still trying to fulfill ambitious development plans formulated during their early years of independence, and their needs for capital were rising. Also, many of the new governments had fallen to military coups in the 1960s and 1970s, and the new military regimes, eager to expand their arsenals, were borrowing heavily to buy foreign military hardware (see Figure 6-19). These capital demands coincided with an excess of oil funds in the hands of private lenders. The oil-rich states generally deposited their enormous earnings in relatively secure Western banks, and the banks recycled the petrodollars as loans to the oil-importing nations of the Third World, whose costs rose sharply after the crisis of 1973. The private banks were willing to increase their exposure in the Third World because growth rates there were relatively high and the rate of default on foreign loans was

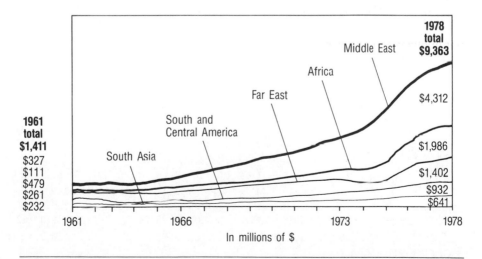

FIGURE 6-19
THIRD WORLD ARMS IMPORTS, 1961–78

significantly lower than on domestic loans. The loans were attractive to the Third World borrowers because high inflation and low interest rates contrived to make the actual cost of the money negative; in effect, the LDCs were borrowing when their purchasing power was strong and repaying later in devalued currency. The strategy worked well between 1973 and 1979, as long as commodity prices were stable and Third World exports and economies were growing. However, the second oil shock of 1979 and the global recession that followed had far more severe effects for both lenders and borrowers than either could have imagined.

Steeply rising interest rates and plunging commodity prices demonstrated just how vulnerable the Third World was to basically adverse terms of trade (see Figure 6-20). Because the North was not as dependent on imported raw materials as the South was on imported finished goods, prices and demand for manufactured goods both remained high, while commodity prices fell. Although its export earnings were declining, the Third World's development needs remained as pressing as ever. Poor countries could not simply tighten their belts or stop importing; they had to go on borrowing to make up their shortfalls. In two decades, Third World debt owed to the World Bank and UN loan agencies tripled, and private banks in Europe, Japan, and America sent tens of billions of dollars to Argentina, Brazil, Mexico, Peru, the Philippines, Indonesia, and fifteen other major Third World borrowers. By 1984, international lending had expanded six-fold, and the largest share of Third World debt was now held by private banks, rather than by official agencies like the World Bank. The combined pressure of high interest rates (which doubled in half a decade) and falling exports had plunged Third World economies into an intolerable situation. In Mexico, the peso lost 80 percent of its value in a single year.

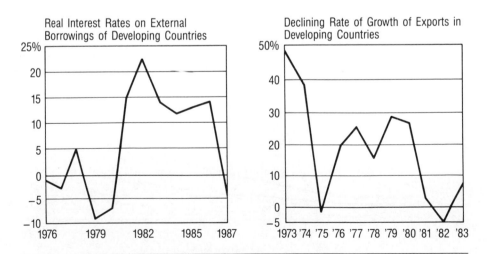

FIGURE 6-20
DECLINING EXPORTS VERSUS RISING INTEREST RATES

FIGURE 6-21

WHO OWES WHAT?

	Total External Debt, End 1982[a] (Billions of U.S. Dollars)	Debt Service in 1983[b] (Percent of Exports) Total	Debt Service in 1983[b] (Percent of Exports) Excluding Short-Term Debt
Latin America	299.4	117	56
Argentina	38.7	154	88
Brazil	89.1	117	67
Chile	18.0	104	54
Colombia	10.4	95	38
Ecuador	8.3	102	58
Mexico	86.1	126	59
Peru	12.8	79	47
Venezuela	36.0	101	25
Asia	121.0	36	14
Indonesia	25.7	28	14
South Korea	37.3	49	17
Malaysia	8.6	15	7
Philippines	24.5	79	33
Taiwan	12.7	19	6
Thailand	12.2	50	19
Middle East & Africa	117.6	58	16
Algeria	16.6	35	30
Egypt	21.7	46	16
Israel	27.6	126	26
Ivory Coast	8.6	76	34
Morocco	13.2	65	30
Nigeria	11.8	28	14
Turkey	18.1	65	20
21 major third-world borrowers	538.0	71	30

[a] Unofficial U.S. estimates
[b] Source: Morgan Guaranty Trust Co.

In Argentina, the inflation rate hit 627 percent; in Bolivia, it reached an almost incredible 2,300 percent.

Growth fell sharply, as did living standards, which dropped as much as 30 percent in some countries. For Latin America as a whole, per capita income fell about 9 percent between 1980 and 1985. Balance-of-payments deficits and increasingly unfavorable terms of trade were restricting access to essential technology. Export economies made possible by Western capital began to collapse, and indebtedness, which had been encouraged by capital-intensive development strategies, reached such high levels that it could not be serviced. Soon the LDCs were using 30 to 80 percent of their export earnings just to repay their enormous debts (see Figure 6-21). According to Peter Worsley's *The Three Worlds,*

> The vulnerability of Africa, by far the poorest part of the world economy, to capitalist economic crisis was reflected, in 1982, in outbreaks of protest in Morocco, the Sudan and Tanzania at drastic increases in food prices as a result of IMF pressure. Africa's external public debt had grown to more than four times what it had been nine years earlier, and whereas only two African

countries had credit agreements with the World Bank [in 1977], twenty-one of the forty-eight African members had called on the Bank for credit by the end of 1981. Globally, the debt burden grew from $19 billion in 1960 to $376 billion in 1976. (p. 317)

By 1983, the debt of the LDCs (except for the oil states) had ballooned to an astronomical $664 billion. By 1988, it was $1.32 trillion.

The biggest debtors were in Latin America: Brazil ($90 billion), Mexico ($86 billion), Argentina ($39 billion), Venezuela ($36 billion), Chile ($18 billion), Peru ($13 billion), Colombia ($10 billion), and Ecuador ($8 billion). Altogether, Latin America accounted for roughly half of Third World indebtedness, and it was now *exporting* capital to the United States in the sum of $30 billion a year in interest payments. The net capital flows between the developed and the Third World actually reversed, so that we have been witnessing the irony of the poor subsidizing the rich. Every year since 1982, total debt service payments from the Third World have exceeded the total of all investments, development aid, grants, and export credits there. The net outflow from poor to rich countries between 1982 and 1988 totaled $249 billion. By 1983, over forty countries had found it impossible to meet their scheduled debt payments. The big banks were also in trouble, since many of them had loaned incautiously, and some held Latin American debt that exceeded their net worth. If there should be massive defaults, the banks (which included the ten largest in the United States) could collapse. The fragile interdependence of the international banking system forced many of the large private banks into offering financial rescue packages to all the big Third World borrowers. Brazil and Mexico were particularly successful in using the threat of default to gain favorable new loans and a rescheduling of payments.

In exchange for debt rescheduling, the creditors (a group known informally as the Paris Club) were able to force on the debtor states stringent austerity programs that would be policed by the IMF, with new loans contingent on the adoption of internal reforms. The Northern governments also refused any bilateral assistance that was not similarly tied to the IMF's conditions. The IMF loan policies reflected the interests of the large industrial economies, whose proportionally larger quota shares give them effective control. By 1983, the IMF was supervising stabilization programs in forty-seven countries under conditional lending agreements whose terms typically required a government to cut spending, eliminate price subsidies, devalue its currency, and raise taxes and interest rates. The brunt of the adjustments has been borne by the poor people in each country. In Brazil, Chile, the Dominican Republic, and Venezuela, riots occurred after the adoption of IMF-approved austerity measures. In 1989, Venezuela's president, Carlos Andres Perez, linked civil unrest in his country directly to cuts in government spending and services made necessary to repay foreign debt, which he said was consuming 70 percent of oil revenues in interest alone. In Brazil, short-term interest rates soared to more than 1,000 percent. Even the middle classes of the Third World have seen the benefits of two decades of growth stripped away in a few short years. (Figures 6-22 and 6-23 show the overall growth in debt and trade

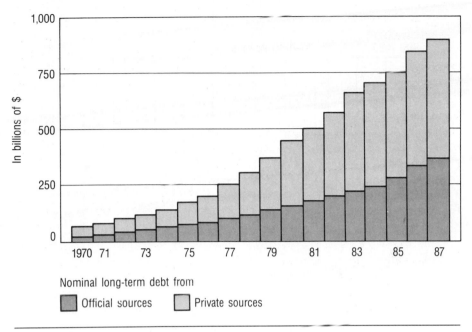

FIGURE 6-22
LONG-TERM EXTERNAL DEBT OF DEVELOPING COUNTRIES, 1970–87

imbalances during this period.) As governments undertake the recessionary steps that are required to reorganize their external debt and correct payment imbalances, such basic services as education and health care are neglected, and malnutrition and infant mortality rise.

The deflationary solutions imposed by international lending agencies like the International Monetary Fund and the World Bank carry a considerable political risk for both global financial institutions and Third World countries. The latter have already suffered more from the global recession than have the advanced countries, whose policies did so much to bring on the deflationary cycle. If the IMF and the Paris Club press too hard, Third World economies could collapse, or a political explosion could trigger a default. Some analysts have suggested that the threat of default on its massive debt is the one lever of influence the Third World holds in the international economy. With more than $1 trillion in loans outstanding, national and international banking systems alike are extremely vulnerable to disruption. Again, the outcome rides on the ability of diverse Third World regimes to adopt a coordinated strategy. Peru's then president, Alan García, became the spokesman for a moratorium policy, although Peru's debt is tiny compared to that of Brazil, Mexico, and Argentina. But his proposal for a debt service limit of 10 percent of a country's foreign exchange earnings brought fire from the U.S. government and from international bankers because it is a self-conscious attempt to unite the Third World on the debt question.

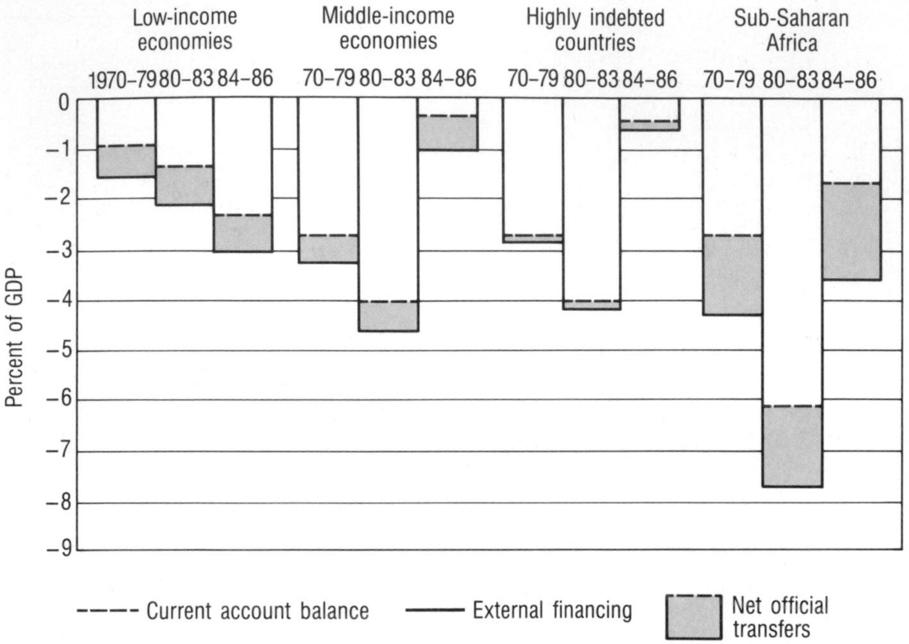

Low-income economies
Middle-income economies
Highly indebted countries
Sub-Saharan Africa

1970–79 80–83 84–86   70–79 80–83 84–86   70–79 80–83 84–86   70–79 80–83 84–86

Percent of GDP

0
−1
−2
−3
−4
−5
−6
−7
−8
−9

–––– Current account balance   ——— External financing   ▨ Net official transfers

FIGURE 6-23
EXTERNAL BALANCES OF DEVELOPING COUNTRIES

In the long run, the Third World is unlikely to repudiate its debt altogether, and the industrialized countries, whose exports to the LDCs have suffered, are likely to provide enough resources so that everyone can muddle through the current crisis. Default or destitution is a no-win set of choices, harmful to lender and debtor alike. The debt problem is probably best managed by renewed growth, stimulated by new loans and by repayment schedules more realistically linked to domestic performance. Some relief has been forthcoming through debt swaps—transfers of Third World assets in exchange for the liquidation of loan obligations at substantial discounts. The banks themselves have also absorbed some of the costs and have begun to write off those portions of the debt that are unlikely to be repaid.

At the root of the debt problem has been the LDCs' poor use of the capital funds they borrowed, which makes an enduring solution impossible without political and economic reforms in the Third World. Such a restructuring will require much more than realistic loan criteria and IMF stabilization measures. Debts and export dependency are not bad in themselves, if the loan funds and export earnings are invested wisely rather than squandered on military hardware, nonessential consumer goods, inappropriate technologies, and an uncoordinated laundry list of politically motivated projects. It is no accident that the bulk of the Third World debt was incurred by military governments, many of whom have abandoned the field now that the painful consequences of their profligate policies are being felt. But waste and corruption are not unique to military regimes. Civilians have also headed the so-called soft states, those that have proved most incapable of managing development or even of effectively absorbing foreign assistance. Huge sums have been embezzled, stolen, or misappropriated, and more has been lost in the form of capital flight, which effectively transfers the risks of development from Third World nationals to the international banks. Data from the IMF and the Morgan Guaranty Bank estimate that 50 percent or more of the borrowed money has flowed right out again through the back door, in the form of private capital concentrated in the hands of a tiny, wealthy, and well-connected elite. Such funds have flowed primarily into U.S., British, and Swiss banks, whose profits from their Third World depositors (with a return-on-equity ratio of up to 200 percent a year) have more than offset their losses on Third World loans.

Some ruling groups have been willing junior partners in the arrangements that have put loan funds and profits in the hands of this select few, while local labor groups or other organizations that could benefit from genuine national development suffer. Many governments are swollen with sinecured but incompetent bureaucrats, originally appointed as a temporary device of political stability. Some Third World governments are so inept that the Asian Development Bank, for one, has sharply decreased lending for lack of qualified projects (as measured by conservative criteria).

Even to service the existing burden of debt will likely depend more on political reforms than on some serendipitous shift in global markets. Oil profits come and go, export prices rise and fall, but nothing can replace honesty, competence, and legitimacy in Third World governments. They cannot expect to weather the debt crisis except on the basis of real economic performance, a large degree of popular support, and a sincere commitment to authentic development. If the Northern governments and international bankers are to stay in touch with the realities of Third World development, they will learn to judge creditworthiness in such political terms, not simply in econometric measures of the strength of exports or return on capital.

Foreign Aid

The debate over foreign aid is highly polarized for and against. Advocates argue that aid is necessary for helping capital-poor countries acquire the new skills and technology they need for development. Taiwan and South Korea, for example, have had notable success in diversifying their economies and stimulating exports through help they have received from international sources. U.S. aid was important in increasing both the amount and the quality of their physical and human capital. In Taiwan, the Sino-American Joint Commission for Rural Reconstruction funded land reform, rural health improvements, forestry and soil conservation, livestock production, water use and control, rural electrification, and communication, with 25 percent of the aid going for education and other investments in human resources. In the 1950s, Taiwan was a heavy importer, running annual trade deficits of $100 million that were almost completely financed by the United States. But all these investments in infrastructure yielded handsome development dividends. In two decades, Taiwan became one of the leading exporters among the Pacific Rim nations, with an economic growth above 10 percent annually. South Korea's aid experience closely paralleled that of Taiwan. In both cases, as with the Marshall Plan aid to Europe after World War II, the foreign assistance was successful because it gave an added boost to countries that were already investing heavily in their own development.

These are not the only success stories. Foreign technical assistance has been an important vehicle for disseminating the benefits of scientific research, most of which is conducted in the North. The U.S. Atoms for Peace program has provided small nuclear reactors and fissionable materials to more than fifty countries for use in power generation and other peaceful applications. U.S. agricultural research on the Third World's behalf paved the way for the Green Revolution in Mexico, India, Pakistan, Sri Lanka, China, and the Philippines, all of whom ended their dependency on food imports by adopting the high-yielding "miracle" grains. And the U.S. Agency for International Development (AID) has had significant success with population control programs in India, Pakistan, Taiwan, Korea, Indonesia, Colombia, and the Philippines.

Foreign aid has generated a significant flow of goods, services, and capital to the Third World. (Figure 6-24 shows funds provided in 1983 by the Development Assistance Committee, the advanced market economies that make up the major foreign aid donors of the Organization for Economic Cooperation and Development.) In addition, government-to-government loans and UN multilateral assistance programs have financed many projects at lending rates below commercial levels. Between 1970 and 1981, the flow of public or publicly guaranteed loans to the Third World increased from $10.3 billion to $78.6 billion. The largest lender, the World Bank, has followed a policy of giving seed money for major projects, with the aim of attracting private or local government investment for ventures that do not fit commercial criteria. Since potential profitability is not the only consideration for foreign-aid loans, they can spare the LDC from a sole reliance on private investment, which usually can be negotiated only on highly concessionary terms. The World Bank's loans have a nearly flawless record of repayment, and 94 percent of the projects have achieved their prescribed objectives, including a 10 percent minimum rate of return. Aid funds are often used to help establish leading sectors of the economy, which can then, through linkages to less developed sectors, pull along the development process. The impact of the aid funds is thus multiplied many times over, without the costly leakage of capital that occurs with the repatriation of profits from private investment. In Thailand, to take one example, the World Bank has funded major projects in irrigation and flood control, electric power, transportation, and education; has helped in the management of external debt; and has set up a National Economic Development Board to oversee the development planning process.

FIGURE 6-24

OFFICIAL DEVELOPMENT ASSISTANCE BY DAC MEMBERS, 1983

Member	% of GNP	Net Disbursements ($ millions)
Netherlands	1.08	1,195
Sweden	1.02	754
Norway	.99	584
Denmark	.76	395
Belgium	.59	480
Australia	.56	753
France	.49	2,500
Germany, Federal Republic of	.48	3,176
Canada	.41	1,429
United Kingdom	.37	1,605
Austria	.35	157
Finland	.30	153
Japan	.28	3,761
New Zealand	.28	61
United States	.27	7,992
Switzerland	.25	320
Italy	.24	827
Total DAC		**26,142**

Former colonies have argued that, out of simple fairness, rich states ought to assist the poor wherever the colonizers' industrial wealth was created with Third World resources. Even when the South's exact contribution is in doubt and the demand for restitution less easy to justify, compassion would call for the rich to take some responsibility for relieving the heavy burdens of global poverty. And the North's foreign aid has indeed been a major force in keeping the poorest economies of Africa afloat. In 1986, foreign aid accounted for 28 percent of the collective gross product of seven sub-Saharan nations — Burkina Faso, Cape Verde, Gambia, Mali, Mauritania, Niger, and Senegal — and provided 41 percent of the GNP in São Tomé, 43 percent in the Comoros, and 50 percent in Cape Verde, according to a report of the Organization for Economic Cooperation and Development (OECD).

Partisans of foreign aid say it is not to blame for the failings of the past few decades in the Third World, where conditions would be worse still without it. In this view, the major shortcomings of the development process are due to structural problems in the global economy, over which the LDCs have little control. They suffered the most from the rising cost of oil and are at the mercy of adverse terms of trade that have prevented them from importing all the capital goods they need. Foreign aid has been a small step toward the redistribution of assets and economic power that are necessary to overcome the injustices and inequities of imperialism and dependency. Though foreign aid is more than the simple palliative that some view it as being, it cannot be expected to compensate all by itself for the basic faults in the international economy that frustrate legitimate development.

In an interdependent world, the LDCs are an important export market for the industrial countries, and foreign aid has helped to sustain this market. When the debt crunch hit, for example, sales of U.S. construction equipment in Latin America experienced a sharp decline. U.S. farmers, autoworkers, and the balance of payments all suffered as Third World economies contracted and overseas customers stopped buying American goods. The Export-Import Bank, a U.S. agency that underwrites loans when credits cannot be secured from commercial banks, stepped in to assist many Third World countries in financing imports, at the same time keeping alive American industries that depended on a vigorous export market. Another successful U.S. aid measure is the Public Law 480 food assistance program, which distributes the agricultural surpluses of American farmers to needy Third World peoples.

Multilateral lending agencies suppported by the contributions of individual governments have made possible a full range of assistance untainted by narrow political considerations (see Figure 6-25). The United States pledges roughly $2 billion a year to such international institutions as the UN Development Program, the World Bank, the International Finance Corporation, the International Development Association, and the Inter-American Development Bank. Lending has been channeled through a variety of regional development banks, like the EEC's European Investment Bank, the African Development Bank, the Asian Development Bank, and the Caribbean Development Bank. The OPEC countries jointly established three separate assistance agencies that have sent approximately $7 billion annually to the Third World, an amount that in 1983 equaled one-quarter of the total development assistance distributed by the OECD countries. Communist states have contributed about $2 billion a year, or about 6 percent of the total. Rich states have channeled more and more of their aid through international agencies, indicating a growing commitment to a nonpolitical development agenda.

There is no doubt that these funds have made a difference. The list of projects is impressive: irrigation in Sri Lanka and the Philippines; rural electrification in Egypt and Brazil; road construction in Honduras; education and adult literacy in Pakistan; fish production and animal husbandry in Burma and São Tomé; improved farming techniques in Tanzania, Guatemala, and Rwanda; potable water and community health measures in India and El Salvador. And, with few exceptions, they have been no-frills basics that have substantially improved the quality of life for millions. Under President Carter, the United States began to focus its aid on bilateral assistance to the poorest countries, and today nations with a GNP of less than $550 per capita receive about 85 percent of the U.S. funds. Food and nutrition programs make up the greater part of this aid. International agencies have been particularly helpful in working with refugee populations, which have no means of support and no government to look after their interests; the UN Relief and Works Agency (UNRWA) has assisted millions of refugees in the Middle East and Southeast Asia. It has been conservatively estimated that a fifth to a third of the growth in GNP in low-income countries is due to official development assistance, which constitutes about three-quarters of all foreign funds this poorest group receives. By contrast, commercial loans and direct private investment in these countries

FIGURE 6-25

MULTILATERAL DEVELOPMENT ASSISTANCE

Agency	Year Established	Form of Aid	Expenditures or Authorizations, 1982 ($ millions)
World Bank Group			
International Bank for Reconstruction and Development (World Bank)	1944	Near-commercial-rate and some concessional loans for specific projects	10,309
International Development Association	1959	Concessional loans for projects in poorest developing countries	2,687
International Finance Corporation	1956	Loans to and equity investment in private enterprises	612
Regional Development Banks			
African Development Bank	1963	} Near-commercial-rate and concessional loans for specific projects	428
Asian Development Bank	1965		1,661
Inter-American Development Bank	1959	}	1,947
Agriculture and Food Aid			
Food and Agriculture Organization of the United Nations	1945	Technical assistance in farm production and marketing	172
International Fund for Agricultural Development	1976	Concessional loans for projects to raise food production and reduce rural poverty	290
World Food Program	1962	Emergency food donations	505
Consultative Group on International Agricultural Research	1971	Techniques to improve crops and eliminate crop diseases	171[a]
UN Development Program	1965 (first predecessor, 1948)	Technical assistance in all fields in cooperation with other agencies	859
UN Fund for Population Activities	1972	Grants for all areas of population and family planning	106
World Health Organization	1946	Technical assistance for national health programs and emergency aid	180
			TOTAL: 19,927

[a] Includes special projects.

account for only about 15 percent of their investment resources. Without foreign aid, the bottom third of the world's population would be considerably worse off than it already is.

Critics of foreign aid have advanced a multiplicity of reasons to explain why it has not been effective in promoting Third World development. In the first place, they say the amounts are pitiful, given the magnitude of the problem. In the 1980s, the total volume of official development assistance from both bilateral and multilateral sources was about $35 billion annually, a sum that, when corrected for inflation, represented a decline over the levels of previous decades, despite the growing Third World population. Although the United States accounted for the largest share in absolute dollars, its commitment as a percentage of GNP was smaller than that of any other industrial nation except Italy, Austria, and the USSR. The U.S. average was about one-fifth of 1 percent (0.2%) of GNP; the international standard established by UNCTAD is 0.7 percent. Only the United Arab Emirates, Saudi Arabia, Kuwait, the Netherlands, Sweden, Norway, and France have exceeded the UNCTAD goal. After three decades of official UN development efforts, the gap between rich and poor is wider than ever.

Furthermore, much of the aid has been in the form of military goods, which contribute nothing to economic productivity. (See Figure 6-26 for data on U.S. security assistance and arms exports.) Of almost $300 billion in U.S. foreign aid dispensed since World War II, more than half has gone for military aid. (For example, the U.S. exported weapons and materiel in 1970 to 131 countries worth $4.3 billion and in 1980 to 126 countries worth $17.5 billion. Between 1971 and 1980, the U.S. exported a total of $123.5 billion of military aid.) By buttressing the power of the armed forces in many Third World states and encouraging the military to play an active political role, these security-assistance dollars may actually have served to undermine democracy, political stability, and economic development. Should advanced countries be sending military aid to developing countries that have already spent more than $1 trillion on their armed forces since 1973? In this period, military expenditures have been rising at a faster rate than economic growth, and the typical LDC spends two or three times as much on arms imports as it receives in foreign nonmilitary assistance. Such practices constitute *dis*investment in development, which is dragged down by the nonproductive military burden.

Another criticism is that foreign-aid funds tend to be concentrated on a few key allies and strategically located states. Out of seventy-odd governments that received almost $34 billion in U.S. bilateral economic assistance in the first half of the 1980s, just ten countries got over half of the aid, and Israel and Egypt together got almost a third. In fiscal 1985, thirty-one low-income LDCs received about $1 per person, compared to $28 per person for high-income LDCs; in politically sensitive Central America, Honduras, El Salvador, and Costa Rica got $69 per person. The world's ten poorest countries, mostly politically insignificant African states, have received less than 5 percent of all U.S. bilateral aid. Overall, 80 percent of U.S. aid has gone to less than 10 percent of the LDCs, and U.S. assistance has been doled out largely on the basis of security perceptions, not need. Very poor countries, in which the funds

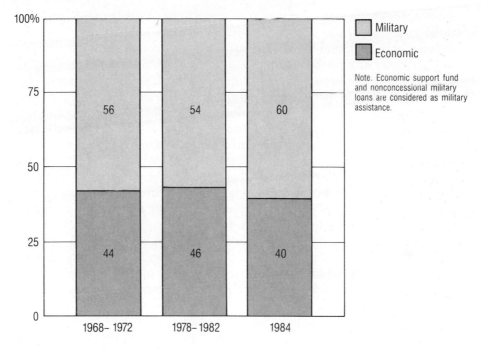

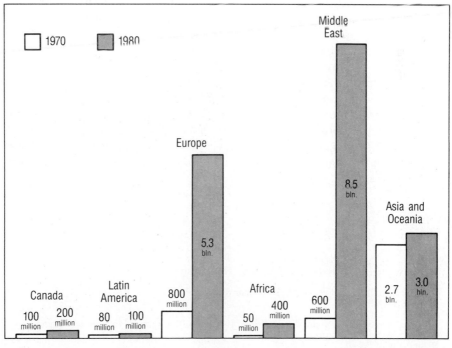

In dollars

FIGURE 6-26
U.S. SECURITY ASSISTANCE

might have been put to the best use, have gotten little. The bulk of U.S. postwar aid has gone to the politically sensitive states of South Korea, South Vietnam, Thailand, India, Pakistan, Israel, Jordan, and Egypt, countries in the containment perimeter around the conflict zones of the Cold War (see Figure 6-27).

Aid funds often have been misallocated, wasted, or simply diverted by corrupt politicians in the recipient governments. Because the money is paid directly to governments, it also can reinforce inefficiency in a state bureaucracy that is already top-heavy and politically unresponsive. Too little of the aid filters down to the masses or into the agricultural sector, where it is most desperately needed. In Tanzania, which has received the highest aid per capita of any nation, output per worker declined 50 percent and the government bureaucracy grew 200 percent during the decade of heaviest foreign assistance. At the same time, mismanagement in industry and agriculture forced more than 300 nationalized companies into bankruptcy and converted Tanzania into a net importer of food. In Bangladesh, aid funds that were allocated for cheap agricultural loans failed to increase the net pool of capital available to farmers because the farmers had to pay out in bribes to corrupt officials as much as they were receiving in credits. When there is not outright corruption, there tends to be gross mismanagement and waste.

Donor governments have not helped the situation by their policy of tying most aid to purchases of their goods. In effect, the LDCs do not get funds that they are free to spend on the cheapest or most appropriate technologies; they get credits that they can spend in only one country. The donors impose such requirements in order to stimulate exports and job growth at home, as well as to tie the recipient more fully into their own economies. In Canada, for example, more than 80 percent of the bilateral aid dispensed by the Canadian International Development Agency is tied to the purchase of Canadian goods.

In the view of its critics, foreign aid reinforces dependency and often works against the growth of indigenous capacity. An example is the U.S. Food for Peace program (PL 480), which has distributed about $1.5 billion in surplus farm products to starving Africans each year. It would seem to be an ideal form of assistance: it goes directly to the most needy; it is a grant, not an interest-

---

FIGURE 6-27

U.S. GRANTS AND LOANS, 1945–82

Middle East and South Asia $35.1 billion
   Principally to Egypt, Israel, India, Pakistan, and Turkey
   Europe $20.5 billion
   Principally to Britain, France, West Germany, and Italy
   Africa $9.0 billion
Far East $24.4 billion
   Principally to South Vietnam, South Korea, Indonesia, Philippines, Taiwan, and Japan
Latin America $10.9 billion
   Principally to Brazil
Oceana $0.9 billion
Aid not allocated by region $29.5 billion
Total U.S. economic aid $130.2 billion

bearing loan; it is economic, not military assistance; it has no strings attached. But it has led to a dependency on cheap food from abroad, pushing out local producers who might have been able to survive economically and contribute toward a self-sufficient, sustainable agriculture. In short, free or cheap U.S. grain can hurt Third World farmers by depressing the prices they get for their own crops. For aid to have any long-term impact, it must be concentrated on the development of local infrastructures and productive capacity. To paraphrase President Reagan, "Let's not give them fish, let's give them a fishing pole and teach them how to fish for themselves."

Foreign aid also can contribute to cultural imperialism and the tyranny of foreign tastes and values. Security aid comes complete with foreign technicians, advisers, and, in many cases, officer training in the donor country that is heavily larded with indoctrination. Many members of the Third World political classes, foreign educated and tending to imitate foreign models, spend a disproportionate share of their aid money on capital-intensive showpieces or, out of national pride and prestige, buy high-technology foreign goods that are not necessarily appropriate to their nations' needs. Aid funds often support national airlines, urban high-rises, and massive hydroelectric dams, instead of practical, labor-intensive, village-based projects such as sanitation, soil conservation, or reforestation. Humanitarian aid can establish a pattern of consumption that increases dependence on imports, as happened in Tanzania, where Canadian aid funds established wheat farming and a taste for factory-made white bread. Much of this aid reflects the lobbying power of export industries at home, not the expressed needs of developing nations; it serves as a foot in the door for foreign investors, advisers, advertisers, and others. Too often, foreign-aid packages are sold to the reluctant taxpaying public as a means for bolstering the home economy and stimulating investment abroad.

Aid often serves the political interests of the donor state. The United States has publicly declared that states seeking its assistance will be appraised on the basis of their willingness to support American positions in the United Nations. Not even the multilateral aid channeled through international agencies is entirely free of political constraints, since many of the agencies are controlled by their leading contributors. Both the World Bank and the IMF reflect the perceptions and priorities of the rich states, and the International Finance Corporation was expressly established to aid in the development of private enterprises with links to the advanced capitalist states. Communist aid follows a similar political trajectory; 99 percent of the Soviet and East European funds have gone to countries with centrally planned economies, mainly North Korea, Vietnam, Laos, Kampuchea, Afghanistan, Cuba, and Nicaragua. OPEC aid has gone primarily to Arab states or those with sizable Muslim populations. Britain and France have favored their former colonies. In short, the military and political objectives that dominate the foreign policy agendas of the great powers carry over into their aid giving.

It is naive to think that any government will act against its own interests in its foreign-aid policies. First World firms and governments need markets for their products and access to foreign resources, which they seek by any means that will promote their growth, profits, security, and autonomy. But these goals often conflict with Third World development. To take one example, Bangladesh is a very poor country desperately in need of development resources, but its aid from the United States has been largely guided by American security and economic interests. U.S. assistance has focused mainly on the upper 10 percent — military officers brought to the United States for training, funds for nuclear power reactors (the most capital-intensive and expensive of energy technologies), and highways serving mostly those rich enough to own a motor vehicle. The compelling need for the bottom 90 percent is agricultural goods, especially seeds and fertilizer, which have only recently received priority in U.S. funding. America did assist in developing a garment industry, but then, just when the industry was beginning to become self-supporting, the U.S. proceeded to erect trade barriers to Bangladeshi textiles. No amount of official pleading by the Bangladeshis could induce the United States to raise the textile quota even to the level of such countries as Sri Lanka, South Korea, and Taiwan. The latter apparently had greater bargaining power with Washington by virtue of their political complexion and strategic location.

The United States is not unique among rich nations in attaching careful strings to its foreign assistance and loan packages. Realists will argue that of course no state is going to give money away for nothing. But this is only another way of saying that development is not the true aim of foreign aid, or, perhaps more accurately, that rich states will support development only if it is compatible with their own power and well-being. They therefore foster capital-intensive growth, indebtedness, and economic dependency in the Third World states. International financial institutions, commercial banks, multinational firms, and parasitic political and economic elites in the LDCs all cooperate in maintaining these dependency relationships, which have proved not to be the most productive or in the best long-term interests of the poverty-stricken majorities in the Third World. In short, genuine altruism in international affairs is rare, and the Third World cannot rely on unrestricted foreign aid to meet its basic development needs.

In response, advocates of foreign aid note that it has suffered from inflated expectations. Within the realistic limits of the present system of national sovereignty, foreign aid has accomplished a great deal. Its main purpose, after all, is not to engender development single-handedly but to cement friendly relations between nation-states, to serve as a tool of diplomacy, not as a handout or an instrument of economic development. In the United States, aid is administered by the Agency for International Development (AID), a division of the Department of State, and its activities naturally reflect a long list of U.S. political and economic objectives: arms aid and defense funds to key allies; economic assistance to strategically placed states vulnerable to outside attack or subversion; promotion of private enterprise; stimulation of U.S. exports; sponsorship of development loans to friendly countries; reform programs aimed at democratization; feasibility surveys designed to stimulate new foreign investment; programs that insure U.S. companies against expropriation or political violence. Measured in these traditional foreign policy goals, aid has been very effective.

Whatever modest development that may occur in the course of protecting American economic and security interests abroad is simply icing on the cake. Aid transfers, after all, are transactions between sovereign states; if the benefits were not genuine and mutual, the recipient states could simply refuse to accept the aid. The fact that they do not is the strongest testimony to the efficacy of aid, or at least its political attractions.

Aid supporters do not deny that there are problems. An AID report issued in 1989 called for a radical reshaping of U.S. programs. Foreign aid was no longer fulfilling its original mandate of helping poor countries make the transition from dependency to self-sufficiency, the study said, but was "simply postponing the day of reckoning for governments unwilling or unable to take the politically painful steps needed for their own development." The report criticized Congress, too, for piling up a "dizzying" array of contradictory goals — more than thirty-three separate statutory objectives, from winning friends, countering the Soviet Union, and alleviating poverty to finding markets for American farm products. Clearly, foreign aid cannot do everything, and judgments about its value likely depend on which of the objectives takes priority.

Dilemmas of the Development Process

Development efforts have been seriously impeded by the lack of agreement over its goals. A peasant woman does not think in terms of industrialization, democracy, or development models, but in terms of family, land, work, bread, dignity, and perhaps a rudimentary sort of personal and cultural autonomy. The revolutionary nationalist leader thinks of development as a radical process of equitable social change and political self-determination. Technical experts and entrepreneurs define it as economic growth. The aid-giving industrial states see economic development as an antidote to revolution and a means of bringing political stability to the Third World and integrating it into the prevailing system of Western political-economic values. The meaning of development is itself politically contested.

In fact, the rich and powerful states of the North have pursued two essentially contradictory goals in the South: speeding the development process, and reducing social turmoil and political instability. They have been frustrated in reaching either goal by the immensity of the poverty and their apparent inability to make any dent in it. They have been unable to impose order on the development process or to limit the unpredictable and often destructive consequences of outside intervention. Instability still abounds because no amount of good intentions has been able to erase the centuries of exploitation or the fundamental asymmetry in power between North and South. The best-laid plans of twentieth-century development experts have not succeeded in erasing the historical fact that the first comers to development, with their new technology, were able to place the rest of the world in political and economic subjugation.

The wisdom of imitating the Western model of the early industrializers is called into question by the vastly different conditions the new nations of the Third World confront today. The early stages of European development were authoritarian, mercantilist, and often revolutionary—qualities that are decried when found today in Third World regimes; it took the rich states three hundred years to achieve democracy, free trade, stability, and economic interdependence. The European powers are dominant in arms technology, in science and its economic applications, in fertile land and an abundant resource base—all of which the majority of new states lack. Finally, the new nations are entering the international economy without the trade protection that the imperial powers gave their colonial dependencies. They have had to compete with developed economies that are well established in the world market and command skills and resources far beyond those of most Third World countries.

The degree of global inequality is apparent in the simple but overwhelming fact that the United States alone, with 6 percent of the world's population, consumes roughly 40 percent of the world's nonrenewable resources. An industrialization that is based on such an inflow of nonrenewable resources may be impossible to reproduce worldwide. In this sense, the era of development may be over, limited to that imperial epoch when the emerging political institutions of the European state system were interacting with new military, scientific, and economic technologies in a global context of abundant resources and weak states. The era of development may be only a hump on the time line of civilization during which a few societies reached a remarkable affluence through extractive technologies and colonial ties that were not sustainable over the long run and that the latecomers to development cannot utilize.

Even if the ingenuity of science should find new sources of abundance in the planetary resource base, the contemporary organization of the international economy poses immense obstacles to development in the Third World. It is an article of faith among many Americans that the free market is an arena in which all parties to a transaction stand to benefit; the market presumably harnesses greed and generates jobs and goods that "trickle down" to the lowliest. The joint benefits and the political indifference of the marketplace presumably make it possible to reconcile the economic interests of rich and poor states. All this might be true for the Third World if markets were more free, if its exports had unfettered access to world markets, and if governments everywhere did not have such a heavy stake in economic outcomes. It might also be true if the typical Third World state possessed a sizable middle class with managerial skills and a government with independent bargaining power. But the conditions of Western industrialization, which harnessed the self-interested impulses of a rising middle class to the needs of national development, cannot invariably be reproduced in the Third World today. Both colonialism and the dominating presence of foreign multinationals have stunted the growth of strong governments and native business classes. Accumulative impulses in the Third World states are concentrated not in an investment-oriented, liberally inclined, mercantile middle class, but in a conservative landowning elite or a bureaucratic (and often corrupt) middle class of military officers and politicians.

Since North and South differ in their historical experiences and their definitions of development, it is not surprising that they disagree about the virtues of integration into the international market system. The North tends to view its ties to the South as benign interdependence and an important vehicle for technology transfer and economic growth. The South views its ties to the North as chains of dependence forged by inequity and impotence. The two sides make conflicting judgments about *what* should be developed and *for whom.* A growing capacity to attract foreign capital and increase exports is a goal that international bankers and IMF planners have pressed on the Third World, but this kind of growth does not necessarily raise the real standard of living among the impoverished masses or provide agricultural resources for feeding the people. Export-oriented growth might be considered an index of progress if the export earnings were high enough to indicate an efficient specialization in the market according to the principle of comparative advantage — as may be the case for a lucky few, like South Korea, Taiwan, Hong Kong, and Singapore. But the majority of Third World states export primary products, and the terms of trade have worked consistently to their disadvantage, placing most of the disposable income in the hands of rich landowners and plantation managers while the caloric intake of their displaced laborers goes down. Even this might be justified by the logic of the market if the earnings were invested to improve the lot of the next generation, instead of being squandered on luxuries or invested outside the country. A thriving export economy and rising aggregate growth rates do not automatically mean more bread for the poor or genuine national development, but may simply indicate an increased consumption by the few who control the export trade and the many who sit at the tables of Europe enjoying their imported goods at rock-bottom prices.

Economic growth and integration into the international market may not be the best index of national development. As E. F. Schumacher has remarked, in *Small Is Beautiful: Economics As If People Mattered,* we should desire growth only of those things that are worth increasing, within an economic framework in which growth has some hope of benefiting those in greatest need. But the political leaders of poor states do not invariably aim to make their own people self-determining or free from poverty. We cannot understand the development process, and especially its failures, until we abandon the naive notion that development is the main priority of Third World elites. Their common struggle seems much more to be over who controls the existing wealth than how to create new sources of wealth. The debate over development is eclipsed by a preoccupation with hanging on to present arrangements of privilege.

For political leaders of all stripes, poverty also appears to be a lesser concern than political instability, which has made security a central policy goal of both aid givers and receivers. Among the LDCs — including those that are not surrogates in the global power struggle — a large fraction of their budgets goes into military spending, which requires expensive arms imports that bleed the nation of precious foreign exchange earnings. The development agendas of most Third World states are held hostage to their political and military insecurity, itself a product of imperialism past and present.

Rich states do not want to raise the poor ones to equal status in wealth and power. The advanced states have more interests in the Third World than simply distributing development assistance. They also sell arms, intervene militarily, seek regional allies in the global power struggle, promote multinational investments, protect their property rights and access to resources, and influence the ideological preferences and consumer tastes of Third World citizens. These practices are probably not compatible with economic development by anyone's definition. They do indicate, however, that global inequalities in wealth are matched by global inequalities in power. If development means not only technical mastery but also political control of one's own fate, then it is predictable that the dominant powers will resist a Third World nation's development, for all their professed desire to supply technology and promote self-determination.

Once we have recognized the political dimension in the development process and have acknowledged that security concerns have overshadowed economic ones, we can see that the problem is less one of a scarcity of capital than of conflicting political interests and mistaken priorities. The United Nations has estimated that roughly $250 billion would fill the shortfall in resources needed to meet the minimum basic requirements of the entire population of the globe. This is one-quarter of the $1 trillion that is spent annually on military goods. Obviously, if states could resolve their quarrels and repressive regimes of both right and left could abandon their militarism, the economic needs of the LDCs could be addressed more effectively. Relieving the problems of poverty does not call for massive technology transfers via the marketplace, spartan schemes of socialist redistribution, or any kind of sacrifice by the rich for the poor so much as it calls for an end to wasteful state spending for nonproductive military purposes. This is the most stifling kind of spending for any economy, and spending in which both superpowers, with their big defense budgets and military aid packages, are as fully implicated as the Third World states are. What is needed is to transform the present exploitative and conflictual relations into relations of justice, cooperation, or at the least coexistence. That is a mammoth task, and one that realists might say is impossible. But a refusal to address this fundamental issue condemns all development efforts to the status of mere palliatives.

Conflicts of interest and inequalities in power between North and South remain the main obstacles to Third World development. Concentration of power in the hands of a few states and the global competition for resources make it difficult for poor states to prosper economically. Alliance concerns supersede development goals, causing the superpowers to support parasitic and unproductive client regimes. Caught in this power bind, the Northern states may find that the best contribution they can make to Southern development is the potentially liberating policy of leaving the poor countries alone to work out their own fates.

DISCUSSION QUESTION (PRO AND CON)

Should the United States intervene in the domestic affairs of Third World states?

☞ **PRO**

Melvin Gurtov, a critic of American military actions in the Third World, defines intervention as "the calculated and partisan use of national power — military, economic, political — to influence the domestic politics of another state" (*The United States Against the Third World*, p. 2). By this definition, intervention is the essence of foreign policy, which can be nothing other than the concerted effort of one state to persuade other states to conform to its will and serve its interests. In such an effort, it is pointless to draw the line at another state's national borders, as if foreign policy were something separate from domestic politics. One state cannot alter another's behavior except by influencing the perceptions and judgments of its leaders, and this can happen from a distance by the most risky of means — military threats — or it can happen close up, by political-economic efforts within the state to alter the very character of the regime. The latter is in fact preferable, when it is possible, since timely influence on a country's domestic train of events can avoid costly military intervention there later on. But both tools are essential to U.S. foreign policy in the Third World in a revolutionary era, and neither should be avoided in the name of diplomatic niceties. Without the capacity to exert power on a regime, internally and externally, diplomacy is nothing but polite and irrelevant conversation.

When it comes to understanding instability in the Third World, there is still some logic to the old domino theory that one revolutionary success leads to another, whetting the appetite for more defiance or subversion. If we do not pull up undesirable governments when they first take hold, then they grow roots that make for more difficult problems later. This is what happened in Cuba and Nicaragua, where the United States took a neutral, wait-and-see attitude in the early years. The radical Marxists were able to consolidate their grip, and both the options of diplomacy and counterinsurgency were effectively foreclosed. It is also clear that the falling of the dominoes can be reversed. The momentum of democratic movements around the globe has forced rollbacks of Communism in Afghanistan, Nicaragua, Angola, Cambodia, and elsewhere. The successes of American-supported freedom fighters have made the Soviets much more cautious. They reduced their aid to Nicaragua, particularly on the military front, and were forced into an early withdrawal from Afghanistan, even though the local situation was worse than when Soviet troops entered in 1979. The lesson: with boldness, patience, and an abiding commitment to resistance, the cause of freedom can be spread around the globe. So why should we settle for containment or a tolerant attitude toward anti-American regimes?

Nowhere is it more necessary for a great power to exercise its influence than in the disorderly politics of the Third World. The fragility of new states, the incoherence of their regimes, and their vulnerability to subversion and instability — all these require a great power to act. We must maintain contact with possible opposition leaders, support friendly movements, and constrain those regimes that, in a moment of political vulnerability, would forsake their commitment to us. America must intervene in the Third World to promote the following national security goals, as outlined by former U.S. Defense Secretary Caspar Weinberger: prevent the coercion of the United States, its allies and friends; protect U.S. interests and citizens abroad; maintain access to critical resources around the globe; oppose the geographic expansion of Soviet control and military presence worldwide, particularly where such presence threatens America's geostrategic position.

The threat of outside intervention by one's adversary or the rise of an independent regime forces every great power to take an active role in the Third World, to protect its sphere of influence. A hands-off policy might be preferable at times, but the realities of global competition do not permit this luxury. (Figure 6-28 lists some of the recent Third World conflicts in which outside involvement has played a decisive role.) We need only show that we are responding to a Soviet threat, for example, to be justified in acting forcefully on behalf of our own national interests. Moreover, any restraint we display in exercising our power in the Third World is perceived as weakness. We must stand firm against radical, independent regimes in order to render the local situation more favorable to American ideology, investment, and strategic access. We must also stand firm to dispel any illusions that America suffers from a Vietnam syndrome. Foreign governments must not think that because we failed once, we can ever be bullied or bluffed into backing down again.

Why should a great power have to apologize for using force self-interestedly? No body of international law forbids it; indeed, war itself is not illegal, but is an instrument available to any party for the protection of its vital interests. As Gregory Foster has suggested, in a 1983 article entitled "On Selective Intervention," the use of military force is likely to be even more prevalent in the future than in the past. He writes:

> There is general agreement today among strategists, defense planners and futurists alike that the evolving international environment will be ever more complex and dangerous. We are already witnessing the revolutionary consequences of soaring population growths, increased urbanization and widening disparities between rich and poor nations. The harbingers point to a tightening economic interdependence, but also to an intensified competition for vital resources amid shifting alliances. In the military arena, the portents are for the modernization of armies even of otherwise backward nations, along with a proliferation of nuclear, chemical and biological weapons.

Consequently, Foster argues, "the United States needs a strategy of selective intervention — one that is designed not only to safeguard and advance U.S. interests in specific situations but also, and even more importantly, to signal the resolve that alone can deter a broader range of unwanted contingencies."

FIGURE 6-28

MAJOR THIRD WORLD CONFLICTS, 1980–86[a]

Conflict	Outside Military Involvement[b]
Middle East	
Afghanistan, civil war and Soviet occupation	USSR[c], Pakistan, USA, China, Saudi Arabia, Egypt
Iran vs Iraq	China, Syria, Israel, Libya, Saudi Arabia, Jordan, Egypt, Morocco, USSR, France
Iran internal challenges	Iraq
Lebanon civil war	Syria[c], Israel[c], PLO[c], USA[c], France[c], Italy[c], USSR
Syria vs Sunni fundamentalists	USSR, Jordan
Africa	
Western Sahara independence vs Morocco	Mauritania[c], Algeria, Libya, USA, France
Chad civil war	Libya[c], France[c], Sudan
Ethiopia vs Somalia and Ogaden secessionists	Cuba[c], USSR, USA, Italy, China, E Germany
Ethiopia vs Eritrean secessionists	Cuba[c], USSR, Iraq, Syria, Saudi Arabia, Sudan, E Germany
Ugandan civil war	Tanzania[c], Libya
Angolan civil war	S Africa[c], Cuba[c], USSR, USA, E Germany
Namibian independence war	S Africa[c], Angola
Mozambique civil war	S Africa, Cuba, USSR
Asia	
China vs Vietnam	USSR
Kampuchea, Vietnamese occupation, and civil war	China, Thailand, USSR, USA
Laos internal challenges	Vietnam[c], China, Thailand, USSR
Indonesia vs East Timor	USA
Philippine civil war	USA
Latin America	
El Salvador civil war	USA, Israel, France, Nicaragua
Guatemalan Indian suppression	USA, Israel
Nicaragua vs antigovernment rebels	USA, Honduras, Costa Rica, Cuba, USSR

[a] Includes only those conflicts causing more than 5,000 deaths between 1980 and 1985.
[b] Includes combat troops, command and logistic support, military advisers, direct military aid, and arms sales to a principal combatant exceeding 20% of combatant's total arms imports.
[c] Indicates combat troops.

Hesitation, inaction, half measures, and outright failures have marked U.S. behavior in a variety of Third World encounters: North Korea's 1968 seizure of the American spy ship *Pueblo,* the debacle in Vietnam, our refusal to respond in Angola, the abortive Desert One raid during the Iranian hostage crisis, our acquiescence in the Soviet invasion of Afghanistan, the abandonment of the *contras* in Central America. Such a record of weakness and indecision invites defiance from our clients and aggression from our adversaries. But we can reverse the risk, according to Foster, by a strategy of selective intervention that applies American power at times and places of our own choosing, thus presenting an image of overall strength where real strength exists, rather than applying power only as a last resort, and often in situations where we are relatively weak. If coercive measures are applied early and successfully, they visibly demonstrate an American resolve that enhances our prestige, deters our enemies, and lessens the likelihood that a higher level of force will have to be used in other times and places. Thus, our initial timidity in confronting General Noriega's anti-American stance in Panama eventually forced a full-scale invasion. Above all, if America is to avoid damage to its superpower reputation and its image of strength, we must be willing and able to respond decisively to hostile acts by third- and fourth-rate powers. In this we should follow the example of two of our closest allies, the British, whose defense of the Falklands restored their international stature, and the Israelis, whose consistent policy of reprisal has dramatically reduced incidents of terrorism against them.

One must avoid stigmatizing force or the exercise of power in international affairs. Instead, we should measure the worthiness of interventions by their political and economic outcomes. When an intervention leads to oppression or an unwanted occupation force, as so frequently has been the case with the Soviet Union, the intervention is naturally to be deplored. Soviet interventions yield no evidence that the promises of Communism have ever been fulfilled, even in Marxist-Leninist terms, and the prospects for reversing a revolution that devours its own children are extremely dim. On the other hand, U.S. interventions in Japan and Germany, to remake their constitutions and their domestic order, bore extremely beneficial results. The tiny island of Grenada is considerably better off politically and economically from the U.S. intervention. The thoroughgoing U.S. involvements in South Korea and Taiwan have boosted their economies and maintained political stability. The Dominican Republic is a democracy today thanks to the U.S. intervention against antidemocratic forces in 1965. The same can be said for our backing of Corazón Aquino and the withdrawal of our support from Ferdinand Marcos in the Philippines in 1986. The problem is with involvements that are half-baked or halfhearted, as in Lebanon, where America had neither the time, the troops, nor the opportunity to rebuild the country. Or in Vietnam, where political constraints permitted the war to drag on so long that public support for it finally eroded. America's resistance to the Sandinista regime in Nicaragua was hamstrung by the same kind of halfheartedness, and the vacillating opposition of Congress robbed the president of effective control over U.S. policy there.

We must face up to the facts of an integrated, international economy: that liberal free-enterprise industrial societies are trading societies that depend on a free exchange of resources. In our modern era, access to the Third World's strategic minerals and other raw materials is essential. Also, its markets are a major outlet for U.S. manufactured goods. The price of economic interdependence is the risk that we may have to intervene if a nation tries to coerce us by withholding something that is necessary to our economic survival. The United States has a national interest in policing the peace in the Middle East because that region holds two-thirds of the free world's petroleum reserves. If America is weak in responding to Soviet initiatives or anti-American activities in Central America, it will put at risk U.S. control of the Panama Canal and our maritime routes in the Caribbean. If we permit the spread of radical regimes in Africa, we risk losing control of a region that is the single most important supplier of strategic minerals, in particular South Africa, where the United States obtains sizable percentages of its chromite, industrial diamonds, manganese, vanadium, and the platinum-group metals — all vital to our high-technology military defenses and our industry. Clearly, America's global economic security is directly related to its ability to exercise military power in the Third World. For this reason, a Democratic Congress (in spite of a budget crunch) was quite willing to accede to President Reagan's request and spend $40 billion for two new aircraft carrier groups — forces designed expressly to police the waters of the Third World and keep open the sea lanes that are so vital to an international trading power.

But how do we answer the critic who says that our defense of American economic interests is constantly forcing us into alliances with right-wing dictators? Realism leaves us no other choice, for the competition in destabilized Third World regimes is usually between dictatorships of the right and of the left. With these as the stark alternatives, our choice has to be the right-wing regimes, which retain some respect for the principles of private property and free trade, although they challenge our democratic values. Left-wing dictatorships attack liberty, democracy, capitalism — all the values we hold dear — and once they are in the grip of totalitarian parties, these radical leftist regimes rarely return to the democratic fold. Critics may point to the restoration of democracy in Nicaragua, but the Chamorro regime has a tenuous grip on power that radical politics is sure to upset, either by renewed revolution or military reaction, in the same manner that the democratic regime was destabilized in Peru. Right-wing regimes are more likely to preserve some sectors of private activity (such as freedom of religion), to develop a prosperous middle class, and to evolve in a liberalizing direction. This has already happened in Germany, Japan, Spain, Portugal, and dozens of Third World states, particularly in Latin America. Even when liberalization does not occur, right-wing dictatorships tend to align with the West in defense of capitalist principles and of America's economic position globally. South Korea, Taiwan, and Brazil have achieved high rates of growth under tutelary dictators, and by their example they also offer hope that the trickle-down effect might be able to transform the conditions of the poor. By providing safe and stable investment climates that have attracted foreign resources, they have alleviated the need for a more radical, and repressive, policy of forced savings at home.

The United States must vigorously exercise its influence in the Third World by whatever means are necessary to defend against radical nationalism or the possibility of subversion. If this includes active intervention, we should not hesitate out of misguided respect for democratic values. The Third World provides an opportunity not so much to maximize American values as to minimize anti-American activities. If we want American power to be respected in the Third World, we have to look like winners, and when we exercise our military might we have to be sure we are winners. To that end, we must use our power to ensure that ruling classes remain sympathetic and durable, or we must intervene decisively to install regimes that we can count on as friends and allies.

☞ CON

U.S. interventionism represents the self-righteous intolerance of a country that does not understand much about the societies it is trying to alter. Americans have a tendency to impose their model on the rest of the world, assuming, with the false optimism of technocrats, that a developed society can be engineered overnight out of interchangeable parts stamped "Made in America." We have repeatedly viewed civil turmoil in the Third World as Communist aggression and have leaped in with arms, aid, and sometimes troops. Instead of a rational policy based on calculations of whether force can bring a timely and satisfactory result — and sometimes it can — we have rashly waded into the swamp of Vietnam and the morass of Central America on the strength of the threat alone. Communism may indeed pose a threat and provide a clear justification for American action, but that does not ensure that an intervention will be successful. A sound foreign policy must still make the cost-benefit calculations and consider the possible negative consequences of any intervention scenario. The latter includes the recognition that a direct foreign presence often inflames nationalist sympathies and that large-scale military conflict tends to compound the disorganization of a revolutionary society in transition.

U.S. policy has been slow to recognize the differences between Communism in Europe, which was Soviet dominated, antidemocratic, and retrograde, and Communism in the Third World, which has frequently been a progressive nationalist force with strong popular support. Communist regimes have been among the few to adopt some measure of economic democracy — the only kind of democracy most poor, illiterate countries can afford in their early stages of development. In the Third World, to cite Bernard Kiernan's *The United States, Communism, and the Emergent World,* "Communism is a process of nation-building, of political centralization, of state-building, of economic growth, of social organization, of intellectual awakening, which parallels, in a speeded up version, the modernization of the West" (p. 18). It is a product of exposure to Western ideas under the difficult constraints of colonialism and dependency, not a symptom of the ultimate historical triumph of either the Soviet Union or Marxist-Leninist ideas. We have carried a conspiratorial image of a monolithic Communism that fits the Stalinism of the 1930s better than it does conditions in the Third World today, where socialist ideas display immense diversity and an outright opposition to any Marxist orthodoxy dictated by Moscow.

We should abandon the notion that nationalist leaders who have adopted radical ideas are morally depraved, "evil," or dupes of the Soviets. They are hardheaded political leaders seeking practical solutions to human problems. Socialism is attractive to them because it explains something about the imperialist experience and because conditions in their societies do not permit the free play of the capitalist marketplace. We cannot change these conditions with a contingent of Marines, a surgical coup, surreptitious support for one party, a generous supply of bribes and arms, or any amount of propaganda. The Soviets can't either. We can reduce the appeal of Communism only by altering the realities of backward societies and giving them tangible development assistance.

Radical nationalism in the Third World is a natural stage in the decolonization process. Revolutionary policies are a necessary instrument of rapid social change in societies controlled by traditional elites that will not relinquish power peacefully. The fundamental changes of modernization cannot come without significant political and social upheaval. This was true of the development process in Europe, Russia, and America, and it is equally true in the Third World today. To fight against progressive social change because we think it anti-American or marked by "adolescent" excesses, is to condemn backward societies to the continuing oppressive grip of tradition. Far better that we should learn to be more tolerant of the growing pains of new states, which are just as eager to be independent of the Soviet Union as of the United States.

Most Third World revolutions are nationalist, not basically socialist or Communist. If Marxist-inspired leaders turn to the Soviet Union, it is not because they are taking orders from Moscow or particularly admire the principles of state socialism. Soviet support often is a lesser-of-two-evils policy for a weak state locked in the middle of a superpower competition. When we act aggressively toward radical nationalist regimes, we only push them all the more firmly into an anti-American posture. If we can defuse the superpower rivalry and show our willingness to coexist peacefully with neutral regimes (though they may be guided domestically by principles quite different from our own), then nationalist regimes will be much less likely to need or want Soviet support.

The U.S. interventions in Grenada and the Dominican Republic were successful because those countries were in our hemisphere and clearly within the American sphere of influence. The nations were small and incapable of resisting overwhelming force, and military measures were followed by political and economic support. We were able to reshape the leaderships and improve the standard of living of the masses. The regimes we opposed there had no guerrilla supporters or grass-roots revolutionary parties, nor any sanctuaries into which the defeated radicals could retreat. None of these conditions were true of Vietnam, Cuba, Angola, Lebanon, or Nicaragua, in all of which the United States was supporting reactionary minorities or so-called democratic leaders with no widespread bases of support. In the case of Amin Gemayel in Lebanon, factions were so polarized that he was regarded with suspicion by all but his own Christian Phalangist party. In the cases of Ngo Dinh Diem, General Nguyen Cao Ky, and General Nguyen Van Thieu in Vietnam, their defense of democracy was purely fictitious, and our choice was in fact between a right-wing and a left-wing dictatorship — with the Communists, under Ho Chi Minh, having the most authentic nationalist credentials and a more genuine concern for the fate of the poor majority. Elsewhere, when factions with democratic potential did exist, American arms aid tended to polarize and militarize the situation, and prospects for democracy quickly vanished.

The U.S. government has supported many status quo regimes more committed to protecting their acquired wealth than to encouraging national development. We have supported elitist dictatorships because they were reliable allies in our anti-Communist containment policy, although indifferent to development. This is the reason American aid has been mainly in the form of arms, not food, technology, or development expertise. And the poor bear the costs of such arms imports, in the sacrifice of their economic needs to pay for foreign military goods. America has launched a kind of state-directed economic warfare against much of the Third World. Security concerns have caused the U.S. government to intervene, officially or semiofficially, to prevent Western firms, banks, and even multilateral development agencies from having to deal with such politically unacceptable governments as Castro's Cuba, Allende's Chile, and the Sandinistas' Nicaragua. In all three of these cases, frustrated development and economic hardships caused the regimes to shift further left and become still more dependent on Soviet assistance.

American military might has often been used to protect American multinationals, positions of monopoly, and privileged access, not free markets. Third World businessmen, confronted with official government interference in the free market and in their political affairs, will naturally become economic nationalists. They turn to their own governments for help, using political leverage and patriotic appeals to bolster their positions vis-à-vis the unfair foreign competition. Although condemned as socialist, such policies closely resemble the quasimercantilist strategies of the rich states. Ironically, American multinationals, and foreign capital in general, have little difficulty in dealing with Third World states organized around a great variety of political-economic principles. The U.S. government might do better to adopt the same evenhandedness.

As Richard Feinberg has pointed out, in *The Intemperate Zone,* the United States' ability to dictate winners and losers in the internal power struggles of the Third World is declining. The Third World is less controllable today, and America's influence has suffered—but, to a still greater extent, so has the USSR's. The Soviet Union, more constrained in the aid it can give, is no longer viewed by the Third World as a promising developmental model.

The United States is not — or at least it should not be — an imperial policeman. Every crisis does not call for American action or suspicions of Soviet skulduggery. The vast majority of the Third World's problems are due to the instability of local elites, intraregional rivalries, indigenous revolutionary nationalism, and the play of international economic forces. Efforts to solve these problems by direct or covert intervention or by sending more arms only serve to perpetuate internal instability, the nonproductive diversion of resources, and repressive attempts to preserve social inequality and antimodernizing power arrangements. The intensity of nationalist feelings makes active American support the kiss of death for any would-be reformer who might otherwise be able to claim legitimate popular support. Our analysis points toward the importance of acts of political restraint, of what we must *stop* rather than start doing. If we can refrain from those acts of manipulation or intervention that promote militarization and political decay, the LDCs are likely to have an easier time of putting their own economic houses in order. A hands-off policy would also give the Soviets time to make their own mistakes in a Third World environment that has proved hostile to control by any outside power.

The potential economic costs of the (unlikely) proliferation of radical regimes will not be heavy. The Third World share of our investment and trade has been decreasing, while socialist regimes have shown no reluctance whatever to continue trading with the West (witness the growing role of foreign capital in Angola, China, Yugoslavia, Hungary, Poland, and the Soviet Union itself). Radical nationalist states like Iraq, Algeria, Ethiopia, Iran, Syria, Jamaica (under Manley), Libya, Mozambique, South Yemen, and Nicaragua have all had strong anti-imperialist foreign policies; yet they have maintained intimate economic relations with the advanced capitalist states, trading at ratios of 50 to 90 percent with the industrial West, while their trade with the Soviet Union languishes at around 2 percent. Socialist states have scrupulously honored their debts to Western banks — even revolutionary Nicaragua, which, despite the U.S. economic boycott, has faithfully made payments on the $1.6 billion in debts inherited from Somoza. With respect to oil, the United States should strive for energy self-sufficiency as a policy that is more secure, cheap, and just — and likely more successful — than the maintenance of an expensive Rapid Deployment Force or a permanent naval presence in the Persian Gulf.

The high cost of U.S. constabulary forces (one-half to three-quarters of our $300 billion defense budget) indicates the logical flaw in an interventionist policy that resists the revolutionary social forces of the twentieth century at the price of a reduction in America's own standard of living. When a society with high economic throughput must employ repressive means to survive, its costs for access to resources will escalate continuously. Why not get off the treadmill, cut military costs, and abandon the dubious policy of trying to control resources by coercion? Only a policy of coexistence and strict respect for self-determination will win us friends in the Third World and permit us to maintain economic relations at an acceptable cost. Only effective programs of development (in which socialism may initially play a constructive role) can bring the Third World to an economic condition that makes global interdependence and free international markets a reality. If Third World governments are to become authentic democracies, they must change from within, and if this means they must undergo a revolutionary transformation in their archaic or exploitative social systems, we should leave well enough alone.

SOURCES AND SUGGESTED READINGS

On Development and Underdevelopment

American Academy of Arts and Sciences. "A World to Make: Development in Perspective." *Daedalus.* vol. 118, no. 1 (Winter 1989).

Andrain, Charles F. *Political Change in the Third World.* Boston: Allen & Unwin, 1988.

Apter, David E. *The Politics of Modernization.* Chicago: University of Chicago Press, 1965.
——— *Rethinking Development: Modernization, Dependency, and Postmodern Politics.* Newbury Park, Cal.: Sage, 1987.

Balassa, Bela. "Development Strategies and Economic Performance: A Comparative Analysis of Eleven Semi-Industrial Economies" in B. Balassa, ed. *Development Strategies in Semi-Industrial Economies.* Washington, D.C.: Johns Hopkins University Press, for the IBRD, 1982, pp. 38–62.

Baran Paul.. *The Political Economy of Growth.* New York: Monthly Review Press, 1957.

Becker, David, et al. *Postimperialism: International Capitalism and Development in the Late Twentieth Century.* Boulder, Colo.: Lynne Rienner, 1987.

Berger, Peter. *Pyramids of Sacrifice: Political Ethics and Social Change.* New York: Basic Books, 1975.

Black, C. E. *The Dynamics of Modernization: A Study in Comparative History.* New York: Harper & Row, 1966.

Blomstrom, Magnus, and Bjorn Hettne. *Development Theory in Transition — The Dependency Debate and Beyond: Third World Responses.* London: Zed, 1984.

Boserup, Ester. *Women's Role In Economic Development.* New York: St. Martin's, 1970.

Cammarck, Paul, David Pool, and William Tardoff. *Third World Politics: A Comparative Introduction.* Baltimore: Johns Hopkins University Press, 1988.

Caporaso, James A. "Dependency Theory: Continuities and Discontinuities in Development Studies." *International Organization,* vol. 34, no. 4 (Autumn 1980), pp. 605–28.

Cardoso, Fernando H., and Enzo Faletto. *Dependency and Development in Latin America.* Berkeley, Cal.: University of California Press, 1979.

Chaliand, Gerard. *Revolution in the Third World,* rev. ed. New York: Penguin, 1989.

Charlton, Susan. *Women in Third World Development.* Boulder, Colo.: Westview, 1984.

Chilcote, Ronald. *Theories of Development and Underdevelopment.* Boulder, Colo.: Westview, 1983.

Chilcote, Ronald H., and Joel Edelstein. *Latin America: Capitalist and Socialist Perspectives of Development and Underdevelopment.* Boulder, Colo.: Westview Press, 1986.

Clapham, Christopher. *Third World Politics: An Introduction.* Madison: University of Wisconsin Press, 1985.

Critchfield, Richard. "Realities Counter Dire Vision of Third World Disaster." *The Oregonian.* (Nov. 30, 1980), p. D1.

Crow, Ben, and Mary Thorpe. *Survival and Change in the Third World.* New York: Oxford University Press, 1988.

Davidson, Basil. *Can Africa Survive? Arguments Against Growth Without Development.* Boston: Atlantic/Little, Brown, 1974.

De Soto, Hernando. *The Other Path: The Invisible Revolution in the Third World.* New York: Harper & Row, 1989.

Degregori, Thomas R., and Oriol Pi-Sunyer. *Economic Development: The Cultural Context.* New York: Wiley, 1969.

Deyo, Frederic C., ed. *The Political Economy of the New Asian Industrialism.* Ithaca, N.Y.: Cornell University Press, 1987.

Erb, Guy F., and Valeriana Kallab, eds. *Beyond Dependency: The Developing World Speaks Out.* Washington, D.C.: Overseas Development Council, 1975.

Escobar, Arturo. "Discourse and Power in Development: Michel Foucault and the Relevance of His Work to the Third World." *Alternatives,* vol. 10 (Winter 1984–85), pp. 377–400.

Evans, Peter. "After Dependency." *Latin American Research Review,* vol. 20, no. 2 (1985), pp. 149–59.

Finkle, Jason L., and Richard W. Gable, eds. *Political Development and Social Change,* 2nd ed. New York: John Wiley, 1971.

Gamer, Robert. *The Developing Nations: A Comparative Perspective,* 2nd ed. Boston: Allyn & Bacon, 1982.

George, Vic. *Wealth, Poverty, and Starvation.* New York: St. Martin's, 1988.

Goulet, Denis. *The Cruel Choice.* New York: Atheneum, 1978.

——— *Incentives, the Key to Equitable Development.* New York: New Horizons Press, 1988.

Griffin, Keith. *Alternative Strategies for Economic Development.* New York: St. Martin's, 1988.

——— *The Political Economy of Agrarian Change.* Cambridge: Harvard University Press, 1974.

Gurr, Theodore. *Why Men Rebel.* Princeton, N.J.: Princeton University Press, 1970.

Hamalian, Leo, and Frederick Karl, eds. *The Fourth World.* New York: Dell, 1976.

Harris, Nigel. *The End of the Third World: Newly Industrializing Countries and the End of Ideology.* New York: Penguin, 1987.

Harrison, Lawrence. *Underdevelopment Is a State of Mind: The Latin American Case.* Lanham, Md.: Madison Books for the Center for International Affairs, Harvard University, 1985.

Harrison, Paul. *Inside the Third World: The Anatomy of Poverty,* 2nd ed. New York: Penguin, 1985.

Heeger, Gerald A. *The Politics of Underdevelopment.* New York: St. Martin's, 1974.

Hicks, Norman. "Growth vs. Basic Needs: Is There a Trade-Off?" *World Development,* vol. 7, no. 11 (1979), pp. 985–94.

Higgott, Richard. *Political Development Theory*. New York: St. Martin's, 1983.

Hoogvelt, Ankie. *The Sociology of Developing Societies*, 2nd ed. New York: Macmillan, 1978.

Hunter, Guy. *Modernizing Peasant Societies*. New York: Oxford University Press, 1969.

Huntington, Samuel P. *Political Order in Changing Societies*. New Haven, Conn.: Yale University Press, 1968.

Huston, Perdita. *Third World Women Speak Out: Interviews in Six Countries on Change, Development, and Basic Needs*. New York: Praeger, 1979.

Illich, Ivan. "Outwitting the 'Developed' Countries." *New York Review of Books* (November 6, 1969).

Janowitz, Morris. *The Military in the Political Development of New Nations*. Chicago: University of Chicago Press, 1964.

Kautsky, John H. *Communism and the Politics of Development*. New York: John Wiley, 1968.

———— *The Political Consequences of Modernization*. New York: John Wiley, 1972.

Klarén, Peter, and Thomas Bossert, eds. *Promise of Development: Theories of Change in Latin America*. Boulder, Colo.: Westview, 1986.

Kling, Merle. "Toward a Theory of Power and Political Instability in Latin America." *Western Political Quarterly*. vol. 9, no. 7 (Mar. 1956), pp. 21–35.

Kurian, George. *Encyclopedia of the Third World* (3 vols.). New York: Facts on File, 1982.

Leiden, Carl, and Karl Schmitt. *The Politics of Violence: Revolution in the Modern World*. Englewood Cliffs, N.J.: Prentice-Hall, 1968.

Levy, Marion J., Jr. *Modernization: Latecomers and Survivors*. New York: Basic Books, 1972.

Leys, Colin, ed. *Politics and Change in Developing Countries*. New York: Cambridge University Press, 1969.

Loup, Jacques. *Can the Third World Survive?* Baltimore, Md.: Johns Hopkins University Press, 1983.

Martin, Michael T., and Terry Kandal, eds. *Studies of Development and Change in the Modern World*. New York: Oxford University Press, 1989.

Midgal, Joel. *Peasants, Politics, and Revolution*. Princeton, N.J.: Princeton University Press, 1978.

Mittelman, James H. *Out from Underdevelopment: Prospects for the Third World*. New York: St. Martin's, 1988.

Moore, Barrington, Jr. *The Social Origins of Democracy and Dictatorship: Lord and Peasant in the Making of the Modern World*. Boston: Beacon Press, 1966.

Myrdal, Gunnar. *Asian Drama: An Inquiry into the Poverty of Nations* (3 vols.). New York: Pantheon, 1968.

Nordlinger, Eric. *Soldiers in Politics: Military Coups and Governments*. Englewood Cliffs, N.J.: Prentice-Hall, 1977

Novak, Michael. "Why Latin America Is Poor." *The Atlantic Monthly*. (Mar. 1982), pp. 66–75.

O'Donnell, Guillermo. *Modernization and Bureaucratic-Authoritarianism: Studies in South American Politics*. Berkeley, Cal.: Institute of International Studies, University of California, 1973.

Paige, Jeffrey. *Agrarian Revolution: Social Movements and Export Agriculture in the Underdeveloped World*. New York: Free Press, 1975.

Palmer, Monte. *Dilemmas of Political Development*, 3rd. ed. Itasca, Ill.: Peacock, 1985.

Perlmutter, Amos. *The Military and Politics in Modern Times: On Professionals, Praetorians, and Revolutionary Soldiers*. New Haven, Conn.: Yale University Press, 1977.

Powelson, John P., and Richard Stock. *The Peasant Betrayed: Agriculture and Land Reform in the Third World*. Boston, Mass.: Oelgeschlager, Gunn & Hain, 1988.

Prosterman, Roy, and Jeffrey Riedinger. *Land Reform and Democratic Development*. Baltimore: Johns Hopkins University Press, 1987.

Randall, Vicky, and Robin Theobald. *Political Change and Underdevelopment*. Durham, N.C.: Duke University Press, 1985.

Rostow, W. W. *The Stages of Economic Growth: A Non-Communist Manifesto*. New York: Cambridge University Press, 1960.

Roxborough, Ian. *Theories of Underdevelopment*. New York: Macmillan, 1979.

Rustow, Dankwart A. *A World of Nations: Problems of Political Modernization*. Washington, D.C.: The Brookings Institution, 1967.

Schumacher, E. F. *Small Is Beautiful: Economics as If People Mattered*. New York: Harper & Row, 1973.

Schwartz, Benjamin. "Modernization and the Maoist Vision." *China Quarterly*, vol. 21 (1965).

Scott, James C. *Comparative Political Corruption*. Englewood Cliffs, N.J.: Prentice-Hall, 1972.

———— *The Moral Economy of the Peasant: Rebellion and Subsistence in Southeast Asia*. New Haven, Conn.: Yale University Press, 1976.

————— *Weapons of the Weak: Everyday Forms of Peasant Resistance*. New Haven, Conn.: Yale University Press, 1985.

Seligson, Mitchell, ed. *The Gap Between Rich and Poor*. Boulder, Colo.: Westview, 1984.

Sen, Gita, and Karen Grown. *Development: Crises & Alternative Visions*. New York: Monthly Review Press, 1987.

Sigmund, Paul E., ed. *The Ideologies of the Developing Nations*, 2nd. rev. ed. New York: Praeger, 1972.

Smith, Tony. "Requiem or New Agenda for Third World Studies?" *World Politics*. (July 1985), pp. 532–61.

————— "The Underdevelopment of Development Literature: The Case of Dependency Theory." *World Politics*, vol. 31 (Jan. 1979), pp. 247–88.

Sowell, Thomas. "Second Thoughts about the Third World." *Harper's* (Nov. 1983), pp. 34–42.

Staudt, Kathleen, and Jane Jaquette. *Women in Developing Countries: A Policy Focus*. Binghamton, N.Y.: Haworth Press, 1983.

Stepan, Alfred. *The State and Society: Peru in Comparative Perspective*. Princeton, N.J.: Princeton University Press, 1978.

Tetreault, Mary Ann and Charles F. Abel, eds. *Dependency Theory and the Return of High Politics*. Westport, Conn.: Greenwood Press, 1986.

Thompson, Mary Anderberg, and Joan Antell. *The Current History Encyclopedia of Developing Nations*. New York: McGraw Hill, 1982.

Todaro, Michael P. *Economic Development in the Third World*. New York: Longman, 1985.

Toynbee, Arnold. *Civilization on Trial* and *The World and the West*. New York: Meridian, 1958.

Uri, Pierre. *Development Without Dependence*. New York: Praeger, 1976.

Valenzuela, Samuel and Arturo. "Modernization and Dependency: Alternative Perspectives in the Study of Latin American Underdevelopment." *Comparative Politics*, vol. 10, no. 4 (July 1978), pp. 535–57.

Weiner, Myron, and Samuel Huntington, eds. *Understanding Political Development*. Boston: Little, Brown, 1987.

Weisband, Edward, ed. *Poverty Amidst Plenty: World Political Economy and Distributive Justice*. Boulder, Colo.: Westview, 1989.

Welch, Claude E., Jr., and Arthur K. Smith. *Military Role and Rule: Perspectives on Civil-Military Relations*. North Scituate, Mass.: Duxbury Press, 1974.

Welch, Claude E., Jr., ed. *Political Modernization*, 2nd ed. Belmont, Cal.: Wadsworth, 1971.

Wilber, Charles K., ed. *The Political Economy of Development and Underdevelopment*, (2nd, 3rd, and 4th eds.). New York: Random House, 1979, 1984, 1988.

Wilkinson, Richard G. *Poverty and Progress: An Ecological Perspective on Economic Development*. New York: Praeger, 1973.

Wolf, Eric. *Peasant Wars of the Twentieth Century*. New York: Harper & Row, 1969.

Wolf-Phillips, Leslie. "Why 'Third World'? Origin, Definitions and Usage." *Third World Quarterly*, vol. 9 (Oct. 1987), pp. 1311–27.

World Bank. *World Development Report*. New York: Oxford University Press, published annually.

Worsley, Peter. *The Three Worlds: Culture and World Development*. Chicago: University of Chicago Press, 1984.

Wriggins, W. Howard. *The Ruler's Imperative: Strategies for Political Survival in Asia and Africa*. New York: Columbia University Press, 1969.

On Colonialism and Anti-Colonialism

Bergesen, Albert, and Ronald Schoenberg. "Long Waves of Colonial Expansion and Contraction, 1415–1969." In Albert Bergesen, ed. *Studies of the Modern World-System*. New York: Academic Press, 1980.

Chase-Dunn, Christopher. "Interstate System and Capitalist World-Economy: One Logic or Two?" *International Studies Quarterly*, vol. 25 (Mar. 1981), pp. 19–42.

Clark, Robert. *Power and Policy in the Third World*, 3rd ed. New York: John Wiley, 1988.

Clough, Shepard. *European Economic History: The Economic Development of Western Civilization*, 2nd ed. New York: McGraw-Hill, 1968.

Cohen, Benjamin J. *The Question of Imperialism*. New York: Basic Books, 1973.

Doyle, Michael. *Empires*. Ithaca, N.Y.: Cornell University Press, 1986.

Dunn, John. *Modern Revolutions*. New York: Cambridge University Press, 1972.

Emerson, Rupert. *From Empire to Nation: The Rise to Self-Assertion of Asian and African Peoples*. Boston: Beacon Press, 1960.

Emerson, Rupert, and Martin Kilson, eds. *The Political Awakening of Africa.* Englewood Cliffs, N.J.: Prentice-Hall, 1965.

Fanon, Frantz. *The Wretched of the Earth.* New York: Grove Press, 1968.

Fieldhouse, D. K. *Economics and Empire, 1830–1914.* Ithaca, N.Y.: Cornell University Press, 1973.

Guha, Ranajit, and Gayatri Chakravorty Spivak, eds. *Selected Subaltern Studies.* New York: Oxford University Press, 1988.

Kilson, Martin. *Political Change in a West African State: A Study of the Modernization Process in Sierra Leone.* New York: Atheneum, 1969.

Langer, W. L. *The Diplomacy of Imperialism.* New York: Knopf, 1950.

McGowan, Patrick J., and Bohdan Kordan. "Imperialism in World-System Perspective." *International Studies Quarterly,* vol. 25 (Mar. 1981), pp. 43–68.

Nehru, Jawaharlal. *The Discovery of India.* Garden City, N.Y.: Anchor/Doubleday, 1960.

Rhodes, Robert I., ed. *Imperialism and Underdevelopment.* New York: Monthly Review Press, 1970.

Rosecrance, Richard. *The Rise of the Trading State: Commerce and Conquest in the Modern World.* New York: Basic Books, 1986.

Smith, Tony. *The Pattern of Imperialism: The United States, Great Britain, and the Late-Industrializing World Since 1815.* New York: Cambridge University Press, 1981.

Stein, Stanley and Barbara. *The Colonial Heritage of Latin America.* New York: Oxford University Press, 1970.

Von der Mehden, Fred R. *Politics of the Developing Nations,* 2nd ed. Englewood Cliffs, N.J.: Prentice-Hall, 1969.

Wallerstein, Immanuel, ed. *Social Change: The Colonial Situation.* New York: John Wiley, 1966.

Weatherby, Jr., Joseph, et al. *The Other World: Issues and Politics in the Third World.* New York: Macmillan, 1987.

Wolf, Eric R. *Europe and the People Without History.* Berkeley: University of California Press, 1982.

On North-South Relations and the Third World in International Politics

Brandt, Willy. *Common Crisis North-South: Cooperation for World Recovery.* Cambridge, Mass.: MIT Press, 1983.

Calvert, Peter. *The Foreign Policy of New States: International Conflict and Superpower Politics.* New York: St. Martin's, 1986.

Calvocoressi, Peter. *World Politics Since 1945,* 4th ed. New York: Longman, 1982.

Cassen, Robert, et al., eds. *Rich Country Interests and Third World Development.* London: Overseas Development Council, 1982.

Crabb, Cecil V., Jr. *The Elephants and the Grass: A Study of Nonalignment.* New York: Praeger, 1965.

Cripps, Edward J. "A New World Order?" *America.* (Oct. 11, 1975), pp. 200–04.

Crowder, Michael. "Whose Dream Was It Anyway?: Twenty-Five Years of African Independence." *African Affairs* (Oxford), vol. 86 (Jan. 1987), pp. 7–24.

Deger, Saadet, and Ron Smith. "Military Expansion and Growth in Less Developed Countries." *Journal of Conflict Resolution,* vol. 27 (June 1983), pp. 335–53.

Doran, Charles F., et al, eds. *North-South Relations: Studies of Dependency Reversal.* New York: Praeger, 1983.

Gasiorowski, Mark J. "The Structure of Third World Economic Interdependence." *International Organization,* vol. 39 (Spring 1985), pp. 331–42.

Handel, Michael. *Weak States in the International System.* London: Frank Cass, 1981.

Hanson, Roger D. *Beyond the North-South Stalemate.* New York: McGraw Hill, 1979.

——— "North-South Policy—What Is the Problem?" *Foreign Affairs,* vol. 58 (Summer 1980), pp. 1104–28.

Haq, Mahbub Ul. *The Poverty Curtain: Choices for the Third World.* New York: Columbia University Press, 1976.

——— *The Third World and the International Economic Order* (Development Paper no. 22). Washington, D.C.: Overseas Development Council, 1976.

Hart, Jeffrey A. *The New International Economic Order: Conflict and Cooperation in North-South Economic Relations, 1974–1977.* New York: St. Martin's Press, 1983.

Jacobsen, Harold K., et al. "Revolutionaries or Bargainers? Negotiations for NIEO." *World Politics,* vol. 35 (April 1983).

Jalee, Pierre. *The Pillage of the Third World*. New York: Monthly Review Press, 1968.

Keohane, Robert O. "Lilliputian Dilemmas: Small States in International Politics." *International Organization*, vol. 23 (Spring 1969).

Korany, Bahgat. *How Foreign Policy Decisions Are Made in the Third World*. Boulder, Colo.: Westview, 1986.

Krasner, Stephen D. *Structural Conflict: The Third World Against Global Liberalism*. Berkeley, Cal.: University of California Press, 1985.

Luckham, Robin. "Militarisation and the New International Anarchy." *Third World Quarterly*, vol. 6 (Apr. 1984), pp. 351–73.

Malhotra, Inder. "Non-Aligned Movement: Case for the Defence." *Far Eastern Economic Review* (Hong Kong), vol. 133 (Aug. 21, 1986), pp. 28–29.

Martin, Laurence W., ed. *Neutralism and Nonalignment: The New States in World Affairs*. New York: Praeger, 1962.

Matthews, Allan F. "World North-South Issues at the Cancun Conference." *Developing Country Courier* (Nov. 1981).

Mullins, A. F., Jr. *Born Arming: Development and Military Power in New States*. Stanford, Cal.: Stanford University Press, 1987.

Murphy, Craig N. "What the Third World Wants: An Interpretation of the Development and Meaning of the New International Economic Order Ideology." *International Studies Quarterly*, vol. 27 (Mar. 1983), pp. 55–76.

Rangel, Carlos. *Third World Ideology and Western Reality: Manufacturing Political Myth*. New Brunswick, N.J.: Transaction Books, 1986.

Rothstein, Robert L. "Epitaph for a Monument to a Failed Protest? A North–South Retrospective." *International Organization*, vol. 42, no. 4 (Autumn 1988), pp. 725–48.

———— *Global Bargaining: UNCTAD and the Quest for a New International Economic Order*. Princeton, N.J.: Princeton University Press, 1979.

———— *The Weak in the World of the Strong: The Developing Countries in the International System*. New York: Columbia University Press, 1977.

Singer, Hans W., and Javed A. Ansari. *Rich and Poor Countries*, 4th ed. London: Unwin Hyman, 1988.

Singer, Marshall R. *Weak States in a World of Powers: The Dynamics of International Relationships*. New York: Free Press, 1972.

Stavrianos, L. S. *Global Rift: The Third World Comes of Age*. New York: Morrow, 1981.

Thomas, Caroline. *In Search of Security: The Third World in International Relations*. Boulder, Colo.: Rienner, 1987.

Tucker, Robert W. *The Inequality of Nations*. New York: Basic Books, 1977.

Wiarda, Howard. *Ethnocentrism in Foreign Policy: Can We Understand the Third World?*. Washington, D.C.: American Enterprise Institute, 1985.

Willetts, Peter. *The Non-Aligned Movement: The Origins of a Third World Alliance*. London: Frances Pinter, 1978.

On Trade

Biersteker, Thomas. "Self-Reliance in Theory and Practice in Tanzanian Trade Relations." *International Organization*, vol. 34, no. 2 (Spring 1980), pp. 229–64.

Boulding, Kenneth, and Tapan Mukerjee, eds. *Economic Imperialism*. Ann Arbor: University of Michigan Press, 1972.

Brock, William E. "Trade and Debt: The Vital Linkage." *Foreign Affairs*, vol. 62 (Summer 1984), pp. 1037–57.

Cline, William R. *"Reciprocity": A New Approach to World Trade Policy?* (Policy Analyses in International Economics, no. 2). Washington, D.C.: Institute for International Economics, 1982.

———— ed. *Trade Policy in the 1980s*. Washington, D.C.: Institute for International Economics, 1983.

Coppock, Joseph D. *International Trade Instability*. Westmead, Eng.: Saxonhouse, 1977.

Emmanuel, Arghiri. *Unequal Exchange: A Study of the Imperialism of Trade*. New York: Monthly Review Press, 1972.

Gray, Peter H. *Free Trade or Protection? A Pragmatic Analysis*. New York: St. Martin's, 1985.

Higgins, Benjamin, and Jean Downing Higgins. *Economic Development of a Small Planet*. New York: Norton, 1979.

Krueger, Anne O. *Foreign Trade Regimes and Economic Development: Liberalization Attempts and Consequences.* Cambridge: Ballinger, 1978.

Krugman, Paul R. "Trade, Accumulation, and Uneven Development." *Journal of Development Economics,* vol. 8, pp. 149–61.

Moran, Theodore. "New Deal or Raw Deal in Raw Materials." *Foreign Policy,* vol. 5 (Winter 1971–72), pp. 119–36.

Mytelka, Lynn. *Regional Development in a Global Economy.* New Haven, Conn.: Yale University Press, 1979.

Pease, Don J., and J. William Goold. "The New GSP: Fair Trade with the Third World." *World Policy Journal,* vol. 2 (Spring 1985), pp. 351–66.

Prebisch, Raul. *Towards a New Trade Policy for Development.* New York: United Nations, 1964.

Raffer, Kunibert. *Unequal Exchange and the Evolution of the World System: Reconsidering the Impact of Trade on North-South Relations.* New York: St. Martin's, 1987.

Sanderson, Steven E., ed. *The Americas in the New International Division of Labor.* New York: Homes & Meier, 1984.

Sewell, John W., and Stuart K. Tucker. *Growth, Jobs, and Exports in a Changing World Economy.* New Brunswick, N.J.: Transaction Books, 1988.

Streeten, Paul. "World Trade in Agricultural Commodities and the Terms of Trade with Industrial Goods." In Nurul Islam, ed. *Agricultural Policy in Developing Countries,* pp. 207–23. London: Macmillan, 1974.

Vernon, Raymond. "International Trade Policy in the 1980s: Prospects and Problems." *International Studies Quarterly,* vol. 26 (Dec. 1982), pp. 483–510.

Winham, Gilbert R. *International Trade and the Toyko Round Negotiations.* Princeton, N.J.: Princeton University Press, 1986.

Yoffie, David B. *Power and Protectionism: Strategies of the Newly Industrializing Countries.* New York: Columbia University Press, 1983.

On Food & Population

Bauer, Peter T. "Population Scares." *Commentary,* vol. 84 (Nov. 1987), pp. 39–42.

Benería, Lourdes, and Gita Sen. "Accumulation, Reproduction, and Women's Role in Economic Development: Boserup Revisited." *Signs: Journal of Women in Culture and Society,* vol. 7, no. 2 (1981).

Faaland, Just, ed. *Population and the World Economy in the 21st Century.* New York: St. Martin's, 1982.

Glaeser, Bernhard, ed. *The Green Revolution Revisited: Critique and Alternatives.* New York: Allen & Unwin, 1987.

Gupte, Pranay. *The Crowded Earth: People and Politics of Population.* New York: Norton, 1984.

Harrison, Paul. *The Greening of Africa: Breaking Through in the Battle for Land and Food.* New York: Penguin, 1987.

Hollist, W. Ladd, and F. Lamond Tullis, eds. *Pursuing Food Security: Strategies and Obstacles in Africa, Asia, Latin America, and the Middle East.* Boulder, Colo.: Lynne Rienner, 1987.

Hopkins, Raymond F., et al. *Food in the Global Arena.* New York: Holt, Rinehart & Winston, 1982.

Kent, George. *The Political Economy of Hunger.* New York: Praeger, 1984.

Lappé, Frances Moore, and Joseph Collins. *World Hunger: Twelve Myths,* rev. ed. New York: Grove Press, 1988.

Lappé, Frances Moore, Rachel Schurman, and Kevin Danaher. *Betraying the National Interest.* New York: Grove Press, 1988.

Linowitz, Sol M. *World Hunger: A Challenge to American Policy* (Headline Series no. 252). New York: Foreign Policy Association, 1980.

Lipton, Michael. *New Seeds and Poor People.* Baltimore: Johns Hopkins University Press, 1988.

Marden, Parker, G., et al *Population in the Global Arena.* New York: Holt, Rinehart & Winston, 1982.

McCoy, Terry L., ed. *The Dynamics of Population Policy in Latin America.* Cambridge, Mass.: Ballinger, 1974.

McNamara, Robert S. "Time Bomb or Myth: The Population Problem." *Foreign Affairs,* vol. 62 (Summer 1984), pp. 1107–31.

Morson, Jamie, and Marian Kalb. *Women as Food Producers in Developing Countries.* Los Angeles: African Studies Association, 1985.

Murdoch, William. *The Poverty of Nations: The Political Economy of Hunger and Population.* Baltimore: Johns Hopkins University Press, 1980.

Oppong, Christine, ed. *Sex Roles, Population and Development in West Africa: Policy-Related Studies on Work and Demographic Issues.* London: Heinemann/ILO, 1987.

Pearse, Andrew. *Seeds of Plenty, Seeds of Want: Social and Economic Implications of the Green Revolution.* London: Clarendon Press, 1980.

Piotrow, Phyllis T. *World Population: The Present and Future Crisis* (Headline Series no. 251). New York: Foreign Policy Association, 1980.

Sachs, Carolyn. *Invisible Farmers: Women in Agricultural Production.* London: Rowman & Allanheld, 1983.

Sen, Amartya. *Poverty and Famines: An Essay on Entitlement and Deprivation.* New York: Oxford University Press, 1981.

Simon, Julian L., and Herman Kahn, eds. *The Resourceful Earth.* Oxford: Basil Blackwell, 1984.

Staudt, Kathleen. "Uncaptured or Unmotivated: Women, Farmers, and the Food Crisis in Africa." *Rural Sociology.* (1987).

Tullis, F. Lamond, and W. Ladd Hollist, eds. *Food, the State, and International Political Economy: Dilemmas of Developing Countries.* Lincoln: University of Nebraska Press, 1986.

Weller, Robert, and Leon Bouvier. *Population: Demography and Policy.* New York: St. Martin's, 1981.

Wolf, Edward. *Beyond the Green Revolution: New Approaches for Third World Agriculture.* Washington, D.C.: Worldwatch Institute, 1986.

Yesilada, Birol A., Charles Brockett, and Bruce Drury, eds. *Agrarian Reform in Reverse: The Food Crisis in the Third World.* Boulder, Colo.: Westview, 1987.

On Oil, Energy, and Resources

Barnet, Richard. *The Lean Years.* New York: Simon & Schuster, 1980.

Castle, Emery N., and Kent Price, eds. *U.S. Interests and Global Natural Resources.* Washington, D.C.: Resources for the Future, 1983.

Deese, David A., and Joseph S. Nye, eds. *Energy and Security.* Cambridge, Mass.: Ballinger, 1981.

Dolman, Antony J. *Resources, Regimes, and World Order.* Elmsford, N.Y.: Pergamon Press, 1981.

Gourevitch, Peter. *Politics in Hard Times.* Ithaca, N.Y.: Cornell University Press, 1987.

Hatfield, Mark. *Running on Empty: United States Oil Policy* (Hatfield Backgrounder No. 307, January 1988). Washington, D.C.: U.S. Senate Office.

Krasner, Stephen. "Oil Is the Exception." *Foreign Policy,* vol. 14 (Spring 1974), pp. 68–90.

Levy, Walter. "Oil and the Decline of the West." *Foreign Affairs,* vol. 58, no. 5 (Summer 1980), pp. 999–1015.

Maguire, Andrew, and Janet Welsh Brown, eds. *Bordering on Trouble: Resources and Politics in Latin America.* Bethesda, Md.: Adler & Adler, 1986.

Mikdashi, Zuhayr. *Transnational Oil: Issues, Policies, and Perspectives.* New York: St. Martin's, 1986.

Morse, Edward. "After the Fall: The Politics of Oil." *Foreign Affairs,* vol. 64 (Spring 1986), pp. 792–811.

Odell, Peter R. *Oil and World Power,* 8th ed. rev. New York: Penguin, 1988.

Ophuls, William. *Ecology and the Politics of Scarcity.* San Francisco: Freeman, 1977.

Pearce, Joan, ed. *The Third Oil Shock: The Effects of Lower Oil Prices.* London: Royal Institute of International Affairs, 1983.

Penrose, Edith. "The Development of a Crisis." In Raymond Vernon, ed. *The Oil Crisis.* New York: W. W. Norton, 1976.

Pirages, Dennis. *Global Ecopolitics: The New Context for International Relations.* North Scituate, Mass.: Duxbury Press, 1978.

———— *Global Technopolitics: The International Politics of Technology and Resources.* Pacific Grove, Cal.: Brooks/Cole, 1989.

Renner, Michael G. "Shaping America's Energy Future." *World Policy Journal,* vol. 4 (Summer 1987), pp. 383–414.

Sampson, Anthony. *The Seven Sisters.* New York: Bantam Books, 1975.

Simon, Julian L. *The Ultimate Resource.* Princeton, N.J.: Princeton University Press, 1981.

Simon, Julian L., and Herman Kahn, eds. *The Resourceful Earth: A Response to Global 2000.* Oxford: Basil Blackwell, 1984.

Skeet, Ian. *OPEC: 25 Years of Prices and Politics.* New York: Cambridge University Press, 1988.

Westing, Arthur, ed. *Global Resources and International Conflict.* New York: Oxford University Press, 1986.

Willrich, Mason. *Energy and World Politics.* New York: Free Press, 1975.

Yergin, Daniel, and Martin Hillenbrand, eds. *Global Insecurity: A Strategy for Energy and Economic Renewal.* New York: Penguin, 1982.

On Debt

Aggarwal, Vinod K. *International Debt Threat: Bargaining Among Creditors and Debtors in the 1980s.* Berkeley: Institute of International Studies, University of California, 1987.

Ayres, Robert. *Banking on the Poor.* Cambridge, Mass.: MIT Press, 1983.

Bauer, Peter T. "Accounts Receivable." *New Republic,* vol. 196 (June 15, 1987), pp. 10–12.

Carvounis, Chris. *The Foreign Debt/National Development Conflict.* Westport, Conn.: Quorum Books, 1986.

Castro, Fidel. "Avoiding a 'Crash': A Radical Proposal for Solving the Debt Crisis." Interview excerpted in *World Press Review,* vol. 32 (Aug. 1985), pp. 23–26.

Cavanaugh, John. "Debt and Development: An Action Agenda." *Christianity and Crisis,* vol. 45 (Oct. 14, 1985), pp. 394–397.

Chinweizu, A. "Debt Trap Peonage." *Monthly Review,* vol. 37, no. 6 (Nov. 1985), pp. 21–36.

Cline, William R. *International Debt and the Stability of the World Economy.* Washington, D.C.: Institute for International Economics, 1983.

Cohen, Benjamin J. *In Whose Interest? International Banking and American Foreign Policy.* New Haven, Conn.: Yale University Press, 1986.

Dornbusch, Rudiger, and Stanley Fischer. "Third World Debt." *Science,* vol. 234 (Nov. 14, 1986), pp. 836–41.

Farnsworth, Clyde. "Financial Drain Reaches Record in Third World." *The Oregonian.* (Dec. 19, 1988), p. A11

Foreign Policy Association. "International Debt Crisis." *Great Decisions '84.* New York: Foreign Policy Association, 1984.

Frieden, Jeff. "Third World Indebted Industrialization: International Finance and State Capitalism in Mexico, Brazil, Algeria, and South Korea." *International Organization,* vol. 35 (Summer 1981), pp. 407–31.

Gallon, Gary. "The Aid Fix: Pushers and Addicts." *International Perspective.* (Nov./Dec. 1983), pp. 11–14.

George, Susan. *A Fate Worse Than Debt: The World Financial Crisis and the Poor.* New York: Grove Press, 1988.

Griffith-Jones, Stephany, ed. *Managing World Debt.* New York: St. Martin's, 1988.

Hartland-Thunberg, Penelope. "Sources and Implications of the Global Debt Crisis." *Washington Quarterly,* vol. 9 (Winter 1986), pp. 95–108.

Kahler, Miles. "Politics and International Debt: Explaining the Crisis." *International Organization,* vol. 39, no. 3 (Summer 1985), pp. 357–82.

——— ed. *The Politics of International Debt.* Ithaca, N.Y.: Cornell University Press, 1986.

Kaufman, Robert R. "Democratic and Authoritarian Responses to the Debt Issue: Argentina, Brazil, Mexico." *International Organization,* vol. 39, no. 3 (Summer 1985), pp. 473–504.

Krueger, Anne O. "Developing Countries' Debt Problems and Growth Prospects." *Atlantic Economic Journal,* vol. 14 (Mar. 1986), pp. 8–19.

Kuczynski, Pedro-Pablo. *Latin American Debt.* Baltimore: Johns Hopkins, 1988.

Macewan, Arthur. "Latin America: Why Not Default?" *Monthly Review,* vol. 38 (Sept. 1986), pp. 1–13.

Makin, John. *The Global Debt Crisis.* New York: Basic Books, 1984.

Payer, Cheryl. *The Debt Trap: The IMF and the Third World.* New York: Monthly Review Press, 1974.

Pool, John C., and Stephen Stamos. "The Uneasy Calm: Third World Debt—The Case of Mexico." *Monthly Review,* vol. 36, no. 10 (Mar. 1985), pp. 7–19.

Sampson, Anthony. *The Money Lenders.* New York: Penguin, 1981.

Sidell, Scott R. *The IMF and Third World Instability: Is There a Connection?* New York: St. Martin's, 1988.

Stewart, Frances. "The International Debt Situation and North-South Relations." *World Development* (Oxford), vol. 13 (Feb. 1985), pp. 191–204.

Weinert, Richard S. "Swapping Third World Debt." *Foreign Policy,* vol. 65 (Winter 1986/87), pp. 85–95.

Wood, Robert E. "Making Sense of the Debt Crisis: A Primer for Socialists." *Socialist Review,* vol. 15 (May/June 1985), pp. 7–33.

On Foreign Aid

Attwood, Donald, Thomas Bruno, and John Galaty, eds. *Power and Poverty: Development and Development Projects in the Third World,* Boulder, Colo.: Westview, 1988.

Barry, Tom, and Deb Pruesh. *The Soft War: The Uses and Abuses of U.S. Economic Aid in Central America.* New York: Grove Press, 1988.

Bauer, P. T. *Equality, the Third World, and Economic Delusion.* Cambridge: Harvard University Press, 1981.

Bauer, P. T., and John O'Sullivan. "Foreign Aid for What?" *Commentary,* vol. 66 (Dec. 1978), pp. 41–48.

Bovard, James. "The Continuing Failure of U.S. Foreign Aid." *USA Today* (Sept. 1986), pp. 10–15.

Brooke, James (New York Times News Service). "São Tomé's Lifeline Hangs on Thin Thread of Foreign Aid." *The Oregonian.* (Mar. 12, 1988), p. A2.

Cassen, Robert. *Does Aid Work? Report to an Intergovernmental Task Force.* New York: Oxford Univerity Press, 1986.

Chambers, Robert. *Rural Development: Putting the Last First.* New York: Longman, 1983.

Doan, Michael, et al. "Foreign Aid: Reaching the Bottom of the Barrel." *U.S. News and World Report* (Dec. 13, 1982).

Gedda, George. "Report Decries U.S. Foreign Aid Policy as Obsolete." *The Oregonian* (Feb. 21, 1989), p. A7.

Hayter, Teresa. *Aid as Imperialism.* Baltimore: Penguin, 1971.

———*Aid: Rhetoric and Reality.* London: Pluto Press, 1985.

Krueger, Anne O. "Aid in the Development Process." *World Bank Research Observer,* vol. 1 (Jan. 1986), pp. 57–78.

Lappé, Frances Moore, and Joseph Collins. *Aid as Obstacle.* San Francisco: Institute for Food and Development Policy, 1980.

Marsden, Keith, and Alan Roe. "The Political Economy of Foreign Aid: A World Bank Perspective." *Labour and Society,* vol. 8, no. 1 (Jan./Mar. 1983).

Office of Technology Assessment. *Enhancing Agriculture in Africa: A Role for U.S. Development Assistance.* Washington, D.C.: U.S. Gov't Printing Office, 1988.

Overholt, Catherine, et al., eds. *Gender Roles in Development Projects.* Hartford, Conn.: Kumarian Press, 1985.

Packenham, Robert. *Liberal America and the Third World: Political Development Ideas in Foreign Aid and Social Science.* Princeton, N.J.: Princeton University Press, 1973.

Poats, Rutherford M. "Development Lessons Learned." *OECD Observer,* vol. 137 (Nov. 1985), pp. 3–9.

Reid, Walter. *Bankrolling Successes: A Portfolio of Sustainable Development Projects.* Washington, D.C.: Environmental Policy Institute, 1988.

Riddell, Roger. *Foreign Aid Reconsidered.* Baltimore: Johns Hopkins University Press, 1987.

Sewell, John, and Christine Contee. "U.S. Foreign Aid in the 1980s: Reordering Priorities." In John Sewell et al., eds. *U.S. Foreign Policy and the Third World: Agenda 1985–86.* New Brunswick, N.J.: Transaction, 1985.

Sommer, John G. *Beyond Charity: U.S. Voluntary Aid for a Changing Third World.* Washington, D.C.: Overseas Development Council, 1977.

On U.S. Intervention in the Third World

See also sources cited in the sections on "Containment" and "Soviet-American Rivalry in the Third World" in Chapter 5).

Acker, Alison. *Honduras: The Making of a Banana Republic.* Boston: South End Press, 1988.

Barnet, Richard. *Intervention and Revolution,* rev. ed. New York: New American Library, 1972.

Bull, Hedley, ed. *Intervention in World Politics.* New York: Oxford University Press, 1984.

Cable, James. *Gunboat Diplomacy, 1919–1979,* 2nd ed. New York: St. Martin's, 1985.

Chomsky, Noam. *Turning the Tide: U.S. Intervention in Central America and the Struggle for Peace.* Boston: South End Press, 1986.

Coleman, Kenneth M., and George C. Herring, eds. *The Central American Crisis: Sources of Conflict and the Failure of U.S. Policy.* Wilmington, Del.: Scholarly Resources, 1985.

Cottam, Richard W. *Iran and the United States: A Cold War Case Study.* Pittsburgh: University of Pittsburgh Press, 1988.

David, Steven R. "Soviet Involvement in Third World Coups." *International Security,* vol. 11 (Summer 1986), pp. 3–36.

Feinberg, Richard E. *The Intemperate Zone: The Third World Challenge to U.S. Foreign Policy.* New York: Norton, 1984.

Feinberg, Richard E., and Kenneth A. Oye. "After the Fall: U.S. Policy Toward Radical Regimes." *World Policy Journal,* vol. 1, no. 1, pp. 201–15.

Foster, Gregory D. "On Selective Intervention." *Strategic Review,* vol. 11 (Fall 1983), pp. 48–62.

Franklin, David, and James Chace. "The Lessons of Vietnam?" *Foreign Affairs* (Spring 1985), pp. 722–46.

Gurtov, Melvin. *The United States Against the Third World: Antinationalism and Intervention.* New York: Praeger, 1974.

Gutman, Roy. *Banana Diplomacy.* New York: Pantheon, 1988.

Hahn, Walter F., ed. *Central America and the Reagan Doctrine.* Washington, D.C.: U.S. Strategic Institute, for the Center for International Relations at Boston University, 1987.

Hamilton, Nora, et al., eds. *Crisis in Central America: Regional Dynamics and U.S. Policy in the 1980s.* Boulder, Colo.: Westview, 1988.

Hoffmann, Stanley. "Muscle and Brains." *Foreign Policy* (Winter 1979/80), pp. 3–27.

Hosmer, Stephen T. *Constraints on U.S. Strategy in Third World Conflicts.* Philadelphia: Crane Russak, 1987.

Huntington, Samuel P. "Patterns of Intervention: America and the Soviets in the Third World." *The National Interest,* vol. 7 (Spring 1987), pp. 39–47.

Immerman, Richard H. *The CIA in Guatemala: The Foreign Policy of Intervention.* Austin: University of Texas Press, 1982.

Kiernan, Bernard. *The United States, Communism, and the Emergent World.* Bloomington: Indiana University Press, 1972.

Klare, Michael T. *Beyond the "Vietnam Syndrome": U.S. Interventionism in the 1980's.* Washington, D.C.: Institute for Policy Studies, 1981.

Klare, Michael T., and Cynthia Arnson. *Supplying Repression: U.S. Support for Authoritarian Regimes Abroad,* rev. ed. Washington, D.C.: Institute for Policy Studies, 1984.

Lafeber, Walter. "The Reagan Administration and Revolutions in Central America." *Political Science Quarterly,* vol. 99 (1984), pp. 1–25.

Lake, Anthony. *Third World Radical Regimes: U.S. Policy Under Carter and Reagan* (Headline Series no. 272, Jan./Feb.). New York: Foreign Policy Association, 1985.

Lane, Charles. "Death's Democracy." *The Atlantic Monthly* (Jan. 1989), pp. 18–25.

Little, Richard. *Intervention: External Involvement in Civil Wars.* Totowa, N.J.: Rowman and Littlefield, 1975.

Pearce, Jenny. *Under the Eagle: U.S. Intervention in Central America and the Caribbean.* Boston: South End Press, 1983.

Pearson, Frederic S. "Geographic Proximity and Foreign Military Intervention." *Journal of Conflict Resolution,* vol. 18, no. 3 (Sept. 1974), pp. 432–60.

Ravenal, Earl C. "Doing nothing." *Foreign Policy* (Summer 1980), pp. 28–39.

Ray, Ellen, et al., eds. *Dirty Work: The CIA in Africa.* Boston: Zed Press, 1980.

Rubin, Barry. *Paved with Good Intentions: The American Experience and Iran.* New York: Penguin, 1980.

Schlesinger, Stephen, and Stephen Kinzer. *Bitter Fruit: The Untold Story of the American Coup in Guatemala.* New York: Doubleday, 1983.

Schoultz, Lars. *National Security and United States Policy Toward Latin America.* Princeton, N.J.: Princeton University Press, 1987.

Scott, Andrew M. *The Revolution in Statecraft: Intervention in an Age of Interdependence.* Durham, N.C.: Duke University Press, 1982.

Sick, Gary. *All Fall Down: America's Tragic Encounter with Iran.* New York: Penguin, 1986.

Sklar, Holly. *Washington's War on Nicaragua.* Boston: South End Press, 1988.

Solarz, Stephen J. "When to Intervene." *Foreign Policy,* vol. 63 (Summer 1986), pp. 20–39.

Stockwell, John. *In Search of Enemies: A CIA Story.* New York: W. W. Norton, 1978.

Tillema, Herbert K. *Appeal to Force: American Military Intervention in the Era of Containment.* New York: Thomas Crowell, 1973.

Tucker, Robert. "Isolation and Intervention." *The National Interest.* (Fall 1985).

Ullman, Richard H. "At War with Nicaragua." *Foreign Affairs,* vol. 62, no. 1 (Fall 1983), pp. 39–58.

Walker, Thomas W., ed. *Reagan Versus the Sandinistas: The Undeclared War on Nicaragua.* Boulder, Colo.: Westview, 1987.

Welch, Richard. *Response for Revolution.* Charlotte: University of North Carolina Press, 1985.

White, Richard Alan. *The Morass: United States Intervention in Central America.* New York: Harper and Row, 1984.

Zelikow, Philip. "The United States and the Use of Force: A Historical Summary" in George K. Osborn et al., eds. *Democracy, Strategy, and Vietnam,* pp. 31–81. Lexington, Mass.: Lexington Books, 1987.

III

ACTORS

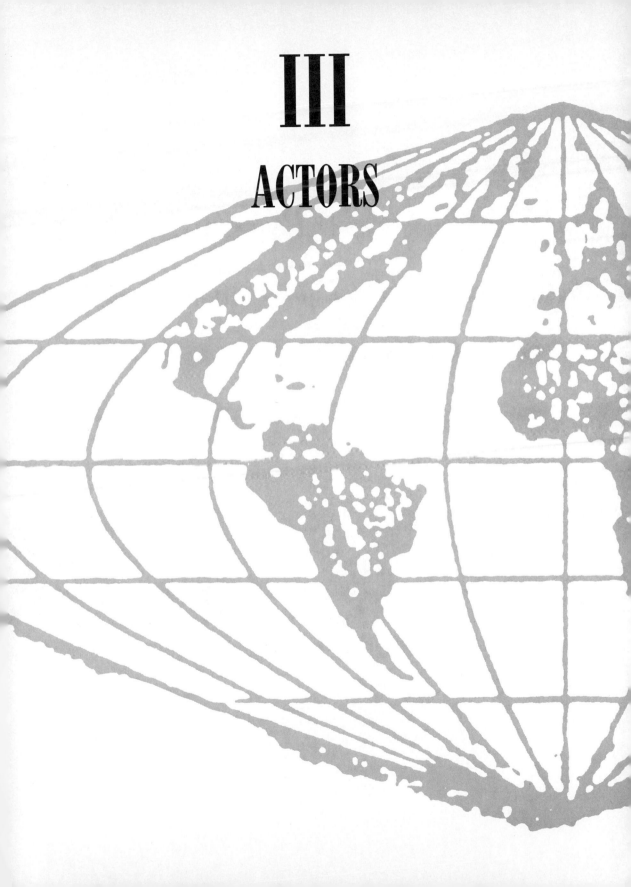

NATION-STATES

The nation-state is the most cohesive and powerful actor in world politics. It is the primary focus of political loyalty, and nationalism remains the most potent political belief system. The citizens of a nation share a common language, race, culture, or historical experience and a tangible sense of geographic community. They interact in the national economy and participate in the state's political institutions. States control the earth's territory and resources, and in the modern era only the state can provide reliable security. Only it can command the decision-making power and tax monies necessary to the maintenance of military protection. In short, the nation-state is the one entity in the international system with an overarching capacity to provide a sense of membership, to ensure physical safety, and to promote economic welfare.

A powerful and cohesive state endows its citizens with a distinctive national identity and a set of national interests. (New or culturally divided states tend to be less powerful because they lack this cohesive national identity.) Each nation-state's foreign policy embodies the cultural characteristics of its people, its prominent institutions, its geographical location and physical endowments, and the interests of its political and economic elites — elements that tend to give the state's behavior a degree of consistency and predictability. The members of a nation-state eventually come to share a common worldview that expresses their habits, their sense of place, their ideology, their interpretation of history, and their orientation to other states. In short, the foreign policy of each nation-state is shaped by its personality, or national style, and its national perspective.

NATIONALISM AND THE STATE

The primary unit of international affairs is the state, a legal and physical entity that meets three criteria. First, the state operates within a *territorial* framework. Its authority resides inside fixed borders, which confer citizenship on all those who are born there or live there permanently. It polices these borders, regulates the adjacent seas and airspace, provides passports to its citizens for travel abroad, and controls the passage of goods and persons into and out of its territory. Second, the state has *sovereignty,* or the power to maintain order within its declared territory. The state is politically independent, recognizing no authority superior to its own, and it has the right to suppress violent internal challenges to its authority and to reject foreign interference. All sovereign states have equal legal status in the international community. Third, the state has some degree of *legitimacy,* both internal and external. Internally, it must command the loyalty, or at least the passive consent, of a sizable majority of its citizens, so that it can exercise its political authority in reliable and durable ways. Without internal legitimacy, civil war is likely. Externally, a state must be recognized by other states as being a legitimate member of the international community. A group or party may be in de facto control of a territory, but that group is not viewed as legitimate until it receives the de jure recognition of other states, who thereby agree to exchange ambassadors, acknowledge territorial claims, conclude trade agreements, and conduct all the other official transactions of normal interstate relations.

These three characteristics — territory, sovereignty, legitimacy — are often imperfectly realized. Territorial boundaries are a frequent matter of dispute. In new states, borders may have been drawn arbitrarily by the former colonial authorities. Wars leave many borders contested, especially if the language or culture of the conquered people is distinct from that of the conquering state. The French and the Germans disputed over Alsace and Lorraine for more than a century. The breakdown of the Austro-Hungarian and Ottoman empires left many borders ill defined, and the aggrandizement of the Russian imperial state led to territorial disputes with China, Japan, Poland, Hungary, and others. Israel, after five major wars, holds disputed territory in the Sinai, the Gaza Strip, the West Bank, Lebanon, and the Golan Heights.

Contemporary disputes over sovereignty have involved fishing rights in territorial waters and the right of free emigration. Even the United States, despite its power, has been unable to control the flow of immigrants entering illegally, particularly Latinos coming across its southern border.

Political and economic sovereignty are relative, since all states are dependent to some degree on others for markets or resources, and many smaller states need great-power protection. Sovereignty and legitimacy are constantly under attack in countries that are politically unstable, like Lebanon, Angola, El Salvador, Afghanistan, and Cambodia, all of which are beset by warring internal factions contesting the jurisdiction of the central authority.

Sovereign equality is a legal fiction. In reality, the great powers dominate international politics and dictate in a variety of ways to the smaller states. Steven Spiegel, in *Dominance and Diversity: The International Hierarchy,* divides states into seven tiers of sovereignty: superpowers (U.S., USSR), secondary powers (Japan, Germany, China, France, the United Kingdom), middle powers (India, Brazil, Argentina, Mexico, Canada, Australia, South Africa, and the small industrialized states of East and West Europe), minor powers (thirty-one more-developed Third World states and the smallest and least-developed European states), regional states (twenty-five, mostly non-Western, whose influence is strictly regional), microstates (fifty-four Third World countries too small to enjoy all the attributes of sovereignty), and dependent states (fifty trust territories or de facto dependencies of other powers). The United Nations formally recognizes all states as being equal by giving each a vote in the General Assembly, but its pragmatic founders were realistic enough to give a veto on certain matters to the permanent members of the Security Council — the great powers of the United States, the Soviet Union, Britain, France, and China.

The periodic changes in a state's government or administration that occur by normal constitutional or other peaceful means do not affect its legitimacy. In such cases, like the election of President George Bush and the ascension to power of Mikhail Gorbachev, the new regime's recognition by foreign governments is pro forma. But a violent change of government, especially a revolutionary overturn that is strongly contested or incomplete, often generates dispute over recognition. The Bolshevik takeover in Russia in 1917 was not recognized by the other great powers for several years — not until 1933 by the United States. The United States withheld formal recognition from Communist China for thirty years. China's case is also unusual in that two governments, the Nationalist Chinese on Taiwan and the Communist Chinese on the mainland, both claim to legitimately represent China, and each hopes someday to regain the irredentist territories lost during the Chinese civil war. A similar situation has existed between North and South Korea and, until recently, between East and West Germany. They are united by language and culture but have been divided as the result of their wartime occupation by rival ideological powers. World War II brought on a three-way contest for recognition in Poland, as different exile groups — sponsored by the British, the Nazis, and the Soviets — vied for control. More recently, military coups in Panama, Haiti, and elsewhere brought to power governments that the United States refused to recognize.

But it is awkward to conduct relations for very long with states that have been refused recognition. When a regime's de facto control has lasted for a few years, it usually is granted official recognition, even by states that were initially hostile on ideological grounds. Two of the rare exceptions are Fidel Castro's Cuba, which the United States has not recognized since it severed relations in 1961, and Israel, founded in 1948 but still unrecognized by most of the Arab states. The case of the Homelands, tribal enclaves set up by South Africa between 1976 and 1979, illustrates the importance of recognition. Three of them, the Republics of Transkei, Bophuthatswana, and Venda, declared themselves independent states and were recognized as such by South Africa. But no other states have recognized them because their creation was motivated by South Africa's policy of apartheid, or racial segregation, and they are economically and politically dependent on their sponsor. Lacking the legitimacy of international recognition, they cannot be considered independent states.

For all these qualifications in their formal status, states are fairly durable and well-defined international actors. The *nation* is less tangible, a loose cultural entity — a kind of community of consciousness or constellation of loyalties. Its members usually share demographic characteristics, such as language, race, or religion. But group affiliations can also develop in heterogeneous populations, through common historical experience, regular economic and social interaction, or the inculcation of shared values through education or political socialization. This is the case with an immigrant melting-pot society like that of the United States. Nations are also defined by a group's desire to be separate and self-governing. A state may be composed of many nationalities (as the United States is), but this ethnic diversity becomes politically salient only if the various constituent communities have nationalist ideals that push them toward political autonomy or independence. Often, the modern state can manage over time to homogenize a multiethnic society. But enduring ethnic and linguistic tensions in such countries as the Soviet Union, Spain, Belgium, Canada, Cyprus, Nigeria, and Lebanon testify to the strong separatist appeal of nationalism.

In fact, most states are not ethnically or linguistically pure, and many nationalities are not politically independent. Less than 10 percent of all countries fit the ideal concept of the nation-state, and almost 30 percent have no ethnic majority. Great Britain has large Welsh, Irish, and Scottish minorities. Spain has Basque and Catalan separatist movements. Canada is divided between English- and French-speaking groups, Belgium between Flemings and Walloons, Yugoslavia between Croatians, Serbs, and half a dozen smaller groups. One study has estimated that sixty-one national minorities have aspirations to be self-governing — with an immensely explosive potential for altering existing political boundaries. The Soviet Union is only 50 percent ethnic Russian; the remainder of the population consists of hundreds of minority nationalities, many of them conquered peoples harboring separatist desires. Nigeria is made up of three main tribal groups (Ibo, Yoruba, and Hausa) and hundreds of smaller tribes. The Ibos, a majority in the oil-rich southeastern region, tried to set up the independent state of Biafra in 1967, but they were suppressed after a four-year civil war. In 1971, the Bengalis of East Pakistan declared their independence from ethnically distinct West Pakistan, forming the new state of Bangladesh. Though both East and West Pakistanis are Muslim, their common religion was not enough to overcome other cultural differences. Cyprus has been in constant turmoil as the result of frictions between a Greek Cypriot majority and a Turkish Cypriot minority — frictions further enflamed by irredentist claims from Greece and Turkey, whose cultural affinities to their respective Cypriot peoples give them a large emotional stake in the outcome. Nationalist sentiment has an especially powerful impact when a cultural or linguistic group overlaps several states. This is true of the Palestinians, who are dispersed throughout the Middle East, mainly in Israel, Lebanon, Jordan, and Egypt, and of the Kurds and the Armenians, both occupying regions in Iran, Iraq, Turkey, Syria, and the Soviet Union. Significant numbers within each of these groups aspire to cultural unity and self-government.

There is no doubt that nationalism has become the most powerful legitimizing force in the modern state. Defense of the nation and its values is the transcendent goal of a state, allowing it to command the loyalty, the resources, and even the lives of its citizens. When the Soviet Union rallied its population for war after Hitler invaded in 1941, it was not Communism but Great Russian nationalism that was the foundation of Joseph Stalin's appeal to his people. However, the notion of the state as a homogeneous group sharing a common race, culture, language, or religion is a recent political ideal. Nationalism was completely alien to traditional concepts of the state, either the ancient empires of Rome and Byzantium or the more recent monarchies, whose authority derived from divine right, personal loyalties, and a cosmopolitan royal kinship that recognized no national or cultural boundaries. Imperial families frequently intermarried, and monarchs freely exchanged peoples and lands. These old empires were held together by dynastic ties, patronage, religious legitimacy, the feudal loyalty of a lord's followers, and military conquest.

Nationalism did not take hold until after the Renaissance. Then, expanding literacy and improved communications began to break down village society and increase contacts among culturally distinct peoples. The Reformation and growing secularization cut traditional religious ties, while changes in technology destroyed the economic insularity of feudalism. Gunpowder and transoceanic navigation extended the power and range of the state, and the economics of the early industrial era pointed up the virtues of an enlarged political entity. Nationalism was a creed that could expand the horizon of political loyalties and fill the void left by the breakdown of traditional affiliations. The rise of democracy, with its belief that legitimacy proceeds directly from the people, also reinforced nationalist appeals. The consolidation of self-governing national communities has gone furthest in Europe, where nationalism first challenged religious and dynastic ties as a legitimate basis for state power. A patriotism born of the French Revolution in 1789 soon spread to the rest of Europe, partly in reaction to Napoleon's conquests, partly as a consequence of the growth of liberal-democratic ideals. Italy and Germany, which for centuries had been divided among small independent principalities and city-states, were consolidated into large nation-states, uniting most of those who spoke the common tongue. In the Austro-Hungarian domains, however, nationalism had a divisive effect, breaking a cosmopolitan empire into its constituent language groups.

Nationalism subsequently animated the drive to self-determination that accompanied the breakup of the colonial empires throughout the Third World. In this non-Western context, Western-educated elites adopted the European idea of nationalism as a rallying focus for the anticolonial struggle and as an ideology for cementing the loyalties of disparate tribal and linguistic groups. But, because the boundaries of the new states were set by European fiat, Third World nationalism was more politcal aspiration tha cultural reality. When independence removed the powerful defining distinctions between white and nonwhite, alien and indigenous, the new states were as often divided by nationalism as united by it, since community identities were still largely rooted in village, tribe, and region. Still, nationalism retains much potency in the Third World because of its anti-imperialist appeal to peoples with long histories of colonial rule. Also, it has assuaged some of the pains of a rapid transition to modernization by encouraging peoples to search out their traditional cultures and resurrect lost historical identities. Though this is a largely synthetic nationalism, its re-creation of the glories of such old empires as Ashanti, Mali, and Benin has helped to establish national unity and an affiliation with the state.

Modern nationalism, at first an extension of liberal and democratic ideas, later became more parochial. In certain circumstances it took on a conservative and aggressive cast that fueled enthnocentric notions of national or racial superiority. German nationalism was the pretext for Adolf Hitler's aggressions against neighboring states with German-speaking minorities, and it became the justification for Germany's domination of "inferior" peoples, and its extermination of Jews, Gypsies, and others. Nationalism can lead to the exclusion of ethnic groups, their forced assimilation into the majority culture, and other forms of discrimination, pushing aside all other values, including those of democratic liberalism.

The balance sheet on the positive versus the negative impact of modern nationalism is difficult to calculate. On the plus side, it has fostered democracy and self-determination, replacing the old concept of ruler and subject with the notion of popular sovereignty and citizenship. Nationalism preserves cultural diversity and political pluralism, which are positive values so long as they do not become so extreme as to cause political instability. In many settings, nationalism has had a modernizing and integrative impact, facilitating economic development and the growth of the modern state. On the destructive side, nationalism can lead to ethnocentrism, insularity, and xenophobia (suspicion or fear of foreigners). Such attitudes increase the likelihood of conflicts between states and lead to the persecution of foreign nationals or resident minorities, such as Mexicans in the United States, Pakistanis in Britain, Turks in Europe, Chinese in South Asia, and Indians in Africa. Nationalism can also support imperialistic foreign policies and a self-righteous and belligerent jingoism. Nationalism encouraged the political unification of Europe, but its impact on the Third World has been largely divisive. Whether nationalism's liberal, creative, and unifying influences are outweighed by its impulses toward subversion, aggression, and conflict is still an open question.

Some theorists argue that the standardizing and homogenizing influences at play throughout the world will curb the evils of nationalism. In theory, increased cross-cultural communication should lessen nationalistic sentiments and we-versus-they stereotypes. But such contacts can also strengthen ethnocentrism, in the same way as the spread of education and communication at the beginning of the modern era originally stimulated national and ethnic consciousness. The excesses of nationalism are often condemned, but no other loyalty seems more powerful — not religion, profit, class affiliation, or a cosmopolitan international identity. Global interdependence, problems of ecology and resource management, collective security — all these argue for commitments that transcend national perspectives. Yet the personal tie to place and people remains a vital ingredient of political solidarity and legitimacy.

NATIONAL ATTRIBUTES

An important determinant of a state's foreign policy is its national character. A state's internal characteristics, values, interests, and motivations shape its self-image and its perceptions of others. Social makeup, ideology, political-economic organization, historical experience, stage of development, and manner of making decisions all affect a nation's outlook and its role in the world.

The personality of a nation-state shows a distinctive and consistent style that appears to transcend changes of regime. Many historians have commented on the similarities between Czarist Russia and the Soviet regime in their conduct of foreign policy: intense secretiveness and suspicion of foreigners, orthodoxy in political outlook, centralization in diplomacy, strict obedience to authority, preoccupation with security, heavy reliance on military means, expansionist tendencies fed by messianic thinking, and what Bismarck called "elementary force and persistence." Monarchical and republican France showed the same kind of continuity, which Alexis de Tocqueville's *The Old Régime and the French Revolution* has traced to ingrained habit, institutional vestiges, and the cultural disposition of the French people.

The enduring attributes that make up national character fall into three categories, which we will look at in detail: geography, economy, and society; political culture and ideology; formative experiences and historical crises. But it is important to remember that these elements are subjective and changeable. The broad concept of national character is a convenient way to summarize a variety of long-term cultural and historical influences on foreign policy, but it is not to be regarded as deterministic or as a single predictive variable. Knowledge of a state's political culture or a decision maker's general belief system will assist our understanding of a particular issue, but we still need to analyze the specific situation, external determinants, idiosyncratic variables, and institutional and political pressures. The personalities, normative beliefs, and acts of individual leaders also make a big difference. On several occasions, a change of president has reshaped American foreign policy substantially, particularly when the new leader showed charisma and historical vision. In the Soviet Union, Joseph Stalin's paranoid tendencies emphasized the hostile and conflictual side of the Bolshevik worldview; Nikita Khrushchev was more flexible and open-minded; and Mikhail Gorbachev has altered policy fundamentally— though only by directly attacking old habits and those very elements of the national character that have resisted change.

Thus, in explaining an event by reference to national character, it is always necessary to specify what element in the national character caused the outcome. Otherwise, national character can easily become a catchall analytic basket into which we dump anything we cannot explain more precisely. It is best used descriptively, not prescriptively—as a means of rendering the background environment within which national decision making takes place. National character defines a state's stylistic differences, limits its range of instruments and options, and describes tendencies or habits, but by itself it does not determine anything.

National patterns of behavior change over time as nations pass through cycles of growth and stagnation, expansion and contraction, intervention and isolation. New ideologies arise, and societies may undergo a gradual evolution in their culture or their political attitudes. Major crises often are turning points, new generations come to the fore, and creative political leadership can reconfigure practically anything. All these factors have the potential for trans-forming national character. National style is always something of a caricature of stereotyped behavior that is constantly evolving.

Tensions exist within the national character and between subcultures, just as they do in the individual personality. Not all members of a ruling group will invariably agree, and the composition of an elite (and its beliefs) can change significantly over a period of time. New external circumstances may engage a different part of the national tradition, or a new chief of state may emphasize one value or subcultural style over another. If a nation does not encounter any profound foreign policy crises, however, it tends to persist quite unconsciously in the same attitudes and routine patterns of conduct, and that is why a study of national attributes is important for our understanding of the international behavior of states.

Geography, Economy, Society

Geography is a unique and usually permanent feature of a nation's character. International affairs have been affected for centuries by the distinctive outlooks of landlocked and seafaring peoples, the vulnerable and the impregnable, the insular and the expansionist. The capitalist societies of Switzerland, Austria, and Finland, for example, nonetheless adopted a posture of neutrality in the East-West struggle largely due to their topography and location. Colin Gray, in *The Geopolitics of the Nuclear Era* , points to the lasting impact of geographical factors on the Soviet-American rivalry:

> East-West political relations may fruitfully be considered as a long-term and inalienable struggle between the insular *imperium* of the United States and the "Heartland" *imperium* of the Soviet Union. In terms of physical geography, Eurasia (with Africa) may be conceived of as a centrally-placed island (the "World-Island" of geopolitical literature), surrounded (loosely) by an "outer crescent" of islands (the Americas, Australia). The interface between the power of the Heartland and the maritime *imperium* of North America are the "Rim-lands" of Eurasia-Africa and the marginal seas which lap the shores of those "Rimlands.". . . In geopolitical terms, superpower conflict may be character-ized as a struggle between a substantially landlocked Heartland superpower, and the substantially maritime dependent (in security perspective) insular su-perpower for control/denial of control of the Eurasian-African "Rimlands." (p. 14)

These rimlands form the zones of competition — Western Europe, Africa, the Middle East, Southeast Asia, Taiwan, Korea, and Japan — in the U.S.-Soviet struggle. Add to this geography such factors as trade ties, industrial potential, and access to strategic minerals, and the United States and the Soviet Union cannot help but be engaged in a contest for influence in these vital areas. In this perception, their conflict is not a product of alliance commitments, ideological rivalry, preference for a forward defense, or adherence to domino or contain-ment theories. It is a result of their different geopolitical perspectives — perspectives that any countries in the same geographical circumstances would have, no matter what their ideology. (A fuller discussion of geopolitical theories is to be found in Chapter 9.)

Britain's position as an island, insulated from the open plains of the continent, is what led it to take the role of balancer in European power struggles, quite apart from any monarchist or republican, Whig or Tory preferences of its government. Geography also dictated that Britain's instrument of power had to be its navy, that it had no need for a large standing army. The seafaring habits of the islanders contributed to the development of a commercial culture, and the growth of a sizable independent mercantile class led to a liberal society marked by democratic habits and a pragmatic spirit. All these gave the British an aversion to militarism and great skill in diplomacy, but also a foreign policy that was largely reactive.

Conversely, the Germans, occupying the center of the vulnerable landmass of Europe, required large standing armies to ensure their security. From this came a tendency toward militarism and the famous Prussian qualities of order and discipline. The authoritarian structure of German society reinforced these tendencies, which took form in a series of external aggressions and a crude and immoderate diplomacy. At the same time, the Germans became distinguished for their brilliance in war planning, in mobilizing the nation's resources, and in commanding the disciplined obedience of the population amid great hardship. The division of Germany after World War II introduced a new geopolitical reality. West Germany's position on the front line of defense, along with the threat from the rival East German government, kept it firmly within the NATO alliance and made it a far more compliant ally than, say, France was. The governments of South Vietnam, South Korea, and Taiwan were similarly shaped by the geopolitical impact of postwar division.

Despite NATO's ideological bonds, geography has created significant tensions within the alliance. The French (under de Gaulle) and later the West Germans (under Chancellor Willy Brandt) were less wed to the rigidities of the Cold War than the Americans were, largely because of their closer proximity to the Soviet Union, their desires for reunification or for trade relations, and their historic ties to regimes in Eastern Europe. They initiated moves toward détente and a defusing of the Soviet threat through diplomacy well ahead of the Americans. Nor have the Europeans ever been as keen as the Americans were on nuclear-war-fighting doctrines, because they knew that a war employing the first-use strategy and tactical nuclear weapons would be fought on their soil. Also, small states do not have much space in which to hide their nuclear missiles or an extensive landmass that can diffuse a nuclear strike. The French, in particular, mistrusted the extended deterrence strategy that the Americans professed was both necessary and adequate for the defense of Europe. Consequently, they developed an independent nuclear force — the *force de frappe* — for reasons of geography as well as national pride.

Japan, like England and America, is geographically insular. Its isolation from the industrial revolution in Europe meant that its modernization came late and with a correspondingly larger role for the state. Racial tensions and feelings of inferiority stemming from contact with the West, plus the warlordism and martial discipline of the samurai tradition, fed a xenophobic and imperialist pattern of development. An imperial government and a collectivist society gave further impetus toward militaristic nationalism. Japan's different social patterns and the late-modernizing push toward recognition as a great power, laid over the template of an insular geography, gave Japanese foreign policy a much more authoritarian cast than that of the Anglo-American democracies.

National character is markedly affected by a state's stage of political or economic development and the degree to which its diplomacy is institutionalized and subject to domestic constraints. The Soviet Union has mellowed considerably in its evolution from a radical, ideologically driven young state to a more pragmatic superpower. Partly this has been the result of economic development and bureaucratic entrenchment. But it is also due to the Soviet Union's passage to great-power status and its "domestication" within the international system, which have given the Soviets a stronger stake in the status quo.

Other significant elements of national character are a folk image and shared historical experiences. Kenneth Boulding, in an article entitled "National Images and International Systems," argues that new states will inevitably have weak self-images and display erratic behavior. In most Third World states, the sense of national identity tends to be concentrated in the powerful state-building or modernizing elite, which often merely imitates other nations or imposes a self-consciously constructed image on the masses. Such images are fragile and likely to be inconsistent with underlying folkways.

In Iran, for example, Shah Muhammed Reza Pahlavi attempted to impose modernization from above, in his "White Revolution" of the 1960s and 1970s. Despite rapid urbanization, massive imports of arms and technology, and the growth of a sizable middle class, his regime collapsed in the face of the traditional Muslim appeals of the Ayatollah Ruhollah Khomeini.

Another argument, advanced by Harry Eckstein in *A Theory of Stable Democracy,* is that states are unstable when the patterns of authority in family, in workplace, and in government are not congruent. This could explain why the democratic norms of the Weimar Constitution adopted in Germany after World War I had little impact on the foreign policy of the Nazis: the Weimar government's reforms were not accompanied by any fundamental alterations in the German economy or society. The reconstruction of Germany and Japan after World War II was more successful because the reforms went well beyond the drafting of new constitutions; the trauma of war, a sense of guilt, and a broad-based perception of the catastrophic consequences of past conduct speeded the shift to new patterns of conduct.

Lucian Pye's *Politics, Personality, and Nation Building* categorizes the stages of national development in terms of parochial versus participant political cultures. In developed states, the participation of the masses in political life, even in authoritarian societies, imposes certain restraints on the political leadership, and their societies also are sufficiently integrated to engender common national values and attitudes. In underdeveloped states, the political cultures are parochial. The elites and the masses are quite distinct, with greatly fragmented or autonomous subcultures, and one can hardly speak of the influence of a single national character. These conditions make Third World behavior less predictable and often more aggressive. Since the political culture is still forming, generational perspectives differ sharply. Because there is no domestic consensus, either on fundamental values or on transitory policy issues, revolutionary challenges, civil war, and changes of leadership are frequent. Elites have great freedom to determine policy, which allows leaders to treat world affairs as a stage on which to perform. Scapegoating is common, and foreign wars serve to distract public attention from domestic difficulties. These distinctive features of Third World foreign policy are due, in large part, to the unformed character of their economy and society.

Political Culture, Ideology, and Constitution

A state's domestic political character has a profound impact on its foreign policy. The three most significant influences are the general values of the state's political culture, its ideology, and its constitution. (Discussion of the differences between democracy and dictatorship is reserved for the treatment of the foreign policy decision process later in this chapter.)

Political culture is the framework within which the citizens of a state become socialized to common habits of thought and feeling. National policy makers, though they may come from a wide variety of professional backgrounds and have quite different personalities, all have acquired, by virtue of their upbringing in a specific historical and national context, a common set of attitudes about politics and an ethnocentric view of their world. Ethnocentrism can sometimes be modified, through empathy, intellectual sophistication, or a self-conscious attempt to overcome national bias — qualities that wise statesmen and skilled diplomats cultivate in order to communicate more effectively. But many national attitudes are unconscious, and a person's very language and categories of thought are bound to reflect the "cognitive map" of his or her political culture. Lucian Pye calls political culture "an ordered subjective realm of politics which gives meaning to the polity, discipline to institutions, and social relevance to individual acts" (*Political Culture and Political Development,* p. 7). A nation's political culture sums up the collective history of the political system and the histories of the individuals who act on its behalf; public and private events converge to give the individual and the state a common sense of identity.

We can trace the impact of political culture on foreign policy through the contrasting experiences of Germany and France in the period between 1848 and 1958. Although the French achieved a constitutional synthesis with the founding of the Third Republic in 1871, underlying tensions between the egalitarian and the monarchical strands in the French tradition left their society fragmented and their politics unstable. This made for great vacillation in foreign policy and a general sluggishness in the development of France's industrial potential and in its responses to the changing realities of power, as manifested in the Maginot Line mentality of the French general staff between the two world wars and, under the Fourth Republic, in the resistance to decolonization. Periods of leaderless political torpor and military conservatism alternated with crises in which the nation escaped stalemate by turning to a rescuing hero or a Napoleonic-style leadership. These foreign policy attitudes have made it impossible for France to live up to its traditional image, cultivated ever since Louis XIV, as the leading power in Europe.

On the other hand, from Bismarck to Hitler, Germany had the advantage of strong leadership and a relatively united political culture. Its vigorous industrial growth was matched by an energetic exercise of power in foreign affairs. Indeed, many social psychologists have argued that Hitler was successful in rallying the German people to fascism, with its extreme nationalism and aggressiveness, because his policy appealed to the authoritarian personality that characterized the German political culture. Certainly a glorification of war and racist thinking were attributes of the Nazi ideology that shaped German foreign policy between 1933 and the German defeat in 1945. But most important, German power after 1871 was rooted in a sense of national unity that the French lacked in many respects.

Different political cultures have also influenced the international communist movement, forcing ideology to compete with national tradition. As early as 1948, Marshal Tito defected from the Stalinist camp and took Yugoslavia on an independent path. China and Albania followed suit in the 1950s and '60s. At the same time, Hungarian, Polish, and Czech Communists were struggling to achieve greater national autonomy within the Soviet bloc; though armed rebellions were suppressed, Communist rule in these three countries became more flexible and took on a distinctly nationalist flavor. In the 1970s, the Communist parties in Spain, Italy, and France split from their allegiance to Moscow. These Eurocommunists have argued ever since that the dictatorship of the proletariat is an obsolete concept and that Communism is compatible with parliamentary rule. Indeed, in many European cities (Marseilles, Milan, Bologna), Communist administrations have governed efficiently within prevailing democratic norms.

Common elements in the political cultures of Britain and America have created an ideological solidarity and a strong convergence of interests in their foreign policy dating back to the end of the War of 1812. The two nations share a liberal-capitalist ideology, strong social and cultural similarities, and a common language and political tradition. The Atlantic partnership was the backbone of the wartime alliance and of the postwar reconstruction of the international system along liberal lines consistent with Anglo-American values. It was this special relationship that so vexed General de Gaulle when he sought to be recognized as an equal in the wartime leadership and that prompted him to oppose Britain's entry into the Common Market — a move that de Gaulle feared would subordinate Europe, and especially France, to American ideas and interests. Thus, national political traditions have affected the liberal as well as the Communist ideological camp.

A common belief in capitalism and democracy has not erased tensions in Japanese-American relations. Strong cultural differences and historic resentments persist, even though Japan has been firmly in the democratic camp since the signing of the Japanese-American Security Treaty of 1951 and relies on the protection of the U.S. nuclear umbrella. In the early part of the century, power in Japan was divided between a civilian faction and a military-oriented expansionist faction. The former signed the Washington Treaties of 1922 providing for a balance of interests in China, restrictions on naval armaments, and other stabilizing measures; the latter resented America's efforts to restrict Japanese influence in Asia. The nationalist military faction felt that Western interference had robbed Japan of the fruits of conquest in 1885, in 1905, and in 1918, and it particularly resented the refusal of the Western allies, at the Paris Peace Conference of 1918, to recognize Japan's claims to a sphere of influence in China or to include a declaration of racial equality in the Covenant of the League of Nations. In the 1930s, the military advocates of expansion gradually gained the upper hand, leading to Japan's invasion of Manchuria, its withdrawal from the League of Nations, and its decision to join Germany and Italy in the Axis Alliance.

After World War II, memories of Japan's defeat amidst horrific firebombings and nuclear devastation put the moderate civilians back in control and left the Japanese with a permanent allergy to both militarism and nuclear weapons. But they have remained bitter over the American demand for unconditional surrender. Only three weeks before Hiroshima, the Japanese had offered to surrender on the sole condition, largely out of cultural pride, that their emperor be permitted to preserve his traditional sovereignty. Most Japanese continue to view the atomic bombings as unnecessary excesses unleashed from motivations of revenge, racism, and America's desire to demonstrate its strength to the Soviet Union. Japanese xenophobia was further aroused by the Soviet Union's opportunistic behavior at the close of the war, when Stalin's declaration of war, on the eve of the second atomic attack, overturned five years of formal Soviet-Japanese nonbelligerency. The Soviet Union quickly seized parts of Manchuria, Korea, and the Japanese northern islands, the latter under Soviet jurisdiction to this day.

All these events fed a strong current of Japanese nationalism, which fortunately has found its expression in economic competition rather than a renewed quest for military dominance. But Japan's ideological realignment from fascism and militarism to constitutional democracy has not completely altered the national character. The rise to economic superpower status has brought new domestic pressures to rearm and has revived the old tensions between nationalist and antimilitarist factions. A growing Soviet economic and military presence in the Far Eastern provinces spurred Japan to expand its defense forces rapidly in the 1970s and '80s. The Japanese economy, dependent on foreign sources of fuel and raw materials, is extremely vulnerable without military means to ensure access to resources. For now, Japan must rely on American forces to protect its trade routes and interests, just as it must depend on the markets and economic policies of the advanced states to sustain its export-oriented economy. Nonetheless, outsiders and economic competitors fear that Japan's export surpluses and its growing investments in the Third World may be a new kind of imperial thrust. The fact that America retains an extensive network of military bases in Japan, long after the termination of the occupation in 1948, adds to Japanese resentments, as do the growing U.S. demands that Japan bear a larger share of the costs of its defense. With Japanese domestic opinion again shifting toward a more assertive role abroad, exclusionary trade policies have further fanned the flames of Japanese-American economic rivalry. These nationalist forces, at times virulent and at times subdued, have run straight through Japanese foreign policy for the last century. They account for much of the continuity in Japanese conduct, just as the crisis of World War II helps explain the radical realignment from military to economic competition.

Formative Experiences and Historical Crises

The formative experiences and historical crises a country goes through, which alter old habits and set new patterns, add a dynamic element to national character. The events surrounding the birth of a nation are often a powerful shaper of national values and perceptions. A new state's character is strongly affected by the violence or the peaceableness attending its formation. In the United States, an immense symbolism attaches to the Declaration of Independence, the Constitution, and the celebration of the Fourth of July. The Soviets have an equally powerful set of myths and historical memories associated with the October Revolution and the Great Patriotic War, so traumatic an event that it amounted to a kind of rebirth of the Soviet peoples.

The trauma that surrounds a great power's loss of empire or defeat in war can bring significant shifts in self-image and national orientation. Germany's feelings of national remorse, after the revelation of the immense Nazi atrocities of World War II, were important in bringing postwar West Germany into a united Europe and in allowing its leadership to cooperate in the events that led to the formation of the European Economic Community. Throughout the continent, popular feeling was strong that something should be done to prevent further bloodshed on the battlefields of Europe, leading to a softening of national attachments and making possible significant advances in international organization. Also, defeat in war gave the Germans a pragmatic inducement for transnational diplomacy; only within a peaceful and united Europe could a divided and disarmed Germany hope to become a great power again.

Defeat in war and the traumas of Hiroshima and Nagasaki marked a dramatic shift in Japanese foreign policy as well. The Japanese adopted a peace constitution prohibiting the development of nuclear weapons or the basing of nuclear forces on Japanese soil and strictly limiting the military budget, with rearmament permitted only for self-defense. These changes, which occurred under the influence of the American occupation, marked the ascendancy of a more pacific foreign policy. The rise of a strong trading orientation pulled Japan out of its regional isolation and integrated it fully into the world market economy. The postwar economic reorganization also reconstructed Japan's ties with China, which has become one of its principal trading partners (the total value of their trade rose ten-fold in the decade between 1970 and 1980). In its normalization of relations with China, Japan was well ahead of the United States, which was still preoccupied with the containment of Communism. Japan's nonnuclear status was formally ratified by its signing of the Nuclear Non-Proliferation Treaty in 1976. Japan's history of war, defeat, and foreign occupation initiated significant changes in its foreign policy.

France's experiences in World War II also affected its foreign policy. Early defeat and subsequent collaboration with the Nazis doomed France to a secondary role in the war and in the postwar international order. President Charles de Gaulle's pretensions, his unreconstructed nationalism, his perceived haughtiness, his insistence on an independent Europe and a separate French nuclear force, his opposition to British entry into the EEC, and his well-publicized, even high-handed, diplomatic initiatives with Moscow were all aimed at restoring French pride and great-power status. France's attempt to regain its leadership in Europe lay at the root of many postwar Franco-American differences, which resulted in France's withdrawal from NATO and its criticisms of U.S. policy toward the Soviet Union, the EEC, and Vietnam. The desire to restore French *grandeur* and resistance to the image of France as a declining power also explain the diehard opposition to decolonization in Indochina and Algeria and the Gaullist determination to preserve the French Empire, in its cultural and economic manifestations, in the form of the French Community. The whole of postwar French foreign policy must be seen in terms of France's difficulty in adjusting to its diminished international stature.

Britain's great historical trauma came over the loss of its empire. The misadventure in Suez in 1956, when the British and the French invaded Egypt in answer to Nasser's nationalization of the canal, was a throwback to colonialism. The strong British response to Argentina's attempted takeover in the Falkland Islands also represented Britain's deep emotional investment in its overseas possessions. Prime Minister Margaret Thatcher's rallying of strong nationalist sentiment among those with a hankering for the old glories of empire, and her strongly chauvinistic language, generated immense popular support for a military solution that was very costly in relation to the economic and strategic value of the Malvinas Islands. But the Falklands became a symbol of Britain's national will to resist Third World challenges and protect the rights of British citizens everywhere in the world. It was a turning point for the Thatcher administration, reversing a decline in the public opinion polls and giving her Tory party a new lease on office.

SOVIET AND AMERICAN WORLDVIEWS COMPARED

How national character affects policy can be seen clearly by comparing the elite attitudes and foreign policy styles of the United States and the Soviet Union. American liberal thought typically assumes that there is a potential harmony of interests among peoples and nations and that individuals, free will, and the free market all play a part in realizing this potential. Disruptions in international affairs are due to the wickedness or weakness of particular individuals or to the lack of appropriate institutions or established legal norms for arbitrating disputes and regulating the use of force. But wicked leaders can be removed, authoritarian systems reformed, and misunderstandings rectified, leaving no permanent obstacles to peace. If structural constraints are present, they reflect the problems of anarchy, not class conflict. Nations want peace, but they are trapped in a "prisoner's dilemma": cooperation can benefit everyone, but disaster will strike the side that behaves altruistically when the other is acting out of self-interest. The safest course is to assume the worst of an adversary, even if this means forgoing a joint gain because the strategy for realizing it seems too risky. The American approach to conflict resolution therefore becomes a search for the lowest common denominator and the adoption of a cautious "satisficing" strategy; conflict is avoided through compromise and the scaling down of one's objectives. Long-term cooperation and a strong level of trust among nations are possible, however, through mutual concessions, trade relations, treaties, alliances, and the establishment of institutions to prevent violations.

The Soviet Marxist has a more deterministic and strategic (that is, long-range) worldview that regards acute conflict as inevitable. Trust, good will, and individual initiative cannot overcome objective forces and fundamental class conflicts. Conflict is restrained only by the rules of prudence ("retreat before superior force") or by the employment of less ambitious means in incremental (though persistent) steps toward otherwise incompatible goals. Traditional Marxism has tended to rule out any intermediate positions between annihilation and world hegemony. To the orthodox Marxist, peaceful coexistence is a tactic, a breathing spell in which to gather one's forces for a new phase in the struggle. Concessions are signs of weakness, not peace offerings, and testimonials of good will are an ideological smokescreen to cover the capitalist's implacable hatred of communism. Since Marxist thought minimizes the role of chance, unfortunate outcomes are attributed not to accident but to the moves of a powerful and calculating opponent. Americans muddle through; the Soviets seek out the one correct line or policy. When the correlation of forces is favorable, a weakening opponent can be intimidated, and daring, risky, or rude behavior can bring a big payoff. Hence, the Soviets have often adopted an optimizing strategy of pressing for the maximum gain. Their foreign policy goals have been limited only by what is objectively possible and by the necessity of avoiding adventures and provocations.

In their nuclear strategy, Americans employ tactics of bluff and gamesmanship that are suited to a psychological model in which individual perceptions and actions can make a difference. Russian thinking adopts a more methodical strategy that emphasizes positions of strength and the objective forces on the field of action. Soviet strategy has not regarded nuclear war as a brief episode whose payoff is predictable in advance by computer calculations and a matrix of rational decision making. As Fritz Ermarth notes, in his article "Contrasts in

Soviet and American Strategic Thought," the Soviet style of doctrinal thinking does not accommodate the kind of bargaining and risk management that go with a strategy of controlled nuclear exchanges. These are more characteristic of the American worldview, with its technological optimism and its emphasis on "makeability" and personal control of one's actions. The formation of American nuclear doctrine is dominated by lawyers, economists, and engineers, not soldiers. Its simplified scenarios display a quantitative orientation and the style of a pluralistic policy process, with bargains struck on the basis of the players' skills and calculations of short-term gain. American strategy also tends to treat nuclear weapons as unique and omnipotent technological tools and to set deterrence theory quite apart from other military doctrine, in a theoretical world all its own. The Soviets view nuclear warfare and weapons as being very much within traditional military doctrine and Marxist thought. The weapons' destructiveness may prompt decision makers to act cautiously, but nuclear power does not change the forces of history or the fundamental politico-military equation.

The two contrasting worldviews also shape different attitudes toward the use of force and the practice of diplomacy. The United States sees war and peace as mutually exclusive; the Soviet Union sees world politics as an endless and continuous struggle. Americans depreciate power politics, treating policy made on the basis of calculations of force as a "dirty" business. The Russians know no other way but armed struggle for staying alive, as a people and as a state. The two nations' completely opposite experiences of war and development left the United States feeling optimistic and invincible, the Soviet Union pessimistic and vulnerable. And the diplomacy of the superpowers reflects the domestic environment out of which it comes: American policy zigs and zags according to who is speaking and what outcome of the moment the pluralist process has decreed. Soviet policy is monolithic and slow to change, the product of a highly centralized bureaucracy and a political elite that rules by consensus.

There are some similarities in attitude, however. Both nations were fundamentally isolationist and xenophobic before they became superpowers. They were frontier societies, for whom foreign policy was somewhat of a distraction from their vast internal development needs. Both are messianic states, with universalistic creeds, and both subscribe to materialist philosophies that celebrate the controlling influence of the laws of economics — although the creeds and philosophies themselves are so at odds that they are actually a source of intense competition. Both nations have had trouble reconciling the conflicting impulses of missionary zeal and xenophobic isolation. Each has undergone a recent crisis of confidence stemming from a traumatic defeat (Vietnam and Afghanistan), the loss of bloc solidarity, and the rise of polycentrism. They have paid the costs of messianism, not only in inflamed bilateral relations with one another but in strained relations with allies that resisted strict ideological conformity or the subordination of nationalist feelings to the superpower's self-proclaimed leadership. Both nations have come to appreciate their mutual interest in managing the nuclear threat, just as each has learned that the possession of such weapons sets limits to their involvement in secondary conflicts. Certainly each has learned that it cannot remake the world in its own image.

Both superpowers have had their preeminence challenged and have suffered crises in their respective spheres of influence. Soviet foreign policy has been indelibly marked by transformative events in its East European sphere, the corridor for repeated invasions and more recently the focus of nationalist dissent from Soviet hegemony. Postwar shifts in Soviet foreign policy are traceable to a number of dramatic crises. The Kremlin leadership became more aggressive after the suppression of the Hungarian uprising of 1956, the *Sputnik* space launch of 1957, and the downing of Gary Powers's U-2 reconnaissance plane over Russia in 1960. It became more moderate after the Cuban Missile Crisis of 1962 and a second intervention in Czechoslovakia in 1968. Although these policy moves came too swiftly to be attributed to changes in national character, such an accumulation of traumatic events can eventually alter fundamental attitudes. There is no doubt that the repeated uprisings in Eastern Europe, along with the failed policy in Afghanistan, have changed the Soviet leadership's perceptions about the universal applicability of the Soviet model and the utility of military force in achieving revolutionary transformation. Some argue that Gorbachev is slowly incorporating the liberalizing experiments of Eastern Europe into the Soviet system itself. If his domestic reforms are brought to fruition, they will surely have a long-term moderating impact on Soviet foreign policy. If they fail, the inertia of authoritarian practices will doubtless be traced to resistant elements of Russian national character, overlaid with an encrusted Marxist ideology.

In like manner, U.S. foreign policy, which has revolved for a century and a half around the special hemispheric relationship with Latin America, has been powerfully affected by events that threaten to disturb this private preserve. Ever since 1823, when the Monroe Doctrine declared the Western Hemisphere off limits to European intervention, the United States has enjoyed hegemony there. But that hegemony was shaken by the victories of revolutionary Marxist regimes in Cuba and Nicaragua. These losses, as well as the still more traumatic defeat in Vietnam, forced a fundamental reassessment of America's power position and ideological appeal. The loss in Cuba led to the preemptive Alliance for Progress, on the one hand, and to more interventionist policies in the Dominican Republic and Chile, on the other. Then the Sandinista victory in Nicaragua, plus the Soviet invasion of Afghanistan, the Iranian hostage crisis, and a general perception of declining U.S. power, brought forth the assertive policies of President Reagan.

As with the Soviet Union, American foreign policy has been affected by domestic perceptions of strength and weakness. The Soviets have responded to stalemate at home and declining power abroad by a turn to liberalization and a call for détente. The Americans have reacted to their diminished economic performance and challenges to their preeminence with a posture of greater assertiveness, even belligerence. Partly these attitudes were the result of the different generational perspectives of the older Reagan, a true Cold Warrior, and the younger Gorbachev. Partly they reflect different national styles — the Americans impatient and inclined to the quick technological fix, the Soviets inclined to take the long view while making a temporary strategic retreat. And partly they point up the different lessons the two elites drew from their foreign policy defeats. To many Americans, the fiasco in Vietnam was due to political weakness at home, a malady that a crusading president could cure by showing he was not afraid to flex America's military muscle. The Soviets, on the other hand, seem to have found the domestic costs of the arms race unacceptable and to have acknowledged the inevitability of socialist pluralism, which no longer allows the Soviet Union to dictate to its neighbors or allies. By 1990, a majority of Muscovites, according to a Soviet public opinion poll, had responded to economic stagnation and the Communist collapse in Eastern Europe by abandoning their belief in Marxism in favor of market principles and parliamentary democracy.

We can readily see that both U.S. and Soviet foreign policy has undergone long-term changes in outlook and style. Traditional U.S. isolationism has rapidly decayed under the impact of superpower status and global responsibilities. Feelings of invincibility and theories of manifest destiny have been shipwrecked on the shores of Cuba, Vietnam, Lebanon, and Nicaragua. U.S. moralism and liberalism's assumptions of natural harmony between self-determining systems were more true of President Woodrow Wilson than of, say, President Richard Nixon and Henry Kissinger, who represented a new postwar strain of realism in the political culture of America's foreign policy elite. In Russia, the Bolshevik operational code, which describes a black-and-white world of stark contrasts and inevitable conflict, has softened considerably as the Soviet Union has moved further and further from its revolutionary Marxist roots. The fear of annihilation, the vigilance against concessions, the aggressive exploitation of every opportunity to expand, the stereotyping of capitalist opponents, the confidence in socialism's inevitable victory have all been modified in the light of Soviet experience. Their superpower status and the protection afforded by nuclear arms have made the Soviets more secure and more flexible. The long period of bilateral diplomacy and an appreciation of the virtues of America's scientific-technical revolution have given the Soviets a more pragmatic and realistic assessment of the United States. And greater independence and pluralism within the international Communist movement have forced the Marxists to revise their assumptions about the nature and future of socialism.

NATIONAL INTEREST

Every nation-state's foreign policy is said to serve the national interest — but national interest is an extremely ambiguous and much-debated concept. Political leaders invoke it repeatedly to justify actions ranging from the most vital to the most trivial. The concept is of limited use in explaining, predicting, or prescribing the behavior of foreign policy decision makers. Nonetheless, an attempt to define a nation's interests can reveal a great deal about the guiding principles of its foreign policy and how it coordinates means and ends.

The National Interest as Diplomats Define It Objectively

Diplomats, the professionals of foreign policy, take an objective approach to the national interest; politicians take a more subjective approach, as discussed in the next section. The objective school looks on foreign policy as a science practiced by professional diplomats, who are the guardians of a nation's vital and enduring interests. The primary interest of every nation is its territorial security, its survival as a political unit, and the preservation of its core values and cultural identity. Other national interests, specific to each country, derive rationally from the geopolitical realities, the nature of the political-economic system, the structure of alliances, and the strategic requirements for protecting, above all else, the nation's security and power resources. In this conception, foreign policy is a nonpolitical or bipartisan endeavor that responds logically to the requirements of the international arena. Democratic nations differ little from dictatorships: the price of sovereignty is the same for all. The only significant variables are whether a state is big or small, rich or poor, interdependent or self-sufficient, seafaring or landlocked, secure or vulnerable. Once they are factored into the power equation, a good diplomat can calculate a rational foreign policy for any government.

In the diplomat's conception, the national interest is best defined by a *synoptic-comprehensive* process, by which policies are formulated in accordance with a formal *plan* or *strategy*. Decision making passes through organized stages of problem recognition and definition, the selection of goals, identification of alternatives, and, finally, choice. The plan is articulated by the chief of state, in cooperation with the foreign secretary and national security advisers. They weigh the vital interests of the nation in a comprehensive process that establishes priorities among the various aims and carefully judges which instruments of policy are most likely to achieve each aim. Choices are based on core values, which determine the hierarchy of interests, and on cost-benefit calculations, which measure the feasibility and the risks of all the options. To the professional, domestic politics is largely a source of confusion and inefficiency and is best excluded. A democracy can conduct a successful foreign policy in competition with autocratic regimes if it will leave matters in the hands of its president or prime minister, the only official in a position to act in a prudent, prompt, and informed manner. The implication of this view is that the failures of American foreign policy are largely the result of a meddling Congress, the inflammatory and irresponsible rhetoric of politicians, and the volatility of a divided and ignorant populace.

The objective school holds that the chief executive and his or her staff of foreign policy professionals are the only proper repositories for the national interest. The professional diplomat, by virtue of interacting in a setting that requires an intimate understanding of the interests of other states, is the best judge of the value of various policy trade-offs. The professional is uniquely situated to see any positive connections between the national interest and wider human or global interests. He or she can afford to take the long view politically, ignoring short-term or selfish demands from private interests. The career diplomat is the most likely of all those who are politically accountable to appreciate that the long run will become the short run eventually; chief executives who refuse to face hidden long-term security issues will undoubtedly be confronted with them later, under much less favorable crisis conditions. A rational policy will consequently plan prudently for the future, shaping alternatives as the opportunity arises rather than being purely reactive. When crises do occur, the national security apparatus of the executive branch is the appropriate locus of decision, for only it has the requisite tools to take speedy and effective action. Only the head of state can reconcile competing private interests with an overarching conception of the common good. A president or secretary of state acting as chief diplomat has both the power and the responsibility for taming the domestic bureaucracy and educating the public. In a rational diplomacy, the national interest is something to be dispassionately defined and defended by those who possess the expertise and the perspective to speak for the whole nation.

The National Interest as Politicians Define It Subjectively

The second school of thought offers a more subjective definition of the national interest, based on the assumption that political values stand above the science of means and ends. This school argues that even the planner's hierarchy of interests is derived from political choices, which cannot be objectified. What is vital to one political party or leader may not seem so to another. All important foreign policy choices flow from the character of the system whose security the diplomat is pledged to protect. And who but the people or the party can say how much or what kind of security is enough, and at what price? The diplomat may be able to say which instruments of policy will gain what results, but it is the political leadership that defines the vital interests and guiding purposes. A nation's foreign policy must represent a balance among competing domestic interests as much as between competing states, armies, or strategies.

This political conception presumes that the national interest cannot be defined in the abstract or for all time, since a nation is constantly evolving, and the needs and desires of its constituent elements change. The national interest consists of whatever principles, guidelines, or claims the current decision makers may advance to justify their actions. Although the definition will change with a shift of regime or administration and in reaction to current needs or international circumstances, it does reflect the values and political perceptions of the citizens and their foreign policy leadership. It is responsive to the political adjustments and consensus building that occur among diverse elements of the political leadership and the foreign affairs bureaucracy. In a democratic society, a subjective national interest will accommodate the subnational and pluralistic interests that are always present. A degree of consistency is provided through the influence of national character, the sum of the nation's historical experiences, ideology, and underlying habits and values — though the latter, too, are subjective and difficult to quantify, predict, or analyze scientifically.

Particularly in a democracy, it is unrealistic to expect foreign policy to conform to a planner's or a diplomat's ideal model. Democracy, by definition, represents a multiplicity of voices and perspectives, and its policies cannot be formulated in an ivory tower by a professional elite or be imposed on an unwilling public. As even the Soviets discovered in Afghanistan, a head of state cannot act effectively if he or she does not enjoy the full support of the populace.

Moreover, no formal plan or strategy can predict which policies will work in specific circumstances. The most experienced of diplomats can never foresee all the hazards in the way of implementing a policy. In an environment of competition and uncertainty, policy is best made in *incremental* steps that are arrived at through a process of *partisan mutual adjustment* and constant *political feedback*. Judgments about what is valuable and vital are incorporated into the debate over the various marginal adjustments, in what Charles Lindblom, in *The Intelligence of Democracy,* calls a process of "successive limited comparisons." Each incremental step is reversible if domestic support is not forthcoming or if international circumstances prove unfavorable. Competing interests and priorities are automatically reconciled during the consensus-building process.

In principle, there is general agreement that the primary national interest is the protection of a nation's security and the promotion of its political values and economic welfare. Policies that preserve national cohesion, territorial integrity, and the stability of the regime presumably are always desirable, as is the establishment of a world order favorable to the regime's ideology. What is more difficult is to make a judgment about whether a particular policy will further these general aims. The U.S. national interest can be articulated in terms of broad propositions, but how they are to be implemented is always open to question. A policy designed to promote one vital interest may conflict with a policy designed to promote another that is equally important.

To take one example, it is certainly in the U.S. national interest to prevent nuclear war, contain communism, protect international trade, maintain key alliances and important spheres of influence, promote democracy abroad, and sustain economic welfare at home. These goals can be embodied in a series of policy commitments. In the area of nuclear arms, it could be U.S. policy to maintain a credible deterrent threat, seek arms control or reductions when they can be reliably verified, and prevent nuclear proliferation. To contain communism, the United States might decide to oppose radical regimes and revolutionary change, while embracing as allies any governments that opposed the Soviet Union. In alliance relations, America could seek to preserve NATO solidarity and secure strategic allies in Central America, the Middle East, and the Persian Gulf. The deployment of a 600-ship navy and economic sanctions against any nation that engaged in unfair trade practices are measures that would protect trade. Promoting democracy might involve support for liberation movements in Eastern Europe and the Third World, the withdrawal of support for repressive regimes, the encouragement of self-determination, protection of human rights, and perhaps aid in the global redistribution of wealth. To enhance economic welfare, the United States could seek a favorable balance of payments, access to cheap raw materials abroad, and the protection or even expansion of foreign investment.

But the moment we set out foreign policy goals so specifically, the internal contradictions immediately become apparent. Is the economic welfare of Americans better served by tariff barriers that keep jobs at home and restore a favorable balance of trade, or by free-trade policies that bring them a greater variety of inexpensive imports? Should the United States have intervened, in the name of democracy and anti-Communism, to assist Hungarian, Polish, or Lithuanian nationalists trying to rid their countries of Soviet domination, even at the risk of war? Should the United States court the favor of a repressive Chinese Communist government because China offers trade or can help to contain Soviet power, even though the ideologies of China and America are incompatible? Does military intervention to preserve the traditional U.S. sphere of influence in Latin America promote democratic values or undermine them? These are questions that have no clear-cut answers in terms of a general set of national interests. Policies aimed at securing human rights in South Africa or Chile collide with policies for protecting or promoting U.S. investments. Sanctions against right-wing regimes that torture and left-wing regimes that nationalize foreign assets violate the principle of self-determination to which the United States is also committed. Foreign aid intended to cement an alliance or encourage economic democracy may be detrimental to domestic welfare and to the balance of payments. Deployments of arms designed to reassure nervous NATO allies or to aid a breakaway Soviet republic may antagonize the Russians and stand in the way of an arms control agreement. Controls on nuclear proliferation may conflict with arms export policies aimed at restoring a positive trade balance or beefing up U.S. influence abroad. Within a single category — say, preventing nuclear war or containing communism — judgments will vary on which policies best serve the national interest. One side will maintain that war and communist expansion can be prevented only by modernizing deterrent forces, taking a tough anti-Soviet stance, and adopting strong counterrevolutionary measures in the Third World. Another side will argue that peace and democracy are best promoted by a policy of détente, arms control, and accommodation with the radical nationalist revolutions of the Third World.

In light of such wide differences of opinion, the subjective approach holds that foreign policy must be guided by political considerations and that the locus of decision making must be at the lowest and broadest level possible. America's most serious foreign policy crises have occurred when an imperial president, in disregard of the democratic process, has tried to impose a policy on a reluctant Congress and public. The Bay of Pigs invasion of Cuba, covert intervention in the Angolan civil war, and CIA support for the *contras* in Nicaragua have all been fiascos precisely because they were conceived in secrecy. Their flaws would surely have emerged if they had undergone the scrutiny of vigorous public debate. The United States failed in Vietnam because the war was managed secretly by two presidents who refused to bring the facts of the conflict to the American people. Unrealistic rhetoric about the domino theory and democratic South Vietnam standing firm against communism was for too long protected from a healthy partisan dialogue that could have exposed its misguided assumptions. When dissenting voices did speak out, they were squelched by both presidents' abuses of constitutional power and by the concentration of decision making in the hands of a foreign policy elite out of touch with the mood of the country. A rational foreign policy, must proceed from the people and from an essentially political definition of the national interest.

A Realist View

It is the realist school that has made the fullest use of national interest, particularly its objective elements, as a guide to policy. The most able proponent of this approach, Hans Morgenthau, while acknowledging that it is difficult to specify the content of the national interest, believes that the concept is useful in setting priorities and developing guidelines for a prudent and rational foreign policy. He argues that national decision makers should distinguish between permanent and variable, primary and secondary, and long-term and short-term interests. Only by keeping an eye on its permanent, primary, and long-term interests can a state make a rational ordering of priorities and appropriately allocate its resources, since it cannot pursue all desirable aims at once. For example, the United States' primary interest in avoiding nuclear war with the Soviet Union has taken priority over the secondary interest of promoting the liberation of Eastern Europe. On the other hand, the presence of Soviet missiles in Cuba was judged enough of a threat to the primary security interest to be worth the risk of nuclear confrontation. Similarly, a short-term gain in the balance of trade from the imposition of tariff barriers must be measured against possible long-term damage to the principles of free trade.

The realists say this approach also protects the national interest from being usurped by subnational or supranational interests. Policy can be subverted by selfish economic, ethnic, or other special interests masquerading as the national interest, or it can be held to overly idealistic international standards like those of the United Nations (even though such norms do not restrain anyone's conduct). The national interest must also be disentangled from the narrow bureaucratic interests of the foreign policy elite and its agencies. Morgenthau argues that a self-conscious calculus of means and ends will protect a nation from policies influenced by partisan, wishful, or moralistic thinking, that a rational ordering of priorities will prevent the national interest and foreign policy from becoming prisoners of the political process.

In Morgenthau's theory, certain rules of rational diplomacy follow from placing the national interest at the center of policy. First, the hierarchy of priorities will control the choice of means, since a nation is not likely to employ armed might in support of any interests save the most vital. Many a war has been lost because a nation entered it carelessly, without measuring whether the stakes were worth the long-term costs. Second, the priority of national over supranational interests will determine alliance partnerships, since common interests must lie at the base of all formal pledges and treaty obligations or they will be stillborn. Many bilateral treaties and multilateral UN declarations have amounted to nothing because they did not reflect such a convergence of interests. Third, a clear-sighted view of the national interest will expedite diplomatic negotiations by establishing a distinction between secondary interests, which can be traded off, and primary interests, which must be guarded forcefully.

In addition, the realists, pessimistic about human nature and the potential for international anarchy, believe every nation should observe certain caveats, or rules of prudence: (1) To guard against unrestrained power, every nation should strive to maintain the balance of power. (2) No statesman has the right to sacrifice the national interest in pursuit of moral principles that may not be realizable; a prudent foreign policy will always seek the attainable gain in preference to the unattainable absolute good. (3) A nation should make no commitment beyond its means; a foreign policy not backed by the power to implement it is worthless. (4) A nation should opt for the temporary stability of an imperfect peace over the risky pursuit of all-out victory; an effective diplomacy always involves compromise and the adjustment of competing interests. Two other cautionary rules of the nuclear age reflect the declining utility of traditional force and the overriding interest of all nations in avoiding nuclear war. Because it may no longer be in the national interest to be allied with any state that has the potential for precipitating a nuclear war, states should avoid an unnecessary association with a nuclear-armed superpower patron. And the superpowers themselves should avoid commitments to unstable clients that may involve them in conflict.

An Idealist Critique

Though the realist's rules take us further down the road toward a rational diplomacy, they still do not tell us which particular policies are the best ones. In fact, the rules of prudence for nuclear diplomacy may conflict directly with the rules for defending vital interests by force or for seeking balance-of-power alliances with states that share common interests. On the basis of Morgenthau's theory, we cannot say whether the United States should reinforce its ties with NATO allies or withdraw its nuclear umbrella from Europe. In the case of Vietnam, Morgenthau argued persuasively that the United States should not have become involved: Southeast Asia was not an area of vital interest, and the United States did not possess the appropriate means for defending such interests as it did have. But other realists strongly supported the Vietnam War, maintaining that the United States failed because its policy, a rational one, came under contradictory domestic political constraints. The realists resolve all such confusions about what the national interest is by applying one universal principle: a policy is in the national interest if it increases a nation's power and autonomy, which presumably will increase the range of means available to the state and its overall freedom of action. As Morgenthau concludes, "interest is defined as power."

The idealist points out that such a definition of the national interest, solely in terms of power, risks the abandonment of a prudent search for appropriate, attainable ends in favor of a highly imprudent pursuit of unlimited means. As Arnold Wolfers has remarked, in his *Discord and Collaboration* (pp. 89 – 90), it is meaningless to argue for the expansion (or the abolition) of power outside the context of ends. National security is the protection of values previously acquired; national interest is the extension or application of those values in the international domain. Power is justified, and civilized, only in terms of the moral purposes it serves. However, the degree of power available or attainable frequently affects the choice of ends. As a nation's armed power alternatives increase, its ambitions may swell or it may resort more frequently to the readily available tool of armed might. A powerful state may define its national interest so expansively that it ends up policing all the world to protect its interests. The quest for security then slowly turns into policies of intervention or domination, which may embroil the nation in a fruitless arms race and the expenditure of resources that could better be used in pursuing other national values or interests. In an era of interdependence, such a search for autonomy may be self-defeating or achievable only at too high an economic cost.

The realist, while assuming that reason can be applied to national affairs, does not grant the equally logical proposition that it is also possible to rationally define and pursue common global interests. Indeed, the idealists say, the avoidance of nuclear war is only one of several interests common to all states. Just as a state has geopolitical constraints that determine prudent policy, so the planet has geophysical limits, which are exceeded at a cost to everyone. The realist's focus on power as the means of resolving conflict may rob nations of their ability to recognize a community of interests and nonviolent paths to peace. A wise national security policy will always take into account the interests of other states and the security interests of the international system as a whole. The idealist definition of the national interest seeks to maximize the opportunity for win-win solutions that will leave all parties satisfied, rather than win-lose situations that protect the national interest but sow the seeds of future conflict. The image of international affairs as a Darwinian fight for survival also obscures the fact that most of the contested issues are far short of threats to a nation's existence or core values. They tend to be disputes over elite interests, credibility, prestige, access to resources, protection of a nonessential ally, extension of a sphere of influence, and other intermediate interests. Whether these should be defended by force is not something to be decided apart from political considerations, for which the realist's definition of the national interest provides no guidance. Probably the best answer is a subjective choice by majority vote — though such a referendum on the "interests of state" is rare.

Lacking an infallible guide to the national interest, a decision maker's own conscience, value preferences, and judgment about the limits of force have a legitimate role to play.

To sum up the idealist position, a nation cannot define its primary interests or order national priorities except by reference to politics and fundamental values. Geopolitical requirements and the disposition of power cannot by themselves tell a statesman what is the right thing to do, which means are consistent with national values, or which policy is likely to succeed. The protection of the status quo and an efficient matching of means and ends are no substitute for the process of moral choice — the only true basis for a hierarchy of national interests.

NATIONAL DECISION MAKING

An immense range of variables, domestic and international, influences the decisions of national policy makers. To understand how states come into conflict or resolve their differences, it is necessary to examine not just their external statements and actions, but their internal decision-making processes. The making of foreign policy represents a complex interplay of internal forces in which no one individual appears to play the central role. Decisions must be made in light of what is both politically feasible at home and permissible in the larger international context. The foreign policy process, lying on the boundary between domestic and international politics, is an arena in which national leaders strive to fulfill personal, political, organizational, and national interests, all the while seeking to reconcile the desirable with the possible and to arbitrate between internal and external demands. The national actor is always limited by international circumstances, including power considerations and such systemic influences as the structure of alliances and the degree of economic interdependence. Internally, decisions reflect a consensus within the political elite, the application of common goals and principles to a process of political accommodation. National character, as we have already seen, gives the political elite its perspective and foreign policy its underlying motive forces.

But the domestic forces at work in national decision making also include the mechanisms by which the national interest is defined and decisions made, and this is the primary focus of the following sections. To describe how the foreign policy machinery works, we enlist the aid of several models of the decision process, in an analysis heavily indebted to Graham Allison's seminal work, *Essence of Decision: Explaining the Cuban Missile Crisis.* Allison employs three models, or conceptual frameworks, of the decision-making process: the *rational actor* model, the *organizational process* model, and the *governmental politics* model, all of which emphasize problem solving and governmental processes. However, since the policy process is often distorted — and occasionally transformed creatively — by individual acts, elite attitudes, crowd behavior, and other psychological influences, we will supplement Allison's institutional approach with additional models that focus on the social-psychological elements of *leadership, perceptions,* and *group dynamics.*

Rational Action

Our first model treats national decision making as analogous to the rational actions of a purposive individual. It personifies the state, as though it were a unitary actor — as we do when we say that "the Soviet Union" did this and "Israel" did that. In this model, the actor takes the detached perspective of the armchair analyst and asks: "What is the rational thing to do in a certain situation to meet a specified objective?" But such a shorthand way of speaking is a great simplification of the decision process. The actor is really engaging in a theoretical reenactment, or vicarious problem solving, rather than accurately describing how an actual decision was reached. Nonetheless, every one of these attempts at analysis reveals additional assumptions about which questions are most important, what types of evidence are relevant, and which variables are the controlling ones. Taken together, the assumptions constitute an implicit or explicit conceptual model that establishes the categories within which a problem will be considered. The model of the state as a unitary, rational actor helps us see what the internal and external incentives and pressures are that lead a government to adopt a particular course of action. The logical approach gives a strategic perspective on the problem and a way of calculating the costs and benefits of alternative courses of action. Treating the nation as a unit helps in identifying the influence of national character — those common values and behavioral tendencies that create a propensity to respond in certain ways.

The rational actor model explains foreign policy conflicts in terms of competing objectives and national styles. Actions are not haphazard or random, but the result of self-conscious, rational choices between alternatives related to a specified goal. Policies reflect the clear intentions of those who do the deciding and their judgments about the consequences of alternative choices. Strategies are selected by measuring available means against international constraints. The decision to purchase certain weapons, say, would be justified logically by a stated national objective or military doctrine.

Most of the strategic thinking exemplified in nuclear scenarios and war games follows this classical method of analytic simplification, which treats a nation as responding to a given set of interests in a consistent, value-maximizing way, without regard for irrational acts or internal contradictions. Deterrence theory assumes that national decision makers act on the basis of rational calculations of costs and benefits and that a stable nuclear balance can therefore be achieved by deploying an invulnerable second-strike force. An adversary that launched a first strike against such a force would find the costs, as measured by the risk of retaliation, all out of proportion to any possible gain. Under these conditions of rational deterrence, national decision makers will never choose nuclear war except under the most extreme provocation or when the most vital national interests are at stake. Limited military actions and crises that could lead to general war can presumably be managed by a rational thinking through of the problem and its alternative solutions. Leaders of all nations will communicate clearly, bargain reasonably, and select logical means appropriate to the threatened interests.

Organizational Process

Our next model treats national decisions as unintended outcomes produced by competing interests in a highly differentiated decision-making structure. National policy is the result of "innumerable and often conflicting smaller actions by individuals at various levels of bureaucratic organizations in the service of a variety of only partially compatible conceptions of national goals, organizational goals, and political objectives" (Allison, p. 6). In this organizational process model, decisions are the output of large organizations whose goals are parochial and who function according to preexisting bureaucratic repertoires and standard operating procedures. Governments are not centrally controlled, completely informed entities pursuing consistent objectives but, rather, are conglomerates of loosely allied, quasi-independent organizations. Leaders can coordinate the work of these organizations somewhat, but they are only partially successful in controlling them. The agencies collect, manage, and transmit information not so much with an eye to effective problem solving as to perpetuate the organization and protect its budget and routines. The power of such bureaucratic organizations lies in their ability to determine the options that come to higher officials for decision. The organizations prejudice policy by resisting options that fall outside familiar horizons and by acting in line with existing programs and procedures. The behavior of bureaucratic personnel follows well-established patterns of role expectations.

Top decision makers, who have limited time and attention to give to the complex and innately risky business of foreign policy, must rely on the bureaucratic agencies to make and carry out policy. The policy makers split up problems into their several parts and turn them over to separate agencies with specialized concerns. The United States has a Department of State, a Department of Defense, a Central Intelligence Agency, an Arms Control and Disarmament Agency, a National Security Council, and dozens more organizations with overlapping jurisdictions, and each agency makes policy according to its own perspective and interests. (For a comparison of the American and Soviet foreign affairs bureaucracies, see Figures 7-1 and 7-2.)

An agency rarely searches among all possible options for the best policy. Typically, it focuses on the problems that are pushed onto its agenda by crisis, the agency's interests, or the annual budget review. Problems other than the standard ones are often dealt with sluggishly or inappropriately. Uncertainty is avoided, whenever possible, by delay, by deal making, by short-term solutions, by management according to a familiar plan or repertoire. Contingencies are handled in accordance with standard prefabricated scenarios. Most

FIGURE 7-1
ADMINISTRATION OF U.S. FOREIGN AFFAIRS

Constitutional Responsibility/Policy Leadership

President
(Head of government/Head of state)

Interagency Policy Coordination/Policy Advice

National Security Council

(Flexible system of interagency committees at various levels and of varying composition depending on subject matter)

Departments and Agencies and Their Functions

Department of State (Responsibilities in all foreign affairs branches)	Department of Defense, Arms Control and Disarmament Agency	Departments of Agriculture, Commerce, Energy, Labor, Treasury; Export-Import Bank; International Trade Commission; Overseas Private Investment Corporation; U.S. Trade Representative; International Development and Cooperation Agency; Agency for International Development	United States Information Agency	Intelligence Community

Foreign Affairs Function

Political Affairs (General foreign policy and conduct of relations with foreign countries)	Politico-Military Affairs (Mutual defense, strategic policy, arms control)	International Commercial and Economic Affairs (Trade, investment, monetary affairs, foreign aid)	Information and Educational and Cultural Exchange (Contact with foreign audiences through government media; promotion of people-to-people relations)	Intelligence (Collection and analysis of information bearing on the conduct of foreign relations)

FIGURE 7-2
ADMINISTRATION OF SOVIET FOREIGN AFFAIRS

Constitutional Responsibility/Policy Leadership

President	General Secretary/Communist Party of the Soviet Union (CPSU) Politburo/Central Committee of the CPSU
Council of Ministers of the USSR	Supreme Soviet Committees on International Relations, State Security and Defense

Interagency Policy Coordination/Policy Advice
Presidential Council

Departments and Agencies and their Functions

	Departments and Agencies and their Functions		Foreign Affairs Function
Foreign Ministry International Affairs Commission of the Central Committee/CPSU	Ministry of Foreign Economic Relations Foreign Ministry	State Committee for Science and Technology State Committee for Cultural Relations with Foreign Countries Secretariat/CPSU: International Department Propaganda Department Union of Soviet Societies for Friendship and Cultural Relations with Foreign Countries	Secretariat/CPSU: Department for Liaison with Communist and Workers' Parties of Socialist Countries International Department
Defense Ministry Defense industry ministries Secretariat/CPSU: Department of Defense Industry		Committee for State Security (KGB)	
Military Affairs			
Political Affairs	International Commercial and Economic Affairs	Information, Educational and Cultural Exchange	Intelligence Relations with Communist Parties and International Fronts

Note: Soviet policy institutions are in rapid flux. This chart incorporates the 1990 constitutional changes, which have created a cabinet-style Presidential Council and elevated the role of the Supreme Soviet (and the Congress of People's Deputies) while downgrading party organs. Still, there exists a parallel bureaucracy of party-state control, as reflected in Gorbachev's joint position as president and general-secretary of the CPSU.

bureaucrats seek not to maximize national values but to satisfy urgent demands by coming up with minimally acceptable solutions. Trade-offs — hard choices between goals — are avoided, and conflicting demands are addressed in sequence, without any attempt to relate them or to reconcile incompatible elements. With power fractionated and centralized supervision of every action impossible, competing policies are often implemented simultaneously in different parts of the bureaucracy: "The right hand does not always know what the left hand is doing." Decisions may depend not at all on what is rational, but on which organization has the responsibility for defining the problem or finding a solution: "If the principal tool one possesses is a hammer, there is an overpowering temptation to treat everything like a nail." An organization's operating style is relatively inflexible. An agency's capabilities set practical limits to what the top leader can do, and a decision triggers an organizational routine that may have little resemblance to what the leader wants or "chooses." Continuity is the primary characteristic of organizational behavior, and existing practice is the best predictor of future performance. Policies that diverge too greatly from existing norms and routines are especially likely to fail. In short, outcomes frequently do not coincide with the formal decisions of a nation's leaders.

Bureaucratic organizations, basically parochial in outlook, tend to focus their attention on the needs of their own personnel and constituents. Institutional loyalty, role expectations, and group pressures are powerful in shaping their behavior. Operational priorities are not tailored to the various decisions or problems, but are established in accordance with work routines, habitual patterns of association, existing information channels, the distribution of rewards within the organization, and prevailing interest-group pressures. The organization's health is defined not by effective performance but by the number of persons assigned and the dollars appropriated. Areas of responsibility are jealously guarded and interagency relations governed by budget-splitting formulas, established practices, and informal but powerful "rules of the game." Organizations are interested in controlling choices, in limiting rather than maximizing options. Alternatives outside existing organizational goals are simply not considered, and an "orphan" policy that falls between jurisdictions has almost no chance unless an agency advocate adopts it. Policies that are hostile to an agency's goals or difficult to implement are simply ignored, for the most part. With political leaders usually too busy to follow up and in office for relatively short terms, the tenured bureaucrat often is acting on behalf of the nation after the politician is long gone.

The tactics of the foreign affairs bureaucracy are aptly described by Leslie Gelb and Morton Halperin in an article entitled "The Ten Commandments of the Foreign Affairs Bureaucracy." Bureaucrats protect a favored policy option from political interference by claiming that it is a matter of "national security" — too sacred to be tainted by crass domestic political considerations. They curtail opportunities for public scrutiny by the claim that a wide airing would reveal "extremely sensitive information." They typically present options as two ridiculous extremes framing a jumbled, inconsistent, but politically palatable middle course that makes every bureaucrat a winner. An agency pleads "infeasibility" to disqualify an undesired option or insists on an all-or-nothing choice that leaves the agency free to implement the policy as it sees fit. Predictions of dire consequences are employed to motivate a president's decision in the face of little information and high risk. Since indecision might erode an agency's credibility and persuasiveness, close decisions within the agency are portrayed to outsiders or higher-ups in the most stark and compelling terms. To get around the tendency of policy makers to delay making controversial decisions, appeals to action often have a now-or-never quality. Bureaucrats resist policy proposals by agreeing in principle but appealing for delay until the timing is more propitious. Other opposition strategies include resisting orders and leaking information in the hope of appealing to a more sympathetic audience. Bureaucrats also try to prevent issues from reaching the president, especially when there is an existing authorization that permits them to act on their own. If an issue must pass to the top, they make every effort to present it as a fait accompli. Finally, they offer only those options that will be persuasive within the present policy framework. Rarely do bureaucrats advocate steps that differ more than incrementally from existing policies.

In the organizational process model, it is not the logic of deterrence that controls the decision about nuclear war. When bureaucratic mechanisms and standard operating procedures make it possible for intragovernmental agencies to initiate a launch decision, then the probability of war goes up, regardless of what the strategic balance is. If the routines for putting a nation's nuclear forces on alert are loose or unpracticed, the risk of accidental launch rises. If the plans and procedures of subordinate organizations, particularly the armed forces, have a tendency to function autonomously, on a kind of automatic pilot, then top decision makers can lose control of events in a nuclear showdown. In the midst of crisis, certain options may be unavailable to a president or a general-secretary simply because the bureaucracy has not foreseen them and is not prepared to implement them. Big organizations cannot carry out complex tasks without practicing at least some of the elements in advance. Military deployment, training, and weaponry typically are planned to meet a limited number of scenarios. When ordered to do something quite unexpected, the military bureaucracy generally delivers from its existing repertoire only an approximation of the desired policy. Often the favored scenarios are controlling: bureaucrats and decision makers respond to their habitual image of the enemy or to the familiar war scenario, not to the reality they are confronting. And the scenarios themselves may have been selected for purely organizational reasons — to enhance the mission of a particular agency or facilitate a desired procurement decision. Weapons decisions in the arms race have rarely been rational countermoves with clear strategic justification, but more often have been choices from the preferred menu of a military service, a defense industry, a research and design lab, or a congressional committee — menus that reflect personal preferences, careerism, interest-group pressures, logrolling, interagency bargaining, and bureaucratic imperialism.

Allison gives this summary of the organizational model's implications for nuclear war:

The lesson: nuclear crises between machines as large as the United States and Soviet governments are inherently chancy. The information and estimates available to leaders about the situation will reflect organizational goals and routines as well as the facts. The alternatives presented to the leaders will be much narrower than the menu of options that would be desirable. The execution of choices will exhibit unavoidable rigidities of programs and [standard operating procedures]. Coordination among organizations will be much less finely tuned than leaders demand or expect. The prescription: considerable thought must be given to the routines established in the principal organizations before a crisis so that during the crisis organizations will be capable of performing adequately the needed functions. In the crisis, the overwhelming problem will be that of control and coordination of large organizations. (p. 260)

Governmental Politics

A third model of the decision-making process focuses on governmental politics. In this perspective, foreign policy decisions are neither rational choices nor bureaucratic outputs. They are the result of various bargaining games among the players in the national government. The perceptions, motivations, positions, power, and maneuvers of the players determine outcomes. What gets decided depends very much on which bargaining arena or action channel the issue arises in, who gets into the political game, and how skillful the players are. The political pressures of the job, past stances and public commitments, and the personalities of the central players influence decisions. The selection of issues is itself politically determined or contested, with political relevance and the urgency of demands for action more important than an issue's bearing on the national welfare or the long-term interests of the state. Issues are forced to a resolution by elections, the pressure of public opinion, and deadlines imposed by crisis, budget review, a scheduled speech, or some other point of pressure (and hence decision) in the political process. In the political model, competing groups with a diversity of goals and values identify with different policies. As Roger Hilsman has pointed out, in *The Politics of Policymaking in Defense and Foreign Affairs,* the relative power of these competing groups is as relevant to the final decision as is the appeal of their goals or the cogency of their arguments:

> The test of a policy is not whether it is in fact the most rational means for achieving an agreed-upon objective or whether the objective is in the true national interest. The test of a policy is whether enough of the people and organizations having a stake in the policy and holding power agree to that policy. Policy faces inward as much as outward, seeking to reconcile conflicting goals, to adjust aspirations to available means, and to accommodate to one another the different advocates of competing goals and aspirations. It is here that the essence of government and policy seems to lie, in a process that is essentially political. (p. 65)

The political decision-making elite is not a monolithic group. Even a highly autocratic system has factions, competing personalities, informal coalitions. Sovietologists have spent much of their time looking for hidden nuances in public speeches and actions that will reveal the political fissures in the facade of Communist party unity. In every government, individuals in the leadership group are separate players in a competitive game. Although distinctly positioned in the hierarchy of the established decision-making circuit, each has an independent political stake, and each bargains to realize national, organizational, and personal goals as he or she sees them. Many games, or sets of political negotiations, are going on at once, over a wide range of issues. Power struggles intersect, and gains or losses in one game affect the outcome of others. Political debts from one bargaining context may be called due by a powerful player on another issue. Responses do not further a consistent set of strategic objectives, but are the compromise — and often inconsistent — outcomes of political pulling and hauling. A decision will often be not the most rational one but the preference of the most powerful player. In the competitive atmosphere, players are less concerned about the best solution than they are about selecting an option for which they can mobilize a winning coalition or that has a high probability of being successfully implemented. Government action is not to be construed as always representing government intentions. Policy is the sum of the behaviors of various national representatives and often has little relationship to a single national objective, a unity of preferences, agreement on doctrine or strategy, or the desire of any one player to set policy or send a consistent message.

Foreign policy is no different from any political problem in that reasonable persons will always disagree about appropriate solutions. Individual members of the political elite carry various responsibilities and have distinct vantage points. Different positions confer different power resources, advantages, and obligations. The president, who bears the final responsibility, wants to keep his options open, but competing cabinet members want to tie the president's hands and force him to embrace their preferred options. What each player sees and what each judges to be important varies tremendously. Players conflict in personality and operating style. They come into office with political baggage: sensitivities on certain issues, commitments to various projects, personal standing with key support groups, political debts. All are presumably committed to some notion of the common good or an overarching national interest and to avoiding a wrong choice that could damage the nation and their own political careers. But each sees this interest in a different way and feels obliged to fight for what he or she believes is right. Foreign policy decisions either ratify the political victors in these intramural struggles or, more often, embody a mixture of conflicting preferences and unresolved power plays. A nation's foreign policy is very often not what any one person desires or intends. It is not shaped just by

> the reasons that support a course of action, or the routines of organizations that enact an alternative, but the power and skill of proponents and opponents of the action in question. . . . Thus the character of emerging issues and the pace at which the game is played converge to yield government "decisions" and "actions" as collages. Choices by one player (e.g., to authorize action by his department, to make a speech, or to refrain from acquiring certain information),

resultants of minor games (e.g., the wording of a cable or the decision on departmental action worked out among lower-level players), resultants of central games (e.g., decisions, actions, and speeches bargained out among central players), and "foul-ups" (e.g., choices that are not made because they are not recognized or are raised too late, misunderstandings, etc.) — these pieces, when stuck to the same canvas, constitute government behavior relevant to an issue. (Allison, pp. 145 – 46)

The governmental politics model of decision making makes us aware that political conflict, diplomacy, alliances, and coalition building are as much present within a government as between competing nation-states. Political leaders emerge on the basis of professional reputation, public prestige, and their power to persuade. Richard Neustadt's *Presidential Power* shows that U.S. presidents have been able to control foreign policy less by the formal powers of the office than by their skill in convincing other players that what the president wants them to do is in their own best interests. The power to command is rare, as President Harry S Truman recognized in his comment about the president-elect, General Dwight D. Eisenhower: "He'll sit here and he'll say, 'Do this! Do that!' *And nothing will happen.* Poor Ike — it won't be a bit like the Army. He'll find it very frustrating" (cited in Neustadt, p. 9). Only under special conditions will even a direct presidential command be carried out: his personal prestige must be directly and unambiguously committed; his words must be clear and not subject to conflicting interpretation; the order must be widely publicized; the organization to which it is directed must be in control of every factor necessary for carrying it out; and the organization must not question the wisdom of the decision or doubt the president's authority to issue it. Such politically straightforward circumstances yield self-executing orders — but few problems are so clear-cut, and fewer presidents are able to muster the time, the attention, or the political capital for a sustained exercise of command. Presidents invest their power resources on a few carefully picked issues; all the rest they must bargain over or leave to other political players to resolve.

Every foreign policy decision has domestic political consequences for the players. Some issues are taken up because they can make a player's reputation, and others are ignored because they are no-win propositions politically, regardless of their importance for the nation's long-term welfare. The losers in a policy battle may go away disgruntled and ready to make trouble in the future. The policy may turn out badly and have political repercussions, or the right decision may be a gamble on which no leader will risk his political hide. So leaders hedge their bets. They search the political horizon for cues from opinion makers and attentive members of the public. They lead much like Charlie Chaplin did when he saw which way the crowd was running, grabbed a flag, and got out in front. They adopt policies that they hope will please all their important constituencies. They make "paper" policy and then do nothing but wait for the problem to go away or the political dust to settle. Or they make deals, promising the losers a favorable outcome on some other issue. They disclaim responsibility, act covertly, and discreetly keep records to prove they were "misunderstood" or actually had opposed a "misguided" policy. All the decision makers may even agree on what should be done, but the issue is so controversial or the outcome so uncertain that no one wishes to be acknowledged as the author of the policy. So we get a leaderless policy, or none at all.

Finally, the political rules of the game vary from nation to nation. These rules constrict the range of government actions and bargaining strategies that are acceptable. Rewards and punishments for success or failure vary enormously. In some systems of arbitrary power, players can lose their lives or their positions overnight if they oppose the winning coalition; in others, the members of a one-party elite who are not immediately accountable politically may have more freedom to take risks or adopt unpopular policies than elected officials do. In pluralist systems, coalitions are more difficult to put together, leading to delayed responses to issues and resistance to departures from a consensus, once one has been hammered out. On the other hand, when consensus building is the norm, a decision stands a better chance of actually being implemented. When an elite with a monopoly of power tries to impose an unpopular decision, reluctant subgroups may ignore or alter the policy radically in the process of implementing it. In the case of authoritarian leaders whose positions are not constitutionally ratified, their tenure in office is very directly linked to their success in policy making. Struggles over policy cannot be separated from an ongoing struggle over power, especially when there is a collective leadership or when a once dominant leader is ill, aging, or losing his grip.

On nuclear war, the governmental politics model raises these questions: Are there any circumstances in which political pressures might lead a decision maker to take unjustified risks? Could one member of a government solve his or her political problems by launching a nuclear attack? Could political miscalculations, confusion, or a foul-up among decision makers bargaining under stress cause a nuclear attack? The most skilled and powerful player is not always the most rational, as the example of Adolf Hitler well attests. A chief of state may be guided by concern over self-image ("Did I act tough enough?"), political reputation ("Will I be perceived as selling out my country?"), reputation in history ("Did my actions mark the end of modern civilization?"), or reputation in the eyes of the adversary ("If I yield on this point, will I be bullied forever after?"). Answers to these questions will add up to a policy radically different from what might be the best policy for preventing nuclear war or preserving the power of the nation. Allison summarizes the nuclear lessons of the political model as follows:

> (1) the process of crisis management is obscure and terribly risky; (2) the leaders of the U.S. government can choose actions that entail (in their judgment) real possibilities of escalation to nuclear war; (3) the interaction of internal games, each as ill-understood as those in the White House and the Kremlin, could indeed yield nuclear war as an outcome. (p. 260)

Leadership and Irrational Actors

Decisions in a nation-state are not made by anonymous agencies or leadership groups. Individuals occupy all the offices of state, and their personalities, prejudices, talents, and ideas make a difference. At every turn in the history of the twentieth century we can see an individual statesman whose initiative or imagination put its mark on policy: Woodrow Wilson, Vladimir Lenin, Mao Tse-tung, Mohandas Gandhi, Adolf Hitler, Joseph Stalin, Franklin Delano Roosevelt, Charles de Gaulle, Winston Churchill. In every case, the entry of one of these leaders onto the international stage marked a dramatic turn in events. All of them came to power during the great crises of our time — the world wars and social revolutions that have made international affairs so turbulent. And it is no accident that such individuals come forward at times when ordinary routines and traditional institutions have broken down. Dramatic social change calls forth a search for new attachments, a willingness to surrender to authority, and a desire for reassurance that the vision and charisma of a great leader can provide. Crisis leaders become the repositories of sovereignty and national identity, the source of hope, the living symbol of salvation. Their personal prestige provides an anchor for allegiance at a time when a system's fundamental values have been called into question. Their ideologies, principles, or programs promise a solution, a sense of direction, a blueprint for a new social order or a new international system. Systemic forces and historical configurations set the stage, and bureaucracies and political institutions provide channels for action. But nothing happens without the players — those dominant actors who put political-economic forces in motion, who speak for the nation, who articulate the compelling ideologies, fight the wars, and raise the revolutionary fervor. The story of foreign policy is more than descriptions of the fixed scenery of institutions, states, and systems or plots outlining the collision of abstract forces. What gives drama, purpose, animation, and exaltation to international affairs is the flesh and blood of political leaders struggling to fulfill themselves and their peoples.

A focus on individual leadership reminds us that decision making is not all problem solving and rational discourse. It is also an emotional act that creates ties between leader and followers. Decisions arise from a leader's private agenda of psychic satisfactions as well as from a public agenda of issues. Leaders are idiosyncratic as well as purposive. That is why the quality of foreign policy decisions depends very much on the character of the individual in charge. The leadership model is sometimes called the "hero in history" — a helpful phrase for seeing foreign affairs as a series of dramatic events unfolding in time. Dankwart Rustow's *Philosophers and Kings: Studies in Leadership* defines leadership as a four-fold relationship between leaders, followers, circumstances, and goals, which Rustow puts in the form of this question: who is leading whom, from where, to where? The personality and ideas of the leader, the only resources he or she fully controls, are only one of the ingredients. The others are the expectations of followers and the opportunities afforded by the particular predicament in which the nation finds itself. A leader's messianic vision and charisma must be couched in the symbols of the culture and must conform to the mood of the masses. Then, all this must coincide with a crisis or some other dramatic opportunity for the leader to take power, amalgamate a movement, or initiate new policies. Routine decisions are adequately explained by Allison's three models, but the unusual event and the great moment in history require an analysis in terms of the influence of charisma, the expectations of the crowd, political crisis, and the symbolic power of ideology.

Sidney Hook's *The Hero in History* calls the great leaders "event-making" individuals, as distinguished from the merely "eventful" figures, who express the dominant social forces of the moment but do not alter them in any significant way. A heroic leader's ability to shape events depends on personal qualities of intelligence, will, and character, rather than on the accident of position. The distinction between event-making and eventful is another way of saying that heroes are great not merely by virtue of what they do but by virtue of who they are. Great leadership is more than opportunism, or a capitalizing on public expectations that already exist. It is genuinely creative, offering solutions hitherto unconsidered, calling on the public to transcend limited alternatives, and often going outside traditional institutional norms to achieve what the leader desires. Mikhail Gorbachev has been such a transformative figure in Soviet foreign policy, just as Mao Tse-tung and Charles de Gaulle initiated radical change in the foreign policies of China and France.

Mao Tse-tung was only one among many Westernizing reformers caught up by the currents of revolution that swept through China after the overthrow of the Manchu dynasty in 1911. But Mao was uniquely able to adapt Western ideas to a peasant society and to transform the urban, industrial bias of theoretical Marxism into practical programs suited to a rural-based guerrilla movement. Similarly, France's traumatic defeat by the Nazis in 1040 created both the need and the opportunity for new leadership. Marshal Philippe Pétain, a hero of World War I, stepped forward as an eventful man and took the role he was handed—president of the collaborationist Vichy regime. Charles de Gaulle, on the other hand, an obscure French colonel, was one of the few to believe that France could retrieve its pride and power through the formation of an independent resistance movement. He flew off to London, rallied a handful of followers, and returned in triumph four years later as the liberator of Free France.

Mao and de Gaulle shared a philosophy of voluntarism, a belief that it was possible to alter the course of history by reshaping the consciousness of the masses, and they were able to instill this belief in their followers. In this spirit, Mao tells the following story:

> There is an ancient Chinese fable called "The Foolish Old Man Who Removed the Mountains." It tells of an old man who lived in northern China long, long ago and was known as the Foolish Old Man of North Mountain. His house faced south and beyond his doorway stood the two great peaks, Taihang and Wangwu, obstructing the way. He called his sons, and hoe in hand they began to dig up these mountains with great determination. Another greybeard, known as the Wise Old Man, saw them and said derisively, "How silly of you to do this! It is quite impossible for you few to dig up these two huge mountains." The Foolish Old Man replied, "When I die, my sons will carry on; when they die, there will be my grandsons, and then their sons and grandsons, and so on to infinity. High as they are, the mountains cannot grow any higher and with every bit we dig, they will be that much lower. Why can't we clear them away?" Having refuted the Wise Old Man's wrong view, he went on digging every day, unshaken in his

conviction. God was moved by this, and he sent down two angels, who carried the mountains away on their backs. Today, two big mountains lie like a dead weight on the Chinese people. One is imperialism, the other is feudalism. The Chinese Communist Party has long made up its mind to dig them up. We must persevere and work unceasingly, and we, too, will touch God's heart. Our God is none other than the masses of the Chinese people. If they stand up and dig together with us, why can't these two mountains be cleared away? (Quoted in Myrdal and Kessle, pp. 14–15)

Event-making leaders may not be well suited to the routine processes of democratic politics, but the force of their personalities can be decisive in the context of crisis, mass politics, or revolutionary transformation.

James Barber, in *The Presidential Character,* has classified American presidents as active or passive, depending on whether they displayed great energy and initiative or were mere custodians of power. Similarly, James MacGregor Burns's *Leadership* contrasts transformative and transactional leaders, or those who energize and mobilize others as opposed to those who are agents or officeholders exercising routine functions. Almost all the great world leaders fall heavily on the active side of the spectrum, as might be expected, since they are more likely to be crisis rather than routine leaders. There also appears to be a rough correlation between activism and idealism; the more passive types tend to have a pragmatic orientation. Personality, philosophy, and style often have a relationship to the leader's *role.* The idealists and the agitators are the revolutionary ideologues and the crisis leaders, while the pragmatists and the passive or detached personalities play the part of officials or diplomats. The latter perform important leadership functions and are in the majority among those who conduct the day-to-day business of international politics, but they are much less active, less visible, and less distinctive in personality than the event-making leaders. On the other hand, a heroic leader's activity by itself is no measure of whether the energy has been used for good ends or for compulsive power seeking.

Another important dimension is the leader's *psychic adaptation* and its effect on the achievement of his or her goals. Leaders whose psychological health and orientation to power are compulsive or rigid often meet with defeat. In Barber's classification, presidents were rated as negative or positive depending on whether they found their responsibilities a burden or a joy. Invariably those who enjoyed exercising power and displayed a sense of humor about themselves were more adaptable, flexible, and successful in office. Franklin Roosevelt's secretary of war, Henry L. Stimson, wrote that the Roosevelts "not only understood the use of power, they knew the enjoyment of power, too. . . . Whether a man is burdened by power or enjoys power; whether he is trapped by personal responsibility or made free by it; whether he is moved by other people and outer forces or moves them—that is the essence of leadership" (cited in Barber, p. 8). Conversely, grim ambition and a heavy or sad aspect often marked those who sought leadership as a means of psychic compensation rather than to render public service. Such persons were more likely to display pathological or neurotic characteristics, as opposed to integrated personalities, and they tended to be self-defeating and at the center of the fiascos of foreign policy.

A leader such as Adolf Hitler was extraordinarily gifted: in terms of sheer impact, he was one of the greatest leaders of all time. One might even say that his pathological and fanatic qualities contributed to his charisma and assisted him in acquiring power. But he used his gifts, in the crisis of the Great Depression, to revive traditional German nationalism and authoritarianism — a reversion to an old pattern whose palliative psychological effect was achieved at the price of aggression against the world and a war of extermination against the Jews. Another leader, Franklin Delano Roosevelt, though he had fewer natural gifts, used the same events to reform his nation, renew its institutional foundations, and, in the crisis of world war, propose an entirely new system of collective security, later embodied in the United Nations. The New Deal and the UN were not just expedient responses to old habits and new conditions, but were attacks on the underlying structural causes of the crises and involved institutional innovation as well as personal creativity. Finally, we must judge leaders on the basis of their contributions to international affairs. Did a leader bring war or peace? Were the nation and the world better off or worse off? This is one case where a moral judgment about the rightness of a leader's cause cannot be avoided.

Rigidities of personality sometimes cause decisions to go awry. Foreign policy is as often derailed by irrational actions geared to the emotional needs of the immediate participants as by bureaucratic distortions, governmental politics, or institutional interests. Leaders who are creative and have well-integrated personalities will be able to perform their roles flexibly. Their political causes will not be subordinated to the unconscious demands of their own psyches. Instead, their inner strengths will give them added political resources, as they did for such leaders as Dag Hammarskjöld, Mohandas Gandhi, and FDR. However, when leadership is synonymous with a neurotic pursuit of power, the leader's commitment will be compulsive and the requirements for success rigid. The leader's actions will be tied to a psychic need for power, success, or recognition, to the point that inner drives may hamper performance and leave the leader out of touch with reality. This was apparently the case with Woodrow Wilson's desperate, self-destroying campaign to save the League of Nations and with Hitler's monomaniacal, and ultimately self-defeating, drive to conquer the world. Harold Lasswell, in *Power and Personality,* speaks of compulsive power seeking as the compensatory acts of individuals who are trying to overcome low self-esteem, and he gives Hitler as the most dramatic instance of a compulsive power seeker. In this psychological model, leaders displace their private motives on public objects and rationalize the motives as being in the public interest. Often such figures come to a point at which their inner needs get in the way of their political judgment — as happened with Lyndon Johnson on the Vietnam War and Richard Nixon on Watergate.

The sociopolitical setting can influence the likelihood of idiosyncratic or irrational leadership. In underdeveloped societies, in which roles are new and expectations unformed, decision making tends to be more erratic and more susceptible to the power and perceptions of particular individuals. In closed societies, less constrained by public opinion and the influence of interest groups, individual decision makers will more frequently diverge from standard role expectations. Officials who are not constrained by checks and balances or the pressures of election or promotion have more opportunities to express their personal idiosyncracies. So also in crisis settings — highly threatening situations, in which information about a potentially hostile act is either too scarce or too abundant — individuals resort to the use of images, projections, simplifying assumptions, and screening mechanisms, which amplify the role of personality.

Erik Erikson's *Young Man Luther* suggests that a psychohistorical dynamic lies behind every act of great social innovation: what cannot be solved on the personal level becomes easier to resolve when it is placed in a higher institutional-cultural framework. In other words, great leaders will solve for the nation as a whole the very problems they cannot solve for themselves. National self-assertion can often be the route through which individual statesmen achieve a personal sense of potency and recognition. War and revolution can be the arena in which the leader slays inner and outer demons simultaneously and, both psychologically and ideologically, arrives at a clear definition of good and evil. For the freedom fighter, rebellious instincts and the search for self-mastery can both find expression in a revolutionary struggle for national self-determination. For the exploited peasant, an act of violence against the alien colonizer can, as the Algerian psychoanalyst Frantz Fanon has suggested in *The Wretched of the Earth*, erase feelings of personal inferiority at the same time as it brings political liberation. An act of sacrifice or public service and the gaining of military victory, independence, national integration, or some other political success can all lead to a deep sense of personal esteem and efficacy. In this conception, the story of the individual and the nation or the cause become intertwined, with leadership the vehicle whereby each — person and nation — solves its problems and achieves greatness or is brought down in flames by the rigidities of a leader who could not adapt to circumstances.

Elite Attitudes and Misperception

The perceptions of individuals have an invisible but powerful impact on foreign policy and on the routines of decision making. Regardless of whether they are outstanding leaders or ordinary personalities, all decision makers are subject to psychological distortions that can lead to *misperceptions:* wishful thinking that reflects certain desires or fears; repression and denial; scapegoating and stereotyped ideas; anxiety produced by the contradiction between image and information (cognitive dissonance); projection or displacement of aggression; rationalization; and many other defense mechanisms that result in selective perception. Many decision makers carry closed images that resist change; they ignore contradictory information or assimilate it to preexisting beliefs. Several studies of Secretary of State John Foster Dulles have confirmed that his general image of the Soviet Union as atheistic, evil, and aggressive overrode specific information about changing Soviet capabilities and actions. Our values control what we pay the closest attention to: we see only what we think is important. Through what Robert Jervis, in *Perception and Misperception in International Politics*, calls the impact of the "evoked set," decision makers organize their perceptions according to what they are concerned about at the moment: "Issues that are very important to a decision-maker take up so much of his time and intellectual resources that he not only sees most events in terms of these issues but cannot realize that others do not share these preoccupations" (p. 211). Decision makers also tend to overgeneralize from firsthand experience — such as an encounter at a summit or a brief acquaintanceship in time of war or crisis — about the customary behavior of a person, agency, or state.

Images of the enemy are particularly subject to psychological distortion. It is common to perceive an enemy as behaving in a more united, organized, and intentional way than is really the case. A negative outcome will be attributed to the adversary's hostile aims rather than to accident or bureaucratic bungling. Such distortions arise because the decision makers, viewing the field of diplomatic action from close range, are prone to overestimate their own importance and to acquire an exaggerated image of their power to control events. When things go badly, they tend to blame an enemy that is more clever and better organized, not chance or their own mistakes. As detailed studies of the events leading up to World War I have confirmed, the gap between intentions and subjective perceptions can be gigantic, and the space is likely to be filled by fears, wishful thinking, and the false assumptions that these generate. Scapegoating, or blaming an internal or external enemy for failings the decision makers cannot admit to, is a convenient way for them to evade responsibility or rally support. Another common distortion is black-and-white or we-versus-they reasoning, which exaggerates the morality and good intentions of one's own nation and denigrates the behavior of the perceived enemy. In the Cold War, elites on both sides celebrated the virtues of their brand of democracy while accusing the adversary of exploiting the masses for profit or power.

Foreign policy decision makers experience the world through a *belief system* and a set of *images* that serve to filter information and yield a selective interpretation of events. Generational perspective illustrates this selective effect. The Depression generation in America and the generation that survived Stalin's terror in Russia both went through hardships that left them with worldviews of life as a grim struggle. Gorbachev's new policy of *glasnost* was more due to his belonging to a younger generation than to changes in the climate of the Cold War, and Ronald Reagan's crusading anti-Communism of the early 1980s was a carryover in his generational perspective, hardly justified by any rise in militancy on the part of an aging Brezhnev or a moribund Soviet elite. Depression, war, revolution, an independence struggle, and other powerful events confer historical lessons that tend to persist in the perceptions of a nation and its foreign policy elite.

Nathan Leites and Alexander George, in separate studies on the systematic influences that go into the formation of elite attitudes, have utilized the concept of the *operational code*. The foreign policy elite's code, the belief system that national decision makers hold in common, includes the rules of conduct or norms of behavior that influence the actors' choices of strategy and tactics, their perceptions of alternatives, and their approach to risks. It embodies, as well, attitudes stemming from the national character, the influence of the leader's personality and experiences in office, and the prevailing orientation to foreign policy that the party elite or bureaucratic establishment inculcates.

Different policy orientations accompany important differences in worldview, as captured in the contrasting styles of idealism and realism. First, the idealist tends toward an active, crusading, universalistic, or revolutionary orientation, while the realist is more passive or pragmatic, often employing balance-of-power tactics to protect the status quo. Second, decision makers favor either an optimistic or a pessimistic outlook on the prospects for realizing the nation's political values and aspirations. Third, the elite tends to see the world as either harmonious or conflictual. Fourth, the political future will be perceived as predictable or indeterminate, and events will be seen as amenable to mastery or subject to chance. Finally, elites have different outlooks on risk taking and risk management, some adopting an optimizing strategy, which seeks to maximize gains, and others adopting a more conservative, "satisficing" strategy of paring down goals to those that seem most feasible.

George's study, "The 'Operational Code': A Neglected Approach to the Study of Political Leaders and Decision-Making," distinguishes between a general set of attitudes, or philosophical beliefs, and a set of "instrumental" beliefs, which affect tactics, risk taking, the calculation of means and ends, and the actor's estimates of particular situations. It is important for foreign policy decision makers to have instruments for dealing with subjective components because their information is typically incomplete, predictions about consequences are unreliable, and it is often uncertain what criteria should be followed in choosing a course of action. The operational code provides a means of managing such uncertainties. Its rules for selecting, ordering, and simplifying the complex data the decision maker receives allow judgments to be made in accordance with national political values, assumptions, and habits of thought. In this sense the code is an aid to problem solving — although it can also impede rational decision making if the code is too far removed from reality. For instance, it may inappropriately apply lessons distilled from previous generations to novel circumstances. However, national styles or codes also make international politics more predictable, so long as diplomats take the trouble to study the style of an adversary or alliance partner.

The Soviet Union and the United States display the most striking contrasts in operational codes and perspectives, as we have already seen. But different elite perspectives have also been at the root of tensions between Western Europe and the United States. Two studies by Stanley Hoffmann, "Perceptions, Reality, and the Franco-American Conflict" and "The Western Alliance: Drift or Harmony?," list several factors of elite culture and national character that have caused cleavages within the Atlantic alliance. First, the Americans prefer simple policies, with clear-cut enemies, options, and outcomes, over complex ones that pose difficulties in sticking to the defined path. West European states-men are skeptical about such simplicity. They are inclined to take a more ambiguous view of their adversaries and to treat them with a mix of rewards and punishments, reflecting their historical experience with the nuances of balance-of-power diplomacy. In Hoffmann's words:

> The West Europeans look at international affairs less as a duel with swords, more as a game played with a whole range of cards; they are more concerned with the overall correlation of forces than with the balance (or imbalance) of military force; and they are more Clausewitzian, i.e., more interested in the variety of ways in which force can serve political objectives. ("The Western Alliance," p. 120)

These differences were apparent in contrasting attitudes toward the Soviets. The Americans initially approached the Cold War in black-and-white terms and with a single-minded reliance on military containment. The policy of détente, however, brought a near-euphoric one-dimensional view that the SALT process and trade liberalization could erase all conflicts, which oversold the prospects for peace. When détente failed, great disillusionment set in, and the U.S. reaction was rearmament and the renewal of forceful interventions. The Europeans, who have always had a more balanced view of the Soviets, were less prejudiced against the normalization of relations before détente and more skeptical afterward about how much reconciliation the policy could achieve.

A second difference is the American and West European attitudes toward conflict. Americans hope for ultimate harmony and tend to react forcefully against those who seem to thwart it. To them, conflict is a symptom of evil and aggressive intentions, and they employ military means in a crusading spirit, as the privileged tool of a nation whose mission is peace. Americans are thus strongly wed to stability, or the preservation of the status quo. Europeans view conflict as a natural, and often inevitable, result of ideological or national differences and are less inclined toward avoiding changes in the status quo at all costs. They will accept change, even violent change, so long it does not destroy the vital interests and values of the West.

Third, the United States still views itself as having a unique mission of leadership in the world, as being the only nation with the power, morality, free institutions, and fair-mindedness to stand up to the Soviets and speak for the free world. American statesmen see the higher interests of humankind as identical to those of the United States, which is the secular arm of a universal moral ideal. This makes the United States at once more arrogant and more insecure, for it causes Americans to interpret conflicts, including those within the Western alliance, as challenges to their primacy and mission. The United States is reluctant to share responsibility, even with its allies, and tries to project democracy and free enterprise everywhere, without having much understanding of other peoples' quite different national or revolutionary experiences. The Western Europeans are more cosmopolitan, more intimately acquainted with a long history of conflict and change, and more concerned about sheer survival. In their view, the world is more multipolar than bipolar and the root conflicts more national than ideological. Consequently, they have had less trouble dealing pragmatically with Moscow when their autonomy was threatened, even at the risk of seeming soft on Communism. And they are more tolerant of Third World revolutions and less inclined to advocate the wholesale transfer of Western models.

Group Dynamics

Irving Janis, in *Groupthink,* offers another way to look at the policy-making process — the group dynamics model. In this theory, decisions are the product of social-psychological pressures that flow from *group cohesiveness* and *conformity to group norms* of the small circle of top decision makers. These pressures are frequently detrimental to rational decision making because they encourage stereotyped images of the enemy and riskier courses of action and discourage critical thinking. Group dynamics particularly affect foreign policy because its crucial decisions are usually made by a few individuals operating under high stress and with little time for thought. Group solidarity markedly increases in the face of external threat or when the decision entails a high probability of deadly risk. Psychologists have long been aware that crowd behavior is radically different from the behavior of single individuals. Members of groups, crowds, committees, or large organizations may not feel a sense of individual responsibility. They are subject to a variety of informal (often unconscious) pressures and inducements to support group goals, along with a sort of monitoring or censoring that discourages nonconformity. Such social-psychological forces quickly generate a hidden agenda that is aimed at preserving friendly intragroup relations. Individuals become concerned with maintaining their image, status, or effectiveness in the group, without respect to the group's formal problem-solving mandate, and "groupthink" follows, diminishing the decision makers' mental efficiency, reality testing, and capacity for moral judgment.

In charting dozens of foreign policy fiascos associated with groupthink, Janis has identified six major defects in the decision making process: (1) The group's discussion becomes limited to a few alternatives. (2) The group fails to evaluate the less obvious risks and drawbacks of the majority's preferred course. (3) It rejects without reevaluation those courses that it has initially found unattractive. (4) It makes little effort to obtain information from experts or outsiders. (5) It shows a selective bias toward information and judgments from experts, the mass media, and outside critics, accepting only facts and opinions that reinforce the existing consensus. (6) Members fail to consider all the potential problems of implementation, substituting wishful thinking for contingency plans that might be more realistic. In addition, such concurrence-seeking behavior appears to stimulate overoptimism, a lack of vigilance, and stereotyped thinking about the weakness and immorality of out-groups. The greater the amiability and esprit de corps within the group, the more likely it is to behave in an irrational or dehumanizing manner toward those with whom it comes into conflict.

A prime illustration of such flawed decision making is the Bay of Pigs fiasco of 1961, during the administration of John F. Kennedy. The CIA had developed a covert plan to invade Cuba and overthrow the government of Fidel Castro, but the operation, beset by problems, failed almost immediately, stranding a brigade of Cuban exiles on the beach at the Bay of Pigs and politically embarrassing the administration. The plan had been approved by an outstanding group of experienced and intelligent men, but their judgment was based on many unrealistic assumptions that would likely have been uncovered if group dynamics had not interfered with critical thinking. One assumption was that the operation could be kept completely secret and that therefore a CIA cover story would conceal the U.S. involvement. Another was that the Cuban air force was ineffectual and could be knocked out before the invasion began. The 1,400 Cuban exiles were thought to be an effective enough military force to carry out the invasion without support from U.S. forces. The invasion would touch off immediate armed uprisings in Cuba that would topple Castro's weak government. If the Cuban exile brigade failed in its prime military objective, the men would retreat to the Escambray Mountains and join anti-Castro guerrilla units holding out there. Each one of these assumptions was based on faulty information or wishful thinking that the Kennedy advisers neglected to scrutinize carefully. By the time the operation was ready for launching, the cover story had been blown, amid rampant press speculation, and the site of the invasion was changed, making any retreat to the mountains impossible. No evidence beyond the assurances of the CIA was ever solicited on the military readiness of the exile force or on the Cuban defenses. A plan based on sloppy thinking and unexamined assumptions was put in motion.

Some analysts blame the decision on political pressures for the Democrats to do something, no matter if it was reckless, to counter Republican accusations that Kennedy was soft on Communism. Others point to agency politics, particularly the role of the CIA in foisting a pet project on a new administration. Bureaucratic procedures also were significant, since the requirement for extreme secrecy led to the screening out of important information and reduced opportunities for consultation with outside experts. Several of the advisers admitted afterward that they had been caught in an "effectiveness trap." As members of a new foreign policy team, they had been concerned over establishing their personal reputations and status and had therefore hesitated to voice objections to the majority opinion. Very likely all these factors contributed to the failure.

But, as Janis notes, these problems of the Bay of Pigs decision might still have been overcome if the group had not shared a number of illusions and norms that contributed to groupthink. Many members of the Kennedy team displayed a self-confidence, even a euphoria, that fed an illusion of invulnerability and an unquestioned belief in the group's inherent morality. They belittled enemies and treated them in stereotypes. There was an atmosphere of assumed consensus, an illusion of unanimity, that caused individuals to suppress their personal doubts. Potential critics were censored by members of the majority acting as self-appointed "mindguards." The group became insulated from contact with outsiders, new information, and fresh thinking. The president established ground rules and a restricted agenda that no one wanted to question, and suave leadership and a "cowering effect" fostered docility and deference to those in authority. Taboos sprang up against antagonizing anyone in the group. The same kind of decision-making defects have contributed to other faulty decisions: intelligence information warning of the Japanese attack on Pearl Harbor was ignored; General Douglas MacArthur's "intoxication with success" led to his decision to invade North Korea; conformity among President Johnson's inner circle of advisers pushed out all the "doves" and led to unrealistic hopes for a military victory in Vietnam.

It should be noted, however, that group processes can sometimes improve the quality of a decision, if the group is appropriately constituted and conducts its deliberations self-consciously and responsibly. As Aristotle said, "many heads are better than one." The framers of the U.S. Constitution believed in the deliberative powers of the Senate, as a check on a president's tyrannical, idiosyncratic, or irrational behavior. Thus, none of the decision-making models we have discussed can be taken as an infallible guide or a unique and complete explanation of the process. Clearly, national policy making is affected by many variables — rational, bureaucratic, political, social-psychological, and undoubtedly others not yet modeled. Each approach gives us a conceptual slice of reality, but only of what is exposed by cutting along that particular analytic plane. To gain a more complete view, we must treat the models as complementary and take several analytic slices through the complex foreign policy process. We must also remember the important role of accident, fate, luck — what Karl von Clausewitz called the "friction" in all foreign policy outcomes. Bureaucratic and psychological distortions explain the limits of rationality in the decision process, but there also are limits to logical explanations for most kinds of foreign policy behavior. Some outcomes may always escape the capacity of our analytic models.

DILEMMAS OF A DEMOCRATIC FOREIGN POLICY

Democracies and dictatorships supposedly vary tremendously in the effectiveness of their foreign policy. Critics of the democratic decision-making process point to all the irrelevant political considerations that distort outcomes. As Alexis de Tocqueville wrote in *Democracy in America:*

> Foreign politics demand scarcely any of those qualities which a democracy possesses; and they require, on the contrary, the perfect use of almost all those faculties in which it is deficient. Democracy is favourable to the increase of the internal resources of a State. . . . But a democracy is unable to regulate the details of an important undertaking, to persevere in a design, and to work out its execution in the presence of serious obstacles. It cannot combine its measures with secrecy, and it will not await their consequences with patience. . . . The propensity which democracies have to obey the impulse of passion rather than the suggestions of prudence, and to abandon a mature design for the gratification of a momentary caprice, [can be] very clearly seen in America.

Particularly maddening to the professional diplomat is the tendency of democracies to behave erratically. Public opinion is fickle and often ill informed. Ordinary citizens are preoccupied with domestic affairs and reluctant to support long-term strategies or timely action abroad. Elected officials are confined by short-term horizons and resist acting until a crisis presses their backs to the wall. In the words of George Kennan, in *American Diplomacy, 1900–1950:*

> I sometimes wonder whether in this respect a democracy is not uncomfortably similar to one of those prehistoric monsters with a body as long as this room and a brain the size of a pin: he lies there in his comfortable primeval mud and pays little attention to his environment; he is slow to wrath — in fact, you practically have to whack his tail off to make him aware that his interests are being disturbed; but, once he grasps this, he lays about him with such blind determination that he not only destroys his adversary but largely wrecks his native habitat. You wonder whether it would not have been wiser for him to have taken a little more interest in what was going on at an earlier date and to have seen whether he could not have prevented some of these situations from arising instead of proceeding from an undiscriminating indifference to a holy wrath equally undiscriminating. (p. 59)

Authoritarian systems can reach decisions relatively quickly. There are no leaks, no press investigations, no organized public opinion to which dissenters in the inner circle can appeal. Once a decision is made, it can be implemented immediately, without any elaborate ratification or consensus-building maneuvers among parties, parliaments, or interest groups. The nation's allies and adversaries alike can count on a relatively high degree of consistency. Beyond the deceptive public statements inherent in all diplomacy, authoritarian systems can usually be relied on to do what they say. Democracies are notorious for giving mixed signals, speaking with a dozen voices, and directing policies at several different audiences. What they publicly declare may have little correspondence to what is implemented. What one administration says may not hold for the next. And when democracies do act quickly and effectively, as the United States did in the Cuban Missile Crisis, the decisions likely are made very much as they are in an authoritarian system — by the chief executive or a small elite of top decision makers.

One of the great weaknesses of a democratic foreign policy is its inability to keep secrets. The openness of the decision-making process invites the exposure and abuse of confidential information. Congressmen routinely leak classified documents to the press in order to embarrass an administration politically. Members of the president's team go on "deep background" with reporters to reveal secret security details, in the hope that such briefings will elicit public support for a desired objective. The free press has often disclosed covert operations and thereby altered their outcomes. Congressional investigations of the CIA or the Pentagon can reveal reams of government secrets to foreign agents, who merely need to read about them in the daily newspaper. During the vigorous debate over Vietnam policy, one disgruntled Department of Defense official, Daniel Ellsberg, gave the "Pentagon papers," a mass of classified security documents, to the *New York Times.* Defenders of democracy point out that public debate and criticism have often saved the government from dangerous and costly policies. Dictatorships may enjoy brilliant successes and be able to change policies quickly, but they also can go on making the same blunders for decades because they are not accountable to the public for their mistakes.

It is said that democratic foreign policy displays all the vices of private interests but all the virtues of public debate. Policy cannot be held hostage to the arbitrary actions or foolish decisions of one person — Hitler, Stalin, Pol Pot, Idi Amin, Moammar Khadafy, or the Ayatollah Khomeini — because there is time and opportunity for debate, criticism, and collective deliberation. But these very virtues open the door to private interest groups or bureaucratic agencies looking out for their own narrow concerns. Decisions bog down in a swamp of political demands, and nothing happens until every important constituency has climbed on board. Policy is watered down to please a fringe group whose consent is essential for political reasons. To be sure, the constitutional separation of powers prevents abuses by the U.S. executive, but it also can leave a president without the clout to act for the nation in times of crisis. When the democratic process is exercised to the fullest, the timeliness and the substance of policy are often compromised. When representation and participation are maximized, diplomatic expertise is often in short supply. Hans Morgenthau captures the dilemma in his *A New Foreign Policy for the United States:*

> A democratic government must accomplish two tasks: On the one hand, it must pursue policies which maximize the chances for success; on the other hand, it must secure the approval of its people for these foreign policies. . . . The necessity to perform these tasks simultaneously faces a democratic government with a dilemma; for the conditions under which popular support can be obtained for a foreign policy are not necessarily identical with the conditions under which such a policy can be successfully pursued. A popular foreign policy is not necessarily a good one. (pp. 150–51)

These problems of a democratic foreign policy are widely bemoaned, not least by the practitioners themselves. But the record of the Iran-Contra scandal of the Reagan years ought to lend skepticism to any move to separate the decision-making machinery from the strings of democratic accountability. Many critics of U.S. policy in Central America and the Middle East have accused John Poindexter, Oliver North, and others in the Reagan national security team of circumventing Congress and the law of the land in order to run a private foreign policy that conformed to their personal values and a narrow conception of the national interest. According to these critics, the National Security Council lost a proper sense of its accountability to Congress, to the people, and even to the president to whom it reported. The flaws were both moral and practical. Constitutional checks and balances were undermined and democracy subverted, and the covert policy made by a small group never underwent the public scrutiny and debate that can give policy clarity and consistency. And all this leaves aside crucial questions of legitimacy, popular support, and the commitment of public resources. The covert Iran-Contra policy, which required members of the administration to systematically mislead Congress and lie to the American people, raised another serious problem for American foreign policy. It showed how an "imperial" president and his close advisers could use executive privilege to pursue hip-pocket wars and covert operations, which inflated their egos and put them in control of "the action." They were able to substitute their narrow, militaristic conceptions of security and patriotism for what should have been a broader, more representative, and more carefully prepared diplomacy.

Behind Iran-Contra is a larger debate over how to make rational policy. In testimony at the congressional "Irangate" hearings, former White House operatives articulated a kind of diplomat's definition of rational policy that conflicts quite profoundly with the democrat's definition. The professional foreign policy establishment, staffed largely by career military officers and foreign service bureaucrats, holds that policy is unduly influenced by popular perceptions and parochial demands. As a result, they say, the president and his advisers, the only persons in a position to know what should be done, are hamstrung by congressional interference from rising above partisan politics. Checks and balances certainly operate, but at the expense of clear policy and timely action. At present, American foreign policy is made by a hydra-headed monster of competing politicians, bureaucracies, and interests that speak with a million voices and advocate dozens of contradictory policies reflecting constituency demands but no coherent overall conception of the national interest. The inconstant and ill-defined character of American policy has often been a source of frustration to the Soviets as well as to America's allies, who maintain that they never know what policy really is, no matter what the president says, because it is amended and reinterpreted daily. American foreign policy is swayed by private interests, special pleading, political grandstanding, pork-barrel politics, and legislative logrolling—all the pluralistic voices of the democratic process. Unfortunately, to be governed by this process means sacrificing the larger, long-term interests of the nation to selfish, short-term demands.

What approach to American foreign policy is the best one? Is there too little democracy or too much? Many of the criticisms of pluralism are legitimate. It is an abuse of democracy when foreign policy becomes a monopoly of special interests rather than a rational response to external circumstances. For example, U.S. policy in the Middle East tends to be a contest between the oil companies and the pro-Israel lobby, each of which has its special reasons for favoring the Arab or the Israeli bent. The position on South Africa is a tug-of-war between liberal and black constituencies concerned about human rights and multinational companies afraid of losing their investments. Central America policy oscillates between the conservative interests of wealthy Cuban and Nicaraguan émigrés and the aims of the sanctuary movement and liberal political exiles in the Spanish-speaking immigrant community. In each of these cases, the issues may be debated vociferously, but the debaters certainly do not represent the sum of America's interests. Partisan policies are not necessarily wrong, but who will speak for the interests that have no paid lobbies or voting constituencies?

The constitutional division of powers has made it difficult for the various arms of the decision-making apparatus to compose their policy differences on arms control, for example. Congress imposed on President Reagan a ban on the testing of antisatellite weapons, an underground testing moratorium, several freezes on procurement, and a variety of other restraints, which the president powerfully resisted. Within the executive branch, the Departments of State and Defense, the Joint Chiefs of Staff, the Arms Control and Disarmament Agency, and the National Security Adviser were unable to agree on provisions for a proposed strategic arms reduction treaty. Such bickering, inside and outside an administration, is typical. Congress and the president have differed fundamentally over the conduct of the Vietnam War, support for the *contras* (or "freedom fighters") in Nicaragua, sanctions on South Africa, Star Wars, and the interpretation of the Anti-Ballistic Missile Treaty. Such confusions undoubtedly contribute to the fragmentation of policy and leave it with no clear sense of direction, no bipartisan continuity, and no controlling strategy or rational set of concepts and assumptions against which policy can be measured.

But the national interest comes in a thousand guises. It is very nearly impossible to distinguish the higher national interest, as articulated by an allegedly objective policy maker, from one more special interest with its own view and values. Who is in a position to speak for the entire nation? In theory, only the president has a uniquely national constituency and so possesses the requisite detachment. The chief executive is vested with the voice, the vantage point, the media coverage, the information, the special leverage that will make his message heard in other nations and among the American public as a whole. Only the president can arbitrate between competing bureaucracies or give both voice and discipline to a consensus. When a president lacks vigor, foreign policy is leaderless and slow to adapt. But when a president takes seriously his role as publicizer, legitimizer, communicator, he can readily focus public attention on key issues and on congressional foot-dragging or partisan legislation that may make for a successful election campaign but is bad foreign policy. To do so effectively, the president cannot ignore or subvert Congress. He must take his democratic powers seriously. Too often in the past, chief executives have mistakenly attempted to control foreign policy by restricting the locus of decision, attacking the press as an adversary and every security leak as an opposition tactic. Instead, the president must function as the chief educator and use his special vantage point, skills, and access to sell his policies to the people. By appealing to a wider arena, he makes the press his ally, not his enemy. And if he fails to convince the public, then he must bow to the wisdom of democracy, no matter how irrational this may seem to the professional policy maker. For the president is a politician, too, with his own prejudices and pet issues. Who is to keep him honest and ensure that his functions as chief of state remain separate from his decisions as a politician and party leader? Only the Congress and the press can do so. Congress may not be very good at making foreign policy, but it still must be permitted to second-guess the president, to investigate, and to put his policies to the test of public approval. If a foreign policy cannot be made palatable to that large and diverse constituency on Capitol Hill, then it is not a good policy.

The media are ever more important in American foreign policy, as a kind of fourth branch of the government. They poll public opinion, provide key news from abroad, shape public perceptions, help set agendas, criticize government officials, and generally serve as a transmission line between the political class in Washington and a wider audience. The media are a kind of perennial loyal opposition, and their role in foreign policy is critical, in the double sense of the word. The press and opinion makers can control the arena of decision making and contribute to the level of public arousal. One reason foreign policy so often falls into the hands of special interests is that many of us tend to be indifferent to foreign events. Particularly when a distant country is involved, popular interest and participation are intermittent. Good investigative journalists can play an important role as gadflies and fact finders, prodding the public into a civic awareness more lasting than momentary attention to periodic crises or politically inspired leaks.

Democracies do not make foreign policy very speedily or neatly. They do not have a single individual or an elite with the requisite wisdom or the infallible capacity for discerning the national interest. But dictatorships may provide unity and dispatch without acting more wisely; they frequently embroil their nations in unwanted wars or erode the nation's power and reputation in pursuit of policies that benefit only the egos or the interests of the elite. Whenever an American president or a small group in the executive branch has hatched a secret operation or pursued an unpopular war by covert means, the results have been disastrous for the nation. On the other hand, when the republic has been in real danger, the people have come together and rallied to the cause. The press and Congress have fallen in behind, supportive and responsible. When important national interests are at stake, a skilled president can bring the public along without violating the Constitution or the spirit of democracy.

QUESTION FOR DISCUSSION (PRO AND CON)

Is American foreign policy controlled by an elite? In particular, does a military-industrial complex dominate decisions about weapons and war?

☞ PRO

A power elite lies at the center of the foreign policy process in the United States. It consists of corporate and military elites who share common interests and values and whose profits and careers depend on the maintenance of a vigorous military establishment and the steady purchase of advanced weaponry. This military-industrial partnership is complemented by a political elite that holds key posts in the national security decision-making apparatus of the executive branch and in the congressional committees that deal with the armed forces and procurement. These elites are bound together by a common social back-ground, a pro-business ethos, and a propensity toward the military as the instrument of foreign policy. All three groups have an anti-Communist philoso-phy, a commitment to the arms race, common strategic doctrines, and a con-ception of the national interest that emphasizes narrow economic and security concerns at the expense of democracy at home and peace abroad. The institu-tional power of these elites facilitates their intercommunication and permits them to control information, shape public opinion, and take decisions over the heads of an uninformed and politically indifferent citizenry. Though the groups may not always be monolithic, conscious, or coordinated, their common inter-ests and attitudes are reflected in all the baseline decisions of doctrine, budget, political orientation, and strategic commitment. Once these fundamental deci-sions have been made, it matters little which weapon is purchased or what particular policy is adopted. Who, when, and where we fight and how much we spend all flow logically from the broad parameters that this political-military-industrial elite — the "iron triangle" — imposes on the policy process. Each individual decision does not need to be debated if the political alternatives available to the Congress or the people have been predetermined by an elite in control of all the large-scale institutions. Individuals — even whole administrations — can shuffle in and out of power endlessly without affecting the fixed ideology or the definition of institutional needs.

Some concrete facts support the validity of these assertions. The Depart-ment of Defense (DOD) owns more property than any other organization in the world and consistently disposes of 40 percent to 60 percent of the national budget (if we exclude social security, which is taxed and disbursed separately). (See Figure 7-3.) The DOD joins with a few dozen big businesses — all oligopo-lies dependent on defense contracts — in transactions worth hundreds of bil-lions of dollars each year. Eighty-five percent of the contracts are awarded without competition to the 100 corporations that control three-fourths of all defense business. The federal government's dependence on such corporations for key weapons systems helps explain why we bailed out Lockheed and Chrysler, whose economic fortunes are tied in turn to the decisions of service chiefs, Washington politicians, and Pentagon bureaucrats. In 1982, 87 percent of the sales of General Dynamics, 81 percent of Lockheed's, 79 percent of McDonnell Douglas's, and 92 percent of Grumman's were to the DOD or the National Aeronautics and Space Administration (NASA). Such spending holds the larger economy hostage, since military expenditures directly or indirectly generate over one-third of the total volume of production and services in the United States. By 1982, total military spending was *twenty* times the prewar level (in constant dollars), a per capita increase from $75 to $885. From 1946 to 1980, the United States spent a total of $2 trillion on defense. Between 1980 and 1988, the Reagan military buildup accounted for another $2 trillion, if we count the obligations and cost overruns that were passed on to the next admin-istration.

As early as 1960, when the defense establishment was a fraction of its present size, President Dwight Eisenhower, a former five-star general, warned

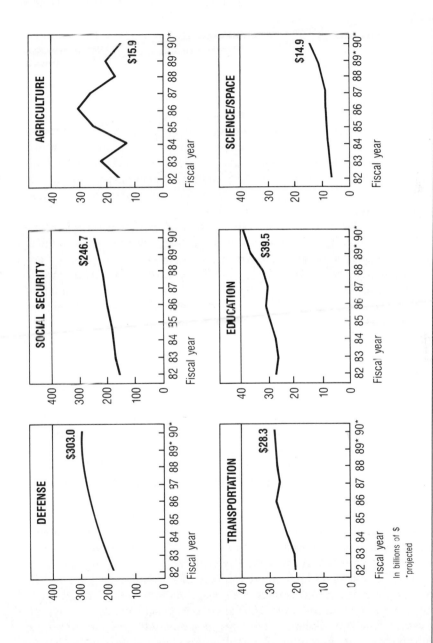

FIGURE 7-3
OUTLAYS BY FUNCTION IN THE REAGAN YEARS

447

that "we have been compelled to create a permanent arms industry of vast proportions." He argued that "we must guard against the acquisition of unwarranted influence, whether sought or unsought, by the military-industrial complex. The potential for the disastrous rise of misplaced power exists and will persist." As Eisenhower predicted, behind all the statistics lies a group of institutions that have acquired a vested interest in defense spending and in a foreign policy posture that justifies an on-going practice of excessive military procurement. This has led to an exaggeration of the Soviet threat; to military doctrines that justify the continued expansion and modernization of our strategic nuclear forces; and to the casting of our national interest in such broad terms as to leave us policing the stability of the entire world with hugely expensive conventional forces. Those who set defense policy and budgets also control the boom-and-slump cycle of the American state-capitalist economy. They have become planners exerting enormous hidden control through a kind of Pentagon socialism — the world's third largest concentration of economic power outside the free market (after the national economies of the Soviet Union and China).

No wonder the Pentagon and defense industries experience chronic waste and fraud. Cost overruns on major weapons systems — fighter planes, tanks, missiles, submarines, bombers, cruisers, helicopters — which generally are two to four times over original estimates, constitute "negotiated" profits for the defense companies, whose contracts guarantee them a fixed percentage of profit over their costs. Then there is the kind of graft and corruption revealed so dramatically in the Pentagon scandals of 1988: favoritism encouraged by secret payoffs, personnel circulating from private industry to the Pentagon and back, the selling of information, fraudulent weapons tests, hidden charges, jacked-up prices (two to five times more than comparable civilian items). These are only the most flagrant instances of the waste and fraud that have recurred periodically over the whole of the postwar era. Such abuses occur because all the systems of accountability have broken down. The separation of wealth from power that is at the root of the liberal conception of countervailing systems has been completely compromised by the relationships of influence in the iron triangle of the "procurement culture." It is not surprising that the states with the largest number of defense industries and military installations are also those that are best represented on the House and Senate armed services committees.

Pentagon capitalism is a special kind of monopoly economy very different from the old stereotype of arms merchants and Wall Street moneybags pulling the strings of government. It more often works the other way around, with national security managers and career military officers managing subsidiary corporations, to their mutual benefit. This state management of the defense economy draws resources away from social welfare programs, which the military-industrial elite opposes on ideological grounds. At the same time, the elite's conservative bias is reinforced by the enlargement of its decision power and the resources under its control. As in all bureaucracies that have escaped democratic controls, success comes to be defined in essentially imperialistic terms. The building of military careers and bureaucratic empires at home requires an expansion of the nation's imperial reach abroad. By pumping up fears of enemy attack and waving the threat of lost defense jobs in key constituencies, the Pentagon can exert a powerful influence on public opinion. By making "sweetheart" deals with private industry—often the same multinationals that have large investments abroad—the Pentagon can generate immense support in the private sector for a more powerful military presence in the Third World. Also, the armed forces tailor their weapons orders at least partially to the needs of favored contractors, and weapons of questionable performance frequently are bought just to keep important production lines operating.

Defenders of the system will point to all the political conflicts and policy disputes as evidence that there is democracy in the decision making. But the disputes are mostly bureaucratic infighting and interservice rivalry over shares of the pie. If anything threatens the size of the whole pie or the basically military cast of America's superpower policies, the groups join to defend the status quo. The power of this elite consensus manifests itself in these core beliefs: (a) realism is preferable to idealism, efficacy to principle, military means to nonviolent alternatives; (b) private property in a system of managed capitalism is preferable to economic democracy in a true free-enterprise system; (c) a limited democracy that protects the privileged access of the military-industrial complex is preferable to any other kind of government. In short, there must be no political infringement on defense monopolies, corporate profits and prerogatives, or the Pentagon empire.

The military-industrial consensus effectively rules out certain foreign policy options. First, it views real disarmament as a political and economic disaster, the ridiculous dream of Utopians. To disarm, the U.S. government and economy would have to go through a conversion—a kind of withdrawal from the addiction to defense spending—that would be extraordinarily radical and painful. It would require the kind of coordinated planning and state intervention on behalf of welfare priorities and reindustrialization that the corporate sector has steadfastly opposed as socialist (while benefiting enormously from the Pentagon's own version of a planned economy).

Second, the consensus resists any form of international regulation or peacekeeping operations that might infringe on sovereignty or the prerogatives of the national security managers. The elite says this policy is in the national interest, but it is often at the expense of peaceful relations and a more cooperative attitude toward international regimes. The elite considers it almost treasonous to suggest that the United States consent to international jurisdiction or arbitration in the settlement of claims deriving from the nationalization of American overseas holdings or the removal of U.S. military installations abroad.

Finally, any commitment to economic development or equitable social change in the Third World is opposed as unrealistic. To the foreign policy elite, it does not matter that we will be spending a thousand times more on arms to police global stability and protect American investments and access to resources than we would spend in foreign aid. (Figure 7-4 shows how little of the military dollar has been spent on the direct defense of the United States.) Since these global policing responsibilities enhance the power, the profits, and the careers of the elite, it is only too willing to substitute military interventions and repressive policies for real justice.

One can argue that changes of administration and foreign policy personnel make it impossible to speak of a ruling class. But there is a constantly circulating supply of elite personnel to fill the positions. Generals and admirals retire from the military and go to work for munitions companies; corporate executives take leaves of absence to serve as Pentagon managers. In the early 1970s, over 2,000 retired military officers were serving as executives of major defense contractors. In 1978, over 1,660 former high-ranking Department of Defense personnel worked for private defense firms. No one company or group is guaranteed a permanent grip on power, but no one can effectively oversee all those who participate in this self-serving recruitment cycle. The core institutions act together to manage the media and public opinion. Executive privilege is invoked to keep information from the press. Agencies reward "good" journalists and punish those who are critical. Public relations firms buff the images of the armed forces, help sell high-tech weapons, and put a "spin" on the news so that it will appear to favor those in political control. The elite also systematically excludes any whose social backgrounds are too different, who are too critical of Pentagon capitalism, who appear too soft on Communism or too socialist in philosophy. Studies by Suzanne Keller *(Beyond the Ruling Class)*,

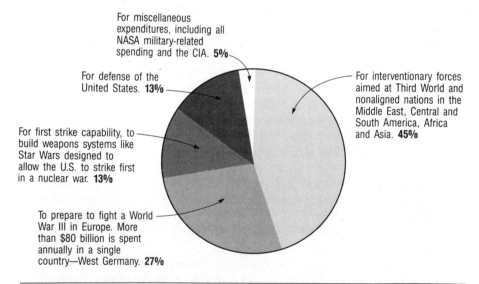

FIGURE 7-4
BREAKDOWN OF THE PENTAGON BUDGET

Richard Barnet *(The Roots of War)*, and G. William Domhoff *(Who Rules America?)* have all confirmed the homogeneous character of America's ruling groups. Finally, certain policy alternatives are never considered at all because they would be too damaging to the prevailing interests of the elite and its definition of national security. If this kind of control does not constitute a perfect model of government by elite, no one can deny that it represents a serious infringement on democratic norms.

Such a concentration of decision-making power may exist in America simply by virtue of our superpower role. In the Soviet Union, elite control is made still more flagrant by authoritarian habits and Marxist-Leninist philosophy, which justifies both the role of elites and the role of violence in social change. The Russian bureaucracy has traditionally funneled power to the few. Events of history have fed a sense of insecurity and a habit of seeking out military solutions. The rise to superpower status and the arms race have expanded the Soviet military sector, which spends twice (as a proportion of GNP) what the United States does to outfit itself as a world-class military power. Neither class divisions nor capitalism are essential to the military-industrial complex, in Russia or in America. But they exist in both countries, in the form of bureaucratic power and an unopposed Defense Unlimited agenda. However, the Soviet political elite has two advantages. It exercises a self-conscious monopoly over the socialist economy, and it has a powerful self-interest in controlling the defense establishment on behalf of civilian goals, especially if it is to provide a starved country with the tangible fruits of *perestroika*. This does not necessarily make Soviet policy any less belligerent or Soviet security concerns any less global. But it does make the military-industrial complex less autonomous that we might imagine it to be in such an authoritarian setting.

These brief reflections on a common U.S.-Soviet predicament should give us pause when we are tempted to dismiss talk of a military-industrial complex as the fabrication of radicals and ideologues. The permissiveness of American society, along with our lack of understanding or vigilance, is precisely what makes possible the arrogation of power by a few.

☞ CON

There are a number of straightforward reasons why we can say that American foreign policy is not under the control of a power elite or a military-industrial complex. In the first place, the scope of the decisions made by any interest group or bureaucratic agency, no matter how powerful it may be, is too narrow to govern anything so broad as the whole of foreign policy. Second, many interest-group complexes — agriculture, health, and others — compete avidly with the military complex for slices of the federal budget. Third, the individuals who head up the various parts of the foreign policy establishment are not a united and self-conscious entity that is capable of coordinating all the vital elements of policy. American foreign policy is so complex that the top decision makers can scarcely keep track of all the parts. Subordinate agencies compete fiercely for their share of the budget. Any abuses that occur are the result of a lack of coordination and supervision, not of conspiratorial direction from a central power elite. In the fourth place, even in those areas most subject to decision by a small group—nuclear strategy, weapons procurement, covert operations, crisis management—public opinion and democratically elected political representatives play a powerful role. When a policy involves routine or uncontested matters, the decision is naturally left to individuals or groups with a special interest or expertise. But no so-called military-industrial complex can exercise power against the interests of an aroused public or without regard for external circumstances. Finally, most large American corporations derive only a small percentage of their profits from defense production. Many large defense contractors have diversified interests. Also, wars disrupt business operations and contribute to inflation. All these factors tend to offset any promilitary bias in corporate America.

Critics of U.S. defense policy point to the large slice of the national budget that goes into foreign and military spending. But this is quite proper in a federal system, which gives state and local governments the primary responsibility for health, education, welfare, and other social services. The amount of defense spending says nothing about who controls policy. It is simply a barometer of the global responsibilities the United States has assumed as the leader of the free

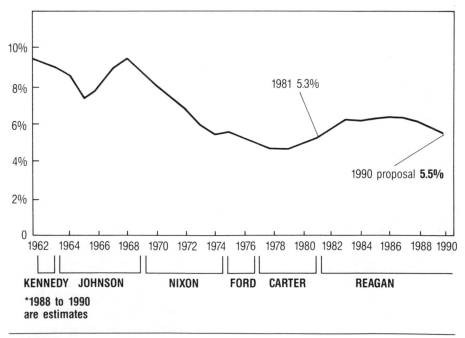

FIGURE 7-5
DEFENSE SPENDING AS A PERCENT OF GNP

world. Defense expenditures as a percentage of GNP have *fallen* steadily since World War II, reflecting the economy's greater capacity to carry the defense burden (see Figure 7-5). Moreover, congressional votes on foreign policy issues (beyond narrow procurement decisions) do not bear a close correlation with the number of military facilities in members' districts.

Nor are cost overruns an indicator of elite control or profit gouging by an economic aristocracy. Government contracting is on a sole-source, cost-plus basis because that is the only possible way of getting weapons systems that cost billions to develop in prototype and tens of billions to produce and deploy. Without such contracts, private businesses would simply refuse to bid on government work, and the Pentagon would have to manufacture its own weapons, via a state-owned military industry that would be still more vulnerable to bureaucratic distortion. Inflation over the ten-year research-and-development cycle and changing program requirements imposed by Congress account for a large part of the cost overruns. Moreover, no one can set an exact price on a technology that has not been invented yet. If the American people want the very latest in military technology, they must be prepared to pay a premium for it. That is the price of survival in an era of technological dynamism and advanced weaponry.

Accusations that an elite is recruited according to exclusionary criteria are also misplaced. Our foreign policy leadership is fairly homogeneous, but that is because it pursues a consensus position and holds common values that are widely shared by ordinary Americans. Fringe elements are excluded because they do not reflect popular opinion, not because the system is closed. The majority of Americans are anti-Communist, probusiness, committed to military preparedness, and in favor of protecting American bases and investments abroad because they help bring us cheap resources and a high standard of living. These policy preferences follow naturally from widely held American values, without the slightest prompting from any elite.

The Vietnam War is a perfect illustration of the power of an aroused public to redirect policy. Here was an occasion when a president and his small group of advisers *did* control policy, for a time. But as mistakes became apparent, the locus of power inevitably shifted outward, in wider and wider circles. Criticism was strong, more and more groups voiced opposition, and President Johnson was actually forced to stand down from reelection. A message was being sent to Washington: bring the boys home. And America did wind down the war, cutting defense budgets drastically between 1973 and 1978. When the political leadership is making wise decisions, the public is content to leave foreign policy to the executive and to the key committees in Congress. But when someone fouls up, more players become involved and the public finally gets to have its say. Nor should we forget the role of congressional investigations. The Pentagon, the CIA, the National Security Council have all been subjected to intense scrutiny: the Gaither report, the Church committee, Team A and Team B, the Kissinger report on Central America, the Scowcroft commission, the Tower report, the Iran-Contra investigative committee, the *Challenger* commission — the list is practically endless. Anyone who reads these volumes of testimony, analysis, and criticism will see that Washington is far from being populated with chummy, like-minded political leaders.

To appreciate the diversity and the democracy of American foreign policy, one has only to compare the administrations of Jimmy Carter and Ronald Reagan. It would be hard to find two leaders further apart on basic policy, both at home and abroad. Carter supported the Sandinista regime in Nicaragua; Reagan financed the *contras* to overthrow it. Carter signed a SALT II arms control treaty that Reagan opposed. Carter championed human rights and embraced radical black nationalist regimes in Africa; Reagan stuck with conservative regimes that backed capitalism at the expense of human rights, and he adopted a policy of "constructive engagement" with the white racist government in South Africa. Carter led the way in establishing an international nuclear nonproliferation regime and put severe restrictions on arms sales; Reagan relaxed nuclear controls and boosted arms sales markedly. Carter initiated the peace process in the Middle East, including an approach to the Palestinians; Reagan backed away from it. Carter supported the Convention on the Law of the Sea and had his ambassador sign the draft treaty; Reagan refused to ratify it. Carter canceled the B-1 bomber and the MX missile, two major weapons systems each worth $30 billion or $40 billion; Reagan reinstated them. Such fundamental differences cannot be overlooked by anyone who claims that a military-industrial complex is running everything. The two administrations did share a get-tough attitude toward the Soviets, because Soviet behavior warranted it. There is an American national interest that provides continuity to policy, but it is hardly the product of an elite. It results from a common perception of the problems the United States confronts abroad.

Finally, we should recognize that there is a need for professionalism in foreign policy, for trained and experienced personnel. These professionals are of necessity an elite, but an elite playing its proper role in protecting national security and one that is ultimately accountable to our elected officials. The American defense community should be measured against practical standards of performance, not against some ideal of perfect efficiency and perfect democracy. America still produces the best weapons in the world. The defense industry can respond to its critics in the same words Winston Churchill used to defend democracy: it may seem like the worst system, except when you compare it with all the others. Comparative analysis reveals that the American system is vastly more competent and productive than, say, the Soviet defense industry, which is famous for its privileged status in the Soviet economy. We have been able to stay ahead of the Soviets in the arms race by virtue of our greater competitiveness, technological ingenuity, and productivity. Attempts to make the procurement process more competitive will simply bring an expensive overlap of research-and-development efforts, duplication of productive capacity, and a greater risk that Soviet industrial espionage will uncover military secrets. Democratizing reforms are not likely to succeed, and the kind of government intervention and bureaucratic restraint that the Pentagon bashers propose is just what has made the Soviet planned economy so inefficient. The system isn't perfect. Allowing some discretion to the defense industry and to foreign policy professionals is the price of a limited partnership between free enterprise and government. When there is discretion, it will sometimes be abused. But democracy has a good record of ferreting out mistakes, waste, and corruption. Our system of making foreign policy is still superior to any conceivable alternative.

SOURCES AND SUGGESTED READINGS

On Nationalism, National Attributes, and National Interest

Akzin, Benjamin. *States and Nations.* Garden City, N.Y.: Doubleday/Anchor, 1966.

Anderson, Benedict. *Imagined Communities: Reflections on the Origin and Spread of Nationalism.* London: Verso Editions and NLB, 1983.

Armstrong, John A. *Nations Before Nationalism.* Chapel Hill: University of North Carolina Press, 1982.

Beard, Charles. *The Idea of National Interest.* New York: Macmillan, 1934.

Boulding, Kenneth. E. "National Images and International Systems." In Wolfram F. Hanrieder, ed., *Comparative Foreign Policy,* New York: David McKay Company, 1971. Pp. 90–107.

Clinton, W. David. "The National Interest: Normative Foundations." *Review of Politics,* vol. 48 (1986), pp. 495–519.

Connor, Walker. "Self-Determination: The New Phase." *World Politics,* vol. XX, no. 1 (1967), pp. 30–53.

Eckstein, Harry. *A Theory of Stable Democracy.* Princeton, N.J.: Princeton University Press, 1961.

Gellner, Ernest. *Nations and Nationalism.* Ithaca, N.Y.: Cornell University Press, 1983.

Gray, Colin S. *The Geopolitics of the Nuclear Era: Heartland, Rimlands, and the Technological Revolution.* New York: Crane, Russak/National Strategy Information Center, 1977.

———. "National Style in Strategy." *International Security,* vol. 6, no. 2 (Fall 1981), pp. 21–47.

———. *Nuclear Strategy and National Style.* Lanham, Md.: Hamilton Press, 1986.

Haas, Ernst B. "What is Nationalism and Why Should We Study It?" *International Organization,* vol. 40, no. 3 (Summer 1986), pp. 709–52.

Herz, John. "Political Realism Revisited." *International Studies Quarterly,* vol. 25 (1981), pp. 182–97.

Holsti, K. J. "National Role Conceptions in the Study of Foreign Policy." *International Studies Quarterly,* vol. 14 (September 1970), pp. 233–309.

Holsti, Ole R. "The Belief System and National Images: A Case Study." In William D. Coplin and Charles W. Kegley, Jr., eds., *Analyzing International Relations,* New York: Praeger, 1975. Pp. 22–33.

Kamenka, Eugene, ed. *Nationalism: The Nature and Evolution of an Idea.* New York: St. Martin's Press, 1976.

Kautsky, John H. *Political Change in Underdeveloped Countries: Nationalism and Communism.* New York: Wiley, 1966.

Kedourie, Elie. *Nationalism.* New York: Praeger, 1960.

Kohn, Hans. *The Idea of Nationalism.* New York: Macmillan, 1960.

Kratochwill, Frederick. "On the Notion of 'Interest' in National Relations." *International Organization,* vol. 36 (1982), pp. 1–22.

Morgenthau, Hans J. "Another 'Great Debate': The National Interest of the United States." *American Political Science Review,* vol. 46 (1952), pp. 961–78.

———. *Politics Among Nations: The Struggle for Power and Peace,* 6th ed., rev. by Kenneth W. Thompson. New York: Knopf, 1985.

Neuchterlein, Donald E. "The Concept of 'National Interest': A Time for New Approaches." *Orbis,* vol. 23 (1979), pp. 73–94.

Pye, Lucian W. *Politics, Personality, and Nation Building.* New Haven, Conn.: Yale University Press, 1962.

Pye, Lucian, and Sidney Verba, eds. *Political Culture and Political Development.* Princeton, N.J.: Princeton University Press, 1965.

Robinson, Thomas W. "National Interests." In James N. Rosenau, ed., *International Politics and Foreign Policy,* rev. ed., New York: Free Press, 1969. Pp. 182–90.

Rochester, J. Martin. "The 'National Interest' and Contemporary World Politics." *Review of Politics,* vol. 40 (1978), pp. 77–96.

Rourke, John T. *International Politics on the World Stage.* Monterey, Calif.: Brooks Cole, 1986.

Seers, Dudley. *The Political Economy of Nationalism.* New York: Oxford University Press, 1983.

Shafer, Boyd C. *Faces of Nationalism.* New York: Harcourt Brace Jovanovich, 1972.

Smith, Anthony D. *Nationalism in the Twentieth Century.* New York: New York University Press, 1979.

———. *Theories of Nationalism.* New York: Harper & Row, 1971.

Snyder, Louis L. *Varieties of Nationalism.* Hinsdale, Ill.: Dryden Press, 1976.

Sondermann, Fred A. "The Concept of the National Interest." *Orbis,* vol. 21 (1977), pp. 121–38.

Spiegel, Steven L. *Dominance and Diversity: The International Hierarchy.* Boston: Little, Brown, 1972.

Terhune, Kenneth W. "From National Character to National Behavior: A Reformulation." *Journal of Conflict Resolution,* vol. 14 (June 1970).

Van Alstyne, Richard W. *Genesis of American Nationalism.* Palo Alto, Calif.: Pacific Books, 1987.

Waldron, Arthur N. "Theories of Nationalism and Historical Explanation." *World Politics,* vol. 37 (1985), pp. 416–41.

Wolfers, Arnold. *Discord and Collaboration: Essays on International Politics.* Baltimore: Johns Hopkins Press, 1962.

On the United States

Almond, Gabriel A. *The American People and Foreign Policy.* New York: Holt, Rinehart & Winston, 1960.

Ambrose, Stephen E. *Rise to Globalism: American Foreign Policy Since 1938,* 5th rev. ed. New York: Penguin, 1988.

Armacost, Michael H. *The Foreign Relations of the United States.* Belmont, Calif.: Dickenson, 1969.

Bartlett, C. J. *The Rise and Fall of Pax Americana: U.S. Foreign Policy in the Twentieth Century.* New York: St. Martin's, 1975.

Blanchard, William H. *Aggression American Style.* Santa Monica, Calif.: Goodyear, 1978.

Bliss, Howard, and M. Glen Johnson. *Beyond the Water's Edge: America's Foreign Policies.* Philadelphia: Lippincott, 1975.

Brown, Seyom. *The Faces of Power: Constancy and Change in U.S. Foreign Policy from Truman to Johnson.* New York: Columbia University Press, 1968.

———. *On the Front Burner: Issues in U.S. Foreign Policy.* Boston: Little, Brown, 1984.

Coates, James, and Michael Kilian. *Heavy Losses: The Decline of American Defense.* New York: Penguin, 1985.

Crabb, Cecil V., Jr. *American Foreign Policy in the Nuclear Age,* 4th ed. New York: Harper & Row, 1983.

———. *Policy-Makers and Critics: Conflicting Theories of American Foreign Policy.* New York: Praeger, 1976.

Dallek, Robert. *The American Style of Foreign Policy: Cultural Politics and Foreign Affairs.* New York: Knopf, 1983.

Davis, Tami R., and Sean M. Lynn-Jones. "City Upon a Hill." *Foreign Policy,* vol. 66 (1987), pp. 20–38.

Destler, I. M., et al. *Our Own Worst Enemy: The Unmaking of American Foreign Policy.* New York: Simon & Schuster, 1984.

Devine, Donald J. *The Political Culture of the United States.* Boston: Little, Brown, 1972.

Englehardt, Tom. "Ambush at Kamikaze Pass." In Steven L. Spiegel, ed., *At Issue: Politics in the World Arena,* New York: St. Martin's, 1973. Pp. 27–43.

Ermarth, Fritz. "Contrasts in American and Soviet Strategic Thought." *International Security,* vol. 3, no. 2 (Fall 1978), pp. 138–55.

Farer, Tom J. *The Grand Strategy of the United States in Latin America.* New Jersey: Transaction Books, 1987.

Fulbright, William. *The Arrogance of Power.* New York: Vintage, 1967.

Gardner, Lloyd C. *Architects of Illusion: Men and Ideas in American Foreign Policy.* Chicago: Quadrangle, 1970.

Gelber, Lionel. *Crisis in the West: American Leadership and the Global Balance.* New York: St. Martin's, 1975.

Goldstein, Martin F. *America's Foreign Policy: Drift or Decision.* Wilmington, Del.: Scholarly Resources, 1984.

Graebner, Norman A. *America as a World Power: A Realist Appraisal from Wilson to Reagan.* Wilmington, Del.: Scholarly Resources, 1984.

Halle, Louis J. *Dream and Reality: Aspects of American Foreign Policy.* New York: Harper Colophon, 1959.

Hartmann, Frederick H. *The New Age of American Foreign Policy.* New York: Macmillan, 1970.

Hartz, Louis. *The Liberal Tradition in America.* New York: Harvest Books, 1955.

Hoffmann, Stanley. *Gulliver's Troubles, or The Setting of America's Foreign Policy.* New York: McGraw-Hill, 1968.

————. *Primacy or World Order: American Foreign Policy Since the Cold War.* New York: McGraw-Hill, 1978.

Holsti, Ole, and James Rosenau. *American Leadership in World Affairs: Vietnam and the Breakdown of Consensus.* New York: Allen & Unwin, 1984.

Hughes, Barry B. *The Domestic Context of American Foreign Policy.* San Francisco: Freeman, 1978.

Hunt, Michael H. *Ideology and U.S. Foreign Policy.* New Haven, Conn.: Yale University Press, 1987.

Hyland, William. *The Reagan Foreign Policy.* New York: New American Library, 1987.

Isaacson, Walter, and Evan Thomas. *The Wise Men: Six Friends and the World They Made.* New York: Simon & Schuster/Touchstone, 1986.

Kegley, Charles W., Jr, and Eugene Wittkopf. *American Foreign Policy: Pattern and Process,* 3rd ed. New York: St. Martin's, 1987.

Kegley, Charles W., Jr, and Eugene Wittkopf, eds. *The Domestic Sources of American Foreign Policy: Insights and Evidence.* New York: St. Martin's, 1988.

Kennan, George F. *American Diplomacy, 1900–1950.* New York: New American Library, 1951.

————. *Memoirs, 1925–1950.* Boston: Little, Brown, 1967.

————. *Realities of American Foreign Policy.* New York: Norton, 1966.

Kissinger, Henry. *American Foreign Policy,* exp. ed. New York: Norton, 1974.

Kwitny, Jonathan. *Endless Enemies: The Making of an Unfriendly World.* New York: Congdon & Weed, 1984.

Landau, Saul. *The Dangerous Doctrine: National Security and U.S. Foreign Policy.* Boulder, Colo.: Westview, 1988.

London, Herbert I. *Military Doctrine and the American Character.* New York: National Strategy Information Center, 1984.

Masters, Roger D. "The Lockean Tradition in American Foreign Policy." *Journal of International Affairs* (Columbia University), vol. XXI, no. 2 (1967), pp. 253–77.

May, Ernest. *Lessons of the Past: The Use and Misuse of History in American Foreign Policy.* New York: Oxford University Press, 1973.

McCormick, James M. *American Foreign Policy and American Values.* Itasca, Ill.: Peacock, 1985.

Mead, Walter R. *Mortal Splendor: The American Empire in Transition.* Boston: Houghton Mifflin, 1987.

Morgenthau, Hans J. *A New Foreign Policy for the United States.* New York: Praeger, 1969.

Morley, Morris H., ed. *Crisis and Confrontation: Ronald Reagan's Foreign Policy.* Lanham, Md.: Rowan & Littlefield, 1988.

Nathan, James, and James Oliver. *United States Foreign Policy and World Order,* 3rd ed. Boston: Little, Brown, 1985.

Nye, Russell B. *This Almost Chosen People.* East Lansing: Michigan State University Press, 1966.

Osgood, Robert E. *Ideals and Self-interest in America's Foreign Relations.* Chicago: University of Chicago Press, 1953.

Oye, Kenneth, Robert Lieber, and Donald Rothchild. *Eagle Defiant: United States Foreign Policy in the 1980s.* Boston: Little, Brown, 1983.

Oye, Kenneth, et al, eds. *Eagle Entangled: U.S. Foreign Policy in a Complex World.* New York: Longman, 1979.

————. *Eagle Resurgent: The Reagan Era in American Foreign Policy.* Boston: Little, Brown, 1987.

Parenti, Michael. *The Sword and the Dollar: Imperialism, Revolution, and the Arms Race.* New York: St. Martin's, 1989.

Paterson, Thomas G. *Major Problems in American Foreign Policy.* Vol. II, *Since 1914,* 3rd ed. Lexington, Mass.: D. C. Heath, 1989.

Perkins, Dexter. *The American Approach to Foreign Policy.* Cambridge: Harvard University Press, 1962.

Schlesinger, Arthur M., Jr. *The Cycles of American History.* Boston: Houghton Mifflin, 1986.

————. "Foreign Policy and the American Character." *Foreign Affairs*, vol. 62, no. 1 (Fall 1983), pp. 1–16.

Schloming, Gordon C. *American Foreign Policy and the Nuclear Dilemma*. Englewood Cliffs, N.J.: Prentice-Hall, 1987.

Serfaty, Simon. "Lost Illusions." *Foreign Policy*, vol. 66 (1987), pp. 3–19.

Spanier, John. *American Foreign Policy Since World War II*, 10th ed. New York: Holt, Rinehart & Winston, 1985.

Steel, Ronald. *Pax Americana*. New York: Viking, 1967.

Thompson, Kenneth W. *Political Realism and the Crisis of World Politics: An American Approach to Foreign Policy*. New York: Wiley/Science Editions, 1960.

Tocqueville, Alexis de. *Democracy in America*, ed. by John Stuart Mill. 2 vols. New York: Schocken Books, 1961.

Tucker, Robert W. *Nation or Empire?: The Debate Over American Foreign Policy*. Baltimore: Johns Hopkins University Press, 1968.

————. *The Purposes of American Power: An Essay on National Security*. New York: Praeger, 1981.

Ungar, Sanford J., ed. *Estrangement: America and the World*. New York: Oxford University Press, 1985.

Van Alstyne, Richard W. *The Rising American Empire*. New York: Quadrangle Books, 1960.

Vlahos, Michael. *Strategic Defense and the American Ethos*. Boulder, Colo.: Westview, 1986.

Wilkinson, Rupert. *The Pursuit of American Character*. New York: Harper & Row, 1988.

Williams, William Appleman. *The Tragedy of American Diplomacy*, 2nd ed., rev. and enl. New York: Dell (Delta), 1972.

Yost, Charles. *The Conduct and Misconduct of Foreign Affairs: Perceptions on U.S. Foreign Policy Since World War II*. New York: Random House, 1972.

On Western Europe

Barnet, Richard J. *The Alliance*. New York: Simon & Schuster, 1983.

Beer, Francis A. *Integration and Disintegration in NATO*. Columbus: Ohio State University Press, 1969.

Beloff, Max. *The Future of British Foreign Policy* . New York: Taplinger, 1969.

————. *The United States and the Unity of Europe: Political, Social, and Economic Forces, 1950–57*. Stanford, Calif.: Stanford University Press, 1968.

Buchan, Alastair. *Europe's Future, Europe's Choices: Models of Western Europe in the 1970's*. New York: Columbia University Press, 1969.

Deutsch, Karl W., et al. *France, Germany, and the Western Alliance*. New York: Charles Scribner's Sons, 1967.

Feld, Werner J. *West Germany and the European Community*. New York: Praeger, 1981.

Feld, Werner J., and John K. Wildgen. *NATO and the Atlantic Defense: Perspectives and Illusions*. New York: Praeger, 1982.

Grosser, Alfred. *French Foreign Policy Under de Gaulle*. Boston: Little, Brown, 1967.

Hahn, Walter F., and Robert L. Pfaltzgraff, eds. *Atlantic Community in Crisis*. Elmsford, N.Y.: Pergamon Press, 1979.

Hanrieder, Wolfram, and Graeme Auton. *The Foreign Policies of West Germany, France, and Britain*. Englewood Cliffs, N.J.: Prentice-Hall, 1980.

Hoffmann, Stanley. "Heroic Leadership: The Case of Modern France." In Lewis J. Edinger, ed., *Political Leadership in Industrialized Societies: Studies in Comparative Analysis*, New York: John Wiley, 1967. Pp. 108–54.

————. "Perceptions, Reality, and the Franco-American Conflict" in John Farrell & Asa Smith, eds., *Image and Reality in World Politics*. New York: Columbia University Press, 1967, pp. 57–71.

————. "The Western Alliance: Drift or Harmony?" *International Security*. Vol. 6 (Fall 1981), pp. 105–125.

Hoffmann, Stanley, et al. *In Search of France*. New York: Harper Torchbook, 1963.

Kaiser, Karl. *German Foreign Policy in Transition*. New York: Oxford University Press, 1968.

Kissinger, Henry. *The Troubled Partnership: A Reappraisal of the Atlantic Alliance*. New York: McGraw-Hill, 1965.

Kolodziej, Edward A. *French International Policy Under de Gaulle and Pompidou*. Ithaca, N.Y.: Cornell University Press, 1974.

Landes, David S., ed. *Western Europe: The Trials of Partnership*. Lexington, Mass.: Lexington Books, 1977.

Link, Werner, and Werner J. Feld. *The New Nationalism: Implications for Transatlantic Relations*. Elmsford, N.Y.: Pergamon Press, 1979.

Macridis, Roy C., ed. *Modern European Governments: Cases in Comparative Policy Making*. Engle wood Cliffs, N.J.: Prentice-Hall, 1968.

Osgood, Robert E. *NATO, the Entangling Alliance*. Chicago: University of Chicago Press, 1962.

Tocqueville, Alexis de. *The Old Régime and the French Revolution*. Garden City, N.Y.: Doubleday Anchor, 1955.

Van Der Beugel, Ernst H. *From Marshall Aid to Atlantic Partnership*. Amsterdam: Elsevier, 1966.

On the Soviet Union

Arbatov, Georgi, and Willem Oltmans. *The Soviet Viewpoint*. New York: Dodd, Mead, 1983.

Bialer, Seweryn. *The Soviet Paradox: External Expansion, Internal Decline*. New York: Vintage, 1986.

——— . *Stalin's Successors: Leadership, Stability, and Change in the Soviet Union*. New York: Cambridge University Press, 1980.

Bialer, Seweryn, ed. *The Domestic Context of Soviet Foreign Policy*. Boulder, Colo.: Westview Press, 1981.

——— . *Politics, Society, and Nationality Inside Gorbachev's Russia*. Boulder, Colo.: Westview, 1988.

Braun, Aurel. *The Warsaw Pact: Change and Modernization in the Gorbachev Era* . Boulder, Colo.: Westview, 1989.

Clubb, O. Edmund. *China and Russia: The "Great Game."* New York: Columbia University Press, 1971.

Cockburn, Andrew. *The Threat: Inside the Soviet Military Machine*, rev. ed. New York: Vintage, 1984.

Cohen, Stephen F. *Rethinking the Soviet Experience: Politics and History Since 1917*, 2nd ed. New York: Oxford University Press, 1989

Colton, Timothy J. *The Dilemma of Reform in the Soviet Union*. New York: Council on Foreign Relations, 1986.

Conte, Francis, and Jean-Louis Martres, eds. *The Soviet Union in International Relations* . New York: St. Martin's, 1987.

Dinerstein, Herbert S. *Fifty Years of Soviet Foreign Policy*. Washington: Washington Center of Foreign Policy Research, 1968.

Doder, Dusko. *Shadows and Whispers: Power Politics Inside the Kremlin from Brezhnev to Gorbachev*. New York: Penguin, 1988.

Gehlen, Michael P. *The Politics of Soviet Coexistence: Soviet Methods and Motives*. Bloomington: Indiana University Press, 1967.

Gray, Colin S. "Reflections on Empire: The Soviet Connection." *Military Review*, vol. 62 (Jan. 1982), pp. 2–13.

Hassner, Pierre. "Soviet Foreign Policy: Ideology and Realpolitik." *Problems of Communism*, vol. 26 (Sept.-Oct. 1977), pp. 82–89.

Hauner, Milan, and Robert L. Canfield, eds. *Afghanistan and the Soviet Union: Collision and Transformation*. Boulder, Colo.: Westview, 1989.

Herrmann, Richard K. *Perceptions and Behavior in Soviet Foreign Policy*. Pittsburgh: University of Pittsburgh Press, 1985.

Hoffmann, Erik P., and Frederic J. Fleron, Jr., eds. *The Conduct of Soviet Foreign Policy*, exp. 2nd ed. New York: Aldine, 1980.

Hough, Jerry F. *Soviet Leadership in Transition*. Washington: Brookings Institution, 1980.

Joyce, John M. "The Old Russian Legacy." *Foreign Policy*, vol. 55 (Summer 1984), pp. 132–53.

Keeble, Curtis, ed. *The Soviet State: The Domestic Roots of Soviet Foreign Policy*. Boulder, Colo.: Westview, 1985.

Kennan, George F. *Russia and the West Under Lenin and Stalin*. Boston: Little, Brown, 1961.

Kolkowicz, Roman. *The Roots of Soviet Power*. Boulder, Colo.: Westview, 1989.

Leites, Nathan. *A Study of Bolshevism*. New York: Free Press, 1953.

Lewin, Moshe. *The Gorbachev Phenomenon: A Historical Interpretation*. Berkeley: University of California Press, 1988.

Light, Margot. *The Soviet Theory of International Relations*. New York: St. Martin's, 1988.

Lukacs, John. "The Soviet State at 65." *Foreign Affairs*, vol. 65 (Fall 1986), pp. 21–36.
Meyer, Alfred G. *Communism*, 4th ed. New York: Random House, 1984.
Mikheyev, Dmitry. "The Soviet Mentality." *Political Psychology*, vol. 8, no. 4 (December 1987), pp. 491–523.
Nogee, Joseph L., and Robert H. Donaldson. *Soviet Foreign Policy Since World War II*, 2nd ed. New York: Pergamon, 1984.
Rubinstein, Alvin Z. *Soviet Foreign Policy Since World War II*. Cambridge, Mass.: Winthrop, 1981.
Rubinstein, Alvin Z., ed. *The Foreign Policy of the Soviet Union*, 3rd ed. New York: Random House, 1972.
Schwartz, Morton. "The 'Motive Forces' of Soviet Foreign Policy: A Reappraisal." (Paper delivered to the American Political Science Association, September 1969).
Shinn, William T., Jr. "On Russians and Their Ways." *Washington Quarterly*, vol. 8, no. 1 (Winter 1985), pp. 3–18.
Sivachev, Nikolai, and Nikolai Yakovlev. *Russia and the United States: U.S.-Soviet Relations from the Soviet Point of View*. Chicago: University of Chicago Press, 1979.
Smith, Gordon B. *Soviet Politics: Continuity and Contradiction*. New York: St. Martin's, 1988.
Taubman, William. "Sources of Soviet Foreign Conduct." *Problems of Communism*, vol. 35 (Sept.-Oct. 1986), pp. 47–52.
Tucker, Robert C. *The Soviet Political Mind*, rev. ed. New York: Norton, 1971.
Ulam, Adam B. *Dangerous Relations: The Soviet Union in World Politics, 1970–82*. New York: Oxford University Press, 1983.
————. *Expansion and Coexistence: Soviet Foreign Policy, 1917–73*, 2nd ed. New York: Praeger, 1974.
Valenta, Jiri, and W. C. Potter. *Soviet Decisionmaking for National Security*. Winchester, Mass.: Allen & Unwin, 1984.
Veen, Hans-Joachim, ed. *From Brezhnev to Gorbachev: Domestic Affairs and Soviet Foreign Policy*. New York: St. Martin's, 1987.
Von Beyme, Klaus. *The Soviet Union in World Affairs*. New York: St. Martin's, 1987.
Zimmerman, William. *Soviet Perspectives on International Relations, 1956–67*. Princeton, N.J.: Princeton University Press, 1969.

On the Foreign Policy Process

Allison, Graham. *Essence of Decision: Explaining the Cuban Missile Crisis*. Boston: Little, Brown, 1971.
Anderson, Patrick. *The Presidents' Men*. New York: Anchor Doubleday, 1969.
Berman, Maureen, and Joseph Johnson, eds. *Unofficial Diplomats*. New York: Columbia University Press, 1977.
Bloomfield, Lincoln. *The Foreign Policy Process*. Englewood Cliffs, N.J.: Prentice-Hall, 1982.
Crabb, Cecil B., Jr., and Pat M Holt. *Invitation to Struggle: Congress, the President, and Foreign Policy*, 3rd ed. Washington: Congressional Quarterly Books, 1988.
Destler, I. M. *Making Foreign Economic Policy*. Washington: Brookings Institution, 1980.
————. *Presidents, Bureaucrats, and Foreign Policy*. Princeton, N.J.: Princeton University Press, 1974.
Franck, Thomas M., and Edward Weisband. *Foreign Policy by Congress*. New York: Oxford University Press, 1979.
Gelb, Leslie, and Morton Halperin. "The Ten Commandments of the Foreign Affairs Bureaucracy." *Harper's Magazine*, June 1972.
Halperin, Morton. *Bureaucratic Politics and Foreign Policy*. Washington: Brookings Institution, 1974.
Hilsman, Roger. *The Politics of Policymaking in Defense and Foreign Affairs: Conceptual Models and Bureaucratic Politics*. Englewood Cliffs, N.J.: Prentice-Hall, 1987.
Inderfurth, Karl F., and Loch K. Johnson, eds. *Decisions of the Highest Order: Perspectives on the National Security Council*. Pacific Grove, Calif.: Brooks/Cole, 1988.
Jensen, Lloyd. *Explaining Foreign Policy*. Englewood Cliffs, N.J.: Prentice-Hall, 1982.
Kanter, Arnold. *Defense Politics: A Budgetary Perspective*. Chicago: University of Chicago Press, 1979.
Lindblom, Charles. *The Intelligence of Democracy*. New York: Free Press, 1965.
Neu, Charles E. "The Rise of the National Security Bureaucracy." In Louis Galambos, ed., *The New American State*, Baltimore: Johns Hopkins University Press, 1987.

Neustadt, Richard. *Presidential Power: The Politics of Leadership from FDR to Carter*, rev. ed. New York: Wiley, 1980.

Neustadt, Richard, and Ernest R. May. *Thinking in Time: The Uses of History for Decision-Makers.* New York: Free Press, 1986.

Rourke, John. *Congress and the Presidency in U.S. Foreign Policy-Making: A Study of Interaction and Influence, 1945–1982.* Boulder, Colo.: Westview Press, 1983.

Spanier, John. *Games Nations Play*, 5th ed. New York: Holt, Rinehart & Winston, 1984.

Spanier, John, and Eric Uslaner. *Foreign Policy and the Democratic Dilemmas*, 3rd ed. New York: Holt, Rinehart & Winston, 1982.

On Leadership, Psychology, and Misperception in Foreign Policy

Axelrod, R., ed. *Structure of Decision: The Cognitive Maps of Political Elites.* Princeton, N.J.: Princeton University Press, 1976.

Barber, James David. *The Presidential Character: Predicting Performance in the White House*, 3rd ed. Englewood Cliffs, N.J.: Prentice-Hall, 1985.

Burns, James MacGregor. *Leadership.* New York: Harper Colophon, 1978.

Derivera, Joseph. *The Psychological Dimension of Foreign Policy.* Columbus, O.: Merrill, 1968.

Erikson, Erik H. *Young Man Luther: A Study in Psychoanalysis and History.* New York: Norton, 1962.

Etheredge, L. *A World of Men: The Private Sources of American Foreign Policy.* Cambridge, Mass.: MIT Press, 1978.

Falkowski, L. ed. *Psychological Models in International Politics.* Boulder, Colo.: Westview Press, 1979.

Fanon, Frantz. *The Wretched of the Earth.* New York: Grove Press, 1963.

Farrel, John C., and Asa P. Smith, eds. *Image and Reality in World Politics.* New York: Columbia University Press, 1967.

Frank, Jerome D. *Sanity and Survival: Psychological Aspects of War and Peace.* New York: Vintage, 1967.

George, Alexander L. "The 'Operational Code': A Neglected Approach to the Study of Political Leaders and Decision-Making." *International Studies Quarterly*, vol. 13, no. 2 (June 1969), pp. 190–222.

Gladstone, Arthur L. "The Concept of the Enemy." *Journal of Conflict Resolution*, vol. 3 (1959), pp. 132–37.

Hermann, Margaret G. "Leader Personality and Foreign Policy Behavior." In James Rosenau, ed., *Comparing Foreign Policies*, New York: Halsted, 1974. Pp. 201–33.

Holsti, Ole R. "The Belief System and National Images: A Case Study." *Journal of Conflict Resolution*, vol. 6 (1962).

Hook, Sidney. *The Hero in History: A Study in Limitation and Possibility.* Boston: Beacon, 1943.

Hopple, G. W. *Political Psychology and Biopolitics: Assessing and Predicting Elite Behavior in Foreign Policy Crises.* Boulder, Colo.: Westview, 1980.

Hopple, G. W., and L. S. Falkowski, eds. *Biopolitics, Political Psychology and International Politics: Toward a New Discipline.* New York: Frances Pinter, 1982.

Isaak, Robert. *Individuals and World Politics*, 2nd ed. Monterey, Calif.: Duxbury Press, 1981.

Janis, Irving L. *Groupthink*, 2nd ed. New York: Houghton Mifflin, 1982.

Janis, Irving L., and Leon Mann. *Decision Making: A Psychological Analysis of Conflict, Choice, and Commitment.* New York: Free Press, 1977.

Jervis, Robert. *Perception and Misperception in International Politics.* Princeton, N.J.: Princeton University Press, 1976.

Kelman, Herbert C., ed. *International Behavior: A Social-Psychological Analysis.* New York: Holt, Rinehart & Winston, 1965.

Klineberg, Otto. *The Human Dimension in International Relations.* New York: Holt, Rinehart & Winston, 1965.

Lasswell, Harold. *Power and Personality.* New York: Norton, 1976.

Leites, Nathan. *The Operational Code of the Politburo.* New York: McGraw-Hill, 1951.

Mendershausen, Horst. *The Diplomat as a National and Transnational Agent: A Problem in Multiple Loyalty.* Morristown, N.J.: General Learning Press, 1973.

Mitchell, C. R. *The Structure of International Conflict.* New York: St. Martin's, 1981.

Myrdal, Jan, and Gun Kessle. *China: The Revolution Continued—the Cultural Revolution at the Village Level.* New York: Vintage, 1970.

Rustow, Dankwart A., ed. *Philosophers and Kings: Studies in Leadership.* New York: Braziller, 1970.

White, Ralph K. *Nobody Wanted War: Misperception in Vietnam and Other Wars,* rev. and exp. ed. New York: Anchor Doubleday, 1970.

———. *Preventing Nuclear War: A Psychological Perspective.* New York: Free Press, 1984.

On the Military-Industrial Complex

Adams, Gordon. *The Iron Triangle: The Politics of Defense Contracting.* New York: Council on Economic Priorities, 1981.

Aspaturian, Vernon V. "The Soviet Military-Industrial Complex—Does It Exist?" *Journal of International Affairs,* vol. 26, no. 1 (1972), pp. 1–28.

Barnet, Richard. *The Roots of War: The Men and Institutions Behind American Foreign Policy.* New York: Atheneum, 1972.

Domhoff, G. William. *Who Rules America?* Englewood Cliffs, N.J.: Prentice-Hall, 1967.

Donovan, John C. *The Cold Warriors: A Policy-Making Elite.* Lexington, Mass.: Heath, 1974.

Fallows, James. *National Defense.* New York: Random House, 1981.

Gansler, Jacques. *The Defense Industry.* Cambridge, Mass.: MIT Press, 1980.

Keller, Suzanne. *Beyond the Ruling Class.* New York: Random House, 1963.

Koistinen, Paul. *The Military-Industrial Complex: A Historical Perspective.* New York: Praeger, 1980.

Luttwak, Edward N. *The Pentagon and the Art of War.* New York: Simon & Schuster, 1985.

Melman, Seymour. *Pentagon Capitalism: The Political Economy of War.* New York: McGraw-Hill, 1970.

———. *The Permanent War Economy: American Capitalism in Decline,* 2nd ed. New York: Simon & Schuster/Touchstone, 1985.

Mosley, Hugh G. *The Arms Race: Economic and Social Consequences.* Lexington, Mass.: Heath, 1985.

Pilisuk, Marc, and Tom Hayden. "Is There a Military-Industrial Complex That Prevents Peace?" In Charles R. Beitz and Theodore Herman, eds., *Peace and War,* San Francisco: Freeman, 1973. Pp. 288–315.

Rosen, Steven, ed. *Testing the Theory of the Military-Industrial Complex.* Lexington, Mass.: Lexington , 1973.

Russett, Bruce. *What Price Vigilance?* New Haven, Conn.: Yale University Press, 1970.

Yarmolinsky, Adam. *The Military Establishment.* New York: Harper Colophon, 1971.

TRANSNATIONAL ACTORS

O ur analysis of international actors has concentrated so far on nation-states and their leaders. But the state's traditional monopoly of influence has been challenged in the twentieth century by a variety of transnational actors — multinational corporations, terrorist groups, intergovernmental organizations like NATO, the European Community, and the United Nations, and other nonstate actors.

Richard Mansbach, Yale Ferguson, and Donald Lampert, in *The Web of World Politics: Nonstate Actors in the Global System* (pp. 1–45), have charted the shift from a state-centric model to what they call a "complex conglomerate" International system. Before the relatively recent era of state sovereignty (which began in 1648), independent groups and individuals — mercenaries, bankers, religious authorities, trading companies, tribes, clans, imperial monarchs — were free participants in world politics. They had autonomous decision-making power, even without the collective attributes of sovereignty, territoriality, and national identity that we associate with the modern state. After the Napoleonic Wars, when nineteenth-century nationalism hardened boundaries and made states almost the exclusive focus of political loyalty, these nonstate actors declined in number and influence. Now, however, global economic interdependence and the power deadlock of nuclear deterrence have encouraged their resurgence. The Palestine Liberation Organization, the Viet Cong, the Mafia, the Colombian drug cartel, and the Irish Republican Army have all exerted power internationally without having any formal sovereignty or defined territorial bases. Economic cartels like OPEC and multinational corporations like IBM are more powerful and independent than many governments. Such private organizations as the Ford Foundation and the International Red Cross make significant contributions to development and refugee assistance. Transnational loyalties — to the Roman Catholic church, the Zionist movement, the Muslim faith — are more important than national identity to many individuals. Functions that were once concentrated in the nation-state — the maintenance of group identity and status, economic development, physical protection — are now dispersed among a variety of cultural, economic, and defensive units. States that were once impermeable and in control of all transactions across their borders no longer have a monopoly on allegiance, economic regulation, or the use of force.

One important factor in the rise in influence of nonnational actors is that the international system has become more diverse and complex, with a multitude of cross-national ties and many conflicts of political allegiance. The same nationalism that helped to consolidate the European states had a subversive and fractionating impact when it spread into regions that lacked state-sized and homogeneous linguistic or ethnic groups. Peoples with different cultural traditions or levels of economic development were being brought into intimate contact — and friction — by the explosive growth in communications and trade. Sovereign equality among states was being undermined by the rapid industrial growth of a few and the rise to independence of many weak Third World countries.

A second factor is that warfare, whether conventional or nuclear, has become more destructive and expensive and the technologies of destruction more mobile and dispersed. This has reduced state reliance on the use of force but has made destructive means increasingly available to terrorists and guerrillas. Also, nonmilitary weapons of power and influence — public opinion, economic boycotts, political propaganda, control of advanced technology, regulation by intergovernmental organizations — have become more important.

Third, the nation-state has proved unable to meet the rising demand for universal standards of justice, equality, prosperity, and security. Statesmen disillusioned by war have turned to organizations like the United Nations as a means of regulating conflict. Ethnic groups like the Palestinians, disappointed by the failure of separate Arab governments to protect their rights and interests, have formed their own liberation organizations. Companies that have found tariff barriers and state regulation too costly have transferred their operations to a multinational level. States that are not viable as independent units have joined in common markets, regional organizations, and collective security blocs.

The fourth factor is technology, which impinges on outer space, the atmosphere, and the oceans in ways that call out for new forms of international law and regulation. Radio transmission, satellite communications, radioactive fallout, acid rain, ozone depletion, seabed mining, fishing rights, and disposal of toxic wastes are only a few of the problems that defy the principles of territoriality and sovereignty. Also, the internationalization of production and the global dissemination of science have brought the need for new means of regulating corporate practices, patent rights, the licensing of technology, and information sharing, traditionally the province of the nation-state.

The Growth of International Organization

Both interstate governmental organizations (IGOs) and international nongovernmental organizations (INGOs) have grown rapidly since World War II.

Though new nations were born at a record rate during that period, international organizations increased still faster, in numbers, activities, personnel, and budgets. In 1969, the Union of International Associations listed about 2,000 intergovernmental, semiofficial, and private agencies organized across national boundaries. By 1981, the number had reached almost 15,000. IGOs are established by formal government agreement to operate in stated areas, and the first modern IGO was the Central Commission for the Navigation of the Rhine, created at the Congress of Vienna in 1815. Today, the United Nations and its affiliated organizations make up the largest network of IGOs. INGOs have a membership of individuals or private associations, rather than states, and are formed by some means other than government agreement. Many INGOs are independent of any strictly national constituency. These include charitable organizations (the Oxford Committee for Famine Relief, the International Red Cross), religious orders (the Rosicrucians, the Catholic church), and multinational corporations. Others, like the World Federation of Trade Unions, the Socialist International, the International Chamber of Commerce, and the World Alliance of YMCAs, are made up of delegations from their respective national organizations. INGOs often have a consultative relationship with IGOs, much like that of lobbyists with national governments. Both INGOs and IGOs have permanent secretariats, hold regular meetings of their memberships, and have specified procedures for decision making.

INGOs have varying degrees of autonomy and nonpartisanship. When the organization is nonpolitical or highly professional, it can often remain independent of national influence. The International Air Transport Association is free to formulate binding rules for its constituent units, and the International Commission of Jurists, an organization of professionals, serves as an official adviser to the United Nations on human rights. National delegations to INGOs sometimes have latitude in the positions they can adopt. In 1980, for example, the national Olympic Committees of Britain, France, Italy, and Australia refused to comply with their governments' official request that they boycott the Moscow Olympic Games — although this was possible largely because the governments were internally divided and unwilling to apply strong pressure. Multinational corporations also fall into a quasi-independent status. Within limits, they have relative freedom to act, and they certainly exert a powerful lobbying influence on their governments. But if a vital national interest is in jeopardy, a government is quite capable of disciplining a recalcitrant corporation by nationalizing its assets or subjecting it to other controls. As compared to states, the resources of the typical INGO (multinational corporations excepted) are extremely small. The average annual budget does not exceed $1 million, and the average number of paid staff workers is less than ten.

IGOs also lack autonomy in decision making, although their member governments may have granted them some formal authority. Typically, states treat IGOs as forums within which they can more effectively employ the traditional instruments of foreign policy, extending them into areas of growing interrelatedness in which multilateral consultations are necessary. The growing number of IGOs is not, therefore, a sign that international conflict is lessening or that states are sacrificing their sovereign decision-making powers. Many of these organizations, like the UN, NATO, and the EEC, have sprung up because states have concluded that unregulated economic and military conflict has become too costly. But the number of conflicts remains high, as does the penchant of states to exploit the international organizations in furtherance of their own interests. IGOs, made up of member states, generally can act only in those areas in which there is a broad international consensus.

International organizations lack the authority to levy taxes, conscript armies, or impose their rulings. They depend on voluntary funding and implementation and on enforcement by the member states. The assets of even the most powerful IGOs are minuscule in comparison to those of national governments. The funds available to the entire UN system equal less than 1 percent of the U.S. national budget, and the highly successful European Community commands a budget that is less than 2 percent of the combined budgets of its member states. The United Nations relies on voluntary contributions from members for all its funding and its peacekeeping forces. The UN-sponsored forces in Korea, the Congo, the Middle East, and Cyprus, for example, were all military units from various nations on loan to the UN. As Harold Jacobson points out, in *Networks of Interdependence* (p. 84), the UN General Assembly apportions expenses among the member states, but the only penalty for a state that fails to pay its assessment is the loss of its vote in the Assembly, and that only after the state is more than two years in arrears. In the period 1956–60, the Soviet Union, to show its opposition to the conduct of UN peacekeeping forces in the Middle East and the Congo, refused to pay its share of the cost of the forces. By 1962, the accumulated arrears amounted to $100 million, and the UN was in jeopardy of financial collapse. The United States bailed it out, through voluntary payments that brought the U.S. share of the UN budget close to 50 percent. In President Reagan's first term, when support for the UN was unusually low (America actually withdrew from UNESCO), the United States withheld its entire assessed contribution. Since the normal U.S. share amounts to about 25 percent of the UN's regular operating budget (in the early years, it was as high as 47 percent), the United States can exert powerful financial leverage on the organization. Of a total UN budget of roughly $2 billion, less than half is raised through so-called mandatory assessments. The remainder — which supports such vital programs as the peacekeeping force in Cyprus, the UN International Children's Emergency Fund (UNICEF), the UN Development Program, the World Food Program, the Fund for Population Activities, and the Relief and Works Agency for Palestine Refugees — comes from the strictly voluntary contributions of interested states.

The lack of independent financing and enforcement limits the power and scope of international organizations. Jacobson (pp. 88–90) classifies their functions into five major categories — informational, normative, rule-creating, rule-supervisory, and operational — with most of their activities revolving around the first two. The informational function involves the gathering, analysis, exchange, and dissemination of data on a great variety of subjects, representing many points of view. In the security area, for example, the UN is an important forum for publicizing acts of aggression, clarifying positions, determining military capabilities, and gathering facts about a crisis or ongoing conflict. On economic issues, the Organization for Economic Cooperation and Development (OECD) and the UN regularly convoke conferences, collect and publish statistics, and make economic forecasts. In the areas of human rights and environmental protection, such INGOs as Amnesty International and Greenpeace publicize violations and monitor the performance of governments.

The normative function involves the definition of standards and declarations of international principles and goals. While not legally binding, such statements can affect diplomacy by altering perceptions of what is acceptable conduct on the world stage. The Hague Peace Conferences of 1899 and 1907, various League of Nations declarations after 1919, the Briand-Kellogg Pact of 1928, and several articles of the UN Charter have helped to change the perception that wars of aggression — regarded as inevitable in traditional balance-of-power diplomacy — are morally acceptable. UN declarations and findings have served to delegitimize slavery, racial discrimination (especially in the form of South African apartheid), and colonialism. The Universal Declaration of Human Rights, adopted by the UN in 1948, has helped to establish general criteria for evaluating violations of human rights. The World Conference of the International Women's Year (in Mexico City in 1975) and subsequent declarations from the UN Decade for Women have set international norms on women's rights and needs. In economic and technical fields, INGO standards facilitate commerce and scientific exchanges.

The rule-creating function is the enactment of formal treaties that are binding on the states that ratify them. Various disarmament committees of the UN were instrumental in the negotiation of the Partial Test Ban Treaty of 1963, the Nuclear Non-Proliferation Treaty of 1968, and other multilateral arms control measures. INGOs have established many regulatory codes in the areas of communications and transport. The General Agreement on Tariffs and Trade (GATT) sets rules governing international trade, and the OECD has drawn up codes covering capital transactions and direct foreign investment. The International Labor Organization (ILO) has adopted more than 140 conventions regarding working conditions, the EEC has legislated on antitrust regulations, and the World Health Organization (WHO) formulates rules on the collection of health data and control of communicable diseases.

Under the rule-supervisory function, some international organizations are authorized to monitor compliance with certain rules. The International Atomic Energy Agency (IAEA) is responsible for ensuring that fissile materials from nuclear power plants are not diverted to weapons production. The International Chamber of Commerce has set up a Court of International Arbitration to settle business disputes in foreign commerce. The International Telecommunications Union (ITU) monitors the use of radio frequencies so as to reduce transmission interference. The Trusteeship Council of the United Nations supervises decolonization in certain specified non-self-governing territories. The

International Narcotics Control Board, created in 1961, helps to monitor the production and distribution of narcotic drugs, in an effort to limit them to medical and scientific uses.

An international organization with an operational function might, for example, administer financial and technical assistance or deploy military forces. The International Monetary Fund (IMF), the International Bank for Reconstruction and Development (IBRD, or World Bank), the International Development Association (IDA), and the International Finance Corporation (IFC), all UN-affiliated agencies, distribute loans that total more than $5 billion annually. The World Bank alone is now the largest source of development loans to the Third World. Such INGOs as Caritas Internationalis (the International Confederation of Catholic Charities) and OXFAM (the Oxford Committee for Famine Relief) provide substantial technical assistance and private aid funds. The UN Development Program (UNDP) offers fellowships and sends technical experts to developing nations. NATO and the Warsaw Pact make military expenditures and deploy troops. And from time to time the United Nations fields peacekeeping forces in hot spots around the world.

The success of an IGO is closely related to its type of membership, the type of issue it addresses, and its degree of specialization and integration. Membership may be universal, regional, or alliance related. Issues range from political and security concerns to economic or technical cooperation. Purposes may broadly encompass the entire field of international affairs or be narrowly confined to a specific issue or jurisdiction. The United Nations, like its predecessor, the League of Nations, is a universal, general-purpose organization. But many of its agencies, such as WHO, UNICEF, and the United Nations Educational, Scientific, and Cultural Organization (UNESCO), while sharing the global scope and membership, are specialized in their functions. Agencies can be highly formal, integrated organs of international decision making, like the International Court of Justice (ICJ), or they can be loosely integrated, cooperative instruments, like the UN Conference on Trade and Development (UNCTAD).

As might be imagined, membership has proved crucial to the effectiveness and legitimacy of IGOs. Those with universalist pretensions have suffered when their membership has not included all the great powers. The League of Nations was flawed at birth by the inability of President Woodrow Wilson, its architect, to convince his own country to join. The League was further crippled by the resignation or expulsion of Germany, Japan, Italy, and the Soviet Union in the 1930s, following their censure for acts of aggression. It was left with little capacity to forestall the coming world war. The United Nations was divided and ineffective on many issues because of its refusal, for more than two decades, to seat a delegation from Communist China, a nation vast in size and military potential and with an important stake in UN-mediated disputes in Korea and Vietnam. Then, when Communist China finally was admitted, as a permanent member of the Security Council with the right of veto, the Republic of China (Taiwan), a powerful force in the Pacific Rim economy, was effectively excluded. Caught up in the disputes of the Cold War, North and South Korea have both been refused admission, though South Korea is a rising economic power. The Democratic Republic of Vietnam, with the fourth largest standing army in the world, was excluded until 1977. East and West Germany, industrially developed powers in the center of Europe, were excluded from UN deliberations from 1945 until 1973.

On the other hand, the high number of new members from the Third World has dramatically altered the balance of power in the United Nations and in many other international organizations. (Figure 8-1 shows the growth in UN membership.) The sharp bipolar divisions of the Cold War were generally diffused after 1962, and the great powers no longer could monopolize the conduct of international affairs. It became much more difficult to muster a UN consensus for peacekeeping actions in the Third World, and more emphasis was given to economic and social development. An institutional matrix that once favored Europe and North America has now become much more responsive to the concerns of Third World and non-Western states.

Alliance-related organizations like NATO and the Warsaw Pact have been among the most successfully integrated IGOs, precisely because they reflect a consistent ideology. Especially in the early years, the threat of the rival alliance served to strengthen their unity and operational effectiveness. International economic organs took a similar, though unintended, alliance-related orientation. The UN framers had hoped that such organizations as the IMF and the World Bank would be universally accepted, but their commitment to free trade and private capital markets made them better suited to the Western free-market economies than to the planned economies of the Soviet Union and Eastern Europe—and Cold War suspicions also made the Communist states reluctant to join. Consequently, an exclusively Western IGO, the OECD, evolved out of the Marshall Plan, the scheme for Europe's economic reconstruction, and the Soviets organized a rival economic arm among the Warsaw Pact states, the Council for Mutual Economic Assistance (CMEA, or Comecon). Communist states also have generally refused to join the Food and Agriculture Organization (FAO) and GATT.

Many general-purpose IGOs are, like NATO and the Warsaw Pact, organized on regional lines—the Organization for African Unity (OAU), the Organization of American States (OAS), the Arab League, and the Association of Southeast Asian Nations (ASEAN). Other important IGOs are both regional and functionally specialized, such as the EEC, the Andean Group, the Caribbean Community and Common Market (CARICOM), the Arab Monetary Fund, and the Economic Commission of West African States (ECOWAS). On the whole, the regional organizations appear to be better integrated than those of global scope. This is particularly true of the EEC and CARICOM; both have confined themselves largely to economic and technical domains, in which it is much easier to enlist the cooperation of national units. Modest successes in regional cooperation and integration should not be viewed, however, as inevitable steps toward a broader international consensus. Firm regional ties often

FIGURE 8-1

GROWTH OF UN MEMBERSHIP, 1945–85

	Americas	Europe	Asia/Oceania	Africa
1945 Original Members	Argentina, Bolivia, Brazil, Canada, Chile, Colombia, Costa Rica, Cuba, Dominican Republic, Ecuador, El Salvador, Guatemala, Haiti, Honduras, Mexico, Nicaragua, Panama, Paraguay, Peru, United States, Uruguay, Venezuela	Belgium, Belorussia, Czechoslovakia, Denmark, France, Greece, Luxembourg, Netherlands, Norway, Poland, Turkey, Ukraine, U.S.S.R., United Kingdom, Yugoslavia	Australia, China, India, Iran, Iraq, Lebanon, New Zealand, Philippines, Saudi Arabia, Syria	Egypt, Ethiopia, Liberia, South Africa
1945–1965	Jamaica, Trinidad and Tobago	Albania, Austria, Bulgaria, Finland, Hungary, Iceland, Ireland, Italy, Malta, Portugal, Romania, Spain, Sweden	Afghanistan, Burma, Cambodia, Cyprus, Indonesia, Israel, Japan, Jordan, Kuwait, Laos, Malaysia, Maldives, Mongolia, Nepal, Pakistan, Singapore, Sri Lanka, Thailand, Yemen (Sanaa)	Algeria, Benin, Burkina, Burundi, Cameroon, Central African Republic, Chad, Congo, Gabon, The Gambia, Ghana, Guinea, Ivory Coast, Kenya, Libya, Madagascar, Malawi, Mali, Mauritania, Morocco, Niger, Nigeria, Rwanda, Senegal, Sierra Leone, Somalia, Sudan, Tanzania, Togo, Tunisia, Uganda, Zaire, Zambia
1965–1985	Antigua and Barbuda, The Bahamas, Barbados, Belize, Dominica, Grenada, Guyana, St. Christopher and Nevis, St. Lucia, St. Vincent and the Grenadines, Suriname	German Democratic Republic, Germany, Federal Republic of	Bahrain, Bangladesh, Bhutan, Brunei, Fiji, Oman, Papua New Guinea, Qatar, Solomon Islands, United Arab Emirates, Vanuatu, Vietnam, Western Samoa, Yemen (Aden)	Angola, Botswana, Cape Verde, Comoros, Djibouti, Equatorial Guinea, Guinea-Bissau, Lesotho, Mauritius, Mozambique, Sao Tome and Principe, Seychelles, Swaziland, Zimbabwe

make states less sensitive to the interests of those outside the region. A number of ideological blocs and regional military organizations are united by their very hostility to outsiders, and the EEC was founded on decidedly protectionist principles aimed at keeping out foreign goods.

The most successful of the regional IGOs have suffered from divisive national tendencies. France withdrew from NATO in 1962, and the French president, Charles de Gaulle, twice vetoed Britain's entry into the Common Market. (The UK eventually joined in 1972, after Georges Pompidou replaced de Gaulle.) Disputes over farm subsidies and associate membership for former colonies have caused serious national differences within the EEC. Most regional economic organizations are also besieged by pressures from the international market. In the Third World, common market arrangements among primary producers, which trade mainly with the more advanced states, have been ineffective in furthering regional integration. On the other hand, the very economic dynamic and incentives of free exchange that integrated the advanced industrial states of Europe eventually pushed the EEC away from its inward-looking customs union and toward greater global interdependence. Strategic considerations have impelled even the CMEA to abandon its regional focus and associate with a broader community of socialist states. Cuba, Vietnam, North Korea, Laos, Afghanistan, Angola, Mozambique, Ethiopia, and South Yemen are all affiliated in one way or another with the CMEA. As Philip E. Jacob has remarked, in "Organizing Nations in the 1970s," regionalism has not replaced nationalism as the dominant political force in the world today. Nor has regional integration changed the essentially global character of the economic and security problems that international organizations are trying to solve.

We can conclude that the effectiveness of international organizations and the degree of integration or independence they display are inversely related to the size and diversity of their membership and the scope of their assigned functions. Some universal IGOs, such as the IAEA and the International Civil Aviation Organization, are successful regulatory bodies because their activities are narrow in scope and all the subscribing members view their function as a vital one. An organization with a more general purpose, like the EEC, is successful because its concerns are those of a relatively small number of like-minded states. The ideological cohesion and similar political-economic systems of member states make the European Court of Justice and the Commission of the EEC almost unique among international bodies in being able to hand down binding rules and regulations that do not require the consent of member states. Still, European economic cooperation has not spilled over into political integration—at least, not on any scale that holds out hope for an effective supranational authority going beyond a limited economic sphere. Plans for the creation of a single, fully integrated market in Europe by 1992 have brought attendant pressures for more political coordination and greater sovereignty for the European Parliament, but it remains to be seen whether any truly transnational governmental functions will arise or endure. International organizations are subject to two contradictory pulls—economic, social, and ideological impulses toward integration, offset by the traditional resistance to the surrender of national sovereignty. They tend to go through pendulumlike swings between periods of regional or global cooperation and periods of state rivalry and institutional disintegration. The proliferation of organizations certainly testifies to the rise of a global agenda, but it by no means signifies greater global unity. Indeed, the world may have been more united and its conduct more coordinated during the nineteenth-century Concert of Europe, when a few great powers dominated, than it is today, when greater economic interdependence exists alongside a global pluralism that emphasizes sovereign equality among states.

International organizations are not supergovernments. As Jacob's article suggests, their role is to reconcile political pluralism and a decentralized state system with technological and social interdependence. They are something more than short-term security-minded alliance systems, which tend to divide the world, and something less than an incipient world government. They are a useful, and even unique, instrument for collaboration within the framework of sovereign states. In Jacob's words, they are "the great political innovation of our times, an instrument of political integration accomplishing what federalism set out to do two centuries ago, but by different processes, and much more extensive in scope." However, we cannot expect them to legislate, adjudicate, or enforce decisions—all the jealously guarded prerogatives of nation-states. International organizations come to grief if they try to force a state to do something it has not agreed to or if they let themselves become smokescreens to hide a government's evasion of its responsibilities. Many of them also suffer from being bureaucracies without a constituency to enforce accountability.

On the other hand, international organizations that embody a true consensus among their member states can be effective regulators and mobilizers of social and economic resources. As neutral third parties, IGOs can mediate disputes, serve as impartial observers, and police cease-fires. They can engage in what UN Secretary-General Dag Hammarskjöld called "preventive diplomacy," intervening to defuse an impending conflict or help the parties reach an accommodation of interests. They are a forum for negotiating informal "rules of the game" and realizing convergent interests. There has emerged what Jacob calls a body of "convenience law" to deal with the problems of increased interdependence. Moreover, the decisions of international organizations are more open to public scrutiny than those of traditional diplomacy. The positions of nongovernmental actors can be introduced with greater regularity, since the horizon of decision is not limited to that of the nation-state. Small, weak, and poor states are better represented. All these features make world politics more rational and more equitable. International organizations are a vital, positive, and permanent force in world affairs.

The following section examines in detail the United Nations, the most important IGO of this century. Then we study terrorist movements, as an example of a transnational, nonterritorial actor, and, finally, multinational corporations, the most important of the INGOs.

THE UNITED NATIONS

The United Nations, founded in 1945 in response to the calamity of two successive world wars, reflected the hope that the wartime cooperation of the Allies
could be institutionalized as the basis for an enduring system of collective
security. Its architects were anxious to avoid the failings of the League of
Nations, which lacked the power to respond effectively to quell aggression.
Consequently, they endowed the United Nations with stronger enforcement
powers, which they lodged in an eleven-member Security Council that could
authorize the use of peacekeeping forces as well as economic sanctions. A
permanent Secretariat would carry out the daily routine, under a secretary-
general whose role was defined as truly transnational. The Secretariat was to
be staffed by tenured civil servants hired on the basis of merit, constituting an
impartial international bureaucracy that would stand above national pressures. To counter another failing of the League, the weakness of its preventive
powers, the United Nations was given several new functions addressing the
social and economic causes of war. A Trusteeship Council was established to
speed an orderly and peaceful decolonization. An Economic and Social Council
would supervise a network of specialized agencies dealing with such issues as
health, nutrition, education, human rights, economic development, working
conditions, the status of women, refugees, and child welfare. An International
Court of Justice was set up to strengthen international law and adjudicate
disputes among nations (provided they accepted the court's jurisdiction) on any
matters covered by the UN Charter.

The General Assembly was the parliamentary hub for all this. The largest
and most representative body, it would exercise deliberative, supervisory,
financial, elective, and constituent functions, and all member states would be
treated as sovereign equals in the Assembly. (Figure 8-2 is a diagram of the
UN's six basic organs, with their various subcommittees and specialized agencies.) All this added up to a potentially powerful mandate embodying an array
of responsibilities in the areas of justice, security, economic development,
social welfare, and human rights that no previous international organization
had ever taken on.

The specialized agencies have proved particularly effective at carrying out
the mandate. For one thing, they have focused on less controversial technical
issues. For another, from the beginning they were given an autonomous or
semi-independent status that has stood them in good stead. Some IGOs, such as
the ILO, predated the UN. The founders wanted their participation, as well as
that of various citizens' organizations and INGOs, and so they made provision
for organizations whose membership might be different from that of the UN
itself to affiliate with the Economic and Social Council. Also, certain agencies,
such as the IMF and the IBRD, would receive most of their funds from the
developed capitalist states and thus did not lend themselves to majoritarian,
one-state–one-vote practices. A weighted voting scheme that favored the major
economic powers was adopted for these agencies, much like the great-power

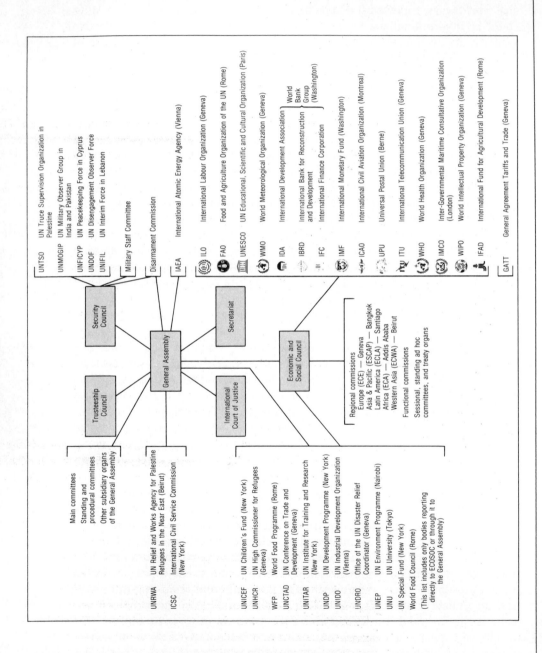

FIGURE 8-2
THE UNITED NATIONS

474

veto in the Security Council reflecting military dominance. The UN's founders thought it prudent to separate nonpolitical agencies from the sensitive areas of peacekeeping and collective security. This good judgment helped to keep such specialized agencies as WHO, FAO, the International Civil Aviation Organization, and the ITU functioning throughout the Cold War—at a time when the Soviet Union and its allies were refusing to support peacekeeping efforts in the Congo and the Middle East and had declined to join the IMF, the World Bank, the FAO, and a number of other UN organs. As the General Assembly grew in size and political fractiousness, this organizational scheme kept economic and social functions somewhat insulated from the immobility, political divisions, and ideological posturing of the parent body.

The UN's biggest weakness lay in the central area of conflict resolution, where little could be done without the unanimous support of the Big Five, the permanent members of the Security Council. The framers had been unduly optimistic about postwar unity, failing to foresee the dramatic rupture between the Soviet Union and the United States or the imminent collapse of Chiang Kai-shek's Nationalist government in China. The great powers of the time— the United States, the Soviet Union, Great Britain, France, and China—had consented to an expanded and more independent role for the UN's executive arm only because each of them would have a veto in the Security Council on all substantive matters. These included enforcement actions against aggressors, proposals for the peaceful settlement of disputes, admission of new members, election of the secretary-general, and amendments to the UN Charter. The earliest disputes were over membership issues, which precipitated frequent Soviet vetoes. Membership for Germany, Korea, and Vietnam, divided by cold war or hot, was particularly contested between the two superpowers. Then, as decolonization brought strife to the Middle East and Africa, rival blocs began to use the United Nations as an ideological forum, and the Security Council became further divided. The United States controlled a majority of the votes on most proposals, but the Soviet Union and its East European allies cast repeated vetoes to block action. (The Soviets cast nearly 80 percent of the Security Council vetoes in the first decade.)

UN Peacekeeping Efforts

When North Korea invaded South Korea in 1950, the Cold War deadlock threatened to stall any action in the United Nations. However, the Western powers were able to get around Soviet opposition by a maneuver that eventually was formalized (during the 1956 Suez crisis) in the "Uniting for Peace" resolution. This procedure gave the General Assembly the power to recommend collective security measures in the event that the Security Council was unwilling or unable to act. The United States and its allies, with an overwhelming majority in the General Assembly in these early decades, could effectively bypass the Soviet veto, and the strategy permitted ongoing UN sponsorship of allied intervention in Korea and in the Middle East. Critics have noted that the measure also bypassed the framers' intentions that the United Nations should never interfere in members' internal affairs or take any military actions without the consent of all five permanent members of the Security Council. The founders presumed that the principle of collective security, and with it the UN's prestige, was based on a common perception of aggression and a united response to it by the leading members of the international community. The Korean action gained for the United States the prestige of being approved by the United Nations, but it was at the expense of the UN's reputation for impartiality.

Nevertheless, the General Assembly's augmented peacekeeping functions proved helpful in subsequent crises. (For an overview of peacekeeping operations, see Figure 8-3.) When Belgium withdrew from the Congo in 1960, plunging that new nation into political turmoil, the United Nations was once again called on to intervene militarily, and Secretary-General Dag Hammarskjöld interpreted the General Assembly's peacekeeping mandate in broad and activist terms. At its height, the UN Congo Operations (ONUC) involved over 20,000 troops from thirty-four countries. However, UN forces could not remain without securing the approval of a sovereign government in the Congo, and the infant administration of Joseph Kasavubu was under challenge from Patrice Lumumba and radical secessionist forces in the provinces of Katanga and Kasai. Any consensus on UN mediation quickly vanished in civil war, tribal conflict, and accusations of neocolonialist intervention, plunging the ONUC into deep controversy and precipitating the Soviet refusal to fund its share of the peacekeeping costs. Nonetheless, the UN forces were able to contain the worst excesses of the civil war, save innocent civilian lives, carry out some administrative functions, and prevent great-power intervention. By 1964, when it was disbanded, the ONUC had succeeded in stabilizing the Congo and preventing the conflict from escalating into a general war.

In 1964, another peacekeeping mission was launched in Cyprus, where the Greek and Turkish communities were embroiled in civil conflict. The mission included a UN-appointed mediator, to assist in the negotiation of a political settlement, and the UN Force in Cyprus (UNFICYP), which has been supported by voluntary contributions and has had its authorization renewed by the Security Council more than forty times. It has maintained its strict neutrality over more than two decades and has helped to reduce the level of violence in the long-standing struggle.

In the series of Middle East wars between the Arabs and the Israelis, the United Nations negotiated cease-fires during the Suez crises of 1956 and 1973, which were monitored by a UN Emergency Force (UNEF), and it sent Disengagement Observer Forces (UNDOF) to the Middle East in 1973, 1974, and 1978. A UN Observer Group played an important mediating role in the Lebanese civil war of 1958, and a UN Interim Force in Lebanon (UNIFIL) was sent in 1978 to supervise Israel's withdrawal from southern Lebanon. Composed of 1,000 French paratroopers and 5,000 soldiers from other neutral nations, the UNIFIL has been trying to keep peace in Lebanon for more than a decade, outlasting the more partisan multilateral forces organized by the United States.

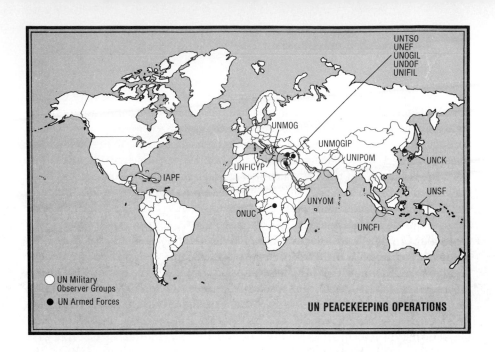

FIGURE 8-3

UN PEACEKEEPING OPERATIONS

Latin America

IAPF   Inter-American Peace Force, 1965–66; Dominican Republic   5

Africa

ONUC   UN Operation in the Congo, 1960–64   34

Europe

UNMOG   UN Military Observers in Greece, 1952–54   7
UNFICYP   UN Force in Cyprus, 1974–present   10

Middle East

UNTSO   UN Truce Supervision Organization in Palestine, 1948–present   17
UNEF   UN Emergency Force, 1956–67, 1973–79; Sinai and Gaza   10
UNOGIL   UN Observer Group in Lebanon, June–December 1958   21
UNDOF   UN Disengagement Observer Force, 1974–present; Israeli-Syrian border   17
UNIFIL   UN Interim Force in Lebanon, 1978–present   9
UNYOM   UN Yemen Observation Mission, 1963–64   13

Asia/Pacific

UNMOGIP   UN Military Observer Group in India and Pakistan, 1948–present   14
UNCFI   UN Commission for Indonesia, 1949–51   6
UNCK   UN Command in Korea, 1950–present   17
UNSF   UN Security Force, 1962–63; West Irian   6
UNIPOM   UN India-Pakistan Observation Mission, 1965–66   20

  Number of states that contributed forces

Over the UN's five decades, the balance of power in the Security Council and the General Assembly has shifted dramatically. After 1960, many newly independent Third World states became members, expanding membership from the original 51 members to over 150 states. In response to pressures from the nonaligned movement and the Group of 77, the Security Council was enlarged from eleven to fifteen members. The ten nonpermanent seats, filled every two years by vote of the General Assembly, are now apportioned (by informal agreement) geographically and ideologically: five for Africa and Asia, two for Latin America, one for the Eastern bloc, two for the Western bloc. The seating of Communist China as a permanent member of the Security Council further altered the political balance by strengthening the Third World voice, and the traditional East-West bipolar division became a more complex triangular one. It now was difficult for the United States to control a majority on the Security Council, and it began to cast a greater number of vetoes, mainly on Middle East and South African issues. For example, when a growing radical majority in the General Assembly took up the Palestinian cause and gave observer status to Yasir Arafat's Palestine Liberation Organization (PLO), the United States continued its staunch defense of its client, Israel, by vetoing a 1983 resolution that condemned Israeli settlements in the West Bank and, in 1988, by refusing to recognize the diplomatic status of the PLO delegates, which forced the closure of the Palestinian UN mission. On South Africa, the United States has condemned apartheid but has used its veto to block the use of force and the imposition of full economic sanctions.

Meanwhile, the General Assembly was splitting along North-South lines, as manifested by the growing practice of bloc voting and by the call, at the Sixth Special Session of the General Assembly in 1974, for a New International Economic Order (NIEO). To the cohesive Communist bloc (9 votes) and the Atlantic community (18 votes) was now added a new, and more outspoken, Third World bloc (commanding roughly 120 votes). Though the bloc periodically broke down into various subdivisions — the nonaligned group, the Group of 77, the Islamic Conference, ASEAN, the Latin American states, and small regional blocs — the overall strength of its voice changed the tenor of UN politics. The United States, regarded as a status quo power and the inheritor of Europe's colonial mantle, became the target of heavy criticism. Anti-Western and anticolonial sentiment spilled over into the specialized agencies as well. The General Conference of UNESCO, for example, adopted a number of resolutions unfavorable to Israel and reorganized the agency's information procedures to get them out of the control of the allegedly "imperialistic" Western media. In 1976, Secretary of State Henry Kissinger announced that the United States would reduce its economic assistance to any country that voted against it in the UN, and in the following decade the United States withdrew from the ILO and UNESCO, on the ground that Third World states were consistently sponsoring anti-Western resolutions and employing the agencies' machinery for their own narrow purposes. The Third World states responded that this was exactly what the superpowers had done during the first decades of the Cold War. Although the United States has been able to maintain its influence in most of the specialized agencies and can still command a General Assembly majority on most of the issues it considers vital, the radical tone of General Assembly debate and the strenuous diplomacy required to muster support have eroded America's confidence in the United Nations. For a time, the acrimony led the great powers to conduct some of their important business outside the UN framework, where they did not have to woo votes or worry about censure. Britain, for one, spurned the UN's mediation efforts in the 1982 Falkland (Malvinas) Islands War. However, the value of the UN as a neutral forum, and of the good offices of the secretary-general as a mediator, was reaffirmed when, in the late 1980s, the UN sponsored talks and negotiated the deescalation of conflicts in Afghanistan, Kampuchea, Angola/Namibia, and other hot spots in the Third World. This revitalization of the peacekeeping function was the result of a convergence of interests between the two superpowers and of the Soviet Union's desire to withdraw from exposed positions in the Third World, which were becoming too expensive both militarily and diplomatically.

The Struggle for an Independent Transgovernmental Role

Rarely in its history has the United Nations been able to escape the limitations of a body composed of sovereign states, all working zealously to enlist the organization on behalf of their national concerns. Power politicking is as much present at the UN's New York headquarters as in any other diplomatic forum, and the various impasses in East-West and North-South relations involve the very issues on which the UN has been most impotent. It was unable to act against the Soviet invasions of Hungary in 1956 and Czechoslovakia in 1968, and it could not mediate the long and bloody contest in Vietnam. The General Assembly did condemn the Soviet invasion of Afghanistan and the Iranian seizure of American diplomatic personnel in 1979, but Soviet vetoes prevented economic sanctions or any other effective action. More than half the resolutions passed by the General Assembly since 1980 (and well over half the U.S. vetoes) have dealt with the Arab-Israeli dispute and with South Africa, with no apparent contribution to a peaceful settlement. (Recent progress has been made in dismantling apartheid in South Africa, but the UN contribution to these new developments has been minimal.)

The restraining effect of national loyalties becomes clear in the functioning of the World Court, ostensibly one of the most international and independent of the UN bodies. The judges who sit on the International Court of Justice are chosen as individuals, but the court's statutes permit a balancing of nationalities by the appointment of special judges from each of the states that are parties to a dispute. Not surprisingly, the votes of the judges tend to correspond to the voting blocs in the General Assembly, lending force to the argument that national points of view do influence the interpretation of international law. Another case in which the national interest prevailed over the UN's commitment to a global outlook occurred in the 1950s, at the height of Senator Joseph McCarthy's anti-Communist witch-hunt. The U.S. government forced the UN secretary-general to dismiss some American employees of the Secretariat who had refused to take loyalty oaths or cooperate in a Senate investigation of alleged Communist activities at the UN. An administrative tribunal, the General Assembly, and the World Court all ruled that the dismissals violated the integrity and neutrality of the UN's civil service, but Congress remained adamant, refusing to compensate the officials or allow them to be reinstated. Similarly, in 1961, during the UN's vigorous intervention in the Congo, the Soviet Union tried to curb the organization's independence by proposing to replace the secretary-general with a troika arrangement that would represent the three prevailing ideological blocs — socialist, neutralist, and Western. Though the proposal failed, it epitomized the national opposition that the UN can arouse when it tries to act independently.

The changing conceptions of various secretaries-general about the responsibilities of the office illustrate the delicate balance the UN has had to strike between national interests, an international consensus, and transnational values. The first secretary-general, Trygve Lie of Norway, used his political powers freely and often took positions that brought him into conflict with the great powers. He got in trouble with the United States by advocating the admission of Communist China, and then he alienated the Soviet Union by supporting the police action against North Korea. He saw himself as an international statesman speaking for the world community, but his outspoken independence finally forced his resignation in 1952.

Dag Hammarskjöld of Sweden, who replaced Lie, adopted a strategy of anonymity and quiet diplomacy, although he occasionally interpreted his peacekeeping mandate broadly and was committed to the principles of the UN Charter above all else. His low-key style and his scrupulously nonpartisan public demeanor earned him the confidence of a majority, and he was reelected to a second five-year term. When Soviet Premier Nikita Khrushchev challenged his neutrality, in the midst of the Congo crisis, Hammarskjöld replied eloquently: "It may be true that in a very deep human sense there is no neutral individual, because everyone, if he is worth anything, has to have his ideas and ideals. . . . But what I do claim is that even a man who is in that sense not neutral can very well undertake and carry through neutral actions because that is an act of integrity." Hammarskjöld's repeated initiatives on behalf of peace, in the face of the Cold War stalemate, demonstrated that the secretary-general did have the authority to act when the superpowers were deadlocked, and he claimed for the UN a kind of residual power in international affairs.

Hammarskjöld's successor, Burma's U Thant, carried forward this conception of the secretary-general as an international statesman and neutral mediator who could offer both discreet diplomacy and a reservoir of good will in moments of crisis. U Thant was somewhat less active, however, consistent with the gradual decline of the UN's influence. Lack of Soviet support in the U Thant years and, later, the growing disaffection of the United States in the early Reagan years handicapped UN peacekeeping and mediation efforts between 1960 and 1986. An Austrian, Kurt Waldheim, who became the fourth secretary-general in 1971, continued the role of moderate activism mixed with impartiality, taking initiatives on international terrorism, famine relief, and peacekeeping. He was followed by Javier Perez de Cuellar, a professional diplomat from Peru, who has served as secretary-general since 1982. Perez de Cuellar, more of an activist, criticized the world community in 1983 for not making better use of the United Nations as a framework for settling international disputes, and he has presided over its modest revitalization in the years since 1986.

The intergovernmental character of the UN and the still-powerful influence of national perspectives limit its role as a transnational actor. One domain that does display truly transnational qualities is the international terrorist movement.

INTERNATIONAL TERRORISM

Shortly before Christmas in 1975, a group of gunmen broke into the OPEC building in Vienna, seized a dozen oil ministers as hostages, and held them prisoner for several days, compelling the Austrian media to broadcast a revolutionary manifesto on behalf of Palestinian liberation. Despite their claim to be acting on behalf of the Palestine liberation movement, however, only a few of the gunmen were Arabs, and it is not certain that there was a single Palestinian among them. They appeared to be led by Germans and Latin Americans, principally Ilyich Ramírez Sánchez, a Venezuelan trained in Moscow and supported by the Cuban intelligence apparatus in Paris. The Egyptian press said that Libya's Colonel Moammar Khadafy had paid for the whole operation. Whatever the facts of the matter, the episode dramatizes the extent to which terrorism has become truly international; its membership, financing, organization, arms, and ideology span national boundaries as easily as a hijacked jetliner does.

Terrorism is not new to world politics. Before World War I, anarchists and revolutionaries, using assassination as a weapon, assaulted a number of heads of state in Europe and America, and the assassination of the Austrian heir-apparent, Archduke Franz Ferdinand, by Yugoslav terrorists in 1914 set World War I in motion. The Irish Republican Army has a history of terrorism stretching back into the last century and continuing right to this day. But modern terrorism is both more frequent and more widespread, more threatening to innocent people, and, through its manipulation of the mass media, more capable of arousing political consciousness and inspiring fear. Over 80 percent of terrorist attacks are directed at people rather than property, and the death rate has been growing along with the lethality of the weapons employed. There were more than 8,000 terrorist incidents between 1968 and 1982, with the number steadily rising from about 150 per year to 800 per year and with more than 3,600 deaths. Western Europe was the most frequent locale, because of its open borders and free democratic societies. In Latin America and the Middle East, the primary targets have been Western officials and businessmen, said to represent the existing power structure. Typical terrorist techniques include hijacking, kidnapping, assassination, sabotage, bombing, and sniper attacks.

The Growth of International Terrorism

The spread of international terrorism is due, first, to technology, which has transformed its every aspect. Modern weapons are highly lethal and mobile. Bombs made of plastic explosives and sophisticated timing devices are easy to plant in cars, airliners, and elsewhere and can even be used for assassinations through the mail. Jet aircraft facilitate contacts among terrorists, offer fast getaways, and are highly visible targets in themselves. Technologically advanced societies are in many ways more fragile, their interdependent networks susceptible to disruption at many points, and nuclear technology is a particularly vulnerable and potentially devastating target for sabotage. Louis René Beres, in "The Nuclear Threat of Terrorism," reports that U.S. nuclear facilities alone experienced more than 175 instances of violence or threatened violence between 1969 and 1978. And nuclear fission may provide the terrorist of tomorrow with the ultimate weapon: without too much difficulty, a very small amount of plutonium can yield a primitive but highly lethal nuclear device. Also, modern technology's worldwide communication networks make it easy for terrorists to coordinate covert actions, and, above all, radio and television give them a mass media to exploit and an international public opinion to appeal to.

In the second place, political, ideological, and religious fragmentation, along with rising national consciousness, has multiplied the number of aggrieved minorities seeking self-determination, and the weakest and most frustrated of these groups may turn to terrorist tactics. Ironically, the rise in liberation movements may be a reaction to the centralizing power of the modern state, which has forced groups that had been relatively autonomous into obedience to a higher sovereignty. Among the minorities are those that wish to found their own new states (Croatians in Yugoslavia, Basques in Spain, Kurds in Iran and Iraq, the Quebecois in Canada); those that aim to destroy an existing state (the Popular Front for the Liberation of Palestine); and those that wish to liberate territory from the control of others (the Irish Republican Army, the Palestine Liberation Organization, and the Armed Forces for National Liberation of Puerto Rico). The most effective and enduring terrorist groups are those with an ethnic base and nationalist aspirations. But many of the groups have broader political, economic, or religious agendas. Some desire to overthrow existing regimes (Tupamaro guerrillas in Uruguay, anti-Castro Cuban exiles); others seek to revolutionize the entire world order (the Italian Red Brigade, the West German Baader-Meinhof group, the Japanese Red Army, and the American Weather Underground); some reflect the growing power of Islamic fundamentalism (Islamic Jihad, Hezbollah, or Party of God, and a multitude of Shi'ite Muslim movements in Lebanon, Kuwait, and elsewhere).

Third, terrorism has multiplied because it has been remarkably effective in the short term. In their study of seventy-five kidnappings, entitled "Numbered Lives," Brian Jenkins, Janera Johnson, and David Ronfeldt enumerate the following results:

- an 86 percent probability of actually seizing hostages
- a 77 percent chance that all members of a kidnap team will escape punishment or death, whether or not they successfully seize hostages
- a 39 percent chance that at least some demands will be met when more than just safe passage or exit permission is demanded
- a 26 percent chance of full compliance with demands
- an 86 percent chance of success when a safe exit for themselves or others is the sole demand
- a 60 percent chance that, if the principal demands are rejected, all or nearly all the kidnappers can still escape by going underground, accepting safe passage, or surrendering to a sympathetic government
- an almost 100 percent probability of gaining major publicity

In Latin America, terrorist organizations have collected ransoms ranging from $1 million to $60 million for foreign businessmen held hostage. Before the introduction of more stringent airport security in the mid-1970s, airline hijackers routinely escaped without punishment. Such highly publicized events have a "demonstration effect" that has led other terrorists to carry out similar acts of political extortion.

The Difficulty of Defining a Terrorist

Judgments about the success of international terrorism depend very much on what we mean by terrorism. If it is defined in the broadest terms as the clandestine use of politically motivated violence or threats of violence against noncombatants, terrorism would have to include the guerrilla tactics of national liberation movements, covert acts of violence by the secret services and surrogate armies of the Soviet Union or the United States, and death-squad killings by the likes of Hitler, Stalin, the Ayatollah Khomeini, Khadafy, and the right-wing governments of Chile, Argentina, El Salvador, Nicaragua, and Guatemala. In these terms, terrorism is commonplace and often "successful"; it has installed many a government in power or kept it there. Some events, by their exceptional nature, are labeled as terrorist acts — such as the suicide truck bombing of the U.S. Marine Corps barracks in Beirut in 1983 — when in fact they are attacks on military personnel in a declared war zone. Other groups are called terrorist because of their extremism or fanaticism, as the Indian government has labeled its Sikh opposition. Some people regard the nuclear bombings of Hiroshima and Nagasaki or the massive firebombing of Dresden as terrorist acts because the sacrifice of innocent civilian lives was so horrifying

as to alter the will of the Japanese or the Germans to continue fighting. Terrorism tends to become a label of opprobrium attached to any allegedly immoral
means and any allegedly illegitimate or overzealous groups.

One group's terrorist can be another group's freedom fighter. As Conor
Cruise O'Brien has written, in "Liberty and Terrorism":

> Those who are described as terrorists, and who reject that title for themselves,
> make the uncomfortable point that national armed forces, fully supported by
> democratic opinion, have in fact employed violence and terror on a far vaster
> scale than what liberation movements have as yet been able to attain. The
> "freedom fighters" see themselves as fighting a just war. Why should they not
> be entitled to kill, burn, and destroy as national armies, navies and air forces do,
> and why should the label "terrorist" be applied to them and not to the national
> militaries?

The ambiguity in terms was particularly apparent during the Reagan years,
when the United States supported governments as diverse as those of Israel,
Zimbabwe, Mozambique, and Chile—all of which had come to power by
guerrilla struggle or had retained power by terrorist means—but denounced
the oppression of freedom fighters in Afghanistan, Angola, and Nicaragua. The
president's vocal opposition to the PLO's terrorism and to the hostage-taking
Shi'ite factions in Lebanon was difficult to square with his condoning of semiofficial relations with Iran and with the various clandestine terrorist acts of the
CIA and the Nicaraguan *contras*. Given the frequency of civil war, the extent of
authoritarian violence, the historical complexity of cross-cutting territorial
claims, and the vacuum in authority brought about by decolonization, it is
extremely difficult to make a moral distinction between repression by an existing authority and revolutionary acts by those being repressed. The terror is
certainly real on both sides.

A more narrow definition of terrorism limits it to *random* acts of violence
employing *fear* or intimidation and aimed at coercing, persuading, or gaining
public attention. This would exclude acts of violence against official or military
targets in an ongoing conflict between two declared opponents, no matter how
unconventional the means or supposedly illegitimate the cause. What makes
terrorism distinctive is its use of symbolic acts of violence to gain publicity and
thereby alter the perceptions or loyalties of persons not directly involved. It is
"propaganda by the deed"—dramatic acts aimed at mobilizing popular revolutionary energies and harassing existing regimes. Sometimes terrorists sacrifice their own lives as a statement of principle, or they deliberately provoke
repression in the hope of polarizing a society. A terrorist can often unravel a
few threads of the social fabric by the mere threat of acting; a telephoned bomb
threat usually achieves the desired effect of publicity and disruption.

International terror, strictly speaking, always involves "acts of violence
across national boundaries, or with clear international repercussions, often
within the territory or involving the citizens of a third party to a dispute. Thus it
is to be distinguished from domestic terrorism of the sort that has taken place in
Ulster, the Soviet Union or South Africa," writes Andrew J. Pierre in "The
Politics of International Terrorism." However, the difficulties of distinguish-

ing domestic from international terror, "legitimate" covert intelligence operations from "state-sponsored terrorism," acts of "national liberation" from "criminal" conduct, have hampered all efforts to cope with terrorism. Some acts—the slaughter of Israeli athletes by Palestinian commandos at the Munich Olympics in 1972, the 1981 assassination attempt on Pope John Paul II, the 1985 airport massacres in Rome and Athens— have evinced near-universal revulsion; others have received a mixed response in the international community.

At the Twenty-seventh Session of the UN General Assembly, the United States submitted a draft treaty on terrorism in the hope of fashioning a diplomatic consensus. According to this Convention for the Prevention and Punishment of Certain Acts of International Terrorism, violence against third countries or innocent parties could be curtailed if nations would apply sanctions in the following cases: if the act is committed or takes effect outside the territory of the state of which the alleged offender is a national; if it is committed or takes effect outside the territory of the state against which the act is directed; if it is committed neither by nor against a member of the armed forces of a state in the course of military activities; if it is intended to damage the interest of or obtain concessions from a state or an international organization. Even this limited definition, which clearly excluded freedom fighters engaged in a war of national liberation in their own country, failed to receive widespread support. The difference in political views was simply too great: Yasir Arafat of the PLO, in speaking against the convention, likened himself to George Washington in the American colonies' revolution against Britain, remarking that under the proposed definition, Lafayette, the Frenchman who aided the American cause, would have been considered a terrorist. A second draft treaty, an International Convention Against the Taking of Hostages, was submitted in 1979 and eventually signed by more than forty countries. But it did not deter the Iranians from taking American diplomatic personnel as hostages after the ouster of the Shah in 1979. Nor did a unanimous decision of the International Court of Justice against the taking of diplomats as hostages persuade the Iranians to set them free. However, the treaty may well have contributed to a universal condemnation of the Iranian action, and that could deter future transgressions of the codes of diplomatic conduct.

Antiterrorist Measures in the International Community

Strategies for coping with terrorism vary. Some emphasize the underlying causes and some the prevention and punishment of overt acts. A long-term strategy would focus on the economic, social, and political grievances of terrorists. Many Third World countries argue that giving the PLO recognition and a legitimate place in Middle East negotiations would go far toward alleviating its frustrations and disarming the more radical of the Palestinians. Other nations follow a stern policy of no concessions and tough sanctions. They argue for stricter laws, stiffer punishments, and military or economic sanctions against countries that shelter hijackers or sponsor terrorism. There has been some cooperation in the sharing of intelligence data through international police agencies like Interpol. But the only consensus on enforcement concerns airliner hijackings; every state has an interest in avoiding disruptions in air traffic and losses of life and property, and no state wishes to deal with the political consequences of harboring a hijacked airliner on its territory. Governments as estranged as those of Cuba and the United States have agreed on rules for the extradition of hijackers. The 1963 Tokyo Convention, the 1970 Hague Convention, and the 1971 Montreal Convention, all instigated by the International Civil Aviation Organization, are widely supported moves to prevent terrorist skyjackings.

Nonetheless, formidable obstacles remain to the control of terrorism through international law. States disagree over who has a right to political asylum and what is a criminal and what a political act. Jurisdictions are disputed and extradition legally complex. The hijackers of the *Achille Lauro,* captured in a dramatic midair intercept with the cooperation of the Egyptian government, were set free in Italy (against the wishes of the United States) because of problems of jurisdiction. In another case, the West Germans refused to extradite a convicted terrorist to the United States because they feared the terrorist organizations fighting the extradition order would retaliate against German hostages they held. The U.S. involvement in an arms-for-hostages deal with Iran (accompanied by an illegal diversion of funds to the Nicaraguan *contras*) and France's payment of ransom for hostages (despite a public policy to the contrary) make it clear that national foreign policy concerns often override a nation's commitments to combat terrorism.

The very nature of terrorist organizations makes it difficult to enforce sanctions against them. Conventional military weapons are of little use because terrorists possess no territory (except for temporary sanctuaries) to attack. Often perpetrators are difficult to identify. Terrorist groups — even those that have formally acknowledged responsibility — are often sheltered by sympathetic governments (such as Iran, Libya, Syria, Iraq, South Yemen, Somalia, and North Korea); or they install themselves in countries too weak to expel them (as the PLO did in Lebanon in the 1970s). The diplomatic costs and the military risks of directly attacking such sanctuaries have usually prevented retaliation. Israel is one of the few nations that has consistently attacked terrorist redoubts, no matter whose sovereignty is violated, but the policy has lost the Israelis much international support. And in Lebanon it entangled Israel in a costly and draining war. By virtue of their transcendent goals and fanatic commitment to a cause, some groups, like the Arab fedayeen ("self-sacrificers"), are relatively immune to any rational cost-benefit calculations of the effects of violence. Terrorists also seem to defy all the norms of international law and diplomacy, making it difficult for anyone to conduct traditional negotiations with them. This defiance of diplomatic rules was vividly clear in the seizure by a radical Shi'ite faction in Lebanon of Terry Waite, an Anglican emissary who had been serving for years as a mediator and neutral party in hostage disputes.

Suppression of terrorism within a state's own boundaries inevitably leads to restrictions on personal freedom and political rights. Authoritarian regimes can readily abridge freedom in exchange for security, but for democratic societies it is a costly strategy. In both Israel and Northern Ireland, strict and prolonged antiterrorist police measures have not removed either the root problem or the ongoing threat, and both societies have become militarized and considerably less democratic. In 1988, after decades of police repression of its Palestinian population, Israel experienced large-scale political unrest so severe that it has threatened to erode the constitutional base of Israel's free society. It may someday be said that Israel's rigid and discriminatory antiterrorist policies contributed more to the unmaking of the regime than terrorism itself did.

The issue is made more complex by established governments' ready use of terrorist tactics or support of terrorist groups. The United States has frequently accused the Soviet Union, Cuba, Libya, and Iran of sponsoring terrorism. The United States in turn has been accused of supporting terrorist operations in Vietnam, Chile, Central America, and elsewhere. The Bulgarians were directly implicated in the assassination attempt on Pope John Paul II, and the Iranians have been open in their support for a wide variety of terrorist groups. In 1988, after President Reagan's extension of American naval protection to shipping in the Persian Gulf, Iran threatened direct terrorist retaliation against the United States for the sinking of two Iranian frigates and a number of patrol boats. That same year, the PLO military commander, Khalil Wazir, was assassinated at his residence in Tunisia by Israel's Mossad intelligence service. Wazir, the number-two man in the PLO, allegedly had masterminded the Palestinian uprising in Israel's occupied territories. Though Israel did not officially admit responsibility, its informal acknowledgment was widely circulated, perhaps to deter further PLO efforts to destabilize the volatile West Bank and Gaza Strip. By all appearances, for some states terrorism has become just one more instrument of foreign policy.

As Brian Jenkins has noted, in his study entitled "High Technology Terrorism and Surrogate War":

> Finding modern conventional war an increasingly unattractive mode of conflict, some nations may try to exploit the demonstrated possibilities and greater potential of terrorist groups, and employ them as a means of surrogate warfare against another nation. A government could subsidize an existing terrorist group or create its own band of terrorists [or covert operatives] to disrupt, cause alarm, and create political and economic instability in another country. It requires only a small investment, certainly far less than what it costs to wage a conventional war, it is debilitating to the enemy, and it is deniable. . . .
>
> We are likely to see more examples of war being waged by groups that do not openly represent the government of a recognized state: revolutionaries, political extremists, lunatics, or criminals professing political aims, those we call terrorists, perhaps the surrogate soldier of another state. Increasingly, there will be war without declaration, war without authorization or even admission by any national government, war without invasions by armies as we now know them, war without front lines, war waged without regard to national borders or neutral countries, war without civilians, war without innocent bystanders.

The only difference between this state-sponsored terrorism and the more spectacular sort is that states do not seek publicity, claim formal responsibility, or openly challenge international norms.

The adoption of terrorist tactics by some states does not mean that terrorism has become an important avenue to international power and influence. In fact, it is likely to be a sign of weakness, not strength. It is often a tactic of last resort for groups or states that have not achieved their aims by more conventional means. Most terrorists are frustrated or failed revolutionaries who turn in desperation to dramatic but isolated acts of violence. Furthermore, tactics that worked well enough in the context of peasant guerrilla struggles are not much good in a highly urbanized context, in either Western Europe or Latin America. As the fate of the Tupamaros in Uruguay indicates, urban guerrillas cannot succeed except where public order has completely collapsed — in which case the military or a police state usually takes over. As Regis Debray, the apostle of the Latin American guerrillas, said of the Tupamaros: "By digging the grave of liberal Uruguay, they dug their own grave." Urban terrorists do not have the same mobility or opportunities for clandestine activity as rural guerrillas do. They survive because they are few in number and are organized into separate "cells" that are difficult for the police to crack — the source of their operational strength, but also of their political weakness. They can cause a great deal of damage, but they cannot be the leaders of a successful mass movement that could effect authentic revolutionary change. Terrorism played a role in some of the anticolonial liberation struggles, but the movements ultimately succeeded because of their ability to win over the general population, mount conventional armies, and project meaningful programs of reform. Terrorism can win only where the state has already lost its legitimacy and the authorities are too weak to use their full powers. But by the time it becomes a real menace to the state, terrorism is more likely to have incited emergency measures for its suppression or to have escalated into a conventional war.

Multinational Corporations

A far more effective and legitimate transnational actor than the international terrorist is the multinational corporation (MNC). In fact, as the global economy has grown in size and interdependence, the MNC has become the dominant transnational actor. David Blake and Robert Walters's *The Politics of Global Economic Relations* defines transnational corporations as "those economic enterprises — manufacturing, extractive, service and financial — that are headquartered in one country and that pursue business activities in one or more foreign countries" (p. 95). A national firm becomes multinational when it makes a direct foreign investment (as distinct from a portfolio investment through shareholding) by establishing a branch or subsidiary within another national jurisdiction. Multinational firms, operating within the integrated global market, move their capital and resources around the world to maximize profits, gain a market for their products, and achieve other objectives of the central organization. According to the United Nations Centre on Transnational Corporations, in 1980 there were more than 10,000 multinational firms with roughly 100,000 subsidiaries around the world. The total book value of these firms' direct foreign investment was $546 billion in 1981, as against $158 billion in 1971 — an increase of almost 250 percent in only one decade. Today, more than four-fifths of world trade is conducted by transnational enterprises. Although estimates vary, the current number of MNCs may well exceed 20,000, and some analysts predict that by the turn of the century MNCs will control more than half of all the industrial production in the world.

The internationalization of production has been increasing rapidly. Between 1950 and 1984, total direct foreign investment by U.S. multinationals rose from $11.8 billion to $232.7 billion (see Figure 8-4). At the same time, U.S. multinationals diversified their holdings (which had tended to be concentrated in extractive industries in Canada and Latin America) by tripling their investments in Western Europe and Asia. Yet in this period, Japanese and European firms made even more rapid gains. U.S. multinationals still command the largest share of total sales (about 50 percent), but their dominance has been gradually eroded by firms headquartered in eighteen other First World countries. Overall, economic power is concentrated in the hands of just a few companies; the 500 largest multinationals control about 80 percent of the global subsidiaries. Of the thousands of American companies operating abroad, 10 percent account for about two-thirds of all sales. Between 1960 and 1980, the top 200 firms increased their share of the world's gross domestic product from 18 percent to 29 percent. International banking also expanded rapidly. In 1981, the combined assets of the world's 100 largest banks reached

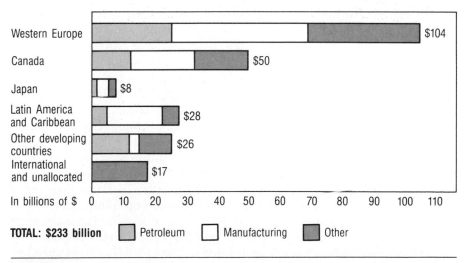

TOTAL: $233 billion ▨ Petroleum ☐ Manufacturing ▧ Other

FIGURE 8-4
U.S. PRIVATE DIRECT INVESTMENT ABROAD

$4.38 trillion, more than double the annual sales of the 200 largest MNCs, with Japanese and U.S. banks controlling about 40 percent of the assets. In 1981, Exxon and the Royal Dutch/Shell Group each generated an annual economic output greater than that of all but 22 nation-states, and General Motors' sales of $62.7 billion exceeded the GNP of more than 110 countries. Almost half of the top 110 economic entities in the world in 1987 were multinational corporations (see Figure 8-5). The most powerful of the MNCs have come to rival nation-states as international political-economic actors.

Multinational corporations vary markedly in size, organization, and type of business activity. The handful that dominate global production operate in dozens of countries, but MNCs more typically are small enterprises with only one or two overseas affiliates. Such corporate giants as Pfizer and IBM depend on international activities for more than 50 percent of their profits, and this makes them active lobbyists with both their headquarters and their host governments for a favorable climate of investment and trade. Several hundred MNCs operate in twenty or more nations and have a special stake in reducing national trade barriers and preserving the stability of the international market. Some conglomerates and industrial firms, like International Telephone and Telegraph (ITT), Ford, Caterpillar, and General Electric, whose investments are primarily in the developed world, are less politically and economically vulnerable. Others, such as Kennecott and Citibank, have a heavy concentration in a few highly unstable Third World states. The subsidiaries of British and American firms are 75 percent wholly owned by the parent or under its majority control, while only 29 percent of Japanese firms' affiliates are wholly owned. This makes the Japanese, whose host countries have a 37 percent minority participation (as compared to only 8 percent for U.S. firms), better able to accommodate the political requirements of nationalist regimes and to penetrate foreign markets through joint ventures.

Howard Perlmutter's study, "The Tortuous Evolution of the Multinational Corporation" (in Modelski, *Transnational Corporations and World Order*, pp. 34 – 44), classifies MNCs as ethnocentric, polycentric, or geocentric, based on ownership, organizational structure, and managerial orientation. The ethnocentric firm maintains ongoing national ties, and decision makers in the headquarters country tend to exert central control over its foreign subsidiaries. Overseas operations are managed for the benefit of the parent corporation in its home market. Key personnel are recruited from the home country and rewarded disproportionately. Profits are repatriated rather than reinvested. Technology is developed in the home country and transferred outward, along with orders and advice, with little adaptation to the subsidiaries or response from them. Ethnocentric managements often have little experience in overseas markets and poor language skills; they retain their strong cultural differences and tend to distrust host governments and foreign managers. The majority of multinational corporations probably fall into the ethnocentric category.

The polycentric firm has a decentralized management that is oriented to a variety of host settings. The parent corporation, functioning as an international holding company, gives subsidiaries great autonomy in setting goals and making operational decisions. Personnel are recruited locally and are subject to a minimum of central direction. Technology and marketing strategies are flexible and adapted to the local culture, making these firms able to survive under circumstances of extreme diversity or economic nationalism. Polycentric firms tend to be concentrated in the consumer goods industry, in which local tastes are paramount in the establishment of markets.

The geocentric firm, complex and interdependent, is a collaborative enterprise between headquarters and subsidiaries marked by a strong two-way flow of communications. Regional or global objectives take priority over national goals. The company recruits the best managers and assigns them anywhere in the world, without regard for nationality. It takes advantage of international mobility and the growing integration of transport and telecommunications to establish universal transnational standards of decision making. Such firms' technology is truly global in application, and their international customers are widely dispersed. Geocentrism generally reflects a management judgment that the best way to maximize growth and minimize economic risk is through the global diversification of production and distribution. Many of the more progressive and successful multinationals have adopted a geocentric orientation —a trend that is likely to grow as competition becomes more intense, the international market more interdependent, and advanced technology more broadly diffused.

Government policy is one important factor in the rapid rise of the multinational corporation. Many governments have encouraged the development of their export sectors by giving tax benefits to firms with foreign subsidiaries. The U.S. tax code, for example, contains deferral provisions under which a corporation can leave its earnings abroad and avoid their being taxed until the profits are actually repatriated. This tax feature was partially responsible for an increase in American multinationals' reinvestment of foreign earnings from $3 billion in 1970 to nearly $11 billion in 1984. Japan has followed a policy of actively promoting foreign investment and the internationalization of business, as a means of guarding against oil and raw material shortages and of enhancing its international position in the absence of military power. Governments also seek direct control over foreign resources as a hedge against disruptions in supply or as a preemptive strategy for denying key assets to potential competitors. Such policies, reflecting nationalist or neomercantilist motivations, enlist multinationals as agents of traditional national security interests.

More often, however, multinationals have arisen for simple economic reasons and are more authentically international. Investment capital is a highly mobile commodity that seeks the highest rate of return it can find in an unrestricted market. In extractive industries, firms go abroad because that is where the oil, minerals, and other natural resources are. In manufacturing, local subsidiaries can ease servicing problems and better adapt the product to local conditions or desires. A national firm may enter the international market to reduce production costs, suppress foreign competition, or maximize the potential for growth. It may subsequently establish an overseas branch to reduce transportation and labor costs. As well-organized unions in the more

FIGURE 8-5

RANKING OF COUNTRIES AND CORPORATIONS ACCORDING
TO SIZE OF ANNUAL PRODUCT, 1987

Countries are ranked according to GNP. Corporations (headquarters in parentheses) are ranked according to
total sales. While not exactly comparable, they are sufficiently close to illustrate size relationships.

Rank	Economic Entity	U.S. Dollars (billions)
1	United States	4,497.22
2	Japan	2,376.42
3	Soviet Union	2,356.00
4	West Germany	1,117.78
5	France	873.37
6	Italy	748.62
7	United Kingdom	575.74
8	Canada	373.69
9	Brazil	299.23
10	China	293.38
11	Spain	287.97
12	People's Republic of China	286.00
13	Poland	259.80
14	India	220.83
15	Netherlands	214.42
16	East Germany	187.50
17	Australia	183.28
18	Switzerland	170.88
19	Yugoslavia	145.00
20	Czechoslovakia	143.90
21	Belgium	142.30
22	Mexico	141.94
23	Rumania	138.00
24	Sweden	137.66
25	South Korea	118.00
26	Austria	117.66
27	*General Motors* (US)	101.78
28	Denmark	85.48
29	Hungary	84.00
30	Norway	83.08
31	*Royal Dutch/Shell Group* (Neth./UK)	78.32
32	Finland	77.99
33	*Exxon* (US)	76.42
34	South Africa	74.26
35	*Ford Motor* (US)	71.64
36	Argentina	71.53
37	Saudi Arabia	71.47
38	Indonesia	69.67
39	Algeria	64.60
40	Bulgaria	61.20
41	Turkey	60.82
42	*International Bus. Machines* (US)	54.22
43	*Mobil* (US)	51.22
44	Venezuela	49.61
45	Thailand	48.20
46	*British Petroleum* (UK)	45.21
47	Peru	45.15
48	*Toyota* (Japan)	41.46
49	*IRI* (Italy)	41.27
50	Greece	40.90
51	*General Electric* (US)	39.32
52	*Daimler-Benz* (W. Ger.)	37.54
53	Hong Kong	36.53
54	Israel	35.00
55	Philippines	34.50

Rank	Economic Entity	U.S. Dollars (billions)
56	Egypt Arab Republic	34.47
57	*Texaco* (US)	34.37
58	Portugal	34.39
59	*American Tel. & Tel.* (US)	33.60
60	Colombia	31.94
61	New Zealand	31.85
62	Pakistan	31.65
63	Malaysia	31.23
64	*E. I. Du Pont De Nemours* (US)	30.47
65	*Volkswagen* (W. Ger.)	30.39
66	*Hitachi* (Japan)	30.33
67	*Fiat* (Italy)	29.64
68	*Siemens* (W. Ger.)	27.46
69	*Matsuhita Electric Industrial* (Japan)	27.33
70	*Unilever* (Neth./UK)	27.13
71	*Chrysler* (US)	26.26
72	*Philips' Gloeilampenfabrieken* (Neth.)	26.02
73	*Chevron* (US)	26.02
74	*Nissan Motor* (Japan)	25.65
75	*Renault* (France)	24.54
76	*ENI* (Italy)	24.24
77	Syrian Arab Republic	23.90
78	United Arab Emirates	23.72
79	*Nestle* (Switzerland)	23.63
80	*BASF* (W. Ger.)	22.38
81	*Philip Morris* (US)	22.28
82	Ireland	21.91
83	*CGE (Cie Generale D'Electricite)* (Fr.)	21.20
84	*Elf Aquitaine* (France)	21.19
85	*Samsung* (Korea)	21.05
86	*Bayer* (US)	20.66
87	*Hoechst* (W. Ger.)	20.56
88	*Toshiba* (Japan)	20.38
89	*Amoco* (US)	20.17
90	Singapore	19.90
91	*Peugeot* (France)	19.66
92	North Korea	19.00
93	Chile	18.95
94	Cuba	18.70
95	*Imperial Chemical Industries* (UK)	18.23
96	Kuwait	17.94
97	Bangladesh	17.60
98	*Honda Motor* (Japan)	17.23
99	*United Technologies* (US)	17.17
100	*Occidental Petroleum* (US)	17.10
101	*Procter & Gamble* (US)	17.00
102	Morocco	16.75
103	*Atlantic Richfield* (US)	16.28
104	*RJR Nabisco* (US)	15.87
105	*Petrobras* (SA)	15.64
106	*Boeing* (US)	15.36
107	*NEC* (Japan)	15.33
108	*Tenneco* (US)	15.10
109	*Nippon* (Japan)	14.64
110	*Volvo* (Sweden)	14.58

Sources: GDP data for OECD countries from World Development Report 1989 (Washington: World Bank, 1989), pp. 168–69; GNP estimates for socialist countries from *The World Factbook 1988* (Washington: Central Intelligence Agency, 1988); sales data from *Fortune*, Aug. 1, 1988.

developed economies bid up wages, firms go in search of cheap labor in the Third World. This is particularly true of such relatively low-skilled, labor-intensive industries as textiles, electronic components, footwear, and small appliances. As industry has gone international, services like banking, consulting, and advertising have also become transnational. Overseas subsidiaries are an effective mechanism for circumventing national trade and tariff barriers. These protective measures are intended to keep out foreign goods, and firms often can penetrate protected markets only through direct investment there. The EEC's imposition of a common external tariff in the 1950s set off an explosive growth in U.S. investment in Europe to take advantage of the European market's increasing wealth, size, and stability.

Marxists view multinational firms as the transmission belts of an inherently expansionist capitalism and attribute their growth to falling profits at home and the international capitalist class's impulse to aggrandizement. Non-Marxist interpretations, such as the one Raymond Vernon offers in *Sovereignty at Bay* (pp. 65 – 77), suggest that multinationalism is a response to the economic imperatives of the product cycle, whereby industries whose technological advantage at home is declining export the technology to foreign countries. This overseas expansion protects the industry from foreign competition and reduces the risk that the technology responsible for its domestic success will become diffused or imitated abroad. Both of these explanations regard the MNC as an independent entity motivated largely by economic criteria, rather than by the patriotic or national security considerations that are important in the economic nationalist's view. We turn now to a more detailed examination of these three perspectives of the MNC—liberal, Marxist, and mercantilist.

The MNC as an Agent of Development and Integration

Many analysts see corporate international expansion as a logical and rational stage in the evolution of capitalism. According to this liberal view, both technology and the free market favor the internationalization of production, for reasons of efficiency and economies of scale. Advances in communications, transport, and management have made complex international enterprises possible. Business enterprises can take advantage of differing costs and investment climates around the world, and an international division of labor allows each nation to specialize in the products in which it has a comparative advantage. Multinationals are simply the transmission belts of such a system. Far from symbolizing capitalism's alleged drive for monopoly control, the rise of international business represents a stage of greater competition. The U.S. auto industry, for example, which in its national phase was highly concentrated (or oligopolistic), has been made more competitive and efficient by the import of German and Japanese products and management styles. As the South Koreans and the Yugoslavs have cracked the market, the auto industry has become highly dispersed and truly global in scale. Intense competition has forced U.S. firms to become more transnational, with an increasing number of subsidiaries and sources abroad, joint ventures with foreign firms, and more efficient production techniques copied from overseas competitors. Even Soviet and East European trading companies, and some European-based multinationals, like Renault, that are fully or partially state owned have expanded into the international market — evidence that the drive for foreign investment is not unique to private capitalism.

The presence of foreign subsidiaries is not necessarily a sign of a country's economic exploitation or dependency, as many leftist ideologues would suggest. The type of MNC and the strength and legitimacy of the host country's political and economic institutions determine how much economic influence the MNC will have. The operations of American multinationals in Western Europe do not conflict with national economic agendas (and bring no accusations of dependency) because the European governments are powerful and autonomous enough to strike mutually profitable bargains and are democratic enough to keep their own economic elites from arranging exclusive deals. Very often this is not so in the Third World, where beneficial economic investment is dependent on significant political and social reforms. But it is hardly the place of the multinationals to sponsor such reforms, and no one can blame them for profiting from the economic and political chaos they often encounter. Still, to judge by their shift toward greater investment in the developed economies, the MNCs appear to prefer a stable economic and political climate. Economic criteria, much more than politics or ideology, seem to be the deciding factors. When socialist leaders can provide stable conditions, as they have in Algeria, China, and (to an extent) Angola, then foreign capital will invest, regardless of ideology.

Another sign that multinationals are not by nature exploitative is the growth of foreign investment in the United States and other advanced economies. Between 1973 and 1985, foreign direct investment in the United States rose from $20.5 billion to $183 billion, making America the world's largest host to overseas capital. At the same time, the United States has remained the world's largest source of investment funds, although the money has flowed increasingly into the manufacturing sector in other advanced economies. Thus, the image of the multinational as an extractive giant preying on the resources of the Third World is not a very accurate one. As early as 1950, the developed areas were receiving 48 percent of the U.S. direct investment abroad, a figure that had leaped to 74 percent by 1985. Investment also has gradually shifted away from extractive industries, even in the Third World. Between 1960 and 1985, the U.S. share of investment in these industries decreased from 43 percent to 25 percent (though absolute investment quadrupled, as a result of the dramatic rise in multinational activity overall). Today, more than a third of all direct foreign investment is in service industries and financial institutions.

Nothing attests to the benefits of multinational enterprise more than the competition between nation-states for investment funds. Third World countries routinely advertise in Northern business journals to extol the virtues of their investment climate. Many nations, even the advanced ones, offer substantial incentives to attract foreign capital. Canada gave IBM a $6 million nonrepayable grant for constructing a large computer facility in a depressed area of Quebec. The state of Pennsylvania offered more than $58 million in incentives to Volkswagen to build an assembly plant near Pittsburgh. In the 1980s, when the economy of the U.S. northwest was unusually depressed, the state of Oregon gave tax incentives to several large Japanese computer firms to entice them to locate in the region. Tax concessions, job training, land, and infrastructure elements are among the many inducements used to attract foreign investment. Host governments, far from discouraging foreign investment as exploitative, actively court it. More than a quarter of the foreign affiliates of U.S. corporations have received at least one incentive from the host country.

Long-term private investment by profit-seeking firms brings many benefits to the host country. It accounts for about 20 percent of total financial flows to developing countries and has played a vital role in the industrialization of such economies as Brazil, Singapore, South Korea, and Taiwan. Jobs are created for the indigenous work force, at an average ratio of about 120 local employees for every manager sent in by the multinational. In 1977, according to a U.S. Commerce Department study, American-owned multinationals employed in their foreign operations approximately 7.3 million persons, whose compensation amounted to $78.1 billion. When technology is transferred, much of the know-how spills out into the local economy through subcontractors. Training programs spread important skills among the local population. Local manufacturing can help a country lower its balance-of-payments deficit by reducing its dependence on imports. Multinationals expand a country's export possibilities as well by integrating it into the international market. For example, about half of all Latin American exports are produced by MNCs. Typically, a third or more of a multinational's production in a host country is exported, generating valuable foreign exchange for the local government. Foreign companies also are major taxpayers in their host countries. In 1977, U.S. firms paid more than $54 billion in taxes to host states, three-quarters of it to developing countries. Adding together wages, direct transfers of capital, taxes, and reinvested profits, multinational investment substantially exceeds the total of direct foreign assistance monies flowing into Third World economies. (Figure 8-6 shows the sources and recipients of direct foreign investment in the Third World by the member countries of the OECD's Development Assistance Committee.)

Multinationals often bring in organizational and managerial skills that a host country has been lacking. Peter Drucker, in "Multinationals and Developing Countries: Myths and Realities," has argued that developing countries often have sufficient capital but cannot productively employ it because they do not know how to mobilize their resources effectively. In such circumstances, multinational investment can trigger development even without bringing to bear large sums in new capital. Foreign firms also can catalyze local enterprise through a kind of "demonstration effect": local firms imitate the more efficient techniques and management practices of the foreign firms. In addition, the international investor performs the valuable planning function of identifying those lead sectors in which local production enjoys a comparative advantage.

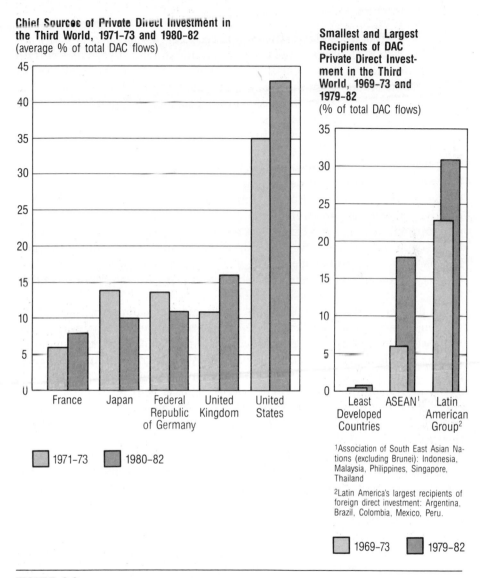

Chief Sources of Private Direct Investment in the Third World, 1971–73 and 1980–82 (average % of total DAC flows)

1971–73   1980–82

Smallest and Largest Recipients of DAC Private Direct Investment in the Third World, 1969–73 and 1979–82 (% of total DAC flows)

[1]Association of South East Asian Nations (excluding Brunei): Indonesia, Malaysia, Philippines, Singapore, Thailand

[2]Latin America's largest recipients of foreign direct investment: Argentina, Brazil, Colombia, Mexico, Peru.

1969–73   1979–82

FIGURE 8-6
FOREIGN DIRECT INVESTMENT IN DEVELOPING COUNTRIES

Even the Third World, which often views MNCs as a threat, recognizes their importance as sources of investment. An Andean group of nations has formed a common market that allows foreign investors to produce and sell in five states (Bolivia, Colombia, Ecuador, Peru, and Venezuela) with a combined population of more than 70 million. But it has set stringent guidelines and controls. The Andean code prohibits foreign investment in banking, insurance, broadcasting, publishing, and internal transportation. It has guidelines and "fade-out" provisions for reducing the number of foreign-controlled firms and boosting the participation of national investors. It limits annual repatriation of earnings to 20 percent of investment and restricts compensation upon with-drawal to a sum no greater than the original investment. It regulates certain transfer pricing practices between parent and subsidiary that can be used to restrict competition, disguise earnings, or inflate the cost of technology. All these measures have, over time, ameliorated some of the more exploitative features of multinational enterprise.

The predatory image of multinationals does not hold up in light of the growing participation of less-developed countries (LDCs) in the global market. In 1983, 42 of the 500 largest industrial corporations outside the United States had their headquarters in developing countries. The spectacular economic success of Taiwan, South Korea, Hong Kong, and Singapore attests to the positive role foreign investment can play in helping Third World states to develop their own vigorous export sectors. More recently, China and the Soviet Union have opened themselves to foreign investment and have sought to estab-lish permanent markets abroad. The growth of the interlocking Pacific Rim trading community is further evidence that multinational enterprise can bene-fit both rich countries and poor, capitalist and socialist.

A final argument on behalf of the multinational corporation is its role in allaying international conflict. MNCs have been an important force in the European Community's integration and its development of a transnational perspective among both management and labor. Multinationals are the cement of economic interdependence, which provides tangible incentives for nationals to reconcile their differences without resort to force. They also contribute to a common culture and life-style by carrying modern values to every part of the planet. Marxists may call this "Coca-Cola imperialism," but such moderniza-tion is central to the development process.

Multinationals also have stimulated cooperation among nongovernmental actors by creating an international "regime" that provides stability without the coercive apparatus of a central political authority. The integrated worldview of the international manager stands above national or ideological differences, counteracting the divisive tendencies of the traditional state system and supple-menting the still meager cooperative efforts of existing international organiza-tions. Profit may not be a more noble goal than national security, but the pursuit of it requires peaceful conditions in which free exchange can flourish.

The MNC as an Agent of Exploitation and Dependency

The Marxist assumption is that the growth of multinational corporations re-flects the inherent imperialism of advanced capitalism, which must find outlets for the surplus capital generated by a system of privilege in which workers do not share. Penetration of international markets also expresses the capitalist impulse for monopoly control. A variety of econometric studies (see especially Richard Newfarmer's "Multinationals and Marketplace Magic in the 1980s") confirm a strong correlation between concentration (four firms accounting for

50 percent or more of production) and foreign participation. Stephen Hymer and Charles Kindleberger both argue that market imperfections and higher profit margins are necessary accompaniments of foreign investment, that without monopoly control the disadvantages of operating in a foreign environment would be so great as to favor local entrepreneurs.

Consequently, foreign investment generally results in a less competitive marketplace as well as a loss of local control over resources. Profits on such oligopolistic transactions have risen from 17 percent in the 1960s to 29 percent in the 1980s; in some industries, the profit stands at 100 percent or more. When competition does exist, it is a temporary condition of an industry in transition. Eventually, corporate interests dictate a vertical integration in which "monopoly rents" (unfair profits) are extracted in exchange for the transfer of advanced technology. For example, 80 percent of the U.S. technology going to the Third World flows through subsidiaries that purchase it at inflated transfer prices. At the same time, over a third of export commodities are first sold internally by the subsidiaries to their parent companies at artificially low prices. Technology-importing, raw-material-exporting countries lose between $50 billion and $100 billion a year in such monopoly practices of vertically integrated firms.

If host governments attempt to exert reasonable controls over foreign investment, however, the multinationals often enlist the support of their home governments to maintain control of their overseas markets. In this respect, international capitalism is a contributor to interstate conflict. Rich states fight for access to the markets and resources of poor states, forcibly reducing them to the status of economic vassals. Global competition between their respective multinationals has heightened frictions between Japan and the United States, and at the same time those MNCs have been appealing to their governments for subsidies, trade protection, and other intervention on their behalf in the Third World. ITT, for one example, urged the United States to oust the Marxist president of Chile, Salvador Allende, when he threatened to nationalize American firms. Multinationals are able to exert influence on governments partly because business and political elites tend to overlap, and also because complex societies are increasingly dependent on multinational sources of production. In the case of oil and strategic minerals, multinationals have sometimes pulled their governments into policies that went against the national consensus. During the OPEC oil crisis, MNCs were instrumental in causing U.S. policy to shift toward the Arab states, despite strong popular support for Israel, and the dominating presence of U.S. companies in Saudi Arabia has become the basis for a special relationship between the two nations. In short, international capital disregards national concerns when they interfere with profits, but it is quick to enlist the diplomatic and coercive tools of the state when economic interests need defending.

It is debatable whether multinational investments in the Third World bring all the benefits the liberal theorists allege. Often profits are exorbitant, with returns on investment running two or three times higher than the rate of return in the developed world. Manipulation of royalties, management fees, and the like permits the multinationals to avoid taxes and get around legal restrictions on excess profits. MNCs are also notorious for exploiting their size and power to soak up local capital and push out local entrepreneurs through unfair business practices. Ronald Müller's "Poverty Is the Product" says that in Latin America more than 80 percent of the MNCs' total finance capital has come from local sources, not the parent firms, and that in 45 percent of the cases, the MNCs used this local capital to buy out domestic competitors rather than start up new production facilities. Not surprisingly, the capital flowing out of Latin America in the 1950s and '60s exceeded the capital going in by as much as three to one.

Overall, multinationals have come to control 40 percent of the LDCs' industrial production and 50 percent of their external economic exchange. In 1977, U.S. companies abroad had a total income of $680 billion, compared to U.S. export earnings of only $120.8 billion. As a result of this increased offshore production, profits repatriated from direct U.S. investment rose from $3.6 billion in 1960 to $41 billion in 1981. During the 1970s, U.S. multinationals increased their investments abroad from $78 billion to $193 billion (a gain of 150 percent), and their net profits rose from $9 billion to $38 billion (a gain of 300 percent). During the recession of the 1980s, U.S. foreign investment continued to be highly profitable for the corporations. Workers, both foreign and domestic, bore the brunt of the downturn; real wages steadily declined practically everywhere. According to the U.S. Department of Commerce, profits from foreign investment in 1984 were $23.1 billion, compared to a capital outflow of only $4.5 billion. Regardless of the state of the global economy, MNCs take more capital out of host countries than flows in. Nothing demonstrates more clearly their monopoly power.

Foreign multinationals often dominate a local economy without serving its real needs. A typical firm in an extractive industry operates within an enclave, with benefits rarely passing beyond a few privileged workers. In consumer goods, there may be some exposure in local urban economies, but it is often in the form of sales and advertising of luxury products that cater to Western tastes — a disguised form of cultural imperialism. In manufacturing, capital-intensive technologies suitable for rich countries (where labor is scarce) are transferred to poor countries (where labor is plentiful), resulting in forms of production that provide few new jobs for poor people and skew income toward those who already possess skills or capital. Half or more of the patented technology multinationals employ in the Third World is foreign controlled, making the host countries permanently dependent on it. In agriculture, foreign investment routinely introduces technologies that work well for large, plantation-style operations raising cash crops for export but are no good for meeting the food needs of the local population.

MNCs maintain their presence in LDCs by allying themselves with local elites, who become a kind of satellite class: a few garner privileges and profits at the cost of national dependency. For example, the United Fruit Company, whose sales revenues dwarfed the national budgets of the Central American states in which it operated (Guatemala, Honduras, El Salvador, Nicaragua, and

Panama), was able to make and unmake governments by currying favor with local bureaucrats and enlisting a dependent class of merchants and bankers willing to do its bidding.

The economic strength of MNCs has a number of negative political consequences for both the host countries and the home governments. Control is foreign based, and the loyalties of executives are with the corporation and most likely the home country; even locally recruited executives tend to develop a company loyalty that supersedes patriotic concerns. The MNCs make important economic decisions whose political impact the host governments cannot control, making it difficult for them to undertake meaningful national planning. Multinationals often corrupt local officials. A series of bribery scandals exposed in the 1970s (involving million-dollar payoffs to heads of state) brought down the governments of Japan and Italy. Investigations by the U.S. Congress and the Securities and Exchange Commission have disclosed that over a hundred American firms made improper foreign payments totaling more than $100 million. Many multinationals are powerful enough economically to pursue a private foreign policy, sometimes directly opposed to the policies of the home government. In Libya, Occidental Petroleum defied President Reagan's economic boycott of the Khadafy regime; in Angola, Gulf Oil supported the Moscow-backed MPLA, believing it the group most likely to bring stability. MNCs often abandon the workers in their home countries and take their jobs to authoritarian Third World states that can guarantee a low-wage, strike-free work force. Or, if the parent country imposes burdensome regulations on pollution control, worker safety, or product standards, the MNC will simply take its business elsewhere, to a country that is desperate for investment and too weak to impose comparable restraints. After the banning of DDT in the United States and Europe, the dangerous pesticide reappeared in fruit imported from Chile and Morocco, where the MNCs were still marketing it.

Dependency theory and the Marxist school regard the multinational corporation as a significant agent of exploitation, the instrument by which capitalist elites in the metropoles have enmeshed the entire world in a process of uneven development, for the benefit of the rich at the expense of the poor. When necessary, the corporate ruling classes have enlisted the power of the state to maintain their privileged position. In the words of Peter Evans, in *Dependent Development: The Alliance of Multinational, State, and Local Capital in Brazil:*

> Simply put, imperialism is a system of capital accumulation based on the export of capital from advanced countries to less developed regions (or more precisely, center capital's acquisition of control over the means of production in those regions) accompanied by the utilization of political and military resources to protect and maintain the means of production over which control has been acquired. (p. 16)

If their bald-faced imperialism threatens to destabilize a country or incur an unacceptable political cost, the multinationals turn to more sophisticated or indirect strategies of domination that leave the polarized center-periphery relations untouched. They employ neocolonial mechanisms to create a growing marginal population and a dependence of the countryside on the city; the city is in turn controlled by a local elite tied to the capitalist economy. This local bourgeoisie, no matter how sizable, remains dependent on the international market (dominated by the MNCs) and plays junior partner to the high-profit, high-technology, oligopolistic foreign firms. Caught in such a pattern of dependency, the elite does not care at all about policies that might encourage indigenous entrepreneurs, widen local markets, redistribute income, or bring the masses into fuller participation in national life. Its economic fortunes are tied to the foreign corporations, whose preoccupations are profit and the maintenance of an essentially imperialist international order.

The Political-Economic Context for Foreign Investment

The argument of economic nationalists is that multinational corporations can be either a positive or a negative force, depending very much on the political-economic context within which they operate. When local governments are powerful and domestic industry well established, the MNC is just another economic actor. In developed societies, governments can bargain effectively to maximize the domestic gain from foreign investment and generally are able to exercise regulatory control. Since the economic environment remains competitive — without dependent elites, enclaves, technological monopolies, or special concessions — the market itself is a powerful controlling influence. In underdeveloped societies, MNCs account for a greater proportion of GNP and of economic activity in the more advanced economic sectors. Multinational investment often is virtually the only avenue of access to new technology for countries whose domestic research and development capabilities are scarce or nonexistent. But an urgent need for capital can reduce the bargaining power of local governments and make local officials susceptible to corruption. Any weak government is vulnerable to economic penetration, whether or not there is a class alliance between a local elite and foreign capital. When they must have foreign technology to exploit a resource, Third World regimes are caught in a special bind: the resource may have a high potential value to future generations, but the regime's immediate need for funds is overwhelming. The royalties paid by a multinational may be paltry, but they represent immediate revenue, funds that would not be available by leaving the resource in the ground. Also, MNCs require a high rate of return on many Third World investments to justify the risks from political instability, possible nationalization, and the underdeveloped nature of the market.

Direct foreign investment often offers the prospect of mutual gain to both the MNC and the host government. The two parties negotiate over their relative shares, and in a surprising number of cases the outcome is a fair one, representing roughly equal bargaining power on each side. Dependence cuts both ways, in other words. Many parent governments are vulnerable to cutoffs in their supplies of raw materials, and many multinationals are in competition with one another for access to scarce factors of production. Balance-of-payments problems affect both advanced and less-developed economies. Repatriated profits or export revenues may be insufficient to cover the import needs of a state, whether parent or host. In spite of America's continued dominance in foreign investment, the United States has a balance-of-payments deficit, an external debt problem, and a dependence on foreign capital flows that are every bit as significant as those of many LDCs.

A concern about the political consequences of overseas investment has led the U.S. and other governments to exert more control over their multinational corporations. In 1977, Congress passed the Foreign Corrupt Practices Act, which assesses severe penalties on companies that offer bribes to officials of foreign governments. Several U.S. administrations have endorsed the Sullivan principles, voluntary guidelines that call for American firms operating in South Africa to resist apartheid and work for desegregation of the workplace by giving nonwhites equal pay, training, and representation in management. Although many opponents of U.S. investment in South Africa have called the Sullivan principles too tame, the assumption behind radical calls for economic withdrawal is that such sanctions will force South Africa to end apartheid — a clear indicator that foreign investment has been a boon for the host country. Even some of South Africa's black nationalist leaders have discouraged the disinvestment campaign, in recognition that it hurts black workers as much as white owners. The UN, the ILO, UNCTAD, and the OECD have sponsored other voluntary codes of conduct for multinationals. Advanced states have monitored compliance with the OECD guidelines, and some of the latter have found their way into state laws and international jurisprudence.

Efforts to regulate the multinationals indicate that governments are wary of their capacity for independent action. But the neomercantilist school of thought argues that the nation-state is quite capable of protecting its economic sovereignty and national interests. Contrary to what both liberals and Marxists say, MNCs usually are dependent on and responsive to the political interests of their parent states. ITT may have been trying to protect its stake in the profitable Chitelco telephone company in Chile by seeking the overthrow of the Marxist government, but its actions were only a small part of a coordinated U.S. government effort to destabilize a regime that was perceived to be a serious political and ideological threat. Multinationals exert their greatest power when they act in concert with their parent governments. Or the interests of the MNC and the parent government may coincide, as when the Johnson administration withheld aid to Peru before a 1968 coup in order to give the International Petroleum Company bargaining leverage in its negotiations with the Peruvian government. But when an MNC's actions threaten national security interests, the government will play an active constraining role. The Trading with the Enemy Act and the Export Administration Act, for example, impose restraints on U.S. multinationals' exports of certain sensitive technologies. The United States tried to impede France's development of an independent nuclear force by prohibiting IBM from selling the needed equipment. More recently, the Reagan administration intervened with Dresser Industries of Dallas, Texas, to prevent its French subsidiary from exporting to the Soviet

Union energy-related technology for a European pipeline project; in a clear contest of national wills, the subsidiary, acting under orders from the French government, defied the American prohibition. The U.S. government has also imposed balance-of-payments guidelines on American multinationals in order to increase the net capital inflow, regardless of the effect on the companies' or the host governments' reinvestment policies. Japanese and French multinationals very closely conform to the interests of their governments. In all these ways, the nation-state is a vigorous actor in the international economy.

David Leyton-Brown, in "The Nation-State and Multinational Enterprise: Erosion or Assertion," lists several ways in which nationalist forces counteract the power of MNCs. The multinationals' size, geographic spread, and international scope make them subject to divisive tendencies and diseconomies of scale. The executives of subsidiaries often develop a parochial outlook and become advocates for local interests. Diversity in cultures and life-styles still prevails over global efficiency and international integration. A vertically integrated multinational is vulnerable to disruption in any of the several states that are linked in the production and marketing chain. A large and valuable subsidiary can become a hostage to threats from a host government, aware that fixed assets are not easily transferred to another country. And tariff barriers and trade agreements negotiated government to government are still the primary determinants of access to national or regional markets.

As Third World states become more sophisticated in their planning and in their capital import strategies, and as the number of multinationals increases, the LDCs will grow less reliant on any one firm's bundle of capital, technology, and management. Governments are paying more attention to their initial screening and are extracting more specific commitments before they permit multinationals to enter a market. In particular, they are scrutinizing the direct impact on employment and the balance of trade, and have stopped assuming that technology transfers and economic growth automatically bring good results. Even the more permissive host governments are sometimes employing an "obsolescing bargain" that permits a high return for the MNC in the risky early stages but calls for renegotiation once the enterprise has proved profitable. Over time, host governments are proving able to alter tax liability, land use, and labor practices, improve linkages to the local economy, and increase their participation in ownership and management without having to decide between the drastic alternatives of losing the investment or nationalizing it.

With certain commodities, such as oil, producing nations have taken control of decisions about pricing and production, with the multinationals following along. A multinational that operates in several conflicting jurisdictions typically must make concessions to both governments or else accommodate the stronger party, at a loss in its own position. This was what happened to Coca-Cola, which had to abandon almost the entire Arab market when its decision to enter the Israeli market became embroiled in Middle East politics. In sum, multinational penetration has set off a powerful nationalist reaction and a reassertion of state prerogatives. States left vulnerable to foreign investment have moved strongly to regulate the multinationals and reestablish control over their national markets.

It should be remembered that the Third World states passed through an unusually vulnerable period in the aftermath of decolonization. Nominal sovereignty, neocolonial vestiges, and concessionary agreements were commonplace. Dependence on foreign capital was the best some of the smaller LDCs could make of their economically untenable situations. The multinationals themselves benefited when, during the intense Cold War competition, the United States was pressed to extend its economic grip on the LDCs. As Benjamin Cohen argues, in *The Question of Imperialism* (pp. 204–05, 241–45), such imperialism is entirely rational, given the anarchic nature of the international system. Nations yield to the temptations of economic domination for reasons of power and prestige, not out of any class orientation or the materialistic needs of capitalism. Imperial powers are concerned with maintaining their national security, which they can bolster by economic alliances, guaranteed access to vital raw materials, and the subordination of the periphery to the center. Multinational business, with selfish interests of its own, encourages dependency out of the pursuit of profit. But the system of dominance and dependence is the creation of nation-states, for power-political reasons. When the balance of power shifts or the costs of imperialism become too high, the interests of the leading powers diverge from those of multinationals. The recent dispersion of power among the leading nation-states and the rising costs of military intervention have led them to withdraw from the MNCs the protective cover that was common in the early postcolonial era. Wherever the forces of independence and Third World nationalism have made themselves felt, the multinationals have been put on the defensive.

In the end, it is impossible to make an abstract judgment about the virtues or vices of multinational corporations. Unquestionably they are important transnational actors—perhaps the most important nonstate actors on the international stage. But how much independent power they possess is an open question. The political-economic context in which they operate and the prevailing international balance of power determine the answer.

QUESTION FOR DISCUSSION (PRO AND CON)

Does the United Nations play an important role in world politics? In particular, is it in the U.S. national interest to continue its support of the UN?

☞ **PRO**

There is no question that the overall impact of the United Nations on world affairs has been positive. The only question open to debate is whether it has accomplished enough to satisfy its critics. For these nay sayers, the main problem has been unrealistic expectations. Many people imagined that the UN would bring permanent peace, redistribute the global economic product more equally, and introduce an era of internationalism, if not world government. Since these were never very realistic goals, the UN should not be faulted for failing to achieve them. Properly viewed as an experiment in multilateral diplomacy rather than an attempt at world government, the United Nations has fundamentally transformed international relations.

Some of its specific accomplishments are significant. First, the Trusteeship Council and peacekeeping efforts overseen by the secretary-general have promoted peaceful decolonization, which has been far less bloody than it might have been had the UN not steadily encouraged the imperial powers to relinquish control.

In the second place, the United Nations has contributed heavily to the codification of international law. Over 20,000 treaties have been negotiated in the last forty years through the work of the International Law Commission, the Commission on International Trade Law, the Conference on the Law of the Sea, the Disarmament Committee, and other UN bodies. The most notable include the Antarctic Treaty (1959), the Limited Test-Ban Treaty (1963), the Outer Space Treaty (1967), the Treaty for the Prohibition of Nuclear Weapons in Latin America (1967), the Nuclear Non-Proliferation Treaty (1968), the Seabed Arms Control Treaty (1971), the Biological Weapons Convention (1972), and the Convention on the Law of the Sea (1982).

Third, the UN has fostered behavioral norms and standards that have changed political consciousness throughout the world on the issues of human rights, the status of women and children, the threat of nuclear war, the plight of refugees, working conditions, health, and the environment. For example, the UN's global Conference on the Status of Women, held in 1975 in Mexico City, inaugurated the UN Decade for Women, which called attention to the crying need for an end to discriminatory practices against women worldwide. This was but one in a series of UN-sponsored international conferences that have drawn attention to key issues and pooled the expertise to manage them. The first of them was the World Conference on the Human Environment, held in Stockholm, Sweden, in 1972. In 1974, the Sixth Special Session of the General Assembly addressed problems of economic development, commodity price stabilization, balance of trade, and access to raw materials. In that same year, the UN convened a Conference on the Law of the Sea (Caracas), a World Population Conference (Bucharest), and a World Food Conference (Rome). Collectively, these UN forums have developed a new North-South agenda and have helped to shift the focus of international diplomacy away from its preoccupation with the East-West struggle. International norms on human rights have been codified in an important series of multilateral conventions, the most significant of which are the Convention on the Prevention and Punishment of the Crime of Genocide (1948), the Convention on the Political Rights of Women (1952), the Slavery Convention (1953), the International Convention on the Elimination of All Forms of Racial Discrimination (1965), the International Covenant on Civil and Political Rights (1966), and the International Covenant on Economic, Social and Cultural Rights (1966).

A fourth accomplishment of the United Nations has been in the area of crisis management. In 107 instances between 1945 and 1968, the UN succeeded in halting a war or averting a potential conflict. Roughly two-thirds of international disputes today are brought before the UN, the World Court, or another international governmental organization. Since the advent of UN mediation, the number of conflicts that have ended in forcible conquest or annexation has dropped from 42 percent to only 15 percent. The efforts of the UN and similar organizations have substantially reduced the likelihood of military aggression against the territory of another state. Though nuclear weapons have done much to reduce the risk of escalation, the UN has also played a prominent role in preventing local crises from flaring out of control. Peacekeeping operations have made a real difference in more than a dozen cases: Korea, Lebanon, the Arab-Israeli dispute, the Congo, Cyprus, Kashmir, Yemen, Namibia, Angola, and others. UN mediation was pivotal in gaining an agreement between Afghan and Pakistani leaders that made possible the Soviet withdrawal from Afghanistan in 1988. At the same time, Costa Rica's president, Oscar Arias, was presenting a peace plan for Central America that called on the neutrality and good offices of the secretary-general to monitor compliance with a cease-fire. The UN has helped to curb the flow of arms to Iran and Iraq, and it worked strenuously for a cease-fire in the critical Persian Gulf region. North and South Korea have agreed to submit to the UN proposals for the reduction of tensions. These are but a few of the many ways in which the UN is helping to make the world a more peaceful place. To honor such accomplishments, the UN's international peacekeeping troops were collectively awarded the Nobel Peace Prize in 1988.

Equally important is the United Nations' status as the one permanent, central, multilateral organization in which heads of state and foreign ministers can carry on a regular dialogue. For many small states, unable to afford diplomatic missions throughout the world, it is the only place where they can conduct international business. The UN has encouraged the democratization of international relations by taking diplomacy out of the sole control of a few big powers. It has provided a neutral ground on which disputing parties can exchange views informally, without the need for observing the cumbersome rules of protocol and without exposing themselves to possible embarrassment, public scrutiny, or loss of face. Drawing on its diverse membership and reputation for neutrality, the UN can usually provide disinterested personnel to patrol, monitor, investigate, and mediate in matters too sensitive for the great powers or the disputing parties to handle. As an international debating society, the UN also serves as an important safety valve for aggrieved parties, who can vent their anger knowing that at the least their views will be heard.

Even within the narrow framework of national interest, there are compelling and pragmatic reasons for nations to bring their disputes to the United Nations. The most obvious reason is to avoid war, with its costs in lives and resources. By expanding the debate beyond short-term political objectives, the UN often can make it possible for a government to take an action under UN auspices that might otherwise have been politically embarrassing or unpopular at home. For small nations, the UN is one of the few forums in which they can safely exert pressure against a great power with overwhelming military strength. Security Council action on a dispute can avoid the need for all nations to take sides. Cease-fire arrangements are more reliable when they are policed by the UN, and agreements signed there are more likely to receive the public scrutiny that encourages compliance.

Finally, the United Nations has contributed splendidly to economic development. Often criticized for its visible failures in peacekeeping, the UN in fact devotes almost 90 percent of its resources to less dramatic work in international trade, finance, investment, environmental protection, and other areas of economic, social, cultural, and scientific cooperation. It supplies loans and technical assistance to almost every LDC. In the decade of the 1970s, its concessional aid to developing countries more than tripled. The efforts of GATT and UNCTAD have revolutionized global economic relations, making the world trade regime at once more liberal, more stable, and more fair. The UN has responded to short-term political and economic disasters by providing relief to refugees in Thailand, Pakistan, and the Middle East and by supplying food to millions of starving Africans. In the long term, UN-sponsored research has increased world food production dramatically and has assisted in the eradication of some communicable diseases. The UN has provided technical coordination and set standards in such fields as air transportation and international postal service. It has promoted education and the preservation of cultural heritages. It has fostered environmental improvements, assisting, for example, in a regional effort to clean up pollution in the Mediterranean Sea. UN initiatives have made it possible for nations to address the sensitive issues of fishing rights, the definition of territorial waters, and common utilization of seabed mineral resources. One can hardly name an international arena that the UN has not touched to good effect. Without doubt, its contributions to development have sped the South on a pace of growth that exceeded that of the North for the period 1960–83. It also has helped to curb the demagogues and tyrants who are prone to feed on economic desperation. UN assistance has made for better neighbors, customers, borrowers, and trade partners. The United Nations is indispensable to our present era of global interdependence and multilateral diplomacy; if we did not have a United Nations, we would have to invent one.

As for America's membership and financial support, the United Nations is one of the cheapest investments we can make in both national and global security. At a time when the gross world expenditure on arms is approaching $1 trillion annually and the U.S. defense budget alone is almost $300 billion, the U.S. contribution to the UN—a little over $1 billion, or less than $4 for each American—amounts to practically nothing. Critics have complained about anti-American voices and vetoes in the UN, but when the chips are down the United States has always been able to muster support for the defense of freedom. This is because the principles of the UN Charter embody so well our own values and political ideas. As Donald Puchala has pointed out, in "American Interests and the United Nations," self-determination, the illegitimacy of armed intervention, the promotion of peaceful change, the protection of human rights, respect for international law, and the resolution of conflict through mediation, conciliation, and adjudication are all central principles of both American and UN diplomacy. If we are occasionally taken to task in the UN, it is usually because our narrow pursuit of a national interest has brought us into conflict with our avowed ideals. When the United States intervenes unilaterally, as it did in Vietnam, Chile, and Grenada, or when it defies international law, as it did in rejecting the International Court's judgment against the CIA for mining Nicaragua's harbors, such actions work against the long-term interests of both the United States and the United Nations.

If we want an international body that will fight consistently against imperialism, totalitarianism, and the excesses of power politics, then we will have to abide strictly by the UN Charter and place some limits on our own power as well. If other nations cynically manipulate the organization, that is no reason for us to do the same. It is precisely why we should not withdraw from such organs as the ILO and UNESCO, which are mismanaged and admittedly have been politicized by illiberal, anti-American elements. We should demand accountability and reform and insist on an end to profligate budgets. But our withdrawal only weakens the larger UN organization and leaves the making of labor and education policies worldwide to our Marxist critics. Besides, for every radical abuse, we can point to an instance in which the UN blocked the radicals' capacity to work mischief. The UN facilitated the peaceful assumption of black majority rule in Zimbabwe, it laid the groundwork for the successful Camp David negotiations between Egypt and Israel, and it paved the way for a just settlement of the dispute with South Africa over Namibia.

It must also be said that the tone of UN debate has grown much more sober and decorous in recent years. The Soviets have ceased to harangue and to employ the jargon of class war. In April of 1989, they even consented to a Canadian NATO officer's taking command of the UN peacekeeping force in Cyprus — cooperation that would have been unthinkable in the depths of the Cold War, when Nikita Khrushchev was criticizing the secretary-general himself for partisanship. Soviet President Mikhail Gorbachev has advocated "a greater role and efficiency of the United Nations" and has called the secretary-general an "authoritative figure enjoying universal trust who must be encouraged in his missions of mediation, conciliation and good offices" (as quoted by Richard Hottelet in the *Los Angeles Times*). Gorbachev has urged wider use of military observers and UN peacekeeping forces, has proposed a UN tribunal to investigate and help eradicate international terrorism, and has spoken of a more vigorous UN role in attacking the problems of environmental protection, economic development, and disarmament. And he has started paying the Soviet Union's delinquent dues, while supporting U.S. attempts to reform the UN's budget and administrative practices, in the face of Third World misgivings about the loss of aid and jobs. It can no longer be said that lack of Soviet support handicaps the work of the United Nations. In fact, the United States, $401.7 million in arrears in its dues (as compared to the Soviets' $181.2 million), is now perceived as the more reluctant partner in international peacekeeping and multilateral diplomacy.

Some criticism of the United States within the UN is the product of growing multipolarity and the passing of American global dominance and Western cultural universalism. (Figure 8-7 illustrates the rather low correlation between U.S. aid given to selected countries and their support for U.S. positions in the UN.) The UN is no longer an American oyster, and world politics is no longer monopolized by Western capitalist regimes peopled by Caucasians. But we cannot restore America to its golden age of preeminence by withdrawing from the UN or abolishing it altogether, nor can we reduce the degree of global diversity or make the world any safer for American values by doing so. In fact, without the UN, we would be worse off in every respect. The evidence is clear that the UN acts only when it has a consensus, meaning that it can do little of substance without U.S. cooperation or U.S. resources — so long as America is present to express its preferences. In the past, Security Council resolutions frequently were modified to court the approval of the United States. The International Development Strategy proposals of the Third UN Development Decade were significantly revised to allay American concerns about free trade, open markets, and the priority of agricultural development. Portions of the NIEO agenda put forth by the Group of 77 were softened through UN diplomacy. The UN Codes on Restrictive Business Practices and the Conduct of Transnational Corporations were modified to meet American criticisms. Without America's strong voice and the moderating influence of the UN forum, the global majority might have proved even more antagonistic. The UN needs the United States as a constructive critic, sympathetic to its goals but realistic about its shortcomings. The United States needs the UN as its voice of conscience, to keep us from succumbing to the great-power temptation to slide down that slippery slope of Machiavellianism and the diplomatic double standard.

Finally, there are tasks that the United States cannot accomplish alone, for all its power and wealth. If we are to limit global population growth, which threatens to add more than 2 billion inhabitants by the year 2000, we need an

---

FIGURE 8-7

AID DOLLARS AND VOTES IN THE UN

Ten Nations Receiving the Most U.S. Aid in 1983	Amount of Aid (in Millions)	Percentage of Votes Cast for U.S. Positions
Israel	$2,485	93%
Egypt	2,344	23
Turkey	689	41
Pakistan	542	23
Spain	415	42
El Salvador	327	30
Greece	281	27
Costa Rica	218	31
India	210	16
Sudan	206	21

organization like the United Nations. If we are to attack the global food deficit, curb the depletion of fisheries, limit the emission of fluorocarbons and carbon dioxide, preserve the tropical forests, manage the enormous and destabilizing debt problems of the Third World, we cannot do without the UN, as an intermediary and a forum for coordinating a united effort. All these are every bit as much problems of collective security as the threat of war is — save that no amount of arms can substitute for the need to cooperate in rescuing a planet that is becoming depleted, despoiled, and unmanageable. Potential economic, social, and ecological catastrophes are simply waiting to happen. We can ignore them now and then cope as best we can when the catastrophes are long past preventing. Or the United Nations can rally the resources and the consciousness of the global community to try for timely solutions. For what it has done and can do, for America and the world, the United Nations is indispensable.

CON

The United Nations is largely irrelevant to the conduct of international affairs. Whatever influence it may have had in the first bloom of the postwar decades has long since wilted. Yet it continues to absorb resources that could be better spent by individual nations in the forthright pursuit of their own purposes. As distasteful as the naked reality may be, false expectations of UN action and the figleaf of multilateral diplomacy only impede a rational foreign policy and a timely response to crisis.

The United Nations is so flawed in conception, in institutional design, and in policy implementation that it can never be effective. At the most fundamental level, it cannot do anything to alter the inequalities of wealth and military capability that define power relations between states. The high-flown language of the UN Charter and the illusion of cooperation do not change the primacy of national interests or the propensity of states to resort to violence in protecting their security or improving their position in the international power hierarchy. Moreover, the progress of events since the UN's founding at the Dumbarton Oaks Conference in 1945 has rendered its structure obsolete. First, the character of war has changed: international terrorism, covert operations, undeclared wars, and low-intensity conflicts make it relatively easy for states and individuals to bypass the UN's peacekeeping mechanisms, which were designed to cope with the old kind of interstate conflict. Second, states have multiplied to such a number that the General Assembly has turned into an unwieldy and impotent body of bickering blocs. Third, the great powers, whose control was supposedly institutionalized in the Security Council, have been steadily declining in influence, making the Council unable to fulfill its functions of mounting peacekeeping operations and initiating preemptive or preventive diplomacy. Fourth, the economic institutions of Bretton Woods no longer enjoy legitimacy. In the context of the debt crisis, the IMF is viewed as a tool of the Western creditor nations. The growth of MNCs and the internationalization of production have permitted private enterprise to escape state regulation, making government-to-government negotiation in the UN largely irrelevant. In sum, the UN is fatally flawed in at least two respects: it has not overcome the enduring reluctance of states to sacrifice their sovereignty in any vital matters; and it has shown no ability to adapt its rigid structure to the dynamism of international affairs.

The United Nations' problems at the policy level are many. There is such a lack of consensus on priorities that the organization feels compelled to dabble in everything while concentrating on nothing. But symbolic participation and token sums of money will not make the serious problems go away. The rigidity of bloc voting and the politicization of the specialized agencies hamper operations. Problems in planning, financing, and personnel have grown more severe over several decades. The Secretariat, weighed down by partisan appointments, unqualified staff, and a bloated bureaucracy, is unable to perform its coordinating tasks. Some 75 percent of the budget goes for personnel expenses to support almost 12,000 positions. Operations budgets, on the other hand, especially those for peacekeeping, are starved because states withhold their assessments as a means of blackmailing the UN into conforming with their ideological preferences or national demands. There are too many outdated programs and too many budget add-ons, both due to inadequate program evaluation. UN bureaucrats, not directly accountable to a political constituency, tend to be fiscally irresponsible. During the global recession of the early 1980s, when nation-states were cutting their budgets to the bone, UN agencies were continuing to project budget growth — another sign that the United Nations does not operate on real-world assumptions.

The United Nations has become irrelevant because it can offer states little incentive for bringing it their serious disputes. Typically, nations do not come to the UN until a problem has reached crisis proportions, even though disputes are best addressed early, before the stakes have risen and positions polarized. Many states fear they will lose control over the resolution; armed conflict particularly reinforces thousand-year-old habits of national sovereignty. Of course, many states do not bother with the UN because they already know they are in violation of international law or norms, and they do not appear to care. Another risk is that UN intervention may politicize, complicate, prolong, or exacerbate an issue. Time pressures and stress put a premium on quick decisions; circumstances on the battlefield can change within hours, making it dangerous to hazard a time-consuming appeal to an international body. In the Cuban Missile Crisis, President Kennedy deemed an immediate response so crucial that he acted first and then consulted the UN. After the naval blockade was in place, the issue went before the Security Council, and the respective UN delegations were able to facilitate communication between the superpowers. But the crisis was resolved by direct negotiation between the United States and the Soviet Union. In other cases, nations may perceive that the outcome of UN debate is predetermined, regardless of the merits. Anti-Zionist feeling has so strongly permeated the Third World bloc that the Israelis do not believe the UN can ever reach a just solution on the Palestinian question. Likewise, the United States has long mistrusted the ideologically determined votes of the socialist and nonaligned blocs.

For all these reasons, none of the major conflicts of the postwar era have come before the United Nations. The UN played no role in the various Berlin crises, or in any of the coups and invasions that secured Eastern Europe as a Soviet political-military preserve. The U-2 crisis and the KAL 007 incident brought no UN response. The erection of the Berlin Wall, the fight over Quemoy and Matsu, the North Korean seizure of the *Pueblo*, the Sino-Soviet border clashes, the invasions of Cambodia (by the United States and by the Vietnamese Communists), the Cuban-Soviet military presence in the Horn of Africa, the American military presence in Central America and the Caribbean, the Persian Gulf war — all involved violations of the UN Charter, yet none led to UN action. The world has seen 150 wars with 20 million deaths since the UN's creation. This is hardly the success story of an organization committed to collective security. The UN's only successful peacekeeping operations have been those that suited the great powers, which sometimes, in the interests of deescalation, have imposed peacekeeping on states whose own best interests were not always served by it. For example, the Israelis, nearly defeated by the surprise attack of Egypt and Syria in the October War of 1973, nonetheless recovered, crossed the Suez Canal, and established a military footing on Egyptian territory. Only then, when Israel was on the verge of dictating terms of surrender that might have established its security in the area once and for all, did the superpowers intervene, through the UN, to protect the status quo ante. Though done in the name of justice, it was an action that, by definition, preserved the interests of the great powers in the Middle East. Such an exercise of the rights of condominium echoes the balance-of-power practices of the nineteenth century. It hardly furthers international law or Israel's prospects for security to camouflage such an act as the peacekeeping of an international body.

The dominance of the great powers in the UN and in international relations generally is disguised by the fiction of sovereign equality embodied in the General Assembly's voting procedures. Microministates exercise the same voting right as continental powers like the Soviet Union and the United States, though the latter foot most of the bills. States with a population of under a million have voting privileges equal to those of India or China, with populations approaching a billion each. Nuclear superpowers are denounced by a majority made up of states whose military capabilities belong to the Stone Age. A few impoverished African states can outvote the economic giants of Japan and the European Community. The discrepancy between voting power and financial contribution is appalling: the United States and the USSR together provide 38 percent of the UN's budget; the entire Group of 77, now numbering more than 120 states, pays only 9 percent. It is theoretically possible to have a controlling majority in the General Assembly of states that together contribute less than 3 percent of the UN budget. Nation-states that are so unequal in the most decisive factors — size, population, power, and wealth — can scarcely be expected to arbitrate historical claims or perceived injustices by consistent reference to UN principles. Such pretense results in irresponsibility by small powers, which use the UN framework to abuse the great states verbally and waste their money on futile attempts to overturn the international status quo. Through its disproportionate power in the General Assembly, the Third World bloc has succeeded in separating the United Nations from military and economic reality and in discouraging middle powers and superpowers alike from taking their problems to the organization. Instead, states all around confine their participation to exploiting the UN and its agencies for propaganda purposes.

The socialist bloc's abuse of the UN has been equally damaging to the organization's legitimacy and effectiveness. According to Soviet defector Arkady Shevchenko, a former undersecretary of the UN, a large percentage of the Soviets serving as delegates to its UN mission and as Secretariat employees are KGB agents. The delegations of many Communist countries, notably those of Cuba and the USSR, are inexplicably large, presumably to facilitate espionage. The United States insisted in 1985 that the Soviets reduce the size of their UN mission in New York, which was larger than the U.S. contingent by almost three to one. But this only set off a corresponding wave of restrictions on U.S. diplomats in Moscow, turning a serious problem into a kind of comic opera of counteraccusations. The Soviets have never been reluctant to ignore the principles of the UN Charter when they have gotten in the way of expansionist or chauvinist interests. Conversely, the United States' commitment to the UN has sometimes prevented us from acting more vigorously in pursuit of our interests. We are bound by conscience, while less scrupulous regimes are not. Radical Marxist regimes have colonized the UN's special agencies, which feel free to funnel aid to such terrorist organizations as the PLO and SWAPO and make policies that curtail the free flow of information and restrict the activities of Western businessmen. These agencies, now in the hands of radical leaders pursuing their own ideological agendas, are racked by incompetence, misallocation of resources, indoctrination, and fraud. Inflammatory resolutions in the General Assembly have accused the United States of colonialism, imperialism, racism, and crimes against humanity and have condemned Zionism as a form of racism and likened Israeli policies to those of fascism. A double standard has operated for communist and capitalist regimes. The United States has been accused of human rights violations, but the UN remained silent about the 3 million Cambodians killed by the Pol Pot regime and the thousands of Soviet political dissidents denied the right of emigration or equal protection of the law. Western "neocolonialism" has been denounced regularly, but not a word has been said about the 116 million East Europeans, 46 million Central Asians, and countless others who have suffered under Soviet imperial dominion.

In light of this double standard of the UN's anti-American majority, it no longer makes sense for the United States to participate in good faith or to continue paying a disproportionate share of the UN's costs. At a time when deficits are forcing us to cut our own budget, how can we justify the wasteful expenditure of funds on an inconsistent and ineffective international organization? Besides, UN policies are often directly opposed to U.S. interests. The Convention on the Law of the Sea discriminates against private mining enterprises, inadequately protects development investments made before the treaty took effect, fails to provide for the arbitration of disputes between the mining industry and governments, and subjects our interests to a Seabed Authority in which the United States is poorly represented. UN codes regulating pharmaceutical companies, the maritime industry, and other multinational businesses are blatantly hostile to the principles of free enterprise and a fair return on investment. The NIEO agenda launched at the UN's Sixth Special Session is openly aimed at the unjustified transfer of wealth from North to South. To call for such "reparations" by the "imperialist" powers makes no allowance for the productivity that has made America wealthy quite apart from any alleged exploitation of the Third World.

The United Nations' disarmament activities also work against U.S. interests. The West has kept the peace through NATO and nuclear deterrence. But disarmament campaigns launched in the UN have threatened to erode this deterrence, especially by a disproportionate impact on Western public opinion. The Soviets, by suppressing all independent peace movements, are immune to such international lobbying, but free societies can be weakened by them. On the peacekeeping front, many disputes are brought to the UN not in the hope of settlement but with the express intent of embarrassing one party or another. America's ally, Israel, has been repeatedly subjected to unfair, one-sided criticism. These tactics have converted the UN from a haven of neutrality and rational argument into a forum for the pursuit of hostile ideological ends. The United States, the main target of such hostility, is foolish to continue acting as if the United Nations is contributing to international peace, freedom, and justice. Even the UN's spirit of compromise works against American values. A compromise between the ideals of the Charter (many of them lifted directly from the U.S. Constitution) and the contradictory morality of Marxism-Leninism is still halfway to totalitarianism. As champions of democracy and free enterprise, Americans can hardly afford to be neutral, even though the dynamic of the UN's bloc politics tends to assume that all systems are morally equivalent. We should lay to rest this stillborn child of the misbegotten wartime alliance between the great powers. The United Nations has long since lost any real power or relevance it might once have had. To perpetuate the United Nations in its contemporary form is to mislead the public into thinking that it actually does something important in international affairs, when in fact the peace that it claims to keep can best be defended by the vigilance of individual nation-states.

SOURCES AND SUGGESTED READINGS

On International Organizations and Transnational Actors

Archer, Clive. *International Organizations*. London: Allen & Unwin, 1983.

Bennett, A. LeRoy. *International Organizations*, 4th ed. Englewood Cliffs, N.J.: Prentice-Hall, 1988.

Bertelsen, Judy, ed. *Nonstate Nations in International Politics: Comparative-System Analyses*. New York: Praeger, 1977.

Claude, Inis L., Jr. *Power and International Relations*. New York: Random House, 1962.

————. *Swords into Ploughshares: The Problems and Progress of International Organization*, 4th ed. New York: Random House, 1971.

Cosgrove, Carol, and Kenneth Twitchett, eds. *The New International Actors: The United Nations and the European Economic Community*. New York: St. Martin's, 1970.

Cox, Robert W., et al. *The Anatomy of Influence: Decision-Making in International Organization.* New Haven: Yale University Press, 1973.

Diehl, Paul F., ed. *The Politics of International Organizations: Patterns and Insights.* Chicago: Dorsey Press, 1989.

Feld, Werner J., and Robert S. Jordan. *International Organizations: A Comparative Approach.* New York: Praeger, 1983.

Gardner, Richard N. *In Pursuit of World Order: U.S. Foreign Policy and International Organizations.* New York: Praeger, 1964.

Haas, Ernst B., Robert Butterworth, and Joseph S. Nye, Jr. *Conflict Management by International Organizations.* Morristown, N.J.: General Learning Press, 1972.

Jacob, Philip E. "Organizing Nations in the 1970s." *Orbis,* Spring 1971, pp. 28–53.

Jacobson, Harold K. *Networks of Interdependence: International Organizations and the Global Political System,* 2nd ed. New York: Knopf, 1984.

Keohane, Robert O., and Joseph S. Nye, Jr., eds. *Transnational Relations and World Politics.* Cambridge: Harvard University Press, 1971.

Krasner, Stephen D., ed. "International Regimes." *International Organization,* vol. 36 (Spring 1982), special issue.

Kratochwil, Friedrich, and John G. Ruggie. "International Organization: A State of the Art on the Art of the State." *International Organization,* vol. 40 (Autumn 1986), pp. 753–75.

Luard, Evan. *International Agencies: The Emerging Framework of Interdependence.* London: Macmillan, 1977.

Mansbach, Richard W., et al. *The Web of World Politics: Nonstate Actors in the Global System.* Englewood Cliffs, N.J.: Prentice-Hall, 1976.

Taylor, Paul, and A.J.R. Groom, eds. *International Organization: A Conceptual Approach.* London: Francis Pinter, 1978.

———. *International Organizations.* London: Allen & Unwin, 1983.

———. *International Organizations at Work.* New York: St. Martin's, 1988.

Taylor, Phillip. *Nonstate Actors in International Politics: From Transregional to Substate Organizations.* Boulder, Colo.: Westview, 1984.

Union of International Associations. *Yearbook of International Organizations.* Brussels: Union of International Associations, published annually.

Wooley, Wesley T. *Alternatives to Anarchy: American Supranationalism Since World War II.* Bloomington: Indiana University Press, 1988.

On the United Nations

Barros, James., ed. *The United Nations: Past, Present, and Future.* New York: Free Press, 1972.

Claude, Inis L., Jr. *The Changing United Nations.* New York: Random House, 1967.

Coate, Roger A. *Unilateralism, Ideology, and U.S. Foreign Policy: The United States in and out of UNESCO.* Boulder, Colo.: Lynne Rienner, 1988.

Crozier, B. "Who Needs the UN?" *National Review,* Nov. 28, 1980, p. 1442.

Finklestein, Lawrence S., ed. *Politics in the United Nations System.* Durham, N.C.: Duke University Press, 1988.

Franck, Thomas. *Nation Against Nation: What Happened to the UN Dream and What the U.S. Can Do About It.* New York: Oxford University Press, 1985.

Gati, Toby Trister, ed. *The U.S., the UN, and the Management of Global Change.* New York: New York University Press, 1983.

Goodrich, Leland M. *The United Nations in a Changing World.* New York: Columbia University Press, 1974.

Gordenker, Leon, ed. *The United Nations in International Politics.* Princeton, N.J.: Princeton University Press, 1971.

Haas, Ernst B. *Why We Still Need the United Nations: The Collective Management of International Conflict, 1945–1984.* Berkeley: University of California Press, 1986.

Harrod, Jeffrey, and Nico Schrijver, eds. *The UN Under Attack.* Vermont: Gower, 1988.

Hazzard, Shirley. *Defeat of an Ideal: A Study of the Self-destruction of the United Nations.* Boston: Little Brown, 1973.

Henkin, Louis. *How Nations Behave: Law and Foreign Policy,* 2nd ed. New York: Columbia University Press, for the Council on Foreign Relations, 1979.

Hottelet, Richard. "New Mood at U.N." *Los Angeles Times,* March 17, 1989.

Keyes, Alan L. "Fixing the UN." *National Interest* (Summer 1986), pp. 12–23.

Kim, Samuel S. *China, the United Nations, and World Order.* Princeton, N.J.: Princeton University Press, 1979.

———. "The United Nations, Lawmaking, and World Order." *Alternatives,* vol. 10, no. 4 (1985), pp. 643–75.

Krauthammer, Charles. "Let It Sink." *New Republic,* vol. 197 (Aug. 24, 1987), pp. 18–23.

Lewis, Stephen. "The Defensible United Nations." *International Perspectives* (Ottawa), Sept.-Oct. 1985, pp. 3–6.

Luard, Evan. *A History of the United Nations: The Years of Western Domination, 1945–1955.* New York: St. Martin's, 1982.

———. *The United Nations: How It Works and What It Does.* New York: St. Martin's, 1985.

McCall, Richard L. "The United Nations and U.S. Policy." *Department of State Bulletin,* Feb. 1981, pp. 60–62.

Morello, Ted. "United Nations Regaining Lost Influence As Global Peacemaker." Christian Science Monitor News Service. *Oregonian,* Sept. 15, 1987, p. A6.

Moynihan, Daniel Patrick, with Suzanne Weaver. *A Dangerous Place.* Boston: Little Brown, 1978.

Murphy, John F. *The United Nations and the Control of International Violence.* Totowa, N.J.: Allanheld, Osmun, 1983.

O'Brien, Conor Cruise. "UN Theater." *New Republic,* vol. 193 (Nov. 4, 1985), pp. 17–19.

Osmanczyk, Edmund Jan. *Encyclopedia of the United Nations and International Agreements.* Philadelphia: Taylor & Francis, 1985.

Parsons, Anthony. "The United Nations and International Security in the 1980s." *Millennium,* vol. 12 (Summer 1983), pp. 101–09.

Perez de Cuellar, Javier. "The United Nations and World Politics." In Charles W. Kegley, Jr., and Eugene Wittkopf, eds., *The Global Agenda,* New York: Random House, 1984.

Pilon, Juliana Geran. "The United States and the United Nations: A Balance Sheet." *Backgrounder,* no. 162 (Jan. 1982), Heritage Foundation, Washington.

Pines, Burton Yale, ed. *A World Without a UN: What Would Happen If the United Nations Shut Down.* Washington: Heritage Foundation, 1984.

Puchala, Donald J. "American Interests and the United Nations." In Steven L. Spiegel, ed., *At Issue: Politics in the World Arena,* 4th ed., New York: St. Martin's, 1984.

Reeves, Richard. "Battered United Nations Shows Signs of New Life." Universal Press Syndicate. *Oregonian,* Oct. 30, 1987, p. C13.

Riggs, Robert E. "The United States and the Diffusion of Power in the Security Council." *International Studies Quarterly,* vol. 22 (Dec. 1978), pp. 513–44.

Riggs, Robert E., and Jack C. Plano. *The United Nations: International Organization and World Politics.* Chicago: Dorsey Press, 1988.

Rikhye, Indar Jit. *The Theory and Practice of Peacekeeping.* New York: St. Martin's, 1984.

Roberts, Adam, and Benedict Kingsbury, eds. *United Nations, Divided World: The UN's Role in International Relations.* New York: Oxford University Press, 1988.

Rowe, Edward T. "Changing Patterns in the Voting Success of Member States in the United Nations General Assembly, 1945–1966." *International Organization,* vol. 23 (Spring 1969), pp. 231–53.

Ruggie, John G. "The United States and the United Nations: Toward a New Realism." *International Organization,* vol. 39 (Spring 1985), pp. 343–56.

Sherry, George L. "The United Nations, International Conflict, and American Security." *Political Science Quarterly,* vol. 101, no. 5 (1986), pp. 753–71.

Stanley Foundation. *Peace and Security: The United Nations and National Interests.* Muscatine, Iowa: The Stanley Foundation, 1984.

———. *UN Budgetary and Financial Impasse.* 17th UN Issues Conference. Muscatine, Iowa: The Stanley Foundation, 1986.

———. *The United Nations and the Future of Internationalism.* 22nd UN of the Next Decade Conference. Muscatine, Iowa: The Stanley Foundation, 1987.

———. *The United Nations' Impact on International Relations.* Muscatine, Iowa: The Stanley Foundation, 1985.

Stoessinger, John G. *The Might of Nations,* 8th ed. New York: Random House, 1986.

———. *The United Nations and the Superpowers: China, Russia, and America,* 4th ed. New York: Random House, 1977.

Tugwell, Maurice. "The United Nations as the World's Safety Valve." In Burton Yale Pines, ed., *A World Without a UN.,* Washington: Heritage Foundation, 1984. Pp. 157–74.

United Nations. *Everyone's United Nations,* 9th ed. New York: United Nations, 1979.

Waldheim, Kurt. *The Challenge of Peace.* New York: Rawson Wade, 1980.

————. "The United Nations: The Tarnished Image." *Foreign Affairs*, vol. 63 (1984), pp. 93 – 107.

Williams, Douglas. *The Specialized Agencies and the United Nations: The System in Crisis*. New York: St. Martin's, 1987.

Wiseman, Henry, ed. *Peacekeeping: Appraisals and Proposals*. Elmsford, N.Y.: Pergamon Press, 1983.

On Terrorism

Alexander, Yonah, David Carlton, and Paul Wilkinson, eds. *Terrorism: Theory and Practice*. Boulder, Colo.: Westview, 1979.

Beeman, William O. "Terrorism: Community Based or State Supported?" *American-Arab Affairs*, vol. 16 (Spring 1986), pp. 29 – 36.

Bell, J. Bowyer. *Transnational Terrorism*. Washington: American Enterprise Institute and Hoover Institution, 1975.

Beres, Louis Rene. "The Nuclear Threat of Terrorism." *International Studies Notes*, vol. 5 (Spring 1978), pp. 14 – 17.

————. *Terrorism and Global Security: The Nuclear Threat*. Boulder, Colo.: Westview, 1979.

Cline, Roy S. *Terrorism: The Soviet Connection*. Philadelphia: Crane Russak, 1986.

Cline, Roy S., and Yonah Alexander. *Terrorism: The Shi'ite Connection*. Philadelphia: Crane Russak, 1988.

Crenshaw, Martha, ed. *Terrorism, Legitimacy, and Power*. Middletown, Conn.: Wesleyan University Press, 1983.

Decter, Moshe. "Terrorism: The Fallacy of 'Root Causes.'" *Midstream*, vol. 33 (March 1987), pp. 8 – 10.

Dobson, Christopher, and Ronald Payne. *The Terrorists: Their Weapons, Leaders, and Tactics*, rev. ed. New York: Facts on File, 1982.

Fontaine, Roger W. *Terrorism: The Cuban Connection*. Philadelphia: Crane Russak, 1988.

Freedman, Lawrence Z., and Yonah Alexander, eds. *Perspectives on Terrorism*. Wilmington, Del.: Scholarly Resources, 1983.

Herman, Edward S. *The Real Terror Network: Terrorism in Fact and Propaganda*. Boston: South End Press, 1988.

Jenkins, Brian. "High Technology Terrorism and Surrogate War: The Impact of New Technology on Low-Level Violence." In Geoffrey Kemp, Robert L. Pfaltzgraff, Jr., and Uri Ra'anan, eds., *The Other Arms Race*, Lexington, Mass.: Lexington Books, 1975.

Jenkins, Brian, Janera Johnson, and David Ronfeldt. "Numbered Lives: Some Statistical Observations from 75 International Hostage Episodes." *Conflict*, vol. 1 (1978).

Johnson, Paul. "The Seven Deadly Sins of Terrorism." *NATO Review*, Oct. 1980, pp. 28 – 33.

Kegley, Charles W., Jr., ed. *International Terrorism: Characteristics, Causes, Controls*. New York: St. Martin's, 1990.

Kennedy, Moorhead. "The Root Causes of Terrorism." *Humanist*, vol. 46 (Sept.-Oct. 1986), pp. 5 – 9.

Kupperman, Robert H., and Darrell M. Trent. *Terrorism: Threat, Reality, Response*. Stanford, Calif.: Hoover Institution Press, 1979.

Laqueur, Walter. *The Age of Terrorism*. Boston: Little, Brown, 1987.

————. "The Futility of Terrorism." *Harper's Magazine*, March 1976, pp. 99 – 105.

————. *Terrorism: A Study of National and International Political Violence*. Boston: Little Brown, 1977.

Laqueur, Walter, ed. *The Terrorism Reader*. Philadelphia: Temple University Press, 1978.

Lynch, Edward A. "International Terrorism: The Search for a Policy." *Terrorism*, vol. 9, no. 1 (1987), pp. 1 – 85.

McForan, Desmond. *The World Held Hostage: The War Waged by International Terrorism*. New York: St. Martin's, 1987.

Morris, Eric, and Alan Hoe. *Terrorism: Threat and Response*. New York: St. Martin's, 1988.

Netanyahu, Benjamin, ed. *International Terrorism: Challenge and Response*. New Brunswick, N.J.: Transaction Books, 1981.

Norton, Augustus Richard. "Review Essay: International Terrorism." *Armed Forces and Society*, vol. 7 (Summer 1981), pp. 597 – 627.

O'Brien, Conor Cruise. "Liberty and Terrorism" *International Security*, vol. 2 (Fall 1977), pp. 56 – 67.

Phillips, Robert L. "The Roots of Terrorism." *Christian Century,* vol. 103 (April 9, 1986), pp. 355–57.

Pierre, Andrew J. "The Politics of International Terrorism." *Orbis,* vol. 19 (Winter 1976), pp. 1251–69.

Pyle, Christopher. "Defining Terrorism." *Foreign Policy,* vol. 64 (Fall 1986), pp. 63–78.

Ra'anan, Uri, et al, eds. *Hydra of Carnage: International Linkages of Terrorism—The Witnesses Speak.* Lexington, Mass.: Lexington Books, 1986.

Raynor, Thomas. *Terrorism: Past, Present, Future.* New York: Franklin Watts, 1982.

Schamis, Gerado. *War and Terrorism in International Affairs.* Brunswick, N.J.: Transaction, 1980.

Slater, Robert O., and Michael Stohl, eds. *Current Perspectives on International Terrorism.* New York: St. Martin's, 1988.

Sloan, Stephen, and Richard Kearney. "Non-Territorial Terrorism." *Conflict,* vol. 1, no. 1, (1978), pp. 131–44.

Sterling, Claire. *The Terror Network.* New York: Holt, Rinehart & Winston, 1981.

———. *The Time of the Assassins.* New York: Holt, Rinehart & Winston, 1984.

Stohl, Michael, ed. *The Politics of Terrorism,* 3rd ed. New York: Marcel Dekker, 1988.

Stohl, Michael, and George A. Lopez, eds. *The State as Terrorist.* Westport, Conn.: Greenwood Press, 1984.

———. *Terrible beyond Endurance: The Foreign Policy of State Terrorism.* Westport, Conn.: Greenwood Press, 1988.

Wardlaw, Grant. *Political Terrorism: Theory, Tactics, and Counter-Measures.* Cambridge: Cambridge University Press, 1982.

On Multinational Corporations

Akinsanya, Adeoye A. *Multinationals in a Changing Environment: A Study of Business-Government Relations in the Third World.* New York: Praeger, 1984.

Ball, George. "Cosmocorp: The Importance of Being Stateless." *Columbia Journal of World Business,* vol. 2, no. 6 (Nov.-Dec. 1967), pp. 25–30.

Baranson, Jack. *Technology and the Multinationals. Corporate Strategies and a Changing World Environment.* Lexington, Mass.: Lexington Books, 1978.

Barnet, Richard, and Ronald Müller. *Global Reach: The Power of Multinational Corporations.* New York: Simon & Schuster, 1974.

Becker, David. *The New Bourgeoisie and the Limits of Dependency: Mining, Class, and Power in Revolutionary Peru.* Princeton, N.J.: Princeton University Press, 1983.

Behrman, Jack N. *National Interests and the Multinational Enterprise.* Englewood Cliffs, N.J.: Prentice-Hall, 1970.

Bennett, Douglas. *Transnational Corporations Versus the State: The Political Economy of the Mexican Auto Industry.* Princeton, N.J.: Princeton University Press, 1985.

Bennett, Douglas, and Kenneth Sharpe. "Agenda Setting and Bargaining Power: The Mexican State Versus Transnational Automobile Corporations." *World Politics,* vol. 32, no. 1 (October 1979), pp. 57–89.

Biersteker, Thomas J. *Distortion or Development: Contending Perspectives on the Multinational Corporation.* Cambridge, Mass.: MIT Press, 1978.

Blake, David H., and Robert S. Walters. *The Politics of Global Economic Relations,* 3rd ed. Englewood Cliffs, N.J.: Prentice-Hall, 1987.

Bornschier, Volker, and Christopher Chase-Dunn. *Transnational Corporations and Underdevelopment.* New York: Praeger, 1985.

Buckley, Peter J., and Mark Casson. *The Economic Theory of the Multinational Enterprise.* New York: St. Martin's Press, 1985.

Caves, Richard E. *Multinational Enterprise and Economic Analysis.* New York: Cambridge University Press, 1983.

Clairmonte, Frederick, and John Cavanagh. "Transnational Corporations and Global Markets: Changing Power Relations." *Trade and Development: An UNCTAD Review,* vol. 4 (Winter 1982), pp. 149–82.

Cohen, Benjamin J. *The Question of Imperialism.* New York: Basic Books, 1973.

Commission on Problems of the Class Struggle in Industrialized Capitalist Countries. "Transnationals in the Capitalist World." *World Marxist Review,* vol. 25 (April 1982), pp. 56–62.

Cox, Robert. "Labor and the Multinationals." *Foreign Affairs,* vol. 54 (January 1976), pp. 344–65.

Cutler, Lloyd N. *Global Interdependence and the Multinational Firm.* Headline Series No. 239. New York: Foreign Policy Association, 1978.

Dixon, C. J., D. W. Drakakis-Smith, and H. D. Watts, eds. *Multinational Corporations and the Third World.* Boulder, Colo.: Westview, 1986.

Drucker, Peter F. *Managing in Turbulent Times.* New York: Harper & Row, 1980.

———. "Multinationals and Developing Countries: Myths and Realities." *Foreign Affairs,* vol. 53 (October 1974), pp. 121–34.

Evans, Peter. *Dependent Development: The Alliance of Multinational, State, and Local Capital in Brazil.* Princeton, N.J.: Princeton University Press, 1979.

Feld, Werner. *Multinational Corporations and U.N. Politics: The Quest for Codes of Conduct.* Elmsford, N.Y.: Pergamon Press, 1980.

Fry, Earl. *The Financial Invasion of the USA.* New York: McGraw-Hill, 1980.

Gereffi, Gary. *The Pharmaceutical Industry and Dependency in the Third World.* Princeton, N.J.: Princeton University Press, 1983.

Gilpin, Robert. *U.S. Power and the Multinational Corporation: The Political Economy of Foreign Direct Investment.* New York: Basic Books, 1975.

Goodman, Louis W. *Small Nations, Giant Firms.* New York: Holmes & Meier, 1987.

Grosse, R. *The Multinational Enterprise in Latin America.* London: Croom Helm, 1988.

Heilbroner, Robert L. "The Multinational Corporation and the Nation-State." In Steven L. Spiegel, ed., *At Issue: Politics in the World Arena,* New York: St. Martin's, 1977. Pp. 338–52.

Hennart, Jean François. *The Multinational Enterprise.* Ann Arbor: University of Michigan Press, 1982.

Hymer, Stephen. *The International Operation of National Firms: A Study of Direct Foreign Investment.* Cambridge, Mass.: MIT Press, 1976.

———. "The Multinational Corporation and the Law of Uneven Development." In Jagdish N. Bhagwati, ed., *Economics and World Order: From the 1970's to the 1990's,* New York: Macmillan, 1972. Pp. 113–40.

Kaempfer, William, James Lehman, and Anton Lowenberg. "Divestment, Investment Sanctions, and Disinvestment: An Evaluation of Anti-Apartheid Policy Instruments." *International Organization,* vol. 41, no. 3 (Summer 1987), pp. 457–74.

Kindleberger, Charles. *American Business Abroad: Six Lectures on Direct Investment.* New Haven: Yale University Press, 1969.

Kobrin, Stephen. "Foreign Enterprises and Forced Divestment in the Less Developed Countries." *International Organization,* vol. 34, no. 1 (Winter 1980), pp. 65–88.

Krasner, Stephen. *Defending the National Interest.* Princeton, N.J.: Princeton University Press, 1978.

Krauss, Melvyn B. *Development without Aid: Growth, Poverty and Government.* New York: McGraw-Hill, 1983.

Kurdle, Robert. "The Several Faces of the Multinational Corporation." In W. Ladd Hollist and Lamond Tullis, eds., *An International Political Economy,* Boulder, Colo.: Westview Press, 1985. Pp. 175–97.

Lall, Sanjaya. "The Rise of Multinationals from the Third World." *Third World Quarterly,* vol. 5 (July 1983), pp. 618–26.

Leyton-Brown, David. "The Nation-State and Multinational Enterprise: Erosion or Assertion." Canadian Institute of International Affairs. *Behind the Headlines,* vol. 50, no. 1 (September 1982), pp. 1–20.

Marton, Katherin. *Multinationals, Technology, and Industrialization: Implications and Impact in Third World Countries.* Lexington, Mass.: Lexington Books, 1986.

McMillan, Carl H. *Multinationals from the Second World: Growth of Foreign Investment by Soviet and East European Enterprises.* New York: St. Martin's, 1987.

Menshikov, Stanislav. "Transnational Monopoly and Contemporary Capitalism." *Political Affairs,* vol. 45 (June 1986), pp. 29–37.

Modelski, George, ed. *Transnational Corporations and World Order.* San Francisco: W. H. Freeman, 1979.

Moran, Theodore H. *Multinational Corporations: The Political Economy of Direct Foreign Investment.* Lexington, Mass.: Lexington Books, 1985.

———. "Multinational Corporations and Dependency: A Dialogue for Dependentistas and Non-Dependentistas." *International Organization,* vol. 32, no. 1 (Winter 1978).

———. *Multinational Corporations and the Politics of Dependence: Copper in Chile.* Princeton, N.J.: Princeton University Press, 1974.

Müller, Ronald. "Poverty Is the Product." *Foreign Policy,* vol. 13 (Winter 1973/74), pp. 71–103.

Mytelka, Lynn Kreiger. "Knowledge-Intensive Production and the Changing Internationalization Strategies of Multinational Firms." In James Caporaso, ed., *A Changing International Distribution of Labor,* Boulder, Colo.: Lynne Reinner, 1987. Pp. 43–70.

Newfarmer, Richard. "Multinationals and Marketplace Magic in the 1980s." In Charles Wilber, ed., *The Political Economy of Development and Underdevelopment,* 3rd ed., New York: Random House, 1984. Pp. 182–207.

Nye, Joseph S., Jr. "Multinational Corporations in World Politics." *Foreign Affairs,* vol. 53 (October 1974), pp. 153–75.

Robinson, John. *Multinationals and Political Control.* New York: St. Martin's, 1983.

Russett, Bruce. "International Interactions and Processes: The Internal vs. External Debate Revisited." In Ada Finifter, ed., *Political Science: The State of the Discipline,* Washington: American Political Science Association, 1983. Pp. 541–68.

Safarian, A. E. *Governments and Multinationals: Policies in the Developed Countries.* Washington: British-North American Committee, 1983.

Salehizadeh, Mehdi. "Multinational Companies and Developing Countries: A New Relationship." *Third World Quarterly,* vol. 5 (January 1983), pp. 128–38.

Sampson, Anthony. *The Sovereign State of ITT.* Greenwich, Conn.: Fawcett, 1974.

Servan-Schreiber, Jean-Jacques. *The American Challenge.* New York: Atheneum, 1968.

Slad, David R. "Foreign Corrupt Payments: Enforcing a Multinational Agreement." *Harvard International Law Journal,* vol. 22 (Winter 1981), pp. 117–55.

United Nations Centre on Transnational Corporations. *Transnational Corporations in World Development: Third Survey.* New York: United Nations, 1983.

Vernon, Raymond. "Ethics of Transnationalism." *Society,* vol. 24 (March-April 1987), pp. 53–56.

——— . *Sovereignty at Bay: The Multinational Spread of U.S. Enterprises.* New York: Basic Books, 1971.

——— . *Storm over the Multinationals: The Real Issues.* Cambridge, Mass.: Harvard University Press, 1977.

Wells, Louis T. *Third World Multinationals.* Cambridge, Mass.: MIT Press, 1983.

IV
INSTRUMENTS

POWER

The Nature of Power

Power is central to all of world politics, and yet it is not easy to define precisely. Realists believe that power underlies all relations between states and that military power, or war, is the ultimate means of resolving all conflicts. Power is the instrument by which states come into existence and protect their independence. States use it to gain their liberty or deprive other states of resources and territory. Power has played a dominant role in nearly all international crises, and the realists ascribe scant influence to any other instrument of policy. To them, power is a kind of universal currency that nation-states accumulate and spend to "purchase" security, welfare, allies, territory, or any other "goods" they desire. Whatever the cultural or ideological differences between states, or the foreign policy objectives of the moment, power is a medium of exchange that all accept. Hans Morgenthau, in *Politics Among Nations*, describes a rational foreign policy as one made by a statesman who "thinks and acts in terms of interest defined as power" (p. 5). Power resources come in many forms, but the most sought after is military might, along with the economic infrastructure to support it.

The nation with great power potential does not possess influence, however, unless the potential is mobilized to a high state of readiness and backed by the will to use military force. The United States, for example, with the greatest potential for power of any nation on earth from 1914 on, was discounted by Germany prior to both world wars because the power was at a low level of readiness and the United States appeared disinclined to become involved. America's eventual mobilization of its economic potential, plus its insulation from direct destruction, proved decisive to Allied victory in both wars. To assess a nation's position, the prudent statesman must add up the military and economic potential and multiply it by the ability of the leadership to mobilize and use it. One CIA analyst, Ray Cline, in *World Power Assessment, 1977*, sets out a formula that equates state power with critical mass (population and territory), plus economic and military capability, modified by strategic purpose, coherent planning, and the will to implement strategy. Realists assume

that is it possible to predict the outcome of any international dispute by analyzing the relative power capabilities of the adversaries, much as a physicist
calculates interacting vector forces. The United States and the Soviet Union
have both become great powers by virtue of their large populations and great
size, their accumulation of industrial capacity and armed might, and their
reputations for acting with efficiency and determination. But when America's
will and purpose faltered (as they did in Vietnam), or the Soviet economy's
technological growth slowed (as it did in Leonid Brezhnev's years), each superpower lost status in the international hierarchy. The United States found it
more difficult to dictate outcomes in other Third World conflicts, such as those
in Angola and Nicaragua, and the Soviet Union could not keep pace in the arms
race or continue subsidizing its Eastern European allies.

Idealists think of power in broader terms, adding the intangibles of legitimacy, diplomatic finesse, moral suasion, ideological appeal, and other, more
positive forms of power to the tangible instruments of military and economic
coercion. They also view power as a relationship of influence, rather than a
fixed quantum of coercive capacity. To them, a state's power is conditioned not
only by its will and the adversary's countervailing power, but also by each
side's motives, perceptions, and responses. Germany could have secured a
more favorable peace in either world war by capitulating earlier, but once it
had aroused the hatred of its adversaries and extracted extreme sacrifices,
nothing would satisfy the victors except unconditional surrender, reparations,
and complete disarmament. Ideology, too, plays a role in raising the power
stakes of conflict, independent of military force. The Soviets fear America's
accumulation of military might, but the British do not, because they have a
close relationship with the United States. France, a great power and the former
colonial master of Chad, might be expected to dictate policy to that weak and
impoverished government, yet the latter has managed to gain costly French
subsidies and military protection, for reasons of cultural affinity and colonial
history. Communist China and the socialist states of Eastern Europe got economic assistance from the Soviet Union past the point at which it was justified
by pure power considerations, largely because of ideological ties. All these
examples point to influences in interstate relations going beyond the narrow
calculus of raw power potential. The prediction of outcomes in any power
competition must be based not only on the accumulated economic assets and
military attributes of each side, but on the history of the relationship and the
dynamic of the interaction.

The spectrum of power ranges from persuasion to deterrence to compellence with the object always being to influence other states to behave in accordance with one's objectives. Although war may have as its immediate objective
the destruction, disarming, or defeat of an enemy, its ultimate purpose, in the
words of Karl von Clausewitz's *On War* (Book I, Chapter 1), is "to compel our
opponent to fulfill our will." The means for doing so are manifold, and military
compulsion should not be mistaken for the only or even the most direct route.
Arrogance and insults may generate resistance, whereas a more diplomatic or
persuasive appeal might win a friendly response. Indeed, good diplomacy is

often defined as the art of getting what one wants without resort to threats or compulsion. Indeed, when conflicting parties share at least a limited range of interests and values, arms and threats may only reduce one side's influence on the other. Persons and states respond not only to threats of deprivation — the costs and punishments associated with coercion — but also to positive inducements and rewards. Even a realist like Morgenthau recognizes that power derives from three sources: the fear of disadvantage, the expectation of benefits, and the respect or love men and institutions command. Although the latter is often thought to be influential only in settled relations within the nation-state, statesmen who have discounted the effects of legitimacy, leadership, or ideology have more than once lost wars with states that were inferior in purely objective military terms. If the differences between adversaries are extreme — as when contested values are mutually exclusive or resources scarce — the conflict may not yield to anything but force and a zero-sum solution (one in which the gains of one party exactly equal the losses of the other). On the other hand, many conflicts are amenable to cooperative, or positive-sum, solutions, in which everyone gains something — though the parties may struggle mightily over the distribution of the gains. To the idealist, power should always be viewed in mixed terms, as a combination of carrot and stick strategies.

Realist and idealist definitions aside, power has dynamic, contextual, and multidimensional characteristics. Its *dynamic* nature is especially evident in the rapid changes in our military technologies. America's explosion of a nuclear device instantly transformed its power position, the nature of warfare, and the very conduct of international relations. The Soviet launch of an artificial satellite — Sputnik — on a rocket booster of intercontinental range instantly changed U.S. perceptions of Soviet power. Over the entire course of the arms race, both superpowers have lived in fear of a technological breakthrough by the other side that would give a decisive military advantage. But technology is not the only factor that keeps power in flux. A war or a revolution can destroy or elevate a nation. The two world wars devastated Europe and set the Third World on the road to decolonization, which in only fifty years dismantled a system that had been in existence for over three centuries. In the midst of war, power relations shift according to wins and losses — as U.S. power did before and after Pearl Harbor, and German power between May of 1941 and May of 1945. Economic growth can quickly change a nation's power position, as was the case with Japan and the Soviet Union. The discovery of new resources, or their depletion, can change the balance of power. Certainly OPEC's control over a diminishing supply of oil, and its effectiveness as a cartel, caused a dramatic shift in power relations after 1973. If world food shortages continue, or are exacerbated by erosion and climatic change, nations with a food surplus will rise in influence. Dynamic political leadership can augment a nation's power, as in the case of Mao Tse-tung in China, Fidel Castro in Cuba, Charles de Gaulle in France, and Mikhail Gorbachev in the Soviet Union. Similarly, the fall of an important leader can contribute to a decline in a nation's perceived power, as happened in the United States with President Richard Nixon's resignation after Watergate, in Egypt with the assassination of Anwar Sadat, and in

Iran with the removal of the Shah in the revolution that brought the Ayatollah Khomeini to power.

Power is *contextual* in that it can be measured only in relation to the adversary and the situation in which it is being exercised. A nation may appear powerful because it possesses large military assets, but the assets may be inadequate against those of a potential enemy or inappropriate to the nature of the conflict. One must always ask: power over whom, and with respect to what? In the first place, perceptions of power are constantly being modified in light of intentions and alliance relations. The military gains of an adversary are viewed with suspicion, but those of an ally strengthen all members of the alliance. An ambitious peace proposal launched in the midst of the Cold War is dismissed as propaganda, but the same proposal in a period of détente is likely to be perceived as genuine. Second, power has a context of national culture and personality, which affect a state's propensity toward force or peace. A nation with a history of militarism or aggressive leadership is viewed differently than a peace-loving state is, though they may be equal in numbers of weapons. Another context is the political-economic one. Rapid population growth, say, may be an asset for a developed country with an industrialized economy but a terrible burden for an underdeveloped society. The Soviet Union was relatively free to exercise power within its recognized sphere of influence in Eastern Europe, just as the United States has been in Latin America. But a state's power to intervene outside its immediate region is at once less potent and less legitimate. Power is also conditional on the nature of the military conflict itself. Nuclear weapons may be useful in deterring an attack by another nuclear-armed power, but they are useless in a guerrilla war or in suppressing revolutionary ferment. Soviet military power may have effectively deterred U.S. nuclear attack, but it proved to be a very poor weapon for pacifying the Afghan population. Military threats are one of the least effective instruments against fanatical terrorists or freedom fighters, who value their ideals more than their lives.

A nation's power is always related to its goals and the context of the competition. A neutral country like Switzerland might actually jeopardize its security by pursuing a power-maximizing strategy. Force might be highly effective against one adversary but not another, or in achieving one purpose but not another. Military power could easily have seized the oil fields in the Middle East, through the bombing of wellheads and refineries, the blowing up of the Suez Canal, or a blockade of the Strait of Hormuz. But that would have been useless in keeping the supply of oil flowing because oil fields are very vulnerable to sabotage by the simplest means. In the Iranian hostage crisis, the objective of freeing the hostages unharmed could not have been achieved by any amount of American military power. Against a poor country that is highly dependent on the world market, economic inducements or sanctions work very well; against a wealthy or a self-sufficient economic power, they do not. In a civil war, moral suasion and claims of legitimacy often count for more than terrorism or a thousand armed battalions. A strong ideological commitment can be a powerful factor in rallying a nation's power; opposing that power militarily may only reinforce the commitment.

The *multidimensional* quality of power is best understood by looking at all its separate elements, and that we will do in the next section.

THE ELEMENTS OF NATIONAL POWER

The dimensions of state power are geopolitical, economic, military, and political. Some, like geography, population, resources, industrial capacity, technology, troops, and weapons, are tangible and can be measured with a degree of objectivity. Others—more subjective and volatile—are the intangibles of strategy, communications (propaganda and intelligence), efficiency (logistics and organization), national morale and will, political cohesion, and the quality of leadership and diplomacy.

Geography

Geography is an immutable dimension of power. All its features—location, topography, size, climate—influence a nation's outlook and capabilities. Throughout their history, the United States, Britain, and Japan have been shielded from easy invasion by large bodies of water. Each became a great power through a large navy and the vigorous pursuit of overseas trade. Thanks to its oceanic moats (3,000 miles wide on the Atlantic side, 6,000 on the Pacific), the United States could heed George Washington's advice to stay free of entangling alliances and European power politics, and for almost a century, it developed peacefully, free of outside interference. Moreover, its expansion came largely without costly conquest, through the purchase of immense tracts of land from France, Spain, and Russia, which found the lands too remote to defend easily. Switzerland, Italy, and Spain have profited from the natural mountain barriers along their frontiers. Switzerland's forbidding and impregnable Alps are the foundation for its longtime neutrality. The Pyrenees have kept Spain apart from the intellectual, cultural, and economic influences that stimulated the development of the European continent, but they also have protected the country from Europe's great political and military conflagrations. Russia, Poland, Germany, France, and the Lowlands have all been invaded repeatedly across the easily accessible plains of central Europe. The vulnerability of Germany's and Russia's frontiers has led them to maintain large standing armies and their attendant bureaucracies, which encourage militarism and autocracy. Poland, precariously situated between the two, has suffered frequent invasions and partitions.

Geography has been just as critical in other parts of the world. In the Middle East, it led to Israel's seizure of the Golan Heights, the Suez Canal, the West Bank of the Jordan River, and the Strait of Tiran to preserve its security. Mountainous or jungle terrain can supply sanctuary to guerrilla fighters, as it has in China, Afghanistan, Vietnam, and Central America. Yet other geographical factors have been equally important in these regions. Afghanistan's smallness and proximity to European Russia and the Middle East, with its volatile elements of Islam and oil, encouraged the Soviets to invade. But China's vast size, its 4,150-mile border with the Soviet Union, and its location at the eastern extremity of the Soviet lines of communication and supply have made it a less inviting object of Russian conquest, in spite of historical and ideological animosities much deeper and more long-standing than those with Afghanistan. Vietnam's distance from the United States and its common borders with Communist or neutral regimes in China, Laos, and Cambodia helped make the war unwinnable. Central American insurgencies, on the other hand, are occurring only a few hundred miles south of Texas, and the United States is better able to fight them by means of counterinsurgency operations run from the territory of friendly regimes like Honduras and Costa Rica.

Russia's vast size and severe winter weather have saved it several times from foreign conquest. Napoleon and Hitler both succeeded in reaching the outskirts of Moscow, but their overextended lines of supply left them stranded in the killing winter. But sheer distance has hampered the Russians, too. Their defeat in the Russo-Japanese War of 1905 was partly due to the difficulty of sustaining land and naval forces in the Pacific region. Even today, the Soviet Union has been slow to exploit its vast eastern frontier, largely because Siberia is so remote and its climate so forbidding. The Soviet Union suffers chronic agricultural problems because so much of its immense territory lies outside the temperate zone; the country occupies one-seventh of the world's landmass, yet all but a small part falls north of the forty-ninth parallel (the latitude of the U.S.-Canadian border). In modern times, all the great powers have been located in the temperate climate zones, and the poorest and weakest either in the tropics or the frigid zones nearest the polar caps. Climatic factors like inadequate rainfall, monsoon cycles, and other conditions inhospitable to agriculture have without doubt contributed heavily to the problems of the underdeveloped countries. Technology may one day be able to mitigate some of these factors, just as accurate intercontinental missiles have reduced the importance of an insular location. But geography still poses many obstacles to the acquisition of power that are costly or impossible to overcome. In the nuclear era, the primary geographical prerequisite for superpower status has been continental size, with only the United States and the USSR large enough to permit the dispersal of their industry, population, and weapons systems. This factor also works in favor of China, but against Britain and France, both small enough to be wiped out by only a few warheads.

Many traditional theories of geopolitics have emphasized the importance of geostrategic location, by which a nation can gain worldwide power through its control of certain vital areas. Alfred Thayer Mahan, a nineteenth-century American naval officer and military theorist, believed this required control of the seas and, to maintain that control, the acquisition of colonies with access to important sea passages, vital coastlines, port facilities, and other strategic waterways. Consistent with this theory, the Russians have steadily sought warm-water ports, and America has traditionally been concerned with controlling sea-lanes and choke points like the Persian Gulf, the Mediterranean Sea, the Panama Canal, the Cape of Good Hope, the Indian Ocean, and the Moluccan straits. Even today, landlocked powers are at a disadvantage in trade and defense and must rely on friendly neighbors for access to the sea and protection from sea-borne invasion.

A British geographer of the early twentieth century, Halford Mackinder, argued that technology favored land power over sea power. In his theory, the railroad, the internal combustion engine, and the concentration of key resources for necessary industrial development put a premium on control of the "world island" (Europe and Asia), which depended in turn on control of the Eurasian heartland (Russia and Eastern Europe). Mackinder saw World War I as a contest between the two great land powers, Germany and Russia, for control of Eastern Europe. A later theorist, Nicholas Spykman, followed Mackinder's belief in the "world island" as the key to the security of the "offshore" states, but Spykman located the strategic zone of control not in Russia and Eastern Europe but in the surrounding rimlands (Western Europe, the Middle East, South and Southeast Asia, China, Korea, and Japan). And it is interesting that Soviet-American rivalry and the battle for containment after World War II have been played out in this unstable but strategically located rimland that Spykman defined. More recent interpretations by Saul Cohen, Colin Gray, and others have emphasized the conflict between land-based and sea-based powers and between the Old World of Eurasia and the somewhat insular New World of the Western Hemisphere and the Pacific.

Population

A large population is important to national power. It gives a country a pool of manpower for its military forces and its industry and a potentially sizable and self-sufficient domestic market. In combination with industrial development, an appropriate age distribution, and a high level of health and education, a large population is a formidable national asset. Of the fourteen nations with populations in excess of 50 million, eight of them are the countries traditionally classified as great powers (the United States, the Soviet Union, China, Japan, Germany, England, France, and Italy). Four others (India, Indonesia, Brazil, and Nigeria) are possible great powers of the future. Prussia's unification of the German-speaking peoples in 1870 instantly catapulted Germany into the ranks of the great powers, and the shift of power in Europe between then and 1940 can be charted on a population graph; in this period, Germany gained 27 million new citizens and France only 4 million. America's growth in power is partly the result of the massive immigration that swelled its population by more than 100 million in the century between 1824 and 1924. In the same period, Canada and Australia, comparable in landmass and level of development but with populations less than a tenth that of the United States, remained secondary powers, and so did the Russian and Austro-Hungarian empires, which had large populations but were divided ethnically, weak politically, and at a very low level of industrial development.

The education and age distribution of a population are significant factors in its power potential. The Soviet Union, though relatively underdeveloped in comparison to the rest of the industrial world, has a highly educated population of 280 million; it has more scientists and engineers than any other nation and competes on a par with the United States in many areas of high technology. Israel's small population has always been a weakness in relation to her more populous Arab neighbors, and the civilian work force is further depleted by the need to field a large army. Israel has therefore put a premium on sophisticated weaponry, mobility, air power, and the preemptive strike as means of avoiding a drawn-out land war that would be costly in manpower. However, superior education has given the Israeli forces an edge in every war. The Arab armies, though equipped and trained by the Soviets in their most advanced weaponry, have not had the skilled military personnel to put the sophisticated equipment to good use. The immense populations of Bangladesh and Pakistan are poor and concentrated in a youthful age bracket that has not yet reached its productive years. In today's Germany, an aging population absorbs more resources that it produces, canceling some of the benefits of a large population. Any nation with a sizable segment of retired persons and generous social welfare benefits is likely to face difficult choices between guns and butter and possible limits to its national power and potential for investment and economic growth.

Thus, a large population must be combined with other factors before it can represent a significant source of national strength. (For a comparison of population and gross national product, see Figure 9-1.) But this is true of all the elements of national power. Treating a single factor in isolation is always risky, whether it is population, geopolitics, or nuclear weapons, each of which various theorists have alleged to be the one decisive determinant. We have seen how much depends on context and have already noted that a large population is a serious problem, not an asset, for a poor country, which must divert scarce resources from development into feeding and educating its citizenry. A large population was once considered of great strategic importance as a source of military manpower, but today no country needs vast numbers of troops to serve as cannon fodder in an old-fashioned land war. The geopoliticians once posited decisive roles for sea power, an insular location, and continental size, but advanced technology and nuclear weapons have made them less important. Then came the arrogant assumption that nuclear weapons made all other forms of power obsolete — until the superpowers had to confront guerrilla war, terrorism, economic boycott, and domestic subversion. Indeed, the second half of the twentieth century has seen an evolution away from military force as the decisive power factor, and in the process population has again become salient.

So long as it remains politically united, a large population is still a serious obstacle to the conquest of a nation, even by a nuclear-armed power, for conquest is not just destruction, but also involves occupation and control. Large markets are important to today's global economy, and the untapped markets of China and Russia, extremely attractive by virtue of their sheer size, offer considerable power leverage to the governments that control access to that trade. A large domestic market protects a nation from the worst consequences of an interruption in overseas supplies, as can be seen in the relative economic independence of the two superpowers and the vulnerability of the small trading states of Europe and Asia. Rapid growth of Muslim and nonwhite populations in the Third World has great significance for the North-South conflict, with the prospect that the Northern Caucasian populations will someday be a tiny minority. The rising number of Muslims in the Soviet Union and of Hispanics in the United States likely will lead to a considerable reorientation of their foreign policies.

Natural Resources

Natural resources—food, sources of energy, strategic minerals—fuel the modern economy, and a nation's self-sufficiency in important raw materials greatly increases its power potential. Arable land, vital for self-sufficiency in food, is increasingly scarce and, like coal, oil, and iron, is very unevenly distributed around the globe. Dramatic gains in agricultural productivity, making it possible to feed a large urban labor force, preceded industrial development in all the great nations. Industrial countries also have typically possessed abundant domestic energy supplies. Those that lack sufficient food, energy, and raw materials, like Britain, Germany, and Japan, have been affected in various ways by their need for overseas supplies. Britain built up its naval supremacy and an extensive network of colonies and trading partners. Germany's resource dependency determined a number of its objectives in wartime: to seek a speedy victory, before food reserves were exhausted; to conquer the great food-producing regions of Eastern Europe; to destroy Britain's monopoly of the seas and gain access to overseas supplies. In both world wars, Germany's failure to reach these objectives brought demoralization, privation, and ultimately defeat. For Japan, which has no oil sources of its own, access to oil is a matter of life or death. Japan is heavily dependent on imports of bauxite (aluminum), nickel, chromium, tin, copper, iron, manganese, zinc, lead, wool, cotton, wheat, timber, and grain. In short, Japan can neither feed its population nor fuel its high-technology economy without access to overseas sources. Highly vulnerable to boycotts and wartime interdiction, Japan relies strongly on its alliance with the United States to ensure its supply of key resources and protect its access to such products as Persian Gulf oil.

Rapid industrial growth and the increasing depletion of global resources have converted the world economy from a buyer's to a seller's market and given powerful economic leverage to nations that control a vital commodity. Modern weapons and high technology require exotic minerals that are in short supply. OPEC's control of oil gave its member states much greater influence than their economic and military power warranted. (OPEC and the oil crisis were discussed at length in Chapter 6, "North-South Conflict.") South Africa, a middle-sized power ostracized by the international community for its racist policy of apartheid, has not suffered unduly from economic sanctions because it is an important source of such key minerals as diamonds, platinum, vanadium,

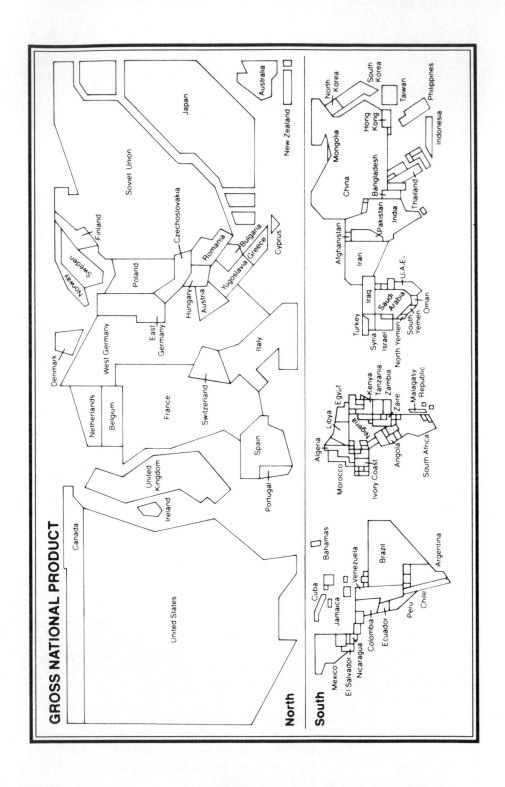

GROSS NATIONAL PRODUCT

North

South

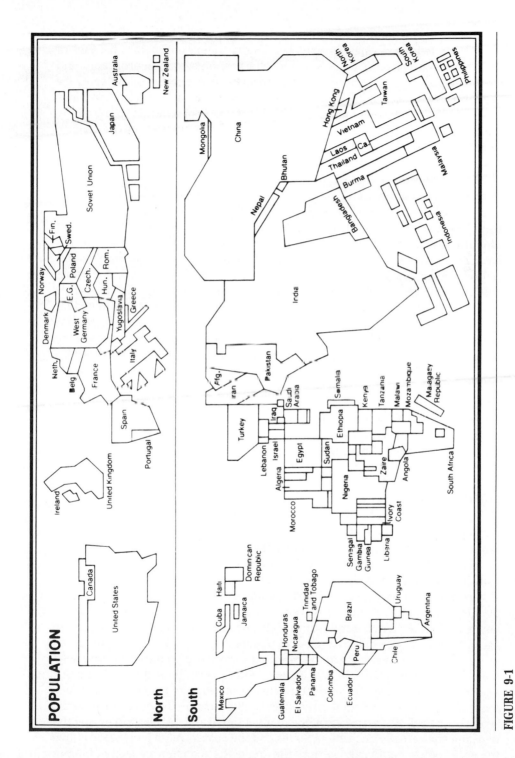

POPULATION

North

Ireland
United Kingdom
Canada
United States
Norway
Denmark
Neth.
Belg.
Fin.
Swed.
E.G. Poland
West Germany
Czech.
Hun. Rom.
France
Yugoslavia
Greece
Italy
Spain
Portugal
Soviet Union
Japan
Australia
New Zealand

South

Mexico
Guatemala
Honduras
El Salvador
Nicaragua
Panama
Cuba
Haiti
Jamaica
Dominican Republic
Trinidad and Tobago
Colombia
Ecuador
Peru
Brazil
Chile
Uruguay
Argentina
Morocco
Algeria
Senegal
Gambia
Guinea
Liberia
Ivory Coast
Nigeria
Lebanon
Israel
Egypt
Sudan
Ethiopia
Somalia
Kenya
Tanzania
Zaire
Angola
Malawi
Mozambique
Malagasy Republic
South Africa
Turkey
Iraq
Saudi Arabia
Iran
Afg.
Pakistan
Nepal
Bhutan
India
Bangladesh
Burma
Mongolia
China
Hong Kong
North Korea
South Korea
Taiwan
Vietnam
Laos
Thailand
Camb.
Malaysia
Indonesia
Philippines

FIGURE 9-1

THE DISTRIBUTION OF THE WORLD'S GROSS NATIONAL PRODUCT AND POPULATION chromium, and uranium. Countries richly endowed with natural resources, like the United States, may nevertheless be dependent on imports because of their voracious consumption. Import surcharges, conservation programs, and the development of substitute products and alternative energy technologies are common practices for increasing self-sufficiency, and a nation can also enhance its power position by accumulating extensive reserves of strategic resources — the reason the United States stockpiles enough petroleum to serve the defense economy for several years.

Africa has been an arena for great-power rivalry throughout the twentieth century because it is one of the last domains of unexplored and untapped resources. The copper-rich Katanga province's attempted secession during the Congo crisis of 1960 – 61 brought superpower intervention, and copper is what has kept the United States steadfastly behind the authoritarian regime of Mobutu Sese Seko in Zaire ever since. Chad, otherwise destitute, has been a battlefield because of its important uranium deposits. The countries of southern Africa are suppliers of key minerals, which made the prospect of a Soviet challenge in Angola, in the 1970s, all the more threatening. The seabed is becoming another arena of international competition. Geologists estimate that offshore reserves of oil are greater than those on land. The United States has pioneered in the mining of manganese nodules from the seabed (one reason the Reagan administration refused to sign the Law of the Sea), and such nodules may also yield important supplies of nickel, copper, and cobalt. Other minerals that can be obtained in significant quantities from the sea are coal, iron, tin, limestone, sulphur, diamonds, and barium. As traditional sources of these strategic resources are exhausted, national competition for control of international waters is likely to become fierce, and nations with long coastlines and extensive territorial waters will have a strong head start.

Economic Capacity

Perhaps the most important measure of a nation's basic power potential is economic capacity — its industrial strength and technological innovation. A nation may be richly endowed with natural resources but lack the ability to convert them into military hardware, high-technology exports, and other instruments of power. The Congo has valuable supplies of high-grade uranium but none of the other economic ingredients that go into the making of a nuclear power. India has vast resources and a highly developed industrial sector, but its agriculture struggles to feed a massive population, and other economic needs are so desperate that few capital resources can be committed to advanced military production. Britain and France, which have the technological skills and industrial capacity to produce nuclear warheads and their delivery systems, do not have the size, the resource sufficiency, or the overall economic strength to field the vast array of both conventional and nuclear forces that the two superpowers do. The United States and the Soviet Union have stood above the other powers militarily because they have the economic capacity to maintain large armed forces, to invest in extensive research and development, to produce and test highly sophisticated weapons, to conduct constant maneuvers and training, and to subsidize costly networks of overseas bases. Their economies also are productive enough to support trade and financial assistance to their allies abroad. The recent collapse of the Soviet economy has called into question the Soviets' superpower status precisely because it can no longer afford to sustain an extensive array of arms and aid relations. In general, there is a direct correlation between a nation's economic capacity (as measured in gross output) and its military strength.

There are exceptions, however. A number of poor Third World states, by employing political organization, ideological motivation, and the techniques of guerrilla war, have developed strong war-making potentials. The United States consistently underestimated the North Vietnamese in this respect. States with imperial ambitions or great-power aspirations, particularly those that have authoritarian governments, are often able to devote a relatively large share of their productive capacity to the military sector. Between 1934 and 1942, the fascist governments of Japan and Germany mounted a significant challenge to an economically superior Allied coalition by putting their entire economies on a war footing and extracting the maximum for military production. Today, Japan has a GNP more than three times that of the People's Republic of China, yet the latter has equal stature as a great power because it has mobilized the military sector of its economy to produce nuclear weapons, guided missiles, and submarine launchers. The Soviet Union, with a GNP only about a third that of the United States, has remained competitive in the arms race by spending 12 to 15 percent of its GNP in the military sector, as opposed to only about 5 percent for the United States. Most Third World countries spend a disproportionately large percentage of their national budgets on military goods, because they are politically unstable, often are governed by a military elite, and regard modern weapons as a prominent measure of their sovereignty and status. In 1983, Saudi Arabia had the highest per capita military expenditures in the world. It purchased arms valued at almost $20 billion to protect a population of less than 10 million, nearly twice the rate of the second-ranked state and clearly made possible by its enormous oil wealth. By comparison, Japan, with a population of about 120 million, spends only about $10 billion on arms annually. Israel spends the highest percentage of GNP on arms, almost 30 percent, followed by Syria and Jordan, at about 16 percent each — levels kept high by the ongoing tensions in the Middle East. (Figure 9-2 shows the various nations' share of world military expenditures.)

A high level of military spending comes at a cost to a nation's larger economy and reduces its ability to invest in future economic growth. Defense spending represents a noneconomic allocation of scarce resources, especially for Third World countries already short of development funds, but even advanced states are regularly forced to choose between guns and butter. (Figure 9-3 compares military spending as a share of GNP by income and by region.) Since a state's political stability and the legitimacy and durability of its leadership are increasingly tied to domestic economic performance, excessive

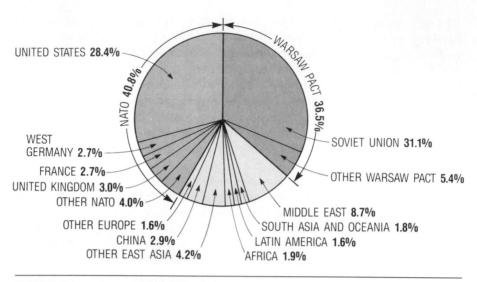

FIGURE 9-2
SHARES OF WORLD MILITARY EXPENDITURES, 1984

spending in the military sector is dangerous, for a less-developed country and a superpower alike. It is not surprising that Japan and Germany, which spend only 1 percent and 3 percent, respectively, of their GNP on defense, have booming export sectors, high rates of savings and innovation, and high levels of productivity. The United States and the USSR are the lowest among the industrial states in these areas, largely because military production siphons off resources that might stimulate overall productivity. A weak agrarian sector is a particular burden for the Soviet Union, almost 30 percent of whose labor force is in agricultural production, as compared to only 5 percent for the United States. A quarter of the Soviet work force is essentially wasted in making up shortfalls in agricultural productivity, and a disproportionate share of Soviet investment capital also goes to agriculture, without noticeable improvement. Data on overall GNP show a large strategic advantage for the Western alliance, which controls well over 50 percent of the world's productive capacity, as compared to only about 20 percent for the Communist states.

In sum, industrial states are powerful because they can convert GNP to military goods, but if they do so to excess, they erode the underlying basis of their own power. The inability of the Soviet economy to match the United States in computers, space weaponry, and other high-technology fields is one of the motives for Gorbachev's push toward détente and his shift of resources from military to civilian production. China has also awakened to the retrogressive effect of defense spending on other indexes of economic strength. It slashed its military budget from $18 billion in 1980 to $14 billion in 1981 and reorganized its seven military ministries under civilian control. In the following decade, China's military spending dropped to about 8 percent, less than half what it had been in 1979, and the military staff was reduced by one-half and overall troop strength by one-quarter, putting more than a million workers back into the civilian economy between 1985 and 1988. In the United States, lagging export performance and low productivity are the more visible signs of the economic distortions associated with a large military-industrial complex.

Large economies generate power independent of military capacity by giving states financial clout in the international arena. Rich states supply much of the aid, investment capital, and loans for less-developed nations. Leading industrial powers wield economic weight through foreign trade and by the impact of their domestic policies on the world economy. A nation's power is weakened by high inflation, a large external debt, or a chronic balance-of-payments deficit. The stronger the economy, the more varied, resilient, and credible are a state's international economic options. Sanctions, for example, are effective only if the country that imposes them controls economic assets

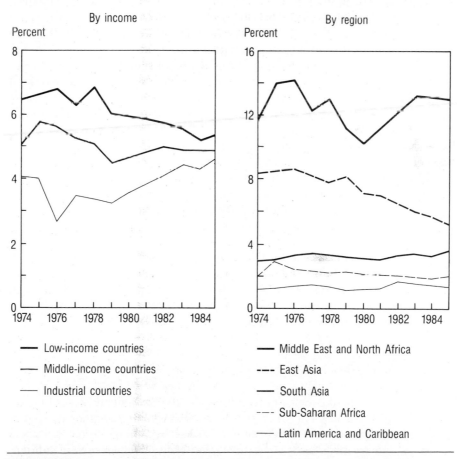

FIGURE 9-3
MILITARY SPENDING AS A SHARE OF GNP, 1974–1985

essential to others, and they are useless against an economy powerful enough to endure the temporary deprivation of a boycott.

Innovativeness in technology is increasingly important, both in raising productivity in the civilian sector and in developing an array of advanced weaponry. Crude nuclear devices are no longer enough. To be powerful today, a state must have sophisticated delivery systems, accurate warheads, and mobile or invulnerable launchers. It must be able to gather intelligence by satellite and other advanced means and to harden its communications facilities so they can withstand a destructive nuclear attack. It must have a massive research and development effort that will keep the nation ahead in the techniques of production (and destruction). High-technology goods are also the backbone of the most aggressive export economies, and the sale of high-technology arms abroad is an important source of security, export revenues, and political influence.

The strategic role of technology is manifest in the Soviet Union's extensive efforts in industrial espionage and in its outright stealing of advanced weapons designs. Clandestine industrial information and data that its spies gathered from America's nuclear weapons industry assisted immeasurably in the rapid Soviet development of a nuclear capability between 1946 and 1949. More recently, the Soviets acquired silent submarine technology through the surreptitious purchase of computerized milling equipment for the manufacture of propellers. Between 1980 and 1984, some highly sensitive military-related technologies were sold illegally to the Soviet Union through third parties — Norway's state-owned armaments manufacturer, Kongsberg, and Japan's Toshiba Machine Company. Of course, such activities are also indicative of the backwardness of the Soviet economy and of how its scientific and technical inadequacies were holding down its power potential.

When introduced into a Third World conflict, high-technology weapons have been decisive. Chinese Silkworm missiles assisted an otherwise weak Iran in staving off defeat in the Persian Gulf. American-built Stinger antiaircraft missiles enabled the Afghan *mujahedeen* guerrillas to neutralize Soviet air power and hasten the Soviet withdrawal. Since these recently developed shoulder-fired antiaircraft missiles cost only about $36,000 apiece, as against $20 million to $100 million for one tactical combat plane, such new technology can tip the balance significantly. Naval warfare was certainly revolutionized when the Argentines, during the Falklands War, sank a multibillion-dollar British battleship with a relatively inexpensive French-made Exocet missile.

Military Strength

Military strength has historically been the means of national power (see Figure 9-4). The appearance of a new power has usually been accompanied by victory in battle, and the decline of a great power signaled by military defeat. Numbers of troops and weapons have constituted the traditional measure of military power and, all other things being equal, can be decisive in establishing a nation's place in the international hierarchy. Soldiers and military hardware,

FIGURE 9-4
MILITARY RANKINGS OF THE WORLD'S TOP THIRTY, 1988

Rank	Defense Expenditures[1] ($ millions)		Defense Expenditures[2] (as % of GDP/GNP)		Regular Armed Forces (thousands)
	ISS	SIPRI	ISS (1987)	SIPRI (1988)	
1. United States	260,268	267,765	6.4	6.0	2,163.2
2. Soviet Union	231,000	(252,000)[3,5]	12.0	(17.0)[3]	5,096.0[4,5]
3. China	5,283	(34,500)[3,5]	1.9		3,200.0[5]
4. United Kingdom	22,637	26,103	4.7	4.4	316.7
5. France	21,903	29,056	4.0	3.8	456.9
6. West Germany	20,870	28,167	3.0	3.0	488.7
7. Japan	15,298	21,554	1.0	1.0	245.0
8. Saudi Arabia	14,444	15,006	22.7		72.0
9. Italy	11,178	15,244	2.4	2.3	386.0
10. India	8,247	8,830	3.8		1,362.0
11. Canada	7,985		2.1	2.0	84.6
12. East Germany	7,256	5,571	8.0	5.0	172.0
13. Iraq	7,051	11,579 (1986)	26.8		1,000.0
14. South Korea	6,309	5,896	5.7	2.4	629.0
15. Australia	4,221		2.7		70.5
16. Czechoslovakia	4,182	3,479	4.9		197.0
17. Spain	4,181	5,475	2.4	2.1	309.5
18. Netherlands	4,014	5,420	3.1	3.0	102.2
19. Taiwan	3,961	6,593	6.3		405.5
20. North Korea	3,943	1,734	9.3	12.3 (1983)	842.0
21. Israel	3,666		14.8		141.0[6]
22. Egypt	3,326		8.0	6.2 (1987)	445.0
23. Sweden	3,052	3,448	3.0	2.5	67.0
24. Iran	2,736	5,960 (1986)	3.0		604.0
25. Pakistan	2,649		7.4		480.6
26. Belgium	2,509	3,372	.5	9.6 (1985)	180.0
27. South Africa	2,376		4.1	4.1	125.5
28. Greece	2,192		6.2	6.6	214.0
29. Turkey	2,158		4.3	4.1	635.3
30. Switzerland	1,869	2,380	1.9	1.7	3.5

[1] The ISS figures are 1985 U.S. dollars; the SIPRI figures are 1986 U.S. dollars.
[2] GDP = Gross domestic product, i.e., the value of domestically traded goods and services only. The values are in local currencies, with GNP used when GDP unavailable, and estimated where official figures unavailable.
[3] U.S. CIA estimates. Chinese and Soviet expenditures are subject to extensive debate and disagreement. The USSR does not categorize defense budgets as in the West, and reports its own figure of $120 billion. It is difficult to price the value of products in a Communist economy, and the CIA's estimates are disputed.
[4] Includes roughly 1 million railroad construction, labor, and general support troops.
[5] Being reduced.
[6] Israel's armed forces can be quickly expanded to over 500,000 by total mobilization.

the most visible and most easily counted elements of a nation's defense, strongly influence the perceptions of others. Quantitative calculations of the military balance serve as an index of the arms race and indirectly influence negotiations between adversaries. Nations with a high level of military production can increase their power leverage by selling arms overseas or giving arms aid to allies or clients. Arms suppliers can station technical advisers abroad, train foreign officers at home, and manipulate flows of ammunition, spare parts, and replacements in such ways as to achieve foreign policy objectives. Military training programs, a main avenue of political indoctrination, are a useful means for the donor regime to gain political support and educate a sympathetic foreign elite. The two superpowers' control of arms supplies to the Middle East and Central America has been the key to their influence in these regions, permitting them to foment or reduce conflict as it suits their interests. In some cases, like Saudi Arabia, Iran, and Libya, arms sales have made military powers of desert countries otherwise incapable of supporting a modern army or air force.

A wide variety of military factors can compensate for numerical inferiority: quality, mobility, versatility, readiness, organization, communications, strategy, tactics, leadership, training, and morale. The quality of arms technology has become vital, in an era in which every decade brings important design breakthroughs. In any test of arms, victory is likely to go to the nation with the best and most reliable weapons. In the past, such timely inventions as the stirrup, the crossbow, gunpowder, the steam engine, the machine gun, the tank, the submarine, the airplane, the nuclear bomb, and the guided missile have revolutionized warfare and often spelled the difference between victory and defeat. The intensity of the arms race has been largely due to both superpowers' fears that technology would make their weapons obsolete. The quality of troops is also vital. An elite corps superior in training and organization can defeat a larger but poorly trained force of conscripts. Alarmists often cited the Warsaw pact's greater numbers of troops, artillery, and tanks as a point of Western vulnerability, but NATO was always able to compensate by the higher quality of its weapons and troops.

Versatility in its armed forces allows a great power to confront a full range of possible military conflicts, from nuclear attack to guerrilla war and terrorism. In 1960, President John F. Kennedy judged America to be militarily weak because it was overly reliant on its nuclear arsenal and was unable to respond to more limited military challenges, either in Europe or in the Third World. He augmented conventional forces to permit a more "flexible response" and began to train American troops in counterinsurgency warfare. Later, the United States expanded its navy, deployed a more sophisticated array of intermediate and tactical nuclear forces, and acquired cruise missiles and other counterforce weapons, making it able to respond more appropriately to almost any type of attack.

Vulnerability to attack is another element of military power, made ever more crucial by the fast delivery time and destructive potential of modern weapons. Nuclear forces are typically made invulnerable by mobility, concealment, dispersal, and hardening. Just as the fighting forces of old used stealth and defensive fortifications to their advantage, the United States today can secrete nuclear missiles in submarines, shuffle them around on railcars, or fortify them within reinforced steel and concrete silos that will withstand all but a direct hit. The United States' widely dispersed strategic triad — manned bombers, land-based intercontinental ballistic missiles (ICBMs), and submarine-launched ballistic missiles (SLBMs) — is aimed at keeping its nuclear forces invulnerable and preserving a second-strike capability. A ballistic missile defense system such as President Reagan's proposed Star Wars space shield is likewise aimed at reducing vulnerability. However, excessively sophisticated weaponry and overly specialized defense systems introduce problems of complexity, coordination, centralized command, logistic support, and resource dependency that could well make them more vulnerable than traditional military forces. Guerrilla fighters and terrorists using very simple technologies can readily disrupt a complex modern defense system by attacking its weakest or most strategically located link.

Mobility and the projection of force are also vital to military effectiveness. In the opening months of World War II, the Germans' blitzkrieg tactics, which employed mechanized armor and close air support, quickly overran the entrenched fortifications of the French Maginot Line. Later in the war, however, long-range strategic bombing by the British and the Americans was a projection of their power that the Germans could not match. America's overwhelming superiority in aircraft carriers, along with the Rapid Deployment Force (RDF) created by President Jimmy Carter, gives it an unmatched capacity for projecting power in the Third World today. Both superpowers have a vast airlift and sealift capability that extends their influence throughout the world. The NATO alliance defended the freedom of West Berlin by airlifting supplies into the city when the Soviets cut off all rail and road access in 1949. The Soviets tipped the outcomes of the Angolan civil war and the conflict between Ethiopia and Somalia by their massive airlifts of arms, advisers, and supplies. Special forces teams, with their superb mobility and communications, can spearhead surgical interventions, like the U.S. invasion of Grenada, or can launch or respond to terrorist attacks, as Israeli commandos did in rescuing a hijacked plane at Entebbe, Uganda, and in assassinating a leader of the Palestine Liberation Organization (PLO), Khalil Wazir. The mobility of the multiple independently retargetable reentry vehicle (MIRV) has increased the firepower and effectiveness of nuclear missiles.

Military readiness and the potential for rapid mobilization are another element in the calculation of force. Israel's permanent army numbers only 164,000, but the forces are highly trained, are instantly ready, and can be supplemented by 400,000 additional combat-ready soldiers within twenty-four hours. Switzerland can mobilize more than half a million troops, about one-twelfth of its population, in less than two days. Similarily, Sweden can raise a force almost overnight that equals the standing army of many a European power. The Soviet Union, on the other hand, has Europe's largest standing army, but, according to the Pentagon's 1988 edition of *Soviet Military Power,* only about 40 percent of Soviet army divisions are combat ready. More than 130 divisions lack their full complement of troops and equipment, training is woefully inferior to that of the NATO alliance, and the majority of the Russian troops are short-term conscripts. Availability of fuel and spare parts, opportunities for engaging in maneuvers or training with live ammunition, and other readiness factors also must be taken into account in the power assessment.

Strategy and tactics determine how a military force is used—that is, whether the force is properly matched to the task and the operational environment. Is there an appropriate balance between the various branches, and are they effectively coordinated? The U.S. invasion of Grenada was nearly a fiasco, due to poor coordination between air, land, and sea forces. An attack was launched inadvertently on a hospital, and the incompatibility of the communications equipment of the various forces compelled one officer to use a pay phone to convey an urgent message. Interservice rivalries cripple decisions about weapons acquisition, and service favoritism has foisted on the United States weapons that are impractical, ineffective, and redundant. Since exotic technologies and hypothetical nuclear scenarios cannot be realistically tested, there is ample opportunity for all modern armed forces to embrace erroneous or wishful strategies and to acquire weapons that do not perform up to expectations—weaknesses that could prove fatal if war ever actually occurs.

Does a nation's military strategy correctly anticipate the nature of a future war, or will it simply fight the next war with the strategy and tactics of the last one? Frederick the Great's genius in military strategy and tactics made Prussia supreme in the eighteenth century. However, Napoleon defeated these same Prussian forces after 1800 by his introduction of still more effective techniques, including conscript armies and systematic, state-sponsored weapons production. Many World War I generals were surprised to find their cavalry and mobile offenses overcome by artillery, the machine gun, and other new tactics of trench warfare. In World War II, the French general staff saw its Maginot Line and two decades of careful planning circumvented in three weeks by the innovative German blitzkrieg strategy. In 1967, the Egyptians prepared their defenses to counter an expected Israeli air attack across the Sinai desert to the east. But the Israelis destroyed the bulk of the Egyptian air force on the ground and won the war virtually overnight by launching a surprise attack from the west. American air force generals incorrectly applied a lesson from World War II to the unconventional war in Vietnam in their assumption that strategic bombing and tactical air superiority would break the North Vietnamese. Errors in strategy and tactics have shaped the outcome of almost every war.

The complexity of modern war gives high priority to matters of organization, such as communications, intelligence, and logistic support. Command, control, and communication—called C^3—have become so important that military planners have devised special "decapitation" strategies to knock out the enemy's control of its forces in the first hours of a war. The superpowers have spent much effort in hardening their command centers against the disrupting atmospheric effects of electromagnetic pulse, and in setting up alternative communication channels with commanders in missile silos and submarines. Intelligence is crucial in targeting, in obtaining advance warning of attack, and in understanding an adversary's strategy and intentions. Good intelligence data, particularly the ability to crack enemy codes, gave the Allies a huge advantage in World War II, allowing them to predict Hitler's movements and to mislead him about the timing and exact location of the Normandy invasion in 1944. The CIA and the KGB, the secret services of the United States and the USSR, are infamous for their ability to spy on one another and to control information and events in various Third World conflicts.

A final category of military strength is the intangibles of leadership, morale, motivation, and discipline, which greatly affect the efficiency and cohesion of a fighting force. The Soviet army was crippled in World War II by Joseph Stalin's purges of the 1930s, which had decimated the officer corps and deprived the armed forces of their most professional leaders. Political interference or the slow infection of incompetence, waste, corruption, and cronyism have weakened many armies. The low morale of the Soviet-trained Afghan army, and the failure of its officers to communicate well with ordinary soldiers led to a high rate of desertions. Though both the regular and the guerrilla armies in Afghanistan came from the same population, well-equipped government soldiers proved no match for the poorly armed but highly motivated rebels. The Soviet army itself is experiencing problems with its predominantly Russian officer corps and a growing number of Muslim conscripts from the eastern republics. The United States has turned to an all-volunteer army, hoping to avoid the morale problems it had with Vietnam-era conscripts by the introduction of more highly paid and better trained career professionals.

Political Qualities

The final element of national power that we will consider is the political dimension, with its ingredients of leadership, national morale, social cohesion, political reputation, and the quality of a government and its diplomacy. Such leaders as Woodrow Wilson and Vladimir Lenin clearly put a personal stamp on the foreign policies of their countries. Winston Churchill and Charles de Gaulle rallied the national morale and the will to resist in England and France during World War II. Adolph Hitler's charisma and political acumen were responsible for the rise of German power (just as much as his excesses were responsible for its fall). American presidents have brought to the office varying degrees of leadership and foreign policy skills. Franklin Delano Roosevelt combined a sense of history and the insights of wide experience with effective organization, superb negotiating skills, and a great personal touch. Jimmy Carter arrived in the White House with almost no foreign policy experience and a tendency to vacillate. Rather than educate the public on the issues of the day, the Carter administration more often mirrored the shifting public moods and drifted from the naive peace efforts of its early months to paranoid and bellicose overreactions to the events in Afghanistan and Iran. Still, Carter's leadership assets of moral suasion and his reputation for great personal integrity were invaluable in convincing Anwar Sadat and Menachem Begin to sign an Egyptian-Israeli peace accord.

National morale is measured by the popular support a nation's citizens are willing to give to their government's foreign policy. Particularly in times of war or prolonged crisis, public opinion can affect dramatically the success of leaders in carrying forward their policies. For example, Russia before World War I and France before World War II were politically unstable and internally divided. Popular unrest over czarist policies brought on the Bolshevik Revolution in 1917 and Russia's subsequent withdrawal from the war. In France, class divisions and collaborationist sentiment abetted the extremely rapid Nazi conquest in 1940 and the creation of the Vichy puppet state. In both Great Britain and the Soviet Union, on the other hand, an enormous upsurge of patriotic feeling during World War II made it possible for their people to endure tremendous military losses without losing hope. In Germany, the popular will to pursue the war was surprisingly resilient, even in the closing months, when a number of top generals and high officials had given up. Japanese soldiers also displayed a tenacious loyalty, even to the point of carrying out suicidal kamikaze attacks, and Japan's high national morale was one of the factors in convincing President Harry S Truman that the nuclear bombings of Hiroshima and Nagasaki were necessary to induce Japan to surrender.

National morale can spell the difference in a military occupation or a prolonged campaign of passive or active resistance. The Danes and the Norwegians resisted the German occupation in World War II with admirable fortitude, and Mohandas Gandhi's campaign of nonviolent resistance in India in the decades after 1920 united the Indian nationalists and hastened the British departure. In Indochina, North Vietnamese General Vo Nguyen Giap's strategy of prolonged unconventional war against France and the United States in the 1950s and '60s was based on his judgment that French and American public morale would not sustain a long war in so distant and peripheral an area of national concern. Giap's 1968 Tet offensive against the cities of South Vietnam, a risky move that was almost certain to fail tactically, was aimed strategically at altering American public opinion, and in that it succeeded greatly. The splash of negative headlines had a powerful demoralizing effect, forcing President Lyndon Johnson to withdraw from the presidential contest and begin to wind down the war. Of course, a more fundamental problem in Vietnam had always been the inability of the South Vietnamese government to attract popular support and unite the country behind the war. In Israel, national morale has affected both internal stability and external conflict. Public opinion was largely united through four wars with the radical Arab states of the Middle East, but it split over the invasion of Lebanon in 1982, generating protests in Tel Aviv stronger than any in the Arab world. The Israeli public was further divided over the question of antiterrorist policies and the management of Palestinian dissent in the West Bank and Gaza. The fundamental disagreements over Palestinian self-rule and approaches to peace and security in the Middle East made it impossible for the coalition Labor-Likud government of Shimon Peres and Yitzhak Shamir to conduct an effective foreign policy.

Problems of national morale are compounded when a nation lacks social cohesion because of underlying class, ethnic, or religious differences. Such disunity has undermined the foreign policies of India (Muslim dissenters in Kashmir), Pakistan (Pathan tribes on the Afghan border), Iraq (Kurdish nationalism), Lebanon (religious factionalism), Ethiopia (contests over Eritrea and the Ogaden), Chad (Muslim minorities sympathetic to Libya), Nicaragua (treatment of the Moskito Indians), Northern Ireland (Catholic sympathy with the Irish Republican Army secessionists), Spain (Basque separatists), and dozens of other states. The question of popular support is crucial for assessing Soviet strength in newly liberated Eastern Europe, where any war or intervention raises the prospect of a strong anti-Soviet, nationalist reaction. Certainly the value of Czech or Polish divisions must be discounted in calculations about troop strength in the event of a clash between NATO and Warsaw Pact forces. The Soviet Union itself has dozens of national minorities (for example, in Armenia, Azerbaijan, and the Baltic states) that are politically restless. The potential disloyalty of its large Muslim minority was certainly a factor in the Soviet response to Islamic fundamentalist revolutions in Iran and Afghanistan. The Soviets have good reason to be concerned about nationality problems; large contingents of Ukrainians and Tartars deserted to the Germans during World War II. Finally, special problems arise for partitioned nations like Germany, China, and Korea, in which common cultural ties and hopes for reunification conflict with ideological divisions. As these examples show, the nature of a political culture affects national unity and morale and the capacity of the state to act with clarity and continuity.

The political reputation of a regime or an administration contributes to its effectiveness. A government's power is enhanced if it is perceived as consistently able to make decisions with dispatch, gain popular approval for its policies, and carry through on its commitments. A reputation for fairness and honesty is bound to improve the quality of a state's alliance relationships. But a government that has a credibility problem, at home or abroad, and that routinely speaks in two or three policy voices, will have diminished power. If it is perceived as duplicitous or wavering from one administration to the next, allies and enemies alike will tend to discount or disregard its foreign policies. A country whose methods are at variance with its national values will have a lessened ideological appeal. Modern diplomacy is very much a propaganda contest for the hearts and minds of uncommitted states, and a nation's reputation for consistency and fidelity to its principles counts. Such perceptions are also central to power calculations, since a reputation for strength is what makes a deterrent threat credible. The failed appeasement policies of British Prime Minister Neville Chamberlain prior to World War II, which allowed Hitler to pursue his aggressions, caused a "Munich syndrome" to infect Western diplomacy during the Cold War — a belief that any concessions to the Soviets would be perceived as a sign of weakness. A similar "Vietnam syndrome" has been at work since the debacle in Indochina. Some have concluded that the Soviet-Cuban aggression in Africa was due to America's loss of prestige and its perceived failure of will in Vietnam; in Central America, others have reached the contrary conclusion that the United States cannot afford any more prolonged guerrilla conflicts, because the public would not support them. Historians draw different lessons from the traumatic experience of Vietnam, but they agree that it has an enduring impact on America's image of itself and on its reputation for power.

Most important in the political dimension of power is the quality a nation gives to its direction of foreign policy. Power resources mean nothing if they are not efficiently employed or serve purposes that are fundamentally misconceived. A good statesman will always distinguish between the desirable and the possible, and will not put sound policy at the service of impractical or illusory aims. A prudent nation will set priorities, adopt policies that are appropriate to the power available, and pursue them by means that do not contradict the original intentions. Hans Morgenthau's *Politics Among Nations* summarizes well the central contribution that good diplomacy makes to a nation's power:

> Diplomacy, one might say, is the brains of national power, as national morale is its soul. If its vision is blurred, its judgment defective, and its determination feeble, all the advantages of geographical location, of self-sufficiency in food, raw materials, and industrial production, of military preparedness, of size and quality of population will in the long run avail a nation little. A nation that can boast of all these advantages, but not of a diplomacy commensurate with them, may achieve temporary successes through the sheer weight of its natural assets. In the long run, it is likely to squander the natural assets by activating them incompletely, haltingly, and wastefully for the nation's international objectives. . . . Often in history the Goliath without brains or soul has been smitten and slain by the David who had both. Diplomacy of high quality will bring the ends and means of foreign policy into harmony with the available resources of power. It will tap the hidden sources of national strength and transform them fully and securely into political realities. (p.159)

In short, the sheer quality of a government affects its foreign policy decision making, both in the setting of goals and in their implementation. Overbureaucratization, personalism, and arbitrary shifts in policy are likely to afflict the diplomacy of authoritarian states. Foreign policy in democracies often suffers from disorganization, stalemate, political division, inconstancy, popular stereotypes, excessive moralizing, and the undue influence of special interests. A foreign policy that is wise, steady, and farsighted is a rare source of strength to a nation.

One last element in a nation's power to protect itself against global anarchy and insecurity is the role of chance or accident. No matter how rich a nation may be in resources or how well organized to exercise its power, "the slings and arrows of outrageous fortune" can decisively alter circumstances. No nation can ever be sure of complete security, nor will analysts ever be able to predict with certainty the outcomes of conflicts, even apparently lopsided ones. James Fallows, in *National Defense,* attributes the essential unpredictability of international affairs to the rapid pace of change as against the slow and cumbersome responses of diplomats and defense planners. "Friction" is what Karl von Clausewitz called the ingredient of uncertainty in war. To it, and to the intangibles of leadership, morale, and motivation, he attributed many a victory or defeat. Friction—the difference between plans and reality—is the bad weather, the fear and confusion, the faulty information, an unexpected break-down, a bit of dumb luck, the intervention of some other unforeseen factor. As Clausewitz wrote in his *On War:* "So in War, through the influence of an infinity of petty circumstances, which cannot properly be described on paper, things disappoint us and we fall short of the mark" (p. 164).

THE PERCEPTION AND CALCULATION OF MILITARY POWER

Hardly any of the myriad contested issues of international affairs are resolved by the actual use of force. More often, the threat of war or a lesser sanction persuades one of the parties to back down, or negotiations uncover a basis for cooperation. The United States and the Soviet Union passed from Cold War to détente between 1984 and 1988 without any shift whatever in the underlying disposition of force. What changed? Many things, including the Soviet leader-ship (Mikhail Gorbachev became general-secretary of the Communist party in 1985), mounting budget deficits in both countries, judgments about the utility (or futility) of the arms race, and an impending change of administration in the United States (which has pushed many presidents with one eye on the history books toward peacemaking). Most fundamentally, we can say that perceptions changed, in the context of repeated summit dialogues and diligent arms control diplomacy. To repeat a point made earlier, judgments about an adversary's intentions conditioned our assessments of power, and such judgments often are fluid and highly subjective. The human ingredient of perception is one of the factors that make power relations so unpredictable.

A nation's reputation for force is a part of this perception, for the deterrent capacity of power lies in the eye of the beholder. Just as a bank robber can get away with using a toy gun if the tellers believe it is real, so bluff and threats can gain the ends of a state so long as others are sufficiently awed by them. Of course, periodic demonstrations of force help to reinforce a reputation for power — the reason "gunboat diplomacy" remains popular among the great powers. But a state wastes its credibility if these means fail to achieve the declared objective. Britain's inept use of force during the 1956 Suez crisis and America's hapless intervention in Vietnam reduced both nations' power by the effect their ineptitude had on the perceptions of others.

The history of warfare is full of underestimates or overestimates of a state's power based on the miscalculation of one or more factors — often the intangibles — apart from the actual military balance. In Vietnam, the United States consistently underestimated the capacity of the North Vietnamese to resist aerial bombing and to circumvent the interdiction of their supply routes. The psychology of the conflict proved especially unpredictable. Air force strate-gists thought that saturation bombing of Hanoi and other urban centers would demoralize the North Vietnamese leadership, but it had the contrary effect of strengthening their will. The United States also made the critical misjudgment that the main support for the South Vietnamese insurgency was coming from the North, and it discounted the intangible but potent force of indigenous South Vietnamese nationalism, which local Viet Cong leaders were able to rally behind an "anti-imperialist" war. America realized only too late that it had stepped into the much-despised colonial role vacated by the French. It did not matter that the U.S. intention was to create democracy and defend freedom; America was perceived as an imperial master and an oppressor. Because of these perceptions, in combination with the crucial role of legitimacy and ideology in an unconventional civil struggle, the political "power to persuade" did not equal military "power to hurt." Armed force is aimed at altering an opponent's will and perceptions, but the path from instrument to object is not always direct or predictable. Vietnam was a case in which American military planners, succumbing to crackpot "realism" and reductionist thinking, mistakenly assumed that U.S. military power was self-evident and that the path between threat and implementation would be short and cheap.

Personality and ideology also contribute to misperceptions of force. Hitler's racism and megalomania caused him to discount the military power of the Soviets, and resulted in his fatal decision to open a second front against the Russians. In the Korean War, General Douglas MacArthur's arrogance and low opinion of the Chinese led him to press his offensive right to the Chinese border, precipitating China's intervention in a counteroffensive that pushed the American forces back to the thirty-eighth parallel. Presidents Johnson and Nixon both showed a disdain for the Vietnamese that was rooted in racism and great-power chauvinism — yet this "bunch of peasants" and "gooks" from a "half-country" that was a "fourth-rate power" handed the United States its first wartime defeat ever.

Intentions Versus Capabilities

One of the tragic dimensions of international diplomacy is the difficulty of communicating peaceful intentions, especially in a situation in which war seems imminent and the adversaries have a history of hostility and ideological rivalry. Interacting misperceptions contributed heavily to the outbreak of World War I — as if the accuracy of the perceptions could be determined only by the acid test of war. It is difficult to make others believe that one's reassurances are unambiguous when each state has the capacity for taking independent military action, and it is easy to disguise hostile intent when so many peace treaties and acts of appeasement have littered the path to war. This is why great-power rivalries have ended so often in arms races and war. But Britain's power went unchallenged throughout the nineteenth century, only partly because of its strong military forces. Just as important was the widespread perception that the British exercised their strength with moderation, and therefore their predominance did not threaten the security of rival powers. David Singer, in *Quantitative International Politics,* has reduced the question of perception to a simple formula: threat equals intentions multiplied by capabilities. Applying the formula to the growth of American military power after World

War II, U.S. power was viewed in many quarters as benign because the intention was to maintain world peace. The Soviets, of course, perceived the U.S. containment policy as encirclement and American police actions as intended to protect the world capitalist order, to the detriment of progressive socialist forces and planned economies — clearly an instance of ideological considerations shaping differing perceptions.

A sustained military buildup by a great power always raises the crucial problem of assessing intentions. The example of Hitler's actions before World War II, and the Soviet Union's expansion of its strategic forces after 1962 are instructive. Many statesmen concluded that Germany's rearmament was inevitable and necessary because of its unfair treatment under the punitive terms of the Versailles peace treaty. Germany had been disarmed and the Ruhr demilitarized, but no other European powers had reduced their military forces. The principle of self-determination had been widely applied throughout Central Europe, but not in the Sudetenland, for security reasons, and that appeared to discriminate against the Germans. Because many thought Germany had a legitimate right to a sovereign and equal position, it became difficult to assess how far Hitler should be permitted to press his nationalist claims. Actions motivated by German patriotism and restored pride could not be clearly separated from those motivated by expansionism and world domination. Many of Hitler's ambitions could be fulfilled only at the expense of his immediate neighbors — but World War I had been a frightfully costly disaster that no one wanted to repeat. The appeasement of Hitler at Munich in 1938 represented a hope that his ambitions could be held in check and general war avoided. Hitler also had adopted the clever strategem of pursuing his goals piecemeal, all the while declaring himself an ardent defender of peace. Until he attacked Poland, no one action seemed serious enough to be worth a war, or so aggressive as to indicate how insatiable his appetite for power was. Hitler's behavior points to a common dilemma: If we treat a potential adversary as aggressive and expansionist when his intentions are largely defensive, we arouse his distrust and risk self-confirming behavior. Treating him as an enemy and mobilizing against him gives him both the incentive and the justification for turning to force. In short, we bring about the very aggressive response we fear. On the other hand, if we assume the best but the enemy harbors hidden ambitions, he is likely to take advantage of our good will to aggrandize himself, slowly, secretly, step by step. By the time we see that his intentions are aggressive, it may be too late. In Hitler's case, appeasement only whetted his appetite and led to his mistaken conclusion that Britain would not oppose by force further German expansion.

A later generation has applied the analogy of Munich to the Soviet arms buildup. Stalin and his successors steadfastly claimed that they were only seeking security and strategic parity with the United States. But Stalin was perceived as a dictator in the mold of Hitler, presiding over a totalitarian system whose goal was world conquest. Every step that brought the Soviets closer to arms equality appeared to be aimed toward their eventual superiority. Though they started from far behind, the rapidity of their nuclear buildup after the Cuban Missile Crisis raised Western fears about the "momentum" of their gains. Despite Russia's long history of geopolitical vulnerability in both Eastern Europe and Asia, the size of the Soviet conventional force aroused suspicions about aggressive intentions. In such circumstances, counting arms could never resolve the debate; Soviet military capability had to be assessed from the standpoint of one's overall view of Soviet intentions. Those who saw the USSR strictly in terms of the revolutionary aspirations of a Marxist-Leninist ideology concluded that the United States must maintain a margin of superiority at all costs. Those who saw the USSR as a partially domesticated, pragmatic power caught up in xenophobia and a passion for secrecy concluded that the acceptance of arms parity and the recognition of the Soviet Union's great-power status would promote moderation and a more cooperative atttitude. Because perceptions are partly the product of the way great powers treat one another, either conclusion could ultimately prove to be correct.

Assessing the Military Balance

Intentions and perceptions aside, accurate calculations of military forces are hard to arrive at, as a look at the Soviet-American strategic nuclear balance will illustrate. There are three ways of measuring nuclear force: by the number of launchers, the number of warheads, and the payload of the weapon system as a whole (the weight of the bomb or warhead package plus that of its booster and reentry vehicle). But these numerical factors give only the grossest measure of equivalence. Left out are considerations of strategy, mode of deployment, and some judgment about which types of weapons are more suitable for a nation's purposes. Also missing are calculations of quality, accuracy, reliability, and other performance characteristics related to weapons design. In 1972, at the first round of the Strategic Arms Limitation Talks (SALT I), the two superpowers in fact agreed to unequal numerical limits because of other offsetting considerations. The Soviets were permitted to have more ICBMs (1,618 to 1,054) and more SLBMs (740 to 656) than the United States, and modernization provisions allowed the Soviets to expand their 40 percent numerical advantage in launchers. But the United States remained well ahead in the total number of warheads, in missile accuracy, and in the deployment of launchers on silent, difficult-to-detect submarines. Bombers, in which the United States had a 450-to-150 advantage, were excluded from the agreement, and no limit was placed on multiple-warhead technology, which left the United States considerably ahead in the number of MIRVs.

In the SALT II treaty, signed in 1979, the total number of launchers and warheads was made equal, but critics on each side complained that the other was getting hidden advantages. The SALT talks, both rounds of which were bilateral Soviet-American negotiations, did not consider the British and French nuclear systems, which totaled 144 SLBMs, 18 intermediate-range missiles, and 150 nuclear-armed bombers, and the Soviets objected because these weapons, all aimed at the Soviet Union, were not counted on the American side. They also complained about the omission of cruise missiles, in which the United

States had a substantial lead. U.S. critics objected about there being no limit on Soviet heavy ICBMs, particularly the SS-18, whose accuracy, high megatonnage warheads, and MIRVed payload gave them a possible first-strike or counterforce capability. The U.S. critics also were concerned about the Soviets' Backfire bomber and their growing number of SS-20s (a cold-launch, reloadable mobile missile) — designated in SALT II as theater weapons but with the range to reach all of Europe and parts of the United States. U.S. opponents of the SALT process objected so strongly to the assymmetries that they were able to prevent Senate ratification of SALT II, and it never came officially into force.

Agreement on the SALT treaties had been possible only because the proposed weapons ceilings were far above existing levels and allowed for a large amount of redundancy. By 1988, however, the total number of warheads on long-range missiles and bombers had risen to 12,252 for the United States and 10,896 for the Soviet Union — though the Soviets retained a slight advantage in the number of launchers and the size of payloads. Under Reagan, Strategic Arms Reduction Talks (START) were begun and were pursued throughout the eight years of his administration, but they too foundered on the problem of measuring equivalence. Reagan and Gorbachev had agreed in principle at the Reykjavík summit to cut long-range nuclear weapons by 50 percent, but disagreements persisted on the definition of sublimits. "Counting rules" were proposed that would treat each bomber equipped with nuclear gravity bombs and short-range attack missiles as one warhead, no matter how many weapons it carried (but air-launched cruise missiles were to be counted separately). Under this rule, which favored the U.S. because of its large number of bomber weapons, the advertised 50 percent reduction actually came closer to 35 percent. The Soviets were anxious for START to include limits on sea-launched cruise missiles and Star Wars space technology, two more areas in which the United States had a large numerical and technological lead. The Americans, for their part, were concerned about the number of powerful and accurate land-based ICBMs that the Soviets would be permitted to keep, even under the proposed ballistic missile warhead ceiling of 6,000. A still more restrictive sublimit of 1,540 on heavy missiles would permit the United States to deploy its new MX and Midgetman missiles but force the Soviets to cut some of their most modern weapons — the 10-warhead, rail-mobile SS-24, the truck-mobile SS-25, and a large number of SS-18s. Thus, the numbers did not control everything; the force structure, or mix, was just as important to both sides. Also, weapons modernization could create significant differences in quality that could offset reductions in quantity, and the Soviets were particularly fearful of provisions that might channel U.S. arms production into areas of demonstrated technological prowess.

The most difficult calculations came over the attempt to distinguish between offensive and defensive weapons. President Reagan insisted that ballistic missile defense — his celebrated Star Wars, or Strategic Defense Initiative (SDI) — was wholly defensive and should be excluded from the START talks altogether. But American critics of SDI, and the Soviets too, pointed out that SDI could nullify the retaliatory threat that had made the deterrent relationship a stable one. By acquiring ballistic missile defenses ahead of the Soviets, the United States would have the ability, and very likely a strong incentive, to launch a preemptive first strike against Soviet missiles — and START's reductions in the number of offensive weapons would only make such a strike easier. If the Soviets were not confident of their ability to compete in Star Wars technology and did not trust Reagan's promises to share the technology or refrain from attack, then the only way they could defeat SDI would be to overwhelm it by an increased number of offensive warheads. Calculations of offense and defense are complex and interrelated.

Antisatellite (ASAT) weapons offer another example. Although space-based missile defense systems like SDI are currently banned by the anti-ballistic treaty, ASAT weapons are not. And yet the technology of these two classes of weapons is so similar that President Reagan was able to conduct a number of SDI experiments under the guise of ASAT tests without technically violating the ABM treaty. Thus, even if the Soviets should persuade the United States to accept limits on Star Wars or any other new weapons technology, similar loopholes on counting and control can likely be found. Indeed, any unforeseen "exotic" weapons technologies will raise problems of definition, control, and verification, making it impossible to establish airtight counting rules for preserving military symmetry between the superpowers.

Assessments of the military balance also depend very much on what strategic doctrine is being applied. Some analysts embrace the strategy of a minimum nuclear deterrent that is sufficient to guarantee mutual assured destruction (MAD). In this strategy, any number of U.S. warheads in excess of 400 — enough to wipe out 70 percent of Soviet industry and 35 percent of the Soviet population — is overkill, weapons acquired out of the momentum of the arms race or in a fruitless search for a symbolic or psychological advantage. From the perspective of MAD, arguments over numbers are stupid. According to George Kennan, a respected political scholar and former U.S. ambassador to the Soviet Union, the nuclear arsenal on both sides is so bloated that cuts of 90 percent could be made without serious risk of vulnerability to either. Advocates of nuclear-war-fighting strategies, or nuclear utilization targeting strategy (NUTS), counter that versatility in the strategic arsenal is necessary, in order to preserve counterforce options, control escalation, limit damage, and gain other objectives that require limited nuclear options or weapons with a hard-target-kill capability. A complex array of weapons, besides providing redundancy, would offer the option of a symmetrical response, would limit damage if deterrence broke down, and would allow for the targeting of various adversaries to meet all possible contingencies. From the perspective of NUTS, the size of the arsenal helps to shape power perceptions; a nation unwilling to challenge an adversary in numbers of weapons would be open to other challenges on a wide range of diplomatic and military fronts.

Another area of controversy in the measurement of military strength has been the power balance in Europe. SALT II placed no limits on either side's intermediate-range nuclear weapons (either missiles or nuclear-capable aircraft), even though these posed a potential nuclear threat to vital allies. By 1982, President Reagan was claiming that the Soviets had gained a six-to-one superiority in European nuclear forces. He called for a zero-zero option, which would remove everyone's intermediate missiles, on the threat that the United States would deploy cruise missiles and Pershing II rockets — theater weapons, but with the range and accuracy to wipe out hardened missile silos on Soviet territory. The Soviets, by counting French and British weapons and the more than 2,000 warheads that American medium-range aircraft based in Europe could deliver, countered that the balance was substantially equal. By the time the Intermediate Nuclear Forces Treaty (INF) was signed, in December of 1987, the missile forces on the American side amounted to 240 ground-launched cruise missiles, 72 Pershing IAs, and 108 Pershing IIs, and the Soviets had 112 SS-4s, 120 SS-12s, 441 triple-warhead SS-20s, and 36 SS-23s. Supporters of the INF treaty argued that the Soviet Union had accepted, in all essentials, Reagan's zero-zero option by agreeing to remove nearly 1,000 more warheads than the U.S. side was removing, in order to rid Europe of all medium-range nuclear missiles. But the treaty left untouched the French and British nuclear forces, which had doubled their number of SLBM warheads since 1979. Also untouched was the American contingent of 330,000 troops stationed in Europe, with their strong array of tactical nuclear weapons like short-range rockets, land mines, and nuclear-tipped artillery. U.S. critics of the INF treaty argued that the reduction of nuclear forces in Europe opened the door to an invasion by the Warsaw Pact's conventional forces. They also worried about the effect of INF on perceptions, fearing it would give impetus to American troop withdrawals and the decoupling of Western Europe from the NATO alliance. The critics also pointed out that nuclear weapons were a relatively cheap means of defending Europe, as compared to the enormously costly conventional forces that might be required in a nuclear-free Europe.

So the INF agreement on nuclear forces immediately led to squabbling over conventional forces. U.S. critics pointed out that the Warsaw Pact forces exceeded NATO by 1.2 million troops (6.3 million to 5.1 million), 15,560 tanks (29,260 to 13,700), 1,382 armed helicopters (1,694 to 312) , and 35 attack aircraft (1,745 to 1,710). Supporters of INF said that the conventional threat was greatly exaggerated, since roughly half the Soviet troops and tanks included in the aggregate totals were deployed along the borders with Afghanistan and China. The Soviet count also included large numbers of military personnel serving in border patrols, internal security forces, and clerical and technical duties — noncombatant positions that either did not exist in NATO or were filled by civilians. The Soviet superiority in tanks (an offensive weapon) was matched by NATO superiority in antitank weapons (defensive) and small-yield tactical nuclear warheads. These strategists also pointed out that conventional warfare requires roughly a two-to-one numerical advantage for the offense and that NATO, a defensive force, therefore did not have to match the Soviet forces, whose military objectives presumably were offensive. It was enough for NATO to possess the minimum 50 percent necessary for countering aggression — especially because the West would be waging a spirited and united defense of its free system, against an aggressive and expansionist Soviet tyranny whose unreliable conscript troops and satellite armies would be mere cannon fodder in an imperialist war (see Schloming, *American Foreign Policy and the Nuclear Dilemma*, pp. 64–65). Finally, the breakdown of Soviet control in Eastern Europe and the decay of orthodox Marxism-Leninism in the Soviet Union itself has caused many analysts to question the significance of any kind of numerical calculation, since rapidly changing events have altered Soviet aims and strategies so fundamentally as to make an invasion of Western Europe unthinkable.

These two case studies in the calculation of the Soviet-American military balance illustrate how difficult it is to quantify power, especially when doctrinal assumptions make the numbers subjective. Allies themselves disagree, as the NATO allies have over their shares of the financial burden. Americans regularly accuse their NATO allies of freeloading on U.S. defense spending, which allows them to shift resources into civilian goods and outsell U.S. products in the international market. The Europeans answer that the American figures are inflated because of the higher pay of the all-volunteer army, versus the low pay the European conscripts earn, and that the United States counts everything it would have to spend, with or without NATO. Moreover, the United States does not take into account the hidden subsidies that the Europeans pay in the form of facilities for bases, maneuvers, and various support services. Finally, the relative shares change with the exchange rate: when the dollar is weak, the Europeans appear to be spending much more; when it is strong, the situation is reversed. All in all, the student of military affairs needs to exercise caution in reducing the power of any nation or military coalition to numbers.

THE CHANGING CHARACTER OF WAR

The dynamism of military force as an instrument of power expresses itself plainly in the changing character of warfare, which has been modified by four military revolutions in the modern era (see Michael Mandelbaum, *The Nuclear Revolution*, Chapter 1, and Martin Van Creveld, *Technology and War*). The first of these revolutions was the nationalist fervor of Napoleon's conscript armies. War was no longer a chess match or diplomatic minuet between kings. The limited, semiritualized battles of mercenary soldiers and aristocratic warriors were replaced by national crusades in which citizen-soldiers sacrificed their own blood. This ideological trend has carried forward into the fanatic patriotism of German fascism, the crusading rhetoric of democracy-in-arms, and the revolutionary nationalism of guerrilla armies in the Third World.

The second revolution was the introduction of mechanized warfare and its increase in destructiveness. Machine guns, tanks, artillery, aerial bombardment, and other weapons of mass destruction raised casualties immensely. Between 1815 and 1914, fatalities in war numbered 5 million. In World War I they totaled 10 million, and in World War II they mounted to 50 million. Casualties as a percentage of population, which had been declining after 1648, suddenly quadrupled in the twentieth century. In fact, the first quarter of the century saw more deaths by war than in all preceding recorded history. Warfare, which had become total in ideological terms, now was total in its destructive impact. Entire economies were mobilized, arms races sprang up (even in peacetime, spurred by state-sponsored weapons research), and war visited its violence on entire civilian populations.

The third military revolution was the introduction of nuclear weapons and their extremely rapid transcontinental delivery systems. Nuclear fusion, in combination with the technology of computers and electronics, brought warfare to the outer limits of explosive fire-power and accurate, instantaneous targeting. Nuclear weapons have destroyed the hard shell of the territorial state and erased the distinction between soldier and civilian, holding whole populations hostage and making military success dependent on the permanent mobilization of the economy. They have pushed the crucial decisions of war ever further in time and space from the battlefield. Technical complexity has brought anonymity and impersonality to modern warfare. Plans and decisions — even attacks — are made by persons who may not personally experience the horrors or bear the costs. War, formerly an enterprise of patriotism, personal bravery, and leadership, has become a technical exercise in the remote planning, projection, and execution of nuclear threats.

The stalemate of nuclear deterrence established the preconditions for the fourth revolution in warfare — limited war and unconventional means of fighting it. The weapons of war now include blackmail, civil disobedience, boycotts, and other forms of economic and psychological coercion. Where the prevailing rules and a nuclear monopoly once favored the great powers, revolutionary challengers have changed the rules of strategy and the tactics of conflict. Superpowers that no longer dare to fight openly resort to clandestine means. Wars are not declared, nor do terrorists or guerrillas respect the neutrality of the innocent bystander. Politics and war are mixed more thoroughly than ever, propaganda and terror working side by side. The state has lost its monopoly on force and seen its claims to sovereignty challenged simultaneously from within and without. Revolution and interstate conflict freely mingle. Arms flow from the superpowers to sustain nearly constant upheavals and low-intensity conflicts in the Third World. Covert operations allow a state to influence the domestic politics of an adversary and to apply continuous, if limited, force on behalf of its foreign policy objectives. The growing militarization of international affairs might be said to have erased any formal distinction between war and peace.

Nuclear war and unconventional war, the two most recent transformations in warfare, are the ones that most powerfully affect international relations today, and for that reason we will take a closer look at each.

UNIQUE FEATURES OF THE NUCLEAR REVOLUTION

The Destructive Effects of Nuclear Weapons

The overwhelming feature of nuclear weapons is their unparalleled destructivness. One U.S. Trident submarine carries 19 megatons, six times the firepower of all the bombs dropped in World War II. A "war within a warhead" can be carried in a single B-52 bomb, a single Titan II ICBM, or a single Poseidon submarine-launched missile (see Figure 9-5). Three hundred megatons can destroy every large- and medium-sized city in the world. The world's current nuclear weapons inventory is 20,000 megatons.

The Hiroshima bomb, the first ever dropped on a civilian population, gave the world some idea of the devastating effects of fission weapons. It had an explosive power of about 12.5 kilotons (equivalent to 12,500 tons of TNT) and created a fireball three miles across, which instantly vaporized persons within its radius. The shadows of Hiroshima victims were burned onto sidewalks and the walls of buildings. Patterns from the victim's clothes were burned into their

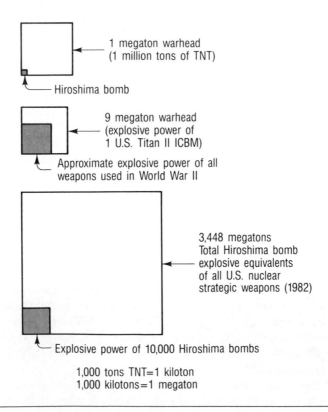

FIGURE 9-5
EXPLOSIVE POWER OF NUCLEAR VS. CONVENTIONAL WEAPONS

skin. Within ten seconds, 100,000 people were killed or fatally injured. Tens of thousands were mutilated severely by flying glass and debris, some of the injuries so grotesque that it was not possible to tell whether one was looking at a person from the front or the back. Intense overpressures immediately flattened all buildings save those of reinforced concrete. All the city's hospitals were destroyed, along with 90 percent of the medical personnel. The blast's intense heat created a huge firestorm lasting six hours, with gale force winds and ground temperatures exceeding 1,400 degrees Fahrenheit. Anything or anyone in the center city that managed to survive the immediate blast was consumed by these thermal effects. Persons miles away who saw the fireball as it exploded were permanently blinded. Two hours later, drops of black rain the size of marbles pelted the city with radioactive fallout. Two weeks later, survivors' wounds began to open, their hair fell out, skin came off in patches. Internal hemorrhaging, nausea, vomiting, diarrhea, bleeding from the gums and intestines, all indicated the presence of advanced and ultimately fatal radiation sickness. An additional 30,000 died from these lingering aftereffects. Thousands more suffered from cancer, infertility, and miscarriages, or bore babies deformed from the mutation of cells and genes exposed to heavy doses of radiation.

The 12.5-kiloton Hiroshima bomb, which represents less than one-millionth of the destructive power of the current inventory of nuclear arms, gives substance to the world's terror of nuclear holocaust, but it does not come close to conveying the level of social disorganization and irreversible damage to civilization that would occur with even a so-called limited nuclear strike. The kind of bomb dropped on Hiroshima and Nagasaki in 1945 would today be considered a tactical device. Strategic warheads now average about 1 megaton (1 million tons of TNT). In 1982, the U.S. nuclear inventory contained about 3,448 megatons; the Soviet Union, with larger payloads and bigger bombs, had considerably more. The United States and the Soviet Union together have enough nuclear weapons to destroy the world 67 times. At such a level of overkill, the notion that one nation has a nuclear "advantage" is ridiculous. Even with anti-ballistic missile and air defenses that could knock out nearly 100 percent of incoming delivery vehicles — and the United States is several decades and hundreds of billions of dollars away from such an airtight defense, if it is possible at all — the penetration of only two or three warheads would bring a catastrophe of unparalleled proportions.

Present nuclear weapons have effects that were not known at Hiroshima or Nagasaki. Those first atomic bombs were exploded in the air, and their radioactive fallout was actually quite small in today's terms. The ground burst from a 1-megaton warhead would spread radioactive debris over thousands of square miles, and a single 20-megaton bomb could wipe out the population of New York or Washington instantly. The Soviets have at least 113 bombs of this size, carried by Bear bombers and SS-18 missiles. A 20-megaton blast would create a scorched desert almost 50 miles across and its radioactive fallout could, if the winds were unfavorable, kill as many as 20 million people. A 1954 test explosion of an American thermonuclear bomb of 15 megatons, conducted under nearly windless conditions, spread contamination over an area of 7,000 square miles (about the size of New Jersey); with moderate winds, the fallout could have covered 100,000 square miles or more. In 1962, a test in the Pacific of a 1.4-megaton bomb caused electrical malfunctions in Hawaii, 800 miles away. Physicists subsequently discovered that this was due to electromagnetic pulse, an atmospheric effect that is likely to disable nearly all communications at the moment of detonation. To all the devastation of the blast and its thermal and radioactive aftereffects must be added the utter chaos of a nation with no means of communication and most likely unable to control or coordinate its own defenses. Another recently discovered effect of high-megaton bombs is the damage they do to the ozone layer, a protective layer in the upper atmosphere that filters out harmful ultraviolet radiation and without which all living creatures would be blinded and the food chain irreparably damaged. Finally, studies in the 1980s showed that a nuclear exchange as low as 100 megatons could trigger the environmental disaster that has been termed "nuclear winter" (see Figure 9-6). Massive clouds of dust and smoke spreading across the globe would obscure the sun and cause surface temperatures to plunge to 13 degrees below zero Fahrenheit over a large part of the Northern Hemisphere. It would be too dark and cold for plants to carry on photosynthesis, and virtually all crops and farm animals would perish. Any human survivors would face the prospect of starvation during a dark and cold radioactive winter stretching over several years and threatening all of the planet's biological support systems.

And we have not begun to chronicle the psychological and political disorganization of nuclear war, or to calculate the social and economic costs of the arms race — what Lester Kurtz, in *The Nuclear Cage*, calls "destruction without detonation." Many Hiroshima survivors went insane from having their reality collapse suddenly around them. No matter how extensive the civil defense measures, recovery from any level of nuclear war is sure to be long and difficult, economically and socially. If the destruction has been widespread, no outside assistance will be available. Sociologists predict anarchy, martial law, rationing, forced requisitioning, and "triage" schemes, which would allocate scarce resources to a small elite and leave the weak to fend for themselves. Among the first victims would be democracy and the free market — already damaged by the arms race's disruptive impact on society and by the resource-gobbling military-industrial complex. The arms race has encouraged monopoly and perverted economic priorities. Children growing up in the shadow of extermination have become fearful. An enormous amount of energy has been wasted in imagining an evil and hated enemy terrible enough to justify the costly sacrifices. Finally, the secrecy, the specialization, and the bureaucratic entrenchment associated with nuclear war planning have eroded democracy and put decisions about war and peace in the hands of a few, whose narrow technological expertise is necessary but hardly justifies their being made custodians of the commonweal.

In nuclear strategy, the offense completely overwhelms the defense, and the same is true of chemical-bacteriological weapons. National security, if

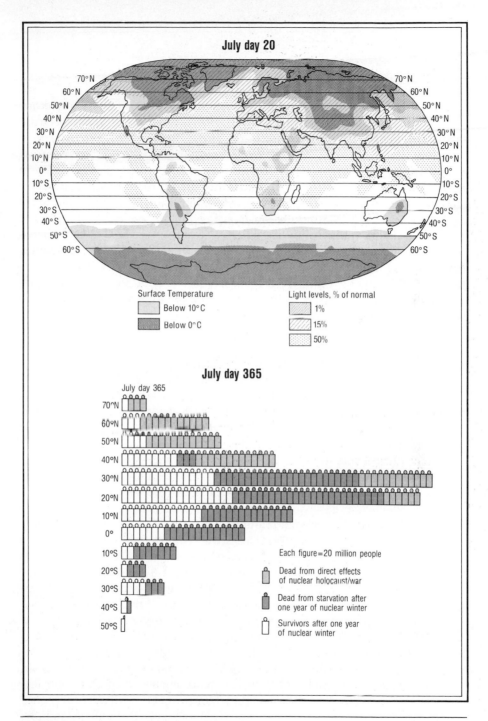

FIGURE 9-6

NUCLEAR WINTER: NOWHERE TO HIDE

Note: The map shows the extent of climatic disruption 20 days after the summer outbreak of war. The graph shows the impact on the world's population 365 days after the holocaust.

defined as territorial impregnability, is destroyed. The loss of any reasonable sense of proportion between military means and political goals makes obsolete Clausewitz's traditional definition of war as the extension of politics by other means. It may be rational for a nation to protect itself from nuclear attack by the threat of retaliation in kind, so long as the bluff is never called. But to think of initiating an attack is near-suicidal. Even if the adversary does not respond, or is too crippled to respond, "nuclear winter" is likely to carry destruction to every corner of the earth. And to follow through on the threat of retaliation after an attack has devastated one's own society is equally irrational. Once deterrence breaks down, retaliation is a pure act of revenge and will only compound the magnitude of the global aftereffects. No political purpose imaginable can be worth the risk of planetary destruction, and a rational diplomacy may have to remove nuclear conflict from the category of war altogether. A nuclear conflagration would be a macabre spectacle of death bearing final witness to the utter failure of politics and the end of international relations as we know them.

Crisis, Credibility, and Nuclear War Planning

The incredible destructiveness of nuclear weapons has introduced new elements into the calculation of power relations between states. Mistaken perceptions become vastly more crucial because they risk mutual annihilation. And yet the potentially suicidal outcome of a nuclear strike makes it almost impossible to take nuclear threats seriously. The dilemma for the superpower is how to convince its adversary that it rationally and deliberately intends to do the irrational. Of course, the deterrent threat must be reserved for the most vital interests. The further it is extended to cover secondary interests, the less likely it is to be believed. So a second dilemma arises: how to communicate to the adversary which interests or objectives are so vital as to be worth the risk of nuclear war. Nations customarily indicated the value of a contested interest through incremental steps in an escalating conventional conflict. Today, vital interests and political will are clarified largely through crises or through surrogate conflicts that substitute for direct clashes between nuclear-armed adversaries. Conflicts are indirect or symbolic; hot wars are contained in peripheral areas and fought there at the conventional level, to avoid the immense risk of crossing the nuclear threshold. Each of these arenas of conflict has its own dynamic and its own political-military objectives, but each also may send signals about the larger contest of wills involving nuclear credibility. Nuclear stalemate has prevented war between the superpowers for half a century, but it has also made proxy wars and crises more frequent and has channeled military competition into a ferocious arms race and a search for allies and arms clients in the Third World.

International crises often are a forum for testing national will, intentions, and perceptions short of the definitive test of war. Glenn Snyder and Paul Diesing, in *Conflict Among Nations,* define crisis as "a sequence of interactions between the governments of two or more sovereign states in severe conflict, short of actual war, but involving the perception of a dangerously high probability of war" (p. 6). Charles F. Hermann's *International Crises* describes a crisis situation as one that "(1) threatens high-priority goals of the decision-making unit, (2) restricts the amount of time available for response before the decision is transformed, and (3) surprises the members of the decision-making unit by its occurrence" (p. 13). Decision-making analyses emphasize the factors of uncertainty and unpredictability, but for our present purpose, an examination of deterrence credibility, we will concentrate on the painful choices states must make during a crisis about which of their interests are vital.

A crisis occurs when an adversary's behavior threatens to upset the status quo. Crises are often precipitated by changes in military capability, which might tempt a rising power to test its new potential, but just as often they are the result of altered judgments or expectations. Nikita Khrushchev's attempt to introduce nuclear missiles into Cuba in 1962 was the result of his new assessment of American resolve following his summit encounter with Kennedy, from which he concluded that the president was weak and inexperienced. There was also Kennedy's apparent failure of nerve during the Bay of Pigs fiasco in 1961, when he did not follow through on the promise of American air cover for the invasion force. And the West had passively accepted the erection of the Berlin Wall in that same year. Khrushchev's calculation was that he could end the Soviet inferiority in strategic capability in one fell swoop, by a single act of daring and resolve. All crises test nations' commitments to their declared purposes and their determination to resist infringement on vital interests. In the nuclear age, which virtually prohibits the adjustment of the superpower balance through war, crises have become the means for nations to establish their credibility and define and protect their vital interests. If a nation proves willing to risk nuclear war, by a direct confrontation or by escalation of a smaller conflict, then its vital interests have indeed been threatened, and the only rational response for a challenger is to retreat. When the crisis clarifies a nation's determination to resist, as it did in the Cuban Missile Crisis, it can serve as a substitute for war. Such crises also allow inferences to be made about the strength of an adversary's military forces, since military weakness usually brings concessions.

But crisis conditions introduce their own distortions and are a dangerous way to test capabilites. Decision makers act in haste, giving stereotyped or preprogrammed responses based on incomplete information. Passions are aroused and the situation becomes a test of wills marked by bravado and bluff, often leading to war by miscalculation. The psychology of conflict also enters in. Nuclear-armed nations tend to "hang tough" in order to reinforce the credibility of their threats, both nuclear and nonnuclear. The administration of Dwight D. Eisenhower, for instance, pursued a policy of "brinksmanship" to extend a nuclear umbrella over remote allies and secondary security commitments. Its threats of retaliatory nuclear attack to protect less than vital interests represented what Thomas C. Schelling has called the "manipulation of risk." Political leaders want to appear more fanatical and less prudent than they really are, in order to intimidate an opponent into backing down. Herman Kahn calls it the "rationality of the irrational." Crises become dangerous psychological duels or games of "chicken," in which prestige itself is the stake and states are tempted into rash conduct just to protect their reputations.

Nuclear weapons have led to more frequent crises and have widened the gap between actual and perceived power. In nuclear war, the power to destroy does not translate directly into the power to persuade, since the destructiveness of the weapons makes them a last resort and believable as a threat only when the most fundamental interest is involved. The risk of escalation, the mutual features of deterrence strategy, and the likely suicidal outcome of a nuclear war all compound the problem of credibility. This is why the nuclear giants have given much emphasis to demonstrations of will; they want their nuclear capacity to be perceived as making them stronger, rather than tying their hands. It is uncertain whether they have succeeded in this game of massaging perceptions. What is certain is that the realities of nuclear destruction have induced extreme caution once a crisis has erupted, even if the posturing and the search for credibility have made the crises more frequent.

The nearly instantaneous character of nuclear attack has forced states to narrow the gap between potential and mobilized power, and this has turned the great-power rivalry into a kind of continuous crisis. Technical dynamism has also made it an ongoing test of economic potential. The ten-year research and development cycle for high-technology weapons requires defense planners to keep their production and scientific establishments on a permanent war footing. The constellation of special interests — the "iron triangle" or the military-industrial complex — constantly lobbies the political system on behalf of additional weapons procurement. When a ballistic missile attack can erase a nation's industrial infrastructure overnight, a premium is put on permanent mobilization. A nuclear war will be fought with the forces that exist at the moment it breaks out. Consequently, the superpowers feel compelled to maintain their forces in a high state of readiness and to introduce new weapons as rapidly as possible. This is what has made the nuclear balance so delicate and the arms race so relentless.

Nuclear weapons also tend to introduce hyperbole and exaggerated perceptions of hostile intent. The Soviet threat has not been the greatest in history; in terms of traditional issues, the Soviet Union and the United States have fewer competing interests than most other great-powers have had. Of course, ideological differences have greatly inflamed the rivalry. But most of all, it is the destructiveness of the weapons that has caused the United States to project its fears of annihilation on the Soviets and to exaggerate their threat to the American way of life. The total nature of the threat is assumed to reflect the depth of conflict and the intensity of the Soviet aggressive intent, when in fact it is a technological consequence of the introduction of nuclear means.

The tendency of defense planners to estimate the enemy's strength and intentions in terms of worst-case scenarios heightens misperceptions. Nuclear strategy cannot be played out except hypothetically; the weapons are too destructive to be realistically tested. In practice, this makes nuclear-armed states

cautious about using arms in any conflicts with each other. But the war planners, with less need to show caution, dismiss any evidence of peaceful intentions and focus "prudently" on the many potential risks of attack. George
Kennan's *The Nuclear Delusion* describes how their worst-case planning leads
to the projection of evil intentions on an adversary:

> The planner has to assume an adversary. In the case at hand, the Russians,
> being the strongest and the most rhetorically hostile, were the obvious candi-
> dates. The adversary must then be credited with the evilest of intentions. No
> need to ask *why* he should be moved to take certain hostile actions, or whether
> he would be likely to take them. That he has the capability of taking them
> suffices. The mere fact that they would be damaging to one's own side is re-
> garded as adequate motive for their execution. In this way not only is there
> created, for planning purposes, the image of the totally inhuman and totally
> malevolent adversary, but this image is reconjured daily, week after week,
> month after month, year after year, until it takes on every feature of flesh and
> blood and becomes the daily companion of those who cultivate it, so that any
> attempt on anyone's part to deny its reality appears as an act of treason or
> frivolity. Thus the planner's dummy of the Soviet political personality took the
> place of the real thing as the image on which a great deal of American policy, and
> of American military effort, came to be based. (p. 33)

The defense establishment's need for long-term peacetime funding also encourages the self-conscious manipulation of public opinion and the image of the
enemy as an ideological rival. Through such means have Americans gotten an
artificially inflated picture of the Soviet threat.

Laypersons are unable to question the judgments of defense professionals
about the adversary's intentions and capabilities because they are largely based
on secret information, and Americans have a hard time finding out about even
their own government's nuclear policies. Ordinary citizens are also handicapped by the insularity of nuclear research and the specialization involved in
high-technology warfare. The two earliest military revolutions we have cited
included forces that affected the general population and had positive as well as
negative consequences. The French Revolution brought democratization and
greater accountability to foreign policy, and the industrial revolution brought
affluence, economic growth, interdependence, and an abundance that could
serve in part as a solvent of conflict. Each contained the self-administered
antidote of a broad social transformation that gave the average citizen a better
understanding of foreign policy and war and a greater stake in the outcome.
The nuclear revolution has no positive side effects commensurate with its
destructiveness, except perhaps the caution that comes with the risk of annihilation. Nuclear weapons put every citizen's way of life at risk daily, but by
means of forces, strategies, and theories that the average person does not
understand and cannot control.

So nuclear weapons have brought a new professional elite of nuclear
warriors and renewed tensions between democratic accountability and "aristocratic" control. To succeed in the gamesmanship of hypothetical wars and
preprogrammed attacks, modern generals must be part scientist, part psychol-
ogist. They must have engineering skills, but they must also have an empathy

and cultural understanding that will enable them to predict accurately how the adversary is going to behave in a crisis. They also should have some moral scruples and a healthy awareness of their own capacity for acting irrationally, so that they do not take their decision-making responsibility lightly. They must have the logical skills to decipher complex scenarios, but also the humanistic perspective to know when to step outside the scenario and use common sense. This combination of skills and qualities is rare in defense planners, most of whom are occupationally handicapped by their specialized training and a narrow perspective. Matters of nuclear strategy and weapons procurement tend to fall outside the arenas of humanistic criteria and effective public control.

Technical complexities and the impersonality of nuclear war encourage a war-games mentality and the loss of cultural and biological inhibitions against violence (see Schloming, pp. 3–6). Strategy is conjured by specialists working in the isolated hothouses of universities or think tanks. Weapons are produced by teams of engineers who see only a few components of a vast technical ensemble. Destruction is wrought at the press of a button or the turn of a key in response to an array of electronically filtered data and complex release codes. The sight of blood, the "whites of their eyes," the terror of attack are reduced to a blip on the radar screen. Except for the chief executive, no one is made to feel personally responsible. No one confronts, immediately and directly, the human consequences of the violence. Single individuals play such small parts in the design, manufacture, and assembly of components and in the long and complex chain of procurement and command that few of them feel a need to take moral responsibility for the creation or use of the immensely destructive weapons. Millions of people can be obliterated from within the antiseptic confines of an air-conditioned office; modern warriors no longer have to insert the bayonets or watch their victims bleed. The human dimension of the ugliness of war is lost, and with it much of the horror that might serve as a restraint.

The technical complexity of nuclear weapons increases the probability of mechanical failure and accidental war. Hiroshima is still vivid enough in memory to restrain all but the most irrational from launching a deliberate attack; miscalculation, accident, or out-of-control technology is the more likely route to Armageddon. Decisions that must be made in a matter of minutes rely on data from computers and other failure-prone products of modern technology whose responses are typically preprogrammed and difficult to alter at the last minute. Short lead times, complex targeting, the size of arsenals, and the sophistication of new technologies all compound the problem of maintaining adequate control over the decisions of war. American military computers have initiated several high-stage nuclear alerts whose accidental origins took precious minutes to decipher, and Soviet computers are much inferior to those of the West — which leaves security riding on the questionable competence of the adversary's technology. The complicated Star Wars defense, designed to reduce U.S. vulnerability to Soviet attack, would surely increase the vulnerability to technical failure and accidental war. Weapons deployments aimed at enhancing security may actually decrease it, the more so as weapons become ever more rapid, efficient, and technologically advanced. Most defense experts rate the probability of a Soviet first strike as extremely low, and America's misguided efforts to secure a foolproof technological fix for its ultimate fears may accidentally bring on the war it dreads.

The nuclear revolution has given the world novel instruments of war, new theories about their use, and unprecedented problems in maintaining control over them. There is a new kind of tension between technology and politics. Military technologies, satellite communications, mass media, trade, and scientific knowledge have penetrated national borders and created a single interdependent security community, planetary in scope. But political consciousness and security arrangements remain predominantly national. Changes in psychology, culture, and politics have not kept up with changes in economics, communications, and weaponry. The nuclear security dilemma has been exaggerated by the lack of political contact and cultural understanding between the two superpowers. Forces of ideology and nationalism, the political devices mobilizing the public in support of arcane nuclear strategies and costly defense budgets, have tended to exacerbate hostility. Public accountability has become the selling of stereotyped views of the enemy to a population that is, by virtue (or vice) of secrecy, ill informed. Defense professionals are part of an isolated "procurement culture" of military specialists who have little contact with public needs and interests, and sometimes with everyday realities. Nuclear strategies tend to insulate leaders from the refreshing influence of democratic debate and public scrutiny. At the same time, many hidebound generals and politicians may still view nuclear war in the inappropriate categories left over from the last great war and an earlier era of international relations. This is a risk that also attaches to our responses to terrorism, guerrilla insurgency, and unconventional war, which have likewise introduced new elements of power and new strategies of conflict.

UNCONVENTIONAL WAR AND LOW-INTENSITY CONFLICT

The gap between the stalemate of nuclear means and the hostility of incompatible ideological ends is filled by various forms of limited, unconventional, and low-intensity conflict, set off by the Cold War competition, the breakdown of colonialism, and the challenge of democratic values to systems of dictatorship, racism, or repression. These conflicts share certain characteristics.

First, the war is typically undeclared. Guerrilla insurgencies, the covert actions of superpowers, terrorist bombings, and economic boycotts all occur outside the framework of a formal declaration of belligerency. Although they are de facto wars, the conflicting parties prefer to disguise their acts of aggression or to deny that they are trying to overthrow an existing state authority. Sometimes the parties to a conflict cannot be clearly identified or are not politically recognized, and that makes traditional bargaining between the adversaries, and therefore a political settlement, difficult. This is so with the PLO, which neither the United States nor Israel recognizes. Israel, in turn, is not recognized by many radical Arab states. In the case of Nicaragua, the United States' unacknowledged sponsorship of the *contras* prevented it from becoming a formal party to peace negotiations. Yet, the Sandinista government was, for almost a decade, unwilling to accept any cease-fire or peace treaty not explicitly guaranteed by the Americans. In such ways are undeclared wars often prolonged ones as well.

Second, unconventional conflicts are limited in some manner. Primarily, military means are not employed as directly or as fully as possible, or the geographical scope is confined, with sanctuaries nearby that are safe from attack. The key limiting factor is the implicit assumption that the war will not escalate to the nuclear level. If a superpower is involved, this means that it must have a limited political aim. Or the war is limited just because no superpower is involved. The actors commonly are few in number; neighboring states usually do not become drawn into a more general war, but provide zones of neutrality or sanctuary for one of the conflicting parties. Guerrilla armies and nonstate actors like terrorists often occupy no identifiable territory against which conventional retaliation can be directed.

A third characteristic of unconventional war is that the adversaries are typically unequal in size and military strength. Consequently, the weaker side tends to rely on economic, psychological, and other unconventional types of coercion. These may include boycotts, strikes, disinformation and propaganda, terrorism, sabotage, assassination, hostage taking, hijacking, blackmail, attacks on noncombatants, hit-and-run guerrilla tactics, and chemical-bacteriological warfare. The strategy of guerrilla fighters is to avoid confronting the full strength of the adversary. They are weaker and on the defensive, but tactically they are always on the offensive, striking swiftly where the adversary is weakest or least expects an attack and then retreating quickly, to renew the battle at a time and place of their choosing. Front lines do not exist in guerrilla war; mobility and surprise are everything. Military victories are important, but mostly for their demoralizing effect on the enemy's will to fight. Propaganda and the selective use of terror are the guerrilla's devices for winning over a population or cutting their ties with an existing government. Just as important are those factors that set the liberation movement apart from the oppressors of the old order — the guerrilla leadership's ideological platform, program for social reform, nationalist credentials, and reputation for honest administration. Economic sanctions were used by the militarily weak OPEC states to defeat the nuclear-armed giants in the Middle-East oil crisis. OPEC selected as its instrument of coercion its control of a key asset to which its adversaries were especially vulnerable. Yet, OPEC was careful to avoid confrontation with the great powers in those arenas in which the latter were superior.

Fourth, new military technology has enhanced the ability of unconventional forces — SWAT teams, paramilitary forces, guerrillas, and terrorists — to achieve the mobility, secrecy, surprise, and concentration of firepower their operations require. Miniaturization of weapons, remote-controlled explosive devices, hand-held antiaircraft and antitank missiles, relatively inexpensive antiship weapons (such as the Exocet and Silkworm missiles), and small but lethal automatic rifles offset some of the inequalities in military power. Jet aircraft, small speedboats, and radio communications are some of the other forms of advanced technology that enable a small force to strike anywhere with maximum impact and minimum risk.

A fifth characteristic is that the two parties do not operate in the same diplomatic-strategic framework. They belong in different systems — for example, the state versus nonstate actors — and follow different "rules of the game." Typically, one party is a defender of the existing international order or the domestic status quo, and the other is a revolutionary challenger. This has clearly been the case in the United States' confrontations with the Ayatollah Khomeini in Iran and with the various Muslim terrorist factions that have seized hostages in the Middle East. Iran's defiance of the principle of diplomatic immunity in the 1979 hostage crisis, along with its rejection of the World Court ruling against the action, indicated that the two parties did not share the same morality or speak the same diplomatic language.

A sixth factor is a sharp discrepancy in the stakes or interests in conflict, making victory or defeat far more significant for one side than the other. The challenger or small power may be struggling for liberation and independence, at the risk of starvation and annihilation if it is defeated. The defender or great power desires greater profits, access to resources, control of a strategic location, or a marginal gain in power or prestige. The one has a strong propensity toward violence; the other is subject to domestic political constraints on the permissible costs of war. Freedom fighters or guerrilla insurgents struggling for survival are more powerfully motivated than a great power that is dabbling in local politics or a corrupt government elite that can retire into a comfortable exile paid for out of its Swiss bank accounts. The intensity of the commitment is asymmetrical, one side's ideological zeal, fanaticism, and will exceeding the other's. Since military force is effective only if decision makers possess the will to use it, differences in political will and commitment can often outweigh a gross inequality in military power.

The seventh characteristic is a disproportion on both sides between political ends and military means. The great power has a limited interest and unlimited means; the small state, the insurgent, or the nonstate actor has limited means and unlimited aspirations. The disproportion gives each side incentives for keeping the conflict limited in one respect or another — in the intensity of violence, political aims, number of actors involved, geographical scope, range of means, degree of moral or diplomatic restraint. Unconventional war is always conducted with an eye to the risk of escalation; each side is likely to fear the intervention of other powers and the consequent possibility of escalation to general or even nuclear war. Because the adversaries are unequal and the political ends and military means disproportionate, motives are mixed on both sides: each desires to win, but also to avoid the potentially greater costs of escalation or further intervention. For the stronger power, escalation risks general or nuclear war, with a military cost out of proportion to the political gain. For the weaker power, escalation risks the fuller brunt of military force that would accompany a wider intervention or a declared war. The parties therefore engage in tacit bargaining and observe informal restraints on the use of violence. This dynamic, along with the fact that the war is undeclared, helps explain why any escalation of unconventional conflicts typically occurs in small, incremental steps.

Another factor is that internal and external conflict are mixed. Revolution, irredentism, and other internal wars of liberation or independence become entangled with interstate conflict, so that the sovereignty of the state is contested from within and without. Outside powers participate in struggles for political control of a population and for the maintenance or subversion of domestic authority. Insurgent forces within the state appeal for outside assistance from ethnic compatriots, ideological allies, or economic patrons. Because of the mixed character of such wars, which lack traditional belligerent acts such as the crossing of frontiers, it is difficult to identify an aggressor.

Finally, unconventional war is much more a struggle of political aims and ideologies than of arms, and the outcome is more dependent on claims to legitimacy than on military capability. Political factors are paramount, purely military solutions impossible. Insurgents aim at altering the enemy's intentions, perceptions, will, and morale. Counterinsurgents aim at gaining the allegiance of neutrals and buttressing existing authority through the reinforcement of ideological orthodoxy or the promulgation of palliative social and political reforms. The intensely political complexion of unconventional war gives the noncombatant audience as much significance as the military adversary. The conflicting parties seek to win public opinion abroad and popular support at home and carefully calculate the impact of military action on neutral parties and on the superpowers. It is always a two-front war—the military battleground and the political or propaganda forum.

THE CONTINUUM OF WAR AND PEACE

The strategy and tools of limited conflict have tended to blur the line between war and peace. Unconventional war lies somewhere between the deterrence of nuclear stalemate and the compellence of all-out war, and its means of guerrilla operations, covert intervention, and indirect coercion have come to play a larger role in modern warfare. Superpowers employ gunboat diplomacy or put their nuclear forces on alert status as devices to signal their serious intent. They stage coups d'état, arm guerrilla forces, and intervene by proxy, rather than courting the costs of conventional war or risking the escalation that may follow a direct challenge to another superpower. If they employ direct means at all, it is likely to be a "surgical strike" or a short-term military intervention. And they supplement all these military means with a host of economic sanctions, such as oil or grain embargoes, prohibitions on the sale of advanced technology, currency manipulation, tariff wars, and other forms of economic intimidation.

At the same time, nuclear stalemate and the rising costs of the arms race have forced the superpowers into limited cooperation simply to work out the rules of coexistence. Even President Reagan, with his "evil empire" view of the Soviets, came to see the wisdom of regular summit diplomacy. Both super-powers have tried to isolate their areas of disagreement and build on the areas of common interest. Among those powers whose economies are complementary and mutually vulnerable, global economic interdependence has also produced strong incentives for the peaceful resolution of conflict, and this has led to a working peace between great powers that, like Japan and the United States, might easily have fallen into renewed rivalry. And the advanced industrial states continue to send economic assistance to the Third World, where they sell almost 40 percent of their exports and secure a still higher percentage of their raw materials. So various forms of stalemate and "undeclared peace" have filled in the continuum between war and peace. The gap between the temporary stability of a balance of power and the greater security of formal alliance, economic integration, and political confederation has grown smaller (see Figure 9-7).

The continuum has an important breakpoint in the center, where stalemate and crisis face each other as two sides of the same reality. Here systems and conditions balance unsteadily on the edge between war and peace. They may show a temporary or apparent stability, but it is a negative peace brought about by threats, the equipoise of arms, and the repression of conflict, not its resolution. It is a condition of stalemate prone to challenge or decay and to sudden transition into crisis. Enduring stability emerges only with conditions of disarmament and positive peace, or peace with justice. Without reconciliation or mutual satisfaction between adversaries, peace cannot be maintained except through constant threat of violence, which inevitably breeds counterviolence. Arms races tend to spiral out of control. The balance of power breaks down, tipped by a shift in technology, alliances, or intentions, or it remains in equilibrium only through the use of arms. Deterrent threats are routinely tested, credibility questioned. Cold War is accompanied by peripheral hot wars that probe the solidity of an alliance or nibble at vulnerable parts of a competing bloc. Repression invites subversion or rebellion. Imperial exploitation and structural violence lead to passive resistance or revolutionary attempts to overthrow racism, inequality, and injustice.

Nonetheless, these crisis-prone systems may contain some features of incipient peace systems. Prolonged stalemate and an equilibrium of social forces are often the precursors to compromise and inducements toward democracy or another arrangement for sharing power. Conquest can lead to pacification if the initial repression and exploitation are gradually replaced by inducements and concessions pointing toward greater equality and interdependence. Power balancing, deterrence, and colonialism all presume some limited cooperation between the adversaries or some elements of codependence, although the roles may be grossly unequal. Deterrence assumes rationality in the opponent and a shared interest in avoiding fruitless conflict. As two powers interact over time in managing their competition, good diplomacy and tacit bargaining can sometimes evolve into détente. The dependency relations of colonialism can move toward interdependence if the weaker party can take control of its resources

FIGURE 9-7

THE CONTINUUM OF WAR AND PEACE

War	Undeclared War	Crisis/Stalemate	Undeclared Peace	Peace
		Interstate Conflict		
Declared war between states/Total war	Show of force ("Gunboat diplomacy")/ Terrorism/ Hostage-taking/ Military intervention/Covert operations/ Unconventional war	Cold War/ Deterrence/ Balance of power/Arms races	Détente/Entente/ Summit diplomacy/ Tacit bargaining/ Arms control	Formal alliance/ Peace treaty/ Disarmament
		Economic Conflict		
Interdiction of supply routes/ Seizure of resources/ Destruction of economic assets	Embargo/ Boycott/ Economic sanctions/Tariff wars/Blackmail	Imperialism/ Colonialism	Economic interdependence/ Trade/Aid	Common market/ Economic integration
		Internal Conflict		
Civil war/ Revolution	Coup d'état/ Rebellion/ Communal violence/ Guerrilla insurgency	Dictatorship/ Martial law/ Apartheid/ Structural violence/Passive resistance/Militant nonviolence	Ideological or ethnic polarization of a party system/Ritual combat (non-lethal)	Political confederation

Compellence	Subversion	Deterrence	Coexistence	Reconciliation
		Methods of Aggregating or Neutralizing Power		
Physical annihilation of a rival/Seizure of the state or its economic assets	Subversion/Indirect coercion/ Divide-and-rule tactics/Mobilization of power/ Intimidation/ Extortion	Repression/ Appeasement/ Partition of weak states or disputed territories/Shifts in alliances or resources/ Economic exploitation	Compromise/ Arbitration/ Economic inducements to collaboration/ Neutralization of issues, actors, or zones	Persuasion/ Electoral contest/Justice/ Sharing of values and interests

and exploit market relations to its advantage. Even militant nonviolence as a tactic of peaceful revolution is based on an appeal to the conscience of the oppressor; if oppressor and victim did not share at least a few moral assumptions, there would be no restraints on the use of repressive violence against the nonviolent resisters.

Systems can move in either direction, and the propensity of aggrieved or oppressed parties to use violence in seeking justice expresses the continuous flux between war and peace. To repeat Clausewitz's dictum, war is the continuation of politics by other means. Rational adversaries always fight with an eye to the policies in conflict and the prospects for peaceful negotiation of a resolution. War itself is subject to certain unwritten rules, limits established in the joint interests of the combatants. Conversely, the institutionalized pluralism of alliance systems and democracy always confronts the prospect of resistance, secession, or communal violence by groups that feel their interests are not fairly represented within the prevailing peace system.

METHODS OF ACCUMULATING OR NEUTRALIZING POWER

Across the continuum of war and peace are many methods of aggregating or neutralizing power. Peace systems are power systems as well, though they have ritualized conflict, monopolized violence, and accumulated state power in a manner that serves the common interests of the community. Groups pool their power or consent to having power exercised over them when doing so promises greater benefits, better security, a higher standard of living, and the like. The prospect of cooperative action and common gain is what has permitted the modern positive state to grow so powerful without being threatening to those over whom it exercises power. Of course, it is consent and legitimacy that give state power a benign aspect, but this simply underlines the point that some power relationships are threatening and others are not. Systems at the peaceful end of the spectrum employ the positive instruments of power or devise techniques for neutralizing it. These include the political methods of persuasion, consensus building, power sharing, and ideological appeal. In essence, aggrieved parties are exhorted to give up violence as a means of conflict resolution in favor of the peaceful means of electoral contest, arbitration, or judicial settlement. Whenever states negotiate a political confederation, as the original thirteen American colonies did, they are thereby establishing a peace system.

Another positive method of accumulating power is through the marketplace. States come together in a common market or expand their trade relations in a way that brings mutual benefit, economic growth, and technological development. Economic aid can sometimes serve as an inducement to collaboration. Economic strategies presume, however, that the gains will be mutual, that the market power of the participants is roughly equal and the system of exchange unconstrained by other forms of power. This is often not the case, as with the dependency relationships of colonialism or the state-motivated economic acts of mercantilism, which are as likely to cause conflict as resolve it. A mercantilist or imperialist economic strategy is an indirect means of accumulating power through the use of the market to camouflage unequal or exploitative relations. Such relations are created by force and must be maintained by the intermittent use of force, although the imperial power can conserve its resources by sharing benefits with an indigenous client elite, which then assists in the maintenance of order over the colonized majority.

When states or groups cannot be politically reconciled or bound together by economic ties, they can sometimes avoid a power competition by a strategy of neutralization. This might be an agreement to set certain issues, actors, or zones outside the bounds of conflict. The English Civil War was settled by the Grand Compromise of 1688, an agreement to set religion outside politics. At different times Belgium and Switzerland have enjoyed a status of neutrality, by which they escaped attack and avoided becoming belligerents in a number of European wars. Latin America has been declared a nuclear-free zone, which has reduced pressures for arms proliferation there and kept the continent free of superpower nuclear bases. The Antarctic Treaty has made that continent a demilitarized zone. Attempts also were made to solve the conflicts in Laos in the 1960s and Afghanistan in the 1980s through treaties of neutralization supported by superpower guarantees, although these ultimately failed.

Power also can be neutralized through proportionate reductions in armaments or through the negotiation of arms limits that establish an equilibrium of power and expectations. The Washington Naval Treaty of 1922 mandated proportionate reductions and limitations of naval armaments by the United States, Great Britain, France, Italy, and Japan. Periods of Soviet-American détente have always begun with important arms control treaties, such as SALT I and the INF treaty. Summit negotiations, exchange agreements, trade liberalization, and all the other devices of détente are aimed at reducing incentives to resort to arms and at providing common interests to counterbalance areas of rivalry. Arms control has rarely succeeded in curbing the arms race, but it has helped to make it more predictable and less threatening.

Power can sometimes be neutralized through appeasement, although this often is only a temporary solution. Concessions tend to be made not in the spirit of agreement but at the demand of the potential aggressor. The threat of forcible appropriation is usually what motivates the appeasement, which is then disguised as an act of justice — that is, a response to legitimate grievances rather than to the underlying threat. The Munich agreement Chamberlain negotiated in 1938, which ceded the German-speaking areas of Czechoslovakia to Germany in the hope of satisfying Hitler, was an act of appeasement in response to what Chamberlain judged to be authentic nationalist claims, as well as an attempt to ensure the maintenance of the status quo — a peace by satisfaction. When long-standing grievances have generated violent dissatisfaction, such palliative measures may be preferable to revolution or war. And if the claims are just and are met by genuine reform or compensation, agreement can remove the motivation for force. But once an aggrieved or oppressed party has been able to compel changes by armed threat, it is rarely satisfied with simple reforms or marginal gains. The dynamic of power has its own momentum. In the case of the Munich settlement, Hitler's appetite for power outweighed the claims that justice had been done.

Neutralization may reflect a more competitive arrangement whereby power cancels out or counterbalances power. The checks and balances of constitutional systems, the pluralism of multiparty politics, and economic differentiation within a society, all of which fractionate or disperse power among many groups, are means of preventing the polarization of conflict or the accumulation of power in the hands of a few. The balance of power in the international system operates on this same principle — that no one party should accumulate enough power to overwhelm an opposing coalition.

Alliances are the classic method by which independent states preserve their security. Nations that feel threatened by the growing power of a rival can alter the balance by banding together, thereby neutralizing the military forces of the possible aggressor. The most enduring alliances are those that arise naturally out of common values, interests, and objectives, as they are the least likely to arouse suspicion in nations that feel excluded. Alliances of strange bedfellows, on the other hand, which usually are born out of desperation or necessity, tend to last — as did the Soviet-American alliance of World War II — only so long as the common danger persists. Alliances that go against ideological principle, such as the Nazi-Soviet Nonaggression Pact, are also perceived as serving short-term power interests, not long-term security. The one recent exception appears to be the tacit entente between the United States and Communist China, which is held together partly by China's hostility to the Soviet Union.

Some alliances are formed between unequal partners that have complementary interests, such as those between a superpower and smaller states seeking its protection. During the Cold War, when both sides were vigorously expanding their spheres of influence and nuclear weapons had made everyone feel vulnerable, alliances were a common means of extending military protection to weak states in the zones of competition. An alliance could also cement a superpower's traditional sphere of influence by extending over it the nuclear umbrella. A hegemonic power sometimes presses a one-sided alliance on a vulnerable state, but these tend to be alliances in name only. An unequal distribution of benefits and burdens in such a lopsided affair can be avoided only if the weaker party offers some key asset. Oil has been the equalizer in relations between Saudi Arabia and the United States, and valuable basing rights have given Spain and the Philippines leverage. Portugal's strategic location, at the entrance to the Mediterranean Sea, has cemented its alliance with the more powerful Great Britain since 1703, because of Portugal's complementary interest in protecting its ports on the Atlantic.

Unable to make an advantageous alliance, a state may turn to deterrence as a strategy for neutralizing a rival's power. It will augment its own military potential, with the aim of forestalling attack by threatening the adversary with retaliation, which neutralizes, or deters, the attacker's power to do harm. But this strategy has costs and risks. Military preparedness has to be paid for, and it can bankrupt a domestic economy or deprive it of resources essential for long-term peaceful development. And when such a self-sufficient, arms-dependent strategy operates in an environment of competing states, it incurs risks. Because it is very hard to tell defensive from offensive weapons, the arming state's intentions are unclear, and its acquisition of arms may lead rival states to arm as well. This is the perennial security dilemma of international affairs — one nation's actions, intended to make it more secure, arouse the suspicions of others and end up making everyone less secure. It is a dynamic typical of arms races. One nation seeks a margin of safety, which its enemy perceives as the first step in a drive for superiority. The enemy compensates, for purposes of self-defense in an environment of anarchy, and sets off similar reactions in other states. The overall level of armaments rises, but collective security recedes still further.

The same dynamic can occur with alliances that are reactive or negative — that is, are directed against another nation or group of nations. Alliances that do not take into account the potential for compensatory action by a rival alliance or power frequently are self-defeating. During the Cold War, each superpower scrambled for allies in the Third World in order to deprive the other of any potential gains. But the competing alliances proved costly to the superpowers, in economic and arms aid, and they turned every square inch of the globe into a strategic piece of turf. The superpowers' attempt to neutralize one another via competing alliances robbed many states of the choice to remain neutral and raised the level of hostility and fear, just as the European alliances had done in their jockeying for power before World War I. The decision to establish the NATO alliance after World War II had the same negative consequences. Intended to increase European security, NATO had the effect of militarizing the continent by precipitating the formation of the Warsaw Pact and formalizing the division of Germany. The latter may secretly have been a desired result, to guard against a future German threat, but its military costs, in standing armies and nuclear arms, have been high. A structure of competing alliances may be unavoidable, and certainly it is preferable to war, but it is no substitute for reconciliation, or for deeper economic and ideological attachments that can make alliances more than mere tools of diplomacy or temporary power-balancing tactics.

Another tool for balancing power is partition, or compensation, by which great powers divide among themselves a weak state or disputed territory in order to preserve an equilibrium. Poland was partitioned three times between 1772 and 1795 to preserve the balance between Prussia, Austria, and Russia. At the Berlin Colonial Conference of 1884–85, the leading nations of Europe sat down and carved up Africa to adjust their competing interests there. A similar, if less formal, process of annexation and partition took place at about the same time in China, during the declining decades of the Manchu dynasty. The Treaty of 1906 established spheres of influence in Ethiopia to adjust the rival claims of France, Great Britain, and Italy. Iran was likewise divided by the Anglo-Russian Treaty of 1907. Partition serves to sanction aggression in the name of peace by allowing rivals to accumulate power and neutralize the gains of their adversaries both at once. It is the most Machiavellian and negative of all peace strategies. Divide-and-rule tactics are another common device when an aggressor does not desire peace at all but simply wants to aggrandize power or gain access to resources. Like appeasement, partition often backfires as a peace strategy. The scramble for colonies after the Berlin conference was one of the principal contributors to the breakdown of the European balance of power that led to the conflagration of World War I.

Dictatorships that sustain their rule by martial law and repression represent systems of armed "peace" that are particularly prone to breakdown. They are civil wars waiting to happen. The same is true of such systems as apartheid and colonialism, which perpetuate racial and economic inequality by force of arms. A power system based on structural violence can control an underdeveloped, weak, and politically disorganized population. Power can be accumulated and the threat of rebellion neutralized through a superior technology, a monopoly of economic resources, or policies of divide and rule that keep a people warring among themselves. But the monopolies decay, the military technologies become dispersed, and the oppressed peoples eventually unite and turn the implements of war against the common oppressor, as happened in the wars of decolonization that have dotted the last two centuries. The techniques of insurgency become more advanced than the techniques of repression, and the idea of freedom overpowers the fading claims of race, king, colony, and dictatorial authority.

Finally, we come to war and various acts of intervention and economic coercion as instruments for accumulating power—tactics that may be attractive to nations that are already powerful. But the active mobilization of power has costs, which must somehow be compensated for. In the days of the traditional balance of power, when war was less costly, nations could better afford to fight in the name of maintaining the balance, or they could profitably conquer territory and resources. Today, war is so costly that one can scarcely imagine it except on behalf of liberation or self defense. Only in such inflamed circumstances as the Arab-Israeli conflict or the Iran-Iraq struggle does war appear to be "justified"—but justified only to those ideologues who have long ago refused a rational calculus of costs and benefits. Sober statesmen question whether, given the global character of the balance today and the intensity with which territories are defended, the aggressive accumulation of power can any longer be a successful or a profitable strategy. It appears to be most effective as an adjunct to neocolonialist strategies for protecting economic domains or spheres of influence. Even here, force is not likely to succeed except in an area where it is infrequently used and is not seriously contested. Great powers may continue to seek limited aims by means of limited wars in the periphery—but what is peripheral to the superpower is not at all peripheral to the local combatants. Such local wars often involve insurgent elements whose goals are political autonomy and self-government and for whom the prize is control of the state—the ultimate justification for the accumulation of power. But this is revolution via legitimization, not the simple aggrandizement of one state at the expense of another. The spread of nationalism and democratic norms have made it nearly impossible for an imperialist state to conquer foreign territories and pacify their populations. Even an old empire that has long been consolidated into a modern state, the Soviet Union, is coming apart at the seams as the result of renascent nationalism and separatism.

Apart from gunboat diplomacy and covert interventions, which can keep a lingering colonialism alive, and revolutions and guerrilla struggles, which attempt to terminate it forever, modern warfare promises relative gains at best. Britain and France were winners in World War II, but they were so exhausted by it that they lost their roles as leading powers. The Soviet Union also was devastated and could be said to have won only in the sense that it ended up in control of the dominant land forces in Europe. Left with a crippled economy that has scarcely recovered yet (and has never approximated the vitality of its American rival, which suffered no domestic destruction in the war), the Soviet Union won an altogether Pyrrhic victory. The benefits of the war are better described by what the Allies avoided—conquest by fascism—than by what they gained. War in its modern form is no longer a rational means for states to aggregate power. A general resort to arms can never be justified except in self-defense or when an armed aggressor cannot be neutralized by less drastic means.

In short, power aggrandizement by military means has lost much of its utility. In our modern era of complex interdependence, power is more accurately a relationship of relative gains and losses, many of them hard to manipulate, than a quantum of coercive capacity by which one state dictates to another. Even the use of economic sanctions requires a preexisting relationship of mutual benefit, else one state would not be able to harm another by refusing to buy or sell. Sanctions are illustrative of the complexity of power relationships: an act of coercion against one part of an interdependent whole has some negative costs for everyone, even the aggressor. Sanctions have little utility except as devices of popular resistance, or for rich states that can afford the losses accompanying an interruption in their trade relations. However, the United States did not find it economically tolerable to pursue its embargo on chromium from Southern Rhodesia or its grain embargo against the Soviet Union. Nor did the power of the Arab states' oil weapon endure past the glut of the early 1980s. At some point the Arabs realized that the industrial societies were their principal customers (and investors) and that they did not want to kill the goose that laid the golden egg.

The most powerful states today are those that have well-developed economic systems and that maintain their power advantages largely through long-term, ideologically based alliances and the indirect exercise of their influence, or the relatively nonthreatening power they command in the marketplace. States that have tried to preserve their great-power status by accumulating arms at the expense of economic development, like the Soviet Union, are losing their capacity to compete. They echo the strategic error of militarism, which mistakenly conceives of power primarily (if not exclusively) in terms of the military assets at a nation's disposal. The militarist equates national power with material force, forgetting that power has positive aspects and can only be preserved, in the long run, by legitimate, peaceful strategies. Nuclear weapons are symbolic of this attitude. Power fetishists amass them in the expectation that they will guarantee security or confer the potential for world dominion. And they certainly give an unlimited destructive capacity to the state that possesses them. But they have no power to create a dynamic trading economy, to finance foreign debt or balance-of-payments deficits, to occupy or subdue a foreign territory, or to legitimize a nation's principles of government or political economy in the eyes of its own citizenry or the world. A nation that thinks too narrowly about power or seeks it too self-servingly ends up surrounded by enemies and dependencies that will ultimately — by war, arms race, revolution, or economic coercion — sap it of its strength.

Of course, we have no absence of wars today. But many of them are fought among the weak and within parameters that the superpowers can police. The majority are wars of liberation or civil wars whose aims are national and political self-determination. Some are old-fashioned border wars, fought by new states using old military technologies that make the violence tolerable. When the two sides are really mismatched, as with India's seizure of Portugese Goa, naked aggrandizement may succeed. More often, however, armed interstate conflicts in the Third World are the narcissistic acts of arbitrary leaders, the pyrotechnic expression of ethnic or religious differences, or an explosive response to frustration and powerlessness, not rational strategies for the management of power.

QUESTION FOR DISCUSSION (PRO AND CON)

Is nuclear deterrence still a viable policy? Can any state fight and win a nuclear war?

☞ PRO

The fearful, the fainthearted, and the Utopian have cried in the streets that we should abolish nuclear weapons as irrational and immoral. These peaceniks paint vivid pictures of holocaust. But they are trying to frighten us into abandoning the most important device of national security that we possess, one that has enforced the peace between the superpowers for more than forty years. There is no doubt that the prospect of assured destruction has kept the Soviets from risking aggression against the American homeland or any of our vital interests in Europe. The definitive statement on deterrence came from Defense Secretary Robert McNamara in 1967: "The cornerstone of our strategic policy continues to be to deter deliberate attack upon the United States, or its allies, by maintaining a highly reliable ability to inflict an unacceptable degree of damage upon any single aggressor or combination of aggressors at any time during the course of a strategic nuclear exchange — even after our absorbing a surprise first strike." No statement could be plainer. However irrational it might seem for us to carry out the threat, the Soviets have to assume that we are serious, given the enormous destructive consequences of a miscalculation. They are made correspondingly cautious, which, after all, is the aim of deterrence.

To achieve deterrence, however, we must deploy nuclear forces in sufficient variety that there can be no doubt about their survivability, or about our
ability to respond to any type of Soviet attack at a symmetrical, and therefore
credible, level of destruction. Deterrent threats do not come out of thin air: they
are based on the availability of appropriate military hardware. But the weapons
do not deter by themselves; they must be managed by decision makers who are
prepared, under the proper circumstances, to *use* them. All the weak-willed
talk about nuclear war being too horrible to contemplate is not helpful to
American national security. Their immense destructive capacity is what makes
nuclear warheads both dangerous and effective as tools of deterrence — if we
can accept the hardheaded requirement that American retaliation is inevitable
in the event of an attack. Otherwise, our foreign policy has lost any relationship
between military means and political ends. Assured retaliation is outlined in
the preprogrammed Single Integrated Operational Plan (SIOP), which defines
the president's options in case of a Soviet attack. Retaliation requires a presidential decision, which is by no means automatic. But possible responses have
been carefully rehearsed, and the Soviets can be certain that no president is so
lacking in options as to simply throw up his hands in surrender.

The apocalyptic character of nuclear war is exaggerated. Nuclear weapons
have not spelled the end of the principles of territorial sovereignty. On the
contrary, they have enhanced the importance of a well-organized national
security community able to mobilize the massive resources necessary for preventing an attack by a nuclear-armed adversary. Neither will nuclear weapons
destroy the planet. Hypotheses of "nuclear winter" are just that — hypotheses
— which of themselves will hardly restrain the Russians. The risk of nuclear
winter may in fact *reinforce* the deterrent credibility of our strategic forces.
Besides, many defense experts (like T. K. Jones and Eugene Rostow, in the
Reagan administration) have testified that we could recover from a general
nuclear war in as little as two to four years. Much depends on the measures we
take in civil defense, stockpiling, and the hardening of industry. Such measures
are simple prudence, as protection against accident or limited attack, and
would go far toward convincing the Soviets that a preemptive nuclear strike
against us would be futile. They have taken many civil defense measures,
including the construction of deep shelters to protect their leaders and command centers, and the United States should do likewise.

On the other hand, we should not assume that American decision makers
are, or have to be, some class of maniacs playing war games. Our national
security managers have a powerful sense of how much is at stake, including the
day-to-day dangers. We have careful procedures for screening out the emotionally or psychologically unstable from any position in the nuclear chain of
command. All missile-firing sequences must be initiated by at least two persons
acting simultaneously and with the proper authorization codes. Any decision
for war will be made not by any one person, not even the president, but by a
team of advisers, who will pass along the order for attack after careful confirmation from a variety of warning systems. The absence of armed conflict
between the superpowers testifies to the extreme caution nuclear weapons

have induced, notwithstanding the intensity of the rivalry and the constant danger of escalation through involvement in various proxy wars and peripheral conflicts in the Third World.

A critic might ask: if deterrence is working so well, why do we need to keep on acquiring weapons and developing new nuclear-war-fighting strategies? Answer: the Soviets are not standing still, and neither is the state of technology. The Soviets may have embraced the doctrine of mutual assured destruction when all they had were a few bombers and some multimegaton warheads. But the disposition of their forces over the last decade—including many large, accurate MIRVed ICBMs—has given them the capability for a counterforce attack that leaves America's land-based missiles highly vulnerable. This counterforce strategy aims at ensuring the survival of Soviet society by destroying the enemy's weapons or by threatening its most potent forces so severely as to pressure it into terminating hostilities on terms favorable to the Soviets. The Soviet defense minister, Marshal A. A. Grechko, stated the doctrine in 1971: "The Strategic Rocket Forces, which constitute the basis of the military might of our armed forces, are designed to annihilate the means of the enemy's nuclear attack, large groupings of his armies, and his military bases; to destroy his military industries; and to disorganize the political and military administration of the aggressor as well as his rear and transport." Although grave damage to our civilian population is likely to result from such counterforce attacks, their primary mission is to disable the U. S. military forces as quickly as possible and force our leadership to submit rather than risk more devastating damage. In short, should deterrence fail, the Soviets are prepared to fight and win a nuclear war. In the event of a crisis, they are also prepared to launch a preemptive strike if they judge there is a serious risk of American attack.

In 1980, America's nuclear forces could not have launched an effective counterforce, damage-limiting, or preemptive strike, nor was our strategy capable of managing a nuclear war in a rational and controlled manner if deterrence failed. Committed to massive retaliation against the Soviet civilian population, we were limited to a few nuclear options, and we could only cross our fingers and hope that no other options would be needed. This is why President Reagan sought additional counterforce weapons and launched his "countervailing" strategy—to close the "window of missile vulnerability." That vulnerability can best be understood in terms of the following scenario: A crisis occurs between the Soviet Union and the United States in Europe or the Persian Gulf, and fighting breaks out between Soviet and American conventional forces. The prestige of both sides becomes fully engaged, and each views the confrontation as vital. The Soviets have the superior conventional strength and use it to good advantage, forcing the United States into a position in which it must either turn to tactical nuclear weapons or threaten a direct strategic attack on the Soviet homeland. In desperation, we explode a small tactical device, in line with our first-use policy in Europe, hoping this will convince the Soviets that we are not going to back down. They reach the correct conclusion, but they also see the crossing of the nuclear threshold as a sign of American recklessness. They fear that escalation to the strategic level is inevitable, and the Soviet leadership decides to strike first. They launch 200 of their heavy missiles, carrying ten warheads each, and target two weapons on each of the 1,000-plus American missile silos. Between 90 percent and 100 percent of the American land-based missiles are destroyed, and the Soviets still have in reserve 85 percent of their rocket forces (about 1,200 missiles).

If it is ever possible for the Soviets to wipe out all our counterforce weapons, as this 1980 scenario imagines, the president will face a terrible dilemma. The most reliable and accurate U.S. weapons will have been destroyed, leaving us with our sea-launched missiles on submarines, which are less accurate and pose communication problems in the midst of crisis. The slow, aged fleet of B-52s would be practically useless. The president could not retaliate with a similar counterforce attack; he could only threaten massive destruction of Soviet cities and industries. And this would not be a rational move since the Soviets could still retaliate in kind, bringing wholesale destruction to both societies. The president would have to choose between suicide and surrender, in the latter case accepting the loss of American ICBMs and a lower death rate (anywhere from 5 million to 20 million). Neither choice is palatable, but anything is preferable to suicide.

Moreover, once the conditions for such a scenario are in place, the Soviets can achieve what they want simply by *threatening* to launch a counterforce attack. The president and his advisers will be able to predict the outcome and will be intimidated into making concessions, rather than risking 5 million American lives in a nuclear showdown that the United States cannot possibly win. The Soviets, with their superiority in prompt hard-target kill capability at each projected level of conflict, will be able to dominate at each rung of the escalation ladder, detering any possible American response. They will be able to force a cease-fire on their terms. The Soviet's supremacy in counterforce capability not only will prove critical to the nuclear victory, but also will give them the diplomatic clout to dominate international affairs generally. As President Reagan well understood, the only way to avoid such an outcome was to restore symmetry and equality to the nuclear balance, especially in counterforce weapons like the MX missile, Pershing IIs, cruise missiles, accurate Trident II submarine warheads, and, eventually, the mobile Midgetman. For the same reasons, he advocated additional measures for strengthening our ability to prevail in a nuclear war. These included federal emergency planning and a renewed emphasis on civil defense; the strengthening of our command, control, and communications facilities to endure a prolonged nuclear attack; the upgrading of our global navigation satellite network and our low-frequency communication link to missile submarines; and the revision of SIOP to include a wider range of limited nuclear options. In addition, we must expand our conventional military forces significantly and end American inferiority in this area. We must match the Soviets in every theater of potential conflict. This will strengthen overall deterrence and also will widen the firebreak between conventional and nuclear war.

Keeping our nuclear forces modern and versatile achieves other objectives. First, it demonstrates to the Soviets our resolve. The arms race is where

America establishes its credibility. If the Soviets see that a society so wealthy as ours is not willing to spend money on the arms race and the competition for influence, they will conclude that we are weak. Only a steady stream of new deployments can convince them that we have the determination to stay the course in the face of their own buildup. In the nuclear era, the balance of resolve counts for as much as the balance of power does. And the decision to buy a weapons system affects the perceptions of a rival, independent of the system's place in military strategy or its effectiveness as an instrument of coercion. Weapons systems have become bargaining chips in the superpower relationship, even systems that do not work very well, or are redundant, or (as with SDI) have not been invented yet. Strategic weapons development is important symbolically for the margin of quantitative superiority it indicates, which translates into prestige and influence, even in the Third World.

In the second place, modernization of the nuclear arsenal prevents our deterrent capability from becoming degraded through technological obsolescence or the loss of reliability. Keeping our land-based missiles viable is important for maintaining forces that can respond accurately and instantaneously. Critics of the missile vulnerability scenario say that our bomber and submarine forces are sufficient. But bombers are not counterforce weapons that can be targeted on the Soviet command and control centers, where the Soviet elite will be in the event of a nuclear crisis. The Soviet military command might just be willing to sacrifice the lives of Soviet citizens (in addition to several million American lives) for the chance to achieve world domination, and if such an elite is to be deterred, we must have accurate weapons that can threaten them, directly and promptly, in their hardened shelters. Submarines may eventually be this weapon, but communication with them in the midst of crisis is undependable, and the oceans may not remain impenetrable forever. A Soviet breakthrough in satellite reconnaissance, sonar technology, or some other antisubmarine warfare technique could make our SLBM force vulnerable almost overnight. Accurate land-based weapons targeted on Soviet missile forces and military installations are both more effective and more moral, since they do not leave the American deterrent threat at a level at which an American president would have to issue the unbelievable order that would willfully destroy the lives of tens of millions of Soviet citizens.

Anyone who expects we can turn the clock back to old-fashioned deterrence — mutual assured destruction via blunderbuss nuclear attacks against cities — is not living in the real world. Like it or not, we live in a technologically dynamic environment in which accurate and mobile miniaturized weapons already exist and new versions, developed at considerable public expense over the course of a decade, are coming forward. To stop this momentum would require the complete reorganization of the military-industrial sector in the two largest powers on earth. Moreover, since America's highly innovative and productive economy is better equipped than the Soviet's to win the arms race, we probably should not try. More important, there appears to be no alternative to the arms race. Arms control agreements have been pathetically unable to put the brakes on technology, and the agreements we have signed have been widely disregarded on both sides. The record of violations is such that no great power can afford to trust its fate to one of these flimsy pieces of paper. Significant reductions in nuclear arsenals raise the risk of breakout, of one power covertly violating an agreement and suddenly showing a nuclear trump card. The lower the level of nuclear arms, the more likely it is that just a few contraband weapons can spell a decisive difference. Traditional Soviet secrecy makes it easier for them to cheat, but there are serious doubts about whether a complete ban on nuclear warheads and delivery systems could be verified even in America's open society. When a hundred cruise missiles can be secreted in a good-sized barn, in Minnesota or in Siberia, have we not already reached a level of technology that makes arms control a hopeless illusion?

This is why President Reagan pressed forward with his Strategic Defense Initiative. He posed the key question: how can we switch from an offensive to a defensive technology, to a strategy that offers some hope of crisis stability in place of the terror and the trigger-happy approach of a strategy rewarding the side that strikes first? SDI promises to protect our land-based missiles, and perhaps eventually our cities and industry. It is based on the sophisticated technologies in which America is superior, rather than on the heavy offensive rockets that the Soviets have mastered. It will provide us with a means of aborting an enemy's accidental launches due to technical failure. At present, a superpower has no alternative but to absorb them, while listening to its mortal enemy declare, in nearly impossible circumstances, that it was all a mistake. And what if the Soviets say it is not their missile? Already, it could be coming from China or, in the near future, a number of hostile Third World states. SDI will protect us from nuclear missiles launched by an unknown enemy, against whom we might be powerless to retaliate or who might be so fanatic as to be undeterred. Strategic defense resolves all the psychological dilemmas of deterrence: it puts control of American national security squarely in our own hands, rather than subject to the rationality and restraint of the Soviets or some unknown nuclear terrorist. It will put an end to all those questions about what represents a credible threat to the Soviets, how much potential damage will deter them, how long our missiles can remain invulnerable, and so forth. The nuclear genie cannot be put back in the bottle. Deterrence is here to stay. All we can do is find ways to make our weapons more efficient and less vulnerable instruments of national defense.

☞ CON

Nuclear weapons are a grave threat to civilization, the more so because we pretend that deterrence has given us a rational framework within which to manage them. Deterrence theory, particularly as it has evolved into its present exotic nuclear-war-fighting forms, is one of the most expensive, illogical, immoral, and unstable of all military doctrines. First, it is impossible to prove whether any kind of deterrent actually works because the desired outcome — the forestalling of an attack — is a nonevent. Maybe the threat of nuclear retaliation has kept the Soviets at bay — or have they been restrained for other reasons? Maybe they did not need to be kept at bay — were the risks of conventional war sufficient to prevent aggression? Perhaps a trillion-dollar arms race is essential to peace — or could it be a vast, wasteful exercise in paranoia and overkill by which, in President Eisenhower's words, "humanity is hanging itself on a cross of iron"? We have piled one multibillion-dollar weapons system on top of another, on the assumption that they make us safer, without an iota of proof that we need anything more than a few Hiroshima-sized weapons. So we begin with the insight that all the alleged benefits of deterrence are speculative, but the enormous costs and the risk of destruction are quite real.

Second, deterrence of any kind depends on the rationality of one's adversary. Madmen or fanatics cannot be deterred; loss of life, including their own, is insignificant in the face of their commitment to a higher goal or to the destruction of a hated enemy. We think of the leaders of the superpowers as being cautious, but on three or four occasions U.S. presidents have considered ordering preemptive nuclear strikes, on the recommendation of the Joint Chiefs of Staff, according to former Defense Secretary Robert McNamara. Also the Soviets once sought, indirectly, America's acquiescence in a preemptive strike against Communist China's infant nuclear facilities. Our war planning calls for the use of tactical nuclear weapons first off to defend against a Soviet invasion in Europe, though no one has ever been able to explain convincingly how nuclear weapons could defend such a densely populated area without utterly destroying it in the process. If perfectly sane leaders can contemplate the use of nuclear weapons, what would happen if they fell into the hands of someone like Hitler, Khadafy, Khomeini, or Idi Amin? We rationalize that it can never happen, that such leaders cannot arise out of the complex party-bureaucratic politics of countries like Russia and America. But Hitler came to the top, at a time of crisis, in the most advanced country in Europe, and the same could happen in one of the superpowers. Moreover, the longer nuclear weapons remain outside some arrangement of international control, the more likely it is that a fission device will become available to the leader of one of the less stable Third World countries. Is this a risk we want to run?

In the third place, nuclear weapons have robbed our moral categories of their meaning by encouraging practices of warfare that violate all our traditional ideas about right and wrong. Through much of history, conventions and agreements about acceptable conduct have carefully circumscribed the waging of war. These rules have been codified in international law; they are expressed philosophically in the just-war tradition and practically in the United Nations Charter and the findings of the Nuremburg war crimes tribunal. The rules are not always followed (just as civil society is never free of crime), but all nations have affirmed them as the prudent and reasonable moral standards of civilized states. Today, when general staffs plan the systematic extermination of whole cities and societies, such indiscriminate destruction calls into question the meaningfulness of these moral restraints. The just-war tradition, which affirms the principle of utility, holds that force always should be purposeful and aimed at winning defined objectives, not at simply punishing an enemy. The nuclear strategy of massive retaliation violates this principle; a nation would gain nothing except revenge if deterrence failed and it had to make good on its promise to retaliate. A second principle of just-war theory is proportionality, the idea that the harm done by violence should not grossly outweigh the benefits gained. When the destructive power of nuclear weaponry cannot even be calculated in advance, and when the potential costs may include cutting off the very cycle of life, this principle is blatantly violated. Without the explosion of a single device, the domestic costs of the arms race, in perverted priorities and in the loss of resources for dealing with poverty, ill health, and homelessness, are out of all proportion to any gains. The realist may answer that civilization is at stake. This might justify the first few hundred warheads, but certainly not the present 10,000 to 12,000. A third principle of just-war is its prohibition against the killing of noncombatants, with the double-effects proviso that excepts civilian casualties incidental to attacks on industrial and military targets. In a limited nuclear counterforce strike, this double effect would involve tens of millions of civilian deaths. The prohibition against killing innocents is erased altogether when nuclear deterrence holds entire civilizations hostage. Nuclear war will be not a conflict of will between soldiers, but a contest of endurance or annihilation between populations. Taken together, these violations of the just-war tradition show how far back nuclear weapons have returned warfare to a primitive struggle for survival, without morality, rules, or restraint.

Most damning of all, deterrence strategy has become a kind of nuclear theology not fundamentally different from those medieval disputes about how many angels can dance on the head of a pin. When Pentagon experts needed to find an invulnerable basing mode for their new MX missile, for example, they came up with a scheme called "dense pack," in which all the missiles would be clustered together. The assumption was that the incoming Soviet warheads would then knock themselves out in a sort of nuclear fratricide. If the theory did not work, however, we would have put $30 billion worth of eggs in one very vulnerable basket. The dense-pack theory eventually was rejected, but hundreds more just as flimsy have been accepted as the basis for new weapons systems, at $30 billion or $40 billion a crack. With no shred of experience in actual nuclear war to go on, the decisive elements of deterrence strategy are what the U.S. president or the Soviet general-secretary believes they are and what the public can be persuaded to accept. Nothing else matters, however wrongheaded the theory may be, for it cannot be disproved until, for all practical purposes, it is too late. Nuclear theories must be taken on faith, yet, cynically, they are often advanced *after* the technology for a new weapons system is available. Advances in warhead accuracy and MIRV technology gave us superfluous warheads, and then counterforce and nuclear-war-fighting strategies gave us ex post facto justifications for them. Finally, even seasoned military professionals tend to discount the destructive power of nuclear weapons because the planning takes place in an unreal war-games atmosphere. Senior American officers participating in one elaborate computer-simulated war in Europe found they had escalated rapidly to a nuclear level that they thought was tactical, but that proved to be destructive enough to obliterate the entire field of operations. The officers themselves were shocked by the unexpected outcome. In short, the theory did not conform to the (simulated) reality.

We can see the flaws of nuclear deterrence strategy by examining one particular war scenario dealing with the missile vulnerability problem, a scenario the Reagan administration used to justify the acquisition of new counterforce weapons. It is a scenario riddled with false assumptions. First of all, it presumes that America is weak in conventional arms, and therefore must rely on nuclear weapons to deter Soviet aggression in Europe and the Middle East. But the Soviet battle-ready battalions in Europe are not substantially stronger than NATO's, and any slight deficiencies in numbers are compensated for by the superior quality of NATO's troops and weapons, and the advantages that go with defending entrenched positions. In the Middle East, the Soviet logistical problems are formidable, due to their gross inferiority in airlift capacity, marines, aircraft carriers, and rapid deployment capability. The war in Afghanistan took 5 percent of Soviet troops, but more than 25 percent of Soviet airlift capacity. The image of the Soviets as a potent force in the Third World is simply untrue, especially when we take into account American naval superiority and our widespread access to hundreds of bases around the world.

The second false assumption of the scenario is that Soviet aggressive intentions are serious enough to invite a nuclear showdown, which would include a Soviet preemptive strike. All the postwar evidence shows that the Soviets have been far more cautious than the United States has in deploying its military forces overseas, and this is even more true under Gorbachev. No one has provided a reason for Soviet aggression other than a general image that the Soviets are a diabolical and ideologically driven enemy. In fact, a Soviet nuclear attack would go against the Marxist theory that capitalism is internally contradictory and self-destructive. If the Soviets believe fanatically in the scientific inevitability of Marxism, they will hardly want to risk the fate of socialism on "one cosmic roll of the dice," in the words of former Defense Secretary Harold Brown. Since history promises them a victory, they can afford to be patient.

A third assumption of the vulnerability scenario is that a Soviet attack will be technically flawless. Multiple launches will be coordinated perfectly, without logistical or communication failures or any significant number of misfirings. A failure rate of even 10 percent would render the Soviet attack meaningless. But anyone who has experienced firsthand the everyday technological breakdowns that plague Soviet society will find the assumption of technical perfection a joke. Even the United States, with its vaunted technological superiority, has not managed a successful test launch from an operational silo, despite several tries. (We finally gave up and now conduct our missile tests from special silos at Vandenberg Air Force Base.) Other uncertainties abound. Missile accuracy is purely theoretical. The technician's measure, called circular error probability (CEP), is the radius of the circle within which 50 percent of the warheads are projected to fall. But this is a statement of probability, not certainty, and a measure of the consistency with which a group of warheads will strike the same target, not necessarily a prediction about the degree of error, or bias, in the missile trajectory. The latter can be affected by weather patterns and by magnetic interference over a polar route, which neither country has ever tested. The air force claims that our missiles are programmed to account for a twenty-four-hour cycle of variations in atmospheric density, seasonal wind patterns, daily temperatures, and anomalies in the gravitational field, but all these variables are put into the computer by humans who have been known to make mistakes. If the Soviet missiles miss by only 200 feet, ten times more American missiles will survive — and this kind of error can result from a miscalculation as small as three parts per million in mapping the gravitational field of the earth. It is not at all improbable for one or two Soviet warheads to go really haywire and land on Minneapolis, Detroit, or Denver, demolishing at once any idea that the strike was a "surgical" one aimed at limiting civilian casualties. And something unforeseen, like solar flares, could affect missile accuracy by aiming an entire group of warheads at a completely unpredictable target. As defense specialist Richard Garwin has said: "It is the things you don't think of that cause the trouble."

A fourth assumption is that the United States will wait out an attack and respond only defensively. Yet the whole missile vulnerability problem could be solved instantly if we changed to a launch-on-warning policy. This is nuclear war gaming at its most elegant and ethereal: a theoretical threat can be countered by a conceptual shift. Why wait for the Soviet missiles to destroy our most accurate weapons? We can launch out from under their attack and target their remaining missile silos, restoring both countries to symmetry. The Soviets' superiority in counterforce weapons would be canceled and, with it, any hope of their blackmailing America into submission. Even without a launch-on-warning strategy, Soviet intimidation is useless if the president calls their bluff. The Soviets might have the capability for destroying all our land-based missiles, but this cannot *compel* us to evacuate the Persian Gulf, dismantle NATO, or surrender to a Soviet occupation. Only the threat of a massive attack on our cities and industry might do that — except that the United States can deter such a threat by promising to retaliate in kind, from our remaining submarines and bombers. The task of the aggressor will always be compellence, while our task is simple deterrence, to maintain the status quo. Once this is recognized, we can see that counterforce weapons are not good for anything but destroying other counterforce weapons. If we refuse to deploy such weapons, the Soviets will have no rational use for theirs. Nuclear weapons are, by their superdestructive nature, deterrent weapons. They can be used to discourage nuclear attack, but they cannot be used to force an enemy to submit so long as one's adversary retains a bare minimum of retaliatory capability.

Fifth, the advocates of controlled nuclear-war-fighting scenarios assume that leaders will remain rational and restrained throughout the period of crisis bargaining and tit-for-tat nuclear exchanges. They assume that communications will remain intact and escalation under control. What is more likely is that any nuclear attack will sow panic and confusion. Nations will lose control of their nuclear forces, or the political elite will be wiped out, making it impossible to negotiate a cease-fire before an all-out nuclear exchange. The risk of a general breakdown is compounded by the very short warning and decision times (six to thirty minutes), the urgency and inadequate information of the crisis decision environment, the risk of miscalculation, the probable failure of some communications and weapons, and the magnitude of possible destruction. The Reagan administration spent billions to harden communications and develop plans for follow-on attacks, including the deployment of a Poseidon submarine under the polar ice cap. Yet it was unable to solve the most basic problem — an authenticating device that could determine whether radioed orders were coming from a valid authority. We must also remember that smaller and more usable nuclear weapons theoretically will strengthen deterrence before an attack, but they will certainly make it easier to pass up the ladder of escalation once deterrence has broken down. In short, it may not be possible to control the conduct of a nuclear war, and the more we plan and arm ourselves to fight one, the more likely we are to end up doing just what we have planned.

The missile vulnerability scenario incorporates a sixth assumption, that each leg of the strategic triad stands alone. We, in our caution, may think we need to duplicate our means of response, but the Soviets can be killed only once, and that is all the risk they care about. If they see that we still have bombers, cruise missiles, and SLBMs carrying more than 10,000 nuclear warheads, they cannot be hopeful about their chances of making us submit by means of a surgical strike against our land-based forces, even if the strike was technically flawless and avoided extensive civilian deaths.

The seventh assumption of the "victory is possible" school of nuclear strategy is that democracy and capitalism will survive nuclear war. But a postnuclear world is likely to be a living nightmare. If the truth be known, the planners of both sides have adopted a basic strategy of preparing for the worst and hoping for the best. But the language of the planners bears no relationship to the awful reality of war, no matter its scope. Between the Soviet version ("If war comes, we will move to decisively defeat the aggressor") and the American version ("If deterrence fails, we plan to terminate conflict on the most favorable conditions possible"), the differences are largely semantic. Bravado and vague language camouflage the prospect that a few nuclear warriors may, if they are lucky, live long enough to destroy a little more of whatever is left after the initial exchange. At best, politics and economy will return to the Dark Ages. Freedom is fragile. It is easily compromised when coercive means are used in its name, and a war economy is scarcely friendly to the liberal values of our civilization. Even in peacetime, nothing has robbed democracy of its voice or capitalism of its competitive virtues so much as the clubbiness, the dependency, and the corruption of the military-industrial complex. The depression and the New Deal did not socialize our economy or centralize our decision making half so much as have the defense planning and the Pentagon socialism imposed on us by nuclear deterrence and the arms race.

Finally, advocates of nuclear deterrence appear unwilling to make a comparative analysis of the risks of ongoing arms deployments as against the risks of disarmament. They assume that conditions of deterrence can be maintained forever. A more realistic assumption is that arms control must be introduced or nuclear war is inevitable. Kenneth Boulding has likened the risk of deterrence failure to the risk of a catastrophic earthquake in San Francisco. No one regards the danger as very high on any given day or year, but the inevitable is waiting to happen: it is only a question of when. The short-term probability that deterrence will fail is very low, but there must be *some* risk that a superpower will use its nuclear weapons, or else it does not make sense to say that nuclear weapons deter. Yet any probability higher than zero means that one day a nuclear war will be launched, although it may take decades for the odds to catch up with us.

Technological optimists may believe that the future holds a Star Wars weapon, a quick fix for the arms race. But the overwhelming majority of the scientific community is pessimistic. Even the Joint Chiefs of Staff and the Pentagon's own Defense Science Board questioned the sketchiness of the Reagan administration's early deployment scheme for SDI. They cautioned that there had been no analysis of the "desirability of deployment" and raised questions about problems of battle management, vulnerability to attack, the ability of sensors to tell warheads from decoys, and unreliable cost estimates. Besides being ruinously expensive (estimates for a complete system cluster around the $1 trillion mark), SDI can be easily overwhelmed (by increased numbers of warheads), outfoxed (by simple and relatively cheap decoys and other countermeasures), and underflown (by cruise missiles, terrain-hugging bombers, or depressed-trajectory weapons launched from SLBMs). A Star Wars system, to be a real defense against ICBMs, must work perfectly the first time and must accurately track and destroy more than 10,000 warheads in less than five minutes. From this perspective, arms control seems a far cheaper and more reliable route to national security. The growing complexity of new weapons systems and the rising risk of technical failure and accidental nuclear war also make arms control an attractive alternative to an arms race that seems fated to end in disaster.

It is nearly impossible that all the optimistic assumptions of the war planners can prove correct as conditions for maintaining deterrence or successfully fighting a limited nuclear war. If any one of them is wrong, by a factor as small as 5 percent, we court disaster. Defense professionals make highly pessimistic assumptions about Soviet intentions, but they make overly optimistic assumptions about the technical reliability of everyone's weapons and the validity of their theories. If they would apply a little worst-case analysis to their own strategies ("anything that can go wrong, will go wrong"), they could not in good conscience foist their improbable scenario on the public, at the cost of hundreds of billions of dollars. No nuclear strategy is foolproof, especially from the foolish acts of those who occupy high office. Deterrence theory does not make room for the human ingredient, or for what Clausewitz has called "friction" — the uncertainties, the inconsistencies, the accidents, and the unpredictable consequences of human feelings and responses. Deterrence is touted as infallible, but it is not. To embrace such nuclear theology as gospel, rather than as the expedient remnant of a historic wrong turn, is indeed to commit a kind of civilizational suicide. We should not place our national security or the fate of the earth in the hands of such flimsy and completely unsubstantiated propositions.

[Ideas and arguments in this pro-and-con section have been drawn freely from Schloming, *American Foreign Policy and the Nuclear Dilemma*, pp. 77–110, where they appear in a more extended version.]

SOURCES AND SUGGESTED READINGS

On Geopolitics

Cohen, Saul B. *Geography and Politics in a World Divided.* London: Oxford University Press, 1973.

Fairgrieve, James. *Geography and World Power,* 8th ed. London: University of London Press, 1941.

Gray, Colin S. *The Geopolitics of the Nuclear Era: Heartland, Rimlands, and the Technological Revolution.* New York: Crane, Russak/National Strategy Information Center, 1977.

————. *The Geopolitics of Superpower.* Lexington, Ky.: The University Press of Kentucky, 1988.

Mackinder, Sir Halford J. "The Geographical Pivot of History." *Geographical Journal,* vol. 23 (1904), pp. 421–44.

Sloan, Geoffrey R. *Geopolitics in United States Strategic Policy, 1890–1987.* New York: St. Martin's, 1988.

Sprout, Harold, and Margaret Sprout. *Toward a Politics of the Planet Earth.* New York: D. Van Nostrand, 1971.

Spykman, Nicholas J. *The Geography of the Peace.* New York: Harcourt, Brace and Co., 1944.

On Power and Its Assessment

Baldwin, David A. "Power Analysis and World Politics." *World Politics,* vol. 31 (1979), pp. 162–88.

Bretton, Henry L. *International Relations in the Nuclear Age.* Albany: State University of New York Press, 1986.

Brodie, Bernard, and Fawn M. Brodie. *From Cross Bow to H-Bomb.* Bloomington, Ind.: Indiana University Press, 1973.

Bundy, William P. "Elements of National Power." *Foreign Affairs,* vol. 56 (Oct. 1977), pp. 1–26.

Claude, Inis L. *Power in International Relations.* New York: Random House, 1962.

Clausewitz, Karl von. *On War (Vom Kriege)* (ed. by Anatol Rapoport). New York: Penguin, 1968.

Cline, Ray. *World Power Assessment, 1977.* Boulder, Colo.: Westview, 1977.

————. *World Power Trends and U.S. Foreign Policy for the 1980s.* Boulder, Colo.: Westview, 1978.

Collins, John M. *American and Soviet Military Trends Since the Cuban Missile Crisis.* Washington, D.C.: Georgetown University Center for Strategic and International Studies, 1978.

Deyoung, Karen. "U.S. Talks of Pullout, and This Time Europe Is Listening." *The Oregonian* (May 8, 1988), p. A2.

Evans, David. "Military Decline Beginning to Show." *The Oregonian* (May 27, 1988), p. E5.

Fallows, James. *National Defense.* New York: Random House, 1981.

Garthoff, Raymond L. "On Estimating and Imputing Intentions." *International Security,* (Winter 1978), pp. 22–32.

Gervasi, Tom. *The Myth of Soviet Military Supremacy.* New York: Harper & Row, 1986.

Gurtov, Mel, and Dali Yang. "China Integrating Military Industries, Civilian Economy." *The Oregonian,* (May 18, 1988), p. B9.

Hart, Jeffrey. "Three Approaches to the Measurement of Power in International Relations." *International Organization,* vol. 30, no. 2 (Spring 1976).

Hoguet, Marie. "Beancounting and Wargaming: How to Analyze the Strategic Balance" in Robert Travis Scott, ed. *The Race for Security: Arms and Arms Control in the Reagan Years.* Lexington, Mass.: Heath, 1985.

Holloway, David. *The Soviet Union and the Arms Race,* 2nd ed. New Haven, Conn.: Yale University Press, 1984.

Howard, Michael. "The Forgotten Dimensions of Strategy." *Foreign Affairs,* (Summer 1979), pp. 975–86.

International Institute for Strategic Studies. *Military Balance*. London: International Institute for Strategic Studies, published annually.

Jouvenel, Bertrand de. *On Power*. Boston: Beacon, 1962.

Knorr, Klaus. "Is International Coercion Waning or Rising?" *International Security*, (Spring 1977), pp. 92–110.

————. *Military Power and Potential*. Lexington, Mass.: Heath, 1970.

————. "On the International Uses of Military Force in the Contemporary World." *Orbis* (Spring 1977), pp. 5–27.

————. *Power and Wealth: The Political Economy of International Power*. New York: Basic Books, 1973.

————. *The Power of Nations*. New York: Basic Books, 1975.

Knorr, Klaus, and Frank Tiager, eds. *Economic Issues and National Security*. Lawrence, Kans.: Allen Press, 1977.

Morgenthau, Hans. *Politics Among Nations: The Struggle for Power and Peace*, 6th ed., revised by Kenneth W. Thompson. New York: Knopf, 1985.

Organski, A. F. K., and Jacek Kugler. *The War Ledger*. Chicago: University of Chicago Press, 1980.

Prados, John. *The Soviet Estimate: U.S. Intelligence Analysis and Soviet Strategic Forces*. Princeton, N.J.: Princeton University Press, 1986.

Rourke, John T. *International Politics on the World Stage*. Monterey, Cal.: Brooks/Cole, 1986.

Sanger, David E. "High-Tech Sales to Soviets May Spell Terrible Harm." *The Oregonian* (June 18, 1987), p. A2.

Schelling, Thomas C. *Arms and Influence*. New Haven, Conn.: Yale University Press, 1966.

————. *The Strategy of Conflict*. New York: Oxford University Press, 1963.

Singer, David, ed. *Quantitative International Politics*. New York: Free Press, 1968.

Sivard, Ruth Leger. *World Military and Social Expenditures*. Washington, D.C.: World Priorities, published annually.

Spanier, John. *Games Nations Play*, 6th ed. Washington, D.C.: CQ Press, 1987.

Stockholm International Peace Research Institute. *World Armaments and Disarmament: SIPRI Yearbook*. Philadelphia: Taylor & Francis, published annually.

U.S. Department of Defense. *Soviet Military Power*. Washington, D.C.: Department of Defense, issued annually since 1982.

USSR Ministry of Defense. *Whence the Threat to Peace?* Moscow: Military Publishing House, 1982.

Wendzel, Robert L. *International Relations: A Policymaker Focus*, 2nd ed. New York: Wiley, 1980.

On Deterrence and Nuclear War-Fighting Strategies   (See also references cited in Chapter 5, under the heading "Nuclear Conflict, the Arms Race, and Arms Control.")

Aldridge, Robert. *First Strike: The Pentagon's Strategy for Nuclear War*. Boston: South End Press, 1983.

Ball, Desmond. *Can Nuclear War Be Controlled?* (Adelphi Paper No. 169). London: International Institute of Strategic Studies, 1981.

————. "PD-59: A Strategic Critique." *F.A.S. Public Interest Report*, vol. 33, no. 8 (Oct. 1980), pp. 4–5.

Baugh, William H. *The Politics of Nuclear Balance*. New York: Longman, 1984.

Bearden, Steven L. *The Evolution of American Strategic Doctrine: Paul H. Nitze and the Soviet Challenge* (SAIS Papers in International Affairs, no. 4). Boulder, Colo.: Westview, 1984.

Beres, Louis René. "Presidential Directive 59: A Critical Assessment." *Parameters—The Journal of the US Army War College*, vol. 11 (Mar. 1981), pp. 19–28.

Betts, Richard K. *Nuclear Blackmail and Nuclear Balance*. Washington, D.C.: Brookings Institution, 1987.

Bobbitt, Philip. *Democracy and Deterrence: The History and Future of Nuclear Strategy*. New York: St. Martin's, 1988.

Bracken, Paul J. *The Command and Control of Nuclear Forces*. New Haven, Conn.: Yale University Press, 1983.

Brodie, Bernard. *Strategy in the Missile Age*. Princeton, N.J.: Princeton University Press, 1959.

Buzan, Barry, ed. *The International Politics of Deterrence*. New York: St. Martin's, 1987.

Carlton, David, and Carlo Schaerf, eds. *The Arms Race in the Era of Star Wars: Studies in Disarmament and Conflict*. New York: St. Martin's, 1987.

Carter, Ashton B. "The Command and Control of Nuclear War." *Scientific American,* vol. 222 (Jan. 1985), pp. 32–39.

Cimbala, Stephen J. "Forever MAD: Essence and Attributes." *Armed Forces and Society,* vol. 12 (Fall 1985), pp. 95–107.

Clark, Ian. *Limited Nuclear War: Political Theory and War Conventions.* Oxford: Martin Robertson, 1982.

David, Charles-Philippe. *Debating Counterforce: A Conventional Approach in a Nuclear Age.* Boulder, Colo.: Westview, 1987.

Drell, Sidney, and Frank Von Hippel. "Limited Nuclear War." *Scientific American,* (Nov. 1976), pp. 27–37.

Dyson, Freeman. *Weapons and Hope.* New York: Harper & Row, 1984.

Dziak, John J. *Soviet Perceptions of Military Doctrine and Military Power: The Interaction of Theory and Practice.* Philadelphia: Crane Russak, 1981.

Ehrlich, Paul, and Carl Sagan. *The Cold and the Dark: The World After Nuclear War.* New York: Norton, 1984.

Ehrlich, Robert. *Waging Nuclear Peace: The Technology and Politics of Nuclear War.* Albany: State University of New York Press, 1985.

Fallows, James. *National Defense.* New York: Random House, 1981.

George, Alexander, and Richard Smoke. *Deterrence in American Foreign Policy: Theory and Practice.* New York: Columbia University Press, 1974.

Gray, Colin S. "Nuclear Strategy: The Case for a Theory of Victory." *International Security,* vol. 4 (Summer 1979), pp. 54–87.

———. "Presidential Directive 59: Flawed But Useful." *Parameters—The Journal of the US Army War College,* vol. 11 (Mar. 1981), pp. 29–37.

Gray, Colin, and Keith Payne. "Victory is Possible." *Foreign Policy* (Summer 1980), pp. 14–27.

Gregory, Donna, ed. *The Nuclear Predicament: A Sourcebook.* New York: St. Martin's, 1986.

Griffiths, Martin. "A Dying Creed: The Erosion of Deterrence in American Nuclear Strategy." *Millenium: Journal of International Studies,* vol. 15 (Summer 1986), pp. 223–48.

Haley, P. Edward, and Jack Merritt, eds. *Nuclear Strategy, Arms Control, and the Future,* 2nd ed. Boulder, Colo.: Westview, 1988.

Harris, John, and Eric Markusen, eds. *Nuclear Weapons and the Threat of Nuclear War.* San Diego: Harcourt, Brace, Jovanovich, 1986.

Harvard Nuclear Study Group. *Living with Nuclear Weapons.* New York: Bantam, 1983.

Jastrow, Robert. "Why Strategic Superiority Matters." *Commentary.* (Mar. 1983).

Jervis, Robert. *The Illogic of American Nuclear Strategy.* Ithaca, N.Y.: Cornell University Press, 1984.

———. "Why Nuclear Superiority Doesn't Matter." *Political Science Quarterly,* vol. 94, no. 4 (Winter 1979–80), pp. 617–33.

Kahn, Herman. *Thinking About the Unthinkable.* New York: Horizon, 1962.

Kaiser, Karl, et al. "Nuclear Weapons and the Preservation of Peace." *Foreign Affairs,* vol. 60 (Summer 1982), pp. 1157–70.

Kaplan, Fred M. *The Wizards of Armageddon.* New York: Simon & Schuster, 1983.

Katz, Arthur M. *Life After Nuclear War.* Cambridge, Mass.: Ballinger, 1982.

Kegley, Jr., Charles, and Eugene Wittkopf, eds. *The Nuclear Reader: Strategy, Weapons, and War.* New York: St. Martin's, 1985.

Kennan, George F. *The Nuclear Delusion: Soviet-American Relations in the Atomic Age.* New York: Pantheon, 1983.

Kissinger, Henry A. *Nuclear Weapons and Foreign Policy.* New York: Harper & Row, 1957.

Kistiakowsky, George B. "Can a Limited Nuclear War Be Won?" *Defense Monitor,* vol. 10, no. 2 (1981), pp. 1–4.

Krepon, Michael. *Strategic Stalemate.* New York: St. Martin's, 1984.

Kurtz, Lester R. *The Nuclear Cage: A Sociology of the Arms Race.* Englewood Cliffs, N.J.: Prentice-Hall, 1988.

Lambeth, Benjamin S. "Deterrence in the MIRV Era." *World Politics* (Jan. 1972).

Lawrence, Philip K. *Preparing for Armageddon: A Critique of Western Strategy.* New York: St. Martin's, 1988.

Lebow, Richard Ned. *Nuclear Crisis Management: A Dangerous Illusion.* Ithaca, N.Y.: Cornell University Press, 1987.

Leebaert, Derek, ed. *Soviet Military Thinking.* London: Allen & Unwin, 1981.

Lewis, Kevin N. "The Prompt and Delayed Effects of Nuclear War." *Scientific American,* vol. 241 (July 1979), pp. 35–47.

Mandelbaum, Michael. *The Nuclear Future.* Ithaca, N.Y.: Cornell University Press, 1983.
────── . *The Nuclear Revolution: International Politics Before and After Hiroshima.* New York: Cambridge University Press, 1981.
Marullo, Sam. "The Ideological Nature of Nuclear Deterrence: Some Causes and Consequences." *Sociological Quarterly,* vol. 26, no. 2 (1985), pp. 311–30.
McGwire, Michael. "Deterrence: The Problem—Not the Solution." *International Affairs* (London), vol. 62 (Winter 1985/86), pp. 55–70.
McNamara, Robert S. "The Military Role of Nuclear Weapons: Perceptions and Misperceptions." *Foreign Affairs,* vol. 62 (Fall 1983), pp. 59–80.
Morgan, Patrick. *Deterrence: A Conceptual Analysis.* Beverly Hills: Sage, 1977.
Office of Technology Assessment. *The Effects of Nuclear War.* Montclair, N.J.: Allenheld, Osmun & Co., 1979.
Panofsky, Wolfgang, and Spurgeon M. Keeny, Jr. "MAD vs. NUTS: Can Doctrine or Weaponry Remedy the Mutual Hostage Relationship of the Superpowers?" *Foreign Affairs,* vol. 60, no. 2 (Winter 1981/82), pp. 287–304.
Payne, Keith B. "The Deterrence Requirement for Defense." *Washington Quarterly,* vol. 9 (Winter 1986), pp. 139–54.
Pipes, Richard. *Survival Is Not Enough.* New York: Simon & Schuster, 1984.
────── . "Why the Soviet Union Thinks It Could Fight and Win a Nuclear War." *Commentary,* vol. 64 (July 1977), pp. 21–34.
Porro, Jeffrey D. "The Policy War: Brodie vs. Kahn." *Bulletin of Atomic Scientists.* (June 1982), pp. 16–19.
Powers, Thomas. "Choosing a Strategy for World War III." *The Atlantic Monthly.* (Nov. 1982), pp. 82ff.
────── . "Is Nuclear War 'Impossible'?" *The Atlantic Monthly,* vol. 254 (Nov. 1984), pp. 53–64.
────── . *Thinking About the Next War.* New York: Knopf, 1982.
Pringle, Peter, and William Aiken. *SIOP: The Secret U.S. Plan for Nuclear War.* New York: Norton, 1983.
Quester, George H. *The Future of Deterrence.* Lexington, Mass.: Lexington Books, 1986.
"The Rational Deterrence Debate: A Symposium." *World Politics* (Special Issue), vol. XLI, no. 2 (Jan. 1989).
Rhodes, Edward. "Nuclear Weapons and Credibility: Deterrence Theory Beyond Rationality." *Review of International Studies,* vol. 14 (Jan. 1988), pp. 45–62.
Roberts, Adam. "The Critique of Nuclear Deterrence" in *Defence and Consensus: The Domestic Aspects of Western Security, Pt. II* (Adelphi Paper 183). London: International Institute for Strategic Studies, 1983, pp. 2–18.
Russett, Bruce. "The Calculus of Deterrence." *Journal of Conflict Resolution,* vol. 7, no. 2 (June 1963), pp. 97–109.
Sagan, Carl. "Nuclear War and Climatic Catastrophe: Some Policy Implications." *Foreign Affairs,* vol. 62 (Winter 1983–84), pp. 257–92.
Scheer, Robert. *With Enough Shovels: Reagan, Bush & Nuclear War.* New York: Random House, 1982.
Schell, Jonathan. *The Fate of the Earth.* New York: Knopf, 1982.
Schelling, Thomas C. *The Strategy of Conflict.* Cambridge, Mass.: Harvard University Press, 1960.
Schloming, Gordon. *American Foreign Policy and the Nuclear Dilemma.* Englewood Cliffs, N.J.: Prentice-Hall, 1987.
Scott, Harriet Fast, and William F. Scott. *Soviet Military Doctrine: Continuity, Formulation, and Dissemination.* Boulder, Colo.: Westview, 1988.
Smith, Michael J. "Nuclear Deterrence: Behind the Strategic and Ethical Debate." *Virginia Quarterly Review,* vol. 64 (Winter 1987), pp. 1–22.
Smoke, Richard. "Extended Deterrence: Some Observations." *Naval War College Review,* vol. 36 (Sept.-Oct. 1983), pp. 37–48.
Snow, Donald M. "Realistic Self-Deterrence: An Alternative View of Nuclear Dynamics." *Naval War College Review,* vol. 39 (Mar.-Apr. 1986), pp. 60–73.
Speed, Roger. *Strategic Deterrence in the 1980's.* Stanford: Hoover Institution, 1979.
Steinbruner, John. "Beyond Rational Deterrence: The Struggle or New Concepts." *World Politics.* (Jan. 1976), pp. 223–45.
Stockton, Paul. *Strategic Stability Between the Superpowers* (Adelphi Paper 213). London: International Institute for Strategic Studies, 1986.
Thompson, Stanley L., and Stephen H. Schneider. "Nuclear Winter Reappraised." *Foreign Affairs,* vol. 64 (1986), pp. 981–1005.
Utgoff, Victor. "In Defense of Counterforce." *International Security,* vol. 6, no. 4 (Spring 1982).

Van Creveld, Martin, *Technology and War. From 2000 B.C. to the Present*. New York: Free Press, 1989.

Van Oudenaren, John. *Deterrence, War-Fighting, and Soviet Military Doctrine* (Adelphi Paper 210). London: International Institute for Strategic Studies, 1986.

Wohlstetter, Albert. "The Delicate Balance of Terror." *Foreign Affairs*, vol. 37 (Jan. 1959), pp. 211–34.

Woolsey, R. James. "The Politics of Vulnerability: 1980–83." *Foreign Affairs*, vol. 62 (Spring 1984), pp. 805–19.

Zagare, Frank C. *The Dynamics of Deterrence*. Chicago: University of Chicago Press, 1987.

On Limited War, Economic Coercion, and Low-Intensity Conflict

Ameringen, Otto Wolff von. "Commentary: Economic Sanctions as a Foreign Policy Tool?" *International Security* (Fall 1980), pp. 159–67.

Bayard, Thomas O., Joseph Pelzman, and Jorge Perez-Lopez. "Stakes and Risks in Economic Sanctions." *World Economy* (London), vol. 6 (Mar. 1983), pp. 73–88.

Cabwell, Robert. "Economic Sanctions and Iran." *Foreign Affairs* (Winter 1981/82), pp. 247–65.

Chaliand, Gerard, ed. *Guerrilla Strategies*. Berkeley: University of California Press, 1982.

Elowitz, Larry, and John Spanier. "Korea and Vietnam: Limited War and the American Political System." *Orbis* (Summer 1974), pp. 510–34.

Evans, David. "Success of Stingers Can Haunt U.S., Too." *The Oregonian* (Apr. 12, 1988), p. B5.

Griffith, Samuel B. *Mao Tse-Tung on Guerrilla Warfare*. New York: Praeger, 1961.

Halperin, Morton H. *Limited War in the Nuclear Age*. New York: Wiley, 1963.

Hermann, Charles F., ed. *International Crises: Insights from Behavioral Research*. New York: Free Press, 1972.

Hufbauer, G. C., et al. *Economic Sanctions Reconsidered: History and Current Policy*. Washington, D.C.: Institute for International Economics, 1985.

Klare, Michael T., and Peter Kornbluh, eds. *Low Intensity Warfare: Counterinsurgency, Proinsurgency, and Antiterrorism in the Eighties*. New York: Pantheon, 1988.

Leyton-Brown, David, ed. *The Utility of Economic Sanctions*. New York: St. Martin's, 1987.

Lindsay, James M. "Trade Sanctions as Policy Instruments: A Re-examination." *International Studies Quarterly*, vol. 30 (June 1986), pp. 153–73.

Losman, Donald L. *International Economic Sanctions: The Cases of Cuba, Israel, and Rhodesia*. Albuquerque, N.M.: University of New Mexico Press, 1979.

Mack, Andrew J. R. "Why Big Nations Lose Small Wars: The Politics of Asymmetric Conflict." *World Politics* (Jan. 1975).

Mayall, James. "The Sanctions Problem in International Economic Relations: Reflections in the Light of Recent Experience." *International Affairs* (London), vol. 60 (Autumn 1984), pp. 631–42.

Miller, Norman, and Roderick Aya, eds. *National Liberation: Revolution in the Third World*. New York: Free Press, 1971.

Minter, William. "South Africa: Straight Talk on Sanctions." *Foreign Policy*, vol. 65 (Winter 1986/87), pp. 43–63.

Olson, Richard S. "Economic Coercion in World Politics: With a Focus on North-South Relations." *World Politics* (July 1979), pp. 472–79.

Osgood, Robert E. *Limited War: The Challenge to American Strategy*. Chicago: University of Chicago Press, 1957.

———. *Limited War Revisited*. Boulder, Colo.: Westview, 1979.

Paarlberg, Robert L. "Food, Oil, and Coercive Resource Diplomacy." *International Security* (Fall 1978), pp. 3–19.

———. "Lessons of the Grain Embargo." *Foreign Affairs* (Fall 1980), pp. 144–62.

Paret, Peter, and John W. Shy. *Guerrillas in the 1960's*, rev. ed. New York: Praeger, 1962.

Snyder, Glenn H., and Paul Diesing. *Conflict Among Nations: Bargaining, Decision Making, and System Structure in International Crises*. Princeton, N.J.: Princeton University Press, 1977.

Thomas, Walter. *Guerrilla Warfare: Causes and Conflict*. Washington, D.C.: National Defense University Press, 1981.

Weintraub, Sidney, ed. *Economic Coercion and U.S. Foreign Policy*. Boulder, Colo.: Westview, 1982.

Williams, Phil. *Crisis Management*. New York: Wiley, 1976.

Young, Oran R. *The Politics of Force: Bargaining During International Crises*. Princeton, N.J.: Princeton University Press, 1968.

10

DIPLOMACY AND INTERNATIONAL LAW

Diplomacy, in its broadest sense, is the entire process through which states conduct their political relations. It is the means for allies to harmonize relations and for adversaries to resolve conflicts without force. Nations communicate, bargain, influence one another, and adjust their differences through diplomacy. Serious confrontations between the great powers since 1815 have ended in force only about 10 percent of the time, and in the entirety of interstate actions, physical conflicts are still less frequent. The routine business of international affairs is conducted through the peaceful instrument of diplomacy.

In a narrower sense, diplomacy is the implementation of foreign policy, as distinct from the process of policy formation. Diplomats may influence policy and have input in the councils of government, but their main task is to negotiate with the representatives—plenipotentiaries—of other countries. Ambassadors, ministers, and envoys are official spokespersons for their nation abroad and the instruments through which states maintain regular direct contact. Though messages are rapidly transmitted from one state to another today, personal, face-to-face encounters can put a stamp of privacy and authenticity on diplomatic exchanges. Formal diplomacy is a regularized system of official communication between states: the exchange of ambassadors, the maintenance of embassies in foreign capitals, the dispatch of messages through officially accredited emissaries, participation in conferences and other direct negotiations.

The foreign ministry is the nerve center of a nation's diplomacy. In the United States, it is called the Department of State, and it has the responsibility for collecting and evaluating information from abroad, giving the president advice on foreign policy, and interpreting and defending U.S. policy before Congress and the American public. Equally important in the United States is the National Security Council (NSC), which, in this time of multiple bureaucracies and executive dominance, has come to be the central coordinating mechanism for foreign affairs, performing many of the Department of State's more traditional functions. Thus, Henry Kissinger rose to his position of leadership in the Nixon administration while serving as the president's national security adviser. Still, the secretary of state remains the official representative of the United States in its external relations.

The State Department's top staff includes a deputy secretary, four or five undersecretaries (political, economic, security assistance, science and technology, management), and twelve or more assistant secretaries (see Figure 10-1). Five of the assistant secretaries have geographical areas of concern, and the others specialize in functional areas, such as international organization, economic affairs, environmental and scientific affairs, human rights, and intelligence and research. Other high-ranking officials of the State Department are the legal adviser, the director of the policy planning staff, and the inspector general of the Foreign Service.

The State Department is the management center for all the nation's diplomats and official foreign representatives. It issues decisions and instructions to ambassadors, coordinates their conduct, and supervises the Foreign Service, which staffs the embassies. Every nation's ambassadors serve as personal representatives of the nation and observe elaborate ceremonial courtesies, as officials who symbolically embody the nation's sovereignty. Rules of protocol, diplomatic immunity, and noninterference, which have developed over centuries, sustain mutual respect for sovereignty, reduce disagreements over status and rank, and permit regular communication even in times of considerable stress. The diplomatic corps is the instrument through which states constantly and discreetly adjust their differences and establish mutual confidence.

An overseas embassy (or legation) is headed by an ambassador (or minister), who typically oversees the work of a large number of officials or attachés. Most nations have embassies in all foreign capitals throughout the world, but some poor Third World countries that cannot afford to staff large foreign service bureaucracies depend principally on their delegations to the United Nations, where there is ample opportunity for multilateral contacts. An American ambassador coordinates (at least in theory) the activities of dozens of officials representing the Agency for International Development (AID), the U.S. Information Service (USIS), the Central Intelligence Agency (CIA), and the Departments of State, Defense, Commerce, Treasury, and Agriculture, to name but a few. Economic interdependence and the complexity of interstate relations have increased the number of agencies with various responsibilities in foreign affairs. The U.S. embassy in London, for example, must coordinate the activities of over 44 agencies. In 1979, the U.S. embassy in Cairo had 61 Foreign Service personnel and 111 additional staff members, mostly from AID.

The demands of conducting relations with more than 150 states have given increased discretion to those charged with implementing policy. Every day the Department of State receives and transmits literally thousands of cables, out of which the Secretary of State will read, at best, a few dozen. All else is left to the country desk officer and the ambassador. Junior officers today deal with matters that before World War II would have come to the secretary. One

FIGURE 10-1
DIVISION OF RESPONSIBILITIES IN THE U.S. DEPARTMENT OF STATE

Duties							
Leadership and overall direction	Policy development and coordination	Development of policy toward and conduct of relations with foreign countries and international organizations	Policy development and conduct of relations in special fields	Policy development in and conduct of consular affairs (passports, visas, citizens' services overseas)	Specialized support	Congressional, media, and public liaison	Management of the Department
Responsible Officers							
Secretary of State	Under Secretaries for Political Affairs, Economic Affairs, and Security Assistance, Science and Technology	Assistant Secretaries for African Affairs, Inter-American Affairs, East Asian and Pacific Affairs, European Affairs, Near Eastern and South Asian Affairs, and International Organization Affairs	Assistant Secretaries for Economic and Business Affairs, Oceans and International Environmental and Scientific Affairs, International Narcotics Matters, and Human Rights and Humanitarian Affairs	Assistant Secretary for Consular Affairs	Legal Adviser	Assistant Secretary for Congressional Relations	Under Secretary for Management
Deputy Secretary of State	Counselor of Department		Directors of Bureaus of Politico-Military Affairs and Refugee Programs, and of the Office for Combatting Terrorism		Director of Bureau of Intelligence and Research	Assistant Secretary for Public Affairs and Spokesman of the Department	Inspector General
	Chairman of Policy Planning Council				Chief of Protocol		Assistant Secretary for Administration
							Director General of the Foreign Service and Director of Personnel
							Comptroller of the Department
							Director of Management Operations

gargantuan task for them is to collect accurate and relevant information on all the governments of the world, half of whom will have an election or other change of regime in any given year (and almost all have opposition parties that may become the next government). Flaws in this most basic task of diplomacy can compromise a nation's entire foreign policy — as happened when the United States failed to detect the weakening position of the Shah of Iran in 1979 and knew almost nothing about the political and religious forces behind the revolution that ousted him. Modern technology has speeded communications and produced new intelligence-gathering devices, but in the process it has created a mountain of information for the foreign affairs bureaucracy to digest. And the multiplication and fragmentation of sovereign entities over the past fifty years have compounded the problem of obtaining timely information on the internal politics and foreign policies of other states.

The importance of diplomacy arises from the fact that most foreign policies are stated very generally, without spelling out measures for implementation. A good diplomat must adapt such policy mandates to the circumstances of the moment. Moreover, power and principle frequently clash, so that a diplomat must decide when to sacrifice a secondary interest in order to protect the nation's basic security and when to press for the implementation of core values at the risk of conflict. Many problems in foreign affairs come from the application of policy to particular situations. A nation's broad objectives can generally be deduced from its well-established values and its domestic political practices. The basic principles of democratic capitalism that guide U.S. foreign policy are deeply rooted in a bipartisan consensus favoring the maintenance of international stability, the expansion of trade and investment, the protection of human rights, and respect for international law and the UN Charter. However, in a far-distant foreign setting it may not be possible to carry out a policy that simultaneously promotes stability, democracy, and capitalism. Then it often falls to diplomacy to decide which policy or principle shall get priority. Moreover, there are a thousand occasions when the demands of a particular situation might justify an exception to policy, and for this a nation must rely on the wisdom of its diplomatic officers in the field. Occasionally this judgment is abused, as when, say, covert CIA operations are at odds with the peacemaking or information-gathering functions of other U.S. agencies abroad. Such conflicts reflect internal political differences within the elite that has framed the policy. Few governments pursue a perfectly consistent policy that is enunciated with a single voice. It falls to the diplomats to reconcile the competing voices and to give coherence, emphasis, and interpretation to their nation's foreign policy.

THE TASKS OF DIPLOMACY

Diplomacy has two, often opposite, faces, like the masks of tragedy and comedy of classical Greek drama. It is the vehicle through which a nation openly asserts itself and articulates its concerns to the world; it is also the principal means of conciliating competing national interests. Diplomacy aims to further a nation's primary interests while preserving international order. It is the tool that states use to get their way without arousing the opposition or animosity of other states. Diplomats must constantly balance the need to protect their nations vigorously and the need to avoid conflict with others and retain their confidence. The ambivalence is captured well in these quotations from traditional statesmen:

> Diplomacy is the art of avoiding the appearance of victory.
>
> (Prince Klemans von Metternich)

> An ambassador is an honest man sent abroad to lie for the good of his country.
>
> (attributed to Sir Henry Wotton)

> Diplomacy is the ability to say or do the nastiest thing in the nicest way.

Diplomats are often characterized as hypocrites who waste their time on elaborate charades and social functions that curry favor without dealing in substance. But the stereotypes miss the point. Inconsistency and ambiguity often are unavoidable in smoothing over differences or in representing faithfully a government whose views can shift with bewildering rapidity. Two-facedness is built into an ambassador's job. In the face diplomacy presents to the world, flexibility, modesty, discretion, the artful use of language, and cosmopolitan social graces are called for. By such means do diplomats ingratiate themselves with all parties and engender smooth relations. When acting on behalf of the nation, however, diplomacy requires patriotic loyalty, tenacity in negotiations, keen powers of observation, candor in its assessments, and clarity of expression; ambassadors must be skillful reporters and trustworthy custodians of the nation's interests. Diplomats blend the roles of peacemaker and intelligence agent, social butterfly and hard-bitten haggler, in simultaneously promoting the national interest and peaceful relations.

Diplomacy has two functions that contribute to international order — *cross-cultural communication* and *conflict resolution.* One of its tasks is to build relationships of trust, good will, and understanding. Its elaborate social rituals serve this purpose, by helping to sew together a fabric of mutual confidence in a brutally competitive and suspicious environment. The ceremonial function serves well as a vehicle for informal exchange and for acquiring knowledge of another nation's society and manners. As the famous French diplomat Jules Cambon wrote in 1926, in *Le Diplomate:*

> To know a country is to penetrate its spirit, live in the atmosphere of its ideas and be in a position to understand the relations between its external and internal policy. To do so the ambassador will not be content to carry on relations with ministers and political personalities alone. On occasion, conversations frivolous on the surface will teach him much more than discussions of high policy. (p. 14)

Diplomatic communication facilitates economic, cultural, and scientific exchanges between countries. Information is collected and disseminated, and cues or signals are sent that indicate an understanding of another nation's desires, concerns, and interests. When hostility, isolation, or a break in diplomatic relations prevents such signaling or causes the cues to be misinterpreted, the prospects for interstate conflict rise dramatically. If the messages are threatening, it is especially important to international order for diplomats to understand them correctly.

Diplomats address problems of mutual concern through formal negotiations. They conclude treaties and agreements regulating areas of actual or potential conflict. When an action of another nation arouses suspicion, they seek reassurance about that nation's intentions. When their nation's reputation or interests are damaged, they try to win an apology or compensation. When misunderstandings arise, it is the task of diplomats to seek the facts, solve the problem, and salve the sense of national outrage. If armed conflict breaks out, good diplomacy can limit the damage, negotiate a settlement, and restore relations between the aggrieved parties.

Three functions of diplomacy serve the national interest—*intelligence gathering, image management,* and *program implementation.* An embassy abroad is a kind of sophisticated spy organization that gathers information on the thinking of the local political leadership, the state of the local economy, the nature of the political opposition, and the size and strength of the armed forces—all of it critical for predicting internal upheaval, anticipating changes in foreign policy, and deterring potential threats. Diplomatic representatives are the eyes and ears of their government. Their cables and reports are the raw material from which almost all foreign policy is molded. Clearly, the accuracy of the information and the quality of the diplomat's judgment directly affect the success or failure of a state's actions abroad.

Diplomacy also aims at creating a favorable image of the nation. Modern communications make it possible, as never before, to shape perceptions and attitudes around the globe. States today have vast public relations apparatuses whose purpose is to place their actions and policies in a favorable light. Foreign embassies supply local news media with official interpretations and a stream of positive images, and try to avoid negative publicity or explain it away. They select or manipulate information to foster the desired attitudes, and diplomats sometimes maneuver to influence popular opinion in order to bring pressure on a recalcitrant government. In 1983, for example, the Soviet Union withdrew from arms control negotiations with the United States and launched a diplomatic campaign in Europe to convince the NATO allies that the deployment of Pershing II and cruise missiles would increase the risk of nuclear war. Many negotiations are aimed not at settlement but at influencing third parties. The Soviet-American disarmament negotiations of the 1950s were largely a propaganda exercise to court world public opinion in the midst of the Cold War. Arkady Shevchenko, in *Breaking with Moscow,* reports this remark of Soviet Premier Nikita Khrushchev to a diplomat: "Never forget the appeal that the idea of disarmament has to the outside world. All you have to say is 'I'm in favor of it,' and it pays big dividends." Recent U.S. diplomacy toward China has been conducted always with an eye to its impact on the Soviet Union.

Diplomatic stances are taken in order to impress or frighten an opponent and also to sway opinion among the nonaligned. Positions on UN resolutions frequently are not a response to substance so much as an attempt to burnish a nation's reputation, garner allies, or reassure third parties. The Soviet and American delegations to the UN lobby constantly for a sympathetic response from Third World regimes.

The final task that diplomacy performs on behalf of the nation-state is the administration of its overseas programs. Foreign representatives negotiate military basing rights and recruit officer trainees, facilitate investment, trade, and arms sales, supervise the distribution of economic aid, and provide information and technical assistance. An official alliance relationship calls for frequent joint consultations and decision making. The NATO countries regularly brief one another in advance, through diplomatic channels, about coming actions or changes of policy. Through its embassy, a dominant state may dictate to a dependent ally, as happened routinely during the Vietnam War, when instructions were issued through the American embassy in Saigon. In many of the so-called banana republics of Central America, during the era of dollar diplomacy and Teddy Roosevelt's big-stick policies, local governments were practically run out of the American embassy. In Eastern Europe, the Soviet representatives used to be a kind of proconsul, issuing directives to local party leaders. In many cases, an embassy coordinates a variety of covert operations aimed at influencing or intervening in domestic politics — unofficial programs that sometimes last for decades, spend tens of millions of dollars, and employ hundreds of undercover operatives. The ambassador, in conjunction with the foreign ministry and the headquarters office of, say, the CIA or KGB, must see that these operations run smoothly, without embarrassment to the home government.

An ambassador would list the immediate, practical tasks of day-to-day diplomacy as follows: (1) to cultivate friendly relations with the host government and thereby persuade it to respond favorably to a nation's foreign policies; (2) to collect information about the government to which he or she is assigned and interpret it for the home country; (3) to facilitate the regular exchange of communications and commerce; (4) to expedite on-the-spot negotiations on issues of mutual concern; and (5) to protect the lives and property of the home country's citizens when they are traveling, residing, or doing business abroad. As diplomacy has become more complex, these tasks have come to be performed by an increasingly bureaucratized foreign service staffed by professionals trained in specific functions: information officers (public relations and propaganda), consular officials (legal assistance and travel requests), commercial attachés (trade and economic interests), economic development specialists (the administration of foreign aid), military attachés (military training and arms transfers), and intelligence officers (the monitoring of local politics).

However, diplomacy involves much more than these routine functions performed by overseas embassies. Hans Morgenthau, in *Politics Among Nations* (pp. 563–65), speaks of the broader responsibilities that fall to the makers of policy back home in the national capital. A foreign ministry must oversee the whole of the nation's diplomacy. It must (1) set goals consistent with the state's power to implement them; (2) assess accurately the power and objectives of other states; (3) determine when its vital interests are incompatible with those of another state; and (4) choose the appropriate means of implementing national strategy, whether by persuasion, compromise, or the threat of force. The art of diplomacy lies in knowing when to compromise and when to stand fast, when negotiation can solve a problem and when it cannot, and which national interests are secondary (and can therefore be sacrificed) and which are not.

OLD AND NEW DIPLOMACY

In the days when travel and communications were primitive, ambassadors had a great deal of authority and discretion in the making of foreign policy. They might be stationed abroad for as long as five years without receiving new instructions or returning home. Nowadays, overseas envoys receive floods of cables and minute-by-minute instructions. Heads of state communicate directly with each other by telephone or by hot-line connections. With foreign capitals only hours apart by jetliner, top policy makers tend to negotiate directly (summit diplomacy) or to send special envoys (shuttle diplomacy)—often the foreign minister, who can be absent from the capital for weeks and still remain in constant contact or, if necessary, return within hours. U.S. Secretary of State James F. Byrnes, for example, logged about 77,000 miles in traveling to high-level conferences between the Yalta Conference, in January 1945, and the Paris Peace Conference, in July 1946. In a two-year period, John Foster Dulles (President Dwight D. Eisenhower's secretary of state) traveled more than double that distance—178,749 miles. Kissinger, in three years as secretary of state, covered more than 650,000 miles in making diplomatic visits to fifty-seven countries. When we add all the time that foreign ministers must spend on duties like receiving visiting dignitaries and briefing Congress, Parliament, or the Politburo, it is no wonder that a nation's foreign policy sometimes appears ill coordinated. Many matters must be delegated to undersecretaries and assistants, and the primary tasks of policymaking—analyzing information, formulating options, briefing the chief of state, coordinating the foreign ministry and its embassies—often receive less attention than they are due.

Today's speedy communications have deemphasized the ambassador's importance—although not as much as some modern analysts have suggested. Dean Rusk, secretary of state in the administrations of both John F. Kennedy and Lyndon Johnson, has pointed out, in "The Uses of Diplomacy" (in Hartmann, *World in Crisis*), that rapid communications, by greatly increasing the pace of events, make the judgment of the person on the spot just as important today as in the days of the clipper ship. For a superpower like the United States, today's ambassadors have responsibilities many times greater than those of their nineteenth-century predecessors. They must refer back to Washington constantly, to ensure that the nation's worldwide commitments are in balance one with another and that policies do not outrun available resources. Domestic interests, particularly in a democracy, are important in dictating what a nation can do in its foreign policy, and the wishes of legislatures and public opinion cannot be ignored. In the days when diplomats were personal representatives of the king and needed to know only what was in the mind of the sovereign, their actions, while they could commit the country to war, infrequently impinged on domestic politics. States could consequently give their ambassadors relatively free rein. Today, foreign policy has a strong "intermestic" dimension. Decisions on oil imports or textile quotas, say, affect domestic and international affairs at one and the same time. Decisions on taxes, deficits, and interest rates influence foreign exchange rates and the flow of capital from abroad. Security conditions in a region that harbors major investments or produces a vital resource — oil, chrome, copper, bauxite, uranium — must be carefully monitored. When a nation's security and economic welfare are so dependent on stable relations with overseas allies and suppliers, frequent consultation with ambassadors is a necessity. But this is due more to interdependence and consensus-building coalition politics than to any loss of faith in the judgment of the ambassador.

The changing role of the ambassador is part of a broader shift away from traditional diplomacy. Democratization, improved communications, and the expansion of the old Eurocentric state system into a global community have brought a more open and multilateral style of diplomacy. The secrecy and aristocratic style of nineteenth-century diplomacy came under attack after World War I, accompanied by a general depreciation of power politics. Woodrow Wilson called for an end to the secret treaties and behind-the-scenes machinations that had aroused suspicions and fed power rivalries before the war. Wilson outlined his plan for a reconstructed world order in his famous Fourteen Points speech, whose preamble reads as follows:

> It will be our wish and purpose that the processes of peace, when they are begun, shall be absolutely open, and that they shall involve and permit henceforth no secret understandings of any kind. The day of conquest and aggrandizement is gone by; so is also the day of secret covenants entered into in the interest of particular governments, and likely at some unlooked-for moment to upset the peace of the world. It is this happy fact, now clear to the view of every public man whose thoughts do not still linger in an age that is dead and gone, which makes it possible for every nation whose purposes are consistent with justice and the peace of the world to avow, now or at any other time, the objects it has in view. The first point reads: "Open covenants of peace, openly arrived at, after which there shall be no private international understandings of any kind, but diplomacy shall proceed always frankly and in the public view."

International organizations like the United Nations have given the new, open diplomacy its multilateral footing. Decisions are increasingly the result of majority rule, and multilateral management is essential for many issues that involve cooperative arrangements among governments. This is true in such areas as nuclear testing, nuclear proliferation, and arms control; trade, tariff, and currency regulation; control of technology and pollution; regulation of air travel and communications; and the suppression of terrorism. The UN and other intergovernmental organizations convene periodic conferences to deal with problems of food, population, the environment, and other issues of global concern. Since most of the less-developed countries make the greater part of their official diplomatic contacts at the UN, many issues of modern diplomacy are addressed in this multilateral forum. Before 1900, U.S. diplomats attended an average of one multilateral conference per year; now the average is closer to three per day. As Gilbert Winham has observed, in "Negotiation as a Management Process":

> Modern international negotiation represents a machine of great systems. It is commonplace today to observe that the world is becoming more interdependent. . . . Today, negotiators function as an extension of national policymaking processes rather than as a formal diplomatic representation between two sovereigns. . . . It is now more akin to the art of management as practiced in large bureaucracies than to the art of guile and concealment as practiced by Cardinal Mazarin.

However, this kind of institutionalized diplomacy, with positions taken and votes cast under the scrutiny of the press and the entire world community, has introduced a certain rigidity into the negotiating process. When an interstate conflict is highly political, propaganda concerns become paramount, if a state's public prestige is visibly and heavily invested, it may pay more attention to assigning blame than to solving the dispute. When the emphasis is on outvoting or embarrassing an adversary, rather than on cooption or persuasion, diplomacy becomes name-calling and ideological posturing.

As a consequence, many of the most important disputes are never brought before the UN, the Organization of American States (OAS), or any of the other public multilateral forums. Increasingly, the superpowers have resorted to secret bilateral diplomacy and periodic summit encounters. The Cuban Missile Crisis of 1962 was resolved by fast-moving, behind-the-scenes exchanges, which led to a solution in which neither power lost face. Formal debate in the UN might well have hardened positions. In the end, the Soviets agreed to withdraw only after Kennedy gave a private oral pledge that the United States would never invade Cuba — a promise that, in view of the inflamed feelings of the moment and with elections upcoming, the president could probably not have given in public. The United States and the Soviet Union came to an agreement on the first strategic arms control treaty only after extensive secret bargaining. The first U.S. proposals for normalizing relations with Communist China were all launched covertly, through informal channels. Likewise, secret negotiations facilitated the settlement of such important matters as the Vietnam War, U.S. relinquishment of control of the Panama Canal, and the Iranian hostage crisis. Had any of these negotiations, or the SALT talks, been exposed to full public scrutiny, they very likely would have come under pressure from opposition elements raising the cry of "appeasement."

Democracies are particularly susceptible to partisan second-guessing, which greatly reduces their diplomatic flexibility. If the parties are left alone to haggle, make concessions, and arrive at a quid pro quo, the chances for agreement are much improved. But when domestic interests look on concessions as traitorous, governments become frozen in fixed positions and start making public declarations about not settling for less than their original demands. Or public opinion arouses the expectations of a quick result and stampedes the negotiators into hasty concessions or a dangerous "agreement in principle." With such public pressures, any sense of a negotiating strategy is lost. Lord Salisbury, a noted British statesman, once likened a foreign minister in a democracy to a man playing a card game while a very noisy "helper" stood behind his chair and loudly called out every card he ought to play. Democratic accountability requires that the results of diplomacy be made public, so that the basic commitments of the nation are clear. But prudence argues that the negotiating process should be shielded from excessive publicity, so that professional diplomats can talk candidly and, when necessary, modify their positions with an eye to substance rather than show. Only then is there likely to be a sound and lasting agreement satisfactory to all parties.

From this perspective, the accomplishments of the old-style diplomats at the Congress of Vienna in 1815 look pretty good. The leading states composed their differences and signed an agreement that ushered in nearly a century of peace. Their diplomatic practices, as John Stoessinger has noted, in *The Might of Nations* (pp. 244–53), could serve as the criteria for successful diplomacy today. First, the negotiating powers accepted the existing structure of the international system as legitimate; no state was refused diplomatic recognition or treated as a pariah. Second, each of the participants advanced limited objectives; no state sought ideological aims beyond its power capabilities or attempted to impose through the negotiating process a result that it would not have been able to achieve or enforce by arms. Third, each of the great powers had a reasonably satisfactory and secure relationship with the others. The Vienna settlement did not make anyone absolutely secure and left some claims unsatisfied, but no state harbored such a large grievance that it was tempted to overturn the system rather than seek adjustment within it. Fourth, all the important negotiations took place in private and involved only the ministers and their most trusted aides. Finally, the plenipotentiaries in attendance were allowed great powers of discretion, and so they were able to address all substantive matters and to craft compromises, even on central questions affecting territory, sovereignty, and security.

Such uses of diplomacy have declined in the twentieth century because conditions have changed. The ideological rivalry between the superpowers reduced diplomatic flexibility, and both the United States and the Soviet Union objected to traditional practices of power politics. America's isolationism and Wilson's moral crusade had put U.S. diplomacy largely in the hands of amateurs, and the Bolshevik Revolution had destroyed Russia's diplomatic service, making both nations relative newcomers to balance-of-power diplomacy. Democracy and totalitarianism alike were antipathetic to traditional bargaining strategies and insisted on their ambassadors being strictly accountable to political direction from the home government. The emissaries therefore lacked opportunities to practice the diplomatic arts of persuasion, flexibility in adapting to novel circumstances, quick response to psychological openings or shifts in mood, and adeptness at pressing or conceding as the situation demanded. For reasons of morality or ideology, neither superpower was willing to compromise and neither regarded the other as a legitimate negotiating partner. Both sought to impose universalist claims on an international system that neither could control by force. Many of the Third World states, also newcomers to diplomacy, added their own strident voices and ideological claims to the international melee. The rise of terrorism and the refusal of some states, like Iran, to recognize the principles of diplomatic immunity are indicators of the modern world's fragmentation among actors with differing conceptions of foreign policy, morality, and diplomacy. These violations of the traditional "rules of the game" testify to the strength of existing grievances and to the intensity of the pressures that revolutionary forces have put on the practice of diplomacy.

Still, diplomacy has achieved its greatest successes in the second half of the twentieth century by returning to the time-honored principles of the nineteenth. In the emerging multipolarity of the early 1970s, President Richard Nixon and his secretary of state, Henry Kissinger, championed an updated version of the classical balance of power, and the Nixon Doctrine, formulated on the eve of the American defeat in Vietnam, was a self-conscious attempt to gain order by diplomacy instead of arms. It imagined a world divided into five power centers—the United States, the USSR, Western Europe, China, and Japan. Each would maintain stability in its regional sphere of influence, and all would commit themselves to coexistence in a global power balance reconstructed on a nonideological basis. Coexistence was made feasible through the diplomatic leverage offered by the Sino-Soviet split and the emerging triangular balance between Russia, China, and the United States, as well as by the relatively conservative, revisionist tendencies of the highly bureaucratized Soviet state. Integral to the success of the new balance was the expectation of détente in Soviet-American relations, with the United States trading its recognition of the Soviet Union's great-power status and legitimacy for a Soviet willingness to abandon its ideological pretensions and its active support for Third World revolutions. Arms control (SALT I) would be both the symbolic cement holding the new relationship together and the pragmatic limit to the destabilizing, immoderate arms race between the superpowers.

It was no coincidence that Kissinger, the architect of détente, was a noted scholar of the Congress of Vienna era. He applied the insights of his historical study, *A World Restored,* to guide his pragmatic statesmanship. If, as his studies showed, peace results from a negotiated equilibrium rather than a quest for total victory, then the superpowers ought to exercise joint restraint in their competition in the Third World. The imbroglio in the Middle East could be solved if the United States adopted a more evenhanded policy toward the Arabs and the Israelis. If a stable international order is created by the co-option of potentially revolutionary powers, then the Soviet Union could be pacified by a U.S. recognition of legitimate Soviet interests and offers of trade and credits, which would give the Soviets a stake in the preservation of the existing system. If the best guarantee of peace is a flexible balance of power free of moral or ideological considerations, then the United States could not refuse to deal with China, a potent counterweight to the Soviet Union. Kissinger's pragmatism led to a number of historic arms control agreements and to a fundamental realignment of U.S. alliance relationships, to take advantage of the growing multipolarity and economic interdependence. One criticism of his realpolitik approach was over the question of Jewish emigration from the USSR, an issue on which he sacrificed moral and humanitarian considerations to the strategic requirements of the balance of power. Diplomatic flexibility may be a great virtue, but in exercising it a statesman often must set aside moral absolutes in favor of the expedient act, the lesser evil, or the temporary good. Kissinger was a brilliant diplomat who engineered dramatic short-term successes in U.S. relations with the USSR, China, and the Middle East while protecting American interests in the withdrawal from Vietnam. Although Kissinger fancied himself a kind of Metternich who was inaugurating a new post-Cold War global order, in the end he had to settle for being a Bismarck: in a one-man tour de force, he erected an edifice that was too complex to be sustained by the average statesman and that relied too much on traditional balance-of-power diplomacy, which historical forces had rendered partially obsolete.

NEGOTIATION

Diplomatic bargaining involves appeals to emotion, principle, rational arguments, promises, and rewards; it also involves threats, punishments, and the manipulation of perceptions through flattery, propaganda, and bluff. Negotiations always exhibit tension between the desire to reach agreement and the desire to win. They are a debate, whose aim is to persuade, but they are also a game in which each party tries to coerce or outwit the other. Of course, a state can rarely win objectives at the bargaining table that it could not obtain by force. Although clever diplomacy can sometimes score gains that do not reflect the underlying distribution of power, such agreements tend to be temporary and susceptible to challenge by the power that feels it has been cheated, duped, or outmaneuvered. As Anatol Rapoport has noted, in *Fights, Games, and Debates,* conflict resolution is most often successful when states treat the bargaining as a debate rather than a game. At some point in any successful negotiation, the common interest of the two parties in reaching an agreement must outweigh the desire to win concessions. The issues at stake must also present opportunities for compromise or clarification, so that common ground can be reached. Misunderstandings and suspicions can be dispelled in the course of bargaining, but objective incompatibilities are almost never composed. The Palestinian question, for example, which involves competing claims to the same territory, has long resisted peaceful settlement. But such irreconcilable conflicts are relatively few. States generally prefer to bargain rather than fight.

The negotiating process entails a series of strategy choices, the first of which is whether the negotiations will be *formal* or *tacit* and will be conducted in *public* or in *private*. Public diplomacy has high symbolic value, engenders a strong commitment toward reaching agreement, and increases the credibility of threats, claims, and concessions. Secret diplomacy introduces flexibility and may permit a fuller exploration of the respective positions. The matter of visibility is often the deciding factor between direct formal negotiations and bargaining tacitly or through an intermediary. Summit diplomacy reflects a strategy choice for negotiations at the highest level and with a high degree of public commitment. Bargaining toward an explicit outcome also tends to be more formal and public. Thomas Schelling and Morton Halperin, in *Strategy and Arms Control,* list these five levels: formal treaties with detailed provisions, executive agreements, explicit but informal understandings, tacit understandings, and simple self-restraint consciously contingent on each side's behavior.

A second strategy choice is over *procedural matters.* Who shall participate in the negotiation? Where will it take place? What will be on the agenda? Debate over these preliminaries can be fierce because they deal with prestige and frequently control the outcome of the bargaining. Postwar negotiations over the status of Berlin became embroiled in the procedural question of recognition for the German Democratic Republic (East Germany). In both the Vietnam and Middle East peace talks, one party to the conflict (the Vietcong and the Palestinians) was excluded because its participation might have implied recognition of its legitimacy. Procedural debates have occurred over such details as the shape of the table and who should enter the room first. (At more than one summit encounter, extra doors were installed so that the various heads of state could enter simultaneously.) The location of negotiations is thought to confer a psychological advantage, so neutral sites are frequently picked. The SALT I negotiations alternated between Helsinki and Vienna. The first Reagan-Gorbachev summit took place in Geneva, the second in Reykjavík, Iceland, and then they alternated between Washington and Moscow. The defining of alternatives for discussion is something of an exercise of power, and the Reagan-Gorbachev summits were plagued by disputes over the agenda. The Soviets wanted to restrict the discussion to nuclear arms limitation, but they insisted on the inclusion of Star Wars. The Americans declared Star Wars nonnegotiable, and wanted to link the discussion of arms control to issues of human rights and regional conflicts like Nicaragua and Afghanistan. Sometimes a narrowly defined agenda can facilitate agreement by concentrating the discussion on one essential facet of a subject. If the agenda does not allow room for compromise, however, risks of failure escalate. Widening the agenda to include unrelated items can sometimes make it possible for the sides to trade concessions by balancing a loss in one issue area with a gain in another.

A third choice is the *goals* of the negotiation. Sometimes the purpose is not agreement but delay or propaganda. Negotiations can be a delaying tactic, forestalling the application of severe sanctions while the threatened or weaker party awaits more favorable circumstances. Or they can have the propaganda goals of embarrassing the other party, appealing to world opinion or a third party, promoting one's own position, making oneself appear to be the reasonable party, or simply avoiding the stigma of refusing to negotiate (see Jack Sawyer and Harold Guetzkow, "Bargaining and Negotiation in International Relations"). Negotiations can also serve the purpose of probing an adversary's intentions and will, gathering intelligence, or deceiving the enemy. Sometimes a state enters negotiations and then sabotages them to give it an excuse for military action. As Fred Iklé points out in *How Nations Negotiate*, such nonagreement objectives pervaded negotiations during the Suez crisis of 1956. Following Egypt's nationalization of the Suez Canal, which risked British and French military intervention, U.S. Secretary of State John Foster Dulles urged negotiations on a proposal for international control, although he privately thought there was little likelihood that Egyptian President Gamal Abdel Nasser would agree. Dulles was stalling for time, in the hope that keeping the British and the French focused on a possible peaceful settlement would lead them to reject force. Meanwhile, the leaders in London and Paris, already planning an invasion, decided to bring the issue before the United Nations first so that they would be on record as having attempted to obtain peaceful redress. Similar negotiating deceptions marked the conflict in Vietnam. The French signed an agreement with Ho Chi Minh's Communist forces in 1946 only to buy time until they could install a puppet government in what was then called Cochin China. The United States repeated the maneuver when it signed the Geneva Accords of 1954 and then violated them by recognizing the Ngo Dinh Diem regime in South Vietnam. And the North Vietnamese played the same game. They signed the 1973 Paris Peace Agreement with the sole objective of getting the American forces out and then used the brief respite the peace talks provided to prepare for a full-scale invasion of South Vietnam. The Nazi-Soviet Nonaggression Pact of 1939 and the U.S.-mediated cease-fire agreement of 1946 between the Chinese Communists and the Kuomintang were similar nonsolution agreements, which simply delayed war rather than addressing underlying grievances. Negotiations like these underline the point that bargaining cannot succeed — even when skillful negotiators put their signatures to paper — if the conflicting parties do not want an agreement or are fighting over irreconcilable interests and objectives.

But when there is room for agreement, one of the goals of negotiation can be to alter an adversary's perceptions of the situation. Talks can also be an avenue through which the parties redefine their alternatives or devise new options that offer a payoff to each side. Some goals, such as tariff or arms reductions, cannot be achieved except through joint agreement; a competitive framework discourages the rational actor, choosing independently, from making unilateral reductions. The collective decision dilemma is common in international affairs: in a climate of suspicion, each of two parties chooses a self-protective option, an outcome neither party prefers; however, if a negotiated agreement can be reached, both sides gain. These collaborative, positive-sum solutions are the principal aim of most international bargaining.

A fourth decision is the *means* to be used to secure an agreement. States can choose among such instruments as threats, promises, bluffs, and faits accomplis. Realists frequently argue that states must negotiate from strength and issue credible threats to punish an adversary that refuses to accept a reasonable offer. But such a resort to coercion is costly to both parties and usually signifies that the state's influence is ineffective. States generally do not threaten coercive action unless they think they can successfully implement it — in which case concessions tend to be forthcoming without the threat. Threats mainly arise out of misunderstood intentions, tests of credibility or will, power miscalculations, or conflicts of interest so fundamental as to be nonnegotiable — all conditions under which negotiations are likely to fail. Military force can be useful in deterring an opponent from taking an unwanted action, but negotiations are the typical instrument for persuading the opponent to do something. To use force or the threat of force as the instrument of persuasion is an act of compellence, which is costly and difficult to achieve. Few states will alter their behavior at the dictate of another unless the force is overwhelming and the issue fundamental to the security of the compelling state. Changes of behavior between roughly equal adversaries come about mainly through inducements and compromises.

The most successful negotiations generally proceed without coercive means. They are marked by the development of cooperative strategies that interrupt the dynamic of competition. The offer of concessions is one way of establishing good will, so long as the concessions are met in a reciprocal spirit. When strong conflicts of interest are present, rewards — diplomatic recognition, territorial concessions, arms aid, trade benefits, economic subsidies — can often bring an aggrieved or reluctant state to the point of compromise. Israel's promise to return the Sinai peninsula (Egyptian territory it had occupied since the Yom Kippur War of 1973) was a powerful bargaining lever in gaining Egyptian recognition of Israel in 1978, as were President Jimmy Carter's promises of security guarantees and greatly increased economic aid. Appeals to precedent, to international law, or to other shared principles of legitimacy can also speed agreement. Good negotiators are skilled at putting themselves in the adversary's shoes and appealing to the opponent's values, to make their positions appear sensible and legitimate in the eyes of the bargaining partner.

Negotiators often can combine carrots and sticks in such a way as to make a settlement doubly attractive. One side seeks to increase its bargaining chips and reinforce its credibility while simultaneously altering the opponent's preferences and "utilities" — that is, changing the stakes or the perception of them. Arms control talks between the superpowers have invariably been preceded by arms buildups, giving both sides more chips to bring to the table. Once there, each side has employed a variety of tactics to increase its credibility and convince the opponent it will not retreat — invoking domestic political pressures, alliance obligations, historic precedent, world public opinion, and the like. To show their resolve, statesmen also may publicly proclaim the righteousness of their cause, invoke the national honor, or mount military demonstrations of the state's strength and commitment. Or, if belligerent tactics are judged unwise, the negotiators may stress their basic good will and the limited nature of the state's goals. They can propose face-saving devices and offer avenues of retreat, or they can invoke community values or international law, in the hope of finding common principles of legitimacy. But the latter strategies do not work very well in the face of threats.

Diplomats must generally choose from the beginning between a hard or a soft approach and must calculate how essential an agreement is and how much the state will sacrifice for it. In the last analysis, there can be no agreement without some recognition of common interests and the political will to embrace them, even at a cost to the nation's power or sovereignty. Wise statesmen are willing to bear the costs of accommodation because they also see the costs of nonagreement, like war, an arms race, tariff barriers, or some other of the invisible taxes states pay to maintain their independence of action. A negotiated agreement, however, involves quite visible sacrifices, in the form of pledges, payments, concessions, or restraints, and statesmen cannot negotiate them unless they are also very skilled at negotiating with their domestic political opponents. This is why every major initiative in arms control has been accompanied in the United States by a major public relations campaign and concessions to the Pentagon and other domestic critics. For example, President Kennedy secured the support of the Joint Chiefs of Staff for the atmospheric Test Ban Treaty of 1961 by promising to pursue a vigorous program of underground testing. Key military-industrial constituencies were brought on board in the SALT I negotiations by the promise to exclude MIRV technology, and President Carter, to get support for SALT II, placated the Pentagon by agreeing to deploy the MX missile.

Another means of facilitating agreement is to break the linkage between large and small issues — fractionate the conflict — in order to show good faith and make progress on less contentious matters. This was the strategy of those who advocated U.S.-Soviet arms control negotiations free of any linkage to human rights or Third World problems. It also was Kissinger's approach to the Middle East peace negotiations, in which he followed a step-by-step bilateral diplomacy in trying to build up momentum toward a final settlement between parties that would not get together to negotiate. When direct negotiations fail, agreement can sometimes be reached through third-party arbitration, adjudication in international courts, a multilateral conference, or appeal to an international organization. Occasionally, negotiations are indirect, conducted by means of a tacit diplomacy in which one side's limited concession is matched by a reciprocal concession from the other. Though no formal agreement may be struck, the posture of restraint and the repetition of constructive acts build mutual confidence — a kind of gamesmanship that creates a positive feedback mechanism. Charles Osgood's *An Alternative to War or Surrender* calls this tacit bargaining strategy "true GRIT" (Graduated Reciprocal Initiatives in Tension-Reduction).

Other bargaining tactics employ bluff and the fait accompli. Bluffing is a highly risky maneuver, and costly if the bluff is called. Hitler managed it in his remilitarization of the Rhineland in 1936, when, in direct violation of the

Treaty of Versailles, he occupied the region and threatened war, although his generals had orders to retreat if fired upon. This success added greatly to Hitler's reputation and the credibility of his later threats. However, when Khrushchev tried the same kind of bluffing tactics in Berlin and Cuba, his humiliating diplomatic failures lost him support within the Soviet political elite, and he eventually was removed because of his "harebrained scheming." A common negotiating tactic involving a degree of bluff is the claim that "our hands are tied." Publicly commiting onself to an action or threatening that it is irreversible can convince an adversary that it has no choice but to comply. While burning one's bridges in this way can add greatly to the credibility of a threat, it can also lead a state into taking an undesired action simply to protect its image of firmness. A reputation for honesty and fidelity is very important to a state in preserving its bargaining power, but that reputation is best protected over the long run by the avoidance of bluffs. Another way to secure a bargaining advantage is to present the adversary with a fait accompli, as Khrushchev attempted to do with his secret placement of missiles in Cuba. In essence, this is a preemptive strategy designed to limit the options open for discussion.

Negotiations are typically plagued by a variety of communication problems. Information about an adversary may be incomplete or incorrect. In arms negotiations, accurate estimates of military strength are crucial, yet one or both sides may choose to conceal the true state of their defenses. Efforts to collect information tend to be viewed as espionage; efforts to provide information are considered propaganda. If misperceptions have been an important contributor to a conflict, they also will be an obstacle to its resolution by negotiation. For example, Khrushchev's famous statement "we will bury you" — a literal rendering of the Russian — was interpreted in the West to mean "we will destroy you," rather than being taken in the boastful sense that "we will outlive you" (that is, history favors the triumph of socialism over capitalism). The problem of communication is especially knotty in the matter of interpreting treaty terms. Manipulation of language and images is central to the bargaining process, and compromise can often be reached only by making the language of a treaty purposely vague. Yet effective compliance requires that the language be precise. This is what lies behind much of the diplomatic wrangling over the most minute and seemingly inconsequential matters. As former Secretary of State George Shultz has said: "The devil is in the details." The ambiguous definition of democracy in the Yalta accords engendered strong disagreements about the fairness of the postwar elections in Soviet-occupied Eastern Europe. Differences of interpretation led the Egyptians to feel betrayed when Israel began building new settlements in the occupied territories — something that Egypt thought had been outlawed in the 1978 Camp David accords. The Soviets cried foul when the Reagan administration "reinterpreted" the Anti-Ballistic Missile Treaty as permitting the testing and deployment of Star Wars weaponry, and even the U.S. Senate, in its debate on the matter, could not agree on the meaning of the treaty language.

Diplomacy sometimes involves communication by deeds as well as documents. States may try to signal their credibility or concern by a military mobilization or by some such symbolic act as President Kennedy's trip to Berlin in the midst of the 1961 crisis. These actions may speak louder than words, but they are hard to deny or undo and are not always self-interpreting. What one side intends as an act of firmness may seem to the other like an act of aggression. A signal designed to give a strong, clear message to an adversary may be misinterpreted by a neutral party or by the political opposition at home. One example of a misinterpreted message was President Nixon's order for the invasion of Cambodia at the same time as he was trying to launch peace talks with the North Vietnamese. The invasion was aimed at solving an acute military problem — the sanctuary that neutral Cambodia was offering to the Vietcong — but undoubtedly Nixon also thought that the invasion would communicate America's resolve to the North Vietnamese and strengthen its negotiating position in the upcoming talks. However, an unforeseen consequence of the invasion was to tarnish Nixon's political image among antiwar critics at home and to alienate many European allies. The intended message had been diluted, for lack of a direct channel and an explicit statement. On the other hand, signals that are subtle enough to avoid such political repercussions can easily be lost in the "noise" of the random or unrelated daily occurrences of the complex international arena. Often there is no substitute for direct, face-to-face talks that conclude with a specific, unambiguous agreement.

Finally, negotiations are very much affected by *background factors* that are out of the parties' control, like a crisis or the climate of public opinion. A crisis can arouse nationalist sentiments that are impervious to reason, and no negotiator wants to appear to be making concessions under pressure. Timing also is critical; a proposal that seems sensible at one moment in history might be nonnegotiable the next. Public opinion inclines toward simple alternatives and is difficult to change once it has been aroused; this has the effect of narrowing the range of options that can be considered, even though the negotiators themselves may wish to formulate new alternatives. For example, the informal bargain struck during the famous "walk in the woods" at the INF talks in Vienna in 1982 was subsequently repudiated by both the Soviet and the U.S. governments largely for political reasons unrelated to the worthiness of the proposal.

Personalities and *negotiating styles* also are significant. Individuals can affect outcomes, independent of merit, because of such idiosyncracies as laziness, a belligerent or a paranoid personality, absence from sessions or social functions, personal affection for or dislike of another negotiator, vanity, deafness, ill health, or poor command of a foreign language. The negotiating team's style is influenced by the national character. The Soviet and American styles contrast markedly. As George Kennan has noted, in *American Diplomacy, 1900–1950,* American diplomats, many of them trained in the law, often resort to legalistic practices and, following American business customs, bargain in the expectation that give-and-take and compromise are the norm. This has resulted in an impatient search for agreement for its own sake, with the emphasis on verbal compromises and statements of principle that often sidestep concrete political interests or the underlying power realities. Soviet negotiators are constrained by the need to consult with party authorities at home and are less inclined to think that good will can be translated into shared interests between ideologically incompatible states. They are reluctant to accept suggestions for compromise from opposing delegations, which are by definition ideologically tainted. In the past, rigid Soviet positions have made Western diplomats skeptical about the Kremlin's motivations: are the Soviets seeking mutual accommodation, or are they carrying on their subversive struggle against capitalism in a different forum? The cautious realism of the Reagan years and the forthrightness of Gorbachev's *glasnost* have helped to narrow the national differences, but they must still be taken into account in the dynamic of the negotiating process.

INTELLIGENCE, PROPAGANDA, AND SUBVERSION

Not all diplomacy is conducted through official, accepted channels. Spying, propaganda, and subversion have become routine means of achieving a national goal apart from formal negotiations. As state boundaries have become more permeable and transparent, formal interstate relations are increasingly accompanied by information gathering and acts of manipulation within other nations. Because domestic political pressures heavily influence every state's foreign policy, it is advantageous for a state to keep itself informed about the internal politics of others and to do what it can to ensure sympathetic leadership and a favorable climate of opinion in an adversary.

A major task for the professional diplomat today is to collect and interpret information about the assets and intentions of other states. The rapid pace of technological change can alter a nation's economic or war-making potential in a matter of months. The acquisition of advanced weaponry can quickly promote a minor power to dominant status in a regional balance of power. A technological breakthrough for one of the superpowers raises the fear that it might launch a surprise attack. The discovery of oil or a crop failure can alter world market conditions dramatically. An impending nationalization of foreign assets can threaten access to a vital raw material. Events like these must be carefully monitored for their potential impact on a nation's foreign policy.

Advanced societies, whose political, economic, and military activities entail the transmission of vast amounts of information, are especially vulnerable to electronic intelligence gathering. In the United States, 70 percent of all domestic telecommunications and 60 percent of all information sent abroad are transmitted via satellites or microwave towers and are easily intercepted by electronic eavesdropping methods. Advanced intelligence techniques like sonar and seismic monitors, high-resolution optics, infrared sensing equipment, and various reconnaissance measures are among other technical means of gathering information. Satellites, high-flying spy planes, and ground stations just outside another country's borders make it possible to gather very sophisticated intelligence even from a closed society like the Soviet Union. Computers have become a valuable tool for processing, sorting, assembling, and interpreting the vast quantities of material. A nation also may place hidden microphones, or bugs, in foreign embassies to eavesdrop on face-to-face conversations. And the new intelligence capabilities have led to the increased use of encrypted messages, jamming, and other countermeasures to protect the security of communications.

Human intelligence gathering is still important—often performed by spies posted abroad under the diplomatic cover of the foreign service. It has been estimated that roughly a third of the 2100 Soviet bloc diplomats stationed in the United States actually are engaged in covert intelligence, and the United States routinely stations intelligence officers abroad in the same manner. Although spying can give access to facilities or top decision-making circles that could not be penetrated in any other way, it is dangerous work and only rarely yields dramatic results. There is also the risk of spies becoming double agents or unwittingly being fed disinformation. For all the glamour of spying as depicted in novels, the vast share of intelligence activity takes place in the open and deals with information from public sources. Systematic monitoring of a country's print and broadcast media can provide a highly accurate profile of a society and of the thinking of its political leadership. For every field operative abroad, there are nine back home reading the foreign press, receiving routine information, analyzing political changes, and making policy recommendations.

In the United States, intelligence tasks are principally in the hands of the National Security Agency (NSA) and the CIA. The NSA has a staff of about 50,000 civilians, augmented by about 100,000 U.S. servicemen and women around the world who supply it with information. It has an annual budget of about $4 billion. The CIA employs about 15,000 people and spends in excess of $2 billion a year. (The exact figure is secret, since a large slice of the budget goes into covert activities.) Other important agencies are the National Reconnaissance Office (which manages satellite intelligence programs), the Defense Intelligence Agency, the State Department's Bureau of Intelligence and Research, and the intelligence arms of the military services. The U.S. intelligence community as a whole employs at least 150,000 and spends more than $8 billion annually. In the Soviet Union, internal security and foreign intelligence are both managed by the Committee for State Security—better known by its Russian initials of KGB. The KGB's budget is estimated at about $2 billion annually, and it employs close to a million in carrying out a wide variety of functions. A second important body, the Chief Intelligence Directorate of the General Staff (known as the GRU), specializes in military intelligence.

Propaganda has come to play a large role in diplomacy, as the result of the intense Soviet-American ideological rivalry and the tendency to conduct modern diplomacy in ever more public and multilateral forums. It is a relatively recent outgrowth of mass politics, popular (if not always democratic) standards of legitimacy, and global media networks, which have given rise to a potent world public opinion. The public reputation and credibility of a nation have become a sensitive barometer of its international power, supplanting pure military preponderance. Despite the pejorative connotation of the word, propaganda in one form or another is used by every nation to project a favorable image abroad. The United States easily spends $1 billion a year on propaganda, and the Soviet Union probably five times that. Propaganda can be nothing but lies and distortions, but more often it is a selective rendering of the facts packaged in such a way as to appeal to the desired target audience. Allies and domestic public opinion are frequently the targets since propaganda is more effective with groups that are already favorably inclined.

Propagandists are skilled at manipulating media events and telling half-truths to their side's advantage. Soviet leaders, for example, in responding to a letter from an American schoolgirl, Samantha Smith, took her on a "peace tour" that painted a favorable image of their country. American propagandists tried to discredit various peace movements by depicting them as Communist fronts, because a few prominent Communists had endorsed their goals. The defense departments of both countries have published slick-cover military assessments of the enemy filled with hyperbole, color graphics (arrows signifying lines of attack slash across the world map), and artists' renderings of the latest dread technology. They do not so much lie as exaggerate, omit, and extrapolate, following the rules of effective advertising — simple, active, repetitive images that are plausible and emotionally charged in a way that will generate the desired response.

At its worst, propaganda can be self-deluding and an impediment to an accurate appraisal. America's World War II propaganda about "Uncle Joe" Stalin and its public relations hype over détente both aroused unrealistic optimism among Americans about the prospects for U.S.-Soviet friendship, and when tensions reemerged the American public was disillusioned and bitter. Cold War propaganda had the same kind of impact, in the opposite direction, through its exaggeration of the negatives — the evil nature of the enemy and differences that were irreconcilable. Systematic distortions of the Soviet threat have led to a series of false alarms and alleged arms race "gaps": the bomber gap, the missile gap, the spending gap, the window of missile vulnerability, the Star Wars gap, the chemical-bacteriological weapons threat, and many others. Long-standing propaganda distortions, suspicions, and misperceptions became determining factors in the arms race and in arms control negotiations. American political leaders who have sought friendlier relations with the Soviets have had to deal with strong public resistance at home — frequently a mindless anti-Communism they themselves had done much to create. One unfortunate dimension of the manipulation of public opinion is that a state begins to believe its own propaganda. In 1985, Vladimir Lomeiko, chief of the Soviet foreign ministry's press department, publicly accused human rights advocates in the West of being "slave traders" running "big-capital networks of houses of prostitution" where they "debauch young girls of developing countries," and he also claimed that Jews had difficulty leaving the United States, but not the Soviet Union. These irrational comments spilled out, with apparent spontaneity, during an emotion-filled moment at a press conference on Soviet compliance with the Helsinki accords.

Still, hypocrisy is the homage that the devil pays to virtue. So long as a state publicly espouses noble causes, there is hope that it can be pressured into making its foreign policy conduct consistent with its official statements. If the new Soviet government signs human rights declarations, writes a new constitution containing a full panoply of democratic guarantees, and proclaims itself in favor of freedom, equality, and social justice, there is hope that the transformation is real. After all, the enlightenment ideals embodied in the Declaration of Independence ("all men are created equal") eventually subverted the slaveholding beliefs of those signers. Words do have power, not only to deceive but to uplift.

The greatest danger of propaganda is the cynicism it breeds in those who manufacture it. Soviet society before Gorbachev was notorious for a kind of Orwellian doublethink in which there was an official version and the real version. Everyone knew the difference, but the agitprop officials and the consumers of the party line both agreed to carry on the charade. In democratic societies, propaganda is more subtle but no less invidious. Any gap between domestic standards of truth telling and Machiavellian diplomatic behavior brings the temptation to cloak foreign policy in convenient fictions. Several U.S. presidents suffered from a credibility gap over their conduct of the Vietnam War because it was reported to the American public, in the glowing camouflage of official lies, as a fight to save "democracy" in South Vietnam. Rather than giving the public a straightforward rationale for the war based on America's great-power role, the United States was seeking to legitimize its intervention under the halo of a selfless ideal, a civilizing mission. The British and the French had justified their imperialism in substantially the same terms.

The more the public comes to realize that it cannot always count on hearing the truth from public officials, the more disillusioned it becomes. This breeds a vicious cycle of propaganda and cynicism in which a government keeps producing more and more propaganda to mobilize the consensus it needs to make a democratic foreign policy function. Just as covert operations have frequently slipped over the line into investigations and harassment of domestic critics, so propaganda designed to mislead the enemy can slip over the line and hide the truth from a nation's own citizens. Propaganda is not just a device for convincing the world; it is also a way of hiding the truth from ourselves. We play with words: an invasion or act of aggression is an "incursion," a "rescue mission," or a "protective reaction." Multimegaton nuclear attacks, because they employ a few hundred missiles instead of tens of thousands, are described as "countervailing," "surgical," or "limited" — a kind of antiseptic or deceitful language that glosses over the fact that the strategists are talking about millions of deaths. The pervasive use of propaganda raises fundamental questions for a democracy. Is a nation's reputation better protected by disinformation and fabrications (at the risk of hypocrisy) or by truth telling (at the risk of exposing its mistakes)? Does truth telling have any real power in international affairs, or do we get better results by telling strategic lies in a professional manner?

A similar dilemma attaches to covert operations of penetration and subversion. Payments to political parties, subsidies to the opposition press, bribes to induce unions to strike, arms and logistical support, intelligence information that abets a military coup — these are but a few of the ways in which one nation can covertly influence the domestic politics of an adversary. Corrupt and unstable Third World governments are particularly susceptible to such penetration. Both superpowers have actively supported insurgencies against governments they found undesirable, and assassinations and other forms of state-sponsored terrorism have become more common tactics. Even democratic societies have come to defend their interests by these questionable clandestine means, but they do so at considerable risk to the integrity of their principles and the accountability of the foreign policy process.

ELEMENTS OF AN EFFECTIVE DIPLOMACY

The frequency of international conflict might lead us to believe that modern diplomacy has failed. But much of the problem lies in the growing incompatibility of beliefs, attitudes, and goals, not in the failure of the diplomatic process. The gravest lapses of diplomacy have been those occasions when ideological animosity caused a state to sever relations with another. United States foreign policy has been particularly hampered by the tendency to treat revolutionary regimes as international outlaws. Unfortunately, such differences are only made more rigid by the refusal of the governments to communicate. The United States' nonrecognition of Cuba, Vietnam, the Soviet Union (from 1919 to 1933), and Communist China (from 1949 to 1972) has stood in the way of improved relations without having any effect on the principles these states espouse. Today, when authoritative information about all the major actors is essential if a state is to protect its own interests, diplomatic recognition is a matter of common sense rather than moral approval.

Some commentators say diplomacy has declined because of the growing hardships (and diminished attractions) of a diplomatic career. Many diplomatic personnel also lack the requisite experience and training. The United States often employs political appointees as ambassadors, instead of those with professional training. President Nixon appointed Walter Annenberg, the publisher of *TV Guide*, as U.S. ambassador to the Court of St. James (Great Britain), and President Reagan appointed John Gavin, a movie star of Hispanic heritage, as ambassador to Mexico. About 50 percent of Reagan's ambassadorial choices were political appointees with no professional diplomatic training. On many occasions, such appointees, particularly when they do not speak the language of the host country, have contributed to miscommunication and the perpetuation of the "ugly American" stereotype. Sometimes the State Department bypasses ambassadors who are incompetent political apppointees, and at other times ambassadors who are career officers are cut out of the decision loop because the policy is politically sensitive and the president does not trust them to carry it out. Or the president, the national security adviser, and the secretary of state may all agree to bypass the formal channels in order to make a covert operation "deniable" or to free a diplomatic initiative from potentially deadening red tape.

The failure to use professional diplomacy in a timely way is dramatically illustrated by an episode in U.S.-Chinese relations that the historian Barbara Tuchman has recounted in "If Mao Had Come to Washington in 1945." In 1945, four years before they rose to national power in China, the Communist leaders Mao Tse-tung and Chou En-lai offered to come to Washington to meet in person with President Franklin D. Roosevelt and establish a working relationship with the United States. However, communication failures, diplomatic bungling, and political pressures all conspired to prevent the United States from responding to the offer. At the time, America's China policy was based on an unrealistic view of the internal situation and an overestimation of America's ability to shape events. The American ambassador, Patrick Hurley, was a vain, ambitious political appointee who knew nothing about the history or nature of the Chinese civil war. (He once made the remarkably ill-informed statement that "there is very little difference, if any, between the avowed principles of the Kuomintang and the Communists; both are striving for democratic principles.") He refused to call on the considerable expertise of an experienced diplomatic staff; instead, he tended to improvise amateurishly on the spot, displaying a typical American businessman's naive confidence in his own powers of negotiation and personal persuasion. He was unwilling to concede that some international problems might not have a single and achievable solution.

Roosevelt was preoccupied with preparations for the Yalta Conference. Strongly influenced by the political atmosphere and diplomatic concerns of the moment, he viewed the situation strictly in terms of what would bring the Chinese into the fight against Japan; immediate matters erased any consideration of long-term interests. Roosevelt also thought, incorrectly, that the Soviets, with whom he was planning to negotiate a deal at Yalta, could control the Chinese Communists. And stereotyped thinking led to American misperceptions about the relative strength of the two Chinese factions. The Nationalist leader, Chiang Kai-shek, was regarded as a "Christian patriot," but the Communist leadership suffered from the typical stereotypes about revolutionary fanaticism. Roosevelt could not believe that these ideological zealots were interested in a rapprochement with the United States. Political leaders, like everyone else, tend to see or hear only what conforms to their expectations. When professional diplomats suggested that the United States respond positively to the Maoist initiative, Ambassador Hurley vigorously attacked the "Communist subversives" in the State Department.

It was the first note in what was to become a cacophony of accusations of Communist influence in the era of Joseph McCarthy. Anti-Communist undercurrents in American public opinion were clearly among the political pressures that caused Roosevelt to dismiss any consideration of cooperation with the emerging Communist Chinese regime. In retrospect, it was a costly lapse in diplomacy. Another course might have changed the whole history of events in Asia, including wars in Korea and Vietnam. The mishandling is a case study in the obstacles to effective diplomacy.

Policy makers can avoid such fiascos by following a few rules of good diplomacy (see Morgenthau, *Politics Among Nations,* pp. 576–94): (1) It is important for government to be realistic and adopt goals that match the state's power resources. Rather than being formalistically defined in terms of abstract principles, the goals should be tailored to historical circumstances, power realities, and specific objectives that will confer a substantive advantage. (2) A government must be well informed, and have an understanding of the other side. In particular, stereotyped thinking and preconceived attitudes should not impair its thinking and prevent all options from receiving serious consideration. (3) It must give attention to long-term national interests and not become a prisoner of current alliance ties, immediate political pressures, or short-term crises. (4) Negotiations should be in the hands of professionals, who can protect the nation's policy against ignorance, amateurism, the quirks or whims of personality, and the tendency to negotiate without reference to an overarching strategy or a clear-sighted, dispassionate evaluation of risks and opportunities. (5) The nation should avoid taking rigid positions and be willing to compromise on all nonvital issues. Good diplomacy's aim is peace, and it always must be conducted in relative terms, with one objective weighed against another in a calculation of political risks and costs. Conflict in one area should not rule out the search for common interests in another. (6) Above all, diplomacy should avoid dogmatism or crusading. An attitude of moral superiority must not interfere with the state's ability to remain flexible and negotiate effectively with all parties. Since the essence of diplomacy is a fluid adjustment to changing realities, a nation should never get itself into a position from which it cannot retreat without loss of face or from which it cannot advance without grave risk. A wise diplomacy will have the foresight to anticipate entirely novel circumstances and the moral courage to terminate mistakes and abandon a failed policy. Theodore Sorenson, in "Superpower Symmetry," suggests that political leaders can pursue a successful diplomacy if they are "able to take the long view, to acknowledge error, to prevent the perfect from driving out the good, to narrow the gap between the desirable and the possible, to bargain, to compromise, to defer and occasionally to take 'yes' for an answer."

THE SOURCES OF INTERNATIONAL LAW

One instrument of diplomacy and conflict resolution that is available not only to states but to other political actors is international law. Its origins go back to the Roman Empire's *jus gentium,* or "law of the peoples," the body of law that governed relations among the conquered peoples and the citizens of the empire. It was a compilation of common ideas of justice found in the laws and customs of all the peoples encompassed by Roman rule, and its principles of equity and right were considered universally applicable, making the code adaptable to a wide range of circumstances and changing conditions. The natural law of medieval times added another component to international law, carrying forward the Greek notion of *jus naturale,* or principles of right reason. To the norms of conduct deduced from the rational and social side of human nature, the medieval Christian philosophers added universal moral standards. Jurists of the early modern age — such as Hugo Grotius, in his key work, *On the Law of War and Peace* — identified a body of customary law, treaties, and legal rules that governed relations between the sovereign states of Europe. Their more positivist orientation, which deemphasized natural, universal, or divine principles, stressed the creation of a set of mutually agreed upon rules establishing the fundamental rights and obligations of states. If all these schools of thought could be united under a single legal principle, it might be the one framed by Montesquieu in 1748 and offered to Napoleon by Talleyrand in 1806: "that nations ought to do to one another in peace, the most good, and in war, the least evil possible" (cited in Mark W. Janis, *An Introduction to International Law,* p. 2).

The most important segment to survive from Christian thought was the just war tradition. The early church fathers, trying to identify the conditions under which it would be morally permissible to take up arms, held that a war was just if it restrained or corrected the wrongdoing of others on behalf of the public good. Ralph Potter, Jr., in "The Moral Logic of War," lists the following examples of just causes: (1) the protection of innocents from unjustified attack; (2) the restoration of rights wrongfully denied; (3) the reestablishment of civil order necessary for a decent human existence. The early just-war theorists also attached moral conditions to the conduct of a war, lest the violence spiral out of control and defeat the just end it was seeking. Their rules of warfare, aimed at limiting the violence to what was necessary and effective, included, first, a rule of proportionality — the good to be accomplished must exceed the harm a war would do. Second, the intentions must be just, with no motives of vengeance, hatred, cruelty, greed, or hysteria. Third, war must be the last resort, after every peaceable means of redress had been exhausted. Fourth, wars must be conducted by lawful authorities to assure that they were politically purposeful and subject to clear procedures and responsibilities, rather than the result of arbitrary personal rule or vigilante justice. Fifth, there should be a clear public declaration of the causes and aims of the war, to let the enemy know what conditions of settlement could avoid the war, and to let potential allies judge for themselves the justice of the cause. A sixth rule was that there must be a reasonable hope of success. Finally, just means must be employed both in combat and in conquest. Noncombatants must be protected from indiscriminate violence, and human life, including that of the enemy, must be respected. A state should employ the least amount of force necessary for restraining the adversary or restoring order.

But warring states began to deviate significantly from this rather elaborate codification, as the moral consensus of medieval Christendom broke down. In the brawling secular atmosphere of the Italian city-state, Niccolò Machiavelli enunciated rules of statecraft that relied little on common morality or natural law. With papal authority declining, Protestant and Catholic monarchs turned to warring with one another in the name of religion, and no common rules arbitrated these conflicts. It took the bloody, frenzied lawlessness of the Thirty Years' War (1618–48) to inspire Grotius, the "father" of international law, to articulate his famous principles of conduct, which drew equally on ancient custom (the *jus gentium*) and on natural law (self-evident rules of "right reason"). The secular code that he elaborated in *De jure belli ac pacis (On the Law of War and Peace)* came to be accepted as the standard among all the newly sovereign states then arising in Europe.

Political and economic conditions made such a code necessary. The rapid expansion and consolidation of the European states had created many legal problems regarding territorial control, treatment of foreigners, restraints on trade, and freedom of navigation. International law early established the rights and privileges of diplomatic agents operating in territories outside the control of their sovereign. Rules also evolved to deal with foreign nationals residing in another state and with the encounters of ships of different sovereignty on the high seas. International law regulated the validity of titles to territories and defined the conditions under which treaties came into effect or were terminated. Sovereign states, which could not exercise the same authority abroad that they did at home, thus acquired a stable and predictable (which is to say, peaceful and lawful) means of adjusting their interests on a reciprocal basis.

Modern international law, because it came into being at a time of preoccupation with the rights and duties of states, paid little attention to the rights of individuals. States made some provision for the protection of their citizens' rights and property when outside home jurisdiction, but the principal accent was on rules of sovereignty relating to territorial rights and state prerogatives. However, diplomats and consular personnel, along with their property and official papers, were declared immune to seizure and entitled to safe transit through third countries. There were also laws covering neutral and belligerent status, wartime treatment of civilians and prisoners of war, and the use of certain types of weapons.

In the twentieth century, as emphasis has shifted from rules of warfare to conditions of collective security, international law has codified peacekeeping responsibilities, has defined the rights, duties, and privileges of international organizations, and has established arbitration mechanisms. With the growth of global trade, rules of commerce and communication have expanded and a large body of law has sprung up that regulates coastlines, territorial waters, international straits, rights of passage on the high seas, and exploitation of fisheries, seabed minerals, and other ocean resources. More recently, with the Antarctic Treaty of 1959 and the Outer Space Treaty of 1967, the protection of international law has been extended to domains outside the realm of national sovereignty. Through the United Nations, universal human rights also are slowly coming to be recognized, although at the cost of some tension over the traditional claims of state sovereignty.

The content of international law today is quite diverse in its origins. The body of rules that almost all states accept as legally binding derives from five main sources, as outlined in Article 38 of the International Court of Justice Statute of the UN Charter: (1) international treaties and conventions whose rules are expressly recognized by the signatory states; (2) international custom, or the universal practices that all states accept as lawful; (3) general principles of law recognized by civilized nations; (4) the judicial decisions of national and international tribunals; and (5) the writings of legal scholars and qualified publicists.

Treaties, the most important element of international law, have an authority that is unambiguously recognized by all signatories. Consequently, much effort has been expended on devising multilateral pacts that set out universally accepted norms and obligations. The Covenant of the League of Nations and the UN Charter are the preeminent examples of such treaty law. But there are hundreds of other multilateral conventions, such as the Hague Convention for the Pacific Settlement of International Disputes (Hague Arbitration Convention, 1899), the Treaty Providing for the Renunciation of War as an Instrument of National Policy (Kellogg-Briand Pact, 1928), the General Agreement on Tariffs and Trade (GATT, 1947), the Vienna Convention on Diplomatic Relations (1961), the Biological Weapons Convention (1972), and the UN Convention on the Law of the Sea (UNCLOS, 1982), to name only a few. They have succeeded best in specialized nonpolitical spheres, in which technical or economic cooperation is essential. On human rights, laws of war, and arms restraints, neither the League of Nations nor the UN has been able to establish a body of law enjoying universal acceptance. Key conventions lack the signatures of one or another great power; the International Court of Justice is not used frequently enough nor are its rulings universally recognized; peacekeeping functions have repeatedly failed; and many international bodies fall short of a universal membership.

Treaty law also includes numerous bilateral treaties, as the growing volume and complexity of foreign interactions have led many governments to formalize their dealings with both allies and adversaries. The Anti-Ballistic Missile and SALT treaties of 1972 were attempts by the United States and the USSR to control the arms race by the imposition of stabilizing mutual legal restraints. The increasing regulation of interstate relations by treaty is apparent in Great Britain's official compendium of its treaties, which grew from 190 pages in 1892 to over 2,500 pages in 1960. Bilateral agreements are themselves regulated by a treaty on treaties — the Vienna Convention on the Law of Treaties of 1969. It codifies the custom of *pacta sunt servanda,* the stipulation that once a state has become a party to a treaty, it shall honor the commitment until such time as the treaty is legally terminated. This can be through various escape clauses or notification procedures built into the original treaty or through appeal to the general principle of *rebus sic stantibus,* which permits withdrawal from a treaty if conditions have changed so radically that it is impossible for a signatory to honor the original terms. Official repudiation of treaties is rare. More often, they are made moot by conflicting interpretations or mutual noncompliance, which occur when the wording is vague, judicial precedents are unclear, the treaties are at variance with domestic law or tradition, or national interests are in open conflict.

Custom, the second main source of international law, embodies longstanding practices of mutual convenience that have acquired legal status. For example, since the seventeenth century states have recognized a three-mile limit on a state's territorial waters — the range of a cannon fired from shore. Customary observance has given this the status of law, although technology has long since made the reason for the limit obsolete. Such rules were unwritten, but states became bound by habit and, having repeatedly observed a particular rule or invoked it for their advantage, they could not lightly discard it. Rules of custom may be the single most reliable element of international law. They are accepted by the international community at large and are uniformly practiced, which gives them validity. Customary law provides a basis for regulating the conduct of states in the absence of special agreements and defines the procedures by which treaties, codes, and more specific rules of international law are made, interpreted, validated or invalidated, and terminated.

When custom or treaty provide no guidance, states can arbitrate their differences by reference to common principles of equity, reason, and logic. Professionals in international law play a prominent role in creating such a consensus. As Terry Nardin writes, in *Law, Morality, and the Relations of States:*

> Although customary international law is a distillation of state practice, the interpretation of what constitutes state practice belongs to a community of professional interpreters whose judgments, if unofficial, are nevertheless extremely influential. To a significant extent international law exists in the practice of states because it exists as an idea in the minds of a class of legal professionals, and because what these professionals understand to be international law is accepted by others. (p. 173)

These professionals invoke UN resolutions, precedents, judicial findings, and arguments by analogy from common principles of domestic law to give authority to international law when express or tacit consent to a written or customary code is lacking.

In sheer numbers of disputes settled, domestic courts and national administrative decisions are the most important interpreters and enforcers of international law. This is particularly true of private international law, which governs individuals and corporations, as opposed to public international law, which concerns the legal relations of states. Indeed, actions within domestic jurisdictions defined the whole content of international judicature for some 250 years, before there existed a Hague Tribunal or a World Court. Although the rulings vary from country to country and hence frustrate the development of entirely uniform principles, these domestic instruments are one of the main avenues for interpreting international law to meet particular situations.

When the opinions of statesmen, legal commentators, and national courts and officials converge — and this happens more often than not — international law is created and its binding power confirmed. Although enforcement is largely a matter of choice, the society of states nonetheless has passed beyond legal anarchy. Acts of reciprocity, comity, judicial deference, and custom have proved able to generate conformity and to extend judgments in particular cases into general legal opinion applicable to the international community.

CONFLICTING PERSPECTIVES ON INTERNATIONAL LAW

The Idealist Approach

The wide range of opinion on the status and utility of international law may be grouped, for simplification, into two perspectives roughly representing the idealist and the realist approaches. The idealist most often embraces the *naturalist* theory, which sees law as rooted in a divinely ordained social order and in universal norms of human conduct drawn from natural laws. The dictates of religion, nature, and custom converge in a kind of higher law, of which the actual laws of nations are a crude approximation. All peoples share a common standard of justice, which is progressively revealed in the unfolding events of history through the common faculty of reason. As the Nuremberg War Crimes Tribunal argued, national policy makers are accountable to these standards of civilized conduct, no matter what political pressures or ideological fictions a state may attempt to superimpose.

The idealist is also typically a *monist,* for whom domestic and international law are but different aspects of a single system of justice. International law therefore ought properly to take precedence over domestic laws and over any claims of sovereignty that might invalidate it. The idealist sees human rights as an important part of the international domain, whose laws must be observed by all nations, regardless of the nature of the regime or the content of its domestic law. National sovereignty does not exempt the South Africans or the Soviets from the obligation to respect universal standards of human dignity. Similarly, idealists often oppose nuclear weapons, chemical-bacteriological warfare, the use of torture, and capital punishment, believing them indiscriminate, cruel, and inhumane instruments of state policy, which should be forbidden everywhere.

To the idealist, international law is a necessary instrument for managing a world order that transcends the territorial bases of the traditional state system. Such international entities as the European Community, multinational corporations, and certain international oranizations possess supranational powers that cannot be regulated except on a consensual, transnational basis. For the idealist, the state is not the sole subject of international law or the protection of sovereignty its sole aim. It must recognize the interests of the global "commons" and the individual as well. The UN Convention on the Law of the Sea is but one legal manifestation of a common interest, as the early rules of navigation were a response to the intrusion of state interests on the high seas. As commerce has spread and communications have made the planet more interdependent, there has sprung up a rational need for international regulation. The unintended consequences of selfish, sovereign state actions — pollution, resource depletion, climate alteration — place an obligation on states to create an international regime that can legislate on and manage their joint problems. As with human rights, these rights of the community are obligations that fall on all states by virtue of the common human condition, not from any sovereign consent. Whether states enter into formal treaty agreements or not, they are bound by these higher laws, which make up the universal core of international law. No one can escape the claims of conscience, reason, and morality or the functional requirements for global cooperation by pretending they do not exist.

According to the idealist, systems of law are more than explicit rules backed by the promise of coercion. They are, in the words of William Coplin's "Law and International Politics," "authoritative . . . modes of communicating or reflecting the ideals and purposes, the acceptable roles and actions, as well as the very processes of the societies" (p. 616). International law affects the perceptions and behavior of states and individuals by presenting an image of world order, by prescribing procedures for the peaceful resolution of conflict, by demanding reasons for state actions, by socializing states under community norms, and by sensitizing states to the requisites of international order. The power of this law lies in the moral authority of the community of states, in the customs it observes, in the self-evident reasonableness of international standards of conduct, and in the expectation of reciprocity (that a state will grant to others the same rights it claims for itself). These are the reasons states and their citizens generally obey the law, even without enforcement procedures or coercive sanctions. International law represents a higher set of norms to which states will gradually accommodate their long-term behavior, despite repeated temptations to lawlessness. The impulse to law-abidingness is a natural product of the search for order among states, which, in our modern economy and international society, tends toward an ever higher degree of self-regulation and mutual cooperation.

The Realist Approach

The realist tends to take a *positivist* approach to international law, generally viewing it as limited in scope and importance (though some positivists oppose this realist conception). Norms of international behavior are set by specific agreement between states; there is no natural justice or universal morality, nor are there any innate qualities of human order waiting to be discovered. No legal obligations exist in international affairs save those that states formally ratify, and no guidelines beyond the actual behavior of states. No power — whether natural, divine, or human — exists outside the jurisdiction of the sovereign state. International laws are in this sense a convenience: they are conventions states adopt for reasons of mutual self-interest, not out of any sense of moral obligation. To the realist, the domain of international law is relatively narrow and its jurisdiction limited. It cannot prescribe political behavior, but can only adjust to the realities of power and mutual interest.

International law is deficient, in the realist view, because it lacks any effective means of adjudication or enforcement. In matters of public order, the law is presumed to be a system of coercive norms to control disruptive behavior. But when the sole agent of enforcement is the state, international norms have limited utility. The traditional aim of the state is the preservation of its security and independence and the maximization of its power, and realists oppose a conception of international law that would infringe on these prerogatives. Treaties are for giving recognition to states, legalizing boundaries, ratifying transfers of authority, and establishing alliances — all aimed at reinforcing the security and legitimacy of the participating states, not infringing on their powers.

The realist is most often a *dualist,* one who believes that domestic legal systems and the law of nations are separate and distinct. Individuals possess legal standing by virtue of their citizenship, and each state establishes what those conditions of citizenship shall be. Under international law, only states are properly subject to the law, and only their external behavior may be regulated, not their domestic practices. Moreover, the prevailing multiculturalism precludes any worldwide moral consensus that might provide a universal foundation for law. Religious and ideological pluralism dictates that justice shall always be related to the value system of a particular nation-state. International law does not express a fixed content or a transcultural essence; it is what the signatories say it is. Its authority comes from the joint enforcement powers of states that share common aims and that impose upon themselves those standards that they wish the law to promote or defend. The rules of law binding on states emanate from their own free will, as expressed in the treaties they negotiate with coexisting independent communities. It is wrong to presume restrictions on the independence of states, the realists say. In fact, protection of the rights and powers of sovereign states is the central purpose of international law.

Idealists point to all the areas in which nations look to international law to provide a stable and predictable environment. A domain of reciprocal concerns and community tasks in which resort to force is not even remotely contemplated may define the vast majority of international transactions. Nonetheless, the realists respond, a system of law that fails to regulate the most significant class of actions at a point of crisis is a fatally flawed system. As Stanley Hoffmann has pointed out in "The Functions of International Law": "the problem of war and peace is both the distinctive feature of international politics, and the test of any legal system. A legal system that breaks down in the area of greatest importance for its subjects is like a house without foundations. The solidity, scope and intensity of regular legal transactions is dependent on the preservation of moderation at the higher level of the states' essential interests." Moreover, the modern system, though more functionally interdependent, is also more crisis-prone, due to a complex global balancing system that includes "a bewildering variety of units, regimes, ideologies, economic systems and class structures, with countless opportunities for conflict over territory, principles of legitimacy, or resources" (p. 432). The idealist may argue that ecological and economic interdependence have altered states' interests fundamentally, but the realist answers that this mutual vulnerability also encourages transgressions of treaty obligations and legal norms in the name of national security. As nations become more dependent on foreign sources of supply, their economic interests offer ample excuses and incentives for intervention overseas. To the realist, the character of the modern world order does not automatically lend itself to collective decision making, nor does the growing need for transnational coordination and legal restraints on force translate into the adoption of universal codes of conduct.

THE COMPETING FUNCTIONS OF INTERNATIONAL LAW

The realist and idealist approaches to international law are mirrored in its various functions. Stanley Hoffmann's "International Systems and International Law" identifies three classes of law, the most basic of which, *laws of reciprocity*, is close to the realist conception. These laws govern those traditional functions and attributes of state sovereignty that are not politically contested (except by a revolutionary transformation of the entire system). They delimit the rights and privileges of states in their mutual relations (diplomatic recognition, rules of protocol, treatment of foreign residents in peace and noncombatants in time of war). They also constitute the rules of cooperation that regulate such areas as commerce, communications, and other routine interactions. Because the benefits are reciprocal and the domain does not extend beyond areas of converging self-interest, these laws are largely self-policing.

A second category of international law is *laws of community*, which deal with those problems of the global "commons" that individual states cannot manage. Typically, these are environmental, technical, or scientific problems for which national borders are irrelevant. They require community action, often in disregard of political considerations. Because laws of the community by their very nature infringe on the sovereign prerogatives of the state, they are entered into only when the matter is nonpolitical or noncontroversial, the need for cooperation is urgent, or a sense of common interest has already formed, through processes of community building among consenting parties.

The third class of international law is *laws of the political framework*. These regulate political decision making, the use of force, and power relations among states and are roughly analogous to the constitutional framework of a domestic regime. In their weakest form, such laws include treaties of alliance, peace agreements that redefine borders or obligations, and "rules of the game" among the major powers as established by international conferences. In stronger form, these laws find expression in the United Nations, the European Community, and other international institutions that aspire to install authoritative conflict-regulation procedures in place of the traditional right of states to employ their own power resources.

As Hoffmann points out, international law works best when it simultaneously serves the interests of national policy makers and those of world order. When it is an instrument of communication and a joint frame of reference for normal interstate transactions, realists and idealists alike support it. Also, when statesmen need an alibi for shunning force, or when they are looking for an alternative to a costly conflict, international law can provide a channel for conflict resolution.

However, states are notorious for cynically manipulating international law to make it support whatever position the state chooses to advance. Then, the law becomes one more tool of policy in the competition between states, rather than an arena for articulating common norms and negotiating cooperative solutions. It is one of the numerous chessboards on which states maneuver to maximize their interests and defeat an adversary. States invoke international law as a device for mobilizing world support behind their position, often for self-serving reasons. And Machiavellian statesmen pay lip service to international law for fear of leaving a propaganda forum open to others even more devious and skilled in managing world public opinion.

But this profusion of legal rationalizations and escalating claims and counterclaims, which devalue international law, can create a credibility gap for a state that employs the law too opportunistically. The British (during the Suez crisis) and the Americans (in Vietnam, the Dominican Republic, and Grenada) advanced debatable legal arguments to justify their military interventions, considerably undermining their credentials as champions of international law. But the world has entered an era in which legal claims are more prominent and propaganda more important to state power, and legal rationalizations have accompanied most of the questionable acts of the great powers throughout the twentieth century.

Still, despite the occasional cynical acts of states, international law has grown in scope, in substance, and in authority. States cannot help but depend on international law for the smooth functioning of a society of states and the regulation of literally millions of routine transactions. Even the Marxist states, which typically start from a bias against the capitalist presuppositions (and the great-power control) of much of international law, have found it practical to participate in the international legal order and follow most of its rules. With international law growing in prestige and the use of force increasingly stigmatized, states have turned more often to the international courts to protect their sovereignty and their traditional rights. New states, especially those so small or weak that they would have been gobbled up by the great powers in an earlier era, have come to rely on international law for their very independence.

Yet states cannot always control the invoking of legal norms. If an international law serves to legitimize a state's interests on one occasion, it can be invoked by an adversary on another occasion. For example, Nicaragua took the United States to the World Court and won a judgment condemning U.S. economic warfare and its mining of Nicaraguan harbors. In rejecting the World

Court's right to adjudicate on this matter, however, the United States gave up considerable leverage that might have been useful in its attempt to have the Marxist dictatorship of Nicaragua branded as an outlaw state under international norms. The U.S.-Nicaraguan dispute also points up international law's strong bias toward the protection of national sovereignty. States therefore use it to increase their power or protect their autonomy, even though this does not invariably lead (as the idealist might hope) to justice at home or abroad.

Realists maintain that the main function of international law is to protect sovereignty and define the laws of reciprocity. To ask for more, they say, is to place on it a burden that it cannot bear under present anarchic conditions and the primitive level of development of international society. Idealists say that international law should also articulate the laws of community and the political framework, even if they are imperfectly obeyed. One long-time advocate of an international oceans regime, Elizabeth Mann Borgese, argues that the world is at a point where the functional and the constitutional approaches to order are coming together to support a more vigorous system of international law. The rationale for such a legal regime lies in the urgent need for regulation of political-economic and environmental matters that fall outside exclusively national jurisdictions. Transnational economic relations bring the need for an international political regime, however informal, that can provide machinery for resolving the inevitable disputes. Weapons of mass destruction and guerrilla warfare have erased the protective insulation of national boundaries, making the old laws of war obsolete. National uses and abuses of fisheries, the seabed, outer space, and the atmosphere are so extensive as to risk irreversible damage to the ecosphere and the depletion of resources beyond the capacity of the planet to renew them. In all these areas, international law promises to transcend its traditional functions.

Another factor favoring the establishment of new laws of the political framework is modern technology. Modernization is nearly universal, and industrialization has had a homogenizing social impact. So far, the scientific-technical revolution has led to unprecedented cooperation among the advanced states, without the need for formal political instruments. Among the membership of the Organization for Economic Cooperation and Development (OECD), this takes the form of informal leadership and extensive consultations as exemplified by the periodic economic summits of the Group of Seven. And there are growing networks of international codes and regulations. But in many areas, including pollution controls, patent law, trade, currency regulation, control of transnational investments, and technology transfers, the current body of international law has proved inadequate. The benefits of standardization are another argument for greater transnational codification and regulatory powers. For the optimist, it is only a matter of time before these needs find expression in a more rigorous regime of international law, though it may not yet take on peacekeeping functions or play an expressly political role.

The pessimist points to the frequency of revolutionary challenges to the existing body of law. Communist ideology is quite at variance with the Western liberal tradition of law, with its focus on property rights and national

sovereignty. Marxists see the state as an instrument of oppression whose prerogatives they hardly wish to enshrine in international law. Like all other
systems of law, international law does have a class bias, and it is one of the tools
by which the advanced capitalist states gained their imperialist domination.
The United Nations in its quasi-legislative role may have helped end formal
colonialism, but it has hardly made a dent in the traditional body of international law that permits transnational corporations to work their will in the
Third World. The Soviets, under Gorbachev, have identified some common
human interests — peaceful coexistence, control of weapons of extermination,
protection of the biosphere, economic and technological development, cooperative utilization of the resources, and (to a limited extent) human rights — that
comprise a legitimate domain for international law, and one that transcends
ideology. But the Communists continue to resist anything that might intrinsi-
cally favor the capitalist states or seem to meddle in the internal affairs of
sovereign socialist states. They are also sensitive to the fact that Western states
have historically been able to use international law to their advantage, as the
United States used the UN peacekeeping function to further its interests in
Korea and the Congo. For this reason, the Communist states have tended to
favor bilateral agreements and the expressly limited jurisdictions of treaty law.

Although many Third World states are dependent on the international
legal order for the protection of their sovereignty, they often attack international law as biased in favor of the rich and established powers, in particular
catering to neocolonial economic interests. International law does reflect the
legal preferences of the European actors that were dominant when its basic
rules were being formulated. The new postcolonial states, disinclined to accept
its customs, claim that they have entered the system of sovereign states without
preexisting commitments or obligations. When the traditional practices codified in international law work to their disadvantage, the revolutionary have-not
states of the Third World feel free to disregard them. Also, many of the weak
states on the global periphery have suffered great-power interventions, and to
them international law appears to be something of a double standard, applied
or ignored at the convenience of the powerful. In addition, most of the international organizations with legislative or regulatory power have voting schemes
weighted to favor the wealthy and powerful states, making them an unpromis-
ing venue for new, late-modernizing states to pursue their claims.

Where the established powers emphasize precedent and process, the new
states look for equity and economic substance. Where jurists in the advanced
capitalist states see international law as a nonpartisan device of integration and
cooperation, Third World and Communist jurists see it as a political tool that
one bloc or another can mobilize on behalf of its interests. Neither Communist
nor Third World states see any overriding virtue in the status quo, or any
inevitability in the prospect of benefiting from peaceful relations. They have
instead launched ideological and economic challenges to existing international
law, which have eroded the regulatory power of legal norms. Outside of a few
privileged OECD states, the international order is also not particularly homogeneous, ideologically, culturally, or economically. Attempts to enforce interna-

tional law in the absence of widespread consensus may lead only to further divisions between the "satisfied" states, which advocate a strong regulatory and peacekeeping role, and the "dissatisfied" states, which see the UN, the World Court, and the so-called international norms as additional means for the powerful states to oppress the weak.

PROBLEMS OF ADJUDICATION AND ENFORCEMENT

One of the greatest weaknesses of international law has been the absence of authoritative mechanisms to arbitrate and adjudicate disputes. The framers of the League of Nations, recognizing this deficiency, created a Permanent Court of International Justice in 1922. Under the UN Charter, this court was replaced in 1945 by the International Court of Justice (ICJ), or the World Court. The court is made up of fifteen judges who are elected by a concurrent majority vote in the Security Council and the General Assembly. Judges are chosen for their "high moral character" and "recognized competence in international law." They serve nine-year terms and often are reelected, giving the court great continuity in membership and largely insulating it from short-term political pressures. This encourages impartiality, as does a requirement that "the main forms of civilization and the principal legal systems of the world" be represented. One seat each is reserved for the United States and the Soviet Union, and a state involved in a case before the court is permitted to name one of its nationals as an ad hoc judge for that particular case. No two members of the court may be of the same nationality.

The World Court recognizes only states as "international legal persons" with rights and obligations under international law, meaning that private individuals and nongovernmental organizations must submit their grievances to national courts (unless they can persuade a government to carry their case before the World Court). Since 1945, the court has laid down more than 115 decisions, covering both contentious cases and advisory opinions, on a broad range of issues. Thomas Franck's *Judging the World Court* reviews some of them:

> The World Court has handled numerous disputes over title to territory (border towns between Holland and Belgium; islands in the English Channel; enclaves or splinters of land on the Swiss-French border, on the Thai-Cambodian boundary, and in West Africa). It has dealt with disputes over the waters of rivers and over the resources on the ocean floor and in fishing grounds off Norway, Iceland, and Maine. It has ruled on property matters as disparate as a whole country (Namibia and the Spanish Sahara) and the rights of individual aliens. It has considered the duties of a state toward foreign enterprises conducting business on its territory and those of a UN senior official running a peacekeeping operation in the Middle East. It has handled cases dealing with ships on public waters that were blown up by mines, and diplomats who were taken hostage. Its opinions have been sought as to whether French nuclear testing in the Pacific violates the environmental rights of Australia and New Zealand, and whether

UN members are legally bound to pay the annual assessments fixed by the
General Assembly when they disagree with an activity for which they are used.
(p. 10)

Unfortunately, major disputes are rarely submitted to the World Court.
Only about fifty contentious cases have been heard; of these, only a handful
involved armed conflict between states, and in roughly a third of the cases the
court did not render a judgment. However, when states do accept the court's
jurisdiction, they generally accept its judgment as binding and resolve the
dispute in accordance with the court's order. More than 140 states are signatories of the ICJ Statute, although only about one-third of them have accepted
compulsory jurisdiction. Even those states that have agreed in advance to
submit certain types of disputes to the court have hedged, giving themselves
reservation clauses that allow them to escape the court's judgment. The United
States, for example, attached to its ratification of the statute the Connally
Amendment, which exempts from compulsory jurisdiction those disputes
"which are essentially within the domestic jurisdiction of the United States as
determined by the United States of America." Such reservations indicate that
most states approach international law with conflicting motives: they want the
benefits of order that come from a global mechanism for resolving conflict, but
they are unwilling to give up absolute sovereignty. As Franck notes (p. 9), the
World Court has been widely criticized as an expensive, do-nothing institution
that wastes its time on such frivolous cases as the disposition of a Belgian-Cana-
dian electricity franchise in Barcelona. Then, when the court does take up a
significant case — the Iranian hostages or the U.S. covert war against
Nicaragua — it is condemned for trespassing on sacrosanct political precincts.
However, there is greater hope for the court following United States and Soviet
agreements, in 1988 and 1989, to cooperate with one another in accepting the
court's compulsory jurisdiction in several specific kinds of disputes.

But the power of international law does not depend exclusively, or even
principally, on the World Court. Regional courts (such as the European Court
of Justice) and national courts play a vital role in applying international law to
domestic suits with a transnational dimension. Most states recognize treaty law
and the basic principles of international law as coequal (if not superior) to
domestic law. International law also decides questions of jurisdiction, assigning legal competence to various subordinate courts, and its guidelines are
helpful in sorting out who is liable for what in a dispute involving several states
or nationals. Frederic S. Pearson and J. Martin Rochester, in *International
Relations* (pp. 304–05), dramatize the jurisdictional dilemma with this question: what happens if a Frenchman kills a Pole on a ship owned by a Canadian
flying the Panamanian flag in U.S. territorial waters? Their summary of the
principles of international law applicable to this case appears in Figure 10-2.

It must also be noted that the body of international law based on multilateral conventions and treaties has never grown so rapidly as in the last thirty
years, despite the lack of an authoritative mechanism for arbitrating differences or interpreting the rights and duties of signatory states. So ambitious a

---

FIGURE 10-2
DETERMINING JURISDICTION IN THE WORLD

"Jurisdiction" refers to the competence of a state to prosecute certain acts of individuals in its courts. The subject of jurisdiction is sufficiently complicated to fill hundreds of pages in most international legal casebooks. We will try here to summarize briefly the basic aspects of the problem.

One must first understand that any given country is composed of a multitude of individual persons, most of whom are citizens, or *nationals,* of that state. However, also traveling or residing within each state are *aliens,* persons who are nationals of another state or may even be stateless (if their citizenship has been lost for some reason). In general, a "national" refers to a person owing permanent allegiance to a particular state, and it is a status acquired either through birth or through naturalization. Regarding birth, some countries, such as the continental European states, stress the *jus sanguinis* principle, whereby a child automatically acquires the nationality of the parents regardless of where the child is born. Other states, such as the United States, utilize not only the *jus sanguinis* principle but also the *jus soli* principle, whereby any child (with a few minor exceptions) who is born on their soil is eligible for citizenship regardless of the nationality of the parents. Hence, a child born to Belgian parents in the United States would be eligible for both American and Belgian citizenship. The conflicts inherent in dual, and sometimes multiple, citizenship are usually resolved through residency requirements imposed by most states. Nationality can also be gained through naturalization, the process whereby a foreigner attains citizenship after complying with the application procedures stipulated by the state.

Jurisdiction can be claimed by states on five possible grounds:

1. The *territorial* principle, whereby a state may exercise jurisdiction over the acts of anyone — nationals or aliens (except for certain classes of aliens such as foreign diplomats) — committed within its territorial borders (e.g., U.S. courts trying an Englishman for a theft committed in New York City);

2. The *nationality* principle, whereby a state may exercise jurisdiction over any acts perpetrated by its own nationals, no matter where they are committed in the world (o.g., U.S. courts trying an American for a murder committed in Egypt);

3. The *protective* principle, whereby a state may exercise jurisdiction over the acts of any persons — nationals or aliens (with a few exceptions) — committed anywhere in the world, if such acts threaten a state's national security (e.g., U.S. courts trying a Hungarian for counterfeiting U.S. currency in Mexico);

4. The *universality* principle, whereby a state may exercise jurisdiction over the acts of any persons — nationals or aliens (with a few exceptions) — committed anywhere in the world, if such acts constitute crimes against the community of nations (e.g., U.S. courts trying a Belgian for engaging in an act of piracy on the high seas by seizing a French fishing vessel, or trying a Palestinian for skyjacking a Jordanian jetliner);

5. The *passive personality* principle, whereby a state may exercise jurisdiction over any person who has injured one of its nationals, no matter where in the world the act was committed (e.g., U.S. courts trying a Syrian for killing an American in Lebanon).

The first two principles are the most commonly invoked and accepted bases of jurisdiction, with the territorial principle being most adhered to by states in the Anglo-Saxon legal tradition and the nationality principle most recognized by states in the continental European tradition. The other three principles, only occasionally invoked, are exceptions to the general notion that states should not seek to prosecute in their national courts those acts committed by aliens abroad. It is clearly possible for more than one state to have legitimate grounds on which to claim jurisdiction over some act, as in the case of a person shooting across a national frontier and killing a person on the other side. As a practical matter, one state — namely the one that has the offender in custody — is usually in a position to determine whether to exercise jurisdiction itself or to *extradite* that person to another state seeking jurisdiction.

In the hypothetical case we have cited here, it is conceivable that France could invoke the nationality principle, Poland the passive personality principle, and the United States or Panama the territorial principle. As a general rule, if the "good order" of the port of the coastal state (here, the United States) were not disturbed by the incident — if a wild shooting spree did not ensue — then the coastal state ordinarily would be willing to defer to the authority of the flag state (Panama), which in turn could decide to hand over the perpetrator to his government (France) for trial. In any event, it is not likely that the Frenchman would go scot-free.

---

measure as the UN Convention on the Law of the Sea was endorsed in 1982 by 155 nations, with only the United States, Turkey, Israel, and Venezuela opposed. Thousands of diplomats met nearly 200 times between 1974 and 1982 to negotiate agreement on its 320 articles and 9 annexes, which established a uniform international standard defining territorial waters, the extent of the continental shelf, and exclusive rights to economic zones. It also declared ocean resources to be the inalienable common heritage of humankind, set up an international authority to supervise deep seabed mining, and contained an unprecedented provision for the sharing of royalties among all nations.

In this one case, a huge majority of states was able to muster the legal ingenuity and political will to negotiate a complex international convention. Overall, however, international law remains weak and subject to frequent violations. Matters of domestic political practice, national honor, security, independence, and vital national interest simply are not brought before international courts. It is not because applicable principles of law are lacking (they have proliferated mightily in the twentieth century), but because the right of a state to be self-determining is still viewed as paramount. Moreover, states have still not passed beyond the point at which resort to force is considered an essential means of resolving their most fundamental disputes.

Violations of international law occur for a great variety of reasons (see A. Sheikh, *International Law and National Behavior*, pp. 281–87). Often there is genuine uncertainty about how general norms apply to a specific situation. A large body of law may exist, but frequently it is ambiguous and subject to multiple interpretations — many of them self-serving ex post facto rationalizations given plausibility by an ingenious foreign office determined to pursue a questionable course for pragmatic reasons. In other cases, there may be two legitimate but conflicting views of the rights, duties, or restraints laid out in an international code. When no judicial body has the authority to interpret a code, or jurisdiction is disputed, every state will make its own interpretation in light of its special concerns.

Second, the law is particularly vulnerable at points of revolutionary transformation in the international system. Drastic changes in the membership of international organizations (as happened in the UN after decolonization) will bring many of the traditional norms of behavior under attack from new members. A revolutionary challenger aspiring to great-power status (Napoleonic France, Soviet Russia, Maoist China) often violates international law. Ideologically inspired movements for radical change (Islamic fundamentalism in the Middle East, Marxist-Leninist influenced insurgencies in the Third World) challenge the rules of the international status quo. The Ayatollah Khomeini's invasion of the U.S. embassy in Iran in 1979 and the taking of diplomatic hostages was a violation of one of the oldest and best observed of all international laws, the principle of diplomatic immunity. (But it must be said that the Iranian action was universally condemned — a sign of the ongoing strength of international law.) If the balance of the world political economy shifts, prevailing principles of trade and investment come into question. France, Britain, and the United States, when they were rising powers, legislated their liberal economic principles into international law, only to violate them later, when their economic dominance began to decline. Also, certain protections and property rights of private overseas investment came under attack by the New International Economic Order, the Third World's strong challenge to the imperialism, dependency, and underdevelopment perpetuated by international capitalism. If a revolutionary challenge appears to have a good chance of success, defenders of the status quo will frequently violate international law in the process of trying to contain the threat. Many of the excesses of U.S. foreign policy in the depths of the Cold War were due to the overzealous reactions of anti-Communists against what they believed was an archrevolutionary and potentially mortal threat to the entire international system. A period of revolutionary change can spawn violations of international law by both the challengers and the defenders of the prevailing order.

Reasons of state *(raisons d'état)* are a third category of violations of international law. These are the knowing acts of governments on behalf of the national interest. Armed force may be the only means for a state to acquire or protect a disputed territory. Coercive sanctions may be judged essential in retaliating against an enemy or persuading it to enter negotiations. Illegal intelligence operations may be deemed necessary to collect information vital to national security. Expropriation of foreign enterprises may be politically attractive or economically profitable. In such cases, a rational calculus of gains and losses to the state overcomes moral scruples. Again, the absence of legal organs to adjudicate or enforce the law tends to encourage states to fall back on this pragmatic determination of the national interest. Or a state acts in a manner it considers prudent, without much concern for the legal implications of a policy. If international law is violated, it is purely accidental or is incidental to the pursuit of an important foreign policy goal—a relatively minor factor in the calculation of state power.

Finally, the gains of aggression, national aggrandizement, and other violations of international law are specific, tangible, and immediate, but the costs of the violation are general, remote, and not clearly defined—though the long-run costs may sometimes exceed the gains. Short-term success becomes the important criterion for most foreign policy makers, beset as they are by intense political pressures and a sense of urgency. Duty, honor, statesmanship, and personal honesty may call for fidelity to international law, but leaders who sacrifice the national interest to international order leave themselves open to political accusations of being unpatriotic, weak, idealistic, or susceptible to manipulation by an opposing state. A violation of international law may have a high cost for the international system and, in the long run, for the nation, but a hard-boiled realist policy brings immediate political gains. The competitive dynamic within which most decisions are made favors preemptive action over lawful restraint and sober, patient consideration. When international law can be violated with impunity, moral standards quickly fall to the level of the least scrupulous, since a nation unwilling to act in a Machiavellian manner is likely to be outmaneuvered by one that is. At the extreme are those emotional or irrational leaders who let nothing stand in the way of their ego needs or power drives. International law is a fragile bulwark against such powermongering.

This raises one of the major problems of international law: the absence of any central mechanism for disciplining violators. The law may clearly identify the rights of one state or the wrongdoing of another, but whether sanctions are applied or punishment evaded depends on how powerful the contending states are. Adherence to international law is based on: (1) the importance of the issue to each state's security and independence; (2) the degree to which the issue has become politicized and therefore controversial in national or world public opinion; (3) the degree to which a state's legitimacy, both domestic and international, is tied to the rule of law; and (4) the extent to which a state can violate the law — that is, act independently — without suffering adverse consequences or a loss of influence. When a state's survival is directly threatened or its identity and core interests politically challenged, international law is often pushed aside by the demands of national interest. When the issue is technical or when a state is relatively weak, is enmeshed in trade and alliance relations that constrain its freedom of maneuver, or is committed to principles of legitimacy that emphasize comity and law-abidingness, it has more powerful motives for observing the sanctity of international law.

In spite of the self-policing and contingent character of international law, it must be noted that most states choose to obey international law most of the time. Given the lack of enforcement power, this is reason for considerable optimism about the state of international society. Precisely because the law is limited, flexible, open to amendment or unilateral interpretation, and impossible to force on a state, it is operative only in areas in which there is a large body of shared interests. Advances in science and technology, the nuclear threat, economic interdependence, worldwide communications and transportation, and the large network of treaties and conventions are expanding the domain of shared interests. In its present form, international law cannot control the megalomaniacal leader, arbitrate the most intense of security concerns, or prohibit the resort to force as the *ultimo ratio*. But its limited scope is the very quality that preserves its relative effectiveness in the many areas it does touch. As Richard Falk has observed, in "The Relevance of Political Context to the Nature and Functioning of International Law":

> No form of law, however much it is supported by the social environment, has been able to eliminate altogether violations of its most fundamental rules of restraint. If one examines the domestic incidence of murder or rebellion in the best-ordered society, the record discloses a frequency of violation that would disappoint any legal perfectionist. . . .
>
> The inability of international law to generate an altogether peaceful world does not imply its inviability to promote a more peaceful world, or to deal adequately with the many aspects of international life having nothing directly to do with war and peace.
>
> Part of the difficulty of accepting international law as a beneficial, albeit imperfect, source of order in world affairs, arises from the fear of a destructive violation of international law culminating in a general nuclear war. Such an

awesome prospect cripples the imagination and inclines observers to conclude that a system of order that cannot offer assurance against such an occurrence is virtually worthless. It is certainly the case that the role of international law in the nuclear age is crucially related to making the system less war-prone or in assisting the transition to a new international system, one where the scale of violence is regulated in such a way that both the incentive and capability to cross the nuclear threshold is dramatically reduced. But while taking account of this nuclear coordinate of world order, it remains possible and necessary to grasp the more moderate, but nonetheless considerable, contributions of international law to the present and prospective attainment of world order, welfare, and justice. (In Deutsch and Hoffman, *The Relevance of International Law*, pp. 190–91)

Falk goes on to list the following as the main contributions of international law to world order: (1) the definition of the "rules of the game," which have set boundaries on conflict; (2) the provision of an avenue for communicating, in the midst of crisis, assertions and counterassertions of claims of right, encouraging the parties to employ limited means to reach limited ends; (3) the establishment of stable expectations for routine transactions, along with procedures for the litigation of nonpolitical disputes; (4) international regimes in such areas as health, transportation, postal service, telecommunications, safety, trade, information, currency regulation, and a host of other fields in which law facilitates cooperation rather than imposing restraints; and (5) guidance on acceptable conduct—that is, a kind of moral yardstick by which to judge deviance from commonly articulated, uniform standards.

Very often states obey international law because they judge it advantageous or prudent to do so. The violation of international norms can be costly; the basis of peaceful intercourse between states is daily acts of reciprocity. Custom and precedent define the bounds of acceptable behavior. In an environment that none but the most powerful can alter, states have strong incentives to get along. In fact, the majority of states are economically and militarily weak and highly dependent on international law for recognition and protection. With no power resources of their own, they look to international law to defend the sanctity of their borders, safeguard their citizens abroad, assure safe transit of their economic goods, and articulate their grievances against the more powerful. Even the strongest nations have an incentive to obey a body of law that they themselves may have to call on in the future. Great powers, which have the widest range of foreign relations, have perhaps the strongest stake in international stability and predictability. A surprising array of international relationships depends on mutual trust and dependability, and international law can help establish this confidence.

Lawless behavior affects a state's credibility and security. It cannot escape the consequences by moving its location or changing its neighbors. Outlaw states place in jeopardy their alliance ties, treaty commitments, trade relations, access to capital and credit, and chances for enlisting others in joint endeavors. Communist China, for example, suffered a dramatic reduction in foreign investment and joint ventures on the heels of its crackdown against the advocates of democracy. In this case, very practical concerns about the stability of the

Chinese government and the predictability of the economic climate may have shaken international confidence, but perceptions are equally shaped by a regime's international behavior. Individuals can ignore disorder and leave law enforcement up to the authorities, but states must zealously scrutinize the behavior of their potential adversaries and adapt themselves to it. Enforcement of international law, against even the most powerful, is not dependent on coercion; many governments respond to lawlessness by taking a negative attitude toward the offending state. When that happens, the offender usually finds it better in the long run to seek an orderly settlement of a dispute rather than to impose a short-run interest by force.

As Roger Fisher says, international law operates as a restraint by making certain courses of action unattractive or counterproductive. A country pays a political cost for engaging in prohibited conduct. Most of us obey the law not primarily because of the threat of coercion, but out of utilitarian considerations (it is safer to stop at a red light) and a sense of moral obligation. Likewise, status as a recognized member of the international system causes most states to identify with the norms of international society and to comply with them as a matter of habit. States routinely obey the law because they have come, over time, to accept it as the right thing to do. Though the sense of duty is still weak in international affairs (as compared to domestic society), the self-interest in restraint is not. The joint stake all states have in avoiding war and settling conflicts peacefully makes mutual interest the regulating principle for international law. It is a principle with distinct limits, but it is far stronger than most critics of international law realize. In the vast majority of cases, utilitarian and moral considerations combine, in the absence of coercive sanctions, to motivate nations to obey international law and preserve the peace.

QUESTION FOR DISCUSSION (PRO AND CON)

Should vital affairs of state and the conduct of negotiations be entrusted to summit meetings between heads of state?

☞ **PRO**

One of the factors that has most impoverished modern diplomacy, and greatly exacerbated the Cold War, is the loss of the human touch. Summit meetings help leaders gain a firsthand impression of their counterparts and provide opportunities for developing cultural understanding and, occasionally, personal friendships. They can dissolve misperceptions and pave the way to better relations. Personal encounters between leading statesmen have been altogether too rare. U.S.-Soviet summit diplomacy is a much-needed antidote to the provincialism of both societies and to the traditional lack of international exposure of both chiefs of state. Ideological stereotypes are broken down only by direct encounters with the object of prejudice, as was shown so profoundly in the growth of President Reagan's warm personal relationship with General-Secretary Gorbachev. Without the opportunity for intimate acquaintance that their series of summits provided, it is unlikely that Reagan would have risked the big shift in arms control policy that occurred in the last years of his administration. The Reagan-Gorbachev summits were an essential element in convincing President Reagan, a determined Cold Warrior, that Mikhail Gorbachev was a new breed of Communist who sincerely wanted to cultivate peaceful relations.

The investment of personal prestige is the very ingredient that can push an entrenched, bureaucratically driven policy onto a new path. Top leaders meeting face-to-face can achieve dramatic breakthroughs, since only they have the authority to make decisive policy changes, commit the nation, and settle disputes on the spot. As Henry Kissinger has noted, a summit conference can make binding decisions more rapidly than any other diplomatic forum. It is the ideal venue for launching a new departure in foreign relations. Kissinger found it so in his implementation of President Nixon's openings to China and the Soviet Union, and he used personal diplomacy to good effect in his own efforts toward peace in Vietnam and the Middle East. Only the heads of state, and their chief foreign policy advisers, could have settled these really intractable disputes; ordinary bureaucrats and low-level negotiators would not have dared to abandon the rigid positions of the Cold War. The summit meeting between Nixon and Chou En-lai in Peking in 1972 marked a big breakthrough in American foreign policy, opening a new era of détente and triangular diplomacy. Similarly, the Carter-Begin-Sadat summit at Camp David in 1978 broke the Middle East deadlock and produced surprising and fruitful steps toward peace.

Personal negotiations at the summit can bypass many of the constraints of professional diplomacy. Members of the foreign affairs bureaucracy typically lack initiative. They are trained to act slowly and cautiously, to analyze thoroughly, to introduce changes incrementally, to avoid risky situations at all costs. But this inevitably leads to lethargy and lack of imagination. Decisions are avoided until a point of crisis, when the only tool for speedy resolution is the personal intervention of the chief executive. Timidity and narrowness of outlook prevent the professional diplomat from making timely innovations or seizing the opportunity for dramatic change. The high risks of the nuclear age have reinforced this cautiousness and the institutionalization of decision making. Planning has overtaken diplomacy, replacing the flexibility of personal encounters with the fixed images of ideology and the planner's worst-case scenarios. Once diplomacy has been abandoned to the bureaucracy, vested interests develop a momentum of their own.

Kissinger, shortly before assuming a diplomatic role himself, commented on the problems of leadership and the negative impact of the administrative structure on foreign policy in his *American Foreign Policy* (pp. 17–43). When everything is done according to routines and standard operating procedures, the bureaucracy is completely unprepared to cope with unexpected problems.

The chief executive either solves them on the basis of personal authority or becomes enmeshed in reconciling what the bureaucracy has expected with what has actually happened. In the latter case, the leader is serving the foreign affairs bureaucracy rather than defining issues independently. Success consists of moving the administrative machinery to the point of decision, with little consideration of the merits of the decision. Presidents are limited to the options delivered by advisers whose horizons do not extend beyond the agency within which they pursue their careers. What passes for planning is the projection of the familiar onto the future. Ideological doctrine is institutionalized, and orthodoxy takes the place of creativity. Decisions arrived at through laborious consensus-building processes become sacrosanct. The more elaborate the administrative structure, the less relevant is one individual's view and the more pervasive the ideological criteria for choice, since one of the purposes of bureaucracy is to remove decision making from the accident of personality. Neither the problems themselves nor the requirements of political survival permit the delays typical of bureaucracy, however, and the executive is inevitably driven toward extrabureaucratic means of decision.

In this context, summit diplomacy is the perfect solution. It provides an impetus for serious negotiation and pressures of publicity and public opinion that can bring both sides to compromise. It gives the bureaucracy a focus for its energies and target dates for decision. It makes room for individuals to put their stamp on policy. It gives the top leaders the leverage for moving their systems to the point of decision. (President Carter once remarked that his toughest negotiations over SALT II were those with the American defense establishment, not the Soviets.)

Summit negotiations leave open the possibility of capricious action or arbitrary decisions, but this is a risk we must run if we want heads of state to have the freedom of maneuver that can bring diplomatic breakthroughs. All the important postwar arms control agreements have been the product of summit diplomacy. The risks of summitry could be reduced significantly by the scheduling of regular meetings between heads of state. This would avoid a lot of the gamesmanship, grandstanding, and inflated expectations that come with infrequent encounters. Whatever one may say about the hazards of mixing policy making and negotiations, no superpower leader has failed to seize the extraordinary opportunity that a summit offers to define options, dramatize priorities, and garner support for movement in a new direction. Given the rigidity of national frames of reference, ideological images, and bureaucratic procedures, we need the creative vehicle of summit diplomacy.

☞ CON

Summit diplomacy has serious disadvantages. Chief executives are seldom experts in international affairs and are often tempted to use summits for their own political advantage, sometimes at a cost to the long-run interests of the nation. The 1960 Paris summit and the Khrushchev-Kennedy summit in

Vienna in 1961 produced rancor and misperceptions, not better understanding. The Reagan-Gorbachev summit at Reykjavík in 1987 was marked by wild improvisation and a kind of one-upmanship in disarmament proposals, leading to the consideration of positions that were neither feasible nor supported by the respective political elites at home. When the smoke cleared, both military establishments attacked their leaders for reckless behavior, and each leader tried to blame the other for bad faith. Summit expectations are so high that failure can have a disillusioning and chilling impact on relations. Presidents who fancy themselves negotiators may make mistakes out of unfamiliarity with diplomatic procedures or a foreign culture, yet their commitments can be disavowed only at a high political cost. Excessive publicity (over 2,000 journalists were present) turned the 1981 North-South multilateral summit meeting at Cancún, Mexico, into an innocuous and frankly ineffective showpiece. Finally, summits can be an enormous waste of a chief executive's valuable time. Preparation alone can take days of briefing. And then, as U.S. diplomat George Ball writes in *Diplomacy for a Crowded World:* "During ten hours of top-level propinquity, one should deduct at least four hours for eating and drinking, another hour or two for small talk and the normal conversational amenities, then divide the remainder by perhaps two and one half for the translation. What is left is about two to three hours in which positions are stated and ideas exchanged" (p. 36).

Sir Harold Nicolson, the esteemed British diplomat and parliamentarian, has said that no mistake is more fatal to good diplomacy than the confusion of policy with negotiations. Precisely because summit negotiations are conducted between politicians with the authority to make immediate commitments and decisions, they are extremely dangerous. The speed with which decisions can be made at a summit increases the risk of hasty or foolish agreement. A summit conference can aid in reconciling opposing points of view when they are based on misunderstanding. But more often the attempt at clarification only deepens the schism between conflicting national interests or ideologically incompatible positions. Also, to commit personal prestige in an atmosphere of extreme publicity and uncritical popular expectations introduces extraneous political considerations, raises the stakes unnecessarily high, and increases the costly consequences of disagreement.

The politician as negotiator suffers from a number of flaws. First, heads of state acting as summit diplomats become so immersed in the process of briefing, bargaining, and dealing with the media that they have little time for the long-term task of formulating sound policy.

Second, the political leader's position, prestige, and future are placed in direct jeopardy at a summit. His performance and the outcome of the negotiations are sure to affect judgments of him by his party, the press, and public opinion. Positions are taken not to protect the national interest or because they are reasonable, but because they will play well in party circles, in the press gallery, in the propaganda forum, or in the history books.

A third flaw is that politicians are often uninformed about the facts of complex issues, such as nuclear arms control, and are still less informed about the psychology of dealing with a foreign power and about bargaining tactics. Heads of state are much more prone to mistakes than are professional experts and trained diplomats.

Fourth, the pomp and circumstance of a summit appeals to the vanity of politicians and often gives rise to false expectations. Lavish hospitality, idealistically worded toasts, and feelings of affability, good will, and gratitude encourage an illusion of agreement. This is more often show than substance, and it does not carry forward the real affairs of state. Worse still, a bruised ego can derail the patient work of decades and go quite against the interests of state. The experiences of Indonesia's President Sukarno illustrate the point:

> In Moscow, 150 musicians playing *"Indonesia Raya"* greeted me at the airport although I arrived in an American plane. It brought tears of pride to my eyes that our land had come to this. Peking welcomes me with tremendous parades and gun salutes. The people with me are proud of me, proud that our downtrodden country has taken its place among the great nations.
>
> And now, people of America, I ask you, why didn't Eisenhower accord me the same respect? Why did your President snub me, deliberately rebuff and insult me? I was invited to Washington in 1960. OK. Eisenhower didn't meet my plane — OK. He didn't greet me at the door of the White House — I guess it's still OK. But when he had me wait outside in the anteroom cooling my heels that is definitely not OK.
>
> . . . Khrushchev sent me jams and jellies every two weeks and handpicked apples, corn, and other vegetables from the best of his crop. So am I wrong to be grateful to them? Who can help being nice to those who are nice to him? I have tried to pursue a neutral policy, yes! But down deep in his soul who can blame me for saying, "Thank you, people from the East, for always showing me friendship, for not trying to hurt me. Thank you for telling your citizens Sukarno is at least trying the best he can for his country. Thank you for your gifts." What I am expressing is gratitude — not Communism! (Cited in Palmer, *Dilemmas of Political Development,* pp. 188–89)

Likewise, America's perceptions of the Soviet Union were shaped more by one impulsive act of Premier Khrushchev — banging his shoe on the table at a formal UN session — than a thousand carefully worded press releases issued by the Soviet foreign affairs bureaucracy.

In the fifth place, politicians typically are trained in advocacy and the arts of argument, skills that make them formidable lawyers, ideologues, and bureaucratic infighters. But they are not the skills of a good negotiator. Bargainers must forget their audience, refrain from the impulse to score debating points, and concentrate on the substance of the issue at hand. Otherwise, diplomatic discussions and consultations simply degenerate into ideological argument.

Finally, a summit meeting burdens the head of state with an enormous workload and immense pressure for results. This means that negotiations are seldom pursued to a precise conclusion, but are likely to be suspended halfway, at the first opportunity for compromise. Suggestions that further study or delay might be needed are set aside, as is any new information that might alter a consensus or prolong the discussion. The summit agreements that result tend to be long on rhetoric and general principles and short on specifics and provisions for enforcement.

Henry Kissinger, also a great diplomat, concurs in Nicolson's skepticism about the value of summit meetings. He notes, in *The Necessity for Choice* (pp.175–217), several factors of contemporary international relations that have reduced the scope of diplomacy and the possibility for individuals to reach agreement. First, the destructiveness of modern weapons has made it difficult for statesmen to introduce believable threats that might bring concessions. Historically, a nation's bargaining position has depended not only on the logic and persuasiveness of its proposals but on the penalties it could exact if the other side failed to agree. Moderate, graduated, and usable instruments of armed force made traditional negotiations more rational, fruitful, and flexible. In the nuclear era, statesmen can be as intransigent as they please and pay no penalty.

The second factor is bipolarity, which has made diplomacy more intractable by reducing the opportunities for maneuver, for limited agreement, or for a change in alliance partners that might produce accommodation. All issues take on the life-and-death proportions of the superpower struggle. Third World conflicts, human rights, trade, espionage, access to technology, and dozens of other issues become bargaining chips that are played every time one chief of state sits down at a superpower summit to negotiate with the other. It becomes impossible to isolate arms control or some other central military concern from the peripheral issues that global polarization has pushed onto the summit agenda.

Third, the clash of opposing ideologies compounds the inherent tensions of a bipolar, nuclear world. Marxists (and realists too) tend to discount the role of individual personalities or the importance of good will, emphasizing instead historical processes and the political-economic realities that individual statesmen are powerless to alter, no matter how eagerly they may approach a summit. The Soviets sometimes give the impression that they think the tensions are due to an unfortunate misunderstanding or the evil machinations of individuals, but they have no realistic expectations that such negotiations will alter the underlying nature of the two societies.

Finally, the United States brings to the summit a philosophy that everything and anything can be negotiated. This reflects the unique blessings we have enjoyed as a people able to solve almost all our domestic problems peaceably, with few really insuperable obstacles. We assume that if a problem has not been solved, it is because we did not attack it with sufficient energy, commitment, perseverance, or good will. Democratic societies are particularly prone to explaining international disputes in terms of mistrust and a conflict of personalities and to reducing diplomacy to good-will gestures and confidence building between heads of state. This optimistic reliance on personalities and agreements is ill founded, in an era of advanced technology, protracted struggle, and ideological conflict. In Kissinger's words,

> It is trivial to pretend that problems of the complexity of those which have rent the world for [half a century] can be solved in a few days by harassed men meeting in the full light of publicity. It cannot be in the interest of the democracies to adopt a style of diplomacy which places such a premium on the authority of a few leaders.

The history of summit negotiations does not speak well for their efficacy. President Eisenhower met with the Soviet leadership in Geneva in 1955 on the assumption that Soviet-American relations could be changed by attention to "the spirit and the attitude" with which problems were approached. The press proclaimed afterward that the personal charm of one man had brought a mellowing to Soviet policy, and expectations sprang up that the Cold War was over, now that the "spirit of Geneva" had taken hold. The hopes were quickly dashed. In 1960, the Eisenhower-Khrushchev summit collapsed before it even got under way. A subsequent encounter with Kennedy at the Vienna summit only reinforced Khrushchev's false impression that the American leadership could be bullied into concessions. The Berlin Wall and the Soviet attempt to place missiles in Cuba followed — both consequences of the misapprehensions stemming from personal diplomacy.

Every summit has raised the same problems of politics on both sides. Before the meeting, leaders restate their policies in the sharpest of terms, to enhance their bargaining positions and reassure the public that they are not preparing to "sell out." During the negotiations, they press hard for tangible gains so they can go home with something to show for their efforts. Failure causes each side to depart in an outburst of invective and recrimination that casts blame on the other. Any gains that emerge are no more than could have been achieved in a less public forum, in which the tendency to exaggerate differences would have been significantly less. Summitry, because it is couched in such grand language (though the concrete results may be few), raises expectations unrealistically. The Nixon-Brezhnev summits led everyone to shout dizzily that peace was at hand, but they were followed by the sobering cold bath of Angola and Afghanistan. The second try at détente, in the round of Reagan-Gorbachev summits, produced equally scant results. Reagan negotiated at Reykjavík out of sheer ignorance and recklessness, taking positions that were roundly criticized and solidly rejected by the Pentagon and Congress when he got home. The language of the "evil empire" disappeared when, in the closing months of his administration, he signed the INF treaty and paraded to Moscow to write himself into the history books as a peace president. But he was unable to pass beyond this limited step, taken amidst the ambience of *glasnost* and good will, to concrete and verifiable reductions in strategic nuclear weapons.

Summit diplomacy is inevitably flawed by the atmosphere of haste surrounding it and by the heavy dependence on the limited capacities of a few key individuals. It is best reserved for ceremonial occasions on which the heads of state can ratify agreements concluded through the patient work of professional diplomats. If real negotiations take place at a summit, they should be viewed, in the words of Harold Nicolson, as

> exceptional and dangerous. Such conferences should be entered into only after careful preparation, on the basis of a programme elaborated and accepted in advance, against a background of acute public criticism and with full realisation that many months of discussion will be required. The subjects for debate should moreover be rigidly curtailed to those requiring a decision of policy, and all secondary issues, entailing negotiations only, should be left in expert hands. ("The 'Old' and the 'New' Diplomacy," p. 430)

Without such precautions, summit encounters come to rely on verbal strategy and public posturing, which may massage a few egos but do nothing to solve deep-seated conflicts. If the primary purpose of summit meetings is to foster good will, on the assumption that this will change the climate of suspicion, they are a delusory exercise that actually replaces the hard work of real negotiations. No matter how well prepared and superbly skilled the leaders are, they cannot alter underlying differences in geography, ideology, or power — the structural realities of international affairs. These are shaped by the evolution of basic forces, not by transient understandings between individuals. In short, summit meetings are propaganda events. They should be discarded in favor of quiet diplomacy and attention to the long-term factors of power that may bring states to alter their basic behavior.

SOURCES AND SUGGESTED READINGS

Diplomatic Memoirs

Acheson, Dean G. *Present at the Creation.* New York: Norton, 1969.
Brzezinski, Zbigniew. *Power and Principle.* New York: Farrar, Straus, & Giroux, 1983.
Cambon, Jules. *Le Diplomate.* Paris: Hachette, 1926.
Kennan, George F. *Memoirs: 1925–1950.* Boston: Little, Brown, 1967.
———. *Memoirs: 1950–1963.* Boston: Little, Brown, 1972.
Khrushchev, Nikita S. *Khrushchev Remembers* (translated and edited by Strobe Talbott). Boston: Little, Brown, 1970.
Kissinger, Henry A. *White House Years.* Boston: Little, Brown, 1979.
———. *Years of Upheaval.* Boston: Little, Brown, 1982.
Shevchenko, Arkady. *Breaking with Moscow.* New York: Knopf, 1985.
Thayer, Charles W. *Diplomat.* New York: Harper, 1959.
Vance, Cyrus. *Hard Choices.* New York: Simon & Schuster, 1983.

On Diplomacy

Bailey, Thomas A. *The Art of Diplomacy.* New York: Appleton-Century-Croft, 1968.
Ball, George W. *Diplomacy for a Crowded World: An American Foreign Policy.* Boston: Little, Brown, 1976.
Barston, Ronald P. *Modern Diplomacy.* Essex, U.K.: Longman, 1988.
Bell, Coral. *The Conventions of Crisis: A Study in Diplomatic Management.* London: Oxford University Press, 1971.
Burton, John W. "The Resolution of Conflict." *International Studies Quarterly,* vol. 16 (Mar. 1972), pp. 5–29.
Craig, Gordon A., and Alexander L. George. *Force and Statecraft: Diplomatic Problems of Our Time.* New York: Oxford University Press, 1983.
Deutsch, Morton. *The Resolution of Conflict: Constructive and Destructive Processes.* New Haven, Conn.: Yale University Press, 1973.
Fisher, Roger. *International Conflict for Beginners.* New York: Harper & Row, 1969.
Garrity, Patrick. "The Dubious Promise of Summitry." *Journal of Contemporary Studies,* vol. 7 (1984), pp. 71–79.
George, Alexander, David K. Hall, and William R. Simons. *The Limits of Coercive Diplomacy: Laos, Cuba, Vietnam.* Boston: Little, Brown, 1971.
Harr, John E. *The Professional Diplomat.* Princeton, N.J.: Princeton University Press, 1969.
Hartmann, Frederick H. *The Relations of Nations,* 6th ed. New York: Macmillan, 1983.
Hartmann, Frederick H., ed. *World in Crisis,* 4th ed. New York: Macmillan, 1973.
Kennan, George F. *Memoirs, 1925–1950.* Boston: Little, Brown, 1967.
Kissinger, Henry A. *American Foreign Policy,* Expanded ed. New York: Norton, 1974.

————. *A World Restored: Metternich, Castlereagh, and the Problems of Peace, 1812–1822.* Boston: Houghton Mifflin, 1957.

————. *The Necessity for Choice: Prospects of American Foreign Policy.* New York: Anchor Doubleday, 1962.

Lebow, Richard N. *Between Peace and War: The Nature of International Crisis.* Baltimore, Md.: Johns Hopkins University Press, 1981.

Machiavelli, Niccolo. *The Prince* (Translated & edited by Robert M. Adams). New York: Norton, 1977.

Macomber, William. *The Angels' Game: A Handbook of Modern Diplomacy.* Briarcliff Manor, N.Y.: Stein & Day, 1975.

Mayer, Arno J. *Politics and Diplomacy of Peacemaking: Containment and Counterrevolution at Versailles, 1918–1919.* New York: Knopf, 1967.

Mayer, Martin. *The Diplomats.* New York: Doubleday, 1983.

McCamy, James L. *Conduct of the New Diplomacy.* New York: Harper & Row, 1964.

McDermott, Geoffrey. *The New Diplomacy and Its Apparatus.* London: Plume Press, 1973.

McDonald, Jr., John W., and Diane Bendahmane, eds. *Conflict Resolution: Track Two Diplomacy.* Washington, D.C.: Foreign Service Institute, Department of State, 1987.

Merritt, Richard L. *Communication in International Politics.* Urbana, Ill.: University of Illinois Press, 1972.

Morgenthau, Hans J. *Politics Among Nations: The Struggle for Power and Peace,* 6th ed. (Revised by Kenneth W. Thompson). New York: Knopf, 1985.

Neustadt, Richard E. *Alliance Politics.* New York: Columbia University Press, 1970.

Nicolson, Harold. *The Congress of Vienna: A Study in Allied Unity, 1812–1822.* New York: Harcourt, Brace, 1946.

————. *Diplomacy.* New York: Oxford University Press, 1950.

————. *The Evolution of Diplomatic Method.* New York: Macmillan, 1955.

————. "The 'Old' and 'New' Diplomacy" in Robert L. Pfaltzgraff, Jr., ed., *Politics and the International System,* 2nd ed. Philadelphia: Lippincott, 1972, pp. 425–34.

Nixon, Richard M. "Superpower Summitry." *Foreign Affairs,* vol. 64 (1985), pp. 1–11.

Palmer, Monte. *Dilemmas of Political Development,* 3rd ed. Itasca, Ill.: Peacock, 1985.

Patchen, Martin. *Resolving Disputes Between Nations: Coercion or Conciliation?* Durham, N.C.: Duke University Press, 1988.

Plischke, Elmer. *Diplomat in Chief: The President at the Summit.* New York: Praeger, 1986.

————, ed. *Modern Diplomacy: The Art and the Artisans.* Washington, D.C.: American Enterprise Institute, 1979.

Poullada, Leon P. "Diplomacy: The Missing Link in the Study of International Politics," in D. S. McLellan, W. C. Olson, and F. A. Sondermann, eds., *The Theory and Practice of International Relations,* 4th ed. Englewood Cliffs, N.J.: Prentice-Hall, 1974, pp. 194–202.

Rourke, John T. *International Politics on the World Stage,* 2nd ed. Monterey, Cal.: Brooks/Cole, 1989.

Smith, Steve, and Michael Clark, eds. *Foreign Policy Implementation.* New York: Allen & Unwin, 1985.

Sorenson, Theodore C. "Superpower Symmetry." *The Oregonian* (June 26, 1988), pp. E1, 4.

Spanier, John W., and Joseph L. Nogee. *The Politics of Disarmament: A Study in Soviet-American Gamesmanship.* New York: Praeger, 1962.

Spender, Sir Percy. *Exercises in Diplomacy.* New York: New York University Press, 1970.

Stoessinger, John G. *The Might of Nations,* 8th ed. New York: Random House, 1986.

Tuchman, Barbara W. "If Mao Had Come to Washington in 1945: An Essay in Alternatives." *Foreign Affairs* (Oct. 1972). [Reprinted in Barbara Tuchman. *Notes from China.* New York: Collier, 1972, pp. 77–112.]

Watson, Adam. *Diplomacy.* New York: McGraw-Hill, 1982.

Wendzel, Robert L. *International Relations: A Policymaker Focus,* 2nd ed. New York: Wiley, 1980.

Williams, Phil. *Crisis Management.* New York: Wiley, 1976.

Winham, Gilbert R., ed. *New Issues in International Crisis Management.* Boulder, Colo.: Westview, 1986.

Young, Oran. *The Politics of Force: Bargaining During International Crises.* Princeton, N.J.: Princeton University Press, 1968.

On Negotiations and Bargaining Behavior

Berman, Maureen R., and I. William Zartman. *The Practical Negotiator.* New Haven, Conn.: Yale University Press, 1982.

Fedder, Edwin H. "Communication and American-Soviet Negotiating Behavior." *Background,* vol. 8 (Aug. 1964), pp. 105–20.

———. "Negotiating Among Nations: A Review Article." *Background.* vol. 9 (Feb. 1966), pp. 339–50.

Franck, Thomas M., and Edward Weisband. *Word Politics: Verbal Strategy Among the Superpowers.* New York: Oxford University Press, 1972.

Iklé, Fred C. *How Nations Negotiate.* New York: Praeger, 1964.

Jönsson, C. *Soviet Bargaining Behavior: The Nuclear Test Ban Case.* New York: Columbia University Press, 1982.

Lall, Arthur. *Modern International Negotiation.* New York: Columbia University Press, 1966.

Lockhart, Charles. *Bargaining in International Conflicts.* New York: Columbia University Press, 1979.

Newhouse, John. *Cold Dawn: The Story of SALT.* New York: Holt, Rinehart, & Winston, 1973.

Osgood, Charles E. *An Alternative to War or Surrender.* Urbana: University of Illinois Press, 1962.

———. "Calculated De-Escalation as a Strategy" in Quincy Wright, William Evan, & Morton Deutsch, eds. *Preventing World War III.* New York: Simon & Schuster, 1962, pp. 171–77.

Pillar, Paul R. *Negotiating Peace: War Termination as a Bargaining Process.* Princeton, N.J.: Princeton University Press, 1983.

Rapoport, Anatol. *Fights, Games, and Debates.* Ann Arbor: University of Michigan Press, 1960.

Rubin, Jeffrey Z., and Bert R. Brown. *The Social Psychology of Bargaining and Negotiation.* New York: Academic Press, 1975.

Sawyer, Jack and Harold Guetzkow. "Bargaining and Negotiation in International Relations" in Herbert C. Kelman, ed. *International Behavior: A Socio-Psychological Analysis.* New York: Holt, Rinehart & Winston, 1965.

Schaetzel, J. Robert, and H. B. Malmgren. "Talking Heads." *Foreign Policy,* vol. 39 (1980), pp. 130–42.

Schelling, Thomas. *The Strategy of Conflict.* New York: Oxford University Press, 1963.

Schelling, Thomas, and Morton Halperin. *Strategy and Arms Control.* New York: Twentieth Century Fund, 1961.

Snyder, G. H., and P. Diesing. *Conflict Among Nations: Bargaining, Decision Making, and System Structure in International Crises.* Princeton, N.J.: Princeton University Press, 1977.

Talbott, Strobe. *Deadly Gambits.* New York: Knopf, 1984.

———. *Endgame: The Inside Story of SALT II.* New York: Harper & Row, 1979.

Winham, Gilbert R. "Negotiation as a Management Process." *World Politics,* vol. 30, no. 1 (Oct. 1977), pp. 87–114.

Zartman, I. William. "Negotiations: Theory and Reality." *Journal of International Affairs,* vol. 29 (Spring 1975), pp. 69–77.

———. "The Political Analysis of Negotiation: How Who Gets What and When." *World Politics,* vol. 26 (Apr. 1974), pp. 385–99.

On Intelligence, Propaganda, and Covert Action

Bamford, James. *The Puzzle Palace: Inside the National Security Agency.* New York: Penguin, 1983.

Breckinridge, Scott. *The CIA and the U.S. Intelligence System.* Boulder, Colo.: Westview, 1986.

Flanagan, Stephen J. "Managing the Intelligence Community." *International Security,* vol. 10, no. 1 (Summer 1985), pp. 58–95.

Garthoff, Raymond L. *Intelligence Assessment & Policymaking: A Case Study from the Kennedy Administration.* Washington, D.C.: The Brookings Institution, 1984.

Jeffrey-Jones, Rhodri. *American Espionage: From Secret Service to CIA.* New York: Free Press, 1977.

———. *The CIA and American Democracy.* New Haven, Conn.: Yale University Press, 1989.

Johnson, Loch. *America's Secret Power: The CIA in a Democratic Society.* New York: Oxford University Press, 1989.

———. *A Season of Inquiry: Congress and Intelligence.* Pacific Grove, Cal.: Brooks-Cole, 1987.

Knightley, Phillip. *The Second Oldest Profession: Spies and Spying in the Twentieth Century.* New York: Penguin, 1986.

Laqueur, Walter. *A World of Secrets: The Uses and Limits of Intelligence.* New York: Basic Books, 1985.

Marchetti, Victor, and John D. Marks. *The CIA and the Cult of Intelligence.* New York: Knopf, 1974.

Marshall, Jonathan, Peter Scott, and Jane Hunter. *The Iran-Contra Connection: Secret Teams and Covert Operations in the Reagan Era.* Boston: South End Press, 1987.

Maurer, Alfred C., et al., eds. *Intelligence: Policy and Process.* Boulder, Colo.: Westview, 1985.

Qualter, Terence H. *Propaganda and Psychological Warfare.* New York: Random House, 1962.

Ranelagh, John. *The Agency: The Rise and Decline of the CIA.* New York: Simon & Schuster, 1986.

Ransom, Harry Howe. *The Intelligence Establishment.* Cambridge, Mass.: Harvard University Press, 1970.

Richelson, Jeffrey T. *Foreign Intelligence Organizations.* New York: Ballinger, 1988.

————. *The U.S. Intelligence Community,* 2nd ed. New York: Ballinger, 1989.

Rubin, Barry. *Secrets of State: The State Department and the Struggle Over U.S. Foreign Policy.* New York: Oxford University Press, 1985.

Smith, Anthony. *The Geopolitics of Information: How Western Culture Dominates the World.* New York: Oxford University Press, 1980.

Treverton, Gregory F. *Covert Action: The Limits of Intervention in the Postwar World.* New York: Basic Books, 1987.

Turner, Stansfield. *Secrecy and Democracy: The CIA in Transition.* New York: Houghton Mifflin, 1985.

Whitaker, Urban G., Jr., ed., *Propaganda and International Relations.* San Francisco: Chandler, 1963.

Woodward, Bob. *Veil: The Secret Wars of the CIA, 1981–1987.* New York: Simon & Schuster, 1987.

On International Law

Akehurst, Michael. *A Modern Introduction to International Law,* 5th ed. London: Allen & Unwin, 1987.

Barkun, Michael. *Law Without Sanctions: Order in Primitive Societies and the World Community.* New Haven, Conn.: Yale University Press, 1968.

Boyle, Francis Anthony. *World Politics and International Law.* Durham, N.C.: Duke University Press, 1985.

Bozeman, Adda B. *The Future of Law in a Multicultural World.* Princeton, N.J.: Princeton University Press, 1971.

Brown-John, C. Lloyd. *Multilateral Sanctions in International Law: A Comparative Analysis.* New York: Praeger, 1975.

Clark, Grenville, and Louis Sohn. *Introduction to World Peace Through World Law.* Chicago: World Without War Publications, 1973.

Coplin, William D. "International Law and Assumptions About the State System." *World Politics,* vol. 17, no. 4 (July 1965), pp. 615–34.

D'Amato, Anthony. *The Concept of Custom in International Law.* Ithaca, N.Y.: Cornell University Press, 1971.

Deutsch, Karl, and Stanley Hoffmann, eds. *The Relevance of International Law.* Garden City, N.Y.: Doubleday, 1971.

Devisscher, Charles. *Theory and Reality in Public International Law.* Princeton, N.J.: Princeton University Press, 1968.

Dore, Isaac I. *International Law and the Superpowers: Normative Order in a Divided World.* New Brunswick, N.J.: Rutgers University Press, 1984.

Eide, Asborn. "International Law, Dominance, and the Use of Force." *Journal of Peace Research,* vol. 11, no. 1, pp. 1–20.

Falk, Richard A. *The Status of Law in International Society.* Princeton, N.J.: Princeton University Press, 1970.

Falk, Richard A., Friedrich Kratochwil, and Saul Mendlovitz, eds. *International Law: A Contemporary Perspective.* Boulder, Colo.: Westview, 1985.

Falk, Richard A., Samuel Kim, and Saul Mendlovitz, eds. *Toward A Just World Order.* Boulder, Colo.: Westview, 1982.

Fawcett, James. *Law and Power in International Relations.* Boston: Faber & Faber, 1982.

Finnegan, Richard B., et al. *Law and Politics in the International System: Case Studies in Conflict Resolution.* Washington, D.C.: University Press of America, 1979.

Fisher, Roger. *Improving Compliance with International Law.* Charlottesville: University Press of Virginia, 1983.

Friedheim, Robert L. "The 'Satisfied' and 'Dissatisfied' States Negotiate International Law." *World Politics,* vol. 18, no. 1 (Oct. 1965), pp. 20–41.

Goldie, Louis F. E. "International Law and the World Community: The Meaning of Words, the

Nature of Things, and the Face of the International Order." *Naval War College Review*, vol. 23, no. 6 (Feb. 1971), pp. 8–20.

Gong, Gerrit W. *The Standard of 'Civilization' in International Society*. New York: Oxford/Clarendon Press, 1984.

Goodwin-Gill, Guy S. *International Law and the Movement of Persons Between States*. New York: Oxford University Press, 1978.

Grotius, Hugo. *On the Law of War and Peace* (Francis W. Kelsey, trans.). New York: Carnegie Endowment for International Peace, 1925.

Grzybowski, Kazimierz. *Soviet Public International Law*. Leyden, the Netherlands: A. W. Sijthoff, 1970.

Henkin, Louis. *How Nations Behave: Law and Foreign Policy*, 2nd ed. New York: Columbia University Press, 1979.

Hoffmann, Stanley. "The Functions of International Law" in Lawrence Scheinman & David Wilkinson, eds. *International Law and Political Crisis*. Boston: Little, Brown, 1968.

———. "International Systems and International Law." *World Politics*, vol. 14 (1961), pp. 205–37.

———. "The Study of International Law and the Theory of International Relations" in S. Hoffmann, ed. *The State of War*. New York: Praeger, 1965, pp. 123–33.

Janis, Mark W. *An Introduction to International Law*. Boston: Little, Brown, 1988.

Kelsen, Hans. *The Law of the United Nations*. New York: Praeger, 1950.

Kirkpatrick, Jeane J. "The U.N. and Grenada: A Speech Never Delivered." *Strategic Review*, vol. 12 (Winter 1984), pp. 11–18.

Levi, Werner. *Contemporary International Law: A Concise Introduction*. Boulder, Colo.: Westview, 1979.

———. "The Relative Irrelevance of Moral Norms in International Politics." *Social Forces*, vol. 44, no. 2 (1965).

Lowe, A. V. "Do General Rules of International Law Exist?" *Review of International Studies*, vol. 0, no. 3 (July 1983).

Luard, Evan. *The International Regulation of Wars*. New York: New York University Press, 1972.

McDougal, Myres, and W. Michael Reisman, eds. *International Law in Contemporary Perspective*. Mineola, N.Y.: Foundation Press, 1981.

McKinnon, Fabian M. "The Role of International Law in Inter-State Conflict: Nine Aspects." *Coexistence*, vol. 20 (Apr. 1983), pp. 27–39.

Moynihan, Daniel Patrick. *Loyalties*. New York: Harcourt Brace Jovanovich, 1984.

Nardin, Terry. *Law, Morality, and the Relations of States*. Princeton, N.J.: Princeton University Press, 1983.

Niemeyer, Gerhart. *Law Without Force: The Function of Politics in International Law*. Princeton, N.J.: Princeton University Press, 1981.

Okolie, Charles C. *International Law Perspectives of the Developing Countries*. New York: Nok, 1978.

Onuf, Nicholas G., ed. *Law-Making in the Global Community*. Durham, N.C.: Carolina Academic Press, 1982.

Owens, Mackubin Thomas. "Grenada, Nicaragua and International Law." *This World*, vol. 9 (Fall 1984), pp. 3–14.

Parry, Clive. "The Function of Law in the International Community" in Max Sorensen, ed. *Manual of Public International Law*. New York: St. Martin's, 1968, pp. 1–54.

Pearson, Frederic S., and J. Martin Rochester. *International Relations: The Global Condition in the Late Twentieth Century*, 2nd ed. New York: Random House, 1988.

Potter, Jr., Ralph B. "The Moral Logic of War" in Charles Beitz & Theodore Herman, eds. *Peace and War*. San Francisco: W. H. Freeman, 1973, pp. 7–16.

Russell, Greg. "Soviet International Law and Ideology." *Global Perspectives*, vol. 2, no. 1 (Spring 1984), pp. 7–29.

Schwarzenberger, George. "The Credibility of International Law." *The Yearbook of World Affairs* (London). (1983), pp. 292–301.

———. *International Law and Order*. New York: Praeger, 1971.

Sheikh, A. *International Law and National Behavior*. New York: Wiley, 1974.

Turkin, G. I. *Theory of International Law*. Cambridge, Mass.: Harvard University Press, 1974.

Von Glahn, Gerhard. *Law Among Nations: An Introduction to Public International Law*, 5th ed. New York: Macmillan, 1986.

Watson, J. A. "A Realistic Jurisprudence of International Law." *The Yearbook of World Affairs* (London). (1980), pp. 265–85.

Weston, Burns, Richard A. Falk, and Anthony D'Amato. *International Law and World Order*. St. Paul: West, 1980.

White, Irvin. "International Law" in Michael Haas, ed. *International Systems*. New York: Chandler, 1974, pp. 251–69.

On the Law of the Sea

Alexander, Lewis M., ed. *The Law of the Sea*. Columbus: Ohio State University Press, 1967.

Andrassy, Juraj. *International Law and the Resources of the Sea*. New York: Columbia University Press, 1970.

Borgese, Elisabeth Mann. "The Law of the Sea." *Scientific American*. (Mar. 1983), pp. 42–49.

Buderi, Charles, and David D. Caron. *Law of the Sea: U.S. Policy Dilemma*. San Francisco: Institute for Contemporary Studies, 1983.

Hollick, Ann L. *U.S. Foreign Policy and the Law of the Sea*. Princeton, N.J.: Princeton University Press, 1981.

Luard, Evan, ed. *The Control of the Sea-Bed: A New International Issue*. New York: Taplinger, 1974.

O'Connell, D. P., with I. A. Shearer, eds. *The International Law of the Sea* (2 vols.). Oxford: Clarendon Press, 1982.

Wertenbaker, A. "A Reporter at Large: The Law of the Sea." *The New Yorker*. (Aug. 1 & 8, 1983), pp. 38–65, 56–83.

On the World Court (ICJ)

Falk, Richard A. *Reviving the World Court*. Charlottesville: University Press of Virginia, 1986.

———. "The Role of the International Court of Justice." *Journal of International Affairs*, vol. 37 (Winter 1984), pp. 253–68.

Franck, Thomas M. *Judging the World Court*. New York: Priority Press, 1986.

Gross, Leo, ed. *The Future of the International Court of Justice*. Dobbs Ferry, N.Y.: Oceana, 1976.

Scott, Gary L., and Craig L. Carr. "The ICJ and Compulsory Jurisdiction: The Case for Closing the Clause." *American Journal of International Law*, vol. 81 (Jan. 1987), pp. 57–76.

11

Some Final Thoughts

The Forces of Change

Nothing is more striking about international relations at the end of the twentieth century than the rapid pace of change. Technological advances have revolutionized the art of war and the state of the economy. Weapons have a mobility, a destructiveness, and a capacity to penetrate state borders that would have been unimaginable a century ago. The global economy is knit together by a thick web of trade ties, capital flows, and technology transfers. The global communications grid has intelligence capabilities that have made our societies virtually transparent. Space voyagers have given us a planetary perspective on our fragile global ecology, endangered by worldwide pollution, ozone depletion, deforestation, and the greenhouse effect, which threaten to set off irreversible changes in climate. (Figures 11-1 and 11-2 show the extent of recent damage to our forests.) Changes in social and political organization have created an array of new actors—international organizations, multinational corporations, revolutionary movements, transnational interest groups—that compete with the nation-state for loyalty and control.

The global power configuration has been transformed with amazing rapidity. Decolonization and two world wars destroyed Europe's dominance of the international system. And now bipolarity and the Cold War between the Soviet Union and the United States—the "new" features of international politics after 1945—seem destined for the dustbin of history, irrevocably affected by the disintegration of the socialist bloc, the rise of new economic powers, the intolerable costs of the arms race, and challenges from the Third World. Nuclear confrontation has been replaced by a grudging but clear-sighted acknowledgment of the necessity for coexistence. The superpower spheres of influence are breaking down. The great powers' once unfettered exercise of military might has been hedged in by the restraints of alliance relationships, economic interdependence, and a world public opinion united around the values of self-determination for all—including the small, the weak, and the stateless. We no longer tolerate dictatorship with resignation or complacency; democracy is advancing, in the Third World and the socialist bloc alike.

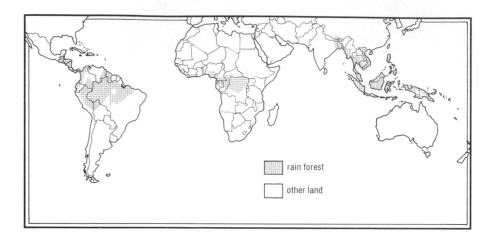

FIGURE 11-1
RAIN FORESTS UNDER THE AX
Almost half the tropical forests have been lost and the rest are being disrupted at the rate of 100 acres a minute.

Relations between the superpowers are more cooperative as the result of a growing awareness of their common problems. Both societies have suffered from the economic bloodletting of excessive arms expenditures and the bureaucratic distortions of a politically entrenched military-industrial complex. Both economies have reached a point of transition; dwindling resources, obsolete technology, and stagnant productivity have seriously eroded their economic leadership of the capitalist or the socialist world. Each society faces the rising social and environmental costs of an urban industrial system. Both political regimes are fighting to escape the dead weight of old vested interests and old ways of looking at the world, to free up the political agenda for major reforms. Bureaucratization and government dependency are problems in both systems, though obviously to a different degree. Many of the problems stem from the unnecessarily competitive superpower rivalry, in which the passion to be number one overcame the good sense of both leaderships and compromised their commitment to the founding principles of their systems. Hegemonic impulses and an overdeveloped arms economy have shackled both constitutional democracy and state socialism. Today's societies also suffer from a common cultural malaise marked by widespread alienation, nonparticipation, and frightening signs of social disintegration (drug and alcohol abuse, rising crime rates, divorce, illegitimate births, mental illness). Problems of materialism and secularization afflict both of these advanced industrial societies. Perhaps an appreciation of their common dilemmas, accompanied by additional successes in arms control, will speed the shift away from a costly military competition toward more mutually beneficial relations.

To be sure, some features of international politics are likely to endure well into the next century. An ideological rivalry between capitalism and socialism

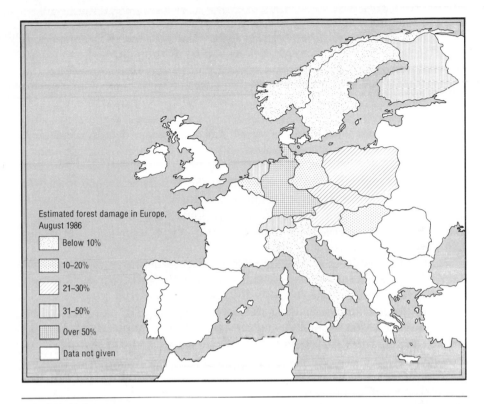

Estimated forest damage in Europe,
August 1986

Below 10%

10–20%

21–30%

31–50%

Over 50%

Data not given

FIGURE 11-2

FOREST DAMAGE IN EUROPE

Atmospheric pollution is being generated in such quantities that it now threatens Europe's forests. Recent assessments suggest that 14 percent, or 19.3 million hectares, are suffering from chemical stress.

will continue, despite some tendencies toward convergence. Balance-of-power politics is here to stay; the nation-state will remain a central actor and its power potential an essential ingredient of state security in a self-help system. But the balance is becoming more complex and more pluralistic, whether in terms of poles and alliance possibilities or in terms of the ingredients that make for an effective exercise of power. Arms will continue to play a powerful role in world politics, but trade, economic growth, productivity, and the capacity for scientific advance have become just as important. The material factors that have encouraged coexistence have been reinforced by moral norms, which, though nowhere practiced with consistency, are increasingly articulated, monitored, and policed by transnational groups and international agencies. Expectations have changed with regard to the status of women, human rights, and economic rights. We now have universally acclaimed minimum standards by which to judge states and persuade them to alter their conduct. Though the world does not yet have common cultural norms to unite it, the forces of economy and science are everywhere breaking down the barriers of cultural prejudice and national identity. The nation-state is being eroded from below as well, by subnational claims for autonomy and by a greater concern for individual rights.

The first steps toward global community were acts of conquest and the penetration of foreign powers and ideas, motivated by national chauvinism, missionary zeal, and impulses to power and wealth. But imperialism dug its own grave when it spread ideals of liberation, technologies of resistance, and the ingredients of world culture along with its conquering armies, its mission schools, and the tentacles of exploitative trade. Political and economic ideologies that went out in the service of great-power ideals came back as subversive doctrines that undermined the monopoly of the few. It happened to liberal capitalism, and it is happening to Leninist thought in the Marxist camp as well.

The problems of the Third World—political instability, revolutionary challenges, economic crises—will be with us for a very long time. The dependent relationships constructed over four centuries of colonialism will not be dismantled in a few decades. But global interconnectedness gives the developed states a high stake in furthering economic growth in the Third World, to sustain both their flourishing trade relations and their access to vital resources. And the politically or technologically dominant states also have strong incentives for ensuring that the process of social and economic change in the Third World is orderly. At the same time, many Third World states have become powerful enough to demand justice and equity as accompaniments to order. East-West tensions will not disappear, but they will be softened by the long-term effects of multipolarity and the relative economic decline of the United States and the Soviet Union. Trade relations, détente, and arms control will dominate the near-term superpower agenda, for reasons of prudence, sanity, and economy. There also will be continuing efforts to contain nuclear proliferation and keep these deadly weapons out of the hands of terrorists and unstable revolutionary states.

The alteration of the international landscape in only a few short decades has been breathtaking, and the pace of change is not likely to slow down. The statesman will find it increasingly difficult to predict or control contemporary events. Students of international affairs will awaken, a few decades from now, to a dramatically different future. Rapid social change and the plasticity of international forces put a premium on the making of wise choices—personal, national, and global. The complexities of the contemporary system force us to be farsighted, to consider the external impact of all our national decisions, to take a global and multilateral approach. Most important of all, we confront a series of trade-offs that we must make if we are ever to escape from the trap of pursuing security by old-fashioned, and possibly self-defeating, means.

As never before, national prosperity is dependent on the continuing cooperation of dozens of states that rely on one another for trade, investment, and vital resources. When the American economy is directly affected by other countries' decisions to tax, spend, invest, raise tariffs, print currency, or withhold resources, U.S. national security can no longer be defined in terms of autonomy — not unless the American public chooses to sacrifice its high standard of living as the price of decreasing its dependence on others. This trade-off between prosperity and security is matched by another: a growth-oriented strategy that seeks protected markets and increases global inequities has a rising political-economic cost. The export-oriented economies of the newly industrializing countries cannot prosper without open markets in the United States, and continuing growth in the Third World increases the market for U.S. exports, which in turn fund America's hefty imports. Punitive tariff policies that respond to national pride or insecurity or reflect the political concerns of a narrow constituency can destroy this circle of prosperity and interdependence. Many Third World states face a different kind of trade-off: if they try to crack the international market through growth strategies that exclude their own poor, they run a significant risk of domestic turmoil down the road. So a state's political stability has a new kind of economic component, and the vitality of its trade requires a political commitment to both open markets and equitable growth.

Policies based on national prestige and one's position in the arms race may no longer be compatible with peace or the maintenance of a secure place in the global economy. The United States and the Soviet Union both have been trapped in an arms race that has degraded their capacity to compete in the global market. They are daily being outflanked by Japan, Germany, France, and other states whose higher productivity is directly related to their smaller defense burdens. The two superpowers have preferred a self-sufficient defense posture and have sought to extend their influence over others by offering military protection. But it is impossible to separate a world power's security from the state of the global economy or global security. Nor can allies accept the protection of the nuclear umbrella unless they stand to gain thereby greater prosperity and an improved position in the international economy.

The international system is divided today between powers that compete through economic productivity and those that rely mainly on arms, and is divided further between the two nuclear-armed policemen, whose security is held hostage by the threat of disorder anywhere on the globe. Both superpowers confront a trade-off between power and prosperity. Neither can dominate globally except by fielding a nuclear and conventional arsenal so immense and costly as to rob the country of its very vitality. Without question, the United States and the Soviet Union were both gaining in national security in the 1980s, if the measure was the size of the defense budget, the number of tanks and planes, and the deployment of new nuclear weapons systems. However, if the measure is position in the international economy or the ability of other nations to affect their way of life, both superpowers were becoming increasingly insecure. Both have incentives for redefining their security in new terms that are less tied to the traditional notion of a competitive, self-contained system of military preparedness. We turn now to a closer look at these competing definitions of security (see Gordon Schloming, *American Foreign Policy and the Nuclear Dilemma*, pp. 230–62).

COMPETING CONCEPTS OF SECURITY

From a National Perspective

Traditionally, national security has been rooted in territorial protection and political autonomy. Independent national units are presumed to possess certain minimum interests that are mutually exclusive and inviolable, and the task of diplomacy is to maximize one's national interest in relation to everyone else's. In a competitive world, conflicts will be frequent and a resort to arms sometimes necessary. Although there is room for limited cooperation, the unregulated character of the international system gives rise to situations in which the gains of one nation are the losses of another. When nations do not agree on fundamentals and there are no restraints on arms, military threats will occur. So the nation must retain its freedom of action and beware of any restraints on its power potential. In this traditional perspective, the interdependence of the modern economy is a source of weakness and vulnerability for individual states. National security requires economic self-sufficiency, reliable access to strategic minerals, and control over sea lanes and trading partners. The "hard currency" of this security is military force and the capacity to mobilize it effectively and speedily. The umbrella of arms protection separates a nation from its neighbors and keeps its people behind a security boundary that cannot be crossed, save through alliance commitments and the export of arms and troops.

This conception presupposes the nation-state as a collective entity whose paramount interest is self-preservation. The state is objectified and its security interests elevated above all other interests, domestic or international. Personal and partisan claims count for little; international appeals are expressions of idealism and good will, to be endorsed cautiously and only at the state's convenience. The state's claims are prior to all others, because if sovereignty is lost, none of the founding principles or constituent interests of the community can be preserved, no matter how important. From this logic, it follows that the statesman and the citizen will have different standards of morality, since the statesman may have to employ deceit and violence in foreign policy to preserve the nation — even if it is a constitutional system that proclaims the virtues of truth telling and nonviolent resolution of conflicts.

But at some point it becomes relevant to ask whether such a means of national security does not compromise the domestic principles it is intended to serve. Armed autonomy can protect a state against external military threats. But we must also consider internal threats to the quality of life and to the domestic conditions that are presumably being protected. Does complete independence of action reduce the freedom and welfare of a nation's citizens? Does an overzealous national security policy subvert a nation from within? Can a state be secure, no matter how well armed, if the majority of its citizens feel economically and personally insecure? Does increasing the power and autonomy of the state necessarily contribute to the immediate welfare of its individual citizens?

The contradiction between means and ends and between external and internal security is apparent in many areas of state action. Militarism and expansionism have deprived more than one state of domestic freedoms, personal security, and consumer goods for its people. The Soviet Union's heavy burden of defense spending has brought its growth to a standstill and forced reforms on the new generation of leaders. Under democratic capitalism, too, foreign policy has often contradicted domestic principle and personal welfare. Despite America's ethos of free enterprise, national security considerations caused the government to bail the Lockheed and Chrysler corporations out of trouble because their economic failure would have brought massive unemployment, economic uncertainty, and the curtailment of key weapons systems. In the name of national security, the United States has subsidized a majority of the top corporations while cutting the flow of federal benefits to individuals. If the challenge to the nation is deemed severe enough, national security can justify a garrison state, wiretaps, the suspension of civil liberties, official lies, secret investigations of "un-American" activities, the falsification of records, and a great range of antidemocratic practices (for example, America's World War II internment of Japanese-Americans, Cold War McCarthyism, the Vietnam War, the Iran-Contra operation). In the name of national security, the American defense establishment can export military aid and launch covert operations to create or prop up regimes that welcome U.S. investment but also tolerate greater poverty, insecurity, and oppression among their masses. These activities may display the power of the state, but it can scarcely be claimed that they make the state safer at home or more secure abroad. In short, great powers frequently pursue foreign policies and institutional interests in the name of the state that appear to be very imperfectly related to an immediate, individual, and human sense of security.

A nation seeks security in at least two domains — international and domestic — but the requirements of these domains are frequently in competition. In its simplest form, it is the classic trade-off between guns and butter. National security is meaningless if it does not bring domestic tranquillity along with external defense. The internal dimension includes access to such basic necessities as food, clothing, and shelter, safety in the streets, a stable economy, secure jobs, a clean and safe environment, freedom from the daily threat of nuclear annihilation, trust in government, a sense of political empowerment, and hope for the future. These elements are threatened less often by foreign governments than by the national security state itself. This perspective weighs the cost of one more bomber or missile against fewer federal dollars for roads and schools, low-income housing, research on alternative energy sources, renewal of antiquated industries, job retraining, crime prevention. As the requirements of external defense have grown — through technological advances, the demands of interdependence, and the growth of state power — the domain of domestic security has declined. To give one concrete example, excessive U.S.

military spending and deficit-driven cuts in government services in the 1980s created a growing "underclass," leaving the poor with less hope and proportionately smaller incomes today than a decade ago. The widening income gap between rich and poor, broken families, joblessness, and homelessness have manifested themselves in social disintegration, rising crime rates, and drug abuse—the latter costing the U.S. economy about $60 billion every year. These are the invisible taxes that come with a misplaced priority on military spending.

A modern defense system typically gobbles up more resources than can be justified in relation to the wider economy. Third World states are notorious for importing the latest weaponry, paid for with scarce foreign exchange earnings that could better be spent on fertilizer, tractors, pharmaceuticals, machine tools, and other goods that the local economy desperately needs. In theory, the American defense establishment protects U.S. trade and access to vital raw materials. But if cheap foreign resources can be secured only by spending hundreds of billions of dollars on a global navy, a rapid deployment force, CIA teams, military aid to friendly regimes, and debt-servicing schemes to protect our overseas investments, how cheap are those raw materials? It is very costly to sustain economic relations based on considerations of power rather than justice or mutual benefit, even when some of the costs are hidden in the defense budget rather than paid over the counter. If the maintenance of dependency and inequitable trade relations in the Third World requires the steady application of U.S. military and political power, then the price of policing stability in friendly regimes may exceed any economic advantage that America presumably enjoys. This is particularly true of a time when both the superpower rivalry and the Third World's resistance to imperial control have raised the cost of maintaining a global power capability.

National security today encompasses much more than superiority in arms, protection of territorial integrity, and political independence. In an era of complex interdependence, threats to the well-being of ordinary citizens are much more widespread and much less visible than traditional military challenges are. We can insulate ourselves from such threats only at a high economic price; or we can gain certain economic benefits at the sacrifice of some political independence. In clinging to a definition of the national interest as a quest for security through power, we lose sight of what security is meant to protect—our values. Security is an instrument, a means for letting us enjoy the fruits of liberty, justice, prosperity, and peace, not an end offering satisfactions in itself. National security is a public "good," but its expensive weapons do not afford any benefit in themselves. As economists remind us, we cannot consume tanks, planes, and warheads; nor do they contribute to investment, industrial expansion, or higher productivity. Military goods are noneconomic; they neither increase our standard of living nor increase the productive capacity of the economy. A nation that seeks autonomy through arms in the traditional manner must often choose between a costly external defense and domestic prosperity and tranquillity. Such a hard choice puts a premium on a national security policy based not on an independent resort to arms but on the cost-conserving strategies of diplomacy, interdependence, alliances, and improved relations with one's adversaries.

From a Global Perspective

The traditional concept of national security has a built-in dilemma: it assumes a well-defined territorial entity whose political unity and economic welfare are not challenged from within or without. But this kind of impregnable, self-sufficient national unit has slowly been disappearing over the past half-century, with the rise of more pluralistic and interdependent societies. Yet old habits persevere. In the words of the Brundtland report, *Our Common Future*, issued by the World Commission on Environment and Development:

> The Earth is one but the world is not. We all depend on one biosphere for sustaining our lives. Yet each community, each country, strives for survival and prosperity with little regard for its impact on others.

In effect, the world has become smaller yet less secure. A great power like the United States has been forced to expand what it means by self-preservation. America's national security has passed beyond the mere preservation of territorial integrity to include the ability to maintain a credible nuclear deterrent, the protection of governments founded on like principles, the extension of economic influence abroad, control over key technologies and resources, and the maintenance of friendly regimes in strategic areas. The latter, which used to mean buffer zones on a state's borders, now include almost any area of economic significance (the Persian Gulf, southern Africa), any theater of potential great-power rivalry (Southeast Asia, Central America), and any region in which one superpower might be able to deny access, vital resources, or allies to the other. Self-preservation in an interdependent world means controlling a state's entire environment of action. For a great power, whose economic ties and alliance relations stretch around the planet, the security arena is truly global. To extend the largely obsolete traditional concept — security equals military control (as means) and national autonomy (as end) — into a world of growing interdependence entails the gargantuan task of policing the entire world.

Just as national security has been hammered and stretched from outside, domestic forces have pulled foreign policy in new directions. Multinational corporations conduct foreign activities independent of the official policies of state. Military-industrial constituencies, with their financial stake in the arms race, push for defense procurement and arms sales abroad. Private interest groups with international concerns lobby on behalf of their special causes. Labor and professional organizations sustain international ties that alter their national perceptions and agendas. Immigrant populations display special sympathies, and workers displaced by runaway industries harbor special animosities. Importers and exporters plead for subsidies or relief from them. Threatened domestic industries plead for special protection. Amidst all these domestic pressures, the national interest and the general welfare often get lost. Ordinary citizens find the world so complex and confusing that they often are unable to form an opinion about a foreign policy issue. Policy falls into the hands of the few who are expert enough, interested enough, or well connected enough to shape it. Or we are left with a dozen foreign policies to satisfy a dozen major constituencies. As the domestic community becomes ever more differentiated and its conflicting stakes or commitments in the international arena grow more diverse, national security loses all coherence. It comes to mean something different to each affected group, with its own perceptions and interests. The breakdown in what is meant by security reflects a diffusion of national unity that has come with participation in the wider global community.

As the world shrinks, the concentration of power and wealth in a few nations becomes more dramatically apparent to their neighbors. They see that many of the components of national power are obtained abroad, and the affluent country's accumulation and enjoyment of wealth invite envy and attack from poorer countries. To sustain their power, the rich must maintain access to resources, but as the advanced economies grow larger, the competition stiffens, in an environment of scarcity and extreme inequality. The accumulation of power can protect the national interest only to a point, for expanding power invites countermeasures from states whose own security appears to be in jeopardy. A policy that focuses only on means is self-defeating; the accumulation of power and wealth at the expense of one's neighbors in a close and competitive world can actually result in attacks on one's security.

Advances in military technology, transportation, and communications make all nations extremely vulnerable to nuclear attack, terrorism, and subversion. For the great powers, their sovereignty is mortgaged to the arms race and the rationality of their adversaries. For the small powers, their sovereignty is hostage to the conditions of the global market and the possibility of superpower intervention, direct or indirect. For all nations, terrorism is a common threat. When even a small power can obtain nuclear weapons, chemical-biological toxins, or other instruments of terror, world peace hangs on the grievances of a few. A lasting peace depends, as never before, on conditions of justice and mutual benefit. When arms were less destructive and nations could fend for themselves, the war system could bring a modicum of security. Now the nuclear-armed superpowers cannot afford to fight, and Third World revolutions must be carefully contained lest they set off a dangerous spiral of escalation. Global communications have put nations at such close quarters, and sovereignty has become so jumbled, that it is hard even to know against whom to direct the military threat that presumably protects the nation. An atomic bomb may not have an identifiable or predictable national origin. If an attack is anonymous, against whom do we retaliate? How does one deter a terrorist who occupies no set territory? We can fill the heavens with Star Wars technology, but what do we do about the suitcase bomb, the cruise missile, or the dozens of miniaturized nuclear devices that scientific ingenuity has yet to invent? The paradox of Star Wars is that it attempts to live out an obsolete concept— protection of territory—with the very technology that has made national boundaries completely permeable.

In such circumstances, a security system must be more than a balance of terror, an equilibrium of armed camps, a temporary absence of war. If security is meant to end our fears, then it must be a system for peace, not a war system that is at rest. True peace is a condition of the "commons," not the product of an equipoise of power. The advanced industrial democracies already have a working peace system among themselves; their economic interdependence and shared principles are sufficiently strong to eliminate war as a means of resolving their conflicting national interests. What chance is there that such a system could be expanded to a global scale? The prospect is uncertain, but there are signs of progress. The Soviet Union and China, huge economies that have been isolated behind economic walls of socialist autarky, are beginning to be integrated into the world economy. With the fresh air of *glasnost* and *perestroika* blowing through the Soviet Union and Eastern Europe, socialist democracy is no longer an unimaginable idea, though it may take decades to come to full expression, and the transition phase must be negotiated without a reversion to separatism, militarism, or dictatorship.

There is also the global "commons" that all nations share, much as the herders of old shared common grazing areas. Environmental problems have come crowding onto the global agenda, making international diplomacy a politics of the "commons" — of resource scarcity, transnational actors, overlapping ecological impacts, and economic interactions (see Figure 11-3). A state cannot make itself secure from acid rain, let alone from intercontinental missiles. The savannas and virgin rain forests of Central Africa show high levels of ozone and acid rain, which are normally associated with industrialization. Fires from African herding, farming, and lumbering activities are releasing magnitudes of carbon dioxide and methane that exceed the pollution in Europe and South America. So nations are trying to create an international law to deal with the common problems of terrorism, pollution, ozone depletion, and resource management.

The warning signs are there, pushing us toward cooperation out of sheer necessity. Scientists worldwide agree that the global warming trend and rising concentrations of carbon dioxide are caused by industrialization and its spendthrift consumption of fossil fuels. Between 1860 and 1985, human activities increased the concentration of carbon dioxide in the atmosphere by 30 percent, from 260 parts per million to 350 (see Figures 11-4 and 11-5). Our ecological interdependence is such that the nuclear winter ensuing from a "limited" war in Europe or the Middle East threatens planetary destruction. The deterioration of the ozone layer — only one sign of more general attacks on the biosphere — was until recently unrecognized or excused in the name of economic growth; now it is universally acknowledged as a global threat. And so is the grim prospect of a catastrophic depletion of global resources, if nations continue to insist on expanding their industrial base as a requisite of military might. Brazil, attempting to develop the economic base that would make it a great power in the old mold, has been destroying its tropical rain forests at breakneck speed; destruction of forests reduces the oxygen content of the atmosphere, and Brazil has recently come under strong international pressure to stop the logging. Pollution — of the seas with oil, of forests and lakes with

---

FIGURE 11-3
EARTH'S VITAL SIGNS

Indicator	Reading
Forest Cover	Tropical forests shrinking by 11 million hectares per year; 31 million hectares in industrial countries damaged, apparently by air pollution or acid rain.
Topsoil on Cropland	An estimated 26 billion tons lost annually in excess of new soil formation.
Desert Area	Some 6 million hectares of new desert formed annually by land mismanagement.
Lakes	Thousands of lakes in the industrial north now biologically dead; thousands more dying.
Fresh Water	Underground water tables falling in parts of Africa, China, India, and North America as demand for water rises above aquifer recharge rates.
Species Diversity	Extinctions of plant and animal species together now estimated at several thousand per year; one-fifth of all species may disappear over next 20 years.
Groundwater Quality	Some 50 pesticides contaminate groundwater in 32 American states; some 2,500 U.S. toxic waste sites need cleanup; extent of toxic contamination unknown.
Climate	Mean temperature projected to rise between 1.5° and 4.5° C between now and 2050.
Sea Level	Projected to rise between 1.4 meters (4.7 feet) and 2.2 meters (7.1 feet) by 2100.
Ozone Layer in Upper Atmosphere	Growing "hole" in the earth's ozone layer over Antarctica each spring suggests gradual global depletion could be starting.

---

acid rain, of soil and groundwater with toxic chemicals and radioactive contamination—is as immediately threatening to security as the risk of direct military aggression is. Soviet Foreign Minister Eduard Shevardnadze, speaking before the UN General Assembly in September 1988, said that environmental problems such as acid rain, the greenhouse effect, and toxic wastes were "gaining an urgency equal to that of the nuclear-and-space threat." He described the problems as "global aggression against the very foundations of life on Earth" and called for all nations to unite behind a global strategy for their solution. U.S. Secretary of State James Baker, meeting with representatives of more than forty countries at the UN-sponsored Intergovernmental Panel on Climate Change, said, in January 1989: "We face the prospect of being trapped on a boat that we have irreparably damaged, not by the cataclysm of war, but by the slow neglect of a vessel we believed to be impervious to our abuse." The global warming trend, he warned, shows "beyond a doubt" that pollution of

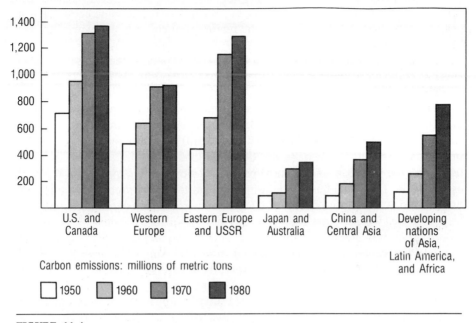

FIGURE 11-4

FOSSIL FUEL CONSUMPTION AND CARBON EMISSIONS

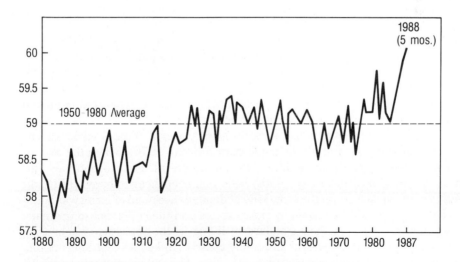

Average global temperatures, on the rise since the 1800s, rose sharply in the 1980s. As a baseline, scientists use the global average from 1950 to 1980.

FIGURE 11-5

VARIATIONS IN GLOBAL MEAN ANNUAL SURFACE TEMPERATURE

the environment is a transnational issue: "We all are in the same boat." (For a graphic depiction of the environmental factors that cause global warming, see Figure 11-6.)

Along with the power of acid rain and ICBMs to penetrate national boundaries has come a loss of sovereignty in the economic realm. Japan has become a principal supplier of cars, computers, and other goods that are staples of America's advanced economy. With their earnings, Japanese investors have purchased a large portfolio of American stocks and real estate, invading Los Angeles, Chicago, and New York in a financial intervention that makes the U.S. military incursions in Grenada and Lebanon look small-time indeed. In Manhattan alone, the Japanese are now parties to more than a quarter of the real estate deals. They also have bought up a substantial portion of the bonds that finance the U.S. national debt. If the Japanese were to lose confidence and stop buying — or, worse, start selling in massive quantities — the U.S. economy would be under catastrophic pressures whose long-term impact would dwarf the destructiveness of the Pearl Harbor attack. In short, America's national security and domestic policies are powerfully affected by conditions and decisions in the wider international political economy.

The same scenario of mutual vulnerability is repeated in the area of Third World debt. Latin American states alone owe the United States more than $1.2 trillion, most of it to highly leveraged commercial banks (that is, banks whose loan portfolios exceed their assets). But the United States, swamped by red ink in 1988 (a $150 billion trade deficit, a $2.5 trillion national debt, and bank failures costing the government tens of billions annually), nevertheless felt compelled to extend a $3.5 billion bridge loan to Mexico, one of the principal debtors. Although pessimists say there is little prospect of the Third World debt ever being paid in full, the short-run risk of financial collapse in the event of a massive default was so frightening as to force both the U.S. government and private banks to keep throwing good money after bad. Optimists argue that the renegotiation of Mexico's debt was a farsighted investment in the future, ensuring Mexican oil supplies and restoring a market for U.S. exports. Both views are based on the premise that U.S. security cannot be separated from the political and economic fate of its neighbors.

Oil supply and energy policy show the same pattern. The United States was one of many nations that hit the panic button in the 1970s, when the two oil crises dramatized the vulnerability of the advanced industrial economies. But since the oil glut of the early 1980s, little has been heard about OPEC and energy shortages. And yet the same kind of dependence on foreign oil was being re-created in the 1980s, fueled by cheap prices and the resistance of ordinary consumers to lowering their standard of living in the interests of achieving energy independence. Political autonomy clearly ranked second to economic affluence — as long as there was no overt crisis. U.S. oil consumption rose 10 percent between 1982 and 1988, and imports rose more than 40 percent. According to a General Accounting Office report, U.S. dependence on foreign oil will surpass the previous high of 1978 by the early 1990s. Meanwhile, America's domestic production is falling, and the British North Sea fields are

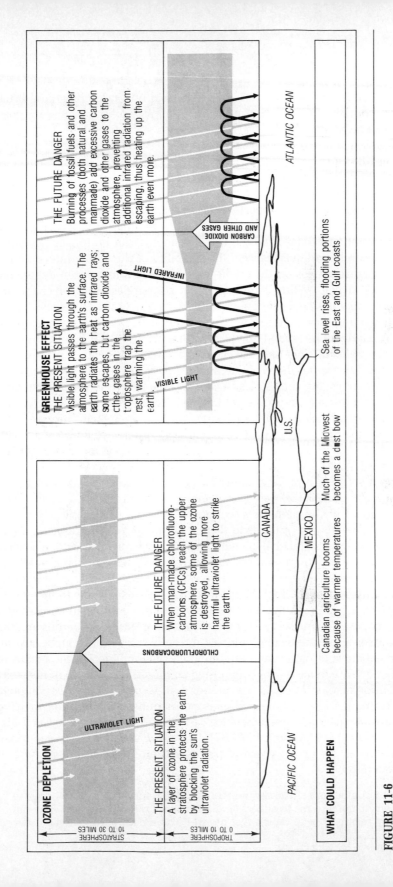

FIGURE 11-6
OZONE DEPLETION AND THE GREENHOUSE EFFECT

being depleted. In addition, the Reagan administration cut funding for alternative energy sources and allowed American automobile manufacturers to postpone their compliance with federal fuel efficiency standards. Before long, the United States will again be vulnerable to an OPEC oil monopoly. The Iraqi invasion of Kuwait in August 1990 and the sharp rise in oil prices that accompanied this Middle East crisis only confirmed predictions of continuing U.S. energy dependence and attendant economic vulnerability.

Global interdependence departs from the traditional assumption that foreign policy stops at the water's edge. Threats to the national interest are as often economic as military today, and the world economy can no longer be subdivided into discrete national markets. The stability of the whole international banking structure hinges on the credit-worthiness of a few dozen debtor nations. A trade deficit, falling commodity prices, or a declining currency can wreak havoc on a national economy within just a few years. Resource dependencies, migrating capital and labor, transnational corporations, trade imbalances, global indebtedness, and fluctuating money markets cancel out any hope of developing self-sufficient national economies. National security is inextricably tied to events around the world that lie far beyond the exclusive power of any one state or coalition of states to control. We live in an interdependent world whose interests (and dangers) are not divisible, but are increasingly shared. Cooperative global solutions offer the only long-term hope for real security and economic viability. To reach these solutions, we must invest with an eye to sustainability and must develop alternative budgets for global security (see Figure 11-7).

National security may be a contradiction in terms, an oxymoron, when defense of the nation requires environmental awareness and cooperation from all the members of the planetary ecosystem. Nations that want to grow in security will have to accept limits to their wealth and power. Capitalism and socialism are caught together in a civilizational predicament in which science and the ideology of progress serve the search for ever-increasing material wealth. Security has been equated with power over nature and, of necessity, over other human beings. Technology has brought us solutions to many economic and social problems, but it has no answer for our political dilemmas, and it cannot save us from ourselves. If the best use of our scientific genius and the ultimate purpose of materialist cultures on both sides of the globe are an unlimited conquest of nature and an unlimited accumulation of the means of power, then we are in danger of committing an unwitting suicide. In his essay "The Abolition of Man," C. S. Lewis reasons that the drive to acquire complete control over nature in the name of affluence or national security ends up being a kind of enslavement of ourselves, since we are a part of nature too (see Daly, *Economics, Ecology, Ethics,* pp. 177–87). In 1854, Chief Seattle, an American Indian, conveyed the predicament of power and environmental privation in these eloquent terms:

> How can you buy or sell the sky, the warmth of the land? The idea is strange to us. If we do not own the freshness of the air and sparkle of the water, how can you buy them? . . . We know that the white man does not understand our

FIGURE 11-7
SUSTAINABILITY AND INVESTMENTS IN GLOBAL SECURITY (in billions of dollars)

Year	Investments Needed for Sustainability							Global Security Defined in Military Terms	
	Protecting Topsoil on Cropland	Reforesting the Earth	Slowing Population Growth	Raising Energy Efficiency	Developing Renewable Energy	Retiring Third World Debt	TOTAL	Current Military Expenditures Continued	Reduced Military Expenditures Necessary for Sustainable Development
1990	$ 4	$2	$13	$ 5	$ 2	$20	$ 46	$900	$854
1991	9	3	18	10	5	30	75	900	825
1992	14	4	22	15	8	40	103	900	797
1993	18	5	26	20	10	50	129	900	771
1994	24	6	28	25	12	50	145	900	755
1995	24	6	30	30	15	40	145	900	755
1996	24	6	31	35	18	30	144	900	756
1997	24	6	32	40	21	20	143	900	757
1998	24	7	32	45	24	10	142	900	758
1999	24	7	32	50	27	10	150	900	750
2000	24	7	33	55	30	0	149	900	751

ways. One portion of land is the same to him as the next, for he is a stranger who comes in the night and takes from the land whatever he needs. The earth is not his brother, but his enemy, and when he has conquered it, he moves on. . . . He treats his mother, the earth, and his brother, the sky, as things to be bought, plundered, sold like sheep or bright beads. His appetite will devour the earth and leave behind only a desert. . . .

Teach your children what we have taught our children, that the earth is our mother. Whatever befalls the earth befalls the sons of the earth. If men spit upon the ground, they spit upon themselves. This we know — the earth does not belong to man, man belongs to the earth. All things are connected like the blood which unites one family. Whatever befalls the earth befalls the sons of the earth. Man did not weave the web of life; he is merely a strand in it. Whatever he does to the web, he does to himself. . . . This earth is precious to him, and to harm the earth is to heap contempt on its Creator. The whites too shall pass: perhaps sooner than all other tribes. Contaminate your bed, and you will one night suffocate in your own waste. But in your perishing you will shine brightly, fired by the strength of the God who brought you to this land and for some special purpose gave you dominion over this land and over the red man. That destiny is a mystery to us, for we do not understand when the buffalo are all slaughtered, the wild horses are tamed, the secret corners of the forest heavy with scent of many men, and the view of the ripe hills blotted by talking wires.

Where is the thicket? Gone.

Where is the eagle? Gone.

The end of living and the beginning of survival.

(Cited in Barnaby, pp. 242–43)

Nuclear weapons are richly symbolic of the deeper problem that afflicts all advanced societies wed to technological fixes and materialist values. These deadly weapons capture the paradox of growing powerlessness in the face of advancing technological prowess: neither superpower can exert its full might without risking suicide, and each superpower's survival depends on the restraint of its adversary. Nuclear weapons are just one illustration of our constant search for technical solutions to human problems — problems that actually must be solved again and again on the basis of the most ancient of wisdom. Unlike the formulas of science, the wisdom we need to compose our political differences is difficult to pass on from generation to generation. We inherit the habits, weapons, and animosities of our forebears, or learn lessons that no longer apply, while the memory of human folly and war fades all too quickly. Should we manage, with some good fortune, to escape nuclear holocaust, we must deal with the underlying problem of the will to power and the absence of limits. Should we fail to do so, we are likely to fall victim to the slower and more insidious technological suicide of pollution, depletion, poisoning, or some other global ecological catastrophe.

From a Personal Perspective

In personal terms, security is a state of mind as much as a collective condition. Traditional approaches to national security mistakenly fix on the tangible and the measurable. But attitude is an important part of our reality and controls many of our actions. Attitude is what could turn many of the worst-case scenarios of the defense planners into self-fulfilling prophecies: when we treat people as if they are aggressive, they often become so, and we inherit the dark future we have imagined. Excessive fear can bring a nation to violate its deepest principles or take actions that actually jeopardize its health. A nation is more secure if its people have confidence in themselves and their system of economy and government. Ironically, peaceful coexistence would have a better chance if capitalists and Marxists would each take seriously their claim that the forces of nature or history favor their ultimate victory. Then they could optimistically commit themselves to peaceful competition. When a nation becomes possessed by fear and concentrates more on what it opposes or what it might lose than on what it stands for, national security is already on a slippery downward slope.

Security is also cultivated by the self-confidence that comes from acting abroad in a manner consistent with one's ideology and national principles. Russia's great-power chauvinism and imperial adventures have done immeasurable harm to Marxist ideas, just as American interventionism and dollar diplomacy have tarnished the ideals of democratic capitalism and political self-determination. Consistency in foreign and domestic policy is a great virtue; a split personality is likely to yield unstable policy and an insecure public. Americans would do well to consider the rationale for many of the U.S. military interventions abroad. Since the days of Woodrow Wilson, our rhetoric has declared that we champion the right of democratic regimes to remain self-governing. Yet U.S. actions in Iran, Guatemala, Chile, Vietnam, and elsewhere have shown a propensity for sacrificing democracy on behalf of security, profits, and the assurance of American control. Nothing has traumatized and divided the American public more than the various crises of conscience set off by interventions that have appeared to contradict our founding principles. Congress was deeply split over support for the Nicaraguan *contras,* and we still confront a tremendous ambivalence over our policies in Central America. Or consider the contradictory rationales we use to justify defense spending. We pass military appropriations to subsidize special interests, to create jobs in key constituencies, to pacify the patriotic cry that we must be number one, to avoid an economic recession by the infusion of new spending. But no one stops to determine rationally how many resources we should be committing to essential military means. A sound national security policy would begin with deciding what we stand for as a nation and then adhering consistently and faithfully to those priorities and principles.

Personal insecurity about international affairs arises from tension between affluent life-styles, national consciousness, and a dwindling global resource base. Americans, with 6 percent of the world's population, consume over 45 percent of the world's nonrenewable resources. Brazilians, Nigerians, Indonesians, and other Third World peoples try to imitate the life-style of the West, but without the resources to permit more than a tiny minority of their people to enjoy a Western level of material affluence. We covet their raw materials; they covet our technology and consumer goods. Both parties want to preserve their cultural identity and national security, but neither side is living within its means. The solution is either a change of consciousness or a change of life-style. Citizens of the developing world could well follow the advice of Ivan Illich and "outwit" the developed countries by ceasing to desire the expensive prepackaged consumer goods and technological fixes of the "advanced" states. They could alter their expectations, embrace more appropriate technologies, and pay closer attention to the basic needs of the majority, rather than the Westernized tastes of an elite. Citizens in wealthy states could live more lightly on the planet, accepting some limits to growth and to their wasteful consumption of nonessential goods. We could curb our relentless demands on political leaders to deliver a cornucopia of progress, which only makes us ever more dependent on Third World resources. We, too, could seek more appropriate alternative technologies that would husband the finite resources of the planet. So long as Americans assuage their existential fears by consuming more, rather than searching for nonmaterial sources of inner security, we will never be free, and we will always feel deprived and powerless, no matter how wealthy our nation is. Krishnamurti, an East Indian sage, understood this well when he said:

> No leader is going to give us peace, no government, no army, no country. What will bring peace is inward transformation which will lead to outward action. Inward transformation is not isolation, not a withdrawal from outward action. On the contrary, there can be right action only when there is right thinking, and there is not right thinking when there is no self-knowledge. Without knowing yourself, there is no peace. (Cited in Barnaby, p. 243)

At a minimum, "Buddhist economics" and the holistic, steady-state assumptions of the "small is beautiful" school teach us this: any nation that wrings more from the world in resources than it gives back in benefits is operating at a deficit and will become, in the long run, increasingly insecure. In an age when all political persuasions are reaffirming the good sense of a balanced budget, it is a wisdom we should heed. It is also an action that is within the power of any individual to take by changing his or her personal life-style and political expectations.

Individuals can enhance their sense of efficacy and security by participating in the political process and trying to make foreign policy conform to their values and desires. Then national policy would less often be something crafted by a distant few or embrace options that violated the principles of so many. All around us are opportunities for self-education, political action on every side of an issue, citizen diplomacy, and the conscientious application in our daily lives of the principles we would like to see lived out in our foreign policy. Foreign policy and peacemaking start in the home, in the workplace, and in the decision-making circles of each citizen's private nation. Peace of mind, if not always world peace, can come from working out one's own answer to the security problems of the day and then pushing hard to be a part of the solution rather than a part of the problem. Ordinary citizens can make a difference, if they abandon old ways of thinking and the habits of denial and political passivity. Many foreign policy matters are highly technical, but basic choices about competing strategies and the path to security are all political questions, and the judgment of the average citizen is just as relevant as that of the defense expert, the economist, or the president. Which values one embraces and which solutions make sense obviously are a matter of personal taste and choice. This book can hardly provide a formula or a prescription, save that personal security comes in part from a deeper understanding of the forces at work in the international arena today and from a capacity to think and decide for oneself.

POWER AND PRINCIPLE

As we bring this dialogue between realism and idealism to an end, we should keep in mind that each perspective captures important elements of truth. The realist sees international affairs from a national perspective, with attention to the animating role of national interest and with a central, and quite natural, preoccupation with security. The idealist sees world politics from a global perspective, with attention to the transnational impact of ideology and to the perennial human cry for liberty, equality, and justice. The realist focuses on the pragmatic demands of security today. The idealist is concerned about the long-term trends that can contribute to world order tomorrow. The realist helps us understand the workings of power and counsels prudence in the face of the unpredictable and often anarchical nature of international affairs. The idealist keeps our eye on the principles that motivate statesmen and give underlying form to the incipient institutions of world order. The picture would be incomplete without both perspectives.

Power and principle are related. Power is a means only. It takes its meaning from the values it serves and the principles it protects. Without the legitimizing halo of political ideals, power is nothing but tyranny, obsession, and aggrandizement. Raw power invites immediate suspicion and challenge. It is quick to erode. It is an ephemeral source of national security. Without the cement of popular support and the justification of an overarching purpose, military forces are nothing but inert matter, rusting equipment, men and women marching aimlessly (and unreliably). But neither can ideals do anything by themselves. They act on history by their power to unleash social forces, to animate leadership, to compel sacrifices of blood and treasure. Ideologies acquire international currency when states promote them with their power assets. Principles are made manifest only by the willingness of ordinary people to commit time and tangible resources to their realization. We need a dose of realism to survive in a sometimes ugly, competitive, and insecure world. We need a dose of idealism to thrive in a world that is fashioned very much by what individuals think is desirable and possible.

SOURCES AND SUGGESTED READINGS

Barnaby, Frank. *The Gaia Peace Atlas.* New York: Doubleday, 1989.
Barney, Gerald O. *The Global 2000 Report to the President.* New York: Penguin, 1980.
Boulding, Kenneth. *The Meaning of the Twentieth Century: The Great Transition.* New York: Harper & Row, 1964.

————. *Stable Peace.* Austin: University of Texas Press, 1978.

Brower, Michael. "The Greenhouse Effect: What Is It, How Bad Will It Get?" *Nucleus,* vol. 10, no. 3 (Fall 1988), pp. 1–4.

Brown, Harold. *Thinking About National Security: Defense and Foreign Policy in a Dangerous World.* Boulder, Colo.: Westview Press (Praeger), 1983.

Brown, Lester. *Building a Sustainable Society.* New York: Norton, 1981.

————. *Redefining National Security.* Washington: Worldwatch Institute, 1977.

————. *World Without Borders.* New York: Random House, 1972.

Brown, Lester, and Pamela Shaw. *Six Steps to a Sustainable Society.* Washington: Worldwatch Institute, 1982.

Brown, Lester, et al. *State of the World 1988.* Washington: Worldwatch Institute, 1988.

Brown, Robert McAfee. *Making Peace in the Global Village.* Philadelphia: Westminster Press, 1981.

Brown, Seyom. *New Forces in World Politics.* Washington: Brookings Institution, 1974.

————. *New Forces, Old Forces, and the Future of World Politics.* Glenville, Ill.: Scott, Foresman, 1988.

Brucan, Silviu. "The Global Crisis." *International Studies Quarterly,* vol. 28 (March 1984), pp. 97–109.

Brundtland, Gro Harlem, et al. *Our Common Future.* Report of the World Commission on Environment and Development. New York: Oxford University Press, 1987.

Capra, Fritjof, and Charlene Spretnak. *Green Politics: The Global Promise.* New York: E. P. Dutton, 1984.

Cornish, Edward, ed. *Global Solutions.* Bethesda, Md.: World Future Society, 1984.

Dahlberg, Kenneth, et al. *Environment and the Global Arena.* Durham, N.C.: Duke University Press, 1985.

Daly, Herman, ed. *Economics, Ecology, Ethics: Essays Toward a Steady-State Economy.* San Francisco: W. H. Freeman, 1980.

Deudney, Daniel. *World Earth Security: A Geopolitics of Peace.* Washington: Worldwatch Institute, 1983.

Durrell, Lee. *The State of the Ark: An Atlas of Conservation in Action.* New York: Gaia Books/Doubleday, 1986.

Falk, Richard A. *The End of World Order.* New York: Holmes & Meier, 1983.

Falk, Richard A., et al, eds. *Toward a Just World Order.* Boulder, Colo.: Westview Press (Praeger), 1980.

Flavin, Christopher. *Slowing Global Warming: A Worldwide Strategy.* Washington: Worldwatch Institute, 1989.

Galtung, Johan. *The True Worlds: A Transnational Perspective.* New York: Free Press, 1980.

Gromyko, Anatoly, and Martin Hellman, eds. *Breakthrough: Emerging New Thinking.* New York: Walker and Co., 1988.

Gurtov, Mel. *Global Politics in the Human Interest.* Boulder, Colo.: Lynne Rienner, 1988.

Hardin, Garrett, and John Baden, eds. *Managing the Commons.* San Francisco: W. H. Freeman, 1977.

Heilbroner, Robert L. *An Inquiry into the Human Prospect: Updated and Reconsidered for the 1980s.* New York: Norton, 1980.

Hollins, Harry B., et al. *The Conquest of War: Alternative Strategies for Global Security.* Boulder, Colo.: Westview, 1989.

Johansen, Robert C. *The National Interest and the Human Interest.* Princeton, N.J.: Princeton University Press, 1980.

Kaufman, Daniel, et al. *U.S. National Security: A Framework for Analysis.* Lexington, Mass.: D. C. Heath/Lexington Books, 1985.

Kegley, Charles W., Jr., and Eugene Wittkopf, eds. *The Global Agenda: Issues and Perspectives.* New York: Random House, 1984.

Kim, Samuel S. *The Quest for a Just World Order.* Boulder, Colo.: Westview, 1984.

Kohr, Leopold. *The Breakdown of Nations.* New York: E. P. Dutton, 1978.

Kothari, Rajni. "Peace in an Age of Transformation." In R. B. J. Walker, ed., *Culture, Ideology, and World Order,* Boulder, Colo.: Westview, 1984.

Mathisen, Trygve. *Sharing Destiny: A Study of Global Integration.* Oslo: Norwegian University Press, 1985.

Mattis, Ann, ed. *A Society for International Development: Prospectus 1984.* Durham, N.C.: Duke University Press, 1983.

McCartney, James. "Soviets Seek to Battle Threats to Environment." *Oregonian*, Sept. 28, 1988, p. A4.

McKinley, R. D., and R. Little. *Global Problems and World Order*. Madison: University of Wisconsin Press, 1986.

Miller, Lynn H. *Global Order: Values and Power in International Politics*. Boulder, Colo.: Westview, 1985.

North, Robert C. *The World That Could Be*. New York: Norton, 1976.

Ophuls, William. *Ecology and the Politics of Scarcity*. San Francisco: W. H. Freeman, 1976.

Oren, Nissan, ed. *When Patterns Change: Turning Points in International Politics*. New York: St. Martin's, 1984.

Orr, David W., and Marvin Soroos, eds. *The Global Predicament: Ecological Perspectives on World Order*. Chapel Hill: University of North Carolina Press, 1979.

Pirages, Dennis. *Global Ecopolitics*. Belmont, Calif.: Duxbury, 1973.

————. *Global Technopolitics: The International Politics of Technology and Resources*. Pacific Grove, Calif.: Brooks/Cole, 1989.

Postel, Sandra. *Air Pollution, Acid Rain, and the Future of Forests*. Washington: Worldwatch Institute, 1984.

Renner, Michael. *National Security: The Economic and Environmental Dimensions*. Washington: Worldwatch Institute, 1989.

Sale, Kirkpatrick. *Human Scale*. London: Secker & Warburg, 1980.

Sarasohn, David. "U.S. Heading for National Insecurity." *Oregonian*, Oct. 21, 1988, p. E10.

Schell, Jonathan. *The Abolition*. New York: Knopf, 1984.

Schloming, Gordon. *American Foreign Policy and the Nuclear Dilemma*. Englewood Cliffs, N.J.: Prentice-Hall, 1987.

Simon, Julian. *The Ultimate Resource*. Princeton, N.J.: Princeton University Press, 1981.

Simon, Marlise. "Acid Rain Caused by Savanna Fires Threatens African Rain Forests." New York Times News Service, *Oregonian*, June 29, 1989, p. A9.

Soroos, Marvin S. *Beyond Sovereignty: The Challenge of Global Policy*. Columbia: University of South Carolina Press, 1986.

Speth, James Gustave. "Now, for a Worldwide Phase-out of CFCs." *Los Angeles Times*, March 29, 1988.

Sprout, Harold and Margaret. *Toward a Politics of the Planet Earth*. New York: Van Nostrand Reinhold, 1971.

Stammer, Larry. "Baker Calls for Action on Global Warming." L.A. Times-Washington Post Service, *Oregonian*, Jan. 31, 1989, p. A3.

Vayrynen, R. *Policies for Common Security*. Philadelphia: Taylor & Francis, 1985.

Vittachi, Anuradha. *Earth Conference One: Sharing a Vision for Our Planet*. Proceedings of Global Survival Conference at Oxford. Boston: New Science Library, 1989.

Copyrights and Acknowledgments and Illustration Credits

Chapter 7

Chapter 9

Chapter 10

Chapter 11

INDEX

Y

Z

A 1
B 2
C 3
D 4
E 5
F 6
G 7
H 8
I 9
J 0

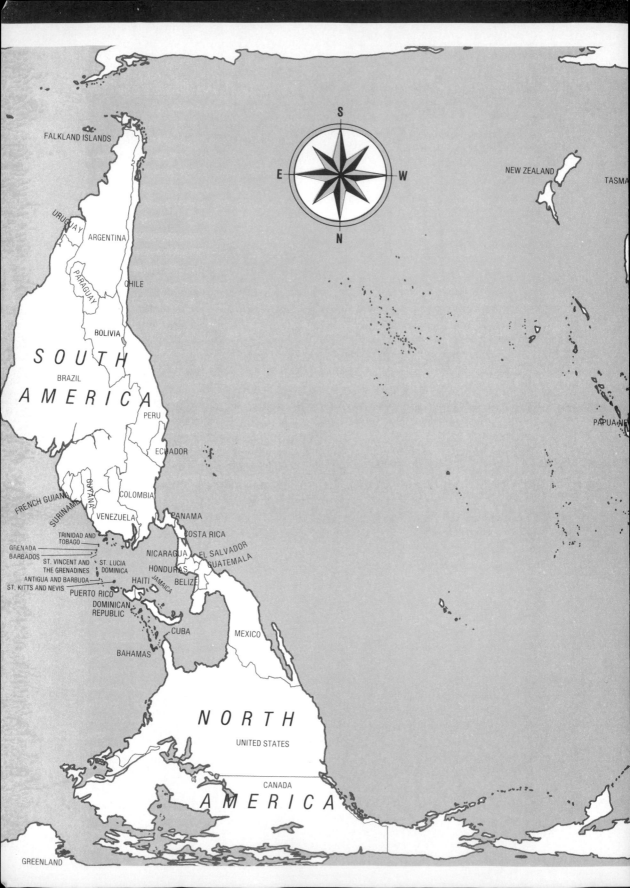